JIMMY SWAGGART BIBLE COMMENTARY

Genesis

JIMMY SWAGGART BIBLE COMMENTARY

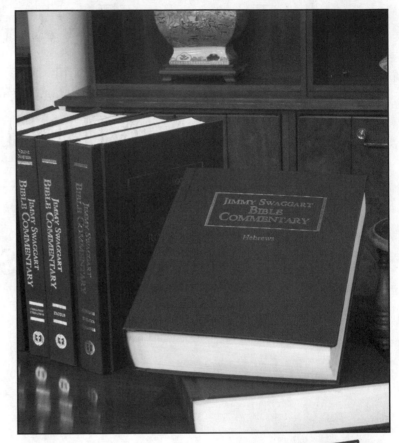

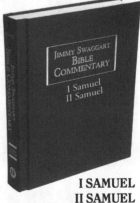

**I SAMUEL
II SAMUEL**

Jimmy Swaggart Bible Commentary

Genesis

WORLD
EVANGELISM
PRESS

ISBN 978-0-9769530-4-3

11-201 • COPYRIGHT © 2003 World Evangelism Press®
Second Printing
P.O. Box 262550 • Baton Rouge, Louisiana 70826-2550
Website: www.jsm.org • Email: info@jsm.org
(225) 768-8300
CW1 0808

TABLE OF CONTENTS

INTRODUCTION

—■—

INTRODUCTION TO THE BOOK OF GENESIS

It is September 3, 2001, Labor Day, as I begin commentary on the Book of Genesis.

Back in 1992 I set out to write a one Volume Commentary on the entirety of the Bible. In fact, the Lord had been dealing with me for some time about this project; however, knowing my inadequacy, which definitely was not imagined, I was loath to attempt such a project. And as well, I wanted to make certain that this was the Lord moving upon me to do such a thing, and not merely something out of my own mind.

I lay no claim to scholarship, which a mere cursory perusal would disprove anyway, but I do claim to ardently love the Word of God. I have read the Bible completely through about 50 times. I never tire of its contents; it always seems to me to be fresh and new, with its great Truths being inexhaustible, which they definitely are.

When I began this effort back in 1992, I quickly realized that I would not be able to do justice to the effort by trying to put everything in one Volume. Mentally I stretched it to three Volumes, but soon realized that would not be sufficient either. At any rate, our first Volume spanned Genesis through II Chronicles. So I'm now rewriting this particular Volume, which will actually stretch into some 13 Volumes, devoting a Volume to each Book, with the exception of joining together Judges and Ruth. At least these are my plans at present.

THE EVANGELIST

Since 1990, the Lord has begun to open up to me at least one of the reasons that He has wanted me to make this effort, regarding these Commentaries. There are very few works of this nature done from the perspective of the Evangelist. I am an Evangelist. That is my Calling; consequently, I see things from that perspective. As a result, these Commentaries contain not only much research as it regards investigation of the Scripture and hopefully their proper exegesis, but as well, the uncompromising, straightforward, presentation of the Gospel, of which an Evangelist alone is capable. As a result, these Commentaries are definitely controversial. The Text pulls no punches. To be frank, the intention is to proclaim the Gospel, and to do so in such clear, concise terms that there be no mistake about what is being said. As a result, I would trust that the theme and spirit of the Text is, *"Thus saith the Lord!"*

THE CROSS

In 1996, after some five years of seeking the Face of the Lord day and night, even with tears, in answer to the seeking of the soul, the Lord began to give me a Revelation of the Cross, which has revolutionized my life and Ministry. In fact, that Revelation continues unto this hour.

He first of all took me to the Sixth Chapter of Romans and then to the Eighth Chapter of that great Epistle penned by Paul. It was as though a new world opened up to me. In the spiritual sense, it was the greatest thing that ever happened to me other than the moment I was Born-Again, and a little later, Baptized with the Holy Spirit. In fact, this Revelation as stated, continues unto this hour, and I personally believe will ever continue.

I have found that the Cross of Christ is not a mere doctrine, but in actuality is the foundation on which the entire fabric of the great Plan of God is built, so to speak. I am positive that Christ looked at His great Work on the Cross as it regarded the giving of Himself in Sacrifice for lost humanity as more than a mere doctrine. It is in fact the foundation of all Doctrine. If we do not see things from the perspective of the Cross, then we do not see them correctly. In fact, if we do not interpret the Word of God, which in effect is the story of the Cross, from that perspective, I personally feel that our interpretation will be flawed.

So, as we go through this great Book of Genesis, I will take every opportunity presented in the Scripture to make the presentation of the Cross. I will do so, even to the point of being repetitious, and possibly some may even think overly so; however, I feel the Holy Spirit is pushing me strongly to underline this particular Message, as no other.

THE IMPORTANCE OF THE BOOK OF GENESIS

Some have said that the Book of Genesis is the most important contained in the Bible. Being the First Book, it definitely contains the Foundation on which everything else is built. It sets the stage for the great Redemptive Work of Christ. In fact, it portrays the Cross in every breath it breathes.

From this Book we have the account of the creation, and of man's place in that creation. The first three Chapters record that event, plus the Fall of man; a Fall of such magnitude incidentally, that it adversely affected the entirety of the Creation of God, at least what man knows of that creation. The remaining 47 Chapters of this great Book record the Plan of God respecting the Redemption of mankind. Love created man, so love must redeem man! In fact, the balance of the entirety of the Bible is the story of Redemption.

Regarding this great Book of Genesis, Joseph Exell says: *"The Book of Genesis contains the history of the world's early progress, as presented in the lives of the most influential men of the times. It is therefore most important, certainly most interesting, and supremely reliable, as the outcome of a Divine inspiration then for the first time given to man. The Book has a doctrinal importance. It narrates the creation of man, with his temporal and moral surroundings. It teaches the Divine origin of the soul; that life is a probation; that communion with God is a reality; that man is gifted with moral freedom; that he is subject to Satanic influence, and that a violation of the Law of God is the source of all human woe.*

"Here we have the only reliable account of the introduction of sin into the world; the true philosophy of temptation, the true meaning of the redemptive purpose of God, the universal depravity of the early race; and we have exemplified the overruling providence of God in the history of all that is good."

As we go through this Book, you will see that God's answer to man's dilemma is the Lord Jesus Christ. He appears on every page, and in every Act of God. He Alone is the theme of all that is said and done. In fact, Jesus Christ and Redemption are synonymous.

But yet, as we will see, it is not merely the Person of Christ which is held up, but as well what He would do to redeem humanity, which is the Cross. He is not presented, but that He is presented in this fashion. Therefore, from the beginning pages, we see the Type, the shadow if you will, of the great Word of the Apostle Paul, *"Jesus Christ and Him Crucified"* (I Cor. 1:23; 2:2). Consequently, if we do not begin our study of the Word of God from that perspective, then as previously stated, our understanding will be flawed.

AUTHORSHIP OF THIS BOOK OF GENESIS

Genesis was written by Moses. Jesus said so! (Lk. 24:27). In fact, Moses wrote all five Books of the Pentateuch, Genesis, Exodus, Leviticus, Numbers, and Deuteronomy. What he wrote is definitely historical, and one might even say that it is definitely scientific; however, it is far more than that. It is Revelation. As a result, it could only be given by inspiration.

The actual happenings of which we read in this Book were passed down from father to son, and by the individuals which are prominent in this account. Moses had access to all of these accounts, and inspiration guaranteed its accuracy.

The object of the writer as inspired by the Holy Spirit was not to present to the world a scientific treatment; however, everything that is said in that vein is definitely correct. The purpose of the Holy Spirit, as He helped Moses write this Book, is overwhelmingly to present the Plan of Redemption. It is from this standpoint that the Book of Genesis was written, and from this standpoint that it should be read. Matthew Henry said: *"The Scriptures were written not to gratify our curiosity, or make us astronomers, but to lead us to God and make us Saints."*

It will be our effort in this Commentary on Genesis to lift up Christ. If we are successful, then the study of this effort will be profitable to you.

"Be Thou exalted, forever and ever,
"God of eternity, The Ancient of Days!
"Wondrous in Majesty, so mighty in wisdom,
"Perfect in Holiness, and worthy of praise."

"Be Thou exalted, O Son of the Highest Gracious
*   Redeemer our Saviour and King!*
"One with the Father, coequal in glory,
"Here at Your footstool our homage we bring."

"Be Thou exalted, O Spirit Eternal! Dwell in
*   our hearts, keep us Holy within;*
"Feed us each day with Your Heavenly Manna
"Healer of wounded hearts Your praises we sing."

THE
BOOK OF GENESIS

—■—

(1) "IN THE BEGINNING GOD CREATED THE HEAVEN AND THE EARTH."
The structure is:

1. *"In the beginning"* refers to the beginning of creation, or at least the creation as it refers to this universe.

2. The phrase, *"In the beginning God,"* explains the cause of all things as it regards creation.

3. Moses does not attempt to prove the existence of God, knowing that creation itself is proof enough.

4. *"The heaven and the Earth"* could be translated *"the heavens and the Earth,"* because God created the entirety of the universe.

THE BEGINNING

The phrase, *"In the beginning,"* speaks of a time in eternity past, when God began the creation of *"the heavens and the Earth."* Williams says: *"Beginning"* is the subject of this Book; it teaches that God is the Beginner of the visible and invisible universe, as He is the Beginner of Salvation in the soul of the sinner.

We aren't told here when this *"beginning"* took place, only that it happened some time in eternity past.

God has always existed, which means that there never was a time when He didn't exist. As such, and knowing that He is a Creator, which is an essential part of His Being (Jn. 5:17), we are made to wonder as to what existed before the heavens and the Earth, however, any idea is speculation at best, and when it comes to God, it's best not to speculate.

GOD

The theory of Evolution puts forth all types of speculation as it regards the creation

of man along with the heavens and the Earth. However, irrespective of the proposals they make, they have absolutely no idea of the first cause. Every hypothesis they put forth is always based on existing materials of some kind; consequently, not having a proper foundation, their hypotheses are always wrong.

The phrase, *"In the beginning God,"* gives the first cause. That first cause is God.

"God" in the Hebrew is *"Elohim."* Its root-meaning is *"strength and power."* *"Elohim"* is a uni-plural noun, which shows the plurality of Persons in the Godhead. Consequently, from the very beginning, we see the Doctrine of three Divine Persons in the unity of the Godhead. There is one God, but manifest in three Persons, *"God the Father, God the Son, and God the Holy Spirit."* To help us understand the Trinity and Creation a little better, perhaps the following may shed some light:

God the Father is the Divine Owner; God the Son is the Divine Architect; God the Holy Spirit is the Divine Builder.

TRINITY

The word Trinity is not found in the Bible. It was used, it is said, by Tertullian in the last decade of the Second Century; however, it did not really find a place formally in the theology of the Church until the Fourth Century. It is, however, the distinctive and all-comprehensive Doctrine of the Christian Faith.

It makes three affirmations: that there is but One God, that the Father, the Son, and the Spirit is each God, and that the Father, the Son, and the Spirit is each a distinct Person. In this form it has become the Faith of the Church (Bible Dictionary).

1

With the Revelation of the Lord Jesus Christ, the Trinity comes much more into view.

For instance, when the Angel Gabriel appeared to Mary, He said that the Holy Spirit would come upon her. He then added that the power of the Most High would overshadow her and that the child born of her would be called *"the Son of God"* (Lk. 1:35). In this we see the Trinity, the Father, and the Spirit functioning in the Incarnation of the Son.

At the Baptism of Christ in the Jordan, three Persons of the Godhead can be distinguished here. The Son is the One being baptized; the Father is speaking from Heaven in recognition of His Son, and the Spirit is descending as a dove upon Jesus (Jn. 1:32-33).

The teaching of Jesus is Trinitarian throughout. He spoke of the Father Who sent Him, of Himself as the One Who reveals the Father, and the Spirit as the One by Whom He and the Father work. In fact, the interrelations between Father, Son, and Spirit are emphasized throughout (Jn. 14:7, 9-10). He declared with emphasis: *"I will pray the Father and He will give you another Counselor (Advocate), to be with you forever, even the Spirit of Truth"* (Jn. 14:16-26). There is thus a distinction made between the Persons of the Godhead, and also an identity. The Father Who is God sent the Son, and the Son Who is God sent the Spirit, Who is Himself God.

In the Commission given by Christ before His Ascension, instructing His Disciples to go into the whole world with His Message, He made specific reference to Baptism as *"in the Name of the Father and of the Son and of the Holy Spirit."* It is significant that the Name is One, but within the bounds of the One Name there are three distinct Persons. In fact, the Trinity as triunity could not be more clearly expressed (Mat. 28:19).

Early Christians knew themselves to be reconciled to God the Father, and that the reconciliation was secured for them by the atoning Work of the Son, and that it was mediated to them as an experience by the Holy Spirit. Thus, the Trinity was to them a fact before it became a Doctrine (New Bible Dictionary).

CREATION

The phrase, *"Created the heaven and the Earth,"* proclaims such being done sometime

in eternity past. Concerning this First Verse in Genesis, Matthew Henry said: *"The First Verse of the Bible gives a surer and better, a more satisfying and useful knowledge of the origin of the universe, than all the Volumes of the Philosophers."* He then went on to say, *"The lively faith of humble Christians understands this matter better than the elevated fancy of the most learned."*

Creation, in its strict sense, carries the meaning of producing something out of nothing. Naturally, that is impossible as it regards man. But it is not impossible with God. In fact, Jesus said, *"With God, all things are possible"* (Mat. 19:26). In fact, God spoke the creation into existence (Heb. 11:3), which we shall see in the following Verses. Why is it so hard for man to believe that?

As stated, Moses did not bother to explain the fact that there is a God. The idea is, creation demands a Creator. Common sense tells us that, but which seems to be in short supply.

(2) "AND THE EARTH WAS WITHOUT FORM, AND VOID; AND DARKNESS WAS UPON THE FACE OF THE DEEP. AND THE SPIRIT OF GOD MOVED UPON THE FACE OF THE WATERS."

The composition is:

1. God did not originally create the Earth without form and void. It became this way after a cataclysmic happening.

2. This cataclysmic happening was the revolt of Lucifer against God, which took place in the dateless past.

3. As a result, darkness was upon the face of the deep.

4. The Moving of the Holy Spirit upon the face of the waters was the beginning of life, done in order to bring the Earth back to a habitable sate.

WITHOUT FORM AND VOID

The phrase, *"And the Earth was without form, and void,"* points to a stupendous convulsion which affected the Earth after it was created by God.

"Without form, and void," in the Hebrew is literally, *"tohu"* and *"bohu,"* which signify, *"wasteness and emptiness."* God did not create the Earth in this fashion. It became that way at a point in time. Many Scholars believe that Lucifer ruled the Earth after it was

originally created, and did so for an undetermined period of time. As well, during that time, he ruled it in Righteousness and Holiness under God. It also seems there was a race of created beings over whom he ruled. Whenever Lucifer led his rebellion against God, one-third of the Angels, plus this race of beings threw in their lot with him. Many think, and it is probably correct, that these particular beings, whatever they might have been, are the demon spirits which presently help Satan.

Some have claimed that demon spirits are fallen angels; however, angels have spirit-bodies, whereas demon spirits have no body whatsoever, and in fact, seek a body to inhabit, whether animal or human.

I think it should be obvious that whatever degree this revolution of Lucifer was, its destructive power was beyond comprehension.

THE MYSTERY OF GOD

Knowing that God is Omnipotent (all-powerful), Omniscient (all-knowing), and Omnipresent (everywhere), and that Lucifer was and is a mere creature, we may wonder as to why the Lord has allowed the Evil One to continue this long. The Scripture refers to this as the *"Mystery of God"* (Rev. 10:7). Why the Lord has allowed this, we are not told; however, we do know that God does all things well, and everything He does is done for a purpose and reason, and is always the right thing to do.

Irrespective of what has happened in the past, and even how it has affected man, this one thing we do know: God has affected Redemption for mankind through the giving of His Son the Lord Jesus Christ, Who at the Cross, by His death, brought about four great judicial results. They are:

1. Calvary affected the acknowledgement in the Person of Christ, the act of the due judgment which the sin-principle required. In other words, Judgment was poured out on Christ instead of on mankind, at least for those who will believe (Jn. 3:16).

2. Calvary made it possible for corrupted self to be placed in Christ, of which Satan is the personal author and representative. As someone has well said, Jesus died on the Cross in order to save man from self as well as from sin (Gal. 2:20-21).

3. Calvary destroyed the organic connection which Satan had brought about between sin and death. While the wages of sin continue to be death, Calvary made it possible for that connection to be assuaged by the Blood of Christ (I Jn. 1:7). In other words, spiritual death as a result of sin, of which all men are guilty, no longer claims its victim, at least as it regards those who have accepted Christ.

4. Calvary made possible the adjudgment of all men to the Redeemer as His Personal possession, that is, those who will believe (I Cor. 6:20).

Thus, by this fourfold achievement, as was carried out at Calvary, the judicial expression of Christ's Work on the Cross extended to the deepest realities of the moral universe. In effect, it anticipated every essential moral issue which the soul need fear in view of its own misgivings concerning destiny. The punishment difficulty with respect to past sin was potentially met. Satan, man's archenemy, was potentially destroyed, the causation between sin and death was potentially broken, and the claim of Christ to the possession of all men was potentially set up.

Thus, Christ's Cross in dealing with the ultimate spiritual realities of the universe was, in effect, the anticipation of the final judgment of all mankind.

In fact, the early triumphs of Christianity were won upon the basis of the conception of Christ's death, as such, a judicial transaction. Actually, this was the heart of Paul's Message (Rom. 6:3-14; 8:1-2, 11; I Cor. 1:17-18, 21, 23; 2:2, 5).

The Mystery of God will be finished at the Second Coming, when Satan will be locked away in the bottomless pit (Rev. 20:1-3). However, the ground was laid for his total defeat, by what Christ did at the Cross, without which, the Evil One would have triumphed. Christ Alone could take the Book from the hand of God the Father, because He Alone was worthy, and He was worthy because of what He did at the Cross (Rev. 5:8-9).

DARKNESS

The phrase, *"And darkness was upon the face of the deep,"* represents the end result of Satanic influence, which is the opposite of light, which latter represents God.

There is what is referred to as the *"gap theory,"* which belongs between Verse 1 and Verse 2. As previously stated, this is the particular time that Lucifer rebelled against God. Actually, the word *"deep"* is from a root signifying, *"to disturb."*

The ruin pictured in this Verse reveals the sinner prior to Regeneration. The remainder of the Chapter describes the renewing power of the Spirit of God introducing light, life, and beauty from out of this ruin. The created energy of the Holy Spirit operates presently in a similar manner in the ruined nature of man. Believers become new creations (II Cor. 5:17) and are created unto good works (Eph. 2:10).

It took the Cross to dispel this *"darkness,"* and because the darkness was more than mere surface. It went all the way to the disturbed deep. In other words, it was total darkness.

The Cross opened up the way to God, making it possible for light to once again shine, of which this Verse is a Type.

THE SPIRIT OF GOD

The phrase, *"And the Spirit of God moved upon the face of the waters,"* presents the beginning of life, i.e., *"re-creation."* Because it is so important, please allow me to say it again:

The Moving of the Holy Spirit is the beginning of life.

We will find that every act of the Godhead carried out on this Earth is done through the Person, Agency, Work, Power, Ministry, and Office of the Holy Spirit. The only exception to that would be the Ministry of Christ in this world, in His First Advent. But even then, the Holy Spirit functioned in every single capacity of His Conception, Birth, Life, Ministry, Death, and Resurrection (Lk. 4:18-19). This corresponds with the statement we have previously made, to use the vernacular, God the Father is the Owner, God the Son is the Architect, and God the Holy Spirit is the Builder. Psalm 33:6 tells us that God made the world by His Spirit. And one might quickly say that by the same mighty Worker the new creation is affected in the soul.

The Holy Spirit works exclusively within the parameters of the Finished Work of

Christ. There is every evidence that in the Mind of God, even before this particular time, God through foreknowledge knew what He would do regarding the creation of man, and He knew that man would fall. But before any of this happened, the creation and the Fall, Redemption's great Plan was already worked out. Peter said:

"Forasmuch as you know that you were not redeemed with corruptible things, as silver and gold . . . but with the Precious Blood of Christ, as of a Lamb without blemish and without spot:

"Who verily was foreordained before the foundation of the world, but was manifest in these last times for you" (I Pet. 1:18-20).

From this moment of re-creation, the Holy Spirit has been in the world. He superintended the giving of the word of a limited reconciliation to the First Family, immediately after the Fall. This is carried out in Genesis, Chapter 4, and is summed up in the sacrifices, which epitomized the coming Christ.

Up unto the time of the Cross, which was about 4,000 years from the time of the Fall, the Holy Spirit was limited in what He could do, and because the terrible sin debt hung over the heads of all of humanity. The blood of bulls and goats could not take away sin, so the debt remained (Heb. 10:4). As a result, when the Saints of God died who lived before the Cross, Satan could still claim them as his captives, which he definitely did; consequently, their souls and spirits went down into Paradise. Because the sin debt was still there, they could not be taken to Heaven when they died (Lk. 16:20-31).

But when Jesus died on the Cross, thereby atoning for all sin, which removed the sin debt, He went down into Paradise, which was in the heart of the Earth, and concerning that visit, Paul said: *"Wherefore He says, when He ascended up on high, He led captivity captive, and gave gifts unto men.*

"Now that He ascended, what is it but that He also descended first into the lower parts of the Earth?" (Eph. 4:8-9).

The term *"He led captivity captive,"* is strange. But it means the following:

As stated, every person in Paradise, which included all the Patriarchs and Prophets of old, were actually held captive there by Satan. He could not put them over into the burning side of the pit, but still they were his captives. But when Jesus paid the price on the Cross, He went down into Paradise, and took those who were captives of Satan, and made them His captives.

Now when Believers die, due to what Jesus did at the Cross, their souls and spirits automatically go to Heaven to be with the Lord (Phil. 1:23).

Concerning how the Holy Spirit works within our hearts and lives as it regards our Sanctification, Paul said: *"For the Law* (a Law devised by the Godhead) *of the Spirit of life* (Holy Spirit) *in Christ Jesus* (this Law is based on what Jesus did at the Cross) *has made me free from the law of sin and death"* (Rom. 8:2).

To sum up, every single thing the Holy Spirit has done in this world, is doing, and shall do, is based entirely on the Cross of Christ. The Cross is what makes everything possible (I Cor. 1:17).

(3) "AND GOD SAID, LET THERE BE LIGHT: AND THERE WAS LIGHT."

The overview is:

1. *"And God said,"* corresponds with Hebrews 11:3.

2. God simply spoke the light into existence.

3. When He spoke the word, instantly, *"there was light."*

THE WORD OF GOD

The phrase, *"And God said,"* presents the manner in which creation or re-creation was carried out. Some ten times this phrase is used, and in the exact manner, with the exception of the last time, where it says, *"And the LORD God said"* (Gen. 2:18).

By the use of the term *"And God said,"* we are given very little information. Probably the phrase, then, is metaphorical, and actually means that God enacted for the universe a law.

However, from these three words, we do learn some things. First of all, we learn from this that God makes no preparation, employs no means, and needs no secondary agency. He speaks, and it is done. His Word alone contains all things necessary for the fulfillment of His Will. God, by speaking, gives to nature a universal and enduring law.

As well, His commands are not temporary, but eternal; and whatever secondary causes were called into existence when God, by a word, created light, those same causes produce it now, and will produce it until God recalls His word. We have, then, here nature's first universal law (Ellicott).

LIGHT

The phrase, *"Let there be light: and there was light,"* presents the first universal law to which we have just alluded.

Are we to understand that this *"light"* now brought into being by God was independent of the sun and the moon, etc.? Calvin and Augustine said that it was; however, I think not! God certainly could have spoken light into existence without the sun, etc.

Nevertheless, I think the light came from the sun, and what we see in Verses 14 through 18 speaks of the regulation of the sun, moon, and stars.

Light travels at the speed of 186,000 miles a second. Incidentally, we are told that the universe is expanding at that particular rate, which means that the Word of God saying, *"Let there be light,"* is still at work.

(4) "AND GOD SAW THE LIGHT, THAT IT WAS GOOD: AND GOD DIVIDED THE LIGHT FROM THE DARKNESS."

The exegesis is:

1. God made a value judgment regarding the light.

2. This *"light"* was designed to do a number of things.

3. He saw that it was good.

4. He then set boundaries for the light and the darkness, for both cannot coexist.

THE LIGHT WAS GOOD

The phrase, *"And God saw the light, that it was good,"* refers to the fact that what it was designed to do it would do.

It was designed not merely for illumination, although that certainly is one of its great purposes, but as well, plants have to have light to survive and grow. So there is a life-giving property of sorts in this light made by God.

LIGHT AND DARKNESS

The phrase, *"And God divided the light from the darkness,"* does not imply that darkness has a separate and independent existence, but that there were now periods of light and darkness.

Taking this particular statement of the dividing of light from darkness into the spiritual sense, we know that light and darkness can never be joined together. As the Scripture says: *"And have no fellowship with the unfruitful works of darkness"* (Eph. 5:11).

In Heaven, there is nothing but perpetual light; while in Hell there is perpetual darkness (Mat. 8:12; Rev. 21:23-25).

This which we are studying is the first day of the week. Likewise, Christ rose from the dead on the first day of the week. It carries the aura of a *"new beginning."*

(5) "AND GOD CALLED THE LIGHT DAY, AND THE DARKNESS HE CALLED NIGHT. AND THE EVENING AND THE MORNING WERE THE FIRST DAY."

The synopsis is:

1. God called the light *"day."*

2. He called the darkness *"night."*

3. By using the phraseology, *"the evening and the morning were the first day,"* we know these were literal, 24-hour days.

DAY

The phrase, *"And God called the light Day,"* is not meant to be a time-measure, but rather a character description. But yet, and as we shall see, at this particular time the word *"day"* is part of a 24-hour period.

NIGHT

The phrase, *"And the darkness He called Night,"* all has to do with the revolution of the Earth. In the manner in which God would make man, the work and rest cycle is figured into this 24-hour revolution of the Earth.

THE FIRST DAY

The phrase, *"And the evening and the morning were the first day,"* seems to me to limit these days to a 24-hour time period. While the word *"day,"* can be used to designate any period of time, and is often used that way, the attaching of the words *"evening"* and *"morning"* seem to nail it down, that in this instance, God is speaking of a literal 24-hour time period.

NOTES

The idea that the word *"day"* as it is used in this Chapter represents some indefinite time period, possibly even thousands of years, is mostly because men doubt the ability of God to bring all of this about in such a short period of time. However long God took to bring the Earth back to a habitable state is really of no consequence. But I think enough Scriptural evidence is given to nail down the 24-hour timeframe. While it's certainly not proper to overstate the case, it's not proper as well to understate it. Understating the case always limits God; while it is virtually impossible to overstate the case as it regards God. He is able to do all things.

(6) "AND GOD SAID, LET THERE BE A FIRMAMENT IN THE MIDST OF THE WATERS, AND LET IT DIVIDE THE WATERS FROM THE WATERS."

The diagram is:

1. *"Firmament"* in the Hebrew means *"expansion."*

2. God divided the waters, making the oceans and the seas on one side, or as one might say, on the bottom, and their clouds with the ability to give rain on the top, with a clear space between.

3. Had not the waters been divided by the atmosphere, human life could not exist.

FIRMAMENT

The phrase, *"And God said, Let there be a firmament in the midst of the waters,"* refers to an expanse between the waters, so to speak, called *"the atmosphere."*

While most probably have never given it much thought, the atmosphere is necessary for the transmission of sound. If there were no atmosphere, the bell could ring, but it could not be heard. The music could play, but it could not be heard. The voices could lift up on high as they sing the anthems of glory, but there would be no sound. So we see that all of this was actually made for man.

DIVIDE THE WATERS

The phrase, *"And let it divide the waters from the waters,"* refers to the fact that before this was done, not only was there water all over the Earth, but as well it seems that water also filled the expanse which we refer to as the atmosphere. The Lord divided these waters, separating the clouds, with some of them filled with water, i.e., *"rain,"* from the waters which covered part of the surface of the Earth.

(7) "AND GOD MADE THE FIRMAMENT, AND DIVIDED THE WATERS WHICH WERE UNDER THE FIRMAMENT FROM THE WATERS WHICH WERE ABOVE THE FIRMAMENT: AND IT WAS SO."

The structure is:

1. God made the expanse between the waters on the Earth and the waters in the clouds.

2. The waters *"under the firmament"* pertain to the oceans, seas, and rivers, etc.

3. The *"waters above the firmament"* pertain to the water that's in the clouds, which comes down as rain upon the Earth.

AND GOD MADE

The phrase, *"And God made the firmament,"* refers to the wide-open expanse above Earth's surface, reaching up to the clouds and beyond, with that marvelous mixture of gases which form atmospheric air, which are necessary for man's existence and activity.

WATERS UNDER AND OVER THE FIRMAMENT

The phrase, *"And divided the waters which were under the firmament from the waters which were above the firmament: and it was so,"* is not contrary to, but in accordance with science.

The creation which God has devised presents the laws by which rain is formed and the Earth watered. This is constantly referred to in the Bible as the chief natural proof of God's wisdom and goodness (Acts 14:17).

Six times the phrase *"and it was so"* is used. It speaks of the resistless energy of the Divine Word. As creation functions accordingly, we should as well function always eager to do the Will of God, so much so in fact that His Word becomes our command.

(8) "AND GOD CALLED THE FIRMAMENT HEAVEN. AND THE EVENING AND THE MORNING WERE THE SECOND DAY."

The composition is:

1. *"Heaven"* as referred to here pertains to the atmosphere around the Earth.

2. God adjusted the firmament on the second day of re-creation.

NOTES

3. The work of the second day is not mentioned as being *"good,"* and because the work of day three had to be carried out before this part was complete.

HEAVEN

The phrase, *"And God called the firmament Heaven,"* is not the same meaning regarding heaven, as in Verse 1.

In Verse 1 *"the heaven"* refers to the entirety of the universe. *"Heaven"* in Verse 8 refers to the atmosphere around the Earth, which goes up about 45 miles from the surface, before it begins to lose its gravitational pull.

THE SECOND DAY

The phrase, *"And the evening and the morning were the second day,"* as well, speaks of a 24-hour timeframe.

(9) "AND GOD SAID, LET THE WATERS UNDER THE HEAVEN BE GATHERED TOGETHER INTO ONE PLACE, AND LET THE DRY LAND APPEAR: AND IT WAS SO."

The construction is:

1. Water had heretofore covered the face of the Earth, but is now gathered into oceans and seas.

2. The dry land, i.e., *"continents,"* now appears.

3. There evidently, at the Word of God, were mighty convulsions on the Earth, which pulled the land mass up, and created a lower mass for the oceans.

OCEANS AND SEAS

The phrase, *"And God said, Let the waters under the heaven be gathered together into one place,"* evidently means that before this, water covered the entirety of the surface of the Earth. God would speak, and the Earth would go into convulsions, which made the mountains and the landmass, which of necessity made the lower mass, where the great oceans and seas were contained.

While the oceans cover a great part of this world, it is evidently only just sufficient to supply the rain necessary for vegetation. Were it less, either the laws of evaporation must be altered, with painful and injurious effects, or much of the Earth's surface would be barren (Ellicott).

In the new Earth to come, the Scripture says, *"There was no more sea."* So, at that time, the evaporation process regarding rain, etc., will have to be changed, which it no doubt will, along with many other things also. In fact, concerning this very thing, the Lord said: *"Behold, I make all things new"* (Rev. 21:5).

CONTINENTS

The phrase, *"And let the dry land appear: and it was so,"* refers to the continents being formed, which, as stated, necessitated great convulsions on the Earth in many and varied forms.

The Psalmist said concerning God: *"Who laid the foundations of the Earth, that it should not be removed forever.*

"You covered it with the deep as with a garment: the waters stood above the mountains.

"At Your rebuke they fled; at the voice of Your thunder they hasted away.

"They go up by the mountains; they go down by the valleys unto the place which You have founded for them.

"You have set a bound that they may not pass over; that they turn not again to cover the Earth" (Ps. 104:5-9).

The Holy Spirit through the Psalmist is referring to this particular work of day three.

(10) "AND GOD CALLED THE DRY LAND EARTH; AND THE GATHERING TOGETHER OF THE WATERS CALLED HE SEAS: AND GOD SAW THAT IT WAS GOOD."

The overview is:

1. God refers to the dry land as *"Earth."*
2. The waters, He calls *"Seas."*
3. God saw that it was good.

EARTH

The phrase, *"And God called the dry land Earth,"* refers to the Supreme Being naming what He had created.

SEAS

The phrase, *"And the gathering together of the waters called He Seas,"* refers to God naming this creation as well, and, incidentally, names which have survived from then until now.

In the Hebrew, Earth is *"shamayim,"* and Seas is *"Yamim."*

IT IS GOOD

The phrase, *"God saw that it was good,"* refers to the finished product, at least at this stage, as being sealed by the Divine approval.

(11) "AND GOD SAID, LET THE EARTH BRING FORTH GRASS, THE HERB YIELDING SEED, AND THE FRUIT TREE YIELDING FRUIT AFTER HIS KIND, WHOSE SEED IS IN ITSELF, UPON THE EARTH: AND IT WAS SO."

The synopsis is:

1. Three types of vegetation are spoken into existence.
2. Grass is brought forth as a carpet.
3. *"The herb"* speaks of vegetables.
4. Various different kinds of fruit trees come forth.
5. *"After his kind"* indicates that the different species of plants are already fixed.

GRASS

The phrase, *"And God said, Let the Earth bring forth grass,"* pertains to the first sprouts of the Earth, tender herbs, in which the seed is so small it's not noticed. It serves as a carpet for the Earth, and at the same time, food for certain animals (Ps. 23:2).

The first creative act of God was the calling of matter into existence, which, by the operation of mechanical and chemical laws, imposed upon it by the Creator, was arranged and digested into a cosmos, that is, an orderly and harmonious whole (Ellicott). These laws are now and ever in perpetual activity, but no secondary or derived agency can either add one atom to the world-mass or diminish aught from it.

The second creative act is the introduction of light, then vegetable, and then animal; and for this nothing less than an Almighty power would suffice (Ellicott).

HERBS

The phrase, *"The herb yielding seed,"* refers to vegetables eaten by man, etc. It is a higher form of plant life than *"grass."*

Nothing here is mentioned about the different types of trees and certain other types of plant life, with the intent seemingly emphasizing that which can be used as food, whether for animals or humans. But one may conclude that the other types of trees, etc., were created at this time as well.

THE FRUIT TREE

The phrase, *"And the fruit tree yielding fruit after his kind, whose seed is in itself, upon the Earth: and it was so,"* presents yet a more advanced creation, one might say.

Expositors say: *"This division is simple and natural. It proceeds from two concurrent marks, the structure and the seed. In the first the green blade is prominent; in the second, the stalk; in the third, the woody texture; in the first (grass) the seed is not conspicuous; in the second it is conspicuous; in the third it is enclosed in a fruit which is conspicuous."*

By the use of the phrase *"after his kind,"* pertains to both vegetables and fruit, indicating that the different species of plants were already fixed. Thus, the modern dogma of the origin of species by development would thus be declared to be unbiblical, as it has not yet been proved to be scientific, and in fact will never be proven in that capacity, simply because a slow development is not actually what happened.

It is God's Word that makes the Earth fruitful. Propagation of fruit, as well as the first being of it, is by God's Word; He makes the seed and enables it to multiply.

(12) "AND THE EARTH BROUGHT FORTH GRASS, AND HERB YIELDING SEED AFTER HIS KIND, AND THE TREE YIELDING FRUIT, WHOSE SEED WAS IN ITSELF, AFTER HIS KIND: AND GOD SAW THAT IT WAS GOOD.

(13) "AND THE EVENING AND THE MORNING WERE THE THIRD DAY."

The composition is:

1. At the Word of God, the Earth brought forth that which God commanded.

2. *"After his kind,"* regards the different species which God ordained.

3. God pronounced it *"good."*

4. The bringing forth of this plant life, which is food for animals and humans, was the work of the third day, a 24-hour period.

AFTER HIS KIND

Verse 12 begins by stating, *"And the Earth brought forth grass, and herb yielding seed*

after his kind, and the tree yielding fruit, whose seed was in itself, after his kind," which proclaims the bringing forth of this foodstuff by the Word of God, and because the atmosphere has been created for its development, brought forth on days one and two.

All of this tells us that the first creation of plant life did not come from seed, but that it came into being through the power of the Word. And continuing with the power of the Word, the seed now has power to grow and reproduce. It is by special Divine power that a kernel, put into soil, comes up in its appointed time, bearing fruit according to its kind. This shows that the creation, according to which every plant is produced after its kind in its proper order, is not a matter of chance, but a preeminent work of Divine providence (Luther).

IT WAS GOOD

Verse 12 further reads, *"And God saw that it was good,"* proclaims not only the fact of creation, but as well the order of creation.

Some have asked the question as to why God would have developed plant life before He brought into being the stars of the heavens, etc.

As we shall see, the heavens, including the stars, along with the sun and the moon, had already been created. This was done *"in the beginning."* On the fourth day, God will regulate them.

God's attention to the Earth is because the Earth is now being re-created for man. He will actually prepare all things for man, even before man is created.

THE THIRD DAY

Verse 13 reads, *"And the evening and the morning were the third day,"* presents the first creation of life, i.e., *"the plants, etc."*

(14) "AND GOD SAID, LET THERE BE LIGHTS IN THE FIRMAMENT OF THE HEAVEN TO DIVIDE THE DAY FROM THE NIGHT, AND LET THEM BE FOR SIGNS, AND FOR SEASONS, AND FOR DAYS, AND YEARS:"

The construction is:

1. God is not creating here the sun, moon, and stars, that having already been done *"in the beginning."*

2. He is here regulating them as to their functions.

3. They will be for signs, seasons, days, and years.

LIGHTS

The phrase, *"And God said, Let there be lights in the firmament in the heaven to divide the day from the night,"* refers to the expanse of the heavens of outer space. In fact, these *"lights,"* i.e., *"sun, moon, and stars,"* had already been created. This was done *"in the beginning,"* whenever that was in the dateless past. The giving forth of these *"lights"* doesn't change. It's the rotation of the Earth which divides the day from the night, but which rotation has to do with the gravitational pull of the planetary bodies.

Some have asked, what is the difference between the *"light"* of Verse 3 and Verse 14? I don't think there is any difference. I think they are one and the same.

The planetary bodies, and especially the sun, are brought back to a serviceable state in Verse 3, and are regulated in Verse 14.

SEASONS

The phrase, *"And let them be for signs, and for seasons, and for days, and years,"* refers in essence to *"time."* The moon by her four quarters, which last each a little more than seven days, measures for us the weeks and the months. The sun, by its apparent path in the sky, measures our seasons and our years, while by its daily rotation through the heavens it measures the days and the hours; and this it does so correctly, never varying, that the Astronauts can depend on it as they make their reentry to Earth from space. Otherwise, they would invite certain death.

It has been well said that the progress of a people in civilization may be estimated by their regard for time — their care in measuring and valuing it. Our time is a loan. It is God's gift to us. We must use it as faithful stewards. And to be sure, we shall have to give an account of its use. *"O Lord, so teach us to number our days, that we may apply our hearts unto wisdom"* (Ps. 90:12).

David said: *"Evening, and morning, and at noon, will I pray, and cry aloud: and He shall hear my voice"* (Ps. 55:17).

NOTES

Concerning this great work of creation, David also said: *"When I consider Your heavens, the work of Your fingers, the moon and the stars, which You have ordained;*

"What is man, that You are mindful of him? And the son of man, that You visit him?" (Ps. 8:3-4).

(15) "AND LET THEM BE FOR LIGHTS IN THE FIRMAMENT OF THE HEAVEN TO GIVE LIGHT UPON THE EARTH: AND IT WAS SO.

(16) "AND GOD MADE TWO GREAT LIGHTS; THE GREATER LIGHT TO RULE THE DAY, AND THE LESSER LIGHT TO RULE THE NIGHT: HE MADE THE STARS ALSO.

(17) "AND GOD SET THEM IN THE FIRMAMENT OF THE HEAVEN TO GIVE LIGHT UPON THE EARTH,

(18) "AND TO RULE OVER THE DAY AND OVER THE NIGHT, AND TO DIVIDE THE LIGHT FROM THE DARKNESS: AND GOD SAW THAT IT WAS GOOD.

(19) "AND THE EVENING AND THE MORNING WERE THE FOURTH DAY."

The overview is:

1. The sun, moon, and stars were to provide light upon the Earth.

2. God brought the sun and the moon, along with the stars, back to a serviceable state.

3. God regulated them to serve a purpose.

4. God saw that it was good.

5. The planetary bodies and their affectation on the Earth were all done on the fourth day.

TO GIVE LIGHT UPON THE EARTH

Verse 15 reads, *"And let them be for lights in the firmament in the heaven to give light upon the Earth: and it was so,"* proclaims the fact that God said it, and His glorious Word contained such power that these planetary bodies will ever carry out their prescribed function.

Though the sun and the planets are so far distant from us, yet this does not interrupt their light and influence. The spiritual lesson we must derive from that is distance cannot hinder us from receiving the benefit of God's care. Though God's influence be in Heaven, His eye beholds the children of men.

So we aren't to allow distance, either in place or condition, to hinder our desires for the good of others.

Verse 16 reads, *"And God made two great lights; the greater light to rule the day, and the lesser light to rule the night: He made the stars also,"* refers to the sun and the moon. In fact, the moon has no light within itself. It is a reflection of the sun, hence much lesser, exactly as the Scripture says.

Modern man scoffs at the idea that God, merely by His Word, could make the sun, plus all the planetary bodies, even the universe. He scoffs as well at God's creation of man, and actually, the entirety of all things as they were created by God. In essence, he denies that there is a God!

The words *"Created"* and *"Made"* should be distinguished when they are read. The difficulties which science, imperfect and limited, finds here have been satisfactorily discussed by able Commentators, and their arguments need not be repeated, except to draw attention to these important and distinctive words *"Created"* and *"Made."*

For example, He *"created"* the sun, moon, and stars at some unknown period of time *"in the beginning,"* and afterwards, when preparing the Earth for man, He *"made,"* i.e., *"pointed them in relation to the Earth (regulated them) as light-holders, as measurers of time, and as vehicles of revelation (Ps. 19)"* (Williams).

GOD

Verse 17 reads, *"And God set them in the firmament of the heaven to give light upon the Earth,"* refers to their function.

GOOD

Verse 18 reads, *"And to rule over the day and over the night, and to divide the light from the darkness: and God saw that it was good,"* proclaims everything now set for animate life.

THE FOURTH DAY

Verse 19 reads, *"And the evening and the morning were the fourth day,"* proclaims the work of re-creation now finished.

The life of man is governed here largely by the order of the material universe. But as he becomes a true Child of God, he rises to a

dominion over the sun, moon, and stars. In fact, the consciousness of fellowship with God is a sense of moral superiority to material things. Man is earthly first, and then heavenly. Human nature is developed under the rule of sun, moon, and stars, but is warped and twisted because of sin. In the world to come, where there shall be no more night, the consciousness of man will then be far more spiritual than material, not unwitting of the material, but ruling it with spiritual freedom and power (Rev., Chpt. 22).

(20) "AND GOD SAID, LET THE WATERS BRING FORTH ABUNDANTLY THE MOVING CREATURE THAT HAS LIFE, AND FOWL THAT MAY FLY ABOVE THE EARTH IN THE OPEN FIRMAMENT OF HEAVEN.

(21) "AND GOD CREATED GREAT WHALES, AND EVERY LIVING CREATURE THAT MOVES, WHICH THE WATERS BROUGHT FORTH ABUNDANTLY, AFTER THEIR KIND, AND EVERY WINGED FOWL AFTER HIS KIND: AND GOD SAW THAT IT WAS GOOD.

(22) "AND GOD BLESSED THEM, SAYING, BE FRUITFUL AND MULTIPLY, AND FILL THE WATERS AND THE SEAS, AND LET FOWL MULTIPLY IN THE EARTH.

(23) "AND THE EVENING AND THE MORNING WERE THE FIFTH DAY."

The overview is:

1. God uses His Word to create animate life.
2. He created all fish and fowls.
3. God saw that it was good.
4. God blessed them.
5. This was the fifth day.

ANIMATE LIFE

Verse 20 reads, *"And God said, Let the waters bring forth abundantly the moving creature that has life, and fowl that may fly above the Earth in the open firmament of Heaven,"* proclaims the creation of fish and birds.

Expositors say, *"Here the creatures of the sea are distinguished from all previous creations, and in particular from vegetation, as being possessed of a vital principle. This does not, of course, contradict the well-known Truth that plants are living organisms. Only the life principle of the animal kingdom is different from that of the vegetable kingdom."*

The way Verse 20 is translated leaves the impression that the fish and the fowl were made from the waters; however, Genesis 2:19 refutes that. The idea is, the *"waters"* (seas, rivers, lakes, oceans) swarmed with every kind of fish. Exactly how God created the fish, for instance, we aren't told. It was probably done by Divine command. As it regards the *"fowl of the air,"* Genesis 2:19 says that the Lord formed these *"out of the ground."*

AFTER HIS KIND

Verse 21 reads, *"And God created great whales, and every living creature that moves, which the waters brought forth abundantly, after their kind, and every winged fowl after his kind: and God saw that it was good,"* emphasizes by the use of the phrases, *"after their kind,"* or *"after his kind,"* the different species which are created.

Some ten times in the First Chapter of Genesis, the phrase *"after his kind,"* or similar is used. This completely shoots down the theory of evolution. Science has never been able to cross that barrier, and in fact, will never be able. In other words, there is no such thing as an animal that is half fish and half land animal. As well, there is no such thing as a fish that is half whale and half shark. The barrier regarding the different *"kinds,"* remains and ever shall remain.

The same can be said for man. There is no such thing as a creature which is half man and half animal. And to be sure, if evolution was a true science, there would be some evidence of such in the world. False science answers that by claiming that the evolutionary process takes many millions or even billions of years; however, even if that were true, which it's not, there would still be some creatures in the world which are part animal and part man. In fact, there would be mutations of every kind. If the rabbit did actually evolve from the frog, or whatever, there would be scores of creatures at different stages. But that doesn't exist, and in fact has never existed, and because the iron barrier of *"after his kind"* as originally created by God, cannot be changed. While man can produce a mule by the crossbreeding of a horse and a donkey, the mule is then sterile and cannot reproduce itself.

NOTES

Actually, the evolutionary process fails in every capacity. Plants, for instance, do not get better and better, but rather tend to degenerate if left on their own, which is the opposite of the so-called evolutionary process. To make plants better, or fruit trees bear more luscious fruit, man has to work with these plants or trees, in order to bring out their best.

It is the same with horses. If the breed is left unattended, it will degenerate. So man has to work with horses in the realm of breeding, to perfect thoroughbreds, etc.

There are at least two processes which debunk evolution:

1. The first is the iron barrier of the species, which cannot be crossed.

2. The second problem is degeneration, even as we have already addressed.

EVOLUTION

Can a person be a Christian and also believe in evolution?

No they cannot. To believe in evolution is to disbelieve the Bible, and to disbelieve the Bible is to disbelieve God.

Some so-called Christians attempt to cover this by claiming that they believe in creation, and that God is the One Who has created all things, but that He did it by evolution.

Once again, this flies in the face of the Word of God.

Not only is evolution unbiblical, but at the same time, it is unscientific.

I read just the other day of the death of a particular man in England, who exposed the Piltdown hoax. This was a skeleton found in a certain part of England, which was supposed to prove the evolutionary process. He found that the skeleton had been doctored with plaster of Paris, or whatever, to make it seem to be something it wasn't. He exposed the fraud, which meant that many school books had to be rewritten.

If the evolutionary conception is true, it naturally follows that the Biblical account cannot be accepted in its literal interpretation. For one of these accounts pictures the different species and general types as coming into existence gradually out of preexisting ones, whereas the other represents them as created by a Divine fiat.

All efforts to harmonize Genesis with evolution lead at best to the negative conclusion that these two are so far different in their purpose and scope as not to involve radical contradiction. A positive agreement between them simply cannot be claimed.

So true is it that the general theories of evolution are not proving true in either the biological or geological field, that one scientific observer has aptly remarked that the present vogue of these theories in the popular and pseudo-scientific mind may be likened to the continued, though dwindling, activities of a central commercial *"trust,"* whose supporting subsidiary companies had all gone into bankruptcy. Furthermore, it is highly significant that many who at first were fascinated by the generalizations of evolution turned from it, after further examination of its proffered evidences and more mature consideration of its claims.

The truth is, evolution is not a fact of science, but a dogma of philosophy. Both its history and its essential nature prove that it belongs primarily to the realm of subjective speculation and not to the field of objective fact.

UNCHRISTIAN

It is significant that the idea of evolution originated in heathen and pagan minds and was not a native product of the Christian intellect, which means that it's not Biblical.

The general run of modern definitions of evolution is also not only completely independent of any thought of a Living God, but for the most part is either directly antagonistic to that thought or irreconcilable with it. In fact, the standard definitions of evolution, which are given by real evolutionists, are, therefore, consistently, and completely in line with anti-God theories. Actually, as it regards evolution, that is if one takes it to its final conclusion, there is no God, and no need for God. In fact, all definitions of evolution, of necessity have to substitute blind force and mere chance for the creative power of a Living God. Those who try to reconcile these theories with the Christian system of truth assert that such is not the case, yet the definitions given, and many others that might be given, prove that God is of necessity ruled

NOTES

out, and that in favor of chance. Evolution must be seen to be diametrically opposed to the Christian system of thought at all essential points.

Some claim that an all-powerful God could have made the world and created man and woman by evolutionary process if He had so desired and willed; but the Bible Revelation tells us that He did not so make the world, man, and woman, and that we may stand upon that Revelation with full assurance. In the words of Professor Mullins, Professor Machen, and Dr. Conrad, evolution leads to a type of religion that is radically different from Christianity, and as well, diametrically opposed to real Christianity.

A final and conclusive consideration in this whole problem of alleged evolution is that there is evidence on all sides, going to prove that the whole world and all that is in it is running down, degenerating, and moving toward some climax of judgment and re-creation, even as the Bible says, instead of ever evolving upward into higher and better forms.

CHEMISTRY

It is most significant that in the science of chemistry, through which we come closest to the deeper facts and forces of both inanimate matter and life, there is no evidence of any resident *"urge"* upward. Not only is it true that the laws of chemical affinity seem to be static and unchangeable as to their operations, but it is now known that there is a disintegrating tendency downward instead of upward that seems characteristic of all matter. In other words, there is a degeneration, even as previously stated.

It is not true that we came up from the slime and the beast through the jungle, and that we pass out into a night of oblivion unlighted by a single star. It is true that *"in the beginning God created the heavens and the Earth"* and that He made *"man in His Own Image."* It is true that we came from God through the Garden, and that we are destined by obedience to Him to an eternity of joy in a land that is *"fairer than day,"* where we will meet again our loved ones who went before, and upon whose blissful shore there falls no shadow and rests no stain.

Again we irrevocably state that a person cannot claim Biblical Christianity and at the same time believe in paganistic evolution. And there is no other type of evolution but that which is paganistic.

(The author is grateful to John Roach Straton for most of the material given above regarding evolution.)

THE BLESSING OF GOD

Verse 22 reads, *"And God blessed them, saying, Be fruitful, and multiply, and fill the waters in the seas, and let fowl multiply in the Earth,"* presents God doing something different. He blesses His creation of fish and fowls.

It may be asked why God did not bless the plant life. Of them Moses simply says that God saw that it was good, but He did not bless them. But here, God begins a new way of propagation, namely, that from living bodies come forth other similar living bodies, which is not true of trees and plants. The pear tree, for example, does not bring forth another pear tree, but only a pear, while a bird produces a bird and a fish a fish. Here, then, is a new creative work, for a living body propagates others out of itself. This indeed is a very marvelous propagation, and there is a marvelous fertility in both the fish and the fowl, especially in the creatures living in the sea.

As humans, when we bless, we can do little more than wish something or someone good, but the Blessing of God means propagation. His Blessing is just as powerful to propagate as His curse is to cut off (Luther).

THE FIFTH DAY

Verse 23 reads, *"And the evening and the morning were the fifth day,"* proclaims the creation of sea life and bird life.

(24) "AND GOD SAID, LET THE EARTH BRING FORTH THE LIVING CREATURE AFTER HIS KIND, CATTLE, AND CREEPING THING, AND BEAST OF THE EARTH AFTER HIS KIND: AND IT WAS SO.

(25) "AND GOD MADE THE BEAST OF THE EARTH AFTER HIS KIND, AND CATTLE AFTER THEIR KIND, AND EVERYTHING THAT CREEPETH UPON THE EARTH AFTER HIS KIND: AND GOD SAW THAT IT WAS GOOD."

The exegesis is:

1. By Divine fiat, God created the animal kingdom.

2. They were originally created out of dust, i.e., *"earth."*

3. All were created *"after their kind,"* which refers to their species, a barrier which has never been bridged.

4. God saw that it was good.

THE CREATION OF ANIMALS

Verse 24 reads, *"And God said, Let the Earth bring forth the living creature after his kind, cattle, and creeping thing, and beast of the Earth after his kind: and it was so,"* proclaims the fact that God leaves nothing empty that He has made, but furnishes all with His store and riches. Thus, when He had created the heavens, He furnished them with stars, the air with birds, the water with fish, and the Earth with herbs, and plants, and now with beasts and men. So the Earth is full of His riches, and so is the wide sea.

Understanding that, we should realize that God likewise will not leave His children empty, the vessels which he has formed for Himself. He desires to fill us with Himself!

Inasmuch as God has created the animal world, we should regard it with appreciation. If we imagine that a tree has as much claim to our attention and regard as a horse, this should not be the case. The latter has a spirit; it possesses animate life. It is a more nobler embodiment of Divine power.

Even though it is Biblically proper for certain animals to be used as food, and as well, for the skin of certain animals to be used for clothing, etc., still, man must show kindness toward the animal kingdom. Men should never manifest an angry spirit toward them. The brute world was designed by God for the use of man, and it renders its high service in the gift of its life for the sustentation of the human family. And the merciful man will be merciful to his beast.

IT IS GOOD

Verse 25 reads, *"And God made the beast of the Earth after his kind, and cattle after their kind, and everything that creeps upon the Earth after his kind: and God saw that it was good,"* tells us unequivocally that God designed each species of the animal kingdom, in such a way that it cannot be crossed.

The difference between the creation of beasts and man cannot be passed over without special observation. Man's body was indeed taken out of the Earth, as well as the bodies of the beast; but his soul was not from the Earth, but from Heaven. But in the creation of beasts, the body, and soul, or life, is wholly out of the Earth; for the Earth is commanded to bring forth the living creatures — that is, the creature, with the life thereof. So that we find no origination of the soul, or life of the beast, but from the Earth only.

As well, there is every evidence that before the Fall, or at least as God originally created the animal kingdom, all were plant eaters, which means that none were carnivorous. The Fall seemed to change some of the animals drastically so, one might say, turning them into killing machines. More than likely, at the Fall, the entirety of the animal kingdom was changed some way, and all in a negative sense. Not knowing or seeing the animal kingdom before that time, we really have little knowledge as to what they must have been like, except a hint here and there given us in the Word of God.

For instance, it is believed that the serpent, before the Fall, had the power of limited speech, and could even reason somewhat. We do know this, when the Bible gives the account of him speaking to Eve in the Garden of Eden, which was actually at the time of the Fall, and with Satan using the body of the serpent, Eve didn't seem surprised that the animal could speak (Gen. 3:1-2). And if this reptile could speak, is it possible that other animals had such limited power as well?

Also, we find in the Book of Isaiah, as the Prophet records the coming Kingdom Age, that the animal kingdom will revert back to its spirit and form before the Fall. We find they all once again become plant eaters, and that all are now docile (Isa. 11:6-8).

When the latter part of Verse 25 speaks of the creation of the animal kingdom, and that *"God saw that it was good,"* to be sure, the creation at that dawn of time was completely different than what we see presently. The Fall affected the animal kingdom terribly so, even though they had no conscious part in

this debacle, unless such blame is to be placed on the serpent.

Paul said: *"For the creature was made subject to vanity* (the Fall), *not willingly* (it was not of their doing) . . . *For we know that the whole creation groans and travails in pain together until now"* (Rom. 8:20, 22).

And the Apostle said: *"Because the creature itself also shall be delivered from the bondage of corruption into the glorious liberty of the Children of God"* (Rom. 8:21).

(26) "AND GOD SAID, LET US MAKE MAN IN OUR IMAGE, AFTER OUR LIKENESS: AND LET THEM HAVE DOMINION OVER THE FISH OF THE SEA, AND OVER THE FOWL OF THE AIR, AND OVER THE CATTLE, AND OVER ALL THE EARTH, AND OVER EVERY CREEPING THING THAT CREEPS UPON THE EARTH."

The diagram is:

1. The creation of man was preceded by a Divine consultation.

2. The pronouns *"us"* and *"our"* proclaim the consultation held by the Three Persons of the Divine Trinity, Who were one in the creative work.

3. Man is created in the Image of God.

4. He is created in the likeness of God.

5. He was given dominion over all the Earth, and over all that was in the Earth.

DIVINE CONSULTATION

The phrase, *"And God said,"* presents the eighth of the ten times this phrase is used in Chapters 1 and 2. (Nine times in Chapter 1 and one time in Chapter 2.) These last three times have to do with man exclusively.

THE CREATION OF MAN

The phrase, *"Let Us make man,"* proclaims, I think I can say without fear of contradiction, the greatest creative act of God. Actually, the very name *"Adam,"* at least from the Arabic root, signifies *"the brilliant one."* Due to the fact that man was created in the Image of God and in His Likeness tells us that man was originally created greater than the Angels.

David said: *"When I consider Your heavens, the work of Your fingers, the moon and the stars, which You have ordained;*

"What is man, that You are mindful of him? And the son of man, that You visit him?

"For You have made him a little lower than the Angels, and have crowned him with glory and honor.

"You made him to have dominion over the works of Your hands: You have put all things under his feet" (Ps. 8:3-6).

As the Holy Spirit asked the question through David concerning man, both the question and the answer concern Christ. In other words, it's speaking of the Incarnation of Christ.

But yet, due to the fact that Christ is *"the Man,"* it answers for man in general also.

The Fifth Verse of this Eighth Psalm was translated, *"For You have made him a little lower than the Angels. . . ."* It should have been translated, *"You have made him a little lower than God."* The Hebrew word translated *"Angels"* is *"Elohim,"* and means *"God."*

As well, God gave man a form of creative powers. While he is not able to create out of nothing as God can do, still, he is able to take that which God has already made and fashion it into many and varied things. In this, he is given a sense of autonomy and independence, which Angels do not seem to have. Therefore, being made or created a little lower than God (Elohim), he is greater than the Angels, etc.

As well, the pronoun *"Us"* proclaims the Trinity, even as the word *"God,"* i.e., *"Elohim."*

Regarding the creation of man, a Divine Counsel is called, which consisted of the Three Persons of the Trinity, God the Father, God the Son, and God the Holy Spirit. Man, when he was made, was to be dedicated to the Father, the Son, and the Holy Spirit. In fact, it is into that great Name that we are baptized, for to that great Name we owe our being.

Matthew Henry says: *"The Three Persons of the sacred Trinity at first concurred in counsel and operation in forming man, as afterwards in his recovery from the Fall."*

A GREAT DIFFERENCE

All of this indicates that there is a great difference between man and all other creatures. Man has much in common with the animals, which live with him, eat the same food, and sleep and rest as he does. But here Moses shows that man is a creature that excels all animals.

And then going to the other end of the spectrum, the Scripture tells us that man will judge Angels (I Cor. 6:3).

NOTES

Of all the things that God has created, as far as we know, man is His last creation. This was done on the sixth day of the bringing of the Earth back to a habitable state.

Day one: God dispelled the darkness with light.

Day two: God brought about the firmament, which separated the water, by putting some on Earth and some in the clouds, and creating an expanse between the two.

Day three: God made the Seas and continents of dry land, and plant life was restored.

Day four: God regulated the sun, moon, and stars.

Day five: Sea life and bird life were brought forth.

Day six: Animal life was created, and then man was created.

Day seven: God rested on this day, signifying the rest that we have in Christ.

It is true that man's body was formed out of the dust, and thus, it is the same as the forms of the mineral, vegetable, and animal creations. In fact, as Oken says, the whole animal world is repeated and represented in man. One might even say that the animal kingdom is man broken up into fragments.

But human nature is not, therefore, to be despised; for though the human body takes all nature into it, it does so to make it a temple for the worship and service of God. And that God designed such a view of the human frame is evident from the fact of the Incarnation. Jesus entered the human body and purified it for His indwelling, making it, in a sense, a palace for the Divine glory and a shrine for the Divine worship.

Concerning the human body, Paul said: *"Know you not that you are the temple of God, and that the Spirit of God dwells in you?*

"If any man defile the temple of God, him shall God destroy; for the temple of God (human body) *is holy, which temple you are"* (I Cor. 3:16-17).

In fact, Jesus was the first one to refer to the human body as a temple of God. He said: *"Destroy this temple, and in three days I will raise it up"* (Jn. 2:19-21).

While it is admitted that the human body is the weakest link in the makeup of man regarding spirit, soul, and body; still, the Holy Spirit through Paul told us to, *"Present your bodies a living sacrifice, holy, acceptable unto God, which is your reasonable service"* (Rom. 12:1).

Paul also said that we are, *"Waiting for the adoption, to wit, the Redemption of our body,"* which refers to the coming Resurrection, when the human body will then be glorified (Rom. 8:23).

The human body is the weakest link, at least at the present, simply because it has been greatly weakened by the Fall. Where man before the Fall was intended to be guided by his spirit, which was in constant communion with God, due to the Fall, he is now guided by the senses (five senses). Due to human nature being corrupted through the Fall, every bent of the senses is toward sin. In fact, the sin nature controls unredeemed man.

(The sin nature is human nature corrupted.)

Upon coming to Christ, everything changes, with the person becoming a new creation (II Cor. 5:17). The spirit of man is once again in contact with the Spirit of God. In fact, the Holy Spirit literally comes into the human body and mind, making it His temple, as we've already stated (I Cor. 3:16). But yet the sin nature remains in the Believer, even as Paul explains in Romans, Chapter 6. Due to being Born-Again, we are dead to the sin nature, but it doesn't say that the sin nature itself is dead. In fact, it is very much alive. And due to the fact that it is very much alive, this is where the problem commences.

THE CROSS

If the Believer doesn't understand God's prescribed order of victory, in other words, how to live this Christian life, he will try to do it the wrong way, even as Romans, Chapter 7 outlines, which guarantees failure, and the ascendancy of the sin nature once again. In fact, this is the great struggle of the Christian.

There is only one way that the Believer can maintain ascendancy over the sin nature, in other words, the Divine Nature ruling rather than the sin nature (II Pet. 1:4). If the Believer doesn't function God's Way, his situation will be, *"O wretched man that I am! Who shall deliver me from the body of this death?"* (Rom. 7:24).

In fact, Romans, Chapter 7 is the example of the Believer attempting to live for God,

but trying to do so in the wrong way. It is Paul's own personal experience.

After Paul was saved and Baptized with the Holy Spirit, and even called to be an Apostle, which means at this time he was an Apostle, not knowing the victory of the Cross, he set out to live for God in the only way he knew. That way was the effort of trying to live for God by his own strength and ability, which he came to refer to as *"the flesh."*

In his defense, there was no one else in the world at that time who knew of the victory of the Cross, for the explanation of the New Covenant had not yet been given. In fact it was given to Paul. Actually, the explanation of the Cross is the explanation of the New Covenant. To simplify the issue, one need only look at the emblems of the Lord's Supper (I Cor. 11:24-25).

So if the great Paul couldn't live this life by his own strength, how do you think you can?

GOD'S PRESCRIBED ORDER OF VICTORY

The Lord has devised a means and a way for the Believer to live a holy, pure, Godly life, meaning that sin will not have dominion over him (Rom. 6:14). It is, as stated, the victory of the Cross, which refers to what Jesus did there.

Some have said that all Revelation is preceded by desperation. Perhaps that is true. I know it was with Paul, and I know it was with me as well!

The Lord gave to the Apostle this prescribed order, which he gave to us in Romans, Chapter 6. Someone has well said that Romans, Chapter 6 is the mechanics of the Holy Spirit, which tells us how He works.

The Apostle explained to us that at the time of conversion, we are literally *"baptized into the death of Christ."* Now of course we were not there when Jesus was crucified; however, when the believing sinner evidences Faith in Christ, in the Mind of God, Jesus Christ becomes our Substitute in all things. When He died, we died with Him, literally baptized into His death (Rom. 6:3). This is all done by faith on our part. In other words, when the sinner expresses Faith in Christ, we are placed by God into the death of Christ.

Now please understand, when Paul said that we are *"baptized into His death,"* he was not speaking of Water Baptism, as many think. He was speaking of the Crucifixion of Christ. But it didn't stop there; it continues. . . .

Paul then said, *"Therefore we are buried with Him by baptism into death,"* meaning that when Jesus was put in the tomb, in the Mind of God we were placed in that tomb with Him. This means that all the *"old man"* is not only *"crucified with Him, that the body of sin might be destroyed,"* but buried with Him, meaning that the old you is gone forever (Rom. 6:4, 6).

But it doesn't stop there; when Christ was raised from the dead by the glory of the Father, we were raised with Him that *"we also should walk in newness of life"* (Rom. 6:4-5).

This which I've just explained to you is the bedrock of the Christian Faith. It is what Christ did for us at the Cross, and is the very reason that Paul also said: *"But God forbid that I should glory, save in the Cross of our Lord Jesus Christ, by Whom the world is crucified unto me, and I unto the world"* (Gal. 6:14).

The Believer is to ever understand that everything he receives from God comes to him exclusively by and through the Cross of Christ. While everything that Christ did is of utmost significance, still, it is what He did at the Cross that redeemed us. In other words, we live *"in the likeness of His Resurrection,"* only as we understand that *"we have been planted together* (Christ and ourselves) *in the likeness of His death"* (Rom. 6:5).

THE OBJECT OF OUR FAITH

The idea is, the Cross of Christ must ever be the object of our Faith. This is so very, very important! While everything that God has and does is of necessity of vast significance; still, it is what He did at the Cross for us, by the giving of His only Son, which *"delivered us from this present evil world"* (Jn. 3:16; Gal. 1:4).

In fact, the Holy Spirit works exclusively within the parameters of the Finished Work of Christ. Paul tells us that in Romans 8:2. He said:

NOTES

"For the Law (a Law made by the Godhead) *of the Spirit of life* (Holy Spirit) *in Christ Jesus* (what Jesus did at the Cross) *has made me free from the law of sin and death."*

The words *"in Christ Jesus,"* tell us how the Spirit of God works within our lives. In other words, all that He does for us, to us, in us, and of us, is done totally and completely within the parameters of the Sacrifice of Christ, which gives Him the legal right to do these great things. In fact, there's only one Law in this world that is greater than *"the law of sin and death,"* and that is *"the Law of the Spirit of Life in Christ Jesus."* In fact, Paul uses this term *"in Christ Jesus,"* or one of its derivatives such as, *"in Him,"* etc., 170 times in his 14 Epistles. More than any other short phrase, the words *"in Christ Jesus,"* define the Christian Faith.

FAITH

For the Holy Spirit to work within our lives, and to do so on a constant basis, which alone guarantees us victory, for He is the only One Who can help us to live this life as we should, we must evidence Faith in Christ and what Christ did at the Cross. Paul said:

"Likewise reckon you also yourselves to be dead indeed unto sin (dead unto the sin nature), *but alive unto God through Jesus Christ our Lord* (what He did for us at the Cross)"* (Rom. 6:11).

We are to reckon ourselves, according to what Jesus did at the Cross, understanding that He did it all for us, and for us exclusively, and that when He died, we died with Him, were buried with Him, and were raised with Him in newness of life (Rom. 6:3-5).

When this is done, we have the promise that *"sin shall not have dominion over us: for we are not under the Law* (that having been satisfied by Christ at the Cross), *but under Grace"* (Rom. 6:14; Col. 2:14-15).

THE METHOD

Perhaps the following, which abbreviates all that I have just said, will be of some help. To live a holy life, this is what the Christian must do, and continue to do:

1. Focus: Our focus must always be on the Cross of Christ, understanding that it is through the Cross that all things come to us from God.

2. The Object of our Faith: Our Faith must ever rest in the Finished Work of Christ. We must understand that what He did was done entirely for us and not at all for Himself.

3. Power Source: Once our focus is on the Cross and remains on the Cross, with the object of our Faith always being the Finished Work of Christ, then the Power Source becomes the Holy Spirit.

4. Results: Victory! (Rom. 6:3-5; 8:1-2, 11; 6:14).

Instead, let me use the same abbreviated formula to show you what happens when the Believer tries to live for God in all the wrong ways:

1. Focus: Works.

2. Object of Faith: Our performance.

3. Power Source: Self.

4. Results: Failure!

Your body is a temple of the Holy Spirit. It can only be kept as such by you functioning in the manner that God intends, which in its simple form refers to what Jesus did at the Cross, all on your behalf, and your Faith in that Finished Work.

THE KEY

Faith is the key to the great treasure house of God. With that statement, most every Christian would agree; however, beyond that simple statement, most have very little understanding. In other words, most Christians don't have the foggiest clue how to put Faith to work.

I suppose that if most Christians had to give a definition of what we're talking about here, their mind would go to various Scriptures, thinking that quoting them by rote would somehow generate Faith, etc.

While quoting the Word of God is always good, that within itself, at least as we have stated it, will never build Faith. While faith definitely comes by hearing, and hearing by the Word of God (Rom. 10:17), we must know what that means, for it to be effective within our lives.

To make it brief, we must understand that the Word of God is actually the story of man's Redemption. This Redemption was carried out by the Lord Jesus Christ, and what He did at the Cross. That's why Paul said, *"We preach Christ Crucified"* (I Cor. 1:23).

NOTES

In the Gospel according to John, we are told:

1. *"In the beginning was the Word, and the Word was with God, and the Word was God"* (Jn. 1:1). This tells us that Jesus is the Living Word.

2. John said: *"And the Word was made flesh, and dwelt among us"* (Jn. 1:14). This speaks of the Incarnation, and then we are told what the Incarnation was all about.

The Apostle then said, as he introduced Christ: *"Behold the Lamb of God, which takes away the sin of the world"* (Jn. 1:29).

In abbreviated form, we have here the total picture of the Word of God. We are introduced to Christ Who is the Living Word. We are then told that this Word was made flesh. We are then told what it was all about, which was the Cross.

So our Faith must be anchored in Christ. But for it to be properly anchored in Christ, we must understand that it is *"Christ Crucified."* We must never separate Christ from His Finished Work, or the Finished Work from Christ. While of course we know that Jesus is no longer on the Cross. In fact, He is presently in Heaven, seated by the Right Hand of the Father (Eph. 2:6; Heb. 1:3). What we are actually talking about are the results of the Cross.

The total meaning of the Crucifixion is something which happened in the past, and was done so well that it will never have to be repeated, and has continued results, and in fact, results which will never be discontinued. It's those results of which we speak.

It's like the Constitution of the United States. We don't go back and rewrite the Constitution constantly, but we do constantly enjoy its benefits.

It is the same with the Cross! It does not have to be repeated, and because what Jesus did there will eternally suffice. That's the reason that Paul referred to it as *"The Everlasting Covenant"* (Heb. 13:20).

So when we speak of Faith, we must always understand that Christ and His Cross must ever be the object of our Faith. If it's not Faith in Christ and what He did for us at the Cross, then it's faith that God will not recognize.

In this manner, and this manner alone, and I speak of functioning according to God's prescribed order of victory, which is the

Cross, can the Believer live a victorious, overcoming, Christian life. In this manner alone can the human body be a proper temple, overcoming every power of darkness (Eph. 2:13-18; Col. 2:14-15).

That's the reason that we must never allow anything else, no matter how holy it might be in its own right, to come between us and our Faith in the Cross. Concerning this, Paul said: *"For Christ sent me not to baptize, but to preach the Gospel: not with wisdom of words, lest the Cross of Christ should be made of none effect"* (I Cor. 1:17).

Was Paul denigrating Water Baptism? No! He was merely stating that we must not allow anything to be preeminent, in other words, to take the place of the Cross. If we do this, the Apostle then says:

FALLEN FROM GRACE

"Christ shall profit you nothing" (Gal. 5:2).

We must remember that Paul is speaking to Believers. He plainly tells us in this Fifth Chapter of Galatians that if we place other things ahead of the Cross, claiming those other things as the way to victory, that *"Christ is become of no effect unto you"* (Gal. 5:4).

And that's the terrible problem which fixes itself to most Christians. They are trusting in things other than the Cross, making Christ of no effect. This guarantees spiritual failure. In fact, when the Believer does this, they *"fall from Grace."* In other words, the goodness of God, which in effect is the Grace of God, can no longer be extended to such a Christian. The end result of such a position is bleak indeed!

But if the Christian doesn't understand the Cross, which means that he is placing his faith in other things, the Grace of God simply cannot come to him. In other words, as Paul also said, such a position *"frustrates the Grace of God"* (Gal. 2:21). And the sadness is, most Christians know almost nothing about the Cross. Actually, almost all Christians think they do, but the truth is, they don't! As a result, they are trying to live this life in all the wrong ways, which frustrates the Grace of God, which guarantees failure.

This is what I was talking about when I mentioned that the focus of such Christians

is on works, with the object of faith being their performance, which means the power source is self, which guarantees defeat.

Total and complete trust in Christ and what Christ has done for us at the Cross guarantees a continued flow of the Grace of God, which guarantees victory. There is no other way, as there doesn't need to be any other way.

IMAGE AND LIKENESS

The phrase, *"In Our Image, after Our Likeness,"* refers to true Righteousness and Holiness.

Ephesians 4:24 says: *"And that you put on the new man, which after God is created in Righteousness and true Holiness."*

The Expositors say that the precise relationship in which the nature of the *"Adam"* about to be created should stand to *"Elohim"* was to be that of a *"tselem,"* which means, *"shadow."* It denotes the shadow outline of a figure.

The *"Image"* and *"Likeness"* also enable us to have fellowship with God. But it does not mean we are gods or can become gods. We were created dependant beings (Ps. 8:5), and even in the new heavens and the new Earth we shall continue to be dependent on the light and energy that God provides through Christ as we both serve God and reign with Christ (Rev. 21:23; 22:3-5) (Horton).

Man created in the *"Image"* and *"Likeness"* of God makes him totally different than the animal creation, and in fact, light years ahead of that creation, and in every capacity. The Bible nowhere links man with animals. In fact, man is not an animal. He is a human being, created, as stated, in the Image and Likeness of God. This is not said about any of God's other creations. In fact, we blaspheme when we put man in the category of animals, because in so doing, we have placed God in the same category.

EXACTLY HOW IS MAN IN THE IMAGE AND LIKENESS OF GOD?

Man created in the *"Image"* and *"Likeness"* of God pertains to the spiritual, and not the physical. In fact, the human body is but a tent or a tabernacle which houses the soul and the spirit, which are indestructible and eternal. While the human body is to be looked at as a temple, even as we've already explained, it is the least of man's triune makeup of spirit, soul, and body (I Thess. 5:23).

This *"Image"* and *"Likeness"* of God in man, and created that way, pertain to man's ability to reason, to love, and to serve. These amazing faculties were meant to function entirely in the realm of service to our Creator. In this Image and Likeness, man is given an amazing degree of latitude. He was created as a free moral agent. But the Fall ruined all of this. Man died spiritually, and as such, he lost at the Fall the Image and Likeness of God.

We must understand that at the Fall, man was not merely wounded in a spiritual sense, or even wounded severely. Spiritually, he died. And we must not forget that dead is dead. This means that man has nothing left in him that pertains to God. He has fallen all the way from total God-consciousness down to the far lower level of total self-consciousness. As a result, he has little regard for others, only that for himself.

Some Preachers misunderstand what seems to be morality evidenced in the lives of unbelievers. But let all know and understand, any and all morality shown in the doings of unbelievers is strictly from the influence of Biblical Christianity. If one looks at the nations of the world which have had little teaching regarding Biblical Christianity, one will find that interest is shown in others, only as it benefits self-interest.

For the spiritual connection of man to once again be reestablished with God, man must be *"born again."* Jesus said: *"Except a man be born again, he cannot see the Kingdom of God"* (Jn. 3:3). And for this great work to be carried out in man, a tremendous plan had to be put into effect, in fact, a plan that originated even before the foundation of the world (I Pet. 1:18-20).

God would have to become man, which He did, and literally die on a Cross, in order for the terrible problem of sin to be properly addressed. When Jesus died on the Cross, He addressed every single thing that man lost in the Fall. Admittedly, at the present we only have the *"firstfruits"* of that which Jesus did, with the balance coming at the Resurrection; however, we must never forget that it took the Cross to address the situation. And only

through Faith in Christ and what He did at the Cross, all on our behalf, can we regain what was lost — the Image and Likeness of God.

DOMINION

The phrase, *"And let them have dominion over the fish of the sea, and over the fowl of the air, and over the cattle, and over all the Earth, and over every creeping thing that creepeth upon the Earth,"* proclaims two things:

1. This dominion was given by God to man.

2. The relationship of man to the rest of creation is now defined to be one of rule and supremacy. The sphere of his lordship is from the lowest to the highest, of the subjects placed beneath his sway.

Incidentally, the word *"man"* in this Verse actually means *"mankind"*; hence, the word *"them."*

This dominion which God gave unto man was meant to be carried on in a responsible way; however, the Fall, while not taking away this dominion, did cause man to warp and twist that which God intended.

Once again, even in this enlightened age, when you go to the nations of the world which little know God, you find a rape of the land and the resources, and irrespective of what kind, to be appalling!

DOMINION AND SELF

When we carry the word *"dominion"* to its full length, it should be understood that it is dominion under God; however, man as a free moral agent could do with this dominion what he liked. The Fall resulted in Satan gaining a dominion over man, which means that man has lost the greater part of this dominion. Satan is now *"the god of this world* (who) *has blinded the minds of them which believe not, lest the light of the Glorious Gospel of Christ, Who is the Image of God, should shine unto them"* (II Cor. 4:4).

At the Fall, man lost dominion over *"self,"* which means that he is no longer ruled by God, but rather by his own passions, and passions, we might quickly say, that are evil. That's why Paul constantly spoke of our own personal strength and efforts as *"the flesh"* (Rom. 8:1, 8).

As someone has rightly said, when Jesus died on the Cross, He did so not only to save us from *"sin,"* but as well to save us from *"self."* The only way that dominion over self, which is the first requirement of all, can be regained is by the person first of all being Born-Again, and then continuing to look exclusively to the Cross for all things. That's what Jesus was talking about when He said:

"If any man will come after Me, let him deny himself, and take up his Cross daily, and follow Me.

"For whosoever will save his life shall lose it: but whosoever will lose his life for My sake, the same shall save it" (Lk. 9:23-24).

TAKING UP THE CROSS DAILY

Most Christians misunderstand this statement made by Christ.

When He spoke of *"denying self,"* He wasn't speaking of asceticism, which is the denial of all things which are pleasurable or comfortable, etc. He was speaking of denying self in the capacity of our own strength and ability, meaning that we understand that we cannot live this life by our own means. We can only do so as Christ lives through us.

When He spoke of taking up the Cross daily and following Him, He wasn't meaning suffering, as most Christians think. He was meaning that every single Blessing we receive from the Lord, every good thing, all and without exception, come through the Finished Work of Christ on the Cross. Consequently, even on a *"daily"* basis, we are to draw down these benefits of what Jesus did at the Cross. That's the way we live and maintain our victory.

When He spoke of saving our life, and thereby losing it, He was meaning if we try to live for God by our own machinations and ability, that instead of saving our life, we will actually lose it. But when we lose our life for His sake, meaning that we give it all to Him, trusting completely in what Christ did at the Cross on our behalf, then we save our life. It's just that simple! It is all in Christ, and if it's not in Christ, there is no proper dominion over self. Paul said:

"I am crucified with Christ: nevertheless I live; yet not I, but Christ lives in me: and the life which I now live in the flesh, I live by the faith of the Son of God, Who loved me, and gave Himself for me" (Gal. 2:20).

NOTES

(27) "SO GOD CREATED MAN IN HIS OWN IMAGE, IN THE IMAGE OF GOD CREATED HE HIM; MALE AND FEMALE CREATED HE THEM.

(28) "AND GOD BLESSED THEM, AND GOD SAID UNTO THEM, BE FRUITFUL, AND MULTIPLY, AND REPLENISH THE EARTH, AND SUBDUE IT: AND HAVE DOMINION OVER THE FISH OF THE SEA, AND OVER THE FOWL OF THE AIR, AND OVER EVERY LIVING THING THAT MOVES UPON THE EARTH.

(29) "AND GOD SAID, BEHOLD, I HAVE GIVEN YOU EVERY HERB BEARING SEED, WHICH IS UPON THE FACE OF ALL THE EARTH, AND EVERY TREE, IN THE WHICH IS THE FRUIT OF A TREE YIELDING SEED; TO YOU IT SHALL BE FOR MEAT.

(30) "AND TO EVERY BEAST OF THE EARTH, AND TO EVERY FOWL OF THE AIR, AND TO EVERY THING THAT CREEPS UPON THE EARTH, WHEREIN THERE IS LIFE, I HAVE GIVEN EVERY GREEN HERB FOR MEAT: AND IT WAS SO.

(31) "AND GOD SAW EVERYTHING THAT HE HAD MADE, AND, BEHOLD, IT WAS VERY GOOD. AND THE EVENING AND THE MORNING WERE THE SIXTH DAY."

The structure is:

1. God created man in His Own Image.

2. God created mankind *"male and female,"* which means that He gave mankind the power of procreation.

3. God then blessed mankind.

4. He gave mankind dominion over everything on the Earth.

5. God gave all the plant life for food.

6. God saw that all that He had made *"was very good."*

7. The creation of animals and the creation of mankind were done on the sixth day.

MALE AND FEMALE

Verse 27 reads, *"So God created man in His Own Image, in the Image of God created He him; male and female created He them,"* represents, at least as far as we know, the first time that God has created the female gender, at least as it regards intelligent beings. There is no record of any female Angels.

The threefold repetition of the term *"created"* should be observed as a distinct rebuttal against the mindless philosophy of evolution.

Evolution teaches that man is gradually evolving into something better and better, while creationism teaches that man has rather fallen from his high beginning.

As well, the Holy Spirit here through Moses not only speaks of creation some three times, but also some three times He makes mention of man created in the *"Image of God."* As stated, that Image, however, was lost at the Fall. Martin Luther said the following, of which I repeat:

"But now it is the purpose of the Gospel to restore this Divine Image. By faith we are born again unto eternal life, or let me rather say, to the hope of eternal life, so that we live in God and with Him, and are one with Him, as Christ says. But we are not only born again unto eternal life, but also unto Righteousness, for our faith receives the merit of Christ, as we steadfastly believe that we are ransomed through His death.

"To this must be added another Righteousness or Image of God, according to which, instructed by the Divine Word, we diligently try, with the help of the Holy Spirit, to render obedience to God. But this Righteousness merely begins in this life; because of the corruption of our nature it can never become perfect. Yet God is pleased with it, not as though it were perfect or an atonement for our sin, but because it flows from a sincere heart, which, endowed by faith, trusts in God's mercy for Christ's sake. Through the Gospel we receive also the Holy Spirit, Who wars against the unbelief, envy and other vices in us and makes us earnestly strive to honor God and His Word.

"Thus there begins in this life the restoration of the Divine Image through the Gospel, though this is never fully accomplished here upon Earth. But when it will be accomplished in the Heavenly Kingdom of God, then our will shall be perfectly free from sin, and perfectly good, and our intellect will be perfectly enlightened, and the memory will be absolutely unfailing."

THE BLESSING OF GOD

Verse 28 reads, *"And God blessed them, and God said unto them, Be fruitful, and*

multiply, and replenish the Earth, and subdue it: and have dominion over the fish of the sea, and over the fowl of the air, and over every living thing that moves upon the Earth," proclaims the Blessing of God, which is the very opposite of the curse.

In the word *"multiply"* we have the meaning of procreation.

When God created the Angels, every evidence is that He created all of them at the same time. In other words, there's never been such a thing as a baby Angel. But when He created mankind, He created them male and female, giving them the power of procreation, which refers to the ability to bring offspring into the world.

In fact, it was the intention of God that these offspring would be *"sons of God,"* thereby continuing in the Image of God. But the Fall ruined that, in that offspring now are brought into the world in the *"likeness of Adam,"* with all of its attendant misery, and not like God (Gen. 5:3).

REPLENISH

The word *"replenish,"* is thought by some to point to a former creation on the Earth before Adam and Eve. According to Isaiah, Chapter 14 and Ezekiel, Chapter 28, Lucifer ruled this world for an undetermined period of time, and did so in Righteousness and Holiness as a beautiful Angel created by God. This was in the dateless past, as stated, before Adam and Eve.

If in fact he did rule this world at that time, and it would stand to reason that there had to be some type of creation on the Earth for him to rule. Some believe that the word *"replenish"* is referring to that creation.

When Lucifer fell, this creation, whatever it was, threw in their lot with him, as did approximately one-third of the Angels. In fact, some think that demon spirits are actually the spirits of this fallen creation.

One thing is certain, demon spirits aren't fallen Angels. Fallen Angels have spirit bodies, and demon spirits have no bodies at all, seeking to inhabit a body whether animal or man.

As is obvious, the Bible doesn't give us much information on this, inasmuch as the Bible is the story of the Creation, Fall, and

Redemption of man and not Angels, etc. But yet, what little it does say in this respect lends credence to the idea of what we have just stated.

FOOD

Verses 29 and 30 read, *"And God said, Behold, I have given you every herb bearing seed, which is upon the face of all the Earth, and every tree, in the which is the fruit of a tree yielding seed; to you it shall be for meat.*

"And to every beast of the Earth, and to every fowl of the air, and to every thing that creeps upon the Earth, wherein there is life, I have given every green herb for meat: and it was so," refers to the fact that both animals and mankind were vegetarians before the Fall. Incidentally, this was changed after the flood (Gen. 9:3).

Of the three classes into which the vegetable creation were divided, grass, herbs, and trees, the last two were assigned to man for food.

We are told in Verse 30 that the green grass was given to the animal kingdom for food. And the term *"Every beast of the Earth, and every fowl of the air, and every thing that creeps upon the Earth,"* tells us that the animals were not originally created as predators. In other words, all animals were then vegetarian as well, which means that all, and not just some, were docile. That means that the lamb and the lion played together, exactly as they will do again in the coming Millennial Reign (Isa. 11:6-8).

VERY GOOD

Verse 31 reads, *"And God saw every thing that He had made, and, behold, it was very good. And the evening and the morning were the sixth day,"* means that it was not simply good, but good exceedingly. It is not man alone that God surveys, but the completed cosmos, with man as its crown and glory.

By using such terminology, God has hereby set us an example of reviewing our works. Having given us a power of reflection, He expects we should use that power. When we have finished a day's work, and are entering upon the rest of the night, we should commune with our own hearts about what we have done that day.

NOTES

But when we come to review our works, we find so often that to our shame, much has been very bad: but when God reviewed His work, all was very good (Henry).

THE SIXTH DAY

In six days, God brought the world back to a habitable state, plus He created plant life, the animal kingdom, and mankind.

However, from this, we are not to think that God couldn't have perfected this work in a much shorter period of time. Actually, due to the fact that He is Almighty, and all-knowing, He could have spoken it into existence in a moment's time; however, He did it in this way, taking some six days, in order that we might see His wisdom, power, goodness, and order.

We find from this that God's government extends even to His creation, and above all to His creation. Government demands order, and God's order is perfect, thereby meaning that His Government is perfect as well.

Matthew Henry said, and I concur: *"Thus ends a Chapter containing the most extensive, the most profound, and most sublime Truths that can possibly come within the reach of the human understanding."*

"We praise Thee, O God, our Redeemer, Creator,
"In grateful devotion our tribute we bring.
"We lay it before Thee, we kneel and adore Thee.
"We bless Thy Holy Name, glad praises we sing."

"We worship Thee, God of our fathers, we bless Thee;
"Through life's storm and tempest our Guide hast Thou been.
"When perils o'er take us, escape Thou wilt make us,
"And with Thy help, O Lord, our battles we win."

"With voices united our praises we offer,
"To Thee, great Jehovah, glad anthems we raise.
"Thy strong arm will guide us, our God is beside us,
"To Thee, our great Redeemer, forever be praised."

CHAPTER 2

(1) "THUS THE HEAVENS AND THE EARTH WERE FINISHED, AND ALL THE HOST OF THEM.

(2) "AND ON THE SEVENTH DAY GOD ENDED HIS WORK WHICH HE HAD MADE; AND HE RESTED ON THE SEVENTH DAY FROM ALL HIS WORK WHICH HE HAD MADE.

(3) "AND GOD BLESSED THE SEVENTH DAY, AND SANCTIFIED IT: BECAUSE THAT IN IT HE HAD RESTED FROM ALL HIS WORK WHICH GOD CREATED AND MADE."

The construction is:

1. The Lord finished the heavens and the Earth, bringing Earth back to a habitable state, and the heavens as well, at least as they affected Earth.

2. On the seventh day, God rested *"from all His work which He had made."*

3. God blessed the seventh day, and sanctified it.

THE HEAVENS AND THE EARTH ARE FINISHED

The First Verse says, *"Thus the heavens and the Earth were finished, and all the host of them,"* proclaims the fact that when the heavens and the Earth were completed, they were a brilliant array.

I think one can say without fear of any Scriptural contradiction, that everything, including the heavens, was affected negatively in some way as a result of the Fall. In fact, Paul said in relation to this: *"For we know that the whole creation groans and travails in pain together until now"* (Rom. 8:22).

So as beautiful as the heavens are presently, what must they have been like before the Fall? As far as our ability to view what presently is there, even that has been greatly impeded in this industrial age.

In the early 1970's, Frances and I, along with Donnie and Debbie and others, were in South Africa in a series of Meetings.

At the conclusion of the Meetings, we had two or three days layover, which we spent at the Kruger Game Preserve, one of the largest in the world.

On the first night we were there, I remember walking outside the little hut in which we were staying that night, looking up at the stars, in fact, at something I had never seen in all of my life.

It seemed as if the heavens were literally blanketed with stars. Because of the pollution in the air, back in the States, I had not seen anything of this nature. I stood there mesmerized, I suppose for nearly an hour, looking at this carpet of stars in the heavens, which was so beautiful as to be beyond description.

So if one can think back in his imagination to before the Fall, the heavens at that time must have been an array of unimagined beauty. They will be that way again. John the Beloved said: *"And I saw a new heaven and a new Earth: for the first heaven and the first Earth were passed away; and there was no more sea"* (Rev. 21:1).

FINISHED

When the Lord said that the creation, or possibly one should say, the re-creation was finished, all is pristine, beautiful beyond compare. About 4,000 years later, His Son hanging on a cruel Cross would again say, *"It is finished,"* and the way back to God was now open. But what a price had to be paid! In fact it was such a price as to make the original creation seem as if it was nothing. Material things, as beautiful as they might be, are still just things; however, the Son of God gave His life on that Cross, and nothing can equal that.

And then, on a coming day, in fact after the Millennial Reign, when the new heaven and the new Earth will be brought into being, and Satan and all of his cohorts of darkness will be placed in the lake of fire forever and forever, and sin is only a bad memory, if that, the final words will then be said, *"It is done"* (Rev. 21:6).

THE SEVENTH DAY

Verse 2 says, *"And on the seventh day God ended His work which He had made; and He rested on the seventh day from all His work which He had made,"* presents an anthropomorphic statement. In other words, it's a statement made about God in the ways and manner of men, that we might understand it better. God cannot be conceived as resting or as needing rest through either exhaustion or fatigue. The Prophet said of Him: *"He Who faints not, neither is weary"* (Isa. 40:28). Cessation from previous occupation is all that is implied in this statement.

Incidentally, a morning here for the Sabbath day is implied, but no evening as with the other days is implied. The Sabbath is actually eternal. It foretells Christ, the True Sabbath, in Whom God rests and in Whom Believers rest. This is *"God's Own rest"* of Hebrews, Chapter 4 (Williams).

When it says that God *"Rested on the seventh day from all His work which He had made,"* I think we can derive from this phrase that He is not creating new universes. Since that time, He has given Himself to the new work of upholding His creation. The Scripture says: *"By Him* (Christ) *all things consist"* (Col. 1:17).

Since the Fall of man in the Garden of Eden, God has given Himself to the carrying out of the Plan of Redemption. Concerning this, Jesus said: *"My Father works hitherto, and I work"* (Jn. 5:17). That's the reason, beginning with Genesis, Chapter 4, and continuing throughout the balance of the Word of God, we have the story of man's Redemption. The whole of this past 6,000 recorded years has been spent in this process.

BLESSING

The Third Verse says, *"And God blessed the seventh day, and sanctified it: because that in it He had rested from all His work which God created and made,"* presents the third Blessing. Williams said, *"Blessing is stamped upon this introduction to the history of God's interest in man and His creatures. He blessed the living creatures (Gen. 1:22); He blessed man (Gen. 1:28), and He now blesses the seventh day."*

If we fail here to see what the Lord is actually doing, then we will miss completely the import of what is being said.

This Sabbath, or seventh day, or Saturday, the last day of the week, is meant by God to be a Type of the Salvation rest which one finds in Christ. That's the reason it was a part of the Ten Commandments.

When an individual accepts Christ, he enters into a Sabbath rest so to speak, which

NOTES

will never end. That's the reason no mention is made of an evening and morning for the seventh day. Read carefully what Paul said:

"Let us therefore fear, lest, a promise being left us of entering into His rest, any of you should seem to come short of it" (Heb. 4:1).

We enter into this *"rest"* not by keeping a certain day. That's not what it means at all. If that's what we seek to do, then we will *"come short of it."*

One enters into this *"rest"* by accepting Christ, making Him the Lord of one's life. And then he said:

"For unto us was the Gospel preached, as well as unto them (Jews before the Cross, and Jews after the Cross)*: but the Word preached did not profit them, not being mixed with Faith in them who heard it"* (Heb. 4:2).

Paul is saying that the Word preached to the Jews before the Cross did not profit them, simply because they tried to make Salvation out of the keeping of the Sabbath day. This meant that they had no faith in the One to Whom the Sabbath day pointed. Paul continues:

"For we which have believed do enter into rest, as He said, As I have sworn in My wrath, if they shall enter into My rest: although the works were finished from the foundation of the world" (Heb. 4:3).

In this Scripture Paul is saying that all the works of God were finished on the sixth day; consequently, there must not be any more works. We enter into this rest, as stated, not by keeping a certain day, but by accepting the One Whom the seventh day typified. Paul continues:

"For He spake in a certain place of the seventh day on this wise, And God did rest the seventh day from all His works" (Heb. 4:4).

This was spoken in Genesis 2:2. Once again, He emphasizes the fact that all the works are now finished. This means that if man tries to find Salvation by works, or maintain Salvation by works, that God has sworn in His wrath that by such efforts man will not enter into His rest. The Apostle then said:

"For he who is entered into His rest, he also has ceased from his own works, as God did from His" (Heb. 4:10).

So we see from all of this that God blessing and sanctifying the seventh day refers strictly to Christ and the rest that He would bring us, by what He did at the Cross on our behalf. We obtain this *"rest"* by exhibiting Faith in Him and His great Sacrifice. If we try to obtain it any other way, which then places us in the position of *"works,"* such activity angers God greatly (Heb. 4:3).

When God finished all His work on the sixth day, and *"He saw everything that He had made, and, behold, it was very good,"* that means that all work and works are finished. To be sure, and even as Paul said in Hebrews, Chapter 4, it pointed to the coming Redemption found only in Christ, which can only be obtained by Faith, and never by works. So the Sabbath was meant to portray Christ and the great *"Rest"* which He would afford, by what He did for the human race in the offering up of Himself on the Cross. Consequently, the Lord *"blessing"* and *"sanctifying"* this particular day carries a meaning far greater than the mere fact that He had finished the creation.

THE RESURRECTION OF CHRIST AND THE FIRST DAY OF THE WEEK

If we are to notice in the Book of Acts and the Epistles, the Sabbath, which is Saturday, gradually fell by the wayside, with the first day of the week, the day of the Resurrection of Christ, taking its place (Acts 20:7; I Cor. 16:2; Rev. 1:10).

Jesus fulfilled all of the Law, which included the Sabbath. As stated, He rose from the dead on the first day of the week, and this was no doubt done purposely. It signals not an ending, but rather a beginning. And so it is!

(4) "THESE ARE THE GENERATIONS OF THE HEAVENS AND OF THE EARTH WHEN THEY WERE CREATED, IN THE DAY THAT THE LORD GOD MADE THE EARTH AND THE HEAVENS,"

The construction is:

1. *"These are the generations,"* occurs 11 times in this First Book of the Bible.

2. *"Generations"* refer to *"Divine divisions."*

3. *"Lord God"* reveals Christ as *"Jehovah Elohim,"* man's Redeemer.

GENERATIONS

The phrase, *"These are the generations of the heavens and of the Earth when they were created,"* refers to the manner in which

all were created, as outlined in Chapter 1. As stated, the Lord has an ordered procedure about all that He does. His Government is perfect regarding creation, as well as all other things. He is a God of order.

In this Government of order, one can much of the time tell what God is going to do, by what He has done in the past. There is no chaos about Him. And at the same time, due to man's fallen nature, there is nothing but chaos about him; consequently, for man to have an ordered existence, he must serve God, and, thereby, learn the ways of the Lord, that he may walk therein. Only in this manner can man walk in a semblance of order. Otherwise, he has disorder.

One can look at the nations of the world, which subscribe at least to a certain extent to the Bible. This means that they have at least a goodly number of their population which serves the Lord. That nation will be orderly, and will prosper. Otherwise, and as we have already stated, there is chaos. As someone has well said, and rightly so, *"No Bible, no freedom! Some Bible, some freedom! Much Bible, much freedom!"*

THE LORD GOD

The phrase, *"In the day that the LORD God made the Earth and the heavens,"* presents the new name of God as *"Jehovah Elohim."*

"Jehovah" is the absolute, Self-existent One, Who manifests Himself to man, and, in particular, enters into distinct Covenant engagements for man's Redemption, which He in due time fulfills.

Concerning this new Name, Williams says: *"This Chapter reveals Christ as Jehovah Elohim, man's Redeemer. The First Chapter reveals Him as Elohim, man's Creator. He first prepares the beauteous world in which man is to dwell and then He creates man, and, as Jehovah, enters into Covenant with him. These two great titles of Christ are distinguished throughout the entire Bible and finally appear in its two closing Chapters, which treat of redeemed man and a new Earth."*

The words *"created and made,"* literally say *"created to make."*

The idea is, God made the world in such a way that it can be almost endlessly developed. This is tied in with man's dominion, which regrettably has been at least partially taken over by Satan. Consequently, that which God originally intended, which is a greater development, has been all but halted in its tracks. However, this will be remedied with the coming new heaven and new Earth.

(5) "AND EVERY PLANT OF THE FIELD BEFORE IT WAS IN THE EARTH, AND EVERY HERB OF THE FIELD BEFORE IT GREW: FOR THE LORD GOD HAD NOT CAUSED IT TO RAIN UPON THE EARTH, AND THERE WAS NOT A MAN TO TILL THE GROUND."

The composition is:

1. The second day of creation is addressed here, which obviously preceded day three when plant life was developed.

2. It seems that rain came to the Earth on day three, which caused the Earth to *"bring forth grass, the herb yielding seed, and the fruit tree yielding fruit after his kind."*

3. All of this was before man was created, showing that he had nothing to do with the creation, that being altogether of God.

THE PLANTS AND THE HERBS

The phrase, *"And every plant of the field before it was in the Earth, and every herb of the field before it grew,"* presents the fact that the Earth did not bring forth vegetation of itself, by any innate virtue of its own; but purely by the Almighty Power of God, Who formed every plant and every herb before it grew in the Earth.

In these few words, the Holy Spirit is informing all and sundry that creation is altogether of God. This completely debunks evolution, and as well, and as we shall see, man's involvement. There is nothing that is created that is a product of man, God always being the first cause. And it is on this one Truth that fallen man runs aground. While man can further develop God's creation, which God originally intended, man cannot bring something out of nothing. That domain lies completely in the realm of God.

HUMOROUS STORY

There is a joke of sorts which says that man approached God, and informed Him that he (man) was now so brilliant that the services of God were no longer needed.

God proposed a little contest, to which man readily agreed. God would create a man, and then it was proposed that man would do the same. Man readily agreed, thinking he could easily clone a specimen.

God reached down and gathered together a little pile of dirt, from which man would be made. Man reached down and did the same thing. God then asked man as to what he was doing.

"I'm getting a pile of dirt in order to make man, exactly as You have done," man replied!

"Get your own dirt," the Lord answered!

RAIN

The phrase, *"For the LORD God had not caused it to rain upon the Earth,"* proclaims the fact that there had not yet been any rain, even though God had divided the waters, putting some in clouds, and leaving some on the Earth, with an expanse between, called *"the firmament"* (Gen. 1:6-8).

The insinuation is, God did cause it to rain upon the Earth on day three, thereby causing the Earth to *"bring forth grass, the herb yielding seed,"* etc.

This shows us that all of creation is subject to God, and God is subject not at all to creation. We must never forget that! When all the seed in the Earth had been placed there by God, and were properly ready to bud and bring forth, then God caused it to rain.

Even though everything has been somewhat perverted due to the Fall, which means that it doesn't quite function properly, still, that which God originally created continues to function exactly as He originally created it to do so, with the exception of the perversions. By *"perversions"* we're speaking of droughts, hurricanes, earthquakes, storms, floods, etc. All of these type of things were never intended by God to be, but came into being due to the Fall. That's the reason, as we have previously stated, *"that the whole creation groans and travails in pain together until now"* (Rom. 8:22).

THE INVOLVEMENT OF MAN

The phrase, *"And there was not a man to till the ground,"* more than anything else refers to the fact that man had nothing to do with creation. Consequently, man should be very careful about taking credit for anything as it pertains to the works of God. In fact, he is due no credit at all!

When we think of plants growing, we think of man putting seed in the Earth and cultivating the ground. Plant life was developed on day three, some three days before man was even created.

To understand these particular words, we must bear in mind that the object of the narrative is not now the formation of the world, but man's relation to Jehovah, hence the introduction of the new Name of God, *"Jehovah Elohim."*

Man's proper relationship to God is in essence a very simple relationship. In other words, it's not difficult to understand. And if it is complicated, it is that man has complicated the process himself.

We must recognize God as the Creator of all things. As such, we must give Him proper praise and glory. But due to the Fall, man has great problems on both counts.

He doesn't want to recognize God as the Creator, thereby substituting the mindless drivel of evolution to explain creation, and accordingly, refuses to give God praise and glory.

The idea is, if man will not recognize God as *"Elohim,"* his Creator, then he will not recognize God as *"Jehovah Elohim,"* his Redeemer.

(6) "BUT THERE WENT UP A MIST FROM THE EARTH, AND WATERED THE WHOLE FACE OF THE GROUND."

The overview is:

1. This pertains to day two of Creation.

2. At that time, day two, there went up a mist from the Earth, which prepared the Earth for the seed which God evidently planted on the beginning of day three.

3. Once again, we see God as the original cause of all Creation.

A MIST

The phrase, *"But there went up a mist from the Earth,"* was done, as stated, on day two, which prepared the Earth for the seed which was to be applied by God, which the rain would bring forth on day three.

THE GROUND

The phrase, *"And watered the whole face of the ground,"* presents the fact that the

Earth was made ready for that which would take place the next day.

Some Commentators have attempted to use these Passages as proof that the days mentioned in Chapter 1 were not literal, 24-hour days. But once it is understood as to what is actually being said, even as I think we have satisfactorily explained, we are given to understand that the Holy Spirit is portraying here through Moses the manner and the way in which God carried this out, which was done in literal, 24-hour days.

(7) "AND THE LORD GOD FORMED MAN OF THE DUST OF THE GROUND, AND BREATHED INTO HIS NOSTRILS THE BREATH OF LIFE; AND MAN BECAME A LIVING SOUL."

The synopsis is:

1. We are told here how man was created.

2. Man was formed out of the dust of the ground.

3. The *"breath of life"* comes from God, and pertains to the soul and the spirit.

4. Man being *"a living soul,"* means that he will live forever, whether in eternal light, or eternal darkness.

THE WAY MAN WAS CREATED

The phrase, *"And the LORD God formed man of the dust of the ground,"* proclaims the body of clay. To understand and remember this ought to inspire a feeling of genuine humility. It should keep men from pride in reference to their renowned ancestry, their apparel, or their wealth, inasmuch as we are the workmanship of His Hands and, therefore, must not contend with our Maker.

While it is true that the material of which man is made is next to nothing, the One Who made us is the Creator, and thereby able to do all things. Consequently, we should say as David: *"I will praise You; for I am fearfully and wonderfully made: marvelous are Your works; and that my soul knows right well"* (Ps. 139:14).

Men judge the value of an item according to the material of which it is made. The worth of that which God creates pertains to Him. His Hand can make something of nothing.

THE BREATH OF LIFE

The phrase, *"And breathed into his nostrils the breath of life; and man became a living soul,"* pertains to man being unique, in that nothing else in God's creation received the breath of God. This means that life came not as the result of man's bodily organization, nor as derived be evolution from any animal, but as a gift directly from God.

Delitzsch said: *"By an act of Divine Omnipotence man arose from the dust; and in the same moment in which the dust, by virtue of creative Omnipotence, shaped itself into the human form, it was pervaded by the Divine breath of life, and created a living being, so that we cannot say the body was earlier than the soul."*

The *"breath of life"* which comes from God pertains to the soul and spirit of man. This was done with the first man, God breathing the soul and the spirit into man, and thereafter, it comes automatically at conception.

(8) "AND THE LORD GOD PLANTED A GARDEN EASTWARD IN EDEN; AND THERE HE PUT THE MAN WHOM HE HAD FORMED."

The synopsis is:

1. The Lord God planted a garden, which we refer to as the Garden of Eden.

2. It was actually planted before Adam was created.

3. It was planted *"eastward in Eden,"* which some Scholars believe was ultimately the site of the city of Babylon.

4. There He placed the man.

THE GARDEN OF EDEN

The phrase, *"And the LORD God planted a garden eastward in Eden,"* means *"land of delight."*

"Eastward in Eden," no doubt meant east of Israel. Of course, at the time this was written, Israel did not exist; however, the Holy Spirit definitely knew that in time it would exist.

MAN'S HOME

The phrase, *"And there He put the man whom He had formed,"* proclaims the place especially prepared for man.

From this we realize that God began preparing for man even before he was created. After the Fall, the greatest preparation of all was undertaken in respect to Redemption,

which would require a price to be paid that beggars all description. And then Jesus said, concerning the eternal abode, *"I go to prepare a place for you.*

"And if I go and prepare a place for you, I will come again, and receive you unto Myself; that where I am, there you may be also" (Jn. 14:2-3).

So in all of this, we see the tender Love, Mercy, and Compassion of God as it regards His choice creation — man. He prepared a garden for man. He prepared Salvation for man, and then He has prepared a paradise that so far outstrips the Garden of Eden, as to be no contest. As stated, all of this portrays the love of God.

(9) "AND OUT OF THE GROUND MADE THE LORD GOD TO GROW EVERY TREE THAT IS PLEASANT TO THE SIGHT, AND GOOD FOR FOOD; THE TREE OF LIFE ALSO IN THE MIDST OF THE GARDEN, AND THE TREE OF KNOWLEDGE OF GOOD AND EVIL."

The exegesis is:

1. The Garden was beautified with every tree that was pleasant to the sight.

2. As well, there was every type of tree which was fruit bearing, plus also nuts.

3. The Tree of Life was situated in the middle of the Garden.

4. As well, in the garden was the tree of knowledge of good and evil

GOOD FOR FOOD

The phrase, *"And out of the ground made the LORD God to grow every tree that is pleasant to the sight, and good for food,"* refers to every type of beautiful tree for adornment, and every fruit tree imaginable, and even those which bear nuts.

In fact, according to the creation of day three, the entirety of the Earth had these type of trees. So, these particular trees in the Garden of Eden must have been of special type, and given special care by the Lord. The trees no doubt were more beautiful, with the fruit trees bearing fruit that was more luscious, and the trees bearing nuts falling into the same category. Without toil and without labor, everything that man needed was amply provided and then some. The provision of God lacked nothing.

TREE OF LIFE

The phrase, *"The Tree of Life also in the midst of the Garden,"* evidently contained a type of fruit. Genesis 3:22 says as much!

Ellicott said: *"The Tree of Life had the power of so renewing man's physical energies that his body though formed of the dust of the ground, and therefore naturally mortal, would, by its continual use, live on forever."* Christ is now to us the *"Tree of Life"* (Rev. 2:7; 22:2); and the *"Bread of Life"* (Jn. 6:48, 51).

What type of fruit the *"Tree of Life"* did bear we aren't told. There are some who suppose it may have been an apple tree, with Divine properties appropriated for this particular fruit. This is derived from the Song of Solomon 2:3.

Even though man's physical body was formed out of dust, by the properties of the *"Tree of Life"* it was meant to live forever. Death was not in the original plan. That came by sin.

It seems that men with natural bodies will come and go in the New Jerusalem, and live forever by virtue of *"the Tree of Life,"* and the fruit that it will bear every month (Rev. 22:2).

This does not refer to those with Glorified Bodies, who will not need such sustenance in order to live eternally, and which will include all who have part in the First Resurrection (Rev. 20:6).

THE TREE OF KNOWLEDGE OF GOOD AND EVIL

The phrase, *"And the tree of knowledge of good and evil,"* presents the tree of death.

One might say that the tree of death appears at the opening of the Bible, the tree of Calvary (I Pet. 2:24), in the middle of the Bible, and the Tree of Life (Rev. 2:7), at the end of the Bible (Williams).

In the manner in which Adam and Eve were created as free moral agents, this agency had to be tested. The tree of knowledge of good and evil served as the vehicle for that testing. It was not that its fruit contained some type of poisonous property, but it was rather the act of disobedience to God in eating this fruit, which God had said they must not eat, which constituted the Fall.

What is meant here by *"good"* and *"evil"*?

Taking the latter first, Adam and Eve knew nothing about evil whatsoever. At the beginning of their creation, they were in total harmony with God, and knew only Righteousness. So the *"evil"* at that time was only a curiosity, but it was such curiosity which did them in.

Unfortunately, due to Adam's Fall, the entirety of the human race has an expert knowledge of evil. To be sure, it's a knowledge we wish we didn't have, for it has been the bane of society and of humanity in general. But it's the knowledge of *"good"* which stumps most people. What in fact is meant by the word *"knowledge of good"*?

THE KNOWLEDGE OF GOOD

Inasmuch as both of these principles are on one tree, *"good"* and *"evil,"* we then know that the good addressed here carries with it a very negative connotation.

It refers to the *"good"* that men attempt to carry out, which they think earns them Salvation, or favor with God, or most of all, that it atones in some way. Because it is *"good,"* and whatever *"it"* might be, it deceives people. And let the Reader please understand that this type of *"good"* covers a wide spectrum.

It runs the gamut all the way from the unredeemed trying to earn Salvation, which most do, to the Christian attempting to earn victory, both by doing good things.

In the first place, the *"good"* which man does is already polluted, because it's touched by human hands. And once this is done, the good is then sullied. Irrespective, none of this earns anything with God. In other words, the *"good"* which man does will not spend in God's economy. The Scripture plainly says the following:

"For by Grace are you saved through Faith: and that not of yourselves: it is the Gift of God:

"Not of works, lest any man should boast" (Eph. 2:8-9).

Paul further said: *"But God forbid that I should glory, save in the Cross of our Lord Jesus Christ, by Whom the world is crucified unto me, and I unto the world"* (Gal. 6:14).

A man came to Jesus one day and asked Him: *"Good Master, what good thing shall I do, that I may have eternal life?*

"And He said unto him, Why call you Me good? There is none good but One, that is, God" (Mat. 19:16-17).

It may seem at first glance that Jesus was saying here that He Personally wasn't good; however, that's not what He is saying. He is saying that the only One Who is good is God. Considering that Christ is God, then He is good.

But when it comes to man, there is no *"good thing"* that he can do that will give him eternal life. But yet he continues to think that he can arrive at that destination in this manner.

The only way to God is through Christ Jesus and what He did at the Cross, and our Faith in that Finished Work. If we try to come any other way, we will be judged by God as a *"thief and a robber"* (Jn. 10:1). That's where the world runs aground, and regrettably, that's where the Church runs aground! This particular *"knowledge"* whether *"of good or evil,"* we don't want. We only want one kind of knowledge:

"For God, Who commanded the light to shine out of darkness, has shined in our hearts, to give the light of the knowledge of the Glory of God in the face of Jesus Christ" (II Cor. 4:6).

(10) "AND A RIVER WENT OUT OF EDEN TO WATER THE GARDEN; AND FROM THERE IT WAS PARTED, AND BECAME INTO FOUR HEADS.

(11) "THE NAME OF THE FIRST IS PISON: THAT IS IT WHICH COMPASSETH THE WHOLE LAND OF HAVILAH, WHERE THERE IS GOLD;

(12) "AND THE GOLD OF THAT LAND IS GOOD: THERE IS BDELLIUM AND THE ONYX STONE.

(13) "AND THE NAME OF THE SECOND RIVER IS GIHON: THE SAME IS IT THAT COMPASSETH THE WHOLE LAND OF ETHIOPIA.

(14) "AND THE NAME OF THE THIRD RIVER IS HIDDEKEL: THAT IS IT WHICH GOES TOWARD THE EAST OF ASSYRIA. AND THE FOURTH RIVER IS EUPHRATES."

The diagram is:

1. A river went out of Eden.

2. Its name is Pison, and it flows through an area outside of the Garden, which has gold.

3. There was also bdellium and the onyx stone.

4. The name of the second river is Gihon, and it goes through Ethiopia.

5. The third river is Hiddekel, which modern name is Tigris, and which goes through Assyria.

6. The fourth river is the Euphrates, and it still retains its same name.

A RIVER

Verse 10 says, *"And a river went out of Eden to water the Garden; and from there it was parted, and became into four heads,"* could mean the river parted while in Eden, with four streams proceeding forth, or that the river flowed through the Garden, and parted into four streams after leaving the Garden.

PISON

Verse 11 says, *"The name of the first is Pison: that is it which compasseth the whole land of Havilah, where there is gold,"* is said to be India, with the river now called the *"Ganges."*

PRECIOUS METAL AND PRECIOUS STONES

Verse 12 says, *"And the gold of that land is good: there is bdellium and the onyx stone,"* presents gold mentioned here, and in Verse 11, which is the first mention in the Bible of this precious metal. It is mentioned last in the Bible, as it refers to the main thoroughfare of the New Jerusalem, in which we are told is *"pure gold"* (Rev. 21:21).

GIHON

Verse 13 says, *"And the name of the second river is Gihon: the same is it that compasseth the whole land of Ethiopia,"* is believed to be the Nile.

HIDDEKEL AND EUPHRATES

Verse 14 says, *"And the name of the third river is Hiddekel: that is it which goes toward the east of Assyria. And the fourth river is Euphrates,"* proclaims the last two rivers. Hiddekel is believed to be the Tigris, with Euphrates maintaining its name.

These rivers at the present time have their sources far apart. The explanation, no doubt, lies in the flood, which altered the topography of the Earth. The headwaters of the first two were drastically changed, while the last two remain basically the same. In fact, it is believed that the Garden of Eden may have been located at the joining of the Tigris and Euphrates, which is the site of ancient Babylon.

We find this river, which was a literal river, starting to flow in the Garden of Eden. It was soon marred by sin, which necessitated the flood, which wrecked the headwaters.

Spiritually speaking, the river appears again, not from Eden, but from the smitten Rock. Paul said, *"That Rock was Christ."*

Passing onward, we find the river flowing in another channel. *"In the last day, that great day of the feast, Jesus stood and cried, saying, 'If any man thirst, let him come unto Me and drink. He who believes on Me, as the Scripture has said, out of his innermost being shall flow rivers of living water'"* (Jn. 7:37-38).

Finally, we have the River of God presented to us in the last Chapter of the Book of Revelation. The Scripture says: *"And He showed me a pure river of water of life, clear as crystal, proceeding out of the Throne of God and of the Lamb"* (Rev. 22:1).

This is the last place in which we find the river. Its source can never again be touched; its channel never again interrupted. It is based now on the ground of accomplished Redemption, which points to Christ and His Cross. And here we have the Throne of God, which is expressive of eternal stability. It is not God's Throne in creation, nor in providence, but rather in Redemption. When I see *"the Lamb,"* I always know its connection with me is as a sinner. As such, *"The Throne of God,"* would but deter me; but when God reveals Himself in the Person of the Lamb, the heart is attracted, and the conscience tranquilized.

The Blood of the Lamb cleanses the conscience from every speck and stain of sin, and sets it, in perfect freedom, in the presence of a Holiness which cannot tolerate sin. In the Cross, all the claims of Divine Holiness were perfectly answered, so that the more I understand the latter, the more I appreciate the former. The higher our estimate of Holiness, the higher will be our estimate of the work

of the Cross. *"Grace reigns, through Righteousness, unto eternal life, by Jesus Christ our Lord"* (Mackintosh).

(15) "AND THE LORD GOD TOOK THE MAN, AND PUT HIM INTO THE GARDEN OF EDEN TO DRESS IT AND TO KEEP IT."

The structure is:

1. The *"Lord God"* is *"Jehovah Elohim."*

2. He put man into the Garden of Eden to dress it and to keep it.

3. Regrettably, man wouldn't last very long.

THE MAN

The phrase, *"And the LORD God took the man,"* in effect means that the Lord told him to go to the Garden, which had been prepared especially for him. So we see here that God exerts special care for His prime creation. The Lord not only created him, but as well, He prepared for him, and now He will give him responsibility.

TO DRESS IT AND KEEP IT

The phrase, *"And put him into the Garden of Eden to dress it and to keep it,"* presents his particular task for that particular time. So in a very real sense is every man's life occupation appointed by God. *"To every man his work"* is the law of God's world as well as of Christ's Kingdom. This thought should dignify *"the trivial task,"* thereby enabling us, that whether we eat or drink, or whatever we do, to do all to the Glory of God.

Every Believer in the world has a special work designed especially for him, and intended for him to do. Unfortunately, far too many Believers try to do something which God never called them to do, or else through apathy and unbelief, they do nothing. Happy is the man and woman who finds the Will of God for their respective lives, and then carries out that Will.

Unfortunately, many Christians do not think of what they are presently doing as being of any consequence. Such thinking is wrong!

As a Believer, irrespective of what we do, even if it's cooking hamburgers at a McDonald's, we should realize that God put us there, and we should do the very best service that we can do. Quite possibly, the Lord places many of His Children in similar circumstances, in order to be a witness at a proven time. If we're looking for the opportunity, to be sure, the opportunity will definitely present itself.

Nothing happens by chance to the Child of God. All is planned, approved, and carried out by the Lord. If it's a mess-up, so to speak, then the mess-up is all on our part, and never on God's part.

Wherever the Lord puts you, you are to look at the task before you, irrespective as to how menial it may seem to be, and then *"dress it and keep it."*

(16) "AND THE LORD GOD COMMANDED THE MAN, SAYING, OF EVERY TREE OF THE GARDEN YOU MAY FREELY EAT:

(17) "BUT OF THE TREE OF THE KNOWLEDGE OF GOOD AND EVIL, YOU SHALL NOT EAT OF IT: FOR IN THE DAY THAT YOU EAT THEREOF YOU SHALL SURELY DIE."

The composition is:

1. Man had only one command from God to keep.

2. He was not to eat of the tree of the knowledge of good and evil.

3. If he did disobey this command, he would *"surely die."*

THE COMMAND

Verse 16 begins by stating, *"And the LORD God commanded the man,"* which presents a stern warning, which in effect, proclaims the first and only command to Adam before the Fall. Probation is the law of man's moral condition now, and it began in Paradise, only the conditions there were different.

As the Creator, God had the right to issue such a command, and to expect man to obey. In this we learn that man was a free moral agent. In other words, he was not a machine, but had the power of reason, and as well, a *"will."* In other words, he could choose to obey the Lord or disobey the Lord, which is obvious from the command given.

Also, the word *"commanded,"* should not be taken lightly. It was a strong, powerful statement, meant to impress upon Adam the severity of the situation, that is, if he disobeyed!

In a sense, one might say that with this command, the Church was formed here. If in fact that is the case, and it certainly seems

to be, this would mean that the Church was the first of the three great Divine institutions formed by God. With the creation of Eve, the home would have been second, and Civil Government would have come last. This became necessary only when man's nature was corrupted. It is the business of Civil Government to oppose sin, as Paul declares in Romans 13:4. Had Adam not sinned, Civil Government would not have been necessary, for man would have lived in perfect peace, rest, and security, for there would have been no robber, murderer, or thief, etc. So Adam would have needed only the Church and the home.

So in a sense, inasmuch as the Church was the first Divine institution formed, we would have to say that it is more important even than the home or Civil Government. It has well been said, and probably correct, that as the Church goes, so goes the home, and so goes the nation.

THE TREE OF THE KNOWLEDGE OF GOOD AND EVIL

Verse 16 further reads, *"Saying, Of every tree of the Garden you may freely eat."*

Verse 17 begins by stating, *"But of the tree of the knowledge of good and evil, you shall not eat of it,"* which constituted the command.

As stated, Adam was given only one command, and that in a paradise. Jesus, by contrast, as the Last Adam, had to keep every Commandment of the Law, with His probationary period beginning in a wilderness (Mat., Chpt. 4). Jesus was in the wilderness with the wild beasts, while Adam was in Paradise with animals which were docile (Mk. 1:13).

Many would ask the question as to why God placed this tree in the Garden. They reason that, minus the tree of the knowledge of good and evil, there would have been no Fall, and, thereby, no problem.

Let the Reader understand that the tree of the knowledge of good and evil was not the cause of Adam's Fall. It was a failure to heed and obey the Word of God, which is the cause of every single failure.

So why would Adam do such a thing? He had no sin nature as all who followed him have. He had every tree in the Garden of which he could eat of their fruit, and only one tree of which he was commanded not to eat.

As to why he did what he did, I don't think I can answer that question; furthermore, I don't think it can be answered by any human being.

The tree had to be there, for man had to be tested. It wasn't that God had to test Adam in order that He (God) might know what Adam would do, for God already knew. It was that Adam might know!

Some reason that if God had given Adam a willpower that was so strong that he could amply resist, miss the point altogether. For a *"will"* to be that which is proper, it has at the same time to be able to say *"yes"* or *"no."* Otherwise, it's not a *"will."*

Psychology claims that the environment is the answer. In other words, if a proper environment can be provided, this will stop all sin and sinning. Well let me remind the Reader that Adam was in a perfect environment when he sinned. So that's not the cause or the cure!

It comes down to obedience or disobedience. We need to look at that:

THE WILL OF MAN

Almost all Christians misunderstand what the will of man actually is.

While it is true that we are free moral agents, and while it is also true that we have the power of choice, the truth is, we need to understand exactly what is being said here.

Most Christians think that once they have come to Christ, they then have the willpower to either say *"yes"* or *"no,"* to whatever it is they so desire. Nothing could be further from the truth.

While the Believer definitely does have the power to say *"yes"* or *"no,"* it is only in one category. That category pertains to Christ. In other words, the Christian can say *"yes"* or *"no"* to Christ, and that's where his will begins, and that's where his will ends. And to be more particular, this *"yes"* or *"no"* must pertain not only to Christ, but what Christ did at the Cross on our behalf. The essence of this is, we can say *"yes"* to what Christ has done for us at the Cross, relying totally and completely on His Finished Work, or we can say *"no."*

If we say *"no,"* we then close the door to the Holy Spirit, which leaves us facing the

NOTES

powers of darkness with nothing but our own personal strength, i.e., *"willpower,"* which we will find every time to be totally inadequate.

No, the Christian is doomed to failure, if he thinks he can face the sin business, and simply say *"yes"* or *"no."* That's not the way it works. Those who try that, and almost all have, every time will conclude by failing. You may win for awhile, but after awhile you're going to fail. Now stop and think about this for a moment:

If it was possible for us to defeat sin and the attacks of Satan by *"willpower,"* then Jesus would not have had to come down here and die on a Cross. He could have merely taught us how to function within our willpower, and that would have solved the problem. But He didn't do that, did He? The truth is, the problem of sin is so deadly that it took the Cross to defeat this monster, and even then we have to have the help of the Holy Spirit to get this thing done. That's why Paul said:

"But if the Spirit (Holy Spirit) *of Him* (God the Father) *Who raised up Jesus from the dead dwell in you, He Who raised up Christ from the dead shall also quicken your mortal bodies by His Spirit that dwells in you"* (Rom. 8:11).

This tells us sin is so powerful that it takes the same power to overcome this thing as it did to raise Jesus from the dead, which of course is the power of the Holy Spirit. Understanding that, we should come to the conclusion that our personal willpower is totally inadequate.

But most Christians, little understanding the victory of the Cross, try to do this thing on their own, which always results in failure.

The following diagram will be given several times in this Volume, and because it's so very, very important. In this we find the key to victory and the way to failure.

The following, in extremely abbreviated form, are the means by which any and every Christian can walk in victory, and by that, we mean perpetual victory:

FOCUS: The focus of every Believer must always be on the Cross of Christ, realizing that it is through the Cross that everything comes from God to the Believer.

OBJECT OF FAITH: The object of our faith is, as well, very, very important. Without exception, it must always be the Finished Work of Christ. Unfortunately, too many Christians have other things as the object of their faith, which guarantees failure.

POWER SOURCE: With our focus on the Cross of Christ, which means that the Finished Work of Christ is now the object of our Faith, our Power Source is now the Holy Spirit. Considering that the Holy Spirit is God, this means that victory is ours.

RESULTS: Having the Cross as our focus, and the Finished Work as the object of our Faith, which guarantees the Holy Spirit being the Power Source, then we cannot fail. It is victory to victory, or we should say, *"Faith to Faith."*

All of this we've just said is found in Romans, Chapters 6, 7, and 8.

Now let's use the same formula, but yet turn it around, which regrettably, is the place and position of most modern Christians.

FOCUS: Not understanding the Victory of the Cross as it regards Sanctification, most modern Christians focus on *"works."*

OBJECT OF FAITH: Focusing on works, the object of our faith becomes our *"performance,"* which is always inadequate, and because the Holy Spirit will not function in this capacity.

POWER SOURCE: Focusing on works, and trusting in our performance, the power source now is *"self."*

RESULTS: Focusing on works, with the object of our faith being our personal performance, and the power source now being self, the results are predictable — failure. And as stated, this latter diagram is the place and position of most modern Christians.

THE CROSS

The reason for the failure is because of not knowing and understanding the Message of the Cross. Paul said:

"For the preaching of the Cross is to them that perish foolishness; but unto us which are saved it is the Power of God" (I Cor. 1:18).

The Greek word translated here *"preaching,"* is *"Logos."* It should have been translated *"Word"* or *"Message."* It would then have read: *"For the Message of the Cross is to them. . . ."*

Regrettably and sadly, very few Christians know the *"Message of the Cross."* They don't

know it simply because it's not being preached and taught behind their pulpits. Considering that *"Faith comes by hearing, and hearing by the Word of God,"* if the Word of God in this capacity is not taught, then the person can have no faith in that which they do not know (Rom. 10:17).

For one to properly understand the Word of God, one must understand the Word of the Cross. In fact, the story of the Bible is the story of the Cross, simply because it's the story of man's Redemption. So, to try to understand the Bible apart from the Cross simply will not work. That's why Paul also said:

"For I determined not to know anything among you, save Jesus Christ, and Him Crucified" (I Cor. 2:2).

FAITH

I am sure that every Believer knows and understands that *"Faith"* is the currency that spends in God's economy. In fact, it's the only currency that He will accept, so to speak. But let the Reader understand the following:

When Paul spoke of Faith, which he did constantly in one way or the other, without exception, he was always speaking of Faith in Christ and what Christ did at the Cross. In fact, he even referred to this great Christian experience as *"the Faith"* (Gal. 2:20).

However, if the faith of which we speak is not Faith in Christ and Him Crucified, then it's faith that God will not recognize. And regrettably, most Christians presently have faith in about everything as it pertains to the Lord, except the Cross. They claim to have faith in the Word. But they fail to understand that if it's not Faith in the Cross, then it's not faith in the Word. The two *"Faith"* and *"Word"* are synonymous. Listen to this:

John said: *"In the beginning was the Word, and the Word was with God, and the Word was God"* (Jn. 1:1).

This tells us that Jesus was the Living Word.

He then said: *"And the Word was made flesh, and dwelt among us"* (Jn. 1:14).

God became flesh in order to be the Last Adam, and most of all, to go to the Cross.

John then said, when he introduced Christ: *"Behold the Lamb of God, which taketh away the sin of the world"* (Jn. 1:29).

We now know why the *"Word"* became *"flesh."* It was that He might go to the Cross, which was demanded, that is, if man was to be Redeemed.

So, if we claim to understand the Word, or to have our faith based on the Word, which is certainly correct, that is, if we know what we're talking about, then we must understand that the Cross must ever be the object of our faith. Then the Word will begin to come into sharp focus. Now let me make this statement. I know it's controversial, but it needs to be said:

If the Believer doesn't properly understand the Message of the Cross, then in some way, everything he thinks he understands about the Word of God will be perverted more or less.

SPIRITUAL DEATH

Verse 17 further reads, *"For in the day that you eat thereof you shall surely die,"* refers to spiritual death, which is separation from God. In other words, the moment that Adam partook of that particular fruit, whatever it was, at that moment he died, i.e., *"was separated from God."* Regrettably and sadly, spiritual death brought on physical death, and unless one turns to Christ, the concluding result will be *"the second death,"* which is the lake of fire, forever and forever (Rev. 20:14).

We know, as we shall see, that Adam had an amazing intelligence. In fact, I think that no man since has had the intelligence level of Adam, at least that which he had before the Fall. But yet, I'm not sure if he fully understood what the word *"die,"* actually meant. Considering that he was created to live forever, and by virtue of the Tree of Life, death, as it is presently, was not in his thinking.

Even though the Bible doesn't say, I do believe that God explained to him what all of this meant, even as he gave him the command not to eat of the fruit of the tree of the knowledge of good and evil. Knowing the detailed account of the creation, and the meticulous way in which God does things, I must believe that He meticulously explained all of this to our first parent. But regrettably, and as we shall see, he chose to disobey.

(18) "AND THE LORD GOD SAID, IT IS NOT GOOD THAT THE MAN SHOULD BE ALONE; I WILL MAKE HIM AN HELP MEET FOR HIM."

The construction is:

1. God never intended that man should be alone.

2. The plan always had been to make *"an help meet for him."*

3. These statements, as we shall see, are not meant to infer that the creation of woman was an afterthought. There is no Plan of God that is incomplete!

A COMPANION

The phrase, *"And the LORD God said, It is not good that the man should be alone,"* was not an idea that suddenly presented itself to the Lord. God is Omnipotent (all-powerful), Omniscient (all-knowing), meaning that there are no surprises with God, nor any situation which presents itself, of which He doesn't have full knowledge. From the time that the Godhead had made the decision to create man, whenever that may have been in eternity past, at that time, the creation of woman was planned as well.

HELPMATE

The phrase, *"I will make him an help meet for him,"* proclaims the fact that the Lord did exactly that. He made a helpmate for Adam, and made it possible for all men who would follow thereafter to have the same. What a Blessing!

All that Adam's nature demanded for its completion, physically, intellectually, and socially was to be included in this one who was soon to stand by his side. Thus, in man's need, and woman's power to satisfy that need, is laid the foundation for the Divine institution of marriage, which was afterwards prescribed not for the first pair alone, but for all their posterity (Spence).

(19) "AND OUT OF THE GROUND THE LORD GOD FORMED EVERY BEAST OF THE FIELD, AND EVERY FOWL OF THE AIR; AND BROUGHT THEM UNTO ADAM TO SEE WHAT HE WOULD CALL THEM: AND WHATSOEVER ADAM CALLED EVERY LIVING CREATURE, THAT WAS THE NAME THEREOF."

38

The composition is:

1. Out of dust the Lord God formed every beast of the field, and every fowl of the air.

2. Adam gave names to all of these creatures.

3. In the name he gave to each creature we find the entirety of the characteristics of that particular animal or fowl.

BROUGHT THEM UNTO ADAM

The phrase, *"And out of the ground the LORD God formed every beast of the field, and every fowl of the air; and brought them unto Adam,"* pertains to specimens.

We must understand that this Chapter is not intended to be a chronology of creation. The narrative runs according to what is being done at the moment.

LIVING CREATURES

The phrase, *"To see what he would call them: and whatsoever Adam called every living creature, that was the name thereof,"* presents two things:

1. Carried within the name that Adam gave to each one of these creatures are the characteristics of that particular animal or fowl. And let the Reader understand that the name hasn't changed from then until now.

2. This proclaims to us the fact that Adam was of such intelligence as to defy all description. What type of intelligence does it take for one to know all the characteristics of these creatures?!

So I think it should be overly obvious that we aren't speaking here of a dolt, or an animal-crawling primate, suggested by some.

To do all of this, Adam had to have a distinct knowledge of speech, the meaning of all words, and the capacity of attaching words to ideas.

Why not?! Adam had the greatest Teacher that man has ever had, *"the Lord God."*

(20) "AND ADAM GAVE NAMES TO ALL CATTLE, AND TO THE FOWL OF THE AIR, AND TO EVERY BEAST OF THE FIELD; BUT FOR ADAM THERE WAS NOT FOUND AN HELP MEET FOR HIM."

The exegesis is:

1. Adam gave names to all the cattle, fowls of the air, and every beast of the field.

2. As stated, in these names were incorporated all the characteristics of the particular creatures so named.

3. No creation in the animal kingdom provided suitable companionship, at least that which was needed.

NAMES

The phrase, *"And Adam gave names to all cattle, and to the fowl of the air, and to every beast of the field,"* proclaims the amazing degree of intelligence possessed by Earth's first man. When we understand that these names incorporate every characteristic of each particular creature, and that these names come down to us unto this very hour, then we are forced to recognize the amazing intelligence possessed by this man.

If man had not fallen, the world would have been a far different place, which is actually a gross understatement. In fact, there's really no way that we can even remotely comprehend what would have been. We get some idea from the Prophets as they spoke of the coming Millennial Reign; however, even then there will still be sin in the world, despite the fact that Jesus will be Personally ruling from Jerusalem. But yet at that particular time, the world will come close to that which God originally intended.

Man has repeatedly attempted to rebuild this paradise himself. His problem is, he tries to do it without the *"Tree of Life,"* which incidentally is the Lord Jesus Christ, and such simply cannot be done. The hearts of men are far too wicked, and hearts incidentally, which can only be changed by Christ. Even then, He had to pay a terrible price by the giving of Himself in Sacrifice on the Cross, in order that this terrible problem of sin might be properly addressed. Regrettably, the world refuses to understand the terrible malady of sin, although it fills the Earth with hatred, murder, and mayhem. Even the Church, I think, doesn't fully realize the terrible horror of sin, and I'll tell you why I say that:

THE CROSS OF CHRIST

If the Church fully understood the malady of sin as they should, they wouldn't keep advocating foolish things other than the Cross, as its cure. The Cross of Christ is the only answer to sin. That refers to the sinner being saved, or the Christian attempting to walk holy before the Lord. If we look to anything else, our looking is in vain! There is no help in any other direction.

This is why Paul said, *"We preach Christ Crucified"* (I Cor. 1:23). He didn't say merely, *"We preach Christ,"* but rather, *"We preach Christ Crucified."* The problem with the Church is, it preaches Christ, but in many and varied ways other than the Cross. Many preach Him as the great example; others preach Him as the Healer; others preach Him as the great prosperity-giver. In fact, the list is almost endless. But unless Christ is preached as the Saviour, and the Saviour by virtue of what He did at the Cross, lives will never be changed. That's why Paul said what he did.

PSYCHOLOGY

Unfortunately, much of the modern Church world, in fact, virtually all, has opted for the psychological way.

Let the Reader understand first of all that the psychological way and the way of the Cross are so diametrically opposed to each other, so diametrically different, so originating from totally different sources that there is no way the two can be wedded.

As for Preachers to claim that the two can be melded shows either a terrible ignorance of the Cross of Christ, or else gross unbelief.

The Lord began to open up to me the Revelation of the Cross in 1996. That Revelation continues unto this hour. At that time, I felt that the foray of the Church into humanistic psychology was, for the most part, caused by ignorance of the Word of God. While that certainly is the case with some, after several years now of observing the Church scene, with much more knowledgeable eyes, I regrettably must come to the conclusion that the real reason the Cross has been abandoned is because of rank unbelief. And to be sure, that is the most dangerous position of all. Ignorance can be corrected, but it is far harder to correct unbelief.

In fact, for unbelief to be corrected, one has to completely and totally renounce the erroneous way that one is traveling, which is very difficult for most to do.

PERSONAL

In fact, the reason that virtually all of the Church world denounces my person is because

of this very thing which we are presently addressing — the Cross. They may claim other things constitute the reason, but the other things are actually only an excuse. The real reason has always been, and is presently, our stand regarding the Lord Jesus Christ and the Cross upon which He died. We claim this is the answer, and in fact, the only answer for hurting humanity. They claim that other things are the answer, hence the juxtaposition.

Admittedly, in 1988, I did not know and understand the Cross as it regards the Sanctification of the Saint. To be sure, I understood the Cross as it regards the initial Salvation experience, and preached it about as strongly as anyone in the world. As a result, the Lord gave us literally hundreds of thousands of souls, for which we give Him all the praise and all the glory.

But not knowing and understanding the Cross as it regards our everyday walk before God, in fact, I was actually reliving the Seventh Chapter of Romans.

This Chapter catalogs Paul's experience after he was saved and baptized with the Holy Spirit, and actually called to be an Apostle; however, at that time, he did not know the Victory of the Cross, and as a result, was attempting to live for Christ by his own strength, etc. Despite trying so hard, he failed, and the following are his exact words:

"For that which I do I allow (understand) *not: for what I would, that do I not; but what I hate, that do I"* (Rom. 7:15).

And then he said:

"For I know that in me (that is, in my flesh,) dwelleth no good thing: for to will is present with me; but how to perform that which is good I find not" (Rom. 7:18).

He plainly tells us here that he is trying to live for God by the virtue of willpower, but found to his dismay that the will alone wasn't enough.

That's where I was, and that's where millions of Christians are presently. They're trying with all their strength to live as they ought to live, but failing miserably. And the sad fact is, the harder they struggle, the worse the situation actually becomes. They are left very, very confused. So what are such Christians doing?

Strangely enough, many of these particular Christians are some of the hardest workers for the Lord in the world. In fact, some of them are extremely consecrated.

Now an unbelieving Church may not agree with that, claiming that such cannot be. But the truth is, the ones doing the criticizing are in worse shape, spiritually speaking, than the ones toward which they are leveling the criticism.

It doesn't matter what a Believer does, or how hard he tries, if he doesn't know and understand the victory of the Cross, which simply means he is to know that everything comes to him from God by and through what Jesus did at the Cross, and that his faith must ever be in the Finished Work of Christ (Rom. 6:3-5, 11, 14). With this done, and continuing to be done even on a daily basis (Lk. 9:23), the Holy Spirit will then work mightily on behalf of the Believer, guaranteeing victory, and victory on a perpetual basis (Rom. 8:1-2, 11).

But if the Christian doesn't know this, thereby seeking to live for God by other means and ways, he is doomed to failure, and irrespective as to whom he might be.

As stated, in 1988, I did not know this, and despite trying so very, very hard, I failed. And I might quickly add, such failure is inevitable if the Believer doesn't understand the Cross.

And despite the shame, the humiliation, the pain, and the suffering, if the Believer continues in his lack of understanding, the failure will continue as well. Unfortunately, pain and suffering are not the cure that will give victory over the attacks by the powers of darkness.

So my enemies took full advantage of that. But the real reason was that I was preaching the Cross. Admittedly, I was only preaching it as it regards the Salvation of sinners, but at the same time, I was still saying, and saying loudly, and on a worldwide basis, that the psychological way was wrong. That didn't set very well with the leaders of particular Denominations, considering that they had embraced the psychological way in totality. So when an opportunity presented itself for them to exact their pound of flesh, they took full advantage. But again, the reason wasn't what it looked like to the world, but rather what I preached, and I speak of the Cross.

THE OFFENCE OF THE CROSS

Paul said: *"And I, Brethren, if I yet preach circumcision, why do I yet suffer persecution?*

NOTES

Then is the offence of the Cross ceased" (Gal. 5:11).

The Holy Spirit, through the Apostle, plainly tells us here that the Cross of Christ is an offence, not only to the world, but to many in the Church. In other words, if one preaches the Cross, lives the Cross, places his faith and confidence totally and completely in what Christ did at the Cross, that will be an offence to many so-called Christians.

Why?

There are two reasons why this happens:

1. There is something in all Believers which desires to live this life for Christ by our own strength and ability. It is a carryover from the Fall. As a result, it's very hard for us to completely *"deny ourselves,"* and thereby to totally trust Christ (Lk. 9:23). So the tendency is always there as it regards dependence on the flesh.

2. Organized religion always builds up a dependence on the organization. In other words, it little by little pulls Preachers into a dependence on what that organization can do for them, which even carries over to their everyday life and living. In fact, all Believers who belong to that particular Denomination are, much of the time, and little by little, made to believe that the mere association with that organization brings some type of spirituality.

So trust, Faith, and dependence on Christ are little by little eroded, being replaced by faith in the Denomination. It is so subtle that the person hardly knows that it's happening.

When the Believer begins to depend totally and completely on the Cross of Christ, and I speak of what Jesus did there for us, he will run headlong into *"the flesh,"* and organized religion. This is what Paul was talking about as it regards *"the offence of the Cross."*

At the first part of the Verse he mentioned the preaching of circumcision. In effect he was saying that if he continued to preach circumcision, speaking of a dependence on the Law, joining that to Christ, then the offence of the Cross would cease. But when he told the Church that circumcision and adherence to the Law avail them nothing at all, but rather that which Jesus did at the Cross, that struck a nerve. And to be sure, that nerve is still in view presently.

So if the Believer charts a course that takes him strictly to the Cross, and total dependence on the Cross, it's going to rub a lot of fur the wrong way. To trust completely in Christ and what Christ did for us at the Cross, at the same time, means to throw over everything else, all the religious props, denominational attachments, personal strength and ability, everything, etc.

No, this doesn't mean that it's wrong to belong to a Denomination or a Church, etc. It just means that it's wrong to put faith and confidence in these things, considering that they are merely man-made, and man-devised efforts and institutions. But the point I wish to make is this:

Once one begins to trust exclusively in Christ, and what Christ has done for us at the Cross, of necessity, this cuts off everything else. This is actually what Paul was meaning when he said:

"I wish they were even cut off which trouble you" (Gal. 5:12).

In other words, there were Judaizers who were trying to get the Galatians to embrace the Law along with Christ, and Paul, in essence, is saying that these people, plus their influence, must be cut off from these who had embraced the Cross.

FELLOWSHIP

Until the Lord showed me this, it grieved me. Let me explain:

I want and desire fellowship with other Brothers and Sisters in the Lord. Being shunned, ostracized, and rejected are not exactly very pleasant. So I sought the Lord earnestly about the matter.

Ultimately He showed me that it was the Cross which drew the line. In other words, there was no way that fellowship would be forthcoming with those who had rejected the Cross. Fellowship could only be with those who had accepted the Cross. And to be sure, it's not a separation that one has to enforce. The Cross itself will force the separation.

So this means that almost all, and I speak of present times, who associate themselves with Denominations, will little respond favorably to those who place their trust completely in the Cross. Am I saying that one cannot belong to a Denomination and at the

same time place one's Faith totally and completely in Christ and what Christ has done at the Cross?

I'm not saying that at all; however, I am saying that the tendency of Denominations, even as we've already stated, is to foster dependence on the Denomination instead of Christ and Him Crucified. As one might say, it's the nature of the beast.

And then there are those who look to the flesh, in other words, their own ability and strength. They reject the Cross in favor of Commandments. There can be no fellowship in that capacity either!

So the Lord showed me that it was not so much me they were rejecting, but in effect the Cross.

Are they saved?

Some are, and some aren't!

But one thing is certain: For all who reject the Cross, even though they are truly saved, there will be no Spiritual Growth, and failure and defeat in some way will ever be the lot of their spiritual lives. It's impossible for it to be otherwise. The Holy Spirit through Paul plainly stated:

"I do not frustrate the Grace of God: for if righteousness come by the Law, then Christ is dead in vain" (Gal. 2:21).

In other words, if we can walk in Righteousness, and I speak of the Righteousness which comes exclusively from the Lord, by any method other than trusting in Christ and what He did at the Cross, then Jesus didn't need to come down here and die on a Cross. So by the very fact that He had to die on a Cross plainly tells us that this is the way, and there is no other. Righteousness cannot come by the Law, cannot come by our own efforts, ability, or by anything that man may devise. It can only come by and through what Christ did for us at the Cross, and our Faith in that Finished Work, which then guarantees the help of the Holy Spirit.

HELPMATE

The phrase, *"But for Adam there was not found an help meet for him,"* was meant to show the first man that the animal kingdom, as beautiful and helpful as some of them were, would be of no help to Adam, at least the help he needed.

To be sure, the Lord already knew all of this, but He wanted Adam to know this as well. Ellicott said: *"But while he could tame many, and make them share his dwelling, he found among them (the animals) no counterpart of himself, capable of answering his thoughts and of holding with him rational discourse."*

The Lord knew all the time what He would do, for in fact, it had been planned from before the foundation of the world (I Pet. 1:18-20).

I think one can say without any fear of contradiction that the Lord always creates a desire in our heart for something, which He proposes to give, although we may understand little about it to begin with.

Adam had no way of knowing what the Lord would do, but he did know that there was a deep longing within his heart for companionship — but yet a type of companionship which would be completely compatible with himself, but yet would not be exactly the same as himself. That's the reason he inspected the animal kingdom very closely.

There is nothing more important than a proper helpmate for a man, other than his personal relationship with the Lord. And in fact, he can never really know all that the helpmate can be, until he fully knows the Lord as he should.

I thank God every day of my life that He was gracious enough to give me Frances. Truly, she has filled this role, and continues to fill this role, to its utmost. In other words, as far as I'm concerned, it would not be possible for the Lord to have given me anything better.

When the Lord said *"helpmate,"* He meant exactly that. A woman has intuition that a man just doesn't have. She has greater sensitivity to things than he has, and, thereby, is able to discern, I think, to a greater extent.

In view of this, the Holy Spirit, through Paul, said: *"Wives, submit yourselves unto your own husbands, as unto the Lord"* (Eph. 5:22).

This means that the husband is to act and conduct himself as the Lord; consequently, it would not be hard for any woman to submit themselves to a man of that particular character and kindness.

He then said, *"Husbands, love your wives, even as Christ also loved the Church, and gave Himself for it"* (Eph. 5:25).

Christ loved the Church enough to die for it. The husband is to love his wife accordingly.

AN IDEAL MARRIAGE

One of the great problems in marriage, and perhaps the greatest problem, is for the husband or wife, or both, to demand of their partner what only Christ can provide. I am persuaded that this is the cause of most marriage problems, even with Christians.

The human being can only be properly satisfied and fulfilled in Christ. But if the husband tries to make the wife meet this spiritual need, or vice versa, there will be burnout. And regrettably, that is the problem with many, if not most.

Addressing Christians, one cannot really know Christ fully, unless one knows and understands the Cross. Otherwise, they are serving and trusting *"another Jesus"* (II Cor. 11:4), which means that Christ cannot truly and properly be to that person what He wants to be, and because their faith is misplaced. Let's say it in a stronger way:

No Believer can know Christ exactly as he should, unless he knows Him in relationship to the Cross. Only there can he find *"more abundant life"* (Jn. 10:10). In truth, every single Christian in the world has *"more abundant life."* One cannot be saved without having this particular *"life"*; however, most Christians never enjoy this *"Life,"* and because they do not understand the Cross (Col. 2:14-15). And then not really enjoying this Life, and because they don't understand the Cross, they look to their mate to meet the need in their heart, which no human being can possibly do.

(21) "AND THE LORD GOD CAUSED A DEEP SLEEP TO FALL UPON ADAM, AND HE SLEPT: AND HE TOOK ONE OF HIS RIBS, AND CLOSED UP THE FLESH INSTEAD THEREOF;"

The overview is:

1. This Verse records the first anesthesia.

2. The word *"rib"* here actually means *"side."*

3. The woman is not merely of a rib, but actually of one side of man.

DEEP SLEEP

The phrase, *"And the LORD God caused a deep sleep to fall upon Adam, and he slept,"* records, as stated, the first anesthesia.

Quite obviously, the Lord explained all of this to Adam after it was done. And to be sure, He no doubt explained every facet of His creation to the first man, exactly as it is recorded here.

Even though this information, even word for word, was passed down from generation to generation, it was not until Moses, some 2,500 years after Adam, that a complete record was made, in that which we now know as the Book of Genesis.

Incidentally, in the Hebrew, the term *"Lord God,"* is actually *"Yahweh God."*

THE RIB

The phrase, *"And He took one of his ribs, and closed up the flesh instead thereof,"* indicates in the Hebrew far more than a rib. It speaks of the rib with the accompanying flesh, which included the blood, the nerves, etc. This means that woman is one side of man; and though he may have several sides to his nature and character, yet without woman one integral portion of him is wanting (Ellicott).

In a sense, Adam in this procedure was a figure of Him Who was to come; for out of the side of Christ, the Second Adam, His spouse the Church was formed, when He slept the sleep, the deep sleep of death upon the Cross; in order to which His side was opened, and there came out Blood and water, Blood to purchase His Church, and water to purify it to Himself (I Jn. 5:6) (Henry).

(22) "AND THE RIB, WHICH THE LORD GOD HAD TAKEN FROM MAN, MADE HE A WOMAN, AND BROUGHT HER UNTO THE MAN."

The synopsis is:

1. In this manner, God built a woman.

2. He brought her unto Adam to be his helpmate.

3. The word *"brought"* insinuates a formal presentation, i.e., *"wedding."* God was the Best Man, so to speak!

BUILT A WOMAN!

The phrase, *"And the rib, which the LORD God had taken from man, made He a woman,"* in the Hebrew actually says, *"built He a woman."*

Horton says, *"When God created the man the word 'form' was used, which is the same*

word used of a potter forming a clay jar. But the word 'build' here seems to mean God paid even more attention to the creation of the woman."

THE WEDDING

The phrase, *"And brought her unto the man,"* implies a formal presentation.

When Adam awakened from his *"deep sleep,"* the Lord as the attending Physician, was standing over him. He had placed Eve, for that's what her name would be, a distance away, perhaps hidden from view.

And then possibly without further explanation, but with Adam knowing that something had transpired, and something wonderful, He *"presented"* the woman unto the man. This was the first marriage.

All of this implies the solemn bestowment of her in the bonds of the Marriage Covenant, which is hence called the Covenant of God (Prov. 2:17); indicating that God is the Author of this sacred institution (Bush).

As God was present at this *"wedding,"* He desires to be present at all weddings. The reason that over half of the marriages in this nation conclude in divorce is because God is not present at the wedding and is, therefore, little present, if at all, in the union.

If the young man and young lady will earnestly seek the Lord as it regards their mate, earnestly desiring His Will, to be sure, the Lord will answer this all-important prayer. Most marriages, sadly, aren't in the Will of God, so they little hold together. And then after marriage, if Christ is one's Lord, such a marriage will be blessed and, therefore, fruitful.

(23) "AND ADAM SAID, THIS IS NOW BONE OF MY BONES, AND FLESH OF MY FLESH: SHE SHALL BE CALLED WOMAN, BECAUSE SHE WAS TAKEN OUT OF MAN."

The exegesis is:

1. In all of God's creation, before woman was created, Adam had found none that answered to his wants and needs.

2. On waking from his trance, which God had induced, he found one presented to him, whom he recognized as a second self.

3. He welcomed her joyfully, and exclaimed, *"This at last is bone of my bones, and flesh of my flesh."*

4. That is, she is man's counterpart, not merely in feeling and sense — his flesh — but in his solid qualities.

BONE OF MY BONES, AND FLESH OF MY FLESH

The phrase, *"And Adam said, This is now bone of my bones, and flesh of my flesh,"* refers to the fact that this one is proper. None of the animal kingdom would suffice, simply because they were different. But this beautiful woman standing before Adam *"was bone of his bones, and flesh of his flesh."* He was meaning that Eve was man's counterpart, not merely in feeling and sense — his flesh — but in his solid qualities.

In several of the Semitic dialects *"bone"* is used for *"self."* So in essence, he was saying, *"This is now self of my self, and flesh of my flesh."*

Martin Luther said concerning this moment, *"The little word 'now' is very meaningful. It expresses the love of Adam, who longed for communion with a woman so full of affection and holiness. Today the bridegroom still longs for his bride, but his love is no longer pure because of sin. Adam's love for Eve was most pure, cordial, and pleasing to God."*

WOMAN

The phrase, *"She shall be called Woman, because she was taken out of Man,"* presents a beautiful description of marriage. Everything which the man has, the woman has also. Both are of the same mind and good will toward each other so that the man differs in no way from the woman except by the dissimilarity of sex.

As someone has beautifully said, God did not take the woman out of man's feet to be stepped on as an inferior; nor out of his head to be put on a pedestal as a superior; but from his side close to his heart as an equal. She was to take her share of responsibility, and to love him and be loved by him.

(24) "THEREFORE SHALL A MAN LEAVE HIS FATHER AND HIS MOTHER, AND SHALL CLEAVE UNTO HIS WIFE: AND THEY SHALL BE ONE FLESH."

The structure is:

1. This Passage must be viewed as an inspired declaration of the law of marriage.

NOTES

2. It is placed in the heart of a young man and a young woman to leave their parents as it regards habitation, and to cleave unto a wife or husband.

3. *"One flesh"* points to a unity of persons, and not simply to a conjunction of bodies, or a community of interests, or even a reciprocity of affections.

HIS WIFE

The phrase, *"Therefore shall a man leave his father and his mother, and shall cleave unto his wife,"* proclaims the plan and sanction of God regarding marriage. And let it be unequivocally understood that this in no way places a seal of approval upon same sex marriages, which in effect are an abomination in the eyes of God. Homosexuality is a grievous sin, and cannot be condoned under any circumstances. As stated, it is abominable in God's Eyes.

In fact, it is so bad that the word translated *"dogs"* in Revelation 22:15 refers to homosexuals. The Passage says:

"For without are dogs, and sorcerers, and whoremongers, and murderers, and idolaters, and whosoever loves and makes a lie."

Concerning the sin of homosexuality, Paul said: *"For this cause God gave them up unto vile affections: for even their women did change the natural use into that which is against nature:*

"And likewise also the men, leaving the natural use of the woman, burned in their lust one toward another; men with men working that which is unseemly, and receiving in themselves that recompense of their error which was meet" (Rom. 1:26-27).

Whenever Legislators legalize same sex marriages, they are, in effect, blaspheming God. They are making a mockery out of creation, which will ultimately bring upon their heads the Judgment of God. Making sin *"legal"* doesn't make it right; it only exacerbates the problem.

The hope for the homosexual, and any other sinner for that matter, is to come to Christ, Who will deliver such a person from the terrible bondages of darkness, cleanse them, and set them free. It can only be done, however, in Christ.

Coming back to the original thought of the Text, unless God unites the man and the woman, there is no real marriage, but only an unhallowed connection, legitimized by man's laws, but not sanctioned by God's.

ONE FLESH

The phrase, *"And they shall be one flesh,"* pertains to one in unity and essence. In effect, this phrase also explains the Trinity. While there are Three Persons in the Godhead, *"God the Father, God the Son, and God the Holy Spirit,"* They are One in unity and essence.

The *"one flesh"* is at least one of the reasons that premarital sex or extramarital activity is so wrong. Sex is to never be looked at as merely a physical pleasure. While it is that, it definitely is not merely that. It is the joining together physically of what has already been joined together spiritually, and in that sense between a husband and wife who truly love each other, and who truly love God, is a holy thing.

In a broad sense, the sex act between a loving husband and wife, as stated, who truly love the Lord, is typical of one's union with Christ. As marriage is not merely a psychological or philosophical union, but something far deeper, likewise, one's union with Christ is actually likened by the Holy Spirit as marriage.

Paul said concerning this very thing: *"Wherefore, my Brethren, you also are become dead to the Law by the Body of Christ; that you should be married to another, even to Him Who is raised from the dead, that we should bring forth fruit unto God"* (Rom. 7:4).

As well, Believers, in a sense, are referred to by John as, *"the Bride, the Lamb's wife"* (Rev. 21:9).

While the union of husband and wife is *"one flesh,"* the union of Christ and the Believer is in essence, *"one spirit."*

(25) "AND THEY WERE BOTH NAKED, THE MAN AND HIS WIFE, AND WERE NOT ASHAMED."

The construction is.

1. The word *"naked"* referred to an absence of clothing, at least as we understand such.

2. They were actually enswathed in ethereal and transfiguring light.

3. They were not ashamed, because there was nothing of which to be ashamed.

NAKED

The phrase, *"And they were both naked, the man and his wife,"* refers to clothing as we think of such presently.

Concerning God, the Scripture says: *"Who only has immortality, dwelling in the light which no man can approach unto"* (I Tim. 6:16).

This Passage tells us that God is enswathed in light.

Inasmuch as Adam and Eve are made in the Image of God, and in His Likeness, it stands to reason that their original covering was the same as that of God's, which was light. In fact, this will probably be the covering of the Glorified Body at the First Resurrection of Life.

Sadly, the covering of light was lost at the Fall.

ASHAMED

The phrase, *"And were not ashamed,"* is said simply, because there was nothing to be ashamed about.

When we stand one day in the celestial Eden, where they neither marry nor are given in marriage, will garments of such incomparable splendor be ours. In the meantime let us say with Isaiah:

"I will greatly rejoice in the LORD, my soul shall be joyful in my God; for He has clothed me with the garments of Salvation, He has covered me with the robe of Righteousness, as a bridegroom decks himself with ornaments, and as a bride adorns herself with her jewels" (Isa. 61:10).

"There is a name from Heaven given,
  God's matchless love its accents tell;
"It tells of One Who calls us 'Brethren,'
  and this His name Emmanuel!
"The Lord, by Angels worshipped yonder, has stooped to Earth with men to dwell,
"Incarnate God, and man forever Our own beloved Emmanuel."

"Another name there is so precious, it moves the heart with deepest love:
"It is the blessed name of Jesus, the name of all other names above.
"It tells me that He is my Saviour, how on the Cross His life He gave.

*"I love the precious name of Jesus, for I
am one He came to save!"*

*"Though dear to us the name of Jesus,
the name of Christ is also dear!
"It tells of Him Who dwells within us, to
cleanse our hearts and cast out fear.
"It tells me of the Spirit's fullness. It
brings the pow'r of Pentecost.
"O blessed Christ, come in Your fullness,
and fill me with the Holy Ghost!"*

*"These names shall live and live forever,
eternal hope and peace they bring;
"My heart is stirred whenever I hear
them, my Blessed Lord, of You I sing!
"How great You are, You King of Glory!
Lo at Your Feet I humbly fall,
"Oh, make my heart Your Holy Kingdom, that I may crown You Lord
of all!"*

CHAPTER 3

(1) "NOW THE SERPENT WAS MORE
SUBTIL THAN ANY BEAST OF THE FIELD
WHICH THE LORD GOD HAD MADE. AND
HE SAID UNTO THE WOMAN, YES, HAS
GOD SAID, YOU SHALL NOT EAT OF EV-
ERY TREE OF THE GARDEN?"

The construction is:

1. As one of God's creatures, the serpent
was originally good.

2. *"Subtilty"* refers here not to something
negative, but rather positive.

3. The serpent at that time evidently had
the ability of limited speech.

4. Eve did not seem surprised that he
spoke to her.

5. As well, every indication is that the serpent, at that time, moved upright, instead of
on its belly, as it later would be condemned
to do.

6. The serpent evidently lent its faculties
to Satan, even though the Evil One is not
mentioned here.

7. Through the serpent Satan speaks, and
questions the Word of God.

8. He asked the question, *"Yes, has God
said, 'You shall not eat of every tree of the
garden?'"*, intending ultimately to draw

NOTES

attention to the tree of the knowledge of good
and evil.

THE SERPENT

The phrase, *"Now the serpent was more
subtil than any beast of the field which the
LORD God had made,"* draws attention to
the animal which Satan used to carry out his
perfidious intentions.

Due to the fact that this was before the
Fall, and that everything God had created was
good, we know that the word *"subtil"* used
here is not negative, but rather positive. It
describes qualities which in themselves were
good, such as quickness of sight, swiftness
of motion, activity of the self-preserving instinct, and seemingly intelligent adaptation
to its surroundings.

As well, there is every evidence that it
moved upright at that time, consigned to its
belly only after the Fall, as a part of the curse
leveled upon it. Some argue that this is unlikely due to the skeletal make-up of the serpent; however, this could very well have
changed at the Fall, which it no doubt did.

Satan is not mentioned here, but it is obvious that he is the one using the serpent as
a tool.

Of course, the question must be asked
whether Satan was there personally, or in
fact, was using a demon spirit. Actually, it
seems as if he was using an evil spirit.

Satan is a fallen angel, and as such, cannot literally inhabit the physical body of anyone or anything; however, demon spirits definitely can function in this capacity, and do
so commonly. So, the manner of this temptation probably was that Satan was using a
demon spirit to function through this animal, which evidently gave permission in
some way for its body and faculties to be
used. I don't think an evil spirit could have
entered the body of this serpent otherwise.
As well, it seems from all of this that the serpent as well had a limited power of choice,
which means that he had a limited intelligence. If he could speak, and every evidence
is that he could, then he must have had limited intelligence.

If in fact the serpent was an unwitting tool
in the hand of Satan, then I think that the
Lord would not have placed a curse upon this

animal, using the words, *"Because you have done this, you are cursed . . ."* (Gen. 3:14).

SATAN

We would wonder why were Satan or demon spirits even allowed in the Garden, or in fact, on the Earth at all?

There would seem to be two reasons, which have to do with cause and effect:

1. The reason why God allowed Lucifer to continue in a state of freedom after his rebellion, which evidently took place before the world was brought back to a habitable state, and before Adam and Eve were created, has to come under the term *"the Mystery of God"* (Rev. 10:7). We do not know why the Lord allowed this, and as well, He hasn't seen fit to reveal His reasons.

2. We do know that God uses Satan constantly. Of course, Satan's effort is to *"steal, kill, and destroy,"* but naturally, God always has something else in mind (Jn. 10:10).

As an example, man had to be tested, and even though there were no doubt other ways and means that God could have used, He carried out the testing by allowing Satan certain latitude in the Garden. As we all know, this testing didn't turn out too well, resulting in the Fall.

Our knowledge is very, very limited in all of this, for the simple reason that the story of the Bible is not the story of the fall of Lucifer, but rather the story of the Creation, the Fall, and the Redemption of mankind. Even though the Evil One plays heavily into all of this, as would be overly obvious, he is in fact secondary.

The principal player in the entirety of the Bible is the *"Lord Jesus Christ"*; the principal purpose is *"Redemption"*; the principal object of this Redemption of course, is *"man,"* who is God's greatest creation; the principal means by which Redemption is carried out is the *"Cross."*

DISPENSATIONS

The period of time from the Creation of Adam and Eve to the Fall is called the Dispensation of Innocence. There is no way to know exactly how long this period lasted. Some claim that it lasted only a day or so, with others a much longer period of time. It

is my contention that the Dispensation of Innocence lasted for 40 days.

I say that because we find that the number 40 is God's number of probation in the Bible. Moses fasted 40 days and 40 nights before the Law was given. Jesus, as well, fasted 40 days and 40 nights. Israel lingered 40 years in the wilderness. So quite possibly, Adam and Eve existed in innocence for 40 days before the Fall. But again, that is only speculation.

After the Fall, man enters into the age or Dispensation of Conscience. This lasted for approximately 1,600 years, or up to the time of Noah. From Noah to Abraham, a period of about 400 years, we have the Dispensation of Government.

At the time of Abraham, man entered into the Dispensation of Promise. This was due to the great promises made to Abraham as it regarded a number of things, but especially that of the coming Redeemer. This Dispensation lasted about 400 years (I've rounded off the numbers).

At the time of Moses, mankind entered into the Dispensation of Law. This Dispensation continued up unto the Crucifixion and Resurrection of Christ, which was a period of approximately 1,600 years.

Beginning on the Day of Pentecost, mankind entered into the Dispensation of Grace, which continues unto this hour, a period thus far of about 2,000 years.

The next Dispensation will be that of Righteousness, and will commence at the Second Coming, and is labeled as the *"Millennial Reign."* It will last for 1,000 years.

The final Dispensation, that is if one could refer to that coming day in this fashion, is the Dispensation of the Perfect Age. It will commence immediately after the Millennial Reign, and will last forever. It is characterized in Revelation, Chapters 21 and 22.

(The word *"Dispensation"* refers to a system of revealed commands and promises regulating human affairs. In the manner in which we are using the word, it refers to the dealings of God with the human race, and the manner in which these dealings are carried out.)

Other than the final dispensation, declension, not progress, is stamped upon all.

Each period opens hopefully but ends in Judgment. This Third Chapter of Genesis narrates the ruin and judgment of the first Dispensation.

THE FIRST TEMPTATION

The question, *"And he said unto the woman, Yes, has God said, You shall not eat of every tree of the Garden?"*, presents the beginning of the first temptation.

It begins with Satan twisting the Word of God, trying to make it say something that it did not really say. He did the same with Christ in the wilderness of temptation (Mat. 4:6). In fact, every single going astray of a human being is that they ignore the Word of God, as all unredeemed do, or else they misinterpret the Word of God, as do Christians. Admittedly, while it's not misinterpreted intentionally, the end result is the same.

An individual who is lost doesn't take the wrong road intentionally, but irrespective of good intentions, he is still lost, and with negative results.

That's the reason it's absolutely imperative for the Believer to know and understand the Word of God. Knowing the Bible, which certainly can be done if a person will apply themselves, should be a lifelong project. Unfortunately, most Christians presently little know the Word of God; consequently, they take the word of whatever Preacher strikes them in a positive sense. In other words, they look on the outward, which is a poor way to judge the situation. In effect, they have placed their lives in the hands of this individual, and possibly even their souls, taking his word for whatever is done.

Untold millions are in Hell right now because of this very thing. They didn't know the Word of God, and they took the word of somebody else, which proved to be wrong, and caused them to be eternally lost. Nothing could be worse than that!

And remember this, Satan does not so much deny the Word, as he does to pervert the Word.

(2) "AND THE WOMAN SAID UNTO THE SERPENT, WE MAY EAT OF THE FRUIT OF THE TREES OF THE GARDEN:

(3) "BUT OF THE FRUIT OF THE TREE WHICH IS IN THE MIDDLE OF THE GARDEN, GOD HAS SAID, YOU SHALL NOT EAT

OF IT, NEITHER SHALL YOU TOUCH IT, LEST YOU DIE."

The composition is:

1. Satan, through the serpent, had addressed his question to the woman.

2. The woman answered the serpent, seemingly not surprised by his ability to speak, which shows that this animal evidently had at least some powers of limited speech.

3. She allowed, in answering the question, that they may eat of the fruit of all the other trees of the Garden, but not the fruit of the tree which was in the middle of the Garden.

4. She quoted what the Lord had said about the prohibition, but then added, *"neither shall you touch it."*

5. She reiterated the fact that the penalty for eating of this particular tree was death.

THE WOMAN

Verse 2 begins by stating, *"And the woman said unto the serpent,"* which proclaims Satan leveling his attack against Eve, instead of Adam. To be sure, his use of Eve was only a means to get to Adam.

Had the Fall stopped with Eve, which means that it would not have included Adam, the damage would have been confined to Eve. Due to the fact that it is the man who contains the seed of procreation, his partaking of the forbidden fruit would mean that not only would he fall, but the entirety of the human race which would follow after him would be fallen as well! In effect, all of humanity which would ever be born, with the exception of Jesus Christ, were in the loins of our first parent.

Evidently Satan thought that Eve was the more susceptible to his suggestions. Paul said concerning this incident: *"And Adam was not deceived, but the woman being deceived was in the transgression"* (I Tim. 2:14).

Whatever Satan's reasons for using Eve to get to Adam, we learn from this, or at least we should, that the Evil One plays very, very dirty. Honesty and integrity are foreign to this fallen angel. That's the reason that if we attempt to match wits with him, even as Eve did, we as well will do the same as Eve.

In the matter of temptation, we are told to have no dialogue whatsoever with the Evil One, but rather, *"Submit yourselves therefore to God. Resist the Devil, and he will flee from you"* (James 4:7).

Peter also said: *"Be sober, be vigilant; because your adversary the Devil, as a roaring lion, walks about, seeking whom he may devour:*

"Whom resist steadfast in the faith, knowing that the same afflictions are accomplished in your Brethren that are in the world" (I Pet. 5:8-9).

HOW DO WE RESIST THE DEVIL?

If most Christians had to answer this question, they would take their cue from Matthew, Chapter 4, concerning the temptation of Jesus in the wilderness. In other words, they would quote Scripture to Satan.

While the quoting of the Word of God is always good, that's not exactly what Jesus was doing as it regards His temptation by the Evil One.

Jesus was answering Satan's suggestions by quoting what the Bible actually said about the matter, whatever it may have been. While one could certainly say that the Master's approach was definitely a resistance to Satan, more than anything else, it was a presentation of the proper perspective of the Word of God.

In fact, both James and Peter tell us how to resist the Devil. James told us first of all to *"submit ourselves therefore to God."* Peter told us to resist the Evil One *"steadfast in the faith."*

When we submit ourselves to God, as James said, we are, in effect, submitting ourselves to God's Word and Way. What is that Way?

That Way is *"the Faith,"* even as Peter stated (I Pet. 5:9). And what is *"the Faith"*?

In abbreviated form, *"the Faith"* is *"Jesus Christ and Him Crucified"* (I Cor. 2:2). The idea is this:

The Believer is to have his Faith placed exclusively in the Cross of Christ, which then guarantees the help of the Holy Spirit. Listen to what Paul said.

"But if the Spirit (Holy Spirit) *of Him Who raised up Jesus from the dead* (God the Father) *dwell in you, He Who raised up Christ from the dead shall also quicken your mortal bodies by His Spirit that dwelleth in you"* (Rom. 8:11).

The *"quickening of our mortal bodies by His Spirit that dwells in us,"* does not refer to the coming Resurrection, but rather speaks of power at this present time in order to overcome Satan and all temptation.

Paul also said: *"For the Law of the Spirit of Life in Christ Jesus has made me free from the law of sin and death"* (Rom. 8:2).

The words *"in Christ Jesus,"* refer exclusively to what Christ did at the Cross on our behalf. When we place our Faith in this Finished Work, the *"Law of the Spirit of Life in Christ Jesus,"* is effected on our behalf. Trusting in the great Sacrifice of Christ is properly resisting the Devil.

FORBIDDEN FRUIT

Verse 2 further reads, *"We may eat of the fruit of the trees of the Garden."*

Verse 3 reads, *"But of the fruit of the tree which is in the midst of the Garden, God has said, You shall not eat of it, neither shall you touch it, lest you die,"* proclaims the fact that Eve very well knew the prohibition.

The trial of our first parents was ordained by God, because probation was essential to their spiritual development and self-determination. But as He did not desire that they should be tempted to their fall, He would not suffer Satan to tempt them in a way which should surpass their human capacity. The tempted might, therefore, have resisted the tempter.

THE STRANGE WAYS OF TEMPTATION

Many scoff at the temptation of Eve, simply because they do not understand the creation. A serpent who speaks seems to them but idle tales, so they discount it as fable:

1. The Bible is the Word of God, which means that every single word between the covers is true. As well, the Bible doesn't merely contain Truth, it is Truth. Inspiration guarantees the veracity not only of the thought, but even down to the very word. In other words, the Holy Spirit literally searched through the vocabulary of Moses, until the right word was found, and then it was used, as the Lawgiver wrote the Text.

2. Before the Fall, the creation was totally different than it is now. The idea that the serpent could speak seemed to pose no surprise for Eve; consequently, even as previously

stated, it evidently had at least a limited ability to speak.

At any rate, Satan used the most unusual means by which to get the attention of Eve, and ultimately Adam, which he evidently did. Maybe we can say that in the case of every temptation, it comes in a most unusual manner, designed to carry forth its intended purpose. And what is that purpose?

Satan wants you to believe a lie!

(4) "AND THE SERPENT SAID UNTO THE WOMAN, YOU SHALL NOT SURELY DIE:"

The construction is:

1. As God had preached to Adam, Satan now preaches to Eve.

2. The object of Satan was to draw away Eve by what he said, from that which God had said.

3. His second step was to challenge the Divine veracity.

4. Jesus called Satan a liar, which probably refers to this very moment (Jn. 8:44).

THE SERPENT SAID

The phrase, *"And the serpent said unto the woman,"* presents a position which has now gone terribly wrong. Eve should not have answered Satan when he spoke to her the first time. That was her first mistake.

I have to believe that Eve was of vast intelligence along with her husband, Adam. They had God as their Teacher, and however long that was, was of monumental consequence. But despite all of that, she is now on the way to total deception.

This shows us that vast intelligence is not the answer. It does show us that obedience to the Word of God, and in every respect, is the answer. Deception can only come about whenever we leave the Word. And the sad thing about the modern Church is that it little knows the Word.

DENIAL OF THE WORD

The phrase, *"You shall not surely die,"* proclaims an outright denial of the Word of God, but with a subtle twist, as we shall see in the next Verse. Among other things, this is probably what Jesus was referring to when He said to the Pharisees concerning Satan: *"You are of your father the Devil, and the lusts of your father you will do. He was a*

murderer from the beginning, and abode not in the Truth, because there is no truth in him. When he speaks a lie, he speaks of his own, for he is a liar, and the father of it" (Jn. 8:44).

And what does he lie about? The answer is simple, *"everything!"*

So, in Eve's case, the moment she took herself out of the Hands of God — out of the position of absolute dependence upon, and subjection to, His Word — she abandoned herself to the government of sense, as used of Satan for her entire overthrow.

THE ENTRANCE OF DEATH

God never intended for Adam and Eve to die, or any who would come after them. By virtue of the Tree of Life, man was meant to live forever.

It was sin, i.e., *"the Fall,"* which brought on death. The first type of death which occurred was separation from God, which was spiritual death.

With spiritual death having set in, the physical body was likewise affected, and due to the fact that man was driven out of the Garden, therefore, unable to partake of the Tree of Life, physical death would ultimately occur. Even then, the physical body was so wondrously made that it took nearly 1,000 years for our first two or three generations to die.

All life comes from God, and with man cut off from God because of sin, man finds himself cut off from life.

It seems as if God did not explain all of this to Adam and Eve, rather just telling them not to eat of the tree of the knowledge of good and evil. They were to obey without question. But the tragedy is, they did not obey, and in their disobedience, they would then find out the terrible truth which I have just briefly explained. This was the *"knowledge"* of which they sought, but to their chagrin, it was not to be what they thought.

(5) "FOR GOD DOES KNOW THAT IN THE DAY YOU EAT THEREOF, THEN YOUR EYES SHALL BE OPENED, AND YOU SHALL BE AS GODS, KNOWING GOOD AND EVIL."

The overview is:

1. Satan accuses God of lying.

2. The eyes being opened suggested the attainment of higher wisdom.

3. He told them they would be as Elohim.

4. Now they knew only good, then, Satan says, they would know both good and evil.

5. What was it about the *"evil"* which enticed her?

EYES OPENED

The phrase, *"For God does know that in the day you eat thereof, then your eyes shall be opened,"* presents the promise of the impartation of power to perceive physically, mentally, and spiritually, objects not otherwise discernible. It suggested the attainment of higher wisdom, which in effect, claims a higher wisdom than God. Unfortunately, Satan has not stopped peddling that lie from then until now. And worse yet, untold hundreds of millions, even billions of souls have bought it.

Paul addressed this by saying, *"Professing themselves to be wise, they became fools"* (Rom. 1:22).

I'm dictating these notes on September 18, 2001. A week ago, September 11, 2001, the world was stunned and shocked by the senseless suicide bombing of the World Trade Center in New York City, and the Pentagon in Washington, D.C. Thousands lost their lives, and the sorrow of tens of thousands will be felt forever. As shocking and horrible as that was, however, the world is full of such activity, even on a daily basis, although on a smaller scale. It's all the result of the *"higher wisdom"* promised by Satan. That's why Jesus said:

"The thief cometh not, but for to steal, and to kill, and to destroy: I am come that they might have life, and they might have it more abundantly" (Jn. 10:10).

The truth is, all eyes have been blinded as a result of the Fall. They are opened only, and I mean only, as one accepts Christ as one's personal Saviour. This is what Jesus was talking about when He said: *"Except a man be born again, he cannot see the Kingdom of God"* (Jn. 3:3).

KNOWING GOOD AND EVIL

The phrase, *"And you shall be as gods, knowing good and evil,"* in effect says, *"You shall be as Elohim."* It was a promise of Divinity.

God is Omniscient, meaning that He is all-knowing; however, His knowledge of evil, and

that knowledge is thorough, is not through Personal experience. By His very Nature, He is totally separate from all that is evil, and He hates it. The knowledge of evil that Eve would learn would be by moral degradation, which of course, God never experienced, and in fact, could not experience. It would not be by intellectual insight that her ambitions would be fulfilled.

THE PROBLEM WHICH PERSISTS

If we are to notice, whatever happened at the Fall, and I speak of the temptations, and even the manner of these temptations, lingers fully with man even unto this present hour. For instance, deception is a part and parcel of the human make-up. Man deceives others very easily, and is deceived himself very easily. As well, there is an innate desire within man for that which is evil. That's at least one of the reasons for the terrible problems of drug addiction, etc. Young men and young women want to know what that forbidden fruit tastes like.

And then we have the problem which has caused so many wars, privation, and want. I speak of man wanting to be God, and, thereby, acting like God, but in a totally unlawful way. Such spirit characterizes all dictators, and finds lodging in the hearts seemingly of all men.

So we see how that deception, and lies, and ungodly desire characterizes the human race, all coming from the first temptation of our first parents. The lie that man believed is the lie that man is. The deception by which he was deceived is the deception by which he deceives. The unholy ambition which came upon his being is the unholy ambition that continues to drive him to eternal darkness.

EVIL

Let's first of all look at *"evil."*

It is true that evil has an enticement that is unexplainable, except in the spiritual sense. However, evil could not have had an enticement to Eve, so the cause of her Fall had to be a desire to be like God, but rather to be like Him in an unlawful way. But once the deed was done, and the nature of sin implanted itself in the heart and life of the human being, then evil carries a great enticement. This enticement starts early, even with preteen children. That's the reason it's absolutely imperative that a child have Godly parents to steer them in the right direction. The utterly stupid idea of letting a child choose for himself, and stupid it is, is a sure road to destruction.

However, attached to all sin is also an enslaving bondage. Once it is entered into, the thrill of that sin is gone, even its enticement is gone, but by then the victim is held in its clutches, with an iron-like grip.

If the first cigarette isn't smoked, there will be no desire for the cigarette. If the first hit of drugs isn't taken, there will be no desire for drugs. In fact, the list is long, covering every facet of the warped passions of a fallen race.

But let's look at the *"good!"*

Isn't *"good"* what it's all about?

Yes it is, but we find here that even *"good"* can be approached in the wrong way.

Once the evil was entered into, man then began to think that he could overcome the evil by doing *"good."* That's the reason that Cain was so incensed when God wouldn't accept his sacrifice. The things he offered to God were the labor of his hands, on which he had expended much effort, and as well, his offering was attractive. Inasmuch as it was *"good,"* why wouldn't God accept it?

So the entirety of the human race, and I speak of the part which is unredeemed, thinks that *"doing good"* is the answer to the spiritual problem. In fact, almost all who are in Hell at this particular moment are there because they believed this lie.

In fact, this is also the greatest problem which plagues the Church. The answer to the entirety of humanity, whether redeemed or unredeemed, is the Cross of Christ. While everyone who is actually saved has embraced the Cross as it regards their initial Salvation experience; still, when it comes to Sanctification, and we speak of becoming Christlike, and the living of this life on a daily basis, most Christians, as well, attempt to do all of this by *"doing good."* Most may not look at it that way, in fact, claiming to be trusting Christ; nevertheless, that's exactly what most Christians are doing.

While doing good things is not wrong within itself, and actually right, the truth is,

these things must be a result of our experience with the Lord, and never the cause. Once we attempt to make them the cause, we then sin and sin greatly. We are in effect saying, whether we realize it or not, that what Jesus did at the Cross is insufficient and we must, therefore, add our personal efforts, which we deem to be good (Gal. 6:14).

THE PREACHING OF THE CROSS

In 1996, the Lord began to open up to me the Revelation of the Cross. He took me first of all to Romans, Chapter 6, explaining that particular Chapter to me. He then informed me that every single thing that we receive from God comes to us exclusively through the Sacrifice of Christ. He then informed me that this being the case, the object of my faith must always be the Cross.

With that carried out, and continued to be carried out on a daily basis (Lk. 9:23), the Holy Spirit, Who Alone can make us what we ought to be, would then work mightily on our behalf (Rom. 8:1-2, 11).

As I began to preach and teach this, with the Lord opening up this great subject more and more, even on a daily basis, I began to note the struggle that many Christians were having, as they heard this great Message of the Cross, almost all of them for the first time.

Little by little I came to realize that the struggle was over this one thing called *"good."* In other words, they took great pride in the *"good things"* they were doing, whatever they may have been, and as Abraham was loath to give up Ishmael, they were loath to give up these good works. As stated, it was not that they should stop the doing of them. In fact, they should do them even more, whatever they might have been. But it was the trust, the faith, and the confidence they were putting in the doing of these things, thinking that it made them holy, which was so wrong. In other words, those things were and are the object of their faith. As such, whether they realize it or not, they have embraced the *"good side"* of the tree of knowledge of good and evil. But let the Reader understand that whether it's the *"good"* side, or the *"evil"* side, both are on the same tree, and both will bring the same result, which is destruction.

The poor sinner coming to Christ is able to be saved only because of what Jesus did at the Cross. Likewise, the Believer attempting to live this Christian life can do so only by what Jesus did at the Cross. But yet it seems just as hard for the Believer to embrace the Cross in order to be sanctified, as it is for the sinner to be saved.

(6) "AND WHEN THE WOMAN SAW THAT THE TREE WAS GOOD FOR FOOD, AND THAT IT WAS PLEASANT TO THE EYES, AND A TREE TO BE DESIRED TO MAKE ONE WISE, SHE TOOK OF THE FRUIT THEREOF, AND DID EAT, AND GAVE ALSO UNTO HER HUSBAND WITH HER; AND HE DID EAT."

The exegesis is:

1. The woman seeing that the tree was good for food presents the *"lust of the eyes."*

2. That it was pleasant to the eyes proclaims to us the *"lust of the flesh."*

3. That the fruit of the tree was desired to make one wise presents the *"pride of life."*

4. She took of the fruit and did eat, which was in direct disobedience to the Command of God, and at that moment spiritually died.

5. She then gave the fruit to her husband who was with her, and he did eat, and likewise died instantly. We continue to speak of spiritual death.

THE LUST OF THE EYES

The phrase, *"And when the woman saw that the tree was good for food,"* presents to us the first step of the three steps which lead ever downward. The Apostle John mentioned this:

"For all that is in the world, the lust of the flesh, and the lust of the eyes, and the pride of life, is not of the Father, but is of the world" (I Jn. 2:16).

If we are to notice, the *"lust of the eyes"* came first with Eve, while the *"lust of the flesh"* was presented first by John. Why the disparity?

Eve had no lust of the flesh at this stage. She was pure and innocent. So the first assault to her at this time had to be the *"lust of the eyes,"* which would then be followed by the other two.

Once man had fallen, the *"lust of the flesh"* is always first, followed by the *"lust of the eyes,"* and the *"pride of life."*

This is the pattern! More or less, it sets the stage for all spiritual failure.

David's problem is a perfect example, even as recorded in II Samuel, Chapter 11.

The *"lust of the flesh"* was already prevalent in David, and because of a lax spiritual condition.

He then *"saw a woman washing herself; and the woman was very beautiful to look upon,"* which constitutes the *"lust of the eyes."* The *"lust of the flesh"* is already prevalent, so the *"lust of the eyes"* comes easy.

The Scripture then says, *"And David sent messengers and took her; and she came in unto him, and he lay with her,"* which constitutes the *"pride of life"* (II Sam. 11:4). This *"pride of life"* says *"I am king,"* and it makes no difference that she is married to another man, if I want her I will take her.

As stated, in one way or the other, more or less, this is the pattern of all sin.

As stated, Eve at this time, having no *"lust of the flesh,"* came to failure first of all by the *"lust of the eyes,"* when she *"saw that the tree was good for food."*

In the first place, she had no business even being around the tree. There were all types of trees in the Garden, bearing all manner of fruits, which were available to her at any time. But at the bidding of the Evil One, she succumbs to his suggestions, and now she minutely inspects this tree of the knowledge of good and evil.

THE LUST OF THE FLESH

The phrase, *"And that it was pleasant to the eyes,"* constitutes the *"lust of the flesh."*

But let us state that the entirety of this ungodly trio, the *"lust of the eyes,"* the *"lust of the flesh,"* and the *"pride of life,"* were all outward at this stage as it regards Eve, whereas they are all inward following the Fall. Nevertheless, even from an outward position, they were lethal. And if they were lethal even from an outward position, how much more deadly are they inwardly! Then her eyes saw this fruit, and her flesh wanted it. As stated, at the present time it is a little different:

Since the Fall, the flesh wants it, and when the eyes see it, the victim is pretty much helpless because of the *"pride of life."*

THE PRIDE OF LIFE

The phrase, *"And a tree to be desired to make one wise,"* presents the *"pride of life."*

"Pride" is no doubt the foundation sin of all sins. It is the bottom line regarding what caused the Fall. In reality, Eve had no *"pride of life"* before she fell, but did see the potential of such. It was the potential that dragged her down, i.e., *"to be like God,"* but to be like Him in an unlawful way.

Pride is the reason the sinner refuses to come to Christ, or even admit his need for Christ. Pride is also the reason the Christian doesn't walk in victory. This pride makes him think that he can live this life, without subscribing to God's order, which is the Cross.

THE FRUIT

The phrase, *"She took of the fruit thereof, and did eat,"* constitutes the Fall. It was not that there was some type of chemical in the fruit which caused the problem, but rather disobedience to God. In effect, she was saying, as all who sin say, that she was smarter than God.

From that moment, billions have continued to *"take of the fruit thereof, and eat."* They have found, exactly as Eve found, that it didn't bring, and it doesn't bring that which is supposed.

HER HUSBAND

The phrase, *"And gave also unto her husband with her; and he did eat,"* refers to the fact that evidently Adam was an observer to all these proceedings. That being the case, he lifted no hand or voice to stop Eve from this terrible thing. Some claim that he ate of the forbidden fruit which she offered him out of love for her. Let me answer that in this way:

No one ever sins out of love, so the reason he did this thing is even worse than her. She was deceived, but the Scripture plainly says, *"Adam was not deceived"* (I Tim. 2:14).

While he yielded to the temptation, he did not do so out of deception. So the only reason we can give as to why he did this thing is

that he entered, at that time, into unbelief. He did not exactly, at that time, believe what God had said about this situation. So he took of the fruit and did eat, and when he did, he died instantly. We refer to spiritual death, which means separation from God.

THE SIN NATURE

The *"sin nature"* is that man's nature after the Fall is to sin. Every thought he thinks is toward sin, every step he takes is toward sin, and everything he does is toward sin! His human nature is corrupted by the sin nature.

To describe the *"sin nature,"* one could say that it is the *"lust of the flesh, the lust of the eyes, and the pride of life"* (I Jn. 2:16).

All unsaved people have two natures: human nature, and the sin nature.

All Believers have three natures: human nature, the Divine nature, and the sin nature. However, the *"sin nature"* in the life of the Believer is supposed to be dormant. The Scripture doesn't tell us that the sin nature is dead, but it does tell us that we are dead to the sin nature (Rom. 6:11).

Some 17 times in Romans, Chapter 6, Paul uses the word *"sin."* Fourteen times out of the 17, the original Greek carries what is referred to as the definite article before the word *"sin."* Consequently, it actually says *"the sin."*

This means that Paul is not talking about a specific act of sin, but rather the sin nature, which, if not controlled properly, will definitely lead to acts of sin.

The unbeliever is controlled by the sin nature, but Believers are definitely not to be controlled in this manner.

Paul said: *"Let not 'the sin' therefore reign in your mortal body, that you should obey it in the lusts thereof"* (Rom. 6:12). This means that while the sin nature does dwell in the Believer, it is not to rule or reign.

Now some Preachers claim that the Believer no longer has a sin nature. If this were so, why is Paul addressing this subject repeatedly?

He is addressing it, simply because the Christian does have a sin nature, and if he doesn't approach it in the correct way, he will find this terrible sin nature once again ruling and reigning in his life, exactly as it did before he was saved. In fact, one can probably say without fear of contradiction that this is the case, sadly and regrettably, with most Christians.

Why?

THE CROSS OF CHRIST

If the Believer doesn't understand the Message of the Cross, which is God's prescribed order of victory, the Believer will be pretty well helpless to be what he ought to be, and no matter how hard he tries, which means that the works of the flesh will be dominant in his life in some way (Gal. 5:1-2, 4, 19-21).

GOD'S PRESCRIBED ORDER OF VICTORY

God has one means of Salvation, and that is the Cross of Christ. He has one means of Sanctification, and that is the Cross of Christ. The Cross Alone is God's answer to sin. If we forget that, then we are missing completely God's prescribed order of victory.

The following has already been given in Chapter 1, but because of the tremendous significance of what we are saying here, it would be proper I think to give it again. More than likely, we will give it several times in this Volume.

God's prescribed order of victory can be outlined according to the following:

1. Focus: The Believer must focus totally and completely on the Cross of Christ. This is absolutely imperative, understanding that this is the means by which God gives all things unto Believers.

2. Object of Faith: The Cross being our focus, and our focus constantly, the object of our Faith then becomes the Finished Work of Christ. This, as well, is very, very important. Satan will do everything he can to move our Faith from the Finished Work of Christ, to other things. He doesn't really care what the other things are, just so it's not the Finished Work of Christ. So in reality, every attack by Satan is for the purpose of moving our Faith from the Cross to other things, which, if successful, could cause us to become so discouraged that we'll just quit.

3. Power Source: With our focus on the Cross, and our object of Faith being the Finished Work of Christ, our Power Source now becomes the Holy Spirit. The Holy Spirit

works only within the parameters of the Finished Work of Christ, hence the demand for us to ever make that the object of our faith. The Holy Spirit is God! Consequently He can do anything. In fact, there is no way that anything from God can be done within our hearts and lives, unless it's carried out by the Holy Spirit. It is impossible for us to do these things by our own strength and ability. The Divine Spirit doesn't require much of us, but He does require that we have Faith. And that the Faith we have must always be anchored in the Finished Work of Christ.

4. Results: Following God's prescribed order, the results will always be victory (Rom. 6:3-14; 8:1-2, 11; Gal. 6:14; Col. 2:14-15).

Not knowing God's prescribed order, or else having rejected it, the following is the only other place the Believer can go. It is as follows:

1. Focus: Works.
2. Object of Faith: Performance.
3. Power Source: Self.
4. Results: Failure.

As stated, this just given is regrettably the position of most Christians, and simply because they do not know God's prescribed order of victory, which alone is the Cross.

WALKING AFTER THE SPIRIT— WALKING AFTER THE FLESH

What we've just given you in these two diagrams is actually the meaning of *"walking after the Spirit"* and *"walking after the flesh."*

Paul said: *"There is therefore now no condemnation to them which are in Christ Jesus, who walk not after the flesh, but after the Spirit"* (Rom. 8:1).

The Spirit of God always leads to Christ and His Cross. Consequently, the first diagram we gave you constitutes walking after the Spirit.

The second diagram, which refers to one looking to self instead of Christ and the Cross, constitutes *"walking after the flesh."*

Many Christians think that *"walking after the Spirit"* refers to doing spiritual things, whatever that might be. It doesn't! They also think that *"walking after the flesh"* refers to doing carnal things, such as watching too much television, etc. None of that is correct!

Walking after the Spirit constitutes one placing one's Faith totally in Christ and what Christ has done for us at the Cross.

Walking after the flesh constitutes the Believer looking elsewhere, in other words, to his own ability, strength, and machinations. It has nothing to do with watching too much television or being too interested in sports, etc.

Once again we state the Truth that the Cross of Christ is the only answer for hurting humanity, whether the unredeemed or the redeemed.

(7) "AND THE EYES OF THEM BOTH WERE OPENED, AND THEY KNEW THAT THEY WERE NAKED; AND THEY SEWED FIG LEAVES TOGETHER, AND MADE THEMSELVES APRONS."

The exegesis is:

1. Their eyes were opened, but definitely not in the right way.

2. They knew, because of their sin, they were now naked to the Judgment of God.

3. The *"fig leaves"* were the best they could come up with, and symbolize man's efforts to save himself.

OPEN EYES

The phrase, *"And the eyes of them both were opened,"* refers to the consciousness of guilt as a result of their sin.

Sin makes the most excellent and glorious of all God's creatures vile and shameful. It defaces the Image of God. It separates man from God. It disorders all the faculties of the soul.

Once this thing was done, the promised results came, but it was not what they thought it would be. Instead of it making them *"like gods,"* it showed them that they were like beasts, and brought the first sense of shame.

The first thing that their opened eyes saw was themselves, and the immediate result of the sight was the first blush of shame.

NAKED

The phrase, *"And they knew that they were naked,"* refers to the fact that they had lost the enswathing light of purity, which previously had clothed their bodies. They were shamed before God and Angels; disgraced in the highest degree; laid open to the

NOTES

contempt and reproach of Heaven, and Earth, and their own consciousnesses (Henry). Sin is a reproach to any people!

THE JUDGMENT OF GOD

The word *"naked"* as presented here has more to do with them being naked to the Judgment of God, than it does an absence of clothing. God cannot abide sin, and sin must be judged.

Of course we know, and as we shall see, God provided for this Judgment by the giving of His Only Son, Who took the Judgment for us. However, if Christ is refused, there remains no more sacrifice for sin, and Judgment must inevitably fall (Heb. 10:12, 26).

FIG LEAVES

The phrase, *"And they sewed fig leaves together, and made themselves aprons,"* presents the clothing Adam and Eve provided for themselves, which did very well until God appeared, and was then to be found worthless. Sinners clothe themselves with morality, sacraments, and religious ceremony; they are as worthless as Adam's apron of fig leaves.

In this, we see True Christianity and mere religion. The former is founded upon the fact of a person being clothed, and of course with the robe of Righteousness; the latter, upon the fact of him being naked. The former has this as its starting ground, while the latter has it as its goal. All that a true Christian does is because he is clothed with the robe of Righteousness, made possible by Christ and what Christ did at the Cross, and imputed to believing sinners upon Faith in the Finished Work of Christ. All that religion does is in order that he may be clothed. In other words, he is working for his Salvation, while the former is working because of his Salvation.

The more we examine man's religion, and all its phases, the more we shall see its thorough insufficiency to remedy his state.

MAN'S CONDITION

We're looking here at man's condition, and how this condition can be rectified.

Man knows that he is *"naked."* He may not like to admit it, and many may even deny it, but he knows! The question is, how is his condition remedied?

Man has a choice, and it's not really a very complex choice to make. The only way his situation can be remedied is by his acceptance of Christ, and more particularly, what Christ did for him at the Cross. If he does that, he will find that a perfect, pure, spotless, Righteousness will be imputed unto him, and done so instantly. The situation is then resolved.

However, if he refuses God's remedy, and resorts to fig leaves, which regrettably and sadly, characterizes much of the world, and for all time, he will find himself continuing to be *"naked."*

If man has a problem, and this problem seems to affect all, it's the problem of the *"fig leaves."*

COVERING

The following is an actual happening. It is simple and silly, but it adequately defines, I think, that of which I speak.

Donnie was preaching a Meeting in a particular state some time ago. After he had been there a day or so, the Pastor asked him, *"Who is your covering?"*

At first, Donnie didn't know what he was talking about, and the Preacher, seeing the puzzled look on his face, further explained, *"A Preacher or Preachers, who vouch for your integrity."*

While the Laity would have little knowledge of this, it is big, especially among Charismatic Preachers. Along the same vein, the Preachers associated with Denominations think of that particular Denomination as their *"covering."*

Donnie answered, saying, *"The Blood of Jesus Christ is my covering."* He then went on to say, *"I'm really not interested in what some Preacher might say about me, and for the simple reason, as Adam of old, he really cannot even cover his own backside."*

I'll be frank with you: I liked the answer!

This is just one of the *"fig leaves"* which characterizes a whole forest of such.

I want my Brother in the Lord to speak well of me. In fact, I want all Believers to speak well of me; however, whatever it is they do say really won't amount to that much in the final analysis. It's what God knows that counts. To be frank, people say

things about me, and God says things about me. It's really only what God says that actually matters.

(8) "AND THEY HEARD THE VOICE OF THE LORD GOD WALKING IN THE GARDEN IN THE COOL OF THE DAY: AND ADAM AND HIS WIFE HID THEMSELVES FROM THE PRESENCE OF THE LORD GOD AMONGST THE TREES OF THE GARDEN."

The diagram is:

1. *"The voice of the Lord God walking in the garden in the cool of the day,"* had once been a welcomed sound. It no longer was!

2. They heard His Voice. He is still speaking to this lost world.

3. It was the *"cool of the day"* toward nightfall.

4. Because of their guilt and what they had done, they hid themselves from the Presence of the Lord God among the trees of the Garden.

THE VOICE OF THE LORD GOD

The phrase, *"And they heard the voice of the LORD God walking in the Garden in the cool of the day,"* had heretofore been a pleasant sound. Now it is the very opposite. Whereas the sound of His Voice had once been a sound of delight, it is now a sound of dread, fear, and even stark terror.

It is not that the Voice of the Lord had changed, for it hadn't. It was the same voice that they had heard since creation. He hadn't changed, but they had.

Paul wrote, quoting David: *"Today if you will hear His Voice, harden not your hearts"* (Heb. 4:7; Ps. 95:7-8).

We find in this that the Lord seeks the sinner. Actually, He seeks the sinner to a far greater degree than we could begin to imagine. That's why He came down to this Earth, taking upon Himself human flesh, and did so in order that He might die on a Cross, that the debt could be paid — a debt incidentally that we could not pay. He is still saying:

"Come unto Me, all you who labor and are heavy laden, and I will give you rest.

"Take My yoke upon you, and learn of Me; for I am meek and lowly in heart: and you shall find rest unto your souls.

"For My yoke is easy, and My burden is light" (Mat. 11:28-30).

He's still saying, *"Come unto Me!"*

GUILT

The phrase, *"And Adam and his wife hid themselves from the Presence of the LORD God among the trees of the Garden,"* presents our first parents doing so not in humility, as unworthy to come into God's Presence, or through modesty, but rather from a sense of guilt.

Expositors say: *"Here is the dawn of a new era in the history of humanity. The eye of a guilt conscience is now opened for the first time, and God and the universe appeared in new and terrible forms."*

It played out to an alarming dread of God. But yet, there's no way to flee from God, because God is everywhere, i.e., *"Omnipresent."* So we find that guilt blinds the reason of men.

Christ Alone can remove the guilt, which is done instantly upon acceptance of Him as one's Lord and Saviour. Paul said:

"There is therefore now no condemnation to them which are in Christ Jesus, who walk not after the flesh, but after the Spirit" (Rom. 8:1).

The Greek Scholars say that this Verse can be translated, *"There is therefore now no guilt to them which are in Christ Jesus. . . ."*

The unredeemed don't know what it is to be without guilt; consequently, they cannot imagine living without this terrible malady.

Guilt plays a tremendous part in all suicides, nervous breakdowns, emotional disturbances, and actually is a factor in every adverse thing that happens to a human being. But not ever having experienced a time without guilt, the unredeemed have no idea as to what a guilt-free life actually is. It is the most wonderful, the most glorious, the most fulfilling lifestyle that one could ever enjoy, but the unredeemed have no conception as to what that means. It's what Jesus was speaking of when He said: *"I am come that they might have life, and that they might have it more abundantly"* (Jn. 10:10).

With the Fall of our first parents, guilt came into the physical, mental, and spiritual make-up of the individual. As stated, it is not possible for it to be removed, except by

the acceptance of Jesus Christ as one's Lord and Saviour. And we must never forget that what Christ does for us was all made possible by the Cross (Gal. 2:20-21; 6:14; Eph. 2:6-18; Col. 2:14-15).

(9) "AND THE LORD GOD CALLED UNTO ADAM, AND SAID UNTO HIM, WHERE ARE YOU?"

The structure is:

1. The Lord called to Adam, and He has been calling to untold millions of others ever since.

2. The great question, *"Where are you?"*, is just as appropriate now as then.

3. *"Where are you?"*, is the first question in the Old Testament, *"Where is He?"*, is the first question in the New Testament (Mat. 2:2).

THE CALL

The phrase, *"And the LORD God called unto Adam,"* presents God seeking the first man. He has been doing so ever since.

Matthew Henry said: *"This inquiry after Adam may be looked upon as a gracious pursuit, in kindness to him, and in order to his recovery. If God had not called to him, to reclaim him, his condition had been as desperate as that of fallen angels."* He went on to say:

"This lost sheep had wandered endlessly, if the Good Shepherd had not sought after him, to bring him back, and in order to that, reminded him where he was not, where he should not be, and where he could not be either happy or easy."

WHERE ARE YOU?

The question, *"And said unto him, Where are you?"*, presents the question of all questions. To be sure, the Lord knew exactly where Adam was, but He wanted Adam to know where he was.

Williams says: *"Adam hides from God, not because of any change in God, but because of the change in himself, wrought by the entrance of sin. The covering he provided for himself did very well until God appeared and was then found to be worthless."*

Adam's absence was clear proof that something was wrong. Before this, he had welcomed the Divine approach. But now there is dread and fear.

Every Believer should take this question to heart, asked by our Heavenly Father so long ago. *"Where are you?"*

As we've already stated, God knows where each of us is. Being Omniscient (all-knowing) He knows everything about us. But oftentimes, we don't know ourselves exactly where we are. It takes that clarion call to bring us to our senses!

(10) "AND HE SAID, I HEARD YOUR VOICE IN THE GARDEN, AND I WAS AFRAID, BECAUSE I WAS NAKED; AND I HID MYSELF."

The construction is:

1. The Voice of God was once a welcomed sound, but not anymore!

2. The first thing that Adam said after the Fall was, *"I was afraid."*

3. He was naked to the Judgment of God, and all sin must be judged.

4. He tried to hide himself from God, even as untold millions have, but never with any success.

FEAR

The phrase, *"And he said, I heard Your voice in the Garden, and I was afraid,"* presents the first words which came out of the mouth of our first parent after the Fall. He said, *"I was afraid."* Why was he afraid?

Concerning this moment, Calvin said: *"His consciousness of the effects of sin was keener than his sense of the sin itself."*

Lange said: *"This is the first instance of that mingling and confusion of sin and punishment which is the peculiar characteristic of our Redemption-needing humanity."*

Luther said: *"The words, 'Where are you?' are words of Divine Law, directed by God to Adam's conscience. God wanted Adam to know that he who hides himself from Him is never hidden from Him, and that he who runs away from Him can never escape Him."*

The type of fear which characterizes Adam is fear brought on by guilt. That's why guilt is such a hazard; it carries with it a tremendous amount of negative baggage.

This type of fear sees God in a completely erroneous way. It sees Him as someone to be dreaded; someone to be avoided. But let the Reader understand this:

Sin is a horrible business, actually the cause of all sorrow, heartache, and destruction in this world, and as well always brings heavy guilt; however, sin should be taken to the Lord, as distasteful and shameful as it might be. There's no one else who can do anything about one's sin, except the Lord of Glory. And His answer for sin is the Cross, which is the greatest example of love that humanity has ever known.

God forbid that we fail the Lord in any capacity; however, regrettably and sadly, the sin problem plagues the whole of the human race, even at times the Godliest. But as bad as it might be, as shameful as it might be, as the great song says, *"Take it to Jesus, take it to Jesus, He is a friend that's well-known."*

The great mistake made by the human race, and regrettably even by the Church, is that we take the sin elsewhere. We take it to the Psychologist, which to be blunt, and I mean to be blunt, can do nothing! We take it to fellow human beings, and no matter how Godly they may be, still, they can do nothing. Beautifully and wondrously, John the Beloved told us what to do:

"If we confess our sins, He is faithful and just to forgive us our sins, and to cleanse us from all unrighteousness" (I Jn. 1:9).

RESTORATION

The Ministry of Restoration should be the Ministry of every Believer. Sooner or later, each Believer will be called upon to aid a Brother or Sister in distress. I speak of one who has failed the Lord. Paul told us what to do in such a case:

"Brethren, if a man be overtaken in a fault, you which are spiritual, restore such a one in the spirit of meekness; considering yourself, lest you also be tempted" (Gal. 6:1).

So what did he mean by this statement?

There is only one way that one can be restored. The one who is *"spiritual,"* which means that this particular individual knows and understands God's prescribed order of victory, which is the Cross, is to explain to the individual who has failed these two things:

1. Why he failed!

2. What to do so as not to fail again!

The one who is *"spiritual"* should patiently explain to the Brother or Sister that

NOTES

he or she has failed because they took their eyes off the Cross, thereby shifting their faith to other things, which is what caused the problem. When this was done, the Holy Spirit simply will not help the Believer, because He will not work outside of the parameters of the Finished Work of Christ. Consequently, such a person becomes an open target for Satan.

While he might try with all of his strength to overcome, he will find that despite all of his efforts, he has failed.

This is generally very confusing to such a Christian. They don't understand why they have failed, simply because they have tried so hard. In fact, they didn't want to do what was done, and tried not to do it. But they found themselves in the same condition as Paul, before he knew the victory of the Cross. He said:

"For that which I do I allow (understand) *not: for what I would, that do I not; but what I hate, that do I"* (Rom. 7:15).

And for a Christian to be in such a state, and then for a fellow Christian to berate him or to seek to punish him in some way, only adds insult to injury.

What good would it have done to have ridiculed Paul or to punish him, when he was in the Romans, Chapter 7 state? But regrettably, that's what many Christians seek to do.

And please understand as well, God doesn't have two remedies for sin, one for the Laity, and another for Preachers. The remedy is all the same, which is the Cross.

Once the failing one has been told why they failed, which was a departure from the Cross, they are to then be told to get their faith back to the Cross, and keep the Cross as the object of their Faith from now on, which will guarantee victory ahead, simply because the Holy Spirit will now help them.

That is the manner in which Restoration is to be enjoined, and that is the only manner that Restoration can be enjoined (Rom. 6:3-14; 8:1-2, 11, 13).

HIDING FROM GOD

The phrase, *"Because I was naked; and I hid myself,"* presents a foolish effort.

Luther said: *"From this we learn how great is the evil of sin. Unless God helps*

and calls the sinner, he will forever flee God, try to excuse his sin by lies, and add one wrong to another until he ends in blasphemy and despair."

How foolish it is to seek to hide from God. God knows all things; so to hide from Him is impossible. He had heard the Voice of God in the Garden and said that it made him afraid. But had he not heard God's Voice when He had commanded him not to eat of the forbidden tree? Why was he not afraid of God then, and why did he not hide himself at that time?

Believe it or not, men are still seeking to hide themselves from God; however, they do it in strange ways.

Many will not go to Church at all, because they surmise that God is in Church, and that He will then apprehend them. They don't seem to realize that God is everywhere.

Concerning God, David said: *"O LORD, You have searched me, and known me.*

"You know my downsitting and my uprising, You understand my thought afar off.

"You compass my path and my lying down, and are acquainted with all my ways.

"For there is not a word in my tongue, but, lo, O LORD, You know it altogether.

"You have beset me behind and before, and laid Your hand upon me.

"Such knowledge is too wonderful for me; it is high, I cannot attain unto it.

"Where shall I go from Your Spirit? Or where shall I flee from Your Presence?

"If I ascend up into Heaven, You are there: if I make my bed in Hell, behold, You are there.

"If I take the wings of the morning, and dwell in the uttermost parts of the sea;

"Even there shall Your hand lead me, and Your right hand shall hold me.

"If I say, Surely the darkness shall cover me; even the night shall be light about me.

"Yes, the darkness hides not from You; but the night shines as the day: the darkness and the light are both alike to You" (Ps. 139:1-12).

NAKED

We have already addressed ourselves to this, but it is here that the idea seems to project itself that Adam and Eve, before the Fall, had been enveloped in light. With the Fall, the light disappears, and they are left *"naked."*

And let us say again that which we have already stated: The word *"naked"* here carries a far greater connotation than merely being without clothing. They were naked to the Judgment of God. Luther said, not necessarily relating to this one incident, but rather the overall picture, but yet the particulars are the same: *"When Moses says that God called Adam, this means that He hailed him before His Judgment Seat. Eve, too, had sinned and fallen from God so that she also was summoned and had to share in this judgment."*

This is the main problem: Men are concerned about the Judgment of God, and rightly so! Let it ever be known and understood that God cannot tolerate sin in any shape, form, or fashion. Sin must be judged wherever it is found.

Now the Lord has a glorious and wonderful solution for that, Who is His Son, the Lord Jesus Christ, and the price that He paid on the Cross. In other words, Christ took the Judgment that the whole of humanity should have suffered. So man has a choice:

He can accept God's Son, with all Judgment being suspended, and for the simple reason that it is not proper to punish for the same crime twice. Jesus has suffered the stroke of God which is death, all on our behalf, which paid the terrible sin debt. When He said, *"It is finished,"* that meant the debt was forever paid. So if the believing sinner accepts Christ, there is no fear of judgment, and there will never be any fear of judgment.

But if the sinner refuses Christ, the Wrath of God remains on him, and of that one can be certain.

So the die is cast; we either accept Christ or suffer the Judgment of God.

PSYCHOLOGY

Modern man has tried to answer the sure Judgment of God by denying it. In fact, the world has been so psychologized that any more it no longer believes that there will be a judgment.

Psychology teaches that man is inherently good. And if he does something wrong, it is because of outside environment, or events beyond his control. So in this teaching, no

person is ever guilty, but rather society, environment, others, etc.

So in this type of thinking, there can be no judgment, because there is no culpability on the part of the individual.

The Bible teaches the very opposite. It teaches that all men are sinful and wicked, and as a result of the Fall. It teaches that man is responsible for his actions, and will have to ultimately answer to God, i.e., *"the Judgment"* (Rom. 1:18).

So it doesn't really matter what crutch man leans on; the Word of God will prevail, and man will ultimately answer.

As well, if man is not personally guilty as psychology claims, then why is he plagued with guilt?

Psychology claims that the Bible is responsible for that. So if the Bible could be banned, this, they say, would stop the guilt.

What they should understand is, the Bible doesn't make the guilt, but only points out what is already there. Man is not guilty merely because the Bible says he's guilty, but he is guilty because in fact, that's what he is. The guilt is a result of his sinful state. But let it be understood, the Bible not only points out the problem, but it also points out the solution, Who is Christ and Him Crucified (Jn. 3:3, 16; Eph. 6:18; Col. 2:14-15).

(11) "AND HE SAID, WHO TOLD YOU THAT YOU WERE NAKED? HAVE YOU EATEN OF THE TREE, WHEREOF I COMMANDED YOU THAT YOU SHOULD NOT EAT?"

The exposition is:

1. The Lord now asks two questions. The first is, *"Who told you that you were naked?"*

2. The second question is: *"Have you eaten of the tree, whereof I commanded that you should not eat?"*

3. The Lord, of course, knows the answer to these questions, but He is trying to pull Adam to a place of honest confession.

THE FIRST QUESTION

The question, *"And He said, 'Who told you that you were naked?'"*, carries Adam's mind from the effect, to the sin that had caused it. As long as a man feels sorrow only for the results of his action there is no Repentance, and no wish to return to the Divine Presence.

What he had described as a want or imperfection, which was his being naked, was really the result of his own act.

Adam is afraid, because he is naked; not only unarmed, therefore, afraid to contend with God, but unclothed, therefore, afraid even to appear before Him. We have reason to be afraid of approaching God, if we are not clothed and fenced with the Righteousness of Christ; nothing but that will be armor of proof, or cover the shame of our nakedness.

But the sin has grown worse, as all sin grows worse. While Adam did admit that he was naked, untold millions presently deny being naked, even though they are obviously so. Adam did hide from God, or rather tried to do so, but man presently doesn't even actually try to hide. He brazenly confronts God, of which we see the type in Chapter 4, as it regards the actions of Cain.

THE SECOND QUESTION

The question, *"Have you eaten of the tree, whereof I commanded you that you should not eat?"*, carries the answer with the question. That is exactly what Adam and Eve have done! They have eaten of the tree, whereof the Lord commanded that they should not partake.

It is not so much the occasion of the sin of which the Lord inquires, but of the consciousness of nakedness that is addressed here. The Lord then asked the question that points to the true cause of the man's nakedness, which of course, proclaimed the Divine knowledge of the transgression.

The way the question is framed removes the pretext of ignorance, and also points to the fact that the sin had been carried out in direct violation of the Divine prohibition (Calvin).

(12) "AND THE MAN SAID, THE WOMAN WHOM YOU GAVE TO BE WITH ME, SHE GAVE ME OF THE TREE, AND I DID EAT."

The composition is:

1. In effect, Adam is accusing God as being to blame for his problem.

2. He insults Eve as well!

3. He recapitulates the history, as if, in his view, it was a matter of course that he should act as he had done. But if there is blame, it's not his, but rather that of God or Eve, or so he intimates.

ADAM SAID

The phrase, *"And the man said,"* proclaims the course of action that will be taken. Adam then and there could have confessed his sin, but chose another route. Consequently, there is no record in the Word of God that he ever fully made things right with the Lord. He is not listed in Hebrews, Chapter 11, along with the great Faith worthies, and more than likely, he died lost.

There are some who claim that his tomb is in Jerusalem. There is another rumor which claims that his body was placed in the Ark, along with Noah and his family at the time of the flood. Actually, the rumor claims that his coffin is still in the Ark, where it is ensconced on Mount Ararat.

We can get an idea of what God intended for this man to be, our first parent, by the Holy Spirit through Paul referring to Jesus as the *"Last Adam"* (I Cor. 15:45).

THE EXCUSE

The phrase, *"The woman whom You gave to be with me, she gave me of the tree, and I did eat,"* portrays the immediate effects of the Fall:

1. Adam now has, it seems, little sense of responsibility, and no feeling that he had a duty towards Eve, and ought to have watched over her, and helped her when tempted.

2. He in effect blames God for his predicament. He, in fact, insinuates that God was accessory to his sin! God gave him the woman, and she gave him the fruit. So in a secondary way, he blames Eve also!

It is strange that man wants to be like God, but as stated, in an unlawful way, and then when things go wrong, he wants to blame God. He seems to forget that if he is like God, he will have to take responsibility for his actions.

WHAT DOES IT MEAN TO TAKE RESPONSIBILITY?

As we are speaking here of sin, we will address ourselves to that particular problem.

To fail the Lord is an extremely hurtful thing, as should be obvious. In the event of failure, what can one do, and to be more particular, what should one do according to

NOTES

the Word of God, as it regards taking responsibility?

That's the key — the Word of God!

The failing Christian is to confess his sins to the Lord. If he has sinned against particular individuals, he has to confess his wrongdoing to them as well, otherwise, only to God. Upon proper confession of sin, the Scripture plainly says that Christ will be *"faithful and just to forgive us our sins, and to cleanse us from all unrighteousness"* (I Jn. 1:9).

As well, the Believer is to understand that he has failed because he has allowed his Faith to be shifted from the Cross of Christ to other things. When this happens, the Holy Spirit will not help such a Believer, and he is then left to the mercy of his own strength and ability, which are woefully insufficient as it regards the powers of darkness. So he is to get his Faith once again anchored in the great Sacrifice of Christ, looking to the Finished Work, which means to place his Faith and confidence exclusively in what Christ has done for him at the Cross. Doing this, the Holy Spirit will once again begin to help him, and he will walk once again in victory (Rom. 8:1-2, 11).

Unfortunately, there are many in the modern Church who claim that *"taking responsibility,"* means that one must submit one's self to whatever foolish rules and regulations that silly men make up, which are totally unscriptural. In other words, they're speaking of punishment.

And let the Reader understand that those who advocate punishment in such a case had best first look at themselves. And as well, they had best understand that by their actions, they are in fact saying that what Jesus suffered at the Cross is not enough, and more punishment needs to be added. Such, to be sure, is abominable in the Eyes of the Lord.

If it's not Scriptural, it's not right! And that being the case, the Believer who has failed must not yield to such foolishness. To do so will have a serious, adverse spiritual affect upon him, and could even cause him to lose his soul.

The curse of the Church is rules made up by men, which have no Scriptural authority. Such men are wrong to make up such rules, and men are wrong who obey such rules.

(13) "AND THE LORD GOD SAID UNTO THE WOMAN, WHAT IS THIS THAT YOU HAVE DONE? AND THE WOMAN SAID, THE SERPENT BEGUILED ME, AND I DID EAT."

The structure is:

1. The Lord now turns to Eve.

2. He asked the question, *"What is this that you have done?"*

3. Eve blames her predicament on the serpent.

THE WOMAN

The phrase, *"And the LORD God said unto the woman,"* presents the Lord, at least at the moment, not responding to Adam, but now turning to the woman. We will find that her answer is far nobler than that of Adam. But yet she still does not properly repent, actually casting aspersion on the serpent.

THE QUESTION

The question, *"What is this that you have done?"*, places the emphasis on the pronoun *"you."*

Of course, God readily knew what Eve had done, why she did it, how she did it, and all about what had happened. In fact, that was not the point of the question.

Probably the two questions, *"Where are you?"* and *"What is this that you have done?"*, comprise the human problem.

The Lord continues to ask the human race, *"Where are you?"* This implies, as previously stated, a place of trouble, difficulties, guilt, and bondage. But that place and position were not arrived at without culpability on our part. It is because we have done something wrong! In effect, we have sinned against God, which has put us in this place of distress.

As we consider the horror which took place on September 11, 2001, to be sure, that question is being asked of God to the entirety of America. *"Where are you?"* and *"What have you done?"* In other words, even though we don't like to admit it, there is a cause.

The Lord does not *"steal, kill, and destroy."* That is the work of Satan. In fact, Jesus said, *"I am come that they might have life, and that they might have it more abundantly"* (Jn. 10:10).

What happened in New York City and in Washington, D.C., and the crashing of the airliner in Pennsylvania, were all caused by Satan. He is the one who *"steals, kills, and destroys"* (Jn. 10:10).

But yet, the Lord did have to allow the Evil One to do this thing, and that being the case, why would He have allowed such? (Job, Chpts. 1-2).

As America now looks at herself, the Lord would ask the same question that He asked Adam, *"Where are you?"*

We would have to answer that we are in a mess, so to speak! Our economy has been hit hard; our vulnerability is now exposed to the entirety of the world; our institutions are under attack. We find ourselves in a position with tens of thousands, and possibly even hundreds of thousands, grief-stricken, brokenhearted, and hurting, because of the loss of loved ones.

And now the second question comes, *"What have you done?"*

What is our answer?

Even though it was given to Israel a long, long time ago; still, it is appropriate at this time as well! The Lord said:

"If My people, which are called by My Name, shall humble themselves, and pray, and seek My face, and turn from their wicked ways; then will I hear from Heaven, and will forgive their sin, and will heal their land" (II Chron. 7:14).

Are we humbling ourselves? Praying? Seeking the Face of the Lord? Turning from our wicked ways?

That and that alone is the answer to our dilemma. That being done, He has plainly said: *"I will forgive your sin, and will heal your land."*

THE SERPENT

The phrase, *"And the woman said, 'The serpent beguiled me, and I did eat,'"* presents Eve blaming the serpent.

In a sense, she was blaming God as well, simply because God had made the serpent. So in effect, she was saying, *"Lord, if You hadn't made the serpent, I wouldn't be in this predicament!"*

Did Satan through the Serpent beguile and deceive Eve? Yes he did! In fact, Satan is still the great deceiver (II Cor. 4:4). But we should realize that God did not accept this excuse, as Verse 16 shows (Horton).

When she said, *"And I did eat,"* she was in actuality saying, *"It's true I did eat, but it was not my fault."*

(14) "AND THE LORD GOD SAID UNTO THE SERPENT, BECAUSE YOU HAVE DONE THIS, YOU ARE CURSED ABOVE ALL CATTLE, AND ABOVE EVERY BEAST OF THE FIELD; UPON YOUR BELLY SHALL YOU GO, AND DUST SHALL YOU EAT ALL THE DAYS OF YOUR LIFE:"

The composition is:

1. The Lord now turns to the serpent.

2. He places a curse upon him.

3. The curse was that he would be reduced to crawling upon his belly.

THE LORD GOD

The phrase, *"And the LORD God said unto the serpent,"* presents no question or interrogation being posed toward the serpent at all. God judges him, and it is in listening to this judgment that the guilty pair hear the first great Promise respecting Christ.

THE CURSE

The phrase, *"Because you have done this, you are cursed above all cattle, and above every beast of the field,"* refers to this animal being reduced from possibly the highest place and position in the animal kingdom to the lowest.

The very fact that the Lord leveled a curse at this creature lets us know that the animal must have had some intelligence, a limited power of choice, and even the power of limited speech.

The reptile, not being a moral creature, could not be cursed in the sense of being made susceptible of misery. But it might be cursed in the sense of being deteriorated in its nature, and, as it were, consigned to a lower position in the scale of being, which it was.

THE EXTENT OF THE CURSE

The phrase, *"Upon your belly shall you go, and dust shall you eat all the days of your life,"* evidently means that it had previously gone erect. That being the case, it would have possessed a backbone, which would have given it the capability of standing upright, etc. The curse changed its skeletal framework. Crawling on its belly, the eating of dust is not meant to be taken literally, but that its mouth is where the dust is, all referring to its inferior position.

(15) "AND I WILL PUT ENMITY BETWEEN YOU AND THE WOMAN, AND BETWEEN YOUR SEED AND HER SEED; IT SHALL BRUISE YOUR HEAD, AND YOU SHALL BRUISE HIS HEEL."

The construction is:

1. The Lord now actually speaks to Satan, who has used the serpent.

2. Putting *"enmity between Satan and the woman,"* in effect says, *"You used the woman to bring down the human race, and I will use the woman as an instrument to bring the Redeemer into the world, Who will save the human race."*

3. There will be enmity between *"her Seed,"* Who is the Lord Jesus Christ, and *"your seed,"* which pertains to those who follow you.

4. Jesus, the Seed of the woman, would bruise the head of the serpent on the Cross.

5. The serpent would bruise the heel of the Saviour, which speaks of the suffering of the Crucifixion.

ENMITY

The phrase, *"And I will put enmity between you and the woman,"* refers as stated, to the fact that Satan used the woman to bring sin into the world, and the Lord will use the woman to bring the Redeemer into the world, Who will save from sin.

However, in all of this, we are not to think that the Virgin Mary crushed the power of the Devil by giving birth to Christ. While she definitely was greatly honored by the Lord in being able to serve in this capacity, the truth is, Mary only provided a house, so to speak, for the birth of the Redeemer into this world. It is the Lord Jesus Christ, and the Lord Jesus Christ Alone, Who has redeemed us, and He did so by the giving of Himself on the Cross, in the pouring out of His Precious Blood (Eph. 2:13-18).

In fact, Jesus had no similarities to His brothers and sisters, simply because Joseph was not actually His father, and Mary only provided for Him a house, so to speak, for some nine months.

While we certainly hold Mary in high regard, it is, in fact, an abomination that the

NOTES

Catholic Church has attempted to make her a co-redemptress. Such thinking and Mary-worship can be construed as none other than blasphemy.

HER SEED

The phrase, *"And between your seed and her Seed,"* refers to those who follow Satan (your seed) and to those who follow Christ (her Seed).

In fact, this *"enmity,"* which refers to hatred, is played out in graphic detail in Chapter 4 of this Book, referring to Cain and his brother Abel, whom he murdered.

This *"enmity,"* or animosity, is prevalent between the unredeemed and the Redeemed. It shows in the religions of the world which oppose Christ, and the more wicked these religions, the more opposition to Christ. In fact, the religion of Islam is the greatest example of all. It is, without a doubt, the most wicked religion in the world; consequently, it hates Christ, and with a venom, one might quickly add.

Islam hates Israel simply because the Bible proclaims the Truth that Isaac is the one through whom the Redeemer would come (Gen. 21:12). As well, the land of Israel was promised to Abraham's seed, who is Isaac (Gen. 28:13). The Muslims claim that Ishmael is Abraham's seed, and that the land of Israel belongs to them. (Mohammed, as are all Arabs, is a descendent of Ishmael.) This conflict is the reason for the constant war of the Muslim world against Israel, and their hatred for the United States. They hate Israel, and they hate the Lord Jesus Christ. Inasmuch as the Muslims look at America as the greatest citadel of Christianity, we are referred to by them as the *"great Satan."*

Some have tried to claim that Islam is a religion of love and a religion of peace. Nothing could be further from the Truth. It is a religion of hate and a religion of war and violence. In fact, if Islam had its way, in other words, if it had the power to do so, there would be no United States of America. They would blot it off the face of the Earth. That they don't do so is not for a lack of the will, but rather a lack of power.

However, this enmity doesn't stop with those who do not confess Christ versus those who do; it extends greatly to the Church, as proven in this last phrase.

THE CROSS OF CHRIST

The phrase, *"It* (Christ) *shall bruise your head, and you shall bruise His heel,"* refers to what Christ would do to Satan through His death on the Cross, and the sufferings of Christ, which this would entail.

How exactly did Christ bruise the head of Satan on the Cross?

"To bruise," means, *"to crush, trample down."* A serpent bites. If his head is crushed, he can hardly continue to bite. This all speaks of what Jesus would accomplish on the Cross.

As God judges the serpent, it is in listening to this judgment that the guilty pair, Adam and Eve, hear the First Great Promise respecting Christ. We have here the sum of the whole matter, and the rest of the Bible does but explain the nature of this struggle, the persons who wage it, and the manner and consequences of the victory.

In this struggle, man is finally to prevail, but not unscathed. And his triumph is to be gained not by mere human strength, but by the coming of One Who is *"the woman's Seed"*; and round this promised Deliverer, the rest of Scripture groups itself. Leave out these words given in this Verse, and all the inspired teaching which follows would be an ever-widening river without a fountainhead. Necessarily with the Fall came the Promise of Restoration. Grace is no afterthought, but enters the world side by side with sin.

Upon this foundation, the rest of Holy Scripture is built, till Revelation at last reaches its cornerstone in Christ (Ellicott).

The *"enmity"* mentioned here has its greatest force in religion than in anything else. If it is to be noticed, the whole world is religious in one way or the other. Man was created to worship, in reality to worship God; consequently, even those who do not know God, which make up the majority of this world, actually worship something, whether the idol of religion or the idol of themselves.

But in the ranks of Christianity, perhaps one can say this enmity is greater than ever. What do we mean by that?

NOTES

To cut straight through, let us say immediately that the Cross of Christ is the dividing line of which we speak here. The last phrase of this Fifteenth Verse proclaims the Cross of Christ as the manner in which the head of Satan would be bruised. Now let us answer our question as to how it was bruised.

THE BRUISING OF THE HEAD OF SATAN

Let not the Reader think that Jesus has fought Satan in some type of physical combat. To be sure, Satan wants no part of Christ. So how did Jesus bruise the head of the Serpent?

Paul tells us how:

"Blotting out the handwriting of ordinances that was against us, which was contrary to us, and took it out of the way, nailing it to His Cross;

"And having spoiled principalities and powers, He made a show of them openly, triumphing over them in it" (Col. 2:14-15).

Jesus went to the Cross to satisfy the demands of a thrice-Holy God. Man owed a terrible debt to God, all brought on by sin, a debt, incidentally, which he could not even hope to pay. This debt was made very clear and plain by the Law of Moses. In other words, the Law told man what he should do and how he should be. But regrettably, due to man's fallen state, he could not live up to this which God demanded and was, therefore, branded by his own actions as a Lawbreaker. The penalty for the breaking of this Law was death (Rom. 6:23).

So Jesus went to the Cross in order to pay that debt, which He did by the pouring out of His Own Precious Blood (Eph. 2:13-18). This satisfied the demands of the Righteousness of God, which means that the debt was paid in full. Jesus Christ was our Substitute, and, actually our Representative Man (I Cor. 15:45). Simple Faith in Him grants to us a perfect and complete Salvation. At the moment of Faith, a perfect Righteousness is imputed to the believing sinner, and he is *"born again"* (Jn. 3:3, 16; Eph. 2:8-9).

However, as a by-product of what Jesus did at the Cross, Satan was totally and completely defeated. His head was forever bruised, which means that the terrible bite of sin and death was made invalid. So what was that by-product?

"Sin" is Satan's legal claim on humanity. By the word *"legal"* we are referring to the right that Satan has to hold man in bondage because of sin.

In fact, this bondage was so complete, that all Old Testament Saints were taken captive by Satan at death, and taken down into Paradise. Because of their Faith, Satan couldn't put them over into the burning side of the pit, but he definitely was holding them captive (Lk., Chpt. 16).

But when Jesus died on the Cross, thereby paying the sin debt, Satan's legal right was canceled. In that manner, Jesus *"bruised the head of Satan,"* which means that He *"spoiled principalities and powers, making a show of them openly, triumphing over them in it"* (Col. 2:15).

In fact, the moment that Jesus died on the Cross, He went down into Paradise, where Paul said: *"He led captivity captive, and gave gifts unto men"* (Eph. 4:8).

That's a strange term, *"He led captivity captive!"*

It means that all the Old Testament Saints, as stated, were held captive by Satan when they died. This means they couldn't go to Heaven, but were rather taken, as also stated, down into Paradise. But when Jesus paid the price, thereby removing the sin debt, this destroyed Satan's power of captivity, with Jesus then making them His captives, which He did, and as well, taking them with Him to Heaven. From that moment, whenever Believers die, they immediately go to be with Christ (Phil. 1:23).

While Believers before the Cross were definitely saved, and because of their Faith in the coming Redeemer, the truth was, the *"blood of bulls and goats couldn't take away sins"* (Heb. 10:4). But when Jesus came, He was introduced by John the Baptist, by that great Prophet saying of Him: *"Behold the Lamb of God, which taketh away the sin of the world"* (Jn. 1:29).

If it is to be noticed, John used the word *"sin"* in a singular sense, while Paul used it in Hebrews 10:4 in a plural sense (sins). What is the difference?

Animal sacrifices had to be offered up for each sin, hence the word *"sins"* being used.

Even though the animal sacrifices covered the sin, hence the word *"Atonement"* being used often in the Old Testament, it still couldn't take away these sins.

But when Jesus came, while He definitely addressed *"sins"* in the plural, which speaks of every single sin that anyone has ever committed being washed and cleansed, He as well addressed the very cause and principle of *"sin,"* hence John the Baptist using the term in the singular. In other words, Jesus took away the cause of sin, which is Satan and self-will. When He bruised the head of Satan on the Cross, which He did by paying the debt for all sin, it went to the very cause and principle of sin.

But let the Reader understand that this was all done at the Cross. This is why it is called the *"Finished Work"* (Jn. 17:4; 19:30). God using the metaphor *"the heel being bruised,"* refers to Jesus suffering on the Cross. In other words, the bruising of the head of Satan didn't come without price. It cost our Lord His very Life; however, due to the fact that He atoned for every sin, the Resurrection was never in doubt. In other words, had He left one sin unatoned, due to the fact that the wages of sin is death, He couldn't have been resurrected from the dead. But due to the fact that He definitely did atone for all sin, there was no way that death could hold Him. The Resurrection was a foregone conclusion.

That's the reason that at the moment of His death, the Scripture says: *"Behold, the veil of the temple was rent in twain from the top to the bottom"* (Mat. 27:51).

This means that the way into the Holy of Holies, the very presence of God, was now opened to man. Jesus had opened it, by what He did at the Cross. At that moment, the Plan of Redemption was complete.

Yes, there had to be a Resurrection; however, as stated, the Resurrection was never in doubt! It was the shedding of His Blood on the Cross, which paid the terrible sin debt, and, thereby, opened up the way to the Presence of God, and this great Work was totally and completely finished at the Cross. It did not await the Resurrection or the Exaltation. While those things were definitely necessary, as stated, due to the price being paid at the

Cross, and God having recognized that Sacrifice by ripping the veil apart, the Resurrection, and the Exaltation were a guaranteed fact.

When Christians boast about being a Resurrection person, they need to understand that the are such only by what Christ did at the Cross. Paul said:

"For if we have been planted together in the likeness of His death, we shall be also in the likeness of His Resurrection" (Rom. 6:5).

This simply means that we cannot enjoy Resurrection power, which I will explain momentarily, unless we first understand *"the likeness of His Death,"* which refers to our part in that death, as outlined in Romans 6:3-5.

THE CROSS AS THE DIVIDING LINE

This *"enmity"* of which the Lord spoke becomes even more rabid in the Church of the Lord Jesus Christ. Satan tells the world that they can have Salvation without Jesus Christ and Him Crucified. He brings that lie over into the Church, by telling Believers that they can have victory other than by Jesus Christ and Him Crucified. And this is where the Cross is the dividing line.

If the Believer rejects the Cross as it regards the means of not only his Salvation, but as well his Sanctification, he will grow more and more lean in his soul, with even the potential of losing his soul. Paul said so in Galatians, Chapter 5. If he accepts the Message of the Cross, looking strictly to what Jesus did at Calvary as the means of his life of victory and Sanctification, he will grow in Grace and the knowledge of the Lord. The Fruit of the Spirit will then be paramount within his life (Gal. 5:22-23), otherwise, the *"works of the flesh"* will manifest themselves in his life (Gal. 5:19-21).

So the Believer has a choice: A. *"Works of the Flesh"* or B. *"Fruit of the Spirit."* The latter comes by Faith in the Cross, with the former coming by faith in self. Now the upshot is this:

Most of the time, those in the Church who reject the Cross will also, at the same time, persecute those who accept the Cross. Again, Paul said so:

NOTES

"And I, Brethren, if I yet preach circumcision, why do I yet suffer persecution? Then is the offence of the Cross ceased" (Gal. 5:11).

The Cross has always been the dividing line between the Truth Church and the apostate Church. It is because the Cross of Christ is the Foundation of the Gospel, exactly as the Lord says in the Verse of our study, Genesis 3:15.

(16) "UNTO THE WOMAN HE SAID, I WILL GREATLY MULTIPLY YOUR SORROW AND YOUR CONCEPTION; IN SORROW YOU SHALL BRING FORTH CHILDREN; AND YOUR DESIRE SHALL BE TO YOUR HUSBAND, AND HE SHALL RULE OVER YOU."

The overview is:

1. The Lord now speaks to the woman as it regards her judgment.

2. He would multiply her sorrow.

3. Her conception of children would no longer be as *"sons of God"* (Lk. 3:38), but rather as sons, or in the *"likeness of Adam"* (Gen. 5:3).

4. Children would be born into a world of sorrow.

5. Her husband, instead of God, would now rule over her.

THE WOMAN

The phrase, *"Unto the woman He said,"* presents judgment that was bitter to say the least, and which, as well, had to do with the Fall. In other words, it had far-reaching effects.

And yet, even though the Lord placed a curse upon the serpent, He did not do so as it regards Adam and Eve, at least as it regarded them personally. This referred to the fact that human beings are candidates for Restoration.

CONCEPTION

The phrase, *"I will greatly multiply your sorrow and your conception,"* carries forth the idea that with the Fall of Adam, all of humanity in essence fell, and because all were in his loins (I Cor. 15:21-22). Adam was the fountainhead of the human race. What he did, all would do. That's the reason that in order for man to be redeemed, there would have to be another Adam sent into this world, Whom Paul referred to as the *"Last Adam,"* Who was the Lord Jesus Christ (I Cor. 15:45).

The word *"conception"* is used here, and the *"multiplying of sorrow,"* simply because children were originally intended by God to be brought into the world, literally as *"sons of God"* (Lk. 3:38). Instead, and due to the Fall, all children would be conceived in sorrow, referring to the fact that they would be brought into the world in the *"likeness of Adam,"* with his fallen nature (Gen. 5:3). As a result of this fallen nature, i.e., *"the sin nature,"* man's every bent and direction would be towards sin, hence all the pain, suffering, privation, poverty, want, death, dying, and war, etc.

CHILDREN

The phrase, *"In sorrow you shall bring forth children,"* refers to that of what we have just said. How many mothers have wept bitter tears, because their sons and daughters have turned out to be murderers, or thieves, etc.? How many have had their hearts broken by the actions of their children? While Christ has made it possible for all of this to be ameliorated, without Him, and to be sure, the *"sorrow"* definitely prevails.

RULE

The phrase, *"And your desire shall be to your husband, and he shall rule over you,"* refers to the fact that because of Eve being the prime actor in sin, henceforward, she was to live in subjection to him.

Among the heathen, the punishment was made very bitter by the degradation to which a woman was reduced. In fact, this continues unto this hour in the ranks of Islam.

In Christ, thankfully, the whole penalty, as Paul teaches, has been abrogated (Gal. 3:28), and the Christian woman is no more inferior to the man than is the Gentile to the Jew, or the bondman to the free. This was made possible by what Jesus did at the Cross. There, He totally and completely liberated mankind, which of course, included all women. So every iota of freedom which a woman presently possesses, which should be totally and completely equal to that of the man, is owed completely to Christ, and what He did at the Cross.

Prior to the Fall, woman was the helpmate of her husband and his equal. After the Fall,

she was no longer his equal. But now in Christ, she has been restored to that previous position of equality.

In the marriage relationship, the husband is to love the wife as Christ loved the Church and gave Himself for it (Eph. 6:25), and the wife is to respect the leadership of the husband (Horton).

(17) "AND UNTO ADAM HE SAID, BECAUSE YOU HAVE HEARKENED UNTO THE VOICE OF YOUR WIFE, AND HAVE EATEN OF THE TREE, OF WHICH I COMMANDED YOU, SAYING, YOU SHALL NOT EAT OF IT: CURSED IS THE GROUND FOR YOUR SAKE; IN SORROW SHALL YOU EAT OF IT ALL THE DAYS OF YOUR LIFE;"

The exegesis is:

1. Adam hearkened unto his wife instead of God.

2. As his penalty, the ground was to be cursed, meaning that there would be no more Garden of Eden.

3. Instead of God feeding him, he would have to derive his nourishment from a cursed ground.

4. Consequently, his life would be that of sorrow.

ADAM

The phrase, *"And unto Adam He said, Because you have hearkened unto the voice of your wife,"* proclaims the fact that Adam didn't listen to God.

Eve is representative here of people who tend to be used by Satan to draw others away from the Word of God. Man can listen to man, or man can listen to God. He cannot listen to both! The tragedy is, most in the world are listening to men instead of God. In fact, the Holy Spirit in I Timothy 2:14 teaches that Adam sinned more deeply than his wife. She is condemned in Verse 16 to subjection to him; prior to that condemnation she was his helpmeet or equal (Williams).

THE TREE

The phrase, *"And have eaten of the tree, of which I commanded you, saying, You shall not eat of it,"* speaks of the tree of the knowledge of good and evil, as portrayed in Genesis 2:17.

As we have previously stated, the problem with the tree in question was not evil properties in the fruit, but rather disobedience to the Word of God. Because this is so very, very important, please allow us to say it again.

OBEDIENCE

Obedience to the Word of God is the criteria for all things. I think any true Christian would readily agree with that statement; however, the great question pertains to the how of obedience. In other words, we are commanded to obey, and every true Christian wants to obey, but the question is, how do we bring this about?

Regrettably, the answer to this question that would be given by most Christians would be that we just simply obey. Most Christians have the idea that now that we are Christians, we have the capacity to say *"yes"* or *"no"* with ease; consequently, if we say *"yes"* to sin and temptation, it is simply because we want to do that, etc. Nothing could be further from the Truth. And to be frank, millions of Christians have run aground on this very premise.

If that is the case, why did the great Apostle Paul say: *"For that which I do I allow* (understand) *not: for what I would, that do I not; but what I hate, that do I"* (Rom. 7:15). I have asked that in the form of a question, even though I ended it with a period.

Some try to explain away the entirety of the Seventh Chapter of Romans by claiming that this is an account of Paul's experiences before Salvation. Nothing could be further from the Truth.

In the first place, Paul says here that he hates sin. No sinner or unredeemed person hates sin. They may hate the effects of sin, but they certainly don't hate sin. In fact, they love sin.

No, the Seventh Chapter of Romans, which is incidentally one of the most important Chapters in the entirety of the Bible, proclaims the experience of the Apostle Paul after he was saved and Baptized with the Holy Spirit. In fact, he had already been called to be an Apostle, and even then was an Apostle. His problem was this:

At that time, and I speak of the time of the Romans, Chapter 7 experience, Paul didn't know the Message of the Cross. In fact, no one else in the world knew that particular Message either. Actually, this Message was

given to the Apostle Paul, which in reality is the meaning of the New Covenant, which is the meaning of the Cross.

Paul is relating his experiences of trying to live for God by his own strength and ability, which are always woefully insufficient. But the tragedy is, that's where most Christians are presently — in the Seventh Chapter of Romans.

In Verse 18 of that Chapter, the Apostle says: *"For I know that in me (that is, in my flesh,) dwelleth no good thing: for to will* (willpower) *is present with me; but how to perform that which is good I find not."*

He is plainly saying in this Passage that willpower, within itself, which simply refers to saying *"yes"* or *"no"* will not suffice. But yet, that's what most Christians find themselves doing. They're trying to obey the Lord by saying, *"yes"* to Him and *"no"* to temptation. Sooner or later they fail!

There's only one way that the Believer can obey the Lord, which refers to obeying God's Word. That way is as follows:

1. He must understand that everything from God comes to us strictly through what Jesus did at the Cross. It's not our willpower, our own personal strength or ability, or any machinations in which we may engage, but strictly the Cross of Christ. There, every victory was won.

2. Understanding that, the Cross of Christ is to ever be the object of our Faith. And this means that if the Cross of Christ is the total and complete object of our Faith, which it must be, then our own ability and strength, or our Church, or whatever, are not the object of our faith. This is very, very important.

3. Understanding that the Cross is the means by which all things come to the Child of God, and that it must ever be the object of our Faith, this being done, the Holy Spirit will then greatly and grandly help us in all things (Rom. 6:3-14; 8:1-2, 11).

Now the Reader will find that in one way or the other, I will give this little abbreviated formula over and over again throughout this Volume. I do so, because there is nothing more important.

This is the manner, and in fact the only manner, in which the Believer can properly obey the Word of the Lord. If we set out to do it any other way, we will find ourselves, whether we admit it or not, in the position of Paul when he said: *"O wretched man that I am! Who shall deliver me from the body of this death?"* (Rom. 7:24).

THE CURSE

The phrase, *"Cursed is the ground for your sake; in sorrow shall you eat of it all the days of your life,"* presents the cursing of the habitation. What the Earth would have been, in fact was intended to be, which was a paradise, has now been altered, and altered severely.

As well, the phrase *"all the days of your life,"* proclaims the death sentence, which means that life is now terminal, all as a result of *"spiritual death,"* which was and is separation from God.

As well, as *"sorrow"* was to be the end result of the children conceived and brought forth, likewise, *"sorrow"* would be the result of one's labor.

Mathew Henry said: *"Man's business shall from henceforth become a toil to him. Observe here that labor is our duty, which we must faithfully perform; not as creatures only, but as criminals, we are bound to work; it is a part of our sentence, which idleness daringly defies. Uneasiness and weariness with labor are our just punishment, which we must patiently submit to, and not complain of, since they are less than our iniquity deserves."* Henry went on to say: *"Let us not by inordinate care and labor make our punishment heavier than God has made it; but study to lighten our burden, by regarding Providence in all, and expecting rest shortly."*

The Righteousness of God is to be acknowledged in all the sad consequences of sin. Yet, in God's sentence, there is Mercy. Man is not sentenced to eat dust as the serpent, but only to eat the herb of the field.

(18) "THORNS ALSO AND THISTLES SHALL IT BRING FORTH TO YOU; AND YOU SHALL EAT THE HERB OF THE FIELD;"

The structure is:

1. Thorns and thistles were not originally in the creation of God.

2. Thorns and thistles are a result of the curse, which is a result of the sin of man.

3. The *"herb of the field"* would not now grow freely, as originally intended, but only now with great care and labor.

THORNS AND THISTLES

The phrase, *"Thorns also and thistles shall it bring forth to you,"* proclaims the fact that left to itself, the ground will no longer bring forth choice trees laden with generous fruit, such as Adam found in the Garden, but will now rather bring forth *"thorns"* and *"thistles."*

The tendency of the Earth is now toward decay and degeneration, again, all because of the curse. In the renewed Earth, the golden age of Paradise, and we speak of the coming Millennial Reign, will return, meaning that the curse will then be lifted.

HERB OF THE FIELD

The phrase, *"And you shall eat the herb of the field,"* proclaims in the next Verse how that herb is to be brought forth.

Even with modern equipment, the produce of the Earth is brought forth only with great care and diligence. Even then, it is prone to destruction regarding the elements and insects, etc. We can thank original sin for that.

And if it is to be noticed, I think one could also say without fear of contradiction that it's the nations of the world which embrace Christianity, or at least a modicum of Christianity, that serve as the breadbaskets of the world. Nations which do not recognize Jesus as Lord can little feed their people, much less help feed others. One might say, *"Much Bible, much food; little Bible, little food; no Bible, no food."*

(19) "IN THE SWEAT OF YOUR FACE SHALL YOU EAT BREAD, TILL YOU RETURN UNTO THE GROUND; FOR OUT OF IT WERE YOU TAKEN: FOR DUST YOU ARE, AND UNTO DUST SHALL YOU RETURN."

The composition is:

1. Food will be obtained by hard labor.

2. The life-source, which was formerly in God, is now in food, and which is woefully insufficient.

3. Physical death is the result.

4. The Power of God Alone could keep the dust alive, that being gone, to dust man returns.

SWEAT

The phrase, *"In the sweat of your face shall you eat bread,"* proclaims the fact not only of hard labor as it regards the producing of food, but as well presents itself as proof, and we continue to speak of sweat, that man is returning to the Earth. It tells of exhaustion and waste.

Toil is the lot of the human race, that, as stated, which God never originally intended.

DUST

The phrase, *"Till you return unto the ground; for out of it were you taken: for dust you are, and unto dust shall you return,"* perhaps can be explained in the following manner:

To prove the immortality of the soul equally proves the mortality of the body.

Bishop Butler says: *"Death is the division of a compound substance in its component parts; but as the soul is a simple substance, and incapable of division, it is per se incapable of death. The body of Adam, composed of particles of earth, was capable of division, and our first parents in Paradise were assured of an unending existence by a special gift, typified by the tree of life. But now this gift was withdrawn, and henceforward the sweat of man's brow was in itself proof that he was returning to the Earth."*

ADAM AND CHRIST

In one way or the other, men constantly claim that the sentence passed upon Adam was too harsh, too severe. As is usual, man continues to blame God for his dilemma. Even after some 6,000 years of recorded history, he refuses to acknowledge the blame as being his own.

To be sure, the situation is made worse by man ignoring the fact that sin demanded such a sentence, and above all, that Jesus answered that sentence by becoming the Last Adam, which wrought Redemption for man. Note the following:

1. Travailing pain came with sin. We read of the travail of Christ's soul, even though He had no sin (Isa. 53:11), and the pains of death which He suffered (Acts 2:24).

2. Subjection came with sin. In answer to this, Christ was made under the Law (Gal. 4:4).

3. The curse came with sin. In answer to that horror, Christ was made a curse for us, and in effect, died a cursed death (Gal. 3:13).

NOTES

4. The thorns came in with sin. In answer to that, Jesus was crowned with thorns for us.

5. Sweat, as well, came in with sin. The Scripture says of Him that His sweat for us was as it had been great drops of blood.

6. Sorrow came with sin. He was a man of sorrows, acquainted with grief.

7. Death came with sin. He became obedient unto death. Thus is the cure as wide as the cause.

Concerning the Fall, Mathew Henry said: *"Man's soul was ruined by the Fall; the image of God was defaced; man's nature was corrupted, and he became dead in sin. The design of God was to restore the soul of man; to restore life, and the image of God, in conversion; and to carry on this work in Sanctification, until He should perfect it in glory."*

One must also say that man's body was ruined; by the Fall it became subject to death. The design of God was to restore it from this ruin, and not only to deliver it from death, by what He did at the Cross through His Son, the Lord Jesus Christ, but to deliver it as well from mortality itself, in making it like unto Christ's glorious body.

(20) "AND ADAM CALLED HIS WIFE'S NAME EVE; BECAUSE SHE WAS THE MOTHER OF ALL LIVING."

The construction is:

1. God named the man, and called him Adam, which means, *"red earth."*

2. Adam named the woman, and called her Eve, which means, *"life."*

3. Adam bears the name of the dying body, Eve of the living soul.

EVE

The phrase, *"And Adam called his wife's name Eve,"* actually means *"life,"* or the *"mother of all the living."* The idea is, through Eve alone could human life be continued, and the *"woman's Seed"* be obtained, Who was to raise up man from his Fall. While, then, woman's punishment consists in the multiplication of her *"sorrow and conception,"* she becomes thereby only more precious to man (Ellicott).

And yet, Eve did not fully understand what the Lord had said concerning the *"Seed of the woman."* In fact, it would not be fully brought out until the Prophet Isaiah gave clarity to the promise by saying, *"Behold, a virgin shall conceive"* (Isa. 7:14). This prophecy made it clear that the Saviour was not to be the offspring of the union of a man and wife. In the New Testament this fact was revealed still more clearly by the Angel (Lk. 1:26-38). Since, then, there was promised man, through the Seed of the woman, deliverance from the Law, sin, and death, and there was given to him a clear and sure hope of the Resurrection and renewal in the future life, it is clear that he could not by his own power remove sin and its punishment. Nor could he by his own power escape death and make amends for his disobedience. Therefore, the Son of God had to sacrifice Himself and secure all this for mankind. He had to remove sin, overcome death, and restore what Adam had lost by his disobedience (Luther).

MOTHER OF ALL LIVING

The phrase, *"Because she was the mother of all living,"* proclaims the power of procreation. But yet, some believe that Adam in the giving of the name Eve to his wife pertains to the proclamation of his faith. That is possible, but I think not!

Faith in the *"Promised Seed"* was the requirement for Salvation. There is some evidence, which we will later explore more fully, that Adam and Eve may have made a start toward God. In other words, they may have initially expressed faith; however, every evidence is that they soon abandoned their faith.

The Scripture tells us of the faith of Enoch, who was contemporary with Adam, at least for a period of time. But it says nothing about the faith of Adam (Heb. 11:5-6).

(21) "UNTO ADAM ALSO AND TO HIS WIFE DID THE LORD GOD MAKE COATS OF SKINS, AND CLOTHED THEM."

The exegesis is:

1. In the making of coats of skins, God in effect was telling Adam and Eve that their fig leaves were insufficient.

2. From this it seems that Adam, in some way, even immediately after the Fall, must have been taught that without shedding of blood is no remission of sin, and that God would accept a vicarious (substitutionary) sacrifice.

3. In this first sacrifice was laid the foundation of the entire Mosaic Dispensation, as in Verse 15 that of the Gospel.

4. It is important that the promise of the Gospel, which is the Sacrifice of Christ, was given first (vs. 15), while that which represented Moses was given second. The Mosaic Law would be temporary; always pointing to Christ Who would be the great Sacrifice.

COATS OF SKINS

The phrase, *"Unto Adam also and to his wife did the LORD God make coats of skins,"* presents the fact that the first thing that died was a sacrifice, or Christ in a figure, Who is, therefore, said to be the Lamb slain from the foundation of the world (I Pet. 1:18-20).

Let it be known that it is the *"Lord God"* Who furnished these coats, and not man himself. This tells us that Salvation is altogether of God and not at all of man. All Adam and Eve could do was to fashion a garment out of fig leaves, which regrettably, man has been attempting to do ever since.

Sin is not a cheap affair, and cannot be satisfied by a cheap solution. Sin is devastating, and can only be addressed by the Sacrifice of Christ, which was, incidentally, the ultimate Sacrifice.

FROM THE VERY BEGINNING, THE CROSS!

The manner in which the Lord would redeem the human race has never been in question. In fact, that was decided by the Godhead, even before the foundation of the world (I Pet. 1:18-20).

Someone asked me once, *"Was it Who Christ was, or What He did that affected our Salvation?"*

Up front, it was What He did!

While Who He was, namely Deity, was absolutely necessary; still, Jesus Christ, in fact, had always been God. As God, He had no beginning, which means that He was unformed, unmade, uncreated, has always been, always is, and always shall be. But all of that, as wonderful and glorious as it was and is, did not redeem anybody. In fact, His Virgin Birth did not redeem anyone, neither His miracles nor healings! The fact that He spoke as no man ever spoke did not effect any Redemption, even though all of these things were of extreme significance.

It was what He did on the Cross which effected Redemption. That's why Paul said: *"For Christ sent me not to baptize, but to preach the Gospel: not with wisdom of words, lest the Cross of Christ should be made of none effect"* (I Cor. 1:17).

As well, when we're given a vision of Heaven through the eyes of John the Beloved, and I speak of his great vision on the Isle of Patmos, we see there the central theme being *"Jesus Christ and Him Crucified,"* all signified by the constant use by the Apostle of the term *"Lamb"* (Rev. 5:6, 8, 12-13).

So it begins with the Cross, and it ends with the Cross. In fact, John used the term *"Lamb,"* signifying Christ and what He did at the Cross, some 28 times in the Book of Revelation, seven times in the last two Chapters alone.

In fact, the last time in the Bible the term *"Lamb"* is used, and we continue to speak of the Son of God, it is used in relationship to the fact that there is *"no more curse."* In other words, the terrible curse that was leveled at the dawn of time as it regards Adam's Fall, was eliminated by the Lord Jesus Christ at great price, which was the shedding of His Life's Blood on the Cross (Rev. 22:3).

COVERING

The phrase, *"And clothed them,"* proclaims the fact that such a covering came at a price, the death of the animals in question; consequently, these coats of skin had a significance. The beasts, whose skins they were, must be slain, slain before their eyes, to show them what death is, and that they might see that they themselves are mortal and dying (Eccl. 3:18). As well, this Sacrifice would also show them the terrible awfulness of sin. As repeatedly stated, it would typify the coming Redeemer.

Jesus said to the Church at Laodicea: *"I counsel you to buy of Me gold tried in the fire, that you may be rich; and white raiment, that you may be clothed, and that the shame of your nakedness do not appear"* (Rev. 3:18).

The Laodiceans had abandoned the Cross. They were trusting in other things; consequently, the shame of their nakedness was obvious!

All of this becomes even more striking, when we realize that the Laodicean Church typifies the Church of this present time. It is referred to as the apostatized Church. And let the Reader understand that the apostasy addressed here is the abandonment of the Cross.

In the last several decades, all types of things have been suggested as the proper *"covering."* Many think of their Denominations as their covering; others think of particular Preachers, while others think of their own good works.

Irrespective as to what it might be, and how good it might seem to be on the surface, if the *"covering"* is not the Blood of the Lamb, and that exclusively, then it is nothing but fig leaves. It is something that God will not honor, in fact, cannot honor. And that is the sin of the modern Church.

THE CHURCH

While the Church in its purest form belongs to Christ, actually referred to as *"My Church"* (Mat. 16:18), the sadness is, it is seldom left in its purest form.

Millions of so-called Christians have made a particular Church the object of their faith. In other words, they think by their association and their involvement, such is their covering. They may not use that term, but the facts are, that particular Church, whoever it might be, is their object of faith. They might talk about Christ, and might even state that their trust is in Christ, but in reality, it's in that Church. In fact, many equate Christ and the Church as somewhat one and the same.

They aren't!

As a Believer, your Faith is to be anchored totally and completely in Christ; however, for it to actually be anchored in Christ, it must be defined by what He did at the Cross; otherwise, you are serving *"another Jesus"* (II Cor. 11:4).

Millions claim to be serving Christ, when in reality, it is *"another Jesus"* which they are serving. And let me say it again. The reason is because of the following:

To claim Jesus Alone is not enough. One must claim what He did at the Cross as well! That's why Paul plainly said: *"But we preach Christ Crucified"* (I Cor. 1:23).

He also said: *"For I determined not to know anything among you, save Jesus Christ, and Him Crucified"* (I Cor. 2:2).

Satan doesn't really care too very much where one places one's faith, as long as it's not in the Cross. He is perfectly content with you to place your faith in the greatest of Christian virtues. He knows that the Holy Spirit will not honor such an object of faith, which will leave the Believer pretty well helpless. At that juncture, Satan can have his way with such a person. That's the reason for so many failures among Christians, failures incidentally, which run the gamut all the way from the proverbial *"A"* to the proverbial *"Z"* (I Cor. 1:17-18).

The *"covering"* has always been the Cross; the covering is presently the Cross, and the covering will ever be the Cross. There is no other.

(22) "AND THE LORD GOD SAID, BEHOLD, THE MAN IS BECOME AS ONE OF US, TO KNOW GOOD AND EVIL: AND NOW, LEST HE PUT FORTH HIS HAND AND TAKE ALSO OF THE TREE OF LIFE, AND EAT, AND LIVE FOREVER:"

The overview is:

1. The Lord knew evil, not by Personal experience, but rather through Omniscience.

2. The pronoun *"Us"* signifies the Godhead, *"God the Father, God the Son, and God the Holy Spirit."*

3. The properties of the *"Tree of Life,"* i.e., *"its fruit,"* were unlike the fruit of the tree of the knowledge of good and evil, which contained no properties within itself.

4. The fruit of the *"Tree of Life"* carried the properties of eternal life.

TO KNOW GOOD AND EVIL

The phrase, *"And the LORD God said, Behold, the man is become as one of Us, to know good and evil,"* refers to the Lord knowing *"evil"* by the power of Omniscience, which knows all things, but never by Personal experience. The Scripture says: *"For God cannot be tempted with evil"* (James 1:13).

This means that He cannot have anything to do with evil in any regard. He is Perfectly Righteous, actually the thrice-Holy God (Rev. 4:8).

As well, the pronoun *"Us"* proclaims the Trinity. No, when the Lord used the pronoun

NOTES

"Us," He wasn't speaking of Himself and Angels, as suggested by some. As well, fallen angels know what evil is by personal experience, but not by Omniscience, because they do not have that attribute. Such pertains only to Deity.

THE TREE OF LIFE

The phrase, *"Lest he put forth his hand, and take also of the Tree of Life, and eat, and live forever,"* proclaims the fact that the fruit of this particular tree evidently contained certain properties designed by God, which would cause the human body to remain forever young, thereby, living forever. And yet at the same time, we must be quick to say that this tree had such power not because of its peculiar nature, but because of the Divine Word attached to it, which made it a life-giving tree.

At the dawn of time, man is denied access to *"the Tree of Life,"* while at the conclusion of the Dispensations, and due to what Christ has done at the Cross, the *"Tree of Life"* is once again opened to man (Rev. 22:1-2).

(23) "THEREFORE THE LORD GOD SENT HIM FORTH FROM THE GARDEN OF EDEN, TO TILL THE GROUND FROM WHENCE HE WAS TAKEN."

The synopsis is:

1. The Lord sending Adam and Eve away from the Garden and, therefore, from the Tree of Life was a favor to them.

2. The *"Garden of Eden"* would no longer be available, and man would now have to forage a living from the Earth by the sweat of his brow.

3. The reason for this was sin.

EXPELLED FROM THE GARDEN OF EDEN

The phrase, *"Therefore the LORD God sent him forth from the Garden of Eden,"* was in effect an act of mercy. Man is expelled from the Garden lest by eating of the Tree of Life he should perpetuate his misery.

To bring this up to modern times, think of an Adolph Hitler living forever! A Joseph Stalin! Or the Muslims who murdered nearly 7,000 people by their acts of atrocity in New York City and Washington, D.C., etc.! In fact, that list is very long. While being driven from the Garden of Eden and access to the Tree of Life was definitely a punishment, in the long run and because of their state, it was definitely a blessing.

Ellicott says: *"Adam had exercised the power of marring God's work, and if an unending physical life were added to the gift of freewill now in revolt against God, his condition and that of mankind would become most miserable. Man is still able to attain to immortality, but it must now be through struggle, sorrow, penitence, faith, and death. Hence a paradise is no fit home for him. The Divine Mercy, therefore, commands Adam to quit it, in order that he may live under conditions better suited for his moral and spiritual good."*

TILL THE GROUND

The phrase, *"To till the ground from where he was taken,"* refers to a place of toil, not to a place of torment. Matthew Henry said: *"Our first parents were excluded from the privileges of their state of innocency, yet they were not abandoned to despair."*

The word *"till"* as used here is the same Hebrew word rendered *"dress"* in Genesis 2:15. Adam's task is the same, but the conditions are now altered. In other words, it will now be far more difficult than was previously intended.

(24) "SO HE DROVE OUT THE MAN; AND HE PLACED AT THE EAST OF THE GARDEN OF EDEN CHERUBIMS, AND A FLAMING SWORD WHICH TURNED EVERY WAY, TO KEEP THE WAY OF THE TREE OF LIFE."

The overview is:

1. The word *"drove"* implies the idea of force and displeasure.

2. The entrance to the Garden was evidently on the east.

3. Cherubims were placed at this entrance to keep Adam and Eve from reentering and partaking of the Tree of Life.

4. The *"flaming sword"* was emblematic of the Divine Glory in its attitude towards sin.

EXPULSION

The phrase, *"So He drove out the man,"* combined with the word *"sent"* in the previous Verse, implies that Adam and Eve definitely

didn't want to depart paradise. Consequently, the two words, *"sent"* and *"drove,"* convey the ideas of force and displeasure. In other words, God had to force Adam and Eve to leave.

But there is one thing that all men must learn. Whatever God does with us is always and without exception for our best. In other words, if we did what we wanted to do, whatever that might be, to be sure, it would turn out to be destructive not only to others, but also to ourselves. To Adam and Eve, it seemed harsh to be driven out of the Garden, and not allowed access anymore; however, the Plan of God was for their everlasting good, as well as all of humanity. Because in essence, what God did to our first parents was done to the entirety of the human race.

The idea was that they would look to the coming *"Promised Seed"* of Genesis 3:15. Had they partaken of the Tree of Life in their fallen state, such would have consigned them to an eternal life of torment, which would grow worse by the millennia. Only the *"Promised Seed"* could alleviate the dilemma! What does this teach us?

THE CROSS: THE ONLY ANSWER TO SIN

Out of the horror of September 11, 2001, one man made the following observation:

In looking at the rubble of the World Trade Center, the workmen, in endeavoring to untangle the great steel beams so they could be hauled away, had with their cutting torches, fashioned a perfect Cross as it stood outlined against the wreckage.

In looking at this, the man stated, *"I wonder if the Lord is not trying to tell us something?"*

In fact, the Lord most definitely is trying to tell us something. He is telling us, in essence, that the cause of this terrible problem is *"sin,"* with the only solution to this problem being *"the Cross."* There is no other answer for sin; no other answer for disobedience; no other answer for rebellion; the Cross Alone is the answer. Let the Church understand that; let the Preacher proclaim that; let every Believer understand that; let the world know that; the only answer is the Cross!

The idea is this: Even though God was forced to drive Adam and Eve out of the

Garden, the sense of the Text is that He went with them, which in essence said, *"I will bring you back."*

Oh the love of God, how rich, how pure! Yes, He would bring man back, but at such price, a price incidentally, which He would pay Himself.

In 1996, the Lord in answer to years of soul-searching prayer, even travail and with tears, began to open up to me the Message of the Cross. To be sure, I had always preached the Cross and had done so strongly. As a result, the Lord had helped me to see hundreds of thousands brought to a saving knowledge of Jesus Christ, and I exaggerate not!

But even though I knew and understood the Cross as it regards the great Salvation Message, I did not understand the Cross as it regards the Sanctification process; consequently, I attempted to sanctify myself, which cannot be done. God's Righteousness is always set forth in the Cross; man's righteousness is set forth in his own works — the sin-stained works — of his own hands. These are works which God cannot accept.

The closing Verses of this Chapter are full of instruction. Fallen man, in his fallen state, must not be allowed to eat of the fruit of the Tree of Life, for that would entail upon him endless wretchedness in this world. To take of the Tree of Life, and eat, and live forever in our present condition, would be unmingled misery. To be sure, the Tree of Life can only be tasted in death and Resurrection — and I speak of our dying in Christ as it regards His Crucifixion (Rom. 6:3), and then being raised in *"newness of life"* (Rom. 6:4-5). This is the Finished Work of the Promised Seed, and it is by that and that alone that reentry can be gained to the Tree of Life, Who is the Lord Jesus Christ.

CHERUBIMS

The phrase, *"And He placed at the east of the Garden of Eden, Cherubims,"* evidently refers to the entrance to the Garden.

There is some evidence, as we shall see, that a Sanctuary was built here, and we continue to speak of the entrance to the Garden, even as we shall see in the next Chapter.

Who and What are these Cherubims?

There are all types of opinions. Some say they are the fullness of the Deity. Some say

NOTES

they are symbolic of earthly life. Others, of the angelic nature. Still others claim they represent the Divine Manhood of Jesus Christ.

Wordsworth says, and I think he is right: *"The Cherubims are symbolic of redeemed and glorified humanity."*

He went on to say: *"Combining with the intelligence of human nature the highest qualities of the animal world, as exhibited in the lion, the ox, and the eagle (Rev. 4:7), they were emblematic of creature life in its most absolute perfect form. As such they were caused to dwell at the gate of Eden to intimate that only when perfected and purified could fallen human nature return to paradise."*

Carrying forth the same principle, the Veil, which hung between the Holy of Holies where resided the Ark of the Covenant and the Holy Place, had Cherubims embroidered on it (Ex. 26:31-32). In effect, the Cherubims on the Veil said the same thing as the Cherubims at the entrance of the Garden of Eden. Man was not allowed entrance. In fact, only the High Priest of Israel could go into the Holy of Holies, and then only once a year, which was on the Great Day of Atonement, and then not without blood. In other words, he had to offer up the blood of the sacrifice on the Mercy Seat, which covered the Ark of the Covenant, and which as well, carried two Cherubim, one on either end, facing each other, and looking down upon the Mercy Seat. This High Priest was a Type of Christ, Who would one day offer up His Own Blood on the Cross of Calvary, which He did! That alone opened up the way to God, making it possible for man to come into the very Presence of God. But let it ever be known that this could be done, and can be done, only by our Faith in the Finished Work of Christ. The writer of Hebrews tells us:

"Let us (Believers) *therefore come boldly into the Throne of Grace, that we may obtain Mercy, and find Grace to help in time of need"* (Heb. 4:16).

Let us say it again, that the way into Paradise has now been opened by the Lord Jesus Christ, which He accomplished by the shedding of His Own Precious Blood, which was effected at the Cross of Calvary. That's the reason that Paul said:

"For Christ sent me not to baptize, but to preach the Gospel: not with wisdom of

words, lest the Cross of Christ should be made of none effect" (I Cor. 1:17).

THE FLAMING SWORD

The phrase, *"And a flaming sword which turned every way, to keep the way of the Tree of Life,"* served as an emblem of the Divine Glory in its attitude towards sin.

"To keep the way of the Tree of Life," presents itself as an interesting statement. While it pertains to the way being kept shut, it also at the same time states that the way is to be kept open. In other words, the idea is, even as we've already stated, while God did drive Adam and Eve from the Garden, He went with them, with a Promise of bringing them (mankind) back. This was done by the *"Promised Seed"* Who is the Lord Jesus Christ, and Who effected the open way by what He did at the Cross.

In effect, and even as we will later study, the Lord showed to Jacob the way back in, by giving him the dream of the *"ladder set upon the Earth, with the top of it reaching to Heaven"* (Gen. 28:12). *"The Angels of God were ascending and descending on it."*

In fact, that *"ladder"* was symbolic of Christ. Concerning this very thing, Jesus said of Himself, even as He began His public Ministry: *"Verily, verily, I say unto you, hereafter you shall see Heaven open, and the Angels of God ascending and descending upon the Son of Man"* (Jn. 1:51).

When Adam and Eve were driven out of the Garden, they went into a world which everywhere exhibited the lamentable results of the Fall. The Cherubim with the flaming sword did forbid fallen man to pluck the fruit of the Tree of Life, but God's Revelation would point him to the Death and Resurrection of the Seed of the woman, as that wherein life would be found beyond the pallor of death, and so it was!

As a consequence, Adam was a safer man outside the bounds of Paradise than he would have been within in his fallen state, and for this reason: Within, his life depended upon himself; whereas outside, it depended upon another, even a Promised Christ.

If the Cherubim and flaming sword closed up the way to Paradise, which they were forced to do, the Lord Jesus Christ has opened

NOTES

"a new and living way" into the Holiest of all. *"I am the Way, the Truth, and the Life; no man cometh unto the Father, but by Me"* (Jn. 14:6; Heb. 10:20).

In the knowledge of all of this, the Believer now moves onward through a world which is under the curse — where the traces of sin are visible on all hands. He has found his way, by Faith, and we speak of Faith in Christ and Him Crucified, to the bosom of the Father; and while he can secretly repose there, he is cheered by the blessed assurance that the One Who has conducted him thither is gone to prepare a place in the many mansions of the Father's House, and that He will soon come again and receive him unto Himself, amid the glory of the Father's Kingdom (Mackintosh).

"Join all the glorious names of wisdom, love, and power,
"That ever mortals knew, that Angels ever bore:
"All are too poor to speak His worth,
"Too poor to set my Saviour forth."

"Great Prophet of my God, my tongue would bless Your Name:
"By Thee the joyful news of our Salvation came,
"The joyful news of sins forgiven,
"Of Hell subdued and peace with Heaven."

"Jesus, my great High Priest, offered His Blood and died;
"My guilty conscience seeks no sacrifice beside:
"His powerful Blood did once atone
"And now it pleads before the Throne."

"Thou are my Counselor, my Pattern, and my Guide,
"And You my Shepherd are; Oh, keep me near Your side;
"Nor let my feet e'er turn astray,
"To wonder in the crooked way."

"My Saviour and my Lord, my Conquer'r and my King,
"Your scepter and Your sword, Your reigning Grace I sing:
"Thine is the power:
"Behold I sit in willing bonds beneath Your Feet."

CHAPTER 4

(1) "AND ADAM KNEW EVE HIS WIFE; AND SHE CONCEIVED, AND BEAR CAIN, AND SAID, I HAVE GOTTEN A MAN FROM THE LORD."

The structure is:

1. Eve is mentioned by name four times in the Bible (Gen. 3:20; 4:1; II Cor. 11:3; I Tim. 2:13).

2. It had been explained by the Lord to Adam that he was to beget children, especially since the blessing of the command, *"Be fruitful, and multiply"* (Gen. 1:28), was confirmed by the Promise that the Seed of the woman should bruise the serpent's head.

3. The phrase, *"knew Eve his wife,"* is the Biblical connotation of the union of husband and wife in respect to the sex act.

4. Cain was the first child born to this union.

5. By the use of the term *"Lord,"* which means *"Covenant God,"* Eve evidently thought that Cain was the Promised Seed.

ADAM AND EVE

The phrase, *"And Adam knew Eve his wife,"* is explained by the Expositors in the following fashion:

"Exiled from Eden, o'er-canopied by Grace, animated by hope, assured of the Divine forgiveness, and filled with a sweet peace, the first pair entered on their life experience of labor and sorrow, and the human race begins its onward course of development in sight of the mystic Cherubim and flaming sword."

Adam knowing Eve his wife, as stated, is the Biblical connotation of procreation, which refers to the bringing of offspring into this world.

As far as we know, humans are the only ones of God's creation given this privilege. It seems that all Angels were created at the same time. While there are different ranks of Angels regarding power, glory, and prestige, or so it seems, there are no Angels older than other Angels. All being created at one time, and created fully mature, such creation was totally different than that of the human.

The sex act, which was originally meant by God to be a product of love, and a product

of love alone, due to the Fall, has degenerated mostly to an act of lust. While, of course, the love between a husband and his wife remains, the fact of lust has been added to that blessing. So, most of the time when the term is used, *"making love,"* it is rather the satisfying of lust, which ironically is never satisfied. But for the Fall, lust in its evil sense would have never come upon mankind. But now, that which had begun encased in light is now encased, at least for the most part, in lust.

And yet, the Holy Spirit through the Apostle Paul said, that is as it regards the true love between a man and his wife: *"Marriage is honorable in all, and the bed undefiled: but whoremongers and adulterers God will judge"* (Heb. 13:4).

A wealth of information is given in this one Verse. We are told the following:

1. Marriage is honorable and thereby sanctioned before God, even as evidenced by Adam and Eve.

2. This is marriage between a man and a woman, and not in any way meant to imply same sex marriage, which is an abomination before God. As someone has well said, *"God created Adam and Eve, not Adam and Steve!"*

3. Between a husband and his wife, the bed is undefiled, meaning that the sex act is sanctioned by the Lord in the realm of marriage.

4. The statement also means that all sex outside of marriage is prohibited, which is the meaning of whoremongers and adulterers.

5. All sex outside of marriage will come under the Judgment of God, and of that one can be certain.

CONCEPTION

The phrase, *"And she conceived,"* records the first pregnancy and, therefore, the first birth. It would conclude exactly as the Lord said it would, with *"sorrow."* And so has been the lot of the human race from then until now.

It was originally planned by God that Adam and Eve, and all who would follow them, would bring into this world sons and daughters of God, which is proven by the order of begetting.

Concerning the lineage of Christ, the Scripture says, *"Which was the son of Enos, which was the son of Seth, which was the son of Adam, which was the son of God"* (Lk. 3:38).

The phrase concerning Seth being the *"son of Adam,"* concerns Genesis 5:3 where it says: *"And Adam lived an hundred and thirty years, and begat a son in his own likeness, and after his image; and called his name Seth."*

It was planned by God for all to be born in the likeness of God and after God's Image (Gen. 1:27). But due to the Fall, Adam, and all after him, could only bring sons and daughters into the world in the likeness of man and not God.

CAIN

The phrase, *"And bear Cain, and said, I've gotten a man from the LORD,"* presents the first birth, one incidentally who would turn out to be a murderer.

By Eve using the title *"Lord,"* which means *"Covenant God,"* and which refers to the *"Seed of the woman,"* (Gen. 3:15), she thought Cain was the Promised One.

But her faith that Cain was the one who would end the misery of sin was misplaced, for this she believed without a definite sign and Word from God by her own conviction. Just because she was so sure of the Promise she regarded her first son as the one who would carry out what the Lord had promised. Her mistake was that she did not know that from sinful flesh, nothing could be born but sinful flesh, and that sin and death could not be overcome by the flesh of corrupt man.

She did not know of the time and hour in which the blessed Saviour was to be conceived by the Holy Spirit and born of a Virgin. This also the Patriarchs did not know, though in the course of time, the prophecies of the Holy Spirit concerning the Promised Saviour became ever more definite (Isa. 7:14) (Luther).

There are seven great Promises in the Old Testament regarding the manner in which the Redeemer would come, four in Genesis and three in the remaining Books:

1. They predicted that the Redeemer should be of the human race (Gen. 3:15).

2. Of a section of that race, Shem (Gen. 9:26).

3. Of a nation belonging to that section, the Hebrew (Gen. 12:3).

4. Of a Tribe in that nation, Judah (Gen. 49:10).

NOTES

5. Of a family in that Tribe, David (II Sam. 7:16).

6. Of a member of that family, a woman, the Virgin (Isa. 7:14).

7. And lastly in a village belonging to that woman, Bethlehem (Mic. 5:2).

Thus these great Prophetic Circles are narrowed, and finally closed around the Lamb and Son of God (Williams).

THE FALLEN CONDITION

Adam and Eve using fig leaves to cover their nakedness (Gen. 3:7), and now thinking that their fallen union could produce a Redeemer, shows that they did not understand the magnitude of their lost condition. Despite some 6,000 years of recorded history, man still does not recognize or realize the degree of his lostness. We know that from the fact that he keeps trying to save himself, seemingly not realizing that corruption can never produce purity.

Let the Reader understand that we can be nothing, have nothing, do nothing, or come to nothing, without Christ. Even the Believer, the one who is Born-Again, the one who is Redeemed, the one who is a new creation in Christ Jesus, still cannot produce anything Righteous by his own efforts, ability, or machinations. We as Believers tend to forget that.

As Believers, we readily recognize that we are saved by Faith in Christ and Christ Alone (Eph. 2:8-9); however, we then turn around and try to sanctify ourselves by our own pitiful abilities. We find to our dismay that we have no more success in trying to sanctify ourselves personally, than the sinner does in trying to save himself personally. The thundering tones of the Apostle confront us at every turn: *"So then they who are in the flesh cannot please God"* (Rom. 8:8). We learn so slowly, even as Jacob of old, that God cannot give victories to the flesh. He can only give victory to His Son and our Redeemer, the Lord Jesus Christ. Let us fully understand that! And because it's so important, allow me to say it again:

All victory is found in Christ, and Christ Alone! And let the Reader understand, even though we have previously made the statement, and will no doubt make it many times again in this Volume, if we think of Christ apart from His Cross, we're then thinking of *"another Jesus,"* which God can never recognize (II Cor. 11:4).

Sadly and regrettably, much of the modern Church is still in the place of Eve of old. It produces a child, which is a work of the flesh, and it thinks that by pronouncing it as *"from the Lord,"* such is now sanctified; however, even as Eve of old, we find to our dismay that such is never to be. That which is of man, even redeemed man, can only *"steal, kill, and destroy"* (Jn. 10:10). As Abraham and Sarah found out, the flesh brings nothing but trouble, and the true seed cannot come forth until all hope of the flesh has been exhausted. It is the Spirit Alone Who can provide things of God (Rom. 8:1-2).

(2) "AND SHE AGAIN BEAR HIS BROTHER ABEL. AND ABEL WAS A KEEPER OF SHEEP, BUT CAIN WAS A TILLER OF THE GROUND."

The construction is:

1. The second child born to this union is Abel.

2. Abel means *"vanity."*

3. Cain being the oldest, this shows that Eve by now had become disillusioned with her firstborn, undoubtedly seeing traits in him which shouted the fact that he was not the Promised Seed.

4. She was losing faith in God.

5. The occupations of these two men tell us something about their spiritual perception.

ABEL

The phrase, *"And she again bear his brother Abel,"* concerns the second birth to this union.

Inasmuch as she named the child *"Abel,"* which means *"vanity,"* she had by now lost faith, or was in the process of losing Faith in God. Evidently, her hopes had been dashed concerning Cain being the Promised One. Quite possibly she had seen traits in his life which obviously told her that he was the opposite of what she had hoped.

As we have stated, she and Adam evidently did not yet quite know the magnitude of their deception, and the degree of their lostness. Their fallen condition was far worse than they had imagined.

Some would teach us that every man is born with qualities and capacities which, if rightly used, will enable him to work his way back to God. This is a plain denial of the fact so clearly set forth in the history now before us. Cain and Abel were born, not inside, but outside of Paradise — they were the sons, not of innocent, but of fallen Adam. They came into the world as the partakers of the nature of their father; and it mattered not in what phase that nature might display itself, it was nature still — fallen, ruined, irremediable nature. *"That which is born of the flesh is* (not merely fleshly, but) *flesh, and that which is born of the Spirit is* (not merely spiritual, but) *Spirit"* (Jn. 3:6).

If ever there was a fair opportunity for the distinctive qualities, capacities, resources, and tendencies of nature to manifest themselves, the lifetime of Cain and Abel furnished it. If there were anything in nature whereby it could recover its lost innocence and establish itself again within the bounds of Eden, this was the moment for its display. But there was nothing of the kind. They were both lost. They were *"flesh."* They were not innocent. Adam lost his innocence and never regained it. He can only be looked at as the fallen head of a fallen race, who, by his *"disobedience,"* were made *"sinners"* (Rom. 5:19). He became, so far as he was personally concerned, the corrupt source from whence have emanated the corrupt streams of ruined and guilty humanity — the dead trunk from which have shot forth the branches of a dead humanity, morally and spiritually dead.

Consequently, Cain and Abel, of necessity, must partake of the nature of him from whom they have sprung, *"As is the earthy, so are they also who are earthy"* (I Cor. 15:48) (Mackintosh).

FEDERAL HEADSHIP

The Doctrine of federal headship is very, very important. If we would but read Romans 5:12-21, we will find that Paul looks at the whole human race as comprehended under two heads. The Fifteenth Chapter of I Corinthians also furnishes instruction of a similar character. In the first man, we have sin, disobedience, and death: in the Second Man, we have Righteousness, obedience, and life. As we derive a nature, the sin nature, from the former, so do we also derive a nature, the Divine Nature, from the latter (Rom. 5:19; II Pet. 1:4).

As we derive the first nature, sin nature, by physical birth, so we derive the Divine nature from the Second Man by a new birth. That's why Jesus said: *"Except a man be born again, he cannot see the Kingdom of God"* (Jn. 3:3).

This as well is what He was talking about when He said: *"Verily, verily, I say unto you, except a man be born of water and of the Spirit, he cannot enter into the Kingdom of God"* (Jn. 3:5).

He wasn't speaking here of Water Baptism as many teach, but rather of the initial birth, which refers to being born into the world as a baby. That's what He meant by the statement, *"That which is born of the flesh is flesh"* (Jn. 3:6).

When the individual is Born-Again, which is *"of the Spirit,"* such has no connection with the flesh, with Christ using the term, *"And that which is born of the Spirit is spirit"* (Jn. 3:6).

In other words, what Adam produces is *"flesh,"* which cannot even *"see the Kingdom of God."* Only the Holy Spirit can bring about the Born-Again experience, which is carried out through Faith in Christ, and Christ Alone!

It is the *"spirit of man"* which is Born-Again, which at the same time saves the soul. The physical body, through the power of the Holy Spirit, and with one's Faith anchored in Christ and His Cross, is then to be brought in line with the Born-Again spirit. Actually, that's the only way, Faith in the Cross, which refers to what Jesus did there, that can effect this victory (Rom. 6:3-14; 8:1-2, 11).

A KEEPER OF SHEEP AND A TILLER OF THE GROUND

The phrase, *"And Abel was a keeper of sheep, but Cain was a tiller of the ground,"* proclaims two honorable professions. So the fault did not lay here in the fact that Cain was a farmer. But the following may be of consequence:

The Lord had explained to Adam the sacrificial process, and what it meant. Every evidence is that Adam had been offering up

Sacrifices ever since his expulsion from the Garden. In fact, every evidence is, even as we shall see in Verse 7, that a Tabernacle of sorts had been built near the entrance of the Garden of Eden. So it is definitely possible that Abel became a *"keeper of sheep,"* simply because of his Faith in the coming Promised Seed, of which the lambs offered were symbols. Concerning this, Matthew Henry said:

"The early use of Sacrifices confirms the belief that they were appointed by God, and revealed to Adam after his transgression. It is difficult else to account for the general use of Altars and Sacrifices to appease the anger of the offended Deity. But we may conclude that God commanded Adam, after the Fall, to shed the blood of innocent animals, and after their death to consume part or the whole of their bodies by fire. He thus referred to that punishment which sinners merit, even the death of the body, and the Wrath of God, of which fire is a well-known emblem, and also prefigured the sufferings of Christ. So we may observe that the religious worship of God is no novel invention. It was from the beginning."

(3) "AND IN THE PROCESS OF TIME IT CAME TO PASS, THAT CAIN BROUGHT OF THE FRUIT OF THE GROUND AN OFFERING UNTO THE LORD."

The composition is:

1. We have, in the persons of Cain and Abel, the first examples of a religious man of the world and a genuine man of Faith.

2. They were both sinners — both had a fallen nature — neither was innocent.

3. Cain brought of the fruit of the ground an offering unto the Lord.

THE PROCESS OF TIME

The phrase, *"And in process of time it came to pass,"* pertains to the fact that Cain had not been in the habit of bringing any type of offering to the Lord. This may have even been the first offering that he brought, and no doubt was! The phrase used here refers to a long indefinite period.

AN OFFERING

The phrase, *"That Cain brought of the fruit of the ground an offering unto the LORD,"* presents the labor of his own hands, and as well, the fruit of a cursed Earth. Moreover, there was no shedding of blood to remove the curse. He presented *"an unbloody sacrifice,"* simply because he had no faith in that which God had demanded, which was the sacrifice of an innocent animal. Had he possessed that Divine principle, it would have taught him, even at this early moment, that *"without shedding of blood there is no remission"* (Heb. 9:22).

This is a great cardinal truth. The penalty of sin is death. Cain was a sinner, and, as such, death stood between him and Jehovah; but, in his offering, there was no recognition whatsoever of this fact — there was no presentation of a sacrificed life, to meet the claims of Divine Holiness, or to answer to his own true condition as a sinner. He treated Jehovah as though He were altogether such a One as himself, Who could accept the sin-stained fruit of a cursed Earth, and above all, the labor of his own hands, which in effect, stated that he did not need a Redeemer.

THE CROSS

Consequently, upon looking at this, we see at once that had Jesus not died upon the Cross, and despite the glorious Ministry which He practiced in all capacities, all His services would have proved utterly unavailing as regards the establishment of our relationship with God. While it is true that, *"He went about doing good"* all His life; it was His death that rent the Veil (Mat. 27:51). And in fact, nothing but His death could have done so.

Had He continued to the present moment *"going about doing good,"* which the world would have ultimately recognized, the Veil would have remained intact, which barred the worshiper's approach into *"the holiest of all."* Hence we can see the false ground on which Cain stood as an offerer and a worshiper. An unpardoned sinner coming into the Presence of God to present *"an unbloody sacrifice,"* could only be regarded as guilty of the highest degree of presumption.

While it is true that he had toiled, perhaps long and hard, to produce his offering; still, but what of that? Can a sinner's toil remove the curse and stain of sin? Can it satisfy the claims of an infinitely Holy God? Can it furnish a proper ground of acceptance for a sinner? Can

it set aside the penalty which is due to sin? Can it rob death of its sting, or the grave of its victory? No, it can do none of these things! Impossible! *"Without shedding of blood is no remission."* Cain's *"unbloody sacrifice,"* like every other unbloody sacrifice, was not only worthless, but actually abominable, in the Divine estimation. It not only demonstrated his entire ignorance of his own condition, but also of the Divine character.

"God is not worshiped with men's hands, as though He needed anything"; and yet Cain thought He could be thus approached, and every religionist thinks the same. Unfortunately, Cain has had many millions of followers, from age to age. Cain-worship abounds all over the world. It is the worship of every unconverted soul, and is maintained by every false system of religion under the sun (Mackintosh).

THE LEVITICAL OFFERINGS

Let us not confuse this offering as given by Cain with the Levitical Offerings, which would in fact, include such an Offering, consisting of flour and oil, or flour prepared with frankincense (Lev. 2:1). In fact, in this Offering, all tree fruits and garden produce were excluded; it was limited to the productions of agriculture (grain) and vine (grape juice). But this Thanksgiving Offering, for that's what it was, and which would come about approximately 2,500 years later, was normally offered up after Burnt-Offerings and Peace-Offerings were offered (Num. 15:1-16). The Offerings which consisted of blood being shed guaranteed forgiveness of sin, that is if the object of faith was correct, which was what the Sacrifices represented, Who was the Coming Redeemer, the Lord Jesus Christ. That being done, a Thanksgiving Offering would be rendered, which celebrated the joy of forgiveness. For the Covenant meal usually marked a reconciliation after estrangement.

This was altogether different than that which Cain offered. As stated, by offering what he did, he in effect was saying that he didn't need a Saviour. Regrettably, that is the condition of much of the world. Many recognize that there is a God, but they refuse to recognize their sinful, wicked, lost condition, which can only be assuaged by Jesus Christ and what He did at the Cross.

(4) "AND ABEL, HE ALSO BROUGHT OF THE FIRSTLINGS OF HIS FLOCK AND OF THE FAT THEREOF. AND THE LORD HAD RESPECT UNTO ABEL AND TO HIS OFFERING:"

The overview is:

1. Abel brought an Offering, which was a *"firstling of his flock,"* which was what God had demanded.

2. *"The fat thereof,"* speaks to the fact that the lamb which he chose was the very best of the flock.

3. This was a blood sacrifice, which proclaimed the fact that Abel recognized his need of a Redeemer, and that One was coming Who would redeem lost humanity; consequently, *"The Lord had respect unto Abel and to his offering."*

ABEL

The phrase, *"And Abel, he also brought of the firstlings of his flock and of the fat thereof,"* signifies a firstborn animal, which was the choicest and best (Ex. 13:12).

There is no difference between the brothers, but an eternal difference between their Sacrifices. They are both corrupt branches of a decayed tree, both born outside Eden, both guilty, both sinners, with no moral difference, and both sentenced to death. The words *"by Faith"* (Heb. 11:4) teach that God had revealed a way of approach to Him (Rom. 10:17). Abel accepts this way; Cain rejects it. Abel's Altar speaks of Repentance, of Faith, and of the Precious Blood of Christ, the Lamb of God without blemish. Cain's Altar tells of pride, unbelief, and self-righteousness.

Abel's Altar is beautiful to God's Eye and repulsive to man's. Cain's Altar, beautiful to man's eye and repulsive to God's. These *"Altars"* exist today, around the one, that is, Christ and His Atoning Work, few are gathered; around the other, many. God accepts the slain lamb and rejects the offered fruit; and the offering being rejected so of necessity is the offerer (Williams).

THE DOCTRINE OF THE CROSS

The secret of the acceptance of Abel's Sacrifice was that he exercised Faith (Heb. 11:4); however, it was the correct object of his Faith that the Sacrifice represented, which was the

coming Redeemer, the Lord Jesus Christ, Who made both his Sacrifice and Faith valid (Rom. 6:3-14; I Cor. 1:17-18, 21, 23; 2:2, 5).

Every Divinely convicted sinner must feel that death and judgment are before him, as *"the due reward of his deeds"*; nor can he, by ought that he can accomplish, alter that destiny. He may toil and labor; he may, by the sweat of his brow, produce an offering; he may make vows and resolutions; he may alter his way of life; he may reform his outward character; he may be temperate, moral, upright, and, in the human acceptation of the word, religious; he may, though entirely destitute of faith, read, pray, and hear sermons. In short, he may do anything or everything which lies within the range of human competency; but, notwithstanding all, *"death"* and *"judgment"* are before him. He has not been able, nor will he be able, to disperse those two heavy clouds which have gathered upon the horizon. There they stand; and, so far from being able to remove them by all his doings, he can only live in the gloomy anticipation of the moment when they shall burst upon his guilty head.

It is impossible for a sinner, by his own works, to place himself in life and triumph at the other side of *"death"* and *"judgment"* — yea; his very works are only performed for the purpose of preparing him, if possible, for those dreaded realities.

Here, however, is exactly where the Cross comes in. In that Cross, the convicted sinner can behold a Divine provision for all his guilt and all his need. There, too, he can see death and judgment entirely removed from the scene, and life and glories set in their stead.

Jesus Christ, by His Death on the Cross, *"has abolished death, and brought life and incorruptibility to light through the Gospel"* (II Tim. 1:10). He has glorified God in the putting away of that which would have separated us forever from God's Holy and blissful Presence. *"He has put away sin,"* and hence it is gone, incidentally, never to be brought against us again (Heb. 9:26).

All this is, in type, set forth in Abel's *"more excellent sacrifice."* There was no attempt, on Abel's part, to set aside the Truth as to his own condition and proper place as a guilty sinner — no attempt to turn aside the edge of the flaming sword, and force his way back to the Tree of Life — no presumptuous offering of an *"unbloody sacrifice"* — no presentation of the fruit of one's hands — he took the real ground of a sinner, and, as such, set the death of a victim between him and his sins, and between his sins and the Holiness of a sin-hating God. This was most simple. Abel deserved death and judgment, but he found a Substitute.

(The author wishes to express gratitude for the scholarship of Charles Henry Mackintosh for the above material regarding *"the Doctrine of the Cross."*)

THE CORRECT OBJECT OF FAITH

Paul plainly stated: *"By Faith Abel offered unto God a more excellent sacrifice than Cain"* (Heb. 11:4).

Most all of Christendom admits that it is *"by Grace that we are saved through faith; and that not of ourselves: it is the Gift of God:*

"Not of works, lest any man should boast" (Eph. 2:8-9). But most don't understand exactly what the short phrase *"through faith,"* actually means.

If asked, most would answer that having faith refers to faith in God, or God's Word, etc. Some would explain it by trusting in Christ, etc.

All of these statements are correct, at least as far as they go; however, the problem is, the statements don't go far enough; consequently, the *"faith"* of most Christians presents a hodgepodge of beliefs. In other words, most Christians actually don't know what they really do believe.

Considering that we are speaking here of the Foundation of Christianity, it certainly should stand to reason that we not only have faith, but that we understand what the proper object of faith is to be. We learn that from Paul.

The Apostle said:

"Therefore being justified by faith, we have peace with God through our Lord Jesus Christ" (Rom. 5:1).

The key to this particular Passage is the phrase, *"through our Lord Jesus Christ."*

How is this Justification by Faith, and this peace with God brought about *"through our Lord Jesus Christ"?* That is the great question!

NOTES

It refers to what Jesus did at the Cross on our behalf. Paul went on to say:

"For when we were yet without strength, in due time Christ died for the ungodly" (Rom. 5:6).

So when we speak of faith, we must always understand that such Faith must be anchored in Christ. But more particularly, it must be Faith in Christ and what Christ did for us at the Cross. Once again, this is the *"Doctrine of the Cross."* This is the only Faith that God will honor. This is what John was talking about when he said:

"This is the victory that overcometh the world, even our faith" (I Jn. 5:4).

THE SANCTIFICATION OF THE SAINT

Most Christians understand what we have just said as it regards the initial Salvation experience. They are able to link the Cross to the Born-Again experience, but that's about as far as their faith goes in this respect.

The truth is, as the sinner is saved by expressing Faith in Christ, and what He did for us at the Cross, likewise, the Believer is sanctified in the same manner. But the tragedy is, most Christians have no idea as to the part the Cross plays in their ongoing Sanctification experience. As a result, they set about to sanctify themselves by their own machinations, etc. As we've already stated, however, God cannot give victory to the flesh. He can only give victory to His Son and our Saviour, the Lord Jesus Christ. So the victory which belongs to Christ becomes our victory, and is all explained in Romans 6:3-14.

When Christ died on the Cross, expressing Faith in Him and what He has done means that in the Mind of God, we are literally *"baptized into His Death."* We are then *"buried with Him,"* and then raised with Him in *"newness of life"* (Rom. 6:3-5).

As Believers, we are to then *"reckon ourselves to be dead indeed unto sin* (the sin nature), *but alive unto God through Jesus Christ our Lord"* (Rom. 6:11). This is where our Faith comes in as it regards our Sanctification.

In other words, we are to believe that what Jesus did for us at the Cross, when He died as our Substitute and our Representative Man, gives us total and complete victory in every capacity. Even though the sin nature within our hearts and lives has not died, we in effect, are dead to the sin nature, which makes it ineffective. This is all done through what Jesus did at the Cross, and our Faith in that Finished Work. Once again we come to the Passage *"through Jesus Christ our Lord."*

Understanding that, and continuing to express Faith, even on a daily basis as it regards what Christ did at the Cross (Lk. 9:23), we then come to the place that *"sin does not have dominion over us: for we are not under the Law, but under Grace"* (Rom. 6:14).

ROMANS, CHAPTER 7

But the tragedy is, most Christians are still living in Romans, Chapter 7.

This was Paul's experience after he was saved and Baptized with the Holy Spirit, but as of yet not having come to the Truth of the Cross. In fact, that great Revelation was given to him, which referred to the meaning of the Cross, which is actually the meaning of the New Covenant. But let the Reader understand the following:

If the Believer doesn't understand the Message of the Cross, as it concerns both the Salvation of the sinner, and the Sanctification of the Saint, for sure, such a Believer will experience Romans, Chapter 7 all over again. It will be, *"O wretched man that I am! Who shall deliver me from the body of this death?"* (Rom. 7:24).

Due to the great significance of these statements, please allow me to repeat myself:

It doesn't matter who you are. It doesn't matter if you're the greatest Preacher in the world, pastoring the largest Church, or an Evangelist drawing the biggest crowds. If you do not understand the Word of the Cross (I Cor. 1:18), you will live a defeated life. There is only one source of victory, not nine, not five, not two, only one. And that is the Lord Jesus Christ and what He did for us at the Cross. The Holy Spirit will not work outside of the parameters of the Finished Work of Christ. That's the reason Paul also said:

"For the Law of the Spirit of Life in Christ Jesus, has made me free from the law of sin and death" (Rom. 8:2).

This *"Law"* which Paul mentions here is not the Law of Moses, but rather the greatest Law that any Believer could ever know.

It is the *"law"* by which the Holy Spirit works, and by which He works exclusively. This *"Law"* is *"in Christ Jesus,"* which refers to what Christ did at the Cross. Never forget that! That's the key to all victory. It's what He did at the Cross on our behalf.

This is the only *"Law"* which will overcome the *"law of sin and death."* Anything else will fall by the wayside. But yet, and sadly so, not one Christian out of 100, and more than likely, not one out of 1,000, knows or understands this *"Law"* of which Paul speaks here.

THE JESUS DIED SPIRITUALLY DOCTRINE

There is a doctrine presently which repudiates the Cross, actually referring to it as *"past miseries,"* and *"the greatest defeat in human history."* That is the doctrine of the *"Word of Faith"* people, which is referred to as the *"Jesus died spiritually doctrine."*

It is sad that millions of Christians follow these particular Teachers, as false as they might be, without really understanding what they are actually teaching. Let the Reader know and understand that any attack on the Cross is an attack on the very heart of the Gospel. That's the reason that Paul said:

"But though we, or an Angel from Heaven, preach any other gospel unto you than that which we have preached unto you, let him be accursed" (Gal. 1:8).

Pure and simple, the Word of Faith people preach *"another gospel"* (II Cor. 11:4). It must be shunned at all costs, and for the simple reason that such teaching can cause a person to lose his soul, or at least be seriously weakened in his Christian experience. In fact, the shores are littered with the wrecks of Christians who have followed this doctrine, and brought upon themselves sure and swift destruction. Paul also said:

"For many walk, of whom I have told you often, and now tell you even weeping, that they are the enemies of the Cross of Christ:

"Whose end is destruction, whose god is their belly, and whose glory is in their shame, who mind earthly things" (Phil. 3:18-19).

What is the Jesus died spiritually doctrine?

In brief, these people teach that Jesus became a sinner on the Cross, actually taking upon Himself the nature of Satan, and died and went to Hell. They teach that He burned in Hell for three days and nights, with Hell celebrating His defeat. At the end of the three days and nights of burning in Hell, they teach, God said, *"It is enough,"* with Jesus then throwing of the shackles which bound Him, and was there *"born again,"* just like any sinner is Born-Again. He was then raised, they go on to say, from the dead.

Consequently, they teach that the Cross was just an incident in the Life and Ministry of Christ, actually referring to it as we have stated, as *"the greatest defeat in human history,"* etc.

Let the Reader understand that there is not a shred of any of this found anywhere in the Bible. They have made it up completely out of whole cloth, so to speak!

The truth is, no one can be saved by trusting in such a gospel, which in reality is no gospel at all (Gal. 1:6-7). No one can be Baptized with the Holy Spirit, healed, or experience deliverance of any nature, as it regards this perfidious gospel. As stated, these Preachers and Teachers are *"enemies of the Cross."*

So why are their Ministries so popular?

Their major thrust is *"money!"* In other words, they teach that every Christian by using their *"secrets,"* can be rich. To be sure, there is enough covetousness in all of us, enough greed, that makes this doctrine palatable.

The truth is, the only ones getting rich are the Preachers.

While the Lord definitely does bless His people, and while that blessing definitely includes finances, the major thrust of the Gospel has never been money. It is deliverance from sin, which is brought about solely through Jesus Christ and what He did at the Cross.

To place the emphasis on money, or anything of such nature, fulfills Paul's statement that *"their god is their belly, and whose glory is in their shame, who mind earthly things"* (Phil. 3:19).

He also said, *"Whose end is destruction,"*

THE LORD HAD RESPECT

The phrase, *"And the LORD had respect unto Abel and to his offering,"* presents that which God will accept, and only that which God will accept.

We must understand that each individual identifies himself with the offering which he presents. We cannot possibly bestow too much attention upon this. The question, in each case, as we have already stated, was not as to the person of the offerer, but entirely as to the character of his offering. Hence, of Abel we read that *"God testified of his gifts."* He did not bear witness to Abel, but to Abel's sacrifice; and this fixes, distinctly, the proper ground of a Believer's peace and acceptance before God.

There is a constant tendency for the Believer to ground his peace and acceptance upon something in or about ourselves. Hence we are constantly looking *"in"* when the Holy Spirit would ever have us looking *"out."* The question for every Believer is not, *"What am I?"* but, *"What is Christ?"* And as long as such a Believer expresses such Faith in Christ, and does so exclusively, and continues to do so, he cannot be lost. But if he moves his faith from Christ to other things, even as many have done, and even as the entirety of the Book of Hebrews addresses, such a person will definitely be lost. Everything hinges on Faith, and more particularly, Faith in Christ and Him Crucified. Denying that, one denies their Salvation, which puts one into a state of unbelief, which means that *"they crucify to themselves the Son of God afresh, putting Him to an open shame,"* which means that such a one completely misunderstands the Crucifixion, claiming that Jesus deserved to die (Heb. 6:6). Such a person *"counts the Blood of the Covenant, wherewith he was sanctified, an unholy thing, and does despite unto the Spirit of Grace"* (Heb. 10:29).

(5) "BUT UNTO CAIN AND TO CAIN AND TO HIS OFFERING HE HAD NOT RESPECT. AND CAIN WAS VERY WROTH, AND HIS COUNTENANCE FELL."

The exegesis is:

1. Regarding Cain and his *"fruit of the ground"* the Lord had no respect.

2. That which filled Abel with peace, filled Cain with wrath.

3. The carnal mind displays its enmity against all this Truth which so gladdens and satisfies the heart of a Believer.

UNACCEPTABLE

The phrase, *"But unto Cain and to his offering He had not respect,"* refers to the fact that it was unacceptable. And let it be known that all such offerings garner no respect from God. They are all unacceptable, which are not of Christ and Him Crucified.

Paul said, *"We preach Christ Crucified"* (I Cor. 1:23). He also stated:

"For I determined not to know anything among you, save Jesus Christ, and Him Crucified" (I Cor. 2:2).

That and that alone is the Message!

Now we should ask ourselves the question, what is our Pastor preaching? What is the Evangelist preaching?

All too often, people follow Preachers, not because of what they are preaching, but rather for other things. The other things can destroy one's soul! The criteria must ever be what one is preaching, and that alone.

Millions of Christians erroneously have the idea that the Preacher alone is responsible. In other words, if they are faithful to Church, at least to a certain extent, and they claim Christ, then all is well.

To be sure, the Preacher definitely is responsible; however, that in no way alleviates the responsibility of each Believer. As a Believer, you are responsible for what you believe as it regards the Gospel. One day when you stand before the Lord, He will not judge you according to what your Preacher said, but rather what you have personally believed. If you have believed wrong, the blame will be on yourself and not on others. Don't misunderstand; God will definitely hold the Preacher responsible. Of that one can be certain; however, that has no bearing on you.

So if we throw out all that is not of the Cross, what do we have left?

I'm afraid that in most Churches, there wouldn't be anything left. The Cross is not preached in most Churches, which means that whatever is preached is actually not the Gospel. It may contain some Gospel, but overall it is not the Gospel. Let us say it again:

As the Lord had no respect unto Cain and his offering, He has no respect for anything that's not the Cross. This Fourth Chapter of Genesis sets the standard. It's the Cross, or it's nothing!

The offering of Cain being rejected means that Cain is as well rejected! This also means that if our offering is rejected, and every

single offering that's not the Cross is definitely rejected, then we are rejected as well!

THE WRATH OF THE FLESH

The phrase, *"And Cain was very wroth, and his countenance fell,"* presents the fact that the carnal mind displays its enmity against all Truth, which Truth gladdens and satisfies the heart of a true Believer. That which filled Abel with peace filled Cain with wrath.

Cain, in unbelief, despised the only way in which a sinner can come to God. He refused to offer a sacrifice regarding the shedding of its blood, without which there can be no remission; and then, because he was not received, *"in his sins,"* and because Abel was accepted, *"in his gift,"* he was angry, and his countenance fell.

In his offering and in his attitude, there was no sorrow for sin, no spirit of inquiry, no self-examination, no prayer to God for light or pardon.

But yet the Lord, as we shall see, does not abandon this transgressor, but patiently instructs him as to how he too might obtain the same blessing of acceptance which his younger brother enjoyed.

OPPOSITION

The anger expressed here was far more directed at his brother than it was toward God, although there definitely was anger toward God. But not being able to do anything against God, he would take all of this out on his brother. Thus, the stage is set for opposition against the Cross, because in reality, this was the bone of contention. It has not changed from then until now.

There is definitely an *"offence"* attached to the Cross. This offence attracts persecution. Paul said so (Gal. 5:11).

And I might quickly add, most persecution against the Cross, and in reality those who espouse the Cross, will come mostly from the Church. It was Abel's brother who opposed him, and it is mostly our *"brother"* who opposes us.

The opposers of the Cross are not content to merely oppose the Doctrine. They feel at the same time that they must stop the mouth of the messenger, and they will go to any length to do such.

When the Scripture says that Cain's *"countenance fell,"* such is a Hebrew way of saying that he could not rest, but had to show his wrath in his looks. His angry and revengeful heart showed itself in all his actions.

(6) "AND THE LORD SAID UNTO CAIN, WHY ARE YOU ANGRY? AND WHY IS YOUR COUNTENANCE FALLEN?"

The synopsis is:

1. The Lord now addresses Cain, attempting to bring him to the right spirit, but regrettably, to no avail.

2. He asked him the question, *"Why are you angry?"*

3. His anger was so intense that it showed on his countenance.

THE LORD

The question, *"And the LORD said unto Cain, Why are you angry?"*, presents the fact that God loves Cain, and wishes to bless him also.

He either spoke to Cain with His Own Voice from between the Cherubim where the flaming sword, the visible symbol of the Divine Presence, had been established (Ex. 20:24), or else He spoke through Adam, as maybe the first parent attempted to bring his wayward son to the right way.

Anger, in one form or the other, accompanies self-righteousness, for that is what plagued Cain. Righteousness can only come by the Cross, while self-righteousness comes by dependence on works. While anger is always present in such a case, it may take a totally different form than that which plagued Cain. In fact, self-righteousness can put on a very pious attitude, while all the time burning with anger toward those who depend on the Cross.

As well, the evil has spread itself from the time of Cain to the present. While the Cross, in essence, was the object at that particular time, it is very seldom the object at present, even though that's where the real offence actually is. Religious men conjure up all types of excuses, but the real reason is the Cross. They have rejected God's Way, but at the same time, they seem very religious.

As an example, almost all of the modern Church has embraced humanistic psychology as the answer to the perversions of man.

They have done this despite the fact that humanistic psychology was birthed in atheistic minds. They cover this by claiming that *"all truth is God's Truth!"*

ALL TRUTH IS GOD'S TRUTH?

The idea of this statement is that irrespective as to where the truth originates, if it is truth, then it must originally come from God.

In the first place, Truth is not a philosophy, but rather a Person. And that Person is the Lord Jesus Christ. He said of Himself: *"I am the Way, the Truth, and the Life"* (Jn. 14:6). He also said: *"Thy Word is Truth"* (Jn. 17:17). The Scripture also says: *"The Spirit is Truth"* (I Jn. 5:6).

So if that which is labeled as *"Truth,"* doesn't match up with Christ, the Word, and the Holy Spirit, then it's not Truth. And to be sure, humanistic psychology is definitely not truth in any capacity, but rather a *"lie."*

In the acceptance of this nefarious system, the Cross is seldom mentioned, if at all; however, the facts are, if one accepts humanistic psychology as the answer to the aberrations and perversions of man, he is at the same time denying the Cross. The Word of God boldly proclaims that the Cross is the answer to sin, and in fact, the only answer. And to be sure, this covers every aspect of man and his being. The Holy Spirit through Peter said:

"According as His Divine power has given unto us all things that pertain unto life and Godliness, through the knowledge of Him Who has called us to glory and virtue" (II Pet. 1:3).

Now we must understand that the *"all things"* mentioned here refers to the Word of God exclusively. In other words, if it's not in the Word, then it's a *"lie."*

Jesus said: *"You shall know the Truth, and the Truth shall make you free"* (Jn. 8:32).

Concerning all that claims to be Truth, but which is outside the Word of God, Jesus addressed that as well by saying: *"You are of your father the Devil, and the lusts of your father you will do. He was a murderer from the beginning, and abode not in the Truth, because there is no Truth in him. When he speaks a lie, he speaks of his own: for he is a liar, and the father of it"* (Jn. 8:44).

If it's not in the Word of God, and humanistic psychology definitely isn't in the Word of God, then pure and simple it is a *"lie."*

While it is definitely true that all Truth is God's Truth, the simple fact is, humanistic psychology is not Truth, plus anything else spawned by unregenerate hearts.

FALLEN COUNTENANCE

The question, *"And why is your countenance fallen?"*, proclaims Cain's response to the rejection. He was angry that God had not accepted his sacrifice, which obviously the Lord had made known to all concerned. As a result, he entertained no humility whatsoever, but rather anger. To which we've already addressed, his reaction would set the stage for all who would follow thereafter. We refer again to the *"offence of the Cross"* (Gal. 5:11).

(7) "IF YOU DO WELL, SHALL YOU NOT BE ACCEPTED? AND IF YOU DO NOT WELL, SIN LIES AT THE DOOR. AND UNTO YOU SHALL BE HIS DESIRE, AND YOU SHALL RULE OVER HIM."

The diagram is:

1. The Lord tells him, *"If you do well,* (which refers to offering up the correct sacrifice), *you shall be accepted."*

2. The word *"sin"* here should have been translated *"Sin-Offering,"* because that's what it is. In other words, he could go get a lamb and offer it up.

3. The *"door"* mentioned here probably refers to some type of Tabernacle, which had been built by Adam and Eve at this particular place.

4. If Cain will do the right thing, which is to offer up the correct Sacrifice, he will function in the realm of the firstborn, meaning that the Messiah would come through his lineage.

ACCEPTED

The question, *"If you do well, shall you not be accepted?"*, proclaims the fact that God will accept any and all who come to Him by the way of Faith, and we speak of Faith in the Crucified Lord. Otherwise, and irrespective as to what the other sacrifice might be, the person is unaccepted. As stated, the offering being rejected, the offerer is rejected as well! The offering being accepted, the offerer is accepted!

NOTES

That's the reason that the Holy Spirit told Paul to *"preach Christ Crucified"* (I Cor. 1:23). The Cross and the Cross Alone is the answer to man's dilemma. So if we preach anything else, if we believe anything else, we are providing no solution. The Lord will accept nothing else. It is only of Christ that He said: *"This is My Beloved Son, in Whom I am well pleased"* (Mat. 3:17). Consequently, He is well-pleased with us, only as we are *"in Christ Jesus,"* and Christ Jesus Alone!

THE SIN-OFFERING

The phrase, *"And if you do not well, sin lies at the door,"* should have been translated *"Sin-Offering."* The Hebrew word is *"chattath,"* which can refer either to *"sin"* or *"Sin-Offering,"* depending on the context. Here it refers to the *"Sin-Offering."*

The *"door"* refers to the door of the Tabernacle that evidently had been constructed close to the entrance to the Garden of Eden. The Lord is telling Cain that a Sin-Offering, i.e., *"a lamb,"* is nearby the door of the Tabernacle. *"Go get the lamb and offer it up,"* is in essence what is being said.

It was so simple for him to do what the Lord had commanded, but yet he refused.

Why?

The only answer that one could possibly give is the problem of self-will. This problem didn't die with Cain. It plagues the entirety of the human race, and is no doubt the Christian's greatest problem.

That's what Jesus was speaking of when He said concerning Believers: *"If any man will come after Me, let him deny himself* (deny self-will), *and take up his Cross daily, and follow Me.*

"For whosoever will save his life shall lose it (refuse to put his life into Christ)*: but whosoever will lose his life for My sake* (place his life in Christ), *the same shall save it"* (Lk. 9:23-24).

Under the New Covenant, the situation is even easier, far easier than under the Old. While then, it was necessary to offer up a lamb as a sacrifice, today all that is required is for us to evidence Faith in the Lamb of God Who has already been offered up, with His Sacrifice of Himself being sufficient for all time.

In other words, it will never have to be repeated. So, simple Faith in Christ and what Christ did at the Cross is all that is required, and yet, most of the world rejects even that!

THE BIRTHRIGHT

The phrase, *"And unto you shall be his desire, and you shall rule over him,"* refers to the real cause of Cain's anger.

I don't think he cared that much that God didn't accept his sacrifice. But when he learned that he was now forfeiting his firstborn rights, and that Abel would now be the chosen one, and we speak of the one through whom the *"Promised Seed"* would come, this angered him greatly regarding his younger brother.

The Lord is telling him that despite the fact of him offering up the wrong sacrifice, that which was unacceptable, if he would turn and do the right thing, which means to repent, he could retain the privileges of his birthright. But this he wouldn't do, and now concocts a plan to eliminate Abel, which he thinks will guarantee him the birthright privileges, and do so on his own terms.

In his fallen state, how little he understood God. And I'm afraid the same is true for most of the world presently. Most concoct and scheme as to how they can obtain what they desire, and do so in their own way. It never works, because it cannot work.

With God, the way up is always down. We speak of humility.

(8) "AND CAIN TALKED WITH ABEL HIS BROTHER: AND IT CAME TO PASS, WHEN THEY WERE IN THE FIELD, THAT CAIN ROSE UP AGAINST ABEL HIS BROTHER, AND SLEW HIM."

The structure is:

1. Cain talking with Abel evidently pertained to the information of Verse 7.

2. In the course of the conversation, it seems that the anger of Cain welled up against his brother.

3. Cain then killed Abel, constituting the first murder.

A CONVERSATION THAT LED TO MURDER

The phrase, *"And Cain talked with Abel his brother,"* evidently concerns what the Lord had said to Cain, as recorded in Verse 7.

Refusal to obey, which characterized Cain, only drives the individual further into disobedience. Sin has no cut off point. Its power is to drive the person to destruction.

The only thing that can stop sin is Repentance before God, which at the same time proclaims Faith in the Cross. Concerning this, Paul said:

"Repentance toward God, and faith toward our Lord Jesus Christ" (Acts 20:21).

Many times, Repentance must include the repenting over good things as well as the bad. In Cain's eyes, his sacrifice was *"good."* In God's Eyes it wasn't good, and because it completely ignored the issue at hand, which was sin. While the sacrifice may have been *"good"* in Cain's eyes, his trust and dependence in this sacrifice was not good, and of that he must repent.

But repenting alone would not accomplish the task. He must also evidence Faith in the Lord Jesus Christ, which was then symbolized by the offering of the Lamb. To be sure, it has not changed from then until now.

RELIGIOUS MURDER

The phrase, *"And it came to pass, when they were in the field, that Cain rose up against Abel his brother, and killed him,"* presents the first murder, and a religious murder at that. Thus has it ever been — the Cain's have persecuted and murdered the Abel's. At all times, man and his religion are the same, faith and its confidence are the same; and wherever they have met there has been conflict.

It is well for us to see that Cain's act of murder was the true consequence — the proper fruit — of his false worship. His foundation was bad, and the superstructure erected thereon was also bad. And so it has been with the entirety of the world from then until now. God has one way and that is the Cross. A few accept that way and receive eternal life. Most reject that way, seeking to devise their own ways, which in one way or the other always leads to murder.

(9) "AND THE LORD SAID UNTO CAIN, WHERE IS ABEL YOUR BROTHER? AND HE SAID, I KNOW NOT: AM I MY BROTHER'S KEEPER?"

The composition is:

1. The Lord speaks to Cain about Abel.

2. He asked the question, *"Where is Abel your brother?"*

3. Cain lied and said, *"I know not."*

4. He tries to pass it off by claiming that he's not responsible for his brother's whereabouts.

THE QUESTION

The question, *"And the LORD said unto Cain, Where is Abel your brother?"*, presents the beginning of the human race which is murder, and God calling it to account. Adam sins against God and Cain sins against man. In their united conduct we have sin in all its forms, and that on the first page of human history.

Cain's religion was too refined to kill a lamb, but not too cultured to murder his brother. God's Way of Salvation fills the heart with love; man's way of Salvation enflames it with hatred. *"Religion"* has ever been the greatest cause of bloodshed.

The sin of murder is horrid to say the least; however, to murder one's own brother is a sin against God, against another human being, and against one's self. To kill one's brother is in some form the sin of suicide.

MY BROTHER'S KEEPER

The question, *"And he said, I know not: Am I my brother's keeper?"*, now proclaims himself a liar.

Willet says concerning this: *"He showed himself a 'liar' in saying, 'I know not'; 'wicked and profane' in thinking he could hide his sin from God; 'unjust' in denying himself to be his brother's keeper; 'obstinate and desperate' in not confessing his sin."*

Cain was not sorry, nor did he repent of his deed, for he denied it. Of such Satanic hatred, which knows no bounds, Christ speaks in John 16:2: *"Whosoever kills you will think that he does God service."* Cain is the father of all murderers who slay God's Saints. As long as there is a spark of life in any Saint, their enemies hate them, as this is proved in the case of Christ.

Who can picture the great grief which Cain inflicted upon his parents by the murder of his brother? Adam and Eve at that time had only two sons; though it is possible they may have also had several daughters.

NOTES

All of this is the result of their own sin in the Garden of Eden when, desiring to be like God, but in an unlawful way, they became like the Devil. They had hoped that their first son would be the one to bruise the head of the serpent, but now he himself has become like Satan by his murder. All this misery stems from their sin (Luther).

The Truth is, we are our brother's keeper, that which Cain denied!

Jesus addressed this when He said: *"You shall love the Lord your God with all your heart, and with all your soul, and with all your mind.*

"This is the first and great Commandment.

"And the second is like unto it, you shall love your neighbor as yourself.

"On these two Commandments hang all the Law and the Prophets" (Mat. 22:37-40).

(10) "AND HE SAID, WHAT HAVE YOU DONE? THE VOICE OF YOUR BROTHER'S BLOOD CRIES UNTO ME FROM THE GROUND."

The composition is:

1. *"What have you done?"*, concerns man's sins, the fruit of his sinful nature.

2. Jehovah tells Cain that the blood he has shed calls aloud for vengeance.

3. Thus, with the first shedding of human blood that ominous thought sprang up, Divinely bestowed, that the Earth will grant no peace to the one who has wantonly stained her fair face with the life-stream of man.

4. *"The Blood of Jesus speaks better things than that of Abel"* (Heb. 12:24). The voice of one cried for justice and retribution: the other for reconciliation and peace.

FRUIT OF THE SIN NATURE

The question, *"And He said, What have you done?"*, proclaims the results of the Fall. The sin nature now dominates the human race. And that nature simply refers to the fact of the individual leaning towards sin in every respect. While it is certainly true that all unredeemed do not commit all types of sins; nevertheless, in one way or the other, the bent is always in that direction, and without fail. In fact, it cannot be otherwise, hence it being called the *"sin nature."*

Paul deals with this constantly in his Epistles. Actually, in Romans, Chapter 6 alone, *"sin"* is mentioned some 17 times. Fourteen of those times the word is prefaced by what is known in the Greek language as the definite article. This means that the original Text actually said *"the sin."* The Apostle was referring to the sin nature. This means that he wasn't referring to particular acts of sin, but the nature of sin which produces these acts, whatever they might be.

In fact, the entirety of the Sixth Chapter of Romans was written to explain to the Believer our place and position in Christ, as a result of the Cross. In fact, it tells us that it is impossible for the Christian to walk in victory over sin, and by that we speak of the sin nature, without his Faith being anchored completely and totally in the Cross of Christ, understanding that it was there that Jesus paid the price and accomplished the Finished Work. If the Believer attempts to overcome the sin nature by any means other than Faith in the Cross, he will find himself being dominated by the sin nature, just as surely as he was before conversion.

THE SIN NATURE

Unfortunately, some Preachers argue that the Believer, who is a new creation in Christ Jesus, no longer has a sin nature. While it is certainly true that all Believers definitely are new creations in Christ (II Cor. 5:17), that in no way means that the sin nature has disappeared. In fact, the Believer, the Scripture tells us, is to be dead to the sin nature (Rom. 6:11); however, it does not say the sin nature is dead. And the way that we stay dead to the sin nature, and in fact the only way, is, as stated, by understanding that everything comes to us through the Cross of Christ, and that our Faith must ever be in that Finished Work.

If it is true that the Believer no longer has a sin nature, why is it that Paul deals with it again and again in his Epistles? There would be no point in dealing with something that doesn't exist!

No, the Scripture plainly teaches that the sin nature is still present within the heart and life of the Believer; however, if we confront it as we should, which refers to Faith in the Crucified Christ, it will cause us no problem. Otherwise, it will cause much problem.

While the sin nature does reside within us, it is not to *"reign"* (Rom. 6:12). In the unbeliever, it resides and reigns. And unless the Believer functions according to God's prescribed order, which is Faith in the Cross, it will *"reign"* in our lives as well. To be sure, that produces a miserable Christian.

THE HOLY SPIRIT

The Believer should understand that there are three key words in his Christian experience, which are more important than anything else. Those words are: A. The Cross; B. Our Faith; and, C. The Holy Spirit.

Some have referred to Romans, Chapter 6 as the mechanics of the Holy Spirit, which tells us *"how"* the Holy Spirit works as it regards Salvation and victory within our lives, while Romans, Chapter 8 is referred to as the dynamics of the Holy Spirit, which tells us *"what"* the Holy Spirit can do, once we understand the *"how."*

The Holy Spirit, without Whom we can do nothing, works exclusively within the parameters of the Finished Work of Christ.

Even though I've already related the following in this Volume, due to the vast significance of what we are discussing here, please allow me the liberty to allude to this previous experience again.

REVELATION

Someone has well said that all Revelation is preceded by desperation. Perhaps that is true. It was with Paul, as evidenced in Romans 7:24, and it was true in my life as well.

The year was 1988. It was the month of March. My world had come to pieces. From being the Evangelist who was drawing the largest crowds in the world, and seeing literally hundreds of thousands brought to Christ, and I exaggerate not, I was reduced to wreckage and shame. The reason was these very things of which we are addressing here.

I understood the Cross of Christ as it relates to the initial Salvation experience and preached it strongly. As stated, God honored the Message, by giving me tremendous numbers of souls. However, I understood not at all the role of the Cross as it regards our Sanctification experience.

The truth is, I had been greatly influenced by the Word of Faith Message, and it almost destroyed me. Not knowing the Message of the Cross as it referred to Sanctification, I, as millions of Christians, tried to sanctify myself. I tried to accomplish this task through Bible reading, prayer, fasting, etc. While the Lord greatly blessed me in these endeavors, in which all true Christians will definitely engage themselves, the Truth is, one cannot find victory over the world, the flesh, and the Devil by this means.

THE CROSS AND OUR VICTORY

I'm going to make a statement that may at first seem to be radical, but in reality it is the Foundation of the entirety of the Word of God.

Unless the Believer understands the Sacrifice of Christ and what it means personally to him, even as Paul explained it in Romans, Chapters 6, 7, and 8, such a Believer cannot walk in victory. Now I want the Reader to read that statement again very carefully.

I didn't say that such a person cannot be saved, for they can. I did say that such an individual cannot walk in victory if they do not understand the rudiments of the Cross. In some way, the sin nature is going to dominate such a person.

To which we've already alluded, most Christians understand the Cross as it regards the initial Salvation process, but they have no idea whatsoever about the Cross as it regards their Sanctification experience. As a result, they try to live for God outside of God's prescribed order of victory. In other words, due to the fact that they are trying to live this life by their own means and not by Faith in the Cross, the Holy Spirit simply will not aid and abet such a process. And without the help of the Holy Spirit, there is no way that we can live this life as it ought to be lived (Rom. 8:1-2, 11, 13).

During the critical time of which I have spoken to you in 1988, the Lord spoke to my heart and said, *"I'm going to show you some things about the Holy Spirit which you do not now know."* Of course, that wouldn't be very difficult, considering that there were many things about the Holy Spirit I didn't know. But that of which the Lord was speaking pertains

to this which we are addressing now, and I refer to our victorious walk or the lack thereof.

What He showed me did not come quickly or easily. Actually, it didn't come until 1996. At that time, and by Revelation, the Lord showed me that the answer to my dilemma, and in fact, the dilemma of the entirety of the world and for all time, was and is the Cross of Christ. He then showed me that the Holy Spirit works exclusively through the Cross, which is the Finished Work of Christ. Let me explain that:

WALKING AFTER THE SPIRIT

The legal means that gives the Spirit the right to work within our lives, which refers to His leading, guidance, empowerment, Anointing, in fact all that He does, is the Finished Work of Christ. In other words, He works entirely and exclusively within those parameters. Listen to Paul:

"There is therefore now no condemnation to them which are in Christ Jesus, who walk not after the flesh, but after the Spirit" (Rom. 8:1).

How does one *"walk after the Spirit"*?

What do you think that answer would be if most Christians had to answer that question? How would it be defined by most Christians?

The truth is, most Christians don't have the foggiest idea as to what it means to *"walk after the Spirit."* That's tragic considering how important all of this is. In fact, if we don't know how to walk after the Spirit, we simply do not know how to live a victorious, Christian life.

While much explanation could be given, I instead will be brief:

Walking after the Spirit simply refers to the Believer placing his Faith exclusively in Christ, because the Holy Spirit always glorifies Christ (Jn. 16:14), and what Christ did at the Cross on our behalf. As we've said repeatedly, Christ and the Cross must never be separated. It is always *"we preach Christ Crucified"* (I Cor. 1:23).

The Cross being the means by which the Holy Spirit works demands that we always and without exception make the Cross of Christ the object of our Faith. Now let's give you Scripture for that:

Paul also said: *"For the Law* (a Law devised by the Godhead) *of the Spirit* (Holy Spirit) *of life* (all life flows from Christ through the Spirit) *in Christ Jesus* (referring to what Jesus did at the Cross) *has made me free from the law of sin and death"* (Rom. 8:2).

This one Verse shows you how the Holy Spirit works. It tells us that this Law, which is devised by the Godhead, will always be adhered to by the Spirit, and that this Law is *"in Christ Jesus,"* which always refers to what Christ did at the Cross.

That's what the Lord showed me about the Holy Spirit. It has revolutionized my life, even as it has revolutionized the lives of untold millions of others, and it will do the same for you.

In those days of years past, I understood what the Holy Spirit did in many and varied things and the way in which He did them; however, I had no knowledge at that time as to how the Spirit worked in our hearts and lives as it regards the Sanctification process, in other words, how to live a victorious life. Not knowing this, Satan took full advantage of my ignorance, and caused me untold heartache and suffering. But prayerfully and hopefully, all of that suffering has not been in vain.

What the Lord has given me as it regards the Cross is actually not something new. It's not new at all. It's the same Message preached by the Apostle Paul, actually that which the Lord gave to him in answer to this very dilemma, which is really the meaning of the New Covenant.

How so much we thank the Lord for His Mercy and Grace, and how we thank Him for what He is doing at this time to help us get this Message of the Cross to others. This is not just one of several answers, but in fact, it is the only answer. That's why Paul said:

"But God forbid that I should glory (boast), *save in the Cross of our Lord Jesus Christ, by Whom the world is crucified unto me, and I unto the world"* (Gal. 6:14).

SPEAKING BLOOD

The phrase, *"The voice of your brother's blood cries unto Me from the ground,"* tells us several things:

Cain had probably buried his brother in the field, after he had murdered him. In regard

to this, Knobel said: *"The blood crying is a symbol of the soul crying for its right to live. In this instance, the cry was a demand for the punishment of the murderer; and that cry has reverberated through all lands and down through all ages, proclaiming vengeance against the shedder of innocent blood. Hence the prayer that the Earth may not drink in the blood shed upon it, in order that it may not thereby become invisible and inaudible."*

Consequently, the sorrow of Adam and Eve would be twofold: one son they lost by murder and the other, as we shall see, by excommunication from the communion of their home.

Concerning the murder of Abel, Luther said: *"It is very comforting to us that God confronted Cain concerning his murdered brother. There is clearly indicated in this the Resurrection of the dead, for by inquiring about the dead Abel, God proved that He was the God of Abel even after his death."*

What Adam and Eve actually thought of Abel beyond him being their son, we do not know. But God regarded Abel as righteous, as Christ, in Matthew 23:35, praises him very highly, calling him the *"righteous Abel."* This means that the dead Abel was declared holy by God, while the living Cain was excommunicated and punished with everlasting damnation. Abel's death was cruel, yet his death was blessed, for he was received into a better life. This glory has been procured for mankind by the Seed of the woman, Who bruised the head of the serpent. The blood of the murdered Abel was precious to God on account of his Faith in the Promised Saviour. This means that the Cross was the deciding factor in all of this.

(11) "AND NOW ARE YOU CURSED FROM THE EARTH, WHICH HAS OPENED HER MOUTH TO RECEIVE YOUR BROTHER'S BLOOD FROM YOUR HAND;"

The structure is:

1. Because of his terrible sin of committing murder, which was a result of his repudiation of the Cross, Cain is now cursed by God.

2. This is the first curse pronounced against a human being. Adam and Eve personally were not cursed, though the serpent and the Devil were.

3. The Earth, which had received the blood of Cain's murdered brother, would now

rebel against Cain, which incidentally continues unto this hour.

THE CURSE

The phrase, *"And now are you cursed from the Earth,"* presents, as stated, the first curse that is leveled by God against a human being.

When God pronounces a curse, it is first of all a denunciation of sin (Num. 5:21, 23; Deut. 29:19-20). As well, it is His judgment on sin (Num. 5:22, 24, 27; Isa. 24:6).

In many ways, the Word of God can go either way. It can be the Word of God's Grace or the Word of God's wrath. In effect, they are the same Word, with the result dependent on obedience or disobedience regarding the individual. The Word, which promises life to the obedient, also promises death and judgment to the disobedient and is, therefore, a curse.

For instance, the Law is a curse to those who fail to obey it (Gal. 3:10), and all have failed, but Christ redeemed us by being made a curse for us (Gal. 3:13), and the very means of His death itself proves that He took our place, for *"cursed be everyone who hangs on a tree"* (Deut. 21:23). This displays the curse of God against sin falling on the Lord Jesus Christ, Who thus became a curse for us.

The idea of this curse as leveled by God against Cain is that it would incorporate the Earth. In other words, Abel's blood had been spilled on the Earth, shed murderously by his brother Cain and, therefore, the Earth would now be against Cain. This meant that everything he tried to do on the Earth, and irrespective as to what it was, would be freighted with difficulties. Every way he turned, and irrespective as to what he did, he would find that the Earth was against him.

THE EARTH AND INNOCENT BLOOD

The phrase, *"Which has opened her mouth to receive your brother's blood from your hand,"* was the beginning of what has proven to be a saturation. From then until now, the Earth has been soaked with the blood of innocent victims. And to be sure, the same curse that was leveled against Cain by God has been leveled against all who have followed in his train.

This is the reason for much of the poverty in the world presently; it is the reason,

I believe, for much of the inclement weather, earthquakes, hurricanes, tidal waves, storms, etc.

Only God knows the untold millions, even hundreds of millions, possibly even billions down through the many centuries, who have been murdered, starved to death, or their lives cut short by despotic individuals. The Earth, consequently, rebels against such action, with the Curse of God continuing in all of its many forms.

To be frank, even though Jesus satisfied the curse on the Cross, taking the penalty upon Himself, still, the full weight of what He did will not be fully felt until the coming Kingdom Age. We now have only the firstfruits of what He carried out, with the entirety coming at that later time. The curse will then be removed from the Earth in totality, with the desert then blossoming as the rose.

THE WORD OF GOD

We must understand that the same God Who said, *"Let there be light, and there was light,"* with light continuing to expand into outer space, at the rate of 186,000 miles a second, also said, *"And now are you cursed from the Earth."* The same power that upholds the former also upholds the latter.

(12) "WHEN YOU TILL THE GROUND, IT SHALL NOT HENCEFORTH YIELD UNTO YOU HER STRENGTH; A FUGITIVE AND A VAGABOND SHALL YOU BE IN THE EARTH."

The construction is:

1. Every resistance of the Earth against Cain in his attempts to grow food would be a reminder of what he had done to his brother.

2. The Earth would not yield to him its strength.

3. He would be a fugitive and a vagabond, which means constantly moving and wandering.

THE GROUND

The phrase, *"When you till the ground, it shall not henceforth yield unto you her strength,"* presents the fact that Cain had polluted man's habitation, and now, when he tilled the soil, it would resist him as an enemy, by refusing *"to yield unto him her strength."*

By rejecting the Cross, Cain, in effect, had chosen the Earth. So he found his punishment there where he had chose his portion, and set his heart. In today's terminology, he would have been called *"a man of the world"*; however, all who strive for that accolade find that the Earth strives against them, and in every way. So what am I saying?

I am saying that all who conduct themselves as Cain suffer the punishment of Cain. It doesn't matter that some of them may get very rich as far as this world's possessions are concerned. The guilt of sin continues to eat them alive. They know no peace, for the Bible says, *"There is no peace, saith the LORD, to the wicked"* (Isa. 48:22).

And again the Scripture says: *"Be not deceived; God is not mocked: for whatsoever a man sows, that shall he also reap.*

"For he who sows to his flesh shall of the flesh reap corruption; but he who sows to the Spirit shall of the Spirit reap life everlasting" (Gal. 6:7-8).

A FUGITIVE AND A VAGABOND

The phrase, *"A fugitive and a vagabond shall you be in the Earth,"* presents the search, not of a better lot, but under the compulsion of an evil conscience.

Matthew Henry said: *"Who knows the extent and weight of a Divine curse, how far it reaches, how deep it pierces? We have all deserved this curse, it is only in Christ that Believers are saved from it, and inherit the blessing."*

This man was condemned to perpetual disgrace and reproach among men, and to perpetual disquietude and horror in his own mind. Yet in this sentence there was mercy mixed, inasmuch as Cain was not immediately cut off, but had space given him to repent: God is longsuffering.

But regrettably, there is no record that Cain ever made things right with God.

In later years this same curse fell upon the Jews, who *"for shedding the Blood of Christ, the most innocent Lamb of God, are vagabonds to this day over the face of the Earth."*

Only in 1948 have they attempted to resettle their land, which has been freighted with difficulties from then until now. In fact, the Jews will never know real peace until they make Christ their Lord, which they most definitely will do at the Second Coming.

(13) "AND CAIN SAID UNTO THE LORD, MY PUNISHMENT IS GREATER THAN I CAN BEAR."

The exposition is:

1. Cain's answer to the Lord was not one of Repentance.

2. Cain is understood as deploring not the enormity of his sin, but the severity of his punishment, as he sees it.

3. Until we properly see the enormity of our sin, we cannot make our way back to God.

THE ANSWER AS GIVEN BY CAIN

The phrase, *"And Cain said unto the LORD,"* as we shall see, can scarcely be considered the language of confession.

Everyone must say something to the Lord. What is it that you are saying?

There is only one statement or petition that the Lord will accept. Jesus told us what it was. He said:

"Two men went up into the Temple to pray; the one a Pharisee, and the other a Publican.

"The Pharisee stood and prayed thus with himself, God, I thank You, that I am not as other men are, extortioners, unjust, adulterers, or even as this Publican.

"I fast twice in the week, I give tithes of all that I possess.

"And the Publican, standing afar off, would not lift up so much as his eyes unto Heaven, but smote upon his breast, saying, God be merciful to me a sinner.

"I tell you, this man went down to his house justified rather than the other; for every one who exalts himself shall be abased; and he who humbles himself shall be exalted" (Lk. 18:10-14). The attitude and prayer of the Publican is really all that the Lord will hear. Every prayer, petition, praise, and in fact all of our supplication to the Lord must be based upon this premise.

PUNISHMENT

The phrase, *"My punishment is greater than I can bear,"* presents Cain, complaining, not of the greatness of his sin, but of the extremity of his punishment, as if disproportioned to his just desserts. Matthew Henry said: *"Impenitent, unhumbled hearts are not reclaimed by God's rebukes, because they think themselves wronged by them. It shows great hardness to be more concerned about our sufferings than our sins."*

There is always a consequence to sin. It doesn't matter if the person is redeemed or unredeemed. Sin must be answered, and to be certain, it definitely will be answered.

In fact, every human being is faced with one of two choices. He can accept Christ, Who took the punishment for our sins, thereby atoning for them, or he can reject Christ, Who is the only solution for sin, and fight against God. The former brings life, while the latter brings death!

(14) "BEHOLD, YOU HAVE DRIVEN ME OUT THIS DAY FROM THE FACE OF THE EARTH; AND FROM YOUR FACE SHALL I BE HID; AND I SHALL BE A FUGITIVE AND A VAGABOND IN THE EARTH; AND IT SHALL COME TO PASS, THAT EVERY ONE WHO FINDS ME SHALL SLAY ME."

The overview is:

1. Adam's sin brought expulsion from the inner circle, Cain's from the outer (Bonar).

2. To be hidden from the Face of God is to be not regarded by God, or not protected by His guardian care.

3. My sentence is that I have to live with my crime, wherever I go.

4. The reference by Cain to other individuals proved that in the some 100 plus years since Adam and Eve were created, the first parents had other children. By this time, there could well have been several thousands of people on the Earth, and no doubt were.

DRIVEN

The phrase, *"Behold, You have driven me out this day from the face of the Earth,"* projects a continuance of complaints, but no Repentance. Would God have forgiven him, had he truly at this time been sorry for his sin?

There has never been a case in human history where an individual went to the Lord pleading for Mercy and Grace, irrespective as to how bad the sin was, but that God didn't hear and willingly and instantly forgive. The Word of God says: *"All who the Father gives Me shall come to Me; and him who comes to Me I will in no wise cast out"* (Jn. 6:37).

THY FACE

The phrase, *"And from Your face shall I be hid,"* refers to the face of blessing, protection, and help. Quite possibly he was referring to the Tabernacle which had been built, if in fact one had been built, near the entrance to the Garden of Eden, where stood the Cherubim with flaming swords, etc. Even though they were outside the Garden, quite possibly they thought that the Promised Seed would come, and allow them entrance once again.

As previously stated, Adam and those after him had not yet come to the full realization as to the degree of their Fall, but little by little the seriousness of the situation becomes more and more real. To be hidden from the Face of God refers to rejection, and because of one's own stubbornness.

Cain did not have to go this route. The sentence could have been suspended at any moment, with the Face of God once again shining upon him. But Cain, as so many others, wanted sin and blessing at the same time. In other words, he wanted God to condone his actions — actions incidentally, which were growing worse by the hour.

He had at first insulted God by bringing to Him a sacrifice of his own choosing, completely ignoring what God had demanded. And then he grows angry with God because the sacrifice is not accepted. He then kills his brother. Sin ever spirals downward!

FEAR

The phrase, *"And I shall be a fugitive and a vagabond in the Earth; and it shall come to pass, that every one who finds me shall kill me,"* could be translated, *"every one who finds me shall seek to kill me."*

Many have concluded that Cain and Abel were the only two children born to Adam and Eve during the past approximately 100 plus years that they had been on this Earth since creation. The Bible says nothing of the sort.

In fact, there could have been many sons and daughters other than these two born to our first parents, with enough time having lapsed for many children to be brought into the world, and then for them to have children, etc. In fact, there were no doubt thousands of people on the Earth at this time.

At the beginning, brothers married sisters, because there was no other way it could be. But soon, as the race expanded, the direct kin lengthened out considerably, as would be obvious.

Cain and Abel are mentioned here because Cain evidently was the firstborn, and Abel had great Faith in God. There could well have been other sons and daughters born to Adam and Eve between the births of Cain and Abel.

So, Cain feared that harm may come to him from some member of this now large family — as stated, by now probably numbering several thousands of people.

(15) "AND THE LORD SAID UNTO HIM, THEREFORE WHOSOEVER KILLS CAIN, VENGEANCE SHALL BE TAKEN ON HIM SEVENFOLD. AND THE LORD SET A MARK UPON CAIN, UNLESS ANY FINDING HIM SHOULD KILL HIM."

The exegesis is:

1. God grants Mercy to Cain.

2. The command is given by the Lord that anyone who kills Cain, vengeance shall be taken on him sevenfold.

3. The Lord set a mark upon Cain, showing God's protection, but we aren't told what that mark was.

PROTECTION

The phrase, *"And the LORD said unto him, Therefore whosoever kills Cain, vengeance shall be taken on him sevenfold,"* presents more questions than it does answers.

Rosenmuller gives these three reasons that God spared Cain:

1. To show that *"vengeance is Mine; I will repay, saith the Lord."*

2. To prove the riches of the Divine clemency to sinful men.

3. To serve as a warning against the crime of murder.

Men were living now in the Dispensation of *"conscience."* The Dispensation of *"government"* would not come in until after the flood, which would be during the time of Noah, some 1,500 years from the time of Cain and Abel. (The flood came about 1,600 years after creation. And Cain and Abel were probably over 100 years old when all of this took place.)

During the Dispensation of government, God would lay down the rule that *"Whoso sheds man's blood, by man shall his blood be shed: for in the Image of God made He man"* (Gen. 9:6). However, the execution for cold-blooded murder, for this is what the term means, was in effect to be carried out by delegated authorities.

During the time of Cain and Abel there was no government; consequently, the Lord did not at all desire that individuals take matters into their own hands, especially considering the state of fallen man. So in effect, the Lord was saying that if Cain was to be killed, He (the Lord) would carry out the task, and not others. The Lord Alone was qualified for this task, as should be obvious.

Due to the Fall of man, the prohibition against self-inflicted justice and vengeance would soon fall by the wayside.

The Scripture says: *"And God saw that the wickedness of man was great in the Earth, and that every imagination of the thoughts of his heart was only evil continually.*

"And it repented the LORD that He had made man on the Earth, and it grieved Him at His heart" (Gen. 6:5-6).

THE MARK

The phrase, *"And the LORD set a mark upon Cain, unless any finding him should kill him,"* does not relate as to what kind of mark it was, or whether it was visible.

The Hebrew says, *"And Jehovah set,"* that is, appointed, *"unto Cain a sign, that no one finding him should slay him."* Maybe the sign was a natural phenomenon, or, the Word of God Alone, which certainly would have been sufficient.

(16) "AND CAIN WENT OUT FROM THE PRESENCE OF THE LORD, AND DWELT IN THE LAND OF NOD, ON THE EAST OF EDEN."

The synopsis is:

1. Cain did not want pardon, because he did not want God.

2. All he wanted was to get out of the Presence of God, and lose himself in the world and its pursuits.

3. He goes to the land of Nod, on the east of Eden, thereby possibly thinking that the curse would not follow him so far.

THE PRESENCE OF THE LORD

The phrase, *"And Cain went out from the Presence of the LORD,"* in effect, means that he withdrew from the neighborhood of the Cherubim.

The meaning of the Text is that Cain willingly renounced God and all that pertained to God, and was content to forego its privileges, so that he might not be under its precepts.

He thought he could live very well without God and he, therefore, set about decorating the world as well as he could, for the purpose of making it a place which he desired, and himself a respectable man therein; however, in God's view, he was under a curse and, therefore, a fugitive and a vagabond.

Such was *"the way of Cain,"* in which way millions are, at this moment, rushing on.

The world is full of people who have some knowledge of God, but most of that knowledge is anything but right. The truth is, they are ignorant of themselves, ignorant of God, but will never admit such. God's remedy is to *"cleanse."* Sadly and regrettably, that is rejected.

Man's effort is to *"improve"* the situation, which he can do somewhat as it regards material things, but not at all as it regards spiritual things. Once again, this is *"the way of Cain"* (Jude, vs. 11).

EAST OF EDEN

The phrase, *"And dwelt in the land of Nod, on the east of Eden,"* refers to Eastern Asia. *"Nod"* means *"wandering."* Some think the Mongol race is the offspring of Cain.

The location of this place is really immaterial. The idea is, Cain wanted to get away from the Presence of God, not seemingly realizing that God was Omnipresent.

As a young boy, five years old, I will never forget my Mother and Dad leaving our hometown of Ferriday, Louisiana, going to Texas. This was immediately before World War II, with the country still in the depths of economic depression. My Dad had planned to go into business in South Texas, but in reality, even as Cain of old, was running from God.

My baby brother had just been born. He was only a few weeks old when we left. He would not come back with us.

NOTES

My parents had started attending the little Assembly of God Church, which had been built in our hometown. They had come under great conviction, but would not yield to Christ. As stated, their leaving constituted them as running from the Lord. As well, they didn't seem to realize that wherever they went, God would be there.

Almost immediately upon arriving at our destination, my Mother came down with pneumonia, and so did my baby brother. My brother lingered for a few days and died. I will never forget that funeral.

I was only a child, but it stands out in my mind. I remember two men helping my Dad out of the car, with him standing over the casket. No one was there but an Assemblies of God Pastor, my Uncle Frank, Dad's brother-in-law, and the mortician. My Mother was too sick to attend the funeral.

I remember my Dad looking down into the casket, and through eyes swollen almost shut from weeping, saying these words: *"Son, I promise you that I will meet you in Heaven."*

I was too young to understand too much of what was happening. But I'll not forget those words. The place was Rio Hondo, Texas. The year was 1940.

The Lord, Who was in Texas, just as well as He had been in Louisiana, took my baby brother home to Heaven, in order to bring my Mom and Dad to their spiritual senses. When my Mother was able to travel, my parents came home, and a few weeks later gave their hearts and lives to Jesus Christ.

Millions have tried to run from God, but none have been successful. Even though there is no record that Cain ever made it back, I have to believe that the Lord of Glory kept reaching out for him. In 1,000 different ways, he would see the handiwork of God wherever he was, and he would always hear that still, small Voice.

(17) "AND CAIN KNEW HIS WIFE; AND SHE CONCEIVED, AND BEAR ENOCH: AND HE BUILT A CITY, AND CALLED THE NAME OF THE CITY, AFTER THE NAME OF HIS SON, ENOCH."

The diagram is:

1. Cain was either married to his sister, or else a cousin, and even possibly one several times removed.

2. *"Knew his wife,"* is Biblical terminology for conception.

3. They had a son whom they named Enoch. This is not the same Enoch of Genesis 5:18.

4. Cain built a city and named it after his son.

THE BUILDING OF A CITY

The phrase, *"And Cain knew his wife; and she conceived, and bear Enoch: and he built a city,"* refers to this man attempting to go ahead with his life, but without God. The term *"built a city,"* actually means *"was building,"* or *"began to build."* The idea is, it was not finished. And so it has been and is with the human race. Nothing is ever quite finished with the unredeemed, simply because what is built doesn't satisfy; therefore, the thought is always projected, if certain other things can be done, then the soul will be satisfied. It never is, simply because, as someone has well said: *"The soul of man is so big that only God can fill it up."*

As we've already stated, Cain had either married his sister, or a cousin, and possibly a cousin several times removed. There were, no doubt, several thousands of people on the Earth at this time. Between 100 and 130 years had passed since the creation of our first parents. It is certain that Adam and Eve continued to have children, and probably at a rapid pace, after the birth of Cain, who was the firstborn (Gen. 5:4).

The name given to this child, *"Enoch,"* means, *"to train,"* as in *"train up a child"* (Prov. 22:6). Whether this meant that the Mother or even Cain desired to train up this child in the ways of the Lord, we aren't told.

Concerning Cain beginning the building of this city, plus other particulars we will see in succeeding Verses, this puts to rest the idea of the human beings of that time being little more than animal crawling primates. In fact, there have never been cave dwellers. While most certainly there have been people who have lived in caves, the general thrust from the very beginning, however, was the accommodation of houses, or tents, etc.

THE NAME OF THE CITY

The phrase, *"And called the name of the city, after the name of his son, Enoch,"* carries

the idea, due to the meaning of the name Enoch, that this city would be a place of education and learning. Whether Cain had this in mind or not, we cannot actually tell; however, the following definitely could apply:

THE INTELLIGENCE OF THE ERA

The intelligence level of Adam and Eve, before the Fall, had to be of tremendous proportions. Without going into detail, I think their ability in just about every capacity was phenomenal.

When they fell, even though a deterioration set in immediately, it is my personal thought, and considering what those early generations were able to do, that this intelligence did not leave immediately, but was a gradual, deteriorating process. In other words, I think there is no doubt that Cain along with all the other sons and daughters of Adam and Eve, and all who were born to these sons and daughters, etc., were of a very high intelligence level. As stated, it immediately began to deteriorate, and has continued with such deterioration through the centuries. It is only with the advent of the Twentieth Century, constituting the last days, that Daniel's prophecy of knowledge being increased, has begun to take place (Dan. 12:4). During this period of time, which has now lasted a little over 100 years, approximately 99 percent of the inventions of modern technology have taken place. And to be sure, more than likely, all of this can be ascribed to the latter rain of the outpouring of the Holy Spirit, prophesied by Joel (Joel 2:23).

THE JEWS

Taking the Jews as an example, even though they as well have suffered nearly 2,000 years of spiritual deterioration; still, the intelligence level of these people as a whole surpasses any other group of people in the world. Think what it was when they were in covenant with the Lord, some 3,000 years ago, etc.

From the Scriptures, we learn, as we shall see in the following Verses, the ability and intelligence level of those particular generations. I think it proves my point that they started out very intelligent, and gradually deteriorated, completely disproving the theory of evolution.

(18) "AND UNTO ENOCH WAS BORN IRAD: AND IRAD BEGAT MEHUJAEL: AND MEHUJAEL BEGAT METHUSAEL: AND METHUSAEL BEGAT LAMECH.

(19) "AND LAMECH TOOK UNTO HIM TWO WIVES: THE NAME OF THE ONE WAS ADAH, AND THE NAME OF THE OTHER ZILLAH.

(20) "AND ADAH BEAR JABAL: HE WAS THE FATHER OF SUCH AS DWELL IN TENTS, AND OF SUCH AS HAVE CATTLE."

The composition is:

1. Some of these names conclude with the letters "el," which means "God." This tells us something!

2. With Lamech taking two wives, we have here the beginning of polygamy.

3. We also see the beginning of the nomadic existence, as it regards shepherds "and of such as have cattle."

GOD

Verse 18 reads: "And unto Enoch was born Irad: and Irad begat Mehujael: and Mehujael begat Methusael: and Methusael begat Lamech."

If it is to be noticed, several of these names end with the letters "el," which in the Hebrew means "God." For instance, Mehujael means, "smitten of God." Mahalaleel means, "glory to God." Methusael means "God's hero." So what does all of this mean?

At this time, which was probably about 300 years after the creation of Adam and Eve, and it definitely could have been longer, God was a strong part of the thinking of these individuals; however, considering the fact that for the approximate 1,600 years between Adam and the flood, during that time there were only two individuals recorded in the Bible as truly living for God (Abel and the Enoch of Genesis 5:18), we must conclude that all the others, whomever they may have been, and whatever their claims, really did not know the Lord. They, as millions since, even billions, devised other ways of proposed Salvation, which of course, God could never accept.

Now, man's ear is filled with sounds other than those which issue from Calvary, and his eye filled with other objects than a Crucified Christ.

NOTES

POLYGAMY

Verse 19 reads: "And Lamech took unto him two wives: the name of the one was Adah, and the name of the other Zillah." This is the first instance of polygamy recorded in the Bible.

Even though polygamy was permitted in those days because of the hardness of men's hearts, it was not so from the beginning. Inglis said: "This was 'a new evil,' without even the pretext that the first wife had no children, which held its ground until Christianity restored the original law" (Mat. 19:4-6).

God's purpose was for a man to cleave or stick to his wife (Gen. 2:24), letting nothing and no one come between. No man can have that kind of relationship with two or more women. Adah means "bright ornament," or "adorned one." Zillah means, "shaded or protected one." Their names show they were loved by their parents, cared about by God, and should not have been abused by Lamech (Horton).

CATTLE

Verse 20 reads: "And Adah bear Jabal: he was the father of such as dwell in tents, and of such as have cattle." This refers probably to the first nomad who introduced the custom of living in tents, and pasturing and breeding sheep and cattle, etc. To find pasture, it was necessary to move quite often, hence the "tents."

We find Cain as the father of shepherds, and as the father of musicians, even as we shall see, but not a father of the faithful. Here is one to teach in brass and iron, but none to teach the good knowledge of the Lord; here are devices as to how to be rich, and how to be mighty, and how to be merry; but nothing of God, of His fear and service. Present things fill the heads of most.

(21) "AND HIS BROTHER'S NAME WAS JUBAL: HE WAS THE FATHER OF ALL SUCH AS HANDLE THE HARP AND ORGAN."

The exegesis is:

1. Adah bear Jabal and Jubal.

2. Jubal was the originator of musical instruments.

3. The grateful sounds of *"the harp and organ,"* drown, to man's ear, the cry of Abel's blood.

MUSIC

Verse 21 says: *"And his brother's name was Jubal: he was the father of all such as handle the harp and organ."* Jubal is recorded as the first inventor of musical instruments, but by no means the last.

As we've already stated, man's ear is now filled with other sounds than those which issue from Calvary, and his eye is filled with other objects than a Crucified Christ.

We know that Heaven is filled with musical instruments (Rev. 5:8; 14:2; 15:2). As well, the Book of Psalms, which actually means *"songs,"* puts forth many and varied musical instruments in the worship of God. Considering that this Book is the largest Book in the Bible, and made that way by the Holy Spirit, we learn from this just how important that music and musical instruments are in the worship of God (Ps. 33:2; 57:8; 149:3; 150:3).

So we know from this that musical instruments are Biblical. But at the same time, we see here how Satan, at the very beginning, seeks to corrupt music and musical instruments, by using them for the glory of evil, instead of the Glory of God.

Satan is still attempting to pervert Sacred Music, by steering it to the Contemporary direction, or to where it has no spirit at all. But used in the manner that God desires that it be used, music and singing are some of the highest forms of worship of God.

When I was eight years of age, I asked the Lord to give me the talent to play the piano. Along with answering that prayer, He also gave me a knowledge of music and singing as it regards worship. It has helped us to reach untold thousands with the Gospel of Jesus Christ.

(22) "AND ZILLAH, SHE ALSO BEAR TUBAL-CAIN, AN INSTRUCTOR OF EVERY ARTIFICER IN BRASS AND IRON: AND THE SISTER OF TUBAL-CAIN WAS NAAMAH."

The diagram is:

1. Tubal-cain was the first one to begin to work with metals.

2. The name of *"Cain"* was probably added to show that these were Cainites.

3. *"Naamah"* means, *"beautiful,"* and probably signifies that beauty had probably now become the chief attraction in women.

METALLURGY

The phrase, *"And Zillah, she also bear Tubal-cain, an instructor of every artificer in brass and iron,"* presents the first metallurgist, one might say.

Considering those who attach the name of *"God"* to their own personal names, we find in all of this an abundance of religion. In fact, man would not be without religion. But what passes for religion is but a screw in the vast machine which has been constructed by man, for man's convenience and man's exaltation.

In reality, the very meaning of the word *"religion,"* pertains to that which is devised solely by man to enable him to reach God, or to better himself, he believes, in some way. This means that it's not originated by God and is, therefore, not sanctioned by God. So man makes religion a part of his daily occurrence, but being of his own devising, it can never reach God.

How different the way of the man of Faith! Abel felt and owned the curse; he saw the stain of sin, and, in the holy energy of Faith, offered that which met it, and met it thoroughly — met it Divinely. He sought and found a refuge in God Himself; but instead of building a city on the Earth, he found but a grave in its bosom. The Earth, which on its surface displayed the genius and energy of Cain and his family, was stained underneath with the blood of a righteous man.

Let the man of the world remember this; let the man of God remember it; let the worldly-minded Christian remember it.

The Earth which we tread upon is stained by the Blood of the Son of God. The very Blood which justifies the Church condemns the world. The dark shadow of the Cross of Christ may be seen by the eye of Faith, hovering over all the glitter and glare of this world. But the Scripture says, *"the fashion of this world passes away."*

It will soon all be over, so far as the present scene is concerned. *"The way of Cain"* will be followed by *"the error of Balaam,"* in its consummated form; and then will come *"the gainsaying of Core"*; and what then? *"The pit"* will open its mouth to receive the wicked, and close it again to shut them up in *"blackness of darkness forever"* (Jude, vs. 13) (Mackintosh).

BEAUTY

The phrase, *"And the sister of Tubal-cain was Naamah,"* is brought out in this fashion for a purpose. *"Naamah"* means *"beautiful."*

It tells us that women were now becoming an object of lust. The terrible results of the Fall are more and more beginning to be felt and seen.

(23) "AND LAMECH SAID UNTO HIS WIVES, ADAH AND ZILLAH, HEAR MY VOICE; YOU WIVES OF LAMECH, HEARKEN UNTO MY SPEECH: FOR I HAVE SLAIN A MAN TO MY WOUNDING, AND A YOUNG MAN TO MY HURT.

(24) "IF CAIN SHALL BE AVENGED SEVENFOLD, TRULY LAMECH SEVENTY AND SEVENFOLD."

The structure is:

1. We find here that Lamech, following the example of Cain, has killed a young man.

2. Evidently, his wives thought that God might strike him down for this sin.

3. He answers them by saying that if Cain shall be avenged sevenfold, truly he should be avenged seventy sevenfold.

4. But what he said of himself was not God's Word, as was that which was said to Cain, but the arrogant and untrue words of an impious murderer.

MURDER

Verse 23 reads: *"And Lamech said unto his wives, Adah and Zillah, Hear my voice; you wives of Lamech, hearken unto my speech: for I have slain a man to my wounding, and a young man to my hurt."*

Lust and lawlessness quickly appear in Lamech; he takes two wives, and he murders a man; but he need not be disquieted thereat, because if God forbad anyone to punish Cain who was so great a sinner, how much safer was he as being less guilty than Cain, or so he thinks!

Evidently, his wives were concerned that God would strike him down for this killing. He attempts to set their mind at ease.

The first recorded poem, therefore, in human history, like so much poetry ever since, glorifies immorality and murder, and denies coming wrath. Lamech, in effect, says that God would be to blame if anything happened to him, i.e., *"that there is no future punishment or judgment."* And so man has attempted to deny the judgment ever since.

THE BOAST

Verse 24 reads: *"If Cain shall be avenged sevenfold, truly Lamech seventy and sevenfold."* With arrogance, he sets himself up as God. With this boastful poem in praise of armed violence and bloodshed, joined with indications of luxury and a life of pleasure, Moses closes the history of the race of Cain.

Quite possibly, this tells us that the situation didn't turn out exactly as Lamech thought it would. Quite possibly, God visited this man with judgment.

(25) "AND ADAM KNEW HIS WIFE AGAIN; AND SHE BEAR A SON, AND CALLED HIS NAME SETH: FOR GOD, SAID SHE, HAS APPOINTED ME ANOTHER SEED INSTEAD OF ABEL, WHOM CAIN SLEW."

The composite is:

1. After dealing with Cain's line and the beginnings of corruption and violence, Moses goes back to the beginning, or somewhere near that time.

2. Adam and Eve now had another son, and they called his name *"Seth."*

3. This is not meant to imply that Adam and Eve had not other children who had grown to adulthood prior to the death of Abel.

4. The Holy Spirit will single out *"Seth,"* because he was in the lineage of Christ.

5. When *"Cain"* was born, Eve said, *"I have gotten a man from the Lord,"* indicating that she believed in the Covenant of Genesis 3:15. Now she uses the term *"God,"* in effect stating that she has lost faith in the Covenant.

6. In reality, this *"other seed,"* which God had appointed her, was indeed the one through whom the *"Seed of the woman"* would ultimately come, namely, the Lord Jesus Christ.

SETH

The phrase, *"And Adam knew his wife again; and she bear a son, and called his name Seth,"* takes us back some years.

Both Cain and Abel were now lost to Adam. Quite possibly Adam and Eve had other sons by this time, but none had been ordained by God to take the place and the position of the firstborn. The name *"Seth"* means, *"appointed, substitute,"* which means that the Lord specifically told Adam and Eve that this child was to assume the rights of the firstborn.

GOD

The phrase, *"For God, said she, has appointed me another seed instead of Abel, whom Cain slew,"* tells us several things:

As stated, Eve now seems to have lost faith in the Promises of God. She had thought that Cain would be the promised one (Promised Seed of the woman), and she had used the Covenant name *"Lord"* (Gen. 4:1). But Cain had turned out to be a murderer.

She didn't put such hopes in Abel when he was born, still thinking that Cain was the one. But now Abel was dead, murdered by the hand of his own brother, and Cain, refusing to repent, was banished by God to distant places.

It seems as if the Lord had revealed to both Adam and Eve that Seth was to be in the lineage as it regards the *"Seed of the woman"*; however, it also seems that Eve had lost faith even though she knew that Seth was the promised one, at least in a sense.

Her statement is tinged with sarcasm. At any rate, by her use of the term *"God,"* it surely isn't said in faith or hope. It seems to be a resignation to the situation, which she now sees as extremely negative.

It's all a matter of faith! Despite her circumstances, does she continue to have Faith in God? It seems she doesn't!

(26) "AND TO SETH, TO HIM ALSO THERE WAS BORN A SON; AND HE CALLED HIS NAME ENOS: THEN BEGAN MEN TO CALL UPON THE NAME OF THE LORD."

The construction is:

1. The scene now changes to an adult Seth, who has evidently married, and now has a son.

2. He called his name *"Enos,"* meaning, *"mortal, decaying man."*

3. The phrase, *"Then began men to call upon the Name of the Lord,"* is probably said in derision. The sons of Cain, it seems, began to fasten upon the others, that is, the

sons of Seth — but in contempt and hatred — the name of Jehovah.

MORTAL MAN

The phrase, *"And to Seth, to him also there was born a son; and he called his name Enos,"* proclaims the fact of dying, decaying man. *"Enos"* means, *"sickly, mortal, decaying man."*

The Scripture indicates that Seth personally gave this name Enos to his newborn. So why would he do such?

By now the human race has learned, and especially the sons of Adam and Eve, the magnitude of their Fall, at least to a certain extent. Without a doubt, the first parents had related to their offspring Who God was and What He was like. They had no doubt, as well, described the Garden of Eden, its beauty, and its glory. In that pristine state, they would never have known death. But now death stares them in the face, and even worse than that, I suppose, the sin nature seems to grow progressively worse, as men become more and more evil.

By now it's a world of killing, murder, rape, stealing, hatred, violence, and strife. In fact, it will become so bad that God will literally repent that He has made man.

Seth sees all of this and sees the constant deterioration, and names his son accordingly.

Even though Seth was in the lineage of Christ, there is no record that he ever really served God. Perhaps he did, and of course one hopes that he did, but he is not listed in the great Eleventh Chapter of Hebrews, and it definitely seems that he would have been placed in that prestigious lineup had faith prevailed within his life.

CONTEMPT

The phrase, *"Then began men to call upon the Name of the LORD,"* probably refers to contempt. Quite possibly the family of Cain, knowing that Seth had now taken the place of Abel, as it regards the *"firstborn"* or *"appointed one,"* contemptuously refers to them as the *"God people,"* or the *"Jehovah people."*

When we look at the Sixth Chapter of Genesis, we do not see men calling upon the Name of the Lord, at least in faith. We see profanity! And so, the phrase as given in this last Verse of this Fourth Chapter of Genesis probably refers to taking the Name of the Lord in vain.

"I have found a wondrous Saviour,
"Jesus Christ, the soul's delight;
"Every blessing of His favor
"Fills my heart with hope so bright."

"Life is growing rich with beauty,
"Toil has lost its weary strain,
"Now a halo crowns each duty
"And I sing a glad refrain."

"Heavenly wisdom He provides me,
"Grace to keep my spirit free;
"In His Own sweet way He guides me,
"When the path I cannot see."

"O what splendor, O what glory,
"O what matchless power Divine,
"Is the Christ of Gospel story
"Christ the Saviour, Who is mine."

CHAPTER 5

(1) "THIS IS THE BOOK OF THE GENERATIONS OF ADAM. IN THE DAY THAT GOD CREATED MAN, IN THE LIKENESS OF GOD CREATED HE HIM;

(2) "MALE AND FEMALE CREATED HE THEM; AND BLESSED THEM, AND CALLED THEIR NAME ADAM, IN THE DAY WHEN THEY WERE CREATED."

The overview is:

1. The phrase, *"This is the Book of the generations of Adam,"* corresponds with the phrase, *"The Book of the generation of Jesus Christ,"* Who was the Last Adam (Mat. 1:1).

2. God created man in His Own likeness.

3. *"Male and female created He them,"* refers to the fact that homosexuality is a grievous sin before God.

4. He blessed them, but the blessing was lost as a result of the Fall.

5. Adam, in the Hebrew, is the word for humankind in general beside the specific name for the first man.

THE FIRST ADAM

The phrase, *"This is the Book of the generations of Adam,"* says it in this manner instead of *"This is the generation of Adam."*

Why is this?

Matthew 1:1 gives the answer. It says, *"The Book of the Generation of Jesus Christ."* Christ is the *"Last Adam"* (I Cor. 15:45).

God intended for Adam and Eve to live for Him, and to bring a race of human beings into the world, which would be sons and daughters of God. In fact, Adam was given extraordinary powers, which included dominion and creative ability. While there is no record that he had creative ability as God, which could bring something out of nothing, still, he definitely had the ability to create many things out of that which God had already made. The indication is that the original Adam was made higher than the Angels, and a little lower than God.

David said: *"What is man, that You are mindful of him? And the son of man, that You visit him?*

"For You have made him a little lower than the Angels, and have crowned him with glory and honor" (Ps. 8:4-5).

The Hebrew word translated *"Angels,"* should have been translated *"God,"* for that's actually what it means. So, the Scripture plainly tells us that God created man a little lower than Himself, which means that man was originally created higher than the Angels.

Unfortunately, man fell! His spiritual fall was so cataclysmic as to ultimately affect every single thing he is and every single thing he touches. Sin is the cause of the ruin, and ruin it is.

For the situation to be rectified, God would have to become man, in effect, and even as Paul stated, become the Last Adam (I Cor. 15:45). The word *"last"* used by Paul tells us that there will never be a need for another in this sense. Jesus paid it all, not only keeping the Law perfectly, all on our behalf, but as well, through the giving of Himself on the Cross, and the shedding of His Life's Blood, He atoned for all sin. Inasmuch as He did all of this totally and completely for us, and I speak of the entirety of the human race, and for all time (Jn. 3:16), simple Faith expressed in Him and what He has done grants the believing sinner eternal life (Eph. 2:8-9, 13-18).

THE LIKENESS OF GOD

Verse 1 further reads, *"In the day that God created man, in the Likeness of God created*

He him," presents the high, glorious, and holy manner in which man was originally created. It was in the *"Likeness of God."*

How do we define the *"Likeness of God"*? Perhaps Paul said it best:

"For God, Who commanded the light to shine out of darkness, has shined in our hearts, to give the light of the knowledge of the Glory of God in the face of Jesus Christ" (II Cor. 4:6).

Consequently, we might say that the *"Likeness of God,"* is the *"Glory of God,"* but more particularly, it is *"the Lord Jesus Christ."*

Through the Fall, man has lost that glory; however, at the First Resurrection of Life, every Believer will then be *"Glorified"* (Rom. 8:17). In other words, what man lost in the Fall, Jesus Christ purchased it back at the Cross. We will then be like Him, Who is the True Likeness of God (I Jn. 3:2).

There is much argument as to what the Atonement includes! However, of necessity, and as stated, it had to include everything. While it is certainly true that we now only have the *"firstfruits"* of what Jesus did there, at the coming Resurrection we will then have it all (Rom. 8:23).

BLESSED

Verse 2 reads, *"Male and female created He them; and blessed them,"* proclaims through the blessing, untold favor. As man lost most of the likeness of God at the Fall, he also lost the blessing. Whereas the *"Likeness of God"* refers to *"God in kind,"* the word *"blessing"* refers to ongoing favor constantly expressed.

It took the Cross to restore the *"Likeness of God,"* as well as the *"blessing."*

It is argued by some that man didn't lose his *"Likeness of God,"* at the Fall; however, man cannot at the same time have the Likeness of God and the Satanic nature, which the latter he most definitely has. God cannot be linked with sin and shame, etc. While unredeemed man might do some good things because of his conscience, he can in no way, by these good things, make himself in the Likeness of God. That can only be done by the unredeemed sinner being *"born again."* Jesus plainly and clearly said: *"Except a man be born again, he cannot see the Kingdom of God"* (Jn. 3:3).

No, the Likeness of God, along with the Blessing, were totally and completely lost at the Fall, with man then being *"dead in trespasses and sins"* (Eph. 2:1). *"Dead"* here refers to being spiritually dead, and as someone has said, *"Dead is dead!"* That means there is nothing remaining of God. The problem with unredeemed man is that he doesn't know how lost he really is, so lost in fact, that there is absolutely nothing he can do to save himself, at least by his own ability, strength, and machinations. Likewise, Believers do not really know or understand to the extent that we are saved. We were completely lost, and now we are completely saved.

FLAWED FAITH!

I happened to read the other day a particular statement made by someone as it regards a Christian who had failed the Lord some years ago, but had Scripturally repented. The individual was referred to as one that was *"flawed."*

I wonder if the individual who made such a statement realizes and understands that by referring to a Believer in such a manner, he has greatly insulted the precious Blood of Jesus Christ which cleanses from all sin (I Jn. 1:9). If any one Christian is flawed, then all Christians and for all time are flawed as well. People who say such things evidently know very little about the Word of God, and, consequently, know very little about their own personal Salvation.

The Truth is, individuals who would say or think such things are flawed themselves. And how are they flawed?

They are flawed because their faith is flawed. In other words, they do not have Faith in Christ and what He did at the Cross on our behalf, but rather have faith in something else. While they may claim Faith in Christ, the truth is, by their own words and statements, they have a flawed faith. If they didn't, they wouldn't make such absurd statements about Christians being flawed, who have Scripturally repented of whatever it was that is in question.

FAITH

The entire Foundation of Christianity is based on Faith. And what do we mean by that?

It refers to Faith in what Christ did at the Cross on our behalf. That's why Paul said:

"Examine yourselves, whether you be in the Faith; prove your own selves. Know ye not your own selves, how that Jesus Christ is in you, except you be reprobates?" (II Cor. 13:5).

If you are to notice, Paul used the term *"the Faith,"* which in effect is a catchall phrase which defines Christianity. It is referred to as *"the Faith!"* However, it refers to what Christ did at the Cross and that exclusively. This means that the object of our faith, that is if it is to be *"the Faith,"* is to ever be the Cross of Christ (Rom. 6:3-5, 11).

While the problem of *"sin"* is the great problem with Christians, it is not exactly sin as we normally think. The sin is the moving of our Faith from the Cross of Christ to other things, hence Paul telling us to *"examine ourselves, whether we be in the Faith."*

And if the Believer allows his faith to be anchored in other things, acts of sin, i.e., *"works of the flesh,"* are definitely going to occur (Gal. 5:17, 19-21).

FIGHTING SIN?

There is no place in the Bible that we are told to fight or conquer sin. Now think about that for a moment! The truth is, many Christians fight sin constantly, which means they are trying to conquer something in their lives which is wrong. That's not the right way to go about it.

The only fight in which we are supposed to engage is *"the good fight of faith"* (I Tim. 6:12). The idea is this:

If you as a Believer try to fight sin or try to conquer sin, you are in essence saying that what Jesus did at the Cross is not enough, and that you must add your part to what He lacked. I would trust that immediately, one would see the futility of such action, even the insulting spirit toward Christ with such thinking. But yet, that is the position of most Christians, simply because they do not understand the Cross.

Jesus totally and completely conquered sin at the Cross. Paul said:

"Blotting out the handwriting of Ordinances that was against us, which was contrary to us, and took it out of the way, nailing it to His Cross;

"And having spoiled principalities and powers, He made a show of them openly, triumphing over them in it" (Col. 2:14-15).

John the Baptist said of Christ: *"Behold the Lamb of God, which taketh away the sin of the world"* (Jn. 1:29).

Paul said: *"But this Man* (Christ), *after He had offered one sacrifice for sins forever, set down on the right hand of God"* (Heb. 10:12).

This means that Jesus, in the offering of Himself in Sacrifice, did so *"for sins,"* and thereby, atoned for all sin, for all time.

So Jesus has already conquered sin in every capacity. Whenever you or I attempt to conquer sin, we are fighting a battle that's already been fought and completely won. But here is the real problem:

THE HOLY SPIRIT

When we do such a thing, and I continue to speak of our attempting to fight sin or to conquer sin, we cut off the help of the Holy Spirit. And please believe me, without the Holy Spirit we're not going anywhere.

The Holy Spirit works entirely within the parameters of the great Sacrifice of Christ. The Finished Work of Christ gives the Holy Spirit the legal right to do all the things which He does for us. He doesn't demand much of us, but He does demand that we evidence Faith in the Cross of Christ at all times. Now Satan will do his best to push our Faith away from the Cross to other things, hence Paul telling us to *"fight the good fight of faith."* There is a fight, but it's a fight to keep our Faith in the right place, which always and without exception is the Cross.

When my Faith is anchored exclusively in the Cross of Christ, I am completely *"in Christ"* (Rom. 8:1). Consequently, His victory is my victory! His overcoming power is my overcoming power! His life is my life!

That's what Jesus was talking about when He said: *"Come unto Me, all you who labor and are heavy laden, and I will give you rest"* (Mat. 11:28). Among other things, he was speaking of the rest that He gives us from trying to fight and conquer sin on our own, which in fact we cannot do. In Him we have rest from all of these things. In Him we walk entirely in victory.

THEIR NAME ADAM

Verse 2 further reads, *"And called their name Adam, in the day when they were created,"* refers to humankind in general being named Adam, beside the specific name for the first man.

(3) "AND ADAM LIVED AN HUNDRED AND THIRTY YEARS, AND BEGAT A SON IN HIS OWN LIKENESS, AND AFTER HIS IMAGE; AND CALLED HIS NAME SETH:"

The exegesis is:

1. Adam was 130 years old when Seth was born.

2. He begat a son in his own likeness, which refers to his fallen nature.

3. In fact, not only Seth, but all of Adam's sons were *"after his likeness,"* which means they were not after the Likeness of God.

BEGAT A SON IN HIS OWN LIKENESS

The phrase, *"And Adam lived an hundred and thirty years, and begat a son in his own likeness,"* presents that which is of extreme importance. As we have previously stated, it was the Plan of God that Adam and Eve, and all who would follow after them, would bring sons and daughters of God into the world (Lk. 3:38). But due to the Fall, Adam can only beget sons and daughters in his own likeness, which refers to his fallen, sinful nature.

These few words we are reading here in this Third Verse give us the reason for all the sin, wickedness, war, pain, sickness, suffering, and man's inhumanity to man, which characterizes the world. Men want to know the cause of evil; well they are looking here at the cause. It's man's fallen, sinful condition, which in effect, is now after his father Satan. In other words, due to the Fall, man now has a Satanic nature, hence all the evil perpetrated in this world.

Jesus said, and speaking to the Pharisees: *"You are of your father the Devil, and the lusts of your father you will do. He was a murderer from the beginning, and abode not in the Truth, because there is no Truth in him. When he speaks a lie, he speaks of his own: for he is a liar, and the father of it"* (Jn. 8:44).

Concerning the September 11, 2001 atrocities, committed by the Muslims against the United States, many called our Radio Network, asking why these Muslims couldn't see the wrong in what they were doing.

The fact is, they don't see the wrong, because they're doing what their father does, and I speak of Satan. He is a murderer and a liar, and his children follow in his footsteps, hence not only the September 11 atrocity, but every evil that takes place in the world, and for all time. The idea that the religion of Islam is a religion of love and peace is a joke! There is no love or peace outside of Christ! In fact, Islam is the very opposite of love and peace. It is hatred, war, and violence, and once again, simply because it is instigated by Satan, as are all religions in the world.

(Bible Christianity is not a religion, but rather a relationship, and with a Person, that Person being the Lord Jesus Christ.)

IMAGE

The phrase, *"And after his image,"* means that Adam no longer had the Image of God. The *"likeness"* and *"image"* are now after Satan.

SETH

The phrase, *"And called his name Seth,"* refers, as previously stated, to the child being given this name, which means *"appointed one,"* not to say that Seth was the Promised One, but through his line, the Promised One would come.

Due to their plight, and knowing to what degree they had fallen, at least to some extent, this child does represent a ray of hope.

However, it would be some 4,000 years before Jesus would finally come. While the lineage would remain intact, the condition of the world would be totally faithless for long periods of time, with the exception of a ray of light here and there. In fact, God would have to raise up an entire people, which He would do from the loins of Abraham and the womb of Sarah, before this *"Promised Seed"* could finally come.

(4) "AND THE DAYS OF ADAM AFTER HE HAD BEGOTTEN SETH WERE EIGHT HUNDRED YEARS: AND HE BEGAT SONS AND DAUGHTERS:

(5) "AND ALL THE DAYS THAT ADAM LIVED WERE NINE HUNDRED AND THIRTY YEARS: AND HE DIED."

The synopsis is:

1. Adam and Eve had many sons and daughters. Exactly how many, we aren't told.

2. Adam lived 930 years on this Earth.

3. Spiritual death finally wore down the physical body, and ultimately *"he died."*

SONS AND DAUGHTERS

Verse 4 reads: *"And the days of Adam after he had begotten Seth were eight hundred years, and he begat sons and daughters."* Some have claimed these numbers to be fictitious; however, such claims are made only because the individuals do not understand what the original intentions of God were.

Man was originally created to live forever. The Tree of Life was placed in the middle of the Garden for that very purpose. In fact, the Tree of Life, after a fashion, will be brought back during the coming Kingdom Age (Ezek. 47:12). It will be brought back eternally during the coming Perfect Age, described in Revelation 22:2.

It is sin which brought on death. When man died spiritually, which he did the moment he sinned, he would ultimately die physically.

Even then, the human body was so wondrously, so miraculously created by God, that even though it was of dust, it took nearly 1,000 years for sin to wear it down. We find up unto the flood, a period of some 1,600 years, and then some years immediately after the flood, men lived to astounding ages. And to be sure, these ages are correct.

By the time of Abraham, about 400 years after the flood, and about 2,000 years after the creation of Adam and Eve, the great Patriarch lived to 175 (Gen. 25:7). As a whole, the ages started gradually dropping until, by the time of David, the great king died at 70 years old. On a worldwide basis, that number hasn't changed much from then until now.

During the coming Kingdom Age, as we've already mentioned, longevity will once again be restored, and because the curse will be lifted from the Earth. In fact, in the Kingdom Age, there will be no death among those who have given their hearts and lives to the Lord Jesus Christ. They will live forever by virtue of the Tree of Life (Ezek. 47:12).

For those who do not accept Christ, and regrettably many won't, a man who dies at

NOTES

100 years old will be looked at as a child (Isa. 65:20).

DEATH

Verse 5 reads: *"And all the days that Adam lived were nine hundred and thirty years: and he died."*

Though he did not physically die the day he ate forbidden fruit, yet in that very day he became mortal; then he began to die; his whole life after was but a reprieve, a forfeited, condemned life; it was a wasting, dying life; he was not only like a criminal sentenced, but as one already crucified, that died slowly and by degrees.

As we look through Chapter 5, we find the humiliating record of man's weakness, and subjection to the rule of death. He might live for hundreds of years, and *"beget sons and daughters,"* but at last it must be recorded that *"he died."*

But whence comes this strange and dreaded thing — death? Paul gives us the answer: *"By one man sin entered into the world, and death by sin"* (Rom. 5:12). Here we have the origin of death. It came by sin. Sin broke the link which bound the creature to the Living God; and, that being done, he was handed over to the dominion of death, which dominion he had no power whatever to shake off. And this, be it observed, is one of the many proofs of the fact of man's total inability to meet God.

There can be no fellowship between God and man, save in the power of life; but man is under the power of death; hence, on natural grounds, there can be no fellowship. Life can have no fellowship with death, no more than light with darkness, or holiness with sin. If man is to meet God, he must do so on an entirely new ground, and on a new principle, even Faith; and this Faith enables him to recognize his own position as *"sold under sin"* and, therefore, subject to death; but at the same time, Faith enables him to apprehend God's character, as the dispenser of a new life — life beyond the power of death — a life which can never be touched by the enemy, nor forfeited by us, as long as our Faith remains intact.

(The author is indebted to C. H. Mackintosh for the material on death.)

(6) "AND SETH LIVED AN HUNDRED AND FIVE YEARS, AND BEGAT ENOS:

(7) "AND SETH LIVED AFTER HE BEGAT ENOS EIGHT HUNDRED AND SEVEN YEARS, AND BEGAT SONS AND DAUGHTERS:

(8) "AND ALL THE DAYS OF SETH WERE NINE HUNDRED AND TWELVE YEARS: AND HE DIED.

(9) "AND ENOS LIVED NINETY YEARS, AND BEGAT CAINAN:

(10) "AND ENOS LIVED AFTER HE BEGAT CAINAN EIGHT HUNDRED AND FIFTEEN YEARS, AND BEGAT SONS AND DAUGHTERS:

(11) "AND ALL THE DAYS OF ENOS WERE NINE HUNDRED AND FIVE YEARS: AND HE DIED.

(12) "AND CAINAN LIVED SEVENTY YEARS, AND BEGAT MAHALALEEL:

(13) "AND CAINAN LIVED AFTER HE BEGAT MAHALALEEL EIGHT HUNDRED AND FORTY YEARS, AND BEGAT SONS AND DAUGHTERS:

(14) "AND ALL THE DAYS OF CAINAN WERE NINE HUNDRED AND TEN YEARS: AND HE DIED.

(15) "AND MAHALALEEL LIVED SIXTY AND FIVE YEARS, AND BEGAT JARED:

(16) "AND MAHALALEEL LIVED AFTER HE BEGAT JARED EIGHT HUNDRED AND THIRTY YEARS, AND BEGAT SONS AND DAUGHTERS:

(17) "AND ALL THE DAYS OF MAHALALEEL WERE EIGHT HUNDRED NINETY AND FIVE YEARS: AND HE DIED.

(18) "AND JARED LIVED AN HUNDRED SIXTY AND TWO YEARS, AND HE BEGAT ENOCH:

(19) "AND JARED LIVED AFTER HE BEGAT ENOCH EIGHT HUNDRED YEARS, AND BEGAT SONS AND DAUGHTERS:

(20) "AND ALL THE DAYS OF JARED WERE NINE HUNDRED SIXTY AND TWO YEARS: AND HE DIED."

The diagram is:

1. As we see, the family history of this, the earthly race which began in Heaven, is marked by death.

2. No matter how long a member of this family lived, yet three words attend his name: *"and he died."*

NOTES

3. In looking at this we are humbled. We say with the Psalmist, *"Teach us to number our days"* (Ps. 90:12).

THE PROMISED SEED

There are some who claim that all of these men listed in Chapter 5 held onto the Promise of God as it regards the coming *"Promised Seed"*; however, other than Enoch, there is no proof of such, and actually, there is proof in the opposite direction. Enoch's Faith, as we shall see, was held up as an example. It stands to reason, if the others had entertained faith, the Holy Spirit would have pointed it out.

In fact, in Chapter 6 the Text points in the totally opposite direction, in other words, a faithless society.

It tells us of fallen angels cohabiting with women, which we will study upon arrival at those Verses. As well, the Lord said, *"My Spirit shall not always strive with man"* (Gen. 6:3).

Many Bible Scholars believe that the *"man"* of which is spoken here refers to Adam. If so, the Lord spoke to him 120 years before he died, in essence pleading with him to get right; however, and as stated, there is no record that he did.

In fact, the Scripture plainly says concerning these days that *"God saw that the wickedness of man was great in the Earth, and that every imagination of the thoughts of his heart was only evil continually."*

In fact, it became so bad that God *"repented that He had made man on the Earth, and it grieved Him at His heart"* (Gen. 6:5-6).

No, there are only two men listed in the Word of God who lived for God before the flood. Those two men were Abel and Enoch. While it is certainly true that Noah and his three sons fall into this category as well, they also lived after the flood. I hope there were more, but the Scripture gives no indication that such people existed.

THE HOLY SPIRIT

By the Holy Spirit having Moses to list this chronology in such a fashion, it is almost as if the Divine Spirit longs for a positive thing to say, especially considering the long lives they were given. But of these long lives, the only record is a name, and the fact *"he died."* Faith alone can be listed, and it seems there was no faith. They no longer believed there was a coming *"Promised Seed."*

Let this be a lesson to all of us. The only thing the Holy Spirit will record is faith, and we speak of Faith in Christ and what He did for us at the Cross. Nothing else matters! How much money we had or didn't have is of no consequence. Our station in life, or the lack thereof, no consequence. Whether we were handsome or homely, no consequence. Faith and Faith alone has eternal consequence.

The other day, I read a short obituary of an English Nobleman who died. All they could say of him was to mention his butterfly collection.

A baseball great died the other day, and his obituary read, *"He played the game well,"* or words to that effect.

Really, it doesn't matter what man has to say. It's what God says that counts. He said that Enoch had Faith! He said nothing as it regards his contemporaries. So let's look at Enoch.

(21) "AND ENOCH LIVED SIXTY AND FIVE YEARS, AND BEGAT METHUSELAH:

(22) "AND ENOCH WALKED WITH GOD AFTER HE BEGAT METHUSELAH THREE HUNDRED YEARS, AND BEGAT SONS AND DAUGHTERS:

(23) "AND ALL THE DAYS OF ENOCH WERE THREE HUNDRED SIXTY AND FIVE YEARS:

(24) "AND ENOCH WALKED WITH GOD: AND HE WAS NOT; FOR GOD TOOK HIM."

The composition is:

1. It seems that Enoch was converted when he was 65 years old.

2. At that age, he *"begat Methuselah,"* which figured prominently in the coming flood.

3. Enoch walked with God for some 300 years, which is the greatest thing that can be said of any person.

4. He was translated that he did not see death, *"for God took him."*

ENOCH

Verse 21 reads: *"And Enoch lived sixty and five years, and begat Methuselah."*

It is believed that Enoch was the first man to receive Heavenly Revelations of the secrets

of the universe in which he transmitted them in writing to later generations. He was also God's Prophet against the fallen angels. Tradition emphasizes his ethical teaching and especially his apocalyptic revelations of the course of world history down to the last judgment. It is believed that he will return to this Earth with Elijah, who was also translated, which will be during the last half of the Great Tribulation (Rev. 11:3-12).

As well, Jude quotes a prophecy attributed to Enoch (Jude, vs. 14).

It is claimed that he wrote five books, which have been placed in one Volume. They are:

1. The Book of Watchers.
2. The Similitudes.
3. The Astronomical Book.
4. The Book of Dreams.
5. The Epistle of Enoch. The complete text survives only in Ethiopic, but sections are also given in Greek.

Some claim that this material was written by various authors a short time before Christ, and circulated under the name of Enoch. Perhaps this is true; however, as mentioned, we do know that he did write some things, for Jude quoted him, and the Holy Spirit would not have sanctioned such had that particular material not been valid.

It seems that Enoch was 65 years old when he gave his heart and life to Christ, so to speak. Whatever happened to him at that particular time, the birth of Methuselah played a definite role. The name *"Methuselah"* means: *"The Deluge shall be sent when he is dead."*

In fact, a few weeks after Methuselah's death, the flood destroyed the world of the ungodly. From the time he was a little boy, Methuselah must have heard his father speak of this coming flood.

Sometime before the birth of Methuselah, perhaps a short time, Enoch gave his heart to God, with great revelations given to him shortly thereafter. Whatever it is that he was told, there are two things of which we are certain, but of which speaks volumes within themselves.

THE REVELATIONS

1. He was told of the Deluge that was coming upon the world, i.e., *"the flood."* Adam

was still alive at this time, probably about 600 to 700 years old. If 700, he would live another 230 years, which means that Enoch would have been a tremendous testimony to him, but seemingly to no avail. Noah was born approximately 100 years after Enoch was translated. No doubt, Methuselah related very graphically so to Noah the great Revelation his father had been given, with such concluding by the Lord commanding Noah to build the Ark, etc. Strangely enough, despite the Godliness of his father, and despite the fact that he was translated that he did not see death, which is one of the most phenomenal things in history, there is no record that Methuselah lived for God. And yet, God allowed him to live longer than any other human being, 969 years. This portrayed the Grace of God in giving man time to repent, but all to no avail!

2. The second Revelation of which we are certain that God gave to Enoch concerns the Second Coming of the Lord. Enoch prophesied, saying: *"Behold, the Lord cometh with ten thousands of His Saints,*

"To execute judgment upon all, and to convince all that are ungodly among them of all their ungodly deeds which they have ungodly committed, and of all their hard speeches which ungodly sinners have spoken against Him" (Jude, vss. 14-15).

So this which Paul mentioned, along with Daniel and John the Beloved in his writing of the Book of Revelation, along with Zechariah and others, was prophesied by Enoch about 3,400 years before the time of Paul, and about 5,400 years from this present time. To be sure, that great Revelation given to Enoch of old is certain of fulfillment, and we're closer today than ever before.

WALKED WITH GOD

Verse 22 reads: *"And Enoch walked with God after he begat Methuselah three hundred years, and begat sons and daughters."*

Enoch was *"the seventh from Adam"*; and it is deeply interesting to find that death was not suffered to triumph over *"the seventh"*; but that, in his case, God intervened, and made him a trophy of His Own glorious victory over all the power of death. The heart rejoices, after reading, six times, the sad

record, *"he died,"* to find that the seventh did not die; and when we ask, how was this? The answer is, *"by Faith."*

Enoch lived in the faith of his translation, and walked with God 300 years. This separated him, practically, from all others. To walk with God must necessarily put one outside the sphere of this world's thoughts.

Enoch realized this; for, in his day, the spirit of the world was manifested; and then, too, as now, it was opposed to all that was of God.

The sons of Cain, and all others for that matter, might spend their energies in the vain attempt to improve a cursed world, but Enoch found a better world, and lived in the power of it. His Faith was not given him to improve the world, but to walk with God. That is a statement that we should read very carefully.

To *"walk with God"* involves the knowledge of God's character as He has revealed it. It involves, too, the intelligence of the relationship in which we stand to Him. It is not a mere living by rules and regulations; nor laying down plans of actions; nor in resolutions to go hither and thither, to do this or that. To walk with God is far more than any or all of these things.

Sometimes it will carry us crossways of even our Brethren, that is, if they are not themselves walking with God. It may sometimes bring against us the charge of doing too much; at other times, of doing too little; but the Faith that enables one to *"walk with God,"* enables him also to attach the proper value to the thoughts of man.

Thus we have, in Abel and Enoch, most valuable instruction as to the sacrifice on which Faith rests, which is none other than the Cross of Christ.

THE CROSS AND THE COMING

It has been remarked that the Cross and the Coming of the Lord forms the termini or concluding point of the existence of the Church, and that in this concluding point is prefigured the sacrifice of Abel and the translation of Enoch. The Church knows her entire Justification through the Death and Resurrection of Christ, and she waits for the day when He shall come and receive her to Himself.

The Church, like Enoch, will be taken away from the evil around and the evil to come. Enoch was not left to see the world's evil rise to a head, and the Judgment of God poured forth upon it. He saw not *"the fountains of the great deep broken up,"* and the world drowned by water. He was taken away before any of these things occurred; and he stands before the eye of Faith as a beautiful figure of those *"who shall not all sleep, but shall all be changed, in a moment, in the twinkling of an eye"* (I Cor. 15:51-52).

Translation, not death, was the hope of Enoch; and as to the Church's hope, it is thus briefly expressed by the Apostle: *"To wait for His Son from Heaven"* (I Thess. 1:10).

(The author is indebted to C. H. Mackintosh for the material on Enoch walking with God.)

LIFE

Verse 23 reads: *"And all the days of Enoch were three hundred sixty and five years."*

Behind his name and his length of years, one will not find the three chilling words, *"and he died!"*

Three statements are made in the Bible respecting Enoch:

1. *"He walked with God"* (Gen., Chpt. 5).
2. *"He witnessed for God"* (Jude).
3. *"He pleased God"* (Heb., Chpt. 11).

Prior to the Fall, God walked with man; subsequent to the Fall, man, at least Enoch, walked with God.

If presently a man walks with God a few years after conversion, it is felt to be an encouraging proof of the power of Christ to save and to keep. But here is a man who walked with God 300 years! The possibility and power of this life of victory is made the more remarkable by the statement that he did not live a life of isolation (though he did live a life of separation), for he was a married man with a family.

Concerning *"all the days of Enoch,"* the first 65 years of Enoch's life were wasted, but the last 300 years present a testimony of unparalleled proportions.

TRANSLATED

Verse 24 reads: *"And Enoch walked with God: and he was not; for God took him."*

Paul would later write and say, *"and was not found,"* meaning that people looked for him

after his translation. But then it was finally concluded that the Lord had translated him *"that he should not see death"* (Heb. 11:5).

Paul also said: *"He had this testimony, that he pleased God."*

What was his testimony?

Paul said: *"But without faith it is impossible to please Him"* (Heb. 11:6).

So we know from this that the testimony which Enoch had was Faith in God.

And knowing that when we speak of Faith that we're speaking of Faith in Christ and what Christ would do for us at the Cross, we then know what type of Faith was possessed by Enoch.

Even though it says nothing about Sacrifices as it regards Enoch; however, in the great Hebrew lineup of Faith, Abel is mentioned immediately preceding Enoch. And it says of him: *"He was righteous, God testifying of his gifts: and by it he being dead yet speaks"* (Heb. 11:4).

So we know from this that Abel's *"more excellent sacrifice"* spoke to Enoch, as it has spoken to untold millions ever since.

(25) "AND METHUSELAH LIVED AN HUNDRED EIGHTY AND SEVEN YEARS, AND BEGAT LAMECH.

(26) "AND METHUSELAH LIVED AFTER HE BEGAT LAMECH SEVEN HUNDRED EIGHTY AND TWO YEARS, AND BEGAT SONS AND DAUGHTERS:

(27) "AND ALL THE DAYS OF METHUSELAH WERE NINE HUNDRED SIXTY AND NINE YEARS: AND HE DIED."

The exposition is:

1. Methuselah lived longer than anyone has ever lived, 969 years.

2. He apparently died just before Noah's flood.

3. Despite his Godly father, there is no record that he lived for God.

METHUSELAH

Methuselah is known for several things:

1. He lived longer than any other human being has ever lived, 969 years.

2. His very name meant, *"It shall be sent when he is dead."*

3. As a result, he was a walking testimony to the warning and the Grace of God, which no one heeded.

4. He was the son of Enoch, and the grandfather of Noah.

5. The year he died, the flood came, exactly as God said it would.

What a sad afterthought, that the Holy Spirit through Moses concluded the account of Methuselah by simply saying *"and he died."* No mention is made of faith. Nothing is said about a testimony which pleased God, as it had been spoken of his father Enoch. He was so close, but seemingly so far away.

If in fact Methuselah did not know the Lord, this is just another proof of the fallacy of generational Salvation. Every human being must be *"born again"* (Jn. 3:3). This means that every individual must have his own, personal experience with God. Enoch did! There's no record that Methuselah did! Have you?

(28) "AND LAMECH LIVED AN HUNDRED EIGHTY AND TWO YEARS, AND BEGAT A SON:

(29) "AND HE CALLED HIS NAME NOAH, SAYING, THIS SAME SHALL COMFORT US CONCERNING OUR WORK AND TOIL OF OUR HANDS, BECAUSE OF THE GROUND WHICH THE LORD HAS CURSED.

(30) "AND LAMECH LIVED AFTER HE BEGAT NOAH FIVE HUNDRED NINETY AND FIVE YEARS, AND BEGAT SONS AND DAUGHTERS:

(31) "AND ALL THE DAYS OF LAMECH WERE SEVEN HUNDRED SEVENTY AND SEVEN YEARS: AND HE DIED.

(32) "AND NOAH WAS FIVE HUNDRED YEARS OLD: AND NOAH BEGAT SHEM, HAM, AND JAPHETH."

The overview is:

1. We are now introduced to Noah, one of the central figures of the Bible, and of all time.

2. The name *"Noah,"* means, *"rest"*; however, Noah brought no rest, but in his days came the flood to punish human sin.

3. From the statements made in Verse 29 by his father Lamech, he seems to have been given a Revelation from the Lord that Noah would be special. Maybe he even thought that Noah would be the Promised Seed. Even though not the Promised Seed, he would be a Type of that coming Blessing.

NOAH

Verses 28 and 29 read: *"And Lamech lived an hundred eighty and two years, and begat a son:*

"And he called his name Noah, saying, this same shall comfort us concerning our work and toil of our hands, because of the ground which the LORD has cursed."

Noah figures prominently in the Biblical narrative in many ways:

1. It is evident that his father Lamech had been given a Revelation concerning this child. It had to do with the *"curse"* placed on the Earth by the Lord at the Fall of Adam and Eve, and seemed to imply that Noah would have something to do with removing this curse, or at the least, alleviating its effect.

2. Noah would be used by God in the preparation of the Ark, which would save the human race as it regards the deluge which God would send on the Earth. Consequently, the entirety of the present Earth goes back to Noah and his three sons, Shem, Ham, and Japheth. While Noah definitely wasn't the Promised Seed, and because sinful man could not produce such; still, he was definitely a Type of the Promised Seed.

The comfort he brought as it regards the curse had to do with the Ark, and the One Who would ultimately come through his lineage, Who would be the Son of God, and Who would remove the greater curse — the curse of the broken Law (Gal. 3:13).

LAMECH

Verses 30 and 31 read: *"And Lamech lived after he begat Noah five hundred ninety and five years, and begat sons and daughters:*

"And all the days of Lamech were seven hundred seventy and seven years: and he died."

As should be obvious, the Lamech introduced here is not the same as the Lamech of Genesis 4:19. The Lamech of Noah sang of prophecy, while the other Lamech sang of lust and vileness.

There is some indication here that this Lamech knew the Lord; however, regrettably, no Faith is mentioned, except in a vague way. At least some Faith was present in that he was given a Revelation of his son Noah, and as well that he gave the little boy a name which means, *"rest."* He died at 777 years old. And even in the years of his life, we find God's perfect number repeated three times. I would like to think that he is now with the One of which he spoke — the Lord.

SHEM, HAM, AND JAPHETH

Verse 32 reads: *"And Noah was five hundred years old: and Noah begat Shem, Ham, and Japheth."*

Due to the fact that every human being on the face of the Earth died in the flood with the exception of Noah and his family, this means that every person in the world today, and in fact every person who has lived since the time of Noah, is a descendant of either Shem, Ham, or Japheth. We will deal with this more fully when we come to the final Verses of Chapter 9.

"We gather together to ask the Lord's Blessing;
"He chastens and hastens His will to make known;
"The wicked oppressing now ceased from distressing,
"Sing praises to His Name: He forgets not His Own."

"Beside us to guide us, our God with us joining,
"Ordaining, maintaining His Kingdom Divine;
"So from the beginning the fight we were winning:
"Thou, Lord, was at our side, all glory be Thine!"

"We all do extol Thee, Thou Leader triumphant,
"And pray that Thou still our Defender will be.
"Let Your congregation escape tribulation:
"Your Name be ever praised! O Lord, make us free!"

CHAPTER 6

(1) "AND IT CAME TO PASS, WHEN MEN BEGAN TO MULTIPLY ON THE FACE

OF THE EARTH, AND DAUGHTERS WERE BORN UNTO THEM,

(2) "THAT THE SONS OF GOD SAW THE DAUGHTERS OF MEN THAT THEY WERE FAIR; AND THEY TOOK THEM WIVES OF ALL THEY CHOSE."

The exegesis is:

1. The events of this Chapter probably begin at about the time of Enoch, which was about 1,000 years before the flood.

2. There were, no doubt, several millions of people on the face of the Earth at that time.

3. The *"sons of God"* here refers to fallen angels.

POPULATION INCREASE

Verse 1 reads: *"And it came to pass, when men began to multiply on the face of the Earth, and daughters were born unto them."*

This is not meant to imply that the births of baby girls were more than that of baby boys, but is rather meant to set up the narrative for that which is about to be said.

As it regards the multiplication of the human race at this particular time, it was probably more rapid in proportion than it is even now. In the first place, sickness was not nearly as prevalent then as now, due to the fact that the human body was still in the process of being worn down. As previously stated, the tremendous ages given as to how long these individuals lived, as recorded in the previous Chapter, were not fables. They actually lived that long. As well, the indication is that their ability to father and bear children went through several hundreds of years for each couple, it seems (Gen. 5:4, 7, 10, 13, 16, 19, 22, 26).

SONS OF GOD

Verse 2 reads: *"That the sons of God saw the daughters of men that they were fair; and they took them wives of all which they chose."*

The *"sons of God"* portrayed here refer to the fallen angels which threw in their lot with Lucifer, who led a revolution against God sometime in eternity past. In order to spoil the human lineage, through which the Messiah would ultimately come, in effect to be the *"Last Adam,"* they would seek to corrupt that lineage and to do so by marrying the *"daughters of men,"* thereby producing a mongrel race, so to speak, of which at least some of these offspring turned out to be *"giants."* At any rate, all who were so affected were tainted in some way. I think the Scriptural evidence for this is replete. It is as follows:

1. Some claim that the term *"sons of God"* refers to the lineage of Seth, versus the lineage of Cain, which could be referred to as the *"sons of Satan."* However, the Bible gives no indication of such. As previously stated, there are only two men recorded who truly lived for God during the some 1,600 years from creation to the flood, who were Abel and Enoch. While there definitely may have been others, the Bible does not record that there were. Every evidence is that the entirety of the human race corrupted itself before God.

2. The term *"sons of God"* in the Old Testament, at least as it is used here, is never used of human beings, but always of Angels, whether righteous or fallen (Job 1:6; 2:1).

3. In his short Epistle, Jude mentions these particular *"angels."* He said that they *"kept not their first estate, but left their own habitation."* He then said what their sin was:

"Even as Sodom and Gomorrha, and the cities about them in like manner, giving themselves over to fornication, and going after strange flesh" (Jude, vss. 6-7).

Concerning this, Jude said that God *"has reserved* (them) *in everlasting chains under darkness unto the judgment of the great day."*

Peter said, and concerning Christ, that after His Crucifixion, and immediately before His Resurrection, He, *"preached unto the spirits in prison."*

He then went on to say: *"Which sometime* (at a particular point in time) *were disobedient, when once the longsuffering of God waited in the days of Noah, while the Ark was a preparing, wherein few, that is, eight souls were saved by water"* (I Pet. 3:19-20).

These *"spirits"* of which Peter speaks here don't refer to human beings, but rather Angels. Again, man is never referred to in the Bible in this fashion.

As well, the word *"preached"* as used here is not the normal word commonly used, which refers to *"good news,"* but rather a particular Greek word which means to *"make*

an announcement." What Jesus said to these fallen angels who were then locked up, and are still locked up, we aren't told. But we know, due to what Peter said about Noah, that these are the same fallen angels spoken of by Jude.

Every evidence is that these are the angels who attempted to corrupt the human race before the flood, and as we shall see, even after the flood, but were not successful in doing so, even though they came perilously close.

4. Some claim that Angels are sexless; however, Jude doesn't imply that, but rather the opposite, even as he used the term, *"giving themselves over to fornication, and going after strange flesh"* (Jude, vs. 7).

Some erroneously interpret Matthew 22:30 in order to buttress their claims: the Scripture says there, *"For in the Resurrection they* (Saints of God) *neither marry, nor are given in marriage, but are as the Angels of God in Heaven."*

This Passage doesn't say that Angels are sexless, but in essence that they never die; consequently, the Saints of God in the coming Resurrection, having Glorified Bodies, will fall into the same category; consequently, there is no need for the Redeemed to have children in order to keep the race in existence.

In fact, every indication is that Angels are of the male variety, hence taking unto themselves the *"daughters of men."* As well, Angels have spirit bodies. That's why Peter mentioned the fact of Jesus preaching to the *"spirits in prison."*

A spirit body is not that of flesh, blood, and bone; nevertheless, it is a body of substance, but on a different plane altogether. In fact, the Glorified Body, which all Saints will have at the First Resurrection, is similar, as far as ability is concerned. However, Glorified Bodies will be totally different in the sense that they will be flesh and bone, but with every indication that they will contain no blood (Lk. 24:39; I Jn. 3:2).

5. We know that all fallen Angels haven't been locked up in prison. In fact, untold numbers of these beings are working presently with Satan in his efforts against Christ and the Kingdom of God (Eph. 6:12). So *"these"* fallen angels were locked up in prison, which incidentally is in the heart of

the Earth, because of some terrible sin they committed, even worse than their rebellion against God with Lucifer. The sin or crime of which we speak can only be that which was addressed by Peter (I Pet. 3:19-20).

(3) "AND THE LORD SAID, MY SPIRIT SHALL NOT ALWAYS STRIVE WITH MAN, FOR THAT HE ALSO IS FLESH: YET HIS DAYS SHALL BE AN HUNDRED AND TWENTY YEARS."

The synopsis is:

1. It is the Spirit of God Who strives with man, in order to persuade him to come to God and to live for God.

2. The *"man"* of which is spoken here is not man in general, but rather Adam.

3. Concerning Adam, the Lord is saying that *"he also is flesh,"* referring to the fact that even though the first man was created personally by God, he still was flesh, and because of the Fall, must ultimately die.

4. From the time of this announcement, Adam was to be given 120 years to repent. There is no evidence that he did.

5. Many think that this 120 years refers to the time limit for man to repent before the flood; however, it has nothing to do with the flood, as we will later prove.

THE HOLY SPIRIT

The phrase, *"And the LORD said, My Spirit shall not always strive with man,"* presents the manner in which men are saved.

Jesus addressed this when speaking to Nicodemus. He said: *"Except a man be born of water* (born as a little baby, which is of the flesh) *and of the Spirit* (Born-Again), *he cannot enter into the Kingdom of God"* (Jn. 3:5).

Concerning the Born-Again experience, and the Holy Spirit, Jesus went on to say: *"The wind blows where it likes, and you hear the sound thereof, but cannot tell from where it comes, and where it goes: so is everyone who is born of the Spirit"* (Jn. 3:8).

Jesus also said: *"He* (the Holy Spirit) *will reprove* (convict) *the world of sin, and of righteousness, and of judgment"* (Jn. 16:8).

"Strive" as used in Genesis 6:3 refers to *"calling to man, contending with man, and pleading with man."*

So we learn from this that the Holy Spirit pleaded with Adam to get right with God, and

which He has been pleading with mankind ever since.

Jesus said: *"And I, if I be lifted up from the Earth* (lifted up on the Cross, i.e., 'the Crucifixion') *will draw all men unto Me"* (Jn. 12:32-33).

The way that men are drawn to Him is that the Holy Spirit does the drawing, and does so on the premise of the Sacrifice of Christ. In other words, what Jesus did at the Cross makes it possible for man to be brought to a right relationship with God, which he is through the Born-Again experience. Before the Cross, men were saved by looking forward to that coming Work, just as they are saved now by looking back to that Finished Work. Before the Cross, Jesus was looked at as prophetical, while now He is looked at as historical.

The Holy Spirit functions on the basis of three things:

1. He functions entirely within the parameters of the Word of God (Jn. 1:1).

2. He functions totally on the basis of the Person of Christ, and what Christ did at the Cross (Rom. 8:2).

3. He functions on the basis of Faith. This refers to Faith exclusively in Christ and what Christ did at the Cross (Jn. 16:8-14).

In fact, the story of the Bible, and the way the Holy Spirit works, can be found in the following three Scriptures; it is all in Christ:

1. *"In the beginning was the Word, and the Word was with God, and the Word was God"* (Jn. 1:1).

2. *"And the Word was made flesh, and dwelt among us, and we beheld His glory, the glory as of the only begotten of the Father, full of Grace and Truth"* (Jn. 1:14).

3. *"The next day John sees Jesus coming unto him, and says, Behold the Lamb of God, which takes away the sin of the world"* (Jn. 1:29).

Jesus Christ is the Living Word, Who became flesh, in order to die on the Cross that men might be saved. In the proverbial nutshell, that is the story of the Bible.

FLESH

The phrase, *"For that he also is flesh,"* speaks exclusively of Adam. While the Spirit of the Lord does strive with all men in general, more or less, it is to a specific man, namely Adam, of whom He speaks here.

Adam is the only man created entirely by God, other than the last Adam, the Lord Jesus Christ, so to speak. Inasmuch as Adam was created Personally by God, as would be obvious, he was looked at as something special. But yet, the Lord says here that because of the Fall and the entrance of sin, Adam must ultimately die. He is but flesh, which means he is not *"spirit"* as Angels. Even though some of the Angels sinned, even as we have been discussing, they did not physically die, and because they aren't physical, but rather spirit. Adam was created *"flesh."* While he would have lived forever had he not sinned, and by virtue of the Tree of Life, which God originally intended, because of the Fall, which instantly resulted in spiritual death, the life force, Who was God, was instantly taken away from Adam. Consequently, even though the body of flesh was originally created to live forever, without that life force, it will die. And so he did! And so have all who have followed him, with the exception of Enoch and Elijah, who will yet die, when they come back to the Earth to witness in Jerusalem, the last half of the coming Great Tribulation (Heb. 9:27; Rev. 11:3-12).

ONE HUNDRED AND TWENTY YEARS

The phrase, *"Yet his days shall be an hundred and twenty years,"* refers to the time that God would give Adam to repent, before he would die. It does not refer to the flood, as most Preachers claim. How do we know that?

The Bible says that *"Noah was five hundred years old: and Noah begat Shem, Ham, and Japheth"* (Gen. 5:32).

Sometime after his 500th birthday, Noah was given instructions to build the Ark, etc. The Scripture then says:

"And Noah was six hundred years old when the flood of waters was upon the Earth" (Gen. 7:6). So we know from this that it was 100 years or less from the time that God told Noah that the flood was coming, until it actually came.

As well, the Scripture also says that Shem was 100 years old when his son Arphaxad was born, which was two years after the flood (Gen. 11:10).

So if Shem was already born when the Lord spoke to Noah about the coming flood, and was only 98 years old when the flood ended, all of these Passages prove that the Lord wasn't speaking of the flood when He said, *"Yet his days shall be an hundred and twenty years."*

As well, the pronoun *"his"* in Genesis 6:3 is personal and not general; therefore, the Passage here is referring to Adam and not mankind as we think of such. In fact, the Hebrew words translated *"with man,"* actually say *"with the Adam."*

(4) "THERE WERE GIANTS IN THE EARTH IN THOSE DAYS; AND ALSO AFTER THAT, WHEN THE SONS OF GOD CAME IN UNTO THE DAUGHTERS OF MEN, AND THEY BEAR CHILDREN TO THEM, AND THE SAME BECAME MIGHTY MEN WHICH WERE OF OLD, MEN OF RENOWN."

The diagram is:

1. The *"giants"* were the product of the union of the *"sons of God"* and the *"daughters of men."*

2. These giants appeared before the flood, and after the flood.

3. The children born to this union *"became mighty men which were of old, men of renown."*

4. This was Satan's effort to corrupt the human bloodline, through which Christ must come, that is if the human race was to be redeemed. In other words, the coming *"Seed of the woman"* had to be of pure human stock, and not a mixture of human beings and Angels.

GIANTS

The phrase, *"There were giants in the Earth in those days; and also after that,"* refers, as is obvious, to two eruptions. *"Those days"* speak of the time before the flood, while *"also after that,"* speaks of the time after the flood. In fact, Goliath, who was killed by David, was one of those specimens. Satan specifically attempted to corrupt the inhabitants of the Promised Land, before the Children of Israel arrived there, and even after they arrived there. That's one of the reasons that the people of Israel were forbidden to intermarry with these heathen tribes, at least in most cases. All of the people of these tribes were not a product of the union between angels and women, but some were. In fact, that is at least one of the reasons that God gave instructions for all of certain tribes to be eliminated, even including the women and children.

Before the flood, there is some evidence that the entirety of the human race was so afflicted. All were not afflicted to the extent that all became *"giants,"* but some definitely were.

MIGHTY MEN

The phrase, *"When the sons of God came in unto the daughters of men, and they bear children to them, the same became mighty men which were of old, men of renown,"* proclaims this ungodly union.

It should go without saying that the lineage of the sons of Seth cohabiting with the *"daughters of men,"* as it refers to the line of Cain, would not produce *"mighty men, men of renown."* So, that among other things shoots down the hypotheses of these terms referring merely to the lineage of Seth and the lineage of Cain. While we always must be careful that we don't read more into the Text than we should, at the same time we must be careful that we do not read into the Text less than we should.

(5) "AND GOD SAW THAT THE WICKEDNESS OF MAN WAS GREAT IN THE EARTH, AND THAT EVERY IMAGINATION OF THE THOUGHTS OF HIS HEART WAS ONLY EVIL CONTINUALLY."

The structure is:

1. These *"men of renown,"* the giants, were developing more and more ways of wickedness.

2. Due to this infestation, the evil began with the very thought processes, and incorporated every human being.

3. This was a continuous action of evil which never let up.

WICKEDNESS

The phrase, *"And God saw that the wickedness of man was great in the Earth,"* refers to the state of man without God, or any influence of God. While the Holy Spirit did strive with men, it was different than His striving presently.

Before the Cross, the sin debt hung over man's head, which prevented the Holy Spirit

from entering into the hearts and lives of individuals. I speak of those who attempted to follow the Lord. To those who didn't know God, thereby having no desire for God, the Holy Spirit could strive with them only in the sense of particular things such as creation. In other words, inasmuch as there was a creation, such demanded a Creator, which should be obvious (Rom. 1:20). But whatever methods the Holy Spirit chose, He was very limited before the Cross as to what He could actually do.

And then on top of that, when we consider the invasion of the human race, so to speak, by fallen angels, with them marrying women and bringing forth a race of giants, which affected the human race in an extremely negative way, the condition of the world becomes obvious. *"Wickedness"* is the apt description!

Due to such increasing evil, and constantly increasing, the only thing that stopped man from destroying himself was the inability to do so. So, when God destroyed the world by water, He, in effect, was performing major surgery on creation. Had it not been done, the evil would have continued to deepen, until man would have ultimately found a way to completely destroy himself from the face of the Earth.

THE HEART AND THE MIND

The phrase, *"And that every imagination of the thoughts of his heart was only evil continually,"* presents a condition that has been accelerated by the union of ungodly angels and women. The idea is, every embodied thought which presented itself to the mind through the working of the heart, that is, the whole inner nature of man, *"was only evil continually."* In the Hebrew, the heart includes the mind. As well, in the Hebrew, the short phrase *"evil continually,"* refers to all the day, from morning to night, without reproof of conscience or fear of Divine justice.

Ellicott says: *"A more forcible picture of complete depravity could scarcely be drawn; and this corruption of man's inner nature is ascribed to the overthrow of all moral and social restraints."*

THE UNITED STATES

The United States of America is looked at by the rest of the world as a Christian nation.

The truth is, the nation is far from being Christian, but it is true that there are probably more professing Christians in this country than in most countries. How many who actually know the Lord is, however, something else again. At the same time, it must be quickly stated that it doesn't take many true Christians to exert great influence. Had there been only 10 Godly people in Sodom and Gomorrha, those twin cities would have been spared. So we see from that how valuable to a city, a nation, even the world in general, is the True Child of God.

Our political leaders and educators of this nation have tried to impress upon the rest of the world the notion of the political structure of democracy. In other words, if every nation in the world, they think, would adopt democracy, then they could enjoy the prosperity and freedom that we enjoy in this nation. However, they're missing the key ingredient:

The political spectrum of democracy without Godliness, without a strong foundation of the Bible, will fall woefully short.

For instance, just yesterday afternoon, I heard former President Clinton proclaim in a television speech how that we must come to terms with Islam, and that this could be done by proper education as it regards learning what Islam is, and them learning what Christianity is. Would to God it were that simple!

The truth is, it is not a matter of education, as much as we would like to think that such is the case, but rather things far deeper and far broader than meets the eye.

Islam is a religion inspired by the powers of darkness. In other words, it is controlled by demon spirits. The only answer for Islam, or any other religion in the world for that matter, and even the corrupt forms of Christianity, is *"Jesus Christ and Him Crucified."* The reason that America is tolerant of Islam, and all other religions for that matter, is because of the influence of true Christianity. To be sure, there is no tolerance in Muslim countries as it regards Christianity.

What makes true Christianity what it is, and we speak of love and peace, is because of the changed heart. Only the power of the Gospel of Christ can change the human heart, and to be sure, the heart of man is the problem. You can't educate that problem away, or psychoanalyze it away. It can only be changed by and through the *"born again"* experience. That alone can come about through the Gospel of Jesus Christ being preached, as it is anointed by the Holy Spirit (Jn. 3:16; I Cor. 1:18; 2:2, 5).

While democracy is a good form of government, it is not this political spectrum which has made this nation great, but rather the foundation on which democracy is built, which is the Word of God. Regrettably and sadly, we are forgetting that as a nation, with our country becoming more and more secular and less and less spiritual.

And why is our nation going in the wrong direction?

THE CHURCH

During the crisis of September 11, 2001, two Preachers made the statement over television that the reason for this horror could be laid at the doorstep of the homosexuals and the abortionists, etc. I beg to disagree!

While those sins are definitely evil and wicked, in truth, they are only symptoms of the real problem. And what is the real problem?

The real problem must be laid at the doorstep of the Church. In other words, the Church is to blame. It's no longer preaching the Cross, but rather every silly thing that man can imagine.

If the Church doesn't make the message of *"Jesus Christ and Him Crucified"* as the foundation of all that it is, then the Church ceases to be an effective instrument for Righteousness. It becomes merely another organization. And let me ask this question!

How many Preachers presently are preaching the Cross? How many Churches are holding up as its banner the Cross of Christ?

The answer is shocking! Almost none!

The Holy Spirit through Peter said: *"For the time is come that judgment must begin at the House of God: and if it first begin at us, what shall the end be of them who obey not the Gospel of God?"* (I Pet. 4:17).

This tells us that when judgment comes, the cause can be laid at the doorstep of the Church. It must *"first begin at us."*

So, instead of us blaming the homosexuals and the abortionists, and others, we had best begin with ourselves.

The Church is responsible for the Light. We are guardians of that Light. If it goes out, it is our fault. Jesus plainly said: *"You are the light of the world. A city that is set on an hill cannot be hid.*

"Neither do men light a candle, and put it under a bushel, but on a candlestick; and it gives light unto all who are in the house.

"Let your light so shine before men, that they may see your good works, and glorify your Father which is in Heaven" (Mat. 5:14-16).

I'm afraid that we haven't held this Light up very high, but have rather allowed it to be dimmed. And remember this, even though I am repetitive, it is the Cross and what Jesus did there that is the Light. Everything else must be subservient to that Message.

The light in the Holy Place of the Tabernacle of old was there for the purpose of the Priests offering up incense on the Altar of Incense, which symbolized Who Christ was, and What Christ would do in order to redeem humanity, which always spoke of the Cross. The coals of fire over which the incense was to be poured were to be brought from the Brazen Altar, which was a Type of the Cross.

The Light was for that alone, and if our message today is anything other than the Cross, it is a wasted message!

EVIL

The *"evil"* mentioned in this Fifth Verse can only be stopped by the Cross. That is the only answer for sin. There is no other.

If we think that psychology is the answer for sin, we're only fooling ourselves. It holds no answer whatsoever, and rather does extreme harm. It leads people away from the true help they can receive in Christ. And God have Mercy on the Churches, which espouse this ungodliness, and ungodliness it is!

Sin is a powerful force, and never remains static. In other words, it only gets worse and worse. The Holy Spirit through Paul likened it to *"leaven,"* which ultimately corrupts the whole (Gal. 5:9).

If we try to hold back sin in any way other than by and through the Cross, we will fail. It is just that simple!

TRUTH

To be sure, Satan always makes it very hard for the Truth to be received. There's always a price attached.

Perhaps Believers don't like the Messenger. In other words, the Messenger whom God has chosen to deliver a particular message is not approved of by much of the Church world. So, for Believers to receive the Truth which this individual is proclaiming will not be easy. They'll have to run the gauntlet of criticism and sarcasm if they accept what this individual teaches and preaches. Regrettably, most are not willing to do that!

In 1996, the Lord began to give me the great Message of the Cross. I use the word *"began,"* because it continues in its Revelation even unto this hour. It is the answer, for which I had sought for so long.

The Lord took me to the Word of God and explained Romans, Chapter 6 to me, and in effect said, *"The answer for which you seek is found in the Cross, and is found in the Cross alone."*

To be sure, this Message has revolutionized my life. It's not new, actually having been given to Paul nearly 2,000 years ago. I know beyond the shadow of a doubt that it is the answer to all spiritual weakness, spiritual declension, backsliding, bondages of sin and darkness, etc. I also know that without a proper understanding of the Cross, the Believer simply cannot live a victorious life. He can be saved, but as far as growing in Grace and the knowledge of the Lord, that he will not be able to do. As well, works of the flesh are going to dominate his life in some way.

The Lord doesn't have several answers, only one, and that is the Cross. If we miss that, we've missed everything. Sadly and regrettably, most of the Church is missing it.

Over the SonLife Radio Network, which covers at this time (2002) approximately 15 million people and will shortly cover the nation, is dedicated to the teaching of the Cross. We have a 90-minute Program every morning at 7 a.m. Central Standard Time, and which is aired again at 7 p.m. We also have a re-airing of programming which is about one year old, at 1 p.m. and 1 a.m., and that as well is aired seven days a week. So, out of a 24-hour period, there are about six hours a day dedicated to the teaching of the Word, of which all the teaching centers up in some way on the Cross. In fact, the Lord has raised up the SonLife Network for several reasons, but with the teaching of the Cross being central.

And yet, I grieve to a certain extent constantly, because I realize that many Christians will not receive this Message simply because they don't like me as the Messenger. However, the one whom God chooses is His business, and His business Alone. Unfortunately or fortunately, whichever way one would look at the situation, man has no choice as to whom the Lord chooses to deliver the Word. But regrettably, to reject the Messenger is at the same time to reject the Message. It is virtually impossible for it to be otherwise.

That's one of the reasons that Paul wrote the Book of Hebrews in the manner in which he did. It has no salutation, as his other Epistles; therefore, the author is not identified.

He was not held in too high regard by the Christian Jews, and inasmuch as this Epistle was written almost exclusively to the Jews, but yet having a great significance for Gentiles as well, the Apostle did all he could to make this Epistle acceptable. But I think it would go without saying that to reject Paul, would be to reject the Message which he preached, which incidentally, was the Cross. And regrettably, many rejected Paul.

As stated, Truth always comes with a price.

(6) "AND IT REPENTED THE LORD THAT HE HAD MADE MAN ON THE EARTH, AND IT GRIEVED HIM AT HIS HEART."

The construction is:

1. The fact that the Lord repents presents the truth that God, in consistency with His immutability, assumes a changed position in respect to changed man (Lange).

2. God repented that He had made man; but we never find Him repenting that He redeemed man (Henry).

3. When God repented that He had made man, He resolved to destroy man. Thus, they

NOTES

who truly repent of sin will resolve, in the strength of God's Grace, to mortify sin, and to destroy it.

REPENTANCE AND GOD

The phrase, *"And it repented the LORD that He had made man on the Earth,"* must be understood as it regards the following:

If we begin with the Omniscience and Omnipotence of God as our foundation, everything on Earth that happens is known beforehand by God. So He knew what man would do when He created man.

At the same time, we must understand and know that man has a free will; therefore, everything depends upon human choice and action. Both these sides are true, though our mental powers are too limited to properly combine them.

In the Word of God, the latter view concerning the will of man is kept more prominently in the foreground, because upon it depends human responsibility. Thus here, the overwhelming of mankind by a flood, and the subsequent abbreviation of life, is set before our eyes as painful to the Deity, and as well, contrary to His goodwill towards men, but necessitated by the extreme depravity of mankind.

DOES GOD PURPOSELY LIMIT
HIS OWN KNOWLEDGE?

I think not! Deity without full knowledge of all things, as well as almighty power, ceases to be Deity. But yet, the truth we must learn is that the ability to know all things, and even the power to do all things, do not at all predestine all things. While certain things are definitely predestined, all things definitely aren't predestined. God being totally Omniscient (all-knowing) and Omnipotent (all-powerful), in no way limits man's free moral agency. While God certainly could limit it all if He so desired, every indication in the Word of God is that He in no way takes such action. So we make a grand mistake if we take the position, *"What will be, will be!"*

While God definitely causes or allows all things, in no way does this limit man's free moral agency.

God knew that man would Fall, even before man was created. He also knew that He would redeem man, by becoming man, and dying on the Cross. This was planned by the Godhead even before the foundation of the world (I Pet. 1:18-20). But this by no means proves that God ordained that man would Fall. Man fell by his own free will. Could God have stopped him? Most definitely He could, but for God to get from man what He wanted and desired, which was to serve Him of his own free will, then God would have to let man follow his desires, even though God knew where all of that would lead.

CAN GOD CHANGE?

The question could better be asked, how do we reconcile the fact that God repented here, which means to change His mind as it regards man, when the Scripture plainly says concerning God, *"For I am the LORD, I change not"*? (Mal. 3:6).

The answer is relatively simple. God does not change as it regards His nature. It is literally impossible for Him to do so. But when it comes to changing as it regards situations developing on Earth, I think it can be said without any fear of contradiction that God is changing constantly in that regard.

He has plainly said over and over again, especially as it regards Israel, that if they did certain things then He would bless them. If they didn't do those things, Judgment would come, and that pure and simple is a change (Deut., Chpt. 28).

But these changes do not constitute a change in His nature. It is only conditions that are changing; therefore, He must change His direction according to those conditions. In fact, if He didn't, everything would be destroyed in a short period of time.

THE GRIEVING HEART OF GOD

The phrase, *"And it grieved Him at His heart,"* pertains to the fact that God is a Person. While He definitely isn't a human being, inasmuch as man was originally made in God's Image and Likeness, God has many of the same traits that man has.

Many Scholars claim that these statements as it regards God are merely anthropomorphic. And what does that mean?

Anthropomorphism is the ascribing of human characteristics to nonhuman things,

NOTES

in this case, to God. In other words, they say that these statements are in the Bible about God simply that we may understand God better. In other words, were He not described in that way, we would not be able to understand Him at all.

However, even though there certainly may be some few anthropomorphic statements in the Word of God regarding the Lord, as it regards the far greater majority of these statements, they aren't anthropomorphic. In other words, if the Holy Spirit, through Moses, said that God grieved in His heart as it regards what had become of man, but that isn't really what happened, then the Holy Spirit lied, which we know is not the case.

I think one can say without any fear of Scriptural contradiction that God has the same sort of emotions and passions as man, with one glaring exception. Whereas these passions and emotions regarding man have been warped and twisted because of the Fall and continued sin, that of course is not true as it regards God. His emotions and passions are perfectly righteous, and righteous in every respect; consequently, while God definitely does get angry, His anger is not the same type of anger which characterizes mankind. The same can be said for every other emotion and passion. If the Scripture here says that God grieved, and it definitely does, then most definitely, God does grieve over certain things.

Matthew Henry says concerning this: *"It speaks of His just and holy displeasure against sin and sinners; against sin as odious to His Holiness, and against sinners as obnoxious to His justice. He is pressed by the sins of His creatures (Amos 2:13); wearied (Isa. 43:24); broken (Ezek. 6:9); grieved (Ps. 95:10); and here, grieved to the heart, as men are when they are wronged and abused by those to whom they have been kind."*

Does God thus hate sin? And shall we not hate it? Has our sin grieved Him to the heart? And shall not we be grieved and pricked to the heart for such?

Henry went on to say: *"O that this consideration might humble us, and shame us, and that we may look upon Him Whom we have thus grieved, and thereby, mourn!"* (Zech. 12:10).

(7) "AND THE LORD SAID, I WILL DE-STROY MAN WHOM I HAVE CREATED FROM THE FACE OF THE EARTH; BOTH MAN, AND BEAST, AND THE CREEPING THING, AND THE FOWLS OF THE AIR; FOR IT REPENTETH ME THAT I HAVE MADE THEM."

The exposition is:

1. In the Hebrew, the destroying of man actually reads, *"I will wipe off man from the Earth."*

2. As stated, the wickedness of man had become so great, if God had not done this, man would ultimately have destroyed himself, although it would have taken much longer.

3. Man is to be destroyed because of sin, and his refusal to repent, irrespective of the strivings of the Lord with him to do so.

4. The animal kingdom was made for man, and if man is destroyed, there is no more purpose or reason for the animal kingdom. So it must be destroyed as well.

THE DESTRUCTION OF MAN

The phrase, *"And the LORD said, I will destroy man whom I have created from the face of the Earth,"* presents the fact that sin cannot be separated from the sinner, except by the Precious Blood of Christ. Sin, which is the ruination of all that is good, must be destroyed, or else the entirety of the creation of God will ultimately be destroyed. As previously stated, sin is like leaven, spreading and growing until it corrupts everything.

Inasmuch as sin had become part and parcel of the human being, and that man would not turn to God for deliverance from this plague, God had no choice then, and has no choice now, but to destroy man who is taken over by this dread malady of sin. In fact, sin ultimately destroys man anyway, so God only shortened the time period. Jesus said: *"The thief cometh not, but for to steal, and to kill, and to destroy"* (Jn. 10:10).

So there we have the end result of sin. *"It steals, it kills, and it destroys."*

So God was not cruel regarding what He did, anymore than a doctor is cruel for removing a cancer from a patient, which is intended to save the patient's life. While the removal of the cancer might cause pain and suffering, it is far better than death.

God performed major surgery on this Earth in the sending of the flood, because not to have done so would have endangered the entirety of his creation, even Heaven itself! So God was definitely not cruel in doing this thing, but rather merciful.

WHAT ABOUT THE CHILDREN?

Many would argue that the children, especially the babies, were innocent. So how can we rectify that?

That is true, in that the children and the babies were innocent; however, the full truth is that the entirety of the human race of that day, including the children and the babies, with the exception of Noah and his family, had been corrupted by the union of fallen angels and women, which produced, among other things, a race of giants, etc. While all were not giants, still all, with the exception of the one family mentioned, had been affected, which means that their bloodline had become contaminated by this union. So the children must be destroyed along with the adults.

DID THESE CHILDREN GO TO HEAVEN OR HELL?

The Scripture plainly tells us in the words of Abraham concerning God: *"Shall not the Judge of all the Earth do right?"* (Gen. 18:25).

It is my personal belief that all children below the age of accountability (and that age varies), which of course includes all babies, if they die, go to Heaven.

Concerning little children, Jesus said: *"Verily I say unto you, except you be converted, and become as little children, you shall not enter into the Kingdom of Heaven"* (Mat. 18:3).

This means, I believe, that all little children, even those of evil and corrupt parents, who die in that state, instantly go to be with the Lord. Children are innocent. They do not have the capacity to judge right and wrong. Even though they are born in sin, as are all, they are protected by God until they reach the age of accountability. As previously stated, that age varies according to the upbringing of the child. With some children, the age of accountability may very well be reached at five years old, or possibly even four years of age. With others, and due to their environment, it may go up to 10 or 12 years of age.

As stated, God is always merciful, and to be sure, He always does that which is right.

So, to answer the question, it is my belief that the children of the antediluvian age who perished in the flood were protected by the Lord, and upon death went to Paradise.

THE ANIMALS

The phrase, *"Both man, and beast, and the creeping thing, and the fowls of the air; for it repents Me that I have made them,"* refers to the overall picture of things.

God made the animal kingdom for man (Gen. 1:28); consequently, if mankind was destroyed from off the face of the Earth, there would be no need for the animal kingdom.

But as we shall see, there was one family that found Grace in the Eyes of the Lord; consequently, the animal kingdom was spared as well.

(8) "BUT NOAH FOUND GRACE IN THE EYES OF THE LORD.

(9) "THESE ARE THE GENERATIONS OF NOAH: NOAH WAS A JUST MAN AND PERFECT IN HIS GENERATIONS, AND NOAH WALKED WITH GOD.

(10) "AND NOAH BEGAT THREE SONS, SHEM, HAM, AND JAPHETH."

GRACE

Verse 8 reads: *"But Noah found Grace in the eyes of the LORD."*

This is the first place that Grace is found in the Bible. Grace refers to the Goodness of God extended to undeserving man. This means that God does good things for man, even though man does not deserve them, and in fact, cannot do anything to deserve them.

So that being the case, why does God show Grace to some, and not to others?

Even though man cannot earn anything from the Lord, cannot merit anything from the Lord, still, God rewards Grace on the principle of man's effort to live a life of obedience to God, even though he falls woefully short. Him falling woefully short means that he didn't earn the Grace, didn't merit the Grace, and in fact did nothing for the Grace. But God looks at the heart and judges accordingly, with Grace being extended or withheld on that premise.

Noah fell into the category of loving God, at least the best that he could, and doing his best to *"walk with God."* That's the reason the Scripture plainly says, *"Whosoever will!"* (Rev. 22:17).

God does not show Grace to those who have no desire for Him, as should be obvious from the Scriptures. As stated, every person is a free moral agent; consequently, God extends Grace or withholds Grace on the premise of what that person wants.

GENERATIONS

Verse 9 reads: *"These are the generations of Noah: Noah was a just man and perfect in his generations, and Noah walked with God."*

The word *"generations"* occurs twice in this Ninth Verse. Hebrew Scholars point out in the original Text the use of different words here, and that the first means *"pedigree"* and the second *"contemporaries"* (Williams).

The statement means that Noah and his family were perfect in their lineage, in that it had not been corrupted by the union of fallen angels and women. The contemporaries of Noah, which refers to all others who lived at that particular time, didn't fall into that category.

Not only was Noah of pure descent from Adam, but he was also pure in his conduct, for he walked habitually with God. The first word *"generations"* points to his natural birth, while the second word *"generations"* points to his spiritual birth (Heb. 11:7) (Williams).

Incidentally, the word *"perfect"* as used here does not mean sinless perfection, but rather that his lineage was perfect in that it had not been corrupted by the union of fallen angels with women.

Even though Noah found favor in the Eyes of God, and because of his hunger and thirst for God, he did not find such with the world; they hated and persecuted him, because both by his life and preaching he condemned the world.

God made more account of Noah than of all the world besides; and this made him greater and more truly honorable than all who were mighty men, and men of renown. Let this be the height of our ambition, to find Grace in the Eyes of the Lord; herein let us labor, that, present or absent, we may be accepted of Him (II Cor. 5:9). Those are highly favored whom God favors, irrespective as to what man says.

JUSTIFICATION

The Scripture says that *"Noah was a just man."* This means that he was justified before God by Faith. And how did this come about?

He was justified before God by Faith in the Promised Seed; for Paul later said that he was an heir of the Righteousness which is by Faith (Heb. 11:7).

But let the Reader understand that Justification by Faith has always come about by and exclusively through the Cross.

At the time of Noah, however, the great Patriarch would not have really known anything about the Cross; nevertheless, by the Sacrificial system in which he engaged, he knew that this Promised Seed would have to give His Life, of which the Sacrifices were a Type. According to the Word of the Lord, the Promised Seed, of which the Sacrifices symbolized, was to be the object of his Faith, and was to be the object of his Faith only. That's why he was referred to by the Holy Spirit as *"just."* And that is the only manner, Faith in the Finished Work of Christ, which brings Justification in the Eyes of God, Whose Eyes Alone actually matter, to the believing soul.

SHEM, HAM, AND JAPHETH

Verse 10 reads: *"And Noah begat three sons, Shem, Ham, and Japheth."*

We learn from the last Verse of the previous Chapter, that these sons were not born to Noah until he was some *"five hundred years old."* Verse 10 is placed here concerning the birth of the three sons of Noah, in order to point out the fact that their birth was without corruption. They were pure Adamite stock, one might say! All of this is very important inasmuch as every single human being on the face of the Earth owes his lineage to one of these men.

From *"Shem,"* we have the Semitic races, which includes the Jews, the Arabs, and some others. From this particular line as well, would come the Son of God, the *"Promised Seed."*

From the lineage of *"Ham,"* we have all of Africa, some of Central and South America, plus some of the Islands of the Sea.

The descendents of *"Japheth"* constitute Europe, Russia, much of the United States, along with China, Japan, and most of the Far East.

To simplify matters, one could probably say that some of the white and some of the brown races descended from Shem; some of the black, some of the brown, and some of the white races descended from Ham; some of the white, the red, and the yellow races descended from Japheth.

(11) "THE EARTH ALSO WAS CORRUPT BEFORE GOD, AND THE EARTH WAS FILLED WITH VIOLENCE.

(12) "AND GOD LOOKED UPON THE EARTH, AND, BEHOLD, IT WAS CORRUPT; FOR ALL FLESH HAD CORRUPTED HIS WAY UPON THE EARTH.

(13) "AND GOD SAID UNTO NOAH, THE END OF ALL FLESH IS COME BEFORE ME; FOR THE EARTH IS FILLED WITH VIOLENCE THROUGH THEM; AND, BEHOLD, I WILL DESTROY THEM WITH THE EARTH."

The overview is:

1. Due to wickedness, the Earth is now filled with violence.

2. *"All flesh had corrupted his way upon the Earth,"* meaning that all were corrupted respecting the lineage concerning the union of fallen angels and women.

3. God is left with no choice but to destroy the entirety of the antediluvian population, with the exception of Noah and his family.

VIOLENCE

Verse 11 reads: *"The Earth also was corrupt before God, and the Earth was filled with violence."*

The more corrupt, the more violence is involved.

To a certain extent, this characterizes all unredeemed; however, a perfect example is the religion of Islam. It nurtures and fosters violence, simply because of its great wickedness. In fact, there is nothing in the world more wicked than that particular religion. It is the most destructive, the most demeaning, and the most damning of all the religions of Satan. While all corruption and all violence are destructive, religious corruption and religious violence are the most destructive of all.

As well, let it be understood that all of this *"corruption"* and *"violence,"* is *"before God."* It is done in His Face, which Satan uses to insult Him.

"Corruption" refers here to the perverting and depraving of the worship of God (Ex. 32:7; Deut. 32:5; Judg. 2:19; II Chron. 27:2).

CORRUPT

Verse 12 reads: *"And God looked upon the Earth, and, behold, it was corrupt; for all flesh had corrupted his way upon the Earth."*

Horton says, *"The Earth was not only corrupt but people were working at making it more and more corrupt. That, too, will characterize the end of the Church Age — with people wanting to be open in their sin, wanting sinful lifestyles to be accepted, and encouraging others to partake of their sins."*

God knows all things, but the short phrase, *"God looked,"* denotes a special observance, as though He had instituted an inquiry into its real condition (Ps. 14:2; 33:13-14).

As previously stated, *"All flesh had corrupted his way,"* refers to the union of fallen angels and women, which resulted in corrupted flesh. In other words, the lineage was now marred. This was the plan of Satan to keep the Redeemer from coming into the world, Who could only function through an uncorrupted lineage.

DESTRUCTION

Verse 13 reads: *"And God said unto Noah, the end of all flesh is come before Me; for the Earth is filled with violence through them; and, behold, I will destroy them with the Earth."*

The phrase, *"For the Earth is filled with violence through them,"* actually says in the Hebrew, *"For the Earth is filled with violence from their faces."* The idea is, the flood of wickedness that comes up before God's Face goes out from their face in the sense of being perpetrated openly. In other words, they knew what they were doing, and, thereby, practice more and more sin, as if daring God to stop them.

They would find to their dismay that they had taken their sin too far, for God said unto Noah, *"I will destroy them from the Earth."*

Never forget, this Earth belongs to God. While Satan now operates its system, the

NOTES

Earth per se doesn't belong to the Evil One. It belongs to God! He Alone is the Creator!

He gave the dominion of it to man, but man forfeited that dominion to Satan, who does nothing but steal, kill, and destroy. We find from this that sin can go too far; evil can become too rampant; wickedness can pile up to an overwhelming degree. That being the case, God is forced to action.

God's fierce wrath over sin is something that human reason can never believe nor understand, and there is no doubt that when Noah spoke of the coming destruction, he was accused of lying. But what was the cause of God's burning anger?

The Earth, as the Text says, was filled with violence. This seems strange indeed, for God here does not say anything about the transgressions against the first table of the Divine Law, which was yet to be given, but mentions only those against the second. He did not take into consideration that the wicked blasphemed His Name, and persecuted His Word, but only that they sinned against one another by violating all that was right and lawful. For that reason, He destroyed all men and with them the whole creation.

There is much Divine Grace and love revealed in this that God complained more about the violence and injustice than about the sins committed directly against Him (Luther).

(14) "YOU MAKE AN ARK OF GOPHER WOOD; ROOMS SHALL YOU MAKE IN THE ARK, AND SHALL PITCH IT WITHIN AND WITHOUT WITH PITCH.

(15) "AND THIS IS THE FASHION WHICH YOU SHALL MAKE IT OF: THE LENGTH OF THE ARK SHALL BE THREE HUNDRED CUBITS, THE BREADTH OF IT FIFTY CUBITS, AND THE HEIGHT OF IT THIRTY CUBITS.

(16) "A WINDOW SHALL YOU MAKE TO THE ARK, AND IN A CUBIT SHALL YOU FINISH IT ABOVE; AND THE DOOR OF THE ARK SHALL YOU SET IN THE SIDE THEREOF; WITH LOWER, SECOND, AND THIRD STORIES SHALL YOU MAKE IT."

The exegesis is:

1. Noah is instructed to build an Ark.

2. Using 18 inches to the cubit, it was to be 450 feet long, 75 feet wide, and 45 feet high.

3. There were to be three floors to the Ark, 15 feet between each floor.

THE ARK

Verse 14 says: *"You make an Ark of gopher wood; rooms shall you make in the ark, and shall pitch it within and without with pitch."*

All stands now in contrast with Eden. There was a realm of life with the tree of death in its midst. This, a realm of death with the *"Tree of Life* (Christ)" in the midst. For of a smitten tree was the Ark made. Then, there was death in the tree; now, life in the Ark.

Regarding the Garden, God then said, *"Away from the tree!"* Satan said, *"Hasten to it!"* God now says, *"Hasten to the Ark and live!"* Satan says, *"Keep away from it!"* Conscience drove Adam from God. Revelation draws Noah to God. Conscience convicts the sinner of what he is. Revelation assures him of what an all-sufficient Saviour Christ is. He is as sure a Saviour to the sinner as the Ark was to Noah (Williams).

The *"gopher wood,"* was most likely Cypress.

The *"pitch"* addressed here was probably *"bitumen"* or *"asphalt."* The Hebrew actually says literally, *"Shall cover it with a covering."*

It carried the symbolism of the covering of sin. It was a Type of the Blood Covering which made expiation for sin.

THE FASHION

Verse 15 reads: *"And this is the fashion which you shall make it of: the length of the Ark shall be three hundred cubits, the breadth of it fifty cubits, and the height of it thirty cubits."*

Using 18 inches to the cubit, which is probably the correct measurement, this would mean that the Ark was 450 feet long, 75 feet wide, and 45 feet high.

However, there are some who claim that the cubit is to be measured at 21 inches, and some with other numbers. At any rate, the cubical content of the Ark was approximately three million feet.

Scientists declare the distinct species of four-footed animals to be about 250. If this number be doubled, and a certain proportion multiplied by seven for the clean animals, and if an equal number of birds be added and 12 cubic feet allotted to each animal and to each bird, the total number of cubic feet so used would be about one million, leaving approximately two million cubic feet for provisions. So I think it should be obvious that there was an abundance of room in the Ark for its inhabitants (Williams).

THE WINDOW AND THE DOOR

Verse 16 reads: *"A window shall you make to the ark, and in a cubit shall you finish it above; and the door of the Ark shall you set in the side thereof; with lower, second, and third stories shall you make it."*

The Hebrew words translated *"window"* and *"door,"* carry a different meaning than appears on the surface.

For instance, the word *"window"* was evidently a means, not merely of lighting the Ark, but also of ventilating it. As well, it could have been an open space one cubit in height (18 inches), running all round the Ark, and formed by not boarding over the upright beams, which would have given a sufficient supply of air, and would have been protected by the overhanging eaves of the roof.

As well, it is believed that the *"door"* probably extended throughout the three floors or stories.

It is believed that the Ark would have displaced about 30 thousand tons or more. Consequently, it was a monstrous ship, about one-third the size of our largest Aircraft Carrier. It is certain that Noah and his sons would have needed much help in the construction of this monster. To be sure, at that time, it was by far the largest vessel ever built.

This means that Noah must have been a man of means to have been able to fund such a large undertaking. How many years it took to build this vessel we aren't told, but we do know, as stated, that it didn't take 120 years.

Even though the information given here in Genesis is very sketchy, I feel certain that the Lord gave to Noah the plans in total detail as to how this vessel was to be constructed. In the first place, in the violence that accompanied the deluge, the spine or back of such a vessel would have been quickly broken, had it not been built according to certain specifications. Considering, as stated, that it was the largest vessel by far which had ever been built, I think the engineering ability prevalent at that particular time would have been woefully insufficient. The Lord had to be the One Who drew the plans in detail, and no doubt even helped Noah and the workers construct this vessel.

(17) "AND, BEHOLD, I, EVEN I, DO BRING A FLOOD OF WATERS UPON THE EARTH, TO DESTROY ALL FLESH, WHEREIN IS THE BREATH OF LIFE, FROM UNDER HEAVEN; AND EVERYTHING THAT IS IN THE EARTH SHALL DIE."

The synopsis is:

1. We learn from this the power of Almighty God, which means that He has almighty power.

2. Everything that was in the Earth died, which included all human beings, all animals, and all birds, with the exception of those with Noah in the Ark.

3. This means that the flood was worldwide.

A FLOOD OF WATERS

The phrase, *"And, behold, I, even I, do bring a flood of waters upon the Earth, to destroy all flesh, wherein is the breath of life, from under Heaven,"* presents the fact by the emphatic statement, that this is a Divine visitation, and not simply a natural occurrence. As we have previously stated, God had to perform major surgery on Earth, that is if mankind was to be saved at all! Sin is the ruination of all that is good. And the Bible plainly tells us that the wickedness in the Earth, resorting to wholesale mayhem and violence, had reached such proportions, that God simply could not allow it to continue. Let all know and understand that God was no less kind, gracious, merciful, and longsuffering in destroying the Earth by water, and all the inhabitants therein, than He was in the giving of His Son to die on a Cross.

Men delight in attributing cruelty to God in such an act, that is, if they believe it at all. However, is government cruel for stopping a serial killer from continuing his rampage? Would those in authority be cruel in the stopping of an individual who was going into a school with bombs strapped

around his body, in order to slaughter scores of little children? I think not! To be sure, if government didn't take proper steps, the world very quickly would go into anarchy.

No! God was not at all cruel in carrying out this act, but was rather merciful. God never takes steps of judgment until there is no more opportunity or chance for the situation to be salvaged. Even then, He measures the judgment in order to bring about a positive purpose.

DEATH

The phrase, *"And everything that is in the Earth shall die,"* refers to all things, with the exception of the fish in the sea (vs. 20). And of course, this was with the exception of Noah, his family, the animals, and fowls which he had been ordered to take with him in the Ark.

The death of the antediluvians was, in effect, a speeded up process. They were ultimately going to die anyway. So the main reason for the deluge was the following:

The fallen angels cohabiting with the daughters of men had corrupted the entirety of the human race, with the exception of Noah and his family. Consequently, the whole of humanity had to be completely blotted out, that is if civilization was to be salvaged.

This was Satan's great effort to stop the coming of the *"Promised Seed."* Dominion had been given to Adam, who had forfeited it to Satan. As a result, God would have to redeem the situation by becoming a man, which He did. Man had lost the dominion, and man would have to win back the dominion, which was done in the Person of the Lord Jesus Christ. If Satan could so sully the pure human strain by a mixture of angels and humans, the Plan of God to send the Promised Seed would be thwarted. As is obvious, the Evil One almost succeeded. But as it is said in many things, almost is not enough.

(18) "BUT WITH YOU WILL I ESTABLISH MY COVENANT; AND YOU SHALL COME INTO THE ARK, YOU, AND YOUR SONS, AND YOUR WIFE, AND YOUR SONS' WIVES WITH YOU."

The diagram is:

1. This is the first time that the word *"Covenant"* is used in the Bible.

2. However, even though the word *"Covenant"* has not been previously used in the Bible, still, a Covenant had been made between God and man. That Covenant is found in Genesis 3:15, concerning the sending of the Promised Seed into the Earth.

3. This Covenant of the Promised Seed would continue with Noah.

4. The *"Ark,"* which was a Type of Christ, would bring Noah and his family through the deluge.

COVENANT

The phrase, *"But with you will I establish My Covenant,"* could be argued that the Covenant mentioned here pertains to the Covenant described in Chapter 9, which God would make with Noah concerning the Earth and man's place in it. However, several things must be said in relationship to that.

The sentence structure of Verse 18 proclaims the fact that the Covenant of which God speaks here has already been established. In other words, it wasn't new with Noah. The idea seems to be that God is, in effect, telling Noah that despite the circumstances, the Covenant originally established with Adam would continue with Noah.

The reason I say that this Covenant was that which pertained to the Promised Seed (Gen. 3:15) is because without this Covenant, all the other Covenants are worthless. Every Covenant in the future would depend upon this particular Covenant.

God had promised the Saviour Who would bruise the head of the serpent. God, in effect, assures Noah that Christ would come from and through his lineage, and that, despite His wrath, He would permit this little band of Noah's family to ultimately become a large Church, so to speak.

The Covenant, therefore, embraced not only bodily protection, but also everlasting life by Faith in Christ.

God expressly said, *"I will establish My Covenant with you."* He did not mention Noah's sons, only Noah himself, by whom the Promise was handed down to Shem. The next great personality in this lineage is Abraham,

with the one following him being David, and from him ultimately to Mary, in whom the Covenant was fulfilled (Luther).

THE ARK

The phrase, *"And you shall come into the Ark, you, and your sons, and your wife, and your sons' wives with you,"* presents the fact that his entire family was saved.

Even though other matters were certainly at stake here, the truth is, Noah guarded his family against the intrusion of evil. Every evidence is, his sons and their wives (no children were yet born to his sons and their wives), heeded the Gospel Message. It is the obligation of the head of every family to lead their family in the ways of the Lord.

Just yesterday, the entirety of our family posed for a group photograph for the December 2001 issue of the Evangelist (front cover). This included Frances and myself, along with Donnie and Debbie, with our three grandchildren, Jennifer, Gabriel, and Matthew. Every member of the family knows Christ, and is Baptized with the Holy Spirit, and in one way or the other, in the Work of the Lord.

If the Lord never did anything else for me, that alone would be worth everything. Frances and I are so proud of our grandchildren, and above all the manner in which Donnie and Debbie have raised them in the fear of the Lord. The Holy Spirit through Solomon gave us the great Promise: *"Train up a child in the way he should go: and when he is old, he will not depart from it"* (Prov. 22:6).

(19) "AND OF EVERY LIVING THING OF ALL FLESH, TWO OF EVERY SORT SHALL YOU BRING INTO THE ARK, TO KEEP THEM ALIVE WITH YOU; THEY SHALL BE MALE AND FEMALE.

(20) "OF FOWLS AFTER THEIR KIND, AND OF CATTLE AFTER THEIR KIND, OF EVERY CREEPING THING OF THE EARTH AFTER HIS KIND, TWO OF EVERY SORT SHALL COME UNTO YOU, TO KEEP THEM ALIVE.

(21) "AND YOU TAKE UNTO YOU OF ALL FOOD THAT IS EATEN, AND YOU SHALL GATHER IT TO YOU; AND IT SHALL BE FOR FOOD FOR YOU, AND FOR THEM.

NOTES

(22) "THUS DID NOAH; ACCORDING TO ALL THAT GOD COMMANDED HIM, SO DID HE."

The structure is:

1. God commanded Noah to bring into the Ark two of every kind of animal and bird, male and female of each kind.

2. He did not have to go out and find them; they would come to him.

3. Noah was to lay up a sufficient supply of food for himself and the animals.

4. Noah minutely obeyed the Lord in all that was commanded him.

TWO OF EVERY SORT

Verse 19 reads: *"And of every living thing of all flesh, two of every sort shall you bring into the Ark, to keep them alive with you; they shall be male and female."*

As we see from this Verse and Verse 20, Noah was to put a male and female of every animal and every bird into the Ark, in order to repopulate the Earth as it would be after the flood.

At this juncture, the question begs to be asked as it regards the dinosaurs, and such like animals, along with types of winged creatures, which definitely existed at some point in time, but no longer do. When did they exist? What happened to them?

There is a possibility that these creatures existed before the flood, but were not included in the list of animals and fowls which were to be saved; however, the terminology of this Verse, *"Every living thing,"* etc., seems to militate against this. While there is very little mention of the animal creation in the Bible as it existed before the flood, however, what little is said militates against the dinosaurs and their kind existing at that particular time.

When the animal kingdom was created by God, the Scripture says that they were all *"brought unto Adam to see what he would call them"* (Gen. 2:19). From the terminology, I don't think that dinosaurs and such like would have been included in these creatures.

In fact, we are given no information in the Bible concerning these particular animals, so anything we say is speculation at best.

It is my personal thought that these animals roamed the Earth during the time that

Lucifer served as its governor, one might say, which was before Adam and Eve. At that time, he ruled under God, and in the capacity of Righteousness and Holiness. At a point in time, he fell, actually leading a revolution against God, which drew away approximately one-third of the angelic hosts. I also believe that Genesis 1:2 is the result of this revolution. In other words, God didn't originally create this Earth *"without form and void,"* but that it became that way because of a cataclysmic upheaval. That upheaval was the revolution of Lucifer.

How long the Earth continued in its original state after the revolution of Lucifer, we have no way of knowing. This we do know! Some of the dinosaur types were ferocious animals, which God did not create in this manner. In other words, they became that way as a result of the Fall of Lucifer and whatever happened on the Earth at that time. In fact, and bringing it up to the time of Adam and Eve and thereafter, all animals, when originally created by God at that time, were grass-eating. But some became flesh-eating as a result of the Fall. The same thing could have happened to the prehistoric animals.

If we try to put the dinosaurs into the antediluvian age, we simply leave too many questions unanswered.

I personally believe the dating methods, as it regards these prehistoric animals, are suspect; however, if in fact the dates given are correct, or even somewhat close, that would fit in perfectly with the explanation I've given as it regards the possible times that dinosaurs existed, etc.

THE ANIMALS WERE BROUGHT TO NOAH

Verse 20 reads: *"Of fowls after their kind, and of cattle after their kind, of every creeping thing of the Earth after his kind, two of every sort shall come unto you, to keep them alive."*

The Spirit of the Lord helped Noah in this endeavor. The Scripture plainly says as it regards their gathering, *"Shall come unto you."* The Lord Who created all things caused these animals to come to Noah, and to come to him in an orderly way, and at the right time. Not only that, they came in pairs, male and female.

From this Verse we also learn that fish were not included. The fish were already in the water; consequently, most of them would not be ill-affected by the flood.

Verse 21 reads: *"Take unto you of all food that is eaten, and you shall gather it to you; and it shall be for food for you, and for them."*

The Lord evidently told Noah how much food to stock, or else Noah just simply filled up the Ark, at least the space set aside for food, which is probably what happened. Inasmuch as God had given him the dimensions of the Ark, it is certain that those dimensions included all necessary space for that which would be placed in the Ark. It is doubtful that the Lord told Noah as to how long the water would be upon the Earth.

We find throughout the Bible, and with personal experience as well, that even though the Lord is very much attuned to fine detail, many times He will purposely leave us in the dark, in order that such may develop faith and trust in Him. He knows exactly what He will do, and is never at a loss as to the proper direction. We are to come to learn that, and to lean on Him, knowing that, proverbially speaking, he knows the way through the wilderness.

OBEDIENCE

Verse 22 reads: *"Thus did Noah; according to all that God commanded him, so did he."*

Martin Luther said, *"Human reason delights in what is extraordinary, but has no pleasure in what is ordinary."*

The obedience of Noah is laudatorial. And it is worthy in the following respect:

Surprisingly, it's easier for some people to obey God in the difficult things, but not so easy, it seems, in the simple things. But yet, for every extraordinary thing that God does for us, or gives us strength to do, there are 1,000 simple things He wants us to do, which do not seem so exciting. There were many things about the Ark which constituted the miracle-working Power of God; however, there were far more things which played out to simple, hard work, but which were necessary,

and were just as much the Commandment of God, as the miraculous things.

For instance, God could easily have spoken an Ark into existence, and could have done it in any variety of ways; however, He instead told Noah to build the thing. He even gave him the dimensions as to how it was to be built.

Far too many Christians get excited only as it regards the miraculous, or as Martin Luther stated, the extraordinary. If those people are to be noticed, little by little the Lord ceases using them for anything. If we're not faithful in the small things, the mundane things, the everyday things, the simple things, then for sure, we're not going to be faithful in the miraculous.

We should realize that every single thing the Lord does with the Believer constitutes a test. In other words, we're being tested as it regards our faith, our obedience, our consecration, our dedication, and in fact, every aspect of our spiritual lives. If we would look at everything in that fashion, understanding that it is a test, even the small things, I would think that we would possibly look at things a little differently.

When the Holy Spirit through Moses wrote of Noah, *"according to all that God commanded him, so did he,"* nothing greater could be said about any man!

One day when I stand before the Lord, and if I hear Him say of this Evangelist, as He said of the Patriarch so long, long ago, I will consider my life to have been worthwhile. We must understand that God hasn't called us to be successful, but rather to be faithful!

"Blessed assurance, Jesus is mine!
"Oh, what a foretaste of glory Divine!
"Heir of Salvation, purchase of God,
"Born of His Spirit, washed in His Blood."

"Perfect submission, perfect delight,
"Visions of rapture now burst on my sight;
"Angels descending, bring from above,
"Echoes of mercy, whispers of love."

"Perfect submission, all is at rest,
"I in my Saviour am happy and blest,
"Watching and waiting, looking above,
"Filled with His goodness, lost in His love."

CHAPTER 7

(1) "AND THE LORD SAID UNTO NOAH, COME THOU AND ALL YOUR HOUSE INTO THE ARK; FOR YOU HAVE I SEEN RIGHTEOUS BEFORE ME IN THIS GENERATION."

The construction is:

1. The Lord speaking to Noah could very well have been from between the Cherubim at the entrance to the Garden of Eden, which we can suppose had not yet vanished from the Earth.

2. *"Come thou and all your house into the Ark,"* shows that God was the first One in the Ark.

3. *"To be righteous before God,"* which God concluded Noah to be, presents the usual Scriptural phrase for Justification.

THE LORD SPEAKS TO NOAH

The phrase, *"And the LORD said unto Noah,"* proclaims the fact that the time had now come. The Ark is finished, and the world is on the very eve of destruction.

And yet the world of Noah's time, and even unto this very hour, saw nothing unusual about events. The prattle of this Preacher was of no consequence to them, and to be sure, Noah definitely preached the Gospel to these people, and did so year in and year out. The Holy Spirit, through Peter, referred to him as *"a Preacher of Righteousness"* (II Pet. 2:5).

The idea of a deluge was a joke to them. It is positive that the saga of Noah building this monstrous boat was known over the entirety of the world of that day. He, no doubt, was the butt of every type of joke. *"A flood was coming, which would cover the highest mountains, and drown every person on the face of the Earth,"* was so much senseless drivel to the inhabitants. Not one single person accepted the Message. Not one single person believed what this Preacher said. Not one single person heeded the call. Even those who helped Noah build the Ark didn't believe a single word that he said.

TERROR-STRICKEN

To be sure, Noah definitely believed what God had said. In fact, the human race owes

its existence to the fact that one man was terror-stricken. The Epistle to the Hebrews states that Noah prepared this Ark because he believed the Divine warning (Heb. 11:7).

"All flesh" had become so bad that it could not be worse; wherefore nothing remained but for God to destroy it totally; and, at the same time, to save all those who should be found, according to His eternal counsels, linked with Noah, the only righteous man then existing. But regrettably, none did cling to Noah.

This brings out the Doctrine of the Cross in a very vivid manner. There we find, at once, God's judgment of nature with all its evil; and, at the same time, the Revelation of His Saving Grace, in all its fullness, and in all its perfect adaptation to those who have really reached the lowest point of their moral condition, as judged by God.

The Scripture says: *"The Dayspring from on high has visited us"* (Lk. 1:78).

Where?

Just where we are, as sinners. God has come down to the very deepest depth of our ruin. There is not a point in all the sinner's state to which the light of that blessed Dayspring has not penetrated; but if it has thus penetrated, it must, by virtue of what it is, reveal our true character. The light must judge everything contrary to itself; but, while it does so, it also *"gives the knowledge of Salvation through the remission of sins."* The Cross, while it reveals God's judgment upon *"all flesh,"* reveals His Salvation for the lost and guilty sinner. Sin is perfectly judged — the sinner perfectly saved — God perfectly revealed, and perfectly glorified, in the Cross (Mackintosh).

THE COMMAND

The phrase, *"Come thou and all your house into the Ark,"* presents the fact that God is the first One in the Ark. Had He been outside, He would have said, *"Go into the Ark!"* Inasmuch as He was in the Ark, He would bid Noah to come.

Methuselah, Noah's grandfather, died the same year that the flood came. He had lived longer than any other human being had ever lived, 969 years. His very life had been a warning of the deluge that was to come, for his name means *"when you are dead, the deluge will come."*

It is for certain that Methuselah had spoken to Noah often concerning the coming catastrophe. And as well, Methuselah no doubt spoke to his grandson about his father Enoch, who was translated that he did not see death. To what degree Methuselah lived for God we do not know. The Scripture does not mention his faith, so we're left with a blank concerning that all-important aspect of his life. And so now the time had come to enter the Ark.

There may have been a crowd there that day that Noah and his family went into the Ark. And then again, maybe they thought so little of his Message that they didn't bother to witness this event.

If a crowd had gathered, no doubt the laughter of sarcasm filled the air, as eight people entered the Ark. If that actually happened, maybe Noah gave a last invitation, but all to no avail.

RIGHTEOUS

The phrase, *"For you have I seen righteous before Me in this generation,"* refers to Noah's Faith in the coming Redeemer, for that is the only Faith that God will recognize. Paul wrote of him:

"And became heir of the Righteousness which is by faith" (Heb. 11:7). The Faith addressed here speaks of Christ and what He would do at the Cross. He only had a dim view of that coming time, but as dim as it was, he placed his past, his present, and his future in the Promise of God to send the *"Seed."*

(2) "OF EVERY CLEAN BEAST YOU SHALL TAKE TO YOURSELF BY SEVENS, THE MALE AND HIS FEMALE: AND OF BEASTS THAT ARE NOT CLEAN BY TWO, THE MALE AND HIS FEMALE.

(3) "OF FOWLS ALSO OF THE AIR BY SEVENS, THE MALE AND THE FEMALE; TO KEEP SEED ALIVE UPON THE FACE OF ALL THE EARTH."

The exposition is:

1. Added information is given here concerning the animals to be taken. Concerning the animals which God labeled as *"clean,"* seven pairs of male and female were to be taken.

2. The animals which God deemed to be unclean, only one pair of each was to be taken, the male and the female.

3. Of the clean fowls of the air, seven pairs of these, male and female, were to be taken as well.

CLEAN BEASTS

Verse 2 reads: *"Of every clean beast you shall take to yourself by sevens, the male and his female: and of beasts that are not clean by two, the male and his female."*

Which were the clean beasts?

There can be no reference here to the Levitical Law, which had respect to human food, etc. Probably the clean animals mentioned were such as from the days of Adam and Abel as had been offered in sacrifice. Thus, provision was made for Noah's sacrifice on his exit from the Ark, when the flood would subside. As well, it would also be for his possession of a small heard of such animals as would be most useful to him amid the desolation which must have existed for a long time after the flood.

The clean beasts would, therefore, be oxen, sheep, goats, and possibly rams. Immediately after the flood, we know that Noah offered up sacrifices, with the animals being used (Gen. 8:20).

The unclean animals would fall into the category of all others beside those named. Only a pair of the unclean were to be taken.

CLEAN FOWLS

Verse 3 reads: *"Of fowls also of the air by sevens, the male and the female; to keep seed alive upon the face of all the earth."*

The birds mentioned here were as well to be of the *"clean"* variety. Seven pairs of these, males and females, were to be taken. Of birds, the dove would especially be clean. Of others, we have no knowledge. The unclean of the *"fowls"* were to be only one pair each, male and female.

(4) "FOR YET SEVEN DAYS, AND I WILL CAUSE IT TO RAIN UPON THE EARTH FORTY DAYS AND FORTY NIGHTS; AND EVERY LIVING SUBSTANCE THAT I HAVE MADE WILL I DESTROY FROM OFF THE FACE OF THE EARTH.

(5) "AND NOAH DID ACCORDING UNTO ALL THAT THE LORD COMMANDED HIM."

The overview is:

1. The announcement was given by God; in seven days, the flood would commence.

2. It would begin with the rain, which would last for forty days and forty nights. As well, *"the fountains of the great deep would be broken up"* (vs. 11).

3. God vows to destroy everything!

4. Once again, the statement is made that Noah did everything the Lord commanded him to do.

SEVEN DAYS

Verse 4 reads: *"For yet seven days, and I will cause it to rain upon the Earth forty days and forty nights; and every living substance that I have made will I destroy from off the face of the Earth."*

The command to enter the Ark was given a week before the rains would begin. It would rain for forty days and forty nights, with the implication being that the Earth had never seen rain such as this. To describe it, the Holy Spirit through Moses used the phrase, *"the windows of Heaven were opened."* This speaks of a deluge, and when it is considered that *"all the fountains of the great deep were broken up,"* we now begin to get the idea as to the magnitude of this thing. To be sure, it will destroy every *"living substance"* from off the face of the Earth, which speaks of a universal flood.

It has been taught by some that it had never rained up to this time, with the Lord watering the ground with *"a mist."* However, Genesis 2:5-6 doesn't say that it did not rain. It was referring to the third day of creation (Gen. 1:11-13). At the end of the six days of creation, and God resting on the seventh, every indication is that the elements responded normally thereafter.

So, while the people of the antediluvian age were accustomed to rain, to be sure, they were not accustomed to the amount of rain that would fall in the coming forty days and forty nights.

OBEDIENCE

Verse 5 reads: *"And Noah did according unto all that the LORD commanded him."*

This is the second time that the Holy Spirit through Moses speaks of Noah's obedience.

The first time that his obedience is addressed (Gen. 6:22), it refers to the building of the Ark, and the preparation of getting the animals ready. The second time refers to further preparation of the animals, and as well, to go into the Ark with his family.

In these two examples of obedience, we have Sanctification and Justification. Sanctification *"prepares"* the believing soul, while Justification *"declares"* the believing soul. If it is to be noticed, in I Corinthians 6:11, Sanctification precedes Justification. It is impossible to legally declare one clean, which is Justification, until one has been cleansed, which is Sanctification.

Sanctification prepares the believing soul to enter Christ, as exampled by Noah preparing the Ark, while Justification portrays the believing soul being in Christ, exampled by Noah and his family now being in the Ark, which is a Type of Christ.

(6) "AND NOAH WAS SIX HUNDRED YEARS OLD WHEN THE FLOOD OF WATERS WAS UPON THE EARTH.

(7) "AND NOAH WENT IN, AND HIS SONS, AND HIS WIFE, AND HIS SONS' WIVES WITH HIM, INTO THE ARK, BECAUSE OF THE WATERS OF THE FLOOD.

(8) "OF CLEAN BEASTS, AND OF BEASTS THAT ARE NOT CLEAN, AND OF FOWLS, AND OF EVERY THING THAT CREEPETH UPON THE EARTH,

(9) "THERE WENT IN TWO AND TWO UNTO NOAH INTO THE ARK, THE MALE AND THE FEMALE, AS GOD HAD COMMANDED NOAH."

The synopsis is:

1. Verse 6 proves that the 120 years of Genesis 6:3 had nothing to do with the time limit unto the flood.

2. Noah obeyed the Lord, and went into the Ark.

3. The animals went in as well.

THE TIME OF WARNING

Verse 6 reads: *"And Noah was six hundred years old when the flood of waters was upon the Earth."*

Genesis 5:32 says that Noah was 500 years old when his three sons were born. The Verse of our study says that Noah was 600 years old when the flood came.

How long it was after the three sons of Noah were born that God gave commandment to Noah to build the Ark, we aren't told. But we do know it wasn't 120 years. As stated, Genesis 6:3 has to do with a warning given to Adam, and doesn't refer to the flood, nor does it refer to the time span that man will live in general.

As we've also said, the phrase *"with man,"* of Genesis 6:3, in the original Hebrew, actually says *"with the Adam."* Therefore, Genesis 6:3 is a warning to Adam, and not to the antediluvians as it regards the flood.

As stated, this was Noah's 600th year. The number six *"is generally a Scriptural symbol of suffering. In the Apocalypse the sixth seal, the sixth trumpet, and the sixth vial introduce critical periods of affliction"* (Wordsworth).

Six is actually man's number, and refers to incompletion, imperfection, and insolvency. If there was ever a time of such on the Earth, this particular period of the flood was that time. Man had refused God's Way, so man would have his way, and it would not be a very pleasant prospect.

So I don't think it was coincidental that this was Noah's 600th birthday.

AT THE COMMANDMENT OF THE LORD

Verse 7 reads: *"And Noah went in, and his sons, and his wife, and his sons' wives with him, into the Ark, because of the waters of the flood."*

At the command of the Lord, Noah, and his family prepared to go into the Ark a full week before the rains would begin. This was *"a proof of Faith and a warning to the world."*

Concerning this time, Paul said in Hebrews 11:7 that they did this thing *"being moved with fear and impelled by faith."* As we've already stated, this man was terror-stricken. Noah built this Ark because he believed the Divine warning. Regrettably, he was the only one that believed that warning.

When Paul wrote, *"By faith Noah, being warned of God of things not seen as yet, moved with fear, prepared an Ark to the saving of his house; by the which he condemned the world, and became heir of Righteousness which is of Faith,"* we should try to understand the world in which Noah lived then,

NOTES

and as well, the solemn, fearful statement as made by the Lord concerning destruction.

The *"fear of God"* is one of the attributes of the Holy Spirit. In fact, the Holy Spirit is referred to as *"the Spirit of knowledge and of the fear of the LORD"* (Isa. 11:2). If men do not have a proper fear of the Lord, which refers to proper awe, respect, and reverence, then they will little serve Him. And one of the terrible sins of the modern Church is that it has very little fear of the Lord.

Preachers routinely stand before congregations, glibly mouthing the words, *"God told me,"* which much of the time is used to wheedle money out of people. While the Lord truly does speak to people, and there are certainly times that *"God told me"* is correct and right, so often it isn't. Listen again to what the Prophet Isaiah said:

"But to this man will I look, even to him who is poor and of a contrite spirit, and trembleth at My Word" (Isa. 66:2).

THE CROSS OF CHRIST

I personally believe that it is absolutely imperative for a Believer to have a proper understanding of the Cross, before they can at the same time have a proper fear of God. In fact, I label all false direction as an improper understanding of the Cross. To the degree that the Cross is misunderstood, or misinterpreted, to that degree will individuals at the same time misunderstand the entirety of the Word of God in some fashion. And regrettably, most of the modern Church world has little understanding of the Cross — and I don't think I exaggerate when I use the word *"most."*

To not understand the Cross as it regards Christianity and the Bible, is like a mechanic who doesn't understand engines, or a pilot who doesn't understand airplanes, or a lawyer who doesn't understand law. It is inconceivable that a Christian wouldn't have a proper understanding of the Cross.

A PROPER UNDERSTANDING

The following will be very brief, but will give you, I trust, at least an elementary understanding of that of which we speak. So let's ask the question:

What do we mean by having a proper understanding of the Cross?

1. We mean that the Message of the Cross of Christ is the Foundation of the Faith, in essence, the foundation of the entirety of the Bible. In fact, it is the story of the Bible. Jesus said: *"And I, if I be lifted up from the Earth, will draw all men unto Me"* (Jn. 12:32).

Jesus using the words *"lifted up,"* refers to being lifted up on the Cross. The Cross, rather the preaching of the Cross, is that and that alone which will draw men to Christ, at least draw men properly to Christ. That's why Paul said:

"For Christ sent me not to baptize, but to preach the Gospel: not with wisdom of words, lest the Cross of Christ should be made of none effect" (I Cor. 1:17).

2. It is what Jesus did at the Cross, and what He did there alone which brings Salvation to believing sinners. He said: *"For God so loved the world, that He gave His only Begotten Son, that whosoever believeth in Him should not perish, but have everlasting life"* (Jn. 3:16).

Whenever it says in the Bible that God *"gave,"* as it regards eternal life, or His Son, without exception, it is always speaking of God giving Christ on the Cross in order that men might be saved.

3. As Jesus Christ and Him Crucified is the Message of Redemption, it is also the Message of Sanctification. In other words, the only way, and I emphasize the word *"only,"* that a Believer can live an overcoming, Christian life after he has given his heart to God, which refers to the Sanctification process, is by making the Cross the object of His Faith. Now many Christians understand the Cross as it regards the initial Salvation process, but have no knowledge whatsoever as it involves the Sanctification process. But what did Paul say?

"Know ye not, that so many of us as were baptized into Jesus Christ were baptized into His death?" (Rom. 6:3).

Jesus is <u>not</u> speaking here of Water Baptism, as most think, but rather the death of Christ on the Cross. He uses the word *"baptized,"* because it is the strongest word that can be used in this particular sense. It has to do with the fact that Jesus Christ was our Substitute. In other words, everything He did was all done for you and me, and not at

all for Himself. He came to this world for us, lived a Perfect Life for us, and then died on the Cross, all for us.

When the believing sinner expresses Faith in Christ, in the mind of God that sinner is placed in the death of Christ. That's why Paul constantly uses the term *"in Christ,"* or one of its derivatives such as *"in Him"* or *"in Whom,"* etc.

But not only did we die with Him, we were also *"buried with Him by baptism into death"* (Rom. 6:4). Once again, this has nothing to do with Water Baptism, but speaks actually of being buried with Christ, which refers to what we once were.

The Lord doesn't try to rehabilitate a person. In fact, the word *"rehabilitation"* or one of its derivatives, is not found in the Bible. That is a word that comes from the world of psychology, and has no Scriptural validity, or in fact, no validity whatsoever.

In Scriptural terminology, the sinner must die. And when we speak of the sinner dying, we're not speaking of the heart ceasing its beating, etc., but rather that he die in a spiritual sense. In other words, we die to what we once were, and it's all done in Christ. As stated, He is our Substitute. Once again as stated, the Lord doesn't rehabilitate anyone, but rather makes of that person a brand-new creation (II Cor. 5:17). But it doesn't stop there:

We are then raised with Christ *"in newness of life,"* which means that we participate in His Resurrection (Rom. 6:4).

All of this refers to the Cross, the death of Christ, His burial, and His Resurrection. All of this was done as our Substitute, which means it was done for you and me.

Understanding that, we are to then *"reckon ourselves to be dead indeed unto sin, but alive unto God through Jesus Christ our Lord"* (Rom. 6:11).

This plainly tells us that our Faith must ever rest in what Christ did for us at the Cross. Concerning this, the Scripture says: *"For in that He died, He died unto sin once: but in that He lives, He lives unto God"* (Rom. 6:10).

This means that Jesus totally and completely atoned for all sin at the Cross, by the giving of Himself, and the shedding of His Life's Blood. So that means that all sin is defeated, which means that you and I can

JIMMY SWAGGART BIBLE COMMENTARY

defeat every sin within our lives, if we will keep our Faith anchored in the Cross. In fact, the Scripture plainly says:

"For sin (the sin nature) *shall not have dominion over you: for you are not under the Law, but under Grace"* (Rom. 6:14).

4. Once your Faith is properly anchored in Christ and what He has done for you at the Cross, in other words that you ever make the Cross the object of your Faith, the Holy Spirit, Who works exclusively within the boundaries and parameters of the Finished Work of Christ, will give you all of His Power, which will then help you to live this life you ought to live. In fact, without the Holy Spirit, you simply cannot be the Christian you ought to be. Here is what Paul said about this:

"But if the Spirit (Holy Spirit) *of Him* (God the Father) *Who raised up Jesus from the dead dwell in you, He Who raised up Christ from the dead shall also quicken your mortal bodies* (give you power to live this life) *by His Spirit Who dwells in you"* (Rom. 8:11).

Now remember, this Eleventh Verse is not speaking of the coming Resurrection, but is speaking of the Holy Spirit living in you, and quickening your mortal body, which means to give you power to live the life you ought to live. But never forget that He does this solely and completely upon your Faith based squarely in the Cross of Christ.

GOD'S PRESCRIBED ORDER OF VICTORY

Continuing to be brief, perhaps the following can give you a foundation on which to stand:

1. You as a Believer must understand that it is through the Cross that every single thing comes to you from God. In other words, the Cross is what made it all possible (Eph. 2:13-18; Col. 2:14-15).

2. Understanding that the Cross is what has made everything possible, it is absolutely imperative that the Cross ever be the object of your Faith. Satan will work harder here than any place else, and I speak of him trying to move your Faith from the Cross to other things. He really doesn't care too very much about what the other things are, just as long as it's not the Cross. In fact, this is the biggest hindrance to the Christian, where

the Christian fails the most. Most don't understand the correct object of Faith and, therefore, believe wrong. The Cross Alone must ever be the object of our Faith (I Cor. 1:17-18, 21, 23; 2:2, 5).

3. Once it is understood that the Cross is the means by which all things come to us from God, and that it must ever be the object of our Faith, the Holy Spirit will then work mightily on our behalf. The Holy Spirit is God; consequently, there is nothing He cannot do. But to have His Power, and to have it working within our lives, which is absolutely essential for us to live a victorious life, we must understand that He works exclusively on the premise of Faith. But at the same time we must also understand that it must be Faith in the Cross, or else the Holy Spirit will not function (Rom. 8:1-2, 11, 13).

THE ONLY WAY OF VICTORY

What I've given you is not one of several ways to live for God, but is in fact, the only way. There is only one Sacrifice for sin, one way to victory, and it is all exclusively in Christ, and what Christ did for us at the Cross. If we miss it here, we have missed it!

Consequently, there are millions of Christians, in fact, almost all, who love the Lord, and are trying hard, but in fact, are living less than victorious lives. And to be frank, these Christians are confused. They try to exercise faith, but in actuality, they don't really know and understand that in which they are attempting to exercise their faith. Most would claim that they are exercising Faith in the Word of God. That is certainly proper, but the truth also is, most of these people don't really know what the Word of God actually teaches. They pick out a Scripture here and there as they've been told to do, quote it over and over again, thinking somehow it's going to work some type of magic with God. They find, to their dismay, that it doesn't!

As stated, the Word of God is the story of the Cross, as the story of the Cross is the Word of God. Once you understand that, and make the Cross the foundation of your Faith, then the Word of God will begin to come into focus as it should. In other words, you will understand it for the first time in your life, as it ought to be understood.

You will find that the entirety of the Word, and in every respect, points to Christ, and most of all, it points to what He did for us at the Cross. In fact, the entirety of the story of the Old Testament is that of pointing to the One Who is to come, the Lord Jesus Christ, and through the Sacrifices, what He would do for us at the Cross.

The New Testament, which is the New Covenant, is in effect the story of the Cross. It's what the Cross means. It was Paul who was given this information, and given to him by the Holy Spirit, with him giving it to us in his 14 Epistles.

So I'll not be misunderstood, let me say it again, and say it plainly.

Unless the Christian properly understands the Cross, he simply cannot live a victorious life. He cannot know and enjoy *"more abundant life"* (Jn. 10:10). He cannot really know Christ as he should, but for the most part, will function in the realm of *"another Christ"* (II Cor. 11:4). And regrettably and sadly, that's the position of most Christians.

ROMANS, CHAPTER 7

Regrettably, Romans, Chapter 7 is by and large ignored by most Christians. In fact, most have been taught that Romans, Chapter 7 is the story of Paul's experience before he was saved. Thinking that, most give little credence to what is being said, because they think it doesn't apply to them, inasmuch as they are now a Christian.

The truth is, Romans, Chapter 7 in no way applies to Paul before his conversion, but rather after his conversion, which means after he was saved and after he was Baptized with the Holy Spirit.

Many Pentecostals and Charismatics deny this, because they cannot see someone Spirit-filled living less than a victorious life. They think this, while all the time, even though Spirit-filled, living a less than victorious life themselves. And that brings up another problem with Christians. Many times we simply aren't honest with ourselves.

No, Romans, Chapter 7 deals with Paul after he was Saved and Baptized with the Spirit, and actually called to be an Apostle, and in fact, was an Apostle.

But at that particular time, Paul didn't know the Message of the Cross. In fact, the meaning of the Cross had not really been given to anyone, so the information was not available at that particular time.

As a result, the Apostle tried to live this Christian life the best way he knew how, which is the manner and way in which most Christians try to live it presently. He tried to do it by his own strength, ability, and will-power, etc. He found he could not do it, no matter how hard he tried. He said:

"For I know that in me (that is, in my flesh,) dwells no good thing (he found that out as surely as we have found it out)*: for to will is present with me* (meaning that he had the willpower, but found it to be insufficient)*; but how to perform that which is good I find not"* (Rom. 7:18).

And as stated, this is where most Christians find themselves.

They know the right way, but they simply cannot live the right way, and no matter how hard they try.

Now let's be honest with ourselves: Are you really living victorious? While some few of you certainly are, the truth is, most of you aren't. You try to live right! You try to be an overcomer! But you're not succeeding.

What is wrong?

That which is wrong is that you are trying to live this life by your own strength and ability. But you are fooled and deceived, simply because your strength and ability are all wrapped up in good things, which you think will bring you victory. That's why Paul also said:

"For sin (the sin nature), *taking occasion by the Commandment, deceived me, and by it slew me"* (Rom. 7:11).

What did he mean by that?

He meant that he was trying to keep the Commandments of the Lord the best way he knew how, which was with his strength and ability, etc. But his thinking that he could live this life in this manner was only deception, and the end result was sin, or moral failure, in which it always will be. Once again, that's where most Christians find themselves.

So what are you to do?

You are to learn Romans, Chapter 6, which we have just briefly addressed. This means you are to learn that your victory is totally and completely in Christ, and not at all in yourself. Now almost all of you would readily agree with that; however, the problem is, most Christians despite knowing that, really do not understand it.

When we say that our victory is in Christ and Christ Alone, with which almost all Christians would agree, we are meaning that it is what Christ did at the Cross, and our Faith in that Finished Work.

IN CHRIST

Just saying that we're trusting in Christ is not really sufficient. While that certainly is the first step, the second step must be enacted as well, which means when we say that we are trusting Christ, or trusting in Christ, we are actually referring to what He did for us at the Cross. Remember, Paul took us to the Cross, and did so in Romans, Chapter 6, when he told us how to live a victorious life. Romans, Chapter 6 is the means by which the Believer lives the victorious, overcoming, Christian life. It is the only means that God has provided. And as most Christians don't understand Romans, Chapter 7, likewise, most don't understand Romans, Chapter 6. In fact, the three Chapters, Romans 6, 7, and 8, actually are, I believe, the three most important Chapters in the entirety of the Bible. These three Chapters sum up everything else that the Bible teaches. They sum up what Jesus did for us, the reason He came, and what He accomplished on our behalf. To fail to understand these three Chapters is in a sense, failure to understand the entirety of the Bible. And let me say it again:

If you don't understand these three Chapters, you simply cannot live a victorious life. It is impossible! If in fact one could do so, then Jesus did not need to come down here and die on a Cross. But the Truth is, other than what He did at the Cross, and our Faith in that Finished Work, which gives the Holy Spirit latitude within our lives, we simply cannot live the life we ought to live. That's why Paul also said:

"But God forbid that I should glory (boast), *save in the Cross of our Lord Jesus Christ, by Whom the world is crucified unto me, and I unto the world"* (Gal. 6:14).

NOTES

In this one Verse, Paul plainly says that the only way you will be able as a Christian to have victory over sin and all the works of the flesh, is by your Faith in what Christ did for you at the Cross, ever making that Finished Work the proper object of your Faith.

THE PRESERVATION OF THE ANIMALS

Verse 8 reads: *"Of clean beasts, and of beasts that are not clean, and of fowls, and of every thing that creepeth upon the Earth."*

Nothing short of Divine power could have effected such a timely and orderly entrance of the creatures into this huge vessel.

AS GOD HAD COMMANDED

Verse 9 reads: *"There went in two and two unto Noah into the Ark, the male and the female, as God had commanded Noah."*

This probably took about seven days to get all of this accomplished.

If it is to be noticed, it says that God *"commanded"* Noah to do all of these things; in other words, this was not a suggestion. To his credit, Noah was very careful to do exactly what the Lord had said that he must do.

(10) "AND IT CAME TO PASS AFTER SEVEN DAYS, THAT THE WATERS OF THE FLOOD WERE UPON THE EARTH.

(11) "IN THE SIX HUNDREDTH YEAR OF NOAH'S LIFE, IN THE SECOND MONTH, THE SEVENTEENTH DAY OF THE MONTH, THE SAME DAY WERE ALL THE FOUNTAINS OF THE GREAT DEEP BROKEN UP, AND THE WINDOWS OF HEAVEN WERE OPENED.

(12) "AND THE RAIN WAS UPON THE EARTH FORTY DAYS AND FORTY NIGHTS."

The exegesis is:

1. When the seven days had passed, even as the Lord had said, the flood began.

2. The flood consisted not only of torrential rain coming down, and without letup, but as well, the Scripture says, *"The fountains of the great deep were broken up,"* which speaks of rivers of water being pushed to the surface of the Earth, and done so constantly.

3. The rain didn't let up for forty days and forty nights.

THE FLOOD

Verse 10 reads: *"And it came to pass after seven days, that the waters of the flood were upon the Earth."*

That which Noah had preached for a number of years was now a reality. Exactly as God stated, the rains now began to fall.

It doesn't really matter where the Ark was situated at this time. Whether down in a valley, or up on the side of a mountain. Noah, no doubt, built the thing, where materials were handy to be attained.

When it began to rain, the people who, more than likely, watched Noah enter the Ark, and no doubt did so with sarcasm, obviously witnessed the beginning of the rain. What were their thoughts then? There is no evidence that this moved them, because unbelief, and we speak of unbelief toward God, is a terrible thing.

Let the Reader understand that as Noah preached for some years about the coming flood, Preachers would do well today to preach about the Second Coming. The first cataclysm, as it refers to the flood, destroyed mankind. The second cataclysm as it refers to the Second Coming, will save mankind. But at the same time, it will slaughter those who are opposed to Christ. Concerning that coming event, the Lord, through the Prophet Ezekiel said: *"And I will plead against him* (the Antichrist) *with pestilence and with blood; and I will rain upon him, and upon his bands, and upon the many people who are with him, an overflowing rain, and great hailstones, fire, and brimstone"* (Ezek. 38:22).

THE FOUNTAINS AND THE WINDOWS

Verse 11 reads: *"In the six hundredth year of Noah's life, in the second month, the seventeenth day of the month, the same day were all the fountains of the great deep broken up, and the windows of Heaven were opened."*

We begin our year now with the month of January. That was not the case during the time of Noah. Although no one knows exactly, at least to my knowledge, when the year began at that time, many think that it was the month of September, at the time of the harvest. In other words, this was the time of the beginning Civil year.

If that in fact was the case, then the flood began in October, which would have been the second month. Since, as Moses tells us, Noah later sent out a dove in the tenth month, which returned with a green olive leaf in its mouth, this seems to speak for the September beginning.

The idea of the fountains of the great deep being broken up, and the windows of Heaven being opened, refers to water coming from above and below.

As well, it is believed by some Scientists, and rightly so, that the waters came with such force from the Earth that it would have taken only a few days to have cut the Grand Canyon, and other such similarities. It has been proven that water rushing fast enough, and with enough force, can cut into solid rock with ease. So the idea that it took millions of years for the Grand Canyon to be formed actually holds no true, scientific validity.

FORTY DAYS AND FORTY NIGHTS

Verse 12 reads: *"And the rain was upon the Earth forty days and forty nights."*

This speaks of violent rain. The actual, literal Hebrew translation is, *"And there was violent rain. . . ."*

To explain this, the Holy Spirit uses the phrase, *"And the windows of Heaven were opened,"* which signals a deluge of unprecedented proportions. I think we can safely say that we're speaking here of it raining as much as several feet an hour, and doing so nonstop for some forty days and forty nights. Coupling that with the fountains of the deep being broken up, and veritable underground rivers being pushed to the surface, and doing so with rapid nonstop force, the topography of much of the landscape must have been drastically changed.

(13) "IN THE SELFSAME DAY ENTERED NOAH, AND SHEM, AND HAM, AND JAPHETH, THE SONS OF NOAH, AND NOAH'S WIFE, AND THE THREE WIVES OF HIS SONS WITH THEM, INTO THE ARK;

(14) "THEY, AND EVERY BEAST AFTER HIS KIND, AND ALL THE CATTLE AFTER THEIR KIND, AND EVERY CREEPING THING THAT CREEPETH UPON THE EARTH AFTER HIS KIND, AND EVERY

FOWL AFTER HIS KIND, EVERY BIRD OF EVERY SORT.

(15) "AND THEY WENT IN UNTO NOAH INTO THE ARK, TWO AND TWO OF ALL FLESH, WHEREIN IS THE BREATH OF LIFE."

The exegesis is:

1. All of this doesn't mean that they entered into the Ark a full seven days before the flood, but rather that Noah then began to carry out the Divine instructions.

2. The key to the types of animals and birds, is the phrase "after his kind."

3. I think one can safely say that the Spirit of the Lord aided in this process, of all these various animals and birds going into the Ark as they did.

THE SELFSAME DAY

Verse 13 reads: "In the selfsame day entered Noah, and Shem, and Ham, and Japheth, the sons of Noah, and Noah's wife, and the three wives of his sons with them, into the Ark."

The idea is, during the previous seven days, the animals were herded into the Ark, and then on the very day that the rains began, Noah and his family entered the Ark.

To be sure, the Ark is a Type of Christ. I think Hebrews 11:7 bears this out very succinctly.

Here is a profound Truth for the heart and conscience of a Believer. "All God's billows and waves" passed over the spotless person of the Lord Jesus, when He hung upon the Cross; and, as a most blessed consequence, not one of them remains to pass over the person of the Believer. At Calvary, we see, in good Truth, "the fountains of the great deep broken up, and the windows of Heaven opened."

Christ drank the cup, and endured the wrath perfectly. He put Himself, judicially, under the full weight of all His people's liabilities, and gloriously discharged them. The belief of this gives settled peace to the soul.

If the Lord Jesus has met all that could be against us, if He has removed out of the way every hindrance, if He has put away sin, if He has exhausted the cup of wrath and judgment on our behalf, if He has cleared the prospect of every cloud, should we not enjoy settled peace? Unquestionably. Peace is our unalienable portion. To us belong the deep

and untold blessedness, and holy security, which redeeming love can bestow on the righteous ground of Christ's absolutely accomplished work (Mackintosh).

AFTER HIS KIND

Verse 14 reads: "They, and every beast after his kind, and all the cattle after their kind, and every creeping thing that creepeth upon the Earth after his kind, and every fowl after his kind, every bird of every sort."

The word "kinds" probably refers to a specimen from each family of animals and birds. For instance, God probably brought a pair of elephants that would become the ancestors of African and Asian elephants, but He did not bring other types such as the hairy mammoth (Horton).

OF ALL FLESH

Verse 15 says: "And they went in unto Noah into the Ark, two and two of all flesh, wherein is the breath of life."

The Hand of the Holy Spirit functions in all of this. As previously stated, the Lord had to do the doing, so to speak, as it regards the animals and the birds, or else it would have been impossible for Noah and his sons to have carried out this command. The idea seems to be that the Lord gave Noah a special sense of attraction, as it refers to these creatures. At the same time, the Lord gave them an instinct to want to go to Noah, hence making it easy for him to gather what was needed.

(16) "AND THEY THAT WENT IN, WENT IN MALE AND FEMALE OF ALL FLESH, AS GOD HAD COMMANDED HIM: AND THE LORD SHUT HIM IN.

(17) "AND THE FLOOD WAS FORTY DAYS UPON THE EARTH; AND THE WATERS INCREASED, AND BEAR UP THE ARK, AND IT WAS LIFTED UP ABOVE THE EARTH.

(18) "AND THE WATERS PREVAILED, AND WERE INCREASED GREATLY UPON THE EARTH; AND THE ARK WENT UPON THE FACE OF THE WATERS.

(19) "AND THE WATERS PREVAILED EXCEEDINGLY UPON THE EARTH; AND ALL THE HIGH HILLS, THAT WERE UNDER THE WHOLE HEAVEN, WERE COVERED.

(20) "FIFTEEN CUBITS UPWARD DID THE WATERS PREVAIL; AND THE MOUNTAINS WERE COVERED."

The diagram is:

1. The Lord Personally shut the door to the Ark.

2. The Ark did not begin to float until forty days and forty nights of rain had passed.

3. The waters continued to rise.

4. All the high hills and mountains were covered. Some Scientists believe that before the flood, the highest mountain on Earth was approximately 10,000 feet, which is far different than some of the mountains today which reach as high as 35,000 feet.

5. The depth of the flood continued to increase, until it was some 22 feet above the highest mountain.

6. The flood was universal, meaning that it covered the entirety of the Earth.

THE LORD SHUT HIM IN

Verse 16 reads: *"And they that went in, went in male and female of all flesh, as God had commanded him: and the LORD shut him in."*

The fact that the Lord shut Noah and his family in the Ark means literally that the Lord Personally closed up the door of the Ark after him. This may have been done to protect him from the rage of the individuals nearby.

The contrast between the two names of the Deity is here most vividly presented. In this one Verse, both *"God"* and *"Lord"* are used. It is *"Elohim"* Who commands Noah about the beasts; it is *"Jehovah,"* the Covenant God, Who ensures his safety by closing the Ark behind him.

Nothing can more fully express the Believer's perfect security in Christ than those words, *"The Lord shut him in."* Who can open what God has shut? None. The family of Noah was as safe as God could make them. There was no power, be it angelic, human, or diabolical, which could possibly burst open the door of the Ark, and let the waters in. The door was shut by the selfsame Hand that had opened the windows of Heaven, and broken up the fountains of the great deep. Thus, Christ is spoken of as the One *"Who has the key of David, He who*

NOTES

opens and no man shuts, and shuts and no man opens" (Rev. 3:7). He also holds in His Hand *"the keys of Hell and of death"* (Rev. 1:18). None can enter the portals of the grave, nor go forth therefrom, without Him. He has *"all power in Heaven and on Earth."* He is *"Head over all things to the Church,"* and in Him the Believer is perfectly secure (Mat. 28:18; Eph. 1:22).

However, as should be obvious, Noah was in that Ark because of his Faith. In other words, he believed God.

Salvation is contingent upon Faith. It has always been that way, it is that way now, and it will ever be that way. *"We are saved by Faith through Grace. It is the Gift of God"* (Eph. 2:8-9). We are justified by Faith (Gen. 15:6). Therefore, if Faith is lost, and Faith can be lost, Salvation is lost as well. God shuts us in only upon the premise of our Faith in Christ and what Christ has done for us at the Cross, and our continued belief in that Finished Work.

THE FLOOD LIFTED UP THE ARK

Verse 17 reads: *"And the flood was forty days upon the Earth; and the waters increased, and bear up the Ark, and it was lifted up above the Earth."*

The first part of this Verse proclaims the fact of Verse 12, where it says that the rain continued for forty days and forty nights. This means that it was torrentially raining, and without letup for this period of time, and did so all over the world. It is described in Verse 11 as *"the widows of Heaven were opened."* On top of that, Verse 11 says as well, *"all the fountains of the great deep were broken up."*

Verse 18 reads: *"And the waters prevailed, and were increased greatly upon the Earth; and the Ark went upon the face of the waters."*

The phrase, *"The waters prevailed, and were increased greatly,"* probably pertains to the fact that the scoffers flattered themselves with hopes that it would abate, and never come to extremity; but still it increased, it prevailed.

As to exactly how many people there were in the world of that particular time, we have no way of knowing; however, it very easily could have been 100 million or more. It had been a little over 1,600 years from the time of Adam and Eve, and multiplication can increase rapidly during such a period of time regarding population.

As well, it is very likely that most everyone, if not every single person on the face of the Earth at that time, heard about Noah's Ark, even if they did not hear him personally. In fact, the greater concentration of the population would have definitely been in the vicinity of the Garden of Eden, which most Scholars believe was in modern-day Iraq. In fact, some believe, and it is probably true, that ancient Babylon was built on the very spot of the Garden of Eden.

Consequently, it is certain that a Message, such as Noah brought to the world of that day, would have been quickly disseminated through the population, perhaps, as stated, reaching every individual. Not knowing God, and living deep in sin, that particular population ignored the message as brought by the Patriarch. As well, more than likely, untold thousands made the trip to the place where the Ark was being built, so they could observe this huge boat for themselves. It had to be the talk, at least at that time, of the antediluvian world.

When the Lord shut Noah and his family in the Ark, along with the animals and birds which had been selected, and then it began to rain, the unbelief no doubt continued in its scoffing, even as unbelief always does.

After the first couple of days, with the rain continuing to come down in torrents, and peculiar things beginning to happen with rivers and streams as they boiled over, literally shooting out mountains of water, and destroying everything in its path, panic now begins to set in. Millions are scrambling for the highest hill, and no doubt, many at that particular time tried to get to the Ark, but it was too late. For years, the opportunity had presented itself, but it was opportunity after opportunity that was laughed off. It is now too late! The door is shut!

There comes a time in every human life when it's too late. That's when death closes in, and let the Reader understand that first, second, and third opportunities are on this

side of the grave. After the night of death falls, there is no more chance to be saved.

THE HIGH HILLS

Verse 19 reads: *"And the waters prevailed exceedingly upon the Earth; and all the high hills, that were under the whole Heaven, were covered."*

This proclaims the fact that the flood was universal, and not merely centered up in a particular locality.

Many Scholars believe that before the flood, the tallest mountain in the world was 10,000 feet or less. In other words, there were no exceedingly high mountains like Mount Everest, which is over 30,000 feet high. In fact, they believe that the flood itself, which had to do with *"the great deep being broken up,"* changed much of the topography of the world, making huge canyons, and at the same time huge mountains. With enough force, this could have all been done, and no doubt was, in just a few days time.

UNIVERSAL FLOOD

Verse 20 reads: *"Fifteen cubits upward did the waters prevail; and the mountains were covered."*

Fifteen cubits translates into about 22 feet. It refers to the fact that the top of the tallest mountain in the world, whatever that was, was about 22 feet underwater. This means, of course, that if the tallest mountain then was about 10,000 feet, the water could have been as much as nearly two miles deep at sea level.

(21) "AND ALL FLESH DIED THAT MOVED UPON THE EARTH, BOTH OF FOWL, AND OF CATTLE, AND OF BEAST, AND OF EVERY CREEPING THING THAT CREEPETH UPON THE EARTH, AND EVERY MAN:

(22) "ALL IN WHOSE NOSTRILS WAS THE BREATH OF LIFE, OF ALL THAT WAS IN THE DRY LAND, DIED.

(23) "AND EVERY LIVING SUBSTANCE WAS DESTROYED WHICH WAS UPON THE FACE OF THE GROUND, BOTH MAN, AND CATTLE, AND THE CREEPING THINGS, AND THE FOWL OF THE HEAVEN; AND THEY WERE DESTROYED FROM THE EARTH: AND NOAH ONLY REMAINED

ALIVE, AND THEY THAT WERE WITH HIM IN THE ARK.

(24) "AND THE WATERS PREVAILED UPON THE EARTH AN HUNDRED AND FIFTY DAYS."

The overview is:

1. Every human being on the Earth at that particular time died. As well, all animals died, along with all birds — except those in the Ark.

2. The fish were not destroyed.

3. The flood took forty days and forty nights to rise to completion. From the time the flood began, to the day the waters began to recede, were 150 days.

THE DEATH OF ALL

Verse 21 reads: *"And all flesh died that moved upon the Earth, both the fowl, and of cattle, and of beast, and of every creeping thing that creepeth upon the Earth, and every man."*

Those who dwelt upon the tops of the highest mountains perished equally with those who lived in the deepest valleys. There was no difference. Many who live presently upon the mountains of morality think themselves secure from the judgment of fire that is now coming, and pity the certain fate of those who live in the depths of vice. But as in the judgment of *"water"* so in the judgment of *"fire,"* all alike will perish who are out of Christ, irrespective of their supposed morality.

Noah illustrates the Scripture terms *"lost"* and *"saved."* Standing without the door of the Ark, he was lost, that is, exposed to the coming judgment and sure to perish. Standing inside the door he was saved, that is, sheltered from the coming doom and sure not to perish. To pass from the one condition to the other he had to take but one step — a step into the Ark — and he was in immediate safety (Williams).

JUDGMENT

Verse 22 reads: *"All in whose nostrils was the breath of life, of all that was in the dry land, died."*

One might say that Noah was saved through the Baptism of the Ark. The Ark was sinless; Noah sinful. The Ark suffered the fierceness of Divine anger — a baptism

NOTES

into death — but not one wave of that judgment reached Noah. He was absolutely safe. Noah could not perish because the Ark could not perish. The Ark could not perish because Jehovah was in the Ark; in effect, the Ark was Christ; therefore, God was in Christ reconciling man unto Himself.

As previously stated, He did not say *"Go into the Ark"* but *"Come into the Ark."*

The Apostle Peter in the Third Chapter of his First Epistle points out that this is how sinners are saved — the Baptism into death, which speaks of the Crucifixion of Christ, which is identical to what Paul said in Romans, Chapter 6.

So in this statement given by Peter, we have both the Baptism into death as it regards Christ and His Resurrection out of death. Peter says that the Baptism and Resurrection of the Ark was a Type of the Death and Resurrection of Christ; he declares that this *"like figure"* saves all who will believe (I Pet. 3:20-21).

Now please understand, Peter is not saying that Water Baptism saves, as some claim, but rather that the Ark was a *"like figure"* of the Salvation process, which was carried out by Jesus Christ on the Cross, when He died as our Substitute. In fact, he uses the word *"Baptism"* exactly as Paul used it. The Apostle of Grace said: *"Know ye not, that so many of us as were baptized into Jesus Christ were baptized into His death?"* (Rom. 6:3).

Paul was not speaking of Water Baptism, just as Peter wasn't speaking of Water Baptism, but rather what Jesus did at the Cross. The Apostle used the word *"baptized"* as it regards what happens when the believing sinner accepts Christ, because that's the strongest word that can be used.

The word *"baptized"* actually means *"to dip under."* To explain it more fully, it means that *"one is in that into which it is baptized, and that into which it is baptized is now in the one being baptized."* Perhaps the following would explain it even better:

Whenever they show a ship that has been sunk, we see the ship in the water, and the water in the ship. That is an excellent description of Baptism.

Whenever the believing sinner accepts Christ as his own personal Saviour, God the

Father actually places that believing sinner into Christ as it refers to the Crucifixion and Resurrection of Christ. That's why Paul uses the term over and over, even some 170 times in his 14 Epistles, *"In Christ,"* or one of its derivatives such as, *"in Him,"* etc.

Let everyone understand that Salvation comes only by Faith in Christ and what Christ did at the Cross. While all the Ordinances of the Church are very important, such as Water Baptism, or the Lord's Supper; however, the truth is, they contribute nothing toward one's Salvation, but stand only as a symbol of what Christ has already done in the heart and life. The symbol is important, even very important, so that we do not forget what Jesus has done for us (I Cor. 11:25).

THE ARK

Verse 23 reads: *"And every living substance was destroyed which was upon the face of the ground, both man, and cattle, and the creeping things, and the fowl of the heavens; and they were destroyed from the Earth: and Noah only remained alive, and they who were with him in the Ark."*

All the men, women, and children who were in the world, excepting those in the Ark, died. We may easily imagine what terror and consternation seized upon them, when they saw themselves surrounded by water.

Our Saviour tells us that till the very day that the flood came, they were eating and drinking (Lk. 17:26-27); they were drowned in sin and sensuality before they were drowned in the water; crying, Peace, Peace, to themselves, deaf and blind to all Divine warnings.

As the rain slashes down and the waters continue to rise, slowly but surely they are convinced of their folly, but it is now too late.

We can certainly suppose they tried all ways and means possible to save themselves, but all in vain. They had no more success than the millions who attempt to save themselves presently, but outside of Christ. Those who were not found in Christ, of which the Ark was a representation, are certainly undone, undone forever (Isa. 10:3).

I would pray that everyone reading these words can see and feel the awfulness of that which transpired so long, long ago. But yet,

its warning should be as clear even as the present danger is clear.

There was no means of safety with the exception of the Ark. Everything else was futile and without success. As stated, those who climbed to the top of the highest mountains, wherever that may have been, perished just as surely as those who were in the lowest valleys. It is the same presently:

If one is not in Christ, one is not saved. It doesn't matter how religious they are, if they do not know Christ as their own personal Saviour, then they are lost.

And when we say *"know Christ,"* we are referring to the fact that total and complete faith must be placed in Him and Him Alone, and what he did at the Cross on our behalf.

THE JESUS DIED SPIRITUALLY DOCTRINE!

If one claims to be trusting Christ and at the same time, trusting Water Baptism for Salvation, pure and simple, that person isn't saved. That would go for one trusting Christ and the Church, or Christ and speaking in other tongues, etc.

As another example, many Charismatics have so twisted and perverted the Atonement, that in their teaching it has no similarity to what the Bible actually says. And please understand, when we deal with the Atonement, we are dealing with the very heart of the Gospel. If we miss it there, we have missed it everywhere.

Many of them teach that Jesus dying on the Cross did not complete the Atonement. They teach that He became one with Satan on the Cross, and that when He died, He went to Hell, and we speak of the burning side of Hell. In other words, when a sinner dies, he goes to Hell. They teach that Jesus did the same thing.

They also teach that for some three days and nights He suffered the agonies of a lost soul in Hell, with demons laughing in hellish glee, because they had defeated Christ. And that at the end of that three days and nights, God said *"It is enough,"* and Jesus was then *"born again,"* they continue to teach, and resurrected from the dead.

Now the problem with all of this is, there is not a shred of this in the Bible. They have made it up out of the figments of their imagination.

The truth is, they demean the Cross, actually referring to it as *"the greatest defeat in human history."*

As a result of this *"born again Jesus,"* they teach that any Born-Again person is now in the *"God class,"* and can, therefore, speak into existence whatever it is that he wants or desires. In other words, he becomes a little god, doing all sorts of miraculous things, and because he is in the *"God class."*

As a result, they completely deny the Sanctification process, which is carried out in the heart and life of the Believer by the Holy Spirit, as the Believer anchors his Faith in the Cross of Christ (Rom. 6:3-14; 8:1-2, 11).

Part of what they teach is true, as is most error. It is true that when the believing sinner comes to Christ, he is at that moment perfectly and totally sanctified, as well as justified (I Cor. 6:11). However, while that is the Believer's *"position"* in Christ, a position incidentally which never changes, we all know that our *"condition"* is not exactly up to our *"position."* This is what the Holy Spirit sets out to correct, which in effect is a lifelong process. As stated, He accomplishes this by and through what Jesus did at the Cross, and our Faith in that Finished Work. That's why Paul said:

"And the Very God of Peace sanctify you wholly: and I pray God your whole spirit and soul and body be preserved blameless unto the coming of our Lord Jesus Christ" (I Thess. 5:23).

In I Corinthians 6:11, Paul is dealing with *"positional Sanctification."* In I Thessalonians 5:23, he is dealing with *"conditional or progressive Sanctification."*

The Jesus died spiritually people teach that there is no such thing as conditional Salvation, that in reality, the Believer is now perfect.

They teach that one's spirit is perfect after being Born-Again, and that his soul is being saved, in other words, being brought into line with his spirit, and that the body is not too very important. But what does the Word say?

"Having therefore these Promises, dearly Beloved, let us cleanse ourselves from all

filthiness of the flesh and spirit, perfecting holiness in the fear of God" (II Cor. 7:1).

Paul has just given a long dissertation concerning the separation process of the Believer, as recorded in II Corinthians 6:14-18. He then goes on to tell us that we must *"cleanse ourselves from all filthiness of the flesh and spirit."* Now if the *"spirit"* of the Born-Again person is perfect, why would Paul be telling us to cleanse ourselves from all filthiness of the spirit?

To deny or pervert the Cross is to deny the very Gospel of Jesus Christ. It is, in effect, and continuing to stay with the spirit of our study, to place one's self outside of the safety of the Ark, which is Christ.

THE WATERS PREVAILED

Verse 24 reads: *"And the waters prevailed upon the Earth an hundred and fifty days."*

This was, no doubt, from the time that it began to rain, until the waters began to recede.

Notice that it says *"the waters prevailed."* This is exactly what God said would happen. It didn't matter that the world of that day met that statement with unbelief. It happened exactly as God said it would happen.

The world today scoffs at the Coming of the Lord. If they don't deny Him outright, they deny that He is coming back to this world. So one might say that as *"the waters prevailed,"* most definitely, the Word of God prevails. Let the whole world know and understand that!

But if we neglect, refuse, or abuse the Salvation of Christ, we shall, notwithstanding whatever advantages we presently have, be overwhelmed in this coming time of judgment. And coming it is, because the Word of God tells us that it's coming.

Peter said: *"Knowing this first, that there shall come in the last days, scoffers, walking after their own lusts,*

"And saying, Where is the Promise of His Coming? For since the fathers fell asleep, all things continue as they were from the beginning of the creation.

"For this they willingly are ignorant of, that by the Word of God the heavens were of old, and the Earth standing out of the water and in the water:

"Whereby the world that then was, being overflowed with water, perished:

"But the heavens and the Earth which are now, by the same word are kept in store, reserved unto fire against the Day of Judgment and perdition of ungodly men" (II Pet. 3:3-7).

"Search me, O God, and know my heart today;

"Try me, O Saviour, know my thoughts, I pray:

"See if there be some wicked way in me:

"Cleanse me from every sin, and set me free."

"I praise Thee, Lord, for cleansing me from sin:

"Fulfill Thy Word, and make me pure within;

"Fill me with fire, where once I burned with shame:

"Grant my desire to magnify Thy Name."

"Lord, take my life, and make it wholly Thine:

"Fill my poor heart with Thy great love Divine;

"Take all my will, my passion, self, and pride;

"I now surrender: Lord, in me abide."

"O Holy Spirit, revival comes from Thee:

"Send a revival, start the work in me:

"Thy Word declares, Thou will supply our need:

"For blessing now, O Lord, I humbly plead."

CHAPTER 8

(1) "AND GOD REMEMBERED NOAH, AND EVERY LIVING THING, AND ALL THE CATTLE THAT WAS WITH HIM IN THE ARK: AND GOD MADE A WIND TO PASS OVER THE EARTH, AND THE WATERS ASSWAGED;

(2) "THE FOUNTAINS ALSO OF THE DEEP AND THE WINDOWS OF HEAVEN WERE STOPPED, AND THE RAIN FROM HEAVEN WAS RESTRAINED;

(3) "AND THE WATERS RETURNED FROM OFF THE EARTH CONTINUALLY: AND AFTER THE END OF THE HUNDRED AND FIFTY DAYS THE WATERS WERE ABATED.

(4) "AND THE ARK RESTED IN THE SEVENTH MONTH, ON THE SEVENTEENTH DAY OF THE MONTH, UPON THE MOUNTAINS OF ARARAT.

(5) "AND THE WATERS DECREASED CONTINUALLY UNTIL THE TENTH MONTH: IN THE TENTH MONTH, ON THE FIRST DAY OF THE MONTH, WERE THE TOPS OF THE MOUNTAINS SEEN."

The exegesis is:

1. The Lord remembers every Promise that He has ever made.

2. As the flood came by the Word of the Lord, the flood will now go by the Word of the Lord.

3. The Ark came to rest upon the mountains of Ararat.

AND GOD REMEMBERED

Verse 1 reads: *"And God remembered Noah, and every living thing, and all the cattle that was with him in the Ark: and God made a wind to pass over the Earth, and the waters asswaged."*

The idea of God remembering as given here does not mean that God had forgotten, or that He could forget. It simply means that He will now give His attention to whatever it is that is being discussed, whether of judgment or of blessing. Here it would be of blessing.

C. H. Mackintosh gives us an interesting thought on both Enoch and Noah, which I feel has great Biblical merit. At this juncture, I think it would be appropriate to relate this man's thoughts. He said:

"I would here mention, for my Reader's prayerful consideration, a thought very familiar to the minds of those who have especially given themselves to the study of what is called 'Dispensational Truth.' It has reference to Enoch and Noah. The former was taken away, as we have seen, before the Judgment came; whereas the latter was carried through the Judgment.

"Now, it is thought that Enoch is a figure of the Church, who shall be taken away before human evil reaches its climax, and

before the Divine Judgment falls thereon. Noah, on the other hand, is a figure of the remnant of Israel, who shall be brought through the deep waters of affliction, and through the fire of judgment, and led into the full enjoyment of Millennial bliss, in virtue of God's everlasting Covenant. I may add, that I quite receive this thought in reference to those two Old Testament fathers. I consider that it has the full support of the general scope and analogy of Holy Scripture."

(Incidentally, in all five Volumes of our Commentaries on the Pentateuch, you will find us quoting C. H. Mackintosh quite frequently. He had an amazing insight into the Word of God. As well, even as we have just given to you, his knowledge concerning Endtime prophetic events was far ahead of its time. While I do not agree with all of his writings, I do find that his interpretation of the great fundamentals of the Faith is, in my opinion, priceless.)

(Charles H. Mackintosh was born October 1820, at Glenmalure Barricks, County Wicklow, Ireland, the son of the captain of a Highland regimen. He was converted at the age of 18 through the letters of a devout sister, and the prayerful reading of J. N. Darby's *"Operations of the Spirit."* When he was 24 years of age, he opened a private school at Westport, but it was not long before he concluded he must give himself entirely to the Ministry of the Word of God.)

JUDGMENT

Judgment is God's *"strange work."* He delights not in it, though He is Glorified by it; however, He is ever ready to leave the place of judgment, and enter that of Mercy, because He delights in Mercy.

If He sends judgment, and to be sure, in one way or the other, He is doing so constantly in this world, whether on a small or large scale, it is always with a purpose in mind, done in order to bring the situation out to a positive conclusion. For instance:

While the Lord definitely did not cause the terrible happenings of September 11, 2001, to be sure, He did allow it. And what do we mean by that?

Everything that happens in this world, God either causes or allows it. While He certainly

doesn't cause sin, destruction, or anything of that nature, because of certain laws that He has Himself formulated, He does allow it. So if He allowed the events of September 11, 2001, and He definitely did, then why did He allow such?

Considering the wickedness of our nation, and it is guilty of gross wickedness, the answer becomes quite simple. God allowed it, because America needs a wake-up call. As a whole, America has long since ceased to worship God. Our gods now are money, entertainment, sports, etc. In fact, the nation has become a materialistic society. And the blame for that must be laid at the doorstep of the Church.

The mission of the Church is to preach the Cross; however, the Church as a whole is not preaching the Cross. In fact, very few Churches are preaching the Cross. We are preaching everything in the world but the Cross, which means that we really aren't preaching the Gospel at all. In fact, even as Paul said so long ago, *"It is another Jesus, another gospel, and another spirit"* (II Cor. 11:4).

So back to the flood, the judgment is now over, and preparations are being made to bring the world back to a habitable state.

THE WORD OF GOD

Verse 2 says: *"The fountains also of the deep and the windows of Heaven were stopped, and the rain from Heaven was restrained."*

The two phrases in this Verse concerning the *"fountains"* and *"windows"* proclaim to us the terrible ferocity of the flood. In fact, it was probably of such ferocity that it literally reshaped much of this world.

Sometime back, I saw part of a documentary over Television addressing the flood.

The Scientists doing the experiments related as to how water pouring forth with great force could cut into solid rock in a very short period of time. In fact, they stated that the Grand Canyon, which I think is the largest canyon in the world, could easily have been cut out of the Earth in a matter of days. As well, the great mountain ranges were probably brought about at that time also.

Let the Reader understand that the flood was no light matter. It was and continues to be the most cataclysmic happening the planet has ever known. It will be surpassed only by the renovation of fire that will take place at the conclusion of the Millennial Reign.

JUDGMENT ENDED

Verse 3 reads: *"And the waters returned from off the Earth continually: and after the end of the hundred and fifty days the waters were abated."*

As God had a key to open, so He has a key to shut up again, and to stay the progress of judgments by stopping the causes of them. The same Hand that brought the desolation must bring the deliverance; to that Hand, therefore, our eye must ever be. He Who wounds is Alone able to heal. When afflictions have done the work for which they are sent, whether killing work or curing work, they shall be removed.

The flood should teach us a valuable lesson.

While it took the Lord only one day to handle the water which covered the Earth during the time of creation (Gen. 1:6-8), it took much longer as it regards the flood of Noah's time. While both of these floods were caused by sin, the first by the rebellion of Angels, and the second by the rebellion of men, we find that the rebellion caused by men required a far greater extent of attention by the Lord. For instance, there was nothing of the sort respecting Calvary as it regarded Angels, but God becoming man and dying on a Cross was definitely essential as it regards the Redemption of mankind. So why the great difference?

Most of the reasons we will probably not know this side of Glory; however, it is my thinking that God gave far greater dominion to Adam, i.e., *"mankind,"* than He did to the Angelic creation. As well, man was created in the image and Likeness of God, which is not said of Angels.

And then again, the Fall of man was great, so great in fact, that there is no way that words could properly explain it. We can only grasp at least a portion of the depths of that ruin, by observing the price that was paid to lift man from that ruin, which was the Cross. The Cross says it all! The worth of something can only be judged by its loss, and then the price paid for it to be redeemed. The Cross is that price!

NOTES

In all of the happenings of the Old Testament, it's almost like every line on every page screams, *"Hold on, He is coming!"*

ARARAT

Verse 4 reads: *"And the Ark rested in the seventh month, on the seventeenth day of the month, upon the mountains of Ararat."*

As the months then were reckoned as to be 30 days each, this makes exactly 150 days.

The speaker's Commentary notices the following remarkable coincidences — *"on the seventeenth day of Abib the Ark rested on Mount Ararat; on the seventeenth day of Abib the Israelites passed over the Red Sea; on the seventeenth day of Abib, Christ, our Lord, rose again from the dead."*

No, I don't think these are coincidences, but rather that God planned it this way for His Own reasons.

There are many summations as to the location of the *"Ararat"* mentioned here; however, it is my personal opinion that the Ararat of Eastern Turkey is the actual resting place of the Ark. In fact, a huge boat high upon the mountain has been observed several times, with even some few people going into the vessel itself. Due to the altitude, which is covered year-round by snow and ice, it can be observed only at particular times when the snow and ice are not so deep.

As well, political problems with the country of Turkey have hindered proper investigation.

But I think if such investigations are ever allowed, they will find that this is actually the Ark built by Noah some 4,400 years ago, with the plans actually given by God.

THE WATERS DECREASE

Verse 5 reads: *"And the waters decreased continually until the tenth month: in the tenth month, on the first day of the month, were the tops of the mountains seen."*

Please notice the exact specification of particular times. On the first day of the tenth month, the tops of the mountains were seen, as the waters continued to decrease. And of course, these were mountains in the vicinity of where the Ark finally came to rest.

I'm sure it's understood that this Ark had no means of propulsion; consequently, it would come to a place of rest where the Lord wanted it to be.

While the Lord had told Noah particularly when the flood would come, even to the very day (Gen. 7:4), yet He did not give him a particular account, at what times and by what steps it should go away. The knowledge of the former was necessary to his preparing the Ark; but the knowledge of the latter would serve only to gratify his curiosity, and the concealing it from him would be the needful exercise of his faith and patience (Henry).

(6) "AND IT CAME TO PASS AT THE END OF FORTY DAYS, THAT NOAH OPENED THE WINDOW OF THE ARK WHICH HE HAD MADE:

(7) "AND HE SENT FORTH A RAVEN, WHICH WENT FORTH TO AND FRO, UNTIL THE WATERS WERE DRIED UP FROM OFF THE EARTH.

(8) "ALSO HE SENT FORTH A DOVE FROM HIM, TO SEE IF THE WATERS WERE ABATED FROM OFF THE FACE OF THE GROUND;

(9) "BUT THE DOVE FOUND NO REST FOR THE SOLE OF HER FOOT, AND SHE RETURNED UNTO HIM INTO THE ARK, FOR THE WATERS WERE ON THE FACE OF THE WHOLE EARTH: THEN HE PUT FORTH HIS HAND, AND TOOK HER, AND PULLED HER IN UNTO HIM INTO THE ARK.

(10) "AND HE STAYED YET OTHER SEVEN DAYS; AND AGAIN HE SENT FORTH THE DOVE OUT OF THE ARK;

(11) "AND THE DOVE CAME IN TO HIM IN THE EVENING; AND, LO, IN HER MOUTH WAS AN OLIVE LEAF PLUCKED OFF: SO NOAH KNEW THAT THE WATERS WERE ABATED FROM OFF THE EARTH.

(12) "AND HE STAYED YET OTHER SEVEN DAYS; AND SENT FORTH THE DOVE; WHICH RETURNED NOT AGAIN UNTO HIM ANY MORE.

(13) "AND IT CAME TO PASS IN THE SIX HUNDREDTH AND FIRST YEAR, AND THE FIRST MONTH, THE FIRST DAY OF THE MONTH, THE WATERS WERE DRIED UP FROM OFF THE EARTH: AND NOAH REMOVED THE COVERING OF THE ARK, AND LOOKED, AND, BEHOLD, THE FACE OF THE GROUND WAS DRY.

NOTES

(14) "AND IN THE SECOND MONTH, ON THE SEVEN AND TWENTIETH DAY OF THE MONTH, WAS THE EARTH DRIED."

The synopsis is:

1. Noah waited forty days after the waters had begun to subside, before he opened the window of the Ark.

2. At the end of the forty days, Noah sent forth a raven. It went to and fro but did not return back to the Ark.

3. After that he sent forth a dove, but she found no resting place, and returned to the Ark.

4. Seven days later, he sent the dove out again. This time it came back with an olive leaf in its mouth. Olive leaves keep green underwater, so once the water was abated, the dove plucked one of the leaves.

5. He waited seven more days, and then sent the dove out again, with it not returning this time, showing that it had found dry land.

6. Noah then removed the covering of the Ark, which pertained to the roof, and was probably covered by skins.

7. Twelve lunar months make 354 days. Considering that the rains began in the six hundredth year of Noah's life, in the second month, and the seventeenth day of the month (Gen. 7:11), and that the waters receded, and were now dried up, *"in the second month, on the twenty-seventh day of the month,"* we find here 11 extra days over the lunar year. However, if we add that 11 days to 354, the result is exactly a full solar year of 365 days. So Noah was in the Ark one year to the day.

THE WINDOW IS OPENED

Verse 6 reads: *"And it came to pass at the end of forty days that Noah opened the window of the Ark which he had made."*

Noah had waited forty days after seeing the mountain heights around him rising clearly into the air, and then, impatient of the slow subsiding of the waters, he sent forth a raven to bring him some news of the state of the Earth.

THE RAVEN

Verse 7 reads: *"And he sent forth a raven, which went forth to and fro, until the waters were dried up from off the Earth."*

The evidence is, the raven flew away and did not fly back to the Ark. Consequently, Noah learned nothing from this fowl.

The raven is an unclean bird. It feeds on death instead of life. Death was not what Noah sought, but rather life, which could only be found by the dove.

The raven is typical of the unredeemed. They feed as well off of death rather than life. In fact, there is no life except in Christ, and even then it must be pointed out by the Holy Spirit. The unredeemed feed on the world, and to be sure, it is a place of death. Their actions lead to death, and because *"the wages of sin is death"* (Rom. 6:23).

THE DOVE

Verse 8 reads: *"Also he sent forth a dove from him, to see if the waters were abated from off the face of the ground."*

The dove is a clean bird, and seeks life. It is similar to the Redeemed who find life in Christ.

The dove at first coming back without finding anything in which to bring, at least anything which was alive, portrays the Believer coming back to Christ. Christ is always the resting place! Always the place of safety and security!

HIS HAND

Verse 9 reads: *"But the dove found no rest for the sole of her foot, and she returned unto him into the Ark, for the waters were on the face of the whole Earth: then he put forth his hand, and took her, and pulled her in unto him into the Ark."*

The raven had no camaraderie with Noah, typical of the unredeemed, while the dove definitely did.

While there were tops of mountains which were protruding out of the water, all on such places were wet and muddy, and in effect, a place of death. The dove could find no resting place in such an area, seeking that which was clean. So she comes back to the Ark.

The Scripture is very detailed and tender, as it portrays Noah putting forth his hand, gently taking her, and *"pulling her in unto him into the Ark."* Such is the gentleness of Christ.

When we as Believers do not find what we want or seek, we then come back to Him, knowing that we will not be reproved or chastened, but rather will be guaranteed His gentleness and kindness. He will take His Hand, extend it to us, and then gently pull us unto Him, with all that this affords.

How many times have all Believers been disappointed in not being able to do what we thought we could do? We find ourselves having to come back to Him, but it is never with trepidation or fear. We know the Gentle Hand will be outstretched, and the entirety of the safety of the Ark will be ours. There is no doubt about that!

In fact, not only is He always available, but He actually bids us to, *"Come unto Me, all that labor and are heavy laden, and I will give you rest.*

"Take My yoke upon you, and learn of Me; for I am meek and lowly at heart: and you shall find rest unto your souls.

"For My yoke is easy, and My burden is light" (Mat. 11:28-30).

And then again: *"The Lord is my Shepherd; I shall not want.*

"He makes me to lie down in green pastures: He leads me beside the still waters.

"He restores my soul: He leads me in the paths of Righteousness for His Name's sake.

"Yes, though I walk through the valley of the shadow of death, I will fear no evil: for You are with me; Your rod and Your staff they comfort me.

"You prepare a table before me in the presence of my enemies: You anoint my head with oil; my cup runs over.

"Surely goodness and mercy shall follow me all the days of my life: and I will dwell in the House of the LORD forever" (Ps. 23).

SEVEN DAYS

Verse 10 reads: *"And he stayed yet other seven days; and again he sent forth the dove out of the Ark."*

Faith doesn't quit, so seven days later, the dove will be sent forth again. Probably Faith is linked to the word *"again"* more than any other word. We keep believing and, therefore, we are *"sent forth again."*

While our patience wears out, the patience of God never wears out, that is if the Believer keeps exhibiting Faith. The Lord has never turned anyone aside, no matter how many or much the failures, and as well, no matter how bad the failures, as long as that person continues to exhibit Faith. Let the Reader always remember that when it comes to the Lord, He will help us *"again."*

THE OLIVE LEAF

Verse 11 reads: *"And the dove came in to him in the evening; and, lo, in her mouth was an olive leaf plucked off: so Noah knew that the waters were abated from off the Earth."*

The dove returning with an olive leaf in her mouth presents a sweet emblem of the renewed mind, which, in the midst of the surrounding desolation, seeks and finds its rest and portion in Christ; and not only so, but also lays hold of the earnest of the inheritance, and furnishes the blessed proof that judgment has passed away, and that a renewed Earth is coming fully into view.

The carnal mind, on the contrary, can rest in anything and everything but Christ. It can feed on uncleanness. *"The olive leaf"* has no attraction for it. It can find all it craves in a scene of death, and hence is not occupied with the thought of a new world and its glories; but the heart that is taught in exercise by the Spirit of God can only rest and rejoice in that in which He rests and rejoices. It rests in the Ark of His Salvation *"until the times of the restitution of all things."*

May it be thus with you and me, that Jesus be the abiding rest and portion of our hearts, so we may not seek them in a world which is under the judgment of God.

The dove went back to Noah, and waited for his time of rest: and we should ever find our place with Christ, until the time of His Exaltation and glory in the ages to come.

The Prophet Habakkuk said: *"And the LORD answered me, and said, 'Write the Vision, and make it plain upon tables, that he may run who reads it.*

"'For the Vision is yet for an appointed time, but at the end it shall speak, and not lie: though it tarry, wait for it; because it will surely come, it will not tarry.'"

The Prophet then said: *"Behold, his soul which is lifted up is not upright in him: but the just shall live by his faith"* (Hab. 2:2-4).

SEVEN DAYS MORE

Verse 12 reads: *"And he stayed yet other seven days; and sent forth the dove; which returned not again unto him any more."*

The frequent repetition of the number *"seven"* clearly points to the division of the *"week."*

Concerning the manner in which Noah did these things, Lewis said: *"The more we examine these acts of Noah, the more it will strike us that they must have been of a spiritual nature. He did not take such observations, and so send out the birds, as mere arbitrary acts, prompted simply by his curiosity or his impatience; but as man of faith and prayer he inquired of the Lord."*

The dove didn't return because this time, it no doubt found a suitable resting place, meaning that the waters were abating.

DRY GROUND

Verse 13 reads: *"And it came to pass in the six hundredth and first year, in the first month, the first day of the month, the waters were dried up from off the Earth: and Noah removed the covering of the Ark, and looked, and, behold, the face of the ground was dry."*

The *"face of the ground being dry"* refers to its surface only. There would be about 57 or 58 more days, according to the next Verse, making a complete solar year of 365 days, from the time the flood began, until it was sufficiently dry.

Someone has well said that mercies restored are much more affecting than mercies continued. Mathew Henry also said, and rightly so, *"The Divine power which then renewed the face of the Earth, can renew the face of an afflicted, troubled soul, and of a distressed, persecuted Church. God can make dry ground to appear, where it seems to be lost and forgotten."*

The Psalmist said: *"He sent from above, He took me, He drew me out of many waters.*

"He delivered me from my strong enemy, and from them which hated me: for they were too strong for me" (Ps. 18:16-17).

THE EARTH

Verse 14 reads: *"And in the second month, on the seven and twentieth day of the month, was the Earth dried."*

As we've already stated, coupling this with Genesis 7:11, we find a full solar year of 365 days.

The old lunar year of Old Testament times did not come out exactly to 30 days to the month, which would have totaled 360 days for a year. It actually came out to about 354. But if to these 354 days we add 11, that is, from the seventeenth to the twenty-seventh of the second month, the result is exactly, as stated, a full solar year of 365 days. As we reckon time presently, Noah was in the Ark exactly one year.

(15) "AND GOD SPOKE UNTO NOAH, SAYING,

(16) "GO FORTH OF THE ARK, YOU, AND YOUR WIFE, AND YOUR SONS, AND YOUR SONS' WIVES WITH YOU.

(17) "BRING FORTH WITH YOU EVERY LIVING THING THAT IS WITH YOU, OF ALL FLESH, BOTH OF FOWL, AND OF CATTLE, AND OF EVERY CREEPING THING THAT CREEPS UPON THE EARTH; THAT THEY MAY BREED ABUNDANTLY IN THE EARTH, AND BE FRUITFUL, AND MULTIPLY UPON THE EARTH.

(18) "AND NOAH WENT FORTH, AND HIS SONS, AND HIS WIFE, AND HIS SONS' WIVES WITH HIM:

(19) "EVERY BEAST, EVERY CREEPING THING, AND EVERY FOWL, AND WHATSOEVER CREEPS UPON THE EARTH, AFTER THEIR KINDS, WENT FORTH OUT OF THE ARK."

The structure is:

1. Noah did not move until the Lord told him to do so.

2. God spoke to Noah saying, *"Go forth,"* not *"come forth,"* showing that the Lord was in the Ark with Noah.

3. All the animals were to go forth with Noah as well.

AND GOD SPOKE

Verse 15 reads: *"And God spoke unto Noah, saying."*

We find from this short Scripture that Noah waited on the Lord. He did nothing here presumptuously. Before he would move, he must hear the Voice of the Lord telling him to move, and what to do.

The biggest problem we have as Christians is getting behind God or ahead of God.

Either way will prove to be the making of trouble. But we are so prone to do that, simply because we do not seek the Face of the Lord enough, as to direction.

The Lord, being God, knows all things. He knows the past, the present, and the future. As well, He has a perfect plan for our lives. The problem with that is that we have plans as well, but which are plans of our own devising. Nothing but trouble constitutes that road.

Paul said: *"Be not conformed to this world: but be transformed by the renewing of your mind, that you may prove what is that good, and acceptable, and perfect, will of God"* (Rom. 12:2).

This plainly tells us that the reason we often do not know the Will of God for our lives is because we're too much *"conformed to this world."* What does that mean?

It means that we are led by events, circumstances, situations, and happenings. In other words, we base our decisions on these things, which are all of the world.

Those particulars have no bearing whatsoever on God. He has a perfect plan for our lives, which is little impacted by events, etc. In fact, He will make circumstances and events work for us, if we will only allow Him to do so.

We must learn that our Source is not Wall Street, or the White House, of the State House. Our Source is God. As Believers, we function on an entirely different basis than the world. We function according to Faith in God, which means the price has already been paid at the Cross. So that means it's not faith in something that possibly will be, but faith in that which has already been.

THE COMMAND

Verse 16 reads: *"Go forth of the Ark, you, and your wife, and your sons, and your sons' wives with you."*

The Lord, being in the Ark with Noah, would tell him *"Go forth of the Ark,"*

If we have the mind of the Lord in all things, in other words, if we seek His direction, and determine to follow that direction, we will always have the Lord with us. Otherwise, we won't!

The same God Who had said, *"Make an Ark,"* and had said, *"Come into the Ark,"* now says, *"Go forth of the Ark."* We see here Perfect Leading and Guidance, which should be an example to all of us. Martin Luther said: *"He who undertakes anything without the Divine Word will labor in vain."*

DIRECTION

Verse 17 reads: *"Bring forth with you every living thing that is with you, of all flesh, both of fowl, and of cattle, and of every creeping thing that creeps upon the Earth; that they may breed abundantly in the Earth, and be fruitful, and multiply upon the Earth."*

This proclaims the fact that the flood was universal. In other words, it covered the entirety of the Earth.

Were that not true, there would have been no necessity of bringing the animals in the first place. If the flood wasn't universal, there would have been animals left in the unaffected places, which most definitely would have migrated over the affected places, after the flood was over, all in a very short time. Yes, the flood was universal!

OBEDIENCE

Verse 18 reads: *"And Noah went forth, and his sons, and his wife, and his sons' wives with him."*

After being in the Ark for one year, it is positive that Noah and his family strongly desired a changed location. That would be obvious; however, as we have seen, the Patriarch didn't move until God said move. What a lesson for us presently!

How the Lord spoke to Noah we aren't told. Maybe it was audibly, or an impression upon his spirit, but the thing is, He definitely spoke.

To be certain, we presently have a more sure witness. We have the Word of God to guide us, which the antediluvians did not have. As well, due to what Christ did at the Cross, we have the Holy Spirit now residing within us, Who will help us to understand the Word, and will give us Leading and Guidance in all things, that is, if we will earnestly seek the Face of the Lord (Jn. 16:13). So if we don't have the Leading of the Holy Spirit within our hearts and lives, then the fault has to be ours.

EVERY BEAST

Verse 19 reads: *"Every beast, every creeping thing, and every fowl, and whatsoever creeps upon the Earth, after their kinds, went forth out of the Ark."*

The idea is, the animals did not leave the Ark in confusion, or at random, one might say, but in an orderly fashion, as they had come in, each one sorting to its kind.

(20) "AND NOAH BUILT AN ALTAR UNTO THE LORD; AND TOOK OF EVERY CLEAN BEAST, AND EVERY CLEAN FOWL, AND OFFERED BURNT OFFERINGS ON THE ALTAR.

(21) "AND THE LORD SMELLED A SWEET SAVOUR; AND THE LORD SAID IN HIS HEART, I WILL NOT AGAIN CURSE THE GROUND ANY MORE FOR MAN'S SAKE; FOR THE IMAGINATION OF MAN'S HEART IS EVIL FROM HIS YOUTH; NEITHER WILL I AGAIN SMITE ANY MORE EVERY LIVING THING, AS I HAVE DONE.

(22) "WHILE THE EARTH REMAINS, SEEDTIME AND HARVEST, AND COLD AND HEAT, AND SUMMER AND WINTER, AND DAY AND NIGHT SHALL NOT CEASE."

The composite is:

1. Civilization, as it sprang from the sons of Noah, has its Foundation in the Cross of Christ, i.e., *"the Altar."*

2. The Lord smelled a sweet savour from the offering up of this Sacrifice, because it spoke of the coming Redeemer, Who would lift man out of this morass of evil.

3. The *"curse"* of which God speaks here refers to the fact that He will not again visit the Earth with a flood.

4. The mention of the *"imagination of man's heart being evil from his youth,"* means that God will take into consideration the results of the Fall, over which man at the time has no control. However, there is a remedy, which is the Altar, i.e., *"the Cross."*

5. The Promise is given here that the seasons of the year will continue forever, because the Earth will remain forever.

THE ALTAR

Verse 20 reads: *"And Noah built an Altar unto the LORD; and took of every clean beast, and of every clean fowl, and offered Burnt Offerings on the Altar."*

The Altar on which sacrifices were offered respecting Old Testament times represented the Cross of Christ. This means that civilization began after the flood, by looking forward to the coming Redeemer, Who would lift man out of this morass of evil.

The *"Burnt Offerings"* offered up by Noah, which consisted of clean animals and fowls, consisted of the idea that God would give His all in order to redeem humanity, which would be in the form of His Son, the Lord Jesus Christ, and that we, in turn, must give the Lord our all as well. It speaks of the fact of consecration. As God has consecrated Himself to the Redemption of man, which was definitely carried out at the Cross, likewise, we must consecrate ourselves to serve Him to the very best of our ability. But as should be obvious, there is a vast difference in *"His all,"* and *"our all."* We really have nothing to offer the Lord, except a *"willing mind and an obedient heart."*

All of this constitutes the obedience of Faith and the worship of Faith: both go together. The Altar is erected where, just before, all had been a scene of death and judgment. The Ark had taken Noah and his family safely over the waters of judgment. It had carried him from the old into the new world, where he now takes his place as a worshipper. It must be observed that it was *"unto the Lord"* he erected his Altar. Superstition would have worshiped *"the Ark,"* as being the means of Salvation. It is ever the tendency of the heart to displace God by His Ordinances. The Ark, to be sure, was a very marked and manifest Ordinance; but Noah's Faith passed beyond the Ark to the God of the Ark; and hence, when he stepped out of it, instead of casting back a lingering look at it, or regarding it as an object of worship or veneration, he built an Altar unto the Lord, which looked forward to the coming Redeemer Who Alone can save, and worshiped Him; and the Ark is never heard of again.

IDOLATRY

This teaches us a very simple, but, at the same time, a very seasonable lesson. The moment the heart lets slip the reality of God Himself, there is no placing a limit to its declension; it is on the highway to the grossest

forms of idolatry. In the judgment of Faith, an Ordinance is only valuable as it conveys God, in living power, to the soul — that is to say, so long as Faith can enjoy Christ therein, according to His Own appointment. Beyond this, it is worth nothing; and if it, in the smallest degree, comes between the heart and His precious Work and His glorious Person, it ceases to be an Ordinance of God, and becomes an instrument of the Devil.

In the judgment of superstition, the Ordinance is everything, and God is shut out; and the Name of God is only made use of to exalt the Ordinance, and give it a deep hold on the human heart, and a mighty influence over the human mind.

Thus it was that the Children of Israel worshiped the Brazen Serpent. That which had once been a channel of blessing to them, because used of God, became, when their hearts had departed from the Lord, an object of superstitious veneration; and Hezekiah had to break it in pieces, and call it *"a piece of copper."*

When used of God, it was a means of rich blessing. Now, Faith owned it to be what Divine Revelation said it was; but superstition, throwing, as it ever does, Divine Revelation overboard, lost the real purpose of God in the thing, and actually made a god of the thing itself (II Ki. 18:4).

A GREAT LESSON

There is a deep lesson in all of this for the present age. We live in an age of Ordinances. The atmosphere which enwraps the professing Church is impregnated with the elements of traditional religion, which robs the soul of Christ and His Divinely full Salvation. It is not that human tradition boldly denies that there is such a person as Christ, or such a thing as the Cross of Christ: were it to do so, the eyes of many might be opened. However, it is not thus.

The evil is of a far more insidious and dangerous character. Ordinances are added to Christ and the Work of Christ. Consequently, the sinner is not saved by Christ Alone, but by Christ and Ordinances, or as one might say, *"Christ plus!"* Thus he is robbed of Christ altogether; for it will assuredly be found that Christ and Ordinances will prove, in the sequel, to be Ordinances and not Christ.

Paul bluntly said: *"If you be circumcised, Christ shall profit you nothing"* (Gal. 5:2). It must be Christ wholly, or not at all.

Satan persuades man that they are honoring Christ when they make much of His Ordinances; whereas, all the while, he knows full well that they are, in reality, setting Christ entirely aside, and thereby, deifying the Ordinance.

(The author is indebted to C. H. Mackintosh for the material on idolatry and Ordinances.)

THE MODERN CHURCH

There are millions who think they are saved because they have been baptized in water. For these people, it is Christ plus Water Baptism. Other millions fall into the same category as it regards the Lord's Supper. Others as it regards speaking with other tongues. Many even think that their Salvation hinges on being baptized in water by a particular formula. And then we have great segments of the Charismatic Church which claims that the Atonement is in two parts. They claim that it's in: A. The Cross and B. Jesus suffering in Hell for three days and three nights, and we speak of the burning side of Hell.

By this action, they have concluded that the Finished Work of Christ on the Cross actually was not finished, and they have added to the Atonement that which they have produced out of a figment of their imagination. It's not in the Word of God, and I continue to speak of this second part to Atonement which they claim, so it has to be something made up out of whole cloth, so to speak. In fact, some of these Teachers claim that the Lord revealed this to them. I would suggest that it was not the Lord Who revealed this error to them, but rather an angel of light (II Cor. 11:13-15).

God's plan of Salvation, and that includes everything we receive from the Lord, is *"Jesus Christ and Him Crucified"* (I Cor. 2:2). If we add anything to that, or take anything from that, we have seriously violated the Word of God. And let the Reader please understand that we are not speaking here of

NOTES

mere semantics. We are rather speaking of the Plan of God for the Redemption of the human race.

A SWEET SAVOUR

Verse 21 reads: *"And the LORD smelled a sweet savour; and the LORD said in His heart, I will not again curse the ground any more for man's sake; for the imagination of man's heart is evil from his youth; neither will I again smite any more everything living, as I have done."*

Several things are said in this Verse which are of tremendous significance.

The Lord *"smelled a sweet savour,"* as it regards the sacrifice which Noah offered up.

Now of course, the question begs to be asked, how can flesh burning on an Altar, and sending its greasy smoke upwards, be constituted a *"sweet savour"*? In the natural it wouldn't; however, it's what it represented which brought about the *"sweet savour."*

The Altar and its sacrifices were Types of Christ offering up Himself as a Sacrifice on the Cross.

To be sure, that means nothing to the world, and regrettably, it doesn't seem to mean much to the Church; however, that which Noah did, and no doubt at the behest of the Lord, proclaimed the fact that he understood that man's only hope was what that Altar and its sacrifices represented. Other things may be important, but they are always subsidiary to the Cross. That's why Paul said:

"For Christ sent me not to baptize, but to preach the Gospel: not with wisdom of words, lest the Cross of Christ should be made of none effect" (I Cor. 1:17).

That's our problem! By placing the emphasis on other things, the modern Church has made the Cross of Christ of none effect. This is the sure road to destruction.

When the Lord said to Noah, *"I will not again curse the ground any more for man's sake,"* in the Hebrew, it doesn't mean a revocation of the curse of Genesis 3:17. The language refers solely to the visitation of the deluge, and promises not that God may not sometimes visit particular localities with a flood, but that another such worldwide catastrophe should never overtake the human race.

When the Lord spoke of the *"imagination of man's heart being evil from his youth,"* whereas He had formerly visited man with judicial extermination on account of his absolute moral corruption, He would now have regard to the circumstance that man inherited his depravity through his birth. Therefore, instead of smiting man with punitive destruction, He would visit him with compassionate forbearance.

Maybe one could say that there was a Divine regret at so calamitous an act as the deluge, although that act was absolutely just and necessary.

SEASONS

Verse 22 reads: *"While the Earth remains, seedtime and harvest, and cold and heat, and summer and winter, and day and night shall not cease."*

We are told here that seasons will remain forever and forever, as it regards the Earth. In essence, what Noah said is that there would be no more deluge, but that the Earth and the seasons of the year were again to return according to their former order. They will continue forever in that order.

The statement, *"While the Earth remains,"* doesn't actually imply that it has but a particular time and then will perish. To be sure, the system of this Earth will definitely perish after the Millennial Reign, but the Earth at that time will be restored to a pristine newness, which it will retain forever. We are given this description in Revelation, Chapters 21 and 22.

"When I saw the cleansing fountain,
"Open wide for all my sin,
"I obeyed the Spirit's wooing,
"When He said, 'Will you be clean?'"

"Tho' the way seems straight and narrow,
"All I claimed was swept away;
"My ambitions, plans, and wishes,
"At my feet in ashes lay."

"Then God's fire upon the Altar
"Of my heart was set aflame;
"I shall never cease to praise Him,
"Glory, glory to His Name!"

"Blessed be the Name of Jesus!
"I'm so glad He took me in;

"He's forgiven my transgressions,
"He has cleansed my heart from sin."

"Glory, glory to the Father!
"Glory, glory to the Son!
"Glory, glory to the Spirit!
"Glory to the Three in One!"

CHAPTER 9

(1) "AND GOD BLESSED NOAH AND HIS SONS, AND SAID UNTO THEM, BE FRUITFUL, AND MULTIPLY, AND REPLENISH THE EARTH.

(2) "AND THE FEAR OF YOU AND THE DREAD OF YOU SHALL BE UPON EVERY BEAST OF THE EARTH, AND UPON EVERY FOWL OF THE AIR, UPON ALL THAT MOVETH UPON THE EARTH, AND UPON ALL THE FISH OF THE SEA; INTO YOUR HAND ARE THEY DELIVERED.

(3) "EVERY MOVING THING THAT LIVES SHALL BE MEAT FOR YOU; EVEN AS THE GREEN HERB HAVE I GIVEN YOU ALL THINGS."

The composite is:

1. The Lord blessed Noah and his family.

2. They were to *"be fruitful, multiply, and replenish the Earth."*

3. The normal condition of the lower creatures will be one of instinctive dread of man.

4. To be delivered into the hand of man refers to the fact that man would be able to tame and reduce certain animals to be of help to him.

5. All the animals could serve as food, as well as could vegetables. Genesis 1:29 implies that man was exclusively vegetarian before the flood.

THE BLESSING

Verse 1 reads: *"And God blessed Noah and his sons, and said unto them, Be fruitful, and multiply, and replenish the Earth."*

Several very significant things are said in this Verse:

The blessing that God gave to Noah was in effect a Covenant. This given to the second father of mankind is exactly parallel to that given to our first father in Genesis 1:28-29 and 2:16-17, with one significant deletion, and as well, with a couple of additions. We'll take those first.

Animals are now given to man for his food, whereas before the flood, man was strictly vegetarian (Gen. 1:29). Connected with this, there is a prohibition against the eating of blood.

Also, there seems to be an added sanction given to human life, with the evident object of guarding against such a disruption of the human race as was the result of Cain's murder of Abel.

The deletion as it regards the Covenant has the removal of the words *"and subdue it,"* which had a place in the Adamic blessing (Gen. 1:28). In the Covenant given to Noah, they are omitted for the obvious reason that the world dominion originally assigned to man in Adam had been forfeited by sin, and could only be restored through the ideal Man, the woman's Seed, to Whom it had been transferred at the Fall. Hence says Paul, speaking of Christ: *"And has put all things under His feet, and gave Him to be the Head over all things to the Church"* (Eph. 1:22).

David said this concerning Christ: *"You made Him to have dominion over the works of Your hands: You have put all things under His feet"* (Ps. 8:6).

As well, the word *"replenish"* is the same Hebrew word here as the one used in Genesis 1:28. As is obvious, it means here to fill back up that which is now empty, but which was once full. In other words, the human race, which perished in the flood, is now to be replenished.

If it means that here, and it definitely does, then it means the same thing in Genesis 1:28, which refers to the fact that there must have been some type of intelligent creation on this Earth before Adam and Eve. Had there not been, I cannot really see how the Holy Spirit would have used the word *"replenish"* as it regards instructions given to Adam.

In all of this, God's command to man, on his entrance into the restored Earth, was to refill the Earth — not parts of the Earth, but the entirety of the Earth. He desired to have men dispersed abroad, over the face of the

world, not relying on their own concentrated energies. We shall see in Chapter 11 how man neglected all this.

THE ANIMAL CREATION

Verse 2 reads: *"And the fear of you and the dread of you shall be upon every beast of the Earth, and upon every fowl of the air, upon all that moves upon the Earth, and upon all the fish of the sea; into your hand are they delivered."*

This does not imply that the animals may not sometimes rise against man and destroy him, which of course does happen occasionally. It does mean that the normal condition of the lower creatures will be one of the instinctive dread of man.

According to the words, *"into your hand are they delivered,"* man has been able to tame most animals, and even to use some of them in the service of labor, such as the horse, the ox, etc.

FOOD

Verse 3 reads: *"Every moving thing that lives shall be meat for you; even as the green herb have I given you all things."*

Man had been completely vegetarian before the flood (Gen. 1:29), but now that restriction is lifted, with animals now serving as food also.

(4) "BUT FLESH WITH THE LIFE THEREOF, WHICH IS THE BLOOD THEREOF, SHALL YOU NOT EAT.

(5) "AND SURELY YOUR BLOOD OF YOUR LIVES WILL I REQUIRE; AT THE HAND OF EVERY BEAST WILL I REQUIRE IT, AND AT THE HAND OF MAN; AT THE HAND OF EVERY MAN'S BROTHER WILL I REQUIRE THE LIFE OF MAN.

(6) "WHOSO SHEDS MAN'S BLOOD, BY MAN SHALL HIS BLOOD BE SHED: FOR IN THE IMAGE OF GOD MADE HE MAN."

The overview is:

1. Man is prohibited from eating blood.

2. Verse 5 condemns suicide, as well as homicide.

3. If man is proven guilty in a court of law for the crime of cold-blooded murder, the state has the right to take his life.

4. This is not meant to deter crime, but rather to impress upon mankind the value

of man in that he was originally created *"in the Image of God."*

THE BLOOD

Verse 4 reads: *"But flesh with the life thereof, which is the blood thereof, shall you not eat."*

The actual words in the Hebrew are, *"Only flesh in its soul, its blood, you shall not eat."*

While the blood is not the soul, there is a close connection. The life of the flesh is in the blood, which is the animation of the flesh. As the blood is to the flesh of man, the soul is as well to the spirit of man. But there is a difference:

The soul is not the life of the spirit, because the soul and the spirit cannot die. Man is a soul, he has a spirit, and both the soul and the spirit inhabit the tabernacle of flesh, called the body.

The blood is God's special gift; for He Alone can bestow upon that aggregation of solids and fluids which we call a body, the secret principle of life. Of this hidden life the blood is the representative, and while man is permitted to have the body of the animal for his food, as being the mere vessel which contains this life, the gift itself must go back to God, and the blood as its symbol be treated with reverence (Ellicott).

The idea of the unity of the soul and the blood, on which the prohibition of blood is based, comes to light everywhere in Scripture. In the blood of one mortally wounded his soul flows forth (Lam. 2:12), and he who voluntarily sacrifices himself pours out his soul unto death (Isa. 53:12). The murderer of the innocent slays the soul of the blood of the innocent (Deut. 27:25).

But the main reason of forbidding the eating of blood was because the shedding of blood in Sacrifices typified the great Atonement which would be carried out by Christ, in the shedding of His life's blood, which He in fact, has already done.

Concerning that, the prohibition is still in force, imposed upon the Gentile converts in the Christian Church by the authority of the Holy Spirit and the Apostles (Acts 15:28-29).

SUICIDE AND HOMICIDE

Verse 5 reads: *"And surely your blood of your lives will I require; at the hand of every*

beast will I require it, and at the hand of man; at the hand of every man's brother will I require the life of man."

This Passage presents a strong prohibition against suicide and homicide. It even goes so far as to claim the life of an animal which kills a man.

This is a solemn proclamation of the sanctity of human life. As well, this prohibition carried over into the Mosaic Law, and is binding on Christians as well (Rom. 13:1-6). The words, *"At the hand of every man's brother will I require the life of man,"* means there will be no exceptions.

As should be obvious here, the Passage is speaking of cold-blooded murder.

As it regards suicide, the Passage states here, *"Your blood of your lives will I require."*

Our lives are not so our own, as that we may quit them at our own pleasure; but they are God's, and we must resign them at His pleasure. If we in any way hasten our own death, we are accountable to God for it (Henry).

ABORTION

The Bible teaches that the person is an eternal soul at the time of conception. David said: *"Behold, I was shaped in iniquity; and in sin did my mother conceive me"* (Ps. 51:5).

David is speaking here of original sin, meaning that all babies are born in a fallen state, in the likeness of Adam (Gen. 5:3).

But as a side issue, this Passage tells us that David was a person at conception. So if that fetus had died in its mother's womb, it would have been David who died. This means that while it is not wrong to prevent conception from taking place to begin with, it is definitely wrong to terminate the pregnancy after conception.

While I see nothing wrong with a pill to prevent conception, I think that a pill taken the morning after, so to speak, to terminate a pregnancy that has just begun is very much wrong. This means that abortion is wrong in any case, unless it would be to save the Mother's life, which very seldom ever happens.

It is not my intention to be unkind or to bring guilt on those who have committed such sin, but at the same time, I personally believe that according to the Scriptures, abortion is murder. I realize that many bridle at that statement; however, if in fact God looks at the conception as a person, which every evidence is that He does, then we would have to say, if in fact that pregnancy is terminated, a person has died, or in such a case, has been killed. Listen to the Prophet Jeremiah:

"Then the Word of the LORD came unto me, saying,

"Before I formed you in the belly I knew you; and before you came forth out of the womb I sanctified you, and I ordained you a Prophet unto the nations" (Jer. 1:4-5). If the pregnancy regarding Jeremiah's Mother would have been terminated, it would have been Jeremiah the Prophet who would have been killed.

The idea that a woman's body is her own, and she can do with it as she likes, is not Scriptural. Ideally, the body is supposed to be the Temple of the Holy Spirit. And as well, the conception in her womb, even though nourished by her body, is in fact, a distinct and separate human being. So I'll ask this question!

Does a woman have the right to kill her child after it is born? Of course the answer to that is a resounding *"no!"* Well, neither does she have the right to abort that same child before it is born. She is responsible for it the moment it is conceived.

It is ironic; it is against the Law in the United States to transport a lobster from one place to another in the third trimester of its pregnancy. (Yes, I said a lobster!) But it's not against the law for a woman to abort a baby.

"Professing themselves to be wise, they became fools" (Rom. 1:22).

CAPITAL PUNISHMENT

Verse 6 reads: *"Whoso sheds man's blood, by man shall his blood be shed: for in the Image of God made He man."*

In this Covenant, we actually have the institution of Government. In other words, for about 1,600 years, from the time of the Fall, man had lived in the Dispensation of Conscience. While conscience remains in vogue, man now enters into the Dispensation of Government, which as well will remain in vogue forever.

NOTES

In the governmental rulings laid down by God, as they were given to Noah, capital punishment for capital crimes is instituted here.

The Passage speaks here of that which we refer to as *"cold-blooded murder."* If such is done, the Lord told Noah that responsible authorities must demand the life of the one who has committed such a crime.

The word *"sheddeth"* literally means *"willfully and unwarrantably."* It does not refer to accidents, or that which is done judicially.

In such a case, responsible authorities, and we speak of Civil Government, are to act as God's instruments and agents.

It must be understood that this command was given long before the Law of Moses was enacted. In fact, it is meant to be a part of Government for all time.

Under the New Covenant, which covers the present time, and all time thereafter, the Holy Spirit through Paul upheld this command. He said:

"Let every soul be subject unto the higher powers (Civil Government). *For there is no power but of God: the powers that be are ordained of God* (God ordains Civil Government).

"Whosoever therefore resists the power, resists the Ordinance of God (meaning that we are to obey the law unless the law is opposed to the Word of God, or it violates our conscience)*: and they that resist shall receive to themselves damnation.*

"For rulers are not a terror to good works, but to the evil (this speaks of responsible Government). *Will you then not be afraid of the power? Do that which is good, and you shall have praise of the same* (in other words, obey the law, whether you like the law or not, unless it violates the Word of God)*:*

"For he is the Minister of God (Civil Authorities) *to you for good. But if you do that which is evil, be afraid; for he bears not the sword in vain: for he is the Minister of God, a revenger to execute wrath upon him who does evil.*

"Wherefore you must needs be subject, not only for wrath, but also for conscience sake (in other words, it's the right thing to do)*"* (Rom. 13:1-5).

If it is to be noticed, Paul mentioned the bearing of the sword. This means that God gives Civil Authorities not only the right to govern, but to put down all those who would seek to disrupt good Government, even to the place and position of using lethal force if necessary.

These Passages not only give Civil Authorities the right to put down crime, etc., and even to engage in capital punishment if the crime warrants such, but as well, it gives righteous nations the Scriptural right to put down rogue nations which would take peace from the Earth.

This means that the Government of the United States is correct in putting down terrorism all over the world, and using whatever force it takes to accomplish this task. In fact, if our nation did not do it, it would be failing God. Now that is not to say that all tactics or strategies are correct, but that the general principle of ridding the world of terrorism most definitely is correct.

In fact, the Holy Spirit through Paul also gave Government the right to levy taxes, and we as Christians are obligated before God to pay taxes. While it is certainly true that Governments at times become excessive as it regards taxes, that is the fault of those in Government, and not Government in general as laid down by God.

While I may not agree with all the ways that Government spends my tax dollars, I'm not personally responsible for that. But I am responsible for paying my fair share of taxes, as is every Christian, and every citizen for that matter (Rom. 13:6).

THE IMAGE OF GOD

Many claim that capital punishment is not a deterrent to crime. They are right, it isn't a deterrent, and in fact, is not meant to be.

Capital punishment for capital crimes was ordained by God because of the inherent worth of man.

Man was originally made in the Image of God. While that image has been woefully marred by the Fall, to be sure, the original intention is still there.

For Instance, the nations of the world who hold to some form of Christianity place a high value on human life. The further away from the Bible a nation gets, even to embracing false religions, etc., the value of human life becomes less and less.

As is obvious, in the Muslim world, human life has very little value. They may claim that it does, but their actions prove otherwise.

(7) "AND YOU, BE YE FRUITFUL, AND MULTIPLY; BRING FORTH ABUNDANTLY IN THE EARTH, AND MULTIPLY THEREIN.

(8) "AND GOD SPAKE UNTO NOAH, AND TO HIS SONS WITH HIM, SAYING,

(9) "AND I, BEHOLD, I ESTABLISH MY COVENANT WITH YOU, AND WITH YOUR SEED AFTER YOU;

(10) "AND WITH EVERY LIVING CREATURE THAT IS WITH YOU, OF THE FOWL, OF THE CATTLE, AND OF EVERY BEAST OF THE EARTH WITH YOU; FROM ALL THAT GO OUT OF THE ARK, TO EVERY BEAST OF THE EARTH.

(11) "AND I WILL ESTABLISH MY COVENANT WITH YOU, NEITHER SHALL ALL FLESH BE CUT OFF ANY MORE BY THE WATERS OF A FLOOD; NEITHER SHALL THERE ANY MORE BE A FLOOD TO DESTROY THE EARTH."

The exegesis is:

1. The population on Earth is to be fruitful and multiply.

2. God continues to speak to Noah, and to Noah's sons as well.

3. The Covenant that God established with Noah was to be extended to all thereafter. In fact, it still stands.

4. This Covenant will also include all the animal kingdom and the fowls of the air, in other words, all of God's creation on Earth.

5. The Covenant that God gives guarantees that the world will never again be destroyed by water.

POPULATION

Verse 7 reads: *"And you, be fruitful, and multiply; and bring forth abundantly in the Earth, and multiply therein."*

As I dictate these notes in October of 2001, there are approximately six billion people on this Earth.

Those who favor abortion claim that it cuts down on the population and is, therefore, valuable and necessary. They are claiming that the population is growing at such a rate that very soon it will not able to feed itself.

What is the truth as it regards the population increase in the world?

There definitely are problems with food, growth, and distribution, but the population has nothing to do with it. Believe it or not, unbiblical religion is the cause of most of the problems in this world. Once again, look at the nations of the world which at least to a degree hold the Bible in high regard. They are able to feed themselves bountifully, plus many others in the world. Look at the nations who ignore the Bible, or do not believe the Bible, and for the most part, you will find countries which cannot feed themselves. There may be an exception here and there, but not many.

The truth is, the world as it is now, if utilized properly, could easily feed 100 billion people.

We talk about the population, but do you realize that the entirety of the population of the world could actually be placed in the rooms in New York City? That means if every room in New York City, with all of its square footage, was utilized totally, every person in this world would fit into those rooms. In fact, the State of Texas would hold every person in the world, and give each family enough room to build a house, and at the same time, have enough room for a nice size garden.

No, population isn't the problem. The evil heart of man is the problem!

THE WORD OF GOD

Verse 8 reads: *"And God spoke unto Noah, and to his sons with him, saying."*

The problem with the world is that it ignores what God has said, and seeks to establish its own way, which always concludes in catastrophe.

God is the Creator of man. And if man will follow God, will seek to obey the Word of God, man can find development, fulfillment, happiness, and in fact, life can be pleasant. But without God, there is no life to speak of.

Jesus said: *"The thief* (Satan) *comes not, but for to steal, and to kill, and to destroy: I am come that they might have life, and that they might have it more abundantly"* (Jn. 10:10).

In a nutshell so to speak, in this one Verse of Scripture, we have the entirety of the cause of the problem, which is Satan and those who follow him, and the cure for the problem,

Who is the Lord Jesus Christ, and those who follow Him.

COVENANT

Verse 9 reads: *"And I, behold, I establish My Covenant with you, and with your seed after you."*

The Covenant between God and man is thus solemnly introduced as Elohim's Personal act. No Covenant is mentioned as existing between the Lord and the antediluvian world, but now, man in a sense is brought nearer to God by being admitted into Covenant with Him.

Now some may look at this Covenant, and conclude it to be inconsequential. But if it's looked at closely, we will see that this Covenant in all capacities is of tremendous magnitude:

1. The Scripture plainly says that *"God blessed Noah and his sons"* (Gen. 9:1). Within itself, that is of such magnitude as to defy all description. To have God bless us is to have anything and everything we need, and all of that in an abundant supply.

2. God has promised that He would not bring another flood upon the Earth. In effect, He is saying that the world will enjoy perpetual generations without fear. And of course, the greatest Promise of all continued in force, that the Seed of the woman would ultimately come, and would take back the dominion that man had forfeited to Satan (Gen. 3:15).

From the time of Noah on, man had every opportunity to follow the Lord, but we soon find that man grossly strayed, thereby forfeiting the blessings, but still enjoying the guarantee of perpetual generations without fear.

THE LOWER CREATION

Verse 10 reads: *"And with every living creature that is with you, of the fowl, of the cattle, and of every beast of the Earth with you; from all that go out of the Ark, to every beast of the Earth."*

Not only is man included in the Covenant, but as well, the lower creation is also included.

Some attempt to claim that the flood was not universal, misreading the phrase, *"And of every beast of the Earth with you; from all that go out of the Ark, to every beast of the Earth."* They claim that the last phrase *"to every beast of the Earth,"* refers to animals which were in places of the Earth that the flood did not reach. That is not the case at all!

If it is to be noticed, the Lord spoke to Noah *"of every beast of the Earth with you,"* which refers to those that were in the Ark. The last phrase, *"to every beast of the Earth,"* refers to the animals which would be born after their parents, so to speak, were released from the Ark. This would go on into perpetuity.

The Lord is saying that the Covenant not only includes man and his seed after him, but also all the animals, and all the animals which would be born or hatched, etc.

As we've already stated, if in fact that flood was not universal, there would have been no reason to put any animals in the Ark. Those in places untouched by the flood would have quickly spread to the parts of the Earth drowned by the flood. No, the flood was universal!

FLOOD

Verse 11 reads: *"And I will establish My Covenant with you, neither shall all flesh be cut off any more by the waters of a flood; neither shall there any more be a flood to destroy the Earth."*

Concerning the part of the Covenant which guaranteed that there would never be another flood, considering the times it is repeated, it would seem that the Words of the Lord are even tediously repeated.

We must understand that the Holy Spirit never heaps words upon another in vain. When we consider how great was the fear of Noah and his family during and after the deluge, we can readily understand why it was necessary for God to say the same things over and over.

Regrettably, man has to be constantly reassured by God. It's almost as if what the Lord has said, He has to say over and over again because of man's faithlessness, weakness, and fear.

As an example, when the Lord gives any of us a Promise, which greatly blesses us, encourages us, and fills our hearts with hope, in just a short time there will be some adversity. During that time of adversity, it is very difficult to hold onto the original Promise of

God. Over and over again, it seems that He has to renew the Promise made to us, which He is kind and gracious enough to do in many and varied ways.

In fact, our faith is never quite what it ought to be. One of the major reasons for that is that the object of our faith is sometimes wrong.

The object of Faith always must be the Cross of Christ. The Lord held out that hope from the very outset of the Fall. It was then prophetical, and it is now historical.

To properly know and understand the Word of God, one without reservation, must have one's faith anchored completely in the Cross. In other words, the Cross must ever be the object of one's Faith. If we don't, discouragement quickly sets in.

(12) "AND GOD SAID, THIS IS THE TOKEN OF THE COVENANT WHICH I MAKE BETWEEN ME AND YOU AND EVERY LIVING CREATURE THAT IS WITH YOU, FOR PERPETUAL GENERATIONS:

(13) "I DO SET MY BOW IN THE CLOUD, AND IT SHALL BE FOR A TOKEN OF A COVENANT BETWEEN ME AND THE EARTH.

(14) "AND IT SHALL COME TO PASS, WHEN I BRING A CLOUD OVER THE EARTH, THAT THE BOW SHALL BE SEEN IN THE CLOUD:

(15) "AND I WILL REMEMBER MY COVENANT, WHICH IS BETWEEN ME AND YOU AND EVERY LIVING CREATURE OF ALL FLESH; AND THE WATERS SHALL NO MORE BECOME A FLOOD TO DESTROY ALL FLESH.

(16) "AND THE BOW SHALL BE IN THE CLOUD; AND I WILL LOOK UPON IT, THAT I MAY REMEMBER THE EVERLASTING COVENANT BETWEEN GOD AND EVERY LIVING CREATURE OF ALL FLESH THAT IS UPON THE EARTH.

(17) "AND GOD SAID UNTO NOAH, THIS IS THE TOKEN OF THE COVENANT, WHICH I HAVE ESTABLISHED BETWEEN ME AND ALL FLESH THAT IS UPON THE EARTH.

(18) "AND THE SONS OF NOAH, THAT WENT FORTH OF THE ARK, WERE SHEM, AND HAM, AND JAPHETH: AND HAM IS THE FATHER OF CANAAN.

(19) "THESE ARE THE THREE SONS OF NOAH: AND OF THEM WAS THE WHOLE EARTH OVERSPREAD."

The synopsis is:

1. In the Covenant, God promises perpetual generations.

2. As a token that there would never be another flood, the Lord set a rainbow in the cloud.

3. Every time the bow would be seen, it was to be a reminder of what God had promised.

4. The Covenant that God was now making was to be *"the Everlasting Covenant."*

5. From the sons of Noah, who are Shem, Ham, and Japheth, would come the entirety of the population of the Earth, and for all time.

PERPETUAL GENERATIONS

Verse 12 reads: *"And God said, This is the token of the Covenant which I make between me and you and every living creature that is with you, for perpetual generations."*

In this Covenant is the guarantee of *"perpetual generations."*

The word *"perpetual"* means, *"continuing forever, everlasting."* So in these two words *"perpetual generations,"* we are told that such will continue forever.

This means that man will not destroy himself with atomic weapons, or some such like inventions, and it also means that the Earth will not be destroyed by a shower of meteorites, etc.

As well, it tells us that even after the Perfect Age to come, which is portrayed in Revelation, Chapters 21 and 22, the perpetual generations will continue forever. This means that alongside the Angels on Earth, which God will then have made His Headquarters, and the Glorified Saints, which includes all who have part in the First Resurrection, at the same time, there will be natural generations of people who are not glorified, but yet are Saved, and will live forever by virtue of the Tree of Life (Rev. 21:24; 22:1, 2). As stated, these generations will go on forever.

THE BOW

Verse 13 reads: *"I do set My bow in the cloud, and it shall be for a token of a Covenant between Me and the Earth."*

The whole creation rests, as to its exemption from a second deluge, on the eternal stability of God's Covenant, of which the bow is the token.

In this context, the rainbow admonishes us to be thankful to God, for whenever it appears, it reminds all men of God's great wrath which once destroyed the world by the flood. But it also comforts us by recalling to our minds that God in His matchless Grace resolved no longer to execute such terrible punishment. Thus it teaches us both the fear of God and trust in God, and these are of all virtues the greatest (Luther).

The question has been asked whether the rainbow existed already before the flood, and as well, did it rain before the flood?

I think there is evidence that it did rain periodically, from the time the creation was finished. So the idea that rain was something the antediluvians had never seen before as it regards the flood is not substantiated by Scripture (Gen. 2:5).

I think the pronoun *"My"* as given in this Thirteenth Verse, says to us that the rainbow did exist before the flood. Had it been otherwise, I think the terminology would have been, *"I do set a bow in the cloud."*

The idea is that God tells Noah, and all who come thereafter, that the rainbow from now on will be a sign of God's pledge to the human race that no such thing as the flood will ever occur again.

THE PROCEDURE

Verse 14 reads: *"And it shall come to pass, when I bring a cloud over the Earth, that the bow shall be seen in the cloud."*

The word *"cloud"* insinuates that at times there will be storms, even with great rain. As well, there will even be flooding at times in some parts of the world; however, periodically, the rainbow will appear, to assure all concerned that God has given His Word, and that He will keep His Word.

REMEMBER

Verse 15 reads: *"And I will remember My Covenant, which is between Me and you and every living creature of all flesh; and the waters shall no more become a flood to destroy all flesh."*

How wonderful to think of what God will, and what He will not, remember! He will remember His Covenant, but He will not remember His people's sins. The Cross, which ratifies the former, puts away the latter. The belief of this gives peace to the troubled heart and uneasy conscience (Mackintosh).

THE EVERLASTING COVENANT

Verse 16 reads: *"And the bow shall be in the cloud; and I will look upon it, that I may remember the Everlasting Covenant between God and every living creature of all flesh that is upon the Earth."*

In this Passage, we are told that this Covenant is everlasting, meaning that it will go on into perpetuity. Literally, in the Hebrew, it is *"the Covenant of Eternity."*

Promises are revocable, and their fulfillment may depend upon man's coagency; a Covenant, however, is irrevocable, and under no circumstances will the Earth again be destroyed by water.

THE TOKEN

Verse 17 reads: *"And God said unto Noah, this is the token of the Covenant, which I have established between Me and all flesh that is upon the Earth."*

This Covenant being universal, the sign is also universal. I've traveled all over the world, and at one time or the other, I've seen rainbows all over the world. They always speak to me of the Grace, Love, Mercy, and Peace of God.

Sometime back, Satan attacked the Ministry, and did so on a worldwide basis. As I dictate these notes, I cannot honestly remember exactly what happened at that time. But I do know that it caused great consternation.

Naturally, I had prayed about the matter very earnestly, doing my best to put it in the hands of the Lord. I do remember that it was something to do with the Media, and I do remember that it was worldwide. Knowing the power of the Media, especially on a worldwide basis, I was attempting to have Faith in the Lord, believing Him that the situation would somehow be rectified.

I remember feeling so helpless, and in fact, in a situation of that nature, one is helpless. What can one do?

I had left the office late that afternoon, going home. Just a few hundred yards before I was to turn off the Interstate to go to our house, to my right there appeared one

NOTES

of the most beautiful rainbows I had ever seen. When I looked at it, the Spirit of God came over me, and I began to weep. Somehow in that bow, I saw the Promises and the Grace of God. As He would not allow the world again to be destroyed by water, neither would He allow me or this Ministry to be destroyed by the efforts of the Evil One. I felt it! I sensed it! And the fear left.

Inasmuch as I cannot remember exactly the occasion of this Media attack, this says plainly that it really did not cause any damage. The Lord did exactly what He said that He would do.

Even as I dictate these notes, I sense the Presence of God, as I think back upon the significance of that time several years ago. Even though the Covenant was meant to guarantee only that the world would never again be destroyed by water, I do believe that Faith could extend it to cover that of which I have spoken. In fact, I know that it can, because I am a recipient of that Promise.

I personally believe that if any Believer will place his Faith and trust in God, in that the enemy will never be able to destroy him, God will allow that rainbow to serve as a sign, which in effect is the Word of God, that Satan will never take best.

THE SONS OF NOAH

Verse 18 reads: *"And the sons of Noah, who went forth of the Ark, were Shem, and Ham, and Japheth: and Ham is the father of Canaan."*

The entirety of the population of the Earth, and for all time since the flood, presents the descendants of Shem, Ham, and Japheth. We will look into this more fully in commentary regarding the following Verses.

The postscript, so to speak, of *"Ham being the father of Canaan,"* was written for the benefit of the Israelites under Moses, who were about to enter the land of Canaan. The Canaanites were to be the bitter enemies of Israel, which, as the Scripture tells us here, originated with Ham.

THE ENTIRETY OF MANKIND

Verse 19 reads: *"These are the three sons of Noah: and of them was the whole Earth overspread."*

This Scripture further tells us that the flood was universal. Were it not universal, there would have been some people who would have been left alive. But this Passage plainly tells us that all the people in the world, then as well as now, are the descendants of the three sons of Noah.

As we have previously stated, the Jews and the Arabs are the descendants of Shem. This would include the Midianites, and possibly some other Tribes. Most of these are settled in the Middle East.

From Ham has come most of the Africans, and as well, the Canaanites, who settled in Canaan, which was later to be *"Israel."*

The descendants of Japheth settled mostly in Europe and the Far East.

(20) "AND NOAH BEGAN TO BE AN HUSBANDMAN, AND HE PLANTED A VINEYARD:

(21) "AND HE DRANK OF THE WINE, AND WAS DRUNKEN; AND HE WAS UNCOVERED WITHIN HIS TENT.

(22) "AND HAM, THE FATHER OF CANAAN, SAW THE NAKEDNESS OF HIS FATHER, AND TOLD HIS TWO BRETHREN WITHOUT.

(23) "AND SHEM AND JAPHETH TOOK A GARMENT, AND LAID IT UPON BOTH THEIR SHOULDERS, AND WENT BACKWARD, AND COVERED THE NAKEDNESS OF THEIR FATHER; AND THEIR FACES WERE BACKWARD, AND THEY SAW NOT THEIR FATHER'S NAKEDNESS.

(24) "AND NOAH AWOKE FROM HIS WINE, AND KNEW WHAT HIS YOUNGER SON HAD DONE UNTO HIM."

The diagram is:

1. Noah planted a vineyard.

2. He drank of the wine, which was fermented, and became drunk.

3. He was so drunk that he failed to dress, and was naked in his tent. Ham saw the drunkenness and the nakedness of his father, and told his two brothers.

4. Shem and Japheth covered the nakedness of their father, without looking at him.

5. The term *"younger son,"* probably refers to Noah's grandson, Canaan.

THE VINEYARD

Verse 20 reads: *"And Noah began to be an husbandman, and he planted a vineyard."*

NOTES

As we see in the Word of God, man fails in about every position in which he is placed by God. Noah falls into the shameful sin of drunkenness; but as always, so here, man's sin provides an occasion for the overabounding Grace of God and at the same time, the sure expression of His abhorrence of evil (Williams).

What is man? Look at him where you will, and in any capacity, and you will by and large see only failure. In Eden, he fails; in the restored Earth, he fails; in Canaan, he fails; in the Church, he fails; in the Presence of Millennial bliss and glory, he fails; he fails everywhere, and in all things: there is no good thing in him. Let his advantages be ever so great, his privileges ever so vast, and his position ever so desirable, he can only exhibit failure and sin.

CONSIDERING THE DRUNKENNESS, HOW DO WE EVALUATE NOAH?

C. H. Mackintosh presented, I think, an excellent statement regarding such a question. He said: *"We must look at Noah in two ways, namely, as a 'type,' and as a 'man'; and while the type is full of beauty and meaning, the man is full of sin and folly; yet the Holy Spirit has written these words: 'Noah was a just man, and perfect in his generation; and Noah walked with God.'*

"Divine Grace had covered all his sins, and clothed his person with a spotless robe of Righteousness. Though Noah exposed his nakedness, God did not see it, for He looked not at him in the weakness of his own condition, but in the full power of Divine and everlasting Righteousness. Hence we may see how entirely astray — how totally alienated from God and His thoughts — Ham was, in the course he adopted; he evidently knew nothing of the blessedness of the man whose iniquity is forgiven, and his sin covered. On the contrary, Shem and Japheth exhibit, in their conduct, a fine specimen of the Divine method of dealing with human weakness; wherefore they inherit a blessing, whereas Ham inherits a curse."

DRUNK

Verse 21 reads: *"And he drank of the wine, and was drunken; and he was uncovered within his tent."*

This is the first mention of wine in the Bible, or any type of intoxicating beverage.

Some have claimed that the fermentation process didn't exist before the flood, and that consequently, Noah was not familiar with the possible product of the grape; however, there is no proof of such a thing, and in fact, the Hebrew language indicates that the Patriarch was familiar with what could be done with the grape as it regards fermentation. As well, Moses does not say this was the first occasion on which the Patriarch tasted fermented liquor.

Since the sin of Noah, and it was sin, cannot be ascribed to ignorance, we can only ascribe it to the weakness of the human being.

Also, we find here that intoxication tends toward sensuality, inasmuch as Noah *"uncovered himself."* Ellicott says, *"It was no accident, but a willful breach of modesty."*

Inasmuch as the first mention of intoxicating beverage in the Bible reveals such a shameful episode, we cannot help but garner from this illustration as given by the Holy Spirit through Moses concerning Noah, the lesson that is being taught here. What should our stand be as a Christian, as it regards alcohol? Is moderate drinking permissible? Is alcoholism a disease or a sin?

Due to the seriousness of this matter, I think it would be proper for us to give it a little more thorough treatment.

ALCOHOL

Back in the 1980's, the news Media seemed inordinately preoccupied with nuclear energy protesters, as if it was their civic duty to convince the American public that nuclear power was extremely dangerous. In view of this constant Media barrage against this particular industry, I'd like to focus on another subject of even more consequence — and I'd like to use the Media's rhetoric regarding nuclear power plants, as they then claimed such to be:

1. What if 40 to 50 people were killed everyday by malfunctioning nuclear power plants?

2. What if such malfunctions seriously injured 1,500 more everyday?

3. What if the presence and influence of nuclear plants causes eight to twenty people per day to commit suicide?

4. What if the secondary effects of nuclear power caused 200 broken homes each day?

5. What if it caused 250 people each day to suffer permanent brain damage — besides the injuries already described?

6. What if it caused some 3,000 parents to abuse their children, or to assault loved ones each day?

7. What if it caused fifty billion dollars a year in direct damages, and an inestimable amount in indirect damages every year?

Awesome and disturbing statistics? Well, if you will *"double"* every figure I have just cited, you will have a fragmented picture of the effects of alcohol on American society today. In view of the fact that after decades of use there hasn't been a single case of a person in the public sector being injured by nuclear power plants, one would have to question why the Media remains silent on alcohol's effects, while carrying on a scathing campaign against other things. I can't answer that, but we can probe the reasons behind the Media's silence on the alcohol question. But first, remember this:

Alcohol is responsible for:

1. Fifty percent of all automobile fatalities.
2. Eighty percent of all home violence.
3. Thirty percent of all suicides.
4. Sixty percent of all child abuse.

WHAT IS THE CAUSE OF ALCOHOLISM?

According to statistics, there are about 20 million alcoholics in this nation, a figure which is equivalent to two out of five heavy drinkers. Actually, I find it hard to see the difference between the alcoholic and the heavy drinker. Think about it:

For every ten automobiles on the road, one is driven by a drunk. It's no wonder that 40 thousand people a year are killed because of alcoholics behind the wheel. In addition, over one million are injured — some never to function normally again.

SICKNESS OR SIN?

I picked up an article sometime back written by a Minister. Unfortunately, his name wasn't credited, so I have no way of acknowledging him for his statement. What he said was excellent, however, and I want to share it with you.

He asked the question, *"What is wrong with the drunkard?"* And then went on to say this:

"Years ago, while holding a citywide Meeting in Salinas, California, I was attracted through an article in the daily paper, to a Convention to be held in a Northern California town. Psychiatrists from all over America were coming out to the coast for this Convention.

"The object of the Convention was the thing that attracted me. They announced as their project . . . the discovery of what causes alcoholism, and then to suggest a cure. Here is a sum of the findings of this body:

"They stated that an alcoholic is not a moral degenerate, but a sick man. He can't help being sick any more than an asthmatic or arthritic." (Notice the lack of personal responsibility.) *"He should not be picked up in a police car and thrown in jail, but should be picked up in an ambulance and put in a hospital. He shouldn't be treated as a moral degenerate, but a respected member of society who is sick.*

"That was the trend of thought all through the deliberation, and not once during the Convention was whiskey mentioned. The closest to it was the word 'alcoholism.' They never said if a man simply didn't drink he would have no problem. No such ugly insinuations were made.

"The final session was the clincher. Headlines in the San Francisco paper stated: 'Psychiatrists decide,' then, in smaller print, 'Alcoholism is caused by an unknown quantity that we shall choose to call "X" . . . until this unknown quantity can be isolated and defined, we have no suggested cure.'"

The Minister went on to state, *"I would hate to be an alcoholic depending on Psychiatrists to help me!"*

I can only say *"Amen"* to that.

I am not a Psychiatrist, but I know what makes men and women alcoholics. I'm certain it is not, as one alcoholic figured it: He railed against God for having done this to him. He shook his fist at his genes, at his heredity, at his father. He felt he had been programmed before birth to be a victim of alcohol.

No, the problem isn't a sickness, and it's not in the genes. It's not heredity, and it's

certainly not God. The problem is *"sin"* — which results in an even more frightening word — *"bondage."*

TODAY THE BIG EXCUSE FOR ALMOST EVERYTHING IS *"SICKNESS"*

Today, everyone is sick: the alcoholic, the thief, the child molester, the rapist, and the murderer. As one august Supreme Court Justice said sometime ago, *"Everybody ought to be turned out of prison, because the prisoners are not really guilty; it's all of society that's responsible."* This statement might be humorous if it weren't so *"stupid."*

You see, the Bible says that men are liars, thieves, drunkards, immoral — and all the other things mankind is inevitably prey to — simply because they are sinners. They've turned their backs on God. Man is a product of the Fall. His Salvation lies not in treatment of a *"sickness,"* but in treatment of his sin — and Jesus took care of this at Calvary. Until men accept this treatment, they will not be cured. If alcoholism is a disease, the individual is not responsible. And Satan's favorite ploy today is to make someone else responsible!

But what does the Bible say? That *"all"* have sinned and come short of the Glory of God. Of course, man doesn't want to hear that. He doesn't want to admit he's a sinner and that he's lost. Most of all, he doesn't want to admit that unless he comes to God he will remain eternally lost. So we give it a new name. We call it a disease or a sickness. Well, listen to this. If it is a disease, it is the only disease:

1. That is contracted by an act of will.
2. That requires a license for distribution.
3. That is bottled and sold.
4. That requires outlets for its sale.
5. That produces revenue for the Government.
6. That promotes crime.
7. That is habit-forming.
8. That is spread by advertising. (Can't you see this in the supermarket's weekly ad? *"Get Coors, it's the best disease we have in the store."*)
9. For which we are fined and imprisoned when we exhibit its symptoms.

10. Which brings death on the highway.

11. Without a bacterial or viral cause, and for which there is no corrective medicine.

12. Last but not least, that bars the patient from Heaven. For the Bible clearly states in I Corinthians 6:10 that no drunkard shall inherit the Kingdom of God. (And I hasten to point out that while no drunkard will inherit the Kingdom of God, the Power of God can set the drunkard free and make him a fit subject for the portals of Glory — just as it can for anyone else.)

No, alcoholism is not a disease. So this crutch that is being used by the medical profession, the Psychiatrists, and many others is merely that — a crutch. It serves to shift blame (and thus remove the responsibility) from the one who is actually to blame, and this is the individual himself.

WHO PROMOTES ALCOHOL?

Constant attention is drawn to the terrible use of such mind-destroying drugs as heroin, marijuana, and cocaine, etc., and this should be done. But very little is being said about the most sinister drug of all — alcohol — the drug that is destroying our nation. It causes untold pain and suffering, and there is scarcely a word said against it. The newspapers are silent, newsmen seem unaware of the problem, and the pulpits (sad to say) are almost silent. As one realizes the tremendous amount of physical, financial, moral, and spiritual damage wrought by alcohol, one can't help but ask, *"Why?"*

Of course, the answer is obvious. Whereas cocaine, heroin, and other drugs are considered to be outside the limits of *"decent society,"* alcohol has been socially accepted. Why is this so?

1. Because it kills a little more slowly than the other types of drugs.

2. Because there are vast amounts of money to be made from alcohol, and the same people who control the distribution of alcohol control the dissemination of the information that influences people to use alcohol.

TELEVISION AND MOVIES PROMOTE ALCOHOL

It is a sad fact that the image of alcohol is tremendously manipulated on television. In

one recent survey it was found that alcohol-related violence was 25 times higher in real life than on television dramas. In other words, the sinister aspects of alcohol are greatly downplayed on TV programming. Again, I ask why? Well, one should keep in mind that the TV networks receive millions of dollars in revenues from beer and wine accounts.

A short time ago one of our Telecasts was censored because we mentioned the name of a specific brewery on one of the Telecasts. Should this shock us? Not if we consider beer and wine accounts that keep TV Stations operating in the black. No one who loves money will bite the hand that feeds him.

Dr. Thomas Radecki of the National Coalition on Television Violence stated, *"With the new research in the past two years, it is increasingly clear that TV advertising and program use of alcohol is playing a major role in the increasing abuse of alcohol."*

Radecki noted that the average child will see alcohol consumed 75,000 times on TV before he reaches the legal drinking age! When he must make his personal decision in regard to drinking, what will the subliminal influences tell him? That the *"in-people,"* those who are bright, sophisticated, and successful on television are almost inevitably seen holding a drink in their hands. In other words, as far as Hollywood and network television people are concerned, if you're bright and smart, you too will have a drink in your hand.

He also observed that on network programming the typical viewer sees 5,000 incidents of alcohol intake per year. Ninety-nine percent of these cases of drinking will be portrayed as favorable, or at least neutral!

THE REAL WORLD

Another question must be asked. Is this what life is like in the real world? The facts show us that 50 percent of real-life violence is associated with alcohol consumption! On television, only one percent of televised violence is associated with drinking. Dr. Radecki believes that TV's benign portrayal of alcohol consumption is one of the major reasons why alcohol abuse and violence are the two most rapidly increasing causes of death in the United States!

A total of 76 percent of those shown drinking any kind of beverage on television will be shown drinking alcohol.

TV characters spend twice as much time drinking alcohol as tea or coffee. They consume 14 times more liquor and beer than soft drinks, and they drink 15 times more alcohol than water. Television viewers will see an average of three incidents of alcohol consumption for each hour they watch during prime time. Those watching daytime TV will see six instances of drinking per hour. (Obviously soap opera characters have a higher percentage of alcoholism than the evening characters have.)

Contrary to what one might expect (if TV is supposed to reflect the real world), it isn't the villains who do the most drinking. The heaviest TV drinkers are well-known stars appearing in regular series where they serve as role models for our children and young people. TV characters seldom refuse a drink — nor do they express disapproval of someone else's drinking. In situation comedies, excessive drinking is often used as a *"good natured"* way to get more laughs.

It is now understandable why over three-quarters of all high school seniors use liquor regularly — with one-half getting drunk at least once a month. It's also easy to understand why the White House Drug Abuse Office states that pressure to drink begins as early as the fourth grade. It might be a fine thing if someone led a crusade to get wine and beer commercials taken from the air as cigarette ads were.

THE MAIN PROMOTERS OF BEER AND WINE ARE THE BREWERS AND DISTILLERS

It certainly isn't hard to imagine the producers of a product as the main promoters of that product. They're in the business of selling the poison they produce. However, it's the manner in which they promote it that's despicable. Let's take a look at this:

We're told that beer in Australia may soon be vitamin-enriched, and probably now is. Researchers at the University of Queensland report that chronic vitamin deficiencies in alcoholics could be offset if brewers were to add vitamin B1 to their products. They assert

that *"a lot of heavy drinkers stand to benefit."* They also said that *"the average person in the Northern Territory (of Australia) consumes 60 gallons of beer yearly!"*

This will, of course, be yet another advertising plus for the breweries. They will suddenly be able to trumpet the nutritional benefits of drinking — trying to divert the consumer's attention from the bondage that comes along with the intake of a little vitamin B.

A California winery has introduced Red Life, a light wine aimed at those soda drinkers who want something *"a little stronger."* The main idea, of course, is to get young people — even children — interested in drinking at an early age so they'll then graduate to something stronger.

You must remember, the breweries have to manufacture customers — and they have to start with the children to do this. I'll give you another example.

In the Oklahoma City Times — containing the report of a speech William Coors (Chairman of the Adolph Coors Company) made to a Convention of security analysts meeting in Denver — he described the advertising of his own company as well as other breweries as *"outrageous"* for its lack of ethics.

He referred especially to the fact that his company pays 250 college students throughout the United States to promote its beer through campus *"Wet T-Shirt Contests,"* *"Get Drunk,"* and *"Chug-a-lug"* parties. He said the other breweries did this so his company followed suit as something *"strictly defensive."*

Coors said, *"We do this — not because we think it is right — but because other brewers do it. They will steal our lunch — if we don't do it."* He added, *"I personally think it's outrageous, and everyone in the company thinks it's outrageous. One way or another, the country's going to stop this because our industry doesn't have the ethics to stop themselves."*

In legal parlance, testimony against self-interest is the most damaging type possible in a court of law. Coors certainly testified against his own self-interest when he confessed the lack of ethics among the brewery owners and managers. And by the way, his company sold nearly 11 million barrels of beer in the first nine months of last year — a 15 percent increase over the same period for the previous year.

At the same time Coors was confessing his sins, he also lashed out at do-gooders who were trying to raise the drinking age from 18 to 21 — questioning the motives of such crusades. He then went on to claim that only five percent of alcohol users are abusers.

However, what he neglected to add is that the other 95 percent of nonabusers are on the way to becoming abusers — in other words, drunks. They will eventually get there if they drink long enough. Simply stated, the five percent who are now abusers were not guilty of drunkenness when they started drinking!

Yes, the boys who make the alcohol are their own best promoters, and they do so in the most hypocritical, perverse manner imaginable.

POLITICIANS ARE SOME OF THE GREATEST PROMOTERS OF ALCOHOL

Legislators in the State of Wisconsin argued recently whether milk or beer should be the state drink. Wisconsin is known for both its dairies and breweries (The Beer That Made Milwaukee Famous) so the competition was intense.

One State Representative declared his choice was alcohol, because, in his words, *"Beer tempers the emotions of our hardworking adults."*

This representative should be reminded that beer murders scores of Wisconsin motorists every year. Alcohol also compels some of those so-called *"hardworking adults"* to beat their wives and deprive their children. To my knowledge, milk has never been cited as a cause of broken homes or bruised bodies.

Since marijuana is the number one cash crop in several sections of the United States, maybe it's only a matter of time before some political opportunist will nominate pot as the official drug for the state.

One cannot help but say and think that the Legislators of Wisconsin ought to have better sense.

One doctor stated the other day that the reason stiffer laws are not enacted for drunk driving (or stiffer sentences not imposed) is because too many of the Legislators and

Judges are drunks themselves. This could well be true.

SAD TO SAY, EVEN SOME PREACHERS PROMOTE THE USE OF ALCOHOL

I know that sounds strange, but it's true. From the majority of American pulpits, there seldom is heard a discouraging word — on the subject of alcohol.

As I write this, I am reminded of a religious periodical that stated (from a teletype news report) that one of the world's noted Evangelist said there was nothing wrong with an occasional drink. Talking to reporters, this particular Evangelist said he didn't believe the Bible-taught teetotalism. After all (this Preacher went on to say) Jesus drank wine, and he pointed to the Biblical account in which Jesus is said to have turned water into wine at a wedding feast. And, as the Evangelist put it, *"That wasn't grape juice, as some try to claim."* I wonder if this statement was made to please and excuse the cocktail-drinking friends of the Preacher.

Not so long ago, one major Missionary Evangelist told me personally that in a great religious conclave (with thousands of Preachers present) he asked all the Preachers (who were Pentecostal incidentally) in the congregation to stand if they did — or would — take a public stand against any and all use of alcohol. He was startled at the number who would not stand!

I had a Preacher tell me just today that our institutions are the way they are because our Churches are the way they are — and our Churches are the way they are because our families are the way they are. I wonder if our families are the way they are because the pulpits are silent.

I want to make a statement. Any Preacher of the Gospel who won't take a public stand against any and all use of alcohol — and be vocal in that stand — is doing his people, his God, and his country a disservice. The position that many Preachers take, that they never mention alcohol because *"their people already know it's wrong,"* is a copout. Many take this position because they don't want to offend the *"sipping Saints"* in the congregation.

The Preacher of the Gospel has always been the one to whip the nation into line.

The Preacher of the Gospel is supposed to address the moral issues. It may not be popular at times, but it is our business. And if we fail to do it — there's no one else to do it. You can be dead-level sure that the Media aren't going to do it, and you can also be certain that the politicians aren't going to do it. (Although, in the last couple of years, a few politicians have stood up and taken a stand on this matter — perhaps as a reaction to the dead, dry sermonizing they hear from the pulpits.)

Preachers — no matter what it costs you — stand up before your congregation and make your position known. Warn the young people of the terrible ravages of alcohol. Make no bones about it, pull no punches, quibble not. And if you don't have strong feelings about seeing death and carnage all around you as a result of America's worst drug — there's something wrong with you!

WHAT SHOULD BE THE CHRISTIANS POSITION IN RESPECT TO ALCOHOL?

Any true Christian in today's society, desiring to set a good example for the Cause of Christ will be a teetotaler. It's just that simple.

All types of arguments are offered to defend social drinking. But let's look and see what the Bible says on this subject:

"Wine is a mocker, strong drink is raging: and whosoever is deceived thereby is not wise" (Prov. 20:1).

"Who has woe? Who has sorrow? Who has contentions? Who has babbling? Who has wounds without cause? Who has redness of eyes? They who tarry long at the wine; they who go to seek mixed wine. Look not upon the wine when it is red, when it gives his color in the cup, when it moves itself aright. At the last it bites like a serpent, and stings like an adder" (Prov. 23:29-32).

"Woe unto them who rise up early in the morning, that they may follow strong drink; who continue until night, till wine enflame them!" (Isa. 5:11).

"Woe unto them who are mighty to drink wine, and men of strength to mingle strong drink" (Isa. 5:22).

"Woe to the crown of pride, to the drunkards of Ephraim, whose glorious beauty is a fading flower, which are on the head of the

NOTES

fat valleys of them who are overcome with wine!" (Isa. 28:1).

"But they also have erred through wine, and through strong drink are out of the way; the Priest and the Prophet have erred through strong drink, they are swallowed up of wine, they are out of the way through strong drink; they err in vision, they stumble in judgment" (Isa. 28:7).

ALCOHOL'S CONSEQUENCES

I was in a Midwestern city in a Meeting, and a tragedy had struck locally that riveted the attention of the whole area.

Service had ended for the night. After almost everyone had left, I walked back to the Pastor's office. I saw him sitting behind his desk, his head in his hands. I asked him what was wrong. He looked at me and asked me if I had heard about the tragedy that had taken place that very day. I had, and then he gave me this background.

The young lady who was murdered was raised in his Church. She had once been Saved and followed Jesus, but had turned her back on God. She and her boyfriend had been to a party and both had been drinking heavily. They left this particular party and went to a bar — and then left it and were on their way to anther bar. The boy made advances toward her, which she repelled. He grew incensed and started beating her with his fists.

He had a large ring on his finger, and in his anger and drunken delirium he beat her to death. She was beaten so badly that they were unable to open her casket for the service.

Some hours later, after he had sobered up, he wandered into a police station and gave himself up. He really didn't know why he did it. He said: *"I was drunk."*

Incidents like this are repeated many thousands of times every year. I can't comprehend how any Christian could see the misery and the heartache that alcohol has caused and not be a teetotaler. Of course, the contention we are told is always this:

It's the abuse of alcohol that is wrong. If you drink moderately, they say, it then becomes a question of *"social relaxation."*

However, who with any sense would question that those who are now abusers (over 20 million in this country) started out as social drinkers, but wound up as falling-down drunks? No, that argument is too thin to skim. Let's go a little further with it.

I don't know how many beers it takes to make a person drunk (or shots of whiskey or glasses of wine for that matter), but for the sake of argument, let's say it takes 10 beers to make a person drunk. If this is the case, it is a scientific fact that one beer then makes the person one-tenth drunk. The vision is impaired by that much, with the motor responses also impaired. The reaction time is also slowed. And this is not the conclusion of a Preacher — this is a scientific fact after exhaustive investigation. Even one drink will affect reflexes and will take two hours to leave the body. That's why it's dangerous to drive after only one drink!

Once again, and because it is so important, let us say it again: it is a scientific fact that after just one drink, your judgment is impaired and your reflexes are slowed. After only one drink, a person is *a little drunk.*

No, alcohol has broken up more homes, murdered more human beings, made paupers of more people, starved more children, started more wars, wrecked more careers, broken more marriages, caused more crimes, sent more souls to Hell, and wrecked more lives than any single factor on the face of the Earth.

In view of this, I must ask the question again: How can any Christian justify even one drink? Alcohol is the most rotten, debilitating, damnable, despicable devil that ever fastened itself upon the human race.

WHAT IS THE ETERNAL FUTURE FOR THE USER OF ALCOHOL?

The Bible is crystal clear on the eternal judgment of the drunkard. Galatians 5:19 begins a list of the works of the flesh, and Verse 21 lists drunkenness among them. Then the conclusion of Verse 21 states, *"They which do such things shall not inherit the Kingdom of God,"*

So the eternal destiny of those who engage in drunkenness is eternal Hell. The Bible is very clear in regard to this. Of course, the answer always comes back, *"But Brother Swaggart, I'm not a drunkard, I only take a social drink now and then, and I can't see where the Bible condemns it."* Let's look at it this way:

As we have mentioned, when a person takes just one drink, he is partially drunk. So the question we must ask ourselves is this: Where will it lead in regard to the road we're traveling? It's not so much that single drink as it is the path the one drink leads to — the example it sets.

When a Christian takes one drink, he's voting in favor of all the broken homes, twisted lives, and twisted dreams caused by alcohol. He's declaring himself in favor of all the hell and horror that alcoholism has caused over the centuries. When you take one drink, you're saying you're in favor of all the world stands for, all the flesh stands for, and all the Devil stands for. No, sir, no Christian who wants to serve his Lord as he should will countenance even one drink. But the Bible has more to say about it than even that.

"Woe unto him who gives his neighbor drink, who puts the bottle to him, and makes him drunken also, that you may look on their nakedness! You are filled with shame for glory: drink you also, and let the foreskin be uncovered, the cup of the LORD's right hand shall be turned unto you, and shameful spewing shall be on your glory. For the <u>violence</u> of Lebanon shall cover you, and the spoil of beasts, which made them afraid, because of men's blood, and for the <u>violence</u> of the land, of the city, and of all who dwell therein" (Hab. 2:15-17).

ONE TRAGIC EXAMPLE

A lot of people have looked with great sorrow, and rightly so, on the terrible tragedies which have befallen the Kennedy family. Despite untold riches, fame, power, and popularity, this family has suffered a jarring succession of tragedies.

Joe, Jr. was killed in an airplane crash in World War II; one daughter was born with serious mental problems. Everyone knows the horror of the terrible assassinations of Jack Kennedy and Bobby Kennedy. Then there was the tragedy of the Chappaquiddick incident with Ted Kennedy — and then the untimely death of David Kennedy from a drug overdose. And then of late, the death of John, Jr. in a plane crash, with his wife and others.

Admittedly, all of these tragedies would not fall under the category of being alcohol induced. But I feel there were too many of them to just be chance. Let's look at the Kennedy background.

When Prohibition ended, President Franklin Delano Roosevelt told Joseph Kennedy, Sr. that the legislation of Prohibition would be repealed. Once again, it would be legal to make and sell alcoholic beverages in the United States. Joseph Kennedy, Sr. bought up the great Haig and Haig Scotch Whiskey Industries in England. The hour Prohibition ended — and it became legal to make and sell alcohol in the United States — Joseph Kennedy had a ready supply of alcohol stored in warehouses in many cities in the United States. He had received permission to store it under the guise of medicinal purposes. So, for a considerable period of time, a good portion of the whiskey sold in the United States came from Joseph Kennedy. That was one of the ways in which multiplied millions of dollars were amassed, which later helped to finance the political aspirations of Jack Kennedy, and his bid for the Presidency.

In short, one might say that whiskey money at least helped buy the presidency for Jack Kennedy. What produced this money?

Multiplied millions of homes enflamed with violence, heartache, dissipation, pain, and death. Multiplied millions were started on the road to ruin. And God said plainly *"Woe unto him who gives his neighbor drink, that puts the bottle to him."* He also said, in the first part of Verse 17 that *"violence . . . shall cover you."* That identifies perfectly what has happened to one of America's most famous and powerful families.

However, this applies not only to people like the Kennedy's who amass great fortunes, but also the bartenders serving it, the grocery store owners selling it, the liquor store distributing it, and the brewery manufacturing it. It also holds for the restaurants that sell it. All are cursed by God. This could be one of the reasons America is the violence capital of the world. It could be the reason that violent crimes are increasing at an unprecedented rate.

LINCOLN'S WORDS

Abraham Lincoln delivered the following words in Springfield, Illinois, on February 22, 1842:

NOTES

"Whether or not the world would be vastly benefited by a total and final banishment of all intoxicating drinks, seems to me not now an open question. Three-fourths of mankind confess the affirmity with their tongues and, I believe, all the rest acknowledge it in their hearts . . . Turn now to the temperance revolution. In it we shall find a stronger bondage broken; a viler slavery manumitted; a greater tyrant deposed. In it, more of want supplied, more disease healed, more sorrow assuaged. By it, no orphans starving, no widows weeping. By it, none wounded in feelings, none injured in interest.

"If the relative grandeur of revolutions shall be estimated by the great amount of human misery they alleviate, and the small amount they inflict, then indeed will this be the grandest the world shall ever have seen.

"And when the victory shall be complete — when there shall be neither a slave nor a drunkard on the Earth — how proud the title of that Land, which may truly claim to be the birthplace and the cradle of both those revolutions, that shall have ended in that victory. How nobly distinguished that people, who shall have planted, and nurtured to maturity, both the political and moral freedom of their species."

A DOCTOR SPEAKS OUT

A doctor wrote this to a newspaper sometime ago:

"Recently we saw another preview of Hell in the Parkland Hospital Emergency Room. A woman was struck down by a drunken driver, a college student lying semi-conscience following a head-on collision with another drunken driver, who was himself critically injured. The drunk's companion was dead. Four other drunks, with lacerations and stab wounds, waiting to be treated.

"Night after night, year after year, the same bloody trail of horror — major auto accidents, stabbings, rapes, and wife beatings. Nightly emergencies, treated and released, are admitted to the hospital or pronounced dead on arrival. And almost always the bloody trail is led to that honored man of distinction — the weekend drinker. Almost always this is the moderate drinker, not the alcoholic. I wonder if there is that much

joy to be gained, from the total consumption of all the beers and whiskeys made, to equal even a small fraction of the innocent suffering, the damaged bodies, the broken marriages, the discarded children, the total brutalities, and crimes that accompany its use.

"What a quiet place our Emergency Room would be if beverage alcohol were ever abolished from our city."

No, sir, alcoholism is not a sickness — it is a sin that results in bondage.

No, sir, the moderate drinker is not socially acceptable — for every alcoholic starts out drinking moderately.

No, sir, no Christian who wants to serve his Lord can even remotely accept the consumption of even one drink.

WAS THE WATER THAT JESUS TURNED INTO WINE IN JOHN, CHAPTER 2 THE KIND OF WINE THAT WILL MAKE ONE DRUNK?

No, and I will explain why:

If the wine is understood to be intoxicating wine, our Lord is automatically placed in the position of providing men who had already "well drunk" (Jn. 2:10) with more wine. If it was intoxicating wine, the Lord would have been breaking His Own Law against temperance. The total amount of water turned into wine that day was about 150 gallon. If this had been an intoxicating beverage, it would have served as an invitation to drink and would have placed our Lord in the unsavory position of providing a flood of intoxicants for the people who had already consumed a considerable amount.

GOOD WINE

The word "good" was used to describe what the Lord had miraculously brought about. It is the Greek word "kalos" and is defined in "Vine's Expository Dictionary of New Testament Words" as denoting what is intrinsically good. Now the pure, sweet juice of the grape could rightly be denoted as "intrinsically good"; but the rotted, fermented, decayed, spoiled, intoxicating kind of wine could hardly be called good. It is easy to think of the term "good" in describing whatever the Lord makes. For example, in describing the creation, Moses said, "And God saw

everything that He had made, and, behold, it was very good" (Gen. 1:31).

It is unthinkable that our Lord would have made corrupted, fermented wine at Cana and called it "good." You see, fermentation is a kind of decomposition, just as are putrefaction and decay. It would be almost blasphemous to call that "good" in connection with our Lord.

Pliny (an ancient Greek Scholar) said that "good wine" was a term used to denote the juice destitute of spirit. Albert Barnes says, "The wine referred to here was doubtless such as was commonly drunk in Palestine." That was the pure juice of the grape; it was not brandied nor drugged wine. Nor was it wine compounded of various substances, such as people drink in this land. The common wine of that day, which was drunk in Palestine, was the simple juice of the grape, i.e., "grape juice."

As well, it is tantamount to blasphemy, in my opinion, to suppose that the first miracle that Christ performed after being filled with the Holy Spirit (compare Mk. 1:9-12; Lk. 4:1) was an act of creating intoxicating wine for a crowd of celebrants, the kind of wine that would make them drunk. It is unthinkable!

Still another fact from the record in John, Chapter 2 is this: those men who had already drunk a considerable amount praised the Bridegroom for having kept the "good wine" until the last. Now, it is a simple fact that alcohol, drunk to any excess, will deaden the taste buds of the drinker. If the wine in Cana of Galilee, that the guests had already been partaking of, was intoxicating wine (and they had already partaken of quite a bit at this point), then when the wine that Jesus had miraculously made was given to them, they could not have detected its taste. Their taste buds would have been deadened. To be honest with you, they would have been drunk by this time, or almost so. Only if they had been drinking the form of the vine's fruit that we know as grape juice, and then had been provided some fresh grape juice would the Governor of the feast have been able to make the observation he did.

WINE IN BIBLICAL TIMES

There are several words in the Bible which describe wine; however, two of these words are the most commonly used. In the New Testament, it is the Greek word *"oinos,"* which can mean either fermented or unfermented wine.

Dr. Ferrar Fenton, a Biblical translator (The Holy Bible in Modern English), lists six different meanings of the word *"oinos"*:

1. Grapes, as fresh fruit.
2. Raisins.
3. Thick grape syrup.
4. A thick jam.
5. Fresh grape juice.
6. Fermented grape juice.

The last type is the only one which would make one drunk.

Dr. Lyman Abbott said that fermented wine in Bible times was the least common of all wines. Even in the fermented kind, the percentage of alcohol was small.

In the Old Testament, the Hebrew word for wine most commonly used is *"yayin."* That word is found 141 times in the Old Testament, and is used interchangeably, depending on the context. In other words, it can mean either grape juice or alcoholic beverage.

I think the reasons given are sufficient proof that Jesus did not change water to the kind of wine that would make one drunk. Instead, it was a sweet, pure grape juice.

Before Prohibition *"wine"* was considered to be exactly as it was in Bible times. However, when Prohibition was enacted in 1929, the term had to be defined more closely. Consequently, *"wine"* was designated to mean something that will make you drunk. The other kind of nonintoxicating beverage was called by whatever name desired, grape juice or whatever. Consequently, many people today confuse the simple word *"wine"* as it was used in the Bible with our understanding of that word, but that is not universally true.

No, Jesus' first miracle was not the making of wine that would make one drunk. It was pure, sweet, fresh grape juice; and I believe that Scripturally, scientifically, and legally we have proof of that.

DID THE SAVIOUR USE INTOXICATING WINE IN THE LORD'S SUPPER?

In the description of the Lord's Supper, the Lord never uses the word *"wine."* We are told, *"He took the cup, and gave thanks,*

and gave it to them, saying, Drink ye all of it" (Mat. 26:27). Mark says, *"He took the cup, and when He had given thanks, He gave it to them"* (Mk. 14:23). Luke says, *"He took the cup, and gave thanks, and said, Take this, and divide it among yourselves"* (Lk. 22:17). Jesus called the drink, *"fruit of the vine"* in Matthew 26:29 and also in Mark 14:25 and Luke 22:18.

It seems the Holy Spirit carried this directive right on through even into the Early Church. The Apostle Paul said, *"After the same manner also, He took the cup, when He had supped, saying, This cup is the New Testament in My Blood"* (I Cor. 11:25). Then, following, He mentioned *"this cup"* and then, later on, *"that cup."*

It becomes clear, when these Passages are read consecutively that God intended for us to use grape juice. I also think the Holy Spirit took particular pains not to use any words that could be construed as referring to any kind of intoxicating beverage. There's not a single reference in the Word of God that a person should use intoxicating wine for the Lord's Supper.

THE SYMBOL OF DECAY

The very meaning of fermented wine makes it unsatisfactory to represent the Blood of our Lord Jesus Christ, and that's exactly what the grape juice of the Lord's Supper is to represent. I do not know a whole lot about fermentation or the wherefores of making alcoholic beverages, but I do know that fermented wine is grape juice in which decay (or rot) has taken place. In other words, the process of fermentation is the breakdown of large molecules caused by the influence of bacteria or fungi. Wine, then, results from the degenerative action of germs on pure substances.

Fermented wine used in Communion would actually symbolize tainted, sinful blood and not the Pure and Perfect Blood of Jesus Christ that had to be made evident to be a perfect cleansing for our sins. Pure, fresh grape juice tends toward life, but fermented wine tends toward death. Alcohol use for drinking purposes is both a narcotic and a poison. It could hardly be used as a symbol for the Blood of the Lord Jesus Christ.

To give you an example, the Jews were required to use unleavened bread with the Passover Feast, and they were commanded that during that time *"there shall no leavened bread be seen with you, neither shall there be leaven seen with you in all your quarters"* (Ex. 13:7). As early as this, bread which had been tainted with bacteria or yeast was considered unsuitable at the religious events celebrated by the Jews. Jesus also used unleavened bread in initiating the Lord's Supper. (Of course, the New Testament made no special issue of the unleavened bread; and as far as that is concerned, any bread made without yeast today would serve as unleavened bread.) Consequently, then, from Exodus to the Gospels, we are told to use only untainted, pure substances in spiritual celebrations.

Consequently, the point that I make is this: If the Lord specifically chose bread that had no bacteria, no fungus spores in kit, to picture His broken body, do you honestly think He would choose alcoholic wine, fermented wine, which is directly the product of fungi or bacteria, to represent His Blood? I hardly think so! The pure Blood of Jesus Christ would be best represented by pure grape juice.

THE MORAL STATUTES

Next, even the High Priests were commanded, *"Do not drink wine nor strong drink . . . when you go into the Tabernacle of the congregation, lest you die: it shall be a Statute forever throughout your generations"* (Lev. 10:9).

You must remember, those Priests entering into the Tabernacle were types of the Lord Jesus Christ, Who is our Great High Priest. Now I ask you a question: Would Jesus, the night He was betrayed, drink intoxicating wine before going to the Crucifixion and entering into His High Priestly Work? I think not. It would have been a rejection and a contradiction of His Own Word given in Leviticus.

I close by saying this: We must always remember that the word *"wine"* in the Bible simply means *"the fruit of the vine."* It can either mean unfermented grape juice or intoxicating wine. So, when the Word is read, whether it is New Testament or Old Testament, this distinction must always be kept in mind according to the context.

No, I do not believe the wine that Jesus used at the Lord's Super was intoxicating wine, nor do I believe it is proper and permissible for us to use such wine in the Lord's Supper today. I think it is a travesty of His Word and a perversion of His intent.

THE CHRISTIAN AND THE CROSS OF CHRIST

Unfortunately, because most Christians do not know or understand God's prescribed order of victory, millions are bound by *"works of the flesh"* in some capacity. Among those works of the flesh is *"drunkenness"* (Gal. 5:19-21).

Yes, and unfortunately, it is possible for a Christian, even one who truly loves the Lord, to be *"hooked"* on alcoholic beverage, gambling, immorality, or one hundred and one other things that we could name. And to be sure, *"works of the flesh"* in some capacity will rule and reign in the Believer's life, if that Believer doesn't understand the Cross of Christ. Let me explain:

Unfortunately, many Christians, not knowing and understanding God's Way, attempt to live this life by means that cannot be approved by the Holy Spirit, which in effect, denies us His help. And to be sure, without the help of the Holy Spirit none of us can live the life we ought to live for Christ and in Christ.

Unfortunately, many in the modern Church, not understanding God's prescribed order of victory, recommend instead humanistic psychology. There is no help from that source! And in fact, there is no help from any source, except through Christ and Him Crucified (I Cor. 1:23).

Quite possibly, some of you studying this Commentary do so with a heavy heart, and because of the bondage in which you now find yourself. You have struggled and fought, all to no avail. In fact, the harder you try to break out of this quagmire of *"drinking secretly,"* or whatever the problem might be, you find yourself getting in deeper and deeper. It has left you without understanding. You love the Lord, and you're trying so very hard, but there is no victory in sight. In fact, it's one failure after the other, and you have despaired of ever knowing or seeing total victory within your life.

On top of that, you hear Preachers constantly speaking of glorious victory, and you have been made to believe that possibly you are one of the very few who somehow cannot find that victory. The truth is, more than likely, the Preacher doesn't have any victory himself. He's preaching what he knows the Word says, but most of the time he really doesn't have the solution to the problem, simply because he knows very little about the Cross. So in some way, it is quite possible that he is hurting just as you are hurting.

What is the answer?

In fact, there is only one answer, and that is *"Jesus Christ and Him Crucified"* (I Cor. 2:2).

Paul also said: *"I am crucified with Christ: nevertheless I live; yet not I, but Christ lives in me: and the life which I now live in the flesh I live by the Faith of the Son of God, Who loved me, and gave Himself for me."*

He then said: *"I do not frustrate the Grace of God: for if Righteousness come by the Law, then Christ is dead in vain"* (Gal. 2:20-21).

Most Christians are *"frustrating the Grace of God,"* which means that they are stopping the help the Holy Spirit can give them, which translates into failure. In fact, it cannot be any other way. Paul plainly says here that if Righteousness could come by the Law, in other words by your efforts and abilities and strengths, then Christ is dead in vain. In other words, Jesus didn't have to come down here and die on a Cross, if victory could be obtained by one's own machinations.

THE CROSS, YOUR FAITH, AND THE HOLY SPIRIT

Almost all of Paul's 14 Epistles are devoted to this particular subject. In fact, he told us in Romans, Chapter 7 what it was like trying to live for God without understanding the Cross. Paul was Saved, Baptized with the Holy Spirit, called to be an Apostle, and in fact serving as an Apostle, and trying with all of his strength and might, but still unable to live a victorious life. It's all there in Romans, Chapter 7. He concludes it by saying:

"O wretched man that I am! Who shall deliver me from the body of this death?" (Rom. 7:24).

Now that's where many Christians are presently. They are trying so hard, but the

end result is *"O wretched man that I am!"* And then the cry comes, *"Who shall deliver me from the body of this death?"*

The Lord gave Paul the answer to that question, which is in reality the meaning of the New Covenant. It is the meaning of the Cross, what Christ actually did there for humanity. You as a Believer must understand that the Cross of Christ has to do not only with your initial Salvation experience, but as well for your Sanctification, which refers to your everyday walk before the Lord. If the Believer doesn't understand the Cross, then the Believer simply cannot walk in victory — and it doesn't really matter what he does otherwise to obtain victory. In some way, the flesh will rule and reign within his life, which will cause untold problems. And regrettably, this is where most of modern Christendom now is.

THE CROSS

You as a Believer must understand that every single thing that comes to you as a Christian does so through what Jesus did at the Cross on your behalf. Always remember, everything He did was for you and me. Understanding the great price that He paid, we should certainly be able to come to the conclusion that He would want us to have the benefits of all that He has done.

Now if you as a Believer have the idea in your mind that victory is achieved by some way other than the Cross, you are going to remain in defeat. So you must understand that totally and completely, everything that you receive from the Lord, and I mean everything, comes to you through what Jesus did at the Cross (Rom. 6:3-5, 11, 14; I Cor. 1:17-18, 21, 23; 2:2, 5; Col. 2:14-15).

YOUR FAITH

Understanding that everything comes to you from God through the Cross, your Faith must ever be in the Cross. In other words, the Cross of Christ must ever be the object of your Faith — not your Church, not your own strength and ability, not your Denomination, not your good works, etc., but the Cross of Christ.

This is why Jesus told us to *"deny ourselves, and take up the Cross daily, and follow Him"* (Lk. 9:23).

Most Christians totally misunderstand this Passage. When He spoke of *"denying ourselves,"* they think that means doing without anything that is pleasurable or good, etc. It doesn't mean that at all!

It simply means that we deny our own strengths and abilities, understanding that they simply aren't strong enough to get the job done. To be sure, the *"flesh"* is always wanting and desiring to do things in order to make us holy. Holiness and Righteousness can never be obtained in that way. Those things are always works of the Spirit.

When He told us to *"take up the Cross daily and follow Him,"* He wasn't speaking of suffering as most Christians think. He was rather speaking of the very opposite, of us taking up the benefits unto ourselves, which His sufferings on the Cross have provided. And please notice; He said that this Cross must be taken up *"daily."*

This means that our Faith must ever be anchored in the Cross, and must never leave the Cross. Paul said:

"But God forbid that I should glory (boast), *save in the Cross of our Lord Jesus Christ, by Whom the world is crucified unto me, and I unto the world"* (Gal. 6:14).

THE HOLY SPIRIT

Anything that we are in the Lord, must be, and without exception, a Work of the Holy Spirit. There is no way that any individual by his own strength and ability can perfect any Work of the Lord within his life. It must always be a Work of the Spirit, and in fact, if it's of the Lord, it definitely will be a Work of the Spirit.

But the sad fact is, even though every single Christian definitely has the Holy Spirit, and to be sure, even many are Baptized with the Holy Spirit, which gives them even more power, still, most Christians get very little help from the Holy Spirit, and it leaves them very confused.

Most Pentecostals think that because they are Baptized with the Holy Spirit and speak with other tongues, this guarantees the help of the Holy Spirit. It doesn't!

Of course, the Holy Spirit will always do all for us that He can; however, the truth is, He works entirely within the parameters of

the great Sacrifice of Christ. In other words, whatever He does must be done within the parameters of the Finished Work of Christ. What Jesus did at the Cross is what gives Him the legal right to do all the things which He Alone can do.

He doesn't demand much of us, but He does demand one thing, and that one thing is Faith (Gal. 2:20). However, when we say *"Faith,"* always and without exception, it must be Faith in the Cross of Christ.

When we place our Faith in the Cross, and keep our Faith in the Cross, the Holy Spirit will then help us, and to be sure, what we could not do by our own strength, He can do easily, and simply because the Holy Spirit is God.

This way and this way alone is the manner in which victory can be obtained, and I speak of victory over all works of the flesh, whatever they might be. Paul said: *"For the Law of the Spirit of Life in Christ Jesus has made me free from the law of sin and death"* (Rom. 8:2).

This of which I speak is actually a *"Law,"* which means that the Holy Spirit will not function outside of this Law. And what is that Law?

It is *"the Law of the Spirit of Life in Christ Jesus,"* which refers to what He did at the Cross. Placing Faith in what Christ did there, we will then be *"free from the law of sin and death."*

In brief, that is God's prescribed order of victory. There is no other.

NAKEDNESS

Verse 22 reads: *"And Ham, the father of Canaan, saw the nakedness of his father, and told his two brethren without."*

Several things are said here:

We see that sin is like leaven; it always spreads. Noah not only gets drunk, but now pulls off all his clothes, and does so intentionally.

There is a form of insanity about sin. The detrimental thing being done makes absolutely no sense, but yet the person, oftentimes otherwise very intelligent, does it, and really does not even know why. This shows us that sin is not merely an act that is the choice of the will. While it is that, it is far more than that. Sin has a power about it, that is so strong, it cannot be broken by man's strength, ability, or his willpower. In fact, the only thing that has ever dealt with sin, and can deal with sin, is the Cross.

We should well understand that if there had been another way to handle sin, Jesus definitely would not have had to come down here and die. But God would have to become man, live a Perfect Life in order to obey the Law, which God demanded, and then would have to address the penalty of the broken Law, of which all were guilty, and do so by dying on the Cross. The wages of sin is death, so Jesus Christ had to die, and did so by the pouring out of His Life's Blood on the Cross of Calvary.

God accepted that Sacrifice, and a Sacrifice it was, as payment for all sin, past, present, and future, at least for those who will believe (Jn. 3:16; Col. 2:14-15).

Sin is the case of all the problems in this world, and what happened to Noah is a perfect example.

"Drunkenness" is an apt description of sin. It is a course and a direction that no one in their right mind would voluntarily travel. But yet almost all do, and because it seems exciting at the beginning.

And then nakedness is the result, which more than all refers to being naked to the Judgment of God. God cannot tolerate sin, inasmuch as it is the cause of all ruination in this world. His judgment must inevitably fall upon sin. So the sinner has one of two choices:

He can accept Christ, and the judgment will be halted. The reason is, Jesus took that judgment at the Cross. Or the sinner can refuse Christ, and if he does, the judgment to be sure, ultimately will come upon him. It's either Jesus or judgment!

The sin of Ham as it regards the nakedness of his father was not so much in seeing his father, as it was in telling his two Brethren, and doing so in a sarcastic way, it seems!

If it is to be noticed, the Holy Spirit through Moses once again refers to Ham as *"the father of Canaan."*

Why?

Verse 24 gives us some indication, which we will address respecting comments on that Verse.

COVERED THE NAKEDNESS

Verse 23 reads: *"And Shem and Japheth took a garment, and laid it upon both their shoulders, and went backward, and covered the nakedness of their father; and their faces were backward, and they saw not their father's nakedness."*

Looking at this episode in one particular way, we have one son attempting to expose the wayward direction of his father, with two sons seeking to cover what had taken place. This is one of the reasons that the Holy Spirit through Peter said: *"And above all things have fervent love among yourselves: for love shall cover the multitude of sins"* (I Pet. 4:8). A lack of love exposes sin, while the Love of God covers sin.

This in no way means that one who has the true Love of God seeks to condone sin, but rather to cover it, and as well, to point out to the one who has failed, the reason that failure has occurred, and how to stop such failure (Gal. 6:1).

As is obvious here, as it regards Ham, to seek to expose sin, thereby holding up the one who has failed to ridicule, cannot in any way claim the Love of God in such action, but rather the opposite.

AN EXAMPLE

Sometime back, there was a young Minister in our congregation who truly had a touch of God on his life. But he had a problem. I won't say what the problem was, but it was quite severe.

Upon it being called to my attention, I prayed with him, and prayed for him.

Regrettably, at the time, I really did not understand the Message of the Cross, so the advice I gave him would not really bring him victory as it regarded his problem. I did the best I could, but simply, as most Preachers, did not know what to tell the Brother to do. To be sure, I told him something to do, but it really would not help as far as victory was concerned.

At any rate, I kept on using him occasionally to minister, and as stated, despite all the problems, there was an Anointing of God upon his life and Ministry.

A short time later, which was inevitable, he fell into the same sin again. We had another Meeting, and I prayed for him again, etc.

At that particular time, I felt that he wasn't making much of an effort. Looking back, I now realize that what I told him to do, if truly engaged, would have been a blessing, but it really would not have seen him through to victory.

At the time, he somewhat rebelled. I said nothing to anyone else about his situation, with the exception of one or two of my Associate Ministers, who I felt needed to know. I didn't use him anymore to preach.

There were several families in the Church who liked to hear him preach, and rightly so. As stated, the Lord, after a fashion, was using him.

One of the families demanded to know the reason why I wasn't using him. In fact, they had some fairly hard things to say about my decision; however, I would not tell them why. My business was to try to restore this Brother. As stated, Scripturally, I really did not know at that time what to tell him to do. But I knew if I spread all over the Church what had happened to him, it would, for all practical purposes, destroy his Ministry, and maybe destroy him as well.

The family in question grew very angry with me, and ultimately quit the Church; however, I would not divulge the situation, because I knew it would be wrong to do so.

I was right! He ultimately gained victory over the problem, and today the Lord is using him to win many souls to Christ. Exposing his spiritual nakedness would not have helped anyone, and as stated, could very likely have destroyed him completely. I'll say it again, *"The true Love of God covers sins, and doesn't expose them."* Let me say it in another way, and perhaps it will be a little more understandable.

When a person is down and cannot defend themselves, and anyone can do any negative thing to them they so desire and not at all be reprimanded but rather commended, then one finds out how many True Christians there really are. One will find there aren't many!

THE GREATER SIN

Verse 24 reads: *"And Noah awoke from his wine, and knew what his younger son had done unto him."*

It is almost positive that Canaan, the grandson of Noah, was with his father Ham

when the drunkenness of Noah was discovered. So whatever happened, it seems that Canaan had part in the act.

The words *"had done unto him,"* carry more weight than a mere observation of Noah's condition. There are some Scholars who believe that either Ham or Canaan, and more likely Canaan, committed an act of homosexuality on the Patriarch. While there is no concrete proof of that, there is definitely some indication in this direction.

The mere looking of Ham and Canaan on the nakedness of Noah, as bad as even that may have been, would not have warranted the curse which resulted. So I think there is more here than meets the eye.

(25) "AND HE SAID, CURSED BE CANAAN; A SERVANT OF SERVANTS SHALL HE BE UNTO HIS BRETHREN.

(26) "AND HE SAID, BLESSED BE THE LORD GOD OF SHEM, AND CANAAN SHALL BE HIS SERVANT.

(27) "GOD SHALL ENLARGE JAPHETH, AND HE SHALL DWELL IN THE TENTS OF SHEM; AND CANAAN SHALL BE HIS SERVANT.

(28) "AND NOAH LIVED AFTER THE FLOOD THREE HUNDRED AND FIFTY YEARS.

(29) "AND ALL THE DAYS OF NOAH WERE NINE HUNDRED AND FIFTY YEARS: AND HE DIED."

The structure is:

1. Noah gives forth one of the most powerful prophecies found anywhere in the entirety of the Word of God.

2. The first part of the prophecy contains a curse on Canaan.

3. The prophecy proclaims blessing upon Shem.

4. In the prediction, the lineage of Japheth shall, in a sense, inherit the blessing of Shem,

5. Noah lived 350 years longer after the flood.

6. Noah lived a total of 950 years, the third longest in history (Gen. 5:20, 27).

CURSED BE CANAAN

Verse 25 reads: *"And he said, Cursed be Canaan; a servant of servants shall he be unto his brethren."*

As stated, Canaan's descendants populated Africa and as well, the land that would eventually be Israel, but was called at first, the land of Canaan.

Before we look deeper into the curse of Canaan, and as well the other parts of this great prophecy, let us look again at the man who gave the prophecy, Noah.

NOAH AND THE PROPHECY

How many Christians presently would wonder how God could use Noah in the realm of Prophecy, especially considering the import of this prophecy, considering the terrible sin into which he had recently fallen?

Christians who would ask such a question do so out of ignorance of the Word of God. First of all, we must understand the following:

God doesn't work or function from the principle of *"good"* or *"evil."* If He did, He wouldn't be able to use anyone. Because the truth is, even in the Godliest of Saints, whoever that might be, they're still coming short of the Glory of God. Paul said: *"For all have sinned, and come short of the Glory of God"* (Rom. 3:23).

Most Christians read that Verse, and interpret it wrongly. They think it refers to their lives before conversion; however, in the Greek Text, it refers to an ongoing condition, which in effect says that all Believers, even the Godliest, are constantly *"coming short of the Glory of God."*

Now please understand, this is not speaking of an individual who is practicing sin, but rather someone who is attempting to live Godly and Holy before the Lord, and trying to do so with all his strength and might. Despite that effort, he is still coming short of the Glory of God.

In fact, the very purpose of the intercessory, High Priestly Work of the Saviour is to presently *"make intercession for us,"* and to do so constantly (Heb. 7:25).

He does so by the fact that even though we are constantly coming short of the Glory of God, at the same time, *"the Blood of Jesus Christ God's Son is constantly cleansing us from all sin"* (I Jn. 1:7). The presence of Christ before God guarantees the effectiveness of the Blood as a cleansing agent.

NOTES

Now once again, we're speaking of individuals who love the Lord with all their hearts, and are living for God to the best of their ability. We're not speaking of individuals who think that they can confess Christ, and at the same time practice sin on a constant basis. In the true Believer is the Divine Nature, and thereby, a hatred for sin. So the idea that a Christian can sin with impunity is facetious! The Scripture plainly says, *"We know that whosoever is born of God sins not* (does not practice sin)*"* (I Jn. 5:18).

Getting back to our original subject, those who think that God functions on the principle of *"good"* and *"evil,"* have in effect, denied the great Sacrifice of Christ. If any person could be *"good"* by his own strength and ability, then Jesus came down here and died needlessly on a Cross. If there is goodness in us, it is all of Christ, and none of ourselves.

So how does God work with Believers?

He works exclusively on the basis of Faith in Christ, and by no other means. Noah had Faith in Christ, which refers at that time to the coming Redeemer.

As we've already stated, though Noah exposed his nakedness, God did not see it, for He looked not at him in the weakness of his own condition, but in the full power of Divine and everlasting Righteousness.

This is proven by what the Holy Spirit said about Noah in the great Chapter of Faith:

"By Faith Noah, being warned of God of things not seen as yet, moved with fear, prepared an Ark to the saving of his house; by the which he condemned the world, and became heir of the Righteousness which is by Faith" (Heb. 11:7).

The Holy Spirit exemplifies the *"Righteousness"* of Noah, which he gained *"by Faith."* The drunkenness and the nakedness aren't mentioned, and not only that, they will never be mentioned.

Not only are our victories in Christ, but our sins are in Him as well, in that He has totally atoned for all sin, past, present, and future — at least for those who will believe (Jn. 3:16).

WHAT WAS THE CURSE WHICH WAS LEVELED AT CANAAN?

It had absolutely nothing to do with the skin of some people being black. In fact, all the descendants of Ham and Canaan were not black, and yet the curse was upon them as well.

Furthermore, although it is not stated, the curse was conditional. And how do we know that?

Canaanites who placed their Faith in God could escape it. Rahab, a Canaanite and a prostitute, is an excellent example. She placed her Faith in God, and after a period of purification, was brought into Israel's camp. She married an Israelite, and became an ancestress of David, and even the greater Son of David, the Lord Jesus Christ (Josh. 6:25; Mat. 1:5; Heb. 11:31).

What a mighty and a merciful God we serve! Any soul who turns to Him, and irrespective as to what the past has been, He will instantly forgive, cleanse, and wash, and that being done, the past and whatever were the curses will never be mentioned again. The Gospel of Jesus Christ and Him Crucified never looks to the past, but always to the future (I Cor. 1:23).

Concerning Canaan, Verse 26 holds what may be an astounding Promise, which we will address next.

THE BLESSING

Verse 26 reads: *"And he said, Blessed be the LORD God of Shem; and Canaan shall be his servant."*

The statement, *"Blessed be the Lord God of Shem,"* as spoken by the Holy Spirit through Noah, blesses God, offering Him Praise and Glory, and not Shem directly. But Shem is greatly blessed indirectly, and because he made the Lord his God. So what would this Blessing be, which would flow over to Shem?

Through Shem would come the Jewish people, who would give the world the Word of God, and would serve as the womb of the Messiah, and nothing could be greater than the two things we have just mentioned. This has enriched the world to such an extent that it defies all description. In fact, the world owes a debt of gratitude to the Jew, which it will never be able to repay.

Every iota of prosperity, freedom, education, advancement, knowledge, etc., which graces this world, has its roots in the Word

of God, given to us by Israel, and above all, their bringing the Son of God into this world, Who would make it possible for mankind to be redeemed, by the great Sacrifice of Himself on the Cross. The *"Blessing"* has been absolutely miraculous, and, thereby phenomenal to say the least!

CANAAN

Williams says that the words *"Canaan shall be his servant,"* may actually read *"Canaan shall become Jehovah's servant."* He is attributing the pronoun *"His"* not to Shem, in that Canaan would be Shem's servant, but rather to God, which means that Canaan would become the servant of the Lord. The idea is this:

The sons of Canaan, after millenniums of slavery, are today becoming servants of Jehovah Jesus. The Grace that much more abounds where sin abounds, and that in this prophecy foretells a Saviour for all men, this we must admit: There are more blacks today coming to Christ, than any other race on the face of the Earth.

So what am I saying? I'm saying that God through Christ has eliminated every curse from off the Earth, at least for those who will believe. The Lord told Abraham:

"I will bless them who bless you, and curse him who curses you: and in you shall all families of the Earth be blessed" (Gen. 12:3).

"All the families of the Earth," definitely includes Ham and Canaan. And thank God, it included my family as well.

JAPHETH

Verse 27 reads: *"God shall enlarge Japheth, and he shall dwell in the tents of Shem; and Canaan shall be his servant."*

From Japheth came the people who populated Europe and the Far East. So how would God enlarge Japheth?

His dwelling in the tents of Shem would be that enlargement. And what does that mean?

Shem was given the Blessing, which regards the bringing of the Messiah into the world, the Saviour of mankind, the Lord Jesus Christ. Shem, i.e., *"Israel,"* rejected her Messiah, and in doing so, rejected the Blessing.

Japheth accepted Christ, and today, virtually all the followers of Christ are descendants of Japheth. Consequently, the figure of speech of Japheth *"dwelling in the tents of Shem,"* means that Japheth has taken and received the forfeited Blessing of Shem. And that is now obvious for the entirety of the world to see.

Today the descendants of Japheth, in effect, rule the world. The prosperity and freedoms which once belonged to Israel, and by rights should have belonged to Israel, have instead been forfeited by the sons of Shem. It was forfeited by unbelief. Japheth accepted Christ, Who was rejected by Israel, and in effect, *"dwells in the tents of Shem,"* i.e., *"takes the forfeited Blessing."*

This triple prophecy foretells a Saviour for all men, as represented in these three great heads of the three families that compose mankind — that Grace appears in the conversion of the *"Ethiopian"* (Ham) (Acts, Chpt. 8), the conversion of *"Paul"* (Shem) (Acts, Chpt. 9), and the conversion of *"Cornelius"* (Japheth) (Acts, Chpt. 10).

THE WORD OF GOD CANNOT FAIL

The prediction respecting Canaan must have, in the days of Moses, upheld the Faith of those who loved the Word of the Lord, and excited the ridicule of those who despised it. For the political position of affairs in the world of that time contradicted the prophecy. The sons of Shem, that is the Israelites, were slaves; the sons of Canaan, that is the Egyptians, were the masters of the world!

But today the truthfulness of that prediction is established; and in the day of Blessing that awaits Israel, and through her the nations, the full glory of this great promise and prophecy will be displayed.

As already pointed out, the conversion of the Ethiopian, of Paul, and of Cornelius foretell the introduction of Shem, Ham, and Japheth into a brighter world than their forefathers looked out upon when leaving the Ark (Williams).

NOAH

Verses 28 and 29 read: *"And Noah lived after the flood three hundred and fifty years.*

"And all the days of Noah were nine hundred and fifty years: and he died."

This means that Noah lived unto the fifty-eighth year of the life of Abraham, and was thus in all probability a witness of the building of the tower of Babel, and of the consequent dispersion of mankind (Pulpit).

One might say that Noah lived in two worlds, before the flood and after the flood. But I think Matthew Henry summed it up pretty well. He said: *"But being an heir of the Righteousness which is by Faith, when Noah died he went to see a better than either."*

*"So precious is Jesus, my Saviour, my
    King,
"His praise all the day long with rap-
    ture I sing;
"To Him in my weakness for strength
    I can cling,
"For He is so precious to me."*

*"He stood at my heart's door 'mid sun-
    shine and rain,
"And patiently waited an entrance to
    gain;
"What shame that so long He entreated
    in vain,
"For He is so precious to me."*

*"I stand on the mountain of blessing
    at last,
"No cloud in the heavens a shadow
    to cast;
"His smile is upon me, the valley is past,
"For He is so precious to me."*

*"I praise Him because He appointed
    a place
"Where, someday, through Faith in His
    wonderful Grace,
"I know I shall see Him, shall look on
    His Face,
"For He is so precious to me."*

CHAPTER 10

(1) "NOW THESE ARE THE GENERATIONS OF THE SONS OF NOAH, SHEM, HAM, AND JAPHETH: AND UNTO THEM WERE SONS BORN AFTER THE FLOOD.

(2) "THE SONS OF JAPHETH; GOMER, AND MAGOG, AND MADAI, AND JAVAN, AND TUBAL, AND MESHECH, AND TIRAS.

(3) "AND THE SONS OF GOMER; ASHKENAZ, AND RIPHATH, AND TOGARMAH.

(4) "AND THE SONS OF JAVAN; ELISHAH, AND TARSHISH, KITTIM, AND DODANIM.

(5) "BY THESE WERE THE ISLES OF THE GENTILES DIVIDED IN THEIR LANDS; EVERY ONE AFTER HIS TONGUE, AFTER THEIR FAMILIES, IN THEIR NATIONS."

The composite is:

1. The order was Shem, Ham, and Japheth; however, the order is now reversed, with Japheth being first, and because of his ascendancy.

2. Japheth had seven sons.

3. From Japheth descended all nations that lived toward the north, as the Medes, Scythians, Tartars, Cimmerians, Poles, Vandals, Danes, Germans, Greeks, Italians, French, and Spaniards.

AFTER THE FLOOD

Verse 1 reads: *"Now these are the generations of the sons of Noah, Shem, Ham, and Japheth: and unto them were sons born after the flood."*

Concerning Chapter 10, Williams says: *"This Chapter sets out the nations as divided in the Earth; the following Chapter gives the cause of that division. This is an instance of one of the 'Laws' or principles to be noticed throughout the whole Bible, exhibiting design on the part of the Holy Spirit in recording facts out of chronological order in order to make prominent a spiritual lesson, or to hold the attention of the Reader to the main subject of the 66 Books of the Bible, which is 'Sin and Salvation.'"*

Verse 2 reads: *"The sons of Japheth; Gomer, and Magog, and Madai, and Javan, and Tubal, and Meshech, and Tiras."*

Japheth, as is obvious here, had seven sons. The name *"Japheth"* means, *"enlargement."* Noah prophesied that God would *"enlarge Japheth,"* and that he would *"dwell in the tents of Shem,"* which refers to receiving the Blessing that should have come to Shem. That Blessing was and is the Lord Jesus Christ. Rejected by the Jews, the sons of Shem, Christ has been accepted by the Gentiles, the sons of Japheth. In fact, his

sons practically govern in the world at present, and have for a long, long time.

EUROPE

Verses 3 and 4 read: *"And the sons of Gomer; Ashkenaz, and Riphath, and Togarmah.*

"And the sons of Javan; Elishah, and Tarshish, Kittim, and Dodanim."

At the outset, the Japhethites showed little promise, while the sons of Ham, who in fact carried the curse, were building mighty cities, etc. But yet, if God says something is going to happen, and He definitely said that He would *"enlarge Japheth,"* then to be sure, what He has said, definitely will come to pass.

Probably one could say that the ascendancy of the sons of Japheth began in earnest with Alexander the Great. From that time on, the descendents of Japheth have, for all practical purposes, ruled the world.

The United States at present is the world's only superpower. Its gross national product is about ten trillion dollars a year. In fact, the GNP of the balance of the world is not much more than that. While this country is made up of every race, the predominate race is white, which sprang from Japheth.

GENTILES

Verse 5 reads: *"By these were the Isles of the Gentiles divided in their lands; every one after his tongue, after their families, in their nations."*

Bishop Watson observes that the Tenth Chapter of Genesis is one of the most valuable records of antiquity. It explains what no other writing does, the origin of nations.

This is the first mention of the *"Gentiles"* in the Bible.

The word *"Gentiles"* originally was a general term for *"nations,"* but gradually acquired a restricted sense by usage. It ultimately came to apply to all nations of the world, and all people, with the exception of the Jews. So in the mind of the Jews, even the Arabs, who were descendants as well of Abraham, are still looked at as *"Gentiles."* The term now refers to everyone in the world other than Jews.

In the eyes of God presently, due to the Advent of Christ and what He did at the Cross, which were equally for all of humanity, the distinction between Jew and Gentile has been erased. And yet, due to the Promises originally made to Israel, this nation and these people will yet be given a very prominent place in the great Work of God; however, it will only be after they have made Jesus Christ their Lord, Saviour, and Messiah. Everything hinges on Christ!

(6) "AND THE SONS OF HAM; CUSH, AND MIZRAIM, AND PHUT, AND CANAAN.

(7) "AND THE SONS OF CUSH; SEBA, AND HAVILAH, AND SABTAH, AND RAAMAH, AND SABTECHAH: AND THE SONS OF RAAMAH; SHEBA, AND DEDAN.

(8) "AND CUSH BEGAT NIMROD: HE BEGAN TO BE A MIGHTY ONE IN THE EARTH.

(9) "HE WAS A MIGHTY HUNTER BEFORE THE LORD: WHEREFORE IT IS SAID, EVEN AS NIMROD THE MIGHTY HUNTER BEFORE THE LORD.

(10) "AND THE BEGINNING OF HIS KINGDOM WAS BABEL, AND ERECH, AND ACCAD, AND CALNEH, IN THE LAND OF SHINAR."

The construction is:

1. We now come to the sons of Ham.

2. These populated Canaan and Africa.

3. Nimrod is introduced here, who engineered the first organized rebellion against God.

4. He is no doubt the builder of the Tower of Babel, which was at the heart of this organized rebellion.

THE SONS OF HAM

Verse 6 reads: *"And the sons of Ham; Cush, and Mizraim, and Phut, and Canaan."*

These, as are obvious, number four, but the one more Biblically important is *"Canaan."* Satan would use these people to do everything possible to hinder Israel from taking the Land of Promise. As well, there would be another eruption of giants among these people, along with the Philistines. The Canaanites were gross idol worshippers, and did everything possible to lure Israel into this base immorality, and succeeded in doing so oftentimes.

NIMROD

Verses 7 and 8 read: *"And the sons of Cush; Seba, and Havilah, and Sabtah, and Raamah,*

and Sabtechah: and the sons of Raamah; Sheba, and Dedan.

"And Cush begat Nimrod: he began to be a mighty one in the Earth."

Nimrod was not the son of Cush, but rather his grandson, or even possibly his great-grandson. When the Scripture says, *"And Cush begat Nimrod,"* it doesn't mean that Nimrod was the son of Cush, but rather that he was in the lineage, possibly several times removed. The word *"begat"* speaks of the lineage, but doesn't give us any clue as to exactly what part of the lineage.

The great figure of this Chapter is Nimrod, and the great city of the Chapter is Babylon. He and his city foreshadow the coming Antichrist and his city.

He may be assumed to have counseled and built the Tower of Babel of the next Chapter. He led the first organized rebellion against God.

BABEL

Verses 9 and 10 read: *"He was a mighty hunter before the LORD: wherefore it is said, Even as Nimrod the mighty hunter before the LORD.*

"And the beginning of his kingdom was Babel, and Erech, and Accad, and Calneh, in the land of Shinar."

"Babel" in the Greek is *"Babylon."* So we know from this that Nimrod founded the city of Babylon. We see the beginning here, but it continues all the way through to the Eighteenth Chapter of Revelation. It appears again and again before us, and always as something decidedly hostile to those who occupy, for the time being, the position of public testimony for God.

Hardly had Israel entered into the Promised Land, when *"a Babylonish garment"* brought defilement and sorrow, defeat and confusion, into the host. This is the earliest record of Babylon's pernicious influence upon the people of God (Josh. 7:21).

Down through the history of the Work of God, whenever God has a corporate witness on the Earth, Satan has a Babylon to mar and corrupt that witness.

When God connects His Name with a city on the Earth (Jerusalem), then Babylon takes the form of a city; and when God connects

His Name with a Church, then Babylon takes the form of a corrupt religious system, called *"the great whore," "the mother of abominations,"* etc. (Rev. 17:1, 5).

In a word, Satan's Babylon is always seen as the instrument molded and fashioned by his hand, for the purpose of counteracting the Divine Operations, whether in Israel of old, or the Church now. Throughout the Old Testament, Israel and Babylon are seen, as it were, in opposite scales — when Israel is up, Babylon is down; and when Babylon is up, Israel is down. Thus, when Israel had utterly failed as a witness for the Lord, *"The king of Babylon broke his bones,"* and swallowed him up. The vessels of the House of God, which ought to have remained in the city of Jerusalem, were carried away to the city of Babylon. But Isaiah, in his sublime prophecy, leads us onward to the opposite of all this. He presents, in most magnificent strains, a picture, in which Israel's star is in the ascendant, and Babylon entirely sunk (Isa. 14:3-8).

THE MIGHTY HUNTER

The Scripture uses the term concerning Nimrod, *"He began to be a mighty one in the Earth."* However, while he may have been mighty on Earth, he was not mighty in Heaven.

As well, the Scripture bearing it out that *"Nimrod was the mighty hunter before the Lord,"* has nothing to do with hunting animals, as most commentators claim. By the use of the phrase *"before the Lord,"* as it concerns this man, it means *"in opposition to the Lord."*

The idea is, Nimrod instituted the first organized rebellion against the Lord and thereby, the ways of the Lord, and thereby those who followed the Lord. He *"hunted"* them down, possibly even killing those who worshipped Jehovah. Consequently, Babylon has always stood for every false religion, every false doctrine, and every false way. That's why it is referred to as *"the great whore . . . the mother of harlots and abominations of the Earth"* (Rev. 17:1, 5).

To which we've already alluded, there are two major cities in the Bible. Those cities are *"Jerusalem,"* where God has chosen to

place His Name, and *"Babylon,"* which is the opposite of all that which pertains to the Lord.

(11) "OUT OF THAT LAND WENT FORTH ASSHUR, AND BUILT NINEVEH, AND THE CITY REHOBOTH, AND CALAH,

(12) "AND RESEN BETWEEN NINEVEH AND CALAH: THE SAME IS A GREAT CITY.

(13) "AND MIZRAIM BEGAT LUDIM, AND ANAMIM, AND LEHABIM, AND NAPHTUHIM,

(14) "AND PATHRUSIM, AND CASLUHIM, (OUT OF WHOM CAME PHILISTIM,) AND CAPHTORIM."

The overview is:

1. Many Scholars believe that Verse 11 should have been translated, *"Out of that land went Nimrod into Assyria,"* etc.

2. Nineveh was the capital of Assyria.

3. *"Philistim"* is the Philistines, who gave Israel so much difficulty.

NINEVEH

Verses 11, 12, and 13 read: *"Out of that land went forth Nimrod in Assyria, and built Nineveh, and the city Rehoboth, and Calah,*

"And Resen between Nineveh and Calah: the same is a great city.

"And Mizraim begat Ludim, and Anamim, and Lehabim, and Naphtuhim."

Many Scholars, if not most, believe that Verse 11 should be translated as I have translated it above. In the first place, Asshur was the son of Shem, and not Ham. So, if we are correct, Nimrod not only founded Babylon, but as well Nineveh.

While it seems that Babylon was founded sometime before Nineveh, the latter city became more prominent at the beginning, and remained that way for quite some time.

It was probably founded about 2200 B.C., and it fell, as predicted by the Prophets Nahum and Zephaniah, in August of 612 B.C. So it was a powerful city for about 600 years.

The Babylonian Chronicle tells how a combined force of Medes, Babylonians, and Scythians laid siege to the city, which fell as a result of the breaches made in the defenses by the flooding rivers (Nah. 2:6-8). The city was plundered by the Medes, and the king Sin-shar-ishkun perished in the flames, though his family escaped. The city was left to fall into a heap of desolate ruin, which it is today (Nah. 2:10; 3:7), and is now a pasturing-place for flocks, which the Prophet Zephaniah predicted would happen (Zeph. 2:13-15).

When Zenophon and the retreating Greek army passed its ruins in 401 B.C., it was already an unrecognizable mass of debris.

Jesus mentioned Nineveh and the great revival which took place there under the Prophet Jonah. He said: *"The men of Nineveh shall rise in judgment with this generation, and shall condemn it: because they repented at the preaching of Jonah; and, behold, a greater than Jonah is here"* (Mat. 12:41).

THE PHILISTINES

Verse 14 reads: *"And Pathrusim, and Casluhim, (out of whom came Philistim,) and Caphtorim."*

"Philistim" refers to the Philistines, who plagued Israel, and did so for many years.

Abraham and Isaac had dealings with a Philistine, Abimelech, the king of Gerar, and his general Phichol (Gen., Chpts. 20-21; 26).

When the Israelites left Egypt, the Philistines were extensively settled along the coastal strip between Egypt and Gaza, and they were obliged to detour inland to avoid *"the way of the land of the Philistines"* (Ex. 13:17). In fact, that particular section of the Mediterranean was in fact referred to as the Sea of the Philistines (Ex. 23:31).

The Israelites after coming into the Promised Land did not at first encounter the Philistines, but by the time Joshua was an old man, these people were established in the five cities of Gaza, Ashkelon, Ashdod, Ekron, and Gath (Josh. 13:2-3). From this time and for many generations, these people were used by God to chastise the Israelites when they went wrong (Judg. 3:2-3).

At times, it seems that the Israelites even adopted the god's of the Philistines, which were an abomination in the eyes of God (Judg. 10:6-7). The great Israelite hero of the period of the Judges was Samson (Judg., Chpts. 13-16).

SAUL AND DAVID

It was probably largely due to the continuing pressure of the Philistines that the need

for a strong military leader was felt in Israel. The Ark was captured by the Philistines in a disastrous battle at Aphek and the shrine at Shiloh was destroyed (I Sam., Chpt. 4), and at this time they probably controlled Esdraelon, the coast plain, the Negeb, and much of the hill-country. They also controlled the distribution of iron, and thus prevented the Israelites from having useful weapons (I Sam. 13:19-22).

Saul was anointed king by Samuel, and after a victory over the Philistines at Michmash, drove them from the hill-country (I Sam., Chpt. 14). His erratic rule, however, allowed the Philistines to continue to assert themselves, as when they challenged Israel at Esphes-dammim, and David killed Goliath there (I Sam., Chpts. 17-18).

When David became king, he drove the Philistines out of the hill-country and struck a heavy blow in Philistia itself (II Sam. 5:25), putting an end to the power of the Philistines as a serious menace.

(15) "AND CANAAN BEGAT SIDON HIS FIRSTBORN, AND HETH,

(16) "AND THE JEBUSITE, AND THE AMORITE, AND THE GIRGASITE,

(17) "AND THE HIVITE, AND THE ARKITE, AND THE SINITE,

(18) "AND THE ARVADITE, AND THE ZEMARITE, AND THE HAMATHITE: AND AFTERWARD WERE THE FAMILIES OF THE CANAANITES SPREAD ABROAD.

(19) "AND THE BORDER OF THE CANAANITES WAS FROM SIDON, AS YOU COME TO GERAR, UNTO GAZA; AS YOU GO, UNTO SODOM, AND GOMORRAH, AND ADMAH, AND ZEBOIM, EVEN UNTO LASHA.

(20) "THESE ARE THE SONS OF HAM, AFTER THEIR FAMILIES, AFTER THEIR TONGUES, IN THEIR COUNTRIES, AND IN THEIR NATIONS."

The structure is:

1. *"Canaan"* is mentioned here, whose lineage would be used by Satan to greatly hinder Israel.

2. Some of these sons of Canaan, such as *"the Jebusite,"* and the *"Girgasite,"* and the *"Hivite,"* are mentioned quite often in the struggle of Israel.

3. These which we have mentioned are types in the literal, physical, and material

sense, of that which Christians struggle against respecting the spiritual.

CANAAN

Verse 15 reads: *"And Canaan begat Sidon his firstborn, and Heth."*

Now we come to at least one of the reasons that the Holy Spirit through Moses addressed Canaan as He did, in the previous Chapter. In fact, He said, *"Cursed be Canaan"* (Gen. 9:25).

Whatever involvement Canaan had with his father Ham, as it regards Noah, his evil bent would continue on in his lineage. Satan would use this lineage to greatly hinder the people of God, in their conquest in the land of Canaan.

Only one city, that is of which we are aware, was named after one of these individuals, and it is Sidon, situated on the seashore, about 30 miles north of Tyre, and still exists today in modern Lebanon.

JEBUSITES

Verses 16, 17, and 18 read: *"And the Jebusite, and the Amorite, and the Girgasite,*

"And the Hivite, and the Arkite, and the Sinite,

"And the Arvadite, and the Zemarite, and the Hamathite: and afterward were the families of the Canaanites spread abroad."

As stated, these tribes mentioned here occupied the Land of Canaan, and were the greatest nemesis to Israel upon her attempts to conquer the land.

These are the names read often in your Bible, as it refers to opposition against the people of God. This was planned by Satan, no doubt from the time of Noah.

How much Satan, who is a fallen angel, knows about the future, we have no way of knowing for sure. But knowing that he has access at times to the Throne of God (Job, Chpts. 1-2), we are led to believe that he has access to some information as it regards the future. To be sure, the Lord gauges just how much He wants the Evil One to know.

As the Reader goes through Joshua, Judges, and I and II Samuel, we are made very much aware of these particular tribes which greatly opposed the people of God. We learn that when Israel was trusting the Lord,

no people could defeat them. We also learn that when they were drifting from God, even at times, sadly and regrettably, blaspheming His Name, then Israel would fall prey to these various enemies.

In a sense, they were physical and material types of the spiritual struggles we as Christians go through presently. However, the following is that which every Believer must know, or else suffer defeat.

VICTORY!

The problem with most Christians, and I especially speak of those who truly love the Lord, is that they attempt to fight battles which Jesus has already fought and won. If Satan can maneuver us into this position and spiritual posture, he will defeat us every time.

To be brief, at the Cross of Calvary, Jesus Christ defeated every enemy, and defeated them completely (Col. 2:14-15). We must understand that every single victory He won, all bought by His Precious Blood, was done entirely for you and me. In other words, He didn't come down to this world for Himself, or for Heaven, but rather for you and me. We must never forget that.

All the great things He did, all of the ministry, healings, and miracles, and all that He accomplished at the Cross, all in totality were done strictly and totally for us, and not at all for Himself.

Therefore, understanding that He did all of this for us, we should surely understand as well that He wants us to have all of the victory which He has purchased, and especially considering that He purchased it at such great price — the giving of Himself on the Cross.

Knowing that He left nothing undone at the Cross, that every single thing Adam lost in the Fall was totally and completely addressed at the Cross, there is no reason for a single Christian to walk in defeat in any capacity. If we do walk in defeat, it's simply because we do not know and understand God's prescribed order of victory.

You don't need to fight battles that Jesus has already fought and won! You don't need to fight the Devil and demon spirits, which Jesus has already defeated at the Cross. There is only one fight in which you should be engaged, and that is *"the good fight of Faith"* (I Tim. 6:12).

THE GOOD FIGHT OF FAITH

To obtain all of these great and wonderful things which the Lord has done for us at the Cross, our only requirement is that we evidence Faith in Christ and His Finished Work (Rom. 5:1-2).

Satan will fight you as a Believer in the realm of your faith, more so than he does in any other manner. In fact, every single attack leveled against a Believer by Satan, whether it be physical, material, financial, domestical, or spiritual is all for one purpose, and that is to destroy, or at least seriously weaken your faith.

He wants you to lose faith altogether, and barring that, at least to get you to shift your Faith from the Cross of Christ to other things. To be sure, he doesn't too very much care what the other things are, just as long as your faith is moved from the Cross. Regrettably, he has been very, very successful with many, if not most, Christians. The faith of most is <u>not</u> in *"Jesus Christ and Him Crucified"* (I Cor. 1:23; 2:2, 5), but rather in Jesus Christ and the Church, or Jesus Christ and our giving of money, or Jesus Christ and the good works that we accomplish, etc.

No, without exception, it's always *"Jesus Christ and Him Crucified,"* or else while it may continue to be faith, it's not faith that God will recognize.

Spiritually speaking, I fought Jebusites, and Girgasites, etc., for years. I fought bravely, and faithfully, but the truth was, I was fighting a battle that had long since been fought and won. In such a conflict, the Holy Spirit will not help the Believer, and to be sure, without the help of the Holy Spirit we simply cannot overcome.

THE HOLY SPIRIT

Whenever we fight correctly, which is to fight the good fight of Faith, which refers to having Faith in Christ and what He did at the Cross, irrespective of what Satan may then try to do, the Holy Spirit will stop him forthwith. Please understand that Satan doesn't mind tangling with us whatsoever, but he wants no part of the Holy Spirit. That

should be obvious, considering that the Holy Spirit is God.

It's a wonderful thing to win battles, but it's even better not to have to fight the battle. And we as Believers do not have to fight that which has already been fought. Jesus Christ is our Champion. He is the Conqueror, and as stated, He did all of this for you and me.

That's one of the reasons that He said: *"Come unto Me, all you who labor and are heavy laden, and I will give you rest"* (Mat. 11:28).

REST

It's sad, but when many Christians think of living for the Lord, they think of a fight, a struggle, etc. And please believe me, I know that feeling.

But haven't we stopped to think that this does not coincide with what Jesus said? He said that He would give us *"rest,"* not more fight or struggle. What did He mean by that?

He simply meant that He would fight for us, which He did at the Cross, and there defeated every power of darkness (Col. 2:14-15).

The way we live, and I refer to our attempts to live for God, I sometimes think that most Christians do not really understand the *"Finished Work of Christ."* What does that mean?

THE FINISHED WORK

On the Cross, even moments before He died, it is fairly certain that the last Words that Jesus said were, *"It is finished: Father, into Your hands I commend My spirit"* (Jn. 19:30; Lk. 23:46).

At the moment He said that, the Scripture says, *"And, behold, the Veil of the Temple was rent in twain from the top to the bottom; and the Earth did quake, and the rocks rent"* (Mat. 27:50-51).

The Veil, as most Bible students know, separated the Holy Place in the Temple from the Holy of Holies. In the latter, the Ark of the Covenant and the Mercy Seat were to reside. It was where God dwelt between the Mercy Seat and the Cherubim. Regrettably, and because of Israel's sins, these articles of Sacred Furniture were not in the Holy of Holies at that particular time. Nevertheless, the Type still presented itself. Consequently, when Jesus died, this signaled the fact that the price had now been paid, and the way was opened up for man to go directly into the Presence of God, with God splitting the Veil, showing that the way was now open.

Before the Cross, only one man, the High Priest, could go into this place, and then only once a year, which was on the Great Day of Atonement, and then not without blood. But when Jesus died, thereby having paid the price, the way was opened that anyone may come, and drink of the water of life freely.

This is what Jesus was speaking of when He cried out on the great day of the Feast, *"If any man thirst, let him come unto Me, and drink.*

"He who believes on Me, as the Scripture has said, out of his innermost being shall flow rivers of living water."

John then said, *"But this spake He of the Spirit, which they who believe on Him should receive"* (Jn. 7:37-39).

The Cross and the Cross Alone made all of this possible (I Cor. 1:17).

Concerning this, Paul also said: *"When He had by Himself purged our sins* (which He did at the Cross), *sat down on the right hand of the Majesty on high"* (Heb. 1:3).

In fact, all the Priests of old, in their duties in the Tabernacle and the Temple, not one time ever sat down, simply because their work was never finished. Their work was not finished because the blood of bulls and goats could not take away sins (Heb. 10:4). Therefore, more and more sacrifices had to ever be offered up. But when Jesus died on the Cross, the Scripture says: *"But this Man, after He had offered one Sacrifice for sins forever, sat down on the right hand of God"* (Heb. 10:12).

Now, there is no more need for earthly Priests, who in fact in Old Testament times, were Types of Christ. That for which they were used and that which they did have forever been finished, and was finished by the Christ of Glory on the Cross. Now we can bank the Altar fires. We can take down the Tabernacle, of which it was but a Type. We can take the little lambs and let them out to pasture, for not another one will ever be needed again, at least for sacrifice. It is done! It is over! It is finished!

Thereby understanding that this Work, this glorious Work, this Work that Christ carried

forth on the Cross, is done and complete. It is finished! Consequently, I must never try to take something from that Work, or add anything to that Work. To do so is tantamount to blasphemy. It is the greatest insult to Christ!

Understanding this, the only thing I'm required to do is to simply place my Faith in this which He has done, understanding that it was completed, and understanding that it was for me. When I place my Faith in the Cross, and keep my Faith in the Cross, the Holy Spirit will then work greatly for me, guaranteeing to me all the great things that Jesus did at the Cross.

That's why Paul said, *"We preach Christ Crucified"* (I Cor. 1:23).

A BANKRUPT MESSAGE!

The other day I received a letter from a Pastor. He told me how much the Message of the Cross had changed his life and Ministry. He then went on to say that most of the preaching done today, and he is exactly right, is rather Preachers preaching a bankrupt message. What did he mean by that?

He was meaning that what most Preachers are preaching is not *"Jesus Christ and Him Crucified,"* but rather something else. And if it is something else, and irrespective as to what the something else is, to be sure, what they are giving to the people is in fact, a bankrupt message. It holds no water; it has no substance; and it will effect no positive results. It might sound good to the natural ear, but it will not do the job. Only the Word, only the Message, only the preaching of Christ and Him Crucified will set the captive free (Eph. 2:13-18).

No, I don't have to fight a battle that's already been fought and won. The Jebusite, the Amorite, the Girgasite, and the Hivite, and all others for that matter, were totally defeated by Christ at the Cross.

THE BORDER

Verses 19 and 20 read: *"And the border of the Canaanites was from Sidon, as you come to Gerar, unto Gaza, as you go, unto Sodom, and Gomorrah, and Admah, and Zeboim, even unto Lasha.*

"These are the sons of Ham, after their families, after their tongues, in their countries, and in their nations."

Satan will do his best to place the enemies of your soul within your promised possession, your inheritance, this which Christ has given to you. In other words, he will make the *"borders"* of his effort your most prized possession.

If you oppose him in the wrong way, to be sure, he can cause you untold problems and difficulties. Most Christians, sadly and regrettably, have to learn that the hard way.

But if you *"fight the good fight of Faith,"* which refers to your Faith being placed strictly in the Cross of Christ, and no other place, and keeping your Faith there, not allowing it to be moved to something else, all that the Evil One brings against you will be to no avail. Jesus said: *"And you shall know the Truth, and the Truth shall make you free"* (Jn. 8:32).

The problem is, far too many Christians are seeking a touch, instead of the Truth. While all of us want to be touched by the Power of God, and while such definitely is a blessing and a help; still, if we do not know the Truth, we will find that the effects of the *"touch,"* soon wears off, and we're back where we began.

Regrettably, Christians are running all over the world, trying to find a Preacher who they believe God is using, hoping that he will touch them, and they will have some type of manifestation, which they think will give them victory.

While the Lord definitely does use Preachers, and while the laying on of hands is Scriptural, and while certain manifestations are definitely of God, still, if we don't know the Truth, we're really not going to make any spiritual headway. Jesus did <u>not</u> say: *"You shall have a touch, and it shall make you free."* He rather said, *"You shall know the Truth, and the Truth shall make you free"* (Jn. 8:32).

What is the Truth?

Once again, we come back to the same thing we have been saying. The Truth is:

"Jesus Christ and Him Crucified." Listen to Paul:

"For Christ sent me not to baptize, but to preach the Gospel: not with wisdom of words, lest the Cross of Christ should be made of none effect" (I Cor. 1:17).

NOTES

Was Paul demeaning Water Baptism? No!

He was in effect saying that the emphasis must always be strictly on the Cross of Christ and nothing else. While Ordinances such as Water Baptism, etc., are definitely important, they must never be placed in the position of preeminence. The Cross must ever have that place.

The following is derived from the Book, *"The Meaning And Message Of The Cross"*, written by Dr. Henry C. Mabie. Dr. Mabie ministered in the latter part of the Nineteenth Century and the first part of the Twentieth Century.

THE CROSS AS A REDEEMING ACHIEVEMENT

"And they overcame Him because of the Blood of the Lamb" (Rev. 12:11).

The Cross of Christ was not only a symbol of the Redeemer's voluntary Sacrificial Work indicating also that He had tasted that spiritual death — that sense of separation from God (from 12 noon until 3 p.m., when He died, when that part of the world turned black), which man's sin incurred; but the Cross represented also an actual triumph over every potency of evil which had come into the world through sin. What the benefits of that triumph were and the principles on which they were secured, we will look at later. It is now important to make clear the matter that the Work of Christ was an actual objective achievement, won on behalf of others.

There are those who contend that the Cross simply marked the tragic end of the greatest of Prophets; they place the emphasis on what Jesus taught, and to what cost to Himself He taught it in His pre-Crucifixion Life, and not on what He achieved in the way of a cure of the moral malady and guilt of the race; thus they imply that He died only as the chief of martyrs; the value of His Cross was in the mere moral influence He acquired through so tragic an endurance of what His persecutors laid upon Him. In this respect He was the consummate Revelation of the real Character of God as Self-sacrificing love; He bore our sins only in the sense that as such incidental cost to the deliverance of His Message, He expressed the intensity of His will to save. On this view there was no penal element whatever in what Christ suffered; His sufferings had no respect to any principle of righteous justice or judgment in the Government of God.

A JUDGMENT DEATH

Now as over against this view, a view which represents only a part of the Truth, I shall point out as I proceed that the death of Christ was really a judgment-death; it could not have accomplished what recovery from the sin-situation in the world demanded without there being such a judgment-death. Before, however, defining in what respect it is such a death, some preliminary considerations will prepare us to apprehend the term, which we grant is somewhat uncommon.

The meaning of this term *"judgment"* has been grossly misconceived as synonymous with a sentence of reprobation, and, in consequence, the most unhappy revolt against it exists in *"the modern mind."*

The existing prejudice is doubtless due to an oversight of a very different and gracious sense and in which the Bible uses the term. The word often is employed in the sense of merciful intervention, vindication. Matthew, quoting from Isaiah, says: *"He shall declare judgment to the Gentiles . . . a bruised reed shall He not break, and a smoking flax shall He not quench, till He send forth judgment into victory, and in His Name shall the Gentiles trust"* (Mat. 12:18-21).

Professor George Adam Smith, commenting on certain gracious uses of the term in Isaiah, says: *"The English word 'judgment' — in the Hebrew 'mishpat' — is a natural but misleading translation of the original, and we must dismiss at once the idea of judicial sentence which it suggests."* He says the word *"judgment"* often means not only *"the civic righteousness and justice, but these with God behind them"*; and I would add, a God Who is filled with Mercy and Grace as well as Truth, and Who intends through His Redeeming Work to use all the strength of His Holiness to uphold His Mercy and give it Divine effect in the recovery of the lost.

Judgment in the Scriptures is never used — not even in the Old Testament — in the vindictive but rather in the vindicatory sense — vindicatory of God's merciful way

of pardoning the sinner, as well as of upholding God's moral rule. When, therefore, the Psalmist cries: *"Save me, O God by Your Name, and judge me in Your might!"* — he is pleading surely not for judicial doom, but for an administration of Mercy harmonious with justice: and again when he says of the coming Redeemer, *"He will judge the poor of the people,"* He means the Redeemer will rescue them from the oppressor.

When Jesus in the Gospel said, after opening the eyes of the blind: — *"For judgment came I into this world that they that see not may see,"* — He was uttering a great generalization concerning His Reign of Grace; as if He had said: — *"For a merciful administration, yet a righteous one, am I come into the world."*

Thus, it is clear that the term *"judgment"* as used in the Scriptures in a fundamental aspect of its meaning, is peculiarly a term of Grace. Nothing could be more tender in character: it offers all the sheltering hospitality of a dovecote to returning aliens whenever they may come flying as clouds, to home themselves in God.

SACRIFICE AND JUDGMENT AS RESPECTING THE CROSS

Be it observed also that this idea of a Redeemer's judgment in the thought of Scripture means far more than sacrifice, or mere altruistic love. In the thought of our time there is much confusion of sacrifice and judgment as respecting the Cross.

Now the Cross was indeed the Divine Sacrifice, but it was more; it looked in two directions: A. It regarded the claims of the Divine Holiness on the one hand and B. It sought to recover the sinner from his ruin on the other. Sacrifice is not a final idea apart from judgment; it is not an end in itself. Sacrifice is only a means; judgment is an end, and Christ's Work must accomplish this end if it is to prove saving.

Judgment is final in its nature, because it is vindication: it establishes both Righteousness and Grace. Appreciation of judgment then is only the appreciation of moral and redemptive quality, but that is at the basis of everything in Faith. If we make light of the idea of judgment we shall necessarily scorn the actual moral and redemptive situation of the world, and that means spiritual anarchy.

Said Jesus, looking straight into the meanings of His Cross: *"Now is the judgment of this world"* (Jn. 12:31): now is a crisis; but such a crisis as involved all that is deepest in the final judgment of mankind.

It is because of this principle of judgment in the very nature of this universe as moral that no statement of the Reconciliation can ever long be satisfying which does not embody in itself the expiatory principle.

EXPIATION

Of course, by expiatory, I do not mean expiatory in any pagan sense of the term — no mere appeasement or placation — God is not irritated nor exasperated that He needs to be won over to a better mood. I conceive of expiation as embracing at least three elements:

THE HOLINESS OF GOD

Expiation is a necessity of the Holiness of God, and Holiness must suffer in view of human sin. It is its nature to do so; and of course it suffers vicariously (as our Substitute). The cry of God in the Garden for the guilty fallen, *"Where art thou?"*, was not as Dr. Henry G. Weston has said, *"The call of a policeman, but the wail of a brokenhearted father."* It was suffering Holiness seeking to Redeem.

THE INSULT DONE TO GOD'S HOLINESS

Sin requires to be expiated in the sense that a public and adequate acknowledgement needs to be made and endured of sin's intrinsic ill-deserved — what one has called *"Christ's apology on behalf of the race for the insult done to God's Holiness."*

This apology needs to be made by one competent in such a matter; by one no less competent than the Son of God, one who has rapport with the Father. Such an acknowledgement was made by Christ on man's behalf, in the responsibilities assumed by His Self-immolation on the Cross.

RIGHTEOUSNESS

Sin needs to be expiated in the sense that a process needs to be instituted within the soul itself, which in the end will destroy the

victimizing power of evil, and instead thereof will establish Righteousness upon sin's ruin, effectually and forever.

This Christ potentially achieved through His corporate identification with the race in His Divine human Life, eventuating in Death and Resurrection, and in the promised Spirit of Pentecost. As risen and living, He waits and yearns to form Himself by His Spirit within the Believer, as *"the hope of glory."*

A DEATH-BEARING BODY AND A LIFE-GIVING POWER

Dr. William Ashmore of China, who, from long contact with Oriental life, has an uncommon insight into the corporate principle which is so prominent also in the Bible, that Oriental Book, has forcefully expressed this saving achievement.

Contending earnestly that no change in God's original plan was involved through the Fall of man, Dr. Ashmore says that God provided for the realization of His saving purposes by sending such a Son into the world as might be incorporated into the race of man.

This Son was *"endowed with a death-bearing body and a life-giving power."* Accordingly, He could die for man, and yet live again; and man in Him could also die and yet rise and live in Him. This was an actual achievement accomplished on behalf of man, and by means of it sin was actually expiated in principle, and so could be put away from all them who believe. (Expiation means to make Atonement or to pay the price.)

It will be seen that by such a view of expiation there is implied no question of willingness or unwillingness on the part of God to save. It is rather a matter of moral consistency that is involved.

The question is how shall the majesty of God's Holy Law, in which the very universe is constituted, be upheld in harmony with His eternal loving disposition to save? The answer in one word is this: the Atonement morally enables God *"to act as He feels."* The problem with God is not in the exercise of the forgiving act, but in so forgiving as to express adequate disapproval of the enormity of sin, and at the same time awaken a new spontaneity in the one forgiven, to loathe and leave his sin.

True, everything that historically came out in the mediating Work of Christ was eternally embraced in the heart and purpose of God. God needed nothing outside Himself to move Him to this. He required indemnity only from Himself and not from another. So to speak, He took the eternal initiative.

In so doing, He disturbed no cosmic order. This, however, is no reason for supposing that God did not have the best of reasons for historically manifesting what was in Him in such self-consistent form as the Bible presents.

REPENTANCE?

Some may ask, if God needed nothing outside Himself to move Him to Redeem, why should He not be able to forgive sin on Repentance alone? Why should any mediatorship at all be necessary?

In a very deep sense, God does forgive the sinner upon his Repentance. If, however, any should feel thus to represent the matter of forgiveness, the terms employed should be used understandingly. We must recognize what implications belong to the Deity as thus conceived, and what is the nature of the penitence contemplated. The God Who can thus forgive is a God Who in Himself, and through His Son from eternity, has entered into responsibility for the sinner's sin through what we call the Reconciliation — His Self-wrought Reconciliation. And the penitence in mind is a right reciprocal attitude of the sinner towards the mediating God in view of a wrongdoing which necessitated such a sacrifice of God's Only Begotten Son.

Thus, if the terms used could only be understood in their true evangelical sense, there would be no objection to saying that God forgives sin in view of real Repentance; for a deep conception of mediatorship on the part of the Divine-human Christ is implied in all the terms employed.

THE CROSS

That man could have repented adequately and easily, with no cross-enactment to reveal God's nature and sin's enormity, we gravely doubt. Even God needs to forgive wisely and man to repent understandingly.

The principles on which God can consistently forgive require to be shown, if man is

to repent deeply: if the sense of his guilt is to be removed, and his conscience put at rest. To say the least, it was a most gracious concession to man's weakness when God concretely revealed in the historic Cross His Way of pardoning and removing the sense of guilt, as well as the measureless cost of it.

In the Reconciliation, God, in the Person of His Son, entered into potential responsibility for the situation created by sin, and with a view of doing the highest justice to all the issues involved. In such an undertaking He could not escape the requirements imposed upon Him by His Own Holy Nature; nor could even man's normal conscience be satisfied with less. And it was important that this should be shown forth openly or publicly in His universe.

If God is to pardon, He must do it in a way which will not legitimize sin. Says the late Principal Cave, *"The death of Jesus was a more splendid vindication of righteous rule than the death of all sinners would have been. Who could say henceforth that sin had been lightly forgiven, and the interests of holy rule in danger?"*

The vindication of God's righteous rule, which took place in the depths of the Divine nature, is a thing more profound than our reason can fully penetrate, it's not strange, since the Bible declares it was a thing so deep that Angels cannot sound it.

This vindication was more than a Truth taught; it was an accomplishment wrought out.

GUILT

A special reason why Repentance alone, in the nonevangelical sense of that term, is not adequate, is that there is in all men the haunting sense of guilt, which, as Dean Freemantle says, *"cannot be pacified by any merely subjective process."*

The reason why Repentance alone, except as evangelical, is not adequate is that the very Repentance admitted to be necessary is itself chiefly conditioned on the realization of the mediating Work of Christ as objective. The truth is, man cannot repent as he needs to do so apart from the Cross; nor can he repent when he will, or without proper motive.

Says Professor Denney: *"All true penitents are children of the Cross. A true repentance* must be towards God; it involves the wakened consciousness of what our sin is to Him, of the wrong it does to His Holiness, of the wounds it inflicts on His love. Repentance is the reaction towards God produced in the soul by Christ's demonstration of what sin is to Him."

One lacks motive to repent till he sees the bearing of his sin upon the suffering Saviour. One most really and deeply repents in view of the horror of the judgment his sin brought on Christ. Repentance is thus vastly more than a mere change of mind; it is a change of care respecting one's responsibility towards the situation created by his sin. This change of *"care"* reaches so far as to wish to have justice done to the whole situation, a matter to which God in Christ's Cross only is equal. Accordingly, when the soul sees the Redeemer thus working in majestic and yet tender self-consistency and on principles of finality, it is touched to the depths by the vision as by nothing else.

THE FINALITY OF THE CROSS

Says Dr. Marcus Dods, *"Mere forgiveness would not make men penitent nor impelled to Righteousness. In order to this, a perception of God's Righteousness is necessary. The Cross exhibits both God's love and Righteousness, and hence is the supreme and perfect instrument for producing repentance."* Thus, we see that the objective death of Christ is itself the means of removing the most radical objective obstacle to that very Repentance, conceded to be necessary.

Says Dr. George Adam Smith in his late work, entitled, *"The Forgiveness of Sins"*:

"At the foot of Christ's Cross, men have known a conscience of sin, a horror of it, and by consequence, a penitence for their own share in it, deeper than anything else has started in human experience. And as thus their whole spiritual nature has been aroused, and they have awakened to the Truth that it would not have been safe, nor in any wise morally well, for them to have been forgiven by mere clemency and without feeling what sin costs, they come to understand that in His sufferings Christ was their substitute."

Says Professor Harnack: *"There is an inner law that compels the sinner to look upon*

God as a wrathful Judge; . . .it tears the heart of man, robs him of peace, and drives him to despair. This conception of God is a false (a misleading) one, and yet not false, for it is the necessary consequence of man's sin.

"How can this conception of God be overcome? When the Holy One descends to sinners, lives with them, and dies for them, then their terror of the awful Judge melts away and they believe that the Holy One is love, and that there is something mightier still than justice . . . mercy!

"The most earnest Christians consider also Christ's passion and His death as vicarious (substitutionary). How can they do otherwise? If they, the sinners, have escaped justice, and He, the Holy One, has suffered death, why should they not acknowledge that which He has suffered was what they should have suffered? In the presence of the Cross no other feeling, no other note is possible. It is a holy secret not understood by the profane, and yet the Power of God and the Wisdom of God."

SIN

In view of the enormous moral difficulty which has been introduced into the universe by the fact of sin, how can anyone object to God's finding and exercising a method of self-consistent action for the Salvation of men, and wholly at His Own costs, is beyond my comprehension. The Cross of the Redemption is morally great, because it so deals with the method of adjudication of the issues between God and the sinner. It has in view a basis of settlement, and a method of moral administration which in the end will approve themselves both to God and to all moral beings.

The Cross of Christ, properly understood, is an anticipation of and expresses the final judgment of the world in at least four respects:

SUFFERINGS?

The Cross was such a judgment in the sense that in and by it Christ acknowledged and met the due judgment of spiritual death, which belongs to the sin-principle, the collective evil, of the race. Christ in His sufferings was not in a commercial sense offering a quid pro quo, a certain amount of pain for a given amount of sin: in no quantitative sense was He offering suffering for sin. While Christ's sufferings were not a mechanical substitution for the judgment we merited, yet there was involved in it a substitutionary, a vicarious principle.

The Atonement, like every other Doctrine of Christianity, is a fact of life; and such facts of life cannot be crowded into our definitions, because they are greater than any definitions that we can frame. The Atonement is a substitution, in that another has done for us what we ought to have done but could not do, and has suffered for us what we deserved to suffer, but could not suffer without loss of holiness and happiness forever.

But Christ's doing and suffering is not that of one external and foreign to us. He is bone of our bone and flesh of our flesh; the bearer of our humanity; yes, the very life of the race.

The life that He lived in Israel and the death that He endured on Calvary were the revelation of a union with mankind which antedated the Fall. Being thus joined to us from the beginning, He has suffered in all human sin; in all our affliction He has been afflicted.

Thus, we are not to think of Christ as one person, and the Believer as another. When Christ is said to die for another, it is upon the presupposition that such an one, a real Believer, is to come into mystical vital union with Christ; so that as thus identified with Christ, the Believer dies with Christ to the life of self and sin, and then lives again in the power of a risen life (Rom. 6:3-5).

SATAN DEFEATED

The Cross of Christ's achievement expresses an aspect of judgment in a further sense, that by the moral attitude which Christ maintained up to the last moment on His Cross; He entirely set at naught the world-principle, or the Satanic philosophy devised and personalized by the Devil.

Christ at the Cross achieved a result, which by virtue of its very nature dealt Satan his death blow. The Bible indeed is mainly the story of an agelong conflict between the old serpent, the Devil, and the Seed of the woman, the Divine Son of Man.

The Word of God opens with the first stage of the onset, in which at first it would appear that Satan is victorious, and it closes with the

proclamation wherein the Devil is overcome and *"cast into the lake of fire"* (Rev. 20:10).

Satan's defeat, and ultimate banishment into the lake of fire is all because of what Jesus did at the Cross.

THE ABOLISHMENT OF DEATH

In a third sense, the Cross of the Redemption expresses its final judgment upon the world, in that it has generated and made available a power whereby the nexus between sin and spiritual death is potentially destroyed.

When Jesus died on the Cross, He dissolved the fateful bond, so that though indeed I am a sinner, yet I need not see death, that is, real doom, spiritual and eternal death; for Christ being in me and I in Him, the relationship between sin and its natural doom has been destroyed. In this sense Christ *"has abolished death"* (II Tim. 1:10).

While the wages of sin is death, yet the free gift of God is eternal life in Christ Jesus our Lord (Rom. 6:23).

A PURCHASED POSSESSION

The fourth and final view of the Cross expresses a new and gracious judgment concerning the world also in this respect, namely, that, by virtue of its achievement, all men have been placed in the relations of a treasure to Christ; they are adjudged to Christ; we belong to Him, potentially, as a precious possession — like the treasure hidden in a field — because of the altered relation in which Christ's Redemptive Work on the Cross has placed us to Himself.

Even though we now belong to Christ, and because of the great price paid for us at the Cross, this Grace will never go into effect against a man's will. God's love having its peculiarity in the fact that it undertakes to deal as the moral situation requires, with the very problem of man's sin and guilt, then a proper reciprocation of that love, even a proper faith in it, requires on man's part that he shall repent of the sin which his Lord has borne, heartily believe in the adequacy and tenderness of such a love, and henceforth surrender himself without reserve to be the property of so complete a Saviour the moment He is known. Refusing to do this is to invite the greater condemnation, even *"the second death."*

But whatever lack of responsiveness in man there may be, it will ever yet remain true that in the gracious work of God's Son all the forces of sin and evil have been adequately grappled with and potentially overcome for man's benefit.

Even though that Salvation be rejected, the rejection will be of something actual, something brought within man's reach — a Divine vicarious achievement — in which God in Christ has done all He consistently could do to save man from moral suicide. He has done it through the giving of His only Son on the Cross, and there could be no greater price than that, and there could be no greater evidence of love than that.

(21) "UNTO SHEM ALSO, THE FATHER OF ALL THE CHILDREN OF EBER, THE BROTHER OF JAPHETH THE ELDER, EVEN TO HIM WERE CHILDREN BORN.

(22) "THE CHILDREN OF SHEM; ELAM, AND ASSHUR, AND ARPHAXAD, AND LUD, AND ARAM.

(23) "AND THE CHILDREN OF ARAM; UZ, AND HUL, AND GETHER, AND MASH.

(24) "AND ARPHAXAD BEGAT SALAH; AND SALAH BEGAT EBER.

(25) "AND UNTO EBER WERE BORN TWO SONS: THE NAME OF ONE WAS PELEG; FOR IN HIS DAYS WAS THE EARTH DIVIDED; AND HIS BROTHER'S NAME WAS JOKTAN."

The composition is:

1. Shem was in the lineage of the Promised Seed. So out of Shem sprang Jesus, the Plant of Renown (Ezek. 34:29; Lk. 3:36).

2. The Earth being divided in the days of Peleg refers to the time of the Tower of Babel, and the confusion of the languages by God. The name *"Peleg"* means, *"division."* It refers here to languages being divided, rather than land being divided.

3. *"Joktan"* is the father of the Arab nations.

SHEM

Verses 21 through 24 read: *"Unto Shem also, the father of all the children of Eber, the brother of Japheth the elder, even to him were children born.*

"The children of Shem; Elam, and Asshur, and Arphaxad, and Lud, and Aram.

"And the children of Aram; Uz, and Hul, and Gether, and Mash.

"And Arphaxad begat Salah; and Salah begat Eber."

In the names under Shem, we find the Semitic races, which make up the Jews and the Arab nations. As stated, through Shem would come the Christ of Glory, even as was prophesied by Noah (Gen. 9:26).

As well, *"Uz"* the grandson of Shem, could well have settled the area, which came to be called *"the land of Uz"* where Job, the grandson of Jacob, ultimately settled (Job 1:1).

The Jews, incidentally, claim that the name *"Hebrews"* is derived from *"Eber."*

PELEG

Verse 25 reads: *"And unto Eber were born two sons: the name of one was Peleg; for in his days was the Earth divided; and his brother's name was Joktan."*

An interesting statement is made concerning *"Peleg."* It says, *"For in his days was the Earth divided."* In the Hebrew language, in which the Old Testament was written, the word *"divided"* means here by languages, rather than the land being divided. Evidently, he is speaking here of the Tower of Babel, which Nimrod built, in order to defy God. As we shall see in the next Chapter, all men were of one language at that time, but in this first organized rebellion against God, which resulted in the building of the Tower of Babel, the Lord foiled their plans, by adding many more languages, which created great confusion.

Incidentally, *"Joktan,"* was the father of all the Arabic nations. So in a sense, the Arabs and the Jews are brothers. So why the great division between them, which continues unto this present hour, and in fact, is the great trouble spot of the world at present, and has been for quite some time?

The consuming chasm between the two peoples is religion. The main problem is Islam.

Bringing it up to the present time, the Jews want their ancient homeland, which is Israel, and which they have occupied for approximately 3,400 years. The Arabs control all the surrounding nations of the Middle East, with the exception of Iraq, which is

Persian, but closely aligned with the Arabs, and bitter enemies of Israel.

The United States at the present time (October, 2001), and as previously stated, is demanding that Israel come to some type of agreement with the Palestinians, who now occupy Gaza and a great part of the West Bank, plus Jericho. But Israel has a problem with this:

How can a settlement be reached, when the charter of the Palestinians calls for the massacre of every single Jew, and the taking of the entirety of the Land of Israel?

ISLAM

As I dictate these notes in October of 2001, the United States has been thrown into the very center of this age-old conflict, and in a dramatic way. The Muslims hate Christianity and the Jews, which they in a sense label as one and the same. They refer to the United States as the *"great Satan,"* and Israel as the *"little Satan."*

To contest the great Satan, the Muslims engineered a plot, which culminated on September 11, 2001, by hijacking four giant airliners. Two of those airliners were flown into the World Trade Center in New York City, and a third was flown into the Pentagon in Washington. The passengers of the fourth airliner evidently wrested control of the plane from the Muslims, which caused it to crash in Western Pennsylvania, killing all on board, but foiling their plans, which some believe were to crash into the Capitol in Washington, D.C. In all of these attacks, over 5,000 people were killed. It was one of the worst blows ever received by this nation.

So since that black day in September, the United States is no longer a detached country, looking from the outside at the Israeli/Islamic problem, but instead, has been thrown into the very middle of this boiling pot.

Our political leaders have vowed to stamp out terrorism in the world, but to do so without offending the Muslims. They have taken the position that the Muslims who would be responsible for such barbaric acts only make up a tiny percentage of the religion of Islam, which President Bush claimed *"is a religion of peace and love."*

NOTES

Nothing could be further from the truth! While all Muslims aren't murderers, the religion they embrace, the religion of Islam, fosters and nurtures the spread of its evil doctrine by the sword. In fact, it is the only religion in the world which advocates evangelism by the means of violence. So even though all Muslims may not be murderers, they are associated with a religion which produces murder, as well as bondage and slavery of every type. Pure and simple, the religion of Islam is not only of Satan, but is Satan's greatest effort in these last days. It is a religion birthed in Hell, and thereby, fomenting Hell on this Earth.

It sees the United States as hindering its world conquest. Unable to match this nation in firepower, it has resorted to terrorism. But please understand the next statement fully. Were it possible for the leaders of Islam to press a button, and to instantly slaughter every single person in the United States, all 280 million, they would do it in a moment's time, and consider that they had carried out a good day's work. They have the will, but they just simply do not have the means — yet!

Therefore, our elected leaders in this nation, setting out on a course which is based on a lie, the lie of Islam being a religion of love and peace, cannot come to any good conclusion. As stated, it is a religion of hate, war, and violence.

FRIENDS?

Claiming that certain Arab nations, such as Saudi Arabia and Egypt, etc., are our friends, we proceed with a policy that is bankrupt to begin with. Whether we like it or not, this is a religious war.

The leaders of Saudi Arabia and Egypt smile at us, take our money and our protection, while all the time spending billions of dollars training young Muslims to be human bombers, or whatever. How can the two, their claim to be our friends, and what they are actually doing, be reconciled?

The truth is, it cannot be reconciled. Islam is not our friend. It hates us, and it hates us because of the Lord Jesus Christ. Again, whether we like it or not, that is the crux of the whole matter — the Lord Jesus Christ.

As I dictate these notes, the United States is bogged down in Afghanistan. We have already spent tens of billions of dollars, trying to *"buy"* friends in the region, and bombing mud huts, which are of no consequence to anyone. We boast that we have knocked out all of their training camps, but neglect to state that the camps were empty when we bombed them. As well, each camp could probably be rebuilt for ten thousand dollars at the most, inasmuch as the buildings are made of mud, etc.

The truth is, it really doesn't matter what happens in Afghanistan. Even if we take the entirety of the country, and ultimately find this man by the name of *"Osama,"* it will change nothing. If we think that Islamic terrorism is wrapped up in Osama bin Laden, we are in for a rude awakening. As stated, Islamic terrorism is not produced by this one man, or others like him, but rather the Islamic religion produces these men and the terrorism.

Refusing to admit the real problem, which is the religion of Islam, we have embarked upon a course that is fraught with peril, and because it's based on a lie.

MOHAMMAD

This conflict actually began some 4,000 years ago with the births of Ishmael and Isaac, both sons of Abraham, but by a different mother.

The Bible proclaims Isaac as the one through whom the Seed of the woman would come, namely the Lord Jesus Christ (Gen. 21:12). Through Isaac, and his son Jacob, came the Jewish people, incidentally raised up by God.

The Koran claims that Ishmael is the promised seed, through whom the Arabs have come, and ultimately Mohammad.

Mohammad, of the tribe of Kuraysh in Mecca, claimed to have received a revelation that God (Allah) was One and that he (Mohammad) was to be Allah's messenger of that truth.

Incidentally, the name *"Allah"* is not another name for God, as is believed by most Christians. It was selected by Mohammad from the some 300 names of idols then worshipped by the Arabs. In fact, the name *"Allah"* goes all the way back to the Babylonian

deities, it being a derivative of Baal, and is actually another name for the moon god, *"Ur."* In fact, the city in which Abraham was born and raised, Ur of the Chaldees, was named after the moon god. That's the reason on many Arab flags, or banners, one will find the crescent or the half moon.

After gathering his first converts from among his family members and close friends, Mohammad encountered severe opposition — so much so that he had to flee to the town of Medina. This flight, or Hejira in Arabic, is now viewed as year one in the Islamic calendar, or A.D. 622.

THE BEGINNINGS

In Medina, Mohammad encountered a large and influential Jewish community. The influence of Judaism on his teaching must have been significant. For example, during this period Mohammad taught that the faithful should pray facing Jerusalem, just as Jewish prayers were always directed there. Only later, after the Jews had rejected his message, did he alter the direction for prayer to Mecca.

Mohammed also taught his followers to fast on the tenth day of Tishri, the same day as the Jewish fast of Yom Kippur. Later, this fast was expanded to include the entire month of Ramadan.

Incidentally, as I dictate these notes on October 28, 2001, there is a controversy going on as to what the disposition of our forces will be as it regards the *"war,"* concerning the Islamic holy month of Ramadan, which begins sometime in mid-November. The insinuation at the present is that we will stop all efforts during this particular month, so as not to offend the Muslims. What course will ultimately be taken, I cannot tell at present; however, for the United States to even consider what the Muslim world likes or doesn't like is a travesty to say the least. What about the 5,000 plus people who were brutally murdered on September 11? Do they have any say in this?

THE BIBLE

In the Word of God, as we've already studied, God ordained Government (Gen., Chpt. 9). In the instituting of such, Government must be given the power to put down crime, and those who would seek to take peace from the land. Government has the right to use lethal force if necessary. Regrettably, there are many evil and corrupt Governments in the world, and as such, they create a climate of oppression; however, bad Government does not negate the idea of the necessity of Government.

As well, if rogue nations seek to take peace from the world, righteous nations have a responsibility under God to put down those nations, and to use whatever force is necessary. This right is given to Government not only in the Old Testament, but in the New as well (Rom. 13:1-6). So it is the obligation of this nation to put down terrorism in the world, and to use whatever force that has to be used to accomplish the task. Not to do so would actually be sin. The Scripture plainly says:

"Because sentence against an evil work is not executed speedily, therefore the heart of the sons of men is fully set in them to do evil" (Eccl. 8:11).

THE KORAN

Mohammad, adopting the Jewish principle of abstaining from pork and circumcising their sons, standard Jewish practices since Biblical days, also accepted the Jewish Prophets Adam, Noah, Abraham, Moses, and David, as well as the *"Prophet"* Jesus, although he strongly rejected the Deity of Christ. Mohammad added that he was himself the *"Seal"* of Prophecy — God's final messenger. While accepting some of the Scriptures of Jews and Christians, Mohammad's *"revelations"* embodied in the Koran, became the authoritative scriptures for his faithful followers. These followers were called Muslims, from the Arabic word *"Islam,"* meaning, *"submission"* to the one God.

Apparently Mohammad thought that Jews would accept his message of a pure monotheism, but the Rabbis ridiculed his illiteracy and his confusion of Biblical traditions. Furthermore, the Jewish people simply could not accept a non-Israelite as God's *"Seal"* of Prophecy.

When the Jews of Medina rejected him and his message, Mohammad turned on them with a vengeance. Then followed the expulsion and exile of two Jewish tribes

from Medina as well as the extermination of a third.

Finally, Mohammad and his fanatical adherents massacred most of the remaining Jews of Northern Arabia and forcibly evicted the rest. The only Jewish community that remained was Yemen, which continued to 1950 when nearly all the Yemenite Jews were airlifted to Israel in *"Operation Magic Carpet."*

THE ARAB-ISRAELI CONFLICT

There is an important contemporary lesson to be learned from this brief historic overview. We cannot fully comprehend the Arab-Israeli conflict unless we understand the attitude of Islam toward the Jewish people. The Land of Israel, or Palestine, as it was called by the Romans and Byzantines, was conquered and ruled more or less by Muslims from the Seventh to the Twentieth Century.

The only interruption came when the *"Christian"* Crusaders ruled the land for less than 100 years.

And incidentally, President Bush inadvertently used the word *"Crusade"* as it regards the present conflict, but quickly changed it, once again, so as not to offend Muslims, which word they do not particularly enjoy hearing, and because of the Crusades so long ago.

Islam finds it unacceptable that the land of Israel, originally conquered for Allah by his followers, is now ruled over by Jews — a people who, according to the Koran, are supposed to be inferior and subservient.

The historic reality, and according to the Bible, the Land of Israel belongs to the Jews; the Muslims find that impossible to acknowledge. As previously stated, the Jews have either controlled the Land of Israel, or else exercised a presence in the land, for some 3,400 years.

This is the real key to understanding the impasse that exists in Israel today. The Arab countries, predominantly Muslim, refuse to accept a foreign, Jewish presence in a land that is supposed to be a part of the *"world of Islam."*

The modern rise of a more fanatical Islam only heightens the tension of this impasse — an impasse that ultimately can be repaired only by the coming of the Messiah, the Saviour of both Isaac's and Ishmael's sons.

PROPHECIES OF THE ENDTIME

The cause of the terrible bloodletting of World War II probably had more to do with the Jews than anything else. Of course, this would not be recognized at all by geopolitical experts, but it is true nevertheless.

Satan, knowing that after nearly 2,000 years, the time had come for prophecy to be fulfilled regarding the establishment of Israel as a nation, would seek to foil that coming event. Consequently, evil spirits would occupy and fill the mind of Adolph Hitler, and others of his henchmen, to exterminate the Jews, which they came close to doing. Over six million were slaughtered by these madmen. If enough can be killed, which was Satan's idea, it will then be impossible for them to form a nation.

However, in 1948, and against all odds, and for the first time that something of this nature had ever happened in history, these people, after wandering the Earth for about 1,900 years, finally once again became a consolidated nation, and as well, in their ancient homeland — the Land of Israel. The Star of David flew over this beleaguered land, and against all odds. But let the Reader understand that what God says will happen, definitely will happen. And He had predicted through the Prophets that they would be brought back to their land (Isa. 11:11-12; 14:2; 27:12-13; 43:5-6; Jer. 3:17-18; 16:14-16; 23:5-8; 24:5-7; 30:3-31; 33:6-26; 46:27-28; Ezek. 11:17-20; 16:60-63; 20:33-44; 28:25-26; 36:6-38; Hos. 1:10-11; 3:4-5; Joel, Chpt. 3; Amos 9:9-16; Zech. 12:10-12; Rom. 11:25-29, etc.).

Understanding this, we see how Satan is using the Muslim world, which religion he raised up, not only to damn many souls to eternal Hell, which this religion does, but as well, to oppose Israel in the last days.

At the present, we're living at the very close of the Church Age. The Rapture is about to take place, which will end this Age, and Israel will be brought back to her proper place and position as predicted by the Prophets. But before this can be done, Israel must go through the Great Tribulation, called by

the Prophet Jeremiah, *"the time of Jacob's trouble"* (Jer. 30:7). In fact, Satan's greatest effort yet to destroy Israel is just ahead, and will take place during the latter half of the Great Tribulation. Jesus said in His Olivet Discourse, *"For then shall be great tribulation, such as was not since the beginning of the world to this time, no, nor ever shall be."*

He then said: *"And except those days should be shortened, there should no flesh be saved: but for the elect's sake those days shall be shortened"* (Mat. 24:12-22).

The word *"elect"* as used here refers to Israel and not the Church, as some think.

The Holy Spirit through Paul plainly tells us in Romans, Chapter 11 that Israel will be brought back. And by that, we refer to her finally accepting Christ as her Lord, Messiah, and Saviour, which she will do at the Second Coming (Zech. 13:1, 6; 14:1-4, 9-11). But before that time comes, Israel will accept the Antichrist, thinking that he is their long-awaited Messiah, but will find to their dismay that they have been deceived. In fact, he will turn on them in the very middle of the Great Tribulation, with Israel suffering at that time her first military defeat since becoming a nation in 1948 (Dan. 9:27).

Their accepting the Antichrist as the Messiah will fulfill the words of Christ when He said: *"I am come in My Father's Name, and you receive Me not: if another shall come in his own name, him you will receive"* (Jn. 5:43).

The *"another"* of whom Christ speaks is the Antichrist.

To attempt to hinder the fulfillment of Bible prophecy, Satan unable to slaughter enough Jews by Hitler, is now using the Muslims. But since 1948, Israel has become very, very strong in a military sense. Consequently, the Palestinians are attempting to wreak havoc in Israel, by the use of human bombs, with most of this being funded by Saudi Arabia.

JEHOVAH OR ALLAH?

Relative to what has been said, the impetus behind the Arab determination to destroy Israel cannot be narrowly defined as a family affair, even though both entities are direct descendants, as stated, of Abraham (Isaac and Ishmael).

Even though Isaac was chosen by God as the one through whom the Promised Seed would come, and to which we have already alluded, Ishmael was also given the Promise of becoming *"a great nation"* (Gen. 21:18) — a nation so great *"that it shall not be numbered for multitude"* (Gen. 16:10). That Promise has been faithfully fulfilled by God. Tiny Israel, about the size of the state of New Jersey, floats in the middle of a sea of Arab nations scattered across a large portion of the globe — some 57.

There are basically two differences between God's Covenants with the Jews and the Ishmaelites. Israel was specifically given the land called Palestine, or Israel (Gen. 13:14-17; 17:6-8, 19-21; 28:3-4).

The paramount difference, however, is discovered in these words: *"And I will bless them who blesses you (Israel), and curse him who curses you: and in you shall all families of the Earth be blessed"* (Gen. 12:3).

The Promise is further defined in Genesis 22:18: *"And in your seed shall all the nations of the Earth be blessed."* That *"Seed"* of blessing delivered through the Jewish people to the Gentile nations — including Arabs — was the Messiah, the Lord Jesus Christ.

"Now to Abraham and his seed were the promises made. He said not, and to seeds, as of many; but as of one, and to your seed, which is Christ" (Gal. 3:16).

Jewry's presence and assigned mission were, therefore, uniquely set apart in marked contrast to those described as characteristic of Ishmael's seed and national legacy.

The *"Seed"* component in God's program for humanity surpasses every other aspect of history. In addition to being the Saviour of men, the Messiah is to as well be King. When His Kingdom finally arrives, He will establish and enforce stability. Delivery of the One Who would so bless mankind was the exclusive province of Abraham's Seed through Isaac. The Promise is specific. The Abrahamic Covenant provided:

1. A King for the Throne: *"And kings shall come out of you"* (Gen. 17:6).

2. A land for the King: *"And I will give unto you, and unto your seed after you, the land wherein you are a stranger, all the land of Canaan . . ."* (Gen. 17:8).

3. A people for the King: *". . . and I will be their God"* (Gen. 17:8).

THE BLESSING

But, unfortunately, it was the *"Blessing"* aspect of the Covenant that developed the animosity in Esau's posterity because the Blessing fell to Jacob rather than to Esau, who fathered their people. Had the Arabs embraced obediently the Saviour and kingly aspects of the Blessing of the Messiah, history would have taken another course.

These residual resentments became deeply engrained in the attitudes of the Arabs toward Israel, and those resentments spun off in manifold and discernable ways as the centuries passed. Scripture is replete with accounts of the heirs of Ishmael who warred against Israel while growling their determination to *". . . come, and let us cut them off from being a nation; that the name of Israel be no more in remembrance. For they have consulted together with one consent . . ."* (Ps. 83:4-5). Their *"one consent"* was and is the extermination of the nation of Israel.

Since the days of the Psalmist, Arab determination has not wavered. However, the entrance of the new religion, Islam (Seventh Century A.D.), refined and sanctified the rationale. It then became incumbent to subjugate or exterminate Jews *"in God's Name."*

A man named Sheikh As'ad Tamini, who claims leadership of *"Islamic Jihad Beit Al-Maqdis,"* focused the issue in a recent statement lauding Iraqi President Hussein's tirade about unleashing chemical weapons against Israel. *"I hope he is as good as his word,"* Tamini said. *"The killing of Jews will continue, killing, killing in God's Name until they vanish."*

Thus, the Allah discovered by Mohammad was a very different god from the God revealed in the Bible. Mohammad's religion, which in his view was to replace Judaism and Christianity, would have a new book (the Koran), a new look, and a new center of worship (Mecca).

JIHAD

The word *"Jihad"* is enshrined in the ecstatic vocabulary of the Muslim believer. To kill in the name of Allah in Jihad (holy war) is a privilege. To die in Jihad is to be assured a place in Heaven. Consequently, military conquests become a theological pursuit, and conquered people became the subjects of Allah.

The religiously driven law of conquest swept Islamic armies in Syria, Israel, Mesopotamia, Egypt, North Africa, and Spain. The advance was finally stopped by Charles Martel, grandfather of Charlemagne, outside Paris in A.D. 732. Later, Muslim hordes encompassed Europe, moving as far west as Austria before being defeated in the late Seventeenth Century.

The manner of evangelism as it regards the Muslim effort is for their army to go into a country, take it over, and kill all people who do not convert to Islam. Under threat of death, most convert. Islamic law is then instituted, which incorporates every part and parcel of human life. In other words, there is no such thing as a separation of Church and State in the Islam religion. They are one and the same. All babies then born from henceforth in that particular area are born into the Muslim religion, and are brainwashed with this religion from the time they are old enough to entertain any type of thinking.

Not having any armies specifically at the present time to speak of, the method of evangelism for the Muslim religion has changed somewhat. For instance, they will go into certain villages or towns in Africa, and will purchase certain things for all the villagers, such as bringing electricity to the village, and then providing refrigerators or television sets, etc., for the village leaders. Of course, they do these things on the premise that the village will convert to Islam.

They claim to be the fastest growing religion in the world; however, their growth is primarily in the fact that the birthrate in Muslim countries is about three times the rate of so-called Christian countries.

There are approximately seven million Muslims in the United States. About five million are among the black population. They have been able to gain this ascendancy among this segment of Americans, by claiming that Christianity is the white man's religion, while Islam is for the black man, etc. In other words, they evangelize by pitting race against race.

NOTES

In countries which are primarily Christian, wealthy Arab nations, such as Saudi Arabia, spend billions of dollars building Mosques in these respective countries.

There are approximately 57 countries in the world at the present time that are classified as *"Muslim."*

One *"defeat"* rankles the world of Islam to no end. This was the deliverance of Jerusalem from the Muslim Ottoman Turks by the *"Christian"* British Expeditionary Force in 1917 and then the return of the Jews to Palestine in 1948, and that area then becoming the State of Israel.

Symbolically, the modern State of Israel stands as a constant reminder to rabid fundamentalist Muslims of their humiliation before infidels — a condition that can only be remedied through conquest.

RELIGIOUS DOMINANCE

This is a fact of life often misunderstood by those restrained by Western beliefs and standards, for the issue of land in the Middle East is not primarily a territorial matter. It is a question of religious dominance — the lack of which is intolerable to the Muslim who is taught that Allah is all and is to possess all.

An abiding tenet of Islam is that all lands are to be subject to Allah. Therefore, once a territory is taken, it must remain under Muslim domination. If land is lost, Jihad (holy war) becomes necessary. Any concessions or treaties made with enemies under conditions making it impossible to restore dominion by force are observed only until means are available to remedy the situation.

A NEGOTIATED PEACE?

For this reason, as Arab spokesmen have repeatedly avowed, any negotiated peace agreement with Israel will only provide a staging area from which to pursue total elimination of the Jewish presence from land claimed to be sacred to Allah.

In other words, peace treaties mean nothing to the Muslims. They are entered into only as it suits their purpose at that particular time, with every intention to proceed forward at the opportune moment, thereby ignoring the agreements previously made.

Hence, the negotiations and peace treaties with the Palestinians regarding the Gaza Strip, Jericho, and the West Bank should be looked at with that understanding.

In such a perpetual state of conflict, Israelis know all too well what the Western world must learn or live to regret — *"survival against the Muslim onslaught means having a superior strength and the will to use that strength."*

MODERN MUSLIM EVANGELISM

Make no mistake about it, Muslims are bent on possessing this planet for Allah, and as I think we are now learning, they are bent on doing this by any means at their disposal, even to the point of committing the most atrocious acts of terrorism. While many years ago, in the first wave, the swords of Islam were wet with blood of vanquished *"infidels,"* a great second wave is now moving across the Western world in the form of Muslim missionary crusaders on one side, and Muslim terrorists on the other, both pushing forward toward the same goal.

To look at the strides they have made in *"Christian"* nations, in France, Islam ranks second only to Catholicism. England has received a massive influx of Muslims, so many that the face of the landscape has literally changed. In 1945, there was one Mosque in England; in 2000, there were over 1,500. London is the site of the largest Mosque in Western Europe.

In mid-October of 2001, outside of this very Mosque in London, hundreds of Muslims were screaming, *"Death to those in number 10 Downing Street"* (seat of government in England), and *"death to Bush"* (President of the United States). In fact, the problem is so bad presently in England that at the time of this writing, the English Parliament is strongly considering the passing of legislation that would make it a crime to foment religious hate.

However, if England does in fact pass such legislation, more than likely, it will do more to restrict Christianity than it does Islam.

As we said some paragraphs back, if the Muslims could push a button and kill every non-Muslim in the world, they would do so instantly, and without regret. We need to

understand that! The only reason they don't do such is simply because they don't have the power to do such. They definitely do have the will.

We in the West can cower behind the foolish notion that the Muslim religion is of love and peace, and that it's only a few fanatics causing all the problem in the world; however, I would remind all concerned that such thinking is based on a lie, and if we continue with such a position, it is going to lead only to more days like September 11. To enter into any type of war on a false premise is foolish indeed! And that's exactly what we are doing presently in the United States.

The first Mosque in the United States was built in Cedar Rapids, Iowa, in 1934. Today, there are over 1,000.

CHRISTIAN CHURCHES IN MUSLIM COUNTRIES?

How many Churches do you think are presently being built in Muslim countries?

If the country is truly Muslim, the answer is *"zero."* In fact, Christianity is outlawed. They may claim it's not, but the truth is, even if Christian Arabs meet in a home to worship the Lord, and the authorities are made aware of such worship, those people are instantly arrested. In fact, this hatred against *"Christians"* is so rabid that many Muslims in the world consider the small area of land in Saudi Arabia occupied by American troops in the Desert Storm War to be contaminated. Never mind that this war was fought to protect the economy of Saudi Arabia, etc.

The fact I wish to project is, wherever Islam rules, there is no freedom of religion; there is no separation of Church and State; there is a strict, controlled form of government, ruled by religion. And if we think Communism is a depressing form of government, Communism is child's play up beside Islam.

ISLAM, A DOMINANT FORCE IN AMERICA

Dr. Ismail Faruqui not too long ago challenged Muslims to pursue a goal of 50 to 75 million new American converts to Islam. *"Only from massive conversions,"* Faruqui said, *"can we hope to elect Muslim politicians, appoint Muslim judges, and incorporate the 'shar'iah' into the judicial system of America. We must transcend our minority status to make Islam a dominant force in America and the West."*

In this regard, a point to ponder is the fact that students from Islamic countries now form the largest group of international students in North American universities and colleges.

For the most part, complacent Christians in North America have taken little or no interest in Islam's advances. Many, in fact, see the strange looking buildings with a curious little crescent that are popping up everywhere as another Denomination — just neighbors who take a strong stand for morality and against some of the things that we, too, are against.

Such is not the case! Islam is not just another religion in town. Islam is not pluralistic. (Pluralism is a state of society in which members of diverse ethnic, racial, religious, or social groups maintain an autonomous participation in and development of their traditional culture or special interests within the confines of a common civilization.) In other words, the intention of Islam is definitely not to go along in order to get along; rather, it ultimately intends to be the only religion left. And again I remind the Reader that it will do anything to attain that end result — and I mean anything!

MUSLIM FANATICISM

While Christians or Jews may lament the loss of one of our own to another religion, for Muslims, conversion to another is a capital offence. For instance, possibly some of you remember Salman Rushdie, a Muslim author who did not convert to another religion, but merely questioned Islam, and for doing such, he now lives under a perpetual death sentence from his brothers in the faith. And, as is being graphically demonstrated in the Middle East, when Muslims perceive that they have sufficient strength to take control, one way, or another, Islam will attempt to seize it.

Louis Farrakhan, of the nation of Islam, is a case in point. While he has been fairly quiet since the September 11 horror, there is no indication, despite the bloodletting of that atrocity, that his feelings have changed. In

NOTES

previous meetings which sometimes drew up to 20,000 mesmerized followers, Farrakhan rails against Jews in general, and Christianity in concept. He calls Christianity *"the white man's religion."* While not taken seriously in many quarters, Farrakhan and his ilk should sound a warning of potential danger and cause people, particularly Christians, to awaken.

Time Magazine warns, *"For them* (Farrakhan's Muslims), *mainstream American values are inherently oppressive and racist, to be rejected at the root."* That leadership has tended to be fringe. It is fringe no longer! Farrakhan's audience and appeal are growing.

He believes Libya's Quddafi is a *"True brother in the struggle." "Zionism is racist . . . Smash Zionism,"* runs his theme. *"God is going to defeat the United States Government!" "If they (black politicians) sell us out, they should be killed"* (The New Republic, July 23, 1990).

Is this the raving of a fringe lunatic? While this man definitely might be a lunatic, what he is saying is the rationale of Jihad. In other words, it is the Muslim way. After experiencing the horror of September 11, 2001, it would seem that Americans ought to now be very well aware of that. If not, what will it take to wake us up?

THE ULTIMATE STRUGGLE

The Word of God has forewarned us of the human heart's capabilities and Satan's bellicose attempts to thwart the Gospel and destroy the Jewish people. Therefore, Muslim intentions — military or missionary so-called — should not surprise, discourage, or distract us.

The point must be made and reconfirmed that in the abiding conflict among the world's three major religions, there is only one transforming option. The Jewish people, in concert with Biblical Judaism's declared directive, saw the Messiah enter the world. Sadly, the Jews missed their Messiah while Islam has missed completely the point of what God accomplished in Him. I speak of the Cross!

The ultimate struggle is not territory, nor is it the satisfaction derived from destroying or subjugating people deemed weaker or inferior. It is, instead, the liberation that comes through Faith in Jesus Christ.

Mohammad sought an alternative to Judaism and Christianity. He succeeded only in leading millions deeper into spiritual darkness. The knowledge that fresh millions are being led along the same path should awaken Christians to the need for increased world missions and intensified evangelistic efforts.

If one ever chances to look at a picture of the thousands of Muslims on their faces around the sacred Kaba in Mecca, surely he will be moved with a deep sense of sadness.

They are kneeling in the wrong place, before an inanimate object that can't bring life, light, or peace. Their only hope of Salvation is that they would bow at the Feet of the Lord Jesus Christ — King of kings and Lord of lords.

"And being found in fashion as a man, He humbled Himself, and became obedient unto death, even the death of the Cross.

"Wherefore God also has highly exalted Him, and given Him a Name which is above every name:

"That at the Name of Jesus every knee should bow, of things in Heaven, and things in Earth, and things under the Earth;

"And that every tongue should confess that Jesus Christ is Lord, in the Glory of God the Father" (Phil. 2:8-11).

PARTICULARS OF ISLAM

• Jerusalem is the third holiest place in Islam after Mecca and Medina — both in Saudi Arabia. Tradition has it that the Prophet Mohammad journeyed at night from Mecca to Jerusalem's Al-Aqusa Mosque and from there ascended to Heaven on a winged horse. (There is no proof that Mohammad ever came to Jerusalem. And of course, the *"winged horse"* claim is only a fabrication.)

• About 90 percent of all Muslims are Sunnis, considered the Orthodox sect. Of the dissident sects of Islam, the largest and most important are Shiites, fundamentalists, as the ones who instigated the September 11 horror. A split came in A.D. 680 over the dreadful manner in which Sunnis tortured and killed Shiite leader Caliphe Yazid.

• Some 70 sects and offshoots of Islam have arisen because of doctrinal differences, which in some cases are irreconcilable.

• Muslims claim to accept the first five Books of the Old Testament, the Psalms, and

the Gospels of the New Testament. However, they believe that only the Koran preserves the truth as it was given by God. It is, therefore, the only true book, they claim!

• The Koran speaks of a line of prophets beginning with Adam and ending with Mohammad. Both Jesus and Moses are part of this line; although, it vehemently denies the Deity of Christ.

• Muslims also vehemently reject the Christian Doctrine of the Trinity as sinful and blasphemous.

• In Islam there is no separation between the religious and the secular. All Islamic nations ostensibly declare their adherence to that concept of total Islamic rule.

• The concept of Islamic Law is all-inclusive. It embraces all aspects of human life and endeavor, both private and public, devotional and secular, civil and criminal.

• Jihad, which means to strive or struggle, is a term that has acquired the Islamic connotation of religious or holy war. Today, however, Jihad has developed into a broader context of striving for the common well-being of Islam and Muslims, but not necessarily exclusively by military terms.

• The birth rate in Islamic countries is 42 per 1,000, while in the Western world it is only 13 per 1,000.

(Most of the information in this article concerning Islam was derived from articles written by Elwood McQuaid, Editor of *"The Friends of Israel Gospel Ministry."* And Will Varner, Dean of the Institute of Biblical Studies of that same Organization.)

There is some evidence that the Antichrist will, at the outset, embrace Islam or, at least, not oppose it. However, there also is evidence that ultimately he will oppose all religions, even Islam, setting himself up as God (II Thess. 2:4). This will take place at the midpoint of the Great Tribulation (Dan. 9:27; Mat. 24:21).

Nevertheless, the whole of all false religions, definitely including Islam, will be totally eliminated at the Second Return of Christ, *"For the Lord has spoken it."*

(26) "AND JOKTAN BEGAT ALMODAD, AND SHELEPH, AND HAZARMAVETH, AND JERAH,

(27) "AND HADORAM, AND UZAL, AND DIKLAH,

(28) "AND OBAL, AND ABIMAEL, AND SHEBA,

(29) "AND OPHIR, AND HAVILAH, AND JOBAB: ALL THESE WERE THE SONS OF JOKTAN.

(30) "AND THEIR DWELLING WAS FROM MESHA, AS YOU GO UNTO SEPHAR A MOUNT OF THE EAST,

(31) "THESE ARE THE SONS OF SHEM, AFTER THEIR FAMILIES, AFTER THEIR TONGUES, IN THEIR LANDS, AFTER THEIR NATIONS.

(32) "THESE ARE THE FAMILIES OF THE SONS OF NOAH, AFTER THEIR GEN-ERATIONS, IN THEIR NATIONS: AND BY THESE WERE THE NATIONS DIVIDED IN THE EARTH AFTER THE FLOOD."

The overview is:

1. As stated, the *"sons of Shem,"* make up the Semitic people of the world, consti-tuting mostly the Jews and the Arabs.

2. From this line would come the Mes-siah, the Saviour of the world, the Redeemer of mankind.

3. It is ironic that even though the Re-deemer came from this line, He is not now recognized as such by the far greater num-ber of this lineage.

JOKTAN

Verses 26 through 29 read: *"And Joktan begat Almodad, and Sheleph, and Hazarmaveth, and Jerah,*

"And Hadoram, and Uzal, and Diklah,

"And Obal, and Abimael, and Sheba,

"And Ophir, and Havilah, and Jobab: all these were the sons of Joktan."

Eber, as stated, was the ancestor of the Hebrews through Peleg and through Joktan came some 13 Arabian tribes.

Even though these names may seem te-dious to those who do not understand their significance, without this history, as given to us in the Divine Word, we could neither understand man's origin nor demonstrate it. This shows how incompetent our reason is. Hence we should regard the Tenth Chapter of Genesis as a mirror in which we see our-selves as so utterly ignorant through sin that we know neither our origin nor our Creator. It is only by God's Word that we possess a spark of Divine Light. So it is utterly foolish

NOTES

for us to boast of our wisdom, wealth, power, and other earthly gifts, which all are perish-able in every way.

We Christians, therefore, do well to regard our beloved Bible as the highest and most precious treasure, which in this Chapter binds together as with a cord all important events, occurring in the world from the be-ginning till the end. This Chapter may seem as though it contains mere words and names which are of no relativity at the present, but what it says is that from Adam the Promise of Christ was handed down to Seth, from Seth to Noah, from Noah to Shem, from Shem to Eber, from whom the people of the Hebrews have their name as the heirs of all the prom-ises of Christ, for to this prerogative it (Is-rael) was appointed before all nations of the world. This is the preeminent wisdom which the Sacred Scriptures teach, and those who are without the Bible live in ignorance, blind-ness, and ungodliness without measure and end. Of themselves they know neither who nor whence they are (Luther).

THE NATIONS

Verses 30 through 32 read: *"And their dwelling was from Mesha, as you go unto Sephar a mount of the east.*

"These are the sons of Shem, after their families, after their tongues, in their lands, after their nations.

"These are the families of the sons of Noah, after their generations, in their nations: and by these were the nations divided in the Earth after the flood."

We know from this record that all the na-tions of the world owe their existence to the *"sons of Noah,"* Shem, Ham, and Japheth. In some way, every single person stems from one of these men. And as we close commen-tary on this Chapter, let us please briefly summarize:

First of all, even though the list is given of these three sons in the order of *"Shem, Ham, and Japheth,"* there is some question as to who actually is the oldest. Some Schol-ars conclude Japheth to be the firstborn, with others claiming Shem. Irrespective, Shem is listed first, because through him the Blessing would come, *"the Plant of Re-nown"* (Ezek. 34:29). The descendants of

Shem include all the Semitic people, mostly centered up in the Jews and the Arabs, but including some others as well.

From Ham we have those who populated the land of Canaan and as well Africa. In this lineage, there is black and white, showing that the color of the skin has nothing to do with the so-called *"curse."*

From Japheth came the occupants of Europe and the Far East. This would include the White, Yellow, Red, and some of the Brown races.

The Bible is the only Book in the world giving this history, which as well is another case in point regarding its authenticity.

"There have been names that I have loved to hear,
"But never has there been a name so dear
"To this heart of mine, as the Name Divine,
"The precious, precious Name of Jesus."

"There is no Name in Earth or Heaven above,
"That we should give and such love,
"As the blessed Name, let us all acclaim,
"That wondrous, glorious Name of Jesus."

"And someday I shall see Him face to face,
"To thank and praise Him for His wondrous Grace,
"Which He gave to me, when He made me free,
"The blessed Son of God called Jesus."

CHAPTER 11

(1) "AND THE WHOLE EARTH WAS OF ONE LANGUAGE, AND OF ONE SPEECH.

(2) "AND IT CAME TO PASS, AS THEY JOURNEYED FROM THE EAST, THAT THEY FOUND A PLAIN IN THE LAND OF SHINAR; AND THEY DWELT THERE."

The synopsis is:

1. Before the flood and after the flood, there was only one language on the face of the Earth.

2. Even though we have no way of knowing specifically, that language was probably Hebrew. We do know that the Lord had the entirety of the Old Testament written in Hebrew, with the exception of a few words, which are in Aramaic.

3. The command of the Lord had been for man to *"replenish the Earth."* We find here that man is tending toward the very opposite, banding together in one large group.

4. The phrase *"from the east,"* can also mean *"in the east,"* and is probably the way it should be read.

5. They elected to settle on a *"plain in the land of Shinar,"* which was probably the site of Babylon.

ONE LANGUAGE AND ONE SPEECH

Verse 1 reads: *"And the whole Earth was of one language, and of one speech."*

The *"whole Earth"* as mentioned here actually concerns only a small part of its surface, the area where the people after the flood were congregated. This particular time frame was probably about 100 to 125 years after the flood. There were probably from five to ten million people on the Earth at this particular time. As stated, before the flood and after the flood, at least up to this time, only one language was spoken among all people. Even though we really have no way of knowing, it was probably Hebrew.

SHINAR

Verse 2 reads: *"And it came to pass, as they journeyed from the east, that they found a plain in the land of Shinar; and they dwelt there."*

The pronoun *"they"* doesn't mean that every single person joined in this particular quest, but rather that the leaders were the instigators, and more than all, they were led by Nimrod.

This Chapter reveals the cause of the divisions recorded in the prior one. The cause was rebellion against the Divine command to replenish the Earth. Men resolve to keep together, to build a city, and to establish a great Temple worship. Nimrod, whose name means, *"rebel,"* headed, according to tradition, this rebellion. God called their city *"Babel,"* that is *"confusion."*

This prince Nimrod, and his city Babylon, and the plain on which it was erected, Shinar, all claim attention. They represent Satan's efforts, using man as his agent, to oppose and destroy God's plans. God has His Prince and His City; so has Satan. And these opposing princes with their cities occupy most of the pages of the Bible — the closing pages of the Book revealing the triumph of Emmanuel and Jerusalem over the Antichrist and Babylon.

In order to bring about man's blessing, God set apart for Himself one day (the Sabbath, a Type of Christ), one land (Israel), one people (the Jews), and wrote one Book (the Bible). Satan's purpose is to degrade the Book, destroy the People, ruin the Land, and desecrate the Day, i.e., *"Christ."*

Satan's first agent raised up after the flood was Nimrod, and the weapon he placed in Nimrod's hand was idolatry. Before the flood, idolatry was impossible. The Garden of Eden, the mysterious Tabernacle at its eastern entrance, with the Cherubim and the sword aflame, made the worship of idols hopeless. After the flood, these no longer existed on the Earth. It was easy, therefore, for Satan to then introduce idols and heroes as representing God. Nimrod, after his death, was worshipped under many names. These names constantly appear in ancient history.

(The Author expresses gratitude to George Williams for the above material regarding the introduction to the first two Verses of Chapter 10.)

(3) "AND THEY SAID ONE TO ANOTHER, GO TO, LET US MAKE BRICK, AND BURN THEM THOROUGHLY. AND THEY HAD BRICK FOR STONE, AND SLIME HAD THEY FOR MORTER.

(4) "AND THEY SAID, GO TO, LET US BUILD US A CITY AND A TOWER, WHOSE TOP MAY REACH UNTO HEAVEN; AND LET US MAKE US A NAME, LEST WE BE SCATTERED ABROAD UPON THE FACE OF THE WHOLE EARTH."

The exegesis is:

1. Considering the materials with which they were to use, they definitely did not plan for this city and tower to be temporary.

2. *"And they said,"* presents the fact that there was no acknowledgment of God, no looking up to, or waiting on Him.

3. The top of this tower reaching Heaven probably signifies the worship of the Zodiac, i.e., *"the planetary bodies."*

4. The human heart ever seeks a name, a portion, and a place and position in the Earth.

5. They had no regard for the command given by God to Noah, to replenish the Earth. So they would seek to keep from being scattered abroad.

SELF-WILL

Verse 3 reads: *"And they said one to another, Go to, let us make brick, and burn them thoroughly. And they had brick for stone, and slime had they for morter."*

"They said" marks the undeniable evil of the human heart. They had no regard for what God wanted. In fact, Noah was still alive at this time. But despite the fact that they owed everything to this man, and that God had seen him through the horrible deluge, as before the flood, these after the flood had no regard for the words of the Patriarch. So he was ignored!

Considering who Noah was, and what had transpired just a few years before, one finds it remarkable that these people had no regard now for him, and no regard for his God. In fact, the very reason they now ignored Noah was simply because they didn't want Noah's God.

The truth is, whether we contemplate man on the plain of Shinar, on the banks of the Tiber, or the banks of the Mississippi, we find him to be the same self-seeking, self-exalting, God-excluding creature throughout. There is a melancholy consistency in all his purposes, his principles, and his ways. He ever seeks to shut out God and exalt himself.

Now, in whatsoever light we view this Babel confederacy, it is most instructive to see in it the early display of man's genius and energies, regardless of God. In looking down along the stream of human history, we may easily perceive a marked tendency to confederacy, or association. Man seeks, for the most part, to compass his great ends in this way. Whether it be in the way of philanthropy, religion, or politics, nothing can be done without an association of men regularly organized.

It is well to see this principle; well to mark its insipient working — to see the earliest model which the page of inspiration affords of a human association, as exhibited on the plain of Shinar, in its design, its object, its attempt, its overthrow.

RELIGIOUS DENOMINATIONS

Associations of religious confederations, or Denominations, aren't wrong within themselves. Ideally they can serve God as a profitable tool to help take His Gospel to the world. However, unfortunately, most religious Denominations do not function in that capacity.

Little by little, these associations take on the spirit of Babel. They want to *"build a city and a tower, whose top may reach unto Heaven; and thereby to make us a name."* As a result, the Denomination takes unto itself a life of its own. In other words, it ceases to be a tool, and by that we refer to pointing toward Christ, and thereby becomes an object of faith within itself.

There are two spirits in the world, and that is the Spirit of God, and the spirit of Satan, with all of his demon hordes. Religious spirits are the most lethal of all, simply because they talk about God, and sound like God, but in reality, as the Pharisees of old, they conclude by crucifying the Lord in the Name of the Lord.

UNHOLY AMBITION

Verse 4 reads: *"And they said, Go to, let us build us a city and a tower, whose top may reach unto Heaven; and let us make us a name, lest we be scattered abroad upon the face of the whole Earth."*

In this one Verse, we find the seedbed of all rebellion against God, whether then or now! Please notice the following:

A. Once again, self-will is the culprit. They do not seek the Will of God, and in fact, have no regard for the Will of God, and further yet, they are purposely planning to violate the Will of God. In fact, the unconverted human heart knows nothing of aspirations after Heaven, Heaven's God, or Heaven's Glory. Left to itself, it will ever find its objects in this lower world; it will ever *"build beneath the skies."* It needs God's Call, God's Revelation, and God's power, to lift the heart of man above this present world, for man is

a groveling creature — alienated from Heaven, and allied to Earth.

In the scene now before us, there is no acknowledgement of God; nor was it the thought of the human heart to set up a place in which God might dwell — to gather materials for the purpose of building a habitation for Him. The truth is, His Name is never once mentioned.

B. They would build a city and a tower, and they cared not what God thought of the enterprise. Did they not stop to think that the God Who sent the flood, could easily foil their plans? How far did they think they could get without His approval?

But yet this spirit of defiance, this spirit of self-will, this spirit of unholy ambition, didn't die with Babel; it continues unto this very hour. And if as Believers we aren't very careful, it is so easy to follow after the same spirit of worldly pride, and because the human heart just naturally gravitates toward that particular power — and a power it is. Only a proper relationship with Christ will keep one in the place that one ought to be.

C. *"Whose top may reach unto Heaven,"* is literally given in the Hebrew, *"And his head in the heavens."* It may well speak of the worship of the Zodiac, i.e., *"the planetary bodies."*

While man does look to the heavens, it is to that which God has created, instead of God Himself. This is what Paul was speaking of when he said, *"Who changed the Truth of God into a lie, and worshipped and served the creature more than the Creator, Who is blessed forever. Amen"* (Rom. 1:25). This could well have been the beginning of *"idolatry."*

D. They would make a name for themselves, which speaks of self-will and selfish pride. They had no regard for the Name which is above every name.

The leader of this rebellion was Nimrod. Even though the whole of the human race of that particular time did not follow him at this moment, he knew that this center of activity would soon draw all the others in this direction. The city would be built, with the *"tower"* at its center. As the builder of all of this, he would be looked up to, aggrandized, even idolized. He would lead the first organized rebellion against God!

E. The Lord, in fact, had commanded that humanity would scatter over the face of the whole Earth, and for many and varied reasons, and not to gather into one group (Gen. 9:1).

(5) "AND THE LORD CAME DOWN TO SEE THE CITY AND THE TOWER, WHICH THE CHILDREN OF MEN WERE BUILDING.

(6) "AND THE LORD SAID, BEHOLD, THE PEOPLE IS ONE, AND THEY HAVE ALL ONE LANGUAGE, AND THIS THEY BEGIN TO DO: AND NOW NOTHING WILL BE RESTRAINED FROM THEM, WHICH THEY HAVE IMAGINED TO DO.

(7) "GO TO, LET US GO DOWN, AND THERE CONFOUND THEIR LANGUAGE, THAT THEY MAY NOT UNDERSTAND ONE ANOTHER'S SPEECH.

(8) "SO THE LORD SCATTERED THEM ABROAD FROM THENCE UPON THE FACE OF ALL THE EARTH: AND THEY LEFT OFF TO BUILD THE CITY.

(9) "THEREFORE IS THE NAME OF IT CALLED BABEL; BECAUSE THE LORD DID THERE CONFOUND THE LANGUAGE OF ALL THE EARTH: AND FROM THENCE DID THE LORD SCATTER THEM ABROAD UPON THE FACE OF ALL THE EARTH."

The diagram is:

1. The Lord observes minutely what men do.

2. *"The Lord said,"* presents the final word! Men rule, but God overrules.

3. The Lord would stop their rebellion in an ingenious way. He would confound their languages, which He did.

4. Whatever language was spoken, those who spoke that particular language, banded together, which ultimately formed nations, all precipitated by language.

5. The whole undertaking, and because of the Lord confounding the language, was referred to by the name of *"Babel."* Quite possibly, the Lord told Noah to ascribe this name to the undertaking.

THE LORD

Verse 5 reads: *"And the LORD came down to see the city and the tower, which the children of men built."*

God is always unquestionably fair and just in all His proceedings respecting His dealings with men, whether redeemed or unredeemed. One might say that He condemns none unheard.

As we have just stated, the flood is not long in the past regarding each of these individuals. Surely, a little forethought would come to the conclusion of the awful power exhibited by Jehovah in this particular judgment; but yet, these individuals have it in their hearts that they will defy God, irrespective of the circumstances. They had no doubt heard Noah say, and probably many times, that God had promised that He would not again destroy the world by water. So in their minds, this evidently gives their rebellion a free pass.

Let all and sundry understand that God takes a vital interest in every single thing that happens on this Earth. Jesus said: *"Are not five sparrows sold for two dollars, and not one of them is forgotten before God?*

"But even the very hairs of your head are all numbered. Fear not therefore: you are of more value than many sparrows" (Lk. 12:6-7).

Even though the Lord in these two Verses is impressing upon Believers the certitude of His love and care on their behalf, still, at the same time, in these statements we are made to realize the degree to which God involves Himself in all things.

Of all the untold millions of birds that are in this world, and the sparrow is one of the least of these birds, not a single one is forgotten before God. And then considering that by the day, even by the hour, even by the minute and less, He numbers the very hairs of our heads, we are presented with a staggering degree of Omniscience.

While God gives man much latitude, still, He always reserves the right to overrule that which He desires to do so. Everything man does is minutely inspected by God, just as this Tower of Babel was inspected. And to be sure, all evil will ultimately receive this just recompense of reward, just as will all righteousness.

The Lord coming down to see this which was being built does not mean that He physically did so, for God is everywhere. It simply means that He stepped in to take a hand in what was being done.

NO RESTRAINTS

Verse 6 reads: *"And the LORD said, Behold, the people is one, and they have all one language; and this they begin to do: and now nothing will be restrained from them, which they have imagined to do."*

The *"one language"* for the entirety of the world and for all time was actually the Will of God. With one language, as would be obvious, commerce is made much easier, and in fact, everything becomes easier.

Even though the adding of many new languages and dialects, which God did instantly, wouldn't stop the evil direction of men's hearts, it definitely did foil the efforts at that particular time as it regards the building of this Tower of Babel.

But the emphasis here is not so much on the addition of languages, as it is the evil imaginations of the hearts of these people, and especially the leaders who were promoting this thing.

As an aside, by this time, which was about 1,700 or 1,800 years after creation, we see how advanced man is as it regards construction and many other things. So the idea of ape-men has no place in the Bible, and in fact, has no place in reality, for such never existed.

It was not until the Twentieth Century that God allowed the entrance of the understanding of most modern technology. A little was given to man in the Nineteenth Century, but I think one can say without fear of exaggeration that 99 percent of all inventions have taken place since the turn of the Twentieth Century, which fulfills Daniel's prophecy about knowledge being increased in the last days (Dan. 12:4). But as it regards the way of living up unto the Nineteenth Century, man possessed most of this knowledge from the very moment of creation.

THE CONFOUNDING OF THE LANGUAGE

Verse 7 reads: *"Go to, let us go down, and there confound their language, that they may not understand one another's speech."*

The pronoun *"us"* as it regards the Lord proclaims the Trinity. There is one God, but manifest in three Persons, *"God the Father, God the Son, and God the Holy Spirit."*

Man's efforts at consolidation were carried out on the premise of rebelling against God's commands. However, God has brought mankind together in a consolidation, that is,

NOTES

those who will believe, all under the banner of Christ.

Whenever a person accepts Christ, they enter into the fellowship of Faith. That's the reason that Missionaries are wrong when they attempt to address various different peoples and their particular countries through the medium of culture. All culture without God is corrupt, ungodly, and wicked. When a person comes to Christ, they actually come into a new culture. It's the Bible culture, the God way of life, all under Christ. So whatever nation in which one might live, or whatever race one might be, all of this is secondary to one's position in Christ. That's the reasons that statements such as *"black is beautiful,"* or *"white is right,"* are totally out of place. In fact, such have no part in the culture of the Word of God. We are all one in Christ, brought together by our acceptance of Christ as our Lord and Saviour, and what He did for us at the Cross.

This is the reason that Christ must come before family, before nationality, before race, before ethnic background, before present culture, before anything for that matter.

As it regards this first organized rebellion, the Lord did this mysterious thing. He instantly instituted, more than likely several hundreds of languages and dialects, which threw everything into confusion. When the languages were given, the idea seems to be that the groups of people given a particular language instantly understood it, but at the same time, instantly forgot the original language. Actually, it seems that it could not be any other way.

SCATTERED

Verse 8 reads: *"So the LORD scattered them abroad from thence upon the face of all the Earth: and they left off to build the city."*

The result of the confounding of the language was that they were then forced to obey the Lord as it regards being scattered abroad. Consequently, the ones who spoke the same language gathered together in a group, with that group going in a certain direction, and other groups according to their particular language going their own way. So the Scripture says *"they left off to build the city."*

If one thinks about it for a moment, with 100 or more languages spoken in one city, nothing much could be done. So whatever was to be done, those with the same language would have to go find their own place, wherever that may have been.

To be sure, this which the Lord did accomplished its purpose, and did so in a remarkable way.

BABEL

Verse 9 reads: *"Therefore is the name of it called Babel; because the LORD did there confound the language of all the Earth: and from thence did the LORD scatter them abroad upon the face of all the Earth."*

The Tower of Babel, and the city itself for that matter, had their origin in deliberate, determined, enthusiastic, exulting hostility to the Divine purpose, that they should spread themselves abroad upon the face of the whole Earth. And herein lies the essence of all rebellion: whatever thought, counsel, word, or work derives its inspiration, be it only in an infinitesimal degree, from antagonism to the mind of God, that is sin. As someone has well said, *"Holiness is but another name for obedience."*

So God gave the name of *"Babel,"* or *"Confusion,"* to this effort. The name of *"Babel"* was an epitome of the foolish aim and end of the builders.

To be frank, the world is full of such efforts — efforts of folly.

"Babel" is also the Hebrew name for *"Babylon."* Later Babylonians rejected this meaning of *"confusion,"* and thereby split up the name arbitrarily, and put a case ending on it to make it *"Bab-ilu,"* which means *"gate of god."* But irrespective, the name of *"Babylon,"* or *"Confusion"* has stuck, and rightly so!

PRESENT CONFUSION

The answer and the only answer to this downtrodden world is *"Jesus Christ and Him Crucified"* (I Cor. 1:23; 2:2). And let the following be understood:

If the Gospel projected in Christianity is not Jesus Christ and His Cross, then in reality, however many good things might be said, it is no better than other religions of the world. And because it is so very, very important, please allow me to say it again:

It is the Cross of Christ which makes Christianity distinct from every other so-called system of faith among men. But if the Cross be removed, then *"another Christ"* is being projected (II Cor. 11:4), and the results are *"zero."* The power of the Gospel is in the Cross. That's why Paul said:

"The preaching of the Cross is to them that perish foolishness, but to we who are saved, it is the Power of God" (I Cor. 1:18).

Then the confusion was in a certain city that was being illegally built; today it's in the Church. Every type of gospel other than that of the Cross is being projected, of which one could ever think. And again we state the fact that if the Cross is not being preached, precious little good will result. In fact, Christianity in such a case is reduced to the same level as the man-made religions of the world. It is the Cross which makes Christianity distinct, and which alone makes it Biblical.

The major problem with the modern Church is attempting to preach Christ and ignore the Cross; however, when this happens, as it most of the time does, in reality the Preacher is projecting *"another Jesus"* (II Cor. 11:4).

The power of the Gospel is in the Cross, and more particularly, in the preaching of the Cross (I Cor. 1:18).

(10) "THESE ARE THE GENERATIONS OF SHEM: SHEM WAS AN HUNDRED YEARS OLD, AND BEGAT ARPHAXAD TWO YEARS AFTER THE FLOOD:

(11) "AND SHEM LIVED AFTER HE BEGAT ARPHAXAD FIVE HUNDRED YEARS, AND BEGAT SONS AND DAUGHTERS.

(12) "AND ARPHAXAD LIVED FIVE AND THIRTY YEARS, AND BEGAT SALAH:

(13) "AND ARPHAXAD LIVED AFTER HE BEGAT SALAH FOUR HUNDRED AND THREE YEARS, AND BEGAT SONS AND DAUGHTERS.

(14) "AND SALAH LIVED THIRTY YEARS, AND BEGAT EBER:

(15) "AND SALAH LIVED AFTER HE BEGAT EBER FOUR HUNDRED AND THREE YEARS, AND BEGAT SONS AND DAUGHTERS.

(16) "AND EBER LIVED FOUR AND THIRTY YEARS, AND BEGAT PELEG:

(17) "AND EBER LIVED AFTER HE BEGAT PELEG FOUR HUNDRED AND THIRTY YEARS, AND BEGAT SONS AND DAUGHTERS.

(18) "AND PELEG LIVED THIRTY YEARS, AND BEGAT REU:

(19) "AND PELEG LIVED AFTER HE BEGAT REU TWO HUNDRED AND NINE YEARS, AND BEGAT SONS AND DAUGHTERS.

(20) "AND REU LIVED TWO AND THIRTY YEARS, AND BEGAT SERUG:

(21) "AND REU LIVED AFTER HE BEGAT SERUG TWO HUNDRED AND SEVEN YEARS, AND BEGAT SONS AND DAUGHTERS.

(22) "AND SERUG LIVED THIRTY YEARS, AND BEGAT NAHOR:

(23) "AND SERUG LIVED AFTER HE BEGAT NAHOR TWO HUNDRED YEARS, AND BEGAT SONS AND DAUGHTERS.

(24) "AND NAHOR LIVED NINE AND TWENTY YEARS, AND BEGAT TERAH:

(25) "AND NAHOR LIVED AFTER HE BEGAT TERAH AN HUNDRED AND NINE-TEEN YEARS, AND BEGAT SONS AND DAUGHTERS.

(26) "AND TERAH LIVED SEVENTY YEARS, AND BEGAT ABRAM, NAHOR, AND HARAN."

The exegesis is:

1. The generations now pick up again with Shem, and because through his lineage the Son of God will be born into the world. However, it stops here with Abraham, and for a specific reason.

2. Not all the names in these genealogies are included.

3. It stops with Abraham, referred to here as *"Abram,"* because it was to this man that the Lord gave the meaning of Justification by Faith. Regarding spiritual things, it was a great step forward.

SHEM

Verses 10 through 13 read: *"These are the generations of Shem: Shem was an hundred years old, and begat Arphaxad two years after the flood:*

"And Shem lived after he begat Arphaxad five hundred years, and begat sons and daughters.

"And Arphaxad lived five and thirty years, and begat Salah:

"And Arphaxad lived after he begat Salah four hundred and three years, and begat sons and daughters."

Considering that Shem lived 500 more years after the flood, that means he was contemporary with Abraham for approximately 75 years; however, that number varies wildly with Commentators. It is almost certain that Shem and Abraham were acquainted, and it is possible that Shem witnessed to Abraham.

Some Commentators have concluded that this particular genealogy concerning Shem means that each one of these men knew the Lord; however, that may well be true, and of course we hope that it is. But there is no proof that even Shem served the Lord, even as much as we would like to think that he did. The fact of being in the lineage of Christ, as wonderful and prestigious as that was, however, did not at all guarantee Salvation. In fact, the only man in this genealogy listed in Hebrews, Chapter 11, the great Chapter of Faith, is Abraham.

EBER

Verses 14 through 21 read: *"And Salah lived thirty years, and begat Eber:*

"And Salah lived after he begat Eber four hundred and three years, and begat sons and daughters.

"And Eber lived four and thirty years, and begat Peleg:

"And Eber lived after he begat Peleg four hundred and thirty years, and begat sons and daughters.

"And Peleg lived thirty years, and begat Reu:

"And Peleg lived after he begat Reu two hundred and nine years, and begat sons and daughters.

"And Reu lived two and thirty years, and begat Serug:

"And Reu lived after he begat Serug two hundred and seven years, and begat sons and daughters."

All of these from Shem constitute the Semitic races; however, it is believed that through Eber the Hebrews had their beginning.

If I had to venture a guess as it regards the spiritual condition of these individuals listed in the genealogy of Shem, I would have to venture the thought that few, if any of them, actually knew God. In fact, when the

Lord revealed Himself to Abraham, then referred to as *"Abram,"* He purposely pulled the Patriarch away from his family. And in fact, even as we shall see, Abraham was an idolater when he was brought to Christ, so to speak.

ABRAHAM

Verses 22 through 26 read: *"And Serug lived thirty years, and begat Nahor:*

"And Serug lived after he begat Nahor two hundred years, and begat sons and daughters.

"And Nahor lived nine and twenty years, and begat Terah:

"And Nahor lived after he begat Terah an hundred and nineteen years, and begat sons and daughters.

"And Terah lived seventy years, and begat Abram, Nahor, and Haran."

The early Verses of this Chapter record man's effort to establish himself in the Earth and to make for himself a name; the Verses now under consideration show God calling a man out of the Earth — Abraham — and giving him a name. Man said, *"Let us make us a name."* God said to Abraham, *"I will make you a name."*

As we have stated, when God called Abraham, he was an idolater (Josh. 24:2); consequently, possessing no moral claim upon God, he was *"a Syrian ready to perish"* (Deut. 26:5). But He Who said to the Publican, *"Follow Me"* (Lk. 5:27), said to Abraham, *"Come with Me and I will bless you, and you shall be a blessing."*

With the family history of Shem, of Terah, and with the call of Abraham is introduced the Divine purpose of blessing families, as such, and bringing them into God's Kingdom upon Earth.

(The writer is indebted to George Williams for the abbreviated account of Abraham.)

(27) "NOW THESE ARE THE GENERATIONS OF TERAH: TERAH BEGAT ABRAM, NAHOR, AND HARAN; AND HARAN BEGAT LOT.

(28) "AND HARAN DIED BEFORE HIS FATHER TERAH IN THE LAND OF HIS NATIVITY, IN UR OF THE CHALDEES.

(29) "AND ABRAM AND NAHOR TOOK THEM WIVES: THE NAME OF ABRAM'S

WIFE WAS SARAI; AND THE NAME OF NAHOR'S WIFE, MILCAH, THE DAUGHTER OF HARAN, THE FATHER OF MILCAH, AND THE FATHER OF ISCAH.

(30) "BUT SARAI WAS BARREN; SHE HAD NO CHILD."

The structure is:

1. Abraham now comes into view, and will prove to be one of the greatest men of God who ever lived.

2. This family lived in Ur of the Chaldees, one of the chief centers of idol worship.

3. Abraham married Sarai. She was barren, and we will soon see why.

TERAH

Verses 27 through 30 read: *"Now these are the generations of Terah: Terah begat Abram, Nahor, and Haran; and Haran begat Lot.*

"And Haran died before his father Terah in the land of his nativity, in Ur of the Chaldees.

"And Abram and Nahor took them wives: the name of Abram's wife was Sarai; and the name of Nahor's wife, Milcah, the daughter of Haran, the father of Milcah, and the father of Iscah.

"But Sarai was barren; she had no child."

We now come to the prelude before the call of one of the greatest men of God who ever lived, Abraham.

As we look back through history as given to us in the Bible, which in fact is the only reliable historic account given, we see that Millenniums or double Millenniums have marked a turning point in this history. For instance, about 1,000 years after creation, Noah was born. His life would mark an episode in history of staggering proportions — the flood. About 1,000 years after Noah, which would be about 2,000 years after creation, we have the account of Abraham. This is another turning point in history, with God giving to this man the meaning of Justification by Faith, which would explain the Salvation process. As well, from the loins of Abraham and the womb of Sarah would come the Jewish people, raised up for the express purpose of giving the world the Word of God, and as well, serving as the womb of the Messiah. So from this, I think we can see how great this man Abraham actually was.

About 1,000 years after Abraham, which would be about 3,000 years after creation, David is called to be the King of Israel. Through his family, the Messiah would come, Who would be called *"the Son of David."*

About 1,000 years after David, making it about 4,000 years after creation, Jesus was born, the Saviour of the world.

From the birth of Christ to this present time, which constitutes the Church Age, we can count approximately 2,000 years, making it about 6,000 years of recorded history from the time of the creation. At this juncture, which should happen very shortly, the Rapture of the Church could take place at any moment, followed by the Great Tribulation, which will conclude with the Second Coming of Christ, which, without a doubt, will be the most cataclysmic moment in history.

The Scripture tells us that Sarai was barren. Satan, knowing that it would be absolutely imperative for a male child to be born to this couple, that is, if the Seed of the Woman was to be born into this world, would consequently make her barren, and God would allow him to do so. In this, we see one of the greatest tests of Faith, which brought about many failures on Abraham's part, but ultimately great victory.

(31) "AND TERAH TOOK ABRAM HIS SON, AND LOT THE SON OF HARAN HIS SON'S SON, AND SARAI HIS DAUGHTER IN LAW, HIS SON ABRAM'S WIFE; AND THEY WENT FORTH WITH THEM FROM UR OF THE CHALDEES, TO GO INTO THE LAND OF CANAAN; AND THEY CAME UNTO HARAN, AND DWELT THERE.

(32) "AND THE DAYS OF TERAH WERE TWO HUNDRED AND FIVE YEARS: AND TERAH DIED IN HARAN."

The composite is:

1. With this family leaving Ur of the Chaldees, we know that by now Abraham has had the great Revelation from God.

2. How this Revelation came to him, we aren't told!

3. The entire family goes with Abraham, which seems to not have been the Will of God.

4. On the way to the land of Canaan, they stopped in Haran, about 600 miles from Ur,

and a little over halfway to Canaan. There the father of Abraham, Terah, died.

UR OF THE CHALDEES

Verses 31 and 32 read: *"And Terah took Abram his son, and Lot the son of Haran his son's son, and Sarai his daughter in law, his son Abram's wife; and they went forth with them from Ur of the Chaldees, to go into the land of Canaan; and they came unto Haran, and dwelt there.*

"And the days of Terah were two hundred and five years: and Terah died in Haran."

It is said that Ur of the Chaldees, located a little north of what is now referred to as the Persian Gulf, was one of the most modern cities in the world of that time. So Abraham and his family would have left these modern conveniences — modern for that time — to go to a land to which they had never been, and to live a nomadic existence for the rest of their lives, and because of a Revelation from God. How many would be willing to do that?

The Jewish Targums (Jewish historical Commentaries of sorts) say that Abraham's family were idol makers. In other words, they made the idol which represented the moon god *"Ur,"* for which the city was named.

Whether this is correct or not, we know that Abraham and his family were idol worshippers, and so we have to venture the thought that whatever Revelation it was that God gave to Abraham, it was so powerful, so obvious, and left such a mark upon the Patriarch, that he would never be the same again. To be sure, this is a conversion that so changes a man, that he will now forsake all that he has known all his life, to reach out by Faith to something that he really could not see — except by Faith.

We know that Abraham had this Revelation when he was in Ur of the Chaldees. But how long he stayed there before he left for Canaan, with a stop in Haran, we aren't told. I suspect it would not have been very long, because as the First Verse of the next Chapter proclaims, the command of the Lord was explicit.

He left Haran when he was 75 years old, as we shall see.

Whether Terah, Abraham's father, accepted the Lord is not clear. There is some evidence that he did, and because he as well left Ur of the Chaldees and got as far as Haran, where he died.

"Nor silver nor gold has obtained my
*   Redemption;*
"No riches of Earth could have saved
*   my poor soul;*
"The Blood of the Cross is my only
*   foundation;*
"The death of My Saviour now makes
*   me whole."*

"Nor silver nor gold has obtained my
*   Redemption;*
"The guilt on my conscience too heavy
*   had grown.*
"The Blood of the Cross is my only
*   foundation;*
"The death of my Saviour could only
*   atone."*

"Nor silver nor gold has obtained my
*   Redemption;*
"The holy commandment forbade me
*   draw near,*
"The Blood of the Cross is my only
*   foundation;*
"The death of my Saviour removes my
*   fear."*

"Nor silver nor gold has obtained my
*   Redemption;*
"The way into Heaven could not thus
*   be bought.*
"The Blood of the Cross is my only
*   foundation;*
"The death of my Saviour Redemption
*   has wrought."*

CHAPTER 12

(1) "NOW THE LORD HAD SAID UNTO ABRAM, GET OUT OF YOUR COUNTRY, AND FROM YOUR KINDRED, AND FROM YOUR FATHER'S HOUSE, UNTO A LAND THAT I WILL SHOW YOU:"

The overview is:

1. In these first three Verses, we have a part of the Revelation given by the Lord to Abraham.

2. He was to leave his home country and his kindred, and even his Father's house.

3. The Lord would show him where to go, and it would be the land of Canaan.

THE REVELATION

The phrase, *"Now the LORD had said unto Abram,"* if it is to be noticed, refers to instructions that had been given to the Patriarch sometime previously.

This Chapter is very important, for it records the first steps of this great Believer in the path of Faith. There were Believers before him (a few), but the Scripture speaks of him as the father of all Believers who would come after him (Rom. 4:16).

While Abraham obeyed, it seems that family ties at first held him back. Though called to Canaan, he nevertheless tarried at Haran till nature's tie was snapped by death, and then, with unimpeded step, he made his way to the place to which *"the God of Glory"* had called him.

All of this is very full of meaning. The flesh is ever a hindrance to the full power of the Call of God. We tend to settle for less than that which God intends.

We are slow to learn that everything we need, and I mean everything, is found totally and completely in Christ. While we are quick to say *"Amen"* to the words I have just dictated, we are slow to actually come to the place of full surrender. *"Self-will"* hinders! The *"flesh"* hinders! However, we make excuses for all of this, by loading the flesh and self-will with religious phraseology.

THE CALL OF GOD

Whatever it is that God calls us to do, it is always beyond what we would at first see or think. Embodied in the Call is not only a work to be done, but as well the ingredients for Spiritual Growth. With the Holy Spirit, it is always growth. And to be frank, the growth must be brought about, or the work cannot be done. And here I would dwell, for a little, on the Cross of Christ. There is only one way all of this can be achieved, and that's by and through the Cross. If we do not understand the Cross, then we cannot really understand the Way of God. In fact, if the Cross is removed from Christianity, Christianity then loses its power (I Cor. 1:18), and for all practical purposes, becomes little more than the religions of the world. While it might have a better ethic, it's an ethic that really cannot be reached without the Cross.

THE CROSS OF CHRIST

The Cross unfolds God as the sinner's friend. It reveals Christ in that most wondrous character, as the Righteous Justifier of the most ungodly sinner.

Someone once asked me, *"Is it Who He is, or What He did, that makes the difference?"*

Only Christ could do what needed to be done to redeem fallen humanity; however, even though Christ is God, and has always been God, on that premise alone, no one was redeemed. God would have to become man and go to the Cross, if man was to be lifted out of his fallen state. So in the final alternative, even though Who He was presents an absolute necessity, in reality, it was What He did, and we speak of the Cross, which guarantees Salvation for even the vilest of sinners.

THE INTRODUCTION OF THE CROSS

The Power of God, with all its wisdom, glory, holiness, and magnitude, but for the Cross, works against the sinner.

How precious, therefore, is the Cross, in this its first phase, as the basis of the sinner's peace, the basis of his worship, and the basis of his eternal relationship with the God Who is there so blessedly and so gloriously revealed.

All that He has said, all that He has done, from the very beginning, indicates that the Cross was ever uppermost in His heart. And no wonder! His dear and well-beloved Son was to hang there, between Heaven and Earth, the object of all the shame and suffering that men and devils could heap upon Him, all because He loved to do His Father's Will, and thereby redeem the children of His Grace.

THE CROSS AND THE WORLD

The same Cross which connects me with God has separated me from the world. A dead man is, evidently, done with the world; and to be sure, every true Believer died with Christ as it regards His death, burial, and Resurrection (Rom. 6:3-5). Having risen with Christ, he is now connected with God in the power of a new life, even a new nature. Being thus inseparably linked with

NOTES

Christ, he, of necessity, participates in his acceptance with God, and in his rejection by the world. The two things go together.

The former makes him a worshiper and a citizen of Heaven, while the latter makes him a witness and a stranger on Earth. If the Cross has come between me and my sins, it has just as readily come between me and the world. In the former case, it puts me into the place of peace with God; in the latter, it puts me into the place of hostility with the world.

THE CROSS AND SEPARATION

The Believer cannot profess to enjoy the former, while rejecting the latter. If one's ear is open to hear Christ's Voice within the Veil, it should be open also to hear His Voice outside the camp; if one enters into the Atonement which the Cross has accomplished, one should also realize the rejection which it necessarily involves.

It is our happy privilege not only to be done with our sins, but to be done with the world also. All this is involved in the Doctrine of the Cross. That's why Paul said:

"God forbid that I should glory, save in the Cross of our Lord Jesus Christ, by Whom the world is crucified unto me, and I unto the world" (Gal. 6:14). This means that Paul looked upon the world as a thing which ought to be nailed to the Cross (Mackintosh).

SEPARATION

The phrase, *"Get out of your country, and from your kindred, and from your father's house,"* proclaims the reason that many cannot be used of God. They refuse to separate themselves from certain things in this world and, therefore, unto God.

This which the Lord demanded of Abraham, He in effect demands of all. It is:

1. *"Our country"*: The true Believer *"seeks a country,"* simply because that which the world offers can never satisfy and, therefore, simply will not do (Heb. 11:14). The things of this world lose their attraction. Money is a means to an end. The old song, *"This world is not my home, I'm just a passing through,"* becomes the song of the Redeemed. If one lays up treasures here, one's heart will be here, and simply because one's heart is where one's treasure is.

2. *"Separate from your kindred"*: Now you belong to Christ. You are bought with a price, and a great price at that, and even though you continue to love your family, even love them very deeply, Christ and what He wants and desires takes precedent over your family and anyone else for that matter. Regrettably, many aren't willing to do that.

3. *"From your father's house"*: This refers to whatever future close loved ones have planned for you. As stated, you now belong to Christ. Anything and everything that might be detrimental in your *"father's house,"* must be laid aside. In effect, you leave everything, and do so for the sake of Christ.

Now as stated, many simply will not do that. And as a result, God simply cannot use them. Or else, they quit altogether, which tragically is the course it seems, for many.

THE WILL OF GOD

The phrase, *"Unto a land that I will show you,"* refers to the fact that Abraham had no choice in the matter. He was to receive his orders from the Lord, and go where those orders led him.

In many ways, living for God is similar to the military. While personally, I've never served in the military, still, from what I see, there isn't a lot of difference, or at least it shouldn't be a lot of difference, in the army of this nation, and the army of our Lord.

(2) "AND I WILL MAKE OF YOU A GREAT NATION, AND I WILL BLESS YOU, AND MAKE YOUR NAME GREAT; AND YOU SHALL BE A BLESSING:"

The composition is:

1. The nation which God made of Abraham has changed the world, and exists even unto this hour. In fact, this nation *"Israel"* still has a great part to play, which will take place in the coming Kingdom Age.

2. God has promised to bless Abraham, and that He did.

3. The builders of the Tower of Babel sought to *"make us a name,"* whereas God took this man, who forsook all, and *"made his name great."*

4. He not only was blessed, but in turn, he has been a blessing.

A GREAT NATION

The phrase, *"And I will make of you a great nation,"* pertains to Israel and all of its people, and for all time. The nation of which God was speaking did not exist at this time. And beside that, Sarah was barren.

And yet, this nation would be totally unlike any nation the world had ever known. Some 400 years later, a wayward prophet would say, and by the Spirit of God, *"For from the top of the rocks I see him, and from the hills I behold him: lo, the people shall dwell alone, and shall not be reckoned among the nations,"* meaning that Israel would be totally unlike any other nation that had ever existed (Num. 23:9).

He then said, *"He shall pour the water out of his buckets, and his seed shall be in many waters, and his king shall be higher than Agag, and his kingdom shall be exalted"* (Num. 24:7).

Under David and Solomon, Israel became the most powerful nation on Earth, and as well, the richest; however, the true riches were in their relationship with God. They would give the world the Word of God, which has blessed the world immeasurably. And even greater than that, they served as the womb of the Messiah, even though they did not know Him when He actually came.

Due to crucifying their Messiah, and the world's Saviour, at their request, the Lord took His Hand of blessing away from them. Consequently, in A.D. 70, they in effect ceased to be a nation, totally destroyed by the Roman Tenth Legion under Titus.

As strangers they wandered the world for about 1,900 years, when once again establishing themselves in their ancient homeland, and once again becoming a nation. And yet, they have some dark days ahead, in fact, darker than anything they have seen in the past. Jesus said so (Mat. 24:21). It will take that for them finally to accept Christ, the One they have rejected. This they will do (Zech. 13:1, 6). Israel will then be restored, never to lose her way again (Rom. 11:26-27).

BLESSING

The phrase, *"And I will bless you, and make your name great,"* proclaims the favor of God. According to Scripture, *"to bless"* means *"to increase."* Abraham would be blessed, and so would Israel.

These words, *"I will bless,"* indicate relations very close between Jehovah and Abraham, whereby the friends and enemies of the one become so equally to the other.

A BLESSING TO OTHERS

The phrase, *"And you shall be a blessing,"* concerns itself with the greatest blessing of all. It is the glory of Abraham's Faith. God would give this man the meaning of Salvation, which is *"Justification by Faith."* This blessing, the great Patriarch would pass on to the entirety of the world.

(3) "AND I WILL BLESS THEM WHO BLESS YOU, AND CURSE HIM WHO CURSES YOU: AND IN YOU SHALL ALL THE FAMILIES OF THE EARTH BE BLESSED."

The overview is:

1. To bless Israel guarantees a blessing from God.

2. To curse Israel guarantees that one will be cursed by God.

3. In this man Abraham, *"all the families of the Earth are blessed,"* at least those who will believe!

THE BLESSING AND THE CURSE

The phrase, *"And I will bless them who bless you, and curse him who curses you,"* holds true not only for Israel, but as well for Spiritual Israel, i.e., *"the Church,"* i.e., *"those who are truly born again."* Let's look first at Israel:

At least part of the reason that America has experienced such blessings is because of our protection of Israel. This promise as given to Abraham by God nearly 4,000 years ago holds true even unto this hour, and in fact will ever hold true.

It holds true for Israel; and it holds true for the Church as well, and I speak of the True Church. All those who bless the Work of God can expect blessings from the Lord, and it doesn't really matter who they are.

As well, if a nation or a people oppose Israel, or the Work of God presently, God has said that He will Personally curse that nation or people. And please understand, if God curses anything, which means to hinder that nation or person, to be sure, trouble will be their continued lot.

Some may ask, why would God continue to bless those who bless Israel, considering that Israel has rejected God's Son and her Messiah? Two reasons:

1. God made a Promise to Abraham, and God keeps His Promises.

2. Israel is going to be restored, and anyone helping her, in a sense, is helping toward that restoration.

ALL THE FAMILIES OF THE EARTH

The phrase, *"And in you shall all families of the Earth be blessed,"* concerns a blessing of unprecedented proportions.

It speaks of Israel giving the world the Word of God, and more particularly, bringing the Messiah into the world. Through Christ, every family in the world who desires blessing from God can have that blessing. While the word *"blessing"* covers a wide territory, the greatest blessing of all would be *"Justification by Faith,"* which would be made possible to every believing soul as it regards the price paid by the Lord Jesus Christ at the Cross of Calvary.

A PERSONAL BLESSING

Every time I read this Passage, I think of the time this *"Blessing"* came to our house.

I was born into a home on March 15, 1935, which did not know God. In fact, until my Dad was 25 years old, he had never been inside of a Church, not one single time. He had never heard a Gospel song, and in fact, had never even seen a Bible, much less having read one. My Mother's experience was very similar.

And then two women, a Mother and her daughter, came to our little town to build a Church. The year was 1939. The lady and her daughter were the Mother and Sister of Lester Sumrall.

A small Church was built. In fact, my Uncle, who was a millionaire, in whose home I was born, loaned the money to build the Church.

My entire family was saved in that Church. And as a result, I accepted Christ when I was eight years old. I was Baptized with the Holy Spirit a few weeks later.

I do not know all the reasons that this great Gospel of Jesus Christ was brought to our town, and ultimately to our family. But by the Grace of God, the Blessing came to us. Consequently, I feel as Paul said so long ago, *"I am debtor"* (Rom. 1:14). I must do everything within my power to help take this glorious Gospel to others. As I had the privilege to hear, they must have the privilege to hear as well!

(4) "SO ABRAM DEPARTED, AS THE LORD HAD SPOKEN UNTO HIM; AND LOT WENT WITH HIM: AND ABRAM WAS SEVENTY AND FIVE YEARS OLD WHEN HE DEPARTED OUT OF HARAN.

(5) "AND ABRAM TOOK SARAI HIS WIFE, AND LOT HIS BROTHER'S SON, AND ALL THEIR SUBSTANCE THAT THEY HAD GATHERED, AND THE SOULS THAT THEY HAD GOTTEN IN HARAN; AND THEY WENT FORTH TO GO INTO THE LAND OF CANAAN; AND INTO THE LAND OF CANAAN THEY CAME.

(6) "AND ABRAM PASSED THROUGH THE LAND UNTO THE PLACE OF SICHEM, UNTO THE PLAIN OF MOREH. AND THE CANAANITE WAS THEN IN THE LAND."

The exegesis is:

1. After some delay, Abraham departs Haran, in obedience to the Lord.

2. He was 75 years old when he started for Canaan.

3. Canaan was the land to which they were to come.

4. However, the Canaanite was in the land.

ABRAM DEPARTED

Verse 4 reads: *"So Abram departed, as the LORD had spoken unto him; and Lot went with him: and Abram was seventy and five years old when he departed out of Haran."*

So Abraham starts for the better land. This was his first surrender: there were seven of them in all:

1. He surrenders here his native land (Gen. 12:1).

2. He surrenders his family (Gen. 12:1).

3. He then surrenders the vale of the Jordan.

4. He then surrenders the riches of Sodom.

5. He surrenders self.

6. He then surrenders Ishmael.

7. And lastly, he surrenders Isaac. Each painful surrender was followed by increased spiritual wealth.

The Holy Spirit through Moses calls attention to the fact that Abram was 75 years old when he departed out of Haran.

Why does He note this?

From the time that God revealed Himself to Abraham, to the time he obeyed the command, might have been several years. Maybe there was a struggle there of which we aren't aware. We know that he did not leave Haran until his father Terah died. That seems to be the lot of many Christians. They go halfway; in other words, while they obey partially, they never quite obey totally. They make it to *"Haran,"* but they never quite make it all the way to Canaan, or else they arrive late.

TO CANAAN

Verse 5 reads: *"And Abram took Sarai his wife, and Lot his brother's son, and all their substance that they had gathered, and the souls that they had gotten in Haran; and they went forth to go into the land of Canaan; and into the land of Canaan they came."*

From Haran to Canaan was approximately 350 miles. Abram had 318 trained men with him (Gen. 14:14), meaning that they were trained to fight as soldiers. They were totally loyal to Abraham, actually born in his household. In fact, there may have been as many as 1,000 people in this entourage.

As well, Abraham was extremely rich in silver and gold, as well as flocks and herds. In other words, he was a mighty man!

THE CANAANITE

Verse 6 reads: *"And Abram passed through the land unto the place of Sichem, unto the plain of Moreh. And the Canaanite was then in the land."*

Abraham now finds himself in the Promised Land. Thus it is presently. The Holy Spirit says, *"Believe on the Lord Jesus Christ and you shall be saved."* The sinner believes and he is saved. Into *"the land of Canaan"* he comes. This is the first step in the life of Faith.

But what an unexpected experience for Abraham! He finds the hateful, impure, and hostile Canaanite in God's land. This was Faith's first trial; his heart would be tempted to question the fact that this was God's land, for how could the Canaanite be in God's land!

So in the present day the young Believer expects after conversion to find nothing in his nature hostile to Christ, but is distressed and perplexed very soon to painfully learn that, alas, the Canaanite is in the land, and that he is now commencing a lifelong battle with what the New Testament calls *"the flesh"* (Williams).

(7) "AND THE LORD APPEARED UNTO ABRAM, AND SAID, UNTO YOUR SEED WILL I GIVE THIS LAND: AND THERE BUILT HE AN ALTAR UNTO THE LORD, WHO APPEARED UNTO HIM."

The synopsis is:

1. The Lord now appears unto Abram. Faith is always rewarded!

2. The Lord promises Abraham a son who will be the progenitor of the Redeemer of all nations.

3. He builds an Altar unto the Lord, and offers up Sacrifice, which portrays what the coming Redeemer would do in order to redeem lost humanity.

THE LORD APPEARS

The phrase, *"And the LORD appeared unto Abram,"* tells us the following:

Though the hostile Canaanite was in the land, the Lord was there as well.

The Bible doesn't say that the Lord appeared to Abraham while he was in Haran, because this was only a partial obedience. God reveals Himself only when the obedience is total.

THE STRUGGLE OF FAITH

All of this is full of instruction for us. The Canaanite in the land is the expression of the power of Satan; but, instead of being occupied with Satan's power to keep us out of the inheritance, we are called on to apprehend Christ's Power to bring us in. This means that the very sphere into which we are is the sphere of our conflict. Should this terrify us? By no means.

We have Christ — a victorious Christ, in Whom we are *"more than conquerors."* We will find that strangely enough, the *"Altar"* is the manner in which Christ gives us the victory.

YOUR SEED

The phrase, *"And said, Unto your seed will I give this land,"* proclaims in this short statement that he will have a son who will be

the progenitor of the Redeemer of all nations. It didn't matter that Sarah was barren, God has promised a son. And as well, this son will lead to the coming of the Messiah. So we're speaking here of something that is outsized regarding importance. In fact, there is nothing in the world more important.

The *"land"* of which the Lord spoke was the land of Canaan. If it is to be noticed, the Lord didn't say that He would give this land to Abraham directly, but rather to *"thy seed,"* which spoke of coming generations. In fact, Stephen stated, and concerning this very moment, *"And He gave him no inheritance in it, no, not so much as to set his foot on"* (Acts 7:5). Therefore, this Promise agreed with that which Abraham had been given before, namely, that he was to become a great people, for the land was promised not to him but, to his descendants.

THE ALTAR

The phrase, *"And there built he an Altar unto the LORD, Who appeared unto him,"* proclaims a step of Faith that tells us several things:

1. That the Canaanites should be dispossessed, and the entirety of their country given to the offspring of a childless man already over 75 years old, demands a great leap of Faith. The apparent improbability of it ever being accomplished presented itself as a constant test of faith throughout the entirety of the life of the Patriarch.

2. The rearing of an Altar in the land was, in fact, a form of taking possession of it on the ground of a right secured to the exercises of his faith (Bush). It is often said of Abraham and the Patriarchs that they built Altars to the Lord; it is never said that they built houses for themselves (Wordsworth).

3. All of this proclaims to us, and we're speaking of the building of the Altar, that the Cross of Christ must ever be the object of our Faith. Nothing is more important than this.

The trouble with the modern Church is not a lack of faith, but rather faith in the wrong thing. Let us say it again, and even more sharply: If one's faith is not anchored squarely in the Cross of Christ, irrespective in what else it might be anchored, and no matter how Scriptural the other thing might be in its own right, the upshot is God will

NOTES

not honor such faith. He honors Faith alone which is in the Cross of Christ.

The Believer must understand, and without reservation that everything we receive from the Lord, and that means everything exclusively, comes to us by the means of the Cross. It is the Cross which has made it all possible. As well, and as equally important, the Holy Spirit, Who we cannot do without, and Whose Power and Help we must have, works entirely within the parameters of the Finished Work of Christ (Rom. 8:1-2, 11).

4. The Altar, and in every case, represented the coming Crucifixion, where the Son of God would give Himself in Sacrifice, in order to atone for all sin, past, present, and future.

The *"Altar"* in essence, said that mankind's most grave problem, in other words, the problem which was the cause of all other problems, was, and is, sin. And sin can only be handled, and in fact was handled at the Cross, and the Cross alone. This means that all of these great Promises given by God to Abraham, his having a son, a great nation being raised up from his loins, all the families of the world being blessed through him, him being a blessing to all nations, his descendants acquiring the entirety of this land of Canaan, all and without exception were for but one purpose, and that was to ultimately pave the way for the Redeemer to come into this world, in order to handle the terrible sin problem.

The problem with the modern Church is, we get our eyes on the temporal aspects of the promise. The *"land"* becomes very important to us, but not in the right way. Even the answers to prayer become very important, but again, all in the wrong way.

The center of gravity as it regards Christianity is always the Cross, and nothing but the Cross. Paul nailed it down when he said:

"Christ Jesus came into the world to save sinners; of whom I am chief" (I Tim. 1:15).

In this short statement, the Holy Spirit through Paul tells us Who the Saviour is, the great problem facing the world which is sin, and that I personally am in need of Redemption, just as much as anyone else, or more!

REVELATION

The Scripture plainly says in this Verse, even two times, that the Lord appeared unto Abraham. Exactly what this means, we aren't told. Taking it at face value, it means that the Lord appeared to him in visible form.

Some may say that if the Lord presently would do that for them, appear in visible form, they could then do great and mighty things, etc.

The truth is, He has done even more. Paul said:

"God, Who at sundry times and in diverse manners spoke in time past unto the fathers by the Prophets,

"Has in these last days spoken unto us by His Son, Whom He has appointed heir of all things, by Whom also He made the worlds" (Heb. 1:1-2).

When we read the four Gospels, and the Epistles for that matter, we're reading what God has spoken unto us by His Son. Jesus went to the Cross and there He atoned for all sin, past, present, and future. He satisfied the demands of the broken Law, by giving of Himself as a Sacrifice. Sin being the legal right that Satan had to hold man in captivity, that legal right is now broken, because all sin has been atoned, at least for all who will believe (Jn. 3:16). When Jesus paid the terrible sin debt, and paid it in full, this put Believers in a brand-new status (Col. 2:14-15).

Due to the sin debt being completely lifted, in other words, man no longer owes a debt to God due to what Jesus did at the Cross, the Holy Spirit Who could only work in a limited way before the Cross, can now come into all Believers, which He does at conversion, and does so to abide forever (Jn. 14:16-17). As well, Believers by the Power of the Holy Spirit can now receive a Baptism of Power, which is always accompanied by the speaking with other tongues (Acts 1:8; 2:4; 10:45-46; 19:1-7). Due to the fact that the Holy Spirit abides within us, and does so forever, He is there to lead us and guide us constantly, giving us the direction that we need (Jn. 16:13-15). Having such constant leadership by the Holy Spirit is far better than having the Lord to appear to us personally at abbreviated times.

CONSECRATION

Even though the Holy Spirit is definitely present at all times with all Believers, even the weakest Saints, His Leadership, Guidance, and Power are seldom known in their fullness, and because of two things. In other words, most Saints experience very little help from the Holy Spirit, when in reality, He desires to do much more, and in fact, will do much more, if we follow God's prescribed order.

The first part of that order has to do with the Cross of Christ. The Holy Spirit works exclusively within the boundaries of the Finished Work of Christ. In other words, every single thing He does for us is done exclusively according to what Jesus did for us on the Cross (Rom. 8:1-2, 11). This is what gives Him, as stated, the legal right to do all the things which He does. As also stated, the sin debt has now been lifted, paid for by Christ at the Cross, which gives the Holy Spirit great latitude in which to work. That's the reason that He couldn't come into hearts and lives to abide forever before the Cross. But after the Cross, it is now an entirely different story (I Cor. 1:17-18, 21, 23; 2:2, 5).

He doesn't ask much of us, but He does demand that we place our Faith exclusively in the Cross of Christ. We as Believers must understand that everything that comes to us from God does so exclusively through and by what Jesus did at the Cross, all on our behalf. In other words, He came to this world for the expressed purpose of going to the Cross. That was His Mission, His Purpose, and in fact, that which had been decided from before the foundation of the world (I Pet. 1:18-20). Actually, the entirety of the Bible, and in every capacity, is the story of man's Fall and Redemption, and the Cross is how the Redemption process was brought about. So the point I'm attempting to make is this:

The Believer needs to understand the Cross, meaning that the Cross was not only necessary for our initial Salvation experience when we were Born-Again, but as well, plays just as much of a part in our everyday living, and in every capacity. In other words, unless you the Believer put your Faith exclusively in the Cross of Christ, ever making it the object of your Faith, you cannot have all the Help, Leading, Guidance, and Empowerment of the Holy Spirit, which means that no matter how hard you try, you're going to fail.

THE OBJECT OF OUR FAITH

It is absolutely imperative that you as a Believer ever make the Cross the object of your Faith (Rom. 6:3-14; 8:1-2, 11; Gal. 1:17-18, 21, 23; 2:2, 5; 6:14). Concerning this very thing, Paul said: *"Blotting out the handwriting of Ordinances that was against us, which was contrary to us, and took it out of the way, nailing it to His Cross;*

"And having spoiled principalities and powers, He made a show of them openly, triumphing over them in it" (Col. 2:14-15).

This Passage bluntly tells us that everything was done at the Cross; consequently, inasmuch as the Lord works exclusively on the basis of Faith, we must understand what the object of faith must ever be.

Every Christian has Faith; in fact, every person in the world has faith. The problem is, it's not faith in God. No unsaved person has Faith in God, while some few may have such in a rudimentary way, it would only be what they were taught by Christian parents, etc. But actually, it's impossible for the unredeemed to have faith, inasmuch as they are spiritually dead.

However, even Christians most of the time do not know and understand what their faith really is. All claim to have faith, and in truth that is correct; but most don't have the faintest idea as to what the object of their faith ought to be. They think they know, but in actuality they don't.

If asked this question, most would claim that they have faith in God, or their faith is in Christ, or they have faith in the Word, etc. While all of these statements are correct, they really don't say very much.

In fact, that which we've just said is not that much different than the type of faith that demons have. Listen to what the Scripture says:

"You believe that there is one God; you do well: the devils also believe, and tremble" (James 2:19).

The entire Foundation of Christianity is the Cross of Christ. So, unless the Christian has as the basis of his Faith the Cross of Christ, it's really not faith that God will recognize.

FAITH IN THE WORD?

In the last several decades, the Church has been inundated with teaching on faith, which claims to be faith in the Word. The adherents to this doctrine, and I speak of the Word of Faith doctrine, do not at all believe in the Cross. In fact, they refer to the Cross as *"past miseries."* They claim that the Cross was the most horrible defeat in human history. So they place no credence in the Cross, which means that what they are teaching is heresy.

They claim to be great students of the Word, to base everything on the Word, etc. Because of making these statements and quoting some Scriptures, most of the Church is deceived into believing that these people truly are sticklers for the Word. But in fact, the very opposite is true.

They teach that the way to *"put the Word to work for you,"* which is the way they label it, is to find several Scriptures which seem to address your problem, whatever your problem might be, and then quote those Scriptures over and over again. They teach that this creates some type of spiritual energy, and I speak of the constant quotation, which then has an effect in the spirit world, and will bring about the answer to your need.

The truth is, this is no more than white magic. It is trying to use the Scriptures as some type of magic formula, which will bring about whatever one desires. Nothing could be further from the truth. God will not honor such foolishness as that.

In the first place, these people teach that whatever they desire is the Will of God. In other words, they teach that they do not now need the Leading of the Spirit, inasmuch as they are new creation people. Whatever they do is right in the eyes of God, whatever that might be. In other words, they totally ignore the Will of God, in effect, claiming that whatever they do constitutes the Will of God. Again, nothing could be further from the truth!

For a Believer to properly know and understand the Word of God, the Believer must realize that the Word is the story of the Cross. Now think about that for a moment! Listen to what John said:

"In the beginning was the Word, and the Word was with God, and the Word was God" (Jn. 1:1). This tells us that Jesus is the Living Word. So, to divorce the Word from Christ, which means to not recognize Who

He is, and What He has done, is to do great violence to the Word. The Scripture then says:

"And the Word was made flesh, and dwelt among us, and we beheld His glory, the glory as of the only Begotten of the Father, full of Grace and Truth" (Jn. 1:14).

Now the story of the Word is the story of Christ, which refers to God becoming man, as the Scripture says, *"was made flesh, and dwelt among us."*

We now learn as to why the Word (Christ) was made flesh. The Scripture now says:

"The next day John sees Jesus coming unto him, and says, Behold the Lamb of God, which takes away the sin of the world" (Jn. 1:29). If it is to be noticed, John the Baptist referred to Jesus as *"the Lamb of God,"* Who would *"take away the sin of the world."*

Now John referred to Jesus as the Lamb of God, simply because His very purpose for coming to this world was to die on the Cross, of which the untold millions of lambs previously offered through the many centuries, were Types and Shadows of this One Who was to come. He would *"take away the sin of the world,"* by what He did at the Cross.

So we have the Word put before us, and we are made to understand that this *"Word"* is Jesus, and that His Purpose was to go to the Cross in order to *"take away the sin of the world."* Now let us bluntly make the following statement, so there will be no misunderstanding.

If the Believer doesn't understand the Word of God according to the Cross, then the Believer really doesn't understand the Word. That being the case, he can claim all he desires that he is a *"Word person,"* but in reality he isn't. Memorizing a few Scriptures, and quoting them over and over doesn't make one a *"Word person."* A true *"Word person,"* is the one who understands the Word in relationship to the Cross of Christ, understanding in effect that they are one and the same. That's why Paul said, *"One Lord, one Faith, one Baptism"* (Eph. 4:5).

ONE LORD, ONE FAITH, ONE BAPTISM

What did Paul mean by the above statement?

Actually, to fully understand this Passage, we must also include Verses 4 and 6. In these three Verses, 4, 5, and 6, Paul deals with the *"one"* aspect, and does so seven times. Let's look at it one by one:

1. *"One body"*: This speaks of the True Church, into which one becomes a part by being *"born again"* (Jn. 3:3). This is done by the believing sinner evidencing Faith in Christ and what Christ did at the Cross, in effect, accepting Christ as one's personal Saviour.

2. *"One Spirit"*: Of course, this refers to the Holy Spirit, Who is the active agent in all that is done as it regards the Godhead, and Their dealing with humanity. In other words, every single thing done by the Godhead on Earth is done through the Person, Purpose, Work, Office, Ministry, and Power of the Holy Spirit (Acts 13:2, 4, etc.).

3. *"One Hope"*: This great hope held by every Saint of God pertains to what Jesus did at the Cross on our behalf. It refers to the fact that we are now washed, sanctified, and justified (I Cor. 6:11). As well, we have the blessed hope that soon we will be *"glorified."* And please understand, the word *"hope"* as used in the Bible is totally different than the way it is presently used. Now it means maybe or maybe not! The Biblical word *"hope,"* means that what is going to happen is guaranteed, but we just don't know exactly when.

4. *"One Lord"*: There is one Christ Who has saved us, and He did so by what He did at the Cross. The title *"Lord,"* in effect means *"Lord of the Covenant."* The Covenant of which it speaks goes all the way back to Genesis 3:15, where it speaks of the Seed of the woman bruising the head of the serpent. This was done by Christ at Calvary. As an aside, this means that all pretenders are just that, pretenders! I'm speaking of Mohammad, Joseph Smith, Confucius, and any other pretended light. There is only *"One Lord,"* not two, just one, and He is the Lord Jesus Christ.

5. *"One Faith"*: If it is to be noticed, I am constantly using the terminology that the Believer must ever have as the object of his Faith the Cross of Christ. In fact, if we place our faith in anything else, we are abrogating the Word of God. There aren't ten faiths, or two faiths, but only *"one Faith,"* and that is, *"Jesus Christ and Him Crucified"* (I Cor. 2:2).

6. *"One Baptism"*: This does not refer at all to Water Baptism as most think. It refers to the Baptism into the death of Christ on the Cross (Rom. 6:3). When He died on the Cross, He did so as our Substitute. Whenever we, as the sinner coming to Christ, or the Believer already in Christ, evidence Faith in Him, in the mind of God, we are literally in Christ, and because of that Faith. We are in Him to such an extent that the Holy Spirit used the word *"baptized into His death"* (Rom. 6:3). It is this Baptism alone which saves.

7. *"One God"*: This speaks of God the Father (Eph. 4:6). We can know Him only by our acceptance of His Son, and our Saviour, the Lord Jesus Christ, and according to what He did for us at the Cross. Jesus said: *"No man comes unto the Father, but by Me"* (Jn. 14:6).

In one way or the other, every single one of these things listed by Paul pertains to the Cross.

HAVING THE LEADING OF THE SPIRIT

An important part to being led by the Spirit is the fact of our consecration. If the Believer is truly looking to the Finished Work of Christ as it regards his daily walk before God, he will then have a prayer life, be dedicated to the study of the Word, without which the Believer can have little relationship with the Lord.

It is tragic, but the modern Church is not a praying Church. In fact, a particular prophecy was given at Azusa Street at the turn of the Twentieth Century, which in essence stated, *"In the last days, My people will praise Me to Whom they no longer pray."* We have seen that come to pass. The modern Church is not only not a praying Church, but as well, it is for all practical purposes, Scripturally illiterate as well! All of this stems from the fact that the Church has been steered away from the Cross, with its faith now scattered in every direction, and incidentally, faith which God will not recognize. Let me give you an example:

The true result of Faith is the *"Fruit of the Spirit"* being manifested in one's life (Gal. 5:22-23). But what is the criterion presently?

Pure and simple, it is material things. In other words, one's faith is now judged, not so much by the evidence of the Fruit of the Spirit in one's life, but rather by the model car the person drives, etc. So Christians are taught that they've got to somehow get a big car, which will show that they have great faith. What a farce! What a travesty? What blasphemy!

Because all of this is so very, very important, please allow me to give the following diagram, even though I've already given it elsewhere in this Volume:

1. Focus: The Cross.

2. Object of Faith: The Finished Work of Christ.

3. Power Source: The Holy Spirit.

4. Results: Victory.

But instead, the following is where most Christians presently are, and sadly so:

1. Focus: Works.

2. Object of Faith: Performance.

3. Power Source: Self.

4. Results: Failure.

Each Believer ought to study both of these diagrams very carefully, and ascertain where, in spiritual reality, is your truthful position?

(8) "AND HE REMOVED FROM THENCE UNTO A MOUNTAIN ON THE EAST OF BETH-EL, AND PITCHED HIS TENT, HAVING BETH-EL ON THE WEST, AND HAI ON THE EAST: AND THERE HE BUILT AN ALTAR UNTO THE LORD, AND CALLED UPON THE NAME OF THE LORD."

The structure is:

1. Abraham is now on a mountain east of *"Beth-el"* which means *"House of God,"* and west of *"Hai,"* which means *"the heap of ruins."*

2. The *"Altar"* and the *"tent"* give us the two great features of Abraham's character. He was a worshipper of God, hence the Cross, and a stranger in the world, hence the tent.

3. Abraham *"built an Altar,"* and there *"called upon the Name of the Lord."* Our prayers are based upon our Faith in Christ and what Christ has done for us at the Cross, of which the Altar was a Type.

THE HOUSE OF GOD AND
THE HEAP OF RUINS

The phrase, *"And he removed from thence unto a mountain on the east of Beth-el, and pitched his tent, having Beth-el on the west, and Hai on the east,"* presents the exact spot in which every Believer finds themselves. Beth-el, the House of God, is on one side, while Hai, the heap of ruins, is on the other.

If the Believer stays with the Altar, *"Christ and Him Crucified,"* their lot will be the House of God; otherwise, it will be the *"heap of ruins."* (Hai is the same city which Joshua would attack some 470 years from this time — Josh., Chpts. 7-8.)

The mention here of the *"Altar"* and the *"tent,"* is very important. This showed where his Faith was.

The Altar represented the fact that he knew that his mission in life was the coming Redeemer. For the Seed of the Woman to come into the world, God would have to raise up a people, which He would do from the loins of the Patriarch and the womb of Sarah. A land would have to be obtained for these people, and that land would be where he was now encamped — Palestine. His business was to claim it and in effect, take it by Faith, which he did! As well, a son would have to be born to he and Sarah, which ultimately would come to pass also.

The *"tent"* which speaks of temporary quarters, proclaimed the fact that Abraham knew all of this. In effect, he was a pilgrim and a stranger (Heb. 11:8-9, 13).

In essence, Abraham is a prototype, so to speak, of every Believer. That's why Paul referred to him as the *"father of us all"* (Rom. 4:16).

We must recognize as well that this world is not our home. We are in effect, only passing through. While it was Abraham's mission in life to prepare for the coming of the Redeemer, even though that coming would be distant years in the future, it is our mission to tell the world that He has come. In one way or the other, every Believer fits into this category. Spiritually speaking, our domicile is to be a *"tent,"* which refers to our roots being in Heaven instead of on Earth. While we may work at particular occupations to make our living for our families, our main business is the Lord Jesus Christ and His Power to save. If the Lord helps us to make sizable amounts of money, we must use it for the Glory of God, and not for selfish purposes. If the *"Altar"* and the *"tent,"* be our characteristic, then the *"House of God"* will be our destination. Otherwise, and there are no exceptions, there will be a *"heap of ruins."*

THE ALTAR

The phrase, *"And there he built an Altar unto the LORD,"* portrays the object of his Faith. The *"Altar"* represents the death of Christ on the Cross, and the giving of Himself in Sacrifice. Abraham would have offered a lamb on this Altar.

He would have slit the throat of this little animal with a knife, with the hot blood pouring out, typifying the Blood that would be shed by Christ on the Cross. He would then remove the skin from its body, showing that sin is more than just a surface problem, but goes to the very vitals.

Inasmuch as this was a Whole Burnt-Offering, quite possibly, he would not have taken the entrails from the body, but would have offered the entirety of the lamb. The Whole Burnt-Offering signified that God would give His all, in reference to the Salvation of our souls, and that we in turn should give Him our all. In effect, it was a consecration offering, the same that we are to give today in our consecration to the Lord. Then it was a lamb and faith, while now it is just Faith, and because the Lamb, the Son of God, has already been offered.

Surely the Reader can see that throughout the Old Testament, we see the Altar. It began, as far as we know, with Abel, as portrayed in the Fourth Chapter of Genesis. It continued unto the Coming of Christ, Who Himself became, and in fact was, that which the Sacrifices represented. He was the Lamb of God Who took away the sin of the world (Jn. 1:29).

THE NAME OF THE LORD

The phrase, *"And called upon the Name of the LORD,"* implies public worship. It is evident, I think, that Abraham's servants joined in the worship as well (Gen. 24:12, 26-27). What Abraham did was also a witness to his Canaanite neighbors, which let them know he was a friend of God (II Chron. 20:6-7; Isa. 41:7-8; James 2:23) (Horton).

The idea of Abraham building the Altar, and calling on the Name of the Lord is that he made known to those around him the Redeemer, Who was to remove the Divine wrath and restore the blessing which man had lost in the Garden of Eden. This was

ever before the Patriarch, and we speak of the terrible need of man, and that the need could be met only by the One Who was to come. And the way that He would meet the need would be to go to the Cross, of which the Altar was a Type.

And thus we have the story of the Word of God. The Fall took only minutes, while Redemption took several millennia.

PARADISE LOST

Sometime ago in a museum in Washington, D.C., I had the occasion to see the famous painting by Milton, *"Paradise Lost."* Milton powerfully portrayed the Fall of man, showing the sublime heights from which he had fallen, and the lowest depths to which he fell. It was the most moving painting I have ever witnessed.

The only manner in which the depth of that Fall can be evaluated is the price that was paid to redeem man from his perilous position. The price was the Cross, and if we attempt to make something else the price, which to be sure is Satan's greatest effort, we blaspheme! I think it cannot be judged in any other fashion. It is ever the Cross! The Cross! The Cross! Cannot we see it in every Book of the Bible? Every Chapter? Every Verse? Even every line? And in reality, every word?

The Church must come back to that which has redeemed us, or else the Church is doomed! The individual Believer must ever make the Cross the object of his Faith, or else he is doomed as well! In fact, if we call upon the Name of the Lord, we can only do so on the basis of the Finished Work of Christ. If we attempt to do so from any other position, even though we may call it faith, or whatever name or label we would choose, the truth is, God will not hear such a petition. He will hear only that which anchors itself in the price that Christ paid at Calvary. The Holy Spirit will work on no other platform or basis (Rom. 8:1-2, 11).

(9) "AND ABRAM JOURNEYED, GOING ON STILL TOWARD THE SOUTH.

(10) "AND THERE WAS A FAMINE IN THE LAND: AND ABRAM WENT DOWN INTO EGYPT TO SOJOURN THERE; FOR THE FAMINE WAS GRIEVOUS IN THE LAND."

The structure is:

1. Abraham journeys further south. It will not be uneventful. Faith has its trials as well as its answers.

2. Faith must be tested, and great faith must be tested greatly.

3. There's a famine in the land, no doubt engineered by Satan, in order to prevent the birth of the Messiah. It would nearly succeed.

4. Better to starve in Canaan, if it should be so, than live in luxury in Egypt.

SOUTH

Verse 9 reads: *"And Abram journeyed, going on still toward the south."*

While there is nothing wrong with the direction of *"south,"* there is definite wrong in where this particular south will lead, which is Egypt. The Lord had told Abraham to come to Canaan, not Egypt!

As Believers, we must be very careful that we have the Mind of the Lord in all things. If one such as Abraham, and he was one of the great Faith giants of the entirety of all time, could go astray, where does that leave us? This shows us that it doesn't matter who we are, or how much faith we might presently have, if we step outside of the Will of God, even to the slightest degree, we are then functioning in Satan's territory, which can lead to disastrous consequences. As Believers, if we feel we do not yet have the Mind of the Lord in a certain thing, we must stand still until we do have the Mind of the Lord, and refuse to move, until that particular direction is perfectly ascertained.

God leaves nothing to chance. The Scripture even tells us: *"The steps of a good man are ordered by the LORD: and he delights in God's way"* (Ps. 37:23). Now if the Lord even minutely orders the steps of His children, well then, we certainly would know that He orders the direction.

THE FAMINE AND EGYPT

Verse 10 reads: *"And there was a famine in the land: and Abram went down into Egypt to sojourn there; for the famine was grievous in the land."*

The famine is engineered by Satan, and done so with a particular goal in mind, which goal was to prevent the birth of the Messiah.

Through the famine he would drive Abraham into Egypt, and with plans already laid for Sarah to be taken into Pharaoh's house, in order that she might become the mother of a child by the Egyptian king, thus defeating the Messianic promise made to Abraham. But for the intervening Hand of God, the plan would have been successful.

A TEST OF FAITH

At the same time, we know that God could have overruled Satan, as it regards the famine. But the Lord didn't do that. Instead, He would use the famine as a test of Faith. In other words, He would allow Satan certain latitude, even as He constantly does with all Believers, all in order that we might grow in Grace and the knowledge of the Lord.

THE MODERN FAITH TEACHING

The Church in the past several decades has been inundated with teaching on faith, but if the truth be known, almost all of this particular teaching is wrong. The modern faith teaching claims that the new creation man, the Born-Again man, can bring anything he so desires into existence. In other words, he now has the power to create. To be sure, there is a touch of truth in this; but here is where the true teaching of Faith parts from the false teaching.

The true Believer, operating on true Faith, which always speaks of the Cross of Christ as its object, can definitely create certain things, but only in the Will of God. The false faith teaching proclaims that the Will of God is whatever the new creation man says it is, in effect, committing the same sin that Adam and Eve committed in the Garden by listening to Satan, and perverting the Word of God. And to be sure, the so-called faith teaching of the *"Word of Faith"* people is definitely a perversion of the Word of God.

They teach that the Believer's power of creation is wrapped up in his confession. In other words, as we have recently stated, whatever problem he thinks he faces, he must choose several Scriptures which seem to address that problem, quote them over and over, which is supposed to create, by the constant recital, some type of energy in the spirit world, which will ultimately bring to pass that which is demanded.

To the carnal ear, such thinking sounds right, and simply because the Word of God is being used; however, and as stated, while it is the Word of God which is being used, it is being used in all the wrong ways.

God will never allow His Word to be used against Himself. And what do we mean by that?

THE WORD OF GOD, THE WISDOM OF GOD, AND THE WILL OF GOD

The Will of God is always the primary objective for the Believer, or at least it certainly should be! But sometimes, due to our own self-will, God's Will cannot be carried out as it ought to, which then His wisdom will dictate another course.

Was it the perfect Will of God for this famine to grip the land of Canaan, which would put Abraham in dire straits? No it wasn't! However, it was definitely His Wisdom that this be done, and for particular reasons. Is it the will of a Godly, loving parent to have to apply corporeal punishment to a wayward child? No it's not; however, it is definitely his wisdom to do so, and because of the prevailing circumstances.

The idea, as taught by the Word of Faith people, that a proper confession can ward off all adverse circumstances is not taught in the Bible. If we judge the rightness of a path by its exemption from trial and tests, this is a great mistake. The path of obedience may often be found most trying to flesh and blood. Thus, in Abraham's case, he was not only called to encounter the Canaanite, in the place to which God had called him, but there was also *"a famine in the land."* Should he, therefore, have concluded that he was not in his right place? Assuredly not. This would have been to judge according to the sight of his eyes, the very thing which Faith never does.

There is no doubt that this was a deep trial to the heart of the Patriarch, even an inexplicable puzzle to nature; nevertheless, all the ways which God leads are not at first easily understood and known.

For instance, when Paul was called into Macedonia, almost the first thing he had to encounter was the prison at Philippi. Thus, to a heart out of communion, this would have seemed to be a deathblow to the entire mission. But Paul never questioned the

rightness of his position; he was enabled to *"sing praises"* in the midst of it all, assured that everything was just as it should be, and so it was; for whatever Satan's plans were, they would not at all succeed.

EVERY ATTACK BY SATAN IS ALWAYS DIRECTED IN ONE WAY OR THE OTHER AT OUR FAITH

It really doesn't matter what Satan's plans were as it regards Paul. The truth is, even as with Abraham, this attack by Satan at Philippi was meant to destroy, or at least seriously weaken the Faith of the great Apostle. In fact, every single attack by Satan, irrespective as to whether it is financial, domestical, physical, or spiritual, is always but for one purpose and reason, and that is, as stated, to destroy our Faith, or at least seriously weaken our Faith.

In the doing of this, Satan is just as satisfied for us to move our Faith from the correct object of the Cross, or in other words, *"Jesus Christ and Him Crucified,"* to something else. While the something else might be good in its own right, and even Scriptural, if we make that, whatever it might be, the primary objective, then we've lost our way. That's why Paul said the following:

"For Christ sent me not to baptize, but to preach the Gospel: not with wisdom of words, lest the Cross of Christ should be made of none effect" (I Cor. 1:17).

That which occasioned Paul to write these words was the emphasis of Faith being shifted from the Cross to something else, and in this case, Water Baptism. While Water Baptism is definitely important, and definitely Scriptural, it, nor anything else for that matter, must ever be the objective, but rather the Cross of Christ.

Abraham should have reasoned accordingly: Despite the famine, he was in the very place (Canaan) in which God had set him; and, evidently, he received no direction to leave it. True, the famine was there; and, moreover, Egypt was at hand, offering deliverance from pressure; still the path of God's servant was plain. *"It is better to starve in Canaan, if it should be so, than live in luxury in Egypt; it is far better to suffer in God's path, than to be at ease in Satan's; it is better to be poor with*

Christ, if such should need be, than rich without Him" (Mackintosh).

CIRCUMSTANCES

Let's look at circumstances for a moment!

Abraham had much responsibility, possibly even as many as 1,000 people to look after. As well, he had great herds of sheep and oxen, etc.

Considering there was a famine in the land, which made it very, very difficult to feed all of these animals, the natural heart would no doubt say that he should take the road to Egypt. But remember this, and it is critically important:

Egypt was not the place of God's Presence. There was no Altar in Egypt, no communion. And the moment we trade the Altar for other things, we have just lost our way, and the end results will never be good.

The fact is, God had put Abraham in Canaan, not in Egypt. And the great problem with the modern Child of God, as well, is that he leaves God's appointed place, and because of circumstances, and he goes elsewhere. Oh to be sure, Egypt always looks enticing and inviting, but this is not where God had told Abraham to occupy himself. It didn't matter that there was a famine, that there was hardship, that there were difficulties, Canaan was where God had brought the Patriarch, and it was in Canaan, hardships or no, where God intended for Abraham to stay.

A WRONG DIRECTION!

Concerning this wrong direction, Mackintosh says:

"Nothing can ever make up for the loss of our communion with God. Exemption from temporary pressure, and the accession of even the greatest wealth, are but poor equivalents for what one loses by diverging a hair's breadth from the straight path of obedience."

He then went on to say, *"Let us, instead of turning aside into Egypt, wait on God; and thus the trial, instead of proving an occasion of stumbling, will prove an opportunity for obedience."*

And then: *"Shall we deny Him by plunging again into what from which His Cross has forever delivered us? May God Almighty forbid! May He keep us in the hollow of His hand, and under the shadow of His wings, until we see Jesus as He is, and be like Him, and with Him forever."*

NOTES

THE TEST OF FAITH

As stated, while every attack by Satan against us, and irrespective of its direction, is always against our Faith, as well, God is always testing our Faith. And to be sure, great Faith always must be tested greatly.

While the Lord always knows our Faith, its strength, its power, its weaknesses, etc., the idea is that we know as well. And to be sure, our Faith is never as strong as we think it is.

Pure Faith always has the pure objective of the Cross! But when the test comes, as it always will, we find to our dismay that there is much *"self-will"* mixed in with our Faith. It is this which the Lord seeks to eradicate in us, exactly as He sought to eradicate such in Abraham.

Since the Lord began to give this Message of the Cross to me, actually, the same Message which he gave to Paul, and which the Apostle gave to us in his 14 Epistles, it has been most interesting, not only to observe myself, but to observe other Christians in this Faith endeavor.

I have watched many embark upon this way of the Cross (I Cor. 1:18), and then meet with tests, even as Abraham, in which they would forsake the land of Canaan, the place where God wants them, and depart for Egypt. Their answer? *"The Cross,"* they say, *"doesn't work for me."* How utterly ridiculous!

No, it's not the Cross which failed, for it can never fail. It is self-will which came into the picture, which caused the failure, whatever it might have been. But always remember this:

The failure was not so much in what you did that was wrong, whatever it might have been, but rather in the departing from true Faith, which is always Christ and Him Crucified (I Cor. 1:23; 2:2). That and that alone is Satan's objective. That and that alone is his goal — forsake the Cross, i.e., *"the Faith"* (Gal. 2:20).

A FAILURE OF FAITH?

Did Abraham's Faith fail? Did Simon Peter's Faith fail regarding the denial of his Lord? Jesus said this of Peter: *"Simon, Simon, behold, Satan has desired to have you, that he may sift you as wheat.*

"But I have prayed for you, that your faith fail not" (Lk. 22:31-32).

Faith does not fail as long as Faith does not quit. While Abraham and Peter, and in fact, every other Believer who has ever lived, had a failure in their Faith, the truth is, their Faith didn't fail. Had their Faith failed, they would have quit. In other words, Abraham would have turned his back on God, and so would have Peter. But they didn't do that!

Faith at times stumbles and falls exactly as unbelief. But the difference is: unbelief stays down, while Faith gets up, and continues on its journey.

There is no such thing as a Believer who hasn't had a failure in his Faith. But one may rest assured that as long as one is believing, one's Faith has not failed. There's an old song that says:

"If you should get to Heaven, before I see that land,
"Listen to the Angels and join their singing band.
"And when you see my Master in the land of endless day,
"Just tell Him when you saw me, I was on my way."

(11) "AND IT CAME TO PASS, WHEN HE WAS COME NEAR TO ENTER INTO EGYPT, THAT HE SAID UNTO SARAI HIS WIFE, BEHOLD NOW, I KNOW THAT YOU ARE A FAIR WOMAN TO LOOK UPON:

(12) "THEREFORE IT SHALL COME TO PASS, WHEN THE EGYPTIANS SHALL SEE YOU, THAT THEY SHALL SAY, THIS IS HIS WIFE: AND THEY WILL KILL ME, BUT THEY WILL SAVE YOU ALIVE.

(13) "SAY, I PRAY YOU, YOU ARE MY SISTER: THAT IT MAY BE WELL WITH ME FOR YOUR SAKE; AND MY SOUL SHALL LIVE BECAUSE OF YOU."

The composition is:

1. Abraham in Egypt presents a repulsive picture of contemptible and abject cowardice.

2. To save himself, he denies his wife, and places her in the home of another man to be his wife.

3. Such is the deep depth to which the Christian readily falls directly when he leaves the path of faith.

EGYPT

Verse 11 reads: *"And it came to pass, when he was come near to enter into Egypt, that he said unto Sarai his wife, Behold now, I know that you are a fair woman to look upon."*

It is not possible to go into Egypt, spiritually speaking, without partaking of Egypt. The Christian who thinks that he can beat this game is only fooling himself. If we go into Egypt, we ultimately become like Egypt.

Much is at stake here, even the great Plan of Redemption. At this time, Sarah is about 65 years old, but yet a very beautiful woman. She would live to be 127 (Gen. 23:1).

Satan's plan was formidable. The entirety of faith on the Earth at this time, at least as far as we know, is wrapped up in Abraham. To be frank, in a sense, it is the same presently.

Faith, and we speak of Faith as it regards leadership, is now ensconced in *"Apostles, Prophets, Evangelists, Pastors, and Teachers"* (Eph. 4:11). Now remember, we are speaking of leadership. All Believers have Faith, but it is not Faith for leadership, that ensconced, as stated, in the fivefold Calling. If this breaks down, and we continue to speak of Faith leadership, then the entirety of the Church breaks down. And regrettably, that's exactly what has happened in the last few decades.

All Faith must be anchored in the Word of God, which in reality is the story of the Cross. To be particular, our Faith must ever have as its object the Cross of Christ (Rom. 6:3-11; I Cor. 1:17-18, 21, 23; 2:2, 5; Gal. 2:20-21; 6:14; Col. 2:14-15; I Pet. 1:18-20).

Satan's plan with Abraham was that he would leave Canaan as a result of the famine, which he did, go into Egypt, where the plan would then be set in motion for Pharaoh to impregnate Sarah, which was meant by the Evil One to thwart the coming of the Redeemer. It was quite a plan, and it almost succeeded. As stated, but for the intervening Hand of God, which we will study more in depth upon arriving at those Passages, it definitely would have succeeded.

THE EGYPTIANS

Verse 12 reads: *"Therefore it shall come to pass, when the Egyptians shall see you, that they shall say, This is his wife: and they will kill me, but they will save you alive."*

NOTES

• God had a plan: That plan was for Abraham and Sarah to bring a son into the world, through whom ultimately the Messiah, the Redeemer of the world would come.

• Satan had a plan: That plan was to foil the Plan of God, and to do so through the weakness of Abraham.

• Abraham had a plan: But Abraham's plan is not now the Plan of God, but is rather a plan of deception, which God can never honor.

DECEPTION

Verse 13 reads: *"Say, I pray you, you are my sister: that it may be well with me for your sake; and my soul shall live because of you."*

Concerning this, Matthew Henry said: *"Observe a great fault which Abraham was guilty of in denying his wife, and pretending that she was his sister. The Scripture is impartial in relating the miscarriages of the most celebrated Saints, which are recorded, not for our imitation, but for our admonition; that he who thinks he stands, may take heed lest he fall. His fault was, disassembling his relation to Sarah, equivocating concerning it, and teaching his wife, and, probably, all his attendants, to do so too, what he said about her being his sister, was in a sense true (Gen. 20:12), but with a purpose to deceive. He concealed a truth, so as in effect to deny it, and to expose thereby both his wife and the Egyptians to sin."*

By this deception, Abraham greatly placed in danger the entirety of the Plan of God. He seemed to think that the great Promise of God concerning *"his seed"* (Gen. 12:7), concerned him alone. In other words, as it regarded his thinking, Sarah didn't matter that much respecting the carrying out of this great prediction. He would merely obtain another woman, which showed up in him sinning regarding Hagar. In fact, the Lord would bluntly tell the Patriarch at a later time, *"As for Sarah your wife . . . I will bless her, and give you a son also of her . . . and she shall be a mother of nations; kings of people shall be of her"* (Gen. 17:15-16).

PRESUMPTION

Abraham erroneously thinks that by offering his wife to the harem of Pharaoh that he will save himself. He didn't seem to realize, at least at this time, that the Plan of God included Sarah, as much as it included him. Perhaps her being barren, not able to bear children, caused him to dismiss her in this capacity. But he was wrong, dead wrong!

All of this was presumption. The Patriarch merely presumed certain things, and because of an imperfect faith.

True Faith will never sell God short, and true Faith will never resort to the deceptive machinations of mere man. True Faith always reaches for the impossible, and will settle for nothing less than God's best. In fact, as it regards true Faith, it is either all or nothing! God would not condone any of the efforts of Abraham. It must be totally of God, or else it is not of Faith. Now let the Reader understand that:

Any time we mix our plans into the Plan of God, His Plan is instantly nullified. True Faith is always all God and none of man. While man is the instrument, it is God Who does the doing, with man intended to be obedient.

(14) "AND IT CAME TO PASS, THAT, WHEN ABRAM WAS COME INTO EGYPT, THE EGYPTIANS BEHELD THE WOMAN THAT SHE WAS VERY FAIR.

(15) "THE PRINCES ALSO OF PHARAOH SAW HER, AND COMMENDED HER BEFORE PHARAOH: AND THE WOMAN WAS TAKEN INTO PHARAOH'S HOUSE.

(16) "AND HE ENTREATED ABRAHAM WELL FOR HER SAKE: AND HE HAD SHEEP, AND OXEN, AND HE ASSES, AND MENSERVANTS, AND MAIDSERVANTS, AND SHE ASSES, AND CAMELS."

The construction is:

1. *"Pharaoh"* was the official title of the kings of Egypt.

2. The particular monarch who occupied the Egyptian throne at the time of Abraham's arrival is believed to have been Necao; with some thinking it may have been Ramessemenes.

3. Sarah is taken into Pharaoh's house in order that she might become the mother of a child by the Egyptian king, thus defeating the Messianic Promise made to Abraham.

4. The riches Abraham acquired in Egypt were nothing by comparison to the riches he stood to lose.

5. The Grace Abraham was most eminent for was Faith; yet he thus fell through unbelief and distrust of the Divine providence, even after God had appeared to him twice.

SARAH'S BEAUTY

Verse 14 reads: *"And it came to pass, that, when Abram was come into Egypt, the Egyptians beheld the woman that she was very fair."*

It is said by some that at this time, Egyptian custom demanded that any foreign Prince coming into Egypt would have to give into the harem of Pharaoh a daughter or a sister. This being done, it was supposed to guarantee the good behavior of such a one while in Egypt. Refusal to do such was considered to be an act of war.

So Abraham would claim that Sarah was his sister, which would make her acceptable for the harem of Pharaoh.

PHARAOH'S HOUSE

Verse 15 reads: *"The princes also of Pharaoh saw her, and commended her before Pharaoh: and the woman was taken into Pharaoh's house."*

Whatever was the custom of those particular times regarding the question at hand, the Text seems to indicate that there was much more to the situation regarding Sarah, than for her to merely become the member of a harem, which means that she was just one of many women.

The Text strongly implies that Pharaoh was looking for a particular woman, one whom he imagined to be of particular quality, who could be the mother of his child and, therefore, the heir to the throne of Egypt. This evidently was Satan's plan, devised to defeat the Promise of God, which would ultimately stop the coming of the Messiah into the world. Consequently, we can see how fully Abraham fell into the trap, which was well laid for him. Even though he was a man of Faith, in fact, one of the greatest men of Faith who has ever lived, still, his present position, strangely enough, is because of unbelief. Despite the famine, he should have remained in Canaan and trusted the Lord for deliverance. Resorting to Egypt is never without its compromise and attendant result.

A FAILURE OF FAITH

I think one can say without fear of Scriptural contradiction that every failure on the part of the Believer is always, in some way, a failure of faith. The criteria has always been, even beginning with Cain and Abel as recorded in Genesis, Chapter 4, that the object of one's Faith, which is always critically important, ever be the Cross of Christ. Regrettably, most modern Christians don't understand this.

When faith is addressed, most Christians merely think of such as faith in God, or faith in Christ, or faith in the Word, etc. While these statements are correct, at least as far as they go, they really don't say much. In fact, one's faith can be solid as it regards these aspects, but yet be unacceptable to God.

It is the object of faith which is so important! While having faith in God, or in Christ, or in the Word, is that which certainly must be done, if it stops there, it will prove to be of little consequence.

The entirety of the story of the Bible is the story of Redemption, and how it was brought about. It centers up on the Cross. It is the Cross which atoned for all sin. It is the Cross which made it possible for guilty man to enter into the very Presence of a thrice-Holy God. It is the Cross which made it possible for sinful man to be washed, sanctified, and justified (I Cor. 6:11).

THE FINISHED WORK

The entirety of the Plan of Salvation was wrapped up in the Words of Christ in His dying moments on the Cross, *"It is finished"* (Jn. 19:30).

This meant that the Plan of Redemption, which was conceived in the Mind of God from before the foundation of the world (I Pet. 1:18-20), was now totally and completely done. This is proven not only by the Words of Christ, which are sufficient within themselves, but as well by *"the Veil of the Temple being torn in twain from the top to the bottom,"* at the time of the death of Christ, which meant that the way to God for all of mankind, at least those who will believe, is now opened up (Mat. 27:51).

All of this means that if anyone stops short of the *"finished,"* or tends to go beyond the *"finished,"* they then nullify the great Plan of Redemption.

For those who would claim that it was the Resurrection which finished the Redemption plan, I would remind them again that God did not wait until the Resurrection of Christ to rent the Veil, but did so upon the death of Christ. In fact, the Resurrection of Christ was a foregone conclusion. Jesus atoned for all sin, past, present, and future. Considering that the wages of sin is death, had one sin been left unatoned, He could not have risen from the dead. The horror of death could have claimed Him forever. But due to fact that He atoned for all sin, this meant that death was defeated as well; consequently, His Resurrection, as stated, was a foregone conclusion. Due to the fact that all sin was atoned, Satan could not keep Him in the death world; consequently, the idea that the Resurrection was in doubt, or that something had to be done by Christ other than the Cross to ensure His Resurrection, holds no Scriptural validity whatsoever. To claim such is at the same time to disavow the *"finished"* aspect of the Sacrifice of Christ. Calvary did it all, which means that nothing else had to be done.

The Resurrection of Christ is certainly important, as is everything about Christ; however, concerning this, Paul didn't say, *"But God forbid that I should glory, save in the Resurrection of our Lord Jesus Christ . . .",* but rather, *"But God forbid that I should glory, save in the Cross of our Lord Jesus Christ"* (Gal. 6:14).

THE JESUS DIED SPIRITUALLY DOCTRINE

This is the reason that the *"Jesus died spiritually doctrine"* is so abominable! It claims that there are two aspects to Redemption, the Cross and Jesus suffering in Hell. In fact, as with all false doctrine, when embraced, the true and the right soon fall by the wayside, as the leaven takes its toll, with nothing ultimately left but leaven (Gal. 5:9).

While those who believe this doctrine claim to believe in the Cross, the truth is, they don't believe in the Cross. The object of their faith, which is the critical aspect, is in some imagined suffering of Jesus in the burning pit of

Hell, where He would be ultimately Born-Again. So, again as Paul said, *"The Cross of Christ is made of none effect"* by such action (I Cor. 1:17). He went on to say, *"Behold, I Paul say unto you, that if you be circumcised* (or believe any other doctrine other than Christ and Him Crucified), *Christ shall profit you nothing . . . Christ is become of no effect unto you . . . you are fallen from Grace"* (Gal. 5:2, 4).

The *"Jesus died spiritually doctrine,"* which is believed by many Charismatics, is an abominable doctrine. It is made up out of whole cloth, which means it has no Scriptural validity. Worse yet, it is an attack on the Atonement, which is the most serious offence of all. In effect, this doctrine disavows the Cross, the Blood, and the Sacrifice. While it claims not to do so, it, in effect, speaks out of both sides of its mouth.

While claiming to believe in the Blood and the Cross, it will at the same time say that this was not enough to atone, but that a second work was needed, which is now inserted by the figment of one's imagination. In other words, it's pure fiction.

This added ingredient claims that Jesus, in bearing the sin penalty on the Cross, actually became a sinner. While many who claim this doctrine would deny the latter aspect, it is impossible for it to be otherwise. If Jesus is going to be condemned to Hell, and there suffer the necessity of being Born-Again, as they claim, then He would have to become a sinner somewhere, and the only logical place, that is if such were true, is while He hung on the Cross.

Whether they admit it or not, in their teaching that Jesus died spiritually, they in effect are claiming that He took upon Himself the Satanic nature, thus becoming one with Satan, and as such, was condemned to Hell, and we speak of the burning side of the pit, to which all unredeemed are condemned. There, they say, He suffered for three days and nights the agony of Hell, being taunted by demon spirits, etc. In effect, they claim that it is this aspect, the burning in Hell for three days and nights, that effects one's Salvation.

They in effect state that what Jesus suffered on the Cross was not enough, and that the sojourn in the burning side of Hell had to be added in order for Him to atone for all sin.

Let us unequivocally say again that this is not in the Bible. In fact, there is nothing that even remotely resembles such found in the Bible. As stated, it is a figment of someone's imagination.

After burning and suffering for three days and nights, which they claim atoned for sin, God then said, *"It is enough,"* and Jesus was then *"born again,"* exactly as any sinner is Born-Again, etc.

Consequently, they have moved the emphasis from the Cross to Hell itself. As a result, the center of Scriptural gravity has been moved to another position altogether, which in effect abrogates the entirety of the Plan of God as carried out in the Bible. They have committed the sin of Cain (Gen., Chpt. 4).

Paul also said: *"Wherefore I give you to understand that no man speaking by the Spirit of God calls Jesus accursed"* (I Cor. 12:3).

The *"Jesus died spiritually doctrine"* claims that Jesus was accursed. There is no other way that it can be explained. If Jesus became a sinner on the Cross, or allowing whatever terminology they may desire to use, and then put in the burning side of Hell to suffer, one can only judge Him as cursed by God. But what does the Scripture say?

The Word of God doesn't say that Christ was cursed by God, but rather that He was *"made a curse for us,"* which is quite different (Gal. 3:13). Christ was made a curse for us, by bearing the sin penalty on the Cross, all on our behalf. He suffered the penalty of the broken Law, which was death. This was the curse He suffered. And He had to be *"made"* that, simply because there was no sin in Him.

Concerning the death of Christ, the Scripture plainly says: *"For Christ also has once suffered for sins, the just for the unjust, that He might bring us to God, being put to death in the flesh, but quickened by the Spirit"* (I Pet. 3:18).

This Passage plainly tells us that Christ died *"in the flesh,"* which means that He did not suffer a spiritual death, which would refer to dying without God. In other words, He did not die spiritually, but physically.

RICHES

Verse 16 reads: *"And he entreated Abram well for her sake: and he had sheep, and oxen,*

and he asses, and menservants, and maidservants, and she asses, and camels."

We find from this Passage that Pharaoh valued Sarah very highly. Even though she was approximately 65 years old, she evidently was beautiful to say the least. It is not unlikely at all that the Lord had a hand in this regarding her beauty, but most definitely which did not pertain to Pharaoh.

In this one Verse of Scripture, we have the position and problem of the modern Church. It, as Abraham at this time, has joined Egypt, and in fact, has been enriched; however, as there was no Altar, or Sacrifice, or Communion with God in Egypt, there is none now as it regards the Church and the world. While it may be able to boast of riches, it can little boast of power with God. Until Abraham went back to Canaan, and back to the Altar, revelation and communion with the Lord were stopped.

Revelation is found only at the Cross, and even then, it comes *"precept upon precept, precept upon precept; line upon line, line upon line; here a little, and there a little"* (Isa. 28:10).

The object of faith for much of the modern Church is riches; however, this is not faith that God will honor. In fact, He will only honor Faith with the Cross of Christ as its object (Rom. 4:25; 5:1-2; I Cor. 1:23; 2:2).

(17) "AND THE LORD PLAGUED PHARAOH AND HIS HOUSE WITH GREAT PLAGUES BECAUSE OF SARAI ABRAM'S WIFE.

(18) "AND PHARAOH CALLED ABRAM AND SAID, WHAT IS THIS THAT YOU HAVE DONE UNTO ME? WHY DID YOU NOT TELL ME THAT SHE WAS YOUR WIFE?

(19) "WHY SAID YOU, SHE IS MY SISTER? SO I MIGHT HAVE TAKEN HER TO ME TO WIFE: NOW THEREFORE BEHOLD YOUR WIFE, TAKE HER, AND GO YOUR WAY.

(20) "AND PHARAOH COMMANDED HIS MEN CONCERNING HIM: AND THEY SENT HIM AWAY, AND HIS WIFE, AND ALL THAT HE HAD."

The overview is:

1. In Canaan Abraham was a blessing. In the land of Egypt he is a curse.

2. In the path of faith the Christian is a blessing to the world, but in the path of self-will a curse.

3. Because of Abraham's wayward path, Pharaoh and his family are plagued with great plagues, and this heathen prince hurries this man of God out of his land as he would chase away a pestilence.

PLAGUE

Verse 17 reads: *"And the LORD plagued Pharaoh and his house with great plagues because of Sarai Abram's wife."*

Concerning this, Matthew Henry said: *"Let us notice the danger Sarah was in, and her deliverance from this danger. If God did not deliver us, many a time, out of those straits and distresses which we bring ourselves into, by our own sin and folly, and which therefore we could not expect any deliverance, we should soon be ruined; nay, we had been ruined long before this. He deals not with us according to our desserts."*

In what manner Pharaoh came to know that the plagues falling on his house were because of Sarah, we aren't told.

Sarah was blameless in this, the fault being that of Abraham. From this Passage, we learn that the Believer can be a blessing or a curse; it all depends upon his faith, and at this time, Abraham was faithless, or he wouldn't have been there to begin with.

The cause of all problems is the Believer leaving the Cross, and the solution to all problems is the Believer going back to the Cross. When Abraham left Canaan to go to Egypt, he left the Altar (Gen. 12:8). When he went back to Canaan, he went back to the Altar (Gen. 13:4). It is always the Cross, of which the Altar is but a Type.

WHAT HAVE YOU DONE UNTO ME?

Verse 18 reads: *"And Pharaoh called Abram and said, What is this that you have done unto me? Why did you not tell me that she was your wife?"*

Abraham had told those who were representing Pharaoh that Sarah was his sister. In fact, this was a half-truth. She was the daughter of his father, but not the daughter of his mother (Gen. 20:12). But because he intended to deceive, God looked at this episode as a *"lie."*

As a Child of God, even a man of Faith, and that despite his present situation, it lay

NOTES

within the power of Abraham to be a blessing or a curse. However, the curse comes only because of wrongdoing on the part of the Believer. It is not possible for a Believer to knowingly and willingly put a curse on anyone. Such activity is always of Satan; however, the Believer will definitely be a curse, if his faith is in the wrong place, even as Abraham.

As we've already stated, in the path of Faith the Christian is a blessing to the world, but in the path of self-will a curse.

QUESTIONS

Verse 19 reads: *"Why said you, She is my sister? So I might have taken her to me to wife: now therefore behold your wife, take her, and go your way."*

Pharaoh had three questions for Abraham:

1. What is this that you have done to me?

2. Why did you not tell me that she was your wife?

3. Why said you, she is my sister?

At this time, Egypt was at least one of the most powerful nations in the world, which means that Pharaoh was one of the most powerful men in the world. Little did he realize the magnitude of these questions.

As he speaks this day to Abraham, little does he know, despite Abraham's present problems, that this is the man the Holy Spirit would refer to as *"the father of us all"* (Rom. 4:16). And yet, the picture that he would get of the Patriarch would be one of subterfuge, chicanery, and deception.

But before we criticize Abraham, we had best look at ourselves. Are we in the path of faith, or that of self-will? According to that answer, we will be a blessing or a curse!

DEPARTURE

Verse 20 reads: *"And Pharaoh commanded his men concerning him: and they sent him away, and his wife, and all that he had."*

Because of Abraham, Pharaoh and his family are plagued with great plagues, and this heathen prince hurries this man of God out of his land as he would chase away a pestilence (Williams).

The implication here is, even though the monarch was very unhappy concerning the turn of events, he knew within his spirit that this man Abraham was more than meets the eye. With anyone else, he would, no doubt, have taken off their head; however, with Abraham, the implication is that he was careful not to do anything to him, or even retrieve the animals which he had given to the Patriarch.

From the Scripture, we're given the bare bones of what actually took place. The mighty Pharaoh saw the Power of God, even though it was in a negative way. What effect it had on him, other than this which we see in the Scripture, we aren't told.

"Down at the Cross where my Saviour died,
"Down where for cleansing from sin I cried,
"There to my heart was the Blood applied;
"Glory to His Name!"

"I am so wondrously saved from sin;
"Jesus so sweetly abides within;
"There at the Cross where He took me in;
"Glory to His Name!"

"Oh, precious fountain that saves from sin!
"I am so glad I have entered in;
"There Jesus saves me and keeps me clean;
"Glory to His Name!"

"Come to this fountain so rich and sweet;
"Cast thy poor soul at the Saviour's Feet;
"Plunge in today and be made complete;
"Glory to His Name!"

CHAPTER 13

(1) "AND ABRAM WENT UP OUT OF EGYPT, HE, AND HIS WIFE, AND ALL THAT HE HAD, AND LOT WITH HIM, INTO THE SOUTH.

(2) "AND ABRAM WAS VERY RICH IN CATTLE, AND SILVER, AND IN GOLD.

(3) "AND HE WENT ON HIS JOURNEYS FROM THE SOUTH EVEN TO BETHEL, UNTO THE PLACE WHERE HIS TENT

NOTES

HAD BEEN AT THE BEGINNING, BETWEEN BETH-EL AND HAI;

(4) "UNTO THE PLACE OF THE ALTAR, WHICH HE HAD MADE THERE AT THE FIRST: AND THERE ABRAM CALLED ON THE NAME OF THE LORD."

The synopsis is:

1. If Abraham went *"down"* into Egypt in Chapter 12, Verse 10, Grace brings him *"up"* out of Egypt in Chapter 13, Verse 1.

2. He went back to the mountaintop where his tent had been at the beginning, *"unto the place of the Altar which he had made there at the first,"* and there, doubtless with tears and shame, he called by Sacrifice on the Name of the Lord.

3. His backslidings were forgiven, his soul was restored, and he resumes his true life as a pilgrim and a worshipper with his tent and his Altar; neither of which he had in Egypt (Williams).

4. In all of this we learn God's Way of Restoration, and God's manner of restoration.

UP

Verse 1 reads: *"And Abram went up out of Egypt, he, and his wife, and all that he had, and Lot with him, into the South."*

Even though the little word *"up,"* refers here to a geographical setting, in this case north, it has a spiritual connotation as well. To go to Egypt, Abraham had to go *"down,"* which as well, even though geographical, presented a spiritual direction also. Whichever way we go as Believers, it is always either *"up"* or *"down."* So the question we must ask ourselves is, *"What direction am I traveling?"* Once again we come back to Faith.

To go *"down"* into Egypt, he did so because of a lapse in faith. To come *"up"* out of Egypt, Faith is now regained, and will be proven by the Altar once again coming into view.

But yet, considering that Lot was with him, Abraham has not fully made the second surrender of leaving his kindred, and his father's house, even as the Lord had demanded (Gen. 12:1). That surrender would come shortly.

RICH

Verse 2 reads: *"And Abram was very rich in cattle, and silver, and in gold."*

Much of the Charismatic world has centered up on this one particular Verse of Scripture. In fact, their gospel, which in reality is *"another gospel,"* has money as its center of gravity (II Cor. 11:4). Some of their Preachers claim that their calling is to tell Christians how to get rich.

Sometime back, I happened to catch a television program featuring one of their premiere Preachers. His subject was Abraham.

He went on to state that the Blessing of Abraham, which Paul mentioned in Galatians 3:14, had nothing to do with Salvation, but rather with money. Pointedly he said, *"The Blessing of Abraham is money."*

It's the only time I can recall finding myself standing in front of the television set screaming at what I was hearing coming forth from the box.

The truth of all of this thing is, this particular *"another gospel"* is pure and simple a scam. The only ones getting rich are the Preachers. But there seems to be enough greed in all of us to keep this *"lie"* going.

While the Lord definitely does take care of His people, and does so in a grand way, Jesus didn't come down here to die on a Cross in order for people to be rich, but rather for people to be Saved. Sin is man's problem, not lack of money. And it's the Cross Alone which addresses the horrible sickness of sin.

While the Lord definitely does bless, and while He does make some rich, even as Abraham, all of this is a side issue as it regards the Gospel. The True Gospel of Jesus Christ is, as the song says, *"Victory over sin and purity within."* The Holy Spirit desires to make us Christlike, and does so by the means of the Fruit of the Spirit. But yet, somebody has rightly said the following:

"It's not what you would do with riches
"Should money ere be your lot;
"But what you're doing at present,
"With the dollar and a quarter you've
　got."

RESTORATION

Verse 3 reads: *"And he went on his journeys from the south even to Beth-el, unto the place where his tent had been at the beginning, between Beth-el and Hai."*

We learn from this the true character of Divine restoration. The first thing we must learn about this is that God does everything in a way entirely worthy of Himself. Whether He creates, redeems, converts, restores, or provides, He can only act like Himself. What is worthy of Himself is, ever and only, His standard of action.

Now the problem of humanity, even redeemed man, is to *"limit the Holy One of Israel."* Mackintosh says, *"And in nothing are we so prone to limit Him as in His restoring Grace."*

From the cowardly escapade in Egypt, Abraham is brought back to where his tent had been *"at the beginning"* . . . unto the place of the Altar which he had made there *"at the first."*

Mackintosh went on to say, *"We, in the self-righteousness of our hearts, might imagine that such an one should take a lower place than that which he had formerly occupied; and so he should, were it a question of his merit or his character; but inasmuch as it is altogether a question of Grace, it is God's prerogative to fix the standard of restoration."*

Mackintosh further said, *"He will either not restore at all, or else restore in such a way as to magnify and glorify the riches of His Grace. Thus, when the leper was brought back, he was actually conducted 'to the door of the Tabernacle of the congregation;' when the prodigal returned, he was set down at the table with his father; when Peter was restored, he was able to stand before the men of Israel and say, 'You denied the Holy One and the Just' — the very thing which he had done himself, under the most aggravated circumstances."*

The idea is, when God brings the soul back to Himself, it is always in the full power of Grace, and the full confidence of Faith.

HINDRANCES TO RESTORATION

The two greatest hindrances to restoration are *"legalism"* and *"license."* Strangely enough, these twin problems prove at the same time to be the greatest danger to the one restored.

It is impossible to restore the soul through legalism, and yet that's where most of the

Church places its efforts. This pertains to the rules of men, rather than the Cross of Christ.

Or else, restoration is looked at in a light way, concluding that sin is of little matter, which pertains to license. If Grace abounds much more than sin, and it definitely does, then we might continue to sin that Grace may abound, some conclude (Rom. 5:20; 6:1).

Continuing with the problem of license, we are not restored in order that we may the more lightly go and sin again, but rather that we may *"go and sin no more."* Mackintosh goes on to say, *"The deeper my sense of the Grace of Divine restoration, the deeper will be my sense of the Holiness of it also."*

Concerning this, David said, *"He restoreth my soul: He leads me in the paths of Righteousness for His Name's sake"* (Ps. 23:3).

John said, and dealing with the same problem, *"If we confess our sins, He is faithful and just to forgive us our sins, and to cleanse us from all unrighteousness"* (I Jn. 1:9).

The proper path for a Divinely-restored soul is *"the path of Righteousness."* To talk of Grace while walking in unrighteousness is, as the Apostle says, to turn *"the Grace of our God into lasciviousness."*

Mackintosh continues, *"If Grace reigns through Righteousness unto eternal life, it also manifests itself in Righteousness, in the outflow of that life. The Grace that forgives us our sins cleanses us from all unrighteousness. Those things must never be separated. When taken together, they furnish a triumphant answer to the legalism and the license of the human heart."*

But possibly an even greater problem than the problem of *"license,"* is the problem of *"legalism."* In simple terms, this is the formulation of laws, rules, and regulations, all made up by men, with the claim that abiding according to such guarantees Righteousness and Holiness, etc. It doesn't!

The greatest example of this was the *"Law of God"* given to Moses, and thereby to Israel. These were Laws designed by God, and which fit the human problem in every capacity. But despite their simplicity, men could not keep them, and because of the fallen nature.

However, Israel turned the effort into a form of Righteousness, better known as self-righteousness. In other words, all of the

efforts at Law-keeping made her feel holy. As someone has said, the *"doing of religion is the biggest narcotic there is."*

Notice that we said *"the doing of religion!"* All of this has to do with legalism. Legalism is always *"doing,"* while Grace pertains to that which is *"done."*

So, men make up rules, and demand that other men live by them, and religious men do this more than all. It is claimed that the doing of such makes one acceptable. But of course, the acceptance is in the eyes of other men, and never in the Eyes of God. He cannot accept legalism in any capacity. Paul plainly said, and bluntly so: *"If you be circumcised, Christ shall profit you nothing."*

He then said, *"Christ is become of no effect unto you, whosoever of you are justified by the Law; you are fallen from Grace"* (Gal. 5:2, 4). I don't know how much clearer it could be.

THE RESTORATION METHODS OF THE MODERN CHURCH

In fact, restoration, as it regards the modern Church, is in name only. There is no restoration. Whenever we forsake the Bible, and begin to devise our own ways, the results, as it regards spiritual things, are always catastrophic. God has a way that's found in His Word, and in His Word only, and if we depart from that, we are then left with the foolishness of man, and foolishness it is.

For instance, in one particular Pentecostal Denomination, if a Preacher has a problem of any nature, he is forbidden to preach behind a pulpit in any Church of that Denomination, for a period of two years. He may preach in jails, prisons, nursing homes, and on street corners, and even preach to children or teens, but he cannot preach behind the pulpit in the main Sanctuary. How ridiculous can we be!

If it's wrong to preach one place, then it's wrong to preach any place. But when man starts to make the rules, thereby forsaking the Word of God, as stated, it becomes more and more ludicrous.

And about all of these Denominations, at least the ones of which I am aware, demand from six months to two years of psychological counseling. Pure and simple, this is a joke! The world of psychology holds absolutely no answers whatsoever to the spiritual needs of man. For anyone to think it does only portrays, in a glaring way, one's spiritual and Scriptural ignorance. I don't mean to be unkind or sarcastic, but I don't know any other way to state the case. When the Church resorts to the likes of Freud to solve its spiritual problems, thereby forsaking the Word of God, it is in serious trouble indeed!

To which we've already alluded, Biblical Restoration is very simple. The reason anyone fails is because they have shifted their faith, whether they realize it or not, from the Cross to other things. Consequently, such a person is to be pointed back to the Cross. Listen to what Paul said:

"*But God forbid that I should glory* (boast), *save in the Cross of our Lord Jesus Christ, by Whom the world is crucified unto me, and I unto the world*" (Gal. 6:14).

Now notice that the Apostle said that the only way to victory over the world, and one might quickly add, "*the world, the flesh, and the Devil,*" is by trusting in what Christ has done for us at the Cross. That is the only solution to any and every problem.

To point anyone in that direction, and I speak of the direction of the Cross, is the only true Restoration there actually is (Gal. 6:1).

ENEMIES OF THE CROSS

Paul also said, "*For many walk, of whom I have told you often, and now tell you even weeping, that they are the enemies of the Cross of Christ:*

"*Whose end is destruction, whose God is their belly, and whose glory is in their shame, who mind earthly things*" (Phil. 3:18-19).

To present to the sinner seeking to be saved anything except the Cross, simply means that the one doing such a thing is an enemy of the Cross.

For the ways of the world to be substituted for those who need restoration in place of the Cross, once again means that those who do such things can be labeled as none other than enemies of the Cross.

When Jesus said that this way was a "*narrow way,*" He meant exactly what He said (Mat. 7:14). In fact, the exact width of this "*way*" which leads to glory is the width of the Cross.

NOTES

If we as Believers point people in any direction other than the Cross, we have to be labeled as none other than an "*enemy of the Cross.*" The Cross is not something which is neutral. As well, it's not one of several ways. It is the only way; therefore, it stands to reason if other ways are presented, that means the Cross has been rejected, which places such a one in the position of being an "*enemy.*"

When the Lord first began to open up to me the Revelation of the Cross, which began in 1996, my immediate thoughts concerning the far greater majority of the Church, and as it regards the Cross, were that ignorance was the culprit. While I'm sure that ignorance is the problem in many hearts and lives, I have since come to the conclusion that the major problem is unbelief.

A PERSONAL EXAMPLE

A Preacher of my acquaintance had a problem a short time ago. Even though I knew him, it was only at a distance.

He happened to be in town (Baton Rouge), and had the occasion to be on our daily Telecast, "*A Study In The Word*". We were teaching on the Cross, actually the Sixth Chapter of Romans.

He was very kind and cordial; however, it quickly became obvious to me that he was not in agreement with what we were teaching.

Now the truth is, the Lord placed him in that particular position that he might hear the Truth, and thereby avoid what was just ahead. But he rejected what he heard, and a very short time later, met with disastrous consequences.

How could anyone reject the Cross? That's a good question!

With preachers, oftentimes it is pride. They are loath to admit that they don't have it all together, so their first reaction is to reject that which they do not presently have, irrespective of its obvious Scripturality.

And then again, many people will reject the Message simply because they don't like the Messenger. As we stated some pages back, were Abraham to have been brought up to the present time, many modern Christians would feel that the debacle in Egypt would have demanded that he step down from his position, whatever that was, and take a lowered or lesser place. And in the meantime, his Message of Justification by Faith would be rejected also.

Now if you will think about that for a moment, the whole situation becomes crystal clear. In effect, the modern Church is rejecting Justification by Faith, and simply because this great blessing cannot come to anyone except through the Cross. They don't like the Messenger, and I speak of myself, so they will reject the Message. Fortunately or unfortunately, whichever way one wants to behold this spectacle, the Lord doesn't ask the permission of the Church as to whom He sends. Consequently, read the following very carefully:

Truth rejected is a lie believed, and more than likely, the individual doing the rejecting will not have another opportunity. It's not that God closes the door to such a person, but that they close it upon themselves.

We have the Holy Spirit bringing about a series of events so the Preacher in question could hear the Truth, but the Holy Spirit, despite the Truth being offered, couldn't make the individual believe the Truth. Therefore, the catastrophe was not avoided.

Even after the problem was made known, I sent for the Brother, knowing that I could help him, if he only would allow me to do so. He refused to come! Where is he now? I don't know; however, even though I pray that his situation will improve, I know in my heart that if he keeps rejecting the Truth, it will be impossible for it to improve. Now please read the following statement very carefully:

It doesn't matter who the person is. It doesn't matter if he's a Preacher and pastors the largest Church in the world, or an Evangelist drawing the largest crowds. If he doesn't understand the Message of the Cross, it is totally and completely impossible for him to live a victorious life. It simply cannot be done. Paul said it very succinctly:

"I am crucified with Christ, nevertheless I live; yet not I, but Christ lives in me: and the life which I now live in the flesh I live by the faith of the Son of God, Who loved me, and gave Himself for me.

"I do not frustrate the Grace of God: for if Righteousness come by the Law, then Christ is dead in vain" (Gal. 2:20-21).

NOTES

Plainly and clearly the Apostle states, *"For if Righteousness come by the Law, then Christ is dead in vain."* This means, as should be obvious, that if man could live a victorious life other than by Faith in Christ and what Christ did at the Cross, then Christ needlessly came down here to die on that Cross. But the truth is, Righteousness cannot come by any method other than Christ and what He did at the Cross, and our Faith in that Finished Work. That's why Paul referred to it as *"the faith."*

THE ALTAR

Verse 4 reads: *"Unto the place of the Altar, which he had made there at the first: and there Abram called on the Name of the LORD."*

Here we have it in black and white. When Abraham was walking in victory, his trust, Faith, and confidence were totally and completely in the Cross (Gen. 12:7). And now Abraham, coming from a place of defeat back to victory, must come back to the Altar. There is no other way!

The Scripture plainly says that Abraham *"called on the Name of the Lord."* One cannot do this, unless it is done in the spirit of the Cross. We must ever understand that every single thing we receive from the Lord comes to us exclusively by and through Christ, and what He has done for us at the Cross. So when we call on Him, it must be with the idea in mind, regarding the price that He paid at Calvary. Prayer is answered only on that basis, and that basis alone! (I Cor. 1:17-18, 23).

VICTORY

I want to make a statement; although very simple, it could very well be one of the most important statements you've ever read, as it regards our living for God. It is as follows:

"God cannot give victories to sinful men. He can only give victories to His Son and our Lord and Saviour, Jesus Christ."

The idea is, the Lord has given total victory, and in every capacity, to the Lord Jesus Christ. In other words, it's already been done. It was done at the Cross. Therefore, whatever victory or victories we might obtain must come exclusively through Him, which demands our Faith in Him, and in what He has done for us.

We must understand that everything Christ did was exclusively for us. He did nothing for Himself! He did nothing for Heaven! He did nothing for Angels! He did nothing for God, simply because God needs nothing. So what He did, and in all its capacity, was done exclusively for you and me.

As well, He paid a terrible price for all that He did. And considering the price that He paid, doesn't it stand to reason that He would want us to have all for which He died? Of course He does! So if we don't have these victories, the fault is ours and not His. That should be understandable from the beginning.

In one way or the other, the whole world, at least for all practical purposes, is calling on the Name of the Lord; however, almost none call on Him correctly. In other words, they call on Him in ways other than the means of the Cross.

That particular Jesus, God will not recognize or honor. Paul referred to such as *"another Jesus"* (II Cor. 11:4). And regrettably, that's where much of the modern Church world presently is. Pure and simple, they are worshiping *"another Jesus."*

(5) "AND LOT ALSO, WHICH WENT WITH ABRAM, HAD FLOCKS, AND HERDS, AND TENTS.

(6) "AND THE LAND WAS NOT ABLE TO BEAR THEM, THAT THEY MIGHT DWELL TOGETHER: FOR THEIR SUBSTANCE WAS GREAT, SO THAT THEY COULD NOT DWELL TOGETHER.

(7) "AND THERE WAS A STRIFE BETWEEN THE HERDMEN OF ABRAM'S CATTLE AND THE HERDMEN OF LOT'S CATTLE: AND THE CANAANITE AND THE PERIZZITE DWELLED THEN IN THE LAND."

The diagram is:

1. Lot was rich, but he wasn't consecrated to the Lord.

2. Worldly substance generally causes problems, even as it did here.

3. There was strife in the Church. In fact, the *"Church"* of that day consisted of the families of Abraham and Lot, at least as far as we know.

LOT

Verse 5 reads: *"And Lot also, which went with Abram, had flocks, and herds, and tents."*

NOTES

As we shall see, the riches seemed to turn Lot's head; however, it didn't have that effect upon Abraham.

It is really never the riches which are at fault, but rather the individual involved. Why is it that Lot would allow such to turn his head from the Lord, even as it does millions today, and it had no such effect on Abraham?

Too oftentimes the Church deals only with the symptom, instead of the real problem. The failure is actually the symptom, whatever the failure might be, but it's not actually the real problem. In fact, it never is!

The Church, for all practical purposes, has borrowed this thinking from the world of humanistic psychology. This nefarious system teaches that man's problem is environment, lack of education, or that which is hereditary. So they think if they can address these issues, man's problem will be solved.

It won't! These are all outward or exterior situations which have no bearing on what the real problem actually is.

The problem is sin, and we must ever understand that sin comes in many and varied forms. The only cure for sin is Christ and the Cross. But instead, we attack the symptom, instead of addressing the real problem. That's the reason that Jesus said:

"You shall know the Truth, and the Truth shall make you free" (Jn. 8:32). Man's problem is, and that includes the Church, he believes a lie. Pure and simple that's the problem.

What is the truth?

The Truth is Christ and what he did for us at the Cross. Listen to what He said:

"I am the Way, the Truth, and the Life: no man comes unto the Father, but by Me" (Jn. 14:6).

He then said: *"And I, if I be lifted up from the Earth, will draw all men unto Me"* (Jn. 12:32).

Being *"lifted up"* spoke of the death that He would die on the Cross. As well, the only way that we can draw men to victory is to draw them to Christ and the Cross. If we attempt to draw them in any other manner, we will draw them to that other than the Lord. And that's what the majority of the modern Church is doing. It's drawing men to Denominations, to Preachers, to the promises of great riches, to all type of things. But it's not drawing men to Christ.

DWELL TOGETHER?

Verse 6 reads: *"And the land was not able to bear them, that they might dwell together: for their substance was great, so that they could not dwell together."*

Abraham had been told by the Lord to leave his kindred (Gen. 12:1). But he brought his kindred with him. It seems that his father Terah slowed him down in his obedience, until death took Terah out of the way: Lot followed him on further, but it seems plain that Lot was, from the very beginning, borne onward rather by Abraham's influence and example, than by his own faith in God. In other words, it seems that Lot functioned on borrowed faith.

It does seem, however, that he made it at last, inasmuch as the Holy Spirit through Peter referred to him as *"that righteous man,"* and *"his righteous soul"* (II Pet. 2:7-8).

In no way do I want to demean Lot, but at the same time, we must not overrate him.

As we've already stated, Abraham and Lot and their families actually constituted the Church of that particular day and time. While this *"Church"* had its problems in the spiritual sense, at the same time it had been blessed abundantly in a financial sense. Please allow me to make this statement:

We preach a prosperity Gospel, but we do not preach a greed gospel. They are two different things. We believe that the Lord blesses and blesses abundantly. We believe that when a person comes to Christ, their entire situation, including the finances, begins to improve. I believe that financial prosperity is just as much a part of the Gospel as Divine Healing. I believe we should preach that, because the Bible teaches that (II Cor. 9:6).

But the primary mission of the Church is not monetary enrichment. The primary purpose of the Church in Abraham's day was certainly not enrichment, even though God abundantly blessed the Patriarch, with Lot *"getting in on"* the blessing. The primary purpose of the Church was the Plan of Redemption, which would be brought about by God becoming man, and dying on the Cross of Calvary. Abraham was to play a tremendous

part in all of this, and that was his mission. The Lord would show the Patriarch the great Doctrine of Justification by Faith (Gen. 15:6). He was to understand what that meant, and more particularly, to Whom it pointed, namely Christ. This was the mission, and nothing else!

I'm afraid that the modern Church has forgotten its mission. In the hearts and lives of far too many, the idea is not Righteousness but rather Rolexes. The idea is not Salvation, but rather secular pleasure. The idea is not the true Moving and Operation of the Holy Spirit, but rather entertainment. The idea is not Holiness, but rather Heaven on Earth.

The *"substance"* of the modern Church is *"great."* It no longer has to say *"Silver and gold have I none."* But the sad fact is, no longer, as well, can it say, *"But such as I have give I thee: in the Name of Jesus Christ of Nazareth rise up and walk"* (Acts 3:6).

STRIFE

Verse 7 reads: *"And there was a strife between the herdmen of Abram's cattle and the herdmen of Lot's cattle: and the Canaanite and the Perizzite dwelled then in the land."*

The outward cause of Lot's foray into Sodom was the strife between his herdmen and those of Abraham. But the fact is, when one is not really walking as one should walk, something will occasion his stumbling. The outward cause is merely the trigger, while the real problem lies elsewhere.

To Abraham, the strife between the herdmen, as distasteful as it was, afforded an occasion for exhibiting the beautiful power of Faith, and the moral elevation on which Faith ever sets the possessor thereof. Mackintosh said, *"However, the strife no more produced the worldliness in Lot than it produced the faith in Abraham; it only manifested, in the case of each, what was really there."*

He then went on to say: *"Thus it is always: controversies and divisions arise in the Church, and many stumble thereby, and are driven back into the world in one way or another. They then lay the blame on the controversy and division, whereas the truth is, that these things were only the means of developing the real condition of the soul, and the bent of the heart. The world was in the heart, and would be reached by some route or another."*

THE CANAANITE AND THE PERIZZITE

The Holy Spirit made mention of these two heathen tribes for a purpose and reason. The idea is, whatever happened between Abraham and Lot was observed by these who knew not God. And the question is, what did they see?

They saw in Abraham a beautiful and gracious spirit. And to be sure, events and circumstances, especially those which are negative, always tend to bring out what is in the spirit of the man. An outward show is one thing; however, pressure reveals what the container really holds.

What did they see in Lot? The details we aren't given; however, I think it is obvious that the spirit of Lot in no way resembled that of Abraham. As we have already stated, Lot, it seems, was functioning on borrowed faith. Regrettably, that is the condition of much of the modern Church presently. It has little faith of its own, but rather borrows from someone else who genuinely has Faith, or else is thought to have faith. Unfortunately, the latter is the situation in most cases. The one being followed has no faith either.

FAITH

The Faith of which we constantly speak, and will continue to do so, is an anchored Faith in the Cross of Christ, i.e., *"the Finished Work of Christ"* (Rom. 6:3-14; 8:1-2, 11; I Cor. 1:17-18, 23; 2:2; Col. 2:14-15). Faith that's not anchored solidly in the Sacrifice of Christ is faith that God will not recognize. In fact, such faith always falls into the category of that possessed by Lot. It doesn't matter whether it's borrowed faith, or whether it's faith in the wrong object; the *"strife"* will always show it up for what it really is. As we've stated, the strife is only the outward symptom, while the real cause is the wrong kind of faith. What is it that the world sees in us presently?

It is ironic that most of the world observes the antics which take place under the guise of Christianity, and automatically know that it's wrong, while at the same time,

most in the Church don't seem to know. How? Why?

This whole debacle, and I speak of the modern greed gospel, or outright erroneous directions, stems from the wrong kind of faith. And to be sure, this wrong type of faith mostly comes under the heading of unbelief rather than ignorance. And that is the greatest tragedy of all!

(8) "AND ABRAM SAID UNTO LOT, LET THERE BE NO STRIFE, I PRAY THEE, BETWEEN ME AND YOU, AND BETWEEN MY HERDMEN AND YOUR HERDMEN: FOR WE BE BRETHREN.

(9) "IS NOT THE WHOLE LAND BEFORE YOU? SEPARATE YOURSELF, I PRAY YOU, FROM ME: IF YOU WILL TAKE THE LEFT HAND, THEN I WILL GO TO THE RIGHT; OR IF YOU DEPART TO THE RIGHT HAND, THEN I WILL GO TO THE LEFT."

The structure is:

1. Abraham sets about to settle the strife.

2. He gives Lot his choice, but lets God choose for him.

3. This is what Faith ever does: it allows God to fix its inheritance, as it always allows Him to make it good.

BRETHREN

Verse 8 reads: *"And Abram said unto Lot, Let there be no strife, I pray you, between me and you, and between my herdmen and your herdmen: for we be brethren."*

Abraham reminding Lot that they were *"Brethren,"* proclaims the fact that the strife had gone beyond the herdmen, and was in Lot's heart as well. The bent toward Sodom is now beginning to exert itself. It demands its *"rights,"* which demands to be able to choose for itself, which at the same time means that it does not trust God to make the choice. This is very important as it regards the Child of God. Do we chart the course, or do we allow God to chart the course? Regrettably, there was contention in the Church of that time, but the contention was only in the heart of Lot; it wasn't in the heart of Abraham.

THE PEACEMAKER

Verse 9 reads: *"Is not the whole land before you? Separate yourself, I pray you, from me: if you will take the left hand, then I will go to the right; or if you will depart to the right hand, then I will go to the left."*

Everything that faces the Child of God, and in whatever capacity, is a test. This was a test for both Abraham and Lot. Lot didn't fare very well, and in fact, his choice would lead to his ultimate ruin.

Mackintosh says: *"Why did not Abraham make the choice of Sodom? Why did not the strife drive him into the world? Why was it not an occasion of stumbling to him?"*

He answers, *"Because he looked at it from God's point of view. No doubt he had a heart that could be attracted by 'well-watered plains' just as powerfully as Lot's heart, but then he did not allow his own heart to choose. He first let Lot take his choice, and then left God to choose for him. This was Heavenly wisdom. This is what faith ever does: it allows God to fix its inheritance, as it also allows Him to make it good. It is always satisfied with the portion which God gives. It can say, 'The lines are fallen to me in pleasant places; yes, I have a goodly heritage.' It matters not where 'the lines' fall; for, in the judgment of faith, they always fall 'in pleasant places,' just because God casts them there."*

Mackintosh continues: *"The man of faith can easily afford to allow the man of sight to take his choice. He can say, 'If you will take the left hand, then I will go to the right; or if you depart to the right hand, then I will go the left.'"*

(10) "AND LOT LIFTED UP HIS EYES, AND BEHELD ALL THE PLAIN OF JORDAN, THAT IT WAS WELL WATERED EVERYWHERE, BEFORE THE LORD DESTROYED SODOM AND GOMORRAH, EVEN AS THE GARDEN OF THE LORD, LIKE THE LAND OF EGYPT, AS YOU COME UNTO ZOAR.

(11) "THEN LOT CHOSE HIM ALL THE PLAIN OF JORDAN; AND LOT JOURNEYED EAST: AND THEY SEPARATED THEMSELVES THE ONE FROM THE OTHER.

(12) "ABRAM DWELLED IN THE LAND OF CANAAN, AND LOT DWELLED IN THE CITIES OF THE PLAIN, AND PITCHED HIS TENT TOWARD SODOM.

(13) "BUT THE MEN OF SODOM WERE WICKED AND SINNERS BEFORE THE LORD EXCEEDINGLY."

The exegesis is:

1. Lot chooses the plain of Jordan, though well knowing the character of the men of Sodom.

2. He lifts up his eyes, and noticing how the plain resembled the land of Egypt, he chooses him that fertile vale, separates himself from God's acknowledged King and Priest, and pitches his tent *"towards Sodom."*

3. His borrowed faith fails, as all borrowed faith sooner or later fails.

THE PLAIN OF JORDAN

Verse 10 reads: *"And Lot lifted up his eyes, and beheld all the plain of Jordan, that it was well watered everywhere, before the LORD destroyed Sodom and Gomorrah, even as the Garden of the LORD, like the land of Egypt, as you come into Zoar."*

Given his choice, what did Lot choose? As stated, everything with the Child of God is always in the form of a test. What will you choose?

He chose Sodom, incidentally, a place which was about to be judged by God, and judged so severely, that there is no trace of it left. That should be a lesson to all of us.

If we choose wrong, and I continue to speak of our life being lived for the Lord, the consequences are never good.

Why select such a spot, as did Lot regarding the plain of Jordan, which was toward Sodom?

It was because he looked at the outward appearance, and not at the intrinsic character and future destiny. The intrinsic character was *"wicked"*; its future destiny was *"judgment"* — to be destroyed by fire and brimstone out of Heaven.

Of course, one could counter by saying that Lot knew none of this. That is correct, and more than likely, Abraham had no knowledge of this sort either. But God knew, and had Lot allowed God to *"choose for him,"* even as did Abraham, the Lord, to be sure, would not have chosen a spot that He Himself was about to destroy. The truth is, Sodom suited Lot, though it did not suit God.

This entire episode presents a perfect picture and as well a perfect example of what happens to the Believer when he allows his senses, i.e., *"the flesh,"* to choose for him.

Outwardly, this looked like the place of prosperity, even though, admittedly, Sodom was a wicked place.

But Lot didn't see the wickedness of Sodom; he only saw the *"well watered plains."* He saw the outward, not the inward.

How many modern Christians are making the same choice presently? How many truly seek the Face of the Lord as it regards direction? How many only assume?

Woe is the Believer who makes his own choices, and is not led by the Lord. And woe is the Believer who thinks he's being led by the Lord, but in reality is being led by something else altogether!

SEPARATION

Verse 11 reads: *"Then Lot chose him all the plain of Jordan; and Lot journeyed east: and they separated themselves the one from the other."*

At long last, that which God had originally told Abraham to do, *"Get thee . . . from thy kindred, and from thy father's house,"* is now done (Gen. 12:1).

From this we learn that the man of true Faith, Faith in Christ and what Christ has done for us at the Cross, must separate himself from those in the Church who have an improper faith. To be sure, this is definitely something that will come to pass without any overt action on the part of the one of true Faith. The two, true Faith and improper faith, cannot in any way mix. They are like oil and water! There must be a separation, even as there is a separation. The man of true Faith looks entirely to God, while the one with improper faith looks to his own senses, mistaking that for faith, when in reality it's something else altogether.

Out of this we have the True Church and we have the apostate Church. It has been that way from the very beginning, with Cain and Abel setting the first example. It has continued thusly ever since. Millions are in the Church, but not of Faith. Millions claim Faith, but in reality it is not faith. And let the Reader properly understand the following:

TRUE FAITH

The entirety of the Bible is the story of the Fall of man, which takes up only one

Chapter (Gen., Chpt. 3), with the remainder devoted to the Redemption of man. The central core of the Redemption Plan is the Lord Jesus Christ, and what He would do at the Cross. Everything in the Bible points to Him. However, it points to Him in the realm of what He would do at the Cross on our behalf. It is always *"Jesus Christ and Him Crucified"* (I Cor. 1:23; 2:2).

It is Faith in that Finished Work which guarantees Redemption for mankind, and Faith in the Finished Work alone which God recognizes as true Faith (Jn. 3:16).

When Paul spoke of *"fighting the good fight of Faith,"* he was speaking of this *"Faith which was once delivered unto the Saints"* (I Tim. 6:12; Jude vs. 3). Satan's greatest effort is to move the Saint away from this Faith, that is making the Cross the object of his Faith, to something else. If he does that, he has succeeded. The Holy Spirit doesn't demand much of us, but He does demand that our Faith be explicitly in Christ, and what Christ has done for us at the Cross. Then and then only will He work within our lives, and do the things which only He can do (Rom. 8:1-2, 11).

The central theme of the Bible is Faith (Jn. 3:16; Heb. 11:6). But as stated, the faith of which we speak is Faith in Christ and what he has done at the Cross. That is *"the Faith"* (Rom. 1:5, 12; 3:3; Gal. 2:20).

SODOM

Verse 12 reads: *"Abram dwelled in the land of Canaan, and Lot dwelled in the cities of the plain, and pitched his tent toward Sodom."*

The first mistake on the part of Lot was the choice of direction, which was toward Sodom. The second mistake was that he *"pitched his tent toward Sodom,"* which means that soon he will be in Sodom, which he was.

The Scripture bluntly says, *"Abram dwelled in the land of Canaan."* The idea seems to be, after the excursion into Egypt, he did not want a repetition of such. He puts his stakes down in Canaan, because this is where God had sent him. In fact, his dwelling in the land had far more to do with the Promises of God, which actually stretched into eternity, than the land itself. Actually, he never personally owned any of the land, except a burial place; however, all of that was of little consequence. How much of it he saw by faith, we really do not know. He knew, of course, what God had told him the future would be, but even then the information was very scarce.

In this land of Canaan, Israel would become a nation. Ultimately the Prophets would come, and through them the Word of God would be given, not only to Israel, but also the entirety of the world. And then the greatest happening of all would take place, and we speak of the coming of the Messiah, which would fulfill the great prediction made by God to Satan through the serpent, concerning the *"Seed of the Woman"* (Gen. 3:15). So Abraham would dwell in Canaan, because that's where God had sent him.

Lot pitching his tent toward Sodom portrays the fact that he little understood the great prophecies concerning the future of Canaan. They seemed to have meant little to him. Were that not the case, he would not have moved toward Sodom, and ultimately into Sodom.

WICKEDNESS

Verse 13 reads: *"But the men of Sodom were wicked and sinners before the LORD exceedingly."*

The Holy Spirit through Moses, as he wrote the Text, is very quick to characterize Sodom and its inhabitants.

The Pulpit Commentary says concerning Sodom, *"Their vileness was restrained neither in quantity nor quality. As it passed all height in arrogance, so it burst all bounds in prevalence."*

The wickedness of the men of Sodom concerned itself, among other things, with the terrible sin of homosexuality. In fact, it is here that the name *"Sodomites,"* concerning homosexuality, came into being (Deut. 23:17; I Ki. 14:24, 15.12, 22.46, II Ki. 23.7). But yet as wicked as this sin is, Jesus proclaimed that the rejection of the Gospel under the New Covenant is far more serious even than the sins of Sodom and Gomorrah (Lk. 10:2-12). Considering the Cross, there is no sin greater than the rejection of Christ. If the *"men of Sodom were wicked and sinners before the*

NOTES

Lord exceedingly," the rejection of Christ presently makes such a person more wicked.

(14) "AND THE LORD SAID UNTO ABRAM, AFTER THAT LOT WAS SEPARATED FROM HIM, LIFT UP NOW YOUR EYES, AND LOOK FROM THE PLACE WHERE YOU ARE NORTHWARD, AND SOUTHWARD, AND EASTWARD, AND WESTWARD:

(15) "FOR ALL THE LAND WHICH YOU SEE, TO YOU WILL I GIVE IT, AND TO YOUR SEED FOREVER.

(16) "AND I WILL MAKE YOUR SEED AS THE DUST OF THE EARTH: SO THAT IF A MAN CAN NUMBER THE DUST OF THE EARTH, THEN SHALL YOUR SEED ALSO BE NUMBERED.

(17) "ARISE, WALK THROUGH THE LAND IN THE LENGTH OF IT AND IN THE BREADTH OF IT; FOR I WILL GIVE IT UNTO YOU."

The structure is:

1. Directly Lot departs, God draws near to Abraham.

2. He gives him a little more detail as to what this land means to the Kingdom of God, and his part in all that is taking place.

3. The Promises were to Abraham; they were not given to Lot.

4. The modern Palestinians should look at the statement, *"And to your seed forever."*

5. Sarah is barren, and yet God promises that the seed of Abraham would be as the dust of the Earth.

6. He was to walk the length and the breadth of the land, knowing that it would ultimately come to his seed. Such speaks of a claim of faith.

REVELATION

Verse 14 reads: *"And the LORD said unto Abram, after that Lot was separated from him, Lift up now your eyes, and look from the place where you are northward, and southward, and eastward, and westward."*

Lot departing from Abraham, and the Lord appearing to the Patriarch after that departure, lets us know that this strife was far more serious than meets the eye. In effect, the Lord was telling the Patriarch that it didn't really matter what Lot or anyone else did, the Promise concerning the land had been given to Abraham, and now God verifies the Promise to an even greater degree. In essence, the Lord abrogated the portion claimed by Lot, and did so by giving it back to Abraham.

The Lord having done this, the Patriarch did not have to fight to defend it, or in fact, to do anything. Let the Reader remember this:

If God gives us something, man cannot take it away. To be sure, even as here, man will try, but he will never be successful.

FOREVER

Verse 15 reads: *"For all the land which you see, to you will I give it, and to your seed forever."*

Not only was the land of Palestine to be given to Abraham and his seed, which it definitely was, but the ownership was to be into perpetuity, i.e. *"forever."*

Now let the Reader look carefully at these simple words *"and to your seed forever,"* for they spell certain doom to anyone or any nation, and irrespective as to how large or powerful they might be, who would seek to abrogate this Promise as given by the Lord.

Some decades ago, mighty Great Britain sought to stop the Jews from claiming their rightful possession. They did not succeed, and today Great Britain is only a shadow of what it once was. The former Soviet Union, with all of its monolithic power set itself against Israel, but instead, saw herself disintegrated. This is an anvil on which many hammers have struck. The hammers break; the anvil remains.

At this present time, the Arab nations are demanding that the United States cease its protection of Israel; however, let the leaders of this nation understand that if we ever lift a hand against Israel, and do so in any manner, we will incur the wrath of Almighty God, a position in which no nation wants to find itself. The statement made by God some 4,000 years ago, *"I will bless them who bless you, and curse him who curses you,"* holds just as much truth at the present, as it did when it was uttered.

And to be frank, as that particular statement was meant for Israel of old, it extends even unto Believers presently. Those who

bless Believers will be blessed; those who curse Believers will ultimately be cursed.

THE SEED

Verse 16 reads: *"And I will make your seed as the dust of the Earth: so that if a man can number the dust of the Earth, then shall your seed also be numbered."*

Not only would the land be given to Abraham and his seed, but as well there would be so many seed that they would not be able to be numbered. Now remember this:

At this particular time, Abraham did not possess one single foot of the land of Palestine, at least as far as personally owning it was concerned. As well, Sarah was barren, so in the mind of the Patriarch, and as we shall see in his later experiences, he wonders how all of this can possibly happen.

We must never forget that there is nothing impossible with God. If He has promised it, to be sure, He will do it — irrespective as to what it might be. He is the One Who opens, and no man shuts; and shuts, and no man opens (Rev. 3:7).

WALK

Verse 17 reads: *"Arise, walk through the land in the length of it and in the breadth of it; for I will give it unto you."*

This is a walk of Faith. His walking the length and the breadth of the land presents his claim regarding this inheritance. It didn't matter to whom it belonged at the present; God said, *"walk it."*

God has the power to give us anything; however, He will only give His treasures to men and women of Faith. And please remember that Faith is always attached to action in some way. We are to take possession of these gifts by Faith. This means, whatever the present circumstances, that we believe God. God said it, we believe it, and that settles it!

There would be many enemies in coming centuries who would try to stop Israel from possessing its land; however, despite their efforts, they were not successful — that is, until the Lord allowed the land to be taken by others, and because of Israel's wayward direction.

(18) "THEN ABRAM REMOVED HIS TENT, AND CAME AND DWELT IN THE

PLAIN OF MAMRE, WHICH IS IN HEBRON, AND BUILT THERE AN ALTAR UNTO THE LORD."

The diagram is:

1. Lot might choose Sodom; but as for Abraham, he sought and found his all in God.

2. There was no Altar in Sodom. All who travel in that direction are in quest of something quite different from that. It is never the worship of God, but the love of the world, that leads them thither.

3. Abraham builds an Altar unto the Lord, which means that his Faith is reestablished in Christ, and what Christ would do to redeem humanity by dying on the Cross.

MOVE THE TENT

The phrase, *"Then Abram removed his tent, and came and dwelt in the plain of Mamre, which is in Hebron,"* proclaims an area some 22 miles south of Jerusalem, on the way to Beer-sheba. Actually, Hebron was built some seven years before Zoan, in Egypt (Num. 13:22). It is elsewhere in the Bible styled *"Kirjath-arba,"* or the city of Arba (Gen. 23:2; 35:27).

The fact of Abraham living in a tent portrayed his pilgrim nature. That which he sought was not to be found on this Earth, but rather in Heaven. *"He looked for a city which has foundations, whose Builder and Maker is God"* (Heb. 11:10). He looked for *"a better country, that is, an heavenly"* (Heb. 11:16).

He moved his tent away from Sodom, even from its direction, bringing it closer to Jerusalem. There are many Believers, spiritually speaking, who desperately need to *"move their tents."* In fact, there are millions, as Lot, who have *"pitched their tents toward Sodom."* There is only disaster in that direction. The blessing is as Abraham did, to move the tent ever toward Jerusalem, i.e., *"the New Jerusalem."*

So I suppose the simple question must be asked, *"Where is your tent?"*

The world's largest *"Christian"* Television Network now specializes in making movies. It ever pitches its tent toward Sodom! The major Denominations resort to humanistic psychology in order to address the needs of man, in which incidentally, there is no help. It moves its tent ever toward Sodom! The

modern greed gospel has repudiated the Cross, therefore, becoming an enemy of the Cross, which means it ever pitches its tent toward Sodom!

When the Church forsakes the Cross, and by and large it has forsaken the Cross, there is nowhere to go but to continue to *"pitch one's tent toward Sodom."*

THE CROSS

The phrase, *"And built there an Altar unto the LORD,"* proclaims the center of gravity as it regards Faith. I speak of the *"Altar,"* which is always a Type of the *"Cross."*

If there is to be victory, if there is to be the Power of God, if there is to be Salvation, if there is to be a mighty Moving of the Holy Spirit, it all must be built on the foundation of the Cross. The Holy Spirit will function and work in no other capacity.

If we try to build faith on Denominationalism, particular Churches, even particular doctrines, on good works, on Preachers, etc., we have just placed ourselves in a position in which the Holy Spirit will not work. He functions alone in the parameters of the Finished Work of Christ. Listen to what Paul said:

"For the Law (a Law devised by the Godhead) *of the Spirit* (Holy Spirit) *of life* (the Holy Spirit Alone brings life; all else is death) *in Christ Jesus* (referring to what He did at the Cross) *has made me free from the law of sin and death"* (Rom. 8:2).

The words *"in Christ Jesus"* proclaim the manner in which this *"Law"* operates and functions. It pertains to what Christ did at the Cross on our behalf, and it is that and that alone in which the Holy Spirit works. As with Abraham, He demands that we place our Faith in the Finished Work of Christ, and that ever be the object of our Faith. As previously stated, He doesn't demand much of us, but He does demand that. If we build on any foundation other than the Cross, as stated a few paragraphs back, He simply will not work in that capacity, and that is exactly what is happening to the modern Church. It desperately needs to go back and *"build there an Altar unto the Lord,"* i.e., *"reestablish our faith in the Cross of Christ"* (Lk. 9:23-24; Rom. 6:3-14; 8:1-2, 11; I Cor. 1:17-18, 21, 23; 2:2, 5; Col. 2:14-15; I Pet. 1:18-20).

"I was lost in sin, but Jesus rescued me,
"He's a wonderful Saviour to me;
"I was bound by fear, but Jesus set me
free,
"He's a wonderful Saviour to me."

"He's a Friend so true, so patient, and
so kind,
"He's a wonderful Saviour to me;
"Everything I need in Him I always find,
"He's a wonderful Saviour to me."

"He is always near to comfort and to
cheer,
"He's a wonderful Saviour to me;
"He forgives my sins, He dries my ev-
ery tear,
"He's a wonderful Saviour to me."

"Dearer grows the Love of Jesus day
by day,
"He's a wonderful Saviour to me;
"Sweeter is His Grace while pressing
on my way,
"He's a wonderful Saviour to me."

CHAPTER 14

(1) "AND IT CAME TO PASS IN THE DAYS OF AMRAPHEL KING OF SHINAR, ARIOCH KING OF ELLASAR, CHEDOR-LAOMER KING OF ELAM, AND TIDAL KING OF NATIONS;

(2) "THAT THESE MADE WAR WITH BERA KING OF SODOM, AND WITH BIRSHA KING OF GOMORRAH, SHINAB KING OF ADMAH, AND SHEMEBER KING OF ZEBOIIM, AND THE KING OF BELA, WHICH IS ZOAR.

(3) "ALL THESE WERE JOINED TO-GETHER IN THE VALE OF SIDDIM, WHICH IS THE SALT SEA.

(4) "TWELVE YEARS THEY SERVED CHEDORLAOMER, AND IN THE THIR-TEENTH YEAR THEY REBELLED."

The composition is:

1. If it is to be noticed, the Spirit of God occupies Himself with the movements of *"kings and their armies,"* only when such movements are in anywise connected with the people of God.

2. We should read all of these illustrations in the Old Testament with the understanding

that these things have to do with the Plan of God, and are always connected with the ever onward thrust of our ultimate Salvation.

3. The conflicts here enjoined will ulti-mately involve Abraham and is, therefore, of our interest.

THE FOUR KINGS

Verse 1 reads: *"And it came to pass in the days of Amraphel king of Shinar, Arioch king of Ellasar, Chedorlaomer king of Elam, and Tidal king of nations."*

Some Jewish Scholars claim that Amraphel was Nimrod; however, that is probably incor-rect, and because by now Nimrod probably had died.

This was about 400 years after the flood, and despite that judgment brought by God which destroyed all of mankind, with the ex-ception of Noah and his family, we find here that man is no better now than he was then. As there was only one family living for God before the flood, and that family was that of Noah, we find now that it has increased very little. At this particular time, the only ones living for God, at least which are recorded are Abraham and his family, and the great Priest-King Melchizedek. Lot could be said to be-long to this number, but only in a limited way.

We find here four kings, led by Chedor-laomer, who sought to put down the rebel-lion of the five kings listed in Verse 2.

And how does this interest us presently?

It interests us simply because it is of in-terest to the Holy Spirit. And it is of interest to Him, simply because it will involve Lot, who was a citizen of Sodom. While Lot is in serious straits spiritually, he is still attended to by the Holy Spirit, even as we shall see. This shows us the security of the Child of God, but it also shows the serious straits in which the Believer can find himself by en-gaging in disobedience.

THE FIVE KINGS

Verse 2 reads: *"That these made war with Bera king of Sodom, and with Birsha king of Gomorrah, Shinab king of Admah, and Shemeber king of Zeboiim, and the king of Bela, which is Zoar."*

These five kings had been ruled by Chedor-laomer for some 12 years, and now they rebel.

The king of Sodom, as we shall see, will be the principle in this confederation led against Chedorlaomer.

This is the first mention of *"war"* in the Old Testament, but without a doubt, many wars had been fought before now.

REBELLION

Verses 3 and 4 read: *"All these were joined together in the vale of Siddim, which is the salt sea.*

"Twelve years they served Chedorlaomer, and in the thirteenth year they rebelled."

This is the first occurrence, as well, of the number *"thirteen"* in the Bible. It is the number of rebellion, and its subsequent occurrences in the Scriptures present the same feature (Williams).

(5) "AND IN THE FOURTEENTH YEAR CAME CHEDORLAOMER, AND THE KINGS THAT WERE WITH HIM, AND SMOTE THE REPHAIMS IN ASHTEROTH KARNAIM, AND THE ZUZIMS IN HAM, AND THE EMIMS IN SHAVEH KIRIATHAIM,

(6) "AND THE HORITES IN THEIR MOUNT SEIR, UNTO EL-PARAN, WHICH IS BY THE WILDERNESS.

(7) "AND THEY RETURNED, AND CAME TO EN-MISHPAT, WHICH IS KADESH, AND SMOTE ALL THE COUNTRY OF THE AMALEKITES, AND ALSO THE AMORITES, THAT DWELT IN HAZEZON-TAMAR.

(8) "AND THERE WENT OUT THE KING OF SODOM, AND THE KING OF GOMORRAH, THE KING OF ADMAH, AND THE KING OF ZEBOIIM, AND THE KING OF BELA (THE SAME IS ZOAR;) AND THEY JOINED BATTLE WITH THEM IN THE VALE OF SIDDIM;

(9) "WITH CHEDORLAOMER THE KING OF ELAM, AND WITH TIDAL KING OF NATIONS, AND AMRAPHEL KING OF SHINAR, AND ARIOCH KING OF ELLASAR: FOUR KINGS WITH FIVE."

The overview is:

1. The four kings of Verse 1 served Chedorlaomer for some 12 years. In the thirteenth year they rebelled, and in the fourteenth year, Chedorlaomer gathered his confederation, in order to bring them back into line.

2. The *"Rephaims," "Zuzims,"* and *"Emims,"* refer to giants. Satan is now doing

NOTES

the same thing he did before the flood, fulfilling Genesis 6:4 which says, *"There were giants in the Earth in those days* (before the flood)*; and also after that* (after the flood)*."*

3. The battle is enjoined, between the four kings of Verse 1 and the five kings of Verse 2.

THE GIANTS

Verses 5 and 6 read: *"And in the fourteenth year came Chedorlaomer, and the kings who were with him, and smote the Rephaims in Ashteroth Karnaim, and the Zuzims in Ham, and the Emims in Shaveh Kiriathaim,*

"And the Horites in their mount Seir, unto El-paran, which is by the wilderness."

In the names *"Rephaims," "Zuzims,"* and *"Emims,"* and possibly even the *"Horites,"* we have once again the entrance of the giants. The last of this particular line, although not the last of the giants, that coming in the time of David, we have *"Og king of Bashan."* His bedstead, the Scripture says, was 18 feet long and six feet wide (Deut. 3:11).

Irrespective of their size, this *"Chedorlaomer"* defeated them.

SODOM

Verses 7 through 9 read: *"And they returned, and came to En-mishpat, which is Kadesh, and smote all the country of the Amalekites, and also the Amorites, that dwelt in Hazezon-tamar.*

"And there went out the king of Sodom, and the king of Gomorrah, and the king of Admah, and the king of Zeboiim, and the king of Bela (the same is Zoar;) and they joined battle with them in the vale of Siddim;

"With Chedorlaomer the king of Elam, and with Tidal king of nations, and Amraphel king of Shinar, and Arioch king of Ellasar; four kings with five."

We have here the mention of Sodom where Lot dwelt, and which causes the interest of Jehovah, and points to the reason for all of this being included in these Passages.

It is obvious from the Text that Lot was not at all in proper relationship with the Lord; however, the Lord, despite that fact, continued to monitor his every move, and in effect, to exercise a form of security and protection for him, despite his having moved in with the Sodomites.

Every Believer should understand the significance of all of this. You are bought with a price; that price is the shedding of the Blood of the Lord Jesus Christ on the Cross of Calvary. As a result, you belong to the Lord. And as a continued result, He minutely watches over you.

To be somewhat mundane, this is why it is so foolish for Believers to fear things. I get amazed at Christians who are afraid of flying, or something of that nature. There is no way that you as a Believer are going to die before the Lord says so.

Now it is quite possible for Christians to be reckless, and to do foolish things, which can shorten their lives; however, the greatest problem of all, the Scripture tells us, is Believers not properly discerning the Body of Christ. And what does that mean?

Concerning our taking that Sacred Ordinance, which we refer to as the *"Lord's Supper,"* Paul said: *"Wherefore whosoever shall eat this bread, and drink this cup of the Lord, unworthily, shall be guilty of the Body and Blood of the Lord.*

"But let a man examine himself, and so let him eat of that bread, and drink of that cup.

"For he who eats and drinks unworthily, eats and drinks damnation to himself, not discerning the Lord's Body."

The Apostle then said, *"For this cause many are weak and sickly among you, and many sleep"* (I Cor. 11:27-30).

"Weak and sickly" explains itself, which refers to bodily sickness. The word *"sleep,"* refers to dying prematurely. While these Believers are saved, their lives are cut short, simply because they are not properly *"discerning the Lord's Body."* And what does that mean?

To take the *"Lord's Supper,"* the Lord doesn't demand perfection. But He does demand Faith; however, the Faith He demands is Faith in Christ, *"and what Christ has done for us at the Cross."* The entirety of the Lord's Supper portrays the broken Body of our Lord and His shed Blood. If we partake of the Lord's Supper, and make something else other than the Body of Christ (Christ giving His Body on the Cross in Sacrifice) the object of our Faith, this means we are not properly discerning the Lord's Body,

which also means that we *"eat this bread, and drink this cup of the Lord, unworthily,"* and thereby incur unto ourselves, *"damnation,"* which in this case refers to harm, and not the loss of the soul.

If the Believer places his Faith exclusively in Christ, and what Christ has done for him at the Cross, depending totally and completely upon that Finished Work, and conduct himself in a forthright, sensible manner, he doesn't have to worry about anything.

But if the Believer, even as Lot, flirts with the world, he definitely can place himself in harm's way, which can cause great problems, even as it did with Lot.

Lot, in a sense, represents the Apostate Church, while Abraham represents the True Church. Lot's attention and direction definitely were not on the Cross of Christ, but something else entirely. And regrettably, that's where most modern Christians are — they have made friends with the world.

(10) "AND THE VALE OF SIDDIM WAS FULL OF SLIMEPITS; AND THE KINGS OF SODOM AND GOMORRAH FLED, AND FELL THERE; AND THEY THAT REMAINED FLED TO THE MOUNTAIN.

(11) "AND THEY TOOK ALL THE GOODS OF SODOM AND GOMORRAH, AND ALL THEIR VICTUALS, AND WENT THEIR WAY.

(12) "AND THEY TOOK LOT, ABRAM'S BROTHER'S SON, WHO DWELT IN SODOM, AND HIS GOODS, AND DEPARTED."

The synopsis is:

1. Lot, in his compromised position, could neither deliver Sodom nor himself.

2. Abraham could deliver both.

3. The only way to help and bless the world is to live apart from it, in fellowship with God.

LOT

Verses 10 through 12 read: *"And the vale of Siddim was full of slimepits; and the kings of Sodom and Gomorrah fled, and fell there; and they that remained fled to the mountain.*

"And they took all the goods of Sodom and Gomorrah, and all their victuals, and went their way.

"And they took Lot, Abram's brother's son, who dwelt in Sodom, and his goods, and departed."

Even though Lot was still under the protection of the Lord, at least to a certain degree, when we take ourselves away from the True Way of God, thereby devising our own way, even as did Lot, we incur upon ourselves great difficulties. The Way of the Lord is the only Way, and to be sure, Sodom was not that way. So the Scripture says, *"They took Lot,"* along with *"his goods,"* etc.

Becoming yoked up with the world, as stated, Lot could neither deliver Sodom nor himself. If we place ourselves in this position as it relates to the world, and that means to become yoked up with its spirit, we will sooner or later be taken captive by the world, just as was Lot. Let the Christian read these words very carefully.

"They took Lot," and sooner or later, they are going to take you.

The Lord demands separation from the world; however, this doesn't mean isolation. Every Believer is *"salt"* and *"light,"* to the world, which speaks of preservation and illumination (Mat. 5:13-14).

Williams says: *"Isolation is not separation. Isolation chills; separation warms. Isolation makes self the center; separation makes Christ the center. Isolation produces indifference to the need of others; separation fills the heart with love and interest for the needy and perishing. So soon then as Abraham hears of the captivity of his relative ('brother'), he immediately sets out to save him. Such is the energy of love. Abraham's was the Faith that not only overcomes the world, but that works by love. Such is the nature of Divine Faith. It purifies the heart; it rescues the perishing; and it puts kings to flight!"*

(13) "AND THERE CAME ONE THAT HAD ESCAPED, AND TOLD ABRAM THE HEBREW; FOR HE DWELT IN THE PLAIN OF MAMRE THE AMORITE, BROTHER OF ESHCOL, AND BROTHER OF ANER: AND THESE WERE CONFEDERATE WITH ABRAM.

(14) "AND WHEN ABRAM HEARD THAT HIS BROTHER WAS TAKEN CAPTIVE, HE ARMED HIS TRAINED SERVANTS, BORN IN HIS OWN HOUSE, THREE HUNDRED AND EIGHTEEN, AND PURSUED THEM UNTO DAN.

NOTES

(15) "AND HE DIVIDED HIMSELF AGAINST THEM, HE AND HIS SERVANTS, BY NIGHT, AND SMOTE THEM, AND PURSUED THEM UNTO HOBAH, WHICH IS ON THE LEFT HAND OF DAMASCUS.

(16) "AND HE BROUGHT BACK ALL THE GOODS, AND ALSO BROUGHT AGAIN HIS BROTHER LOT, AND HIS GOODS, AND THE WOMEN ALSO, AND THE PEOPLE."

The exegesis is:

1. Abraham has little interest in the proceedings, had it not been for Lot.

2. He hears that Lot has been taken captive, and he sets about to rescue him.

3. What the five kings of Verse 2 couldn't do, Abraham did do. He defeated Chedorlaomer.

4. He not only rescued Lot and his goods, but as well he rescued all who had been taken captive, plus all the goods of the five kings of Verse 2.

HIS BROTHER WAS TAKEN CAPTIVE

Verses 13 through 15 read: *"And there came one that had escaped, and told Abram the Hebrew; for he dwelt in the plain of Mamre the Amorite, brother of Eshcol, and brother of Aner: and these were confederate with Abram.*

"And when Abram heard that his brother was taken captive, he armed his trained servants, born in his own house, three hundred and eighteen, and pursued them unto Dan.

"And he divided himself against them, he and his servants, by night, and smote them, and pursued them unto Hobah, which is on the left hand of Damascus."

Mackintosh says: *"The claims of a brother's trouble are answered by the affections of a brother's heart. This is Divine. Genuine Faith, while it always renders us independent, never renders us indifferent; it will never wrap itself up in its fleece while a brother shivers in the cold. There are three things which Faith does: it 'purifies the heart,' it 'works by love,' and it 'overcomes the world' (I Jn. 3:3; 5:4; I Cor. 13:2); and all these results of Faith are beautifully exhibited in Abraham on this occasion."*

What are we to do as Believers, if we hear that our brother has been taken captive by the Devil?

Of course, we are to do exactly as Abraham, set about to rescue him.

However, we must realize that there is only one way that one can be rescued, and that is by taking them back to the Cross.

While there are many things which entered into this situation, the very reason that Lot had been taken captive by these heathen kings is because, in effect, he had left the Cross, i.e., *"the Altar."* And the very reason any Believer is taken captive by the enemy is because he leaves the Cross. In the Cross, and the Cross Alone, is our protection. Our Faith and trust in the Finished Work of Christ is what gives the Holy Spirit latitude within our hearts and lives, and keeps us from *"works of the flesh"* (Gal. 5:16-25). If the Believer is taken captive by the enemy, it is because he has left the Cross, and if he is to be brought back to a place of victory, he must first of all be brought back to the Cross. The reason for failure is departure from the Cross, while regaining the victory is being brought back to the Cross, and remaining there.

It is tragic that the modern Church has, for all practical purposes, forsaken the Cross. As a result, almost all of the Church presently is in the clutches of the enemy. The greater tragedy is, it is so deceived that it doesn't even recognize the position in which it now finds itself. It is only proper Faith in the Cross which keeps one from deception. Paul said:

"Now the Spirit speaks expressly, that in the latter times (the times in which we now live) *some shall depart from the faith* (trust in Christ and what Christ has done for us at the Cross), *giving heed to seducing spirits* (deception), *and doctrines of devils"* (I Tim. 4:1).

Lot departed from the Cross, and Lot was deceived. As a result of his spiritual blindness, he could not see the terrible predicament in which he found himself. And neither can most modern Christians. For all practical purposes, the Church has forsaken the Cross, and for all practical purposes, it finds itself so deceived, that it does not realize the clear and present danger.

Every evidence is Lot was angry with Abraham as a result of the strife between the herdsmen (Gen. 13:7-8). But Abraham wasn't angry with Lot, only hurt by Lot's

actions toward him. Never mind, this did not enter into the situation at present. Abraham must rescue Lot. He is Lot's *"brother."*

THE MODERN CHURCH

Unfortunately, the rescue attempts, if one would call it that, of the modern Church, doesn't include the Cross. It has so adopted the ways of the world, that it uses the ways of the world to try to effect rescue, which in effect, is no rescue at all. Let me ask this question:

Could Abraham have rescued Lot if he had been captive of the kings also? Of course he couldn't have done so. He would have needed rescuing himself. But thankfully that wasn't the case with Abraham; however, it definitely is the case with the modern Church.

To the brother who has been taken captive by the enemy, does the modern Church hold up the Cross as the solution to his problem? Unfortunately it doesn't. It rather holds up humanistic psychology, which provides no help at all. Let me give you an example:

Three or four years ago, someone sent me a copy of the Pentecostal Evangel, the weekly voice of the Assemblies of God. I did not keep the magazine; therefore, I cannot give the exact date of the issue.

Somewhere in the body of its contents, in addressing the problems we are discussing here, the writer of the article I was reading boldly recommended the 12-step programs of humanistic psychology. His statement was, if the Church being attended didn't have a good 12-step program, the individual was to find one that did.

By allowing such an article to be published, this means that the entirety of the Leadership of that Denomination approved of this particular direction.

PSYCHOLOGY

It is impossible to trust in the Cross and humanistic psychology at the same time. To recommend the latter is to deny the former. One cannot have it both ways. To embrace this nefarious system of the world is at the same time to deny the Cross. While of course these religious leaders would deny that, the simple fact is, one cannot embrace the world and its systems, and at the same time, embrace the Lord and His Cross. One or the other must go. Paul plainly said:

"Be ye not unequally yoked together with unbelievers: for what fellowship has Righteousness with unrighteousness? And what communion has light with darkness?

"And what concord has Christ with Belial? Or what part has he who believes with an infidel? . . .

"Wherefore come out from among them, and be ye separate, says the Lord, and touch not the unclean thing; and I will receive you" (II Cor. 6:14-7:1).

Unfortunately, for every Christian who presently has a problem of any nature, the Church is holding up, at least for the most part, humanistic psychology as the answer to that dilemma. It has forsaken the Cross, and as such, it has forsaken all hope of rescue. Concerning this, Jesus bluntly said:

"They be blind leaders of the blind. And if the blind lead the blind, both shall fall into the ditch" (Mat. 15:14).

RESCUE

Verse 16 reads: *"And he brought back all the goods, and also brought again his brother Lot, and his goods, and the women also, and the people."*

Abraham not only rescued Lot, but all of his material possessions as well, along with all of the people who had been taken captive, and their goods also. In other words, every single thing which the enemy had taken was retrieved.

A proper restoration will at the same time retrieve everything that has been lost. As it regards Egypt, which is a type of the world, *"not one hoof must be left behind"* (Ex. 10:26).

Exactly how many others were with Abraham and his 318 trained soldiers, we aren't told. So we must come to the conclusion that the Lord greatly helped Abraham in this excursion. There is no record that he lost a single man.

Victories we win by our own ingenuity oftentimes come at great price. Victories we win by the Power of God come at no price at all on our part, but all on the part of God's Son, and our Saviour, the Lord Jesus Christ.

VICTORY

The Believer must understand that God cannot give victories to sinful man. He can only give victories, even as we've already stated, to His Son, the Lord Jesus Christ. And this victory is given to Christ for us, due to what the Lord did at Calvary's Cross.

Once our faith and trust is solely in Christ and His Cross, then the victory which Christ has won becomes our victory. But if we try to gain victory in any other manner, we will fail every single time. John clearly said:

"This is the victory that overcometh the world, even our faith" (I Jn. 5:4).

But never forget, the faith mentioned here is, without exception, Faith in Christ and Him Crucified (I Cor. 1:23).

(17) "AND THE KING OF SODOM WENT OUT TO MEET HIM AFTER HIS RETURN FROM THE SLAUGHTER OF CHEDORLAOMER, AND OF THE KINGS THAT WERE WITH HIM, AT THE VALLEY OF SHAVEH, WHICH IS THE KING'S DALE."

The diagram is:

1. In the sevenfold surrender of Abraham, he will now face the fourth surrender, *"the riches of Sodom."* The previous three are: *"his country," "his kindred,"* and *"the plain of Jordan"* (Gen. 12:1; 13:10).

2. There is no time so dangerous to the Christian as the morrow after a great spiritual victory.

3. Abraham pursues the king of Elam, but the king of Sodom pursues Abraham.

THE KING OF SODOM

Verse 17 reads: *"And the king of Sodom went out to meet him after his return from the slaughter of Chedorlaomer, and of the kings that were with him, at the valley of Shaveh, which is the king's dale."*

Everything has been retrieved by Abraham. The people who lived in the five cities were wicked; yet for Abraham's sake, most, if not all, of them were saved from death. Thus, God honors His Saints, for He spares the most perverse ingrates on account of one or two Believers. In addition, these people received also their goods, which they could never have otherwise expected.

The same is true today, and in fact, has always been true. Whatever blessings the world enjoys, it enjoys because of God's Saints on Earth. If it were not for His people, and I speak of those who have been washed in the Blood of the Lamb, God would have utterly destroyed the whole world long ago.

All of this should have been a lesson to the Sodomites, which means they definitely should have repented, but they only increased in wickedness until they had to be destroyed, which they were a short time later. This which God allowed Abraham to do in rescuing all of these people and their goods was the greatest sign of all of the supremacy of Jehovah. But the Sodomites seemingly gave it little thought; they were only interested in their worldly goods.

(18) "AND MELCHIZEDEK KING OF SALEM BROUGHT FORTH BREAD AND WINE: AND HE WAS THE PRIEST OF THE MOST HIGH GOD.

(19) "AND HE BLESSED HIM, AND SAID, BLESSED BE ABRAM OF THE MOST HIGH GOD, POSSESSOR OF HEAVEN AND EARTH:

(20) "AND BLESSED BE THE MOST HIGH GOD, WHICH HAS DELIVERED YOUR ENEMIES INTO YOUR HAND. AND HE (ABRAHAM) GAVE HIM (MELCHIZEDEK) TITHES OF ALL."

The structure is:

1. Melchizedek appears on the scene, who is a King and a Priest, and above all who is a Type of Christ (Ps. 110:4; Heb. 5:5-6).

2. Some Scholars believe that Melchizedek could actually have been Shem, the son of Noah. Shem was alive at this time and actually lived for about 60 years more. In fact, some think he died when Abraham was about 150 years of age.

3. Abraham is introduced here to God by a different name than he had previously known, "El Elyon," meaning, "Most High God."

4. Melchizedek gives praise and glory to God Who has given Abraham this great victory. But the victory actually is in Christ; of Whom Melchizedek is a Type.

5. This is the first time that "tithes" are mentioned in Scripture.

MELCHIZEDEK

Verse 18 reads: "And Melchizedek king of Salem brought forth bread and wine: and he was the Priest of the Most High God."

NOTES

Without fanfare or explanation, Melchizedek is introduced into this scenario. Who is he? What is he?

His name means "King of Righteousness," and "King of Peace" (Heb. 7:2).

Some have thought he was a Canaanite, simply because he resided in Canaan, and was in fact king of Salem, an ancient name for Jerusalem. But if he was in fact Shem, the son of Noah, he would not have been a Canaanite.

However, we do not know exactly who he was, and the Holy Spirit meant for it to be that way. He suddenly appears after the slaughter of the kings. Up till now, he has been hidden. The true Melchizedek is now hidden but will appear in blessing after the destruction of the kings of Revelation, Chapter 19. As King of Righteousness, the Lord Jesus Christ, as stated the True Melchizedek, will judge the wicked, and as King of Peace He will bless the Earth. Peace does not displace Righteousness, but is based upon it. These are Millennial glories reserved for Israel and the redeemed nations; but the Church being one with Him will share all His glories whether Heavenly or earthly.

Melchizedek, at this meeting with Abraham, brings forth "bread and wine," symbolic of the coming Crucifixion. At the Last Supper the True Melchizedek brought forth bread and wine, symbolizing His broken Body and His shed Blood, necessary for the Salvation of mankind (Mat. 26:29; Mk., Chpt. 14; Lk. 22:15; Rom. 8:21).

Melchizedek as a "Priest" symbolized the coming Christ, Who is our Great High Priest (Heb. 7:15-17).

Concerning this, David prophesied about 1,000 years after Abraham, "The LORD has sworn, and will not repent, You (Christ) are a Priest forever after the order of Melchizedek" (Ps. 110:4).

Why after Melchizedek and not after Aaron the High Priest of Israel?

The Aaronic Priesthood of Israel was only meant to be temporal, while the Priesthood of Melchizedek was meant to be eternal. The former represented Israel only, while the latter represents the entirety of mankind, both Jews and Gentiles.

The Old Covenant was a Shadow of Heavenly things. Christ is their substance. He fulfilled all of the Old Covenant, thereby replacing it with the New. Consequently, He is the High Priest after the order of Melchizedek, and will be forever.

He was made such by the *"Most High God,"* i.e., *"El Elyon,"* and there is no greater authority than that.

While Abraham knew God in a glorious and wonderful way, he had not previously known Him as *"El Elyon"*; consequently, He now knows Him in even a higher and more blessed way.

THE BLESSING

Verse 19 reads: *"And he* (Melchizedek) *blessed him* (Abraham), *and said, Blessed be Abram of the Most High God, Possessor of Heaven and Earth."*

We find here Melchizedek blessing Abraham, which means that the standing of Melchizedek was greater than that of Abraham. How could this be?

Paul said of this situation, *"Now consider how great this man was* (Melchizedek), *unto whom even the Patriarch Abraham gave the tenth of the spoils."*

He then said, *"And without all contradiction the less is blessed of the better"* (Heb. 7:4, 7).

Melchizedek stood in a higher position, simply because he was raised up by God to be a Type of Christ, and more particularly, the High Priesthood of Christ. Even though Abraham definitely represented Christ, it was this King-Priest who was a Type of Christ.

Concerning this position, Paul further said: *"Without father, without mother, without descent, having neither beginning of days, nor end of life; but made like unto the Son of God; abideth a Priest continually"* (Heb. 7:3).

This Passage in Hebrews doesn't mean that Melchizedek didn't have a father or a mother, or that he wasn't born or that he didn't die, but rather that none of these things are recorded of him, and because he was to be a Type of the eternal Priesthood of Christ.

JEWISH SCHOLARS

It is the common opinion of many Jewish Scholars that Melchizedek was in fact Shem, the son of Noah. As we have stated, Shem

was a contemporary of Abraham for a number of years, with some even thinking that possibly he outlived Abraham, dying just before Jacob went down into Egypt.

Considering that this man was referred to by the Holy Spirit as *"King of Righteousness,"* and *"King of Peace,"* (Heb. 7:2), this means that he preached remission of sins through the coming Seed of the Woman, the Promised Redeemer. Since this Doctrine was unknown to the world, or if known, despised by it, the pious people at Salem (Jerusalem) chose this man to be their King.

Not far from him there ruled the kings of Sodom and Gomorrah, who far surpassed him in riches, honor, and power, and, no doubt, they greatly despised him as a poor, though righteous king. Nevertheless, to the people of Jerusalem at that time, he was Melchizedek, the King of Righteousness. The others were kings of unrighteousness, tyrants, and idolaters, for which reason God in His righteous wrath punished them with war and bloodshed. Shem, on the other hand, was king of Salem, that is, king of peace (Heb. 7:2) (Luther).

BLESSED OF THE BETTER

We find another Doctrine in this particular Verse that should be attended closely.

While all Believers should *"pray for the other,"* as we daily seek the Lord, and while it's perfectly proper for Associate Ministers in the Church to lay hands on the Senior Pastor (Acts 13:1-4), Believers who do not stand in one of the fivefold Callings (Eph. 4:11), should never take it upon themselves to lay hands on a Preacher of the Gospel. All must ever understand that the better is never blessed by the less. Such attitude smacks of pride, and is seldom, if ever, of God.

Unfortunately, the land is full of self-called Prophets, etc., who have an exalted opinion of themselves, and thereby take it upon themselves to administer so-called blessings when in reality, they administer nothing. The truth is, such action grieves the Holy Spirit, and for the simple reason that such individuals are refusing to recognize the Calling that God has placed upon someone.

What if Abraham had haughtily proceeded to *"bless"* Melchizedek, instead of allowing the Lord to lead the situation? Abraham was the one who had been given the Revelation, had been called into Canaan, but the Patriarch never took a haughty, self-imposed position. He always allowed the Lord to lead in these particulars; consequently, the Will of God was always carried out. In fact, had Abraham not had this humble spirit, he would not have even been a footnote in Biblical history, much less the *"father of us all."*

THE MOST HIGH GOD

The Holy Spirit knows that a great temptation is about to fall upon Abraham, so through Melchizedek reveals Himself to the Patriarch in a more exalted manner as *"the Most High God, Possessor of Heaven and Earth."* Abraham would now know him as *"El Elyon,"* which in effect meant, *"the Most High."*

The king of Sodom, as we shall see, will attempt to entice Abraham with riches, but God is telling him here through Melchizedek that the One Abraham is serving is *"Possessor of Heaven and Earth"*; consequently, God can and will give him whatever he needs, which means he doesn't need the ill-gotten gains of the King of Sodom.

"El Elyon" describes God as the High, the Highest, the Exalted, the Supreme, and is sometimes used in conjunction with Jehovah (Ps. 7:18).

We find here that Melchizedek did not come forth when Abraham was in pursuit of Chedorlaomer, but when the king of Sodom was in pursuit of Abraham. This makes a great moral difference. Concerning this, Mackintosh said: *"A deeper character of communion was needed to meet the deeper character of conflict."*

TITHES ✓

Verse 20 reads: *"And blessed be the Most High God, which has delivered your enemies into your hand. And he* (Abraham) *gave him* (Melchizedek) *tithes of all."*

Melchizedek blesses Abraham, and as well, blesses the Lord, giving Him praise and glory, and thereby the credit for delivering Abraham from his enemies. This tells us that the Lord, which should be obvious, greatly helped Abraham in this conflict. In fact, without this help, it would have been impossible for the

small army of Abraham to have defeated the army of the enemy, which no doubt numbered many times their size. So proper praise is given to the Lord.

After this blessing, Abraham gave tithes to Melchizedek, which referred to a tenth, evidently of all the goods he had taken from the enemy.

This is the first recorded instance of tithes being given to the Work of the Lord, but it is obvious that this practice had been carried out for a long, long time.

In Genesis 4:4, where it says that Abel brought *"of the firstlings of his flock,"* some think that this could have meant a tenth of the flock, or a tithe. If in fact that was the idea, then the practice continued, and comes down to us even unto this present time.

Abraham paying the tithe to Melchizedek sets the standard for this practice, and is meant to be continued even now. Many erroneously think that tithing originated with the Law of Moses; however, I think it is obvious that such was not the case. Tithing preceded that Law, and continues unto this hour.

Abraham paid tithe to Melchizedek, who was a Type of Christ. Consequently, Abraham's children, which make up the Church presently, are to continue to pay tithe to those carrying out the Work of God, of which Melchizedek was a Type. So we have two Types here.

Abraham was a Type of the Church (Rom. 4:16). Melchizedek was a Type of Christ (Ps. 110:1-4).

Under the Mosaic Law, which is not incumbent upon the Church, there were actually three particular tithes. They are as follows:

1. The people were to pay their tithe to the Levites who attended the Temple. In fact, this was the support of the Levites, which included the Priests, who attended to all the many duties of the Temple, which was a very involved process, and required many people (Lev., Chpt. 27; Num., Chpt. 18).

2. Each family was to lay aside a second tithe to cover expenses for attending the national feasts, conducted three times a year, and were all carried out at the Temple in Jerusalem (Deut. 14:22-26).

3. There was to be a third tithe of sorts, carried out over three years, totaling three

and one-third percent each year. This was for the strangers, fatherless, and widows. It was a special tithe for the poor, a charity tithe to relieve suffering, etc.

It was, as stated, to be given only every third year.

So all of this made up 23 and one-third percent per year, which was the Mosaic Law.

Presently, it is ten percent of our income, and has been since the Day of Pentecost, which was the beginning, in essence, of the Church. Every evidence is that tithing, as a way and manner of the Lord, had its beginning at the very dawn of time, and continues unto this hour. There is no Passage in the Word of God which abrogates this practice.

In II Corinthians, Chapters 8 and 9, the Holy Spirit through Paul gives the greatest dissertation on giving found in the entirety of the Word of God. And yet in this dissertation, tithing is not once mentioned. Why?

While tithing is incumbent upon the Child of God, that is if he wants to obey the Lord, giving under the New Covenant is to go much further than ten percent. The idea is, everything we have belongs to God. It is at His disposal, and we are to be ever open to His Leading. In all of the teaching that the Apostle gives in these two Chapters, perhaps the entirety can be summed up in the following:

"But this I say, he who sows sparingly shall reap also sparingly; and he who sows bountifully shall reap also bountifully" (II Cor. 9:6).

(21) "AND THE KING OF SODOM SAID UNTO ABRAM, GIVE ME THE PERSONS, AND TAKE THE GOODS TO THYSELF.

(22) "AND ABRAM SAID TO THE KING OF SODOM, I HAVE LIFTED UP MY HAND UNTO THE LORD THE MOST HIGH GOD, THE POSSESSOR OF HEAVEN AND EARTH,

(23) "THAT I WILL NOT TAKE FROM A THREAD EVEN TO A SHOELATCHET, AND THAT I WILL NOT TAKE ANYTHING THAT IS YOURS, LEST YOU SHOULD SAY, I HAVE MADE ABRAM RICH:

(24) "SAVE ONLY THAT WHICH THE YOUNG MEN HAVE EATEN, AND THE PORTION OF THE MEN WHICH WENT WITH ME, ANER, ESHCOL, AND MAMRE; LET THEM TAKE THEIR PORTION."

The construction is:

NOTES

1. Satan will now use the king of Sodom, endeavoring to draw Abraham into his web. He will use money to do so.

2. Abraham answers him by refusing to be enriched by the king of Sodom.

3. How could he think of delivering Lot from the power of the world if he himself were governed thereby? The only true way in which to deliver another is to be thoroughly delivered yourself.

4. The world, in all its various forms, is the great instrument of which Satan makes use in order to weaken the hands and alienate the affections of the servants of Christ.

5. Incidentally, this is the fourth surrender by Abraham to the Lord. The first three pertained to surrendering his country, his kindred, the Vale of Jordan, and now the riches of Sodom.

THE RICHES OF SODOM

Verse 21 reads: *"And the king of Sodom said unto Abram, Give me the persons, and take the goods to yourself."*

Satan's ways are always very subtle. Abraham had performed a valuable service for the five kings, with the king of Sodom evidently being the leading principle. So in effect, Abraham having defeated the four kings who had attacked the five, which the five couldn't do, the five were in his debt.

It's perfectly satisfactory for the world to be in debt to the Believer, but never the Believer to be in debt to the world. Now when I say that, I'm not speaking of the normal and natural courtesy that every Believer should show any and all concerned, whomever they may be, for favors done, etc. It's the snare of which I speak, and that for which the Believer should be on guard.

Sodom was a doomed city, as well as several others of the five. In fact, their time was running out, even as the king of Sodom was speaking to Abraham.

Here was another opportunity for this king to come to know the Lord. Without a doubt he knew that there was something different about Abraham. This man Abraham, as stated, with a small army, had defeated the confederation, of which they had been unable to do. He sought to appease his conscience by offering Abraham money, when the real problem was spiritual.

ABRAHAM'S ANSWER

Verse 22 reads: *"And Abram said to the king of Sodom, I have lifted up my hand unto the LORD, the Most High God, the Possessor of Heaven and Earth."*

Evidently much more went on here than meets the eye. It seems from the terminology used by the Patriarch that the king of Sodom may have proposed an amalgamation of sorts with Abraham. But the Patriarch proclaims to all concerned that his allegiance is totally and completely to *"the Lord the Most High God, the Possessor of Heaven and Earth."* In this, he proclaims the fact that he is beholden to no man, but yet gracious to all men, even as he was in delivering this king and his confederates.

Once again, this goes back to separation. We are in the world, but as Believers we are definitely not of the world. However, separation does not mean isolation. Our lights are to shine before men that they may see our good works and, thereby, glorify the Lord Who is in Heaven.

Abraham definitely performed good works, and definitely glorified God, but absolutely refused any entanglement with the world.

That should be our example!

THE GOLD OF SODOM

Verses 23 and 24 read: *"That I will not take from a thread even to a shoelatchet, and that I will not take anything that is yours, lest you should say, I have made Abram rich:*

"Save only that which the young men have eaten, and the portion of the men which went with me, Aner, Eshcol, and Mamre; let them take their portion."

Abraham lifting his hand to God, and proclaiming to the king of Sodom that he would not take even so much as a thread or a shoelace, proclaims the fact that the Lord had instructed Abraham in this capacity.

What a difference this meeting was than that in Egypt! There, Abraham, functioning from the position of fear, accepted all types of gifts from Pharaoh, which was no credit to the Lord God of Glory. Now he is operating in Faith, and because he is where God wants him to be, and the story is quite different. Faith is never fearful and Faith is never greedy.

NOTES

At the same time, he made it known that the allies with him could be free to take what they so desired, and what the king of Sodom desired to give them.

It is noticeable that Lot is not mentioned in these proceedings. The reasons are obvious.

He has compromised himself with Sodom, and even now he hasn't learned his lesson, even as we shall see. So the meeting with Melchizedek he will miss, and as well the revelation of God as *"The Most High."*

How so much we miss, when we miss God!

In all of this, Melchizedek may never have imagined how great was the dignity put upon him as a Type of Christ. Living a quiet, pure, and devoted life, he becomes accepted by his fellows as a Priest of the Most High, and becomes the Type of Him Who was to be the Saviour of the world.

Faith, which Melchizedek exhibited, is always stronger, bigger, and greater than we could ever begin to imagine. In fact, anything from God always fits that category, but it's always Faith which allows us access to the Most High, and more importantly, Faith in Christ and what Christ has done for us at the Cross.

Everything we see in these Chapters is a prelude to the main event, and that main event is always Christ and Him Crucified. That and that alone would bring mankind out of the terrible morass of evil, which now holds him in a vice-like grip. Jesus broke those chains!

Under the Jewish Dispensation, there was no one who in his person could represent the twofold character of Christ as the only High Priest and universal King. But in Melchizedek, both Offices are proclaimed!

"Loved with everlasting love, led by Grace that love to know;
"Spirit, breathing from above, You have taught me it is so!
"Oh, this full and perfect peace! Oh, this transport all Divine!
"In a love which cannot cease, I am His, and He is mine."

"Heaven above is softer blue, Earth around is sweeter green,
"Something lives in every hue, Christ-less eyes have never seen.

*"Birds with gladder songs overflow,
   flowers with deeper beauties shine,
"Since I know, as now I know, I am
   His, and He is mine."*

*"Things that once were wild alarms
   cannot disturb my rest,
"Closed in everlasting arms, pillowed
   on the loving breast.
"Oh, to lie forever here, doubt and care
   and self resign,
"While He whispers in my ear, I am His,
   and He is mine."*

*"His forever, only His; Who the Lord
   and me shall part?
"Ah, with what a rest of bliss, Christ
   can fill the loving heart!
"Heaven and Earth may fade and flee,
   firstborn light in gloom decline;
"But while God and I shall be, I am His,
   and He is mine."*

CHAPTER 15

(1) "AFTER THESE THINGS THE WORD OF THE LORD CAME UNTO ABRAM IN A VISION, SAYING, FEAR NOT, ABRAM: I AM YOUR SHIELD, AND YOUR EXCEEDING GREAT REWARD."

The composition is:

1. Genesis, Chapter 15 is without a doubt, one of the most important Chapters in the entirety of the Word of God.

2. The Lord appears to Abraham in a Vision.

3. He tells him to *"fear not,"* which shows that fear had been present.

4. He was afraid he would be killed by enemies, before the great Promise of God could come to pass in his life. I speak of him bringing a son into the world, which was necessary as it regards the coming Incarnation of Christ.

5. The Lord promises him that He would be his shield.

6. By the Lord telling Abraham that He would be his *"Exceeding great reward,"* He in effect, was telling the Patriarch not to get his eyes on the Promise, but rather the Giver of the Promise.

THE VISION

The phrase, *"After these things the Word of the LORD came unto Abram in a vision,"* presents one of four ways which God spoke to individuals in Old Testament times (Num. 12:6-8):

1. He spoke in Visions (Amos 7:1).

2. He spoke in dreams (Gen. 41:1; Dan. 2:1).

3. He revealed Himself by speaking directly to the Prophets *"mouth to mouth"* (Dan. 12:8).

4. He spoke through His Word (Mat. 4:4). (The time of the Gospels was still under Old Testament authority.)

How long it was after the events of Chapter 14 that Abraham had this Vision, we aren't told.

The contents of this Vision will include many things; however, the greatest part will be the Revelation of *"Justification by Faith."* While this Revelation would continue to expand the balance of Abraham's life, it was here that the foundation was laid; consequently, it would affect the entirety of the human race, and above all, those who would make Jesus Christ their Lord and their Saviour.

A great foundation had already been laid as it regards the Revelation of Justification by Faith. It is all found in the Altar. In fact, Abraham is known as the *"Altar Builder."* The Vision given here to the Patriarch gives him a much more expanded knowledge of what the Altar was all about.

FEAR NOT

The short phrase, *"Saying, Fear not, Abram,"* proclaims the fact that fear had definitely been present, and to such an extent that the Lord would have to reinforce His Promises to the Patriarch.

From previous manifestations, Abraham knew that a child was to be born to him, and for all of these promises to be carried out, it was absolutely necessary that this child be born. Due to the recent conflict with the four kings, Abraham had made powerful enemies. Most probably, the threats of death to the Patriarch had come to his ears. In that climate, human life was cheap. Even though he had defeated these kings in battle, it was still within their power to hire assassins to take the life of the Patriarch by stealth. What they had failed to do in battle, they may well have threatened to do in another manner.

The humiliation of their defeat must have been great, especially considering that they had been defeated by this stranger and his soldier-herdsmen.

Whatever the reason for the fear, it was not merely that the Lord had appeared to him in the Vision, but rather went far deeper than that. Even though the appearance of the Lord is always a momentous occasion, still, the relationship between Abraham and Jehovah was such that the appearance of the Lord would have evoked no fear, at least in this capacity.

Many might be quick to condemn the Patriarch, wondering as to why he would fear, considering that he has just experienced a tremendous victory!

The answer to that is not as difficult as it at first seems. Great victories in the Lord are often followed by an attack on our faith. The Evil One, jealous of the defeat recently suffered, will renew his efforts, crowding the mind with all type of thoughts. If he cannot stop the victory, he will try to demean the victory, and fear is usually the result.

A PERSONAL EXAMPLE

What I'm about to say is small potatoes by comparison to that of which Abraham experienced; however, the principle is the same.

In November of 2001, it had come to our attention that a powerful Radio Station in East Texas might be possible to obtain. It had a wide coverage, reaching nearly one and one-half million people.

In 1998, the Lord gave me a vision regarding Radio, and what I must do regarding this medium. We set out to do what he had told us to do, and the success was immediate. I had been seeking the Lord for several months as it regards coverage in the major cities, wondering how such could be done, especially considering the price of powerful FM Stations. And now, here was a Station that seemed to be within our reach.

I immediately went to prayer, asking the Lord as to what we should do. In a few minutes time, the Lord told me how much money to offer the people, and on what terms it would be offered. It was so simple that in fact, it seemed to be too simple.

I had my associate, David Whitelaw, to contact the necessary parties, and we made arrangements to go speak with them the very next day. I took three of my associates with me.

We met the Broker and one of the principal owners at a designated place, and discussed the situation for a short period of time.

I then asked the two men to step out of the room, while I consulted with my associates. I related to them what I believed the Lord had told me to do. They immediately gave their approval.

We called the two men back into the room. On a piece of paper, I outlined to them what I would pay for the Station, and the terms that I would like to have.

They looked at my figures for a few minutes, and tried to push the price higher, but finally accepted my offer. And now the point of this illustration.

After we shook hands on the deal, for the next several hours, fear gripped my heart, and seemingly in one hundred different ways. How could we pay for it? I knew the Lord had told me to do this thing, but I also knew that I had to raise the money by going before our audience over Radio, asking for their help. Would they respond favorably?

Now why would I fear, when the situation had worked out exactly as the Lord had told me it would work out?

Incidentally, the Radio audience responded very favorably to my purchase of this Station, supplying the funds for the down-payment, and doing so in a short period of time.

The reason for the fear is, as previously stated, Satan not being able to stop the victory, will now try to demean the victory.

SHIELD

The phrase, *"I am your shield,"* proclaims the Lord informing the Patriarch that irrespective of the threats of these defeated kings, or anyone else for that matter, the Lord would be a shield. In that case, there was nothing on Earth, in Heaven, or under the Earth that could hurt Abraham. And to be frank, if the Lord has told someone that certain things are going to happen, and that he will be included in those things, to be sure, the Lord is a shield for that individual.

If it is to be noticed, the Lord didn't merely say that He would provide a shield, but rather *"I am your shield."* There is no higher power than such a word coming from *"El Elyon, Possessor of Heaven and Earth."*

REWARD

The phrase, *"And your exceeding great reward,"* in effect was telling Abraham that the Lord was his reward, and not these things which the Lord had promised, as exceptional as they might have been.

As Believers, we have a tendency to get our eyes on the reward instead of the Rewarder. In fact, that's what Abraham was doing as well.

When we do this, we see nothing but problems and difficulties, exactly as Abraham saw nothing but problems and difficulties. If we keep our eyes on the Lord, understanding that He Alone is our reward, then the other things take care of themselves, because we know it's the Lord doing the doing, and not man. Eyes on the reward, and the reward only, tend to shift Faith from God to ourselves, which always brings problems.

In October of 1991, the Lord spoke to my heart, telling me to begin two Prayer Meetings each day. After these Prayer Meetings began, which incidentally continue unto this hour, and I trust will ever continue, the Lord spoke to my heart, saying, *"Seek Me, not so much for what I can do, but rather for Who I am."* In essence, that's the same thing that the Lord told Abraham.

(2) "AND ABRAM SAID, LORD GOD, WHAT WILL YOU GIVE ME, SEEING I GO CHILDLESS, AND THE STEWARD OF MY HOUSE IS THIS ELIEZER OF DAMASCUS?

(3) "AND ABRAM SAID, BEHOLD, TO ME YOU HAVE GIVEN NO SEED: AND, LO, ONE BORN IN MY HOUSE IS MY HEIR.

(4) "AND, BEHOLD, THE WORD OF THE LORD CAME UNTO HIM, SAYING, THIS SHALL NOT BE YOUR HEIR; BUT HE WHO SHALL COME FORTH OUT OF YOUR OWN BOWELS SHALL BE YOUR HEIR.

(5) "AND HE BROUGHT HIM FORTH ABROAD, AND SAID, LOOK NOW TOWARD HEAVEN, AND TELL THE STARS, IF YOU BE ABLE TO NUMBER THEM: AND HE SAID UNTO HIM, SO SHALL YOUR SEED BE."

The overview is:

NOTES

1. Verse 2 proves that Abraham's fear was that he would be killed or die, before a child could be born.

2. At the present time, he can only see Eliezer, his servant, as his heir.

3. The Lord rejects this thinking, and tells Abraham that his heir will be a son born to him.

4. He then tells him that while he is now worrying about having one son, in fact, his seed shall be as the stars of the heavens for multitude.

WHAT WILL YOU GIVE ME?

Verse 2 reads: *"And Abram said, LORD God, what will you give me, seeing I go childless, and the steward of my house is this Eliezer of Damascus?"*

Abraham knows that the great statement made to him by the Lord concerns him having a child. He remembers very vividly the Promise made to him by the Lord some years earlier, when the Lord appeared unto him, and said, *"Unto your seed will I give this land"* (Gen. 12:7). So in effect, he is asking, *"How can I have all of these things, seeing I go childless?"* He wonders, *"Can this Eliezer of Damascus, my servant, be my heir?"*

Sarah is now well past 65 years of age, probably about 70, and considering her age, and especially that she had been barren all of her life, how could this thing be?

As all of us, Abraham was trying to figure the thing out? How could it be done? How was it all possible?

With God, questions are useless! Even though Faith is tempted to ask questions, it should not do so. If God has said it, irrespective as to how impossible it might look, He will bring it to pass. He is able to do all things!

THE HOUSE SON

Verse 3 reads: *"And Abram said, Behold, to me You have given no seed: and, lo, one born in my house is my heir."*

Abraham holds a conversation with the Lord, pointing out the fact that he has heard the Promise given to him concerning *"his seed,"* but as of yet, he has no seed, i.e., *"no son."* And as it stands at the present, *"the son of my house,"* not born of me, is of now my heir. Eliezer is his name.

So now in this perplexing situation, even as we will see in the next Verse, the Lord will expand this Revelation to the Patriarch.

YOUR HEIR

Verse 4 reads: *"And, behold, the Word of the LORD came unto him, saying, This shall not be your heir; but he who shall come forth out of your own bowels shall be your heir."*

So now, as stated, the Revelation is expanded. The Lord tells Abraham that in fact, he will have a son, and he shall be the father of that son. It will not be someone adopted, etc.

But the Lord at this time doesn't include Sarah in this mix, actually saying nothing about her. That will come later. That's the way Revelation generally is.

The Lord gives us bits and pieces, so to speak, and does it in this manner for a particular reason. He's teaching us trust and Faith, even as He reveals His Way and Direction to us.

From this we learn that most of the time, we aren't quite as strong in faith as we think we are. So the ways and manners of the Lord are designed with several purposes in mind, all for our good.

THE STARS

Verse 5 reads: *"And He brought him forth abroad, and said, Look now toward Heaven, and count the stars, of you be able to number them: and He said unto him, So shall your seed be."*

While Abraham is pondering the seeming impossibility of having even one child, the Lord takes him outside of the tent, has him look up at the stars, and tells him, *"So shall your seed be."* And so it was, and so it is!

(6) "AND HE BELIEVED IN THE LORD; AND HE COUNTED IT TO HIM FOR RIGHTEOUSNESS."

The composition is:

1. This is one of the single most important Scriptures in the entirety of the Word of God.

2. In this simple term, we find the meaning of Justification by Faith.

3. Abraham was saved by Grace through Faith, not by his good works. There is no other way of Salvation anywhere in the Bible.

4. God demands Righteousness; however, it is the Righteousness afforded strictly by

Christ and Christ Alone. Anything else is self-righteousness, and totally unacceptable to God.

FAITH

The phrase, *"And he believed in the LORD,"* does not refer to the Promises of God, although that is included, but particularly refers to believing in God.

Believed what?

Upon this Text, Paul bases the central article of our Christian Faith, which both the world and the Devil hate, namely, that Faith alone justifies and saves (Rom. 3:28).

It was to Paul that the meaning of the New Covenant was given, which in effect, is the meaning of the Cross. The great Apostle framed the entirety of his teaching around Genesis 15:6. He said:

"Abraham believed God, and it was counted unto him for Righteousness" (Rom. 4:3).

To answer the question as to what Abraham believed, we must point to the Cross. He believed that God would send forth a Redeemer into the world, and that the seed that he (Abraham) would bring forth would have something to do with the coming of this Redeemer. He also believed that this coming Redeemer would give His life in order to redeem the fallen sons of Adam's race, hence the constant demands by God that Abraham build Altars.

Abraham would not have known anything about the Cross; just the death of the One Who was coming. It remained for Moses to be given that Revelation, and by the serpent on the pole (Num., Chpt. 21).

The word *"believed"* as used regarding Abraham simply means to have Faith. But what does that mean?

THE OBJECT OF OUR FAITH

The Cross of Christ must ever be the object of our Faith. This pertains to what Jesus did on our behalf, and actually did as our Substitute. At the Cross, He satisfied the demands of the broken Law, and did so by pouring out His Life's Blood, thereby giving His Life (Eph. 2:13-18). Therefore, when the believing sinner evidences Faith in Christ and what Christ did at the Cross, a perfect, pure Righteousness, the Righteousness afforded by Christ, is instantly imputed to the believing sinner. In fact, God will impart such Righteousness on no other basis than Faith in the Finished Work of Christ.

Christianity is very simple. It's not complicated at all, and if it is complicated, it is because we have made it so. In order to be saved, the Scripture just plainly says to us, *"Believe on the Lord Jesus Christ, and you shall be saved, and your house"* (Acts 16:31). Nothing could be simpler than that. Or whosoever calls on the Name of the Lord shall be saved (Rom. 10:13).

THE CHRISTIAN AND VICTORY

What I've said thus far is readily believed by any True Christian. But as it regards our everyday walk before God, that is, the living of this Christian experience, this is where most Christians go off track. They automatically relegate that which Abraham said about believing God, and how that God imputed it to him for Righteousness, to the initial, Born-Again experience. Most don't think of it at all as it regards our daily walk before God; however, this statement made about Abraham, and that which Paul used as the foundation of his great Gospel of Salvation by Grace, is just as apropos for the Believer as it is for the sinner coming to Christ. But most Christians don't know that. So they cast about, trying to build their own victory, and always conclude by building a house on sand. It looks good for awhile, in fact, just as good as the real thing; however, once the adverse weather begins to come, then the true story is told, and the house is lost.

The truth is, the Cross is just as important to the Believer's ongoing victory as it is for the sinner being saved. This is proven to us in Romans, Chapter 6.

Paul begins that Chapter by saying, *"What shall we say then? Shall we continue in* (the) *sin, that Grace may abound?"*

He answered by saying, *"God forbid. How shall we, who are dead to* (the) *sin, live any longer therein?"* (Rom. 6:1-2).

Paul is dealing here with the sin question, actually the sin nature, as it pertains to Christians. In other words, he is about to tell us how to live a victorious, overcoming, Christian life. So what does he say in regard to that?

Beginning with Verse 3 of Romans, Chapter 6, he immediately goes into a dissertation on the Cross of Christ. He said:

"Know ye not, that so many of us as were baptized into Jesus Christ were baptized into His death?"

Most Christians brush past this Scripture, simply because they misunderstand the word *"baptized,"* thinking it means Water Baptism. It doesn't! They conclude that inasmuch as they have been baptized in water, they do not need to dwell here for any length of time.

The truth is, Romans, Chapter 6, Verses 3, 4, and 5 are some of the most important in the entirety of the Bible.

As stated, Paul is not speaking of Water Baptism, but rather the death of Christ on the Cross, and how that we were baptized into His death, which took place upon our evidencing Faith in Christ. Now of course, the Reader understands that we're speaking here of something spiritual and not physical. The idea is this:

The moment you as a believing sinner expressed Faith in Christ, even though at that time you did not know too very much about Christ, in the Mind of God, you were literally placed in Christ as He died on the Cross. He died as our Substitute, and our Faith in Him places us in His actual Crucifixion.

The Apostle then said: *"Therefore we are buried with him by baptism into death: that like as Christ was raised up from the dead by the glory of the Father, even so we also should walk in newness of life."*

We not only were baptized into the death of Christ when we evidenced Faith, but when Christ was buried, we as well were buried with Him. This means that the old you, the sinful you, the you that you would like to forget, all of its filth, sin, and evil passions, were buried with Christ, meaning that the old you died.

You were then raised with Christ from the dead, and you now *"walk in newness of life."* That's what your Faith gets you.

The Apostle then said: *"For if we have been planted together in the likeness of His death, we shall be also in the likeness of His Resurrection"* (Rom. 6:5).

This Passage plainly tells us that we cannot be in the likeness of His Resurrection, until we first of all understand that we have been *"planted together in the likeness of His death."* Resurrection life is predicated on Faith in the *"likeness of His death."* In other words, we died with Him, and came forth a new man.

FAITH

Now as a Christian, and determined to live a victorious life, the way we do that is to understand that everything we have from God comes to us entirely through the Cross. As stated, Paul explained that to us in Verses 3, 4, and 5 of Romans, Chapter 6. Understanding that, we are to *"reckon ourselves to be dead indeed unto sin, but alive unto God through Jesus Christ our Lord"* (Rom. 6:11).

We are to understand that Jesus Christ addressed every single problem at the Cross, which man incurred at the Fall. We are to believe that, and, thereby, to reckon ourselves to be dead unto the old life. In other words, the old life has no more control over us.

As we keep our Faith in the Cross, understanding what Jesus has done for us, and that our victory is always in the Cross, the Holy Spirit through Paul gave us the guarantee that *"sin shall not have dominion over us, for we are no longer under the Law, but under Grace"* (Rom. 6:14).

However, if we shift our Faith from the Cross to other things, to be sure, sin will once again begin to have dominion over us, which means that the sin nature will then begin to rule us.

Let's look at the sin nature in a little more detail.

THE SIN NATURE

Some 17 times the Apostle Paul refers to *"sin"* in this Sixth Chapter of Romans. Fourteen of those 17 times, he is directly referring to the sin nature. Two of the remaining three times actually means the sin nature, even though it is only inferred. In the original Greek language, before the word *"sin,"* it carries what is referred to as *"the definite article."* In other words, and using the First Verse as an example, Paul actually wrote, *"What shall we say then? Shall we continue in the sin...."* This means that he is not referring to particular acts of

sin, but rather the principle of sin, i.e., *"the sin nature."*

In fact, every Believer has three natures. He has:

1. Human nature: Christ had this as well.

2. Sin nature: Every human being has a sin nature, as a result of Adam's Fall. Jesus didn't have a sin nature, and because He was not born by natural procreation. In other words, He was not the product of Joseph's sperm or Mary's egg. He was actually conceived in Mary's womb as a result of a decree given by the Holy Spirit (Lk. 1:35).

3. Divine nature: Every Believer has this nature, and it is the most powerful nature of all (II Pet. 1:4). The Divine nature comes into the Believer at the moment of Salvation, i.e., *"born again."*

Let's look at the five ways that the sin nature is addressed by the Church, the first four being wrong:

IGNORANCE

I think I can say without any fear of exaggeration that most Christians are totally ignorant of the sin nature. This, which can cause them more problems than they could ever begin to think or realize, is actually, for the most part, an unknown quantity in their lives. This is tragic, but it is true.

Whatever we learn about the Bible, for the most part, has to be taught from behind our pulpits. Regrettably, with most Preachers not understanding the sin nature, almost nothing is said about this subject, when in reality, this is one of the most important aspects of the Christian life. In fact, this is why Paul spent so much time on this particular subject.

Using myself as an example, I cannot remember hearing one single Message on the sin nature, in all the years of my coming up in Church. This fact proved to be extremely hurtful to this Evangelist.

DENIAL

And then we have a great segment of the Church which denies that there is a sin nature. While they might admit that such existed before conversion, they claim it was taken away at conversion.

Once again, I counter with a question, if we have no sin nature as Believers, why did

Paul spend so much time on the subject? To use just one Scripture of many, listen to what he said:

"Let not the sin therefore reign in your mortal body, that you should obey it in the lusts thereof" (Rom. 6:12).

Paul is not speaking here of acts of sin, but rather the sin nature, and simply because he uses the definite article *"the"* in front of the word *"sin,"* making it read, *"the sin."* He's speaking of the sin principle or the nature of sin, that which took place with the Fall of Adam. In other words, after the Fall it became the very nature of mankind to sin.

So if the sin nature does not exist in the life of the Believer, then what is Paul talking about?

The truth is, even as Paul deals with the subject over and over, the sin nature definitely does exist in the Believer. Momentarily, I will address the manner in which it is to be handled by the Believer.

LICENSE

The third way in which many Believers address the sin nature is the *"sin a little bit everyday"* syndrome. In other words, they admit that they have a sin nature, and because they have a sin nature, they are not really responsible for the many failures which they have constantly.

They claim that however much sin abounds, Grace abounds much more (Rom. 5:20).

Paul's answer to that is: *"God forbid. How shall we, who are dead to sin, live any longer therein?"* (Rom. 6:2). The Grace of God gives us liberty, but it definitely does not give us license. To be frank, license is the sin of antinomianism.

In the Greek, *"anti"* means, *"to be opposed."* The word *"nomi,"* means *"law."* So the meaning of the word is that Christians who think this way, and I speak of turning Grace into license, are opposed to any law. In other words, they are lawless, which of course, is unbiblical.

STRUGGLE

Not knowing how to address the sin nature, most Christians, and especially those who fall into the first two categories, struggle against this monster, which means that their

Christian experience is primarily one of *"sinning and repenting."* In fact, the harder the person struggles against this thing, the worse the situation becomes, which leaves the person confused.

Concerning this, Paul said of himself before he understood the Message of the Cross, *"For that which I do I allow not"* (Rom. 7:15). The word *"allow"* should have been translated *"understand."* What he really said is: *"For that which I do I understand not."* As stated, this characterizes most Christians.

They struggle and fight, but not only do they not win this conflict, in fact the situation just continues to get worse, which leaves the Believer in a quandary. What is wrong? Considering that they are trying so hard, why is it that they are not succeeding?

Let the Reader understand that if the sin nature is not approached correctly, and by that we speak of being Scriptural, the Believer is not going to come out successful. It doesn't matter what he does, to what Church he belongs, how much he quotes Scriptures over and over, even how much he prays or fasts, etc., while all of these things are very good in their own way, none will bring victory to the Child of God. Paul plainly addressed this by saying:

"I do not frustrate the Grace of God: for if Righteousness come by the Law, then Christ is dead in vain" (Gal. 2:21).

In other words, if you as a Believer can make yourself Righteous by your struggle, which actually falls out to a law of some nature, then Christ came down to this world and died on a Cross in vain. In other words, He wasted His time.

Well of course we know that He didn't waste His time, so what is the true answer to this dilemma?

GRACE

Paul told us the answer in many and varied ways; however, this one Passage, I think, will explain it properly. The Apostle said:

"I am crucified with Christ: nevertheless I live; yet not I, but Christ lives in me: and the life which I now live in the flesh I live by the Faith of the Son of God, Who loved me, and gave Himself for me" (Gal. 2:20).

Paul takes us back to Romans 6:3-5. He tells us that the secret of our victorious life is that we were *"crucified with Christ."* This means that everything we receive from the Lord comes to us through the Cross; consequently, the object of our Faith as a Believer must ever be the Cross, and not other things.

Regrettably, as it regards victory and our living an overcoming life, the faith of most Christians is anchored squarely in things other than the Cross. I speak of *"good works,"* or belonging to a certain Church, or memorizing certain Scriptures and quoting them over and over, etc. In fact, when it comes to devising ways to live this Christian life, there are about as many different ways as there are Christians; however, none of them will work, with the exception of the Grace of God.

As a Believer, you are to simply place your Faith in Christ and what Christ did for us at the Cross, keep your Faith anchored in the Cross, even renew that anchored Faith on a daily basis (Lk. 9:23), and then you will find the Holy Spirit grandly working within your life, thereby, giving you daily victory. This is God's prescribed order of victory for the Saint. There is no other! (Rom. 8:1-2, 11, 13).

If we try to do other things, and whatever they might be, and however right they may be in their own way, all we succeed in doing is to *"frustrate the Grace of God."* In fact, our efforts in any direction other than the Cross is a gross insult to Christ, as ought to be obvious (Gal. 2:21).

Paul emphatically states that we can't do this thing without Christ, and our Faith in what He did for us at the Cross. If we think we can. We're only fooling ourselves. Now read the following very carefully:

While the *"sin nature"* is definitely not dead in the heart and life of the Believer, the truth is, we are *"dead to the sin nature"* (Rom. 6:7-8, 11). And we are dead to the sin nature, by the fact that we were crucified with Christ, buried with Him, and then raised with Him in newness of life (Rom. 6:3-5). The secret is that we stay dead, and as long as we do, we'll have no problem with the sin nature.

And how do we stay dead to the sin nature?

We stay dead by simply continuing to evidence Faith in what Christ has done for us,

understanding that it all comes through the Cross.

When our Faith is properly placed, and when our Faith is properly maintained, the Holy Spirit gloriously and grandly works for us. Let's look at that:

THE HOLY SPIRIT

Paul also said: *"For the Law* (a Law devised by the Godhead) *of the Spirit* (Holy Spirit) *of life* (there is Spiritual Life in no other means than this) *in Christ Jesus* (what He did for us at the Cross) *has made me free from the law of sin and death"* (Rom. 8:2).

This one Passage plainly tells us that the Holy Spirit works according to a particular prescribed order; and what is that order?

In fact, it is so much an order that it is referred to as *"the law."* Now the Believer certainly should understand that Paul is not speaking here of the Law of Moses, but rather a Law devised by the Godhead. And what is that Law?

It is the work that Christ carried out at the Cross, and is referred to as *"in Christ Jesus."* That means that it is all in Him, and more particularly, in what He did for us at the Cross.

This means that our Faith, which is so very, very important, must ever be anchored in Christ and the Cross. That's why Paul said, *"But we preach Christ crucified"* (I Cor. 1:23).

If it is to be noticed, he didn't merely say *"we preach Christ,"* but rather, *"we preach Christ crucified."*

One of the great problems with the modern Church is that it preaches Christ, but it puts little emphasis on His Finished Work, which pertains to the Cross. Let the Reader understand that it is only *"Christ Crucified,"* which can set the captive free. Everything else falls into the realm of failure.

Christ as God, as necessary as that was, never delivered anyone. It is only *"Christ Crucified,"* which effects deliverance.

That's why the Apostle also said to the Corinthians: *"For I determined not to know anything among you, save Jesus Christ, and Him Crucified"* (I Cor. 2:2).

Understanding that, and functioning from that basis of Faith, the Holy Spirit now has great latitude to work in our lives. He is God; consequently, He can do anything.

Unfortunately, most Pentecostals (and I am Pentecostal) think that merely being Baptized with the Holy Spirit and speaking with other tongues are all they need. The tragedy is, there are millions who fall into that category, and while their experience is definitely real, they are still living lives of spiritual failure. Once again we come back to the synopsis of the struggle, etc.

No, just because one is Baptized with the Holy Spirit doesn't guarantee one victory in any capacity. The potential is there, but unless we function according to God's prescribed order, the Spirit-filled Believer will not really walk in any more victory than the one who is not Spirit-filled.

But if we walk and function according to God's prescribed order, which is to understand that everything comes to us through Christ and what He did at the Cross, and we ever make that the object of our Faith, then the Holy Spirit will do mighty things for us, with us, and within us. Listen again to Paul:

"But if the Spirit (Holy Spirit) *of Him* (God the Father) *Who raised up Jesus from the dead dwell in you, He* (God the Father) *Who raised us Christ from the dead shall also quicken your mortal bodies by His Spirit* (Holy Spirit) *Who dwells in you"* (Rom. 8:11).

Most Christians skim past this Verse, thinking that Paul is speaking of the coming Resurrection. He isn't!

He is telling us that the same Holy Spirit Who raised Jesus from the dead lives within us. And that means the same Power He used to bring Christ from the dead is available to us. And when we think about that a moment, we're thinking about Almighty Power, and to such an extent that it defies description.

But that Power is available to us only if our Faith is properly placed, and I continue to speak of Christ and His Cross. Otherwise, although the Holy Spirit will definitely remain in the heart and life of the Believer, what He can do will be greatly curtailed.

No Believer wants that. We all want to walk in victory, and to be sure, God has a prescribed order. That order is: A. The Cross; B. Our Faith in the Cross; and, C. The Holy Spirit will then work for us.

NOTES

All of this, and much which I have not addressed, is bound up in the statement made of Abraham, *"And he believed in the Lord; and He* (God) *counted it to him for Righteousness."*

RIGHTEOUSNESS

The phrase, *"And He counted it to him for Righteousness,"* presents the place and position which God demands. And this is where the conflict ensues.

The only type of Righteousness which God will accept is a perfect, unspotted, unsullied Righteousness, which He Alone can provide. In other words, the type of Righteousness which God demands is absolutely impossible as it regards humanity. The only thing we can produce in this realm is self-righteousness, which is brought about by our attempting to function outside of God's prescribed order. Tragically, this is where most of the Church actually is — self-righteousness.

The Righteousness which God demands can be found only by the believing sinner expressing Faith in Christ and what Christ has done for Him at the Cross. That being done, the Lord instantly imputes to the believing sinner a perfect, unspotted, unsullied Righteousness. Once again, it is referred to as *"Justification by Faith."* This means that the individual is now justified, which means, *"to be declared just by God."* As repeatedly stated, that can only come about through Christ, and what Christ did for us at the Cross, and our Faith in that Finished Work. If we try to obtain this Righteousness in any other manner, it is always and without exception a manner which God will never accept.

Once the believing sinner is made completely righteous by God, and according to his Faith in Christ, it is to be understood that we maintain that Righteousness by continuing to express Faith in Christ and what He has done for us at the Cross.

Most True Christians would acquiesce completely to the first part of my statement about the believing sinner trusting Christ, and thereby being imputed a perfect Righteousness. But unfortunately, after the initial Born-Again experience, many Christians try to maintain their Righteousness by their own good works, or whatever methods they or someone else comes up with. That's where the problem ensues.

In the same manner that we obtain Righteousness, in that same manner we maintain Righteousness. That's why Paul kept taking us to Christ and the Cross. That's why he stated, *"I am crucified with Christ"* (Gal. 2:20). But sadly and regrettably, millions of Christians refuse to believe that which the Apostle taught. Just as the Judaizers of Paul's day, the modern brand continues to follow the same course of attempting to add some type of law of their own devising to that which Christ has sufficiently done. As always, such efforts only lead to disaster (Gal. 2:21).

CHRISTIAN DISCIPLINES

Some time back on our daily Radio Program, *"A Study In The Word"*, we had two guest Preachers. We were discussing this very thing, and I speak of our living a victorious, overcoming life.

At a given point in the teaching, the younger of the two Preachers spoke up and said, *"Whenever I have a problem of any nature,"* and he was speaking of sin, *"I fast three days, and that takes care of the problem."*

While fasting definitely is Scriptural, and definitely will be a blessing to any Believer, the Truth is, if *"fasting"* is the answer to our sin problem, and whatever that problem might be, then once again I say with Paul, *"Jesus died in vain."* All He needed to have done was to teach us how to fast, etc., and the problem would be solved. Unfortunately, it's not that simple.

I diplomatically remonstrated to him that which I've just said in the above statement about Jesus having to die on the Cross, and he quickly retorted, and with a touch of anger, *"Well, it works for me!"*

The tragedy is, when we put our faith in things other than the Cross, we become blinded to a certain degree. Didn't he stop to think that he was having to repeat this scenario over and over?!

While all Believers should fast as the Lord leads them, it must be for the right reason, which pertains to Christ coming back, etc. (Mat. 9:15). However, to try to use fasting, or any other Christian discipline in the fashion of trying to overcome sin, will always lead

to defeat. Once again we come back to the simple thought that if these things could defeat sin within our lives, then why did Jesus have to come down here and die on a Cross?

The truth is, sin is of such magnitude, such power, that it is only the Cross which could address this monster, which Jesus did there (Col. 2:14-15).

So why did the Brother get somewhat testy? And unfortunately, he's not alone in that attitude.

ABRAHAM AND ISHMAEL

The Doctrine of Justification by works generates religious pride — that of Justification by Faith produces contrition and humility. Nothing gives more Glory to God than simply believing Him. And that's what Justification by Faith actually is. Justification is not actually a change in character, that being effected by Sanctification, but rather a declaration by God as to the Believer's standing before Him.

Isaac and Ishmael symbolize the new and the old natures in the Believer. The birth of the new nature demands the expulsion of the old. It is impossible to improve the old nature. The Holy Spirit says in Romans, Chapter 8 that *"it is enmity against God, that it is not subject to the Law of God, neither indeed can be."* If, therefore, it cannot be subject to the Law of God, how can it be improved?

How foolish, therefore, appears the doctrine of moral evolution!

Williams says concerning this: *"The Divine way of Holiness is to 'put off the old man' just as Abraham 'put off' Ishmael. Man's way of holiness is to improve the 'old man,' that is, to improve Ishmael. The effort is both foolish and hopeless.*

"Of course the casting out of Ishmael was 'very grievous in Abraham's sight,' because it always brings about a struggle to cast out this element of bondage, that is, Salvation by works. For legalism is dear to the heart. Ishmael was the fruit, and to Abraham the fair fruit of His own energy and planning."

But as the Word of God declares, Ishmael had to go, and as well, our own personal ways to holiness must go also. There must be nothing left but pure Faith in Christ and what Christ has done for us at the Cross.

The young Preacher didn't want to give up his dependence on fasting, and because he had put a lot into that effort. Neither do we enjoy giving up our own particular efforts as well. It's a struggle with the flesh when we are told that we must depend solely upon Christ and Christ Alone.

One Preacher remonstrated the other day, when told that his Faith must rest exclusively in the Cross, *"Well I guess that's alright for some people, but not for all."*

Now isn't that a ridiculous statement?!

How could it be right for some, and not for all?

No, the Cross is God's Way for all. None are excluded!

(7) "AND HE SAID UNTO HIM, I AM THE LORD WHO BROUGHT YOU OUT OF UR OF THE CHALDEES, TO GIVE YOU THIS LAND TO INHERIT IT.

(8) "AND HE SAID, LORD GOD, WHEREBY SHALL I KNOW THAT I SHALL INHERIT IT?

(9) "AND HE SAID UNTO HIM, TAKE ME AN HEIFER OF THREE YEARS OLD, AND A SHE GOAT OF THREE YEARS OLD, AND A RAM OF THREE YEARS OLD, AND A TURTLEDOVE, AND A YOUNG PIGEON."

The structure is:

1. The Lord reaffirms the Revelation.

2. Abraham asks two questions, *"What will You give me?"* (Gen. 15:2), and *"Whereby shall I know?"* Christ is the answer to the first question; the Covenant, to the second.

3. The Covenant is founded on Grace, for five living creatures are sacrificed to establish it. Five in the Scripture is the number of Grace; and these five sacrifices set out the fullness of the great Sacrifice of Calvary (Williams).

REAFFIRMING THE REVELATION

Verse 7 reads: *"And He said unto him, I am the LORD Who brought you out of Ur of the Chaldees, to give you this land to inherit it."*

After Abraham proclaimed the statement of Faith given to us in Verse 6, and it was *"counted to him for Righteousness,"* the Lord now reaffirms, and greater yet, expands the Revelation. In this Seventh Verse, He in effect says three things:

NOTES

1. He reaffirms Himself to Abraham as the *"Covenant God,"* by using the name *"Lord."* In other words, He is saying that whatever He has said, it most definitely will come to pass. And Abraham believes that.

2. When He spoke of bringing Abraham out of *"Ur of the Chaldees,"* He is in effect referring to the fact that He had delivered the Patriarch from idolatry, and all the evil of that former lifestyle. There must be a separation from that to the Lord, and only God can bring about such a separation. It involves much more than a geographical change, rather a Spiritual Miracle. This Abraham experienced.

3. He has promised this land of Palestine, which would be later renamed Israel, to Abraham. All of this speaks Volumes.

Even though Abraham would not personally own any of it, at least during his earthly sojourn, the fact is, his seed would own every part of it, with him personally owning it, so to speak, at the Second Coming.

If it is to be noticed, the Lord said He would *"inherit"* it, which means that it actually belongs to God, Who would give it to the Patriarch.

THE QUESTION

Verse 8 reads: *"And he said, LORD God, whereby shall I know that I shall inherit it?"*

In this Vision, and as stated, Abraham asks the Lord two questions. The first one was (vs. 2), *"What will You give me?"* Christ Alone is the answer to this question.

Directly the sinner believes God's testimony about His Beloved Son, He is not only declared righteous, but he is made a son and an heir. *"Sonship"* is introduction into the family; *"heirship,"* is entrance into the Kingdom, hence the second question, *"Whereby shall I know that I shall inherit it?"*

Abraham is then shown the suffering that he must encounter, and which all heirs of the Kingdom must know. The Apostle says, *"If we suffer with Him, we shall also reign with Him"* (Rom. 8:17).

THE FIVE SACRIFICES

Verse 9 reads: *"And He said unto him, Take Me an heifer of three years old, and a she goat of three years old, and a ram of three years old, and a turtledove, and a young pigeon."*

The Lord now has Abraham to offer up five living creatures, which will set out the fullness of the great Sacrifice of Calvary.

Five is the number of Grace. The Covenant which God was making with Abraham was, in a sense, unconditional, simply because God was the One and only contracting party (Gal. 3:20). But its foundation was Grace, as the entirety of the foundation of God is Grace.

That the heifer, goat, and ram were to be three years old signifies the earthly Ministry of the Son of God.

As well, the *"heifer"* symbolized His Priestly Office. The *"she goat"* symbolized His Prophetic Office. The *"ram"* symbolized His Kingly Office. Jesus was Priest, Prophet, and King.

The *"turtledove"* symbolized Him being led and guided strictly by the Holy Spirit, while the *"young pigeon,"* symbolized Him obeying the Spirit in every capacity.

(10) "AND HE TOOK UNTO HIM ALL THESE, AND DIVIDED THEM IN THE MIDST, AND LAID EACH PIECE ONE AGAINST ANOTHER: BUT THE BIRDS DIVIDED HE NOT.

(11) "AND WHEN THE FOWLS CAME DOWN UPON THE CARCASSES, ABRAM DROVE THEM AWAY.

(12) "AND WHEN THE SUN WAS GOING DOWN, A DEEP SLEEP FELL UPON ABRAM; AND, LO, AN HORROR OF GREAT DARKNESS FELL UPON HIM."

The composition is:

1. The dividing of the three larger animals in sacrifice, which means their bodies were literally cut in two pieces, with one piece on one side and the other piece on the other, signified the terrible depth of sin, which the Cross Alone could answer.

2. The fowls represent the opposition to the Cross by demon spirits.

3. As Abraham drove the fowls away, likewise, in the Name of Jesus, we should do the same with demon spirits.

4. The *"horror of great darkness"* which fell upon Abraham, represents the sufferings which would come to God's people Israel, and as well, at times to the Saints.

THE EFFECTS OF SIN

Verse 10 reads: *"And he took unto him all these, and divided them in the midst, and*

NOTES

laid each piece one against another: but the birds divided he not."

The heifer, goat, and ram were literally split open, in effect totally divided, with one side of the carcasses placed on the right and the others on the left. Probably one bird was placed on one side with the other on the other side, for no mention is made of their small carcasses being split.

The carcasses being treated in this manner show the terrible effects of sin. It is far more than a mere surface problem, but rather reaching to the very vitals of each and every individual. Consequently, when Jesus would die on the Cross, He would suffer the full penalty of sin, which was death. That and that alone would God accept as full payment for the penalty of sin.

One need only take a look at these Sacrifices, and their mutilation, to recognize the terrible futility of man attempting to address the sin problem any other way, than by the Cross of Calvary. And to be sure, it was addressed at Calvary in all of its totality, its depth, its destruction, and depravity. Nothing was left unanswered. In reply to this, Paul said:

"In Whom (Christ) *also you are circumcised with the circumcision made without hands* (the circumcision of the heart), *in putting off the body of the sins of the flesh by the circumcision of Christ* (the Crucifixion of Christ).

"Buried with Him in baptism (referring to His death and burial), *wherein also you are risen with Him* (in newness of life) *through the faith of the operation of God, Who has raised Him from the dead."* (This is what Paul said in Romans 6:3-5; 8:11.)

"And you, being dead in your sins and the uncircumcision of your flesh, has He quickened together with Him, having forgiven you all trespasses;

"Blotting out the handwriting of ordinances that was against us, which was contrary to us, and took it out of the way, nailing it to His Cross (meaning that He satisfied at the Cross all the demands of Heavenly Justice);

"And having spoiled principalities and powers, He made a show of them openly, triumphing over them in it"; meaning that

inasmuch as all sin was atoned, past, present, and future, Satan then lost his legal claim upon man, which is sin. Thereby, every demon spirit and fallen angel, along with Satan, were totally and completely defeated at the Cross (Col. 2:11-15).

DEMON SPIRITS

Verse 11 reads: *"And when the fowls came down upon the carcasses, Abram drove them away."*

Satan hates the Cross, represented by the carcasses, as he hates nothing else, as should be obvious. This is where he was totally and completely defeated.

In fact, the defeat which he suffered was total and complete, so total in fact, that he now has no more valid claim on the Child of God.

Sin is his claim, and with all sin atoned, which Jesus did at the Cross, and that speaks of sin in every capacity, whether past, present, or future, the Evil One now has no more claim whatsoever (Jn. 1:29).

Some Christians seem to think that Jesus fought Satan in some type of physical combat. Nothing like that ever happened! In fact, Satan wants no part of Christ in any capacity.

The conflict between Righteousness and unrighteousness has always been in the realm of sin. The fact of sin gives Satan certain legal rights, and to be sure, he has exercised those legal rights in every capacity. Sin is a breaking of the Law of God. When this is done, man finds himself on the side of unrighteousness. Actually, he is born into unrighteousness as a result of original sin, which came about as a result of Adam's Fall. The entirety of the nature of man is completely ruined by the fact of the sin nature.

That's why John the Baptist, in his introduction of Christ, said, *"Behold the Lamb of God, which taketh away the sin of the world"* (Jn. 1:29).

If it is to be noticed, he didn't say *"sins of the world,"* but rather *"sin of the world."* In other words, Jesus addressed the sin question, or the principle of sin, which refers to the very cause of sin, at the Cross. That *"cause"* is the fall of man from total God-consciousness, which existed before the Fall,

to the far lower level of self-consciousness, which took place immediately after the Fall.

At the Fall, man was totally separated from God, and pronounced as *"spiritually dead."* As a result, he is now totally in the domain of Satan, who *"steals, kills, and destroys"* (Jn. 10:10). For this problem to be satisfactorily addressed, God would have to become man, and die on a Cross, which was actually planned from before the foundation of the world (I Pet. 1:18-20).

So it is easy to see how that Satan hates the Cross as he hates nothing else. It was there that his hold on humanity was broken.

Even though demon spirits continue to attempt to attack the Child of God, and in every way, as Abraham drove away the fowls, we as Believers, using the Name of Jesus, can drive away the powers of darkness also (Mk. 16:17-18).

DARKNESS

Verse 12 reads: *"And when the sun was going down, a deep sleep fell upon Abram; and, lo, an horror of great darkness fell upon him."*

Williams says: *"The great horror that descended upon Abraham foretold the suffering of the heirs of Promise."* This pertained to Israel, which we will address to a greater degree momentarily, but as well, it pertains to all Believers.

More particularly, it pertains to *"the offence of the Cross"* (Gal. 5:11). It involves persecution, and strangely enough, the far greater persecution comes from the Church and not the world.

While the world, as well, is opposed to the Cross, not really understanding it, its opposition is limited mostly to a simple but deadly rejection of Christ.

But when it comes to the Church, its opposition is much different. It seeks to devise a way other that the Cross, but as well, seeks to eliminate all who place their Faith and trust in the Cross, of which the murder of Abel by his brother Cain is an example (Gen., Chpt. 4).

Even now, and as it always has been, if the Preacher says that he is going to preach the Cross, and thereby look to the Cross for all victory, the far greater majority of the time, if not always, he will ultimately be ostracized by most other Preachers. The reason is this:

THE TOTALITY OF THE CROSS

The Cross of Christ addresses every capacity of the Biblical experience of Salvation. It leaves out nothing.

It demands first of all that the Believer adhere strictly to the Government of God, which within itself crosses the grain of most religious Denominations. The Government of the Cross demands that total and complete allegiance be given to that which Christ has done for us, placing trust and Faith in nothing else.

Most religious Denominations demand allegiance solely to that particular Denomination, which in a sense demands total control. The Government of the Cross will not allow allegiance to be placed elsewhere. Love yes! Allegiance no!

In Paul's day, some in the Church were attempting to force the Law, i.e., *"physical circumcision,"* upon Believers. In other words, they were claiming that without adhering to the Law, one could not truly be saved (Acts 15:1). Even though the Apostles in Jerusalem opposed this erroneous doctrine, the evidence from Paul's writings is that it didn't die. That's why Paul said, *"For if Righteousness come by the Law, then Christ is dead in vain"* (Gal. 2:21).

In fact, as it was law then, it is law now, but in a different way. While the Law of Moses is now little in vogue, the Church has adopted another type of law, that of its own devising. I speak of humanistic psychology. Not knowing the way of the Cross, or else registering rank unbelief as it regards the Cross, many have turned to this nefarious system of humanistic psychology, which was birthed in the hearts of unbelievers, and actually was birthed by Satan himself. The world, not believing in Christ and His Cross, has to have another solution, which in reality is no solution at all, but building an entire system around this fabrication, it is held up as the answer to man's problems. As stated, one can understand the world going in this direction, but it is quite another matter to see the Church following suit. But follow suit it has! In the two major Pentecostal Denominations, the

Assemblies of God and the Church of God, if a Preacher has a problem of any nature, before he can be reinstated in good standing with either one of these Denominations, he must undergo several months of psychological counseling. This in effect registers a vote of no confidence as it regards the Cross. The reality is, and sadly so, these particular Denominations, and if the truth be known, almost all, have totally and completely departed from the Cross, and in effect, have rejected the Cross. Concerning this very thing, Jesus said: *"The kingdom of Heaven is like unto leaven, which a woman took, and hid in three measures of meal, till the whole was leavened"* (Mat. 13:33).

The *"Kingdom of Heaven"* could be translated *"the Kingdom from Heaven."* It is the True Gospel, which can be summed up in the word *"Jesus Christ and Him Crucified"* (Jn. 3:16; I Cor. 1:23; 2:2).

The *"leaven,"* speaks of false doctrine, with the word *"woman"* used here in an evil sense.

The *"meal"* represents the Word of God, but with *"leaven"* (false doctrine) inserted *"till the whole is leavened."*

In this shortest of the parables as given by Christ, He in effect tells us here that in the last days, the entirety of the Church world would be totally and completely leavened, i.e., *"corrupted."* Regrettably and sadly, for all practical purposes, that has come to pass.

THE CHURCH

The Church, even as Israel of old, is fastly being divided into two segments, so to speak. I speak of the True Church and the apostate Church. In effect, it has been this way, beginning even with Cain and Abel as recorded in Genesis, Chapter 4. But it is more important now, and even more distinct now, simply because the Church is nearing the very end of its particular dispensation. The Rapture is about to take place (I Thess. 4:13-18). In fact, were it not for the Rapture of the Church, the Church as a viable, Scriptural entity, would become extinct. In other words, as the Second Coming of the Lord will save the world from total destruction, likewise, the Rapture will save the Church from total extinction.

The dividing line between the True Church and the apostate Church is the Cross of Christ. In effect, it has always been that way, but serves in this capacity now in a greater way than ever before. This means that Denominations aren't the dividing line, or anything else one might think, but rather the Cross of Christ. In other words, as one views the Cross, so one states their position. If the Cross is opposed, one has to be placed in the position of being *"an enemy of the Cross"* (Phil. 3:18-19). They are, therefore, part of the apostate Church. To place one's Faith, confidence, and trust solely in Christ and what He has done for us at the Cross places one into the True Body of Christ (I Cor. 2:2; Gal. 6:14; Col. 2:14-15).

SONSHIP AND HEIRSHIP

Directly the sinner believes God's testimony about his Beloved Son, he is not only declared righteous, but he is made a *"son"* and an *"heir"* (Rom. 8:14-17).

"Sonship" is introduction into the family; *"heirship,"* into the Kingdom.

The believing sinner is made a *"son"* by his trust and Faith in Christ and what Christ has done for us at the Cross. With Faith thereby evidenced, the Lord imputes a perfect Righteousness to the believing sinner. In fact, this is what Genesis 15:6 actually means. If one understands that particular Verse, then one understands the entirety of the Bible. If one misunderstands that Verse, then one misunderstands the Word of God.

As it regards the Word of God and the Plan of Salvation, all which were shown to Abraham as it regards Justification by Faith, this is where the great controversy lies. This is where Satan fights his hardest, and this is the core of all false doctrine. If we miss it in our faith, then we've missed it completely.

When Genesis 15:6 says that Abraham believed God, it doesn't mean that he merely believed in God, but in effect, believed what God had said, which pertained to a Redeemer coming into the world, Who would redeem fallen humanity. And because Abraham believed in this One Who was to come, God counted it to him for Righteousness, which in effect, made Abraham totally and completely righteous. It was and is imputed Righteousness,

and is the foundation of all Salvation as it regards every person who has ever come to Christ. That's why Paul referred to Abraham as the *"father of us all"* (Rom. 4:16).

There are two keys to Redemption, so to speak. They are *"Faith"* and *"Righteousness."* God demands Righteousness, and the only way that Righteousness can be obtained is by Faith in Christ and His Cross (Jn. 3:16; Rom. 10:9-10, 13).

Paul also said: *"Therefore being justified by Faith, we have peace with God through our Lord Jesus Christ"* (Rom. 5:1).

That settles the *"sonship."*

"Sonship" and *"heirship"* are inseparably connected in the thoughts of God. Sonship is the proper basis of everything; and, moreover, it is the result of God's Sovereign Counsel and Operation, as we read in James: *"Of His Own Will begat He us."*

As it regards *"heirship,"* we enter into that position immediately after entering into *"sonship."* We do so in exactly the same way, as we did by entering into sonship, and I speak of our Faith totally and completely in the Cross of Christ. The great mistake of the Church is to accept *"proper sonship,"* but then, try to attain *"heirship"* in all the wrong ways. It all comes by the Cross, and by nothing except the Cross. As we came to Christ, by that same manner we maintain Christ, and Christ maintains us. As long as the Believer keeps his Faith in the Cross of Christ, understanding that it is through the Cross that we receive all things from the Lord, and that we can receive nothing except by that method, the *"heirship"* will take care of itself. It is only when we go off on tangents that we miss what Christ has done for us.

(13) "AND HE SAID UNTO ABRAM, KNOW OF A SURETY THAT YOUR SEED SHALL BE A STRANGER IN A LAND THAT IS NOT THEIRS, AND SHALL SERVE THEM; AND THEY SHALL AFFLICT THEM FOUR HUNDRED YEARS;

(14) "AND ALSO THAT NATION, WHOM THEY SHALL SERVE, WILL I JUDGE: AND AFTERWARDS SHALL THEY COME OUT WITH GREAT SUBSTANCE.

(15) "AND YOU SHALL GO TO YOUR FATHERS IN PEACE; YOU SHALL BE BURIED IN A GOOD OLD AGE.

(16) "BUT IN THE FOURTH GENERATION THEY SHALL COME HITHER AGAIN: FOR THE INIQUITY OF THE AMORITES IS NOT YET FULL."

The exegesis is:

1. The 400 years mentioned here have to do with the years that Abraham, Isaac, and Jacob spent in Canaan, but basically without owning any of it, plus the years spent in Egypt, before being delivered.

2. The *"nation"* mentioned in Verse 14 refers to Egypt.

3. Abraham, although living to a *"good old age,"* would not personally see this coming time; nevertheless, it would come.

4. Levi, Kohath, Amram, and Moses fulfilled the prediction of Verse 16: they were four generations.

5. God granted to the Amorites a day of Grace that lasted four centuries. They were then destroyed.

FOUR HUNDRED YEARS

Verse 13 reads: *"And He said unto Abram, Know of a surety that your seed shall be a stranger in a land that is not theirs, and shall serve them; and they shall afflict them four hundred years."*

The 400 years pertains to the time from the weaning of Isaac, to the deliverance of the Children of Israel from Egyptian bondage.

From Abraham's arrival in Canaan to the birth of Isaac was 25 years (Gen. 12:4; 17:1, 12); Isaac was 60 years old at the birth of Jacob (Gen. 25:26); Jacob was 130 at his going down to Egypt, which three numbers make 215 years; and as well, Jacob and his children dwelled in Egypt for the same period of 215 years, making a total of 430 years (Ex. 12:40).

The Promises of God at times take awhile before fulfillment. But that being the case, even as here, the Lord in one way or the other will relate this fact.

The Lord couldn't give the entirety of this land to Abraham at the present. How could he hold it, with only a few individuals? First of all, the Lord would have to raise up a people, which would take time to do so, in this case, about 400 years. And there were other particulars which had to be considered, even as we will see in the Sixteenth Verse.

EGYPT

Verse 14 reads: *"And also that nation, whom they shall serve, will I judge: and afterward shall they come out with great substance."*

That particular nation would be Egypt, even though at this time, the Lord does not divulge that information. But in this short Verse, He proclaims what will happen to Israel at that time.

In the first place, the Israelites by this time, and I speak of the last years in Egypt, had become a mighty people, although slaves. As slaves, they were now serving Egypt, exactly as the Lord said they would. But He also promises to judge Egypt, which He definitely did.

What He said was fulfilled in totality. *"They came out with great substance."*

ABRAHAM

Verse 15 read: *"And you shall go to your fathers in peace; you shall be buried in a good old age."*

Once again, quite a number of things are said here with very few words:

1. We learn here that Abraham would not see all of this fulfilled, but would in fact die, before this particular time.

2. This statement is a proof of the survival of departed spirits in a state of conscious existence after death.

3. When the Patriarch would die, which would be at a ripe old age, he would go in *"peace,"* proclaiming the fact that what God had called him to do, he will have done.

So in effect, what the Lord is telling Abraham, is the same thing He had previously said concerning the birth of a son. This miracle child would come forth.

THE FOURTH GENERATION

Verse 16 reads: *"But in the fourth generation they shall come hither again: for the iniquity of the Amorites is not yet full."*

From this statement concerning the *"fourth generation,"* the Lord, it seems, would not begin the countdown until the sons of Jacob were born. Consequently, the first generation began with Levi, with the second being Kohath, the third being Amram, and the *"fourth generation"* being Moses. Thus was fulfilled what the Lord had spoken. Even then, there was another situation at hand, concerning the Amorites.

They seemed to be the most powerful people of the central hill country of Canaan where Abraham lived at this particular time. That being the case, all the other tribes of Canaan would fall under their umbrella.

The simple statement, *"For the iniquity of the Amorites is not yet full,"* proclaims much to us. As the Book of Job teaches, Job's friends were wrong when they thought that God immediately brings judgment on sinners. In fact, He is patient and longsuffering. But He is also just, and the judgment will eventually come, if there is no repentance (Horton).

Discoveries at the ancient Ugarit, north of Tyre in Sidon, have revealed that the Canaanite religion promoted child sacrifice, idolatry, and prostitution, all in the name of religion, with all kinds of occultic and immoral practices. In fact, one Archeologist, after working for years in the Middle East, stated that God, Who gave instructions for entire tribes to be wiped out, did future generations an untold service.

The mental aberrations brought on by these evil practices, along with physical disabilities as well, continue to be rampant in many nations of the world, and definitely present in all nations.

So we find from this that God did not destroy these particular tribes, whomever they may have been, until the cup of their iniquity was so full that He had no choice.

THE CUP OF INIQUITY

We have to ask ourselves the question, what nations at present are looking at a *"full cup"*? How far down the road has the United States gone? And let the Reader understand that this holds true not only for nations, but as well for individuals.

God's nature is to bless. He does not delight in judgment; however, He cannot bless sin, as should be obvious. And if the sin gets bad enough, which it always does unless it's washed away by the Blood of Christ, ultimately, judgment will have to come. The Cross Alone can deal with sin, but yet that simple Truth seems to be beyond most in the

NOTES

modern Church. They keep trying to address this monster, this destructive power, this evil direction, by humanistic methods, which at best are only cheap, surface Band-Aids. Faith in what Christ did at the Cross will totally eliminate sin. John beautifully said: *"The Blood of Jesus Christ God's Son cleanses us from all sin"* (I Jn. 1:7).

(17) "AND IT CAME TO PASS, THAT, WHEN THE SUN WENT DOWN, AND IT WAS DARK, BEHOLD A SMOKING FURNACE, AND A BURNING LAMP THAT PASSED BETWEEN THOSE PIECES."

The overview is:

1. The darkness represents the state of this world, now filled with sin.

2. The *"smoking furnace"* proclaims the furnace of affliction that Israel will have to pass through, and in fact, every Believer.

3. The *"burning lamp"* proclaims the Word of God.

4. The *"pieces"* speaks of the Sacrifices, and portrays the Cross.

THE DARKNESS

The phrase, *"And it came to pass, that, when the sun went down, and it was dark,"* is meant to proclaim the condition of this present world, as it regards sin. The conflict is between light and darkness, and we speak of that in the spiritual sense. That's the reason that Isaiah prophesied of the coming Christ: *"The people who walked in darkness have seen a great light: they who dwell in the land of the shadow of death, upon them has the light shined"* (Isa. 9:2).

THE SMOKING FURNACE

The phrase, *"Behold a smoking furnace,"* refers to the trial and test through which Israel would have to go, as well as all Believers. Isaiah again said:

"Behold, I have refined you, but not with silver; I have chosen you in the furnace of affliction" (Isa. 40.10).

Some of the modern gospel has attempted to escape this particular *"furnace"*; however, the manner in which the Lord gave this to Abraham, and considering that he is the father of us all, proclaims to us the fact that no true Christian can escape this *"furnace of affliction."* It must come, and in fact will come, simply because it is necessary. And why is it necessary?

The problem of *"self"* is a never-ending problem; unfortunately, self cannot be properly placed, which is in Christ, unless it comes by the route mentioned here. The fire is necessary, in order to burn out the dross.

When I was a kid, I worked for a short period of time for a plumber. He taught me how to melt lead, which was poured between the joints of pipes, etc.

He had a small pot which had a gas burner attached under it, which would heat it red-hot. The bars of lead would be placed in the pot, and would be melted. All the impurities would float to the top, with extreme heat being the only way that the separation could be brought about. The impurities would then be siphoned off, and pure lead poured between the joints, which then would not leak. Unfortunately, it is the same with Believers.

We may think there are no impurities; however, whenever the proper heat is applied, i.e., *"the furnace of affliction,"* we then find, to our dismay, that many impurities remain, which can now be removed. It is the Holy Spirit Who authors and engineers all of this. In fact, John the Baptist said the following about himself and Christ: *"I indeed baptize you with water unto repentance: but He Who comes after me is mightier than I, Whose shoes I am not worthy to bear: He shall baptize you with the Holy Spirit, and with fire:*

"Whose fan is in His hand, and He will thoroughly purge His floor, and gather His wheat into the garner; but He will burn up the chaff with unquenchable fire" (Mat. 3:11-12).

The *"unquenchable fire,"* as it regards the Holy Spirit, pertains to the *"furnace of affliction."*

BURNING LAMP

The phrase, *"And a burning lamp,"* has to do with the Word of God. The Psalmist said: *"Your Word is a lamp unto my feet, and a light unto my path"* (Ps. 119:105). Every answer needed in this journey of life, is found in the Word of God.

THE SACRIFICE

The phrase, *"That passed between those pieces,"* concerns the sacrifice. The idea is,

we can make it through the darkness only as the *"burning lamp,"* goes before us, which is the Word of God superintended by the Holy Spirit, but which all is based upon the Sacrifice of Christ. The Word of God will always portray the story of the Cross, and the Holy Spirit will always lead us to the Cross.

If we try to get through this world any other way, the *"burning lamp"* simply will not function, and because we have left the safety and protection of the Sacrifice of Christ. Let the Reader remember that the safe path is only *"between those pieces."*

(18) "IN THE SAME DAY THE LORD MADE A COVENANT WITH ABRAM, SAYING, UNTO YOUR SEED HAVE I GIVEN THIS LAND, FROM THE RIVER OF EGYPT UNTO THE GREAT RIVER, THE RIVER EUPHRATES:

(19) "THE KENITES, AND THE KENIZZITES, AND THE KADMONITES,

(20) "AND THE HITTITES, AND THE PERIZZITES, AND THE REPHAIMS,

(21) "AND THE AMORITES, AND THE CANAANITES, AND THE GIRGASHITES, AND THE JEBUSITES."

The synopsis is:

1. The Promises of God are so sure that they can be spoken of in the past tense here, even though they have not yet been realized.

2. The area promised to Abraham and his seed, which extended from *"the river of Egypt unto . . . the river Euphrates,"* came closer to being fulfilled under David than at any time in the history of Israel. It will be fulfilled in totality in the coming Millennial Reign.

3. It is promised Abraham that all of these tribes listed will be totally defeated in that coming day, even plus others not named here.

THE COVENANT

Verse 18 reads: *"In the same day the LORD made a Covenant with Abram, saying, Unto your seed have I given this land, from the river of Egypt unto the great river, the river Euphrates."*

The *"Covenant"* of which the Lord mentions here is unique in that it is different. Most Covenants, as would be obvious, are between two people or more. But here, God covenants to do the whole work. He would begin it. He would finish it. All Abraham had to do was accept it by Faith. In fact, he actually could not help God fulfill it. In truth, he would not even live to see it fulfilled. But it definitely would be fulfilled.

Normally in the making of a Covenant in those particular times, an animal would be killed, and divided, exactly as the heifer, she goat, and ram were divided, with the two individuals walking between the pieces. By doing this, each would solemnly promise to do his part, in effect saying that if he did not, the other could cut him the way the sacrifice was cut.

But in this Covenant, it was only God Who passed between the pieces, and did so by a symbol of fire. As stated, all Abraham did, and in fact, all he could do, was to evidence Faith in this which God had promised.

And in reality, that is all that God requires of us today under the New Covenant, of which this the Lord showed Abraham, was a Type.

THE RIVER OF EGYPT AND
THE RIVER EUPHRATES

The Covenant at that particular time consisted of the land of Canaan, which the Lord would give to the seed of Abraham, with its borders being the river of Egypt on the south, and the river Euphrates up north.

"River" in both cases is the word for a river or canal with water in it all the year round. Some take the river of Egypt to be the insignificant "Wadi el-Arish" in Northeastern Sinai; however, the Hebrew word for the Wadi is different. The promised southern border is rather a branch of the Nile River in its delta. This promise was nearly fulfilled in Solomon's time (I Ki. 8:65), but will have its complete fulfillment in the Millennium. However, the rule of Christ will extend over the entirety of the Earth, and in fact, He will rule from this land of Israel during the time of the Millennium.

The actual area promised by God to Abraham goes all the way to Egypt, which of course includes the Sinai, includes the Arab Peninsula, includes much of modern Iraq, most of Syria, and all of Lebanon.

Israel, during the times of David and Solomon, made no attempt to take the Arab peninsula, simply because it was nothing but desert. Although it was rich in oil, that particular commodity meant nothing then. But

of course, God knew what the future would hold and the future would need; consequently, during the coming Millennium, Israel will control most of the oil of this world, and because she will then control the entirety of the Arab peninsula, plus most of modern Iraq.

TEN

Verses 19 through 21 read: "The Kenites, and the Kenizzites, and the Kadmonites,

"And the Hittites, and the Perizzites, and the Rephaims,

"And the Amorites, and the Canaanites, and the Girgashites, and the Jebusites."

Ten nations are listed here. Ten is the number of completeness in the Bible, and indicates that the entirety of this land, which would also include other tribes, would be given to Abraham's descendants.

Up to this day in Abraham's life, God would say to him, "I will give you this land," but from the hour of this blood-sealed Covenant, He says, "I have given you this land"; for Promises based upon the Precious Blood of Christ are so absolutely sure that Faith can claim them as already possessed. Hence the Believer in the Lord Jesus Christ is neither ashamed nor afraid to say, "I am saved."

Up to the close of this Chapter attention is directed to God's plans with respect to the blessing of man. From this Chapter on, God's ways in carrying out those plans are recorded (Williams).

"Praise Him! Praise Him! Jesus, our Blessed Redeemer!

"Sing, O Earth, His wonderful love proclaim!

"Hail Him! Hail Him! Highest archangels in Glory,

"Strength and Honor give to His holy Name!"

"Like a shepherd Jesus will guard His children.

"In His arms He carries them all day long:"

"Praise Him! Praise Him! Jesus our blessed Redeemer!

"For our sins He suffered and bled and died;

"He's our Rock, our hope of eternal Salvation,
"Hail Him! Hail Him! Jesus the Crucified."

"Sound His praises, Jesus Who bore our sorrows.
"Love unbounded, wonderful, deep and strong:"

"Praise Him! Praise Him! Jesus, our blessed Redeemer!
"Heavenly portals loud with hosannas ring!
"Jesus, Saviour, reigneth forever and ever,
"Crown Him! Crown Him! Prophet and Priest and King!"

"Christ is coming, over the world victorious.
"Power and glory unto the Lord belong:"

CHAPTER 16

(1) "NOW SARAI ABRAM'S WIFE BEAR HIM NO CHILDREN: AND SHE HAD AN HANDMAID, AN EGYPTIAN, WHOSE NAME WAS HAGAR.

(2) "AND SARAI SAID UNTO ABRAM, BEHOLD NOW, THE LORD HAS RESTRAINED ME FROM BEARING: I PRAY THEE, GO IN UNTO MY MAID; IT MAY BE THAT I MAY OBTAIN CHILDREN BY HER. AND ABRAM HEARKENED TO THE VOICE OF SARAI.

(3) "AND SARAI ABRAM'S WIFE TOOK HAGAR HER MAID THE EGYPTIAN, AFTER ABRAM HAD DWELT TEN YEARS IN THE LAND OF CANAAN, AND GAVE HER TO HER HUSBAND ABRAM TO BE HIS WIFE.

(4) "AND HE WENT IN UNTO HAGAR, AND SHE CONCEIVED: AND WHEN SHE SAW THAT SHE HAD CONCEIVED, HER MISTRESS WAS DESPISED IN HER EYES."

The diagram is:

1. This Chapter begins with a terrible sin about to be committed by Abraham and Sarah.

2. Sin in some way is always a lack of faith.

3. The *"conception,"* was a work of the flesh and, therefore, unacceptable to God.

HAGAR

Verse 1 reads: *"Now Sarai Abram's wife bear him no children: and she had an handmaid, an Egyptian, whose name was Hagar."*

For the Promise of God to be fulfilled, a child would have to be born, through whom ultimately the Messiah, the Redeemer of the world would come. The idea is, God would have to become man in order to redeem man.

Paul said, *"For if by one man's offence* (the Fall of Adam) *death reigned by one; much more they which receive abundance of Grace and of the gift of Righteousness shall reign in life by One, Jesus Christ"* (Rom. 5:17).

He then said: *"And so it is written, the first man Adam was made a living soul; the Last Adam* (the Lord Jesus Christ) *was made a quickening spirit* (One Who makes alive)*"* (I Cor. 15:45).

The child that Abraham and Sarah must have has to do with the Incarnation, God becoming man. In fact, this is what all of this was all about.

Concerning this dark episode in the history of Abraham, Williams says: *"Chapter 15 sets out the faithfulness of God, Chapter 16 the faithlessness of Abraham. The Covenant that secured to Abraham riches far exceeding the wealth of Sodom was the more amazing because it necessitated the death of Him (Christ) Who made it! Such was the faithful love to which Abraham responded with unbelief and impatience. The Apostle says you have need of patience that you may inherit the Promises. The 'flesh' can neither believe nor wait for a Divine Promise.*

"The path of faith is full of dignity, the path of unbelief full of degradation. Abraham, finding that God has failed to give him a son, and tired of waiting, no longer sets his hope upon God, but upon an Egyptian slave girl. The natural heart will trust anything rather than God. Abraham thinks that he can, by his clever plan, hasten and bring to pass the Divine Promise. The result is misery. He succeeds in his plan, Ishmael is born; but better were it for Abraham and the world had he never been

born! It is disastrous when the self-willed plans of the Christian succeed."

THE VOICE OF SARAH

Verse 2 reads: *"And Sarai said unto Abram, Behold now, the LORD has restrained me from bearing: I pray you, go in unto my maid; it may be that I may obtain children by her. And Abram hearkened to the voice of Sarai."*

Sarah saying, *"The LORD has restrained me from bearing,"* proclaims the usual impatience of unbelief; and Abraham should have treated it accordingly, and waited patiently on the Lord for the accomplishment of His gracious Promise. However, we have a problem here, and the problem is the flesh.

The poor heart prefers anything to the attitude of waiting. Concerning this, Mackintosh said, *"It will turn to any expedient, any scheme, and resource, rather than be kept in that posture. It is one thing to believe a promise at the first, and quite another thing to wait quietly for the accomplishment thereof."*

How different it would have been had Sarah said, *"Nature has failed me, but God is my resource."*

GOD'S INSTRUMENT

Receiving the Revelation; however, the Lord most of the time, gives very little information concerning His Leading. He expects us to ardently seek His Face as it regards direction. To be sure, He has planned everything, even down to the minute detail, but most of the time we don't know the details.

All of this is meant to teach us trust and Faith. It, as well, is meant to teach us patience.

Hagar was not God's instrument for the accomplishment of His Promise to Abraham. God had promised a son, but He had not said that this son should be Hagar's; and to be sure, their foray into that direction would only seek to multiply their sorrow.

And to be sure again, Abraham's mission was of such magnitude that we are still suffering the results of that ill-fated direction. In fact, the horror of September 11, 2001 is a direct result of Abraham's lack of faith, i.e., *"sin."*

NOTES

TEN YEARS IN THE LAND OF CANAAN

Verse 3 reads: *"And Sarai Abram's wife took Hagar her maid the Egyptian, after Abram had dwelt ten years in the land of Canaan, and gave her to her husband Abram to be his wife."*

Let the Reader understand, as it regards the morality of this act, we find that marriage with one wife was the original law (Gen. 2:24), and that when polygamy was introduced, it was coupled by the inspired narrator with violence and license (Gen. 4:19). Monogamy was the rule, as we see in the households of Noah, Terah, Isaac, and others; but many, like Esau and Jacob, allowed themselves a greater latitude. In so doing, their conduct falls below the level of Biblical morality, but everyone's actions are strongly influenced by the general views of the people among whom he lives; and in Abraham's case it must be said in his defense that, with so much depending on his having offspring, he took no steps to obtain another wife, but remained content with the barren Sarah. When he did take Hagar, it was at his wife's request, and for a reason which seemed to them adequate, and even sacred (Ellicott).

Abraham and Sarah had now been some ten years in Canaan. Even as we have previously stated, ten being the number of completion, is it possible that at this time, God had planned to bring forth Isaac? Perhaps it would be better to ask the question in another way:

How much do our failures of faith hinder in our lives that which God desires to do? Or worse still, how much does it delay us with what He desires to do?

Of course, only God can answer that; however, I think we must come to the conclusion that failure certainly doesn't help. And if it doesn't help, then in some way it definitely must hurt, and that despite the fact that God is gracious and merciful! Beside the harm that the birth of Ishmael caused, I have to believe that the possibility at least existed that this excursion into unbelief also caused a delay.

DESPISED!

Verse 4 reads: *"And he went in unto Hagar, and she conceived: and when she saw that she had conceived, her mistress was despised in her eyes."*

Hagar now becomes pregnant. Noting, no doubt, the accolades which came her way, she begins to treat Sarah in a haughty manner. Having no grace of faith, she as well, has no regard for Sarah, and thereby, oversteps her position. She looks down on Sarah with contempt.

(5) "AND SARAI SAID UNTO ABRAM, MY WRONG BE UPON YOU: I HAVE GIVEN MY MAID UNTO YOUR BOSOM; AND WHEN SHE SAW THAT SHE HAD CONCEIVED, I WAS DESPISED IN HER EYES: THE LORD JUDGE BETWEEN ME AND YOU.

(6) "BUT ABRAM SAID UNTO SARAI, BEHOLD, YOUR MAID IS IN YOUR HAND; DO TO HER AS IT PLEASES YOU. AND WHEN SARAI DEALT HARDLY WITH HER, SHE FLED FROM HER FACE.

(7) "AND THE ANGEL OF THE LORD FOUND HER BY A FOUNTAIN OF WATER IN THE WILDERNESS, BY THE FOUNTAIN IN THE WAY TO SHUR.

(8) "AND HE SAID, HAGAR, SARAI'S MAID, FROM WHERE DO YOU COME? AND WHERE WILL YOU GO? AND SHE SAID, I FLEE FROM THE FACE OF MY MISTRESS SARAI."

The structure is:

1. Sarah blames Abraham for her situation, even though the fault is actually hers.

2. To handle the situation, Abraham gives Sarah the position of leadership regarding Hagar.

3. We find the Lord Jesus Christ, in a preincarnate appearance, takes the matter in hand.

IT IS YOUR FAULT . . .

Verse 5 reads: *"And Sarai said unto Abram, My wrong be upon you: I have given my maid unto your bosom; and when she saw that she had conceived, I was despised in her eyes: the LORD judge between me and you."*

Concerning all of this, Williams says: *"The Epistle to the Galatians declares that Sarah and Hagar represent the two principles of Law and Grace. Hagar represents Salvation by works; Sarah, Salvation by Faith. These principles are opposed to one another. Ishmael is born as the result of man's planning and energy.*

Isaac is born as the result of God's planning and energy. In the birth of Ishmael, God had nothing to do with it, and as regards the birth of Isaac man was dead. So it is today, Salvation by works entirely depends on man's capacity to produce them; Salvation by Faith upon God's ability to perform them.

"Under a Covenant of works, God stands still in order to see what man can do. Under the Covenant of Grace, man stands still to see what God has done. The two Covenants are opposed; it must be either Hagar or Sarah. If Hagar, God has nothing to do with it; if Sarah, man has nothing to do with it."

SARAH AND HAGAR

Verse 6 reads: *"But Abram said unto Sarai, Behold, your maid is in your hands; do to her as it pleases you. And when Sarai dealt hardly with her, she fled from her face."*

While the Scripture doesn't say exactly what Sarai did, whatever it was, it must have been severe. It is believed by some Expositors that she actually had one of the servants to administer corporeal punishment to her in the form of a whipping. Whatever it was, it was so severe that Hagar fled the premises.

THE ANGEL OF THE LORD

Verse 7 reads: *"And the Angel of the LORD found her by a fountain of water in the wilderness, by the fountain in the way to Shur."*

Every evidence is that the *"Angel of the Lord"* mentioned here is none other than a preincarnate appearance of the Lord Jesus Christ.

The Lord, upon meeting Hagar, promises to bless her, tells her He has heard her affliction and comforts her.

Regrettably, later on, she despised this Grace and sought to murder the Divinely given child, which would later come, who would be Isaac.

She calls the name of the well where she met Jesus the Lord, *"The well of living after seeing,"* for she said, *"Do I live after seeing God?"* She did live, but not as the other woman whom Jesus met at Jacob's well. These wells and these women are contrasted here.

QUESTIONS

Verse 8 reads: *"And He said, Hagar, Sarai's maid, from where do you come? And where will you go? And she said, I flee from the face of my mistress Sarai."*

As we shall see, the Lord will not recognize her marriage to the Patriarch. He will remind her of her original position as a bondwoman, from which liberty was not to be obtained by running away, but rather by submission.

As we found with Lot, we find here as well, even with a servant girl, even one who did not necessarily believe the Covenant, that inasmuch as she was in the household of Abraham, she would receive special attention by the Lord. In fact, He would save her life, inasmuch as had she continued on her journey, she would, no doubt, have perished in the wilderness.

(9) "AND THE ANGEL OF THE LORD SAID UNTO HER, RETURN TO YOUR MISTRESS, AND SUBMIT YOURSELF UNTO HER HANDS.

(10) "AND THE ANGEL OF THE LORD SAID UNTO HER, I WILL MULTIPLY YOUR SEED EXCEEDINGLY, THAT IT SHALL NOT BE NUMBERED FOR MULTITUDE.

(11) "AND THE ANGEL OF THE LORD SAID UNTO HER, BEHOLD, YOU ARE WITH CHILD AND SHALL BEAR A SON, AND SHALL CALL HIS NAME ISHMAEL; BECAUSE THE LORD HAS HEARD YOUR AFFLICTION.

(12) "AND HE WILL BE A WILD MAN; HIS HAND WILL BE AGAINST EVERY MAN, AND EVERY MAN'S HAND AGAINST HIM; AND HE SHALL DWELL IN THE PRESENCE OF ALL HIS BRETHREN."

The composition is:

1. The Lord demands that Hagar place herself back under her mistress who was Sarah, and submit herself under her hands.

2. The Lord promised that the seed of Hagar would be great for multitude, but it says nothing about faith.

3. The Lord told her to name the child *"Ishmael,"* which means *"God will hear."* However, the meaning of the name refers to Hagar instead of Ishmael.

4. The Arab world, which descended from Ishmael, fits the description exactly as the Lord predicted here.

SUBMISSION

Verse 9 reads: *"And the Angel of the LORD said unto her, Return to your mistress, and submit yourself under her hands."*

NOTES

In the case before us in this Chapter, it is evident that Hagar was not God's instrument for the accomplishment of His promise to Abraham. He had promised a son, no doubt, but He had not said that this son should be Hagar's; and, in point of fact, we find, from the narrative, that both Abraham and Sarah *"multiplied their sorrow"* by having recourse to Hagar. Sarah's dignity was trampled down by an Egyptian bondwoman, and she found herself in the place of weakness and contempt.

The only true place of dignity and power is the place of felt weakness and dependence. There is no one so entirely independent of all around as the man who is really walking by faith, and waiting only upon God; but the moment a Child of God makes himself a debtor to nature or to the world, he loses his dignity, and will speedily be made to feel his loss. It is no easy task to estimate the loss sustained by diverging, in the smallest measure, from the path of faith. And now Sarah feels that loss.

However, *"the bondwoman"* cannot be eliminated by hard treatment. When we make mistakes, as Sarah did, and find ourselves called upon to encounter the results thereof, we cannot counteract those results by carrying ourselves with a high hand. We frequently try this method, but we are sure to make matters worse thereby.

If we have done wrong, we should humble ourselves and confess the wrong, and wait on God for deliverance. But Sarah didn't do that. So far from waiting on God for deliverance, she seeks to deliver herself in her own way. However, it will always be found that every effort which we make to rectify our errors, previous to the full confession thereof, only tends to render our path more difficult. Thus, Hagar had to return and give birth to her son, which son proved to be not the child of promise at all, but a very great trial to Abraham and his house, as we shall see.

Grace forgives the sin and restores the soul, but that which is sown must be reaped. Abraham and Sarah had to endure the presence of the bondwoman and her son for a number of years, and then see the separation brought about in God's Way.

There is a peculiar blessedness in leaving ourselves in God's Hands. Had Abraham and

Sarah done so on the present occasion, they would never have been troubled with the presence of the bondwoman and her son; but, having made themselves debtors to nature, they had to endure the consequences, and so do we! (Mackintosh).

DID HAGAR TRULY SUBMIT?

The Lord told Hagar to go back and to submit herself totally and fully to Sarah. While she did this somewhat, she did not fully obey. As we shall see, she submitted outwardly, but never really submitted from her heart.

THE SEED

Verse 10 reads: *"And the Angel of the LORD said unto her, I will multiply your seed exceedingly, that it shall not be numbered for multitude."*

Looking at Hagar, she is like so many in the modern Church. She is in the Church, i.e., *"The Covenant,"* but actually never really a part of it. She never recognized Isaac as the Promised Seed, and in fact, actually plotted the murder of Isaac (Gal. 4:29). And so she represents all who would seek to obtain the Promise *"after the flesh,"* which refers to doing so other than by the Cross (Gal. 4:23-25).

In the natural, the Arab people of this particular time (2001), number 100 million plus. In the spiritual sense, the Church is filled with these *"workers of the flesh,"* so much so in fact that it cannot be *"numbered for multitude."*

Isaac represents the Cross, while Ishmael represents the flesh. These two directions are ever before the Church. One or the other must be chosen. And whichever one is chosen, the other one must be cast out. Regrettably and sadly, the far greater majority of the modern Church has cast out the Cross in favor of the flesh. The true way is to cast out the bondwoman and her son, and in fact if the *"Promise"* is to be obtained (all that Jesus did for us at the Cross), they must be cast out (Gal. 4:30).

ISHMAEL

Verse 11 reads: *"And the Angel of the LORD said unto her, Behold, you are with child and shall bear a son, and shall call his name Ishmael; because the LORD has heard your affliction."*

The fault of her situation did not belong with Hagar, but rather with Abraham and Sarah; however, she ultimately forfeited what the Lord could have done for her, by opposing His Plan, which was Isaac.

The Lord does not condone mistreatment, irrespective as to who does it, or to whom it is done. While Hagar definitely had not treated Sarah right after it was found that she had conceived, still, this gave Sarah no right to mistreat this servant girl. As Believers, we do not return kind for kind regarding evil.

The Lord tells Hagar to name the son that will be born to her, *"Ishmael."* The name means, *"God hears,"* but it has nothing to do with Ishmael, but rather the plight of Hagar.

PERSONALITY

Verse 12 reads: *"And he will be a wild man; his hand will be against every man, and every man's hand against him; and he shall dwell in the presence of all his brethren."*

These predictions describe the Arab people perfectly. They cannot get along with anyone in the world, and they cannot even get along among themselves.

At the present time, they have tried to unite regarding the destruction of Israel, but despite the fact that they are about 25 times larger than Israel regarding population, they have failed to make any inroads in regard to this effort, and mostly because they cannot agree among themselves. Ishmael opposed the Cross in his efforts to kill Isaac, and his descendents have continued in the same vein. So he dwells in the presence of all his brethren (Israel), but does not subdue them, and in fact, never will subdue them.

(13) "AND SHE CALLED THE NAME OF THE LORD WHO SPOKE UNTO HER, THOU GOD SEES ME: FOR SHE SAID, HAVE I ALSO HERE LOOKED AFTER HIM WHO SEES ME?

(14) "WHEREFORE THE WELL WAS CALLED BEER-LAHAI-ROI; BEHOLD, IT IS BETWEEN KADESH AND BERED.

(15) "AND HAGAR BEAR ABRAM A SON: AND ABRAM CALLED HIS SON'S NAME, WHICH HAGAR BEAR, ISHMAEL.

(16) "AND ABRAM WAS FOURSCORE AND SIX YEARS OLD, WHEN HAGAR BEAR ISHMAEL TO ABRAM."

The construction is:

1. Hagar recognized that the Angel was in fact, the Lord, actually the God of Abraham.

2. The well where Hagar received this Revelation was named *"The well of the Living One Who sees me."*

3. The child was born to Hagar, exactly as the Lord said it would be. Abraham was 86 years old when Ishmael was born, and due to the fact of what Hagar told him about this Revelation, likewise named the child *"Ishmael."*

THE LORD

Verse 13 reads: *"And she called the name of the LORD Who spoke unto her, Thou God sees me: for she said, Have I also here looked after Him Who sees me?"*

Hagar gave the name to the Lord of *"El Roi,"* which means, *"You are a God Who permits Himself to be seen."* She then exclaims, *"Do not I still see after seeing?"* According to Elliott, her meaning is this:

"Do I not see, and therefore am alive, and not even blinded, nor bereft of sense and reason, though I have seen God."

As is obvious, she truly had a wonderful Revelation, but sadly and regrettably, her self-will overrode her faith. She wanted her son Ishmael to be the heir of Promise, but that was not to be. She would even go so far, even as we will see, to try to kill Isaac. And so do all who reject the Cross follow in her footsteps.

THE WELL

Verse 14 reads: *"Wherefore the well was called Beer-lahai-roi; behold, it is between Kadesh and Bered."*

"Beer-lahai-roi" means *"Well of the Living-Seeing God."* It was the well where God had been seen, and the beholder still lives. It was a place frequented by Isaac (Gen. 25:11).

ISHMAEL

Verse 15 reads: *"And Hagar bear Abram a son: and Abram called his son's name, which Hagar bear, Ishmael."*

Hagar, without doubt, related to Abraham all that had happened, placed herself under the authority of Sarah, and Abraham was

then careful to name the boy what the Lord had said — *"Ishmael."*

EIGHTY-SIX YEARS OLD

Verse 16 reads: *"And Abram was fourscore and six years old, when Hagar bear Ishmael to Abram."*

Abraham would have to wait some 13 more years before the Promise would begin to be fulfilled, and actually some 14 years before Isaac would be born.

As previously stated, I have to wonder if this lapse of faith did not prolong the waiting period for the Promise to be realized. I would not venture to say that such is always the case, however, I do definitely believe that a lapse of faith does definitely have a negative effect. I cannot really see how it could be otherwise. And I think I can say without any fear of exaggeration or contradiction that every sin in some way can be traced back to a lapse of faith. Of course, we're speaking of Believers.

Perhaps one could better explain the situation by saying that it's not so much a lapse of faith as it is the object of faith being changed. The faith of Abraham and Sarah was switched from God and His Promise, to themselves and the Egyptian girl.

THE GALATIANS

The Holy Spirit through the Apostle Paul uses this scenario in the Epistle to the Galatians, to teach us a tremendous Truth.

The error into which the Galatians, or at least some of them, were being drawn was that of adding something to what Christ had already accomplished for them by the Cross. The Gospel, which Paul had preached to them, was the simple presentation of God's absolute, unqualified, and unconditional Grace. *"Jesus Christ had been evidently set forth, crucified among them"* (Gal. 3:1). A Crucified Christ settled everything, in reference both to God's claims and man's necessities.

However, false teachers came in, telling the Galatians that unless they were circumcised, they couldn't be saved. They were attempting to add *"Law"* to *"Grace."*

Paul countered by telling them that if they attempted to add something to the Cross, *"Christ is become of no effect unto you"* (Gal. 5:4).

The moment anyone attempts to add something to faith, they have nullified the Grace of God, and thereby, have subverted Christianity.

The true Message of Christianity, at least as the Bible teaches it, is that God comes down to me, just as I am, a lost, guilty, self-destroyed sinner; and coming, moreover, with a full remission of all my sins, and then a full Salvation given to me, all perfectly brought about by Jesus having died on the Cross, and my Faith in that Finished Work (Jn. 3:3, 16; Rom. 5:1-2; I Cor. 1:17-18, 23; 2:2, 5; Col. 2:14-15; I Pet. 1:18-20).

Understanding this, Paul does not hesitate to say to the Galatians, *"Christ is become of no effect unto you; whosoever of you are* (seek to be) *justified by the Law. You are fallen from Grace"* (Gal. 5:4).

If it is of Grace, it must be all of Grace. It cannot be half Grace, and half Law. The two Covenants, one of works, and one of Faith, are perfectly distinct. To make it clearer, it cannot be half Sarah and half Hagar: it must be either the one or the other. If it is Hagar, God has nothing to do with it, it all being of man. If it is Sarah, man has nothing to do with it, it being all of God.

The Law addresses man, tests him, sees what he is really worth, proves him a ruin, and puts him under the curse; and not only puts him under it, but keeps him there, so long as he is occupied with it, so long as he is alive.

But once the believing sinner accepts Christ, he is actually baptized into the death of Christ, is buried with Christ, and is raised with Christ in newness of life; consequently, what the sinner once was, he no longer is. He is dead, at least as far as the *"old man"* is concerned. Paul said:

"Knowing this, that our old man is crucified with Him, that the body of sin might be destroyed (its guilt and its power), *that henceforth we should not serve sin.*

"For he who is dead is freed from sin" (Rom. 6:6-7).

I'm certain that the Reader understands that Paul is not speaking here of one dying physically, but rather dying in Christ, which happens when one accepts Christ. That's why we are referred to as a *"new creation"* (II

Cor. 5:17). The Lord cannot accept anything else. He can only accept perfection, which alone is found in Christ. Our Faith in Christ, and what Christ has done for us at the Cross, guarantees us a perfect, imputed Righteousness, i.e., *"the Righteousness of Christ."*

There is no way that man by his own machinations and religiosity can attain to such Righteousness. And whenever he attempts to do so by adding his own rules and regulations, or whatever he may submit, the only thing such tends to do is to insult Christ. It in effect says that Christ did not finish the work at the Cross, and something needs to be added.

Of course, God cannot tolerate such thinking, and cannot tolerate such action. It is all of Christ, or it is nothing!

That's the reason that Ishmael, spiritually speaking, must go. Isaac and Ishmael cannot remain in the same place. The former is a child of promise, while the latter is a work of the flesh. And this is what the Believer faces in his living for God.

He can either resort to his own efforts or the efforts of others, thereby accepting Ishmael, or he can rely totally on Christ and what Christ has done at the Cross, thereby relying on Isaac, so to speak. But let the Reader understand the following, that is if he accepts Ishmael:

Paul said: *"Nevertheless what says the Scripture? Cast out the bondwoman and her son: for the son of the bondwoman shall not be heir with the son of the free woman"* (Gal. 4:30).

If in any capacity we attempt to keep *"Ishmael,"* that is, to depend upon the flesh, which means to reject the Cross, all we succeed in doing is to *"frustrate the Grace of God"* (Gal. 2:21). And that is a frightful place for any Christian. We forfeit the inheritance, for only Faith in Christ and the Cross can inherit the Blessing.

RELUCTANCE TO ACCEPT THE CROSS!

The Cross of Christ is the greatest cause of contention in the Church. Most would deny that, because the Cross is seldom mentioned; however, whenever anything is placed before the Christian as necessary, which is an addition to the Cross, the Cross, whether addressed or not, has just become the focal point of contention.

Considering that the Cross is so prominent throughout the entirety of the Bible, so prominent in fact that it's impossible to escape its center of gravity, why should it raise a question?

Let the Reader peruse the following statements very carefully, and because they are so very, very important:

No human being denies the Cross from a position of theology, but always from a position of morality. And what do we mean by that?

The Message of Christ, that He came to this world and died to save sinners, is about as simple as anything could ever be (I Tim. 1:15). Consequently, no individual can claim that he has rejected the Cross simply because he cannot understand the Cross. If it is rejected, it is always from a position of morality. In other words, whether we're speaking of a Believer or an unbeliever, the cause is always unbelief, pride, self-will, etc. As we've stated, Believers do not give up their Ishmaels easily. It is always a struggle, and because Ishmael is always a fruit, and a fair fruit at that, of our own efforts. As a result of it being such, men do not part such company very easily.

THE OFFENCE OF THE CROSS

Paul said: *"And I, Brethren, if I yet preach circumcision, why do I yet suffer persecution? Then is the offence of the Cross ceased"* (Gal. 5:11).

In Paul's day, circumcision, which was a part of the old Mosaic Law, was the big thing. Many Christian Jews were saying that Gentiles had to be *"circumcised after the manner of Moses,"* that is, if they were to be saved (Acts 15:1). So they were adding circumcision to Grace, which of course cannot be done.

Presently, circumcision is not the problem, but rather other things; however, it doesn't really matter what it is which we attempt to substitute for the Cross, or else add to the Cross; the end result is the same. In such a case, *"Christ shall profit you nothing"* (Gal. 5:2).

Why is it that these other things, whatever they might be, carry no offence, and the Cross does?

That's a good question!

Among other things, the Cross proclaims the fact of how sinful and wicked that man is, so sinful and wicked in fact, that God would have to become man, and die on a cruel Cross, shedding His Life's Blood, in effect, offering Himself for Sacrifice, in order that man might be saved. Man doesn't want to admit that he's that bad. He likes to think that while he might have a problem of sorts, still, he can save himself in some way. So he keeps trying, and he keeps trying, and he keeps trying, all to no avail. But despite the fact that the guilt doesn't leave, because his own efforts never bring about a Born-Again experience, he tries to cover up the emptiness of his soul, by claiming that which he really doesn't have.

Far too often, the Believer who has rejected the Cross, or else doesn't understand the Cross, will also try to cover up his lack of victorious living, by loudly claiming, even as the unbeliever, that which he as well doesn't have.

THE FAÇADE

The modern Church is literally built, at least for all practical purposes, on methods devised by man, which actually will not work. It's another *"Ishmael."*

But instead of tearing down the façade, because that's what it is, instead, the façade is strengthened. In other words, we groom and we dress up Ishmael.

Outside of the Cross, there are probably as many methods of so-called victory as there are people.

I received a letter just the other day from a Preacher who was touting the following:

He was invited to a *"Seminar,"* with only Preachers present, at least that's what his letter seemed to imply, with all being in desperate need of victory.

The method proposed at this Seminar was that each Preacher and his wife, that is if she was with him, should take a piece of paper and write on that paper all of their faults and sins, etc. They were then to pair off with a stranger, men with men, and women with women, and then read their list of faults and failures to each other.

After this was done, they were to then rip up the piece of paper on which their faults and failures had been listed, and throw it all on the floor. They were then to trample the pieces underfoot, and somehow all of this, at least according to the Pastor of a large Church who was sponsoring the Seminar, was to give them victory. Several hundreds of Preachers believed this stupidity, and attended, and did what they were told to do.

The sadness is, all of these Preachers were supposed to be Spirit-filled.

This is just another ridiculous method (and ridiculous it is) of substituting something else in place of the Cross. Not a shred of such foolishness is found in the Bible, but yet it was being touted as a great spiritual breakthrough.

The non-Pentecostal world has attempted to preach the Cross without the Holy Spirit. Now they are, for all practical purposes, preaching neither one. The Pentecostal world has attempted to preach the Holy Spirit without the Cross, and has degenerated into fanaticism, of which I've just given an example. If the Church doesn't return to the Cross, which must always be the Foundation of all that we believe and preach, the situation will only grow worse.

"There is a Name I love to hear,
"I love to sing its worth;
"It sounds like music in my ear,
"The sweetest Name on Earth."

"It tells me of a Saviour's love,
"Who died to set me free;
"It tells me of His precious Blood,
"The sinner's perfect plea."

"It tells me what my Father has
"In store for every day,
"And, tho' I tread a darksome path,
"Yields sunshine all the way."

"It tells of One Whose loving heart
"Can feel my deepest woe,
"Who in each sorrow bears a part
"That none can bear below."

CHAPTER 17

(1) "AND WHEN ABRAM WAS NINETY YEARS OLD AND NINE, THE LORD APPEARED TO ABRAM, AND SAID UNTO

HIM, I AM THE ALMIGHTY GOD; WALK BEFORE ME, AND BE THOU PERFECT.

(2) "AND I WILL MAKE MY COVENANT BETWEEN ME AND YOU, AND WILL MULTIPLY YOU EXCEEDINGLY.

(3) "AND ABRAM FELL ON HIS FACE: AND GOD TALKED WITH HIM, SAYING,"

The composition is:

1. Some 13 years passed before the next Revelation was given to Abraham by the Lord.

2. The Lord now renews the Covenant with Abraham, which greatly enlarges upon the Promises previously made.

3. The Power of God was so great, as God talked with Abraham, that the Patriarch *"fell on his face."*

EL-SHADDAI

Verse 1 reads: *"And when Abram was ninety years old and nine, the LORD appeared to Abram, and said unto him, I am the Almighty God; walk before Me, and be thou perfect."*

It had probably been about 13 years since the Lord had last spoken with Abraham. During this time, he probably continued to think that Ishmael was the Promised Seed. That is indicated from Verse 18. But now he will know different.

The last personal Revelation that Abraham had received from the Lord regarding the Name of the Lord concerned the meeting with Melchizedek. And even then, the Revelation was given by Melchizedek to Abraham, with the Lord referred to as *"El Elyon,"* which means *"Most High God, Possessor of Heaven and Earth."* As well, through Hagar, he had learned of God as *"El Roi,"* which means, *"Thou art a God Who permits Himself to be seen."* But now, he will be given the Revelation of *"Almighty God,"* which in the Hebrew is *"El Shaddai."* It means, *"Strong so as to overpower."* Keil says of this Name, *"As possessing the power to realize His promises, even when the order of nature presented no prospect of their fulfillment, and the powers of nature were insufficient to secure it."*

In the various names given in the Bible of God, we learn of His Nature and His Characteristics. These names define Who He is and as well, what He is.

Concerning this time, Williams says: *"Thirteen years of silence on the part of God follow upon Abraham's folly in the matter of Ishmael; but man's foolish planning cannot undo God's eternal counsels. The time is fulfilled and the child of Promise must be born.*

"But faith must be energized if Isaac is to be begotten; and accordingly there is a new and abrupt Revelation made of Jehovah to Abraham's soul as 'El-Shaddai.' This is the first occurrence of this great Divine title. It assured Abraham that what God had promised, He was Almighty to perform. The first occurrence of this title in the New Testament (II Cor. 6:18) expresses the same truth. Throughout the Chapter therefore, man is dead and God is the Actor; and it was not so much what God was for Abraham, but what he was Himself — not 'I am your shield,' but 'I am El-Shaddai.'"

THE WALK OF THE PATRIARCH

Concerning Abraham's life and living, it is very evident that he had not been walking before Almighty God as he should have walked, when he adopted Sarah's suggestion in reference to Hagar. It is Faith alone that can enable a man to walk before God as he should walk. And above all, it is Faith with its object being the Cross, which it must ever be, or else it is faith which God will not recognize. The Holy Spirit superintends Faith with the Cross as its object, but He will not superintend faith in anything else (Rom. 8:1-2, 11).

With the words, *"I am the Almighty God; walk before Me, and be thou perfect,"* the Lord was telling Abraham two things:

1. He must be perfect in his Faith. It must not waver as it had done regarding the situation with Hagar, but must rest in Almighty God.

2. There is no way that one's *"walk"* can be as it ought to be, without the Power of Almighty God. It is simply impossible otherwise!

We as Believers presently have the Power of the Holy Spirit, Who is Almighty God, and Who will help us, even as He is meant to do. And to be sure, without Him, the task simply cannot be performed.

Unfortunately, most modern Christians do not understand the way and the means by which the Holy Spirit works. They take Him for granted, or else they know next to

nothing about Him, looking at Him as someone or something mysterious. The truth is, He desires to lead us, guide us, empower us, and make of us what we ought to be, which is all done by development of the Fruit of the Spirit, and above all, to glorify Christ within our lives. For us to have His help, and on a constant basis, we must *"walk after the Spirit."* To not walk after the Spirit is to *"walk after the flesh,"* which automatically brings failure (Rom. 8:1).

The modern Christian has a much better Covenant as it regards the New Covenant, by comparison to the Covenant under which Abraham functioned. Our New Covenant is much better, because it's based on a work already done by Christ on the Cross, relative to a work before the Cross, which was only promised.

The Covenants before the Cross were based on animal blood, which was woefully insufficient. The New Covenant is based on the Blood of our Lord and Saviour, Jesus Christ. Whereas the blood of animals could not take away sins, the Blood of Christ definitely could take sin away, and all its effects (Heb. 10:4). So since the Cross, so to speak, we have a much better contract (Jn. 1:29).

WHAT DOES IT MEAN TO WALK AFTER THE SPIRIT?

To give the answer before we deal with the particulars, walking after the Spirit simply means that the Believer places his Faith exclusively in the Cross of Christ, understanding what Jesus did for him there, and thereby placing his Faith in nothing else (Rom. 8:1-2, 11). *"Walking after the flesh,"* is placing one's faith in anything, irrespective as to what it might be, other than the Cross of Christ.

Most Christians don't have the slightest idea as to what *"walking after the Spirit"* or *"walking after the flesh"* actually is. Were they to give an answer, at least as it regards *"walking after the Spirit,"* they would think it refers to doing spiritual things. It doesn't!

By *"spiritual things,"* I'm speaking of faithfulness to Church, giving our money for the Work of the Lord, fasting, having a regular prayer time each day, reading one's Bible, witnessing to souls, etc. These things are what we refer to as *"Christian disciplines,"* and are what every good Christian will always do. And to be sure, those things are deeply spiritual, and will prove to be a great blessing to any and all Believers in the carrying out of these particulars; however, the doing of those things is not *"walking after the Spirit."*

In effect, Paul tells us what it is in Romans 8:2. He said: *"For the Law* (a Law devised by the Godhead) *of the Spirit* (Holy Spirit) *of life* (that which tenders life) *in Christ Jesus* (this Law is made up of what Christ did at the Cross on our behalf) *has made me free from the law of sin and death."* When we place our Faith in Christ and what Christ has done for us at the Cross, in effect, never divorcing Christ from His Cross, and do so on a constant basis, which refers to the fact that we know and understand that everything we receive from God comes to us by and through Christ and what He did at the Cross, such constitutes *"walking after the Spirit."* Such constitutes a perfect walk, and without our faith properly placed, our *"walk,"* (manner of life), will be erratic to say the least. We can walk before the Lord even as God demanded of Abraham, and do so correctly, if we follow God's prescribed order, which is the Cross of Christ.

COVENANT

Verse 2 reads: *"And I will make My Covenant between me and you, and will multiply you exceedingly."*

Concerning this *"Covenant,"* one could say that it is an extension of the Covenant already given to the Patriarch (Gen., Chpt. 15), or because it goes into such great detail, one might even place it in the position of an enlarged Covenant.

In Covenants made by the Lord, we find that the Lord doesn't leave anything undone. He will perfectly settle everything on behalf of those who simply put their trust in Him, and that refers to what Christ has done for us at the Cross. When unerring wisdom, omnipotent power, and infinite love combine, the confiding heart may enjoy unruffled repose. Unless we can find some circumstance too big or too little for *"the Almighty God,"* we have no proper base on which to found a single anxious thought. Now that is an amazing

statement, but it happens to be true. There should be no room for worry, anxiety, or fear in the heart and life of any Believer, who has placed his Faith totally and completely in Christ, and what Christ has done for him at the Cross.

This is an amazing Truth, and one eminently calculated to put all who believe it into the blessed position in which we find Abraham in this Chapter. When God had, in effect, said to him, *"Leave all to Me, and I will settle it for you, beyond your utmost desires and expectations: the seed and the inheritance, and everything pertaining thereto, will be fully and everlastingly settled, according to the Covenant of the Almighty God."*

All of this hinges on Faith, and more particularly, it hinges on Faith properly placed, and Faith properly placed always and without exception refers to the Cross of Christ. If we attempt to place our faith in the Word of God, which is what we certainly should do, without first anchoring it in the Cross, we will find that we will misinterpret the Word. The Word of God is, in effect, the story of Christ and His Cross. That is the tenor and timbre of the Bible from Genesis 1:1 through Revelation 22:21.

The Living Word came to this world (Jn. 1:1). *"That Word was made flesh, and dwelt among us"* (Jn. 1:14).

He did this for a particular reason, and John tells us what that reason was.

When John the Baptist introduced Jesus, he said: *"Behold the Lamb of God, which taketh away the sin of the world"* (Jn. 1:29).

In effect, these three Passages I have just given, give us the story of the Bible.

I made the statement the other night in preaching, *"If one understands Genesis 15:6, then one understands the entirety of the Bible. If that one Scripture is misunderstood, then basically the entirety of the Word of God, in some way, is misunderstood."*

I do not think that any Believer can properly understand the Bible unless he first understands the Cross. Once he begins to properly understand the Cross, then the entirety of the Word of God will begin to come into focus. This is true Faith, and the only way that Faith can be properly expressed and anchored in the Word of God. In fact, even as Jesus and His Cross must never be separated, the Word and the Cross must as well not be separated, and for the simple reason that the story of the Word is the Cross.

THE BLESSING

The phrase, *"And will multiply you exceedingly,"* could be translated, *"And will bless you exceedingly."*

Blessing from God always falls out to increase, with increase explained in the realm of multiplication. It means that the Lord doesn't merely add to, but rather that He multiplies. There is a vast difference!

So, Abraham is concerned about one particular seed, not seeing how in the world it can be brought to pass, considering his age and the age of Sarah, and especially that she has been barren all of her life, and now God tells him that not only will the seed be forthcoming, but He is going to multiply that seed exceedingly, which He most definitely did.

Concerning the Power of God, Paul said: *"Now, unto Him Who is able to do exceeding abundantly above all that we ask or think, according to the power that worketh in us"* (Eph. 3:20). That's the kind of God that we serve, and the reason that if our Faith is properly placed, we need have no occasion for worry, fear, or anxiety.

THE RESPONSE

Verse 3 reads: *"And Abram fell on his face: and God talked with him, saying."*

The Power of God was no doubt expressed here in a tremendous way. So Abraham falling on his face was either because he simply couldn't stand due to the Power, or else he fell on his face in reverence to God. More than likely, both circumstances came into play here. He could not continue to stand because of the Power, and his desire as well, was to prostrate himself before the Lord.

THE NAMES OF GOD

In these three Verses, the Lord reveals Himself by three different names. The name *"Lord"* in Verse 1 means, *"Jehovah."* In the latter part of Verse 1, the Lord refers to Himself as *"the Almighty God,"* Who in effect is *"El-Shaddai,"* the *"All-powerful One."*

In Verse 3, He refers to Himself as *"Elohim,"* which refers to Him being Creator.

The *"Perfection"* demanded in Verse 1 means, *"guileless."*

In effect, the Lord is saying, *"Leave all to Me, let Me plan for you. I am Almighty. No longer scheme to beget an Ishmael, but trust Me to give you an Isaac."* In effect, one might say that this is the meaning of the word *"perfect"* in Verse 1. It does not mean that Abraham was sinlessly perfect, for he wasn't, and neither is there any other individual as well.

(4) "AS FOR ME, BEHOLD, MY COVENANT IS WITH YOU, AND YOU SHALL BE A FATHER OF MANY NATIONS.

(5) "NEITHER SHALL YOUR NAME ANY MORE BE CALLED ABRAM, BUT YOUR NAME SHALL BE ABRAHAM; FOR A FATHER OF MANY NATIONS HAVE I MADE YOU.

(6) "AND I WILL MAKE YOU EXCEEDING FRUITFUL, AND I WILL MAKE NATIONS OF YOU, AND KINGS SHALL COME OUT OF YOU.

(7) "AND I WILL ESTABLISH MY COVENANT BETWEEN ME AND YOU AND YOUR SEED AFTER YOU IN THEIR GENERATIONS FOR AN EVERLASTING COVENANT, TO BE A GOD UNTO YOU, AND TO YOUR SEED AFTER YOU."

The composition is:

1. It was promised Abraham that he would be a father of many nations, and so he was.

2. His name was changed from *"Abram,"* which means *"exalted father,"* to *"Abraham,"* which means *"father of the multitudes."*

3. Nations and kings would come from him.

4. This Covenant would be labeled by the Lord as an *"Everlasting Covenant."*

A FATHER OF MANY NATIONS

Verse 4 reads: *"As for Me, behold, My Covenant is with you, and you shall be a father of many nations."*

From the one seed, i.e., *"child,"* which Abraham was worried about, the Lord takes him to the position of *"father of many nations."* In effect, He was saying to the Patriarch, *"I am Almighty God, and I can do anything."*

Ellicott says that this Fourth Verse is translated poorly. He goes on to say, *"Literally the word, 'of many nations,' signifies a confused noise like the din of a populous city. Abraham was to be the father of a 'thronging crowd of nations.'"*

ABRAHAM

Verse 5 reads: *"Neither shall your name any more be called Abram, but your name shall be Abraham; for a father of many nations have I made you."*

"Abram" means, *"exalted father,"* while *"Abraham"* means, *"father of the multitudes."*

The *"multitudes"* of which are spoken here concern all who have come to Christ. While nations and kings actually came from Abraham, in fact, the entirety of the Arab world, now numbering approximately 100 million, along with the Jews, numbering approximately 20 million, if all are counted in the world, all these would be other than the Body of Christ.

The True Seed, which came from Abraham, is Christ (Gal. 3:16). Consequently, all who are of Faith are blessed with faithful Abraham, being partakers of the same Covenant blessings, secured by the same oath and promise.

All that the Christian world enjoys, or ever will enjoy, it is indebted to Abraham and his Seed. A high honor this is, to be the father of the faithful, the stock from which the Messiah should spring, and on which the Church of the Living God should grow.

This honor Esau despised when he sold his birthright; and here lay the profaneness of that act, which involved a contempt of the most sacred of all objects, the Messiah and His everlasting Kingdom (Henry).

FRUITFUL

Verse 6 reads: *"And I will make you exceeding fruitful, and I will make nations of you, and kings shall come out of you."*

Without a doubt, the two greatest kings to come from Abraham would be David and Solomon. But yet the greatest of all, and Who cannot be classed among mere men, is the Lord Jesus Christ, the King of kings and the Lord of lords. Actually, Christ is referred to as *"the Son of David, the Son of Abraham"* (Mat. 1:1).

THE EVERLASTING COVENANT

Verse 7 reads: *"And I will establish My Covenant between Me and you and your seed*

after you in their generations for an everlasting Covenant, to be a God unto you, and to your seed after you."

This Covenant as made with Abraham, is totally different than the Covenant made with Moses, with the latter being temporary. The Covenant with the Patriarch is everlasting, simply because, even though it involves many things, its end result is Justification by Faith. In fact, its conclusion will be the New Covenant, which in fact was as well referred to as *"the Everlasting Covenant"* (Heb. 13:20).

(8) "AND I WILL GIVE UNTO YOU, AND TO YOUR SEED AFTER YOU, THE LAND WHEREIN YOU ARE A STRANGER, ALL THE LAND OF CANAAN, FOR AN EVERLASTING POSSESSION; AND I WILL BE THEIR GOD.

(9) "AND GOD SAID UNTO ABRAHAM, YOU SHALL KEEP MY COVENANT THEREFORE, YOU, AND YOUR SEED AFTER YOU IN THEIR GENERATIONS."

The structure is:

1. The land of Canaan was to be given to Abraham, and to his seed, for an everlasting possession.

2. His seed was to worship God, and God Alone. In other words, *"You shall have no other gods before Me."*

3. All who followed thereafter were to keep this Covenant, which had only one outward ordinance, and that was Circumcision. The balance was entirely of Faith.

CANAAN

Verse 8 reads: *"And I will give unto you, and to your seed after you, the land wherein you are a stranger, all the land of Canaan, for an everlasting possession; and I will be their God."*

Both the Jewish and Arab worlds point to Abraham as their father, and rightly so. The difference is the seed. The Arabs, which are mostly Muslim, claim Ishmael is the true seed, while the Jews claim Isaac to be the True Seed, which latter corresponds with the Word of God (vs. 21). Because of this contention, the *"land of Canaan"* has been, probably one could say, the world's chief trouble spot. This conflict between the Muslims and the Jews, and especially as it regards the land of Canaan, has raged, more or less, for some 1,400 years. To be frank, the greatest contention is just ahead, as it regards the Antichrist, etc.

THE KEEPING OF THE COVENANT

Verse 9 reads: *"And God said unto Abraham, You shall keep My Covenant therefore, you, and your seed after you in their generations."*

This could well be called a *"Covenant of Grace,"* and as such, is everlasting; it is *"from"* everlasting in the counsels of it, and *"to"* everlasting in the consequences of it.

Israel, upon becoming a nation some 400 years later, recognized the great Covenant as given to Abraham, but instead of making it the foundation Covenant, they placed the Law or Covenant of Moses in the first place, and made the Abrahamic Covenant second place, which means they inverted it. Consequently, they destroyed themselves. Law must never precede Grace. If so, Grace is abrogated.

Regrettably, the Church is, for all practical purposes, doing the same identical thing. Abraham is our father, but in a sense, the modern Church has made Moses their father. While it's done in a subtle way, and thereby not recognizable to all, the facts are, if we look to man-devised law instead of the Cross, we have abrogated, exactly as did Israel, this beautiful and wonderful Abrahamic Covenant. Both, and I speak of the Covenant of Grace, and the Covenant of Law, cannot exist at the same time. One or the other must go. In fact, Jesus has totally and perfectly kept the Mosaic Covenant, and He is the only One Who has done this, and in fact, He did it all on our behalf. We are meant to function only in the Covenant of Grace, which in effect, is the Abrahamic Covenant (Rom. 4:16), of which Jesus is the result. But regrettably, the Covenant of Law seems to be far more enticing!

(10) "THIS IS MY COVENANT, WHICH YOU SHALL KEEP, BETWEEN ME AND YOU AND YOUR SEED AFTER YOU; EVERY MAN CHILD AMONG YOU SHALL BE CIRCUMCISED.

(11) "AND YOU SHALL CIRCUMCISE THE FLESH OF YOUR FORESKIN; AND IT SHALL BE A TOKEN OF THE COVENANT BETWIXT ME AND YOU.

(12) "AND HE WHO IS EIGHT DAYS OLD SHALL BE CIRCUMCISED AMONG YOU, EVERY MAN CHILD IN YOUR GENERATIONS, HE WHO IS BORN IN THE HOUSE, OR BOUGHT WITH MONEY OF ANY STRANGER, WHICH IS NOT OF YOUR SEED.

(13) "HE WHO IS BORN IN YOUR HOUSE, AND HE WHO IS BOUGHT WITH YOUR MONEY, MUST NEEDS BE CIRCUMCISED: AND MY COVENANT SHALL BE IN YOUR FLESH FOR AN EVERLASTING COVENANT.

(14) "AND THE UNCIRCUMCISED MAN CHILD WHOSE FLESH OF HIS FORESKIN IS NOT CIRCUMCISED, THAT SOUL SHALL BE CUT OFF FROM HIS PEOPLE; HE HAS BROKEN MY COVENANT."

The overview is:

1. Circumcision was to be the physical sign of this Covenant.

2. Every boy baby was to be circumcised at eight days old. No boy or man was to be excluded, even slaves.

3. Any child or man who refused to be circumcised, was to be out of the Covenant, and would be *"cut off,"* i.e., *"lost."*

CIRCUMCISION

Verse 10 reads: *"This is My Covenant, which you shall keep, between Me and you and your seed after you; every man child among you shall be circumcised."*

The rite of Circumcision is now introduced. Every male member of the household of Faith must bear in his body the seal of that Covenant. There must be no exception.

We are taught in Romans, Chapter 4 that Circumcision was *"a seal of the Righteousness of Faith."* Abraham believed God, and it was counted unto him for Righteousness. Being thus counted righteous, God set His *"seal"* upon him, and all who would follow him in this principle of Faith.

The seal with which the Believer is now sealed is not a mark in the flesh, but *"that Holy Spirit of Promise, whereby he is sealed, unto the day of Redemption."* This is founded upon our everlasting connection with Christ, and our perfect identification with Him, in death and Resurrection.

Paul said: *"And you are complete in Him, which is the Head of all principality and power: in Whom also you are circumcised with the Circumcision made without hands, in putting off the body of the sins of the flesh by the Circumcision of Christ: buried with Him in Baptism, wherein also you are risen with Him through the faith of the operation of God, Who has raised Him from the dead. And you, being dead in your sins and the uncircumcision of your flesh, has He quickened together with Him, having forgiven you all trespasses"* (Col. 2:10-13).

This Passage as given by Paul, proclaims to us the true idea of what Circumcision was meant to typify. Every Believer belongs to *"the Circumcision"* by virtue of his living association with Him Who, by His Cross, has forever abolished everything that stood in the way of a perfect Justification. One might say that there is not a speck of sin, nor a principle of sin in the nature of God's people, for which Christ was not judged on the Cross; and we are now looked upon as having died with Christ, lain in the grave with Christ, and then raised with Christ, perfectly accepted in Him, all our sins, iniquities, transgressions, and enmity, having been entirely put away by the Cross (Rom. 6:3-5).

CHRIST

Circumcision, in a sense, is a Type of the Cross. Blood is shed and separation is made. This speaks of the shed Blood of Christ, which separates us from our sins, and in fact, the only thing which will separate us from our sins.

So, Christ fulfilled this *"rite of Circumcision,"* by what He did on the Cross, as well as fulfilling all of the Law in totality.

Unfortunately, some of the Christian Jews during the time of Paul were attempting to demand circumcision of all Gentile converts (the boys and the men).

Knowing that Jesus had fulfilled this particular physical act by what He did at the Cross, which now made the physical act meaningless, He addresses this subject by saying: *"Behold, I Paul say unto you, that if you be circumcised, Christ shall profit you nothing"* (Gal. 5:2).

This doesn't mean at all that Paul was opposed to the physical act of circumcision, but he was deadly opposed to this act if it was

claimed that it was necessary in order for a person to be saved. Either what Christ did at the Cross was totally sufficient, or it was not sufficient at all. Inasmuch as what Christ did was definitely sufficient, then neither circumcision, nor any other physical act or rite, were necessary. The idea is, and even as previously stated, it is impossible to have both *"Grace"* and *"Law"* as the object of one's faith. So the Apostle is saying that if any man or boy submits to the physical act of circumcision, thinking that it adds spiritual profit, *"Christ shall profit you nothing."* And regrettably, that is where much of the modern Church is presently. Trusting in law of one type or the other, *"Christ profits them nothing."* As stated repeatedly, one cannot have both the Cross and Law. One or the other must go!

A TOKEN OF THE COVENANT

Verse 11 reads: *"And you shall circumcise the flesh of your foreskin; and it shall be a token of the Covenant betwixt Me and you."*

According to the Pulpit Commentary, Circumcision says several things:

1. It was a sign of the Faith that Christ should be descended from Abraham.

2. Circumcision was to be a symbolic representation of the putting away of the filth of the flesh and of sin in general.

3. It was to distinguish the seed of Abraham from the Gentiles.

4. It was to perpetuate the memory of Jehovah's Covenant.

5. It was to foster in the nation the hope of the Messiah.

6. It was to remind them of the duty of cultivating moral purity (Deut. 10:16).

7. It was to preach to them the Gospel of a Righteousness by Faith (Rom. 4:11).

8. It was to suggest the idea of a Holy or a Spiritual Seed of Abraham (Rom. 2:29).

9. It was to foreshadow the Christian rite of Baptism (Col. 2:11-12).

Verses 12 and 13 read: *"And he who is eight days old shall be circumcised among you, every man child in your generations, he who is born in the house, or bought with money of any stranger, which is not of your seed.*

"He who is born in your house, and he who is bought with your money, must needs

be circumcised: and My Covenant shall be in your flesh for an everlasting covenant."

This Covenant is everlasting, but only in Christ. As the Holy Spirit related through Paul, the time came that Christ finished His Work on the Cross; consequently, physical circumcision, as well as any other ordinance or rite, must be laid aside, that is if it was thought of as pertaining to Salvation. Either the Work of Christ was total and complete, or else it wasn't. If it was total and complete, then nothing else is needed. And to be sure, it definitely was total and complete in every respect.

THE BROKEN COVENANT

Verse 14 reads: "And the uncircumcised man child whose flesh of his foreskin is not circumcised, that soul shall be cut off from his people; he has broken My Covenant."

This simply means that if any Israelite, whether child or adult, refused to follow this Commandment of Circumcision, he would forfeit his standing in the congregation, in effect, would cease to be a part of the Covenant, which means that he was lost.

The same can be said presently for those who disavow the Work of the Cross. That being the case, and irrespective of all other religious activity, that individual is lost. In fact, the entirety of the Book of Hebrews was written for this very purpose.

Particular Christian Jews had grown discouraged, turned their backs on Christ, and had gone back into Judaism, i.e., "Temple worship," etc. To do this, they had to disavow Christ and the Cross, and this being done, and if one remained in this position, they would be eternally lost.

As important as was Circumcision to the Abrahamic Covenant, and even to the Mosaic Covenant, as important is the Cross to the modern Believer. And when I speak of the Cross, I'm not speaking of a wooden beam. I'm speaking of the great Work which Christ carried out on that gibbet, all for you and me. However, there was a great difference in regard to circumcision and the Cross.

THE DIFFERENCE BETWEEN THE CROSS AND CIRCUMCISION

As it regards the ancient rite of Circumcision, a Jewish man could easily come to the

place that he believed the act of circumcision itself constituted Salvation, even as did millions. But of course, that was basely incorrect. The physical act of circumcision afforded no Salvation, but only Faith in what Circumcision represented, namely Christ, brought about saving Grace.

It is not possible, however, for one to place his Faith in Christ and the Cross as a mere form. In fact, the Cross is the only guarantee given in the Bible against mere form (I Cor. 1:17-18, 23; Col. 2:14-15).

(15) "AND GOD SAID UNTO ABRAHAM, AS FOR SARAI YOUR WIFE, YOU SHALL NOT CALL HER NAME SARAI, BUT SARAH SHALL HER NAME BE.

(16) "AND I WILL BLESS HER, AND GIVE YOU A SON ALSO OF HER: YES, I WILL BLESS HER, AND SHE SHALL BE A MOTHER OF NATIONS; KINGS OF PEOPLE SHALL BE OF HER.

(17) "THEN ABRAHAM FELL UPON HIS FACE, AND LAUGHED, AND SAID IN HIS HEART, SHALL A CHILD BE BORN UNTO HIM WHO IS AN HUNDRED YEARS OLD? AND SHALL SARAH, THAT IS NINETY YEARS OLD, BEAR?"

The exegesis is:

1. Sarai's name is changed to "Sarah."

2. The Lord now tells Abraham that the son that will be born will be of Sarah, and no one else.

3. Abraham's laughter at this prediction was not one of skepticism, but rather of Faith.

SARAH

Verse 15 reads: "And God said unto Abraham, As for Sarai your wife, you shall not call her Sarai, but Sarah shall her name be."

The name "Sarai" means, "my princess," referring to the fact that she was Abraham's princess alone.

"Sarah" simply means, "Princes." The idea is, whereas she was formerly Abraham's princess only, she will now be recognized as a princess generally, and in fact, as the "mother of the Church." Actually, she is now to be a "Princess to the Lord."

If it is to be noticed, the letter "h" is taken from the name "JeHovaH," as in the change of Abram into Abraham, with the name Sarai being changed to Sarah.

The very fact of the changing of the name of Sarah spoke volumes to Abraham, or at least certainly should have. Formerly she belonged only to him, but now, in essence, she will belong to the entirety of the world. The very change of her name proclaimed the fact that she was now to be a great part of the Covenant.

As well, the change to a Hebrew form of the name, which the new name, *"Sarah"* proclaims, shows a complete break with the past. She would never return to her birthplace, for she was to focus her life on the Promise of God.

As well, the change of her name proclaims a giant step taken toward the fulfillment of the *"Seed of the Woman"* bruising the head of Satan. As we previously stated in the earlier part of this Commentary, by that prediction given by God in Genesis 3:15, the Lord in essence was saying to Satan, *"You have used the woman to pull down My choice creation, and I will use a woman to lift that creation back to its original status."* All of this portrays the fact that God has so much more for us than our own pitiful efforts can provide. That's the reason that Salvation must be all of God and none at all of man.

THE COVENANT

Verse 16 reads: *"And I will bless her, and give you a son also of her: yes, I will bless her, and she shall be a mother of nations; kings of people shall be of her."*

This is the first time in all of God's dealings with Abraham that He had mentioned the fact that the promised son would be of Sarah, and as one might say *"Sarah's own son."* In effect, the Promise regarding Sarah was very similar to that regarding Abraham, at least as it pertains to entire nations proceeding from her.

The word *"bless"* refers to all the things that God can do, which means that He can do all things, but more particularly, it refers to the culmination of all blessing, Who is the Lord Jesus Christ.

The Covenant of Circumcision was to be in force until the Messiah would come. Inasmuch as this rite was carried out on the male member, and not on women, for they were exempt, showed us several things.

It shows us that man was responsible for the Fall, inasmuch as the seed of procreation

is in him. As well, the foreskin of the male member being removed by circumcision, was to be a reminder to the people of Israel of original sin, which is hereditary one might say, and remains in us till we die. Even though Eve was tempted, and actually fell first, due to the fact that the seed was alone in the man, and not in the woman, we find that women were exempted by God from circumcision. Thus, God foreshadowed in the Circumcision rite the whole theology of Redemption, namely, both sin and Grace.

It reminded the Jews of the fact that all men by nature are children of wrath on account of hereditary sin (Eph. 2:1-3). It also reminded them of Grace, for it indicated the birth of Christ from a virgin who was to abrogate circumcision and save all men from sin and death, and do so by His Own death.

LAUGHTER

Verse 17 reads: *"Then Abraham fell upon his face, and laughed, and said in his heart, Shall a child be born unto him who is an hundred years old? And shall Sarah, who is ninety years old, bear?"*

Concerning that which is recorded in this Verse, Ellicott says, *"The Jewish interpreters regard Abraham's laugh as one of joy, and Sarah's as one of unbelief (Gen. 18:12)."* Actually, that seems to be the case, and our Lord confirmed the view that joy was uppermost in Abraham's heart, as it regards these things (Jn. 8:56).

These questions asked by Abraham were not questions of unbelief or derision. They were really an exclamation of holy wonder. What reason declared impossible was possible to Faith. Paul said of him: *"He considered not the deadness of Sarah's womb"* (Rom. 4:19).

When we read these illustrations, it should make us ashamed of ourselves. If Abraham felt such joy, and expressed it accordingly, as it regarded a Promise, for that's all he had then, how much more should we rejoice presently, when in fact, that Promise has totally and completely been realized in the Lord Jesus Christ?

This Salvation is that which can be felt. It is that which is experienced not only in conduct, but also in joy which fills the soul to overflowing, and doing so, invigorates the spirit. I am persuaded that most stress, worry, anxiety, fear, and all of their attendant woes can be throttled completely by Believers exhibiting expressions of Faith, for this is exactly what Abraham did. So what am I saying?

I'm saying that Faith rejoices, and that Faith always rejoices. When we realize what Jesus has done for us at the Cross, that His Work is not merely a Promised Work, but a Finished Work, then we must shout for joy. How can we do less, considering this great Salvation that fills our hearts? If Abraham laughed in wonder and exclamation, which in essence was a laugh of victory, how can we as Believers presently do less!

I feel that these Passages completely abrogate a cold, lifeless, even one might say, a cold storage faith. A faith that never rejoices, never marvels, never exclaims with joy, I seriously doubt to actually be faith. If it's True Faith, which refers to Christ, and what Christ has done for us at the Cross, then there must be a joy which accompanies such Faith. It must be that which occasions us to marvel constantly, even as did Abraham.

Again I emphasize the fact that he had only the Promise, while we now have the Possession.

(18) "AND ABRAHAM SAID UNTO GOD, O THAT ISHMAEL MIGHT LIVE BEFORE YOU!

(19) "AND GOD SAID, SARAH YOUR WIFE SHALL BEAR YOU A SON INDEED; AND YOU SHALL CALL HIS NAME ISAAC: AND I WILL ESTABLISH MY COVENANT WITH HIM FOR AN EVERLASTING COVENANT, AND WITH HIS SEED AFTER HIM.

(20) "AND AS FOR ISHMAEL, I HAVE HEARD YOU: BEHOLD, I HAVE BLESSED HIM, AND WILL MAKE HIM FRUITFUL, AND WILL MULTIPLY HIM EXCEEDINGLY; TWELVE PRINCES SHALL HE BEGET, AND I WILL MAKE HIM A GREAT NATION.

(21) "BUT MY COVENANT WILL I ESTABLISH WITH ISAAC, WHICH SARAH SHALL BEAR UNTO YOU AT THIS SET TIME IN THE NEXT YEAR.

(22) "AND HE LEFT OFF TALKING WITH HIM, AND GOD WENT UP FROM ABRAHAM."

The structure is:

NOTES

1. Abraham asked the Lord that Ishmael might have some place, and not be completely left out.

2. The Lord tells Abraham that the son who will be born to him and Sarah is to be named Isaac.

3. It is to Isaac that God will establish His Covenant, which in fact, will be *"an Everlasting Covenant, and with his seed after him."*

4. He will also bless Ishmael, but not as it regards the Covenant.

5. The Covenant is to be established with Isaac, and Isaac alone!

ISHMAEL

Verse 18 reads: *"And Abraham said unto God, O that Ishmael might live before You!"*

The prayer that Abraham prays as it regards Ishmael was not that he would be the child of Promise, but that he might receive some measure of Divine blessing, though he was to be set aside in favor of the unseen child now promised.

As should be obvious, Ishmael was very dear to Abraham, but as we shall see, would not prove to be worthy of that trust and love.

THE COVENANT

Verse 19 reads: *"And God said, Sarah your wife shall bear you a son indeed; and you shall call his name Isaac: and I will establish My Covenant with him for an Everlasting Covenant, and with his seed after him."*

Concerning this Everlasting Covenant, Williams says: *"The great subject of this Chapter is the expansion of the Covenant already revealed in Chapters 12 and 15. The new features introduced are the purposes of God as it regards Israel and the Gentiles, pertaining to Salvation. Both of the countless multitudes of redeemed men spring from Abraham as the first vessel of promise and the root of all who should after him believe unto life everlasting.*

"At the same time this Chapter sets out the two principles upon which these Divine purposes are founded. These principles are 'death' and 'Grace.' The sign of circumcision expressed the one, the Divine Promise the other.

"Man must have the sentence of death written upon his flesh, which circumcision

did, and Grace brings to this dead man life and ever-enduring riches. The sign of circumcision, therefore, declared man to be absolutely without moral value, and justly, as a sinner, sentenced to death. Grace which comes in the Covenant, takes up Abraham who was by nature an idolater, declares him to be a righteous man because he believed the testimony of God, and makes him the root out of which Israel and the redeemed nations should proceed."

So we have circumcision, which points to man's sin, and the Covenant, which points to Christ, Who will lift man out of his sin, and will do so by the Cross. For the Covenant must of necessity include the Cross, even as Genesis 3:15 proclaims.

THE EVERLASTING COVENANT

As we have previously stated, this Covenant which God established with Abraham, pointed to Christ, and what Christ would do to redeem humanity; therefore, it could be called an *"Everlasting Covenant"* (Heb. 13:20).

This *"Everlasting Covenant"* is to be established with Isaac, and not with Ishmael.

The world of Islam claims the very opposite, that Ishmael was the promised seed and, therefore, the heir of the Covenant. As well, they claim that Christ is not the fulfillment of the Covenant, but rather Mohammed.

Of course, only a cursory examination of the Koran will prove the fallacy of such claims. Mohammed, in attempting to relate to Bible illustrations, puts people in the wrong generations, which are glaring mistakes, which also is glaring evidence that what he proposed to be Divine, is in fact, not inspired at all, but rather the prattle of an unregenerate man. The Holy Spirit doesn't make mistakes. And Mohammed's futile attempts to rewrite history proclaim the utter foolishness of the claims of inspiration.

At the present time (2001), in America's so-called fight against terrorism, our Diplomats are demanding that Israel come to an agreement with the Palestinians.

The irony of all of this is, it doesn't take a seasoned Diplomat to instantly recognize the futility of such an effort. How can agreements be made with people, who respect agreements not at all? As well, how can

agreements be made with those who have sworn your destruction? And to be sure, the Palestinians aren't attempting to have a *"piece"* of Israel, which they may call their homeland, but rather, they want every Jew dead, and the entirety of the land of Israel to be claimed as their own. So again I ask the question, how can agreements be made with a mindset of that nature?!

No, even as the Word of God broadly proclaims, the Covenant is with Isaac and not with Ishmael. This means that the land of Israel belongs to the Jews, and to no one else. In fact, it belongs to God. And this means that even Israel doesn't have the right to give great portions of it to the Palestinians, or anyone else for that matter.

To be frank, the country of Jordan, which is several times larger than Israel, has plenty of room for the Palestinians. And in fact, the country of Jordan was originally carved out by the British to be a homeland for the Palestinians. But the problem is spiritual and not material, which means that it's not really the land area in question here, but rather the Word of God.

THE BLESSING OF ISHMAEL

Verse 20 reads: *"And as for Ishmael, I have heard you: behold I have blessed him, and will make him fruitful, and will multiply him exceedingly; twelve princes shall he beget, and I will make him a great nation."*

The Lord, of course, kept this Promise as it regards Ishmael (Gen. 25:13-16). He has multiplied exceedingly, and the blessing comes down even unto this hour.

However, the blessing pronounced here is certainly not because of Ishmael, but because of Abraham, and Abraham alone. The blessing should have caused the Arabs to serve God as it regards the Bible; however, most of them have completely gone astray following the Koran, which is a web of deceit, and will lead all of its followers to eternal perdition.

THE COVENANT AND ISAAC

Verse 21 reads: *"But My Covenant will I establish with Isaac, which Sarah shall bear unto you at this set time in the next year."*

In this one Verse, the Lord says several things:

1. For the third time in this dialogue with Abraham, the Lord promises that Sarah would bear a son, and that despite her age.

2. Furthermore, this child would be born within the next year.

3. Even though He would bless Ishmael, it was with Isaac that the Covenant would be established.

COMMUNION

Verse 22 reads: *"And He* (God) *left off talking with him, and God went up from Abraham."*

Communion with God is the most profitable exercise there is. Paul taught us this in his Epistle to the Ephesians. He said:

"Now unto Him Who is able to do exceeding abundantly above all that we ask or think, according to the power that worketh in us,

"Unto Him be glory in the Church by Christ Jesus throughout all ages, world without end. Amen" (Eph. 3:20-21).

It has been said that God's proper name is the *"Hearer of Prayers."* But the problem is, most of the time, we do not know what we ask (Mat. 20:22). Martin Luther said concerning this: *"Our hearts are too weak to understand the great things which God desires to give us. We worry about the time, place, and means for God to help us. We make our goals too narrow and small, for we must always wrestle with unbelief in our hearts."*

He went on to say, *"We poor weak persons can never really understand the exceeding Grace and Mercy of God. We have a God Who wants to give us far more than we ask or think. Therefore since we do not know how and what to ask, the Holy Spirit intercedes for us with groanings which cannot be uttered (Rom. 8:26)."*

And then he said, *"I write this in order that no one may despair on account of his unworthiness, or also on account of the high majesty of God Whom we address in our prayers. Nothing is too great for Him for which we pray, even if we ourselves do not understand the things for which we ask. Abraham received far more than he requested, and in this he left us an example that we should not discontinue our pleadings before the Lord, but surely believe that*

NOTES

they will never be without fruit or benefit. God regards the heart and knows the groanings in us which we cannot utter, indeed, which even we ourselves cannot understand, for we are like the little children who stammer their prayers before meals."

PERSONAL COMMUNION

Just last night in prayer (Dec. 1, 2001), the Lord moved so mightily upon my heart. It concerned the Moving and Operation of the Holy Spirit within my heart and life and in my Ministry.

We have many things we are attempting to do for the Lord, even as He directs us. But the most important thing of all is the working of the Holy Spirit within us. In the last few years, I've learned many things, but I think the two most important things I've learned are:

1. We must be totally and completely led by the Spirit in everything we do, even the small things. He is God, and He has the capacity to do whatever needs to be done. Unfortunately, we far too often only consult Him as it regards very serious matters, somehow thinking we have the ability to handle everything else. The truth is, we really don't have the ability to handle anything. We need His help in all matters and in all things.

2. There must be a Moving and Operation of the Spirit within my life at all times. This refers to prayer and Ministry, for He Alone can move and flow through us, in order to bless the hurting hearts of others.

When I was but a boy, my Grandmother taught me the tremendous value of prayer. To be frank, it has been my mainstay through the many years, but in the last few years has taken on a completely new dimension.

In 1991, at a time of great crisis in my life and Ministry, I determined to seek the Lord to whatever extent it took, in order to find the answer to my dilemma. In fact, it was the same petition and cry uttered by Paul nearly 2,000 years ago: *"O wretched man that I am! Who shall deliver me from the body of this death?"* (Rom. 7:24).

The Lord was some five years in answering that prayer, even as I sought His Face on a daily basis, and with tears. But in 1996, the great Revelation of the Cross began to come to me. I say *"began,"* simply because the Revelation has continued to expand unto this hour.

In fact, it was nothing new, actually that which the Lord had given to Paul, and the great Apostle had given to us in his Epistles; however, and to be sure, this Revelation cannot be understood except the Holy Spirit reveals it to us. And to be sure, He definitely will do that with anyone who will earnestly seek the Face of the Lord, and earnestly desire that which He has for us. Our problem is *"self."* It looms so large, and hinders so greatly, that the Holy Spirit cannot give to us that which He desires.

Self is not something new; it is the problem that every single Believer has faced, even the Bible greats. We will see this even to a greater extent, when we come to Genesis, Chapter 21, where God demanded of Abraham that he part with Ishmael, which is a type of self-will. Since the Revelation of the Cross, prayer, as stated, has taken on a completely new dimension. I now know the correct object of Faith, which is a knowledge of unsurpassed value. That correct object is the Cross of Christ. When Faith is properly placed, and when it is properly maintained in that place, the Holy Spirit will then do great and mighty things within our hearts and lives. But to be sure, *"self"* cannot be properly conquered, and I speak of it being as well placed *"in Christ,"* until we properly understand the Cross. In fact, without a proper understanding of the Cross, one cannot really understand the Bible as one should, and one certainly cannot be led by the Spirit as one should. Everything hinges on the Sacrifice of Christ (Eph. 2:13-18).

(23) "AND ABRAHAM TOOK ISHMAEL HIS SON, AND ALL THAT WERE BORN IN HIS HOUSE, AND ALL THAT WERE BOUGHT WITH HIS MONEY, EVERY MALE AMONG THE MEN OF ABRAHAM'S HOUSE; AND CIRCUMCISED THE FLESH OF THEIR FORESKIN IN THE SELFSAME DAY, AS GOD HAD SAID UNTO HIM.

(24) "AND ABRAHAM WAS NINETY YEARS OLD AND NINE, WHEN HE WAS CIRCUMCISED IN THE FLESH OF HIS FORESKIN.

(25) "AND ISHMAEL HIS SON WAS THIRTEEN YEARS OLD, WHEN HE WAS CIRCUMCISED IN THE FLESH OF HIS FORESKIN.

(26) "IN THE SELFSAME DAY WAS ABRAHAM CIRCUMCISED, AND ISHMAEL HIS SON.

(27) "AND ALL THE MEN OF HIS HOUSE, BORN IN THE HOUSE, AND BOUGHT WITH MONEY OF THE STRANGER, WERE CIRCUMCISED WITH HIM."

The composition is:

1. The obedience of Abraham in circumcising the entirety of his house, servants and all, should be a lesson to us.

2. Even though Ishmael was circumcised, he who was born after the flesh was by his natural birth a rebel, even though he may enter into an outward covenant.

3. The Epistles to the Romans, to the Galatians, and to the Colossians teach that Christians are circumcised in the Cross of Christ, baptized in the death of Christ, and raised in the Resurrection of Christ.

4. The Scriptures continually present Abraham as a pattern of Faith.

OBEDIENCE

Verse 23 reads: *"And Abraham took Ishmael his son, and all who were born in his house, and all who were bought with his money, every male among the men of Abraham's house; and circumcised the flesh of their foreskin in the selfsame day, as God had said unto him."*

The short phrase, *"As God had said unto Him,"* regarding circumcision, presents Abraham obeying the Lord minutely and immediately.

Even though every male, young or old, was circumcised in Abraham's house, which means in a sense that they became a part of the Covenant, did it also mean that they all were saved?

Salvation is never by *"rites,"* *"rituals,"* *"ordinances,"* or *"ceremonies."* Salvation, and without exception, has always been Faith in Christ, and never in the symbols which are supposed to represent that faith.

How many of these people were truly saved, only the Lord knows. I think we can say without any fear of contradiction that most definitely Hagar and Ishmael were not saved.

About 2,000 years after Abraham, the Holy Spirit through Paul said of Ishmael and his mother, *"But as then he* (Ishmael) *who was born after the flesh persecuted him* (Isaac) *who was born after the Spirit, even so it is now.*

"Nevertheless what says the Scripture? Cast out the bondwoman and her son: for the son of the bondwoman shall not be heir with the son of the freewoman" (Gal. 4:29-30).

The word *"persecuted"* in Verse 29 of Galatians, Chapter 4, carries the idea of murder. The Jewish Targums, which are Commentaries of sort, say that Ishmael, when he was about 18 years old, would send Isaac, who at the time was about four years old, running after arrows he (Ishmael) had shot. The idea was, he tried to hit him with one of the arrows, thereby killing him, with it looking like an accident. Because of murder in the heart of his mother and himself, the Lord would dispel them from the home of Abraham, even as Chapter 21 proclaims.

No, the *"rite"* of Circumcision, even though demanded and entered into, didn't automatically mean that the person was saved. That was a matter of Faith, and we speak of Faith in Christ, even as it always has been a matter of Faith.

ABRAHAM

Verse 24 reads: *"And Abraham was ninety years old and nine, when he was circumcised in the flesh of his foreskin."*

As we've already stated, the act of circumcision on the man's private member, which is his reproductive organ, proclaims the fact of original sin. As each baby is born into the world, due to Adam's Fall, each child is born in sin. Concerning this, David said: *"Behold, I was shaped in iniquity, and in sin did my mother conceive me"* (Ps. 51:5).

David here wasn't meaning that his mother had played the harlot, but rather that he, along with every other child that is born, with the exception of Christ, was conceived in original sin. So, the rite of Circumcision proclaims that fact. As well, it also proclaims the fact of the Cross of Christ, in that blood is shed. The foreskin being cut loose proclaims a picture of the person being cut loose from sin, upon acceptance of Christ, and due

to what Christ did at the Cross, by the shedding of His Precious Blood.

ISHMAEL

Verse 25 reads: *"And Ishmael his son was thirteen years old, when he was circumcised in the flesh of his foreskin."*

Even though the male member of Ishmael was circumcised, his heart wasn't. As well, untold millions of individuals have been baptized in water, which is a symbol of Regeneration, but in fact were not saved. As we have stated, outward *"rites"* and *"ceremonies,"* have never saved anyone.

In fact, virtually every Jew thereafter was circumcised, which numbered untold millions; however, many, if not most, Jews were eternally lost, simply because they had no faith in Christ, but rather in outward ceremonies, etc.

ABRAHAM AND ISHMAEL

Verse 26 reads: *"In the selfsame day was Abraham circumcised, and Ishmael his son."*

Two men were circumcised. By that *"rite"* both men entered the Covenant; however, only one of the men, Abraham, was saved.

How many millions presently, simply because they belong to a particular Church, or they engage in some type of religious activity, think that by the doing of that they are saved? The truth is, they have never been Born-Again, which means there has never been a change within their hearts and lives.

Nicodemus is an excellent case in point. He was a ruler of the Jews, and most definitely had been circumcised, which means that he had entered the Covenant. As well, one could certainly say that he was a good man, and in fact was a student of the Word. But the truth is, Nicodemus was not actually saved.

When he approached Jesus about the miracles that Christ had performed, Jesus in essence ignored what he said, and rather said to him, *"Verily, verily, I say unto you, except a man be born again, he cannot see the Kingdom of God"* (Jn. 3:3).

Regrettably, even though Nicodemus was very religious, he did not really understand what Jesus meant.

When Nicodemus asked Him, *"How can these things be?"*, Jesus answered and said unto him: *"Are you a master of Israel, and know not these things?"* (Jn. 3:9-10).

In other words, He was telling Nicodemus that if he was truly saved, he would know what was being addressed concerning being *"born again."*

Unfortunately, there are untold millions presently who claim Salvation, but all on the wrong basis; therefore, they aren't saved. I realize that's blunt, but it cannot be any other way.

One is saved by trusting explicitly in Christ, and what Christ has done for us at the Cross. The moment this is truly done, and anyone can do that if they so desire, that person is then saved, and instantly so (Jn. 3:16; Rom. 10:9-10, 13). It has nothing to do with ceremonies, the joining of Churches, or anything of that nature. As stated, it is all by Faith, and we refer to Faith in Christ, and what He did for us in offering Himself as a Sacrifice on the Cross (Gal. 1:4).

SALVATION IS FOR ALL

Verse 27 reads: *"And all the men of his house, born in the house, and bought with money of the stranger, were circumcised with him."*

This one Passage tells us that every single man in the house of Abraham was saved, whether servants, slaves, or family, that is if they believed. This tells us that all can be saved, and there are no distinctions made by the Lord regarding humanity, and the Salvation of all.

As well, mighty Abraham had to come the same identical way, as the lowliest slave, whomever that might have been. There was no difference, and there were no exceptions.

How fortunate and blessed were these individuals, whomever they might have been, to be in the house of Abraham and, therefore, to be a party to the Covenant. But of course, they had to accept by Faith that which the Covenant represented, but the opportunity was before them. As stated, how many truly accepted in their heart, only God knows. But the facts are, all were given the opportunity to do so, and a grand opportunity it was.

The sadness is, many people in the world, and no doubt we can say most, never really have that opportunity. Even the so-called

Gospel which is preached, too often times is *"another gospel"* (II Cor. 11:4). This being the case, the person cannot be saved, even if they hear such a gospel.

The other day I happened to listen to a Preacher for a few minutes over Television. He closed his Message by stating that it was imperative that a person be baptized in water in order to be saved. Inasmuch as this Preacher was making Water Baptism the object of faith, whoever listened to him would not be able to find Christ.

As another example, the Catholic Church claims that Salvation is in the Church. In other words, they claim that keeping the sacraments of the Church ensures Salvation. Therefore, they have moved the Faith from its true place in Christ to the Church, which means that all who belong to that system cannot be saved. As well, if our Seventh Day Adventists friends make the keeping of the seventh day a requirement for Salvation, they have as well moved the center of gravity, so to speak, from Faith in Christ to something else.

One of the major problems of many Churches is the equating of doing certain things as being the same as Faith in Christ. It isn't, and no matter how important it may be in its own right. One cannot engage in a ceremony, and equate that with Faith in Christ. It never works that way.

True Faith in Christ is the placing of one's total and complete confidence in Him, and in nothing else. Christ plus other things, and whatever those other things might be, abrogates Christ. It's either Christ totally and completely plus nothing else, or it's Christ not at all.

Getting saved is not difficult. In fact, Paul said: *"For whosoever shall call upon the Name of the Lord shall be saved"* (Rom. 10:13). But that doesn't mean to call upon the Church, or one of its many ordinances. It means exactly what is says, to *"Call upon the name of the Lord."*

But after we come to Christ, it is incumbent upon us to understand that all that we receive from Christ and through Christ is received totally and completely by and through what He did at the Cross, and through no other instrument or means. *"Christ and Him Crucified"* is to ever be the center of our gravity as we speak of Faith. If it's in anything else, we will cause ourselves, even though we are Christians, great difficulties.

"Depth of mercy! Can there be
"Mercy still reserved for me?
"Can my God His wrath forbear?
"Me, the chief of sinners spare?"

"I have long withstood His Grace,
"Long provoked Him to His Face,
"Would not hearken to His calls,
"Grieved Him by a thousand falls."

"Lord, incline me to repent;
"Let me now my fall lament,
"Deeply my revolt deplore,
"Weep, believe, and sin no more."

"Still for me the Saviour stands,
"Shows His wounds, and spreads His
   Hands;
"God is love, I know, I feel.
"Jesus weeps, and loves me still."

CHAPTER 18

(1) "AND THE LORD APPEARED UNTO HIM IN THE PLAINS OF MAMRE: AND HE SAT IN THE TENT DOOR IN THE HEAT OF THE DAY;

(2) "AND HE LIFT UP HIS EYES AND LOOKED, AND, LO, THREE MEN STOOD BY HIM: AND WHEN HE SAW THEM, HE RAN TO MEET THEM FROM THE TENT DOOR, AND BOWED HIMSELF TOWARD THE GROUND,

(3) "AND SAID, MY LORD, IF NOW I HAVE FOUND FAVOR IN YOUR SIGHT, PASS NOT AWAY, I PRAY YOU, FROM YOUR SERVANT:

(4) "LET A LITTLE WATER, I PRAY YOU, BE FETCHED, AND WASH YOUR FEET, AND REST YOURSELVES UNDER THE TREE:

(5) "AND I WILL FETCH A MORSEL OF BREAD, AND COMFORT YOUR HEARTS; AFTER THAT YOU SHALL PASS ON: FOR THEREFORE ARE YOU COME TO YOUR SERVANT. AND THEY SAID, SO DO, AS YOU HAVE SAID.

(6) "AND ABRAHAM HASTENED INTO THE TENT UNTO SARAH, AND SAID, MAKE

NOTES

READY QUICKLY THREE MEASURES OF FINE MEAL, KNEAD IT, AND MAKE CAKES UPON THE HEARTH.

(7) "AND ABRAHAM RAN UNTO THE HERD, AND FETCHED A CALF TENDER AND GOOD, AND GAVE IT UNTO A YOUNG MAN; AND HE HASTED TO DRESS IT.

(8) "AND HE TOOK BUTTER, AND MILK, AND THE CALF WHICH HE HAD DRESSED, AND SET IT BEFORE THEM; AND HE STOOD BY THEM UNDER THE TREE, AND THEY DID EAT."

The construction is:

1. The First Verse of this Chapter confirms the experience of the Christian that a fresh Revelation of the Lord to the soul follows upon obedience to a Divine command (Williams).

2. Spiritual activity in the heart of one servant of Christ's stirs up activity in the hearts of other servants.

3. The emphasis here is on how God dealt with Abraham and recognized him as a friend worthy of His confidence.

4. I think it is obvious that Abraham did not recognize at the beginning, who these individuals were. Perhaps Hebrews 13:2 refers to this when it says: *"Be not forgetful to entertain strangers: for thereby some have entertained Angels unawares."*

THE APPEARANCE OF THE LORD

Verse 1 reads: *"And the LORD appeared unto him in the plains of Mamre: and he sat in the tent door in the heat of the day."*

Jewish tradition claims that this visit by the Lord to Abraham was on the third day after the rite of circumcision had been performed, and was for the purpose of healing him from the painful consequences of it. It was on this account, as they think, that Abraham was resting at home, instead of being with his herds in the field (Ellicott).

Of course, this is only an assumption, but the fact remains that the Lord did appear to the Patriarch, which consequences will be striking to say the least.

At this particular time, two momentous events will transpire, the first being the announcement by the Lord of the conception by Sarah. In fact, I think one can say without fear of contradiction that this is one of the most momentous occasions in history. From this beginning will come the Jewish people, who will give the world the Word of God, and who in effect, will serve as the womb of the Messiah, which will bring the Redeemer into the world, which is what this is all about.

All of this must be done in this manner, because Angels could not redeem humanity, and even God as God couldn't redeem humanity. God would have to become man, and as the God-man Jesus Christ, would then redeem Adam's fallen race.

Dominion had been given to Adam, which means that tremendous responsibility had been given to the first man (Gen. 1:26; Ps. 8; Rom. 5:12, 17-19; I Cor. 15:45-47).

As well, in all of the doings, and I continue to speak of the Plan of Redemption being carried out, God would have to do things according to His Personal Nature. When many people think of God, they think of Him in an entirely wrong manner. If God is all-powerful, they think, and in fact He definitely is, then He can do anything.

While it is certainly true that He definitely can do anything, the facts are, He will not do anything against His Nature. So, to bring Redemption into this world, God would have to prepare a people who would evidence Faith in Him, even as He would reveal Himself to them, and because He is a God of Faith (Heb. 11:1-3).

The end result of all of God's workings and dealings with man is Righteousness. But we have a problem here. Man thinks that he can perfect or concoct Righteousness by his own efforts. But of course, that is impossible. The Righteousness which God accepts, which is the Righteousness of Christ, and in fact, the only Righteousness He will accept, could only be brought about in a particular way. As stated, God would have to become man, which He did, keep the Law perfectly, all on our behalf (Gal. 4:4-5), and then die on a Cross, which alone would satisfy the demands of the broken Law.

(When we speak of the Law, we're speaking of the Law of Moses, which moral aspects were centered in the Ten Commandments — Exodus, Chpt. 20.)

THE CROSS

Without the Cross, Christ's Perfect Life would have availed us nothing. In fact, without

the Cross His healings and miracles, as stupendous as they were, would have availed nothing. Only the Cross could address the terrible problem of sin and all of its effects, which it did (Eph. 2:13-18; Col. 2:14-15).

The greatest shame of this modern age is, the modern Church little knows or understands the tremendous significance of the Cross. To most, the Cross is just incidental in their lives and living for God. In fact, whatever credence that the modern Church gives the Cross, which is very little indeed in any regard, is centered up in the initial Salvation experience. Thank God for that; however, the sadness is, most in the modern Church not understanding at all the part the Cross plays in their ongoing Christian experience, try to *"live"* for the Lord in other ways. What do we mean by that?

As Salvation is *"attained"* by Faith in Christ and what He has done for us at the Cross, likewise, it is *"maintained"* by continued exclusive Faith in the Cross, which is the way that we grow in Grace and the knowledge of the Lord. Having such little teaching in this regard, most Christians try to function outside of God's prescribed order, which is always catastrophic, simply because the Holy Spirit will not function in this capacity. While He definitely will remain with us, He demands that we have Faith in Christ exclusively, which refers to what He did for us at the Cross, which will then guarantee His function within our hearts and lives (Rom. 8:1-2, 11).

The Lord works exclusively on the premise of Faith; however, it is always to be Faith in Christ and what Christ has done for us at the Cross. The whole gist of Salvation is Christ Himself. But more particularly, it is what He has done for us regarding His Sacrifice, which makes it all possible.

CHRIST AND HIS CROSS

If we try to divorce Christ from the Cross, which much of the modern Church does, we then have *"another Jesus,"* which is always of *"another spirit,"* which presents *"another gospel"* (II Cor. 11:4).

The Reader needs to peruse these words very carefully. We're speaking here of God's prescribed order for a victorious life. And to be sure, He only has one order, and man has none, and in fact, will never have any. Therefore, the appearance of the Lord to Abraham at this particular time, would ultimately lead to these things of which we have been addressing, which is the Salvation of humanity, and in every capacity.

THREE MEN

Verse 2 reads: *"And he lifted up his eyes and looked, and, lo, three men stood by him: and when he saw them, he ran to meet them from the tent door, and bowed himself toward the ground."*

The energy and intelligence of the Divine life in Abraham's soul is seen in his conduct. He sits, not sleeps, in the heat of the day; he looks, and he recognizes his Divine visitor Who is accompanied by His Angelic servants. He runs to meet them, he bows himself to the ground, he urges them to rest, he hastens into the tent, he presses Sarah quickly to make ready cakes upon the hearth, he himself runs into the herd and fetches a calf, he commands the servant to hasten to dress it, he himself as a servant places the food before his guests, and as a slave ready for further service, stands while they eat.

All is activity, for not only is he active himself, but he makes everybody else active. Here is a great principle that can be a great teacher. Spiritual activity in the heart of one servant of Christ's stirs up activity in the hearts of other servants (Williams).

Several things should be said here about Abraham:

1. The word *"looked"* implies an act of mental perception. In other words, he now knows that one of them is Jehovah.

2. Him *"bowing himself toward the ground"* implies *"worship."* It is more than a mere oriental expression.

3. Abraham's heart was right with God; therefore, he was glad to see the Divine visitor. Such could not be said of many modern Christians.

PETITION

Verse 3 reads: *"And said, My LORD, if now I have found favor in Your sight, pass not away, I pray You, from Your servant."*

Proving that Abraham now knows who one of the three actually is, he addresses Him as *"Lord,"* the same terminology that he used in Genesis 15:2.

The phrase, *"If now I have found favor in your sight,"* implies far more than a mere formal remark, or question. Abraham had found favor in God's sight, but only by and through the Faith which Abraham exhibited, and to be sure, it was Faith in Christ, and what Christ would do to redeem us. Again I refer to the fact that Jesus spoke of Abraham seeing His day and, therefore, being glad (Jn. 8:56).

Favor in God's sight can be obtained in one manner, and in one manner only, and that is by Faith; however, when we speak of Faith, we are speaking exclusively of Faith in Christ and His Cross. Who Jesus is, and What Jesus has done, and again we refer to the Cross, is where all Faith should be anchored and maintained. This alone guarantees the favor of God, and all else guarantees His disfavor.

HOSPITALITY

Verse 4 reads: *"Let a little water, I pray You, be fetched, and wash Your feet, and rest Yourselves under the tree."*

Does Jehovah, or even Angels for that matter, need their feet washed? Do they grow tired and, therefore, require rest?

The answer of course, is *"no"* to both questions. So why did Abraham conduct himself in such fashion, knowing that one of these *"men"* was Jehovah, and the other two were undoubtedly Angels?

I must believe that the Holy Spirit moved upon Abraham as it regards his conduct. If in fact that was the case, and it had to be, then we must also know that the Holy Spirit causes all things to be done for a purpose.

The washing of the feet, which incidentally was a common, oriental practice, also contains a great spiritual meaning. As the Patriarch washed the feet of his Divine guest, and His associates, such would proclaim the fact that all Believers would need their feet washed daily, and we speak of the spiritual sense, which would be typified by Christ washing the feet of the Disciples, as it involves our daily walk before God (Jn. 13:5).

As well, the *"rest"* of which Abraham mentions here refers to the *"rest"* afforded all true

Believers, as their Faith is anchored solely in Christ. In fact, Jesus said, *"Come unto Me, all you who labor and are heavy laden, and I will give you rest"* (Mat. 11:28).

We know that the Lord does nothing, but that it provides for us a lesson, which we are intended to learn.

THE BREAD

Verse 5 reads: *"And I will fetch a morsel of bread, and comfort Your hearts; after that You shall pass on: for therefore are You come to Your servant. And they said, So do, as you have said."*

Bread is at times used as a symbol, to portray the Gospel. Hence, Jesus would say of Himself, *"I am the Bread of Life: he who comes to Me shall never hunger; and he who believes on Me shall never thirst"* (Jn. 6:35).

Abraham giving the Lord bread, along with His Angelic associates, proclaims what the Lord will do for the whole of humanity, and above all, that He would actually be that bread. This is the *"bread"* which satisfies all hunger.

SARAH

Verse 6 reads: *"And Abraham hastened into the tent unto Sarah, and said, Make ready quickly three measures of fine meal, knead it, and make cakes upon the hearth."*

The *"fine meal"* mentioned here should have been translated, *"fine flour,"* for that's actually what it says in the Hebrew.

Flour was used in the Thank-Offering (Meat-Offering), and was meant to represent the perfection of our Incarnate Lord (Lev. 2:1). So, even though Abraham little recognized the situation, it was all planned by the Holy Spirit.

While we can certainly pass off this incident as merely an action of hospitality, I think to do so would belittle the action of the Holy Spirit. While of course, the true reason for the visit of our Lord and the two holy visitors was to announce the conception which Sarah would experience, and as well, the destruction of Sodom and Gomorrah, which also would affect Lot, all which are obvious, at the same time, we must come to the conclusion that everything done by the Lord is never without spiritual significance. There is a lesson in every action, move, and word.

NOTES

While we must not take flights of fancy with that which is done, at the same time, we must not discount that which is done, but rather, do our very best to ascertain what the Holy Spirit is saying to us, and learn thereby.

THE TENDER CALF

Verse 7 reads: *"And Abraham ran unto the herd, and fetched a calf tender and good, and gave it unto a young man; and he hasted to dress it."*

The young calf that was prepared was not a common article of consumption among Orientals.

This shows that Abraham gave his very best on this particular day, even as he should have, which signifies that we are to do the same. As well, the Lord would also give His very best, even His only Son, which would be necessary, if we were to have eternal life (Jn. 3:16). As the calf would be killed, likewise would the Son of God. Also, as the calf would be eaten, Jesus Himself said:

"Verily, verily, I say unto you, except you eat the flesh of the Son of Man, and drink His Blood, you have no life in you.

"Whoso eats My flesh, and drinks My Blood, has eternal life; and I will raise him up at the last day.

"For My flesh is meat indeed, and My Blood is drink indeed.

"He who eats My flesh, and drinks My Blood, dwells in Me, and I in him.

"As the Living Father has sent Me, and I live by the Father: so he who eats Me, even he shall live by Me.

"This is that bread which came down from Heaven: not as your fathers did eat manna, and are dead: he who eats of this bread shall live forever" (Jn. 6:53-58).

What did Jesus mean by all of this?

He would quickly answer by saying: *"It is the Spirit that quickeneth; the flesh profits nothing: the words that I speak unto you, they are spirit, and they are life"* (Jn. 6:63).

To make the explanation brief, Jesus was simply speaking of the absolute necessity of mankind placing their Faith and Trust in Christ and what Christ did for them at the Cross.

There are millions of people who claim to believe in Christ, but they ignore the Cross, which means they've only given a mental assent or acceptance to Christ, which is woefully insufficient. The mention of His *"flesh"* and *"Blood,"* and humanity *"eating"* and *"drinking"* of same, refers to nothing physical, but rather an act of Faith, and above all Faith in what Christ suffered for us, which in effect, Jesus explained in John 7:63.

Of the death of Christ, Peter would say: *"For Christ also has once suffered for sins, the just for the unjust, that He might bring us to God, being put to death in the flesh, but quickened by the Spirit"* (I Pet. 3:18).

The *"flesh"* pertains to Christ giving Himself, which refers to His pure, spotless, unsullied, physical body, which He gave on the Cross. The *"blood"* refers to the shedding of that precious commodity, one might say, on the Cross. This alone atoned for Salvation, thereby paying the terrible sin debt owed by man to God (Eph. 2:13-18).

THEY DID EAT

Verse 8 reads: *"And he took butter and milk, and the calf which he had dressed, and set it before them; and he stood by them under the tree, and they did eat."*

As they did eat, likewise, Jesus told us that we must eat as well. I speak of the *"eating of Christ,"* which in effect, speaks of evidencing Faith in Him and what He has done for us.

Untold millions have the food set before them, but actually do not eat. Let it be known and understood that unless we *"eat,"* which again refers to evidencing Faith in Christ and His Cross, we do not really have Christ.

The world is full of religion. Some time ago, one of the major magazines named Christ as one of the ten most powerful men who has ever lived, etc.

While they may have thought they were being generous, the facts are, they were blaspheming. To even remotely think of comparing other men to Christ, at least as it regards significance, etc., is gross stupidity to say the least! But the problem is, they know about Christ, but they really don't know Christ.

Christ is God! And to think of Him as anything else is to blaspheme.

And as important, we must recognize what He did to redeem humanity, which was to go to the Cross. As we've stated again and again, Christ and the Cross must never be divided.

NOTES

To recognize Christ apart from the Cross is to fail to evidence proper Faith and, therefore, to *"eat Him."* Such plays out, as we've already stated, to *"another Jesus"* (II Cor. 11:4).

It is my feeling that St. John, Chapter 6 portrays the offering up of Christ on the Cross, and our Faith in that Finished Work, as being an absolute necessity. If we attempt to interpret these Passages in any other capacity, we do great violence to the Word of God, and stand in jeopardy even of the Salvation of our souls.

(9) "AND THEY SAID UNTO HIM, WHERE IS SARAH YOUR WIFE? AND HE SAID, BEHOLD, IN THE TENT.

(10) "AND HE SAID, I WILL CERTAINLY RETURN UNTO YOU ACCORDING TO THE TIME OF LIFE; AND, LO, SARAH YOUR WIFE SHALL HAVE A SON. AND SARAH HEARD IT IN THE TENT DOOR, WHICH WAS BEHIND HIM.

(11) "NOW ABRAHAM AND SARAH WERE OLD AND WELL STRICKEN IN AGE; AND IT CEASED TO BE WITH SARAH AFTER THE MANNER OF WOMEN.

(12) "THEREFORE SARAH LAUGHED WITHIN HERSELF, SAYING, AFTER I AM WAXED OLD SHALL I HAVE PLEASURE, MY LORD BEING OLD ALSO?

(13) "AND THE LORD SAID UNTO ABRAHAM, WHEREFORE DID SARAH LAUGH, SAYING, SHALL I OF A SURETY BEAR A CHILD, WHICH AM OLD?

(14) "IS ANYTHING TOO HARD FOR THE LORD? AT THE TIME APPOINTED I WILL RETURN UNTO YOU, ACCORDING TO THE TIME OF LIFE, AND SARAH SHALL HAVE A SON.

(15) "THEN SARAH DENIED, SAYING, I LAUGHED NOT; FOR SHE WAS AFRAID. AND HE SAID, NO; BUT YOU DID LAUGH."

The overview is:

1. One of the greatest announcements ever made in human history is now forthcoming.

2. Regrettably, this announcement is met by Sarah with unbelief, who is the very one through whom the Promise must come.

3. The response was skeptical laughter, to which the Lord did not look kindly.

4. Before this great Promise could be brought to fruition, all hope of the flesh had to die.

SARAH

Verse 9 reads: *"And they said unto him, Where is Sarah your wife? And he said, Behold, in the tent."*

The question, *"Where is Sarah your wife?"*, proclaims the omniscience of the Lord. As there is no evidence that she had previously revealed herself, the Lord could have known her name only by the fact that He knows all things.

It would seem from the following conversation that Abraham had not revealed to Sarah this which the Lord had told him some days, or perhaps some weeks earlier about her having a son (Gen. 17:16). If in fact he didn't tell her, which it seems he didn't, why not?

While there is no evidence that Abraham doubted the Lord, there is evidence that possibly he doubted himself. Had he heard correctly? Did the Lord really tell him this, or did he fabricate it in his own mind?

Sometimes we can want something so bad that we can imagine God telling us all type of things, when in reality, He hasn't.

As well, of all people, Abraham knew the impossibility of Sarah having a child, especially considering that she was now 90 years of age, and he was 100 (Gen. 17:17).

Irrespective as to what Abraham thought, the Lord, it seems, desired at this time that Sarah would also know, and that the information would not be withheld from her. He knew she was listening, so He then tells Abraham what is shortly to come to pass.

A SON

Verse 10 reads: *"And He said, I will certainly return unto you according to the time of life; and, lo, Sarah your wife shall have a son. And Sarah heard it in the tent door, which was behind him."*

It is evident that this statement concerning *"returning . . . according to the time of life,"* denotes some fixed period. Jewish tradition says that it means, *"according to this time next year."*

The statement is emphatic, *"Sarah your wife shall have a son."* As we've already stated, Sarah is now 90 years old, and Abraham 100. Why did God wait this long?

God's timing is just as important as His actions. Among other things, and probably

the most important, all hope of the flesh had to die, before this miracle could be brought about. This should be a great lesson for all of us.

What do we mean by all hope of the flesh dying?

When Abraham and Sarah finally came to the place that they knew and understood that they could not bring about this great Promise of God by their own machinations, and despite how hard they might try, then all hope of the flesh was gone. In other words, they could not, within themselves, do this thing. So when they finally cease from their own actions, God then could perform a work of the Spirit; then and only then would Sarah conceive.

THE FLESH

I think one can say without any fear of contradiction that the *"flesh"* is the biggest hindrance to the Child of God. For the sake of clarity, the *"flesh,"* especially as used by Paul, denotes man's own efforts and ability, which means the Holy Spirit, because of the flesh, cannot function. To clarify it even more, quite possibly one could say that the *"flesh"* is a dependence on ourselves or others, instead of Christ and what He has done for us at the Cross. The Christian must learn that every single work of the Lord carried out within our lives, and irrespective as to what it might be, must without exception be carried out by the Holy Spirit. And He does all His Work, predicated on one premise, and that is according to Who Christ is, and What He has done for us in His suffering (Rom. 8:1-2, 11). So He demands, as we have repeatedly stated, that we as Believers maintain Faith in Christ, with the understanding that everything Christ has done for us has been through the instrument of the Cross.

The sinner cannot be saved except through Faith in Christ and His Finished Work.

The Believer cannot live a victorious life, except he maintains his Faith in Christ and what Christ has done for us at the Cross. It is not possible to overstate the Cross; especially considering that every single thing we receive from the Lord comes to us through that sacrifice (I Cor. 1:17-18; Eph. 2:13-18; Col. 2:14-15).

It seems that despite the fact that the Cross of Christ is now history, we continue to make the mistakes made by Abraham and Sarah. We keep trying to do, in one way or the other, what only the Holy Spirit can do. And the major reason that we have this problem is simply because we do not understand the Cross nor its implications. We claim faith in Christ, in fact, constantly claiming that our trust is in Christ; however, the Jesus in Whom we trust is by and large a fabricated Jesus, or as Paul referred to the situation, *"another Jesus"* (II Cor. 11:4).

The tragedy is, all the time we think we are properly trusting Christ, but the truth is, if we do not understand the Cross, it is impossible to fully understand and trust Christ.

IMPOSSIBLE!

Verse 11 reads: *"Now Abraham and Sarah were old and well stricken in age; and it ceased to be with Sarah after the manner of women."*

The Holy Spirit is quick at this particular juncture to emphasize the point that in the natural, it was impossible for Sarah to conceive. As well, Abraham was also *"well stricken in age."*

As Believers, we must not look at the impossibilities, at least things which are impossible to us; we must look to God with Whom nothing is impossible. Jesus plainly said concerning so-called impossibilities:

"With God all things are possible" (Mat. 19:26).

As well, we should understand that God is no respecter of persons, and that He is the same yesterday, today, and forever.

Now that doesn't mean that God will give children to women who are 90 years old, and their husbands who are 100. If it's God's Will for such to be, then it will be; however, God never functions against His Will and Wisdom.

The Will of God for our lives is of extreme importance, as all of us should understand. True Faith will never circumvent that will, nor will it even desire anything that's not according to God's Will. People who think they can bring anything into being by using some little formula of faith, are in for a rude awakening. God will never allow His Word to be used against Himself. In fact, if

man could do that, he would make himself God, and do so in short order. That's been the great problem with mankind from the beginning, and continues to be the great problem in the Church. Men twist and pervert the Word of God, attempting to make it their servant, when God will never allow such things. In fact, the Word of God and the Will of God go hand in hand. And all of it is tied to the Finished Work of Christ on the Cross.

UNBELIEF

Verse 12 reads: *"Therefore Sarah laughed within herself, saying, After I am waxed old shall I have pleasure, my lord being old also?"*

Upon the announcement that Sarah would have a son, even at her advanced age, the Scripture says that Abraham laughed (Gen. 17:17). But his laugh was the laughter of Faith, while the laughter of Sarah is the laughter of unbelief. It is incredulous to her that she could have a child being 90 years old, or that Abraham could father a child being 100 years old. While her unbelief did not stop the process, it did solicit a mild rebuke from the Lord, even as we shall see.

There are always two ways of receiving God's Promises; the one of which secures, but the other of which imperils, their fulfillment (Mk. 9:23; 11:23).

As we shall see, the Lord will seek to pull Sarah from unbelief to Faith, and He will do so in three different ways:

1. He will proclaim the fact that the thing promised is not beyond the resources of Jehovah to accomplish.

2. He will do so as well, by a further certification of the event.

3. He will also do so by an impressive display of Miraculous Power, first in searching Sarah's heart, and second in arresting Sarah's conscience.

RESPONSE

Verse 13 reads: *"And the LORD said unto Abraham, Wherefore did Sarah laugh, saying, Shall I of a surety bear a child, which am old?"*

We should note several things from this particular Passage.

As should be obvious, God knows all things. He knows the reaction of our spirit, and He knows the things which we say. So, we should be very careful what we say and what we do as it regards the Lord and His Work.

MIRACLES

Verse 14 reads: *"Is anything too hard for the LORD? At the time appointed I will return unto you, according to the time of life, and Sarah shall have a son."*

In Verse 13, one of the Divine visitors announces himself as the *"Lord,"* which in effect, proclaims this as a preincarnate appearance of Christ. He now remonstrates in Verse 14 that nothing is too hard for the Lord. The actual Hebrew rendering is: *"Is anything too wonderful for Jehovah?"*

I think the way the phrase is translated as it regards *"too hard,"* leaves a wrong impression. The truth is, as it regards miracles, there is nothing even hard for the Lord. The idea as presented here in the English version seems to be that while God can do such a thing, it would be difficult. The actual rendering is that not only can He do whatever is necessary, but as well, it's not even hard for Him to accomplish the task. In other words, He does whatever is needed with ease.

The words *"time appointed,"* tell us that God had long since appointed a time for Sarah to have a child. It had been appointed, to be frank, even before Sarah was born (I Pet. 1:18-20).

We are not teaching predestination here as it regards the wills of individuals; we are rather teaching the foreknowledge of God. God being omniscient, that is all-knowing, has the capacity, and in fact, does know the past, the present, and the future. This doesn't mean that He predestines people to act in certain ways, but that, as stated, through foreknowledge, can know what they will do.

For instance, He knew that Abraham and Sarah would accept Him as Lord and Saviour. He also knew that even though they would stumble in their efforts, they wouldn't stumble according to their Faith. In other words, despite the lapses as recorded here, they would always respond favorably to the Lord, with Faith renewed. Therefore, all along it had been appointed that Sarah would ultimately have a son, and irrespective of

circumstances, events, or her advanced age. What had been appointed, God was able to carry it through.

And let me quickly say to the Reader that the Lord has appointed certain things for you also. You must continue to believe, and not allow yourself to be pulled aside by circumstances and hindrances. Despite the occasional setback, you must continue to believe. Remember, *"It is appointed,"* which means it's going to happen.

REBUKE

Verse 15 reads: *"Then Sarah denied, saying, I laughed not; for she was afraid. And He said, No; but you did laugh."*

Unbelief will never stop at skepticism, but will always degenerate into works of the flesh, such as *"lying."*

When confronted, Sarah denied that she had laughed. She now stands in the presence of Jehovah, and the Scripture says, *"She was afraid."*

Unbelief always tenders fear. We need never fear God in a negative way, when we are functioning in Faith. It is always when we are functioning in unbelief that such fear is brought about.

The Lord gently rebuked her, by simply saying, *"But you did laugh."*

The narrative ends there, at least as it regards Sarah; however, it is positive that the rebuke had its intended result. She was smitten in her conscience, knowing that she had doubted God, and was now brought back to a place of Faith.

How many times does the Lord gently rebuke us? Our sin, even as that of Sarah, is far more serious than we realize; but in Grace, the Lord only sets us straight, and doesn't bring judgment on us. When we look at Sarah, and evaluate here her actions, we should do so with the thought in mind that we ourselves have been in the same position, possibly several times. But as with Sarah, the Lord only gently rebuked us, and, thereby, did not bring upon us the judgment which we deserved.

(16) "AND THE MEN ROSE UP FROM THENCE, AND LOOKED TOWARD SODOM: AND ABRAHAM WENT WITH THEM TO BRING THEM ON THE WAY.

(17) "AND THE LORD SAID, SHALL I HIDE FROM ABRAHAM THAT THING WHICH I DO;

(18) "SEEING THAT ABRAHAM SHALL SURELY BECOME A GREAT AND MIGHTY NATION, AND ALL THE NATIONS OF THE EARTH SHALL BE BLESSED IN HIM?

(19) "FOR I KNOW HIM, THAT HE WILL COMMAND HIS CHILDREN AND HIS HOUSEHOLD AFTER HIM, AND THEY SHALL KEEP THE WAY OF THE LORD, TO DO JUSTICE AND JUDGMENT; THAT THE LORD MAY BRING UPON ABRAHAM THAT WHICH HE HAS SPOKEN OF HIM."

The exegesis is:

1. Sin can become so bad that judgment is inevitable.

2. Some sins are worse than others.

3. Only Calvary has kept the world from destruction.

SODOM

Verse 16 reads: *"And the men rose up from thence, and looked toward Sodom: and Abraham went with them to bring them on the way."*

God, as well as the two Angels with Him, are referred to as *"men,"* and simply because they have taken on such an appearance.

They now look toward Sodom, and will divulge to Abraham their intentions.

We note from this as well that the Lord monitors every country, city, and each individual in the world. While Sodom and Gomorrah were destroyed in a most unusual way, I have every confidence that the Lord has likewise destroyed many other cities down through the centuries. He may not have done so in the same manner, but nevertheless, He did bring about their destruction in many and various ways. With some, He used the elements, while with others He used war; nevertheless, the reason for their destruction has always been *"sin,"* and sin to such a degree that their destruction was warranted.

As well, the interest of the Lord in all things concerning this world is predicated more on how it affects His Work in the world, than anything else. Had Sodom and Gomorrah continued, Satan would no doubt have used these twin cities to greatly subvert the land of Canaan, which would have

greatly hindered, if not stopped altogether, the advent of the Israelites into Canaan.

During the period of the Book of Acts, mighty Rome then ruled the world. But as mighty as they were, and as far reaching were their effects, Rome is mentioned only as it impacts the Work of God.

It should go without saying that the Work of God is the singular most important thing in the world, at least as far as God is concerned. Therefore, He is very interested in anything that hinders that particular work in an adverse way.

Sodom and Gomorrah is now the center of that attention.

ABRAHAM

Verse 17 reads: *"And the LORD said, Shall I hide from Abraham that thing which I do?"*

Concerning this, Matthew Henry said: *"The secret of the Lord is with them who fear Him. Whether He be pleased to show them what He intends to do or not, He will cause them to understand and to adore the justice and reasonableness of His dispensations, and show them the glory of His works."*

BLESSING

Verse 18 reads: *"Seeing that Abraham shall surely become a great and mighty nation, and all the nations of the Earth shall be blessed in him?"*

It's one thing for men to say certain things, but quite something else when the Lord says certain things. Both predictions came through exactly as spoken by the Lord.

Abraham became a great and mighty nation as it regards Israel. Second, *"all the nations of the Earth have been blessed in him,"* which refers to Christ. Christ came through the Jewish people, and through His Sacrificial, Atoning Death on the Cross of Calvary, all the nations of the world have truly been blessed, and because Abraham is the father of us all as it regards the Born-Again experience (Rom. 4:16).

THE COMMAND

Verse 19 reads: *"For I know him, that he will command his children and his household after him, and they shall keep the way of the LORD, to do justice and judgment; that* the LORD may bring upon Abraham that which He has spoken of him."

The actual Hebrew says, *"For I have known him in order that he may command his sons,"* etc.

The idea reaches out more so to the knowledge of God instituted in Abraham, than Abraham commanding his family, etc.

The idea is that Abraham should spring forth a nation whose institutions were to be imbued with Divine Truth, whose Prophets were to be the means of revealing God's Will to man, and of whom, as concerning the flesh, the Messiah should come.

It was the unique and high purpose for which this nation was to be called into being (Israel) which brought Abraham into so close a relation to Jehovah.

Israel was the only nation in the world which even remotely carried out the commands of the Lord, as it regards *"justice and judgment."* They could do this because they had the Word of the Lord, which in fact, no other nation in the world possessed at that time. This put Israel the proverbial light-years ahead of all other people. In fact, the Law of God given to Moses was the only fair and equitable law that man ever knew. This is because it was instituted by Jehovah, and not by man. While of course, there were many laws in the world of that day, they were all devised by man, and as such, were fraught with injustice and a lack of judgment on those who would seek to take peace from the Earth.

The old adage is true: *"Much Bible, much freedom; little Bible, little freedom; no Bible, no freedom."*

In a sense, every iota of freedom that's in the world today, every blessing that has come upon humanity, irrespective as to whom the people might be, Abraham more than any other man, has been responsible for all of this under God. And if one wants to put one's finger on the cause and the reason for Abraham being the result of all of this, one would have to point toward his Faith. But in understanding this, one might say that his Faith centered up in *"Jesus Christ and Him Crucified"* (Jn. 8:56).

(20) "AND THE LORD SAID, BECAUSE THE CRY OF SODOM AND GOMORRAH IS

GREAT, AND BECAUSE THEIR SIN IS VERY GRIEVOUS;

(21) "I WILL GO DOWN NOW, AND SEE WHETHER THEY HAVE DONE ALTOGETHER ACCORDING TO THE CRY OF IT, WHICH IS COME UNTO ME; AND IF NOT, I WILL KNOW.

(22) "AND THE MEN TURNED THEIR FACES FROM THENCE, AND WENT TOWARD SODOM: BUT ABRAHAM STOOD YET BEFORE THE LORD.

(23) "AND ABRAHAM DREW NEAR, AND SAID, WILL YOU ALSO DESTROY THE RIGHTEOUS WITH THE WICKED?"

The diagram is:

1. The sin of Sodom and Gomorrah had become so great that it threatened contamination of the entirety of that part of the world; consequently, it had to be destroyed.

2. Before the Lord would dispense such judgment, even though He already knew, He would Personally look into the situation, to see if these cities could be spared.

3. Abraham intercedes for the twin cities, but his real reason is his nephew, Lot.

SODOM AND GOMORRAH

Verse 20 reads: *"And the LORD said, Because the cry of Sodom and Gomorrah is great, and because their sin is very grievous."*

Some 15 years before, due to the efforts of Abraham, Sodom and Gomorrah had been rescued from the hands of a tyrant. By freeing them, this showed that God was willing to forgive their transgressions if they would repent; however, they seem to little inquire after Abraham's God, if at all. So there was no Repentance; consequently, there could be no forgiveness.

The human heart is so altogether corrupt that it seems neither God's threats nor His Mercies seldom lead the wicked to Repentance.

There is evidence that at the beginning, the Sodomites were somewhat grateful to God for His Mercy extended to them. But soon they forgot entirely the help that Abraham had given, and they blasphemed the Divine Message which he and Lot proclaimed.

But at the same time, they were a proud people, and believed themselves to be wise.

Martin Luther said: *"Wherever people are ungrateful to God and despise His Word, there is neither honor nor honesty among them, for these virtues, like good fruits, spring forth entirely from the seed of the Divine Word."* When the Divine Word is no longer proclaimed, or it is erroneously interpreted, blasphemy and extreme wickedness are the end result.

As we go down into the Text, we shall see just how wicked Sodom and Gomorrah had become.

"The cry of Sodom and Gomorrah" was not the cry of the oppressed, as some have claimed. It was the cry of evil and wickedness which came up into the ears of God, and which He always sees. But in this case, it had become so great that it could no longer be ignored. Their sins had become more and more wicked, which, therefore, meant that it grieved the heart of God.

Let the Reader understand that God cannot abide sin in any capacity. A thrice-Holy God cannot condone sin. There is only one remedy for sin, and that is the Cross of Christ. The world may put forth its proposed cures for the situation, but all to no avail. Regrettably, the Church all too often follows suit. In other words, the modern Church little looks toward the Cross.

The answer to sin, which the world has accepted, and regrettably, most of the Church as well, is humanistic psychology. Is there any hope in these claims? Does it hold the answer for hurting humanity?

Perhaps the following illustration will be of some help.

HUMANISTIC PSYCHOLOGY

I happened to see a documentary the other day on the addiction of gambling. The principal in the documentary was a man who had an earned Ph.D. His field of study was psychological counseling. As one should know, a Ph.D. is the highest educational attainment to which one can ascribe. He specialized in counseling alcoholics and drug addicts.

In this state, he had no belief in God, and in fact, ridiculed the Bible, and all for which God stands.

To make the story brief, he and his wife went with some friends to a gambling casino. He had little interest in going, but to please

them, he went. He had promised himself that he would stay only 20 minutes.

He had never gambled in his life, and determined to spend about 20 minutes at the slots, and then go home. Two hours later he was still there, and in two or three days, he was completely hooked.

During the next two years, he went through the entirety of their savings, sold their home, sold his automobile, borrowed every dollar that he could borrow, all in order to continue his gambling habit.

After a period of time, he realized he was in deep trouble, and at one point, planned to take his own life.

As he parked his car under a tree out on a side road, he reached in the glove compartment to get a gun, which he thought was there, but it was gone. His wife had taken it a couple of days earlier, planning to sell it, which she actually did, in order to pay the light bill, so their lights would not be turned off. That's how bad the situation had become.

All the skills of humanistic psychology which he had used as it regards psychological counseling concerning alcoholics and drug addicts, he used on himself, but to no avail. He tried every trick in the book, but the addiction yielded to none of his efforts.

He then realized that what he was promoting was a bankrupt philosophy. It had no power to set anyone free.

At this stage, he began to call on God Whom he had once ridiculed. The miracles at which he had once laughed, he now sought. And as the Lord has met untold millions down through the many centuries, he met this man as well, at the point of his need.

He gave his heart and life to Jesus Christ, with the Lord then breaking the addiction of gambling, which only the Lord could do.

This is one of the most strident illustrations I've ever known as it regards the futility of humanistic psychology. And yet, the Church, which ought to know better, has bought this lie, and has done so in totality.

THE CROSS

As we have stated, the only cure for sin, and we mean the only cure, is the Cross of Christ. And any so-called Preacher of the

Gospel who would recommend psychology is, in effect, placing a vote of no confidence in the Cross. One cannot have it both ways. One either believes in the Cross, or one believes in the world. One cannot believe in both at the same time.

And to be frank, at least as it regards the Church, unbelief is the great problem. Men claim to believe in Christ, but in reality they don't! Preachers claim to present Christ, but in reality they are presenting *"another Christ"* (II Cor. 11:4).

The sin of the Church in rejecting the Cross and accepting humanistic psychology, to put it in Biblical terms, *"is very grievous."*

JUDGMENT

Verse 21 reads: *"I will go down now, and see whether they have done altogether according to the cry of it, which is come unto Me; and if not, I will know."*

All sin is inherently offensive in the Eyes of the Almighty; but some forms of wickedness are more presumptuously daring or more intrinsically loathsome than others, and of such sort were the sins of Sodom. Though God speaks of making investigation into the sins of Sodom, this was really unnecessary. The moral degeneracy of the inhabitants of these twin cities was one of the *"all things"* that are ever *"naked and manifest"* unto His Eyes. So nothing can be hidden from God (II Chron. 16:9; Prov. 15:3; Amos 9:8).

The meaning of these phrases is that though the guilt of Sodom was great, God would not let loose His vengeance until it should be seen to be perfectly just. Nothing would be done in haste, but all with judicial calmness (Exell).

TWO ANGELS

Verse 22 reads: *"And the men turned their faces from thence, and went toward Sodom: but Abraham stood yet before the LORD."*

The idea seems to be, the Lord remained here with Abraham, while the two Angels with Him would go into Sodom, but going there for the purpose of rescuing Lot. They would then bring judgment upon these cities.

Abraham's posture before the Lord refers to a petition he will lay out, all of which concerned

Lot and his family. He would intercede on the part of his nephew.

THE RIGHTEOUS?

Verse 23 reads: *"And Abraham drew near, and said, Will You also destroy the righteous with the wicked?"*

I think the Text bears it out that while Abraham was definitely concerned about the entirety of the population of these cities, his greatest concern was about Lot. When he mentions the word *"righteous"* he could only be thinking of Lot. But the question as posed by Abraham covers a broad waterfront. The answer is as follows:

No, the Lord will not destroy the righteous with the wicked. While the Lord definitely oversees all, and that regards the unredeemed as well as the Redeemed, the Redeemed, to be sure, are in a category all by themselves. The Scripture plainly says that we are *"bought with a price: therefore glorify God in your body, and in your spirit, which are God's"* (I Cor. 6:20). So that means that the Lord monitors every action of the Child of God, and that nothing happens to Believers but that the Lord either causes it or allows it.

For instance, if God in His foreknowledge knows that an airplane is going to crash, killing all on board, He will do one of two things as it regards Believers: A. He will either stop the Believer from getting on the plane, which He can do with no difficulty, or else, B. He will delay the *"accident"* because of the Believer. In other words, because of the Believer being on board, the plane won't go down.

This is the reason that the presence of a Believer is of utmost benefit to all concerned, even the ungodliest; regrettably, most unredeemed don't know that, and would ridicule such a statement if it came to their attention; however, it is nevertheless true.

(24) "PERADVENTURE THERE BE FIFTY RIGHTEOUS WITHIN THE CITY: WILL YOU ALSO DESTROY AND NOT SPARE THE PLACE FOR THE FIFTY RIGHTEOUS WHO ARE THEREIN?

(25) "THAT BE FAR FROM YOU TO DO AFTER THIS MANNER, TO SLAY THE

RIGHTEOUS WITH THE WICKED, AND THAT THE RIGHTEOUS SHOULD BE AS THE WICKED, THAT BE FAR FROM YOU: SHALL NOT THE JUDGE OF ALL THE EARTH DO RIGHT?

(26) "AND THE LORD SAID, IF I FIND IN SODOM FIFTY RIGHTEOUS WITHIN THE CITY, THEN I WILL SPARE ALL THE PLACE FOR THEIR SAKES.

(27) "AND ABRAHAM ANSWERED AND SAID, BEHOLD NOW, I HAVE TAKEN UPON ME TO SPEAK UNTO THE LORD, WHICH AM BUT DUST AND ASHES:

(28) "PERADVENTURE THERE SHALL LACK FIVE OF THE FIFTY RIGHTEOUS: WILL YOU DESTROY ALL THE CITY FOR LACK OF FIVE? AND HE SAID, IF I FIND THERE FORTY AND FIVE, I WILL NOT DESTROY IT.

(29) "AND HE SPOKE UNTO HIM YET AGAIN, AND SAID, PERADVENTURE THERE SHALL BE FORTY FOUND THERE. AND HE SAID, I WILL NOT DO IT FOR FORTY'S SAKE.

(30) "AND HE SAID UNTO HIM, OH LET NOT THE LORD BE ANGRY, AND I WILL SPEAK: PERADVENTURE THERE SHALL THIRTY BE FOUND THERE. AND HE SAID, I WILL NOT DO IT, IF I FIND THIRTY THERE.

(31) "AND HE SAID, BEHOLD NOW, I HAVE TAKEN UPON ME TO SPEAK UNTO THE LORD: PERADVENTURE THERE SHALL BE TWENTY FOUND THERE. AND HE SAID, I WILL NOT DESTROY IT FOR TWENTY'S SAKE.

(32) "AND HE SAID, OH LET NOT THE LORD BE ANGRY, AND I WILL SPEAK YET BUT THIS ONCE: PERADVENTURE TEN SHALL BE FOUND THERE. AND HE SAID, I WILL NOT DESTROY IT FOR TEN'S SAKE.

(33) "AND THE LORD WENT HIS WAY, AS SOON AS HE HAD LEFT COMMUNING WITH ABRAHAM: AND ABRAHAM RETURNED UNTO HIS PLACE."

The synopsis is:

1. Abraham now begins to intercede for Sodom.

2. We find from this narrative how important the righteous are, as it involves the overall scheme of things.

3. While the Lord wouldn't spare the city, and because not even ten righteous could be found there, He would spare righteous Lot.

FIFTY

Verse 24 reads: *"Peradventure there be fifty righteous within the city: will You also destroy and not spare the place for the fifty righteous who are therein?"*

The fifty doesn't include the children. Even though they were destroyed in the judgment, they were not eternally lost, even though their parents were. This we conclude from Jonah 4:11, which tells us of little children who *"cannot discern between their right hand and their left hand."* So I believe and teach that every child below the age of accountability, irrespective of the state of their parents, if they should die in that innocent state, they are protected by the Lord, and in fact, go to be with Him in Heaven. I don't believe there is a single baby or child below the age of accountability in Hell, nor will there ever be.

What the age of accountability is would vary with the child. With some, it could be as young as five or six years old, and with others it could be as much as nine or ten years old. All that would depend on many things, and only the Lord would know the answer as it regards each child.

Abraham now begins to intercede for the city of Sodom, which would probably include all five cities of the plain, with four ultimately destroyed. He asked that if fifty righteous are found in this city or cities, would the Lord spare the place?

Every Believer has the spiritual and Scriptural right to intercede on behalf of whatever it is that is thought to be needed. In fact, it was the Holy Spirit Who prompted Abraham to intercede, and it is the Holy Spirit Who prompts us likewise.

Many Believers have the mistaken idea that God is going to do whatever it is He desires to do, and there is nothing that can stop it. The truth is, the Lord has put great responsibility into the hands of all Believers, which means, if we fall down on the job, whatever it is that needs to be done, simply will not be done.

For instance, if the Church lets down as it regards Evangelism, untold millions in the world will be lost. In fact, God has already done His part. He has given His Son, the Lord Jesus Christ, which makes all things possible. It's up to us now to tell others this greatest story of all.

RESPONSIBILITY

At this very moment, there are Sodoms hanging in the balance. If Saints somewhere in this world don't intercede, these cities will be lost, which could mean that untold thousands or even millions could die and go to Hell.

Even if the areas aren't spared, much good will still be done, even as it was done with Abraham's intercession. While Sodom and Gomorrah were not spared, Lot was spared.

One of the major problems is, most Christians aren't living close enough to the Lord to even hear His Voice. The Holy Spirit attempts to move upon them, but all to no avail. That is the tragedy!

THE JUDGE

Verse 25 reads: *"That be far from You to do after this manner, to slay the righteous with the wicked: and that the righteous should be as the wicked, that be far from You: Shall not the Judge of all the Earth do right?"*

As stated, the Lord doesn't slay the righteous with the wicked. In fact, the righteous aren't like the wicked in any manner, the Precious Blood of Jesus having made the difference.

Of all things, exactly as Abraham said, we can be totally confident that the Judge of the Earth shall do right. That Judge is the Lord!

He is the Judge of all the Earth; He always does right in everything He does and carries out; as well, He has the power to guarantee whatever it is that needs to be done.

THE ANSWER

Verse 26 reads: *"And the LORD said, If I find in Sodom fifty righteous within the city, then I will spare all the place for their sakes."*

We learn from this, and as previously stated, that the righteous are a tremendous boon and blessing to the entire area which they occupy. This means that the more Believers which are in any given place, the more Blessings of God will be poured out on that place, and destruction withheld.

NOTES

Think of it! If only ten righteous had been found in Sodom, the city, despite its wickedness, would have been spared.

While the world doesn't understand this at all, and in fact maligns and even curses the Child of God oftentimes, the truth is, every single blessing, and in whatever capacity, that the unredeemed receive, it is received because of the righteous ones who are in their midst.

Now this is not understood by the world, and in fact never will be; however, it is, nevertheless, true. The Lord has spared untold numbers of people, as well as entire cities, because of the Righteous.

HUMILITY

Verse 27 reads: *"And Abraham answered and said, Behold now, I have taken upon me to speak unto the LORD, which am but dust and ashes."*

In referring to himself as *"but dust and ashes,"* we find here the humility of the great Patriarch. Despite the fact that the Lord had come all the way from Heaven, and on this journey He had visited Abraham, and despite the fact that through the Patriarch all the nations of the world would be blessed, Abraham thought of himself even as he should have done so.

It is very difficult for men and women to be signally honored and blessed by the Lord, and it not affect them in the realm of pride. Consequently, the Lord cannot bless many people, and for the obvious reasons.

As well, spiritual pride is the worst pride of all. Such exists simply because the individual has an improper view of the Cross. In fact, one cannot really know humility unless one knows and understands the Cross.

The knowledge of the Cross humbles anyone who understands it accordingly. In fact, the very fact of the Cross was the greatest act of humility the world has ever known. For God to become man, and to lay aside the expression of His Deity, and then to die upon a Cross, portrays humility as humility has never been portrayed. As well, for the Believer to know and understand this tremendous quality, which incidentally God demands, the Believer must without fail understand the Cross. That alone will bring the Believer to the place we ought to be concerning the opposite of spiritual pride.

FORTY-FIVE

Verse 28 reads: *"Peradventure there shall lack five of the fifty righteous: will You destroy all the city for lack of five? And He said, If I find there forty and five, I will not destroy it."*

If it is to be noticed, Abraham frames his requests in an uncanny manner. He doesn't ask for the city to be spared if there are 45 righteous, but rather if five of the 50 are lacking, throwing the emphasis on *"five,"* which of course plays out to 45, would the city be spared? Instead of putting the emphasis on the 45, he puts it on the five.

FORTY

Verse 29 reads: *"And he spoke unto Him yet again, and said, Peradventure there shall be forty found there. And He said, I will not do it for forty's sake."*

Emboldened now with courage as well as Faith, he lowers the number to 40. Again, the Lord acquiesces to the lower number.

THIRTY

Verse 30 reads: *"And he said unto Him, Oh let not the LORD be angry, and I will speak: peradventure there shall thirty be found there. And He said, I will not do it, if I find thirty there."*

By his constant persistence, Abraham prays that he will not anger the Lord.

While Abraham would not have had the knowledge of the Lord that we presently have, I think it can easily be said that the Lord delights in the Believer pressing, as it regards petitions and desires. While it should be done with humility, and in fact always done with humility, which means that we know and understand that we deserve nothing good, the Believer should press through to the desired results.

If 30 righteous could be found, the Lord would spare the city.

TWENTY

Verse 31 reads: *"And he said, Behold now, I have taken upon me to speak unto the LORD: peradventure there shall be twenty found there. And He said, I will not destroy it for twenty's sake."*

It is obvious that the Patriarch fears that the number of righteous in Sodom, other than Lot, is virtually nonexistent. He asked for 20, and the Lord acquiesces.

However, through foreknowledge the Lord knew exactly how many righteous were in the city, and that Abraham's petition really would not do any good. So why did He not inform him of this to begin with?

This we do know: everything the Lord does is always for our benefit. In other words, He has a prime reason for all things.

I think He allowed Abraham to continue in this vein, in order that this narrative may teach us the practice of intercession, and as well, the position of relationship.

Abraham was the friend of God, and this illustration proclaims that fact. Due to the Cross, we presently carry a higher claim.

When I was a child, my Grandmother taught me a very valuable lesson. She said to me, *"Jimmy, God is a big God, so ask big."*

I've never forgotten that! Abraham asked big! While he did not succeed in his quest for Sodom to not be destroyed, still, he did succeed in once again rescuing Lot.

TEN

Verse 32 reads: *"And he said, Oh let not the LORD be angry, and I will speak yet but this once: peradventure ten shall be found there. And He said, I will not destroy it for ten's sake."*

What the population of this city of Sodom was at this time, we have no way of knowing; it was probably at least 100 thousand strong, if not more. And yet, there were not even 10 righteous people in the city.

We should note in this that Abraham ceased asking before God ceased giving. Such is the power and the value of prayer!

THE LORD

Verse 33 reads: *"And the LORD went His way, as soon as He had left communing with Abraham: and Abraham returned unto his place."*

While the Lord now goes His way, He doesn't do so until Abraham ceases his petitioning. As stated, Abraham ceased asking before God ceased giving. That's quite a statement, and should be looked at very closely.

How so much we miss, simply because we do not take it to the Lord in prayer.

Why? There are two reasons:

1. In many cases, it's unconfessed sin in the person's life, and prayer immediately demands that such sin be repented of, and forsaken. Many Christians simply don't want to forsake their sin.

2. There isn't much faith on the part of most Believers. And to have the necessary prayer life we ought to have, a great deal of faith is required. But I believe the greatest problem of prayerlessness is because of the following:

If the Believer doesn't properly understand the Cross, prayer will not be nearly as important to him as it could be. And that is the condition of the modern Church. There has been so little teaching and preaching on the Cross in the last several decades, that for all practical purposes, the modern Church is all but Cross illiterate. Consequently, without the Cross as the central core of our faith, the Church is splintered in every direction.

A proper understanding of the Cross will give the Believer Faith, simply because the Word of God is the story of the Cross. When we properly understand the Cross, we are properly understanding the Word; therefore, Faith is generated!

"Fairest Lord Jesus, Ruler of all nature,
"O Thou of God and man the Son;
"Thee will I cherish, Thee will I honor,
"Thou my soul's glory, joy, and crown."

"Fair are the meadows, fairer still the
woodlands,
"Robed in the blooming garb of spring;
"Jesus is fairer, Jesus is purer,
"Who makes the woeful heart to sing."

"Fair is the sunshine, fairer still the
moonlight,
"And fair the twinkling, starry host;
"Jesus shines brighter, Jesus shines
purer,
"Than all the Angels Heaven can boast."

"All fairest beauty heavenly and earthly,
"Wondrously, Jesus, is found in Thee;
"None can be nearer, fairer, or dearer,
"Than Thou, my Saviour, art to me."

CHAPTER 19

(1) "AND THERE CAME TWO ANGELS TO SODOM AT EVENING; AND LOT SAT IN THE GATE OF SODOM: AND LOT SEEING THEM ROSE UP TO MEET THEM; AND HE BOWED HIMSELF WITH HIS FACE TOWARD THE GROUND;

(2) "AND HE SAID, BEHOLD NOW, MY LORDS, TURN IN, I PRAY YOU, INTO YOUR SERVANT'S HOUSE, AND TARRY ALL NIGHT, AND WASH YOUR FEET, AND YOU SHALL RISE UP EARLY, AND GO ON YOUR WAYS. AND THEY SAID, NO; BUT WE WILL ABIDE IN THE STREET ALL NIGHT.

(3) "AND HE PRESSED UPON THEM GREATLY; AND THEY TURNED IN UNTO HIM, AND ENTERED INTO HIS HOUSE; AND HE MADE THEM A FEAST, AND DID BAKE UNLEAVENED BREAD, AND THEY DID EAT."

The structure is:

1. While the Lord speaks with Abraham, the two Angels who had come with Him now go into Sodom.

2. The principle of evil, which the Bible calls *"sin,"* and which has wrought such ruin in human nature, painfully appears in this Chapter.

3. The Angels on their part had to be pressed to accept hospitality from the Nephew which they had at once accepted from the Uncle.

THE GATE OF SODOM

Verse 1 reads: *"And there came two Angels to Sodom at evening; and Lot sat in the gate of Sodom: and Lot seeing them rose up to meet them; and he bowed himself with his face toward the ground."*

While Abraham was interceding with the Lord, the two Angels go into Sodom, and do so for the sole purpose of rescuing Lot. As these two Angels entered the city, dressed like men, and looking like men, little did the citizens of Sodom know the power these men held in their possession. They had been sent on a mission, and that mission was to rescue Lot, and this they would do.

Lot sitting at the gate probably denoted position and authority. Inasmuch as Abraham, his Uncle, some time back had saved the life of the king of Sodom, along with the lives of Lot and all who had been taken captive, plus even the material goods, at that time, Lot was probably elevated, and due to these factors, could possibly have even been Mayor of the city, even though that is only supposition.

How Lot knew these two men (Angels) when they came into the city, we aren't told. They definitely knew who he was, so they may well have introduced themselves in some fashion, which is probably what happened. It is even possible that they revealed their true identity to Lot, inasmuch as he *"bowed himself with his face toward the ground."* As well, we will find that he will do everything within his power to protect them, even to the proposal of giving his two daughters to the mob.

THE INVITATION

Verse 2 reads: *"And he said, Behold now, my lords, turn in, I pray you, into your servant's house, and tarry all night, and wash your feet, and you shall rise up early, and go on your ways. And they said, No; but we will abide in the street all night."*

Other than the destruction of this place, whatever else the Angels had in mind, we aren't told. As if they didn't already know, they would see firsthand the terrible wickedness of this place called *"Sodom."*

There are two methods used by the Lord to draw Believers away from the attractions of the world. They are as follows:

1. He first of all reveals to us the stability and eternal value of the *"things above."*

2. He shows us the temporal nature of the things of this world. Thus, if we fully realize the stability of Heaven, we will have no problem rejecting the delusive joys of Earth.

Looking at Lot as he *"sits in the gate,"* we see that he has *"gotten on in the world."* If we look at his situation from a worldly point of view, it seems that he has been successful.

He first of all *"pitches his tent toward Sodom."* He then found his way into the city, and now we find him sitting at the gate — a prominent, influential post.

Concerning Abraham, the Scripture says, *"By faith Abraham sojourned in the land of promise, as is in a strange country, dwelling*

in tabernacles" (Heb. 11:9). We read no such statement as it regards Lot. It could not be said, *"By faith Lot sat in the gate of Sodom."* Actually, he gets no place at all among the Faith notables in Hebrews, Chapter 11.

It should be observed that there was a material difference between these two men, even though they both started together on the same course. The tragedy is, they reached a very different goal, at least so far as their public testimony was concerned.

I think the Scripture is clear that Lot was saved; yet it was *"so as by fire,"* with his works being *"burned up."*

As it regards Abraham and Lot, the Lord remained to commune with the Patriarch, while He merely sent His two Angels to Sodom as it regards Lot.

In fact, the Angels, as we have seen here, didn't even desire to enter into the house of Lot, but rather said, *"We will abide in the street all night."* What a rebuke!

CONDEMNATION

The answer of the Angels to Lot, even though they ultimately did go into his house, contains a most unqualified condemnation of his position in Sodom. The idea is, they would rather stay in the street all night, than to enter under the roof of one in a wrong position. In fact, had it not been for Abraham, every evidence is Lot would not have been spared at all. It was simply for Abraham's sake that Lot was allowed to escape. The Lord has no sympathy with a worldly mind; and such a mind it was that had led Lot to settle down amid the defilement of that guilty city. Faith never put him there; a spiritual mind never put him there; *"his righteous soul"* never put him there: it was simple love for this present evil world that led him first to *"choose,"* then to *"pitch his tent toward,"* and finally to *"sit in the gate of Sodom."*

And look what he chose! A city that was doomed to destruction; a destruction so awful that none would be saved.

Lot no doubt thought that he was doing well when he came into Sodom. And when he was honored to be able to sit in the gate, which insinuates a place of authority and position, he is even more gratified. But that which followed shows how entirely he erred; and it also sounds in our personal ears a voice of deepest solemnity — a voice telling us to beware how we yield to the incipient workings of a worldly spirit (Mackintosh).

HOSPITALITY

Verse 3 reads: *"And he pressed upon them greatly; and they turned in unto him, and entered into his house; and he made them a feast, and did bake unleavened bread, and they did eat."*

The idea seems to be that he would not take no for an answer, as it regards them coming into his house and partaking of his hospitality.

We do know that everything the Lord does, even through His Angels, is always with design and purpose. So their reluctance to enter into his house may have been more of a test than anything else.

While Abraham's intercession was to be greatly heeded, still, Lot could not be spared on that alone. He had to have a personal relationship with the Lord, that is, if he was to be saved.

So quite possibly, they refused his hospitality at the beginning, just to see what he would do. Would he insist, or would he easily take no for an answer, showing little regard and concern?

To his credit, *"he pressed upon them greatly."* Only then did they *"turn in unto him, and enter into his house."* Only then did they partake with him in the feast that was prepared, which speaks of communion, and carries a tremendous spiritual meaning.

Even though he was in sad shape spiritually, still, his righteous soul cried out to God, which became evident by his actions, which meant that they could now commune with him, which they did!

While his faith was too weak to reject Sodom, it was too strong to reject the Angels, and thank God for that!

(4) "BUT BEFORE THEY LAY DOWN, THE MEN OF THE CITY, EVEN THE MEN OF SODOM, COMPASSED THE HOUSE ROUND, BOTH OLD AND YOUNG, ALL THE PEOPLE FROM EVERY QUARTER:

(5) "AND THEY CALLED UNTO LOT, AND SAID UNTO HIM, WHERE ARE THE MEN WHICH CAME IN TO YOU THIS NIGHT?

BRING THEM OUT UNTO US, THAT WE MAY KNOW THEM.

(6) "AND LOT WENT OUT THE DOOR UNTO THEM, AND SHUT THE DOOR AFTER HIM,

(7) "AND SAID, I PRAY YOU, BRETHREN, DO NOT SO WICKEDLY.

(8) "BEHOLD NOW, I HAVE TWO DAUGHTERS WHICH HAVE NOT KNOWN MAN; LET ME, I PRAY YOU, BRING THEM OUT UNTO YOU, AND DO YOU TO THEM AS IS GOOD IN YOUR EYES: ONLY UNTO THESE MEN DO NOTHING; FOR THEREFORE CAME THEY UNDER THE SHADOW OF MY ROOF.

(9) "AND THEY SAID, STAND BACK. AND THEY SAID AGAIN, THIS ONE FELLOW CAME IN TO SOJOURN, AND HE WILL NEEDS BE A JUDGE: NOW WILL WE DEAL WORSE WITH YOU, THAN WITH THEM. AND THEY PRESSED SORE UPON THE MAN, EVEN LOT, AND CAME NEAR TO BREAK THE DOOR.

(10) "BUT THE MEN PUT FORTH THEIR HAND, AND PULLED LOT INTO THE HOUSE TO THEM, AND SHUT TO THE DOOR.

(11) "AND THEY SMOTE THE MEN THAT WERE AT THE DOOR OF THE HOUSE WITH BLINDNESS, BOTH SMALL AND GREAT: SO THAT THEY WEARIED THEMSELVES TO FIND THE DOOR."

The composition is:

1. The sin of homosexuality was the primary sin which occasioned the destruction of Sodom (Jude, vss. 6-7).

2. The men of Sodom would even violate the Angels, that is had they the opportunity to have done so.

3. Though Lot gave in to Sodom in order to enjoy its material advantages, the Scripture says that he was *"vexed with the filthy lifestyle of the wicked"* (II Pet. 2:7-8). In fact, he had spoken out against these things so often that the men of Sodom accused him of wanting to play the judge.

4. The Angels used their power to smite the men with blindness, who were trying to force the door. Their lust knew no bounds!

THE HOMOSEXUALS

Verse 4 reads: *"But before they lay down, the men of the city, even the men of Sodom, compassed the house round, both old and young, all the people from every quarter."*

The lust of the men of Sodom was so great, and we speak of homosexual lust, which seemed to have possessed the entirety of the city, that they would literally force the door, in order to get to the two Angels, who they thought were mere men.

I think we can see from the account given here just how deep into sin Sodom had deteriorated. It was past Redemption, past saving. It was like a cancer that had to be surgically removed, which the Lord would now do.

Whether the sin of homosexuality is the worst sin there is or not, only the Lord knows; however, this we do know, Sodom and Gomorrah are the only cities, plus two smaller ones at this time, which have ever been destroyed in this fashion. While the Lord down through the centuries has no doubt destroyed many, these are the only ones done in this manner and in this way. That being the case, we should understand that the sin of homosexuality is at least one of the worst sins known to man.

Homosexuals are not born in this way, just as alcoholics or thieves, etc., are not born as such. While all are born in original sin, which means that the seed of all sin is present in our hearts and lives, this does not mean that certain ones are predestined for certain particular lifestyles. So how does one become a homosexual?

LIFESTYLES

While some may definitely be more predisposed toward certain directions than others, which I think is obvious, boys are pushed over the edge, at least some of them, when they are molested by a homosexual. The Scripture says: *"But every man is tempted, when he is drawn away of his own lusts, and enticed"* (James 1:14).

Without a doubt, evil spirits enter into this situation, as evil spirits enter into all sin.

Medical Scientists are investigating the possibility of a particular gene being perverted or malformed, which could bring about a homosexual lifestyle, or other problems as well; however, if they in fact do find that this is the case, they will still only be treating the symptoms and not the real cause.

The cause is the sin principle or sin nature, which came upon the human race as a result of the Fall in the Garden of Eden. It takes many forms and many directions, but it is that which is more powerful than man, and which drives him toward evil.

DELIVERANCE

There is deliverance from any and all bondages, and irrespective as to how awful they might be, in Jesus Christ. However, the manner in which deliverance is brought about is through what Christ did at the Cross. As we've said repeatedly, to divorce Christ from the Cross is to make Christ ineffective.

Deliverance from sin is of greater magnitude than a mere display of power, which the Lord readily has. Sin is an affront to God, and for sin to be properly handled, God's Nature and Justice must be totally and completely satisfied. He is the One Who has been offended, and He is the One Who must be satisfied.

The Cross Alone satisfied Him, in that there, all sin, in its totality, was atoned. It was at the Cross that the *"body of sin was destroyed,"* (Rom. 6:6). This means that the *"guilt"* of sin was removed, and the *"power"* of sin was broken. As stated, it was done at the Cross, and it is through the Cross that all victory comes.

If it is to be noticed, Jesus did not say that He came to deliver people, even though He did do that, but rather that He came to *"preach deliverance to the captives"* (Lk. 4:18). What did He mean by that?

What I'm doing right here is preaching deliverance to you. He also stated, *"You shall know the Truth, and the Truth shall make you free"* (Jn. 8:32).

The Truth is Jesus Christ and what He did for us at the Cross. That's why Paul said: *"I determined to know nothing among you, save Christ and Him Crucified"* (I Cor. 2:2).

That's why he also said: *"For the preaching of the Cross* (which is actually the preaching of deliverance) *is to them who perish foolishness; but unto us which are saved it is the Power of God"* (I Cor. 1:18).

The homosexual can be delivered totally and completely; the alcoholic and drug addict can be delivered totally and completely;

the thief and the liar can be delivered totally and completely; in fact, irrespective as to what the bondage or vice might be, one can be totally and completely delivered; however, this can only be done by the Lord Jesus Christ, and the means by which He does this is by and through what He did for us at the Cross. Paul continued to say:

"Who gave Himself for our sins, that He might deliver us from this present evil world, according to the Will of God and our Father" (Gal. 1:4).

This means that the sinner, homosexuals included, must accept Christ as their Saviour. They must then place their Faith totally and completely in Christ, and what He has done for them at the Cross, asking for, and receiving the deliverance which He has already afforded. Millions have been set free, and anyone can be set free, who will so subject his faith.

The idea that one can be saved, and continue on in such a lifestyle of homosexuality, or anything else of that nature, is a fool's hope. It cannot be done! Jesus didn't die on the Cross in order to save us in our sins, but rather *"from"* sin. And to be sure, homosexuality, along with drunkenness, adultery, stealing, lying, and a thousand and one other things, constitute sin. If Salvation doesn't save us from sin, then it's not true Salvation, but rather mere religion, made up by man.

THE ACT OF HOMOSEXUALITY

Verse 5 reads: *"And they called unto Lot, and said unto him, Where are the men which came in to you this night? Bring them out unto us, that we may know them."*

The words *"know them"* as it was used by the men of Sodom, and as it regarded the two men (Angels) in the home of Lot referred to knowing them sexually, i.e., *"in a homosexual way."*

Homosexuality is always, after a fashion, predatorial. Actually, predatorality is the spirit of homosexuality. It is not merely an alternate lifestyle, but rather a perversion of the worst sort.

That all the mass of men gathered at the door of Lot's house without exception were involved in this demand is emphatic, and shows the absolute depth to which the citizenship of

this city had sunk, at least as it regards sexual perversion.

Josephus, the Jewish historian, claims that these two men, who were in reality Angels, had beautiful countenances, which tended to excite the lust of the Sodomites and caused them to assault Lot's house with shameful demands.

The sin of homosexuality was exceedingly prevalent among the Canaanites (Lev. 18:22) and other heathen nations as well (Rom. 1:27). Under the Law of Moses it was punishable by death.

LOT

Verse 6 reads: *"And Lot went out at the door unto them, and shut the door after him."*

As we shall see, Lot, either by pleading or by warning, accomplished nothing. The more he begged this mob, the more irrational, and lustful these reprobates became.

In the first place, it is impossible to reason with lust, and especially this type of lust. As stated, it is predatorial, and will respond to no rational appeal.

BRETHREN?

Verse 7 reads: *"And said, I pray you, brethren, do not so wickedly."*

The Text marks this sin as unspeakably vile, by telling us that they commanded Lot to bring out his guests so that they could seduce them publicly and in the sight of the whole population. They had lost all sense of shame and decency, for they made no attempt at perpetrating this shameful vice in secret. Had the Lord not wiped out this city, and the three others similar in the region, this wretched state of affairs would have put an end to all morality and decency in that area, and could very well have greatly hindered God's Plan for Canaan in the coming years.

Lot refers to them as *"brethren,"* though the correct name would have been *"perverts."*

Why did he refer to them as brethren?

The very fact of this type of terminology shows that Lot had long since compromised his testimony. As a result, these vile individuals had not become like Lot, but rather Lot had become like them, at least in many ways. This is always the shame of compromise. It never remains static, but rather suffers deterioration.

We learn from this that while the Bible does not teach isolation, it definitely does teach separation. The admonition of the Holy Spirit through Paul, *"Be ye not unequally yoked together with unbelievers: for what fellowship has Righteousness with unrighteousness? And what communion has light with darkness? . . . Wherefore come out from among them, and be ye separate, saith the Lord, and touch not the unclean thing; and I will receive you,"* was definitely not being practiced by Lot (II Cor. 6:14, 17). While the record is clear that he did not partake of their evil, and as well, that it vexed his righteous soul (II Pet. 2:7-8), still, he compromised his testimony.

THE RESULT OF COMPROMISE

Verse 8 reads: *"Behold now, I have two daughters which have not known man; let me, I pray you, bring them out unto you, and do to them as is good in your eyes: only unto these men do nothing; for therefore came they under the shadow of my roof."*

This Passage proves that not all the men of Sodom were homosexuals; nevertheless, I think one can say without fear of contradiction that the majority were.

The idea of giving one's daughters to this vile mob is beyond comprehension. Lot seeks to appease these animals by a most humiliating proposition, but all in vain. If a man will mingle with the world, for the purpose of self-aggrandizement, he must make up his mind to endure the sad consequences. We cannot profit by the world and, at the same time, bear effectual testimony against its wickedness.

A JUDGE?

Verse 9 reads: *"And they said, Stand back. And they said again, This one fellow came in to sojourn, and he will needs be a judge: now will we deal worse with you, than with them. And they pressed sore upon the man, even Lot, and came near to break the door."*

The terminology used here tells us several things:

1. Due to Abraham having rescued many Sodomites from Chedorlaomer, evidently these homosexuals had declared him off limits. But now, due to Lot's protection of the two Angels, they are breaking their commitment to him.

2. Who does he think he is, they contemplate, judging them? They will do whatever they so desire, and his appeals will fall on deaf ears. In other words, they were saying, *"You are not our judge."*

And again, by them using the word *"judge,"* there is a slim possibility that Lot was actually a judge in the city of Sodom.

THE ANGELS

Verse 10 reads: *"But the men put forth their hand, and pulled Lot into the house to them, and shut to the door."*

The Angels, observing the situation, now take charge. Evidently, Lot was standing near the door. The Angels opened it, took him by the arm, and pulled him back into the house. They will now take matters into their own hands.

Little did these perverts know as to who these men actually were. Little did they realize that they were hours away from total destruction. And let all who walk accordingly understand the following:

As destruction ultimately came upon Sodom and other cities in that region, likewise, destruction will most definitely come upon all who reject God. As fire came upon Sodom, fire is coming upon this world, and upon every single soul who rejects Christ.

Now men can laugh at that, make fun of that, ridicule and make light of that; nevertheless, that's exactly what is going to happen (II Pet. 3:7).

There is only one way to escape this coming judgment, and that is to accept the Lord Jesus Christ. In Him Alone is Salvation. In Him Alone is Redemption. Addressing this very thing, He said:

"I am the Way, the Truth, and the Life: no man comes unto the Father, but by Me" (Jn. 14:6).

This means that every single person in this world who is following Mohammad will die and go to Hell. It means that all who are following Buddha, Confucius, Joseph Smith, or anyone or anything else, will die and go to Hell. Jesus Christ is the only way, and because He Alone is God, and He Alone paid the price on Calvary's Cross, in the giving of Himself as a Sacrifice, which culminated in the shedding of His Own Precious Blood. Faith in that vicarious, atoning Sacrifice will bring Salvation, and that alone will bring Salvation.

BLINDNESS

Verse 11 reads: *"And they smote the men who were at the door of the house with blindness, both small and great: so that they wearied themselves to find the door."*

The *"blindness"* mentioned here was not total blindness as we think of such. The word really means a disturbance of vision caused by the eye not being in its proper connection with the brain. They could still see, but not see properly. So now, their sight becomes as perverted as their passions, in which it no doubt remained until they were all destroyed a few hours later.

Not desiring to make more of this episode than we should, but at the same time knowing that we should not make less as well, an analogy can be drawn as to the protection of the Child of God.

As Believers, we are in the midst of an evil, wicked, ungodly world. It is ruled by Satan, exactly as Sodom was ruled by Satan. In fact, Paul refers to Satan as *"the god of this world"* (II Cor. 4:4). Whereas the Angels blinded the eyes of these Sodomites, Satan has *"blinded the minds of them which believe not, lest the light of the glorious Gospel of Christ, Who is the Image of God, should shine unto them"* (II Cor. 4:4).

As well, evil spirits working in this maelstrom of iniquity constantly seek to hinder and oppress the Child of God.

However, concerning this very thing, the Apostle John said: *"You are of God, little children, and have overcome them: because greater is He Who is in you, than he who is in the world"* (I Jn. 4:4).

The pronoun *"He"* as used here by John refers to the Holy Spirit Who abides constantly and perpetually in the heart and life of each Believer. However, we must never take Him for granted. Considering how important He is to us, and above all that He is God, and that we have the privilege of having Him to abide with us, we should seek to learn how He functions and works.

THE HOLY SPIRIT

Most Christians, I suppose, think that His work is automatic. In other words, He just

NOTES

does what He desires to do, etc. Nothing could be further from the truth.

Potentially, all things are possible, and potentially, the Holy Spirit can and will do mighty and great things for us, but only on the premise of us doing certain things, and what is that?

The Holy Spirit works entirely on the premise of the Finished Work of Christ on the Cross (Rom. 8:2). In fact, He will not work outside of those premises.

This means that every Believer must ever make the Cross of Christ the object of his Faith. In fact, this is the only thing the Holy Spirit actually requires. He does not require the Saint to be a theologian or a scholar. He only requires that one's Faith be anchored squarely in the great Sacrifice of Christ, for this is where the demands of the Law were satisfied, by Jesus giving His life, to atone for all sin (Jn. 1:29).

If the Believer understands that the Cross of Christ is the means by which God gives all things to Believers, and that the Holy Spirit works exclusively within the parameters of the Finished Work of Christ, and thereby anchors his Faith exclusively in that Finished Work, then total and complete victory will be ours, and in every capacity (Rom. 6:3-5, 11, 14; 8:1-2, 11, 13; I Cor. 1:17-18, 21, 23; 2:2, 5; Gal. 6:14; Eph. 2:13-18; Col. 2:14-15).

What I've just given to you in brief is the single most important thing as a Believer that you could ever hear or read. It is God's prescribed order for victory as it regards His children.

If we place our Faith and confidence strictly in Christ and what He has done for us at the Cross, ever making the Cross the object of our Faith, we can rest assured that total and complete Divine protection will be given unto us in every capacity, and Satan will not be able to touch us. Let the Church understand that the Cross and the Cross Alone is the answer. Unfortunately, far too many Preachers seek to project something else as the answer and the solution. Other than the Cross of Christ, there is no other solution, and because no other solution is needed.

(12) "AND THE MEN SAID UNTO LOT, HAVE YOU HERE ANY BESIDES? SONS IN LAW, AND YOUR SONS, AND YOUR

DAUGHTERS, AND WHATSOEVER YOU HAVE IN THE CITY, BRING THEM OUT OF THIS PLACE:

(13) "FOR WE WILL DESTROY THIS PLACE, BECAUSE THE CRY OF THEM IS WAXEN GREAT BEFORE THE FACE OF THE LORD; AND THE LORD HAS SENT US TO DESTROY IT.

(14) "AND LOT WENT OUT, AND SPOKE UNTO HIS SONS IN LAW, WHICH MARRIED HIS DAUGHTERS, AND SAID, UP, GET YOU OUT OF THIS PLACE; FOR THE LORD WILL DESTROY THIS CITY. BUT HE SEEMED AS ONE WHO MOCKED UNTO HIS SONS IN LAW."

The overview is:

1. Lot is told to get his family ready to depart, at least those who will hear and heed.

2. The command is given, *"We will destroy this place."*

3. The testimony of Lot was so weak that at this news, his sons-in-law mocked him.

THE FAMILY

Verse 12 reads: *"And the men said unto Lot, Have you here any besides? Sons in law, and your sons, and your daughters, and whatsoever you have in this city, bring them out of this place."*

Concerning this, Mackintosh said: *"To attempt to reprove the world's ways, while we profit by association with it, is vanity; the world will attach very little weight to such reproof and such testimony. Thus it was, too, with Lot's testimony to his sons-in-law; 'He seemed as one who mocked.' It is vain to speak of approaching judgment while finding our place, our portion, and our enjoyment in the very scene which is to be judged."*

DESTRUCTION

Verse 13 reads: *"For we will destroy this place, because the cry of them is waxen great before the face of the LORD; and the LORD has sent us to destroy it."*

The Lord sent two Angels to destroy Sodom and Gomorrah, along with two other smaller cities. I wonder at this moment, are Angels being sent to other cities in this world? Or even America?

Perhaps one can say that in every city in this world, and I speak of the present time,

there are at least a few Believers, and in some cities, many. And to be sure, even a few, even as we have seen here, carry great weight. So I think the following is what the world is now facing:

Judgment must come, and for all the obvious reasons; however, before this judgment comes, and we speak of judgment on a scale that is beyond present comprehension, Believers must be taken out of this world, which will be done at the Rapture (I Thess. 4:13-18). So the Church presently should be ardently looking for the Rapture. Is it?

Hardly!

Once again I go back to the Cross. When the Church properly looks to the Cross, then everything as it regards the Word of God begins to come into proper focus. Otherwise, the Believer is *"tossed to and fro, and carried about with every wind of doctrine, by the sleight of men, and cunning craftiness, whereby they lie in wait to deceive"* (Eph. 4:14). In fact, the Cross of Christ is the actual dividing line between the Truth Church and the Apostate Church. It is as one views the Cross that one will view Truth.

THE TESTIMONY

Verse 14 reads: *"And Lot went out, and spoke unto his sons-in-law, which married his daughters, and said, Up, get you out of this place; for the LORD will destroy this city. But he seemed as one who mocked unto his sons-in-law."*

Some claim that the original Hebrew Text addresses these men as the future sons-in-law of Lot, meaning they were only engaged to Lot's daughters, but that the wedding had not yet been consummated. Actually, it doesn't matter!

Irrespective as to whether they were now his sons-in-law or prospective only, they had no confidence in his testimony. In fact, they mocked him, by claiming that he was mocking them.

The nearer the world approaches the end, the more it laughs at the Divine threats pronounced upon the wicked. Similarly, Noah warned his generation in vain. When now we speak, even as I have just spoken, of the last coming of the Son of God to judge the world and cast unbelievers into the eternal fire of

Hell, the ungodly ridicule this as something that is unthinkable. Let us, therefore, beware of despising the warnings of God, as do the Epicureans, who accept only what pleases their flesh and agrees with their reason, though the Divine Truth is manifest to them (Luther).

(15) "AND WHEN THE MORNING AROSE, THEN THE ANGELS HASTENED LOT, SAYING, ARISE, TAKE YOUR WIFE, AND YOUR TWO DAUGHTERS, WHICH ARE HERE; LEST YOU BE CONSUMED IN THE INIQUITY OF THE CITY.

(16) "AND WHILE HE LINGERED, THE MEN LAID HOLD UPON HIS HAND, AND UPON THE HAND OF HIS WIFE, AND UPON THE HAND OF HIS TWO DAUGHTERS; THE LORD BEING MERCIFUL UNTO HIM: AND THEY BROUGHT HIM FORTH, AND SET HIM WITHOUT THE CITY.

(17) "AND IT CAME TO PASS, WHEN THEY HAD BROUGHT THEM FORTH ABROAD, THAT HE SAID, ESCAPE FOR YOUR LIFE; LOOK NOT BEHIND YOU, NEITHER STAY YOU IN ALL THE PLAIN; ESCAPE TO THE MOUNTAIN, LEST YOU BE CONSUMED."

The construction is:

1. As the Angels hastened Lot, likewise, the Holy Spirit is hastening the modern Church as it regards the Rapture.

2. Regrettably, the modern Church, at least as a whole, is as reticent as Lot. As he lingered, they linger!

3. Preachers cannot expect to win their congregations from the wrath to come, if they themselves live as though there were no such wrath to be feared!

THE ANGELS

Verse 15 reads: *"And when the morning arose, then the Angels hastened Lot, saying, Arise, take your wife, and your two daughters, which are here, lest you be consumed in the iniquity of the city."*

Two things are said here:

1. The day now arrives which will occasion the destruction of Sodom and the other cities of the plain. But little did its inhabitants know of such a thing, and neither did they believe such a thing. Their cup of iniquity had reached the overflowing point, and God had no choice but to destroy them.

What He did is the same as a surgeon removing a diseased organ from a patient, in order that his life be spared. While it occasions pain and suffering, the act of surgery must be regarded as positive, as is obvious. It is likewise with the Judgment of God.

The Lord does nothing, but that it is good in the long run, for all involved. In fact, the destruction of these cities was an act of Mercy on the part of the Lord, as far as the Earth was concerned. Wickedness can become so great that destruction is the only answer.

2. The Angels who were sent by God to carry out this task hastened Lot in his preparations to leave, which are slow to say the least.

Is the Holy Spirit presently hastening the Church to get ready for the Rapture? I believe He is.

A PERSONAL EXPERIENCE

In 1998, the Lord began to move on my heart about Radio, but in a different way than I had previously known. Back in the 1970's, the Lord instructed me to begin a 15-minute daily program, which we called *"The Campmeeting Hour."* The Lord blessed it greatly, with us ultimately being on some 600 Stations, and developing, in those days, the largest daily audience for Radio in the field of Gospel.

But the Lord began to move upon my heart in 1998 in a totally different manner. Instead of a 15-minute *"daily,"* we were to own the Stations, which would give us total time on an unending basis.

The Lord instructed me to change the programming on the two Stations the Ministry then owned, which we immediately did. All of the programming, which refers to all of the music, worship, teaching, and preaching, was to come exclusively out of Family Worship Center. Thankfully, the Lord has put together a group of singers, musicians, and engineers capable of putting out a quality product. But above all, it was and is the Anointing of the Holy Spirit upon our efforts, which makes it what it is. Talent and ability can be found in many places; but the Anointing of the Spirit is another matter altogether.

As well, the Church as a whole, and I speak of Family Worship Center, provides an impetus and a spirit which comes through all of the programming, and helps make it what it is. So in essence, the entirety of the Church is what makes the programming applicable to the people, and in fact, a blessing to the people, with above all, the Anointing of the Spirit being prevalent.

The Lord also informed me that we were to apply to the F. C. C. in Washington for available frequencies in order to build Stations, and also, we were to purchase Stations across the country.

This we have begun to do, and with the results being absolutely astounding, and I speak of people being saved, lives being changed, people being delivered by the Power of God, and Believers filled with the Spirit, along with the sick being healed. The True Gospel of Jesus Christ always accomplishes the task.

As I dictate these notes on December 8, 2001, we now have 55 Stations on the air, and will not stop, until we cover the entirety of this nation.

But I've said all of that in order to say this:

I feel an urgency in my heart as I've never felt it before, as it regards getting this job done. It's like the Holy Spirit is telling me to *"hurry,"* and that's exactly what we are attempting to do. I get frustrated at times, when I'm held up because of a lack of funds, but the point I wish to strongly make is that whatever it is the Holy Spirit is having us to do, we don't have long to get it done. And make no mistake about it, the Gospel of Christ, and I speak of the preaching of the Cross, is the only answer for hurting humanity. It's not just one of several answers; it is the only answer. That's why we *"preach the Cross,"* and that's why Paul *"preached the Cross"* (I Cor. 1:17-18, 21, 23; 2:2, 5).

LINGERING

Verse 16 reads: *"And while he lingered, the men laid hold upon his hand, and upon the hand of his wife, and upon the hand of his two daughters; the LORD being merciful unto him: and they brought him forth, and set him without the city."*

Concerning his lingering, Whitelaw says: *"Lot's irresolution would have been his ruin but for his attendants. His heart manifestly clung to the earthly possessions he was leaving. The Angels made no mention of his attempting to save a portion of his great wealth."*

NOTES

The loving insistence of the Angels with this unhappy procrastinator was most touching. Its cause is revealed in the words *"the Lord being merciful unto him."* His folly in lingering, and, further, in preferring his own place of safety to that proposed by the Angels, illustrates the deep unbelief of the human heart (Williams).

The Angels did not let Lot linger long. It seems that they literally took hold of his hand and the hand of his wife, along with his two daughters, and in a sense, pushed them out of the city. To be sure, Lot and his family were not acting in faith or obedience, so bringing them out of the city was pure, unmerited Grace. In essence, it was for Abraham's sake, who interceded on Lot's behalf, thereby serving as a Type of Christ and His intercession for us (Heb. 7:25).

ESCAPE

Verse 17 reads: *"And it came to pass, when they had brought them forth abroad, that he said, Escape for your life; look not behind you, neither stay you in all the plain; escape to the mountain, lest you be consumed."*

Every city in the plain, which obviously numbered about five, was to be destroyed. So they were told to *"Escape to the mountain unless you be consumed."*

As well, it seems that now Jehovah Himself, Who, though not mentioned, has now appeared upon the scene.

The phrase *"Escape for your life,"* actually says in the Hebrew, *"Escape for your soul."* This means that had he stayed, his soul would have been lost.

The command, *"Look not behind you,"* was not given merely to prevent delay, but also showed that God demanded of them a total abandonment in heart and will of the condemned cities, and hence the severity with which the violation of the command was visited.

All of this that we are seeing here in this example given proclaims to us the fact that all that's in this world, all that we count so dear, all which seems to be so valuable, in reality is going to be totally consumed. That's at least one of the reasons that Jesus said:

"Lay not up for yourselves treasures upon Earth, where moth and rust do corrupt, and where thieves break through and steal:

"But lay up for yourselves treasures in Heaven, where neither moth nor rust do corrupt, and where thieves do not break through nor steal:

"For where your treasure is, there will your heart be also" (Mat. 6:19-21).

(18) "AND LOT SAID UNTO THEM, OH, NOT SO, MY LORD.

(19) "BEHOLD NOW, YOUR SERVANT HAS FOUND GRACE IN YOUR SIGHT, AND YOU HAVE MAGNIFIED YOUR MERCY, WHICH YOU HAVE SHOWED UNTO ME IN SAVING MY LIFE; AND I CANNOT ESCAPE TO THE MOUNTAIN, LEST SOME EVIL TAKE ME, AND I DIE:

(20) "BEHOLD NOW, THIS CITY IS NEAR TO FLEE UNTO, AND IT IS A LITTLE ONE: OH, LET ME ESCAPE THITHER, (IS IT NOT A LITTLE ONE?) AND MY SOUL SHALL LIVE.

(21) "AND HE SAID UNTO HIM, SEE, I HAVE ACCEPTED YOU CONCERNING THIS THING ALSO, THAT I WILL NOT OVERTHROW THIS CITY, FOR THE WHICH YOU HAVE SPOKEN.

(22) "HASTE THEE, ESCAPE THITHER; FOR I CANNOT DO ANYTHING TILL YOU BE COME THITHER. THEREFORE THE NAME OF THE CITY WAS CALLED ZOAR.

(23) "THE SUN WAS RISEN UPON THE EARTH WHEN LOT ENTERED INTO ZOAR."

The structure is:

1. Though commanded by the Angels to flee to the mountain, he refuses, and still fondly clings to the idea of *"a little city,"* — some little shred of the world.

2. There is no casting himself wholly upon God. He had too long walked at a distance from Him.

3. As spiritually deficient as was Lot and his family, still, the Lord could not destroy these cities until they had vacated the premises. This shows the significance of the Child of God, even as weak as one like Lot.

THE MOUNTAIN?

Verses 18 and 19 read: *"And Lot said unto them, Oh, not so, my LORD.*

"Behold now, Your servant has found grace in Your sight, and You have magnified Your mercy, which You have showed unto me in saving my life; and I cannot escape

NOTES

to the mountain, lest some evil take me, and I die."

By Lot referring to this One as *"Lord,"* and when we add Verse 24, it becomes obvious that Jehovah has now joined the two Angels, and will direct the judgment. Lot as well, knows that this is the Lord.

But strangely enough, he does not want to obey the Lord as it regards going to the mountain. As we shall see, he wants to go to another city, even as small as it might be.

Lot had functioned in the flesh for so long, that even in the face of impending doom, he must continue to do so. The *"Lord"* told him to go to the mountain, while the flesh steered him toward the city — any city. But fear will haunt him there as well.

To be out of the Will of God is to be away from God. Now let's say that again, and because it is so very important:

If one is in the Will of God, one is at the same time in the Way of God. But to be outside of the Will of God is at the same time to be away from God.

How crass for Lot to question God, especially at a time like this!

Why was he afraid of the mountain? If God had told him to go there, and He definitely had, then most definitely the Lord would protect him; however, the *"flesh"* has no *"Faith."* It has none, simply because it's depending on self, and not on the Lord.

THE CITY

Verse 20 reads: *"Behold now, this city is near to flee unto, and it is a little one: Oh, let me escape thither, (is it not a little one?) and my soul shall live."*

It makes no sense whatsoever for Lot to disobey the Lord in not going immediately to the mountain, but instead desiring to go to another city, as small as it might be. But again, when a Believer attempts to function in the realm of disobedience, what he does makes no sense whatsoever, and because in fact, it is nonsensical. People do not do stupid things when they are in the Will of God. It's when they are attempting to function in the realm of disobedience that they become foolish in their direction.

Lot was wrong in accepting the Plain of Jordan, which was toward Sodom, to begin with.

He should have let Abraham decide for him. He was wrong in pitching his tent toward Sodom, and wrong in moving into Sodom.

For the Believer who is going in the wrong direction, to once again get things straight, he has to first of all cease going in the wrong direction. In other words, he has to make things right with God, and then get in the Will of God. That's not difficult to do, once we tell the Lord that's what we desire. And then, had it not been for the intercession of Abraham, Lot would have been destroyed along with Sodom, etc.

So Lot had been going in a wrong direction for a long, long time. He is accustomed to charting his own course, and he still hasn't repented even at this late hour, so he continues to do the same. Amazingly enough, the Lord will humor him, even as He humors us also.

YOUR REQUEST IS GRANTED

Verse 21 reads: *"And He said unto him, See, I have accepted you concerning this thing also, that I will not overthrow this city, for the which you have spoken."*

Evidently, this small city was one of the towns located in the plain, which had also been marked for destruction. So the Lord gives him that which he desires.

It was a prayer that Lot would have wished had never been answered in a positive way. It would not at all prove to be satisfactory, and Lot would shortly have to leave there, and go to the mountain, where the Lord had originally directed him.

Excursions of the flesh never come to a good end, simply because it's a course that the Lord hasn't charted. So as Lot, we waste our time on these excursions. They may seem right at the moment, but if the Lord hasn't designed them, we will find soon enough that there is no profit in that direction.

THE LORD AND BELIEVERS

Verses 22 and 23 read: *"Haste you, escape thither; for I cannot do anything till you be come thither. Therefore the name of the city was called Zoar.*

"The sun was risen upon the Earth when Lot entered into Zoar."

Marvelously enough, the Lord proclaims the fact that He could not send the judgment

NOTES

until Lot was safely out of Sodom, and had gone to the city of his request. What does it mean, the Lord could do nothing?

I think the answer to that question covers far more territory than meets the eye. First of all, the Lord doesn't need us. In fact, He doesn't need anything. But in His Grace and Mercy, He has allowed us to be a part of His great Plan, as it regards Redemption. This means that whatever it is that He does is based a great deal on what we do.

If the Church goes in the wrong direction, or even if one Believer goes in the wrong direction, to that extent, whether the entirety of the Church, or the lone Believer, the Work of God will be hindered. This makes it imperative that we do our very best to ascertain the Will of God, and to walk therein.

The Lord in essence had given His Word that He would spare Lot. So, until they were safely out of the city, He couldn't bring judgment on the city, which was so desperately needed. It can work the opposite way as well.

If the Believer doesn't function in Faith, the Lord, Who works through Believers, can little function in the capacity of bringing souls to Himself. Perhaps if we understood this properly, we would be more responsible in our daily walk before the Lord.

(24) "THEN THE LORD RAINED UPON SODOM AND UPON GOMORRAH BRIMSTONE AND FIRE FROM THE LORD OUT OF HEAVEN;

(25) "AND HE OVERTHREW THOSE CITIES, AND ALL THE PLAIN, AND ALL THE INHABITANTS OF THE CITIES, AND THAT WHICH GREW UPON THE GROUND.

(26) "BUT HIS WIFE LOOKED BACK FROM BEHIND HIM, AND SHE BECAME A PILLAR OF SALT.

(27) "AND ABRAHAM GOT UP EARLY IN THE MORNING TO THE PLACE WHERE HE STOOD BEFORE THE LORD:

(28) "AND HE LOOKED TOWARD SODOM AND GOMORRAH, AND TOWARD ALL THE LAND OF THE PLAIN, AND BEHELD, AND, LO, THE SMOKE OF THE COUNTRY WENT UP AS A SMOKE OF A FURNACE.

(29) "AND IT CAME TO PASS, WHEN GOD DESTROYED THE CITIES OF THE PLAIN, THAT GOD REMEMBERED ABRAHAM, AND

SENT LOT OUT OF THE MIDST OF THE OVERTHROW, WHEN HE OVERTHREW THE CITIES IN THE WHICH LOT DWELT."

The overview is:

1. The Lord, Whom we now know as God the Son, called judgment from the Lord out of Heaven, Whom we now know as God the Father.

2. All the cities of the plain were destroyed, except Zoar.

3. In disobedience, Lot's wife looked back, and *"became a pillar of salt."*

4. When God destroyed the cities of the plain, He remembered Abraham, and because of Abraham, spared Lot.

JUDGMENT FROM HEAVEN

Verse 24 reads: *"Then the LORD rained upon Sodom and upon Gomorrah brimstone and fire from the LORD out of Heaven."*

Several things are said here:

1. The way the Scripture is structured, we have here a distinction of Persons in the Godhead. Jehovah (the Son) rained down from Jehovah (the Father), the destruction upon Sodom and Gomorrah.

2. The brimstone and fire, that is, burning brimstone, which destroyed the cities, did not burst upon them from Hell beneath, but from Heaven above.

3. The doom of these cities is referred to in the following Scriptures: (Deut. 29:23; Isa. 13:19; Jer. 49:18; Zeph. 2:9; Mat. 10:15; II Pet. 2:6; Jude, vs. 7).

Some claim that it was a violent earthquake which caused this disaster, however, an earthquake can hardly account for the burning of the sulphur. The Bible emphatically attributes the judgment to the Lord. In other words, the cause was supernatural, not natural.

THE PLAIN

Verse 25 reads: *"And He overthrew those cities, and all the plain, and all the inhabitants of the cities, and that which grew upon the ground."*

The entire plain was seared. What was once a verdant garden has now become a desert. This is what sin does!

All the inhabitants of these particular cities died in the inferno. This is proof of their entire corruption.

NOTES

If it is to be noticed, at least as one reads the Bible, the Lord took an interest only in the countries and cities of the world of that time, and actually all down through history, which affected His people. At this particular time, he was preparing the family of Abraham for the possession of Canaan, even though it would be several hundreds of years before this would actually take place. And as Israel finally became a nation, we find the Lord once again dealing with nations which impacted Israel, and especially if they impacted the chosen people in a negative way. There is no record that the Lord dealt with other nations of the world which were too distant, at least at that time, to have had an affect upon the chosen people and the chosen land.

Even during the times of the Early Church, we find the Lord addressing Himself to mighty Rome, which ruled the world of that day, only as it impacted the Church.

The terrible evil of Sodom and Gomorrah was all planned by Satan to hinder, harm, and corrupt the Work of God. He was successful in drawing Lot into his web, and had it not been for Abraham, he would have been eternally lost. But his major effort in all of this evil was to stop the coming of the Seed of the Woman (Gen. 3:15). I doubt very seriously that he knew exactly how all of this was going to happen, but that it would happen, whatever would be the means or the method, and would spell his doom. So he set out in several ways to stop the coming of the *"Seed."*

At this particular time, and I speak of December, 2001, considering the terrorist activity, events are speeding up as it regards the fulfillment of Bible Prophecy. In other words, the Rapture of the Church is near at hand, and because the advent of the Antichrist is already being prepared. And we know from II Thessalonians, Chapter 2, that the Antichrist cannot be revealed until first the Church has been taken out (II Thess. 2:7-8).

Regrettably, a great part of the Church has already apostatized, with the words of Paul already coming to pass. He said:

"Now the Spirit (Holy Spirit) *speaks expressly* (pointedly), *that in the latter times* (the times in which we now live) *some shall depart from the faith* (depart from the Cross),

giving heed to seducing spirits, and doctrines of devils" (I Tim. 4:1).

The Lord has raised up this Ministry (Jimmy Swaggart Ministries) among others, to preach the Cross. The Message of the Cross, and that Message alone, is the very center and core of Christianity. With the Cross removed, Christianity ceases to be Biblical, and becomes no more than the other religions of the world, which at best is a philosophical quest. Without the Cross, there is no power to deliver (I Cor. 1:18). Without the Cross, captives aren't set free (Lk. 4:18). Without the Cross, lives aren't changed (Gal. 6:14). In fact, and as I've already stated, the Cross is the dividing line between the True Church and the apostate Church. That and that alone decides the order. Only that which is on the side of the Cross will stand the acid test, while all else will be *"burned"* exactly as Sodom and Gomorrah.

PILLAR OF SALT

Verse 26 reads: *"But his wife looked back from behind him, and she became a pillar of salt."*

The Seventeenth Verse of this Chapter proclaims the fact that God had pointedly warned Lot and his family not to look back, as destruction was brought to bear upon the cities of the plain. Lot and his daughters obeyed, but his wife didn't. The Scripture says that she *"looked back,"* and when she did, *"she became a pillar of salt."*

The words *"looked back from behind him,"* as it regards this woman, means in the Hebrew that *"she kept looking back steadily, wistfully, and with desire."* Her heart was in Sodom, so her soul was in Sodom as well. Regrettably and sadly, it is now in Hell.

Jesus reminded the world of this episode by pointedly saying, *"Remember Lot's wife"* (Lk. 17:32). Jesus also said:

"No man, having put his hand to the plough, and looking back, is fit for the Kingdom of God" (Lk. 9:62).

ABRAHAM

Verse 27 reads: *"And Abraham got up early in the morning to the place where he stood before the LORD."*

We do not know exactly what Abraham knew at this time as it regards Lot. There is

no indication that the Lord told the Patriarch during the intercessory period that He would spare Lot; however, Abraham's posture at this time proclaims the fact that he believed that the Judge of all the Earth would in fact bring out his nephew.

"Standing before the Lord," indicates that Abraham was in prayer. In other words, the indication is that he was still interceding before the Lord as it regards Lot, even up unto the last minute. As is obvious here, the Lord honored that intercession.

James said: *"The effectual fervent prayer of a righteous man availeth much"* (James 5:16).

This should encourage every Believer to constantly intercede for their lost loved ones, and even for those who are weak in the Faith, even as Lot.

SODOM AND GOMORRAH

Verse 28 reads: *"And he looked toward Sodom and Gomorrah, and toward all the land of the plain, and beheld, and, lo, the smoke of the country went up as the smoke of a furnace."*

It is believed that these cities were situated at the southern extremity of the Dead Sea.

As the Lord rained brimstone and fire upon these cities, the Scripture says that *"the smoke . . . went up as the smoke of a furnace."*

The violence of the fire is indicated by the word *"furnace,"* which is not the ordinary word, but means a kiln, such as that used for burning chalk into lime, or for melting ores of metal. In other words, the heat was so intense that everything melted, which means there was nothing left.

Some may argue that a God Who is referred to as *"love,"* could not do such a terrible thing, which resulted in the deaths of untold thousands of people, even including all the children and babies. My answer to that is as follows:

If God is truly a God of love, as He definitely is, then He had to do this thing, as distasteful as it may have been. Once again I go back to the idea of a surgeon removing a cancer from a patient. Even though it causes pain and suffering, the surgeon is taking such drastic action because if he doesn't, the patient will die. In other words, he performs surgery in order to save the patient.

Many times in history, God has had to perform major surgery on this Earth, in order to save the patient. Sin is the ruination of all that is good. It is the destroyer of all happiness, all peace, all welfare, and all security. It is the most insidious cancer, one might say, that mankind has ever known. It must be stopped, or all will be ruined.

It can be stopped by judgment coming upon the sinner, or by judgment coming upon God's Son, Who took our place. In other words, we accept Christ Who suffered judgment in our place, or we will be judged instead. There is no alternative; sin must be judged, and to be sure, all men are sinners. So there is no alternative to the statement I've just made. It is either Jesus Christ or eternal Hell. That may be blunt, but it just happens to be true!

GOD REMEMBERED

Verse 29 reads: *"And it came to pass, when God destroyed the cities of the plain, that God remembered Abraham, and sent Lot out of the midst of the overthrow, when He overthrew the cities in the which Lot dwelt."*

The words, *"God remembered Abraham,"* proclaim the fact that Abraham's intercessory petition did not go unanswered. This shows that God preserved Lot, not on account of his Righteousness, for Lot sinned by being in Sodom, and further sinned by his delay, but because of the intercession of believing Abraham. God so dearly loved the Patriarch that He spared Lot. In this case, as we have previously stated, Abraham was a Type of Christ. He served as a mediator between God and Lot.

Presently, and forever more, Jesus Christ is our Mediator. The Scripture says:

"For there is one God, and one Mediator between God and men, the Man, Christ Jesus" (I Tim. 2:5).

While presently, we can certainly pray for others, even as did Abraham, actually interceding on their behalf; however, no human being since Christ can serve as a Mediator, that prerogative being that of Christ Alone. When the Holy Spirit said that there is *"one Mediator between God and men,"* He meant exactly what He said. That means there aren't ten, five, or two, only one, and that One is *"the Man Christ Jesus."*

This means that every Catholic Priest, and any other person who might label himself as such, is blaspheming. In effect, by their very actions and supposed office, they are saying that Christ did not accomplish the task at Calvary, and human instrumentation is needed. Such thinking is blasphemy, actually undermining the entirety of the Scriptures.

Furthermore, the Scripture tells us that Christ was not always a Mediator. While He has always been God, He has not always been the Mediator. He became that by becoming *"the Man Christ Jesus."* But as well, that alone did not make Him the Mediator.

He became the Mediator only after He *"gave Himself a ransom for all"* (I Tim. 2:6). This speaks of the Cross, which gave Christ the right to become and be the Mediator between God and men. He atoned there for all sin by the giving of Himself, and did so as our Substitute and Representative Man (I Cor. 15:45-47).

When it says that God remembered, it doesn't mean that God has a tendency to forget. Since God knows everything, He never forgets anything with the exception of the sins He has forgiven and put out of existence.

When the Bible speaks of God remembering, it means God now breaks into the situation to do something about it. God sent His Angels to bring Lot out of Sodom, not because Lot deserved it, but for Abraham's sake. Thus, although Sodom was not spared, the intent of Abraham's intercession was answered (Horton).

(30) "AND LOT WENT UP OUT OF ZOAR, AND DWELT IN THE MOUNTAIN, AND HIS TWO DAUGHTERS WITH HIM; FOR HE FEARED TO DWELL IN ZOAR: AND HE DWELT IN A CAVE, HE AND HIS TWO DAUGHTERS.

(31) "AND THE FIRSTBORN SAID UNTO THE YOUNGER, OUR FATHER IS OLD, AND THERE IS NOT A MAN IN THE EARTH TO COME IN UNTO US AFTER THE MANNER OF ALL THE EARTH:

(32) "COME, LET US MAKE OUR FATHER DRINK WINE, AND WE WILL LIE WITH HIM, THAT WE MAY PRESERVE SEED OF OUR FATHER.

(33) "AND THEY MADE THEIR FATHER DRINK WINE THAT NIGHT: AND THE

FIRSTBORN WENT IN, AND LAY WITH HER FATHER; AND HE PERCEIVED NOT WHEN SHE LAY DOWN, NOR WHEN SHE AROSE.

(34) "AND IT CAME TO PASS ON THE MORROW, THAT THE FIRSTBORN SAID UNTO THE YOUNGER, BEHOLD, I LAY YESTERNIGHT WITH MY FATHER: LET US MAKE HIM DRINK WINE THIS NIGHT ALSO; AND GO THOU IN, AND LIE WITH HIM, THAT WE MAY PRESERVE SEED OF OUR FATHER.

(35) "AND THEY MADE THEIR FATHER DRINK WINE THAT NIGHT ALSO: AND THE YOUNGER AROSE, AND LAY WITH HIM; AND HE PERCEIVED NOT WHEN SHE LAY DOWN, NOR WHEN SHE AROSE.

(36) "THUS WERE BOTH THE DAUGHTERS OF LOT WITH CHILD BY THEIR FATHER.

(37) "AND THE FIRSTBORN BEAR A SON, AND CALLED HIS NAME MOAB: THE SAME IS THE FATHER OF THE MOABITES UNTO THIS DAY.

(38) "AND THE YOUNGER, SHE ALSO BEAR A SON, AND CALLED HIS NAME BENAMMI: THE SAME IS THE FATHER OF THE CHILDREN OF AMMON UNTO THIS DAY."

The overview is:

1. Having disobeyed the Lord, Lot now lives in fear. He will not dwell in Zoar, the city of his request, because he evidently fears that God might smite it as well. So he dwells in a cave with his two daughters.

2. The shameful incest of his two daughters is now recorded. Infected by the spirit of Sodom, they see nothing wrong with their shameful action.

3. The results were the Moabites and Ammonites, who became enemies of God's people, as all works of the flesh must ultimately be.

ZOAR

Verse 30 reads: "And Lot went up out of Zoar, and dwelt in the mountain, and his two daughters with him; for he feared to dwell in Zoar: and he dwelt in a cave, he and his two daughters."

Lot either fled Zoar because the people there threatened to kill him, perhaps blaming him somewhat for the destruction of the other cities, or else he was fearful that God might smite this city as well.

Regarding the latter, he had reason to fear. Even though Zoar was but a small town, it was as wicked as Sodom. It was a center of idolatrous worship for the whole area.

The Scripture says, "He dwelt in a cave." Let's look at that a moment:

His wealth had once been so great that he and Abraham could not dwell together, and because of the size of their herds, but he is now living in a cave, with this being his miserable home.

But wealth or no wealth, there is no profit in living for Satan. Per capita, the suicide rate among the up and out is far greater than it is for the down and out. And let it be understood that all without God, no matter how "up" they may be according to the view of the world, are at the same time, "out." The only satisfaction in life is living for Christ. That's why Jesus said:

"Take heed, and beware of covetousness: for a man's life consisteth not in the abundance of the things which he possesseth" (Lk. 12:15).

The Scripture says that Lot "feared." When one is out of the Will of God, thereby out of the Presence of God, which means they are devoid of the leadership of the Lord, fear rules. It is a terrible, disquieting condition for one to find oneself. In that state, it doesn't matter where one goes, or what one does; the fear remains. The reasons are obvious, or at least certainly should be.

LOT'S DAUGHTERS

Verse 31 reads: "And the firstborn said unto the younger, Our father is old, and there is not a man in the Earth to come in unto us after the manner of all the Earth."

What the two daughters of Lot were about to do constituted a monstrous sin, as is overly obvious; however, family and preservation of the family line were important, very important, in ancient times. Since Lot was old, and now poor, with all his belongings destroyed along with Sodom, his daughters saw no prospect for marriage. As well, and to which we have already alluded, these girls had been adversely influenced by the low morals of Sodom. While they knew God, and in their weak way served the Lord, the entirety of their dilemma is not to be blamed on them, but rather their father. While no sin is excusable, still, at times, there are mitigating circumstances.

Considering all of this, it is not strange that the older daughter suggested incest as the only way they could preserve the family line.

Lot had long since ceased trusting God, but rather his own ingenuity, so his daughters follow suit. The Lord could have given them husbands, but they didn't understand the path of Faith.

WINE

Verse 32 reads: *"Come, let us make our father drink wine, and we will lie with him, that we may preserve seed after our father."*

Despondent and full of fear, Lot succumbs to the lure of alcoholic beverage.

This is at least one of the reasons that the world is sated with alcohol, nicotine, and drugs. It is guilt-ridden, and cut off from God, it seeks a substitute. But alas! Such substitutes always put one in bondage, with their situation now the worse instead of the better. How quickly these things cease to be a crutch, and now become a slave-master.

As we look at all of this, we find the utter degradation of Lot and his family, which thus ends in his intense shame.

Concerning this, Mackintosh said: *"And then see his end! — His own daughters make him drunk, and in his drunkenness he becomes the instrument of bringing into existence the Ammonites and the Moabites — the determined enemies of the people of God. What a volume of solemn instruction is here! Oh, my Reader, see here what the world is! See what a fatal thing it is to allow the heart to go out after it! What a commentary is Lot's history upon the brief but comprehensive admonition, 'Love not the world'! This worlds Sodoms and its Zoars are all alike. There is no security, no peace, no rest, no solid satisfaction for the heart therein. The Judgment of God hangs over the whole scene; and He only holds back the sword in long-suffering mercy, not willing that any should perish, but that all should come to repentance."*

THE FIRSTBORN

Verse 33 reads: *"And they made their father drink wine that night: and the firstborn went in, and lay with her father; and he perceived not when she lay down, nor when she arose."*

This was no drunken orgy, but still, it was a revolting sin. As we look into the entirety of this sordid picture, let us see the cause of it.

The cause is a lack of faith, as the cause of all sin is a lack of faith. Paul said: *"Whatsoever is not of faith is sin"* (Rom. 14:23). What did the Apostle mean by that statement?

FAITH

As stated, if we trace the origin of sin, and in whatever form, we will always find, and without exception, that the cause is a lack of faith.

When Paul speaks of Faith, he is speaking of Christ and what Christ has done for us at the Cross, that ever being the object of our Faith. If that ceases to be the object, while it still may be faith, it's not faith which God will recognize. So let the Reader understand that always and without exception Faith in the Bible always refers to *"Jesus Christ and Him Crucified"* as its object. When the Believer keeps his Faith anchored in the Cross, everything comes into proper perspective. When his faith is moved to other things, then everything is out of place.

When Lot chose the well-watered plains of Jordan, which led toward Sodom, he had moved his Faith from the Cross, to other things such as money, etc. So let us say it again:

Sin always begins with our Faith being transferred from the correct object, which is the Cross, to something else. And it doesn't matter what the something else is.

Having taken this course, Lot ultimately moves into Sodom, because now his faith is in his own ingenuity and ability. So that's what his daughters learned. They know God, but they know nothing about trusting God, and above all, they know nothing of what this is all about, which would ultimately lead to the coming of the Redeemer and the Cross. They could have known, and Lot could have known. They had the greatest opportunity in the world. Few men in history were given revelations from God as was Abraham. So they didn't know, because they had little desire to know.

How many Christians presently are like Lot and his daughters? They know God, but they know little about God.

One can know trust and Faith only as one understands the Cross. Otherwise, what one refers to as faith, while it might be faith, it's not faith which God will recognize. In other words, it's not saving and keeping faith, which alone comes by one's proper understanding of the Cross, which gives one a proper understanding of the Word.

So that night, Lot resorts to alcohol, and because his faith has long since been misplaced. His daughters commit an even more heinous sin by committing incest with him, and even though he was not a party to that crime, it actually was his fault.

THE YOUNGER

Verse 34 reads: *"And it came to pass on the morrow, that the firstborn said unto the younger, Behold, I lay yesternight with my father: let us make him drink wine this night also; and go thou in, and lie with him, that we may preserve seed of our father."*

The details of this account clearly show that Lot, when he went to the mountain cave, endeavored to escape from his problems not by carrying them to God's Throne, where all Believers should carry them, but by drowning them in dissipation. This wretched man, who had once been a Saint in God's Church, lost his way, because he moved his faith from the Cross of Christ so to speak, to other things.

There is one glimmer of light in the whole thing. The daughters apparently believed that unless their father was drunk, he would never be brought to assent as it regards their lewd proposal.

Twice overcome by wine, he is twice in succession dishonored by his daughters; and twice overcome while in his drunken stupor, he allows himself to commit an act which almost out-Sodomed Sodom. To what depths a Saint may fall when once he turns his back on God! (Exell).

DESPAIR, DRUNKENNESS, AND DECEPTION

Verse 35 reads: *"And they made their father drink wine that night also: and the younger*

arose, and lay with him; and he perceived not when she lay down, nor when she arose."

These girls had been in Sodom most of, if not all, of their lives; consequently, they had been greatly influenced by the low moral standards of the city, which if anything, is a gross understatement. So it is not strange that the older daughter suggested incest as the only way they could preserve the family line.

One can see in this the picture of so many modern Christian families. These girls knew about God, but they were far more influenced by the evil of Sodom than they were the Righteousness of Heaven. In fact, their very position proclaimed where their attachments were. And you can lay all of this at the feet of their father, Lot.

They knew nothing of faith, of what it meant to really live for God, of what their purpose in life should have been. So when they find themselves in this dilemma, they turn to their own evil ingenuity, instead of trusting the Lord.

As stated, how many modern Christians fall into the same category? The answer is sadly obvious, almost all.

Some time back, I occasioned to know of a terrible problem which had arisen in a particular family. I suggested to them that they take it to the Lord, especially considering that they loudly proclaimed themselves to be good Christians.

We have two Prayer Meetings a day at the Ministry, and I was hoping they would come to the Prayer Meetings, at least the ones around which they could arrange their schedule. The response was tepid to say the least!

Some days later, it was related to me that the dear lady had actually said in response to my invitation, *"I just don't get anything out of it!"*

That's a strange statement coming from a Christian. What in the world did she mean, that she got nothing out of seeking God? Was she meaning that she did not want to pray with us, or was she meaning that God didn't answer prayer; consequently, it was a waste of time?

I don't know the answer to those questions; I only know her response. I also know that in the not too distant future, the thing of which she was greatly concerned went into total wreckage, with all type of sorrow and heartache.

As we've already stated, it is all a matter of faith. Is our faith anchored in the Cross, or is it anchored elsewhere?

RESULTS

Verse 36 reads: *"Thus were both the daughters of Lot with child by their father."*

After this, Lot disappears from sacred history, not even his death being recorded.

It is believed by some that Abraham took Lot and his daughters into his home, and supported them. There is no record of such; however, one cannot imagine Abraham seeing his nephew homeless and penniless, and not helping him. He had risked his life to save him from the heathen king, who had taken him and his family captive some years before, so it is certain that he would provide help at this time as well.

THE MOABITES AND THE AMMONITES

Verses 37 and 38 read: *"And the firstborn bear a son, and called his name Moab: the same is the father of the Moabites unto this day.*

"And the younger, she also bear a son, and called his name Benammi: the same is the father of the children of Ammon unto this day."

"Moab" means, *"from my father,"* while *"Benammi"* means, *"son of my people."* They are the ancestors of the Moabites and the Ammonites.

Despite their ignoble beginnings, the Lord showed a concern for them as descendants of Lot (Deut. 2:9, 19), but regrettably, they later became enemies of Israel (I Sam. 14:47; II Ki. 3:5; II Chron. 20:1, 22).

As it was then with Sodom and Gomorrah, so it will be soon with this world. The Believer, consequently, must see what Lot failed to see, and, regrettably, many, if not most, modern Christians fail to see as well.

This world and all that it holds is passing, and is for short duration. As stated, the Judgment of God hangs heavily over it.

Furthermore, we're living at the very conclusion of the Church Age. The foundation is already being laid for the advent of the Antichrist, so that makes the Rapture even much closer. While Christ is definitely

going to take over this world, it will not be as many Preachers claim.

It is claimed by many that Christianity is gradually going to take over the entirety of the world, actually coming to terms with other religions. Then, they say, the Millennium will begin. Of course, these individuals believe that the Book of Revelation is now history. In other words, that it's already been fulfilled many centuries ago, and holds no validity for the future. How anyone could come to that conclusion, at least if they read this Book with any degree of honesty at all, is beyond my comprehension.

The truth is, Jesus Christ is definitely going to take over this world, but it will not be by Christianity gradually changing society, but rather in a cataclysmic, even violent way. Some 2,600 years ago, the Lord gave a dream to a heathen king by the name of Nebuchadnezzar. In a great statue, he saw the coming kingdoms of this world, but did not know what it all meant, even as the world presently knows nothing of futuristic events, which the Bible so boldly proclaims. Daniel interpreted the dream for the man, and then said concerning this giant statue, *"You saw till that a stone was cut out without hands* (Jesus), *which smote the image upon his feet that were of iron and clay, and break them to pieces . . . and the stone that smote the image became a great mountain, and filled the whole Earth"* (Dan. 2:34-35).

As stated, it is definitely true that Jesus is going to rule the entirety of this Earth. But this will not take place until the Second Coming, which will be a time of tremendous display of power, as the nations and kingdoms of this world are violently overthrown. So clearly, the Scripture teaches that the rosy picture painted by some Preachers is only a fabrication. It's not Scriptural! In fact, the Holy Spirit through Paul said: *"This know also, that in the last days perilous times shall come"* (II Tim. 3:1).

He also said: *"Now the Spirit speaks expressly, that in the latter times some shall depart from the faith, giving heed to seducing spirits, and doctrines of devils"* (I Tim. 4:1).

So, apostasy is predicted for the Church as it regards its closing days. Regrettably, that apostasy is even now upon us. The world not only tries to build its kingdom on Earth, but at the same time, many in the Church are attempting to do the same thing.

Our business as Believers is not to build an earthly kingdom, but rather to *"preach the Gospel to every creature"* (Mk. 16:15).

"At the Name of Jesus every knee shall bow,

"Every tongue confess Him King of Glory now.

"'Tis the Father's pleasure we shall call Him Lord,

"Who from the beginning was the mighty Word."

"At His Voice creation sprang at once to sight,

"All the Angel faces, all the hosts of light,

"Thrones and dominations, stars upon their way,

"All the Heavenly orders in their great array."

"Humbled for a season to receive a Name,

"From the lips of sinners unto whom He came,

"Faithfully He bore it spotless to the last,

"Brought it back victorious, when from death He passed."

"In your hearts enthrone Him; there let Him subdue

"All that is not holy, all that is not true:

"Crown Him as your Captain in temptation's hour:

"Let His Will enfold you in its light and power."

"Brothers, this Lord Jesus shall return again,

"With His Father's Glory, with His Angel train;

"For all wreaths of empire meet upon His brow,

"And our hearts confess Him King of Glory now."

CHAPTER 20

(1) "AND ABRAHAM JOURNEYED FROM THENCE TOWARD THE SOUTH

COUNTRY, AND DWELLED BETWEEN KADESH AND SHUR, AND SOJOURNED IN GERAR.

(2) "AND ABRAHAM SAID OF SARAH HIS WIFE, SHE IS MY SISTER: AND ABIMELECH KING OF GERAR SENT, AND TOOK SARAH.

(3) "BUT GOD CAME TO ABIMELECH IN A DREAM BY NIGHT, AND SAID UNTO HIM, BEHOLD, YOU ARE BUT A DEAD MAN, FOR THE WOMAN WHICH YOU HAVE TAKEN; SHE IS A MAN'S WIFE.

(4) BUT ABIMELECH HAD NOT COME NEAR HER: AND HE SAID, LORD, WILL YOU SLAY ALSO A RIGHTEOUS NATION?

(5) "SAID HE NOT UNTO ME, SHE IS MY SISTER? AND SHE, EVEN SHE HERSELF SAID, HE IS MY BROTHER: IN THE INTEGRITY OF MY HEART AND INNOCENCY OF MY HANDS HAVE I DONE THIS.

(6) "AND GOD SAID UNTO HIM IN A DREAM, YES, I KNOW THAT YOU DID THIS IN THE INTEGRITY OF YOUR HEART; FOR I ALSO WITHHELD YOU FROM SINNING AGAINST ME: THEREFORE SUFFERED I YOU NOT TO TOUCH HER.

(7) "NOW THEREFORE RESTORE THE MAN HIS WIFE; FOR HE IS A PROPHET, AND HE SHALL PRAY FOR YOU, AND YOU SHALL LIVE: AND IF YOU RESTORE HER NOT, KNOW YOU THAT YOU SHALL SURELY DIE, YOU, AND ALL WHO ARE YOURS."

The synopsis is:

1. Sin is just as hateful in a man of God as in a man of the world, and its guilt is greater.

2. Abraham must have been shocked at the power of unbelief in those of the previous Chapter, but was he equally shocked at the power of evil in himself at this particular time?

3. The sin and misery that resulted years before from journeying *"toward the south country"* should have taught him never again to move in that direction. But man, as such, never learns, nor can he learn spiritual lessons

4. Abraham once more forsakes the path of Faith; and in denying his wife sinks to a depth of moral degradation that is contemptible in the extreme.

5. His fall on this occasion was deeper than on the prior one; for he now had the Divine Promise that within that very year

Sarah should become the mother of a miraculous child.

6. So long as the Christian walks in the path of Faith, he is clothed with dignity and ennobled with courage. But, when directly he leaves that path, he falls lower than even the children of the Evil One.

7. These facts revealed by unsparing truth make it plain that Abraham, by natural disposition and character, was cowardly and false. He was only noble when energized by Faith.

8. Sad as all this is, there is encouragement in it for the weakest; for it teaches that the most abject and contemptible man may become noble and strong, if by Faith he surrenders his broken humanity to Him Who can subdue all things unto Himself. Thus, we find Abraham, so abject here before this heathen prince, reproving him later on with dignity and boldness (Gen. 21:25).

THE SOUTH COUNTRY

Verse 1 reads: *"And Abraham journeyed from thence toward the south country, and dwelled between Kadesh and Shur, and sojourned in Gerar."*

We find Abraham often journeying, which by the Lord he was probably intended to do, in that he was to be ever reminded that Canaan was not intended for a permanent habitation, but for a constant pilgrimage (Poole); however, it seems that Abraham all of the time did not exactly seek the Face of the Lord, as to exactly where the journey should lead him. He will once again go south, which will prove, exactly as it did before, to be the occasion for another sad spectacle. This time he did not go into Egypt, but he went toward Egypt, which he should not have done. As we have stated, man, if left on his own, cannot learn spiritual lessons. Abraham, for reasons known only to him, journeys south, and thereby forsakes the path of Faith. As such, he will once again sink into a degradation that is contemptible.

We will find here that an old sin is an easy sin.

DECEPTION

Verse 2 reads: *"And Abraham said of Sarah his wife, She is my sister: and Abimelech king of Gerar sent, and took Sarah."*

This is the same sin that Abraham committed in Egypt. He, exactly as Lot, left the path of Faith, thereby, trusting in his own ingenuity, which always gets us into trouble. And because it's so important, please allow me to say again what we've said some paragraphs back.

Every sin is always a departure from Faith. Faith in Christ and Him Crucified is the only answer to the sin problem, as it is to every problem. The trouble is, the Church all too often deals with symptoms as it regards sin, instead of the cause. In fact, the Church little knows the cause, so it manufactures its own causes.

One of the primary examples is, if we sin, so the Church says, we do so because that's what we want to do. While sin definitely is a matter of choice, it is not a choice as one thinks.

SIN AND ITS CAUSE

In the first place, there is no true Christian who wants to sin. The Divine Nature is in him, ever propelling him toward Righteousness and Godliness, which means that sin is totally and completely an aberration. In other words, it's something that shouldn't happen as it regards the Child of God, and something that will not happen, that is, if the Believer knows and understands God's prescribed order of victory (II Pet. 1:4).

Once the Believer leaves the path of Faith, his power of choice is now greatly weakened as it regards Righteousness. In other words, on a path of faithlessness, Satan can make a person do something that he doesn't want to do.

I realize that most Christians would disagree with that statement, but it is the truth. Let's see what the Word of God says:

Paul said: *"For that which I do I allow* (understand) *not: for what I would, that do I not; but what I hate, that do I"* (Rom. 7:15). What in the world did Paul mean by this statement?

Romans, Chapter 7 is the account of the experience of the Apostle Paul immediately after he was saved. It is not, as many Preachers claim, the account of Paul before he was saved. In the first place, what good would that do?!

From Romans, Chapter 7, it is easy to understand that Paul is saying here that he is doing things that he doesn't want to do. In other words, he was trying very, very hard not to sin, but was failing just the same. He went on to say:

"For I know that in me (that is, in my flesh,) dwells no good thing: for to will is present with me; but how to perform that which is good I find not" (Rom. 7:18).

He plainly tells us here that willpower, within itself, is not enough. In effect he is saying that if a Believer is trying to live this Christian life by his own power and strength, he will fail every single time, and furthermore, the failures will get worse and worse, and that despite all of his efforts to do and be otherwise.

Consequently, it is very easy to see in these Passages that Christians are not sinning because they want to sin, but rather, because they embarked upon a wrong course, which means their faith is in the wrong place, which means that the Holy Spirit simply will not help in that type of situation, which leaves the individual helpless.

Oh yes, the Believer is definitely responsible for his actions. There is no place or time that he isn't responsible. But he is not responsible in the way that most in the Church claims it to be so. In other words, a true Christian, if he sins, is not sinning just because he wants to sin. He is sinning, simply because he has left the path of true Faith, and is now functioning in the flesh.

TRUE FAITH

That which we are about to say, we have already said many times, and will continue to say it many times in this Volume, because it's so very, very important. In fact, it is the single most important thing that the Christian could ever hear, read, or know.

Jesus Christ and Him Crucified must always be the object of our Faith. If our Faith is anchored in the Sacrifice of Christ, then the Holy Spirit, Whom we must always have as it regards His Power, and all else that He is for that matter, will grandly help us. Otherwise, if we move our Faith from the Cross of Christ to other things, we deny ourselves the help of the Spirit (Rom. 8:1-2, 11), which means that we're left on our own, and that failure is going to be the result no matter how hard we might try otherwise.

So the Church, little knowing the reason for failure, only knows to do what the world

does if there is failure, and that is to engage in punishment. That's not the answer! It is only adding insult to injury. In the first place, the one doing the punishing may very well be in worse spiritual condition, than the one who is being punished. And furthermore, for us to punish someone who has failed is, in essence, insulting Christ, by saying that Christ was not punished enough on the Cross, and we have to add something to what He has already done. Doesn't the Reader understand just how abominable such thinking actually is?

Jesus suffered for us, and His suffering had to do with sin. Furthermore, there is no way that suffering or punishment on our part can atone for sin. Once again, if we think that such is the case, this means that we do not at all understand the Atonement, and in fact, are making up our own Salvation, which is abominable in the eyes of God. It is Jesus Christ and Him Crucified, or it is nothing!

So Abraham leaves the path of Faith, lies about Sarah, and to be sure, his sin this time is far more abominable than it was down in Egypt, because the Lord has recently told him that Sarah is going to bear a child. This means that the entirety of the great Plan of God for the human race is placed in jeopardy.

It may be said that this was Satan's second effort to hinder the birth of the Messiah by the intervention of a heathen father and that, therefore, he would, and could, incite Abimelech to this action.

This means that Abraham's fall on this occasion was deeper than when he was in Egypt. As stated, so long as the Christian walks in the path of Faith, he is clothed with dignity and ennobled with courage. But when directly he leaves that path, he falls even lower than the children of Satan. Nothing but Faith can impart true elevation to a man's character, because it alone connects the soul with God. And please remember, when we speak of Faith, always and without exception, we are speaking of Faith in Christ and His Cross.

There is in the confession of Abraham to Abimelech this painful feature revealed in his character. He starts upon his course with a falsehood, and compels his wife to be the degraded sharer of the lie.

If it is objected that this whole occurrence is incredible, because it is claimed that no heathen prince would desire to marry a woman upwards of 90 years of age, or to conceive such a passion for her that, to secure her, he would murder her husband — the very fate which Abraham feared for himself — we must understand that God undoubtedly had miraculously renewed the youth of Sarah, so that she became sufficiently youthful in appearance to suitably become the wife of this Philistine prince. Even though she was some 90 years of age, she evidently looked like she was 30 years of age, if that, and considering that she was already beautiful, we now see the attraction.

To not believe this is to limit God.

If it is to be noticed, the Holy Spirit through Moses, when this Text was written, was careful to delineate that Sarah was Abraham's wife, and not his sister, at least in the capacity of which he claims. Once again, Abraham sets out to deceive Abimelech, which was the title of the Philistine Prince, exactly as he had tried to deceive Pharaoh in Egypt.

INTERVENTION

Verse 3 reads: *"But God came to Abimelech in a dream by night, and said to him, Behold, you are but a dead man, for the woman which you have taken; for she is a man's wife."*

Three things are said here:

1. God revealed Himself to Abimelech in a dream.

2. What the Lord said to Abimelech greatly scared him. In essence He said, *"If you touch Sarah, you can consider yourself a dead man."*

3. If God had not intervened, Abraham's sin would have been disastrous. If it is to be noticed, Sarah is again referred to by the Holy Spirit as Abraham's wife. The *"sister"* thing was mentioned only by Abraham, and not by the Lord. The truth is, Sarah was Abraham's half-sister, both of them having the same father, but not the same mother.

It had been some 20 years since the episode in Egypt, but an old sin is an easy sin.

ABIMELECH

Verse 4 reads: *"But Abimelech had not come near her: and he said, LORD, will You slay also a righteous nation?"*

The Lord had intervened with the dream, before Abimelech had a chance to come near Sarah.

The Philistine Prince already knowing of the destruction of Sodom and Gomorrah, fears that he and his people are in for the same destruction, unless the Lord is pacified quickly.

He refers to God as *"Lord,"* in effect referring to Him as Deity. The question begs to be asked, considering the power that the Lord had just unleashed as it regards the destruction of the cities of the plain, which were close to Philistine territory to say the least, and that God appears in a sense to this Philistine Prince in a dream, surely that was enough evidence to prove to this man that Jehovah was the True God. Why then he not serve God?

That same question can be asked presently of the untold millions in this world who know about God, but yet refuse to serve Him; however, the major problem with most who live in a so-called Christian nation is that they actually think they are serving Him, when in reality they've never been Born-Again. Deception is an awful thing, and it has many ways in which to plague the human race. Once again we come back to Faith.

Millions have faith in God, but it's in the wrong kind of way. True Faith is always anchored in Jesus Christ and Him Crucified. Otherwise, while it may be very religious, it is not acceptable to God. And regrettably, Faith in Christ and His Cross is not acceptable to much of the world, and even not much of the Church.

CLEAN HANDS

Verse 5 reads: *"Said he not unto me, She is my sister? And she, even she herself said, He is my brother: in the integrity of my heart and innocency of my hands have I done this."*

This heathen Prince pleads his innocence before God, at least as far as the matter of Sarah is concerned. Abraham claimed that Sarah was his sister, and Sarah backed up what he had said, by claiming that Abraham was her brother. So on this basis, Abimelech took her into his harem.

In this matter, the man was innocent. It was Abraham, and Sarah as well, who had done wrong.

Forgetting God's ability to protect his life, he had recourse to the same stratagem which, years before, he had adopted in Egypt. Here we have the father of the faithful carried away by taking his eye off God. He is no longer a man of faith, but rather of craftiness and deception.

How true it is that we are only strong as we cling to God in the sense of our perfect weakness. So long as we are in the path of His appointment, nothing can harm us. Had Abraham simply leaned on God, the men of Gerar would not have meddled with him; and it was his privilege to have vindicated God's Faithfulness in the midst of the most appalling difficulties. Thus, too, he would have maintained his own dignity as a man of Faith.

Concerning this, Mackintosh said: *"It is often a source of sorrow to the heart to mark how the Children of God dishonor Him, and, as a consequence, lower ourselves before the world by losing the sense of His sufficiency for every emergency. So long as we live in the realization of the Truth that all our hope is in God, so long shall we be above the world in every shape and form. There is nothing so elevating to the whole moral being as Faith: it carries one entirely beyond the reach of this world's thoughts; for how can those of the world, or even worldly-minded Christians, understand the life of Faith? Impossible! The springs on which it draws lie far away beyond their comprehension. They live on the surface of present things. So long as they can see what they deem a proper foundation for hope and confidence, so long they are hopeful and confident; but the idea of resting solely on the promise of an unseen God, they understand not.*

"But the man of Faith is calm in the midst of scenes in which nature can see nothing. In fact, none but those who know God can ever approve the actings of Faith; for none but they really understand the solid and truly-reasonable ground of such actions."

PROTECTION

Verse 6 reads: *"And God said unto him in a dream, Yes, I know that you did this in the integrity of your heart; for I also withheld you from sinning against Me. therefore suffered I you not to touch her."*

Not only does Abimelech assert his position, but the Lord admits the plea. And yet this Philistine king indulges in polygamy, and claims the right of taking the female relatives of anyone passing through his territory to add them to his harem.

But his words mean no more than that he was not consciously violating any of his own rules of morality, and thus illustrate the Gospel principle that men will be punished not by an absolute decree, but equitably, according to their knowledge (Lk. 12:47-48).

Abimelech was doing wrong, and was suffering punishment, but the punishment was remedial, and for his advancement in right-knowing and right-doing. It is thus by means of Revelation that men have attained to a proper understanding of the moral law. Though often called *"the law of Nature,"* yet Nature does not give it, but only acknowledges it when given.

The inner light, in fact, is but a faint and inconstant glimmering, for Christ Alone is the True Light; for only by Him does the law of Nature become a clear rule for human guidance (Mat. 6:23; Jn. 1:9; Rom. 2:14-15) (Ellicott).

A PROPHET

Verse 7 reads: *"Now therefore restore the man his wife; for he is a Prophet, and he shall pray for you, and you shall live: and if you restore her not, know that you shall surely die, you, and all who are yours."*

It should be noticed in this Text that even though Abraham has done wrong, very wrong, his position as a Prophet has not been diminished, nor in fact, any part of his calling.

In the history of God's people, whether we look at them as a whole, or as individuals, we are often struck with the amazing difference between what we are in God's view, and what we are in the view of the world. God sees His people in Christ. He looks at us through Christ, and hence He sees us *"without spot or wrinkle or any such thing."* We are as Christ is before God. We are perfected forever, as to our standing in Christ.

But the truth is, in ourselves, we are poor, feeble, imperfect, stumbling, inconsistent creatures; and, inasmuch as it is what we are in ourselves, and that alone that the world takes knowledge of, therefore, it is that the difference seems so great between the Divine and the human estimate. Thus when Balak seeks to curse the seed of Abraham, Jehovah's word is, *"I have not beheld iniquity in Jacob, neither have I seen perverseness in Israel."*

He then said, *"How goodly are thy tents, O Jacob, and thy tabernacles, O Israel"* (Num. 23:21; 24:5).

The outward observance was, and very obvious, that Israel in the natural did not measure up to these things, but that's the way God saw them, simply because He looked at them through Christ. He does the same with all Believers, and again because of Christ.

According to many modern Pentecostal Denominations, Abraham, due to his failure, would have had to cease all ministry for two years, etc. Now while such foolishness may sound satisfactory to the carnal ear, such thinking and action are actually an abomination with God. It belittles the Sacrifice of Christ, actually saying that what He did at the Cross is not enough.

When we cease to be Biblical, we become very foolish!

At the same time, it should be understood that this in no way means that God condones sin in any fashion. It's just that sin and wrongdoing are so evil, so bad, that only Christ and what He did at the Cross can cleanse the stain. Man's foolish efforts at punishment, or his own ways and means of Atonement, are woefully insufficient. And again, I emphasize the fact that when we try to add something to the shed Blood of Christ, we greatly insult the Lord and His Finished Work.

Abraham was a Prophet before the problem, he was a Prophet during the problem, and he was a Prophet after the problem. No, this does not condone the problem, and in fact, great hurt always accompanies sin, as should be obvious. But as we've already stated, sin is so awful, so terrible, and so destructive, that it took the Cross to address this thing, and if we try to use other means or methods to address sin other than the Cross, we sin greatly.

THE OFFICE OF THE PROPHET

In fact, even though Abraham was a Prophet, along with Moses, and in fact, Enoch

was a Prophet as well, it was Samuel who first stood in the office of the Prophet (I Sam. 9:9).

One might say that the office of the Prophet was twofold:

1. To announce the Will of God to men (Ex. 4:15; 7:1).

2. To intercede with God for men (Jer. 7:16; 11:14; 14:11).

Now let's go back to Abraham: He might lower himself in the view of Abimelech, king of Gerar, which he did, and Abimelech might rebuke him, which he did as well, yet when God comes to deal with the case, He says to Abimelech, *"Behold, you are but a dead man"*; and of Abraham He says, *"He is a Prophet, and he shall pray for you."*

Yes, with all *"the integrity of his heart and the innocency of his hands,"* the king of Gerar was *"but a dead man"*; and, moreover, he must be a debtor to the prayers of the erring and inconsistent stranger for the restoration of the health of his household. Such is the manner of God.

God may have many a secret controversy with His Child, on the ground of his erroneous ways, if in fact that be the case, but directly the enemy enters a suit against the Child of God, Jehovah ever pleads His servant's cause — *"Touch not My Anointed, and do My Prophets no harm."* And then, *"He who touches you, touches the apple of My eye."* And then, *"It is God Who justifieth, who is he who condemns?"*

The idea is, no dart of the enemy can ever penetrate the shield behind which the Lord has hidden the very feeblest lamb of His Blood-bought flock (Mackintosh).

(8) "THEREFORE ABIMELECH ROSE EARLY IN THE MORNING, AND CALLED ALL HIS SERVANTS, AND TOLD ALL THESE THINGS IN THEIR EARS: AND THE MEN WERE SORE AFRAID.

(9) "THEN ABIMELECH CALLED ABRAHAM, AND SAID UNTO HIM, WHAT HAVE YOU DONE UNTO US? AND WHAT HAVE I OFFENDED YOU, THAT YOU HAVE BROUGHT ON ME AND ON MY KINGDOM A GREAT SIN? YOU HAVE DONE DEEDS UNTO ME THAT OUGHT NOT TO BE DONE.

(10) "AND ABIMELECH SAID UNTO ABRAHAM, WHAT SAW YOU, THAT YOU HAVE DONE THIS THING?

(11) "AND ABRAHAM SAID, BECAUSE I THOUGHT, SURELY THE FEAR OF GOD IS NOT IN THIS PLACE; AND THEY WILL SLAY ME FOR MY WIFE'S SAKE.

(12) "AND YET INDEED SHE IS MY SISTER; SHE IS THE DAUGHTER OF MY FATHER, BUT NOT THE DAUGHTER OF MY MOTHER; AND SHE BECAME MY WIFE.

(13) "AND IT CAME TO PASS, WHEN GOD CAUSED ME TO WANDER FROM MY FATHER'S HOUSE, THAT I SAID UNTO HER, THIS IS YOUR KINDNESS WHICH YOU SHALL SHOW UNTO ME; AT EVERY PLACE WHERE WE SHALL COME, SAY OF ME, HE IS MY BROTHER."

The exegesis is:

1. It is emphasized in this Chapter that natural goodness and integrity, as in the case of Abimelech, do not necessarily make a man a Child of God, and, on the other hand, a temporary moral lapse through fear does not unmake the Believer a member of the household of Faith.

2. Whatever answer that Abraham gave to Abimelech seemed right to the flesh, but the truth was, his difficulty was the result of his own imperfect faith, as imperfect faith is always our difficulty.

3. Even though God protected Abraham, even as He protects all of His Children, still, wrongdoing in any capacity always brings about humiliation and shame, even as it did here.

THE TESTIMONY

Verse 8 reads: *"Therefore Abimelech rose early in the morning, and called all his servants, and told all these things in their ears: and the men were sore afraid."*

The very next morning after the dream that night, Abimelech sought to rectify the situation.

In all of this, Abimelech is taught that he does not himself hold a near relation to God, but requires someone to speak for him, meaning that he had need of fuller instruction, and that he ought to try to attain to a higher level with God. He certainly had the opportunity to do so; however, the following Verses tell us that He allowed Abraham's previous performance to greatly hinder him as it regards this of which we speak.

This is one of the great hurts of failure. It always causes someone to stumble. To be sure, there is no excuse for the stumbling, as there was no excuse for Abimelech; however, the human spirit is fallen as a result of what happened in the Garden of Eden. As a result, it seldom seeks the higher level, but rather uses any excuse to continue to wallow in the mud hole.

ABIMELECH AND ABRAHAM

Verse 9 reads: *"Then Abimelech called Abraham, and said unto him, What have you done unto us? And what have I offended you, that you have brought on me and on my kingdom a great sin? You have done deeds unto me that ought not to be done."*

We will find here that the questions which Abimelech posed to Abraham were very similar to those posed by Pharaoh, concerning the same sin (Gen. 12:18).

As Abimelech spoke to Abraham, his words were unquestionably designed to convey a severe reproach, which it did.

It seems that Abimelech's conversation stems more so from fear and frustration than anything else.

It is interesting that this heathen king understood the word *"sin,"* which means that he had some knowledge of God, which was greatly increased after the dream which he had.

As well, it is interesting that he really did not accuse Abraham of sin, but rather of Abraham putting him in a position to where that he might have sinned and sinned greatly, which would have affected the entirety of his kingdom. This is what he gathered from what the Lord told him in the dream, and he was right about the matter. When he spoke about what Abraham had done, he merely said, *"You have done deeds unto me that ought not to be done."*

All of this shows that he was greatly afraid of Abraham. And to be frank, he conducted himself exactly as he should have, and God rewarded him by healing him and all of his household of the plague which had caused them great problems.

THE QUESTION

Verse 10 reads: *"And Abimelech said unto Abraham, What did you see, that you have done this thing?"*

Abimelech asked the question as to what was in Abraham's mind, that would have caused him to take this particular position?

He in effect is saying, *"We aren't murderers, and furthermore, we treat people right."*

Abimelech seems to take pride in his just rule. And every indication is, he seems to have been a just king, especially considering that his knowledge of the Lord was very sketchy. Unfortunately, his first contact with one who truly knew God, at least as far as we know, did not present the Lord in the best light.

How guilty all of us are in this respect. We are recipients and projectors of His Light. But how so often what we in fact project is not entirely that which we have received.

FEAR

Verse 11 reads: *"And Abraham said, Because I thought, Surely the fear of God is not in this place; and they will slay me for my wife's sake."*

Abraham speaks of the fear of God, but the truth is, he was operating in human fear and not in Faith. So in his mind, he projected a scenario, which in fact would never have happened.

How so often we modern Believers operate in the same capacity. We operate from the spirit of fear, rather than the power of Faith. Even at our highest, too often we make our plans, and then ask God to bless those plans. Such a position is that which God will not take. He blesses only the Plans which He Alone has instituted.

PROPER FAITH

Even though we have explained it several times already, due to the serious nature of the subject, and due to the fact that much error has been propagated in the last several decades, I think it would be difficult for us to address the subject too much.

When we speak of Faith, it must always be understood that it's Faith in Christ and Him Crucified. This must ever be the object of Faith, or else it will be faith that God will not recognize.

We talk about having faith in the Word, which is certainly correct; however, we should also understand that our claims of having faith in the Word of God are not valid, unless we

first understand that everything is based on the Sacrifice of Christ. In fact, the Sacrifice of Christ is the story of the Bible. It's not the other way around, meaning that the Word of God merely portrays that particular story. The Word is the Story, and the Story is the Word.

The first object lesson as it regards the Word of God and the great Plan of Redemption, which is what the Word is all about, is found in Genesis, Chapter 4. In graphic detail, we have there the illustration of Cain and Abel, and the sacrifices offered by these two men, one which was accepted by God (the blood Sacrifice of Abel), with the other rejected by God (the sacrifice of Cain which was vegetables, or some such work of his own hands). This particular Chapter sets the stage for the entirety of the Bible. It is the Sacrifice of Christ on the Cross, versus every other sacrifice of which one can think, with all others being rejected other than Christ and what He did at the Cross. So when we speak of Faith, we must always understand that Biblically speaking, it must be Faith in Christ and what Christ did at the Cross.

And again, even though I am being very repetitious, Christ must never be separated from the Cross. If in any way we separate Christ from the Cross, we are left with *"another Jesus"* (II Cor. 11:4).

And just what do we mean by that?

ANOTHER JESUS

To be frank, Christ in the modern Church has mostly been separated from the Cross. That means the emphasis is placed on anything and everything as it regards Christ, except the Cross. That's why Paul said:

"For Christ sent me not to baptize, but to preach the Gospel: not with wisdom of words, lest the Cross of Christ should be made of none effect" (I Cor. 1:17).

He also said: *"If you be circumcised, Christ shall profit you nothing"* (Gal. 5:2).

And then: *"Christ is become of no effect unto you, whosoever of you are justified* (seek to be justified) *by the law; you are fallen from Grace"* (Gal. 5:4).

Paul is not knocking Water Baptism, and neither is he saying that it's a sin for little boys to be circumcised, etc. He is meaning that if we emphasize these things, or claim that such has to be in order for one to be saved, then we have made the Cross of Christ, which refers to all that Jesus did there, of none effect. And that's the sin of the modern Church — they have made the Cross of Christ of none effect.

While the healing Jesus is very important, as well as the miracle-working Jesus, and of course, Jesus in any posture in which we can place Him; still, the emphasis must always be on Jesus Christ and Him Crucified. As we've said, He must never be separated from the Cross.

WIFE

Verse 12 reads: *"And yet indeed she is my sister; she is the daughter of my father, but not the daughter of my mother; and she became my wife."*

If it is to be noticed, Abraham dwells on the fact that Sarah is indeed his half-sister, while the Holy Spirit emphasizes the fact of the lady being his wife (vss. 2-3, 7).

As stated, Sarah was apparently Abraham's half-sister, being Terah's daughter by another wife; and we gather from her calling her child Sarai — that is, princess — that Sarah's mother was not a concubine as Hagar, but belonged to some noble race.

Many Christians, I'm afraid, think little of this which Abraham did in referring to Sarah as his sister. However, the motive was deception. And placing Sarah in this very compromising position was what Satan desired. If he could have impregnated her by Pharaoh or Abimelech, the Plan of God would have been seriously hindered, and may have delayed it for a long period of time. In fact, only the intervention of God stopped this effort by the Evil One.

While we expect Satan to do everything within his power to hurt and hinder, he can only bring his plans to fruition if he can get a Saint of God, as Abraham, to cooperate with him. While Abraham did so unwittingly, still, the danger was the same. The real sin was Abraham leaving the path of Faith, as that is always the real sin with us presently.

SARAH

Verse 13 reads: *"And it came to pass, when God caused me to wander from my father's*

house, that I said unto her, This is your kindness which you shall show unto me; at every place where we shall come, say of me, He is my brother."

This deception, it seems, was formulated by Abraham at the very beginning of his sojourn, which of course was many years earlier. It is somewhat understandable at Abraham doing such a thing in his earliest days, even though it was wrong at that time as well, it is harder to understand these many years later.

Abraham had seen God do great and mighty things for him. He and his small band, as the Lord led and guided them, had defeated powerful armies some years earlier, and did so without the loss of a single person, and as well, recovering all that had been stolen and taken. This was a miracle of unprecedented proportions.

As well, the Lord had appeared to him several times, even had visited him, which was the time before the destruction of Sodom and Gomorrah. As well, at this particular time, Abraham had been given almost the entirety of the Revelation concerning the birth of this miracle child. He now knew that it would not be Ishmael, but rather the one who would be born to Sarah, even though she had not been able to conceive all of these years.

So why did he need to lie to Abimelech, especially this late in the day, so to speak?

The answer to this is probably not as complicated as it first seems.

DAILY

The path of Faith is a daily exercise. In other words the Faith we had yesterday, while sufficient for that time, is not sufficient for today. There must be a fresh enduement of Faith each and every day.

Jesus addressed this by saying:

"If any man will come after Me, let him deny himself (deny his own strength and ability), *and take up his Cross daily, and follow Me"* (Lk. 9.23).

If it is to be noticed, Jesus spoke of taking up the Cross *"daily."* It's almost as if we start over again each and every day. The idea is this:

As stated, Faith we had yesterday will not suffice for today. And the Lord has designed it that way. In all of this He is teaching us several things.

They are:

1. He is telling us that the Cross is the answer for everything which we need. In other words, it was there that Jesus paid the price, and made it possible for God to grant us Grace in every capacity.

2. He has so designed it that we will in essence have to appropriate Faith each and every day, and we speak of Faith in the Cross. It is done in this manner, in order to teach us trust, confidence, and a constant looking to Him.

3. All of this is done in this manner that we may learn not to depend on ourselves, but rather to deny our own ability and strength, thereby depending totally and completely on Christ and what Christ has done for us.

This is the big struggle for the Child of God. Whether we realize it or not, we want to discontinue our trust in Christ and what He has done for us at the Cross, and rather depend on other things. But let it ever be understood, if our trust is placed in anything other than Christ and Him Crucified, we have then departed from the true path of Faith, and the faith we now have is a pseudo-faith, which God will not recognize, and which will fall out to grave problems, exactly as it did with Abraham.

The sin is leaving the path of true Faith, which always falls out to wrongdoing in other ways.

(14) "AND ABIMELECH TOOK SHEEP, AND OXEN, AND MENSERVANTS, AND WOMENSERVANTS, AND GAVE THEM UNTO ABRAHAM, AND RESTORED HIM SARAH HIS WIFE.

(15) "AND ABIMELECH SAID, BE-HOLD, MY LAND IS BEFORE YOU: DWELL WHERE IT PLEASES YOU.

(16) "AND UNTO SARAH HE SAID, BE-HOLD, I HAVE GIVEN YOUR BROTHER A THOUSAND PIECES OF SILVER: BEHOLD, HE IS TO YOU A COVERING OF THE EYES, UNTO ALL WHO ARE WITH YOU, AND WITH ALL OTHER: THUS SHE WAS REPROVED.

(17) "SO ABRAHAM PRAYED UNTO GOD: AND GOD HEALED ABIMELECH, AND HIS WIFE, AND HIS MAIDSERVANTS; AND THEY BEAR CHILDREN.

(18) "FOR THE LORD HAD FAST CLOSED UP ALL THE WOMBS OF THE

NOTES

HOUSE OF ABIMELECH, BECAUSE OF SARAH ABRAHAM'S WIFE."

The overview is:

1. Despite the wrongdoing, the Lord blessed Abraham. In fact, He does the same to us. Abraham's heart was right, even though his actions were wrong.

2. The Lord used the unconverted heathen king to reprove Sarah, as well as Abraham. It is sad when the Lord has to use the world to reprove us, but regrettably, it often happens.

3. The Lord healed Abimelech, but He used Abraham to do so.

THE GIFTS

Verse 14 reads: *"And Abimelech took sheep, and oxen, and menservants, and womenservants, and gave them unto Abraham, and restored him Sarah his wife."*

Once again the Holy Spirit calls attention to the fact that Sarah was Abraham's wife.

Abimelech gave these things to Abraham, simply because he recognized the Power of God. In other words, he didn't want to offend the Lord, so he would give His Prophet these gifts, which Abraham took.

Him taking the gifts meant that he accepted the apology of Abimelech, and at the same time, he was saying, *"I am sorry for my actions."* The giving of gifts and the receiving of gifts were very special in those days, and held high meaning.

KINDNESS

Verse 15 reads: *"And Abimelech said, Behold, my land is before you: dwell where it pleases you."*

Abimelech was a smart man, in fact a just ruler. While we have little knowledge as to the exact spiritual condition of this man, we do know that he knew and understood that the Blessings of God were upon Abraham; consequently, he offers him a place in *"his land."* To be sure, this was a smart move on the part of this heathen king, and he no doubt experienced great blessings from God because of this act.

To help the Work of God, which he certainly did, never goes unnoticed by the Lord. And to be sure, even as Jesus said:

"He who receives a Prophet in the Name of a Prophet shall receive a Prophet's reward;

and he who receives a righteous man in the name of a righteous man shall receive a righteous man's reward" (Mat. 10:41). Abraham was both a Prophet and as well was righteous; as a result, Abimelech, even as we shall see, was greatly blessed in his blessing of Abraham.

THE REPROOF

Verse 16 reads: *"And unto Sarah he said, Behold, I have given your brother a thousand pieces of silver: behold, he is to you a covering of the eyes, unto all who are with you, and with all other: thus she was reproved."*

Abimelech reproves Sarah by referring to Abraham as her *"brother,"* when in reality, all knew that he was her husband. In effect, this heathen prince is telling her, *"Don't do that again. It doesn't become you."*

And then by using the phrase, *"Behold, he* (Abraham) *is to you a covering of the eyes* (and), *unto all who are with you, and with all others,"* he is saying, *"If you openly claim Abraham as your husband, this to be sure, will be protection enough for you."*

In other words, he was saying to her that God would protect the both of them. What a rebuke!

HEALING

Verse 17 reads: *"So Abraham prayed unto God: and God healed Abimelech, and his wife, and his maidservants; and they bear children."*

Evidently, Abimelech related to Abraham the physical problem which had beset them. It seemed to have affected himself, and his wife, as well as all who were of his household, however many that may have been. It seems the women could not conceive, and we know from the next Verse that the Lord had instigated this.

We learn from these two Verses that not only can the Lord heal, but as well, He can cause physical problems, if in fact it serves His purpose.

THE MALADY

Verse 18 reads: *"For the LORD had fast closed up all the wombs of the house of Abimelech, because of Sarah Abraham's wife."*

The advent of sickness came about as a result of sin, which caused the Fall. In fact, Satan is the primary author of sickness and

NOTES

disease. God never intended in the beginning for man to be so afflicted. In fact, had there not been the Fall, there would be no such thing as sickness or disease, or dying for that matter. Man was originally created to live forever, and would have done so by partaking of the Tree of Life, if the Fall had not occurred.

But even though Satan is the author of sickness and disease, still, he can do nothing unless he receives permission from the Lord to do so. In fact, Satan, who is the archenemy of God, and who is the author of all evil, is subject to the Lord in everything. So, when it says here that *"the Lord had fast closed up all the wombs of the house of Abimelech,"* it can mean that the Lord either did this Personally, or else He allowed Satan to do so. From the way the Text reads, it seems like the Lord did this Personally.

However, God never chastises men, either by affliction or rebuke, for His pleasure, but rather for their profit. As well, He never pardons sin without bestowing blessing on the sinner. So He blessed Abraham by answering his prayer regarding healing for Abimelech, and He healed Abimelech, irrespective that he was a sinner.

Horton says that in the midst of all of this, *"God was faithfully watching over Sarah as the mother of the promised son, the one who would carry on the blessings of God's Covenant."*

"The trusting heart to Jesus clings,
"Nor any ill forebodes,
"But at the Cross of Calvary sings,
"Praise God for lifted loads!"

"The passing days bring many cares,
"'Fear not,' I hear Him say,
"And when my fears are turned to prayers,
"The burdens slip away."

"He tells me of my Father's love
"And never slumb'ring eye;
"My everlasting King above
"Will all my needs supply."

"When to the Throne of Grace I flee,
"I find the Promise true,
"The mighty arms upholding me
"Will bear my burdens too."

CHAPTER 21

(1) "AND THE LORD VISITED SARAH AS HE HAD SAID, AND THE LORD DID UNTO SARAH AS HE HAD SPOKEN.

(2) "FOR SARAH CONCEIVED, AND BEAR ABRAHAM A SON IN HIS OLD AGE, AT THE SET TIME OF WHICH GOD HAD SPOKEN TO HIM.

(3) "AND ABRAHAM CALLED THE NAME OF HIS SON THAT WAS BORN UNTO HIM, WHOM SARAH BEAR TO HIM, ISAAC.

(4) "AND ABRAHAM CIRCUMCISED HIS SON ISAAC BEING EIGHT DAYS OLD, AS GOD HAD COMMANDED HIM.

(5) "AND ABRAHAM WAS AN HUNDRED YEARS OLD, WHEN HIS SON ISAAC WAS BORN UNTO HIM.

(6) "AND SARAH SAID, GOD HAS MADE ME TO LAUGH, SO THAT ALL WHO HEAR WILL LAUGH WITH ME.

(7) "AND SHE SAID, WHO WOULD HAVE SAID UNTO ABRAHAM, THAT SARAH SHOULD HAVE GIVEN CHILDREN SUCK? FOR I HAVE BORN HIM A SON IN HIS OLD AGE."

The synopsis is:

1. Despite all of Satan's hindrances, Isaac, the progenitor and Type of the Messiah is born.

2. He is born at the *"set time,"* which refers to the exact time of which God had spoken to Abraham.

3. The mention of Sarah's name some four times in the first three Verses is done for purpose and reason; the Holy Spirit is impressing the fact that Sarah was in truth the very mother of this miraculous child.

4. Isaac in the Hebrew means, *"laughter."*

5. That which was impossible with man was entirely possible with God.

THE MIRACLE

Verse 1 reads: *"And the LORD visited Sarah as He had said, and the LORD did unto Sarah as He had spoken."*

This Chapter presents a new creation, the Divine title *"Elohim"* and not *"Jehovah"* appears throughout it, with the exception of Verses 1 and 33. In these Verses, God is *"Jehovah"*

because it touches His Covenant relationship as a Saviour.

The birth of Isaac had to do with the Incarnation of the Lord Jesus Christ. The first Adam had failed and failed miserably, which plunged the human race into an abyss of wickedness and evil, resulting in death. In fact, sin gave Satan a legal right to hold the entirety of humanity in captivity, which he did. The only hope for the human race, the fallen sons of the first Adam, was for God to become man, and thereby die on the Cross. He would be referred to as the *"Last Adam,"* because there would never be a need for another one, and the *"Second Man"* (I Cor. 15:45, 47).

Even though Jesus Christ was God, and in fact had always been God, and would always be God, still, as God He could not redeem humanity. The simple reason was, for man to be redeemed, there would have to be a death, and God cannot die. So God would become man.

But to become man, a line would have to be established, actually beginning with Abraham. As a Prophet, Abraham was a Type of Christ. It would go through the lineage of David, who was king, and would be a Type of Christ in His Kingly posture. Hence the genealogy of Christ opens in Matthew with the words: *"The Book of the generation of Jesus Christ, the Son of David, the Son of Abraham"* (Mat. 1:1).

So this lineage had to begin in the Lord and in the Lord Only. That's the reason that all hope of the flesh had to die, before Isaac could be born. And when that hope or the efforts of Abraham and Sarah totally and completely died, the Lord would miraculously give life to Sarah's dead womb, even though she was 90 years of age, and would empower Abraham, even though he was 100 years of age.

Here we have the accomplished Promise — the blessed fruit of patient waiting upon God. And let it be understood that none ever waited in vain.

FAITH

The soul that takes hold of God's Promise by Faith has gotten a stable reality which will never fail him. Thus was it with Abraham; thus was it with all the faithful from age to age; and thus will it be with all those who are enabled, in any measure, to trust in the Living God (Mackintosh).

And even at the risk of such repetition so as to excite the Reader, let us once again illuminate the fact that the Faith addressed here is Faith in Christ and what Christ would do at the Cross. Even though Abraham may not have understood the Cross as we do presently, he definitely did have a general idea of all that God was doing in order to bring about the Redeemer. Jesus said so (Jn. 8:56). *"This is the victory that overcometh the world, even our faith"* (I Jn. 5:4).

God will always do what He has spoken. Of that we can be certain, and of that we can be sure.

THE SET TIME

Verse 2 reads: *"For Sarah conceived, and bear Abraham a son in his old age, at the set time of which God had spoken to him."*

God's Word gave Abraham strength to beget, Sarah to conceive, and Isaac to come forth. Three times repeated in two Verses, the clause points to the supernatural character of Isaac's birth (Pulpit).

The *"set time"* tells us that God's timing is all a part of His Will, and is just as important as what is done. As we've already stated, the hope of the flesh had to totally and completely die in both Abraham and Sarah before this great miracle could be brought about. It is the same with us presently.

The work that is carried out in our hearts and lives by the Lord must be totally of the Lord. And the biggest problem that He has with Believers, believe it or not, is unbelief. We keep trying to do for ourselves, exactly as did Abraham and Sarah, which only God can do. In this Chapter, we will see exactly as to why it cannot be done by our own ingenuity and ability.

ISAAC

Verse 3 reads: *"And Abraham called the name of his son who was born unto him, whom Sarah bear to him, Isaac."*

A year before, the Lord had told Abraham that Sarah would bear a son, and that his name should be called *"Isaac"* (Gen. 17:19). Isaac means, *"laughter."* And he was named this for a purpose and a reason.

NOTES

As stated, Isaac was to be the progenitor and Type of the Messiah, Who would one day come. As such, He would bring Salvation to this hurting world, which would be the occasion of unspeakable joy. *"Laughter"* speaks of blessing, of increase, of healing, of life, of well-being, of good things, hence Jesus saying, *"I am come that they might have life, and that they might have it more abundantly"* (Jn. 10:10). As Isaac was a Type of Christ, it would not be wrong to say that one of the names of Christ is *"laughter."*

"It is joy unspeakable and full of glory,
"Full of glory, full of glory.
"It is joy unspeakable and full of glory,
"And the half has never yet been told."

CIRCUMCISION

Verse 4 reads: *"And Abraham circumcised his son Isaac being eight days old, as God had commanded him."*

When the Covenant of Circumcision had been given to Abraham, the Lord commanded that little boy babies were to be circumcised at eight days old (Gen. 17:12). The eight days after birth were for physical reasons. It took this long after birth for the blood to properly develop, in that it would properly coagulate.

But other than that, Circumcision was a sign of the Covenant, which in essence proclaimed the fact that God would ultimately send a Redeemer into this world, Who would redeem the fallen sons of Adam's race by going to the Cross of Calvary. Many other things played into this Covenant, and were in their own capacity very important; however, the end result was ever to be Christ.

ONE HUNDRED YEARS OLD

Verse 5 reads: *"And Abraham was an hundred years old, when his son Isaac was born unto him."*

This Verse is placed in the Text so that all may know that Isaac's birth was indeed miraculous. A woman some 90 years old could not conceive, and a man 100 years old could not father a child. So the conception and birth of Isaac were far beyond the boundaries of human possibility; therefore, God was the

One Who brought about this miraculous act, which resulted in this miracle child.

Concerning this, Paul said: *"Who against hope believed in hope, that he might become the father of many nations; according to that which was spoken, so shall your seed be.*

"And being not weak in faith, he considered not his own body now dead, when he was about an hundred years old, neither yet the deadness of Sarah's womb:

"He staggered not at the Promise of God through unbelief; but was strong in faith, giving glory to God;

"And being fully persuaded that, what He had promised, He was able also to perform.

"And therefore it was imputed to him for Righteousness" (Rom. 4:18-22).

While Abraham definitely did not stagger at the Promise of God, knowing that God would ultimately bring this Promise to pass, still, he had some trouble getting there, as the account discloses. The Promise he believed. It was the *"how"* of the Promise which gave him trouble. And it is often the same with us presently. How will He do what He has promised? And then we try to help Him out, all ultimately to our chagrin.

SARAH

Verse 6 reads: *"And Sarah said, God has made me to laugh, so that all who hear will laugh with me."*

The birth of Isaac, as would be obvious, was an occasion of great joy; however, the joy expressed here was of far greater degree, to which we have already alluded, than the mere fact of what had happened, as wonderful as that was. All of this leads to Christ, and Christ brings an unparalleled joy to all who accept Him, and thereby, know Him.

Sarah had once laughed in unbelief; she now laughs in Faith, a laughter incidentally expressing joy which will never end.

THE MIRACLE OF FAITH

Verse 7 reads: *"And she said, Who would have said unto Abraham, that Sarah should have given children suck? For I have born him a son in his old age."*

This is a poem, and could very well have been a song.

NOTES

The question that Sarah asks in her poem or song refers to the fact that what had happened was beyond human reasoning and most definitely beyond human ability. Who would have thought that Sarah, barren all of her life, at 90 years of age would give birth to a baby boy? But that's exactly what happened, because it was a work of the Lord.

(8) "AND THE CHILD GREW, AND WAS WEANED: AND ABRAHAM MADE A GREAT FEAST THE SAME DAY THAT ISAAC WAS WEANED.

(9) "AND SARAH SAW THE SON OF HAGAR THE EGYPTIAN, WHICH SHE HAD BORN UNTO ABRAHAM, MOCKING.

(10) "WHEREFORE SHE SAID UNTO ABRAHAM, CAST OUT THIS BONDWOMAN AND HER SON: FOR THE SON OF THIS BONDWOMAN SHALL NOT BE HEIR WITH MY SON, EVEN WITH ISAAC.

(11) "AND THE THING WAS VERY GRIEVOUS IN ABRAHAM'S SIGHT BECAUSE OF HIS SON.

(12) "AND GOD SAID UNTO ABRAHAM, LET IT NOT BE GRIEVOUS IN YOUR SIGHT BECAUSE OF THE LAD, AND BECAUSE OF THE BONDWOMAN; IN ALL THAT SARAH HAS SAID UNTO YOU, HEARKEN UNTO HER VOICE; FOR IN ISAAC SHALL YOUR SEED BE CALLED.

(13) "AND ALSO OF THE SON OF THE BONDWOMAN WILL I MAKE A NATION, BECAUSE HE IS YOUR SEED."

The diagram is:

1. Isaac was probably about five years old when he was weaned.

2. The effect of the birth of Isaac was to make manifest the character of Ishmael.

3. The end result of the *"mocking"* was that Ishmael actually desired to murder Isaac (Gal. 4:29).

4. Isaac and Ishmael symbolize the new and the old natures in the Believer.

5. Sarah and Hagar typify the two Covenants of works and Grace, of bondage and liberty (Gal., Chpt. 4).

6. The birth of the new nature demands the expulsion of the old. It is impossible to improve the old nature.

7. How foolish, therefore, appears the doctrine of moral evolution!

ISAAC

Verse 8 reads: *"And the child grew, and was weaned: and Abraham made a great feast the same day that Isaac was weaned."*

The custom in those days was to nurse children for two to three years before they were weaned, with some children being as much as five years old. When a boy was weaned, he was then turned over to his father for training, at which time his education began.

Isaac was the son of Promise, and through him would come the Blessing, which would ultimately touch the entirety of the world. That Blessing was and is Christ. In view of this, and as was the custom as well, Abraham made a great feast on the day of the weaning of Isaac.

MURDER

Verse 9 reads: *"And Sarah saw the son of Hagar the Egyptian, which she had born unto Abraham, mocking."*

According to the time that Isaac was weaned, Ishmael would now be anywhere from 17 to 20 years old.

The *"mocking"* by Ishmael of Isaac is mentioned by Paul in Galatians 4:29. He uses the word *"persecuted,"* which carries the meaning in the Greek of a desire to murder. So Ishmael, spurred by is mother Hagar, wanted to murder Isaac.

The Jewish Targums say that Ishmael had planned Isaac's murder by stealth. He would feign that he was playing a game with the young child, would shoot arrows in the distance, and then have Isaac run and fetch them. The plan was for one of the arrows to hit Isaac and kill him, with it then claimed to be an accident. But Sarah saw what was happening, whatever it might have been at that time, and demanded the expulsion of the bondwoman.

Paul used this in Galatians, Chapter 4 as an allegory. (The word *"allegory"* simply means a symbolic representation.)

We have in this example, even as Paul used it, Isaac symbolizing the new nature, i.e., *"the Divine nature,"* which comes into the Believer at conversion, and Ishmael, who represents the old nature. The birth of the new nature demands the expulsion of the old. It

is impossible to improve the old nature. In other words, Ishmael must go.

Paul said in Romans 8:7 that the old nature is *"enmity against God, that it is not subject to the Law of God, neither indeed can be."* George Williams said, *"If therefore it cannot be subject to the Law of God, how can it be improved? How foolish therefore appears the doctrine of moral evolution!"*

Regeneration is not a change of the old nature, but the introduction of a new; it is the implantation of the nature of life of the Last Adam, by the Operation of the Holy Spirit, founded upon the accomplished Redemption of Christ. The moment the sinner believes in his heart, and confesses with his mouth the Lord Jesus, he immediately becomes the possessor of a new life, and that life is Christ. He is born of God, is a Child of God, and as Paul put it, is a son of the free woman (Rom. 10:9; Gal. 3:26; 4:31; Col. 3:4; I Jn. 3:1-2) (Mackintosh).

Mackintosh went on to say: *"Nor does the introduction of this new nature alter, in the slightest degree, the true, essential character of the old."* Concerning this, the Scripture says: *"The flesh lusteth against the Spirit, and the Spirit against the flesh: and these are contrary the one to the other"* (Gal. 5:17).

THE GROUND OF MOST FALSE DOCTRINE

It is in this area which most false doctrine appears. There are some who think that Regeneration is a certain change which the old nature undergoes; and, moreover, that this change is gradual in its operation, until, at length, the whole man becomes transformed. Once again, this is moral evolution, which the Bible doesn't teach.

It rather teaches that it is impossible to improve the old nature. Paul plainly says: *"It is not subject to the Law of God, neither indeed can be"* (Rom. 8:7). And if it's not subject to the Law of God, how can it be improved? But this is where the struggle commences.

If the Believer doesn't understand the Cross, and what Jesus did there, and that his Faith must ever remain in the Cross, which alone is the secret of all victorious living, that Believer will seek to devise means and ways to live a holy life, which God cannot recognize, and in which the Holy Spirit will not function. Therefore, the Believer is left on his own, which guarantees failure. But regrettably, because of having an erroneous understanding of the Cross, most Christians attempt to make Ishmael holy, which means they try to improve the old nature, which is always doomed to failure. It is either Faith in the Cross, or it is failure. God doesn't have ten ways or even two ways of victory, only one, and that is *"Jesus Christ and Him Crucified."*

CAST OUT THE BONDWOMAN AND HER SON

Verse 10 reads: *"Wherefore she said unto Abraham, Cast out this bondwoman and her son: for the son of this bondwoman shall not be heir with my son, even with Isaac."*

Isaac is a Type of Christ, and in Christ we have all life and all victory. The *"bondwoman,"* which of course is Hagar, symbolizes the Law, while her son Ishmael, symbolizes the old nature (Gal., Chpt. 4).

Sarah rightly said to Abraham, even as we shall see, that this bondwoman and her son had to go. Isaac had now arrived, and if Hagar and Ishmael were allowed to stay, they would only seek to do away with Isaac. There is no compromise here, and there is no ground for reconciliation. One or the other must go.

Bringing it over into the spiritual sense, even as Paul did in Galatians, Chapter 4, this means that we must cast out all efforts of the flesh as it regards the living of a righteous and holy life. Our confidence and Faith must totally and completely be in Christ, and what Christ has done for us at the Cross. If we seek to live this life in any other way or manner, we are going against the Bible, and the end result will not be victory, but rather failure, and abject failure at that.

This is not a question of *"maybe,"* or *"hope so,"* or *"maybe so,"* but rather *"do or die."*

Due to the fact that this is very difficult for many to understand, please allow us the freedom of being more specific.

If you as a Believer think that your Righteousness with God, or your holiness, etc., has to do with you belonging to a certain Denomination, or a certain Church, or your doing certain good things, or not doing certain bad things, then pure and simple, you

are harboring Ishmael, which God can never condone. It must always be Christ and Him Crucified, and never anything else.

I had a Preacher some time back to tell me, in effect, that if a person did not belong to a particular Denomination, something was wrong with that person, whomever they might be. In fact, untold millions believe the same way.

Such an attitude proclaims the fact that this Preacher, and others like him, have placed their faith in that Denomination, which means it's not in Christ and Him Crucified. They may claim it is, but it isn't. Any time we make certain things a condition, other than Christ and His Sacrifice, we have told the Lord that we're going to keep Ishmael, etc. That's why the Holy Spirit through Sarah said, *"For the son of this bondwoman shall not be heir with my son, even with Isaac."*

If you as a Believer want to inherit the great Promises of God, in other words you want all that the Lord has for you, you can only obtain this by going God's Way. And if you want to argue that God has ways other than the Cross, please show it to me in the Bible. You can't show it, because it's not there.

THE FRUIT OF THE FLESH

Verse 11 reads: *"And the thing was very grievous in Abraham's sight because of his son."*

Ishmael was the fair fruit of Abraham's efforts, and he was loath to give him up.

George Williams says: *"The Divine way of Holiness is to 'put off' the old man' just as Abraham 'put off' Ishmael. Man's way of Holiness is to improve the 'old man' that is, to improve Ishmael. The effort is both foolish and hopeless. Of course the casting out of Ishmael was 'very grievous in Abraham's sight' because it always brings about a struggle to cast out this element of bondage, that is, Salvation by works. For legalism is dear to the heart. Ishmael was the fruit, and to Abraham the fair fruit of his own energy and planning."* So the Church as a whole doesn't want to give up Ishmael, and Believers as a whole don't want to give up Ishmael.

We have placed a lot of effort, scheming, planning, and sweat, so to speak, in this *"fruit of the flesh,"* and we do not part with it easily. Now what exactly am I talking about?

I'm speaking of us putting our faith in all type of things other than Christ and His Cross, thinking this will bring us Righteousness and Holiness, etc.

Now most Christians, I think, would read these words, and automatically claim that their faith is in Christ and His Sacrifice. But the truth is, for most, it isn't. And how do I know that? There are two reasons:

1. In the lives of most Christians, there is anything but victory.

2. If our pulpits are silent on a particular subject, it is a cinch that the people in the pew are not going to know anything about that particular subject. And to be sure, as it regards the Cross of Christ, the pulpits for the last several decades have been stone silent. Faith comes by hearing, and hearing by the Word of God, but if the Word of God on any subject, as stated, is not taught, then it's impossible for *"Faith to come"* (Rom. 10:17).

Most Christians place their faith and confidence in the Cross as it regards their initial Salvation experience, but when it comes to Sanctification, they don't have the faintest idea as to how the Cross plays into this all-important aspect of their life and living.

In Romans, Chapter 6, when Paul set out to explain the sin nature, he immediately took the Believer to the Cross (Rom. 6:3-5). Now that is all-important. He did that, because that's where it all happens.

When Jesus died on the Cross, was buried, and then rose from the dead, He did all of this as our Substitute. When we exhibit Faith in that great Sacrifice, in the Mind of God, we are literally placed *"in Christ."* Consequently, all the victory that Christ purchased becomes ours. But it is only in Christ and His Sacrifice, and our Faith in that Finished Work, which guarantees the help of the Holy Spirit, which then guarantees victory.

If we maintain our Faith in the Cross of Christ, ever making it the Standard, then the Holy Spirit through Paul plainly states, *"Sin shall not have dominion over you"* (Rom. 6:14).

All too often, we Christians love to hold to our *"works."* When told that we must give them up, and by that I refer to our ceasing to place faith in these things, but rather in Christ and Him Crucified, it becomes very grievous to us. As stated, we put a lot of time,

energy, and labor into these things, and as Abraham loved Ishmael, we love these particular *"works."* As someone has well said, *"The doing of religion is the greatest narcotic there is."*

IN ISAAC SHALL YOUR
SEED BE CALLED

Verse 12 reads: *"And God said unto Abraham, Let it not be grievous in your sight because of the lad, and because of the bondwoman; in all that Sarah has said unto you, hearken unto her voice; for in Isaac shall your seed be called."*

The birth of Isaac did not improve Ishmael, but only brought out his real opposition to the Child of Promise. He might have gone on very quietly and orderly till Isaac made his appearance; but then he showed what he was, by persecuting and mocking the Child of Promise.

What then was the remedy? To make Ishmael better? By no means; but, *"Cast out this bondwoman and her son; for the son of this bondwoman shall not be heir with my son, even with Isaac."* Here was the only remedy. That which is crooked cannot be made straight. Therefore, you have to get rid of the crooked thing altogether, and occupy yourself with that which is Divinely straight. It is labor lost to seek to make a crooked thing straight. Hence all efforts after the improvement of nature are utterly futile, so far as God is concerned.

THE GALATIANS

The entire Book of Galatians deals with this very subject. The error into which the Galatian Churches fell was the introduction of that which addressed itself to works. *"Except you be circumcised after the manner of Moses, you cannot be saved."* Here Salvation was made to depend upon something that man could be, or man could do, or man could keep.

This was upsetting the entirety of the fabric of Redemption, which, as the Believer knows, rests exclusively upon what Christ is, and what He has done. To make Salvation, and we speak of Righteousness, Holiness, Victory, etc., dependent, in even the most remote manner, upon anything in, or done by man, is to set it entirely aside. In other words, Ishmael must be entirely cast out, and all Abraham's hopes be made to depend upon what God had done and given in the person of Isaac.

This, as is obvious, leaves man nothing in which to glory. As well, man has nothing in which he can rightly glory. Salvation is all of God, and must ever remain all of God. He is the Creator, I am the worshipper; He is the Blesser, and I am the blessed; He is *"the Better,"* and I am *"the less"* (Heb. 7:7); He is the Giver, and I am the receiver.

This is what makes Christianity unique, and distinguishes it from every system of human religion under the sun, whether it be Romanism, Hinduism, Islam, Confucianism, Mormonism, Buddhism, or any other *"-ism."*

Human religion gives the creature a place, more or less; it keeps the bondwoman and her son in the house; it gives man something in which to glory. On the contrary, Christianity, that is Bible Christianity, excludes the creature from all interference in the work of Salvation — casts out the bondwoman and her son, and gives all the glory to Him to Whom Alone it is due.

WHO ARE THE BONDWOMAN AND HER SON?

Let us inquire as to who this bondwoman and her son really are, and what they represent. Galatians, Chapter 4 furnishes ample teaching as to these two points.

In a word, the bondwoman represents the Covenant of the Law; and her son represents all who are *"of works of law,"* or on that principle. This is very clear and plain.

The bondwoman only genders to bondage, and can never bring forth a free man. How can she? The Law never could give liberty; for so long as a man is alive, it rules him (Rom. 7:1). I can never be free, so long as I am under the dominion of anyone; for while I live, the Law rules me, and nothing but death can give me deliverance from its dominion. This is the Doctrine of Romans, Chapter 7. But Paul said:

"Wherefore, my brethren, you also are become dead to the Law by the Body of Christ (what Christ did at the Cross), *that you should be married to another, even to Him*

Who is raised from the dead, that we should bring forth fruit unto God" (Rom. 7:4). This is freedom; for *"If the Son shall make you free, you shall be free indeed"* (Jn. 8:36).

So the first four Verses of Romans, Chapter 7 tell us, if the Believer is attempting to live this Christian life by placing his faith in that other than Christ and what Christ has done at the Cross, in effect, God looks at that Christian as committing *"spiritual adultery."* This is what the first four Verses of Romans, Chapter 7 reveal to us.

THE SON OF THE BONDWOMAN

Verse 13 reads: *"And also of the son of the bondwoman will I make a nation, because he is your seed."*

If it is to be noticed, Hagar is never acknowledged as Abraham's wife; however, her child, as Abraham's son, receives a noble promise for the father's sake. Here the allegory breaks down, or at least partially so, even as do all allegories and Types, etc.

However, let us look at this situation in the natural, at least as it regards the *"nation,"* of which the Lord spoke to Abraham. As we have stated over and over, Ishmael was a work of the flesh. He was the result of the scheming and planning of Abraham and Sarah, and by no means was the product of the Holy Spirit, as should be overly obvious. In the natural, in Ishmael we're seeing the beginning of the Arab world. Even though a half-brother to Isaac, i.e., *"Israel,"* it would be Israel's bitter enemy. It continues unto this very hour.

Out of this *"work of the flesh,"* came the religion of Islam, which claims that Ishmael is the promised seed and not Isaac. It also claims that Mohammad is a result of that seed, and not Christ. So any time a work of the flesh is brought forth, it will always bitterly oppose the ways of the Lord, and at the same time, will gender much trouble.

(14) "AND ABRAHAM ROSE UP EARLY IN THE MORNING, AND TOOK BREAD, AND A BOTTLE OF WATER, AND GAVE IT UNTO HAGAR, PUTTING IT ON HER SHOULDER, AND THE CHILD, AND SENT HER AWAY: AND SHE DEPARTED, AND WANDERED IN THE WILDERNESS OF BEER-SHEBA.

(15) "AND THE WATER WAS SPENT IN THE BOTTLE, AND SHE CAST THE CHILD UNDER ONE OF THE SHRUBS.

(16) "AND SHE WENT, AND SAT HER DOWN OVER AGAINST HIM A GOOD WAY OFF, AS IT WERE A BOWSHOT: FOR SHE SAID, LET ME NOT SEE THE DEATH OF THE CHILD. AND SHE SAT OVER AGAINST HIM, AND LIFT UP HER VOICE, AND WEPT.

(17) "AND GOD HEARD THE VOICE OF THE LAD; AND THE ANGEL OF GOD CALLED TO HAGAR OUT OF HEAVEN, AND SAID UNTO HER, WHAT AILS YOU, HAGAR? FEAR NOT; FOR GOD HAS HEARD THE VOICE OF THE LAD WHERE HE IS.

(18) "ARISE, LIFT UP THE LAD, AND HOLD HIM IN YOUR HAND; FOR I WILL MAKE HIM A GREAT NATION.

(19) "AND GOD OPENED HER EYES, AND SHE SAW A WELL OF WATER; AND SHE WENT, AND FILLED THE BOTTLE WITH WATER, AND GAVE THE LAD TO DRINK.

(20) "AND GOD WAS WITH THE LAD; AND HE GREW, AND DWELT IN THE WILDERNESS, AND BECAME AN ARCHER.

(21) "AND HE DWELT IN THE WILDERNESS OF PARAN: AND HIS MOTHER TOOK HIM A WIFE OUT OF THE LAND OF EGYPT."

The structure is:

1. Even though the deed was grievous in his sight, Abraham rose up early in the morning, in order to carry out the commands of the Lord, as it regards sending away Hagar and Ishmael. The Lord expects obedience from us.

2. Even though Hagar and Ishmael were dead wrong in their actions toward Isaac, still, the Lord would have mercy.

3. The Lord spoke to her, and when she evidenced Faith, then she saw a well of water.

4. Ishmael, true to the Promise of God, would be the progenitor of the Arab people, resulting in many Arab nations.

THE DEPARTURE

Verse 14 reads: *"And Abraham rose up early in the morning, and took bread, and a bottle of water, and gave it unto Hagar, putting it on her shoulder, and the child, and sent her away: and she departed, and wandered in the wilderness of Beer-sheba."*

The Holy Spirit through Paul would use this incident to teach a very valuable spiritual lesson; still, these were actual events. Even though Hagar and Ishmael conducted themselves very wrong toward Isaac, and actually desired to murder him; still, the scene before our eyes is one of great sadness.

Due to the command of the Lord, Abraham rose up very early in the morning to carry out that which was demanded of him. It would not be an easy situation for the Patriarch. Whatever he thought of Hagar, he greatly loved the boy, and despite what was happening, that love was not diminished. But yet, he knew that the Lord was exactly right in what was being demanded. For Isaac's sake, he must send them away.

This is Abraham's sixth surrender. First of all, he would have to surrender his *"country,"* then his *"family,"* then the *"vale of Jordan,"* and then the *"gold of Sodom."* Next and fifth would come *"self,"* recorded in Chapter 15. And now the sixth surrender is *"Ishmael,"* with the last one being *"Isaac"* himself.

The sevenfold surrender, which was demanded of Abraham, was a pattern as it regards every single Believer, even unto this hour. These surrenders do not come easily or quickly, as all of us are prone to find out. But yet, if we are to be what the Lord wants us to be, they are surrenders which must be made. Even though they are hard, they are necessary, and then looking back, we always see why they were for the best.

WATER

Verse 15 reads: *"And the water was spent in the bottle, and she cast the child under one of the shrubs."*

Irrespective as to what Hagar and Ishmael had done, it is hard to conceive of Abraham sending her and the boy into the wilderness, as he did. It would seem, considering that he was a very wealthy man, that he would have made provisions for them as it regards another place, and then seen to their needs, etc.

So, even though the Scripture is silent concerning these matters, we have to come to the conclusion that the Lord told Abraham to do as he did. Otherwise, I hardly think he would have done so, especially considering the feelings he had for Ishmael.

All of this is bigger than life, and the Lord was no doubt guiding in all matters, even down to the smallest details.

So now the water that Hagar had been given is gone. The boy is evidently very thirsty, and the woman sees no way out but death.

I'm sure that she knew what the Lord had said concerning Isaac. He was the Promised Seed and, therefore, Abraham's true heir; nevertheless, she had schemed as it regards Ishmael, wanting him to have that portion, and willing, it seems, to do anything to secure her ends. But she was fighting against God, and now she faces death.

DEATH

Verse 16 reads: *"And she went, and sat her down over against him a good way off, as it were a bowshot: for she said, let me not see the death of the child. And she sat over against him, and lift up her voice, and wept."*

Evidently, Ishmael was near fainting, and his mother knew that, without water, he would die very soon. Actually, both of them would die.

Unable to bear the thought of seeing her son die, she leaves him under a shrub, and staggers a distance away, herself as well facing certain death. Out of despair, she lifted up her voice, and wept.

FEAR NOT

Verse 17 reads: *"And God heard the voice of the lad; and the Angel of God called to Hagar out of Heaven, and said unto her, What ails you, Hagar? Fear not; for God has heard the voice of the lad where he is."*

It is not said that either Ishmael or his mother prayed to God in their distress. Hence the Divine interposition on their behalf was due solely to Mercy and to God's love for Abraham. So it seems that the Lord did many things for other people for Abraham's sake (Gen. 19:29).

The Lord called to Hagar and said certain things to her.

ISHMAEL

Verse 18 reads: *"Arise, lift up the lad, and hold him in your hand; for I will make him a great nation."*

Ishmael was between 17 and 20 years old at this particular time. So when Hagar is

told to *"hold him in your hand,"* the Lord is referring to her placing her hand on his shoulder and steadying him, which she did. For the sake of Abraham, the Lord said that he would *"make of him a great nation."* And that He did! As stated, Ishmael was the progenitor of the Arabs.

A WELL OF WATER

Verse 19 reads: *"And God opened her eyes, and she saw a well of water; and she went, and filled the bottle with water, and gave the lad drink."*

The idea seems to be that she, at this juncture, believed the Lord, and when this came about, *"God opened her eyes."* She then saw a well of water. Why she had not seen it before, we aren't told. Perhaps the Lord purposely blinded her to the well, until certain things could be made known to her, and that she would acknowledge them, which required a modicum of Faith.

THE BLESSINGS OF THE LORD

Verse 20 reads: *"And God was with the lad; and he grew, and dwelt in the wilderness, and became an archer."*

Once again, the Lord was with him, which means that He helped him, and despite his murderous attitude toward Isaac, simply for the sake of Abraham. Genesis Chapter 17, Verse 18 records Abraham seeking the Lord as it regards Ishmael, and Verse 20 records the answer given by the Lord, concerning the blessing of Ishmael. And to be sure, God always keeps His Promises.

ISHMAEL

Verse 21 reads: *"And he dwelt in the wilderness of Paran: and his mother took him a wife out of the land of Egypt."*

We have here the beginning of the Arab people.

In all of this, we notice God's care even for an Ishmael, who would appear to be outside all Covenant blessings. He was one whose *"hand was to be against every man, and every man's against him"* (Gen. 16:12). But yet, God manifested care for Ishmael.

(22) "AND IT CAME TO PASS AT THAT TIME, THAT ABIMELECH AND PHICHOL THE CHIEF CAPTAIN OF HIS HOST SPOKE

UNTO ABRAHAM, SAYING, GOD IS WITH YOU IN ALL THAT YOU DO:

(23) "NOW THEREFORE SWEAR UNTO ME HERE BY GOD THAT YOU WILL NOT DEAL FALSELY WITH ME, NOR WITH MY SON, NOR WITH MY SON'S SON: BUT ACCORDING TO THE KINDNESS THAT I HAVE DONE UNTO YOU, YOU SHALL DO UNTO ME, AND TO THE LAND WHEREIN YOU HAVE SOJOURNED.

(24) "AND ABRAHAM SAID, I WILL SWEAR.

(25) "AND ABRAHAM REPROVED ABIMELECH BECAUSE OF A WELL OF WATER, WHICH ABIMELECH'S SERVANTS HAD VIOLENTLY TAKEN AWAY.

(26) "AND ABIMELECH SAID, I WOT NOT WHO HAS DONE THIS THING; NEITHER DID YOU TELL ME, NEITHER YET HEARD OF IT, BUT TODAY.

(27) "AND ABRAHAM TOOK SHEEP AND OXEN, AND GAVE THEM UNTO ABIMELECH; AND BOTH OF THEM MADE A COVENANT.

(28) "AND ABRAHAM SET SEVEN EWE LAMBS OF THE FLOCK BY THEMSELVES.

(29) "AND ABIMELECH SAID UNTO ABRAHAM, WHAT MEAN THESE SEVEN EWE LAMBS WHICH YOU HAVE SET BY THEMSELVES?

(30) "AND HE SAID, FOR THESE SEVEN EWE LAMBS SHALL YOU TAKE OF MY HAND, THAT THEY MAY BE A WITNESS UNTO ME, THAT I HAVE DIGGED THIS WELL.

(31) "WHEREFORE HE CALLED THAT PLACE BEER-SHEBA; BECAUSE THERE THEY SWEAR BOTH OF THEM.

(32) "THUS THEY MADE A COVENANT AT BEER-SHEBA: THEN ABIMELECH ROSE UP, AND PHICHOL THE CHIEF CAPTAIN OF HIS HOST, AND THEY RETURNED INTO THE LAND OF THE PHILISTINES.

(33) "AND ABRAHAM PLANTED A GROVE IN BEER-SHEBA, AND CALLED THERE ON THE NAME OF THE LORD, THE EVERLASTING GOD.

(34) "AND ABRAHAM SOJOURNED IN THE PHILISTINES' LAND MANY DAYS."

The construction is:

1. From the time Ishmael is put away, outwards all is strength and victory.

NOTES

2. Consequently, he no longer fears the prince of this world, but rather reproves him. We speak of Abimelech.

3. Now that the heir is come, Christ in Type, he knows himself to be the possessor of Heavenly as well as earthly Promises.

4. The well of the oath is witness to Abraham's title in the Earth and to Abimelech's confession of the fact.

5. So Abraham now dwells where the power of the world had been; Abimelech as well as Ishmael withdraw from his land.

6. All this is a pledge of what Israel shall have and of the glory and dominion that will be hers in Christ, and with Christ as the Everlasting God.

ABIMELECH

Verse 22 reads: *"And it came to pass at that time, that Abimelech and Phichol the chief captain of his host spake unto Abraham, saying, God is with you in all that you do."*

From the dream that Abimelech had concerning God, and what the Lord told him about Abraham, and Abraham praying for the healing of his household, caused him to stand big in the eyes of this heathen prince. As well, he had no doubt heard of the birth of Isaac, and considered it as well as none other than a miracle. And then he saw the power, strength, and riches of Abraham, and concludes by saying to him, *"God is with you in all that you do."*

He wants to stay on the good side of Abraham, which is not a difficult thing to do, inasmuch as the Patriarch is a kind, gracious, considerate man. He wants to let Abraham know as well that he intends no harm to him, and that he in fact wants the two of them to be friends.

A COVENANT

Verse 23 reads: *"Now therefore swear unto me here by God that you will not deal falsely with me, nor with my son, nor with my son's son: but according to the kindness that I have done unto you, you shall do unto me, and to the land wherein you have sojourned."*

Abimelech desires a Covenant with Abraham that will extend not only to his son, but as well to his grandson.

As we can see from the terminology being used here, from the time of the victorious sixth surrender, which spoke of the expulsion of Ishmael, from this moment onward, all is strength and victory. He no longer fears the prince of this world, in this case represented by Abimelech, but rather reproves him. Now that Isaac has come, who is Christ in Type, Abraham knows himself to be the possessor as well of earthly promises, and conducts himself accordingly. Even the heathen prince confesses that God is with him.

THE MODERN BELIEVER

The spirit now possessed by Abraham is the same spirit that the modern Believer should have. Jesus has now come and suffered on the Cross, thereby providing for us both earthly and Heavenly Promises. But we can have these possessions, only as we know and understand the manner in which they are given to us. Once again we come back to Christ and His Cross.

God hasn't changed, because God cannot change. It is the Cross which has brought about all good things.

Before the Cross, a thrice-Holy God could not allow sinful man to approach Him. Such would have occasioned the death of all who made that attempt. But the Cross settled that problem, by Jesus atoning there for all sin. Due to the Cross, the door is now open for all to come, and actually, the invitation is given (Rev. 22:17).

THE COVENANT IS MADE

Verse 24 reads: *"And Abraham said, I will swear."*

Even though Abraham did swear as it regards that for which the heathen prince asked, there was still a present and personal matter to be settled.

THE WELL OF WATER

Verse 25 reads: *"And Abraham reproved Abimelech because of the well of water, which Abimelech's servants had violently taken away."*

The ownership of wells in that part of the world was as jealousy guarded as the possession of a valuable object. So, the greatest

possible injury that could be done to one, at least of a material kind, was the hindering of his water supplies. It seems the servants of Abimelech had violently taken over a well that had originally belonged to Abraham.

ABIMELECH

Verse 26 reads: *"And Abimelech said, I know not who has done this thing; neither did you tell me, neither yet heard I of it, but today."*

Evidently, one of the reasons that Abimelech, along with his chief captain Phichol came to visit Abraham was because he evidently noticed a coolness on Abraham's part. Not knowing the reason for this, simply because he had no knowledge of the incident of the well, he comes to Abraham in order to ascertain what the problem might be, or in fact if there was a problem.

When Abraham explains the situation, which may not seem like much to us presently, but was quite an affair at that time, Abimelech confesses that he had heard nothing of this situation; consequently, he definitely was not an accomplice in this situation, the deed having been carried out by his herdsmen.

THE COVENANT

Verse 27 reads: *"And Abraham took sheep and oxen, and gave them unto Abimelech; and both of them made a covenant."*

Abraham desired to show this heathen prince, and those with him, and especially his chief captain, that he carried no animosity against anyone, but only sought to live peaceably. Desiring the friendship of Abimelech, and showing that he carried no ill will, he furnished sheep and oxen for both he and Abimelech, in order to offer them in sacrifice before God, so that the Covenant would be binding.

SEVEN EWE LAMBS

Verse 28 reads: *"And Abraham set seven ewe lambs of the flock by themselves."*

The seven ewe lambs are to be a gift to Abimelech. If he accepts them, which he did, this shows that the argument has been settled, and the well is returned to Abraham, who dug it in the first place.

ANOTHER COVENANT OF SORTS

Verse 29 reads: *"And Abimelech said unto Abraham, What mean these seven ewe lambs which you have set by themselves?"*

The word in Hebrew for *"swearing"* is a passive verb, literally signifying *"to be sevened,"* that is, done or confirmed by seven. In this ancient narrative we see a Covenant actually thus made binding.

Seven ewe lambs are picked out and placed by themselves, and by accepting these, Abimelech bound himself to acknowledge and respect Abraham's title to the well. Apparently this matter of ratifying an oath was unknown to the Philistines, as Abimelech asks, *"What mean these seven ewe lambs?"* As soon as the lambs were accepted, the ratification was complete.

A WITNESS

Verse 30 reads: *"And he said, for these seven ewe lambs shall you take of my hand, that they may be a witness unto me, that I have digged this well."*

This is the well, which by now is obvious, that was the cause of the contention. Abraham had dug the well, but the herdsmen of Abimelech had taken it over by force. If Abimelech takes the seven lambs, which he obviously did, this shows that he agrees with Abraham's statements concerning the fact that the well had originally belonged to him, and had been fraudulently taken.

BEER-SHEBA

Verse 31 reads: *"Wherefore he called that place Beer-sheba; because there they swear both of them."*

Abimelech took the seven lambs, signifying that he agreed with Abraham, and that the matter was now settled. *"Beer-sheba"* means, *"the well of the oath."*

The well of the oath is witness to Abraham's title in the Earth and to Abimelech's confession of the fact.

THE COVENANT MADE

Verse 32 reads: *"Thus they made a covenant at Beer-sheba: then Abimelech rose up, and Phichol the chief captain of his host, and they returned into the land of the Philistines."*

NOTES

This area as ruled by Abimelech is called here the land of the Philistines for the first time. However, the main body of the Philistines who established their cities in the south coastal plain of Canaan did not arrive until later.

Abimelech was not as aggressive as the later Philistines, since he was willing to make this treaty and allow Abraham to live in his territory (Horton).

However, there is a difference now in Abraham, as I think is somewhat obvious. Since Isaac has now been born, has been weaned, and Abraham knows that he is the Child of Promise, and Ishmael has been expelled, we now find a man who is operating strictly on the path of Faith.

And yet, when we think of his failures, we should not charge him unduly. Would we have done any better? Would we have done even as well? Considering the fact that the Cross is now history, which means that all that Abraham looked forward to has now come to pass, and as well we have the Holy Spirit abiding with us, we should do much better than Abraham; however, who would be so crass as to place themselves in such a position of superiority?

THE TREE

Verse 33 reads: *"And Abraham planted a grove in Beer-sheba, and called there on the Name of the LORD, the Everlasting God."*

In the Hebrew, the word is *"tree,"* and not *"grove."* Accordingly he takes possession of the land, thereby, planting a tree. He worships Jehovah the Everlasting God; for the God Who gave Isaac must be in truth the Everlasting God. So Abraham now dwells where the power of the world had been; Abimelech as well as Ishmael withdraw from his land.

All of this is a pledge or a sign, of what Israel shall have, and of the glory and dominion that will be hers in Christ, and with Christ as the Everlasting God. This is the Divine definition of Jehovah, i.e., *"Jesus Christ, the same yesterday and today and forever."*

Abraham planted, it is believed, a tamarisk tree; a tree that is loaded with beautiful pink blossoms in the spring.

He refers now to Jehovah as *"El'olam."* In Genesis 14:22, Abraham claimed for Jehovah that He was *"El Elyon,"* the supreme God; in Genesis 17:1, Jehovah reveals Himself as *"El Shaddai,"* the Almighty God; and now Abraham claims for Him the attribute of eternity. As he advanced in Holiness, Abraham also grew in knowledge of the manifold nature of the Deity, and we also more clearly understand why the Hebrews called God, not *"El,"* but *"Elohim."* In the plural appellation all the Divine attributes were combined. *"El"* might be *"'elyon,"* or *"shaddai,"* or *"'olam"*; Elohim was all in one (Ellicott).

SOJOURN

Verse 34 reads: *"And Abraham sojourned in the Philistines' land many days."*

The Patriarch would actually live here until he died.

"Great God of wonders!
"All Your ways are matchless, Godlike,
*   and Divine;*
"But the fair glories of Your Grace,
"More Godlike and unrivaled shine,
"More Godlike and unrivaled shine."

"In wonder lost, with trembling joy,
"We take the pardon of our God:
"Pardon for crimes of deepest dye,
"A pardon bought with Jesus' Blood,
"A pardon bought with Jesus' Blood."

"O may this strange, this matchless
*   Grace,*
"This Godlike miracle of love,
"Fill the whole Earth with grateful
*   praise,*
"And all the angelic choirs above,
"And all the angelic choirs above."

CHAPTER 22

(1) "AND IT CAME TO PASS AFTER THESE THINGS, THAT GOD DID TEMPT ABRAHAM, AND SAID UNTO HIM, ABRAHAM: AND HE SAID, BEHOLD, HERE I AM.

(2) "AND HE SAID, TAKE NOW YOUR SON, YOUR ONLY SON ISAAC, WHOM YOU LOVE, AND GET YOU INTO THE LAND OF MORIAH; AND OFFER HIM THERE FOR A

BURNT OFFERING UPON ONE OF THE MOUNTAINS WHICH I WILL TELL THEE OF.

(3) "AND ABRAHAM ROSE UP EARLY IN THE MORNING, AND SADDLED HIS ASS, AND TOOK TWO OF HIS YOUNG MEN WITH HIM, AND ISAAC HIS SON, AND CLAVE THE WOOD FOR THE BURNT OFFERING, AND ROSE UP, AND WENT UNTO THE PLACE OF WHICH GOD HAD TOLD HIM.

(4) "THEN ON THE THIRD DAY ABRAHAM LIFTED UP HIS EYES, AND SAW THE PLACE AFAR OFF.

(5) "AND ABRAHAM SAID UNTO HIS YOUNG MEN, ABIDE YOU HERE WITH THE ASS; AND I AND THE LAD WILL GO YONDER AND WORSHIP, AND COME AGAIN TO YOU.

(6) "AND ABRAHAM TOOK THE WOOD OF THE BURNT OFFERING, AND LAID IT UPON ISAAC HIS SON, AND HE TOOK THE FIRE IN HIS HAND, AND A KNIFE; AND THEY WENT BOTH OF THEM TOGETHER."

The composition is:

1. The first mention of love in the Bible is found here in the Second Verse.

2. The whole Chapter is Christ in His Death and Resurrection, and the worldwide Redemption which results therefrom.

3. This was Abraham's seventh, and greatest, and last surrender.

4. *"God did test Abraham."* It is a high honor to be tested by God.

5. There are various kinds of trials, but the highest character of trial, and it is full of dignity, is that which comes from God Himself.

6. In his mind and heart, Abraham had already offered up Isaac, and the Patriarch fully believed that God would raise him up from the dead; *"from whence also he received him in a figure."*

7. The word *"Moriah"* is a Hebrew word, and means, *"foreseen by Jehovah."* Here was the threshing floor that David bought, and here Solomon built the Temple.

TEST

Verse 1 reads: *"And it came to pass after these things that God did tempt Abraham, and said unto him, Abraham: and he said, Behold, here I am."*

The word *"tempt"* should have been translated *"test"* or *"prove,"* for that's what it means in the Hebrew. God did not *"test"* Abraham that He (God) might know, as we think of such, for He already knew. God is omniscient, meaning that He knows everything, past, present, and future. He did this that Abraham might know. Faith must always be tested, and great Faith must be tested greatly. And to be sure, this was at least one of, if not the greatest test that any man ever had to undergo.

George Williams said: *"It is a high honor to be tested by God. There are various kinds of trials, some from circumstances or some from the hand of Satan, but the highest character of trial is that which comes from God Himself."*

THE REASON FOR THIS TEST

Most do not understand the cause or reason for this test. Many think that it's because Abraham loved Isaac too much, etc. While Abraham certainly loved his son, even as he should have, this was not the reason for the test.

The entire framework of the Move of God as it regarded Abraham was the part the Patriarch would play, which was great indeed, in bringing the Redeemer into this world. This is the entire Plan of God; He must redeem Adam's fallen race. The way that it would be done, in fact, the way it had to be done, had long since been decided, even before the foundation of the world (I Pet. 1:18-20). God would have to become man, and because it was man who had fallen. God as God couldn't redeem humanity, and neither could Angels or Seraphim or Cherubim. As well, tremendous responsibility had been given to the first Adam, who incidentally failed, so another Adam, so to speak, Whom Paul referred to as the *"Last Adam"* would have to be brought on the scene (I Cor. 15:45).

In all of this, the Bible student must realize that it is not Satan that is in view here, but rather God. It is God Who has been offended; consequently, it is God Who will set the Standard for Redemption, in other words, the price that will have to be paid in order for His thrice-Holy Nature and Righteousness to be satisfied. In fact, the price was so

high that man could in no way meet the terms. So God would have to pay the price Himself, and that price would be death. Inasmuch as God cannot die, He would have to become Man in order to make the supreme sacrifice.

In this object lesson of all object lessons, God will show the Patriarch as to how He will redeem lost humanity. As stated, it will be through death. However, even though He would show Abraham this much, He wouldn't exactly show him the means by which this death would be carried out, and we speak of the Cross. That would later be shown to Moses (Num. 21:8-9). The Reader must remember that anything and everything which God does is always far larger than we can at first contemplate. No, God didn't have Abraham to undergo this tremendous test, merely to prove a point. To be sure, many things entered into that which was done, as it always is with God. But the primary purpose was to show the Patriarch what all of this was all about, and what it would take to redeem the human race. This is at least one of the reasons that Jesus said: *"Your father Abraham rejoiced to see My day: and he saw it, and was glad"* (Jn. 8:56).

The phrase, *"And it came to pass after these things,"* refers to some years after the expulsion of Ishmael. It could have been anywhere from 15 to 25 years after that particular event. In other words, Isaac at this time could have been between 20 and 30 years of age.

The Lord had spoken to Abraham quite a number of times through the years, but this was to be the most momentous of all. When the Lord called his name, and the Patriarch answered, *"Behold, here I am,"* little did he realize what was about to transpire. As stated, this was undoubtedly one of the greatest tests that God ever asked of any man.

Quite possibly the Patriarch thought that every test of his Faith had come and gone. The problem with Lot had finally been settled, even though we are not aware of the end result. The terrible situation with Ishmael had finally come to a head, and had been the source of great hurt; however, Abraham had passed the test with quick obedience. So now he is at ease, having made peace with the Philistines, he and Sarah are enjoying their leisure of old age. And now the Lord speaks again:

HIS SON, A BURNT-OFFERING

Verse 2 reads: *"And He said, Take now your son, your only son Isaac, whom you love, and get you into the land of Moriah; and offer him there for a Burnt Offering upon one of the mountains which I will tell thee of."*

One can only imagine, and that not very successfully, what must have gone on in Abraham's mind, upon first hearing this command. What preliminary remarks were made, if any, before this tremendous announcement came forth, we aren't told. But then again, what was required was of such moment, so absolutely mind-boggling, that really there is no way to soften the blow. So it seems that without preliminary fanfare, the Lord simply uttered the command. This would be the seventh of the sevenfold surrender required of Abraham, and as previously stated, which in one way or the other, is required of every Believer. Inasmuch as the Patriarch is the father of us all (Rom. 4:16), his example serves as a pattern for us.

Abraham is commanded to slay his son. The trial was twofold:

1. Human sacrifice was abhorrent to the nature of Jehovah, so the Patriarch must now prove to himself that what he is hearing is definitely from God. Could such a deed really be enjoined upon him by God?

In fact, in the future, some Israelites would offer up their firstborn in trying to atone for their sin (Mic. 6:7). But instead of such a deed bringing peace, it only brought a deeper condemnation to the soul. Had Abraham as well been moved upon by such means, his conduct would have deserved and met with similar condemnation. But when he convinced himself that this word definitely did come from the Lord, then obedience was required of him.

2. He now was faced with a trial of his Faith. He was being told to destroy the son in whom *"his seed was to be called."* Several things had to be faced, the least certainly not being his love for his son. And even more importantly was the position of Isaac as the appointed means for the blessing of all mankind. All of this stood arrayed against the command.

As a result of Abraham's obedience, there were great blessings for both he and Isaac, for Isaac grandly obeyed as well, in the submitting himself for sacrifice, which we must not overlook.

But there was something even higher than all of this, in that the act, or rather the command for the act to be performed, contained a great typical value. As we've already stated, there was in it the setting forth of the mystery of the Father in the giving of His Son to die for the sins of the world. In that we have the greater purpose. While all things played their part, God would show the Patriarch the reason for all that he had thus far gone through. To be sure, even though this would be the greatest test of his Faith, it was by no means the only test of his Faith, many milestones already having been passed. So now the Heavenly Father will relate to a greater degree the *"why"* of all of this.

Abraham was to go to *"the land of Moriah."* The very name means, *"Jah or Jehovah is Provider."*

As we have stated, it is believed that this mountain where Isaac was to be offered is the same place where the Temple would later be built. Actually, it is believed that the large stone over which the Muslim Dome of the Rock is now built was the actual site of the proposed sacrifice, and as well the site as to where the Holy of Holies was located in Solomon's Temple.

To this command of Isaac being offered up as a *"Burnt-Offering,"* and that the Promise would still in some Divine manner be fulfilled in him, the only answer that Abraham could come up with was that God would raise the boy from the dead.

Concerning this proposed Sacrifice, God used the word *"only"* as it referred to Isaac. *"Only"* means only in the sense of unique, one-of-a-kind, and special. In other words, Isaac was Abraham's only hope for the fulfillment of God's Salvation-Promise. Isaac being Abraham's *"only"* son whom he loved thus became a Type of God's *"only"* Son Who is also called His *"Beloved Son"* (Mat. 3:17).

The *"Burnt-Offering"* or *"Whole Burnt-Offering"* as it was sometimes called, means literally *"an ascent."* It went up completely in smoke, which means it was consumed totally, and was a type or illustration of complete surrender to God and a complete exaltation of Him.

OBEDIENCE

Verse 3 reads: *"And Abraham rose up early in the morning, and saddled his ass, and took two of his young men with him, and Isaac his son, and clave the wood for the Burnt Offering, and rose up, and went unto the place of which God had told him."*

As in the prior Chapter concerning Ishmael, so here, there is as well prompt obedience. Abraham rises early in the morning. There is no record that he told Sarah what he was doing, possibly for fear that she would try to stop him.

Why didn't God tell the Patriarch to take one or even many of his lambs out of his great flocks, and offer them up? Why the human sacrifice, especially considering that God hated such?

As we've already stated, among other things, this was a Type of what God would do in the giving of His Only Son, to redeem lost humanity.

The human sacrifice was demanded, because the blood of bulls and goats cannot take away sin (Heb. 10:4). And as well, God hated human sacrifice, which made the giving of His Only Son an even greater thing. That's why John 3:16 is perhaps the most beloved Scripture in the entirety of the Bible:

"For God so loved the world, that he gave His Only Begotten Son, that whosoever believes in Him, should not perish, but have everlasting life."

What must have been the thoughts of the Patriarch, when he was cutting the wood which would provide the fire for the Burnt-Offering? How his heart must have broken a thousand times over. How so much the stifled sobs choked him, as he endeavored to carry out the command of God. Let me ask the following question.

When we look at the modern faith prima donnas, which in reality is no faith at all, as they boast of their $3,000 suits, claiming that their faith obtained such for them, when in reality the money was wheedled out of stupid Christians, with the lure that the stupid Christians are going to get far more in return, and

then place such abominations up beside the Faith of Abraham, I will ask the Reader as to how it compares.

This stuff which passes today for Faith is, in reality, no more than a con game. It is in street parlance, *"a scam."* And yet millions of Christians fall for these *"scams,"* and simply because there seems to be enough greed in all of us to keep the con game alive.

Let the Reader understand that when we speak of Faith, it must be Faith in Christ and His Cross, or else it's not faith that God will recognize. In other words, any other type of so-called faith is bogus (Rom. 6:3-14; 8:1-2, 11; I Cor. 1:17-18, 21, 23; 2:2, 5; Gal. 6:14; Eph. 2:13-18; Col. 2:14-15).

Concerning obedience, the Scripture says that Abraham, *"rose up, and went."* It is just that simple! As well, he went to *"the place of which God had told him."*

THE THIRD DAY

Verse 4 reads: *"Then on the third day Abraham lifted up his eyes, and saw the place afar off."*

This was no doubt the longest three days of Abraham's life. What were his thoughts, when he *"saw the place afar off"*? How many temptations did he endure, which prompted him to turn around and go back? Did he sleep any during these three days and nights?

Some folk think that perfect Faith never has a question, never has a second thought, never experiences any qualms; however, that is wishful thinking only, and not reality. In fact, were there no struggle, there would be no Faith. What kind of test would it be, if in fact there was no question?

WORSHIP

Verse 5 reads: *"And Abraham said unto his young men, Abide you here with the ass; and I and the lad will go yonder and worship, and come again to you."*

We learn two very important things, from this particular Verse:

1. We learn some things about worship.

Praise is what we do, while worship is what we are. In other words, every part and particle of our life and living should be worship of the Lord. While all worship is not praise, all praise definitely is worship.

If it is to be noticed, even though no one but Abraham knew what actually was to happen at this place of sacrifice, still, he knew what was supposed to happen. His son was to be sacrificed; and yet, he calls it *"worship."*

2. By him using the phrase, *"And come again to you,"* he is stating that he believed that God would raise the boy from the dead. In essence he said, *"I and the lad will go yonder,"* and *"I and the lad will come again to you."*

THE CROSS

Verse 6 reads: *"And Abraham took the wood of the Burnt Offering, and laid it upon Isaac his son: and he took the fire in his hand, and a knife; and they went both of them together."*

In Isaac carrying the wood on which he was to be sacrificed, we discern a Type of Christ carrying His Cross (Jn. 19:17).

This was the seventh of the sevenfold surrender of Abraham, and by far, the hardest. There is no way that we can put ourselves in his shoes. There's no way that we really can even begin to understand what he was going through as he and Isaac walked up this mountain together. Was he having second thoughts?

Whatever his thoughts were, nothing slowed his advancement in his obedience to God. In all of this scenario, he never slacked, nor did he slow. His demeanor seemed to be that of Christ when Isaiah said of him, *"For the Lord GOD will help me; therefore shall I not be confounded: therefore have I set My face like a flint, and I know that I shall not be ashamed"* (Isa. 50:7).

(7) "AND ISAAC SPAKE UNTO ABRAHAM HIS FATHER, AND SAID, MY FATHER: AND HE SAID, HERE AM I, MY SON. AND HE SAID, BEHOLD THE FIRE AND THE WOOD: BUT WHERE IS THE LAMB FOR A BURNT OFFERING?

(8) "AND ABRAHAM SAID, MY SON, GOD WILL PROVIDE HIMSELF A LAMB FOR A BURNT OFFERING: SO THEY WENT BOTH OF THEM TOGETHER.

(9) "AND THEY CAME TO THE PLACE WHICH GOD HAD TOLD HIM OF; AND ABRAHAM BUILT AN ALTAR THERE, AND LAID THE WOOD IN ORDER, AND BOUND

NOTES

ISAAC HIS SON, AND LAID HIM ON THE ALTAR UPON THE WOOD.

(10) "AND ABRAHAM STRETCHED FORTH HIS HAND, AND TOOK THE KNIFE TO SLAY HIS SON.

(11) "AND THE ANGEL OF THE LORD CALLED UNTO HIM OUT OF HEAVEN, AND SAID, ABRAHAM, ABRAHAM: AND HE SAID, HERE AM I.

(12) "AND HE SAID, LAY NOT YOUR HAND UPON THE LAD, NEITHER DO THOU ANYTHING UNTO HIM: FOR NOW I KNOW THAT YOU FEAR GOD, SEEING YOU HAVE NOT WITHHELD YOUR SON, YOUR ONLY SON FROM ME."

The composition is:

1. Isaac, as the unresisting Burnt-Offering, is a striking Type of Him Who said, *"I delight to do Your Will, O My God."*

2. He Who said, *"Abraham, Abraham"* was the Mighty God Who said: *"Martha, Martha," "Simon, Simon,"* and *"Saul, Saul."*

3. It was God Who, from Heaven, was speaking to Abraham.

THE LAMB

Verse 7 reads: *"And Isaac spoke unto Abraham his father, and said, My father: and he said, Here am I, my son. And he said, Behold the fire and the wood: but where is the lamb for a Burnt Offering?"*

Isaac now speaks with his father, inquiring as to where was the lamb. The question must have broken Abraham's heart all over again.

The sacrificial system was obviously explained to Adam and Eve by the Lord, and meant to serve as a Type and Symbol of the coming Redeemer. There is evidence of sacrifices being offered all the way from the beginning, with that of Abel being the first recorded case (Gen., Chpt. 4).

As well, there is every evidence that the ones offering up the Sacrifices knew that they represented the coming Redeemer, with the first prediction being given in the Garden of Eden (Gen. 3:15). Naturally, they would not have had as much knowledge as we presently have, due to the fact that the Cross is now history; however, they were well aware that the sacrifices were a substitute, until the Seed of the woman could come, Who would redeem the fallen sons of Adam's race.

GOD WILL PROVIDE

Verse 8 reads: *"And Abraham said, My son, God will provide Himself a lamb for a Burnt Offering: so they went both of them together."*

What exactly did Abraham mean by the statement, *"God will provide Himself a lamb for a Burnt Offering"*? Was he speaking prophetically of the work of the Father and the Son as it regards Redemption? Or was he, by the use of the word *"lamb,"* meaning Isaac, thus showing that it was not he who chose the victim, but God? I think in a sense it was both.

I think the Holy Spirit, by the mouth of Abraham, predicted the Lamb of God, which would be provided, and which would take away the sin of the world (Jn. 1:29).

I think by now, Abraham knows his own Faith, in order to act on this which God has commanded; he knows not Isaac's to endure it; however, as we shall see, Isaac will pass the test with flying colors.

THE ALTAR

Verse 9 reads: *"And they came to the place which God had told him of; and Abraham built an Altar there, and laid the wood in order, and bound Isaac his son, and laid him on the Altar upon the wood."*

The Lord, as is obvious here, had told him exactly to where he should come. As stated, about 1,000 years into the future, Solomon would build a Temple on this spot.

As Abraham built the Altar, he was drawing ever closer to the fatal moment. Was God asking too much of him? Was it possible for a human being to stand such a thing? Such thoughts must have gone through his mind.

Isaac would yield unreservedly to that which his father was about to do. Sometimes we have a tendency to overlook Isaac. Sandwiched between his father and his grandfather Jacob, he doesn't draw the attention of the other two. Even though his test did not compare with that of Abraham, still, his yielding as he did shows the Faith he had in both God and Abraham. By this time, Abraham had resigned himself to the death of Isaac, and Isaac had resigned himself to serve as the sacrifice.

THE KNIFE

Verse 10 reads: *"And Abraham stretched forth his and, and took the knife to slay his son."*

Isaac, as the unresisting Burnt-Offering, is a striking Type of Him Who said, *"I delight to do Your Will, O My God."*

When Abraham took the knife in his hand and raised his arm, he fully intended to plunge the knife deep into his son's chest. He would then ignite the wood with fire, and thereby reduce Isaac's body to ashes. He then expected the Lord to raise Isaac from the dead. In other words, if there was ever a man committed, this man was committed.

In his mind, how could it be otherwise! The Lord had promised to establish His Covenant with Isaac (Gen. 17:19) and had even said, *"In Isaac shall your seed be called"* (Gen. 21:12). So the only thing that Abraham could see was that God would raise the boy from the dead.

But the Lord wasn't wanting to portray at this time His miracle-working Power to Abraham, but rather the object lesson of the Plan of Redemption, which would require the death of God's Son, and which the entire scenario as well would prove beyond the shadow of a doubt Abraham's love for the Lord, and his trust in the Lord.

ABRAHAM, ABRAHAM

Verse 11 reads: *"And the Angel of the LORD called unto him out of Heaven, and said, Abraham, Abraham: and he said, Here am I."*

He Who said *"Abraham, Abraham"* was the same One Who said: *"Martha, Martha,"* *"Simon, Simon,"* and *"Saul, Saul."* The repetition denotes urgency.

Horton said, *"When Abraham took the knife, his surrender was complete."* His Faith and consecration had now been demonstrated totally and completely, and so God stopped him by calling his name twice.

As the Lord at this time called out to Abraham, to be sure, the Voice of God never was so welcomed, never so sweet, never so seasonable as now. Concerning this, Matthew Henry said: *"It was the trial that God intended, not the act. It was not God's intention that Isaac should actually be sacrificed. In this it was shown that nobler blood than that of animals, in due time, was to be shed for sin — even the Blood of the only Begotten Son of God. But in the meanwhile God would not in any case have human sacrifices used."*

FAITH TESTED

Verse 12 reads: *"And He said, Lay not your hand upon the lad, neither do you anything unto him: for now I know that you fear God, seeing you have not withheld your son, your only son from Me."*

All of this portrays the fact that it's not so much the act, but the intent of the heart which God sees. Abraham didn't have to kill the boy to prove himself to God, but he had to fully intend to do so, and that he did! He did it, even though he did not understand why God would ask such a thing, or why it was necessary for God to ask such a thing. In other words, he knew he had heard the Voice of God, and he knew what God had told him to do. In his mind, even though the questions loomed large, the answer to those questions was not really his affair, that being in the domain of Jehovah. His business was to obey, and obey he did.

OMNISCIENCE

How do we reconcile the words *"For now I know that you fear God,"* with the omniscience of God, which means that He knows all things, past, present, and future?

Some have claimed that God had to know the situation by experience as well as by foreknowledge; however, that would make His Word less than experience, which we know is not the case.

Others have claimed that this is merely an anthropomorphism, which means that the Holy Spirit spoke in human terminology, in order that we might understand. That is not plausible either, because were that the case, that would mean the Holy Spirit is not telling the truth.

The Hebrew word here for *"know"* is *"yada,"* and means, *"to observe, to care, to recognize, to instruct, to designate, or even to punish."*

A root of *"yada"* is *"yiddehonee,"* and means *"the knowing One."* And this is the meaning

of the word *"know"* in Verse 12. So it can be translated to help us understand it better:

"For I the knowing One knew that you feared God, and that you would not withhold your son, your only son from Me."

(13) "AND ABRAHAM LIFTED UP HIS EYES, AND LOOKED, AND BEHOLD BEHIND HIM A RAM CAUGHT IN A THICKET BY HIS HORNS: AND ABRAHAM WENT AND TOOK THE RAM, AND OFFERED HIM UP FOR A BURNT OFFERING IN THE STEAD OF HIS SON.

(14) "AND ABRAHAM CALLED THE NAME OF THAT PLACE JEHOVAH-JIREH: AS IT IS SAID TO THIS DAY, IN THE MOUNT OF THE LORD IT SHALL BE SEEN.

(15) "AND THE ANGEL OF THE LORD CALLED UNTO ABRAHAM OUT OF HEAVEN THE SECOND TIME,

(16) "AND SAID, BY MYSELF HAVE I SWORN, SAYS THE LORD, FOR BECAUSE YOU HAVE DONE THIS THING, AND HAVE NOT WITHHELD YOUR SON, YOUR ONLY SON:

(17) "THAT IN BLESSING I WILL BLESS YOU, AND IN MULTIPLYING I WILL MULTIPLY YOUR SEED AS THE STARS OF THE HEAVEN, AND AS THE SAND WHICH IS UPON THE SEASHORE; AND YOUR SEED SHALL POSSESS THE GATE OF HIS ENEMIES;

(18) "AND IN YOUR SEED SHALL ALL THE NATIONS OF THE EARTH BE BLESSED; BECAUSE YOU HAVE OBEYED MY VOICE."

The overview is:

1. *"In the stead of his son,"* presents the Doctrine of Substitution clearly stated.

2. Jehovah-Jireh means, *"the Lord will provide."*

3. The Lord called to Abraham out of Heaven the second time. The first time was for substitution; the second time, for Revelation.

4. The oath of Verse 16 is the foundation of Israel's Blessings. David's *"sure mercies"* are all founded on it.

5. Abraham's seed being as *"the stars of the Heaven, and as the sand which is upon the seashore,"* is not an exaggeration; for no natural figure could exaggerate the Resurrection Power of God (Williams).

6. Verse 18 proclaims the fact that obedience is better than sacrifice.

THE DOCTRINE OF SUBSTITUTION

Verse 13 reads: *"And Abraham lifted up his eyes, and looked, and behold behind him a ram caught in a thicket by his horns: and Abraham went and took the ram, and offered him up for a Burnt-Offering in the stead of his son."*

As stated, we have the Doctrine here of Substitution plainly laid out. The ram was offered up in Sacrifice instead of his son.

As is clearly observed, the Lord Jesus Christ became our Substitute. It would have done no good to have actually sacrificed Isaac, simply because, as all, with the exception of Christ, Isaac was born in sin. But the ram, which was an innocent victim, could be a Type of Christ, and could be offered up in the place of Isaac, which it was. Faith in what that Sacrifice represented would definitely cover sin, even though the blood of bulls and goats could not take away sin, that remaining until the Cross of Christ (Heb. 10:4).

THE DOCTRINE OF SUBSTITUTION AND IDENTIFICATION

Even though the Doctrine of Substitution, as stated, is clearly set forth here, its corresponding Doctrine of Identification is not so clearly stated, that awaiting Moses (Num. 21:9). But still, we are seeing here the very heart of the Salvation Plan.

Jesus Christ is our Substitute, meaning that He did for us what we couldn't do for ourselves, which refers to satisfying the demands of a thrice-Holy God, which Christ did by dying on the Cross, and then we are to identify with Him in this, which He has done.

All of this is clearly laid out in Romans, Chapter 6. First of all we are baptized into the death of Christ, then buried with Him, and then raised with Him in newness of life (Rom. 6:3-5).

When the Scripture speaks of us being baptized into His death, it is not speaking of Water Baptism, as many believe, but rather our identification with Christ. It means this:

Whenever the believing sinner exhibits Faith in Christ, in the Mind of God, that believing sinner was literally placed into the very Crucifixion, Death, and Resurrection of Christ. He was our Substitute, and our Faith in Him so identifies us with Him, that God looks at us as though what was done was done by us, even though it was done by Christ.

We were then buried with Him, which refers to the old life and all that we once were being buried, which means it is no more, meaning that the old you died (Rom. 6:7-8).

We were then raised with Him *"in newness of life,"* which means that we are now new creations, with old things having passed away, and all things having become new (II Cor. 5:17).

This which we have given is the very heart of Salvation, which pertains to all that we are in Christ. In fact, the very words, *"in Christ,"* portray this great Plan more so than anything else. The Apostle Paul uses *"in Christ,"* or *"in Him,"* or one of its several derivatives, some 170 times in his 14 Epistles. Due to what Christ did at the Cross, all on our behalf, and our Faith and confidence in Him and what He has done, we are literally *"in Christ."* That is the Doctrine of *"Substitution and Identification."*

JEHOVAH-JIREH

Verse 14 reads: *"And Abraham called the name of that place Jehovah-Jireh: as it is said to this day, in the Mount of the LORD it shall be seen."*

As stated, *"Jehovah-Jireh"* means, *"the Lord will provide."* The question may be asked, *"Provide what?"*

He will provide a Saviour, a Redeemer, Who would be, the Lord Jesus Christ, God's only Son, of which both Isaac and the ram were a Type.

While this *"provision"* pertains to everything that the Believer needs, whether it is domestical, physical, or material, it is primarily the spiritual which is addressed here. Man needs a Redeemer, which is his primary need, and that Redeemer is the Lord Jesus Christ.

From all of this, the Jews coined a proverb, which states, *"In the Mount of the Lord it shall be seen,"* which is a prophecy of the manifestation of Christ. It might be said that on this very mountain, the Sacrifice would be offered, which would take away the sin of the world (Isa. 53:5; Jn. 1:29).

Unfortunately, at the present time, this *"provision,"* which incidentally is by far the greatest provision ever known, has been perverted, or one might say *"inverted."* The emphasis at the present time is placed by many on the provision of material things, when the primary cause of this provision pertains to God providing a Saviour from sin. This is what Paul was speaking of when he said:

"For many walk, of whom I have told you often, and now tell you even weeping, that they are the enemies of the Cross of Christ:

"Whose end is destruction, whose god is their belly, and whose glory is in their shame, who mind earthly things" (Phil. 3:18-19).

Paul told us to *"mark those"* who conducted themselves in that fashion, which means to point them out.

The phrase, *"Whose god is their belly,"* points to their own self-will, with the *"earthly things,"* pointing to that which money can buy. Considering this, their *"glory"* is not in the Cross of Christ, but rather in themselves, which is *"their shame."*

These Passages mean that anyone who places other things ahead of the Cross of Christ, or rather looks to other things than the Cross of Christ, they have to be put down as *"enemies of the Cross."* This pertains to those who follow after the psychological way, as well as those who subscribe to the Word of Faith doctrine.

Concerning *"glory,"* Paul also said: *"But God forbid that I should glory, save in the Cross of our Lord Jesus Christ, by Whom the world is crucified unto me, and I unto the world"* (Gal. 6:14).

He also said: *"For Christ sent me not to baptize* (not to place the emphasis on Water Baptism, or anything else for that matter), *but to preach the Gospel: not with wisdom of words, lest the Cross of Christ should be made of none effect"* (I Cor. 1:17).

In truth, and sadly so, the modern Church has all but rejected that which God has provided, which is the Cross of Christ, and has substituted other things to take its place. The modern Church is, for all practical purposes, a Cross-less Church. Consequently, it is *"Christian"* in name only. If we remove the Cross, or ignore the Cross, or fail of belief regarding the Cross, or even shift our faith from the Cross to other things, we have denied that

NOTES

which God has provided, and are substituting other things to take its place. In other words, we blaspheme!

This of which we speak here has been the battleground of the Plan of God from the very beginning. Abel has offered up the lamb as a sacrifice, which God provided, and Cain has offered up something else, and grows very angry because God will not accept it. It hasn't changed from then until now. Religious men keep trying to offer up other things than Christ and Him Crucified, and then when God rejects it, which shows itself up in a lack of victory in their hearts and lives, they seek to kill those who trust in God's Way. It began that way, it continues that way, and will be that way until the Lord comes.

REVELATION

Verse 15 reads: *"And the Angel of the LORD called unto Abraham out of Heaven the second time."*

The first time the Lord spoke to Abraham, at least after they had arrived at the mountain, regarded substitution, as we've already explained. This time, it will be for Revelation, meaning that God will reveal to Abraham what He is going to do for him. However, let the Reader understand that the *"Revelation"* is entirely dependent upon the *"Substitution."* No Substitution, no Revelation! To make it simpler, no Cross, no Revelation!

The modern Church stumbles along with little or no Revelation, or else a borrowed Revelation, simply because it has ignored the Substitution, i.e., *"the Cross."*

All Revelation depends in some way on the Cross of Christ. In fact, anything and everything that God does for us, to us, of us, with us, and in us, is done exclusively by and through Christ and what He did at the Cross. If we deny the Cross in any way, we cut God off, and open ourselves up to deceiving spirits. So, anything and everything that one hears from Preachers who have denied the Cross or ignored the Cross, is not of God, and in fact is made up out of their own minds, or else given to them by angels of light (II Cor. 11:13-15).

FOUNT OF BLESSING

Verse 16 reads: *"And said, By Myself have I sworn, saith the LORD, for because you have done this thing, and have not withheld your son, your only son."*

Taking this statement through to its ultimate conclusion, it in effect is saying exactly what I have just said.

While Isaac wasn't sacrificed, actually in a figure he was, and as well, in a figure raised from the dead (Heb. 11:18-19). This means that although he wasn't Christ, he was a figure of Christ.

But the point of this statement is, the great Blessing that God pronounces upon Abraham and his seed, which in effect includes not only Israel, but also every Believer who has ever lived (Rom. 4:16), comes exclusively by and through the Cross of Christ. In fact, it could not be any clearer.

VICTORY

Verse 17 reads: *"That in blessing I will bless you, and in multiplying I will multiply your seed as the stars of the Heaven, and as the sand which is upon the sea shore; and your seed shall possess the gate of his enemies."*

This Passage tells us three things:

1. First, it is no longer a promise, but a solemn compact ratified by an oath. God said, *"By Myself have I sworn"* (vs. 16).

2. Next, it assures Abraham's seed of ultimate victory. This refers to victory over the world, over the flesh, and over the Devil, which all comes by what Jesus did at the Cross, our Faith in that Finished Work, which gives latitude to the Holy Spirit to exhibit His Power on our behalf.

3. Lastly, it transfers to Abraham's offspring the promise of being the means of blessedness to all mankind, which refers not only to Israel, but as well to the Church, all in Christ.

CERTAIN VICTORY

In the last phrase of this Verse, He didn't say, *"And your seed may possibly possess the gate of his enemies,"* but rather, *"Your seed shall possess the gate of his enemies."*

This pertains to Christ and what He did at the Cross. Paul outlined this by saying:

"Blotting out the handwriting of Ordinances that was against us, which was contrary to us, and took it out of the way, nailing it to His Cross;

"And having spoiled principalities and powers, He made a show of them openly, triumphing over them in it" (Col. 2:14-15).

"Possessing the gate" refers to taking the city, or defeating the enemy. It pertains to certain victory. The idea is this:

If you the Believer go God's Way, which is the way of the Cross, which is perfectly outlined in this Chapter, then you are guaranteed of certain victory over the world, the flesh, and the Devil, as coined by the early Church fathers.

To the contrary, if one's faith, and I speak of Believers, is in anything other than the Cross of Christ, then victory is impossible. The very word *"Believers,"* refers to believing in Jesus Christ and Him Crucified (I Cor. 1:23). Failure to believe in the Cross, which means to put one's faith totally and completely in the Sacrifice of Christ, puts one in the ranks of *"unbelievers."* And no matter how religious the other things may be in which one might place their faith, it is that which God cannot recognize.

REJOICING!

If I remember correctly, it was the winter of 1992. We had gathered for the morning Prayer Meeting, and in the course of the short dissertation I gave from the Scriptures to those assembled, I quoted the verse of an old song, which is as follows:

"I'm rejoicing night and day, since I found this pilgrim way,
"And the Hand of God in all my life I see.
"Oh the reason for my bliss, the reason all is this,
"The Comforter abides with me."

Again if I remember correctly, I only managed to recite the first half of the verse, when the Glory of God fell in the room. I was unable to continue, even as the Spirit of God moved upon me mightily.

A few days ago (December, 2001), while teaching over our daily Radio Program, *"A Study In The Word"*, the Lord brought back to me that morning Prayer Meeting, of nearly ten years ago. He spoke this to my heart:

"I gave you the words of that song nearly ten years ago, and poured out My Spirit upon you as a token of what I was going to do, and today, due to the Revelation of the Cross, you are rejoicing night and day."

That's exactly what I'm doing. Due to this Revelation of the Cross, which is the same as that given to the Apostle Paul, I am literally rejoicing night and day. At the time the Lord gave me that promise, the promise that rejoicing would come, and it would literally flow through me night and day, even as it has, at that time, I did not understand the Message of the Cross as it refers to Sanctification. I understood it as it referred to Salvation, but not at all as it regards Sanctification.

A few months earlier, actually in the Fall of 1991, I had cried to the Lord that He must give me the answer to victory over the world, the flesh, and the Devil. I knew the answer was in the Word of God, but I did not know exactly how to obtain that victory. Sadly and regrettably, most others did not know the answer either, and neither do most others know it presently.

For some five years, beginning in late 1991, I sought the Lord daily, and I do mean daily, and with tears, and then in 1996, He began to give me this Revelation, which has gloriously changed my life. In fact, it has changed the lives of millions of others, and in fact, it is the Cross and the Cross only, which can effect such a change. Now I know what Jesus was talking about when He said, *"You shall know the Truth, and the Truth shall make you free"* (Jn. 8:32). I also know what He was talking about when He said: *"I am come that they might have life, and that they might have it more abundantly"* (Jn. 10:10). I am truly rejoicing night and day, and I want every other Believer to do the same thing.

But alas! I have found to my dismay that there are many enemies of the Cross in the ranks of Christendom.

The Radio Program, which I mentioned a moment ago, is presently being aired in hundreds of towns and cities. It is expanding as well, almost daily. It is devoted exclusively to the teaching and preaching of the Cross. In fact, even though SonLife Radio was raised up by the Lord for many things, its primary purpose is to *"preach the Cross."* And that we are attempting to do, and with all that is within us.

OBEDIENCE

Verse 18 reads: *"And in your seed shall all the nations of the Earth be blessed; because you have obeyed My voice."*

NOTES

Obedience from Abraham, and in every respect, even the most difficult things, was that which the Lord desired.

For the modern Saint we find two things which are absolutely necessary:

1. We are to obey the Word of God in every respect, understanding that it is our guide through life. Truly as the Psalmist said: *"Your Word is a lamp unto my feet, and a light unto my path"* (Ps. 119:105). The first question for anything must be, *"Is it Scriptural?"*

2. On a personal basis, the Lord desires to lead us in all things, and will definitely give us personal guidance and direction, if we will only seek His Face as it regards this of which we speak. Regrettably, many Christians only seek the Lord in times of crisis, and little consult Him, if at all, as it regards the everyday directions of life. But the Lord wants to be involved in every aspect of our lives and living, and unless He is involved in every aspect, He cannot ascertain our obedience.

Everything as it pertains to a Believer, and irrespective as to what it is, has to do with our Faith and our obedience. In fact, Faith and obedience are twins. If there is little faith, there will be little obedience. And of necessity, great Faith demands total obedience.

And once again, even though we are being repetitious, when we speak of *"Faith,"* always and without exception, we are speaking of Faith in Christ and what Christ did for us in His suffering. Those two things are to never be divorced.

Please notice, the *"Blessing"* which was given to Abraham, was all predicated on his obedience. It is no less with us presently.

Incidentally, the Promise that all the nations of the Earth should be blessed in the Promised Seed predicts primarily the Salvation of the Gentiles, as such. This is a proof that the *"mystery"* revealed in the Epistle to the Ephesians, and revealed there for the first time, is not the blessing of the Gentile nations per se, but rather, Christ and the Church (Eph. 3:3-4, 9; 5:32; 6:19).

(19) "SO ABRAHAM RETURNED UNTO HIS YOUNG MEN, AND THEY ROSE UP AND WENT TOGETHER TO BEER-SHEBA; AND ABRAHAM DWELT AT BEER-SHEBA.

(20) "AND IT CAME TO PASS AFTER THESE THINGS, THAT IT WAS TOLD

ABRAHAM, SAYING, BEHOLD, MILCAH, SHE HAS ALSO BORN CHILDREN UNTO YOUR BROTHER NAHOR;

(21) "HUZ HIS FIRSTBORN, AND BUZ HIS BROTHER, AND KEMUEL THE FATHER OF ARAM,

(22) "AND CHESED, AND HAZO, AND PILDASH, AND JIDLAPH, AND BETHUEL.

(23) "AND BETHUEL BEGAT REBEKAH: THESE EIGHT MILCAH DID BEAR TO NAHOR, ABRAHAM'S BROTHER.

(24) "AND HIS CONCUBINE, WHOSE NAME WAS REUMAH, SHE BEAR ALSO TEBAH, AND GAHAM, AND THAHASH, AND MAACHAH."

The synopsis is:

1. The return of Abraham to Beer-sheba with Isaac had to be the happiest journey that Abraham ever took. It was truly a journey of victory.

2. The present brief account of Nahor's descendants is introduced for the sake of showing the descent of Rebekah, who is soon to become Isaac's wife.

3. It should be noted that three of Terah's descendants, Nahor, Ishmael, and Jacob each had 12 sons. The 12 sons of Jacob would form the 12 Tribes of Israel, and would figure greatly in the promised Blessing to Abraham and the world.

THE RETURN TO BEER-SHEBA

Verse 19 reads: *"So Abraham returned unto his young men, and they rose up and went together to Beer-sheba; and Abraham dwelt at Beer-sheba."*

As the leaving of Beer-sheba with Isaac and the others some three days before was, without a doubt, the most horrifying three days' journey that Abraham had ever undertaken, likewise, but in the opposite direction, the three day journey back to Beer-sheba was, without a doubt, the most wonderful journey the Patriarch had ever engaged. He left with Isaac, and he came back with Isaac, and at the same time, he fully obeyed the Lord.

The phrase, *"And Abraham dwelt at Beer-sheba,"* indicates that he probably spent the balance of his life in this place, with the exception, that he may have visited Mamre, near Hebron, from time to time.

Verses 20 through 24 read: *"And it came to pass after these things, that it was told Abraham, saying, Behold, Milcah, she has also born children unto your brother Nahor;*

"Huz, his firstborn, and Buz his brother, and Kemuel the father of Aram,

"And Chesed, and Hazo, and Pildash, and Jidlaph, and Bethuel.

"And Bethuel begat Rebekah: these eight Milcah did bear to Nahor, Abraham's brother.

"And his concubine, whose name was Reumah, she bear also Tebah, and Gaham, and Thahash, and Maachah."

This Chapter concludes with an account of Nahor's family, who settled at Haran (Gen. 12:1-5). None of this would have been given, but for the connection which it had with the Work of God on Earth. From these people mentioned here, both Isaac and Jacob took wives; and preparatory to the account of those events, this genealogy is recorded.

All of this was for the sake of bringing Christ into the world. God must become man, and as Man, He would redeem the human race, and do so by dying on the Cross.

Isaac was a Type of Christ, and had he actually died at this time, the time of the proposed Sacrifice, it would have been with inward peace, and without extraordinary pain. But Christ actually tasted death and all its bitterness. He died surrounded with contempt and insult, treated with indignity and cruelty, and loaded with the weight of our iniquities, while *"It pleased the LORD to bruise Him, and to put Him to grief, and even to make His soul a Sacrifice for sin"* (Isa. 53:10).

Hereby we perceive the love of Christ, in that He gave Himself a Sacrifice for our sins. Behold He dies; yet rises; He lives, ascends, and intercedes for us! And calls to sinners to come to Him, and partake of His Blood-bought Salvation.

Whatsoever is dearest to us upon Earth is our Isaac — happy are we if we can sacrifice it to God. The only way for us to find comfort in any earthly thing is to surrender it in Faith into the Hands of God.

Yet we shall do well to remember that Abraham was not justified by this action regarding Isaac, but by the infinitely more noble obedience of Jesus Christ — his Faith receiving this, relying on this, rejoicing in this, which means that his Salvation was by Faith in Christ and the suffering of Christ. And so is every other soul who has ever made Christ the Lord of their life. It is all by Faith, as it has all been by Faith.

And so the closing Verses of this Twenty-second Chapter, which seem to be insignificant, with the casual reader wondering as to why they were even included, we find are extremely important, and because they ultimately point to Christ. Anything connected with Christ is the single most important thing there is.

"The God of Abraham prays, Who reigns enthroned above;

"Ancient of Everlasting Days, and God of love.

"Jehovah, great I Am, by Earth and Heaven confess;

"I bow and bless the sacred Name, forever blest."

"The God of Abraham prays, at Whose supreme command

"From Earth I rise, and seek the joys at His right Hand.

"I all on Earth forsake, its wisdom, fame, and power;

"And Him my only portion make, my shield and tower."

"He by Himself has sworn, I on His oath depend,

"I shall, on eagles' wings upborne, to Heaven ascend;

"I shall behold His face, I shall His Power adore,

"And sing the wonders of His Grace forevermore."

"The whole triumphant host give thanks to God on high;

"'Hail, Father, Son, and Holy Ghost!' they ever cry.

"Hail, Abraham's God and mine! I join the Heavenly lays;

"All might and majesty are Thine, and endless praise."

CHAPTER 23

(1) "AND SARAH WAS AN HUNDRED AND SEVEN AND TWENTY YEARS OLD:

THESE WERE THE YEARS OF THE LIFE OF SARAH.

(2) "AND SARAH DIED IN KIRJATH-ARBA; THE SAME IS HEBRON IN THE LAND OF CANAAN: AND ABRAHAM CAME TO MOURN FOR SARAH, AND TO WEEP FOR HER.

(3) "AND ABRAHAM STOOD UP FROM BEFORE HIS DEAD, AND SPAKE UNTO THE SONS OF HETH, SAYING,

(4) "I AM A STRANGER AND A SOJOURNER WITH YOU: GIVE ME A POSSESSION OF A BURYINGPLACE WITH YOU, THAT I MAY BURY MY DEAD OUT OF MY SIGHT.

(5) "AND THE CHILDREN OF HETH ANSWERED ABRAHAM, SAYING UNTO HIM,

(6) "HEAR US, MY LORD: YOU ARE A MIGHTY PRINCE AMONG US: IN THE CHOICE OF OUR SEPULCHRES BURY YOUR DEAD; NONE OF US SHALL WITHHOLD FROM YOU HIS SEPULCHRE, BUT THAT YOU MAY BURY YOUR DEAD."

The exegesis is:

1. Sarah is the only woman in the Bible whose age and death and burial are recorded.

2. This is significant, partly, no doubt, because she is the mother of the Hebrew nation, and partly because the promised heir having come, the vessel of the Promise, that is, Sarah, i.e., *"the first Covenant,"* necessarily passes away.

3. Love bent down over her sleeping face, and Faith *"stood up"* from before its dead.

SARAH

Verses 1 and 2 read: *"And Sarah was an hundred and seven and twenty years old: these were the years of the life of Sarah.*

"And Sarah died in Kirjath-arba; the same is Hebron in the land of Canaan: and Abraham came to mourn for Sarah, and to weep for her."

This means that Isaac was 37 years old when his mother Sarah died, and Abraham was 137.

"Arba" is the old name of *"Hebron."* Abraham must have moved here from Beer-sheba temporarily.

Perhaps the phrase, *"in the land of Canaan,"* is given regarding the place of Sarah's death, in order that we might know that she did not die in the country of the Philistines, but rather in the *"Promised Land."* Upon coming into the Promised Land, which took place about 400 years later, Caleb took *"Kirjath-arba"* as his possession (Josh. 15:13-14).

The sadness of Abraham in losing Sarah was, I think, to a greater degree than normal. She had fought this good fight of Faith with him every step of the way. Consequently, in a sense, as he was the *"father of us all"* (Rom. 4:16), Sarah was the *"mother of us all"* (I Pet. 3:6).

FAITH

Verses 3 through 6 read: *"And Abraham stood up from before his dead, and spoke unto the sons of Heth, saying,*

"I am a stranger and a sojourner with you: give me possession of a buryingplace with you, that I may bury my dead out of my sight.

"And the children of Heth answered Abraham, saying unto him,

"Hear us, my lord: you are a mighty prince among us: in the choice of our sepulchres bury your dead; none of us shall withhold from you his sepulchre, but that you may bury your dead."

As we have stated, love weeps for Sarah, but Faith *"stood up from before his dead."*

With Abraham's statement to the sons of Heth, that he was *"a stranger and a sojourner among you,"* was a confession that he sought, as his real inheritance, a better country, even an Heavenly (Heb. 11:13).

The request for a *"burying-place"* for Sarah is the first mention of a grave in Scripture.

The Patriarch's request of the sons of Heth, that he might purchase a gravesite for Sarah was a sign of his right and title to the land of Canaan, of which the sons of Heth would not have understood.

They offered to give him a burying-place without cost, but the Patriarch, for reasons these individuals would never have understood, could not accept their largesse. With perfect courtesy, therefore, though likewise with respectful firmness, he declines their offer.

(7) "AND ABRAHAM STOOD UP, AND BOWED HIMSELF TO THE PEOPLE OF THE LAND, EVEN TO THE CHILDREN OF HETH.

(8) "AND HE COMMUNED WITH THEM, SAYING, IF IT BE YOUR MIND THAT I SHOULD BURY MY DEAD OUT OF MY SIGHT; HEAR ME, AND ENTREAT FOR ME TO EPHRON THE SON OF ZOHAR,

(9) "THAT HE MAY GIVE ME THE CAVE OF MACHPELAH, WHICH HE HAS, WHICH IS IN THE END OF HIS FIELD; FOR AS MUCH MONEY AS IT IS WORTH HE SHALL GIVE IT ME FOR A POSSESSION OF A BURYINGPLACE AMONG YOU.

(10) "AND EPHRON DWELT AMONG THE CHILDREN OF HETH: AND EPHRON THE HITTITE ANSWERED ABRAHAM IN THE AUDIENCE OF THE CHILDREN OF HETH, EVEN OF ALL THAT WENT IN AT THE GATE OF HIS CITY, SAYING,

(11) "NAY, MY LORD, HEAR ME: THE FIELD GIVE I YOU, AND THE CAVE THAT IS THEREIN, I GIVE IT TO YOU; IN THE PRESENCE OF THE SONS OF MY PEOPLE GIVE I IT TO YOU: BURY YOUR DEAD.

(12) "AND ABRAHAM BOWED DOWN HIMSELF BEFORE THE PEOPLE OF THE LAND."

The synopsis is:

1. The sons of Heth offer Abraham the choicest of their sepulchres, but in death as in life the man of Faith would be a pilgrim, and would have no fellowship with the children of darkness, would not be indebted to them even for a grave, and accordingly insisted upon this purchase.

2. They had no idea that Abraham was looking forward to the possession of the whole land; and because he did so look forward, the possession of a grave was by no means a small matter to him.

3. Hebrews, Chapter 11 states, *"These all died, not having received the promise"*; but in dying as in living they found the promises real and satisfying.

ABRAHAM

Verse 7 reads: *"And Abraham stood up, and bowed himself to the people of the land, even the children of Heth."*

The Patriarch feels out these sons of Heth, as to how they felt about him securing a gravesite for Sarah, which was among them. Once he ascertains that they are agreeable, he will now proceed to speak of a specific place. As is obvious, not any place will do. It must be the *"cave of Machpelah."*

THE CAVE OF MACHPELAH

Verses 8 and 9 read: *"And he communed with them, saying, If it be your mind that I should bury my dead out of my sight; hear me, and entreat for me to Ephron the son of Zohar,*

"That he may give me the cave of Machpelah, which he has, which is in the end of his field; for as much money as it is worth he shall give it me for a possession of a buryingplace among you."

In the purchasing of Machpelah for a burying place, Abraham gave expression to his Faith as it regards Resurrection. *"He stood up from before his dead."* Faith cannot long keep death in view; it has a higher object. Resurrection is that which ever fills the vision of Faith, and, in the power thereof, it can rise up from before the dead.

There is much conveyed in this action of Abraham. We want to understand its meaning much more fully, because we are much too prone to be occupied with death and its consequences. Death is the boundary of Satan's power; but where Satan ends, God begins.

Abraham understood this when he rose up and purchased the cave of Machpelah as a sleeping-place for Sarah. This was the expression of Abraham's thought in reference to the future. He knew that in the ages to come God's promise about the land of Canaan would be fulfilled, and he was able to lay the body of Sarah in the tomb *"in sure and certain hope of a glorious Resurrection"* (Mackintosh).

THE HITTITE

Verses 10 through 12 read: *"And Ephron dwelt among the children of Heth: and Ephron the Hittite answered Abraham in the audience of the children of Heth, even of all who went in at the gate of his city, saying,*

"No, my lord, hear me: the field give I to you, and the cave that is therein, I give it to you; in the presence of the sons of my people give I it to you: bury your dead.

"And Abraham bowed down himself before the people of the land."

The sons of Heth knew nothing about Salvation and Resurrection, which means that the thoughts which filled the Patriarch's soul were entirely foreign to them. To them it seemed a small matter where he buried his dead, but it was by no means a small matter to Abraham.

The finest traits and characteristics of Faith are those which are the more incomprehensible to the natural man. The Canaanites had no idea of the expectations which were giving character to Abraham's actions on this occasion. They had no idea that he was looking forward to the possession of the land, while he was merely looking for a spot in which, as a dead man, he might wait for God's time and God's manner.

This is a truly glorious feature in the Divine life. Those *"witnesses"* of whom the Apostle is speaking in Hebrews, Chapter 11 did not merely live by Faith, but even when they arrived at the close of their lives, they proved that the Promises of God were as real and satisfying to their souls as when they first began.

(13) "AND HE SPAKE UNTO EPHRON IN THE AUDIENCE OF THE PEOPLE OF THE LAND, SAYING, BUT IF YOU WILL GIVE IT, I PRAY YOU, HEAR ME: I WILL GIVE YOU MONEY FOR THE FIELD; TAKE IT OF ME, AND I WILL BURY MY DEAD THERE.

(14) "AND EPHRON ANSWERED ABRAHAM, SAYING UNTO HIM,

(15) "MY LORD, HEARKEN UNTO ME: THE LAND IS WORTH FOUR HUNDRED SHEKELS OF SILVER; WHAT IS THAT BETWEEN ME AND YOU? BURY THEREFORE YOUR DEAD.

(16) "AND ABRAHAM HEARKENED UNTO EPHRON; AND ABRAHAM WEIGHED TO EPHRON THE SILVER, WHICH HE HAD NAMED IN THE AUDIENCE OF THE SONS OF HETH, FOUR HUNDRED SHEKELS OF SILVER, CURRENT MONEY WITH THE MERCHANT.

(17) "AND THE FIELD OF EPHRON WHICH WAS IN MACHPELAH, WHICH WAS BEFORE MAMRE, THE FIELD AND THE CAVE WHICH WAS THEREIN, AND ALL THE TREES THAT WERE IN THE FIELD, THAT WERE IN ALL THE BORDERS ROUND ABOUT, WERE MADE SURE.

(18) "UNTO ABRAHAM FOR A POSSESSION IN THE PRESENCE OF THE CHILDREN OF HETH, BEFORE ALL THAT WENT IN AT THE GATE OF HIS CITY.

(19) "AND AFTER THIS, ABRAHAM BURIED SARAH HIS WIFE IN THE CAVE

NOTES

OF THE FIELD OF MACHPELAH BEFORE MAMRE: THE SAME IS HEBRON IN THE LAND OF CANAAN.

(20) "AND THE FIELD, AND THE CAVE THAT IS THEREIN, WERE MADE SURE UNTO ABRAHAM FOR A POSSESSION OF A BURYINGPLACE BY THE SONS OF HETH."

MONEY

Verse 13 reads: *"And he spake unto Ephron in the audience of the people of the land, saying, But if you will give it, I pray you, hear me: I will give you money for the field; take it of me, and I will bury my dead there."*

This is the first time that money is mentioned in the Bible as a medium of exchange.

Why was Abraham so particular about this purchase? Why was he so anxious to make good his claim to the field and cave of Ephron on righteous principles? Why so determined to weigh out the full price *"current with the merchant"*?

"Faith" is the answer. He did it all by Faith. He knew the land was his in prospect, and that in Resurrection-glory his seed should yet possess it, and until then, he would be no debtor to those who were yet to be dispossessed.

THE PURCHASE

Verses 14 through 16 read: *"And Ephron answered Abraham, saying unto him,*

"My lord, hearken unto me: the land is worth four hundred shekels of silver; what is that between me and you? Bury therefore your dead.

"And Abraham hearkened unto Ephron; and Abraham weighed to Ephron the silver, which he had named in the audience of the sons of Heth, four hundred shekels of silver, current money with the merchant."

Abraham was a mighty prince among these people, and they undoubtedly would have been very glad to have done him the favor of giving him the land free of charge; but Abraham had learned to take his favors only from the God of Resurrection, and while he would pay *"them"* for Machpelah, he would look to *"Him"* for the entirety of the land of Canaan, which most certainly one day would be his.

The truth is, looking at things in this light, the cave of Machpelah was worth much more to him than it was to them. Faith conducts the soul onward into God's future; it looks at

NOTES

things as He looks at them, and estimates them according to the judgment of the Sanctuary,

As stated, even though the sons of Heth did not understand these things, Abraham was purchasing this burying-place, which significantly set forth his hope of Resurrection, and an inheritance founded thereon (Mackintosh).

THE POSSESSION

Verses 17 through 20 read: *"And the field of Ephron which was in Machpelah, which was before Mamre, the field, and the cave which was therein, and all the trees that were in the field, that were in all the borders round about, were made sure.*

"Unto Abraham for a possession in the presence of the children of Heth, before all that went in at the gate of his city.

"And after this, Abraham buried Sarah his wife in the cave of the field of Machpelah before Mamre: the same is Hebron in the land of Canaan.

"And the field, and the cave that is therein, were made sure unto Abraham for a possession of a buryingplace by the sons of Heth."

Thus, we may view this beautiful Chapter in a twofold light:

1. As setting before us a plain, practical principle, as to our dealings with the world, that such dealings must always be above board, forthright, and honest.

2. We should do everything with the idea in mind that the blessed hope is ever before us, and should ever animate the man of Faith.

Putting both these points together, we have an example of what the Child of God should ever be. The hope set before us in the Gospel is a glorious immortality; and this, while it lifts the heart above every influence of nature and the world, furnishes a high and holy principle with which to govern all our dealings with those who are without. *"We know that when He shall appear, we shall be like Him, for we shall see Him as He is"* (I Jn. 3:2).

What is the Scriptural affect of this?

"Every man who has this hope in Him purifieth himself, even as He is pure" (I Jn. 3:3) (Mackintosh).

In the cave of Machpelah, his own remains, and those of Isaac, Rebekah, Jacob, and Leah were deposited. Rachel alone of the great Patriarchal family was not buried here.

DISCREPANCY?

Some have claimed that there is a discrepancy in the account given in Genesis, Chapter 23 concerning the cave of Machpelah, and the statement made by Stephen in Acts 7:16. That particular statement says:

"And were carried over into Sychem, and laid in the sepulchre that Abraham bought for a sum of money of the sons of Emmor the father of Sychem."

There is no discrepancy.

The reference here as given by Stephen is to the burial of the 12 Patriarchs, who were Jacob's sons. Jacob was buried in the cave of Machpelah near Hebron where Abraham and Sarah had been buried (Gen. 23:17, 19; 50:13). Joseph was buried in Shechem (Josh. 24:32).

Genesis 33:19 and Joshua 24:32 indicate Jacob did the actual buying of the plot in Shechem; however, Abraham was still alive at the time, and it was undoubtedly purchased in the name of Abraham as the head of the clan, as things were done in those days. So there is no discrepancy in the account given by Moses in Genesis, Chapter 23 and the account given by Stephen in Acts 7:16.

Incidentally, Shechem is about 75 miles north of Hebron where the cave of Machpelah was located.

"Thanks to God for my Redeemer,
thanks for all You did provide!
"Thanks for time now but a memory,
thanks for Jesus by my side!
"Thanks for pleasant, cheerful spring-
time, thanks for summer, winter, fall!
"Thanks for tears by now forgotten,
thanks for peace within my soul!"

"Thanks for prayers that You have an-
swered, thanks for what You did deny!
"Thanks for storms that I have weath-
ered, thanks for all You do supply!
"Thanks for pain, and thanks for plea-
sure, thanks for comfort in despair!
"Thanks for Grace that none can mea-
sure, thanks for love beyond compare!"

"Thanks for roses by the wayside,
thanks for thorns that stems contain!
"Thanks for homes and thanks for fire-
side, thanks for hope, that sweet re-
frain!

"Thanks for joy and thanks for sorrow,
thanks for Heavenly peace with Thee!
"Thanks for hope in the tomorrow,
thanks through all eternity!"

CHAPTER 24

(1) "AND ABRAHAM WAS OLD, AND WELL STRICKEN IN AGE: AND THE LORD HAD BLESSED ABRAHAM IN ALL THINGS.

(2) "AND ABRAHAM SAID UNTO HIS ELDEST SERVANT OF HIS HOUSE, WHO RULED OVER ALL THAT HE HAD, PUT, I PRAY YOU, YOUR HAND UNDER MY THIGH:

(3) "AND I WILL MAKE YOU SWEAR BY THE LORD, THE GOD OF HEAVEN, AND THE GOD OF THE EARTH, THAT YOU SHALL NOT TAKE A WIFE UNTO MY SON OF THE DAUGHTERS OF THE CANAANITES, AMONG WHOM I DWELL:

(4) "BUT YOU SHALL GO UNTO MY COUNTRY, AND TO MY KINDRED, AND TAKE A WIFE UNTO MY SON ISAAC.

(5) "AND THE SERVANT SAID UNTO HIM, PERADVENTURE THE WOMAN WILL NOT BE WILLING TO FOLLOW ME UNTO THIS LAND: MUST I NEEDS BRING YOUR SON AGAIN UNTO THE LAND FROM WHENCE YOU CAME?

(6) "AND ABRAHAM SAID UNTO HIM, BEWARE THAT YOU BRING NOT MY SON THITHER AGAIN.

(7) "THE LORD GOD OF HEAVEN, WHICH TOOK ME FROM MY FATHER'S HOUSE, AND FROM THE LAND OF MY KINDRED, AND WHICH SPAKE UNTO ME, AND WHO SWEAR UNTO ME, SAYING, UNTO YOUR SEED WILL I GIVE THIS LAND; HE SHALL SEND HIS ANGEL BEFORE YOU, AND YOU SHALL TAKE A WIFE UNTO MY SON FROM THENCE.

(8) "AND IF THE WOMAN WILL NOT BE WILLING TO FOLLOW YOU, THEN YOU SHALL BE CLEARED FROM THIS MY OATH: ONLY BRING NOT MY SON THITHER AGAIN.

(9) "AND THE SERVANT PUT HIS HAND UNDER THE THIGH OF ABRAHAM HIS MASTER, AND SWEAR TO HIM CONCERNING THAT MATTER."

The diagram is:

1. Abraham, cherishing the Promises, takes early steps to obtain from the family of Shem a wife for his son.

2. In this Chapter, although veiled before the Day of Pentecost, is an illustration of the mission of the Holy Spirit going forth after the Death and Resurrection of the Son of God, to bring the Church to Christ.

3. Isaac is a Type of Christ. Eliezer is a Type of the Holy Spirit. Rebekah is a Type of the Church.

ABRAHAM

Verse 1 reads: *"And Abraham was old, and well stricken in age: and the LORD had blessed Abraham in all things."*

In fact, the Patriarch was now about 140 years old, and would actually live to the age of 175 (Gen. 25:7). He lived some 35 years after Isaac was married, and lived to see Esau and Jacob nearly grown up.

Chapters 22 through 24 present a startling picture. In Chapter 22, the son is offered up; in Chapter 23, Sarah is laid aside; and in Chapter 24, the servant is sent forth to procure a bride for him who had been, as it were, received from the dead in a figure.

When we turn to the New Testament, we see a remarkable similarity:

1. The rejection and death of Christ.

2. The setting aside of Israel after the flesh.

3. The calling out of the Church to occupy the high position of the bride of the Lamb.

So in this Chapter, we shall see a portrayal of that just mentioned.

Some may ask if we are in fact to view this particular Chapter as a *"type"* of the calling out of the Church by the Holy Spirit. Perhaps, as Mackintosh says, it would be better to look at it as an illustration of that glorious work. He went on to say:

"We cannot suppose that the Spirit of God would occupy an unusually long Chapter with the mere detail of a family compact, were that compact not typical or illustrative of some great truth."

I personally believe that it furnishes us with a beautiful illustration or foreshadowing of the great mystery of the Church. It is important to see that while there is no direct Revelation of this mystery in the Old

Testament, there are, nevertheless, scenes and circumstances which, in a very remarkable manner, shadow it forth, which are portrayed in this Chapter.

ISAAC

Verses 2 through 4 read: *"And Abraham said unto his eldest servant of his house, who ruled over all that he had, Put, I pray you, your hand under my thigh:*

"And I will make you swear by the LORD, the God of Heaven, and the God of the Earth, that you shall not take a wife unto my son of the daughters of the Canaanites, among whom I dwell:

"But you shall go unto my country, and to my kindred, and take a wife unto my son Isaac."

The *"eldest servant"* mentioned here, and who by the way is referred to in that manner throughout the entirety of this Chapter, and done so for a particular reason, if in fact this Chapter is also meant to portray the Holy Spirit seeking a bride for Christ, which is the Church, which I believe it is, then this servant must be none other than Eliezer of Damascus.

The business of the Holy Spirit is not to glorify Himself, even though He is God, but rather to glorify Christ (Jn. 16:13-14).

Before Eliezer went on this all-important journey, he had to swear by the Lord, the God of Heaven, that he would not choose one of the daughters of the Canaanites, as a wife for Isaac. He was instructed to go to Abraham's country, from whence the Patriarch had come, and we speak in this case of Nahor, which was near the city of Haran. It was about a 700 mile journey from Beer-sheba.

The placing of the hand of the servant under the thigh of the Patriarch seems to be an origination of Abraham, inasmuch as nothing similar can elsewhere be found.

The thigh, as the source of posterity, has been regarded as pointing to Abraham's future descendants, and in particular to Christ, the Promised Seed. So the oath was the equivalent to a swearing by Him Who was to come, namely Christ.

Abraham knew that his Calling and purpose in life were to bring about the promised son, which had now been done, through whom the great nation of Israel would come forth, all for the intended purpose of bringing the Son of God into the world. So, not only was Isaac of extreme importance as a person, as would be obvious, but the young lady to whom he would be married would figure prominently in that importance as well. She must not be a daughter of the Canaanites, but rather of his own people.

CANAANITES!

What was the difference between the Canaanite women and those of his own family back in Haran?

There were at least three reasons that Abraham demanded that Eliezer not choose a woman of the Canaanites:

1. It is undoubtedly correct that the Lord moved upon Abraham to do what he did (vs. 7). Abraham's entire family were descendants of Shem, of whom the prophecy declared that the Blessing (Christ) would come (Gen. 9:26).

2. There is a good possibility that the Canaanite races or people were already being infiltrated by fallen angels, bringing forth a race of giants, with the entirety of some tribes totally contaminated in some way. Genesis 6:4 says, *"There were giants in the Earth in those days* (before the flood)*; and also after that* (after the flood), *when the sons of God came in unto the daughters of men, and they bear children to them."* As well, the Canaanites were descendants of Ham who had been cursed (Gen. 9:25).

3. Due to the Revelation given to Abraham by God, the entirety of his family, whomever they might have been, knew God in some fashion, whereas the Canaanites knew Him not at all.

THE COMMAND OF THE LORD

Verses 5 through 7 read: *"And the servant said unto him, Peradventure the woman will not be willing to follow me unto this land: must I needs bring your son again unto the land from where you came?*

"And Abraham said unto him, You beware that you bring not my son thither again.

"The LORD God of Heaven, which took me from my father's house, and from the land of my kindred, and Who spoke unto me, and Who swore unto me, saying, Unto your

seed will I give this land: He shall send His Angel before you, and you shall take a wife unto my son from thence."

Several things are said here:

1. Eliezer, not being the one to whom the Word from the Lord was given concerning this thing, foresees potential problems. But yet he would totally submit to Abraham's Faith, despite these potential difficulties. Blessed is the Pastor who has men like this in his Church, who can recognize Faith.

2. By no means was Isaac to be taken to the particular land where his wife was to be found. The Promised Land was his home, and opportunity for temptation must not be put in his way. His calling is Canaan, even though he, as his father Abraham, will not live to see the Promise brought to pass.

3. According to Verse 7, every indication is the Lord had given Abraham instructions as to what to do.

4. The Lord would send an Angel who would precede Eliezer, and thereby prepare the way.

FAITH

Verses 8 and 9 read: *"And if the woman will not be willing to follow you, then you shall be clear from this my oath: only bring not my son thither again.*

"And the servant put his hand under the thigh of Abraham his master, and swore to him concerning that matter."

Even though Abraham mentions the possibility of the particular woman chosen by the Holy Spirit not being willing to follow, this is said only to placate Eliezer. Abraham knows that the woman chosen by the Lord will, in fact, be willing to follow Eliezer back to the land of Canaan, in order to be the wife of Isaac. But under no circumstances was the idea to be entertained that Isaac himself was to go to Haran, even if the woman demanded she meet him before such a journey be undertaken. The instructions were specific: Isaac was to remain in Canaan, and the woman was to come to Canaan to be with him.

Eliezer realized that such was a tall order, and wondered in his mind if he could get a woman to do such a thing, considering that she had never met Isaac, didn't know what he was like, but yet she would be committing her entire life to this unseen man. But Eliezer had Faith.

Regarding these conditions, Eliezer did as Abraham commanded him, as it regards him putting his hand under the thigh of the Patriarch, and in effect, swearing to an oath.

Far more here was at stake than meets the eye. And I think that Eliezer completely understood what was at stake, at least as much as one could at that particular time. In fact, the entirety of the Plan of God hinged on this being carried out, and being carried out exactly as the Lord had told Abraham that it must be carried out.

(10) "AND THE SERVANT TOOK TEN CAMELS OF THE CAMELS OF HIS MASTER, AND DEPARTED; FOR ALL THE GOODS OF HIS MASTER WERE IN HIS HAND: AND HE AROSE, AND WENT TO MESOPOTAMIA, UNTO THE CITY OF NAHOR.

(11) "AND HE MADE HIS CAMELS TO KNEEL DOWN WITHOUT THE CITY BY A WELL OF WATER AT THE TIME OF THE EVENING, EVEN THE TIME THAT WOMEN GO OUT TO DRAW WATER.

(12) "AND HE SAID, O LORD GOD OF MY MASTER ABRAHAM, I PRAY YOU, SEND ME GOOD SPEED THIS DAY, AND SHOW KINDNESS UNTO MY MASTER ABRAHAM.

(13) "BEHOLD, I STAND HERE BY THE WELL OF WATER; AND THE DAUGHTERS OF THE MEN OF THE CITY COME OUT TO DRAW WATER:

(14) "AND LET IT COME TO PASS, THAT THE DAMSEL TO WHOM I SHALL SAY, LET DOWN YOUR PITCHER, I PRAY YOU, THAT I MAY DRINK; AND SHE SHALL SAY, DRINK, AND I WILL GIVE YOUR CAMELS DRINK ALSO: LET THE SAME BE SHE WHO YOU HAVE APPOINTED FOR YOUR SERVANT ISAAC; AND THEREBY SHALL I KNOW THAT YOU HAVE SHOWED KINDNESS UNTO MY MASTER."

The construction is:

1. Faith is the coin of the realm in this mission, as Faith is always the coin of the realm.

2. *"Ten camels"* portray completeness. The Salvation of our Lord is a complete Salvation.

3. Eliezer is a Type of the Holy Spirit, that is if we use the word *"type"* loosely. All the goods of Abraham being in his hand proclaim

NOTES

the fact that all the goods of our Heavenly Father are in the Hand of the Holy Spirit.

4. Faith never presumes but rather specifies, hence Eliezer seeking the Face of the Lord, as it regarded his mission.

5. When Eliezer came to seek a wife for his master, he did not go to places of amusement, and pray that he might meet one there, but to the well of water, expecting to find one there employed aright.

6. So as not to choose from outward appearance, he would lay down by Faith some specifics, and then ask the Lord to meet those specifics, which the Lord graciously did.

ALL THE GOODS

Verse 10 reads: *"And the servant took ten camels of the camels of his master, and departed; for all the goods of his master were in his hand: and he arose, and went to Mesopotamia, unto the city of Nahor."*

Camels were the largest beasts of burden, at least in that particular area. *"Ten"* in the Bible is the number of completion. So a little bit of everything that Abraham had was placed on those camels. No doubt, Eliezer also had many other servants with him, in order to help him on this long journey.

If we follow the narrative through, believing that this portrays Abraham as a Type of God the Father, and Isaac a Type of Christ, and Eliezer a Type of the Holy Spirit, with Rebekah being a Type of the Church, i.e., *"the bride of Christ,"* then we must come to the conclusion that all that the Father has, actually belongs to Christ, but that it has been placed in the Hands of the Holy Spirit, Who will dispense it as He sees fit. The Reader must remember that Isaac, in a figure, has already been offered up in sacrifice, and resurrected, hence a Type of the exalted Christ, Who has sent the Holy Spirit into the world to seek a bride for the Son of God.

While Eliezer was under strict orders from Abraham, still, He could dispense these goods as He saw fit. But to be sure, the goods would be dispensed only to the right people.

THE CAMELS

Verse 11 reads: *"And he made his camels to kneel down without the city by a well of water at the time of the evening, even the time that women go out to draw water."*

The long journey of some 700 miles, which probably took several weeks, has now been completed. He has arrived at the city of Nahor, which is very near Haran.

Inasmuch as he has now arrived, he will immediately begin his quest for a bride for Isaac.

Where Eliezer would begin his quest, should provide us food for thought. He didn't go to a place of amusement, but rather to a *"well,"* where the women drew water, which needless to say, was a laborious task. In other words, he was looking for a young lady who was industrious, zealous, not afraid of hard work, and who was responsible. He could only find her at such a place as this.

PRAYER

Verses 12 through 14 read: *"And he said, O LORD God of my master Abraham, I pray You, send me good speed this day, and show kindness unto my master Abraham.*

"Behold, I stand here by the well of water; and the daughters of the men of the city come out to draw water:

"And let it come to pass, that the damsel to whom I shall say, Let down your pitcher, I pray you, that I may drink; and she shall say, Drink, and I will give your camels drink also: let the same be she who You have appointed for Your servant Isaac; and thereby shall I know that You have showed kindness unto my master."

Let's look at what is done here:

1. Eliezer is looking to the Lord to lead him and guide him. He does not at all trust his own instincts, or personal wisdom. He needs leading from the Lord, so he will seek the Lord. How much this should be a lesson to all of us as well.

Also, we should understand as Believers that everything that happened to Abraham, and we speak of the spiritual sense, due to the fact that he is the *"father of us all"* (Rom. 4:16), all of these things in some way apply to us.

2. If it is to be noticed, he does not for a moment forget that the mission on which he has embarked is for Abraham.

3. He is specific in his prayer, asking for a certain thing; consequently, it is obvious that he believes that God hears and answers prayer.

4. Camels drink a lot of water; consequently, anyone who would slake their thirst, much less

ten of these animals, would have to draw a lot of water, which within itself is a big task. So he put the following before the Lord:

The young lady to whom he would approach, asking for a drink of water, and she would graciously give it to him, and then as well would offer to give the camels water, this was to be the one *"appointed for Your servant Isaac."*

As is obvious, Eliezer certainly didn't make it easy. Asking that the Lord would impress upon her to water the camels as well, narrowed down the field considerably. What young lady would want to draw that much water, and especially for a stranger?

(15) "AND IT CAME TO PASS, BEFORE HE HAD DONE SPEAKING, THAT, BEHOLD, REBEKAH CAME OUT, WHO WAS BORN TO BETHUEL, SON OF MILCAH, THE WIFE OF NAHOR, ABRAHAM'S BROTHER, WITH HER PITCHER UPON HER SHOULDER.

(16) "AND THE DAMSEL WAS VERY FAIR TO LOOK UPON, A VIRGIN, NEITHER HAD ANY MAN KNOWN HER: AND SHE WENT DOWN TO THE WELL, AND FILLED HER PITCHER, AND CAME UP.

(17) "AND THE SERVANT RAN TO MEET HER, AND SAID, LET ME, I PRAY YOU, DRINK A LITTLE WATER OUT OF YOUR PITCHER.

(18) "AND SHE SAID, DRINK, MY LORD: AND SHE HASTED, AND LET DOWN HER PITCHER UPON HER HAND, AND GAVE HIM DRINK.

(19) "AND WHEN SHE HAD DONE GIVING HIM DRINK, SHE SAID, I WILL DRAW WATER FOR YOUR CAMELS ALSO, UNTIL THEY HAVE DONE DRINKING.

(20) "AND SHE HASTED, AND EMPTIED HER PITCHER INTO THE TROUGH, AND RAN AGAIN UNTO THE WELL TO DRAW WATER, AND DREW FOR ALL HIS CAMELS."

The composition is:

1. We have the first mention here of Rebekah, who will be the wife of Isaac, and who will figure so prominently in the great Plan of God. The Holy Spirit chose wisely, even as He always does.

2. The girl was beautiful, and as well, a virgin. She was that which the Church is to be.

3. She was industrious and responsible, showing again what the Lord expects the Church to be.

REBEKAH

Verse 15 reads: *"And it came to pass, before he had done speaking, that, behold, Rebekah came out, who was born to Bethuel, son of Milcah, the wife of Nahor, Abraham's brother, with her pitcher upon her shoulder."*

Did Rebekah know that when she arose that morning, she was being guided by an Angel, for this is exactly what happened? Maybe the girl had been praying for months that the Lord would give her the right husband. Little did she know and realize how that prayer would be answered, and how important her part and position would be in the great Plan of God — a Plan that pertained to Redemption, and would touch the entirety of the world, and for all time. This was the young lady chosen by the Lord. Incidentally, she was the second cousin of Isaac.

BEAUTIFUL

Verse 16 reads: *"And the damsel was very fair to look upon, a virgin, neither had any man known her: and she went down to the well, and filled her pitcher, and came up."*

The girl was beautiful, and as well, she was a virgin. Also, she was industrious, as is obvious here.

This is a picture of what the Lord expects the Church to be. In His Eyes, the Church is beautiful. As well, the Lord expects the Church to follow Him exclusively, and not depend on self or other people, which He will always look at as *"spiritual adultery"* (Rom. 7:1-4). As well, if in fact Rebekah is a Type of the Church, then it is plain to see that the Lord expects the Church to be industrious, i.e., *"busy in the Work of the Lord."*

Even though this young girl was beautiful, she did not think herself too good to perform this task of drawing water at the well, which was not easy to say the least.

Most of the wells in those days were fed by a spring, with a series of steps that led down to the well; consequently, to walk up those steps carrying one or two goatskins full of water was no easy task.

THE SIGN

Verse 17 reads: *"And the servant ran to meet her, and said, Let me, I pray you, drink a little water of your pitcher."*

Eliezer will now put the first part of his plan into operation. Seeing the girl, but still not knowing who she was, who evidently was the first girl to show up at the well, and apparently came up at the very time he was arriving, he would ask her for a drink of water from her pitcher.

I would say the request was unusual, especially considering that a man was asking such of a woman. She could easily have told him to go draw his own water. But she didn't, responding exactly as he hoped she would.

DRINK

Verse 18 reads: *"And she said, Drink, my lord: and she hasted, and let down her pitcher upon her hand, and gave him drink."*

She not only acquiesced to his request, but she did so gleefully and promptly.

As she gave him to drink, we as members of the Body of Christ are to give the water of life to a hurting, dying world. As she drew from the well, we are to draw from the well, i.e., *"Christ."* Jesus said, *"If any man thirst, let him come unto Me and drink"* (Jn. 7:37).

THE SECOND PART OF THE SIGN

Verse 19 reads: *"And when she had done giving him drink, she said, I will draw water for your camels also, until they have done drinking."*

Without him asking her to do so, she immediately volunteers to draw water for the camels, exactly as he had asked the Lord that the chosen girl would do.

As stated, camels drink a lot of water. So the girl had to make quite a few trips down the stairs to the well, and then bring back those heavy goatskins full of water.

HER CONDUCT

Verse 20 reads: *"And she hasted, and emptied her pitcher into the trough, and ran again unto the well to draw water, and drew for all his camels."*

Eliezer had servants who might have spared Rebekah her labor; but he interfered not, that he might observe her conduct, and await the answer to his prayer.

Her conduct, in itself, so amiable, and so exactly in unison with his wishes, struck him with a kind of amazement, accompanied with a momentary hesitation, whether all could be true.

Recovering from his astonishment, and being satisfied that the Lord had indeed heard his prayer, as we shall see, he now will present her with gifts, which must have been a surprise to her.

(21) "AND THE MAN WONDERING AT HER HELD HIS PEACE, TO WIT WHETHER THE LORD HAD MADE HIS JOURNEY PROSPEROUS OR NOT.

(22) "AND IT CAME TO PASS, AS THE CAMELS HAD DONE DRINKING, THAT THE MAN TOOK A GOLDEN EARRING OF HALF A SHEKEL WEIGHT, AND TWO BRACELETS FOR HER HANDS OF TEN SHEKELS WEIGHT OF GOLD;

(23) "AND SAID, WHOSE DAUGHTER ARE YOU? TELL ME, I PRAY YOU: IS THERE ROOM IN YOUR FATHER'S HOUSE FOR US TO LODGE IN?

(24) "AND SHE SAID UNTO HIM, I AM THE DAUGHTER OF BETHUEL THE SON OF MILCAH, WHICH SHE BEAR UNTO NAHOR."

The overview is:

1. The Lord answers prayer.

2. The gifts given here are Types of *"Gifts of the Spirit."*

3. Everything to be observed here was put together by the Holy Spirit. He's still doing the same thing presently, at least for those who will believe, but if it is to be noticed, He always uses human instrumentation. This demands total consecration on the part of the individuals being used.

THE LORD

Verse 21 reads: *"And the man wondering at her held his peace, to wit whether the LORD had made his journey prosperous or not."*

"Wondering at her," means that he *"eagerly or carefully watched her."*

Eliezer keenly observed all that Rebekah said and did, and then carefully came to the conclusion that this beautiful and kind maiden was the destined bride of the son of his master. The Lord had answered his prayer.

NOTES

It should be noticed here as to the degree that Eliezer sought the Lord, looked to the Lord, and depended on the Lord. I cannot overemphasize the fact that this should be a great lesson to us as Believers. Presently, due to what Christ has done at the Cross, the Holy Spirit gives us this help constantly, or at least He desires to do so, whereas such help afforded in Abraham's day, was sporadic at best. Presently, the Holy Spirit abides permanently (Jn. 14:16-17).

Modern Christians are constantly proclaiming that they wish that the Lord would give them the type of help that He gave Eliezer. The truth is, He will do even more, and because He now has greater latitude, due to the Cross. The problem is not with the Holy Spirit, as the problem is never with the Holy Spirit. The problem is us! Most Christians have very little prayer life, whereas it is obvious that Eliezer had a very personal relationship with the Lord. He had allowed Abraham's Faith to become his Faith. Likewise, Abraham's consecration was also his consecration.

The modern Believer can get as close to the Lord as he so desires. It's never up to the Lord; He is always ready. The slackness is always on our part.

THE CROSS

As I dictate these notes, I have been living for the Lord only about 15 months short of 60 years. I've learned a few things during that period of time. But this I can say, I think, without reservation:

Since the Lord in 1996 began to open up to me the Message of the Cross, in effect, what the Cross actually means, which is actually the meaning of the New Covenant, I think I've learned more in this last five years, than all the rest of my time put together, as it refers to living for God. I have found out that the Cross is the Foundation of all Doctrine. In other words, every single Doctrine in the Word of God must stem from the Cross, which has made it all possible in the first place, or else it will be perverted in some manner. It should be obvious, if the foundation of anything isn't right, then what's built on that foundation cannot be right as well. But if the foundation is correct, irrespective of what is built on the foundation, even if it's wrong, it can be corrected. So it's absolutely imperative that each and every Believer understands the Cross, even as the Word of God sets it forth. In fact, the story of the Bible is the Cross of Christ, even as the Cross of Christ is the story of the Bible.

UNDERSTANDING THE CROSS?

Regrettably, most Believers automatically think they understand all about the Cross. I remember a letter someone sent to me a short time back. It was cryptic and to the point. The man said, *"Why do you keep talking about the Cross? We already understand all about the Cross."* The truth is, this man didn't understand anything about the Cross; unfortunately, most of Christendom falls into the same category.

Many modern Christians dismiss the Cross out of hand, and if they think of it at all, do so only in a sentimental way. Others place value on the Cross as it regards their initial Salvation experience, but it stops there. Precious few Christians understand the Cross as it regards their Sanctification experience, and that can cause the Believer untold problems. Please note the following:

Chapters 1 through 3 of Romans proclaim to us the fact that all men are lost, consequently, desperately needing a Redeemer.

Chapters 4 and 5 proclaim the solution to man's lost condition, which is Jesus Christ and Justification by Faith.

Chapters 6 through 8 explain the Sanctification process of the Holy Spirit as it regards the Child of God. If you'll notice, in Chapter 6, as it regards this process, the Apostle Paul takes the Believer directly to the Cross (Rom. 6:3-5). In effect, the Apostle in this Chapter is explaining the sin nature, which we must understand if we are to understand Sanctification.

In a very abbreviated way, I will attempt to proclaim what the Holy Spirit is telling us through the Apostle Paul regarding this all important aspect of the Believer's life.

As stated, Paul takes us to the Cross, telling us that we as Believers, when we were saved, were *"baptized into His death."* We were then *"buried with Him by baptism into death,"* and as well, raised with Him *"in newness of life"* (Rom. 6:3-4).

NOTES

That is our *"in Christ"* experience. This means that Christ was our Substitute, and all that He did for us at the Cross now becomes ours, upon our simple Faith evidenced in Him. We are, at least in the mind of God, Whose mind Alone actually matters, placed into Christ by our Faith. But please remember, it must be Faith in Christ and what Christ has done for us at the Cross.

Now please remember that Paul is speaking here to Believers, in other words, people who have already been saved, some of them for many, many years. But still, he takes these Believers, plus you and me, to the Cross.

He tells us that when we evidenced Faith in Christ, and I continue to speak of the moment we were saved, at that particular time, we *"died with Christ"* (Rom. 6:7-8). This means that we died to the sin nature. While the sin nature didn't die, we died to it, and the way we stay dead, and this is very important, is to continue our Faith in the Cross, and not allow it to be moved to anything else.

Continuing to anchor our Faith in Christ and His Cross gives the Holy Spirit latitude within our hearts and lives, to work as He Alone can work. In fact, the Holy Spirit, Whom we must have, works entirely within the parameters of the Finished Work of Christ. That's what gives Him the legal means to work with us and in us (Rom. 8:1-2, 11).

WALKING AFTER THE SPIRIT

Paul said: *"There is therefore now no condemnation to them which are in Christ Jesus, who walk not after the flesh, but after the Spirit"* (Rom. 8:1).

Sanctification is *"walking after the Spirit."*

But how does one walk after the Spirit?

We'll give the answer.

Walking after the Spirit is simply placing our Faith totally and completely in Christ, and what Christ has done for us at the Cross. Paul also said: *"For the Law* (a Law devised by the Godhead) *of the Spirit* (Holy Spirit) *of life* (the Holy Spirit guarantees this life to all Believers) *in Christ Jesus* (this Law of the Spirit of life is based on what Jesus did at the Cross, and that entirely) *has made me free from the law of sin and death"* (Rom. 8:2).

In other words, if our Faith is properly placed in the Cross, giving the Holy Spirit latitude to work within our lives, this will give us total victory over the law of sin and death, i.e., *"the sin nature."*

If the Believer has his Faith properly placed in the Cross, ever making that the object of his Faith, he need never worry about the sin nature. He is dead to that particular factor. But if the Believer attempts to live for God by means other than constant Faith in the Cross, the Believer will see the sin nature once again beginning to dominate him, exactly as it did before he was saved, which is a miserable existence for any person to undergo. And regrettably, that's where most modern Christians actually are. They know little about the Cross, if anything, and, therefore, try to live for God by other means.

Chapters 9 through 11 of Romans proclaim to us certain events, mostly the cause of Israel's Fall, and the occasion of their rise, which is just ahead of us.

Chapters 12 through 16 give us the aspects of practical Christianity, in other words, how it ought to be lived, after we understand the Cross. Unfortunately, many Christians try to jump automatically to Chapter 12, without understanding Chapters 6 through 8. Such is not to be!

GIFTS

Verse 22 reads: *"And it came to pass, as the camels had done drinking, that the man took a golden earring of half a shekel weight, and two bracelets for her hands of ten shekels weight of gold."*

The *"golden earring of half a shekel weight"* would be worth presently about $300. And incidentally, it was a nose-ring instead of an earring.

Whether the two bracelets weighed *"ten shekels"* each, or both weighed *"ten shekels,"* we aren't told. At any rate, *"ten shekels weight of gold,"* would be worth, in today's money, about $4,000.

In the spiritual sense, these gifts which came from Eliezer are Types of Gifts of the Spirit, and in fact, all good things which the Lord does for us. The fact that these were items of *"gold,"* proclaims the fact that they are all of God.

I suspect that Rebekah was somewhat taken aback, when she was given these very expensive gifts.

Whenever the believing sinner comes to Christ, the Holy Spirit immediately begins to give good, beautiful, and wonderful things to us, which in fact, never ends all the days of our lives. To be sure, what He gives us is of far greater value than the symbolism of gold suggested here. While He takes care of us financially and materially as well, His greater blessings are in the spiritual sense. And the mature Christian soon finds that out.

As well, the gifts presented to Rebekah by Eliezer were in no way meant to pay her for the work she had done. In fact, Eliezer could have asked someone to water his camels for a small fraction of what he gave Rebekah. No! These were gifts, and because Eliezer suspected that this was the one whom God had chosen. He was right!

We soon learn in living for God that we really cannot earn anything from Him. In fact, the Lord has nothing for sale. If He did, we certainly would never be able to afford such wonders. His gifts are free and freely given. As well, they are lavishly given, and because He is rich in the things we desperately need.

Oh how I sense His Presence, even as I attempt to elaborate on this gesture of Eliezer which took place so long, long ago. How much the Lord wants to give us good things! How much He longs to lavish His largesse on us! And then again, how so very valuable are His gifts. And they just keep on coming. It is like we are admitted into a treasure house. We go into one room, which is filled with all type of riches. But then we see a door, which leads to another room with even more riches, and it seems like the rooms never end, and the riches just keep getting greater and greater.

Rebekah now only has these token gifts. She will soon be wed to Isaac, which means that all he has, and to be sure that is bountiful, will then become hers in totality.

When we come into Christ, we become *"heirs of God, and joint-heirs with Christ"* (Rom. 8:17).

QUESTIONS

Verse 23 reads: *"And said, Whose daughter are you? Tell me, I pray: is there room in your father's house for us to lodge in?"*

Two questions are asked here:

1. *"Whose daughter are you?"* Considering that the signs requested of the Lord by Eliezer have now been granted, he must know who the young lady actually is. The question will gender a positive response, even as we shall see, and at the same time, as it follows the *"type,"* is meant to point to identification with Christ. Rebekah will soon belong to Isaac, who is a Type of Christ, even as the believing sinner is soon to belong to Christ.

2. *"Is there room in your father's house for us to lodge in?"*, presents the question that the Holy Spirit asks of every believing sinner. We must make room for Christ. In fact, the Holy Spirit is constantly asking untold millions around the world, *"Is there room for Me?"*

IDENTIFICATION

Verse 24 reads: *"And she said unto him, I am the daughter of Bethuel the son of Milcah, which she bear unto Nahor."*

Rebekah mentions her father's mother to show that she was descended from a highborn wife, and not from a concubine. But Eliezer would welcome the information as proving that not only on the father's side, but also on the mother's, she was Isaac's cousin, Milcah being the daughter of Haran, Abraham's brother.

This is probably the time that he gave her the jewels which he was holding in his hand.

(25) "SHE SAID MOREOVER UNTO HIM, WE HAVE BOTH STRAW AND PROVENDER ENOUGH, AND ROOM TO LODGE IN.

(26) "AND THE MAN BOWED DOWN HIS HEAD, AND WORSHIPPED THE LORD.

(27) "AND HE SAID, BLESSED BE THE LORD GOD OF MY MASTER ABRAHAM, WHO HAS NOT LEFT DESTITUTE MY MASTER OF HIS MERCY AND HIS TRUTH: I BEING IN THE WAY, THE LORD LED ME TO THE HOUSE OF MY MASTER'S BRETHREN.

(28) "AND THE DAMSEL RAN, AND TOLD THEM OF HER MOTHER'S HOUSE THESE THINGS.

(29) "AND REBEKAH HAD A BROTHER, AND HIS NAME WAS LABAN: AND LABAN RAN OUT UNTO THE MAN, UNTO THE WELL.

(30) "AND IT CAME TO PASS, WHEN HE SAW THE EARRING AND THE BRACELETS UPON HIS SISTER'S HANDS, AND

WHEN HE HEARD THE WORDS OF REBEKAH HIS SISTER, SAYING, THUS SPOKE THE MAN UNTO ME; THAT HE CAME UNTO THE MAN; AND, BEHOLD, HE STOOD BY THE CAMELS AT THE WELL.

(31) "AND HE SAID, COME IN, YOU BLESSED OF THE LORD; WHEREFORE STAND YOU WITHOUT? FOR I HAVE PREPARED THE HOUSE, AND ROOM FOR THE CAMELS.

(32) "AND THE MAN CAME INTO THE HOUSE: AND HE UNGIRDED HIS CAMELS, AND GAVE STRAW AND PROVENDER FOR THE CAMELS, AND WATER TO WASH HIS FEET, AND THE MEN'S FEET THAT WERE WITH HIM.

(33) "AND THERE WAS SET MEAT BEFORE HIM TO EAT: BUT HE SAID, I WILL NOT EAT, UNTIL I HAVE TOLD MY ERRAND. AND HE SAID, SPEAK ON."

The exegesis is:

1. Rebekah said, *"There is room."* The Holy Spirit awaits the same answer from us.

2. Eliezer now thanks the Lord for His Leading and Guidance. We must be very careful to thank Him as well!

3. Laban, Rebekah's brother, assured Eliezer that there was room in their house, not only for him and his servants, but as well *"for the camels."*

4. The Holy Spirit emphasizes the fact that the camels were attended to as well, and despite the fact of their needs, which required much food, etc. The camels carried all the grand and glorious gifts, which had come from Isaac. Spiritually speaking, we as well presently, must make room for the camels.

There are some things about the Holy Spirit which the world doesn't understand. These things not understood, and which at times might seem crude to the world, are necessary, of which the *"camels"* are a type. If we want the gifts, we must make room for the camels.

ROOM TO LODGE IN

Verse 25 reads: *"She said moreover unto him, We have both straw and provender enough, and room to lodge in."*

Her answer was in the positive, exactly that for which Eliezer had hoped. In essence she was saying that they would give Eliezer and those with him everything that they had, regarding hospitality, and as well, would make room for them as it regarded their lodging.

Little did she know or understand the words she was saying, how important they were, how significant they were. Little did she realize to where this invitation would lead, that individuals would be talking about her thousands of years into the future, and because of her saying *"yes"* to the Lord Jesus Christ, for that's actually what she was doing.

When the great invitation comes to us, and in whatever capacity, may our answer be as open and as broad as that of Rebekah.

WORSHIP

Verse 26 reads: *"And the man bowed down his head, and worshipped the LORD."*

It is obvious that Eliezer had a close walk with the Lord. It is obvious that the Faith of Abraham was his Faith as well! It is obvious that he was accustomed to being led by the Lord. His demeanor, his attitude, his response, all point to total consecration.

Abraham had entrusted to his hand the future of the entirety of the Plan of God. What a responsibility he had, and how so much with dignity, responsibility, and forthrightness did he carry out this which he was assigned to do. May we do as well!

In the Hebrew language, the word *"bowed down"* expresses reverent inclination of the head. The second verb *"worshipped,"* proclaims a complete prostration of the body, which means that Eliezer fell prostrate on the ground worshipping the Lord, in thankfulness to Him for the guidance and the leading which had been given at this time.

A PRAYER OF THANKSGIVING

Verse 27 reads: *"And he said, Blessed be the LORD God of my master Abraham, who has not left destitute my master of his mercy and his truth: I being in the way, the LORD led me to the house of my master's brethren."*

This prayer of Eliezer proclaims the fact that this man knew and understood the Grace of God, which he exclaims by mentioning the Mercy of the Lord, and as well, *"His Truth."* Mercy being a product of Grace proclaims the fact that Eliezer understood this great Doctrine. And to be sure, if Grace is properly

understood, *"truth"* as well will be properly understood.

The short phrase, *"I being in the way,"* refers to him being in the way of Mercy and Truth, which is the place that every Believer ought to be, and in fact can be.

As well, if Grace and Truth are properly understood and entertained, there will at the same time be leading and guidance by the Lord, which refers to a place of deep consecration.

THE WITNESS

Verses 28 and 29 read: *"And the damsel ran, and told them of her mother's house these things.*

"And Rebekah had a brother, and his name was Laban: and Laban ran out unto the man, unto the well."

How far Rebekah lived from the well, we aren't told; however, it must have been only a short distance, possible several hundreds of yards.

The indication is that first of all, she went and told her family what had just transpired. Even though this is the logical narration of the story, still, it is that which every Believer should do. We should witness first of all to our family, and then to all others as well. A story so wonderful, so grand, so glorious, begs to be told. And to be sure, the Gospel Message is the grandest story ever told. How right was the songwriter:

"What a wonderful light in my life has been shone,
"Since Jesus came into my heart!"

OBSERVATION

Verse 30 reads: *"And it came to pass, when he saw the earring and bracelets upon his sister's hands, and when he heard the words of Rebekah his sister, saying, Thus spake the man unto me; that he came unto the man; and, behold, he stood by the camels at the well."*

Every true Christian has gifts given to him by the Lord, which should be an obvious sign to the world. The Bible said that Laban *"saw"* and *"heard."* He saw the gifts, and he heard the words which his sister said.

As it regards our lives, the world should *"see"* what the Lord has done for us, and then they will *"hear"* what we have to say concerning that tremendous miracle which has transpired.

Laban then went to Eliezer.

PREPARATION

Verses 31 and 32 read: *"And he said, Come in, thou blessed of the LORD; wherefore stand you without? For I have prepared the house, and room for the camels.*

"And the man came into the house: and he ungirded his camels, and gave straw and provender for the camels, and water to wash his feet, and the men's feet who were with him."

Laban was an idolater (Gen. 31:30); however, by him referring to Eliezer as *"blessed of the LORD,"* we know that he had some knowledge of the Lord. In fact, the original Revelation given by God to Abraham had no doubt instituted the worship of Jehovah in the household. But yet, they were still clinging to their idols, which regrettably, is indicative of many modern Christians.

Many presently serve God, but at the same time, the things of the world prove to be an allurement. In fact, Israel had the same problem, hence the Prophet Samuel saying to them, *"Prepare your hearts unto the LORD, and serve Him only"* (I Sam. 7:3).

The idea was, they were serving the Lord and Baal at the same time. Regrettably, that problem didn't die with Israel.

THE MESSAGE

Verse 33 reads: *"And there was set meat before him to eat: but he said, I will not eat, until I have told my errand. And he said, Speak on."*

We are witnessing here a perfect example of proper responsibility. That which was uppermost on his mind was not his own wants and needs, but rather the very purpose for which he came, which was to relay the message that Abraham had given him to relay.

All of this has to do with the protocol of that day, which was rigidly observed at that particular time.

Continuing to stand on protocol, Eliezer will request that he be given permission to speak, even before the hospitality of food is enjoyed. And if Laban had not conceded, he would not have entered his house. But Laban did concede.

Incidentally, we will hear more of Laban, and I speak of the time of Jacob. He was a man of greed, and through greed he lost Jacob. As well, and as we shall see, it seems to be greed that forces his attention at this present time with his sister Rebekah, and with Eliezer.

(34) "AND HE SAID, I AM ABRAHAM'S SERVANT.

(35) "AND THE LORD HAS BLESSED MY MASTER GREATLY; AND HE HAS BECOME GREAT: AND HE HAS GIVEN HIM FLOCKS, AND HERDS, AND SILVER, AND GOLD, AND MENSERVANTS, AND MAIDSERVANTS, AND CAMELS, AND ASSES.

(36) "AND SARAH MY MASTER'S WIFE BEAR A SON TO MY MASTER WHEN SHE WAS OLD: AND UNTO HIM HAS HE GIVEN ALL THAT HE HAS.

(37) "AND MY MASTER MADE ME SWEAR, SAYING, YOU SHALL NOT TAKE A WIFE TO MY SON OF THE DAUGHTERS OF THE CANAANITES, IN WHOSE LAND I DWELL:

(38) "BUT YOU SHALL GO UNTO MY FATHER'S HOUSE, AND TO MY KINDRED, AND TAKE A WIFE UNTO MY SON.

(39) "AND I SAID UNTO MY MASTER, PERADVENTURE THE WOMAN WILL NOT FOLLOW ME.

(40) "AND HE SAID UNTO ME, THE LORD, BEFORE WHOM I WALK, WILL SEND HIS ANGEL WITH YOU, AND PROSPER YOUR WAY; AND YOU SHALL TAKE A WIFE FOR MY SON OF MY KINDRED, AND OF MY FATHER'S HOUSE:

(41) "THEN SHALL YOU BE CLEAR FROM THIS MY OATH, WHEN YOU COME TO MY KINDRED; AND IF THEY GIVE NOT YOU ONE, YOU SHALL BE CLEAR FROM MY OATH."

The synopsis is:

1. The reason for this journey is faithfully told by Eliezer. He is careful to say exactly what Abraham had said. We as well should be very careful that we faithfully deliver the Word of the Lord, and not err in that delivery.

2. This matter is so serious that Eliezer is sworn to obedience. Is it any less presently with the Gospel?

3. Inasmuch as Abraham is the *"father of us all"* (Rom. 4:16), then everything that

happened to this man presents itself as a lesson for us, and is meant to do so.

THE BLESSING

Verses 34 and 35 read: *"And he said, I am Abraham's servant.*

"And the LORD has blessed my master greatly; and he is become great: and He has given him flocks, and herds, and silver, and gold, and menservants, and maidservants, and camels, and asses."

1. Eliezer identifies himself, but does so by promoting Abraham, which the Holy Spirit always does, as it regards God the Father and God the Son. In fact, it is said of the Spirit: *"Howbeit when He, the Spirit of Truth, is come, He will guide you into all Truth: for He shall not speak of Himself; but whatsoever He shall hear, that shall He speak: and He will show you things to come.*

"He shall glorify Me: for He shall receive of Mine, and shall show it unto you" (Jn. 16:13-14).

This is exactly what Eliezer is now doing!

2. He gives praise and glory to the Lord for all the good things which have happened. He credits the Lord with blessing Abraham with material things, which Laban would have readily understood.

Let the Reader know and understand that the Lord will do the same thing presently, as He did then. He is no respecter of persons, and what He has previously done, He definitely will continue to do.

So every Believer ought to believe the Lord for the Blessings of God regarding all things, as well as financial and material things. Our problem is, *"We have not because we ask not."* And then far too often, *"We ask, and receive not, because we ask amiss, that we may consume it upon our lusts"* (James 4:2-3).

However, if we genuinely desire to bless the Work of the Lord, should the Lord place material things into our hand, to be sure, the Lord will definitely bless. In fact, He desires to bless! He wants to bless! If we will ardently seek His Face, consecrate ourselves fully to Him, look to the Cross for all things, understanding that it was there that the price was paid, to be sure, God will bless us spiritually, physically, domestically, and financially.

NOTES

I can sense the presence of the Lord even as I dictate these words. And I believe that you the Reader can sense the Lord as well. He loves you! He wants to bless you! And He will do so in all things, because He has all things. God is good, and as the song says, *"He's not good just some of the time, but God is good all of the time."*

ISAAC WAS GIVEN ALL

Verse 36 reads: *"And Sarah my master's wife bear a son to my master when she was old: and unto him has he given all that he has."*

In this short sentence, so much is said.

Isaac was the miracle child, born to Sarah when she was 90 years old, and Abraham was 100. This proclaims the miracle-working power of Almighty God.

Even though Eliezer did not mention this here, this *"son"* was to be the seed who would bring the *"Seed of the Woman"* into the world, which had been predicted immediately after the Fall in the Garden of Eden (Gen. 3:15).

Isaac is now a grown man, and Abraham has given to him all of his riches, which means that he was a very wealthy man.

Laban would have been little impressed by the great spiritual riches which in fact had made all the other things possible, so they were not mentioned. But he was greatly impressed by the material riches, so this is what Eliezer addressed. And as a point of information, this is what he should have addressed, because Laban could little have understood spiritual things.

Likewise, the Heavenly Father has given all things unto the *"Son."* And the Son has given all things to us, exactly as everything that belonged to Isaac would be given to Rebekah, who was a Type of the Church.

Some would claim that she was a Type of Israel, in fact being the mother of Israel so to speak. While the latter is true, we must go to Romans 4:16, where the Holy Spirit through Paul proclaims the fact that Abraham is the *"father of us all,"* and He is speaking of Israel and the Church. So I think the ground referring typology is safe regarding my conclusions respecting the symbolism.

A WIFE

Verse 37 reads: *"And my master made me swear, saying, You shall not take a wife to my son of the daughters of the Canaanites, in whose land I dwell."*

As everything was to be a certain way regarding Isaac, likewise, it is the same for the Christian presently. The Lord has a Will for all things, and it's our business to find what that Will is, and then wholeheartedly obey that Will.

THE ANGEL

Verses 38 through 40 read: *"But you shall go unto my father's house, and to my kindred, and take a wife unto my son.*

"And I said unto my master, Peradventure the woman will not follow me.

"And he said unto me, The LORD, before Whom I walk, will send His Angel with you, and prosper your way; and you shall take a wife for my son of my kindred, and of my father's house."

As we have stated, the Lord had already informed Abraham that He would prepare the way before Eliezer, even by sending an Angel to protect him, and to prepare for his arrival. It is obvious that this is exactly what was done.

THE OATH

Verse 41 reads: *"Then shall you be clear from this my oath, when you come to my kindred; and if they give not you one, you shall be clear from my oath."*

The Lord, as is obvious, had so engrained into Abraham the necessity of what was to be done, that he is fearful lest it not be carried out exactly as the Lord wanted. He even made his trusted servant, Eliezer, take an oath that he would strictly follow all directions.

The reason Abraham was adamant in this is because it was the Word of the Lord. Even though they didn't have a Bible in those days, the first Books yet to be written by Moses some 400 years later; still, what the Lord told the Patriarch was very exact, and in fact, would be written by Moses at the later time mentioned.

We should be so zealous presently to follow the Word of the Lord exactly as it is given. The first question that should be asked about anything and everything is, *"Is it Scriptural?"*

(42) "AND I CAME THIS DAY UNTO THE WELL, AND SAID, O LORD GOD OF

MY MASTER ABRAHAM, IF NOW YOU DO PROSPER MY WAY WHICH I GO:

(43) "BEHOLD, I STAND BY THE WELL OF WATER; AND IT SHALL COME TO PASS, THAT WHEN THE VIRGIN COMES FORTH TO DRAW WATER, AND I SAY TO HER, GIVE ME, I PRAY YOU, A LITTLE WATER OF YOUR PITCHER TO DRINK:

(44) "AND SHE SAY TO ME, BOTH OF YOU DRINK, AND I WILL ALSO DRAW FOR YOUR CAMELS: LET THE SAME BE THE WOMAN WHOM THE LORD HAS APPOINTED OUT FOR MY MASTER'S SON.

(45) "AND BEFORE I HAD DONE SPEAKING IN MY HEART, BEHOLD, REBEKAH CAME FORTH WITH HER PITCHER ON HER SHOULDER; AND SHE WENT DOWN UNTO THE WELL, AND DREW WATER: AND I SAID UNTO HER, LET ME DRINK, I PRAY YOU.

(46) "AND SHE MADE HASTE, AND LET DOWN HER PITCHER FROM HER SHOULDER, AND SAID, DRINK, AND I WILL GIVE YOUR CAMELS DRINK ALSO: SO I DRANK AND SHE MADE THE CAMELS DRINK ALSO.

(47) "AND I ASKED HER, AND SAID, WHOSE DAUGHTER ARE YOU? AND SHE SAID, THE DAUGHTER OF BETHUEL, NAHOR'S SON, WHOM MILCAH BEAR UNTO HIM: AND I PUT THE EARRING UPON HER FACE, AND THE BRACELETS UPON HER HANDS."

The diagram is:

1. In Verses 42 through 44, Eliezer repeats his prayer from memory, but inexactly. Who could have written the actual prayer and Eliezer's imperfect remembrance of it but the Holy Spirit? This is a remarkable illustration of inspiration.

2. It is abundantly evident here that the Lord has a particular way that He wants things done. It's our business to find what that Way actually is, and then to follow minutely and distinctly.

3. The Lord Who is able to plan for us is also able to bring that Plan to pass. It is our business to trust Him.

PROSPERITY

Verse 42 reads: *"And I came this day unto the well, and said, O LORD God of my master*

Abraham, if now You do prosper my way which I go."

The prosperity of which Eliezer speaks refers to the petition he will lay before the Lord, and he prays that God will answer his prayer.

THE PETITION

Verses 43 and 44 read: *"Behold, I stand by the well of water; and it shall come to pass, that when the virgin comes forth to draw water, and I say to her, Give me, I pray you, a little water of your pitcher to drink;*

"And she say to me, Both of you drink, and I will also draw for the camels: let the same be the woman whom the LORD has appointed out for my master's son."

Eliezer has reasoned that he will stand by the well, inasmuch as women come during the day to draw water. As men generally did not perform this task, he felt this would be the best place to begin.

However, as it concerned this girl, she first of all had to be a virgin, and second, she had to be a part of Abraham's family. He could not tell by looking at her as it regarded these things. So his petition was this:

He would ask her for a drink of water, and if she willingly gave him the water, and at the same time also offered to draw water for his camels, this would be the woman.

Considering that he had men with him who could easily have drawn the water, and as well, that this was a very hard task, it would have to be the Lord for this young lady to offer her kindness in this regard. But that was the petition he put before the Lord, which anyone would have to agree, if it was met, it would have to be the Lord. No young lady out of the blue, so to speak, would volunteer to make many trips down the stairs to the well, thereby carrying the heavy load back in order to water the camels.

THE ANSWER

Verses 45 and 46 read: *"And before I had done speaking in my heart, behold, Rebekah came forth with her pitcher on her shoulder, and she went down unto the well, and drew water: and I said unto her, Let me drink, I pray you.*

"And she made haste, and let down her pitcher from her shoulder, and said, Drink,

and I will give your camels drink also: so I drank, and she made the camels drink also."

As Eliezer silently prayed, before he had even finished, Rebekah appears on the scene. He asks her for a drink of water, and she immediately acquiesced to his request. She also instantly volunteered to water the camels as well.

But he had one more hurdle to cross.

FAMILY

Verse 47 reads: *"And I asked her, and said, Whose daughter are you? And she said, The daughter of Bethuel, Nahor's son, whom Milcah bear unto him: and I put the earring upon her face, and the bracelets upon her hands."*

Lo and behold, when asked about her family, she is a member of the family of Abraham.

(48) "AND I BOWED DOWN MY HEAD, AND WORSHIPPED THE LORD, AND BLESSED THE LORD GOD OF MY MASTER ABRAHAM, WHICH HAD LED ME IN THE RIGHT WAY TO TAKE MY MASTER'S BROTHER'S DAUGHTER UNTO HIS SON.

(49) "AND NOW IF YOU WILL DEAL KINDLY AND TRULY WITH MY MASTER, TELL ME: AND IF NOT, TELL ME; THAT I MAY TURN TO THE RIGHT HAND, OR TO THE LEFT.

(50) "THEN LABAN AND BETHUEL ANSWERED AND SAID, THE THING PROCEEDS FROM THE LORD: WE CANNOT SPEAK UNTO YOU BAD OR GOOD.

(51) "BEHOLD, REBEKAH IS BEFORE YOU, TAKE HER, AND GO, AND LET HER BE YOUR MASTER'S SON'S WIFE, AS THE LORD HAS SPOKEN."

The structure is:

1. Eliezer worships and thanks the Lord for His Leading.

2. Her brother and father recognize the fact that the entire proceeding was from the Lord; consequently, they saw the wisdom of speaking neither bad nor good, which means they dare not subtract from or add to.

3. They immediately gave their consent, with Laban it seems, being the main spokesman.

WORSHIP

Verse 48 reads: *"And I bowed down my head, and worshipped the LORD, and blessed the LORD God of my master Abraham, which had led me in the right way to take my master's brother's daughter unto his son."*

If it is to be noticed, Eliezer is not at all ashamed to confess before these men his dependence on the Lord. We should presently as well be so forward.

THE ANSWER

Verses 49 through 51 read: *"And now if you will deal kindly and truly with my master, tell me: and if not, tell me; that I may turn to the right hand, or to the left.*

"Then Laban and Bethuel answered and said, The thing proceeds from the LORD: we cannot speak unto you bad or good.

"Behold, Rebekah is before you, take her, and go, and let her be your master's son's wife, as the LORD has spoken."

After Eliezer relates these things to these men, they are quickly made to see that all of this is entirely beyond their scope of comprehension. They do not attempt to elaborate on the subject, or it seems, to even ask any questions. Their statement, *"The thing proceeds from the Lord,"* in effect, said it all. They immediately give their consent for Rebekah to go with this man back to the home of Isaac, some 700 miles distant.

This was a very long journey in those days, and they would probably never see Rebekah again.

(52) "AND IT CAME TO PASS, THAT, WHEN ABRAHAM'S SERVANT HEARD THEIR WORDS, HE WORSHIPPED THE LORD, BOWING HIMSELF TO THE EARTH.

(53) "AND THE SERVANT BROUGHT FORTH JEWELS OF SILVER, AND JEWELS OF GOLD, AND RAIMENT, AND GAVE THEM TO REBEKAH: HE GAVE ALSO TO HER BROTHER AND TO HER MOTHER PRECIOUS THINGS.

(54) "AND THEY DID EAT AND DRINK, HE AND THE MEN WHO WERE WITH HIM, AND TARRIED ALL NIGHT; AND THEY ROSE UP IN THE MORNING, AND HE SAID, SEND ME AWAY UNTO MY MASTER.

(55) "AND HER BROTHER AND HER MOTHER SAID, LET THE DAMSEL ABIDE WITH US A FEW DAYS, AT THE LEAST TEN; AFTER THAT SHE SHALL GO.

(56) "AND HE SAID UNTO THEM, HINDER ME NOT, SEEING THE LORD HAS

NOTES

PROSPERED MY WAY; SEND ME AWAY THAT I MAY GO TO MY MASTER.

(57) "AND THEY SAID, WE WILL CALL THE DAMSEL, AND INQUIRE AT HER MOUTH."

The construction is:

1. If it is to be noticed, Eliezer frequently worships the Lord. We should follow his example.

2. Upon the consent given, the gifts now are abundant, expensive, and lavish.

3. His mission complete, Eliezer asks for permission to leave immediately.

THANKS TO THE LORD

Verse 52 reads: *"And it came to pass, that, when Abraham's servant heard their words, he worshipped the LORD, bowing himself to the Earth."*

For every victory, Eliezer worships the Lord, which speaks volumes of this man. And his worship was not merely a silent *"thank you,"* but he was very physical, even prostrating himself on the ground.

When, of course, we understand how important all of this was, and which I think Eliezer realized its vast significance, at least as far as it was possible then, we can understand his reaction.

THE GIFTS

Verses 53 and 54 read: *"And the servant brought forth jewels of silver, and jewels of gold, and raiment, and gave them to Rebekah: he gave also to her brother and to her mother precious things.*

"And they did eat and drink, he and the men who were with him, and tarried all night; and they rose up in the morning, and he said, Send me away unto my master."

The gifts now were lavish. Considering how rich Abraham was, and how important this event, the worth of all of this was undoubtedly staggering.

TARRY NOT

Verses 55 through 57 read: *"And her brother and her mother said, Let the damsel abide with us a few days, at the least ten; after that she shall go.*

"And he said unto them, Hinder me not, seeing the LORD has prospered my way; send me away that I may go to my master.

"And they said, We will call the damsel, and inquire at her mouth."

Perhaps a little different than the custom, Eliezer wants to depart immediately. His mission is all-important, and he cannot rest until the young lady is safe by Isaac's side.

There is no doubt that the Holy Spirit was working as it regards the situation, not only as it pertained to Eliezer, but as well as it pertained to Rebekah and her family.

(58) "AND THEY CALLED REBEKAH, AND SAID UNTO HER, WILL YOU GO WITH THIS MAN? AND SHE SAID, I WILL GO.

(59) "AND THEY SENT AWAY REBEKAH THEIR SISTER, AND HER NURSE, AND ABRAHAM'S SERVANT, AND HIS MEN.

(60) "AND THEY BLESSED REBEKAH, AND SAID UNTO HER, YOU ARE OUR SISTER, BE THOU THE MOTHER OF THOUSANDS OF MILLIONS, AND LET YOUR SEED POSSESS THE GATE OF THOSE WHICH HATE THEM.

(61) "AND REBEKAH AROSE, AND HER DAMSELS, AND THEY RODE UPON THE CAMELS, AND FOLLOWED THE MAN: AND THE SERVANT TOOK REBEKAH, AND WENT HIS WAY."

The composition is:

1. The great question was posed to Rebekah, *"Will you go with this man?"* Her answer was immediate and positive, *"I will go."*

This is the question that the Holy Spirit is asking every one who would be a part of the Bride of Christ.

2. Her family pronounced a blessing upon Rebekah. Little did they know and realize that the staggering number they spoke, would in fact come true.

3. As well, the second part of the blessing will most definitely come to pass, in that victory through Jesus Christ, and in every capacity, is ours.

4. Eliezer took Rebekah, exactly as the Holy Spirit will one day take the Bride of Christ to meet our Lord. It's called the Rapture of the Church (I Thess. 4:13-18).

THE GREAT QUESTION

Verse 58 reads: *"And they called Rebekah, and said unto her, Will you go with this man? And she said, I will go."*

NOTES

One can certainly understand the feelings of this family, taking into consideration that they would probably never see Rebekah again. This could not be easy for her mother and father, as well as her brother. So they asked for ten days, in order to say their goodbyes, which would include all of the relatives.

But Eliezer felt in his spirit that he must leave immediately, so Rebekah is given the choice as to what she wanted to do.

She was asked the great question, *"Will you go with this man?"* Her answer seems to be without hesitation. She said, *"I will go."*

Whenever we come to Christ, we in effect must give up our families, our friends, and everything for that matter. That certainly doesn't mean that we cease to love them. Not at all. In fact, we love them even more, but Christ comes first.

And to be sure, when the Holy Spirit poses the question to each of us, *"Will you go with this man?"*, and speaking of Christ, our answer must be as quick as was the answer of Rebekah. *"I will go!"* It is a journey that, in fact, will never end.

THE BLESSING

Verses 59 and 60 read: *"And they sent away Rebekah their sister, and her nurse, and Abraham's servant, and his men.*

"And they blessed Rebekah, and said unto her, You are our sister, be thou the mother of thousands of millions, and let your seed possess the gate of those which hate them."

No doubt, the blessing they posed upon Rebekah was standard; however, little did they realize that the staggering numbers they presented would in fact come to pass. Every single person who has ever come to Christ is a part of these *"thousands of millions."*

And as well, through Jesus Christ, victory in every capacity has been won, and victory in every capacity will continue to be won.

FOLLOW THE MAN

Verse 61 reads: *"And Rebekah arose, and her damsels, and they rode upon the camels, and followed the man: and the servant took Rebekah, and went his way."*

Not only did Rebekah's nurse go with her, but other young ladies as well, as represented by the word *"damsels."* This showed that her family was quite wealthy also.

The Scripture says that they *"followed the man,"* speaking of Eliezer.

We are to follow the Holy Spirit in all of His Leading, and always without exception, He will lead us to Christ.

(62) "AND ISAAC CAME FROM THE WAY OF THE WELL LAHAI-ROI; FOR HE DWELT IN THE SOUTH COUNTRY.

(63) "AND ISAAC WENT OUT TO MEDITATE IN THE FIELD AT THE EVENTIDE: AND HE LIFTED UP HIS EYES, AND SAW, AND, BEHOLD, THE CAMELS WERE COMING.

(64) "AND REBEKAH LIFTED UP HER EYES, AND WHEN SHE SAW ISAAC, SHE LIGHTED OFF THE CAMEL.

(65) "FOR SHE HAD SAID UNTO THE SERVANT, WHAT MAN IS THIS WHO WALKS IN THE FIELD TO MEET US? AND THE SERVANT HAD SAID, IT IS MY MASTER: THEREFORE SHE TOOK A VEIL, AND COVERED HERSELF.

(66) "AND THE SERVANT TOLD ISAAC ALL THINGS THAT HE HAD DONE.

(67) "AND ISAAC BROUGHT HER INTO HIS MOTHER SARAH'S TENT, AND TOOK REBEKAH, AND SHE BECAME HIS WIFE; AND HE LOVED HER: AND ISAAC WAS COMFORTED AFTER HIS MOTHER'S DEATH."

The overview is:

1. The idea seems to be that Isaac was in a private place, but not far from the well-traveled road, and had gone there to pray, most probably about the bride he hoped to have.

2. His prayer would be answered in a most startling manner. He would look up, see the camels coming, and know that it was Eliezer. So, Rebekah would meet Isaac at his place of prayer.

3. Rebekah was everything that Isaac had hoped her to be. She was beautiful, a virgin, and above all, she was the Will of the Lord for Isaac. The Lord had arranged this marriage, and all marriages which He arranges are as they should be. He will do the same presently for all who will wait on Him.

PRAYER

Verses 62 and 63 read: *"And Isaac came from the way of the well Lahai-roi; for he dwelt in the south country.*

NOTES

"And Isaac went out to meditate in the field at the eventide: and he lifted up his eyes, and saw, and, behold, the camels were coming."

It is beautiful that Isaac first laid his eyes on his bride-to-be, while in prayer.

Evidently, he had gone out to a place of solitude to seek the Face of the Lord, possibly about the mission of Eliezer concerning the obtaining for him a wife.

It is doubtful that he expected Eliezer back so soon. He knew the long distance to where his father Abraham had sent Eliezer, and about how long it would take to get there, and to get back; however, he had no idea as to how long Eliezer would be once he arrived there. So I doubt very seriously that he was expecting the servant back this soon.

Thoughts no doubt filled his mind. Would Eliezer be successful? If so, what would she look like?

He was not to be disappointed. The Lord would arrange this match, and that which the Lord does so is always beautiful and glorious. While in prayer, he happened to look up, and behold, the camel train was coming.

REBEKAH

Verses 64 and 65 read: *"And Rebekah lifted up her eyes, and when she saw Isaac, she lighted off the camel.*

"For she had said unto the servant, What man is this who walks in the field to meet us? And the servant had said, It is my master: therefore she took a veil, and covered herself."

All the thoughts that Isaac had, no doubt, were present in the mind of Rebekah as well. What would he be like?

In a sense, her commitment was even greater than that of Isaac. While he would be able to remain with his family to the end of his days, she had left her family back in Haran, and actually would never see them again. She had left all for this man, whom she had never seen. But to be sure, she definitely was not to be disappointed.

Again, the Lord has arranged all things, and His arrangements are always perfect.

We aren't told what the thoughts of Isaac were or those of Rebekah at the moment of their meeting. Perhaps it was too personal for the Holy Spirit to divulge this meeting.

But this one thing is certain: both were very pleased at what the Lord had chosen.

ELIEZER

Verse 66 reads: *"And the servant told Isaac all things that he had done."*

After Isaac had met Rebekah, Eliezer then relates to him the Blessings of God upon his journey. God had moved wondrously, and the mother of Israel, for that's actually what Rebekah would be, would be everything that Isaac could ever want. And to be sure, Isaac would be everything that Rebekah would ever want or desire.

HIS WIFE

Verse 67 reads: *"And Isaac brought her into his mother Sarah's tent, and took Rebekah, and she became his wife; and he loved her: and Isaac was comforted after his mother's death."*

Incidentally, in those days, the primitive marriage ceremony consisted solely of the taking of a bride before witnesses.

If it is to be noticed, the word *"death"* is added here by the translators. It was not in the original Text. It is as if the Holy Spirit would not conclude this beautiful and joyful narrative with a note of sorrow (Wordsworth).

Isaac being comforted by Rebekah after his mother's death shows that he did not make comparisons between his mother and Rebekah, which allowed his wife to be the queen of the home, even as she should have been. In other words, she didn't have to compete with Sarah, meaning that Isaac did not constantly compare the two.

And so is told this beautiful love story, which symbolizes Christ and the Church, represented by Isaac and Rebekah. However, the emphasis seems to be on Eliezer, who symbolized the Holy Spirit, as he secured the bride for Isaac. Likewise the Holy Spirit is making up the Church at present as a bride for Christ.

"O magnify the Lord with me, you people of His choice,
"Let all to whom He lendeth breath now in His Name rejoice,
"For love's best Revelation, for rest from condemnation,

"For uttermost Salvation to Him give thanks!"

"O praise Him for His Holiness, His wisdom and His Grace;
"Sing praises for the precious Blood which ransomed all our race,
"In tenderness He sought us, from depths of sin He brought us,
"The way of life then taught us, to Him give thanks!"

"Had I a thousand tongues to sing, the half could not be told,
"Of love so rich, so full and free, of blessings manifold;
"Of Grace that faileth never, peace flowing like a river,
"From God the glorious Giver, to Him give thanks!"

CHAPTER 25

(1) "THEN AGAIN ABRAHAM TOOK A WIFE, AND HER NAME WAS KETURAH.

(2) "AND SHE BEAR HIM ZIMRAN, AND JOKSHAN, AND MEDAN, AND MIDIAN, AND ISHBAK, AND SHUAH.

(3) "AND JOKSHAN BEGAT SHEBA AND DEDAN. AND THE SONS OF DEDAN WERE ASSHURIM, AND LETUSHIM, AND LEUMMIM.

(4) "AND THE SONS OF MIDIAN; EPHAH, AND EPHER, AND HANOCH, AND ABIDAH, AND ELDAAH. ALL THESE WERE THE CHILDREN OF KETURAH."

The composition is:

1. Sarah having waxed old and vanished away (Heb. 9:13), that is, the Jewish Covenant of works, Keturah, the Gentile, now appears with her sons. Thus is the future pictured.

2. This having been accomplished, the nations of the Earth (represented by Keturah and her sons) will be raised up as children of Abraham and receive their inheritance, which of course, speaks of the Church.

3. Abraham not only laid the groundwork for Israel, but as well, for the Church. So everything that happened to him was of utmost significance as it regards the entirety

of the Plan of God, hence Abraham referred to as *"the father of us all"* (Rom. 4:16).

KETURAH

Verse 1 reads: *"Then again Abraham took a wife, and her name was Keturah."*

If it is to be noticed, Sarah, while representing us all, was more so the mother of Israel. Keturah, Abraham's second wife, and we're speaking of this union taking place after Sarah's death, represents the Church and, therefore, the Gentiles. So when Paul said that the Patriarch *"was the father of us all,"* the statement actually covered the entirety of the Plan of God.

Abraham Was 137 years of age when Sarah died. He probably married Keturah not long thereafter. He died at 175. So he was married to her 35 or more years.

GENTILE SONS

Verses 2 through 4 read: *"And she bear him Zimran, and Jokshan, and Medan, and Midian, and Ishbak, and Shuah.*

"And Jokshan begat Sheba and Dedan. And the sons of Dedan were Asshurim, and Letushim, and Leummim.

"And the sons of Midian; Ephah, and Epher, and Hanoch, and Abidah, and Eldaah. All these were the children of Keturah."

Abraham was probably between 140 and 150 when these sons were born.

Of course it would be obvious that it is beyond nature for a man 100 years old to have a son; how much more improbable, then, must it have become after 40 more years had passed! So we must conclude that the rejuvenation given to Abraham by the Lord as it regards the birth of Isaac, carried over for many more years, which it no doubt did. With God all things are possible!

It is believed that Midian is the one son of Keturah who had a great future before him, inasmuch as his race became famous traders. As well, it is believed that Medan and Midian grew together into one tribe. Jethro, the father-in-law of Moses, belonged to this tribe (Ex. 2:15-16).

If it is to be remembered, Gideon won a great victory over the Midianites, as recorded in Judges, Chapters 6 through 8.

(5) "AND ABRAHAM GAVE ALL THAT HE HAD UNTO ISAAC.

(6) "BUT UNTO THE SONS OF THE CONCUBINES, WHICH ABRAHAM HAD, ABRAHAM GAVE GIFTS, AND SENT THEM AWAY FROM ISAAC HIS SON, WHILE HE YET LIVED, EASTWARD, UNTO THE EAST COUNTRY.

(7) "AND THESE ARE THE DAYS OF THE YEARS OF ABRAHAM'S LIFE WHICH HE LIVED, AN HUNDRED THREESCORE AND FIFTEEN YEARS.

(8) "THEN ABRAHAM GAVE UP THE GHOST, AND DIED IN A GOOD OLD AGE, AN OLD MAN, AND FULL OF YEARS; AND WAS GATHERED TO HIS PEOPLE.

(9) "AND HIS SONS ISAAC AND ISHMAEL BURIED HIM IN THE CAVE OF MACHPELAH, IN THE FIELD OF EPHRON THE SON OF ZOHAR THE HITTITE, WHICH IS BEFORE MAMRE;

(10) "THE FIELD WHICH ABRAHAM PURCHASED OF THE SONS OF HETH: THERE WAS ABRAHAM BURIED, AND SARAH HIS WIFE.

(11) "AND IT CAME TO PASS AFTER THE DEATH OF ABRAHAM, THAT GOD BLESSED HIS SON ISAAC; AND ISAAC DWELT BY THE WELL LAHAI-ROI."

The structure is:

1. The child of the Spirit only can be heir to the Promises.

2. Abraham now dies and passes off the scene, making way for the heir of promise.

3. He was born of the Spirit at 75 years of age and departed to be with Christ at 175. He was, therefore, a sojourner for 100 years.

4. It is pleasant to read in Verse 9 that Isaac and Ishmael stood side by side at their father's grave. That, their standing side by side, will yet be fulfilled!

5. The *"Blessing"* which rested upon Abraham will now rest upon Isaac, and because he is the son of Promise.

6. In the Hebrew, the *"well Lahai-roi"* means, *"the well of the living one in the desert."*

HEIR OF THE PROMISE

Verse 5 reads: *"And Abraham gave all that he had unto Isaac."*

That alone which is born of the Spirit can be partaker of the Promises. The flesh cannot inherit such. In the spiritual, what does this mean?

Everything that is truly of God is born strictly of God. This means that all of Salvation, and all of Sanctification, are totally and completely of God. When the Believer understands this, and functions accordingly, the Promises in all of their abundance, and we speak of victory and prosperity, are his.

When man attempts to bypass God's Way, which incidentally is the Cross, and thereby attempts to manufacture his own Salvation as it regards the unsaved, which untold millions do, or his own Sanctification, which regrettably, millions of Christians do, the problem begins.

The *"Cross"* is the means by which God gives all things to the fallen sons of Adam's race. Whether it be Salvation for the sinner, or Sanctification for the Saint, all and without exception come by means of the Cross.

It is only when the Believer takes his eyes off the Cross, thereby placing them on something else, which means that his faith is transferred from the Cross to something else, that the problem begins.

While all of this sounds very complicated, in reality it isn't. Please note carefully what I've already given any number of times in this Volume:

1. Everything comes to the sinner and the Saint by the means of the Cross. And of course, I speak of what Jesus did there (I Cor. 1:17-18, 21, 23; 2:2; Gal. 6:14; Col. 2:14-15).

2. As a result, the Believer must ever keep his Faith anchored in the Cross. It must never be moved to other things. While many other things are definitely important, it is the Cross which makes these things possible. So the object of Faith is always to be the Cross of Christ, and most definitely it will be, if the Believer understands and believes that all things come to him by means of the Cross (Rom. 6:3-14; Eph. 2:13-18).

3. With Faith properly placed in the Cross, and Faith properly continued in the Cross, the Holy Spirit, Who works strictly within the parameters of the Finished Work of Christ, will then grandly help the Believer (Rom. 8:1-2, 11, 13).

Abraham was very, very rich! And if it is to be noticed, he gave everything he had to Isaac, which tells us that the Lord will give

NOTES

everything He has to those who are true heirs of the Promise.

SEPARATION

Verse 6 reads: *"But unto the sons of the concubines, which Abraham had, Abraham gave gifts, and sent them away from Isaac his son, while he yet lived, eastward, unto the east country."*

There is a vast difference in mere *"gifts"* than the entirety of the inheritance.

While the Believer might receive some small *"gifts"* as it regards ways other than the Cross, which to be frank have characterized all Believers, that is a far cry from the inheritance. So the modern crowd regarding the modern Church, who has repudiated the Cross, might receive a few *"gifts,"* but the truth is, what they are getting is a far cry from the inheritance. The *"inheritance"* involves spiritual things, while the *"gifts"* at least as represented here, involve only material things, which are at best temporal. So the Believer can have the inheritance, or he can settle for temporary gifts. I think it is obvious as to the correct way.

As well, Abraham was instructed by the Lord to separate Isaac from the sons born to Keturah. While the Bible definitely teaches separation, as is proclaimed here, it does not teach isolation. Let it be ever understood that the two, and I speak of that which is born of the Spirit and that which is born of the flesh, definitely cannot coexist.

The way of Faith is the way of the Cross, just as the way of the Cross is the way of Faith. In the literal or the spiritual sense, it can have no fellowship with the flesh.

Taking the latter first, *"the bondwoman and her son"* must be cast out, even as Paul used Hagar and Ishmael as an allegory (Gal. 4:30-31). The Holy Spirit in our lives is ever struggling against the flesh in our lives, seeking to cast it out (Gal. 5:16-17).

In the natural or literal sense, the same holds true. Those who follow the way of the Cross can have no fellowship with those who follow the way of flesh. In fact, those who are of the flesh, which refers to trusting in things other than Christ and what He did at the Cross, will always persecute those who are after the Spirit (Gal. 1:23).

So, even though the sons of Keturah are at the same time the sons of Abraham, they are not heirs of the Promise, that alone going to Isaac.

THE DEATH OF ABRAHAM

Verses 7 and 8 read: *"And these are the days of the years of Abraham's life which he lived, an hundred threescore and fifteen years.*

"Then Abraham gave up the ghost, and died in a good old age, an old man, and full of years; and was gathered to his people."

Abraham was born about two years after the death of Noah, and was contemporary with Shem, Noah's son, for many years. So he was in a position to receive the facts affecting the antediluvian world. As stated, he was born of the Spirit at 75 years of age and departed to be with Christ at 175.

Few men in history, if any, have affected the world as did Abraham. That which characterized his person and his life was that of Faith. And by that, we speak of Faith in Christ, and what Christ would do to redeem the fallen sons of Adam's lost race. As with Paul, this giant *"fought a good fight, finished the course, and kept the faith."* And there was definitely laid up for him a Crown of Righteousness.

The phrase, *"Then Abraham . . . was gathered to his people,"* implies the belief in a future life. He was satisfied not merely with life and all its blessings, but with living, which characterizes all who are of Faith. He was now ready for the transition to a higher sphere. He died in the hope of a better country, even an heavenly (Heb. 11:13-16).

Abraham died a natural death, apparently without pain. He simply breathed his last and went to be with his people.

ISAAC AND ISHMAEL

Verse 9 reads: *"And his sons Isaac and Ishmael buried him in the cave of Machpelah, in the field of Ephron the son of Zohar the Hittite, which is before Mamre."*

It is pleasant to read that Isaac and Ishmael stood side by side at their father's grave, which speaks to us of prophetic overtones.

In the year A.D. 2002, the animosity between the two, as it has been all these many centuries, is at fever pitch; however, one day

that's going to change, and we speak of the Coming of the Lord.

On that glad day, when it is obvious to all that Jesus Christ is the Son of God, and as well, the Messiah of Israel, Isaac's *"Seed,"* and as well the True *"Seed of the woman,"* both Isaac and Ishmael will accept Him, Who is Lord of all. It is ironic; the True *"Seed"* is rejected by both Isaac and Ishmael. That will soon be rectified, and both Isaac and Ishmael will stand side by side, with the hate and the war now forever gone. This alone, and we speak of the Coming of the Lord, is the hope of humanity.

THE PURCHASED FIELD

Verse 10 reads: *"The field which Abraham purchased of the sons of Heth: there was Abraham buried, and Sarah his wife."*

This plot of ground in which Abraham and Sarah were buried was that alone which Abraham owned when he died, as far as land was concerned. And yet, that burial place proclaimed to all that one day the entirety of the land, which would ultimately be called *"Israel,"* would belong to him. So his burial place was of far greater significance than the sons of Heth, from whom the land was purchased, ever knew. It signified his Faith in the Promises of God, and yet was far broader than the mere land itself.

Actually, the land was but a means to an end, which would support a people, who would ultimately bring the Messiah into the world, Who would give His life in order that man might be saved. So the greatness of Abraham can be summed up in that short statement:

"He believed God, and God accounted it to him for Righteousness" (Gen. 15:6).

When it says that he *"believed God,"* it is speaking of what God would do to redeem fallen humanity, which would be the giving of His Only Son, of Whom Isaac was a Type, Who would give Himself as a Sacrifice, which would affect the Salvation of all mankind (Gal. 1:4). This is the type of Faith which characterized Abraham. His Faith was in a prophetic Jesus, while ours is in a historic Jesus.

THE BLESSING

Verse 11 reads: *"And it came to pass after the death of Abraham, that God blessed his son Isaac; and Isaac dwelt by the well Lahai-roi."*

If it is to be noticed, it says that God blessed Isaac, but it doesn't mention anything about God blessing the other sons of Abraham. If we desire the Blessing, we can have the Blessing as well. In fact, all who make Christ and His Cross the object of their Faith are guaranteed the *"Blessing of Abraham."* Paul said so:

"That the Blessing of Abraham might come on the Gentiles through Jesus Christ; that we might receive the Promise of the Spirit through faith" (Gal. 3:14).

The *"Blessing of Abraham"* is predicated on what Christ did for us in order to *"redeem us from the curse of the Law."* He did this by *"being made a curse for us,"* which took place by him *"hanging on the tree"* (Gal. 3:13).

The *"curse of the Law"* was death, which means that all who broke the Law were subject to its penalty. Sadly, the whole of the human race, other than Christ, broke the Law and, thereby, came under its curse.

But when Jesus came as our Substitute, and took the penalty for us, which He Alone could do, and because He was the Son of God, thereby the Perfect Sacrifice, the curse, which was death, was satisfied, and satisfied in every respect. In other words, all sin was atoned, both past, present, and future. This made it possible for the *"Blessing of Abraham,"* which incidentally is *"Justification by Faith,"* to come upon the Gentiles, and the Jews as well, for that matter.

As a result of what Jesus did for us at the Cross, and our Faith in that Finished Work, the Holy Spirit now abides permanently within our hearts and lives, which is the present end result of the *"Blessing of Abraham."*

(12) "NOW THESE ARE THE GENERATIONS OF ISHMAEL, ABRAHAM'S SON, WHOM HAGAR THE EGYPTIAN, SARAH'S HANDMAID, BEAR UNTO ABRAHAM:

(13) "AND THESE ARE THE NAMES OF THE SONS OF ISHMAEL, BY THEIR NAMES, ACCORDING TO THEIR GENERATIONS: THE FIRSTBORN OF ISHMAEL, NEBAJOTH; AND KEDAR, AND ADBEEL, AND MIBSAM,

(14) "AND MISHMA, AND DUMAH, AND MASSA,

NOTES

(15) "HADAR, AND TEMA, JETUR, NAPHISH, AND KEDEMAH:

(16) "THESE ARE THE SONS OF ISHMAEL, AND THESE ARE THEIR NAMES, BY THEIR TOWNS, AND BY THEIR CASTLES; TWELVE PRINCES ACCORDING TO THEIR NATIONS.

(17) "AND THESE ARE THE YEARS OF THE LIFE OF ISHMAEL, AN HUNDRED AND THIRTY AND SEVEN YEARS: AND HE GAVE UP THE GHOST AND DIED; AND WAS GATHERED UNTO HIS PEOPLE.

(18) "AND THEY DWELT FROM HAVILAH UNTO SHUR, THAT IS BEFORE EGYPT, AS YOU GO TOWARD ASSYRIA: AND HE DIED IN THE PRESENCE OF ALL HIS BRETHREN."

The overview is:

1. There is no blessing recorded regarding the posterity of Ishmael.

2. Ishmael is the father of the Arab people. Twelve sons of his became princes, that is, the heads of great tribes. But more than likely, Ishmael had other sons also, who did not gain such notoriety.

3. Regrettably, the Arab people, the descendants of Ishmael, although the sons of Abraham, did not enjoy Abraham's Faith. As a result, they have embraced a false way, and I speak of the false religion of Islam.

ISHMAEL, ABRAHAM'S SON

Verse 12 reads: *"Now these are the generations of Ishmael, Abraham's son, whom Hagar the Egyptian, Sarah's handmaid, bear unto Abraham."*

Ishmael had every opportunity to serve God, but regrettably, he chose another path. He or his mother would not yield to Isaac. Ishmael being the oldest, they looked at things in the natural, with no desire as it regards that which the Lord wanted. They were so close, but yet so far away.

The path of faith is open only to those who will walk that path; otherwise it is closed.

A CLOSED ACCOUNT

Verses 13 through 18 read: *"And these are the names of the sons of Ishmael, by their names, according to their generations: the firstborn of Ishmael, Nebajoth; and Kedar, and Adbeel, and Mibsam,*

"And Mishma, and Dumah, and Massa,

"Hadar, and Tema, Jetur, Naphish, and Kedemah:

"These are the sons of Ishmael, and these are their names, by their towns, and by their castles; twelve princes according to their nations.

"And these are the years of the life of Ishmael, an hundred and thirty and seven years: and he gave up the ghost and died; and was gathered unto his people.

"And they dwelt from Havilah unto Shur, that is before Egypt, as you go toward Assyria: and he died in the presence of all his brethren."

Inasmuch as the path of faith was rejected, even though Ishmael was the son of Abraham, he could not have the Blessing of Abraham, that going only to the sons of Promise. Even though Ishmael had no choice over the circumstances of his birth, he definitely had a choice over the circumstances of his life. He chose the way of the world. He was the head of the Arab people, who regrettably chose also, a path of faithlessness. Christ being rejected, as always is the case, a false deity filled the void. That false deity was Mohammad, who has enslaved the Arab people from then until now.

As previously stated, spiritually they live in Satanic bondage. Economically, they are some of the poorest nations on Earth. Socially, they know few freedoms, with their women bearing the brunt of this false direction.

Let it ever be understood, if men reject God, a false god will always fill the void, which always leads to slavery, and in every capacity.

Twelve of the sons of Ishmael became heads of tribes, which, as stated, made up the Arab people. Ishmael undoubtedly had other sons, but they did not head up tribes.

Because he was the son of Abraham, Ishmael did receive some favors from God; however, regrettably he did not allow those favors to lead him to Christ, but rather went deeper into faithlessness.

(19) "AND THESE ARE THE GENERATIONS OF ISAAC, ABRAHAM'S SON: ABRAHAM BEGAT ISAAC:

(20) "AND ISAAC WAS FORTY YEARS OLD WHEN HE TOOK REBEKAH TO WIFE, THE DAUGHTER OF BETHUEL THE

NOTES

SYRIAN OF PADAN-ARAM, THE SISTER TO LABAN THE SYRIAN."

The exegesis is:

1. The generations of Isaac would ultimately lead to the Lord Jesus Christ, and then ultimately the Church.

2. The Lord told Abraham that the wife of Isaac must be chosen from his family, and not the Canaanites. There definitely were several reasons for this.

3. In a sense, Rebekah would pick up where Sarah left off.

THE GENERATIONS OF ISAAC

Verse 19 reads: *"And these are the generations of Isaac, Abraham's son: Abraham begat Isaac."*

God had said to Abraham, *"In Isaac shall your seed be called"* (Gen. 21:12). This meant that it wouldn't be in Ishmael, or anyone else for that matter.

Isaac was born of the Spirit, which means that it was only the Spirit of God Who could have brought Isaac into the world, seeing that his mother was 90 years old and his father was 100 years old. All of this was so very, very important, simply because through this lineage would come the Son of God, Who would redeem the entirety of the world, by His death on the Cross. So it was imperative that this son of Abraham, whom God had chosen, would be totally and completely of the Lord, and not of human ingenuity.

Ishmael had been a work of the flesh as it regards Abraham and Sarah. They shifted their faith from trust in the Lord, to themselves. Ishmael was the result, which the Holy Spirit is quick to point out, *"whom Hagar the Egyptian, Sarah's handmaid, bear unto Abraham."*

THE SUCCESS OF THE FLESH

The worst thing that can happen to a Believer is for plans to succeed which are not of the Spirit. As an example, the entirety of the world is still suffering the results of that which happened between Abraham and Sarah some 4,000 years ago. It was originally Sarah's idea that Abraham father a child by her Egyptian handmaid, which was the custom of that day and time, that is if the legitimate wife could not conceive. But it was not of God, and was strictly of the planning and scheming of Abraham and Sarah.

The Arab people are the result of that particular scheme. They have proven to be exactly what God said they would be: *"And he will be a wild man; his hand will be against every man, and every man's hand against him"* (Gen. 16:12).

REBEKAH

Verse 20 reads: *"And Isaac was forty years old when he took Rebekah to wife, the daughter of Bethuel the Syrian of Padan-aram, the sister to Laban the Syrian."*

"Laban the Syrian," is mentioned here, simply because he will figure very prominently as it regards Jacob, Rebekah's son, who we will study momentarily.

Under Abraham's guidance, the Lord will choose the wife for Isaac. That which the Lord chooses is always right. That which we choose is almost always wrong, and probably one could say without fear of contradiction, that which we choose is always wrong.

As an aside, the Lord will as well choose a wife or a husband for every young man and young lady, who looks to Him for Leading and Guidance. In fact, if we will only ask the Lord to lead us and guide us in all things, He will definitely do such. The problem with most modern Believers is that they very seldom seek the Lord as it regards anything. Such is so foolish, considering Who the Lord is, and what He can do, and then compare that with our own pitiful fallibility.

I need the Leading of the Lord in every single thing which I attempt. Be it little or large, I want His Leading, His Guidance, etc.

A PERSONAL EXPERIENCE

In 1998, the Lord began to move upon my heart concerning Radio. We immediately began to set out to do exactly what he had told us to do, which concerned itself with the programming, which was to come in its entirety from Family Worship Center, and then the securing of Stations all over this nation, in order to propagate the Message of the Cross.

At first we set out to secure Translator frequencies all over this nation. These are small Stations, which cover about a 15-mile distance in all directions. They are called *"Translators,"*

simply because we send our programming from the Mother Station in Baton Rouge to these particular Stations, which means they air the same identical thing as the Mother Station.

However, most of the Translator frequencies had long since been taken up in the major cities. And I knew that for us to get this work done, we were going to have to somehow find a way to get into the major cities.

At first glance, that seemed to be an impossible task, simply because the price of FM Stations was so exorbitant, that such is way beyond our range. So how could this be done?

I took it to the Lord, asking Him to show me a way to get this thing done. It took about six months of seeking the Face of the Lord, when a series of events were brought to pass, and I might quickly add were brought to pass by the Lord, which showed me how we could secure Stations in major cities. This we immediately began to do, and are continuing unto this hour.

The point I'm attempting to make is that whatever it is we need from the Lord, He knows the answer. We must seek His Face, exactly as Abraham did as it regarded a wife for Isaac, which no doubt Isaac was ardently praying about as well.

It is a shame that most Christians do not take advantage of all the things the Lord can do for them. Better yet, He wants to be involved, which means that He wants to lead us and guide us, and because as the song says, *"The Lord knows the way through the wilderness, and all we have to do is follow."*

(21) "AND ISAAC ENTREATED THE LORD FOR HIS WIFE, BECAUSE SHE WAS BARREN: AND THE LORD WAS ENTREATED OF HIM, AND REBEKAH HIS WIFE CONCEIVED."

The synopsis is:

1. Satan hindered the birth of Jacob for 20 years.

2. God overruled all things to emphasize once more the great Truth that He displays the riches of His Grace and Glory where nature is dead.

3. This is a principle in the Spiritual Life which nature is unwilling to learn.

BARREN

As stated, we find that Satan hindered the birth of Jacob, through whom the Lord would work, for some 20 years. And the Lord allowed him to do such.

Why?

Anything and everything that Satan does, he does only by permission from the Lord. To be sure, he is subject to the Lord in every capacity (Job, Chpts. 1-2).

So as it regards Believers, this means that the Lord uses Satan in order to strengthen the faith and trust of Believers. How does He do that?

As mentioned, He allows Satan a modicum of latitude. Of course, Satan means to hurt us and even destroy us. But the Lord's reasons are altogether different, as should be overly obvious.

He wants us to do exactly what Isaac did.

ENTREATED THE LORD

Twenty years is a long time. But Isaac didn't give up. During this time, he kept entreating the Lord to heal Rebekah, that she might be able to conceive, and to bear children.

As well, even though he and his wife naturally wanted children, and wanted them very much, the real reason was far more important. The birth of a son to this union was just as important as his miracle birth had been as it regarded his father and mother, Abraham and Sarah. For the Plan of God to be brought forth, which pertains to the Redemption of all of mankind, Isaac and Rebekah would have to have a son.

As far as Rebekah was concerned, nature was dead. In other words, she could not have a child. But God is able to overrule all of these things. He wanted Isaac to continue to believe Him. In other words, this was a test of faith, as all things as it pertains to Believers are tests of faith.

The answer ultimately came, and because the Lord was entreated of him, and Rebekah conceived.

What was the Lord's reasoning behind all of this, and we speak of the barrenness of both Sarah and Rebekah?

Among other things, it was to show that the children of the Promise were to be not simply the fruit of nature, but the gift of Grace.

(22) "AND THE CHILDREN STRUGGLED TOGETHER WITHIN HER; AND SHE SAID,

IF IT BE SO, WHY AM I THUS? AND SHE WENT TO INQUIRE OF THE LORD."

The composition is:

1. Rebekah's language in this Verse in essence says, *"If in answer to prayer God is about to give me the joy of being a mother, why am I so physically oppressed that I am in danger of death?"*

2. Why should such an answer to prayer be accompanied by such mysterious suffering?

3. Rebekah took her questions to the Lord, which is exactly where we should take them as well!

THE STRUGGLE

The phrase, *"And the children struggled together within her,"* pertains first of all to the fact that there were twins in her womb. However, the *"struggle"* carries with it a tremendous spiritual meaning.

Two energies, the one believing and the other unbelieving, struggled within her, and was present even before they were born. It is like the two natures, sin nature, and Divine nature, within the Believer.

So as we had in the union of Abraham and Sarah the beginning of the Divine Plan, we have with Isaac and Rebekah the opposition to that Divine Plan, which strangely enough, centers up in the same family.

Jacob and Esau, as we shall see, represent the two natures struggling within the Believer. There is only one way that victory can be achieved over the sin nature, and that is by subscribing to God's prescribed order, which is the Cross.

THE QUESTION

The question, *"If it be so, why am I thus?"*, probably means, *"If I have thus conceived, in answer to my husband's prayers, why do I suffer in this strange manner?"*

In answer to this question which plagued her heart, she took it to the Lord.

(23) "AND THE LORD SAID UNTO HER, TWO NATIONS ARE IN YOUR WOMB, AND TWO MANNER OF PEOPLE SHALL BE SEPARATED FROM YOUR BOWELS; AND THE ONE PEOPLE SHALL BE STRONGER THAN THE OTHER PEOPLE; AND THE ELDER SHALL SERVE THE YOUNGER."

The diagram is:

1. If in answer to prayer God was about to give Rebekah the joy of becoming a mother, why the intense struggle?

2. She took the matter to the Lord, exactly as we should take all things to the Lord.

3. The two boys, as stated, represent the two natures in the Christian, the sin nature and the Divine nature. The Divine nature is the younger, but it is to have the victory. Such should be a tremendous consolation to all Believers.

THE ANSWER TO PRAYER

The phrase, *"And the LORD said unto her, Two nations are in your womb, and two manner of people shall be separated from your bowels,"* does not exactly tell us the manner in which the Lord spoke to Rebekah, but just that He did.

The two nations God told her about are the Edomites and Israelites. From her womb, that is, from the time of their birth, Jacob and Esau would be separated, divided, even hostile, for they would have nothing in common, and exactly as the Lord said would happen, the elder people descended from Esau, who was born first, who served the people descended from the younger son, Jacob.

This was fulfilled when the Edomites were made subject to King David (II Sam. 8:13-14).

But the greater fulfillment will have to do with the coming Millennial Reign. Then Israel will be the supreme nation on Earth, and all other nations will look to her, with Jesus Christ at her head.

As well, the descendants of Esau would also fall in with the descendants of Ishmael, both being the Arab people, with the animosity between these people and Israel continuing even unto this hour.

THE SPIRITUAL SENSE

The phrase, *"And the one people shall be stronger than the other; and the elder shall serve the younger,"* while continuing in the material and physical sense, also carries over greatly into the spiritual.

As we have stated, the two boys may represent the two natures in the Christian. We speak of the sin nature and the Divine nature (II Pet. 1:4). In one sense, that was the reason for the struggle between the two

NOTES

unborn babies, while they were yet in their mother's womb.

Esau was born first, and represents the sin nature, with which, due to Adam's Fall, every person is born. This simply means that the nature of the person is bent totally and completely towards sin, disobedience, and rebellion to God.

When the believing sinner is Born-Again, he now has the Divine nature, which is stronger than the sin nature. So when the human being is firstborn, he has the sin nature, and when he is Born-Again, he now has the Divine nature.

However, the sin nature doesn't leave once the believing sinner is Born-Again. And if the Believer doesn't understand God's prescribed order of victory, which speaks of the sanctified life, the sin nature will once again dominate the person, exactly as it did before conversion. This is sad but true! In fact, at this very moment, untold millions of Christians, even though they love the Lord very much, are being dominated by *"Esau,"* i.e., *"the sin nature."*

When the Apostle Paul set out to inform the Believer as to how to walk in victory in this life that we live for the Lord, he began in the Sixth Chapter of Romans, to explain to us the sin nature.

Now some Preachers teach that once the person comes to Christ, the sin nature is forever gone. My answer to that is, that being the case, why did the Holy Spirit through Paul take up so much time explaining to Believers how to have victory over this monster? Listen to Paul:

"Neither yield ye your members as instruments of unrighteousness unto the sin (Paul is speaking here of the sin nature)*: but yield yourselves unto God, as those who are alive from the dead, and your members as instruments of Righteousness unto God"* (Rom. 6:13).

If it's not possible for the Believer to yield themselves to unrighteousness, with the sin nature once again dominating them, why would Paul warn us here of these things?

The truth is, the sin nature, although continuing to abide in the heart and life of the Believer, doesn't have to be a problem at all. As we have explained in past Commentary, the truth is, we are to be dead to the sin nature. And if we are properly *"dead,"* then we'll have no problem with the sin nature. If it is to be noticed, the Scripture doesn't tell us that the sin nature is dead, but that we are to be dead to the sin nature. Again Paul said:

"Likewise reckon ye also yourselves to be dead indeed unto the sin, but alive unto God through Jesus Christ our Lord" (Rom. 6:11).

THE SIN NATURE

In the original Greek Text, there is what is known in their language a term, referred to as *"the definite article."* In fact, in the Sixth Chapter of Romans alone, this definite article is used some 14 times, and is implied two other times. In other words he said, *"How shall we, who are dead to the sin, live any longer therein?"* (Rom. 6:2).

The way the King James translators gave it to us, it makes it seem as though Paul is talking about particular sins; however, he is actually speaking of the sin nature, and we know that because he included the definite article, i.e., *"the sin."*

Once again, he didn't tell us here that the sin nature was dead, but that we were dead to the sin nature.

THE CROSS

It is because of the Cross that we are dead to the sin nature. Paul explains this in Romans 6:3-5. We died with Christ, were buried with Him, and raised with Him in newness of life.

And as far as what we once were, all of that is dead. That's why he said, *"Knowing this, that our old man is crucified with Him, that the body of the sin might be destroyed* (the guilt of sin removed and the power of sin broken), *that henceforth we should not serve the sin"* (Rom. 6:6).

HOW DO WE STAY DEAD TO THE SIN NATURE?

We stay dead by continuing to maintain our Faith in the Cross, understanding that it was there that all victory was won. That's why Paul also said: *"But God forbid that I should glory* (boast) *save in the Cross of our Lord Jesus Christ, by Whom the world is*

crucified unto me, and I unto the world" (Gal. 6:14).

If the Believer constantly maintains his Faith in the Cross, he'll have no problem with the sin nature.

FAITH

But this is where the fight commences, even the struggle between Jacob and Esau, so to speak.

Paul also said: *"Fight the good fight of faith, lay hold on eternal life, whereunto you are also called, and have professed a good profession before many witnesses"* (I Tim. 6:12).

This *"good fight of faith"* is the only fight we are called upon to engage. That's where the struggle is. Satan tries to move our Faith from the Cross to other things, and regrettably, he succeeds with many, if not most, Christians.

And if he does succeed, the sin nature will once again begin to rule in that Believer's life. He'll find himself just as unable to overcome sin, as he was before being Born-Again.

In these cases, the Believer, who is being ruled by the sin nature, sets out to try harder than ever to live for God, but despite all of his efforts, finds himself losing the battle more and more. It leaves him in a confused state, not understanding what is happening, especially considering that he is trying so hard. This is what Paul was talking about when he said: *"For that which I do I allow* (understand) *not: for what I would, that do I not; but what I hate, that do I"* (Rom. 7:15).

As the Believer should understand, this is Paul's account of his struggle, before the Lord gave him the interpretation of the New Covenant, which is the meaning of the Cross. Despite him trying so hard to live right, he found himself failing.

If the Reader should notice, we have the word *"understand"* in parentheses after the word *"allow."* Actually, the Greek word should have been translated *"understand,"* for that's what it actually means. So it would then say:

"For that which I do I understand not." Regrettably, that characterizes most Christians.

In other words, they're struggling with everything within themselves and with all their might to live right, but continue to fail. This they don't understand.

So what is wrong?

Satan has succeeded in pulling the Believer's Faith from the Cross to other things. If he does this, and irrespective as to what these other things might be, the Believer has just been placed in a posture of failure. And it doesn't matter how hard he tries, how hard he labors, how hard he struggles, he is doomed to failure, and simply because no human being can get victory in this manner. The works of the flesh will begin to manifest themselves in one's heart and life, which will cause untold problems (Gal. 5:18-21).

The answer to this situation is for the Believer to put his faith once again in the Cross of Christ, understanding that the Cross is the solution to all of his problems, and he will find little by little, victory will once again be his.

REACTION TO THE SIN NATURE

Even though, if I remember correctly, I've already given the following in this Volume, because of its extremely serious nature, please allow me the liberty of repeating myself.

The following presents to us the various ways in which the sin nature is addressed as it regards the modern Church. The first four constitute wrong directions, and will lead to nothing but failure and extreme trouble. It is only the last one which guarantees victory. Let's look at it carefully. I will use five headings:

IGNORANCE

Due to the fact that almost nothing is preached or taught behind our pulpits on the sin nature, most Christians are ignorant of this which can cause them tremendous problems. When we consider that Paul took so much time and put forth so much effort to explain the sin nature, exactly as he did in Romans, Chapter 6, we are then made to realize just how important this subject actually is. Please look at it in this way.

When the Lord began to give the meaning of the New Covenant to Paul, which incidentally is the meaning of the Cross, the very first thing he did was to explain to Paul the meaning of the sin nature, which he gave to us in Romans, Chapter 6.

DENIAL

Some Preachers claim that even though all of us had a sin nature before we were saved, now that we have come to Christ, we are new creations, with old things having passed away and all things having become new (II Cor. 5:17). So they deny the presence of a sin nature.

If in fact that is true, why did Paul take up so much time explaining something that no longer exists? While II Corinthians 8:17 is definitely correct, that doesn't preclude the fact of the sin nature.

No, the Believer faces this conflict constantly, and because there are two natures within him.

LICENSE

Many Christians claim that due to the fact that they have a sin nature, they simply cannot help but sin. It's called the *"sinning a little bit everyday"* religion. They claim the Grace of God covers all of their sins, and thereby, make little effort to obtain any type of victory.

Paul's answer to that is, *"God forbid! How shall we, who are dead to the sin, live any longer therein?"* (Rom. 6:2).

STRUGGLE

Not knowing God's prescribed order of victory, many Christians are led to believe that this Christian experience is just a long series of struggles, with them fighting the sin nature on a daily basis. That is incorrect. That's not the more abundant life of which Jesus spoke (Jn. 10:10).

While we as Believers definitely are called upon to fight, it's not with the sin nature, but rather *"the good fight of faith."* That's the only struggle we are to have. And it's a good fight, because if we fight it correctly, we're going to come out as the winner.

GRACE

The Grace of God is the only manner in which we can live this life, and live it as we should. And what does this mean?

It means that the Cross is the means by which God gives us all things. In other words, it's the Cross which makes the Grace of God, which is the goodness of God extended to undeserving people, possible in our hearts and lives.

When we look exclusively to the Cross, we are availing ourselves of the Grace of God, which guarantees the help of the Holy Spirit, which guarantees victory.

WHY DOES THE LORD ALLOW THE SIN NATURE TO REMAIN IN THE BELIEVER AFTER CONVERSION?

While there are no doubt many reasons, the primary reason pertains to the fact that our physical bodies are not yet redeemed. This refers to being glorified. Paul said:

"And not only they (the creation), *but ourselves also, which have the firstfruits of the Spirit, even we ourselves groan within ourselves, waiting for the adoption, to wit, the Redemption of our body"* (Rom. 8:23).

All that Jesus did at the Cross is not yet made available to us. Paul said, we now have the firstfruits, which probably speak of about ten percent. The balance will come at the Resurrection, i.e., *"the Rapture."*

Man is created spirit, soul, and body (I Thess. 5:23). The weak link in man's triune makeup is his body.

In fact, the body is neutral. It need not cause us problems, but <u>can</u> cause us severe problems. It is through the body that Satan works his evil passions, i.e., *"works of the flesh."* As a Believer, we have the ability and strength to yield the members of our physical body as instruments of Righteousness or unrighteousness (Rom. 6:13). As stated, the human body is neutral; however, the way that God provides our strength and ability is through the Cross, and not through our own efforts. And this is what causes problems with many Christians.

Millions of Christians are trying to yield their physical body to Righteousness, but despite all of their efforts, are instead yielding themselves to unrighteousness. Now that is tragic, but it happens to be true.

If the Believer looks to the Cross and the Cross exclusively for all that he receives from the Lord, including victory in his daily life and living, he will find himself being able to yield the members of his physical body to Righteousness. Otherwise, he cannot! That is the

NOTES

order that God has devised in order for us to live this life and to be what we ought to be in Christ. It might be summed up as: A. The Cross; B. Our Faith; and, C. The Holy Spirit.

So to answer the question, due to the fact that the human body is not yet glorified, the sin nature remains. Once the trump sounds, and *"this corruptible shall have put on incorruption, and this mortal shall have put on immortality,"* there will be no more sin nature (I Cor. 15:54).

So, the good fight of faith, which is being carried out in our lives daily, guarantees us that the *"elder,"* i.e., *"the sin nature,"* will ultimately serve the younger, i.e., *"the Divine Nature."*

(24) "AND WHEN HER DAYS TO BE DELIVERED WERE FULFILLED, BEHOLD, THERE WERE TWINS IN HER WOMB.

(25) "AND THE FIRST CAME OUT RED, ALL OVER LIKE AN HAIRY GARMENT; AND THEY CALLED HIS NAME ESAU.

(26) "AND AFTER THAT CAME HIS BROTHER OUT, AND HIS HAND TOOK HOLD ON ESAU'S HEEL; AND HIS NAME WAS CALLED JACOB: AND ISAAC WAS THREESCORE YEARS OLD WHEN SHE BEAR THEM."

The structure is:

1. The disposition of Esau was probably the fault of Isaac, as we shall see.

2. The name *"Esau"* means *"hairy one,"* portraying his violent nature. *"Jacob"* means *"heel-catcher,"* or *"supplanter."*

3. Jacob taking hold of Esau's heel at birth portrays the Believer trying to gain spiritual supremacy by means of the flesh and not the Spirit, which characterized Jacob for many years.

ESAU

Verses 24 and 25 read: *"And when her days to be delivered were fulfilled, behold, there were twins in her womb.*

"And the first came out red, all over like an hairy garment; and they called his name Esau."

Esau is a Type of the sin nature which is *"enmity against God: for it is not subject to the Law of God, neither indeed can be"* (Rom. 8:7).

His name means, *"the hairy one,"* which speaks of sensuality. In other words, he was a man of the world, and cared not at all, as we shall see, for the things of God, although he was of the Godly family. How can one be so close to the things of God, and yet be so devoid of spiritual things?

JACOB

Verse 26 reads: *"And after that came his brother out, and his hand took hold on Esau's heel; and his name was called Jacob: and Isaac was threescore years old when she bear them."*

Isaac was 40 years old when he and Rebekah married (vs. 20). He was 60 years old when the two boys were born, showing that they had been some 20 years trying to have children, and succeeded only when the Lord intervened.

Usually there is a considerable interval — an hour or more — between the birth of twins; but here Jacob appears without delay, following immediately after his brother. This means there was absolutely no interval between them. Though very rare, yet similar cases have been chronicled from time to time.

That being the physical explanation, there is a spiritual sense involved here as well, even greatly so.

In later years, Esau would refer to this phenomenon of birth, and because of Jacob's own unworthy conduct (Gen. 27:36).

These boys were named by their mother, and which she was no doubt led by the Holy Spirit, especially considering that their names so very much characterized their dispositions, once grown.

To be at a person's heel is to be his determined pursuer, and one, who on overtaking throws him down, which in a sense, at least in the spiritual, characterizes Jacob. He wanted the birthright, and mostly for spiritual reasons, but went about to get it in all the wrong ways.

To Abraham was given the great Doctrine of *"Justification by Faith."* About thirteen and one-half Chapters are devoted to the Patriarch.

Jacob instead signifies Sanctification, with about twenty-five and one-half Chapters devoted to this Patriarch. This shows us that *"living the Life"* is far more complicated than *"receiving the Life."*

Perhaps in Jacob, as no other personality of the Bible, we find the greatest illustration of the great quest for victory. We see ourselves

in Jacob, and plainly so, even as intended by the Holy Spirit. If not, then you're not looking at yourself properly.

We find the motive of Jacob as being very good, but his actions being very deplorable.

(27) "AND THE BOYS GREW: AND ESAU WAS A CUNNING HUNTER, A MAN OF THE FIELD; AND JACOB WAS A PLAIN MAN, DWELLING IN TENTS.

(28) "AND ISAAC LOVED ESAU, BECAUSE HE DID EAT OF HIS VENISON: BUT REBEKAH LOVED JACOB.

(29) "AND JACOB SOD POTTAGE: AND ESAU CAME FROM THE FIELD, AND HE WAS FAINT:

(30) "AND ESAU SAID TO JACOB, FEED ME, I PRAY YOU, WITH THAT SAME RED POTTAGE; FOR I AM FAINT: THEREFORE WAS HIS NAME CALLED EDOM.

(31) "AND JACOB SAID, SELL ME THIS DAY YOUR BIRTHRIGHT.

(32) "AND ESAU SAID, BEHOLD, I AM AT THE POINT TO DIE: AND WHAT PROFIT SHALL THIS BIRTHRIGHT DO TO ME?

(33) "AND JACOB SAID, SWEAR TO ME THIS DAY; AND HE SWEAR UNTO HIM: AND HE SOLD HIS BIRTHRIGHT UNTO JACOB.

(34) "THEN JACOB GAVE ESAU BREAD AND POTTAGE OF LENTILS; AND HE DID EAT AND DRINK, AND ROSE UP, AND WENT HIS WAY: THUS ESAU DESPISED HIS BIRTHRIGHT."

The construction is:

1. We find here that Isaac loved Esau, which quite possibly characterized something in Isaac which was wrong, which brought about the character of Esau.

2. But the Holy Spirit in the Epistle to the Hebrews calls Esau a *"profane person,"* and, this, because he sold his birthright.

3. He bartered future and eternal wealth for present and temporary need.

4. Jacob on the other hand, gave up present things, poor things no doubt, only pottage; but poor as they were, they had power over Esau's heart.

ISAAC'S LOVE FOR ESAU

Verses 27 and 28 read: *"And the boys grew: and Esau was a cunning hunter, a man of the field; and Jacob was a plain man, dwelling in tents.*

"And Isaac loved Esau, because he did eat of his venison: but Rebekah loved Jacob."

The original language proclaims the fact that Esau was a wild, undisciplined man who lived a wild life seeking sport and adventure. In contrast to him, Jacob was a quiet, mature individual. The Hebrew *"tam"* also means that he was sensible, diligent, dutiful, and peaceful. He could be counted on to carry out the duties of life. He was orderly, and paid attention to business.

But yet Isaac loved Esau, while Rebekah loved Jacob.

While Isaac certainly should have loved Esau, the type of love he manifested toward him was against the Word of God. He was determined to give the blessing of the birthright to Esau, even though his oldest son cared not at all for spiritual things.

Isaac at this stage seems to have forgotten his very purpose and reason for living.

Regrettably and sadly, Isaac is a symbol of the Church. If left to its own devices, it will every time give the birthright to Esau. What was Isaac thinking? What is the modern Church thinking? What do I mean by the modern Church?

I mean that the modern Church all too often places its hand of approval upon an Esau, while altogether ignoring or even opposing Jacob. In other words, it will place its seal of approval on one not chosen by God. And when I say the Church, I am primarily speaking of organized religion.

And yet, if one is not led exclusively by the Spirit, this is what one is liable to do. Even the mighty Samuel would have chosen one of the other brothers in place of David, simply because he looked on the outward appearance as do most (I Sam. 16:6-7).

THE BIRTHRIGHT

Verses 29 through 31 read: *"And Jacob sod pottage: and Esau came from the field, and he was faint:*

"And Esau said to Jacob, Feed me, I pray you, with that same red pottage; for I am faint: therefore was his name called Edom.

"And Jacob said, Sell me this day your birthright."

Even though Esau was hungry, this had little, if anything, to do with him trading the birthright for a bowl of stew.

The first emphasis is on Jacob wanting the birthright.

Exactly what was the birthright? The birthright was:

1. Succession to the earthly inheritance of Canaan.

2. Possession of the Covenant Blessing, which included his seed being as the stars of the sky, and all the families of the Earth being blessed in him.

3. Progenitorship of the Promised Seed, which was the greatest Blessing of all, and spoke of Christ.

The firstborn was to receive the birthright, and Esau was the firstborn.

As it can be seen, the birthright then dealt primarily with spiritual things, of which Esau had no regard or concern.

Under the Mosaic Law, which would come about 400 years later, the privileges of the firstborn were clearly defined:

1. The official authority of the father.

2. A double portion of the father's property.

3. The functions of the Domestic Priesthood.

More than likely, the birthright in Isaac's time included these same privileges.

Jacob, deplorable as was his character, valued Divine and eternal blessings; and had he placed himself in God's Hands, the prophecy made to his mother before he was born, would have been fulfilled to him, and without the degradation and suffering which his own scheming brought upon him.

The Domestic Priesthood meant that the eldest son acted as Priest for the family, and offered the sacrifices which God had commanded Adam and his sons to offer.

PROFIT?

Verses 32 through 34 read: *"And Esau said, Behold, I am at the point to die: and what profit shall this birthright do to me?*

"And Jacob said, Swear to me this day: and he swear unto him: and he sold his birthright unto Jacob.

"Then Jacob gave Esau bread and pottage of lentils; and he did eat and drink, and rose up, and went his way: thus Esau despised his birthright."

The natural heart places no value on the things of God, as we see evidenced in the choices made by Esau. To the natural heart, God's Promises are a vague, valueless, powerless thing, simply because God is not known. Hence it is that present things carry such weight and influence in man's estimation. Anything that man can *"see,"* he values, because he is governed by sight and not by faith. To him, the present is everything; the future is a mere uninfluential thing — a matter of the merest uncertainty. Thus it was with Esau.

His question, *"What profit shall this birthright do to me?"*, characterizes the majority of the human race. The *"present"* is everything, while the *"future"* is nothing. As a result, they abandon all interest in eternity! The things of God did not interest the eldest son of Isaac; so he despised his birthright: thus Israel despised the pleasant land (Ps. 106:24); thus they despised Christ (Zech. 11:13); thus those who were bidden to the marriage despised the invitation (Mat. 22:5).

Think about it! To Esau, a mess of pottage was better than a title to Canaan.

THE THOUGHTS OF FAITH

When a person truly knows God, he will have a true worth of eternal things. As well, he will see present things for what they really are, temporal, vague, slippery and, therefore, of little consequence. The clearer one can see the vanity of man's present, the more he can cleave to God's future. Look at the judgment of faith:

The Scripture says, *"Seeing, then, that all these things shall be dissolved, what manner of persons ought ye to be in all holy conversation and Godliness, looking for and hasting unto the coming of the day of God, wherein the heavens being on fire shall be dissolved, and the elements shall melt with fervent heat? Nevertheless we, according to His Promise, look for new heavens and a new Earth, wherein dwelleth Righteousness"* (II Pet. 3:11-13). These are the thoughts of God and, therefore, the thoughts of faith. The things which are seen shall be dissolved.

THE CROSS

We must judge things as the Lord judges things, and this can only be done by Faith. In fact, *"Faith"* is the key to all things. But

as we have said over and over thus far in this Volume, and due to its great significance, we will continue to repeat this great Truth, proper faith, that is the Faith that God recognizes, can only be found in our understanding of the Cross. In fact, if we attempt to understand the Word of God, without putting the Word in its proper perspective of the Cross of Christ, then we will have a false understanding of what the Word teaches.

The story of the Word of God is the story of the Cross. The entirety of its warp and woof is centered up in the Cross of Christ. In fact, the Cross was the first Promise given after the Fall. The Lord said to Satan through the serpent:

"And I will put enmity (hatred) *between you* (Satan) *and the woman, and between your seed* (humanity without God) *and her Seed* (the Lord Jesus Christ)*; it* (Christ) *shall bruise your head* (the victory of the Cross)*, and you shall bruise His heel* (the suffering of the Cross)*"* (Gen. 3:15).

Immediately, even beginning in Genesis, Chapter 4, we find the symbolism of the Cross given plainly in the Substitutionary Offering of the Sacrifices. The lamb was to serve as a substitute until Christ would come. In fact, the head of each family was to serve as a Priest regarding that family, and was commanded by God to offer up Sacrifices; hence, in essence, Esau was saying that he had no interest in such things, didn't see any use in any of it, and had little, if any, qualms in trading the birthright, which included the Domestic Priesthood, for a bowl of soup. How cheaply he sold out! But isn't it the same with the world today?

As we presently view the situation, we cannot help but come to the conclusion that mankind is doing the identical same thing presently. It really doesn't matter if he sells his soul for a bowl of soup or one billion dollars; the end result is the same. Compared to the worth of his soul, and the degree of eternity, what is one billion dollars?!

But the sad truth is, the far greater majority of the world gets only what Esau got, a little soup for the belly, and that's about it.

The offering up of sacrifices by the head of each family was meant to be continued by God until the Law would be given, which would include the sacrificial system, and in a much more pronounced way, which was given to Moses some 2,400 years after the Fall. All of it typified Christ, and what Christ would do on the Cross as it regards the Redemption of humanity.

BELIEVERS AND THE CROSS

It should be understood that Esau was in the Covenant, but yet, he wasn't of the Covenant. In other words, he was like multiple millions of modern Christians, who are in fact in the Church, but are <u>not</u> in the Lord.

It is my contention, if the Believer doesn't understand the Cross, then he will not truly understand the things of the Lord, with many going in the same direction as Esau. And the sadness is, most modern Christians have little understanding of the Cross of Christ, beyond the fact that Jesus died for them. And great numbers in the modern Charismatic Church are even denying that.

By that statement, I'm referring to the fact that they claim that the Cross is of little consequence, in fact, of no consequence at all. They teach that man's Salvation comes through what Jesus did in Hell.

In other words, they teach that Jesus took upon Himself the Satanic nature while he hung on the Cross, thereby, dying as a sinner and going to Hell, as all sinners do. They teach that He suffered three days and nights in Hell, and we speak of the burning side of Hell, with Satan and all the demon hordes thinking that He was defeated. They claim that this, the three days and nights of suffering in the burning side of Hell is the Atonement. At the end of the three days and nights of suffering, they then claim that God said, *"It is enough,"* with Jesus then being *"born again,"* as any sinner is Born-Again, and then raised from the dead.

Never mind that there is not a shred of Biblical evidence to support such contentions, this is what millions believe. It is called *"the Jesus died spiritually doctrine."* It means that he not only died physically on the Cross, which they account for nothing, but as well that He died spiritually, which means that He died without God.

All of this is done through a twisting of Scripture. It is as Peter said: *"Which they who are unlearned and unstable wrest . . . the . . . Scriptures, unto their own destruction"*

NOTES

(II Pet. 3:16). Let's look at some of these Scriptures which they use to support their fallacious doctrine.

FIRSTBORN

Concerning Jesus being *"born again"* in Hell, their basic Scripture is Romans 8:29. It says: *"For whom He did foreknow, He also did predestinate to be conformed to the Image of His Son, that He might be the Firstborn among many brethren."*

The Greek word for *"Firstborn"* is *"prototokos."* It means, *"the foremost, the beginning, the chief, the best."*

It doesn't mean that Jesus was *"born again,"* but rather that He is the One Who makes it possible for all sinners to be Born-Again.

For instance, Paul also said: *"Who* (Christ) *is the Image of the invisible God, the firstborn of every creature"* (Col. 1:15).

This doesn't mean that the Lord of Glory is a creation such as all other things, but rather that He is the One Who has created all things.

Again Paul said: *"And He* (Christ) *is the Head of the body, the Church: Who is the beginning, the firstborn from the dead; that in all things He might have the preeminence"* (Col. 1:18).

Once again this doesn't mean that Jesus was Born-Again, but rather that He is the One Who has made the Resurrection possible.

In fact, there is no English word, the Greek Scholars tell us, which can adequately explain the Greek word *"prototokos."* The word *"firstborn"* is the closest they can get, but which does not adequately explain what it really is.

MY GOD, MY GOD, WHY HAVE YOU FORSAKEN ME?

Jesus was put on the Cross at about 9:00 in the morning, and died at about 3:00 in the afternoon. The Scripture says that there was *"darkness over all the land,"* from the sixth hour to the ninth hour. And at *"about the ninth hour Jesus cried with a loud voice, saying, 'Eli Eli, lama sabachthani?' That is to say, 'My God, My God, why have You forsaken Me?'"* (Mat. 27:46).

There is evidence that during this three hour period, from noon until 3 p.m., that God actually turned His Face from Christ, because He was bearing the penalty of the sin of the world. To fully carry out that penalty, He would have to die.

This doesn't mean that God forsook Christ because He was now a sinner, but because He was bearing the sin penalty. And the thrice-Holy God cannot look at sin in that fashion, in any manner.

However, moments before He died, He said, *"It is finished"* (Jn. 19:30). This meant that He was about to die and, therefore, the sin penalty would be satisfied. He then said, and this is very, very important: *"Father, into Your hands I commend My spirit."* The Scripture then says, *"And having said thus, He gave up the ghost"* (Lk. 23:46).

As is obvious here, He commended His spirit to God, certainly not to Satan and thereby to Hell.

While Jesus after His death did go to Hell, it was only to the Paradise part of Hell, and not to the burning side (Eph. 4:8-9).

He also *"preached unto the spirits in prison,"* referring to fallen angels (I Pet. 3:19-20). There is no record whatsoever of Him going into the burning side of Hell, much less suffering there for three days and nights, burning in the flames, etc.

And those who believe this are actually repudiating the Cross and, therefore, must be put in the category of *"enemies of the Cross of Christ"* (Phil. 3:18).

No, it's the Cross and the Cross alone which guarantees our Salvation and our Sanctification (Eph. 2:13-18; I Pet. 1:18-20).

"Come, let us join our cheerful songs
"With Angels around the Throne;
"Ten thousand are their tongues,
"But all their joys are one."

"Worthy the Lamb Who died, they cry,
"To be exalted thus!
"Worthy the Lamb our hearts reply;
"For He was slain for us."

"Jesus is worthy to receive
"Honor and pow'r Divine;
"And blessings, more than we can give,
"Be, Lord, forever Thine."

"Let all who dwell above the sky,
"And air, and Earth, and seas,
"Inspire to lift Your glories high,
"And speak Your endless praise."

"The whole creation join in one
"To bless the sacred Name
"Of Him Who sits upon the Throne,
"And to adore the Lamb."

CHAPTER 26

(1) "AND THERE WAS A FAMINE IN THE LAND, BESIDE THE FIRST FAMINE THAT WAS IN THE DAYS OF ABRAHAM. AND ISAAC WENT UNTO ABIMELECH KING OF THE PHILISTINES UNTO GERAR.

(2) "AND THE LORD APPEARED UNTO HIM, AND SAID, GO NOT DOWN INTO EGYPT; DWELL IN THE LAND WHICH I WILL TELL THEE OF:

(3) "SOJOURN IN THIS LAND, AND I WILL BE WITH YOU, AND WILL BLESS YOU; FOR UNTO YOU, AND UNTO YOUR SEED, I WILL GIVE ALL THESE COUNTRIES, AND I WILL PERFORM THE OATH WHICH I SWORE UNTO ABRAHAM YOUR FATHER:

(4) "AND I WILL MAKE YOUR SEED TO MULTIPLY AS THE STARS OF HEAVEN, AND WILL GIVE UNTO YOUR SEED ALL THESE COUNTRIES; AND IN YOUR SEED SHALL ALL THE NATIONS OF THE EARTH BE BLESSED;

(5) "BECAUSE THAT ABRAHAM OBEYED MY VOICE, AND KEPT MY CHARGE, MY COMMANDMENTS, MY STATUTES, AND MY LAWS."

The structure is:

1. It is not difficult for Satan to break down the faith of a Believer. So small a matter as a famine is sufficient.

2. We find here that God blessed Isaac materially, but we also find that there is a vast difference between material blessings and Spiritual Blessings.

3. If it is disastrous to the Spiritual Life for the Christian to go down into *"Egypt,"* it is dangerous to go down unto *"Gerar,"* for it is a half way house to Egypt.

THE FAMINE — THE TEST

Verse 1 reads: *"And there was a famine in the land, beside the first famine that was in the days of Abraham. And Isaac went unto Abimelech king of the Philistines unto Gerar."*

"*Abimelech*" was a title somewhat like "*President*" or "*Pharaoh.*" So this was not the same man who dealt with Abraham, a time of some 80 or more years having now passed.

A famine now grips the land, either caused or allowed by the Lord. It was to be a test of Isaac's faith, even as everything which comes our way is a test of faith.

Isaac was now dwelling at the well Lahai-roi, and the evidence is, the well, due to the famine, had now dried up.

The evidence also is that he now determines to go into Egypt, exactly as his father Abraham had done.

It is positive that Abraham had rehearsed all of these matters with Isaac, and the right and wrong of such, so it would seem that the Patriarch would now know better than to make the same mistake as Abraham had made. But while tests and temptations may seem to be so similar at a distance, oftentimes they seem to be extremely dissimilar in their happenings. To abide in the path of faith is relatively a simple thing; however, the reasons for stepping outside of that path are very simple as well, and seem to us, at least at the time, to be very plausible and right.

We find how serious the situation was by the fact of what happened as recorded in the Second Verse.

THE LORD

Verse 2 reads: "*And the LORD appeared unto him, and said, Go not down into Egypt; dwell in the land which I shall tell you of.*"

Evidence is, the Lord appeared to Isaac while he was still at Lahai-roi. Due to the famine, Isaac planned to go down into Egypt, where he surmised he would find ample pasture, etc. Knowing that he is about to make the same mistake as his father Abraham had made, the Lord appears to him. His directions were specific:

1. He was definitely not to go down into Egypt.

2. He was to dwell where the Lord told him to dwell; however, the evidence is, he didn't earnestly seek the Lord about that exact place, rather went to Gerar, and as someone has said, this was the half way house to Egypt. There he would lie and deny his wife, and suffer even a greater danger, prosperity.

Concerning this, Mackintosh said: "*The trials which meet God's people in their course are very much alike, and they ever tend to make manifest how far the heart has found its all in God. It is a difficult matter — a rare attainment — so to walk in sweet communion with God as to be rendered thereby entirely independent of things and people here.*

"*The Egypts and the Gerars which lie on our right hand and on our left present great temptations, either to turn aside out of the right way, or to stop short of our true position as servants of the true and Living God.*"

He went on to say: "*We are informed that 'from Gerar to Jerusalem was three days' journey.' It was, therefore, as compared with Egypt, an advanced position; but still it lay within the range of very dangerous influences. Abraham got into trouble there, and so does Isaac in this Chapter, and that, too, in the very same way.*

"*Abraham denied his wife, and so does Isaac. This is peculiarly solemn. To see both the father and the son fall into the same evil, in the same place, tells us plainly that the influence of that place was not good.*"

Every evidence is that the Lord told Isaac that He would tell him where he was to dwell; however, it seems that some time would pass before Isaac earnestly sought the Lord regarding this particular place and position, which he should have done at the beginning.

THE PROMISES OF GOD

Verses 3 through 5 read: "*Sojourn in this land, and I will be with you, and will bless you; for unto you, and unto your seed, I will give all these countries, and I will perform the oath which I swore unto Abraham your father;*

"*And I will make your seed to multiply as the stars of Heaven, and will give unto your seed all these countries; and in your seed shall all the nations of the Earth be blessed;*

"*Because that Abraham obeyed my voice, and kept My charge, My commandments, My statutes, and My laws.*"

Basically, the Lord reaffirms the Promise He had already made to Abraham, and which He now makes to Isaac.

Horton says: "*The reason Isaac could inherit the Promise and enjoy God's Presence and Blessing was because Abraham obeyed God, fulfilled the obligations God put on him, kept the requirements, commandments, rules, and instructions God gave him."*

Horton continues: *"The Lord told Isaac this to let him know that if he wanted to continue to enjoy God's Salvation, Blessing, and Presence he needed to continue in the same sort of faith and obedience to all the various aspects of God's instructions to him. While he did not yet have a written law, he did have the example of Abraham, and we can be sure that Abraham trained him well."*

Being Pentecostal, we have the tendency to refer back to our Pentecostal forefathers who greatly enjoyed the Blessings of God. However, to have those same Blessings, we have to walk the same path of faith. These Blessings will not automatically follow. Faith and obedience are always required. No one receives anything from the Lord simply because of who they are. Every person, irrespective as to whom they might be, must as well walk the path of Faith, and render obedience to all that the Lord requires, whatever that might be.

While the Lord operates strictly on the basis of Grace, this in no way means that Grace is arbitrary or automatic. Grace functions on the basis of Faith and obedience. And what do we mean by that?

FAITH AND OBEDIENCE

When we speak of faith, exclusively we are speaking of Faith in Christ and what Christ has done for us at the Cross. That is the story of the Bible, which in essence is the story of Redemption. It is the manner in which God deals with humanity.

When we speak of obedience, it needs to be defined, or it will be misunderstood.

Because Jesus fulfilled all the Law, we aren't bound to any such thing. So our obedience now refers strictly to obeying God as it regards our Faith being placed totally and completely in Christ and what Christ has done for us as it regards His sufferings. Obedience refers to trust in His Finished Work. So in a sense, proper Faith and obedience are relatively the same.

If we think of obedience in the realm of laws, rituals, rules, and regulations, etc., we're

misunderstanding the term altogether. All of that went out with the Law. Our obedience presently is centered up in the object of our Faith, Who is Christ Jesus, and what He has done for us in His great Sacrifice of Himself.

(6) "AND ISAAC DWELT IN GERAR:

(7) "AND THE MEN OF THE PLACE ASKED HIM OF HIS WIFE; AND HE SAID, SHE IS MY SISTER: FOR HE FEARED TO SAY, SHE IS MY WIFE; LEST, SAID HE, THE MEN OF THE PLACE SHOULD KILL ME FOR REBEKAH; BECAUSE SHE WAS FAIR TO LOOK UPON.

(8) "AND IT CAME TO PASS, WHEN HE HAD BEEN THERE A LONG TIME, THAT ABIMELECH KING OF THE PHILISTINES LOOKED OUT AT A WINDOW, AND SAW, AND, BEHOLD, ISAAC WAS SPORTING WITH REBEKAH HIS WIFE.

(9) "AND ABIMELECH CALLED ISAAC, AND SAID, BEHOLD, OF A SURETY SHE IS YOUR WIFE; AND HOW SAID YOU, SHE IS MY SISTER? AND ISAAC SAID UNTO HIM, BECAUSE I SAID, LEST I DIE FOR HER.

(10) "AND ABIMELECH SAID, WHAT IS THIS YOU HAVE DONE UNTO US? ONE OF THE PEOPLE MIGHT LIGHTLY HAVE LAID WITH YOUR WIFE, AND YOU SHOULD HAVE BROUGHT GUILTINESS UPON US.

(11) "AND ABIMELECH CHARGED ALL HIS PEOPLE, SAYING, HE WHO TOUCHES THIS MAN OR HIS WIFE SHALL SURELY BE PUT TO DEATH."

The composition is:

1. Isaac dwells in Gerar, with no indication that this is what God had told him to do.

2. Isaac practiced deception here exactly as did his father Abraham.

3. The Patriarch now functions in fear, also exactly as did Abraham his father.

4. Once again the deception doesn't work, as deception is ultimately always found out.

GERAR

Verse 6 reads: *"And Isaac dwelt in Gerar."*

There is no indication that the Lord told Isaac to go to Gerar. The indication is that he went there according to his own leading and direction. It was not the Lord! Events proved that. As we said in the headings, Egypt is a Type of the world; consequently, such a foray always proves to be disastrous. That being the case, it is also very dangerous to go to Gerar, because that is toward Egypt. We are to shun the very appearance of evil.

DECEPTION

Verse 7 reads: *"And the men of the place asked him of his wife; and he said, She is my sister: for he feared to say, She is my wife; lest, said he, the men of place should kill me for Rebekah; because she was fair to look upon."*

Evidently, Rebekah, as Sarah, was very attractive. Probably the ones who inquired about Rebekah were emissaries from Abimelech. At any rate, Isaac lied to them, telling them that Rebekah was his sister.

It is positive that Isaac knew in detail of his father's episode in Egypt, and the wrongness of the act. So why did he follow the same course?

FAITH

Everything we do as a Believer is either an act of Faith, or else an act of faithlessness. If we veer from the path of Faith, and as always we are referring to Christ and the Cross ever being the object of our Faith, we then submit ourselves to all type of problems. Fear sets in, which leads to erroneous actions, such as these committed by Isaac.

As previously stated, I think we can say without fear of contradiction that all sin is caused by one leaving the path of Faith. Faith in Christ and what He has done for us regarding His Sacrifice provides the means by and through which the Holy Spirit works. Faith properly placed guarantees the help of the Spirit, which guarantees victory. To leave the path of Faith, and for whatever reason, opens ourselves up to Satan, with temptation being the result, and almost invariably, failure following closely on its heels (Gen. 0.14, I Cor. 1:17-18).

FAITHLESSNESS

Verses 8 and 9 read: *"And it came to pass, when he had been there a long time, that Abimelech king of the Philistines looked out at a window, and saw, and, behold, Isaac was sporting with Rebekah his wife.*

"And Abimelech called Isaac, and said, Behold, of a surety she is your wife; and how said you, She is my sister? And Isaac said unto him, Because I said, Lest I die for her."

Deception can succeed only for a short period of time. Isaac forgets himself and kisses his wife, and that in a place where he can be seen, and in fact was seen. So Abimelech calls him on the carpet, so to speak. Then the truth comes out.

Once again, God's primary emissary on Earth is humiliated. And let it be known and understood that sin always humiliates, and irrespective by whom it is committed. In fact, and as should be obvious, the humiliation is even worse according to the position of the individual in question.

ABIMELECH

Verses 10 and 11 read: *"And Abimelech said, What is this you have done unto us? One of the people might lightly have laid with your wife, and you should have brought guiltiness upon us.*

"And Abimelech charged all his people, saying, He who touches this man or his wife shall surely be put to death."

Basically the same questions are put to Isaac by Abimelech, as were put to his father by Pharaoh.

Concerning this, Matthew Henry said: *"There is nothing in Isaac's denial of his wife to be imitated, nor even excused. The impartiality of the sacred historian records it for our warning, and to show that Righteousness comes not by the Law, but by faith in Christ."*

The sin of Isaac was greater than the sin of his father Abraham. While no sin is to be excused, Isaac had this unsavory example before him, so there was no excuse for what he did.

(12) "THEN ISAAC SOWED IN THAT LAND, AND RECEIVED IN THE SAME YEAR AN HUNDREDFOLD: AND THE LORD BLESSED HIM.

(13) "AND THE MAN WAXED GREAT, AND WENT FORWARD, AND GREW UNTIL HE BECAME VERY GREAT:

(14) "FOR HE HAD POSSESSION OF FLOCKS, AND POSSESSION OF HERDS, AND GREAT STORE OF SERVANTS: AND THE PHILISTINES ENVIED HIM.

(15) "FOR ALL THE WELLS WHICH HIS FATHER'S SERVANTS HAD DUG IN THE DAYS OF ABRAHAM HIS FATHER, THE PHILISTINES HAD STOPPED THEM, AND FILLED THEM WITH EARTH.

(16) "AND ABIMELECH SAID UNTO ISAAC, GO FROM US; FOR YOU ARE MUCH MIGHTIER THAN WE.

(17) "AND ISAAC DEPARTED THENCE, AND PITCHED HIS TENT IN THE VALLEY OF GERAR, AND DWELT THERE."

The construction is:

1. A man may, like Isaac, become rich in *"Gerar,"* but it is not recorded that Jehovah appeared to Isaac in Gerar. He appeared to him before he went there and the very night of the day that he left.

2. We can never judge that a person's condition with the Lord is right because of prosperous circumstances.

3. We must always understand that there is a great difference between the Lord's Presence and His Blessing.

4. How many do we see surrounded by God's Blessings, who neither have nor wish for God's Presence?

THE HUNDREDFOLD RETURN

Verses 12 through 14 read: *"Then Isaac sowed in that land, and received in the same year an hundredfold: and the LORD blessed him.*

"And the man waxed great, and went forward, and grew until he became very great:

"For he had possession of flocks, and possession of herds, and great store of servants: and the Philistines envied him."

There is a tremendous lesson to be learned in these Passages, if we only have the spiritual depth to do so.

We're living in an age when the faith of individuals is all too often judged by the price of the suit of clothes they wear, or the model of car they drive. And to be sure, this fallacious doctrine is heady, and simply because there seems to be a modicum of greed in all of us.

Financial prosperity is one thing, while spiritual prosperity is something else altogether. Satan is perfectly happy for us to concentrate our efforts in the realm of material prosperity, while we neglect the spiritual, or

to equate material prosperity with spiritual prosperity.

Some may ask the question, if Isaac's position in Gerar is wrong, how do we read, *"Then Isaac sowed in that land, and received the same year an hundredfold; and the Lord blessed him"*?

Scripturally, the answer is that we can never judge a person's spiritual condition by the light of prosperous circumstances. We make a great mistake if we do so. There is a great difference between the Lord's Presence and His Blessing. Many have the latter without the former; and, moreover, the heart is prone to mistake the one for the other — prone, as stated, to put the Blessing before the Presence, or at least to argue that the one must ever accompany the other. This is a great mistake.

How many do we see surrounded by God's Blessings, who neither have nor wish for God's Presence? It is important to see this.

A man may *"wax great, and go forward, and grow until he becomes very great, and have possession of flocks, and possession of herds, and great store of servants,"* and all the while not have the full unhindered joy of the Lord's Presence with him. Flocks and herds are not necessarily the Lord. They can only be constituted as *"things"*! And Jesus said concerning that:

"Take heed, and beware of covetousness: for a man's life consisteth not in the abundance of the things which he possesseth" (Lk. 12:15).

While we definitely believe that the Bible teaches that God will bless and prosper any Believer who puts and places their Faith and trust in Him; however, the ambition of the Believer must never be that of material things, but rather the Presence of the Lord. If the Lord sees fit in fact, to bless us with material things, we should give Him all the praise and all the glory, and then use those proceeds for His glory, which is to take the message of Redemption to a hurting world.

THE WELLS

Verses 15 through 17 read: *"For all the wells which his father's servants had dug in the days of Abraham his father, the Philistines had stopped them, and filled them with earth.*

"And Abimelech said unto Isaac, Go from us, for you are much mightier than we.

"And Isaac departed thence, and pitched his tent in the valley of Gerar, and dwelt there."

Isaac watered his vast herds from the wells which Abraham had dug many years before. However, the Philistines filled up the wells, thereby destroying his water supply, which was essential, and then requested that he depart from them. So he left Gerar proper, and *"pitched his tent in the valley of Gerar, and dwelt there."*

We will find that Isaac still wasn't in the place where the Lord wanted him, as far as him dwelling in the land was concerned. Sometime before, the Lord had told Isaac, *"Go not down into Egypt; dwell in the land which I shall tell thee of"* (vs. 2).

It seems that Isaac only assumed that he knew where the Lord wanted him at the time, or else he based his conclusions on human reasoning. Either way, as we see, was wrong.

But yet, even though he wasn't in the center of God's Will, the Lord continued to bless him, and continued to do so greatly.

We must understand that the Blessings of the Lord, to which we've already alluded, are not always because of our great Faith, or our goodness, but rather because of the Grace of God. In fact, one must say that the Blessings of the Lord are always because of God's Grace, and never because of any goodness on our part. But we're so prone to think of *"our faith,"* or *"our goodness,"* etc. The truth is, if the Lord withheld Blessings from us because of an improper spiritual condition, etc., more than likely, very few people would experience any blessing at all.

We must understand that whatever way the Lord leads us, it is always for the purpose of drawing us closer to Him. While it may not work, that is not the fault of the Lord, but rather our fault. I think the following would always be very helpful:

If every Believer would look at his present circumstances, and whatever they might be, understand those circumstances as having been brought on by the Lord, whether good or bad, and that the Lord has but one purpose in mind, and that is our spiritual welfare. So we should let our present position, whatever it might be, serve as a lever if you

will, to push us toward the Lord, instead of allowing the circumstances to drive us away.

Jesus told the story of the rich man and Lazarus. The latter was a beggar.

The rich man didn't allow his blessing to draw him to God, which it was intended to do, and Lazarus didn't allow his poverty to push him away from the Lord. Men respond in different ways. But it's God's intention that all would look at their circumstances and respond favorably to the Lord, for the circumstances are brought to bear for that very purpose.

So Isaac moved his tent to the *"valley of Gerar and dwelt there."* But this was not God's place for him, and now contention will begin to rear its ugly head.

(18) "AND ISAAC DUG AGAIN THE WELLS OF WATER, WHICH THEY HAD DUG IN THE DAYS OF ABRAHAM HIS FATHER; FOR THE PHILISTINES HAD STOPPED THEM AFTER THE DEATH OF ABRAHAM: AND HE CALLED THEIR NAMES AFTER THE NAMES BY WHICH HIS FATHER HAD CALLED THEM.

(19) "AND ISAAC'S SERVANTS DUG IN THE VALLEY, AND FOUND THERE A WELL OF SPRINGING WATER.

(20) "AND THE HERDMEN OF GERAR DID STRIVE WITH ISAAC'S HERDMEN, SAYING, THE WATER IS OURS: AND HE CALLED THE NAME OF THE WELL ESEK; BECAUSE THEY STROVE WITH HIM.

(21) "AND THEY DUG ANOTHER WELL, AND STROVE FOR THAT ALSO: AND HE CALLED THE NAME OF IT SITNAH.

(22) "AND HE REMOVED FROM THENCE, AND DUG ANOTHER WELL; AND FOR THAT THEY STROVE NOT: AND HE CALLED THE NAME OF IT REHOBOTH; AND HE SAID, FOR NOW THE LORD HAS MADE ROOM FOR US, AND WE SHALL BE FRUITFUL IN THE LAND."

The overview is:

1. This activity of Isaac called forth anew the opposition of the Philistines.

2. Prosperity does not necessarily guarantee peace, and in fact, most of the time has a tendency, as we shall see, to bring about contention.

3. The Lord allowed the contention, so as to push Isaac to the locality where God wanted him.

ABRAHAM

Verse 18 reads: *"And Isaac dug again the wells of water, which they had dug in the days of Abraham his father; for the Philistines had stopped them after the death of Abraham: and he called their names after the names by which his father had called them."*

The Philistines didn't have any right to stop up these wells for the simple reason that Abraham had made a league or covenant with Abimelech, the king of the Philistines, which allowed him these wells.

So Isaac unstopped these wells, and called them by the names which his father Abraham had called them, whatever that may have been.

However, as we shall see in the next few Verses, these particular wells evidently did not provide enough water for the vast flocks and herds of Isaac, so new wells would be dug.

But still, as we shall see, Isaac was not where the Lord actually wanted him.

STRIFE

Verses 19 and 20 read: *"And Isaac's servants dug in the valley, and found there a well of springing water.*

"And the herdmen of Gerar did strive with Isaac's herdmen, saying, The water is ours: and he called the name of the well Esek; because they strove with him."

The idea as held by the Philistines was that the land belonged to them, and Isaac had no right to be there. They looked at the digging of wells as a claim to the land. So they contended with Isaac's herdmen. So Isaac named the well *"contention."*

While the Lord definitely did not put it into the hearts of these individuals to contend with Isaac, he did use the evil that was already there to further His purpose.

Many times the opposition we receive, while definitely wrong on the part of the one who is doing the opposing, still, the Lord uses these things to further His Cause in our lives. While the Lord never excuses the wrong, and to be sure, the ones doing such will ultimately answer; no wrong, irrespective as to who does it, is ever overlooked by the Lord.

But when it comes to our reaction, we must realize that the Lord is allowing these things to happen, whatever the things might

be; therefore, we must leave the individuals in the Hands of the Lord, and as well try to learn what the Lord is teaching us.

CONTENTION

Verse 21 reads: *"And they dug another well, and strove for that also: and he called the name of it Sitnah."*

As *"Esek"* means, *"contention,"* the word *"Sitnah"* means, *"strife."* We find here that the opposition of the Philistines was developing into bitter persecution. I think now that Isaac is beginning to get the message, but it will take even yet more convincing.

FRUITFUL

Verse 22 reads: *"And he removed from thence, and dug another well; and for that they strove not: and he called the name of it Rehoboth; and he said, For now the LORD has made room for us, and we shall be fruitful in the land."*

The Philistines did not seem to contend for this particular well, with Isaac referring to it as *"wide spaces."*

He says that *"the Lord has made room for us, and we shall be fruitful in the land,"* showing that he knows that the Lord is leading and guiding in all of this. Despite the fact that there is no contention for this particular well, he seems to now understand that he still isn't exactly where God wants him to be. The Lord wanted him in Beer-sheba, but as with all of us, sometimes we have to go through contention and strife before we finally come to the place desired for us by the Lord.

(23) "AND HE WENT UP FROM THENCE TO BEER-SHEBA.

(24) "AND THE LORD APPEARED UNTO HIM THE SAME NIGHT, AND SAID, I AM THE GOD OF ABRAHAM YOUR FATHER: FEAR NOT, FOR I AM WITH YOU, AND WILL BLESS YOU, AND MULTIPLY YOUR SEED FOR MY SERVANT ABRAHAM'S SAKE.

(25) "AND HE BUILT AN ALTAR THERE, AND CALLED UPON THE NAME OF THE LORD, AND PITCHED HIS TENT THERE: AND THERE ISAAC'S SERVANTS DUG A WELL."

BEER-SHEBA

Verse 23 reads: *"And he went up from thence to Beer-sheba."*

Several years of strife and contention could have been avoided, had Isaac earnestly sought the Lord in the beginning as it regarded his dwelling place. But like so many of us, we fail to seek the Lord as we should, and thereby bring upon ourselves hurt and harm.

As to why the Lord wanted the Patriarch in Beer-sheba, we aren't exactly told. And neither is it our business as to why the Lord wants us to do certain things. Our business is simply to know what He wants and desires, and then to obey.

We must always remember that God has nothing but our good at heart. He not only has our good, but He knows what is best for us, and sadly, we don't.

Actually, Beer-sheba was closer to the Philistines than the place he was leaving. But if we're in the Will of the Lord, wherever the place might be, things will work out in one way or the other.

THE PROMISE

Verse 24 reads: *"And the LORD appeared unto him the same night, and said, I am the God of Abraham your father: fear not, for I am with you, and will bless you, and multiply your seed for My servant Abraham's sake."*

In this land of Beer-sheba he finds peace, refreshment, and fellowship with God. So long as he dwelt at Gerar there was nothing but strife and contention. Now that he is at Beer-sheba, where the Lord wants him to be, the Lord appears to him, evidently immediately upon his arriving there.

This appearance by the Lord is to let Isaac know that he is now in the center of God's Will. And never mind that he is very close to the Philistines, he need not fear. And the reason that he need not fear is that the Lord is with him in every capacity. This doesn't mean that the Lord had not been with him all along, for He definitely had. But it does mean that Isaac is now in a new dimension, which can expect the very best from the Lord.

The Lord will bless him, and not only in material things, but above all, even as the next Verse proclaims, in spiritual things, which are by far the most important.

Abraham is held up by the Lord as an example, which means that the Lord intends for Isaac to emulate his father.

If it is to be noticed, Abraham is spoken of, although dead, but not as one who has ceased to be. In fact, Abraham right then was in Paradise, along with Abel, Enoch, Noah, and probably many others.

Again if it is to be noticed, blessing always involves addition or multiplication.

THE ALTAR

Verse 25 reads: *"And he built an Altar there, and called upon the Name of the LORD, and pitched his tent there: and there Isaac's servants dug a well."*

This Verse proclaims four things:

1. The Patriarch built an Altar: This proclaims his Faith in that which the Lord would do as it regards the sending of a Redeemer into this world, Who would die on the Cross. The *"Altar"* was a Type of that Sacrificial Offering.

This is the first instance of Altar building ascribed to Isaac. It is almost certain that those erected by his father were used by him as well to offer Sacrifices.

2. Calling upon the Name of the Lord proclaims the Patriarch publicly celebrating his worship in the midst of his household. There is a difference in calling on the Name of the Lord when one is outside the Will of God, than it is when one is in the center of God's Will. This *"Calling"* is anchored in Faith and victory, and will be rewarded accordingly.

3. He pitched his tent there: This was the place the Lord wanted him, and had in fact, appeared unto him; consequently, it was there that he wanted to domicile, and it is understandable as to why. It had taken awhile to get here, but he definitely now knew that this was the place that God wanted him.

4. Isaac's servants dug a well: The Hebrew word used here has not been previously used in this Chapter. It doesn't refer to a well newly dug, but rather signifies the reopening of the well which Abraham had dug many years before, but which had been stopped or closed by violence or neglect. At any rate, the well was reopened.

(26) "THEN ABIMELECH WENT TO HIM FROM GERAR, AND AHUZZATH ONE OF HIS FRIENDS, AND PHICHOL, THE CHIEF CAPTAIN OF HIS ARMY.

(27) "AND ISAAC SAID UNTO THEM, WHEREFORE COME YOU TO ME, SEEING YOU HATE ME, AND HAVE SENT ME AWAY FROM YOU?

(28) "AND THEY SAID, WE SAW CERTAINLY THAT THE LORD WAS WITH YOU: AND WE SAID, LET THERE BE NOW AN OATH BETWEEN US, EVEN BETWEEN US AND YOU, AND LET US MAKE A COVENANT WITH YOU;

(29) "THAT YOU WILL DO US NO HURT, AS WE HAVE NOT TOUCHED YOU, AND AS WE HAVE DONE UNTO YOU NOTHING BUT GOOD, AND HAVE SENT YOU AWAY IN PEACE: YOU ARE NOW THE BLESSED OF THE LORD.

(30) "AND HE MADE THEM A FEAST, AND THEY DID EAT AND DRINK.

(31) "AND THEY ROSE UP BETIMES IN THE MORNING, AND SWEAR ONE TO ANOTHER: AND ISAAC SENT THEM AWAY, AND THEY DEPARTED FROM HIM IN PEACE."

The exegesis is:

1. Abimelech now seeks peace between himself and Isaac, and because the fear of the Lord is now on him as it regards Isaac.

2. Inasmuch as Isaac is now in the place where God wants him, and that he is in the center of God's Will, the Lord will make even his enemies to be at peace with him.

3. The Philistines saw that the Lord was with Isaac. In modern terminology, it's a shame that many in the world can see the same thing, and the Church cannot.

ABIMELECH

Verses 26 and 27 read: *"Then Abimelech went to him from Gerar, and Ahuzzath one of his friends, and Phichol the chief captain of his army.*

"And Isaac said unto them, Wherefore come you to me, seeing you hate me, and have sent me away from you?"

Concerning this visit, Williams says: *"It is when Isaac definitely separates himself from the men of Gerar that they come to him seeking blessing through him from God. All the time that he dwelt among them it is not recorded that they approached him in this way. This is one of the many lessons in the Bible which teach the Christian that*

he best helps the world when living in separation from it."

THE BLESSINGS OF THE LORD

Verses 28 through 31 read: *"And they said, We saw certainly that the LORD was with you: and we said, Let there be now an oath between us, even between us and you, and let us make a covenant with you;*

"That you will do us no hurt, as we have not touched you, and as we have done unto you nothing but good, and have sent you away in peace: you are now the blessed of the LORD.

"And he made them a feast, and they did eat and drink.

"And they rose up betimes in the morning, and swear one to another: and Isaac sent them away, and they departed from him in peace."

In those days, blessings or judgment were ascribed to the *"god"* of that particular country or people. In fact, in all countries with the exception of Israel, many gods were worshiped.

In some manner, Abimelech recognizes the Hand of the Lord upon Isaac, and although not accepting Jehovah, still, he certainly did recognize the power of Jehovah, at least to a certain degree.

Whether the Philistine king was serious concerning his statements is anyone's guess. We do know that some of his statements concerning peace, etc., were entirely wrong.

In fact, many years before, Abraham had been confederate with the Amorites (Gen. 14:13), and as well, on friendly terms with the Hittites (Gen. 23:6), the two most powerful races of Canaan. So Abimelech may have reasoned that these two powerful tribes may as well be ready to aid the son of Abraham.

But whatever the reason, the Lord used these series of circumstances, whatever they may have been, to bring about peace between the Philistine king, and Isaac.

At any rate, a covenant is made between Isaac and Abimelech, with the Scripture saying, *"they departed from him in peace."*

He will stay in Beer-sheba for some time, but would ultimately move to Mamre, about 35 miles north of Beer-sheba, and would die in Mamre. He would be buried at Machpelah, where Abraham was buried, and where Jacob as well would be buried.

(32) "AND IT CAME TO PASS THE SAME DAY, THAT ISAAC'S SERVANTS CAME, AND TOLD HIM CONCERNING THE WELL WHICH THEY HAD DUG, AND SAID UNTO HIM, WE HAVE FOUND WATER.

(33) "AND HE CALLED IT SHEBAH: THEREFORE THE NAME OF THE CITY IS BEER-SHEBA UNTO THIS DAY."

The synopsis is:

1. The water here is symbolic of the water of life which would be afforded by the Lord Jesus Christ, the *"Seed"* of Abraham, Isaac, and Jacob.

2. *"He called it Shebah,"* which means, *"the well of the oath."* It was symbolic of the Covenant made by the Lord with Abraham concerning Redemption.

3. The entire Chapter pertains to *"a voice to be heard, a charge to be kept, commandments to be obeyed, statutes to be loved, and laws to be followed."*

THE WELL OF THE OATH

Verses 32 and 33 read: *"And it came to pass the same day, that Isaac's servants came, and told him concerning the well which they had dug, and said unto him, We have found water.*

"And he called it Shebah: therefore the name of the city is Beer-sheba unto this day."

It is certain that Isaac perfectly understood that this place had been so named by his father about 75 years before. Considering this, it should be understood that all of this had a spiritual connotation.

Isaac was reaffirming that the Covenant made between God and his father, concerning the land ultimately belonging to Abraham, i.e., *"his seed,"* that this in fact would definitely be done (Gen. 21:27-34).

And so it was!

(34) "AND ESAU WAS FORTY YEARS OLD WHEN HE TOOK TO WIFE JUDITH THE DAUGHTER OF BEERI THE HITTITE, AND BASHEMATH THE DAUGHTER OF ELON THE HITTITE:

(35) "WHICH WERE A GRIEF OF MIND UNTO ISAAC AND TO REBEKAH."

The diagram is:

1. Esau's profanity in selling his birthright was quickly followed by his double marriage with the Hittites. So is it ever, the heart that

despises heavenly things very quickly becomes doubly yoked to this present evil world.

2. In marrying these Canaanite women, Esau renounced all claims to a spiritual inheritance.

3. While Esau was in the covenant family, he was not of the Lord. Millions today are in the Church, but they definitely aren't of the Lord.

ESAU

Verses 34 and 35 read: *"And Esau was forty years old when he took to wife Judith the daughter of Beeri the Hittite, and Bashemath the daughter of Elon the Hittite:*

"Which were a grief of mind unto Isaac and to Rebekah."

Esau at 40 years of age was the same age as his father Isaac when some 60 years before, he had married Esau's mother, Rebekah.

The names of these two women are remarkable, and showing that the Hittites spoke a Semitic tongue. *"Judith"* as the feminine form of Judah, means *"praised."* *"Bashemath"* means, *"fragrant,"* and was the name also of a daughter of Solomon (I Ki. 4:15).

No doubt, Esau reasoned in his mind that these girls were little different, if at all, than the family of Abraham back in Haran. But there was a great difference; the greatest being that God had commanded that wives be taken from the family of Abraham, and not from the Canaanites. Whatever the other reasons, that is enough! (The family of Abraham was in the line of Shem, from whom the Messiah would come. Also Canaan and his line were cursed [Gen. 9:25-26].)

"The spacious firmament on high, with all the blue ethereal sky,
"And spangled heavens, a shining frame.
"Their great original proclaim, the unwearied sun, from day-to-day, does his Creator's Power display,
"And publishes to every land the work of an Almighty Hand."

"Soon as the evening shades prevail, the moon takes up the wondrous tale,
"And nightly to the listening Earth repeats the story of her birth;
"While all the stars that round her burn, and all the planets in their turn,

*"Confirm the tidings as they roll, and
spread the truth from pole to pole."*

*"What though in solemn silence all,
move round this dark terrestrial ball?"*

*"What though no real voice nor sound,
amidst their radiant orbs be found?"*

*"In reason's ear they all rejoice, and
utter forth a glorious voice;"*

*"Forever singing, as they shine, the
Hand that made us is Divine."*

CHAPTER 27

(1) "AND IT CAME TO PASS, THAT WHEN ISAAC WAS OLD, AND HIS EYES WERE DIM, SO THAT HE COULD NOT SEE, HE CALLED ESAU HIS ELDEST SON, AND SAID UNTO HIM, MY SON: AND HE SAID UNTO HIM, BEHOLD, HERE AM I.

(2) "AND HE SAID, BEHOLD NOW, I AM OLD, I KNOW NOT THE DAY OF MY DEATH:

(3) "NOW THEREFORE TAKE, I PRAY YOU, YOUR WEAPONS, YOUR QUIVER AND YOUR BOW, AND GO OUT TO THE FIELD, AND TAKE ME SOME VENISON;

(4) "AND MAKE ME SAVORY MEAT, SUCH AS I LOVE, AND BRING IT TO ME, THAT I MAY EAT; THAT MY SOUL MAY BLESS YOU BEFORE I DIE.

(5) "AND REBEKAH HEARD WHEN ISAAC SPOKE TO ESAU HIS SON. AND ESAU WENT TO THE FIELD TO HUNT FOR VENISON, AND TO BRING IT."

The structure is:

1. The history of Jacob is a treasure house of spiritual instruction for the people of God. Jacob as no other man symbolizes the Sanctification process.

2. Jacob was the most unlovely member of the family: yet Grace chose him to be the head of all the nations of the Earth.

3. Grace heaps everything upon those who deserve nothing.

4. Jacob himself is a sad illustration of the destructive power of fallen human nature.

THE BIRTHRIGHT

Verses 1 through 5 read: *"And it came to pass, that when Isaac was old, and his eyes were dim, so that he could not see, he called*

Esau his eldest son, and said unto him, My son: and he said unto him, Behold, here am I.

"And he said, Behold now, I am old, I know not the day of my death:

"Now therefore take, I pray you, your weapons, your quiver and your bow, and go out to the field, and take me some venison;

"And make me savory meat, such as I love, and bring it to me, that I may eat; that my soul may bless you before I die.

"And Rebekah heard when Isaac spoke to Esau his son. And Esau went to the field to hunt for venison, and to bring it."

As the record will show, if Esau was ready to sell the birthright for a mess of pottage; his father was prepared to sell it for a dish of venison! Concerning this, Williams said: *"Humbling picture of a man of God under the power of his lower sensual nature!"*

Isaac had been told by God at the time of Jacob's birth that he (Jacob) was to possess the birthright. But yet he ignores this Word from the Lord, and proceeds in his determination to give this birthright to Esau, despite the fact that Esau knew the Lord not at all!

So Rebekah overhears the intention of Isaac, and proceeds to manage the affairs herself; therefore, she steps outside the path of faith.

We may wonder about all of this, considering that these people were the Church of that particular time; however, the Lord definitely had and has a Purpose in setting before us all the traits of man's flawed character. We will find that it serves two means. It is to magnify His Grace, and to serve as a warning for you and me.

The truth is, all of this is done, not at all to perpetuate the memory of sins, which in fact, are forever blotted out from His sight. In fact, all the flaws, sins, and wrong directions of Abraham, Isaac, and Jacob, plus every other Believer who has ever lived, have been perfectly washed away, with each of these individuals taking their place amid *"the spirits of just men made perfect."*

In all of this, we see that God has not been dealing with perfect men and women, but with those of *"like passions as we are,"* and that He has been working and bearing with the same failures, the same infirmities, the same errors, as those over which we mourn everyday.

THE POWER OF SIN

In all of this, and most assuredly, we surely should see the terrible power of sin, which shows up in the flaws of humanity, irrespective of the Blessings of God upon our lives. If we forget this, we need only look at the pages of the Holy Bible, and the case is made.

In fact, all of this stands in striking contrast with the way in which the great majority of human biographies are written, in which, for the most part, we find, not the history of men, but of beings devoid of error and infirmity. Such flatteries have the effect of rather discouraging us, than edifying us. They are rather histories of what ought to be, than of what they really are, and they are, therefore, useless to us, not only useless, but for the most part, harmful.

Thus, the Word of God in no way glosses over the flaws, faults, and failures of even its champions. They are laid out in all of their ugliness, with nothing held back, which shows us the terrible degree of man's depravity and lostness.

THE CROSS

Consequently, we see, or most definitely we should see, the terrible need for the Cross. When it's all said and done, when the last roll call has been given, when all the façade is stripped away, when we've tried to explain Justification by Faith, and as well, Sanctification by Faith, plus our understanding of God's Grace, coupled all together with His love, we see — finally we see — that really the only thing that is left, or maybe we can say that all of these great Doctrines are bound together in one symbol, and that symbol is the Cross of Christ. It alone stands between us and eternal Hell! It alone stands between us and eternal darkness! The Cross alone stands as the beacon of light in the midst of a darkened world!

Such is the power of sin, but make no mistake about it, the Cross is greater! If sin has dragged down the entirety of the human race, and done so in all of its putrid ugliness, the Cross has lifted man out of this morass of

evil, and of course when we speak of the Cross, we speak of Christ.

THE NEW CHURCH

The new Church in its modern doctrine strikes at the very foundation of the faith. It understands Christ's death on the Cross as merely God's Way of showing how much He loves us. In this view, Christ does not atone for our sins, since our sins, as one Preacher put it, are merely nothing more than our individual acts of individual wills. Consequently, Jesus, they teach, is not at all our sacrifice; rather, He is our example. He shows us how to love each other. His death on the Cross makes us feel sorry for Him, and when we really realize how much He suffered, it makes us feel God's love. This motivates us, they say, to change our lives and to love others.

So the new Church does not involve itself in proclaiming God's judgment against sinners and His gracious offer of Salvation through Faith in Jesus Christ. Rather, the new Church simply educates people as to how much God loves them. According to the way of thinking of the new Church, God really does not want to punish anyone; He wants all to feel good about themselves, to lead a full life, to be happy. Although this theology of the new Church turns God into a warm, fuzzy therapist, it is essentially a teaching of moralism and despair, focusing on human works. It gives no comfort to tormented souls and includes no provision for the forgiveness of sin. In fact, the words of Paul scream out against this nonsense. He said, *"If Righteousness could be gained through the Law, Christ died for nothing!"* (Gal. 2:21).

Concerning all of this, Michael Horton said: *"Before, God existed for His Own happiness, but this new god exists for ours. Instead of sinners having to be justified before a good and holy God, we are now ourselves the good guys who demand that God justify Himself before us. Why should we believe in Him? How will believing in Him make me happier and more fulfilled than believing in Karma or the latest ideological bandwagon?"*

Gene Veith said: *"Throughout its history, the Church has always had two options — to go along with the times or to counter them. One could argue that the most vital theological movements in Church history have been those that went against the trends of their time."*

RESPONSE TO THE CROSS

As I've already said several times in this Volume, the Lord in 1996 began to give to me the Revelation of the Cross. It was not something new, actually the teaching of the Apostle Paul, as the Holy Spirit gave it to him. But the difference in my own situation was that the Lord helped me to understand this which the great Apostle had taught.

It revolutionized my life, exactly as it has revolutionized the lives of untold millions of others. In fact, there is no deliverance, no victory, no Salvation outside of the Cross of Christ. As the song says, *"All else is sinking sand."*

But I have been amazed at the response of many, even when they were proverbially hanging on by their fingertips. Staring destruction in the face, they say, *"I suppose that's alright for some* (speaking of the Cross), *but it's definitely not for all."*

What could they mean by such thinking?

Does God have ten, or five, or even two ways of Salvation and victory? The answer to that is quite simple; no, He doesn't! He has only one Way, and that is the Cross. That's why Paul said:

"But God forbid that I should glory, save in the Cross of our Lord Jesus Christ, by Whom the world is crucified unto me, and I unto the world" (Gal. 6:14).

Therefore, this brings us to the reason that the Cross is rejected.

THE CROSS IS NEVER REJECTED FOR THEOLOGICAL REASONS, BUT ALWAYS FOR MORAL REASONS

And what do we mean by that?

The great Plan of Redemption, despite its dire cost, is in reality a simple provision. A person doesn't have to be a scholar, a theologian, a genius, or any such like, in order to understand God's Plan of Redemption. He just simply has to believe (Jn. 3:16; Rom. 10:9-10, 13; Rev. 22:17).

So if a person rejects the Cross, he must do so on the basis of moral reasons. This means that the problem is pride, self-will, stubbornness, rebellion against God, or some

NOTES

such sin, which as is obvious, all fall into the morality problem.

When the Lord first began to open up this great truth to me, and I might quickly add after some five years of soul-searching prayer, I at first thought that Scriptural ignorance was the problem. But after nearly six years of observing people, I have now come to the conclusion that while ignorance definitely does abound, the greatest problem of all is *"unbelief."* In other words, the great mass of the modern Church, and again we speak of the *"new Church,"* no longer believes in the Cross. And the striking thing about all of this is, we are not speaking of modernists, but in reality those who claim to be fundamentalists or Pentecostal, etc. In other words, many who are presently rejecting the Cross claim at the same time to be Spirit-filled. I have to wonder, filled with what spirit? The Holy Spirit will always lead to the Cross. Paul also said:

"For the Law of the Spirit (Holy Spirit) *of life in Christ Jesus* (what Jesus did for us at the Cross) *has made me free from the law of sin and death"* (Rom. 8:2).

We learn from this Passage, plus scores of others, that the Holy Spirit works exclusively within the parameters of the Finished Work of Christ. So despite the claims, the truth is, the Holy Spirit has nothing to do with the direction of the new Church.

The problem is, the new Church tries to dress up the *"old man,"* when in reality he must be killed (Rom. 6:6-8).

(6) "AND REBEKAH SPOKE UNTO JACOB HER SON, SAYING, BEHOLD, I HEARD YOUR FATHER SPEAK UNTO ESAU YOUR BROTHER, SAYING,

(7) "BRING ME VENISON, AND MAKE ME SAVORY MEAT, THAT I MAY EAT, AND BLESS YOU BEFORE THE LORD BEFORE MY DEATH.

(8) "NOW THEREFORE, MY SON, OBEY MY VOICE ACCORDING TO THAT WHICH I COMMAND YOU.

(9) "GO NOW TO THE FLOCK, AND FETCH ME FROM THENCE TWO GOOD KIDS OF THE GOAT; AND I WILL MAKE THEM SAVORY MEAT FOR YOUR FATHER, SUCH AS HE LOVES:

(10) "AND YOU SHALL BRING IT TO YOUR FATHER, THAT HE MAY EAT, AND

THAT HE MAY BLESS YOU BEFORE HIS DEATH.

(11) "AND JACOB SAID TO REBEKAH HIS MOTHER, BEHOLD, ESAU MY BROTHER IS A HAIRY MAN, AND I AM A SMOOTH MAN:

(12) "MY FATHER PERADVENTURE WILL FEEL ME, AND I SHALL SEEM TO HIM AS A DECEIVER; AND I SHALL BRING A CURSE UPON ME, AND NOT A BLESSING.

(13) "AND HIS MOTHER SAID UNTO HIM, UPON ME BE YOUR CURSE, MY SON: ONLY OBEY MY VOICE, AND GO FETCH ME THEM.

(14) "AND HE WENT, AND FETCHED, AND BROUGHT THEM TO HIS MOTHER: AND HIS MOTHER MADE SAVORY MEAT, SUCH AS HIS FATHER LOVED.

(15) "AND REBEKAH TOOK GOODLY RAIMENT OF HER ELDEST SON ESAU, WHICH WERE WITH HER IN THE HOUSE, AND PUT THEM UPON JACOB HER YOUNGER SON:

(16) "AND SHE PUT THE SKINS OF THE KIDS OF THE GOATS UPON HIS HANDS, AND UPON THE SMOOTH OF HIS NECK:

(17) "AND SHE GAVE THE SAVORY MEAT AND THE BREAD, WHICH SHE HAD PREPARED, INTO THE HAND OF HER SON JACOB."

The construction is:

1. Jacob's history, as we shall see, teaches the lesson, which the natural will is so unwilling to learn, that planning for self instead of resting in the Hand of God brings sorrow.

2. Rebekah schemes in order to get Jacob the birthright, exactly as Sarah schemed to give Abraham a son. Both were on the path of self-will.

3. Abraham and Sarah attempted to deceive Pharaoh; Isaac and Rebekah attempted to deceive Abimelech; Jacob and Rebekah attempt to deceive Isaac. Such is the path of self-will.

REBEKAH

Verses 6 through 8 read: *"And Rebekah spoke unto Jacob her son, saying, Behold, I heard your father speak unto Esau your brother, saying,*

"Bring me venison, and make me savory meat, that I may eat, and bless you before the LORD before my death.

"Now therefore, my son, obey my voice according to that which I command you."

Here we have the aged Patriarch Isaac, standing, as it were, at the very portal of eternity, the Earth and nature fast fading away from his view, yet occupied about *"savory meat,"* and about to act in direct opposition to the Divine counsel, by blessing the elder instead of the younger.

And Rebekah reasons that if Isaac will do this thing which is against God, she is justified in her actions of deception. But wrongdoing is never justified! It always reaps a bitter result, exactly as it did here.

DECEPTION

Verses 9 through 12 read: *"Go now to the flock, and fetch me from thence two good kids of the goat; and I will make them savory meat for your father, such as he loves:*

"And you shall bring it to your father, that he may eat, and that he may bless you before his death.

"And Jacob said to Rebekah his mother, Behold, Esau my brother is a hairy man, and I am a smooth man:

"My father peradventure will feel me, and I shall seem to him as a deceiver; and I shall bring a curse upon me, and not a blessing."

Rebekah's plan is one of deception, and not pleasing at all to the Lord. But such is the path of the flesh; it always seems right to the natural heart and mind.

We may look at this and think that such chicanery died with Jacob and his mother; however, regrettably that is not the case.

My following statements will be strong, but I feel them to be absolutely correct.

Living for the Lord almost all of my life, and as the writer of Amazing Grace said, *"Through many dangers, toils, and snares, I have already come."* In this I've learned a few things:

From experience, and above all my study of the Word of God, and the Revelations given to me by the Lord concerning the Word, I personally believe, if one doesn't walk the path of Faith, one will practice the life of spiritual deception. There are only two paths, *"faith,"* and *"flesh."*

And to walk the path of Faith, one must ever understand what Faith actually is. The

Holy Spirit through Paul defined it very ably. He said:

"I am crucified with Christ: nevertheless I live; yet not I, but Christ lives in me: and the life which I now live in the flesh (our natural walk) *I live by the faith of the Son of God, Who loved me, and gave Himself for me"* (Gal. 2:20).

Notice the way that Paul used the term *"the faith of the Son of God."*

This refers to what Jesus did for us at the Cross, which was the great Sacrifice of Himself. In fact, Christianity is often referred to as *"the Faith,"* with that latter term always referring to what Christ did at the Cross.

So it's the Cross, or it's deception!

THE CURSE

Verses 13 through 17 read: *"And his mother said unto him, Upon me be your curse, my son: only obey my voice, and go fetch me them.*

"And he went, and fetched, and brought them to his mother: and his mother made savory meat, such as his father loved.

"And Rebekah took goodly raiment of her eldest son Esau, which were with her in the house, and put them upon Jacob her younger son:

"And she put the skins of the kids of the goats upon his hands, and upon the smooth of his neck:

"And she gave the savory meat and the bread, which he had prepared, into the hand of her son Jacob."

It should be understood that Rebekah wanted the Blessing for Jacob, not just because he was her favored son, but because she knew this was the Will of the Lord; however, her means of obtaining this showed a lack of trust, and, thereby, constituted a work of the flesh. In essence, by resorting to trickery, she was doing the same thing that Sarah did as it regarded a son being born to Abraham. Both women would seek to *"help"* God, but which the Lord, and irrespective as to whom the people might be, can never accept.

We are observing here the greatest hindrance to the Christian experience. We do not trust the Lord, or else we do not know how to trust the Lord, which is more often the case than many would realize.

NOTES

If the Believer doesn't understand the following three things, he will invariably seek to do exactly what Rebekah here sought to do. He will resort to the flesh because as stated, if the path of Faith is not properly trod, there is nowhere else to go but the way of the flesh.

These three things are:

THE CROSS

Even though we've already said these very same things several times in this Volume, due to the fact that we're dealing with the very heart of the Christian experience, we dare not say the following too little, with it being virtually impossible to say it too much.

The Believer must understand that everything he receives from the Lord from the time that he is brought to Christ, throughout the entirety of his life and living, comes by the means of the Cross (Rom. 6:3-14; I Cor. 1:17-18, 21, 23; 2:2, 5; Gal. 6:14; Eph. 2:13-18; Col. 2:14-15; I Pet. 1:18-20).

OUR FAITH

The problem is not Faith, but rather the proper object of our faith. In fact, everyone in the world has faith. Even the Scientist, who boasts that he would never think of basing his claims on faith, is in fact, carrying on his work and life by and through faith. Every experiment he performs is done on the basis of faith, whether he realizes it or not.

The nations of the world which have a free market economy are operating on the principle of faith, hence it producing the greatest prosperity in the world, and because it's God's Way. The nations of the world which have a controlled economy, which stifles faith, can scarcely feed their people.

However, all of that, although faith, is not the type of faith which God recognizes. The only type of Faith that He will recognize is that which pertains solely to the Cross, i.e., *"the Sacrifice of Christ."* It is Faith in Christ, and His Finished Work, which God recognizes, and that alone! As previously stated, that's why Paul referred to it as *"the faith"* (Rom. 1:5, 8, 17; 3:3, 22, 25, 27-28; 4:5, 11; I Cor. 2:5; II Cor. 5:7; Gal. 2:16, 20; 3:23).

In fact, the only fight the Christian is supposed to engage is *"the good fight of faith"* (I

Tim. 6:12). We are not told to fight the Devil, or sin, or demon spirits. We are told to *"fight the good fight of faith."* This means that every struggle, every effort, all the wrestling (Eph. 6:12), are all in the realm of faith. Satan tries to move our Faith from the Cross of Christ to other things. And it really doesn't matter how good the other things are, or even Scriptural in their own right. If we are depending on those things, whatever they might be, to give us victory, we will fail, and simply because that's not God's Way. It is faith and faith alone, but more particularly Faith in Christ and what Christ did at the Cross. If your Faith is not anchored in Jesus Christ and Him Crucified, then again allow me to state, it's not faith which God will recognize.

THE HOLY SPIRIT

The Believer must understand that it is the Holy Spirit Who makes possible to us all the great things which Jesus did at the Cross. It really doesn't matter how much faith we have; it's the Holy Spirit Who carries out the task. However, the secret is this:

He will not work except within the parameters of the Sacrifice of Christ. This is what makes it legally permissible for Him to do all the things which He Alone can do.

Before the Cross, the Holy Spirit could work with Believers, and even at times work within them, at least to help them perform a task which God had called them to do. But as far as Him abiding in them, even the great Patriarchs and Prophets, as He does presently, that He couldn't do. And the reason He couldn't do those things is simply because the sin debt still hung over the heads of the entirety of the human race. The blood of bulls and goats, although functioning as a stopgap measure, still couldn't take away sins (Heb. 10:4). So the Holy Spirit was then limited as to what He could do as it regards the Old Testament Saints.

But since the Cross, and because all sin has been taken away (Jn. 1:29), the Holy Spirit can now come into the heart and life of the Believer, which He does immediately at conversion, and abide there forever (Jn. 14:16-17).

So it is the Cross which makes possible the great work the Holy Spirit does within our hearts and lives.

Paul said: *"For the Law* (the Law devised by the Godhead) *of the Spirit* (Holy Spirit) *of life* (all life comes from the Son by the Spirit) *in Christ Jesus* (what Jesus did for us at the Cross) *has made me free from the law of sin and death"* (Rom. 8:2).

So now you have it:

1. The Cross.
2. Our Faith.
3. The Holy Spirit.

The little diagram I've just given you is the only way that the Believer can walk in perpetual victory.

(18) "AND HE CAME UNTO HIS FATHER, AND SAID, MY FATHER: AND HE SAID, HERE AM I; WHO ARE YOU, MY SON?

(19) "AND JACOB SAID UNTO HIS FATHER, I AM ESAU YOUR FIRSTBORN; I HAVE DONE ACCORDING AS YOU BADE ME: ARISE, I PRAY YOU, SIT AND EAT OF MY VENISON, THAT YOUR SOUL MAY BLESS ME.

(20) "AND ISAAC SAID UNTO HIS SON, HOW IS IT THAT YOU HAVE FOUND IT SO QUICKLY, MY SON? AND HE SAID, BECAUSE THE LORD YOUR GOD BROUGHT IT TO ME.

(21) "AND ISAAC SAID UNTO JACOB, COME NEAR, I PRAY YOU, THAT I MAY FEEL YOU, MY SON, WHETHER YOU BE MY VERY SON ESAU OR NOT.

(22) "AND JACOB WENT NEAR UNTO ISAAC HIS FATHER; AND HE FELT HIM, AND SAID, THE VOICE IS JACOB'S VOICE, BUT THE HANDS ARE THE HANDS OF ESAU.

(23) "AND HE DISCERNED HIM NOT, BECAUSE HIS HANDS WERE HAIRY, AS HIS BROTHER ESAU'S HANDS: SO HE BLESSED HIM.

(24) "AND HE SAID, ARE YOU MY VERY SON ESAU? AND HE SAID, I AM.

(25) "AND HE SAID, BRING IT NEAR TO ME, AND I WILL EAT OF MY SON'S VENISON, THAT MY SOUL MAY BLESS YOU. AND HE BROUGHT IT NEAR TO HIM, AND HE DID EAT: AND HE BROUGHT HIM WINE AND HE DRANK."

The composition is:

1. One sin is always followed by a worse sin.

2. As Jacob falsely claimed the help of the Lord, all religious deception does such.

3. A Believer's sin is worse than the sin of an unbeliever, simply because it makes the

Lord, in essence, a part of the sin. Thus, blasphemy is added to disobedience.

THE DECEPTION

Verses 18 through 20 read: *"And he came unto his father, and said, My father: and he said, Here am I; who are you, my son?*

"And Jacob said unto his father, I am Esau your firstborn; I have done according as you bade me: arise, I pray you, sit and eat of my venison, that your soul may bless me.

"And Isaac said unto his son, How is it that you have found it so quickly, my son? And he said, Because the LORD your God brought it to me."

Jacob brings the Lord into his perfidiousness. But so it is with all Believers who fail God. It's bad enough to do wrong, but to attempt to make the Lord a part of our wrong makes it infinitely worse.

Inasmuch as our very bodies are temples of the Holy Spirit (I Cor. 3:16), then the Third Person of the Triune Godhead must observe all we do, whether good or bad. In a sense, even though never touched by sin Himself, it never fails to grieve Him, and to do so to a degree perhaps we will never understand (Eph. 4:30).

THE DEED

Verses 21 through 25 read: *"And Isaac said unto Jacob, Come near, I pray you, that I may feel you, my son, whether you be my very son Esau or not.*

"And Jacob went near unto Isaac his father; and he felt him, and said, The voice is Jacob's voice, but the hands are the hands of Esau.

"And he discerned him not, because his hands were hairy, as his brother Esau's hands: so he blessed him.

"And he said, Are you my very son Esau? And he said, I am.

"And he said, Bring it near to me, and I will eat of my son's venison, that my soul may bless you. And he brought it near to him, and he did eat: and he brought him wine and he drank."

The depth of Rebekah's sin carried out by her son Jacob is labeled very correctly, I think, by Matthew Henry. He said: *"Rebekah wronged Isaac by practicing an imposition*

upon him; she wronged Jacob by using her authority and persuasion to tempt him to wickedness; she sinned against the Lord, and dishonored His power and faithfulness, by supposing He needed such means of effecting His purpose, and fulfilling His Promise.

"She put a stumbling block in Esau's way, and furnished him with a pretext for enmity, both against Jacob and against the Salvation of the Lord, by putting Jacob upon acting such a treacherous part.

"It was one of those crooked measures which have too often been adopted to accomplish the Divine Promises; as if the end would justify, or at least excuse the means."

The entirety of this transaction speaks of fraud. All the parties are to be blamed: Isaac is to be blamed for endeavoring to set aside the Divine Will; Esau for wishing to deprive his brother of the blessing he had himself relinquished to him; Rebekah and Jacob for wishing to secure it by fraudulent means, not trusting wholly in the Lord.

As an aside, how remarkable it is in this wonderful creation of God, that of all the billions of people in this world, every voice is different.

(26) "AND HIS FATHER ISAAC SAID UNTO HIM, COME NEAR NOW, AND KISS ME, MY SON.

(27) "AND HE CAME NEAR, AND KISSED HIM: AND HE SMELLED THE SMELL OF HIS RAIMENT, AND BLESSED HIM, AND SAID, SEE, THE SMELL OF MY SON IS AS THE SMELL OF A FIELD WHICH THE LORD HAS BLESSED:

(28) "THEREFORE GOD GIVE YOU OF THE DEW OF HEAVEN, AND OF THE FATNESS OF THE EARTH, AND PLENTY OF CORN AND WINE:

(29) "LET PEOPLE SERVE YOU, AND NATIONS BOW DOWN TO YOU: BE LORD OVER YOUR BRETHREN, AND LET YOUR MOTHER'S SONS BOW DOWN TO YOU: CURSED BE EVERYONE WHO CURSES YOU, AND BLESSED BE HE WHO BLESSES YOU.

(30) "AND IT CAME TO PASS, AS SOON AS ISAAC HAD MADE AN END OF BLESSING JACOB, AND JACOB WAS YET SCARCE GONE OUT FROM THE PRESENCE OF ISAAC HIS FATHER, THAT ESAU HIS BROTHER CAME IN FROM HIS HUNTING.

(31) "AND HE ALSO HAD MADE SAVORY MEAT, AND BROUGHT IT UNTO HIS FATHER, AND SAID UNTO HIS FATHER, LET MY FATHER ARISE, AND EAT OF HIS SON'S VENISON, THAT YOUR SOUL MAY BLESS ME.

(32) "AND ISAAC HIS FATHER SAID UNTO HIM, WHO ARE YOU? AND HE SAID, I AM YOUR SON, YOUR FIRSTBORN ESAU."

The overview is:

1. There are two grand points brought out in Jacob's history — God's purpose of Grace, on the one hand; and on the other hand, self-will plotting and scheming to reach what that purpose would have infallibly brought about, without any plot or scheme at all.

2. This tells us that in all of us, there is nothing, perhaps, in which we are so lamentably deficient, as in the Grace of patient, self-renouncing dependence upon God.

3. God did not need the aid of such elements as Rebekah's cunning and Jacob's gross deceit, in order to accomplish His Purpose. He had said, *"The elder shall serve the younger."* This was enough — enough for Faith, but not enough for self-will, which must ever adopt its own ways, and as stated, know nothing of what it is to wait on God.

THE BLESSING

Verses 26 through 29 read: *"And his father Isaac said unto him, Come near now, and kiss me, my son.*

"And he came near, and kissed him: and he smelled the smell of his raiment, and blessed him, and said, See, the smell of my son is as the smell of a field which the LORD has blessed:

"Therefore God give you of the dew of Heaven, and the fatness of the Earth, and plenty of corn and wine:

"Let people serve you, nations bow down to you: be lord over your brethren, and let your mother's sons bow down to you: cursed be everyone who curses you, and blessed be he who blesses you."

It is observed by Matthew Henry that the blessing given by Isaac is expressed in very general terms. He went on to say that no mention is made of those distinguishing mercies included in the Covenant with Abraham.

The first part of the blessing is a generalization. It speaks of the blessings of the Earth belonging to the recipient.

But in Verse 29, it becomes much more particular, with even the entirety of the Earth bowing down to him. The idea pertains to Christ.

The Incarnation would bring the Son of God into the world. So this Blessing would only pass through Jacob and many others, and be realized only in Christ. And even yet, it hasn't been fulfilled in totality, but most definitely shall be at the Second Coming. It is ironic; the Blesser is Christ, and the Blessing is also Christ!

ESAU

Verses 30 through 32 read: *"And it came to pass, as soon as Isaac had made an end of blessing Jacob, and Jacob was yet scarce gone out from the presence of Isaac his father, that Esau his brother came in from his hunting.*

"And he also had made savory meat, and brought it unto his father, and said unto his father, Let my father arise, and eat of his son's venison, that your soul may bless me.

"And Isaac his father said unto him, Who are you? And he said, I am your son, your firstborn Esau."

Does not Jacob realize that Esau will soon come upon the scene? Perhaps he thought that Esau cared so little for the birthright, that he would raise no objection; however, if he thought all of this, why did he not say such to his father, without trying to deceive the old man?

The truth is, Esau did want the blessing, but not for the right purpose and reason. As well, he would treat the transaction made between him and his brother as it regards the birthright, as no more than a joke. But he finds to his dismay that he has been outtricked!

Esau represents those in the Church who would walk the path of self-will. Jacob represents those who know the path of Faith, but would leave that path, and suffer greatly. Isaac represents those who are in positions of leadership, and know so little of the mind of God, that they would give the birthright to the Devil instead of to Christ. What an ignominious mess! But I wonder how much the Church has really changed, if any at all?

NOTES

(33) "AND ISAAC TREMBLED VERY EXCEEDINGLY, AND SAID, WHO? WHERE IS HE WHO HAS TAKEN VENISON, AND BROUGHT IT TO ME, AND I HAVE EATEN OF ALL BEFORE YOU CAME, AND HAVE BLESSED HIM? YES, AND HE SHALL BE BLESSED.

(34) "AND WHEN ESAU HEARD THE WORDS OF HIS FATHER, HE CRIED WITH A GREAT AND EXCEEDING BITTER CRY, AND SAID UNTO HIS FATHER, BLESS ME, EVEN ME ALSO, O MY FATHER.

(35) "AND HE SAID, YOUR BROTHER CAME WITH SUBTILTY, AND HAS TAKEN AWAY YOUR BLESSING.

(36) "AND HE SAID, IS NOT HE RIGHTLY NAMED JACOB? FOR HE HAS SUPPLANTED ME THESE TWO TIMES: HE TOOK AWAY MY BIRTHRIGHT; AND, BEHOLD, NOW HE HAS TAKEN AWAY MY BLESSING. AND HE SAID, HAVE YOU NOT RESERVED A BLESSING FOR ME?

(37) "AND ISAAC ANSWERED AND SAID UNTO ESAU, BEHOLD, I HAVE MADE HIM YOUR LORD, AND ALL HIS BRETHREN HAVE I GIVEN TO HIM FOR SERVANTS; AND WITH CORN AND WINE HAVE I SUSTAINED HIM: AND WHAT SHALL I DO NOW UNTO YOU, MY SON?

(38) "AND ESAU SAID UNTO HIS FATHER, HAVE YOU BUT ONE BLESSING, MY FATHER? BLESS ME, EVEN ME ALSO, O MY FATHER. AND ESAU LIFTED UP HIS VOICE, AND WEPT.

(39) "AND ISAAC HIS FATHER ANSWERED AND SAID UNTO HIM, BEHOLD, YOUR DWELLING SHALL BE THE FATNESS OF THE EARTH, AND OF THE DEW OF HEAVEN FROM ABOVE;

(40) "AND BY YOUR SWORD SHALL YOU LIVE, AND SHALL SERVE YOUR BROTHER; AND IT SHALL COME TO PASS WHEN YOU SHALL HAVE THE DOMINION, THAT YOU SHALL BREAK HIS YOKE FROM OFF YOUR NECK."

The exegesis is:

1. Isaac trembled exceedingly at what he had almost done in giving the birthright to Esau, considering that he had been told by God at the time of Jacob's birth that he (Jacob) was to possess the birthright.

2. He trembles exceedingly under a just fear. This fear brings him back into the path of Faith, and directly he returns to that path he steps from self-will to dignity.

3. Although Jacob's actions were wrong, and a wrong for which he would pay dearly, still the birthright belonged to Jacob. It was promised to him by God.

4. Every Believer now has a part in this birthright by and through the Lord Jesus Christ Who rightly is the Blesser and the Blessing.

A JUST FEAR

Verses 33 through 35 read: *"And Isaac trembled very exceedingly, and said, Who? Where is he who has taken venison, and brought it to me, and I have eaten of all before you came, and have blessed him? Yes, and he shall be blessed.*

"And when Esau heard the words of his father, he cried with a great and exceeding bitter cry, and said unto his father, Bless me, even me also, O my father.

"And he said, Your brother came with subtilty, and has taken away your blessing."

Concerning this, Ellicott says, *"The trembling of Isaac was not from mere vexation at having been so deceived, and made to give the blessing contrary to his wishes. What Isaac felt was that he had been resisting God. Despite the prophecy given to Rebekah, and Esau's own unspiritual character and heathen marriages, he had determined to bestow on him the birthright by an act of his own will; and he had failed. But he persists no longer in his sin,"* although he does acknowledge the subtilty of Jacob.

Isaac trembles at what he had almost done, which would have given the blessing of Abraham to this ungodly, unspiritual son, whom the Holy Spirit refers to as a *"fornicator"* (Heb. 12:16).

"The will of the flesh" made Isaac wish to bless Esau, but Faith in the end conquered (Heb. 11:20), and he cries respecting Jacob: *"I have blessed him, and he shall be blessed."*

Hebrews 12:17 recalls Esau's bitter weeping, when he found that he had lost the birthright, and now he failed with his tears to cause his father to change his mind. He found no place of repentance in his father's will (Williams).

As Paul describes this *"repentance"* (Heb. 12:17), he is not speaking of true Repentance, for Esau manifested no such thing. He is referring to Esau attempting to change the mind of his father, Isaac. Esau wanted the material part, but he had no interest whatsoever in the spiritual part, which was, in reality, the substance of the birthright. In fact, Esau little desired the birthright, if at all, but wanted the blessing. How so similar to many in the modern Church!

Millions today are presently being led down the path of Esau. Of the spiritual aspect of the birthright, they have no desire. They only want the so-called double portion of material goods that went with the birthright.

Some time ago, I overheard one of the leading gurus of the *"Word of Faith"* movement claim that the *"Blessing of Abraham,"* had nothing to do with spiritual things, but only with money. It's the only time in my life that I found myself standing on the floor in front of the TV set, screaming at the absolute absurdity of such a statement. The tragedy is, this man pastors a Church in California, which numbers several thousands of people, and has wide influence over untold thousands through Television.

But let it be known, the real *"Blessing"* cannot come to Esau, who desires only material things, but rather to Jacob, even though he is a sad illustration of the destructive power of fallen human nature. Therefore, Psalm 46:11 is very dear to the hearts of all true Believers:

"The LORD of Hosts is with us; the God of Jacob is our refuge. Selah."

Here are brought together into the one Verse the two great titles, *"The Lord of Hosts"* and *"God of Jacob."* The one title presents Him as the God of countless hosts of sinless Angels; the other title proclaims Him as the God of one stumbling, sinning, scheming, planning, and broken man! These Divine titles link Almighty Power with infinite Grace.

JACOB

Verses 36 through 40 read: *"And he said, Is not he rightly named Jacob? For he has supplanted me these two times: he took away my birthright; and, behold, now he has taken away my blessing. And he said, Have you not reserved a blessing for me?*

"And Isaac answered and said unto Esau, Behold, I have made him your lord, and all

his brethren have I given to him for servants; and with corn and wine have I sustained him: and what shall I do now unto you, my son?

"And Esau said unto his father, Have you but one blessing, my father? Bless me, even me also, O my father. And Esau lifted up his voice, and wept.

"And Isaac his father answered and said unto him, Behold, your dwelling shall be the fatness of the Earth, and the dew of Heaven from above;

"And by your sword shall you live, and shall serve your brother; and it shall come to pass when you shall have the dominion, that you shall break his yoke from off your neck."

Only one son could inherit the spiritual prerogatives of the birthright, and the temporal lordship which accompanied it (Ellicott).

Concerning Verse 39, the actual Hebrew reads, *"Thy dwelling shall be of the fat places of the Earth."* But most Expositors consider that the preposition *"of"* should be translated *"from."* Thus, it would read, *"Behold your dwelling shall be away from the fat places of the Earth, and away from the dew of Heaven from above, and by your sword you shall live."*

This is closer to the original intent of the Hebrew language, and as well more aptly describes the descendants of Esau, the Arabs. For the most part, their domicile or dwelling has been the desert and not otherwise. And as well, they have been and are a violent people, thereby fulfilling Verse 40, *"And by your sword you shall live."*

The Edomites were the descendants of Esau. And the prophecy was fulfilled in that they were in subjection to Israel for many, many years. But in the first days of Joram, and then of Ahaz, Edom revolted, and recovered its freedom, exactly as Isaac had prophesied in Verse 40.

So in reality, there was no blessing for Esau, as there can never be a blessing for those who would demean the ways of God, thereby setting their own course.

As we have stated, the Blesser is the Lord Jesus Christ, and the Blessing is the Lord Jesus Christ. In fact, Christ being born into this world and, thereby, redeeming lost humanity by going to the Cross, is what all of this is all about. God had to have a lineage of Faith through whom He could come as a man, and the lineage of Abraham produced these people. It is Jesus Christ or it is nothing! He said of Himself:

"I am the Way, the Truth, and the Life: no man comes unto the Father, but by Me" (Jn. 14:6).

In essence, Jesus Christ is the coin of this spiritual realm. Not the Church, not good works, not good deeds, but Faith in Christ and what Christ has done for us at the Cross.

Jesus Christ Alone was and is the Son of God, and Jesus Christ Alone went to the Cross and paid the price for man's Redemption (Jn. 3:16; Gal. 1:4). So everyone in this world who places their faith and trust in Mohammad, or Buddha, or the Pope, or the Church, or Denominations, or good works, will be eternally lost. And let no one think that faith in the Church, or whatever, equates with Faith in Jesus Christ. It must be Christ, and Christ Alone. And more so, it must be *"Christ and Him Crucified"* (I Cor. 2:2).

(41) "AND ESAU HATED JACOB BECAUSE OF THE BLESSING WHEREWITH HIS FATHER BLESSED HIM: AND ESAU SAID IN HIS HEART, THE DAYS OF MOURNING FOR MY FATHER ARE AT HAND; THEN WILL I SLAY MY BROTHER JACOB.

(42) "AND THESE WORDS OF ESAU HER ELDER SON WERE TOLD TO REBEKAH: AND SHE SENT AND CALLED JACOB HER YOUNGER SON, AND SAID UNTO HIM, BEHOLD, YOUR BROTHER ESAU, AS TOUCHING YOU, DOES COMFORT HIMSELF, PURPOSING TO KILL YOU.

(43) "NOW THEREFORE, MY SON, OBEY MY VOICE; AND ARISE, FLEE TO LABAN MY BROTHER TO HARAN;

(44) "AND TARRY WITH HIM A FEW DAYS, UNTIL YOUR BROTHER'S FURY TURN AWAY;

(45) "UNTIL YOUR BROTHER'S ANGER TURN AWAY FROM YOU, AND HE FORGET THAT WHICH YOU HAVE DONE TO HIM: THEN I WILL SEND, AND FETCH YOU FROM THENCE: WHY SHOULD I BE DEPRIVED ALSO OF YOU BOTH IN ONE DAY?

(46) "AND REBEKAH SAID TO ISAAC, I AM WEARY OF MY LIFE BECAUSE OF THE DAUGHTERS OF HETH: IF JACOB TAKE A WIFE OF THE DAUGHTERS OF HETH, SUCH AS THESE WHICH ARE OF THE

NOTES

DAUGHTERS OF THE LAND, WHAT GOOD SHALL MY LIFE DO ME?"

The synopsis is:

1. Isaac was mistaken as to the proximity of his death (vs. 2); Esau was mistaken as to an early opportunity for murdering his brother (vs. 41); and Rebekah was mistaken (vs. 44) in her expectation to see Jacob soon again, for she died before he returned (Williams). So we have before us the path of self-will.

2. Isaac was 137 years of age at this time. His half brother Ishmael had died at that age. Perhaps it was the fact of his death that made Isaac think that he also was about to die; but he lived for 43 years longer (Gen. 35:28).

3. Esau's hatred of Jacob proved that he was not truly repentant, however disappointed and remorseful he might have been.

4. Rebekah loves Jacob more than Truth, even more than God. This was idolatry!

REBEKAH

Verses 41 through 45 read: *"And Esau hated Jacob because of the blessing wherewith his father blessed him: and Esau said in his heart, The days of mourning for my father are at hand; then will I slay my brother Jacob.*

"And these words of Esau her elder son were told to Rebekah: and she sent and called Jacob her younger son, and said unto him, Behold, your brother Esau, as touching you, does comfort himself, purposing to kill you.

"Now therefore, my son, obey my voice; and arise, flee to Laban my brother to Haran;

"And tarry with him a few days, until your brother's fury turn away;

"Until your brother's anger turn away from you, and he forget that which you have done to him: then I will send, and fetch you from thence: why should I be deprived also of you both in one day?"

Esau had no cause to hate Jacob. He knew that the prophecy had given the birthright to Jacob. As well, he knew that his profligate lifestyle did not warrant such. He had no desire to be the Priest of the family, in fact, no desire for the things of God whatsoever. So his hatred was fueled by ungodliness, and not for any imagined wrong.

It must be remembered that Esau was in the Covenant, but actually not part of the Covenant. Although he was in the sacred family, he was not really a spiritual part of the sacred family. And as previously stated, so are millions of modern Church members. They are in the Church, but not really of the Church. They claim the Lord, but they aren't really of the Lord.

As we have stated, Jacob himself was a sad illustration of the destructive power of fallen human nature, but yet, he truly loved the Lord, and truly wanted the things of the Lord. In fact, Jacob is a Type of the consecrated Child of God, who tries to attain from the Lord by self-will what can only be attained through and by the Holy Spirit. But as Jacob, we have to learn that lesson the hard way also.

How so much his life mirrors my own, and yours! However, even though it will take some time, and pass through many dangers, toils, and snares; and yet, ultimately, Jacob, the deceiver, the supplanter, the heel-catcher, will become *"Israel,"* the *"soldier of God."*

MORE DECEPTION

Verse 46 reads: *"And Rebekah said to Isaac, I am weary of my life because of the daughters of Heth: if Jacob take a wife of the daughters of Heth, such as these which are of the daughters of the land, what good shall my life do me?"*

There is no doubt that Rebekah was concerned about *"the daughters of the land,"* and none of them being a suitable wife for Jacob. She of course, is the very recipient of this which Abraham demanded concerning a wife for his son, Isaac; however, her real reason at this time for sending Jacob away was not that which she told Isaac, but rather because she feared for his life as it regards the anger of Esau.

So we cannot exonerate Rebekah altogether from a charge of duplicity in this. This is what she wanted Isaac to believe, but it is not the real reason.

The *"few days"* of Verse 44 would turn into some 20 years, and she in fact, would never see Jacob again. She would die before his return to the Land of Promise.

And such is the path of self-will. How it must have broken her heart a thousand times over that she never saw her son again.

I think there is no doubt that Rebekah ultimately made all of this right with God, but there was no way she could undo the results

of her act. This would haunt her for the rest of her life.

How different it would have been had she left the matter entirely in the Hands of God! This is the way in which Faith manages, instead of us trying to do it ourselves. Jesus said concerning these very things, *"Which of you by taking thought can add to his stature one cubit?"* We gain nothing by our anxiety and planning; we only shut out God, and that is no gain.

It is always a just judgment from the Hand of God to be left to reap the fruits of our own devices; and I know of few things more sad than to see a Child of God so entirely forgetting his proper place and privilege as to take the management of his affairs into his own hands. The birds of the air and the lilies of the field may well be our teachers when we so far forget our position of unqualified dependence upon God.

Out of this Text, we also learn what a profane person actually is, even as the Holy Spirit described Esau (Heb. 12:16). It is one who would like to hold both worlds, one who would like to enjoy the present without forfeiting his title to the future. It is the person who attempts to use God, instead of God using him. And please understand, we're not speaking here of those of the world, but those in the Church, those who claim Divine privilege.

"Praise to the Lord, the Almighty, the
    King of creation!
"O my soul, praise Him, for He is your
    help and Salvation!
"All you who hear, now to His Temple
    draw near;
"Join me in glad adoration!"

"Praise to the Lord, Who o'er all things
    so wondrously reigneth,
"Shelters thee under His wings, yea, so
    gently sustaineth!
"Hast thou not seen how thy desires
    e'er have been
"Granted in what He ordaineth?"

"Praise to the Lord, Who with marvel-
    ous Wisdom has made thee!
"Decked thee with health, and with lov-
    ing Hand guided and stayed thee;
"How oft in grief hath not He brought
    thee relief,
"Spreading His wings for to shade thee!"

"Praise to the Lord! O let that is in me
　　adore Him!
"All who have life and breath, come
　　now with praises before Him!
"Let the Amen sound from His people
　　again:
"Gladly for aye we adore Him."

CHAPTER 28

(1) "AND ISAAC CALLED JACOB, AND BLESSED HIM, AND CHARGED HIM, AND SAID UNTO HIM, YOU SHALL NOT TAKE A WIFE OF THE DAUGHTERS OF CANAAN.

(2) "ARISE, GO TO PADAN-ARAM, TO THE HOUSE OF BETHUEL YOUR MOTHER'S FATHER; AND TAKE YOU A WIFE FROM THENCE OF THE DAUGHTERS OF LABAN YOUR MOTHER'S BROTHER.

(3) "AND GOD ALMIGHTY BLESS YOU, AND MAKE YOU FRUITFUL, AND MULTIPLY YOU, THAT YOU MAY BE A MULTITUDE OF PEOPLE;

(4) "AND GIVE YOU THE BLESSING OF ABRAHAM, TO YOU, AND TO YOUR SEED WITH YOU; THAT YOU MAY INHERIT THE LAND WHEREIN YOU ARE A STRANGER, WHICH GOD GAVE UNTO ABRAHAM.

(5) "AND ISAAC SENT AWAY JACOB: AND HE WENT TO PADAN-ARAM UNTO LABAN, SON OF BETHUEL THE SYRIAN, THE BROTHER OF REBEKAH, JACOB'S AND ESAU'S MOTHER."

The diagram is:

1. Now we have the commencing of God's special dealings with Jacob. Now begins the *"making of a man."*

2. God will accomplish His Own purpose, no matter by what instrumentality; but if His child, in impatience of spirit and unbelief of heart will take himself out of God's Hands, he must expect much sorrowful exercise and painful discipline. Thus it was with Jacob, and thus it is with us (Mackintosh).

3. Isaac now fully seems to have returned to the path of Faith. There is now no attempt to substitute Esau for Jacob, or to lessen the privileges of the latter, but with hearty cheerfulness he blesses the younger

NOTES

son, and confirms him in the possession of the whole Abrahamic Blessing.

ISAAC

Verses 1 and 2 read: *"And Isaac called Jacob, and blessed him, and charged him, and said unto him, You shall not take a wife of the daughters of Canaan.*

"Arise, go to Padan-aram, to the house of Bethuel your mother's father; and take you a wife from thence of the daughters of Laban your mother's Brother."

It was not the Will of God for Esau or Jacob to marry *"the daughters of the land,"* but now that Jacob was the recipient of the Blessing, thereby the chosen one as it regards the birthright, which had to do with the coming of the Redeemer into the world, it was imperative that he not marry one of the Canaanite girls, as had his brother Esau. These people were idolaters, and even above that, their lineage was of the cursed line of Canaan. So the command by Isaac, and rightly so, was emphatic, *"You shall not take a wife of the daughters of Canaan."* He was rather to take a wife of one of the daughters of Laban, his mother's brother.

THE BLESSING

Verses 3 through 5 read: *"And God Almighty bless you, and make you fruitful, and multiply you, that you may be a multitude of people;*

"And give you the Blessing of Abraham, to you, and to your seed with you; that you may inherit the land wherein you are a stranger, which God gave unto Abraham.

"And Isaac sent away Jacob: and he went to Padan-aram unto Laban, son of Bethuel the Syrian, the brother of Rebekah, Jacob's and Esau's mother."

The appellative *"God Almighty"* means, *"El-Shaddai,"* and promises guardianship and companionship. Concerning this, Williams says: *"This great title, declaring God to be the Almighty One, assured Jacob beforehand of the sufficiency and ability of God to meet and provide for all his needs. This is the more instructive, when it is noticed that God promises to bless him in going obediently to Haran just as He had promised to bless his grandfather Abraham if obediently* leaving Haran. *This illustrates how the life of Faith appears a life of contradictions to human wisdom.*"

The *"Blessing of Abraham"* is mentioned by Paul (Gal. 3:14). It means *"Justification by Faith."* Paul also said: *"And the Scripture, foreseeing that God would justify the heathen through Faith, preached before the Gospel unto Abraham, saying, In you shall all nations be blessed"* (Gal. 3:8; Gen. 12:3).

In its most simplistic form, it simply means that a believing sinner is justified before God by simply having Faith in Christ and what Christ has done for us at the Cross.

The word *"justify,"* or *"Justification,"* is a legal term. It refers to one being declared *"innocent,"* or *"not guilty,"* or *"accepted."*

In the Salvation process, which all is instant, but yet is broken down into three parts, which one might say are done simultaneously, the Scripture says: *"And such were some of you: but you are washed, but you are sanctified, but you are justified in the Name of our Lord Jesus, and by the Spirit of our God"* (I Cor. 6:11).

To be *"washed"* refers to the accomplishment of the blood which was shed by Christ on the Cross. It is not a physical experience but rather a spiritual experience. The moment the sinner evidences Faith in Christ, at that moment the Precious Blood of Christ cleanses from all sin (I Jn. 1:7). The believing sinner is then sanctified, which means to be set apart, which means to be *"made clean."* He is then declared *"justified,"* and all *"in the Name of the Lord Jesus, and by the Spirit of our God,"* which means that all of this was done for us in Christ, and brought about in our lives by the Holy Spirit.

The *"Blessing of Abraham"* was promised not only to Jacob, but as well, *"to your seed with you,"* which includes every single Believer who has ever lived, both Jews and Gentiles.

THE LAND

The *"land"* he was promised, of course refers to the land area of Canaan, which would later be named Israel, and would be the home of the Jewish people, Jacob's *"seed."* All of this was for the purpose of bringing the Redeemer into the world. A people would have to literally be created, which they were, who

would have Faith in God, to whom God could give His Word, and as well, that they would serve as the womb of the Messiah, so to speak. However, when this Redeemer would come, which He did about 1,800 years later, He would come for the entirety of the world, and not for the Jews only (Jn. 3:16).

But whereas the word *"land,"* then referred to an exact geographical location, it now has a spiritual connotation. The *"land"* we now possess is a spiritual inheritance, but just as real in the spirit world, as the actual taking of the physical land by Joshua, when the children of Israel finally possessed that place. Concerning the present time, the song says:

"We are able to go up and take the country,
"And possess the land from Jordan unto the Sea.
"Though the giants may be there our way to hinder,
"Our God has given us the victory."

However, there is a vast difference in the taking of the land by Joshua, which would take place about 300 years into the future, than the taking of the land presently, to use a metaphor.

Jesus Christ, our Heavenly Joshua, has already taken the land for us, which means that He has won every victory, defeated every enemy, and has done it all for us. For us to have this great possession, and to occupy it totally and completely, which refers to having victory over the world, the flesh, and the Devil, all we have to do is to trust in Christ and what He has already done for us in the Sacrifice of Himself. In fact, it is at the Cross where He won this great victory and did so in totality (Eph. 2:13-18; Col. 2:14-15).

The biggest mistake the Christian can make is to try to do all over again what Christ has, in fact, already done. That's why Jesus said: *"Come unto Me, all you who labor and are heavy laden, and I will give you rest"* (Mat. 11:28). This life of Faith, for that's what it is, is now a resting or reposing in Him, for He has already won the battle, and has done so in totality. In other words, the land is yours, right now! All you have to do is believe it, enjoy it, and rest in it. It is truly a land of *"milk and honey."*

(6) "WHEN ESAU SAW THAT ISAAC HAD BLESSED JACOB, AND SENT HIM AWAY TO PADAN-ARAM, TO TAKE HIM A WIFE FROM THENCE; AND THAT AS HE BLESSED HIM HE GAVE HIM A CHARGE, SAYING, YOU SHALL NOT TAKE A WIFE OF THE DAUGHTERS OF CANAAN;

(7) "AND THAT JACOB OBEYED HIS FATHER AND HIS MOTHER, AND WAS GONE TO PADAN-ARAM;

(8) "AND ESAU SEEING THAT THE DAUGHTERS OF CANAAN PLEASED NOT ISAAC HIS FATHER;

(9) "THEN WENT ESAU UNTO ISHMAEL, AND TOOK UNTO THE WIVES WHICH HE HAD MAHALATH THE DAUGHTER OF ISHMAEL ABRAHAM'S SON, THE SISTER OF NEBAJOTH, TO BE HIS WIFE."

The structure is:

1. Esau, understanding spiritual things not at all, now tries to rectify his situation concerning marriage to Canaanite girls, by taking yet another wife of the family of Ishmael.

2. The world, as Esau, who is a Type of the world, does religious things, and thinks that constitutes spirituality. It doesn't!

3. Esau knew nothing of the life of Faith, only that of self-will. To know the life of Faith, one must know Jesus Christ and His Power to save.

ESAU

Verse 6 reads: *"When Esau saw that Isaac had blessed Jacob, and sent him away to Padan-aram, to take him a wife from thence; and that as he blessed him he gave him a charge, saying, You shall not take a wife of the daughters of Canaan."*

Esau, knowing nothing of the path of Faith, concludes erroneously that the reason Isaac gave Jacob the blessing, is because he (Esau) had married Canaanite women.

Esau was like millions in the modern Church presently. He wanted the blessing, but he understood the blessing not at all in spiritual terms, but only in material terms. And that Jacob now had the blessing, which he obtained by Faith, rankles Esau to no end, which he will now try to obtain by self-will.

All of this is a perfect picture of the Church. We have those who trust in Christ and His Cross, symbolized by Jacob, and we have those who trust in other things, symbolized by Esau. But as Cain hated Abel, and murdered him, Esau also hates Jacob, and would have murdered him, if the opportunity had presented itself.

None of this is meant to excuse Jacob's wrongdoing, but the wrongdoing he committed is a wrong that mostly every single Christian commits in attempting to rightly walk the path of Faith. In fact, the Seventh Chapter of Romans describes it perfectly, even as Paul gave there his own testimony. However, the wrongdoing on Jacob's part was in not understanding the path of Faith, while the wrongdoing on Esau's part, was his efforts to ignore the path of Faith altogether.

JACOB

Verse 7 reads: *"And that Jacob obeyed his father and his mother, and was gone to Padan-aram."*

The *"obedience"* mentioned here of Jacob was the opposite of that concerning Esau. While Jacob's going to Syria to obtain there a wife of the family of Abraham was the right thing to do, the way it was brought about was not the right thing. But that is laid aside for the moment, as the Holy Spirit shows us the difference, or at least one of the many differences, between Jacob and Esau.

Concerning disobedience on the part of Esau, the Scripture says, *"And Esau was forty years old when he took to wife Judith the daughter of Beeri the Hittite, and Bashemath the daughter of Elon the Hittite."*

It then says, *"Which were a grief of mind unto Isaac and to Rebekah"* (Gen. 26:34-35).

The path of Faith, which in its total conclusion is Faith in Christ and what Jesus did for us in His Sufferings, has as its intersecting strength, the principle of obedience. The obedience presently demanded is that we not resort to self-will in any capacity, but ever trust Christ for all things, understanding that everything we receive from God comes to us exclusively through the Cross, and because it was there that every victory was won. All of this is referred to as *"the good fight of faith"* (I Tim. 6:12).

THE DAUGHTERS OF CANAAN

Verse 8 reads: *"And Esau seeing that the daughters of Canaan pleased not Isaac his father."*

The truth is, Esau had little understanding as to why the daughters of Canaan did not please Isaac. He had no comprehension of the spiritual issues involved, nor his own spiritual lack.

How typical Esau is of millions of modern so-called Christians, who seek to please man, even as Esau sought to please Isaac, but have no understanding whatsoever of trying to please God. They are two different things altogether! How so similar all of this is to untold numbers of modern Preachers who seek to please Denominational heads, but have no thought of attempting to please God.

Let it be understood that we can please God or we can please man. The simple truth is, we cannot please both.

ISHMAEL

Verse 9 reads: *"Then went Esau unto Ishmael, and took unto the wives which he had Mahalath the daughter of Ishmael Abraham's son, the sister of Nebajoth, to be his wife."*

In fact, Ishmael had been dead now for some years, so it refers to Esau going to the family of Ishmael.

The truth is, Ishmael was no closer to acceptance, than the daughters of Canaan. He had long before been rejected by the Holy Spirit, and had been thrust out of the family of Abraham, even though he was the son of Abraham, but in reality a work of the flesh.

If the modern Believer doesn't understand the true path of Faith, he will always try to build his case on a work of the flesh.

Regrettably, the modern Church has many works of the flesh, exactly as did Abraham have this work of the flesh. Sadder still, it little knows or understands what is or isn't a work of the flesh, exactly as Esau didn't understand. To him, this would surely please Isaac, who at this time was a Type of Christ. His modern contemporaries do the same. Little do they know and realize that anything outside of the parameters of *"Jesus Christ and Him Crucified,"* is unacceptable to God.

(10) "AND JACOB WENT OUT FROM BEER-SHEBA, AND WENT TOWARD HARAN.

(11) "AND HE LIGHTED UPON A CERTAIN PLACE, AND TARRIED THERE ALL NIGHT, BECAUSE THE SUN WAS SET; AND HE TOOK OF THE STONES OF THAT PLACE,

NOTES

AND PUT THEM FOR HIS PILLOWS, AND LAY DOWN IN THAT PLACE TO SLEEP.

(12) "AND HE DREAMED, AND BEHOLD A LADDER SET UP ON THE EARTH, AND THE TOP OF IT REACHED TO HEAVEN: AND BEHOLD THE ANGELS OF GOD ASCENDING AND DESCENDING ON IT.

(13) "AND, BEHOLD, THE LORD STOOD ABOVE IT, AND SAID, I AM THE LORD GOD OF ABRAHAM YOUR FATHER, AND THE GOD OF ISAAC: THE LAND WHEREON YOU LIE, TO YOU WILL I GIVE IT, AND TO YOUR SEED;

(14) "AND YOUR SEED SHALL BE AS THE DUST OF THE EARTH, AND YOU SHALL SPREAD ABROAD TO THE WEST, AND TO THE EAST, AND TO THE NORTH, AND TO THE SOUTH: AND IN YOU AND IN YOUR SEED SHALL ALL THE FAMILIES OF THE EARTH BE BLESSED.

(15) "AND, BEHOLD, I AM WITH YOU, AND WILL KEEP YOU IN ALL PLACES WHERE YOU GO, AND WILL BRING YOU AGAIN INTO THIS LAND; FOR I WILL NOT LEAVE YOU, UNTIL I HAVE DONE THAT WHICH I HAVE SPOKEN TO YOU OF."

The composition is:

1. A lonely wanderer, hated by his brother, and obliged to flee from his home in order to save his life, Jacob learns the very first night of his exile that he is the object of Heaven's love and care, and that the Angels of God were busily employed passing and repassing from Heaven to Earth in ministering to him.

2. He learned that Earth and Heaven were united, and united in his interest and for his temporal and eternal welfare.

3. This wondrous *"ladder"* united him to Jehovah the God of his grandfather, and the God of his father.

4. Jacob merited nothing and God promised him everything. Such is Grace!

HARAN

Verse 10 reads: *"And Jacob went out from Beer-sheba, and went toward Haran."*

Now we might say that this is the beginning of *"the making of a man."* Jacob is alone, but yet God and all the Holy Angels are with him, even as we shall see. Only now, where he is totally dependent on the Lord, which means he had no other resources, could God reveal Himself to the Patriarch.

What a lesson for us!

That's why the great Apostle Paul said: *"Therefore I take pleasure in infirmities, in reproaches, in necessities, in persecutions, in distresses for Christ's sake: for when I am weak, then am I strong"* (II Cor. 12:10).

This is said by the Apostle, because the Lord had said to him: *"My Grace is sufficient for you: for My strength is made perfect in weakness."* The Apostle then said in answer to that: *"Most gladly therefore will I rather glory in my infirmities, that the power of Christ may rest upon me"* (II Cor. 12:9).

While God definitely was not the Author of the manner in which Jacob was to go to Haran, He would definitely use this time to *"make the man."*

A PERSONAL EXPERIENCE

I have some personal knowledge of what it means to go to *"Haran,"* and to do so as Jacob, in fact, exactly as Jacob; but I also know, of the Lord using this experience to bring me to the place of the path of Faith, which rests exclusively in Christ and His Cross.

Since the Fall of 1991, Jimmy Swaggart Ministries has been totally and completely dependent on the Lord, with all other resources completely cut off. Not the least of these would be our financial picture.

Our Ministry is a Media Ministry, which is what God has called us to do. While this type of Ministry reaches tremendous numbers of people, which it is intended to do, even though the cost per person is very low, still, in the aggregate, it takes a lot of money to get this task accomplished.

In that morning Prayer Meeting, in October of 1991, I didn't personally see how in the world we could financially survive. To be frank, I only wanted what the Lord desired that I do. If He wanted me off of Television, or whatever else, that's exactly what I wanted to do. But if He wanted me to remain on Television, again, that's exactly what I wanted to do. I harbored no illusions as to the impossibility of our situation, at least as it regarded our remaining in the Media, especially considering that virtually the entirety of the Church world was clamoring for our demise. I did not know what to do, except to take the thing to the Lord in prayer, which is exactly what I did.

This was the beginning of the daily Prayer Meetings, which have lasted unto this hour. I will never forget that morning.

The night before in another Prayer Meeting, the Lord had moved mightily and graciously, and let me know that what He had called me to do regarding the Media was to be continued. In fact, the following is what He said to me:

"I'm not a man that I should lie, neither the son of man that I should repent. What I have blessed nothing can curse."

In essence He was telling me that He had not changed His mind, and in fact, He never does change His mind as it regards the Callings.

So I knew that we were to continue in Media Ministry, but how in the world could it be done? How could we raise the finances? Who would give to us, considering that virtually the entirety of the Church world was demanding that we get off Television?

While excuses were offered, the main reason was, they didn't like what I preached. Our total dependence on Christ and the Cross rankled them to no end, especially considering, they were loudly recommending other things, such as the world of psychology, etc.

Knowing all of this, I began to importune the Lord as to how we could financially survive. And then the Lord spoke to my heart:

THE LORD WOULD SUPPLY

The Lord, while in prayer that morning, took my mind to the case of the tribute money. The Jews were demanding that Jesus and His Disciples pay taxes.

Peter asked the Lord if, in fact, the taxes were actually owed.

Jesus proclaimed that they, in fact, were not owed; however, He then said:

"Notwithstanding, lest we should offend them, go to the sea, and cast an hook, and take up the fish that first comes up; and when you have opened his mouth, you shall find a piece of money: that take, and give unto them for Me and you" (Mat. 17:24-27).

The Lord was telling me that as He provided the funds that day for the taxes to be paid, so He would provide for our Ministry.

But yet, I knew that this was the most unorthodox way of obtaining funds, that could ever be imagined.

As the Spirit of God fell in that Prayer Meeting that morning, moving mightily upon my soul, as well as all others present, I knew that God had spoken to me. I knew that He would provide for the Ministry, but I also knew that it was going to take my total and complete dependence upon Him for all of this to be done. As I've just stated, this has to be, the finding of a piece of money in the mouth of a fish, the most unorthodox way to raise funds, that possibly has ever been heard of. In other words, my Faith was going to be stretched to the limit.

LOOK WHAT THE LORD HAS DONE!

As I dictate these notes, it is December 31, the last day of 2001. A little over 10 years have passed from that morning Prayer Meeting unto this present time. And the Lord has done exactly what He said He would do.

I have watched Him bring in funds from some of the strangest sources, that one could ever imagine. But the fact remains, irrespective of the unorthodox manner in which it has been done, the Lord has definitely done exactly what He said He would do.

Just last month, we purchased three Radio Stations, one 50,000 watt FM giant, along with two AM Stations, all in East Texas and Arkansas, covering nearly one and one-half million people. We paid over one million dollars for the three Stations, and were able to pay cash the $300,000 down-payment.

This morning, December 31, 2001, I will sign the Letter of Intent to purchase another FM Station, covering the Chattanooga, Tennessee area, reaching approximately one million people. In fact, we hope to purchase at least ten full power FM Stations this year, plus the installation of a number of Translators. Look what the Lord has done!

So instead of being only on Television, we are as well now over Radio, and not merely with a short 30-minute Program each day, but rather programming the Gospel, and especially the Message of the Cross, 24 hours a day, seven days a week. *"If God be for us, who can be against us"* (Rom. 8:31).

TEST OF FAITH

In these last 10 years, there have been countless times that my Faith has been tested to the utmost. In other words, we would

come down to the very wire, financially speaking, when at the last minute, the Lord would help us to find a piece of money in the mouth of the fish. Out of the innumerable times, one stands out.

If I remember correctly, it was sometime in the year 2000. Our financial picture was desperate. We had over one million dollars worth of bills, due for payment now, and with no money to pay them. That particular Friday night was a sleepless night for me. Perhaps I should not have been concerned, but I was.

After having slept almost none at all, I got up that morning, preparing to go to the office, as I always did on Saturday mornings. In working on the Commentaries, I can do so on Saturday mornings for several hours, without interruption.

At any rate, that particular morning I was very discouraged. So discouraged in fact, that a little later I realized that it was a spirit of darkness which was hindering me. Everything looked impossible, and I did not know how in the world these bills could be paid.

I was preparing to shave, when I pushed the little button that turned on the radio, and of course it was tuned to SonLife, 88.5. I forget now which song was being sung, but almost immediately the presence of God filled that room, and came over me greatly.

The Lord began to speak to my heart, saying, *"I have brought you through demons, I have brought you through false brethren, I have brought you through adversity of every kind, and do you think after all I've done for you, that I'm going to let you fall to the ground now?"*

The moment the Lord spoke that to my heart, that spirit of which I mentioned a moment ago instantly left.

As I look back, I don't remember exactly what the Lord did to see us through, but it is obvious that we made it. As stated, the ways in which the Lord has provided during these last 10 years have been very unorthodox. So unorthodox in fact, that at times it has been mind-boggling. But as I look back, I realize that every test has been a test of Faith.

Oh yes! I know what it is to go to Haran. And I also know what it is to *"wrestle with the Lord,"* exactly as did Jacob. And thank

God, I also know what it is for the name to be changed from *"Jacob,"* to *"Israel."*

And incidentally, my name in English is actually *"James."* In Hebrew, ironically enough, it is *"Jacob."*

SLEEP

Verse 11 reads: *"And he lighted upon a certain place, and tarried there all night, because the sun was set; and he took of the stones of that place, and put them for his pillows, and lay down in that place to sleep."*

Nothing could possibly be more expressive of helplessness and nothingness than Jacob's condition as set before us here.

Cut off from his family, running from a murderous brother, going to a place of which he knew nothing, it is here that God will begin to reveal Himself to the Patriarch.

In fact, the sun was setting on stage one of his life, with stage two about to begin.

The *"sleep"* represents him ceasing from his personal activity, and God beginning His Personal activity. Jacob has much to learn, but it will begin here.

And that's exactly where the Lord has to bring most of us, and, perhaps, all of us. We have to be brought to the place where our own resources are dried up; therefore, we must now depend totally upon God. The *"sleep"* represents this dependence. Willingly we seldom come to this place. But spiritually, the Holy Spirit must bring us to this place.

ENGLAND

As an aside, the teaching of British Israelism enters the picture at this juncture. This teaching claims that two tribes of Israel were lost, Ephraim and Manasseh. The teachers of this false doctrine claim that England is one of those tribes, with America being the other.

For many years, there was a stone placed under the chair where the Kings and Queens of England were crowned in Westminster Abby. They claim this is one of the stones that Jacob used for a pillow.

Some years ago I was in Westminster Abby and observed this stone. It has since been given back to Scotland, from where it had been obtained many years ago.

As stated, all of this is false doctrine, for there have never been any lost tribes of Israel. As well, all those in England and America are Gentiles, and not Jews, at least as far as the greater makeup of these two countries is concerned.

While there definitely is supremacy in a rock, to be sure, that

"Rock" is Jesus Christ, and not some stone allegedly having been used by Jacob as a pillow.

THE DREAM

Verse 12 reads: *"And he dreamed, and behold a ladder set up on the Earth, and the top of it reached to Heaven: and behold the Angels of God ascending and descending on it."*

Concerning this, Mackintosh said: *"The ladder 'set on the Earth' naturally leads the heart to meditate on the display of God's Grace, in the Person and Work of His Son. On the Earth it was that the wondrous work was accomplished which forms the basis — the strong and everlasting basis — of all the Divine counsels in reference to Israel, the Church, and the world at large. On the Earth it was that Jesus lives, labored, and died; that, through His death, He might remove out of the way every obstacle to the accomplishment of the Divine purpose of blessing to man."*

The *"top of the ladder reaching to Heaven,"* proclaims the medium of communication between Heaven and Earth. It in fact, would in essence, show the way from Earth to Heaven. That *"Way"* would be Jesus Christ.

In fact, Christ alluded to this when Nathaniel said to Him: *"Rabbi, You are the Son of God; You are the King of Israel"* (Jn. 1:49).

Jesus then said: *"Verily, verily, I say unto you, hereafter you shall see Heaven open, and the Angels of God ascending and descending upon the Son of Man"* (Jn. 1:51).

In essence, one could say that Jesus Christ was and is that ladder.

The *"Angels of God ascending and descending on it,"* proclaim all the resources of God, which are now at the disposal of Jacob. It is the same for every modern Believer, that is, if we properly understand Jesus Christ and look to Him exclusively, according to what He has done for us in the Sacrifice of Himself on the Cross.

THE LORD

Verse 13 reads: *"And, behold, the LORD stood above it, and said, I am the LORD God of Abraham your father, and the God of Isaac: the land whereon you lie, to you will I give it, and to your seed."*

The words *"above it"* in the original Hebrew, actually should read *"beside him."* Not only did the Angels descend by it to him, but God Himself descended this stairway of glory, and, standing beside him, said: *"Behold I am with you and will keep you in all places where you go"* (vs. 15).

When He said to Jacob, *"I am the Lord God of Abraham your father, and the God of Isaac,"* He was in essence telling Jacob that as He had been with them, He would be with him. As well, the Promises that He gave to both, He now gives to him.

The Patriarch, destitute and with a stone for a pillow, literally having to leave this land, is now told by the Lord, *"To you will I give it, and to your seed."*

Only Faith could accept such a Promise, especially considering the condition in which Jacob presently found himself. But most of the time, the great Promises given to us by the Lord come at times when they seem the most unlikely.

THE BLESSING

Verse 14 reads: *"And your seed shall be as the dust of the Earth, and you shall spread abroad to the west, and to the east, and to the north, and to the south: and in you and in your seed shall all the families of the Earth be blessed."*

The first portion of this Verse speaks not only of Israel, but as well, of every single person who has ever been Born-Again. Considering that this seed would be *"as the dust of the Earth,"* we are speaking here of a tremendous multitude.

The spreading abroad in all directions tells us that *"This Gospel of the Kingdom shall be preached in all the world for a witness unto all nations; and then shall the end come"* (Mat. 24:14).

The *"seed"* expressed in the last phrase of this Verse speaks of Christ (Gal. 3:16). And in Him and Him Alone *"shall all the families of the Earth be blessed."*

Thank God my family got in on this great Blessing. As the song says:

"I never shall forget that day
"When all the burdens of my heart, they rolled away.
"It keeps me happy, glad, and free,
"I'll sing it, shout it, for He is everything to me."

THE WORD OF GOD

Verse 15 reads: *"And, behold, I am with you, and will keep you in all places where you go, and will bring you again into this land; for I will not leave you, until I have done that which I have spoken to you of."*

Several things are said in this Verse:

1. I am with you.
2. I will keep you.
3. I will bring you again into this land.
4. I won't leave you, until I have done all that of which I have spoken to you.

As the Lord spoke these great Promises to Jacob, through Christ, He has spoken the same thing to us.

Concerning my own personal life and Ministry, I claim these Promises, exactly as given to Jacob. And I believe I have the spiritual right to do this, and I believe that you do as well!

If the Lord has spoken anything to you, and irrespective as to what it might be, and you are sure of that Voice, if you will only walk in obedience, and continue to look to Christ and His Cross, *"He will not leave you,"* until this thing comes to pass.

As we understand the terminology as given to Jacob, he wasn't personally, at least at that time, to own all of Israel. But his seed definitely would. In fact, this is at least one of the reasons that he charged his sons to *"bury him with his fathers in the cave that is in the field of Ephron the Hittite"* (Gen. 49:29).

(16) "AND JACOB AWAKED OUT OF HIS SLEEP, AND HE SAID, SURELY THE LORD IS IN THIS PLACE; AND I KNEW IT NOT.

(17) "AND HE WAS AFRAID, AND SAID, HOW DREADFUL IS THIS PLACE! THIS IS NONE OTHER BUT THE HOUSE OF GOD, AND THIS IS THE GATE OF HEAVEN.

(18) "AND JACOB ROSE UP EARLY IN THE MORNING, AND TOOK THE STONE

THAT HE HAD PUT FOR HIS PILLOWS, AND SET IT UP FOR A PILLAR, AND POURED OIL UPON THE TOP OF IT.

(19) "AND HE CALLED THE NAME OF THAT PLACE BETH-EL: BUT THE NAME OF THAT CITY WAS CALLED LUZ AT THE FIRST.

(20) "AND JACOB VOWED A VOW, SAYING, IF GOD WILL BE WITH ME, AND WILL KEEP ME IN THIS WAY THAT I GO, AND WILL GIVE ME BREAD TO EAT, AND RAIMENT TO PUT ON,

(21) "SO THAT I COME AGAIN TO MY FATHER'S HOUSE IN PEACE; THEN SHALL THE LORD BE MY GOD:

(22) "AND THIS STONE, WHICH I HAVE SET FOR A PILLAR, SHALL BE GOD'S HOUSE: AND OF ALL THAT YOU SHALL GIVE ME I WILL SURELY GIVE THE TENTH UNTO YOU."

The construction is:

1. How happy and free from care would Jacob's life had been had he let God plan for him! But yet, I'm not so sure, but that all of us have to take the same course, in some way, as did Jacob.

2. The *"vow"* which Jacob vowed is the first recorded vow in the Bible.

3. For the first time, Jehovah reveals Himself to Jacob. There is a distinct possibility that on this very night, Jacob was born from above.

4. In the consecration of the Patriarch, he promises a portion of his yearly gains to the Lord.

5. Isaac and Esau refuse subjection to God; Rebekah and Jacob refuse cooperation with God. The rebellion of the human will is seen in the first pair and its wickedness in the second pair (Williams).

THE PLACE OF THE LORD

Verse 16 reads: *"And Jacob awaked out of his sleep, and he said, Surely the LORD is in this place; and I knew it not."*

What *"place"* was this?

It was not the geography that counted, but rather Jacob's present condition. He was at his weakest here. Whatever the material blessing from his father's flocks would have been, it is now lost. In fact, financially, he is, for all practical purposes, destitute. As well, he doesn't have the comfort of his family on which to lean. Once again the fact is, his

brother is seeking to kill him. But in this lonely, destitute condition, the Lord meets Jacob, and gives him the greatest Promises that could ever be given to any man.

This tells us, as previously stated, that all hopes of the flesh must die, before the Spirit can properly be revealed to us. As long as Christian man has a frail arm of flesh on which to lean, that he will do. So the Lord has to bring us to a place, to where there are no more arms on which to lean, and our dependence is now totally in Him. Regrettably, we do not come to this place and position quickly or easily.

The gist of this particular Verse is, at the very time, moment, and place, where and when Jacob least expects the Lord, is when the Lord appears to him.

PUNISHMENT OR BLESSING?

It is ironic; the Lord never mentions here the wrongdoing of the Patriarch. There is no reprimand, no upbraiding, and definitely no punishment. But yet, I think if this situation was brought into the present, the modern Church would think of nothing but punishment.

It thinks in this vein simply because it little knows the path of Faith, but rather functions in the realm, mostly of Law. And of course, Law demands punishment, while Faith demands Grace.

The modern Church as well, would never even dream of admitting that God would speak to someone, who just a few days before had practiced great deception on his father Isaac and his brother Esau. Once again, such thinking is because the Church functions mostly in Law. Such would shut the door as it regards God speaking to such an individual, but Faith builds a ladder, and on that ladder God descends, along with all His Holy Angels.

As we have previously stated, Jacob merited nothing and God promised him everything. Such is Grace!

THE HOUSE OF GOD AND THE GATE OF HEAVEN

Verse 17 reads: *"And he was afraid, and said, How dreadful is this place! This is none other but the House of God, and this is the Gate of Heaven."*

"How dreadful is this place!" could have been translated, *"How awe-inspiring is this place!"*

Jacob was afraid, and in such a case, rightly so. So were Moses (Ex. 20:18-19), Job (Job 42:5-6), Isaiah (Isa. 6:5), Peter (Lk. 5:8), and John (Rev. 1:17-18), at similar discoveries of the Divine Presence.

Considering what Jacob had experienced, it is no wonder that he refers to this place a *"Beth-el,"* i.e., *"the House of God,"* and *"the Gate of Heaven."*

Presently under Christ, *"the House of God,"* is Believers. Paul said: *"Know ye not that you are the Temple of God, and that the Spirit of God dwells in you?"* (I Cor. 3:16).

Now the *"Gate of Heaven"* is Jesus Christ, as it always has been; however, due to the Incarnation, and what Jesus has done for us at the Cross, the *"Gate of Heaven"* can be found almost anywhere, for Christ can be accepted anywhere.

THE STONE

Verse 18 reads: *"And Jacob rose up early in the morning, and took the stone that he had put for his pillows, and set it up for a pillar, and poured oil upon the top of it."*

The *"stone"* would have been looked at by the Lord, I think, as a Type of Christ, with the *"oil"* serving as a symbol of the Holy Spirit.

Incidentally, the stone we mentioned some time back, claimed by British Israelism to be the stone which served as a pillow for Jacob, could not be such. That particular stone is *"Scottish sandstone,"* and all the stone around Beth-el in Israel is *"limestone."*

BETH-EL

Verse 19 reads: *"And he called the name of that place Beth-el: but the name of that city was called Luz at the first."*

The place that Jacob named as *"Beth-el,"* which means *"House of God,"* was a little ways from the town, then called *"Luz."* It was then a Canaanite town, but came to be called *"Beth-el,"* after the conquest by Israel (Judg. 1:26). *"Beth-el"* is actually a suburb of Jerusalem at present. The last time I was there, a Jewish army base was the principal part of the area.

THE VOW

Verse 20 reads: *"And Jacob vowed a vow, saying, If God will be with me, and will keep*

me in this way that I go, and will give me bread to eat, and raiment to put on."

This is the first recorded vow in the Bible. Williams says concerning these statements by Jacob: *"There is much to make it appear that the word 'if' in this Passage means 'since.' Personal Salvation is not a matter of education, but of Revelation (Mat. 11:27). And Jacob no doubt had received a good religious education from his parents; but, now, for the first time, Jehovah reveals Himself to him."*

The path of Faith has now been opened up to Jacob, and he, for all practical purposes, understands what it is. There is every evidence, as stated, that Jacob truly was *"born again"* this particular night.

In fact, millions are in the modern Church who have never been Born-Again. They have received some religious education, exactly as did Jacob, but they've never had a Revelation from the Lord. And what would that Revelation be?

In its most simplistic form, it is the Holy Spirit dealing with the heart, even as the Word of God is preached, creating alarm in the sinner's soul, and as well, bringing about the need for Christ. This Revelation is a must, if an individual is to be saved. Otherwise, they merely have an education, which definitely will not suffice.

Such a Revelation will always come, and without fail, providing the Word of God is faithfully preached, and the Anointing of the Holy Spirit accompanies such a Word. Without fail, if the heart is open at all, the Revelation will then come!

As well, this Passage proves that Jacob had basically forfeited the double portion which came to the one having the birthright, at least when the father died. In fact, both Jacob and Esau were expecting Isaac to die at this particular time. He didn't, incidentally!

So in Jacob's mind, all of this inheritance was gone. So he asked the Lord to provide for him. As stated, he was now totally dependent on the Lord for everything.

PEACE

Verse 21 reads: *"So that I come again to my father's house in peace; then shall the LORD be my God."*

The Patriarch is asking two things:

1. Would he ultimately be able to come home?

2. Could he come in peace, i.e., *"free from Esau's avenging threats."*?

The Lord did all of this with Jacob, plus much more. He gave him far more than *"bread to eat,"* and *"raiment to put on."*

TITHE

Verse 22 reads: *"And this stone, which I have set for a pillar, shall be God's House: and of all that You shall give me I will surely give the tenth unto You."*

Jacob set up the stone for a *"pillar,"* and designated the place as *"God's House."*

In fact, this definitely was one of the greatest Revelations thus far, that God had given to any man. From this tremendous experience, Jacob claimed his part in the great appellative, *"The God of Abraham, of Isaac, and of Jacob."*

His vow is that he would *"give the tenth,"* or tithe, unto God.

Just exactly as to whom he would give this, we aren't told. So more than likely, when he came into possession of herds, and no matter how large those herds, Jacob gave a tenth unto God, which he no doubt offered in Sacrifice. If that was the case, and it no doubt is, we now find Jacob offering up Sacrifices to a degree as no one else. This would have greatly glorified God, all the sacrifices being a symbol of the coming Redeemer, Who would die on the Cross, shedding His Life's Blood (Eph. 2:13-18).

In effect, if the tithe we now give to the Work of God doesn't go to proclaim the Message of Jesus Christ and Him Crucified, then in reality, we are not giving to God, but to something else entirely.

This is the second time that giving to the Lord in the form of tithes is mentioned in the Bible. On the first occasion, Abraham paid tithes to Melchizedek, who was a Type of Christ as our Great High Priest. Jesus would become this by dying on the Cross as a Sacrifice. So both occasions of paying tithes speak to the Cross; therefore, our tithe presently must go for the same benefit, to proclaim the grand Message of *"Jesus Christ and Him Crucified"* (I Cor. 1:23; 2:2). Otherwise, we really aren't paying tithe!

"All the Saviour's glory mind can never measure,
"Nor the tongue of man define;
"I have come to know Him as Life's dearest treasure,
"Know Him as my Friend Divine."

"Mine in time of trouble when my heart is breaking,
"When my spirit droops with grief,
"He with blessed comfort heals the bitter aching,
"Swift and sure He brings relief."

"He's my strength in weakness, joy in times of sadness,
"My protection from the foe,
"Patient, kind, and loving, heart of all my gladness,
"He dispels my every foe."

"And in Earth or Heaven there is not His equal,
"Saints nor Angels can compare,
"Nor the matchless splendors of the realm supernal,
"He's the fairest of the fair."

CHAPTER 29

(1) "THEN JACOB WENT ON HIS JOURNEY, AND CAME UNTO THE LAND OF THE PEOPLE OF THE EAST.

(2) "AND HE LOOKED, AND BEHOLD A WELL IN THE FIELD, AND, LO, THERE WERE THREE FLOCKS OF SHEEP LYING BY IT; FOR OUT OF THAT WELL THEY WATERED THE FLOCKS: AND A GREAT STONE WAS UPON THE WELL'S MOUTH.

(3) "AND THITHER WERE ALL THE FLOCKS GATHERED: AND THEY ROLLED THE STONE FROM THE WELL'S MOUTH, AND WATERED THE SHEEP, AND PUT THE STONE AGAIN UPON THE WELL'S MOUTH IN HIS PLACE.

(4) "AND JACOB SAID UNTO THEM, MY BRETHREN, WHERE ARE YOU? AND THEY SAID, OF HARAN ARE WE.

(5) "AND HE SAID UNTO THEM, KNOW YE LABAN THE SON OF NAHOR? AND THEY SAID, WE KNOW HIM.

(6) "AND HE SAID UNTO THEM, IS HE WELL? AND THEY SAID, HE IS WELL: AND, BEHOLD, RACHEL HIS DAUGHTER COMES WITH THE SHEEP.

(7) "AND HE SAID, LO, IT IS YET HIGH DAY, NEITHER IS IT TIME THAT THE CATTLE SHOULD BE GATHERED TOGETHER: WATER YE THE SHEEP, AND GO AND FEED THEM.

(8) "AND THEY SAID, WE CANNOT, UNTIL ALL THE FLOCKS BE GATHERED TOGETHER, AND TILL THEY ROLL THE STONE FROM THE WELL'S MOUTH; THEN WE WATER THE SHEEP."

The overview is:

1. Grace Forgave Jacob, and confirmed to him the Promises.

2. We will find in this scenario that even though Jacob has had a great Revelation from the Lord, still, spiritually speaking, he has yet a ways to go.

3. Self is the culprit; no one can really enjoy God until he gets to the bottom of self.

THE JOURNEY

Verse 1 reads: *"Then Jacob went on his journey, and came into the land of the people of the east."*

This *"journey,"* even as we shall see, was to last for some 20 years. In it, Jacob would learn much, but would still need another Revelation before the total change would come. These 20 years, more than anything else, were to make him see the need for change.

God will not really begin to reveal Himself, until the end of flesh is seen. If, therefore, I have not reached the end of my flesh, in the deep and positive experience of my soul, it is morally impossible that I can have anything like a just apprehension of God's Character. Regrettably, it takes a long time to come to the end of self-will.

This is what this *"journey"* is all about!

We will find in the coming scenario that the problem of deception is still with Jacob. An old sin is an easy sin!

Jacob was now in Mesopotamia, about 450 miles from Beer-sheba.

THE WELL

Verse 2 reads: *"And he looked, and behold a well in the field, and, lo, there were*

three flocks of sheep lying by it; for out of that well they watered the flocks: and a great stone was upon the well's mouth."

As we shall see, it is obvious that this well could only be used at fixed times. A great stone covered its mouth, which probably required two or three men to remove it.

From the way the scenario unfolds, more than likely, Laban, the father of Rachel, owned this well. Because immediately upon her arrival with the sheep, the stone is rolled away, and her sheep watered first, while the rest, though they had been there long before her, yet had to bide their time till her sheep are watered.

Considering the value of wells of that particular time, this is probably the truth of the matter.

Jacob comes upon this well, and sees sheep and shepherds gathered by it. They are evidently waiting for the stone to be rolled away, so their sheep can be watered.

WATER

Verse 3 reads: *"And thither were all the flocks gathered: and they rolled the stone from the well's mouth, and watered the sheep, and put the stone again upon the well's mouth in his place."*

This Verse mainly tells us how the sheep were watered, at this particular well. As stated, it probably belonged to Laban, and was only opened at certain times.

HARAN

Verse 4 reads: *"And Jacob said unto them, My brethren, whence be ye? And they said, Of Haran are we."*

In those days, signs were not on every corner giving directions, etc. And as well, one did not ask just anyone concerning distances or directions. Robbers were lying in wait for those who were lost or disoriented.

So when Jacob asked these shepherds where they were from, with their reply being *"Haran,"* which was actually his destination, he knew he was close, and this no doubt reminded him of God's Promise to guide him on his journey.

For the Lord to be with one, to guide one, to lead one, to give direction, to help in that which at first seems to be but small things, but which quickly lead to large things, is the greatest blessing that one could ever know. This which the Lord promised to do for Jacob, as wonderful as it was, is available to every single Believer, irrespective as to whom they might be. Paul quotes the Master when He said: *"I will never leave you, nor forsake you.*

"So that we may boldly say, The Lord is my Helper, and I will not fear what man shall do unto me" (Heb. 13:5-6).

However, such relationship is not automatic with the Believer. The Believer must actively want and desire such relationship, and must ask the Lord to provide such. It is a prayer that the Lord will definitely answer; however, He will not push His way in, always waiting for the initiative to be taken by the Believer.

LABAN

Verse 5 reads: *"And he said unto them, Know ye Laban the son of Nahor? And they said, We know him."*

Laban, it is remembered, is Rebekah's brother. He is the one who primarily dealt with Eliezer, the servant of Abraham, who had come to find a bride for Isaac (Gen., Chpt. 24).

The language spoken then by the shepherds was probably Chaldean. Jacob, who spoke Hebrew, was evidently able to converse with them either because he had learned Chaldee from his mother, or, as is more probable, because the dialects were not then greatly dissimilar (Gosman).

He called Laban the son of Nahor, though he was the grandson. In both Hebrew and Aramaic, there is no separate word for grandson. *"Son"* means any descendant down the line.

RACHEL

Verse 6 reads: *"And he said unto them, Is he well? And they said, He is well: and, behold, Rachel his daughter comes with the sheep."*

This is the first mention of Rachel in the Bible. She will figure very prominently in the great Plan of God, being the mother of Joseph and Benjamin. She was the ancestress of three of the great Tribes of Israel, Benjamin, Ephraim, and Manasseh, the latter two, being the sons of Joseph. She and her sister Leah were honored by later generations as those

NOTES

"who together built up the house of Israel" (Ruth 4:11).

The evidence is that Laban was not so well to do financially. His daughter is serving as a shepherdess. She was evidently raised to do her part in the family, and thereby was taught responsibility and industry. From such the Lord drew the Mothers of Israel.

In all of this, we see the Hand of the Lord working, which is a pleasure to behold. Jacob, who must have a wife in order for the great Plan of God to be brought forth, is led to this particular well, even at the exact time that Rachel appears.

THE SHEEP

Verses 7 and 8 read: *"And he said, Lo, it is yet high day, neither is it time that the cattle should be gathered together: water ye the sheep, and go and feed them.*

"And they said, We cannot, until all the flocks be gathered together, and till they roll the stone from the well's mouth; then we water the sheep."

Knowing that the shepherds had brought the sheep for water, Jacob wonders as to why they are not attending to the task, but seemingly waiting.

More than likely, the reason was that Laban owned the well, and the flocks could not be watered until Rachel first of all had watered her flock.

Wells in those days, especially in the places of hot, dry climates, which this was, were very valuable. So a system for watering undoubtedly was worked out with the various different flocks in the area.

The stone at the well's mouth, which is so often mentioned here, was to secure the water; for water was scarce — it was not there for everyone's use.

(9) "AND WHILE HE YET SPAKE WITH THEM, RACHEL CAME WITH HER FATHER'S SHEEP: FOR SHE KEPT THEM.

(10) "AND IT CAME TO PASS, WHEN JACOB SAW RACHEL THE DAUGHTER OF LABAN HIS MOTHER'S BROTHER, AND THE SHEEP OF LABAN HIS MOTHER'S BROTHER, THAT JACOB WENT NEAR, AND ROLLED THE STONE FROM THE WELL'S MOUTH, AND WATERED THE FLOCK OF LABAN HIS MOTHER'S BROTHER.

(11) "AND JACOB KISSED RACHEL, AND LIFTED UP HIS VOICE, AND WEPT.

(12) "AND JACOB TOLD RACHEL THAT HE WAS HER FATHER'S BROTHER, AND THAT HE WAS REBEKAH'S SON: AND SHE RAN AND TOLD HER FATHER.

(13) "AND IT CAME TO PASS, WHEN LABAN HEARD THE TIDINGS OF JACOB HIS SISTER'S SON, THAT HE RAN TO MEET HIM, AND EMBRACED HIM, AND KISSED HIM, AND BROUGHT HIM TO HIS HOUSE. AND HE TOLD LABAN ALL THESE THINGS."

The synopsis is:

1. We readily see the Hand of the Lord working in this situation regarding the meeting of Jacob with Rachel.

2. I think the Holy Spirit immediately informed Jacob that this young lady was to be his wife.

3. However, as we shall see Jacob's way was fraught with difficulty.

RACHEL, THE SHEPHERDESS

Verse 9 reads: *"And while he yet spake with them, Rachel came with her father's sheep: for she kept them."*

At this point Laban had no sons, although later he would have. As the younger daughter, Rachel was assigned to the task of keeping the sheep, which she did. How old Rachel was at this time, we have no way of knowing.

LOVE AT FIRST SIGHT

Verse 10 reads: *"And it came to pass, when Jacob saw Rachel the daughter of Laban his mother's brother, and the sheep of Laban his mother's brother, that Jacob went near, and rolled the stone from the well's mouth, and watered the flock of Laban his mother's brother."*

Three times the Holy Spirit has Moses to repeat the term *"his mother's brother."* It is not done unintentionally. The idea is, Jacob has met with his own relations, with *"his bone and his flesh."*

This is some proof that Laban owned this well, in that Rachel waters her sheep first, or at least, Jacob waters them for her.

It is highly unlikely that Jacob would have acted here as he did, had he not learned from Rachel, or possibly even the waiting shepherds, that the well belonged to Laban, and

that no sheep were to be watered until Rachel had first watered hers.

The Scripture says, *"When Jacob saw Rachel. . . ."* Every evidence is that it was love at first sight.

RACHEL

Verse 11 reads: *"And Jacob kissed Rachel, and lifted up his voice, and wept."*

The Patriarch is overcome with emotion, and I think mostly, at the joy of seeing the Hand of God working in his life. Truly the Lord was with him. While he was very happy to have met his relatives, which means that his long journey is now over, I think the greatest joy of all was that of a spiritual note. As well, he may have known at that very moment, and informed by the Spirit of God, that Rachel was to be his wife. He of course would not at that moment, have told her that, but more than likely, the Spirit of the Lord definitely informed him of such.

RELATIONS

Verse 12 reads: *"And Jacob told Rachel that he was her father's brother, and that he was Rebekah's son: and she ran and told her father."*

Jacob was actually the nephew of Laban. Terms of relationship were used in a very indefinite way among the Hebrews.

We will find that Jacob's love for Rachel is one of the Bible's outstanding examples of human love — seven years *"seemed to him but a few days because of the love he had for her"* (Gen. 29:20).

When she told her father Laban about Jacob, I wonder if he did not recall when his sister Rebekah, those many years before, had come to him when Eliezer had come on behalf of Abraham, as it regarded a bride for Isaac.

LABAN

Verse 13 reads: *"And it came to pass, when Laban heard the tidings of Jacob his sister's son, that he ran to meet him, and embraced him, and kissed him, and brought him to his house. And he told Laban all these things."*

Laban now did almost exactly what he had done those many years before, when he was told by Rebekah of Eliezer. As he ran then to meet Abraham's servant, he now runs to meet Jacob.

The Patriarch now relates to Laban all the things which had happened between him and Esau, and especially he no doubt gave all the information which Laban required, about his mother Rebekah, who was Laban's sister.

Laban would no doubt have been well over 100 years of age at this time, possibly even about 120.

(14) "AND LABAN SAID TO HIM, SURE-LY YOU ARE MY BONE AND MY FLESH. AND HE ABODE WITH HIM THE SPACE OF A MONTH.

(15) "AND LABAN SAID UNTO JACOB, BECAUSE YOU ARE MY BROTHER, SHOULD YOU THEREFORE SERVE ME FOR NOUGHT? TELL ME, WHAT SHALL YOUR WAGES BE?

(16) "AND LABAN HAD TWO DAUGH-TERS: THE NAME OF THE ELDER WAS LEAH, AND THE NAME OF THE YOUNGER WAS RACHEL.

(17) "LEAH WAS TENDER EYED; BUT RACHEL WAS BEAUTIFUL AND WELL FA-VORED.

(18) "AND JACOB LOVED RACHEL; AND SAID, I WILL SERVE YOU SEVEN YEARS FOR RACHEL YOUR YOUNGER DAUGHTER.

(19) "AND LABAN SAID, IT IS BETTER THAT I GIVE HER TO YOU, THAN THAT I SHOULD GIVE HER TO ANOTHER MAN: ABIDE WITH ME.

(20) "AND JACOB SERVED SEVEN YEARS FOR RACHEL; AND THEY SEEMED UNTO HIM BUT A FEW DAYS, FOR THE LOVE HE HAD TO HER."

The exegesis is:

1. Jacob is now about to begin to reap the bitter fruit of his sin.

2. He is at the outset deceived, exactly as he deceived his father, and was deeply wounded in the deepest affections of his heart.

3. It is a popular mistake to suppose that Jacob did not marry Rachel till the end of the seven years, or even the second seven years. Every evidence is that he took her immediately for his wife.

THE BEGINNING

Verse 14 reads: *"And Laban said to him, Surely you are my bone and my flesh. And he abode with him the space of a month."*

NOTES

After Jacob related everything to Laban, the uncle admitted that Jacob was indeed who he had said he was, and for the simple reason that no one else would have had the knowledge of so many details.

Jacob abiding with Laban for the space of a month means that he lives with Laban for this particular period of time, and then went out and obtained his own place after that.

WAGES

Verse 15 reads: *"And Laban said unto Jacob, Because you are my brother, should you therefore serve me for nought? Tell me, what shall your wages be?"*

Jacob the dealer meets now with Laban the dealer, and they are both seen, as it were, straining every nerve to outwit each other.

Evidently, during the month that Jacob spent in the house of Laban, he applied himself to serve his uncle, even as he had begun, when he watered his flock. So Laban wants to strike up a bargain with him, that Jacob might be in his employ.

Due to the manner in which Jacob had to leave his home, he was destitute of money of any nature, and so, was at the mercy of Laban to a great degree.

THE BARGAIN

Verses 16 through 20 read: *"And Laban had two daughters: the name of the elder was Leah, and the name of the younger was Rachel.*

"Leah was tender eyed; but Rachel was beautiful and well favored.

"And Jacob loved Rachel; and said, I will serve you seven years for Rachel your younger daughter.

"And Laban said, It is better that I give her to you, than that I should give her to another man: abide with me.

"And Jacob served seven years for Rachel; and they seemed to him but a few days, for the love he had to her."

Would the deception that Laban was now planning to carry out on Jacob have been carried out, if in fact Jacob had not tried to practice deception on his father Isaac?

I think not! The Scripture emphatically states, *"that we reap what we sow"* (Gal. 6:7-8). Even though the Passage in Galatians is speaking of sowing to the flesh, or sowing to the Spirit, still, the principle is the same.

SOWING TO THE FLESH

In its most simplistic form, this refers to trying to live this Christian life by means other than Faith in Christ and what Christ has done for us at the Cross.

Even though Believers were not referred to as *"Christians"* during Jacob's time, the principle was the same. Jacob all too often was trying to follow the Lord by the means of self-will, instead of trust in the Lord.

But we have far less excuse today than did Jacob. The Cross, through which everything comes to the Believer from the Lord, is now historical. In other words, it's a fact. The Cross, with Jacob, was prophetic, meaning that it was yet in the future. But still, as we receive everything presently from the Lord by looking back to the Cross, in Old Testament Times, everything was received from the Lord by looking forward to that coming time of the Cross. In fact, the Sacrifices of old represented Christ and His Cross. Faith in those Sacrifices per se would have done little good; however, Faith in Who and What they represented was the secret of all victory and power.

SOWING TO THE SPIRIT

Sowing to the Spirit refers to the Holy Spirit, and refers to placing our Faith and confidence totally and completely in Christ and the Cross, through which the Holy Spirit works (Rom. 8:1-2).

Many Christians have the idea that *"sowing to the Spirit"* refers to doing spiritual things. It doesn't! While those things we do might be good, helpful, instructive, and informative; still, our walk with God is not so much in what we *"do,"* but rather what we *"believe"* (Jn. 3:16).

As we look at Jacob, we might possibly think that we would never do such a thing as Jacob did, as it regards the practicing of deception. While deception may not be our direction, to be sure, some other wrong is. In other words, we don't come to the place of *"walking after the Spirit"* very quickly or very easily. And we can't come there at all, if someone doesn't teach us the Truth.

NOTES

That's the reason these Commentaries, if I may be allowed to say so, are so very, very important. Jesus said: *"You shall know the Truth, and the Truth shall make you free"* (Jn. 8:32).

While it's not possible to eliminate the growing process in the heart and life of the Believer, we can save ourselves much grief, if we are blessed enough to come under correct teaching.

So Jacob loves Rachel, and agrees to serve Laban some seven years for her hand, so to speak.

It would seem from these statements that Jacob served Laban for seven years before Rachel became his wife; however, the terminology employed rather refers to a contract or agreement. Jacob married both Leah and Rachel immediately, the first in which he was deceived into doing so, and the second by intention. Now he must serve 14 years, which he did.

(21) "AND JACOB SAID UNTO LABAN, GIVE ME MY WIFE, FOR MY DAYS ARE FULFILLED, THAT I MAY GO IN UNTO HER.

(22) "AND LABAN GATHERED TOGETHER ALL THE MEN OF THE PLACE, AND MADE A FEAST.

(23) "AND IT CAME TO PASS IN THE EVENING, THAT HE TOOK LEAH HIS DAUGHTER, AND BROUGHT HER TO HIM; AND HE WENT IN UNTO HER.

(24) "AND LABAN GAVE UNTO HIS DAUGHTER LEAH ZILPAH HIS MAID FOR AN HANDMAID.

(25) "AND IT CAME TO PASS, THAT IN THE MORNING, BEHOLD, IT WAS LEAH: AND HE SAID TO LABAN, WHAT IS THIS YOU HAVE DONE UNTO ME? DID NOT I SERVE WITH YOU FOR RACHEL? WHEREFORE THEN HAVE YOU BEGUILED ME?

(26) "AND LABAN SAID, IT MUST NOT BE SO DONE IN OUR COUNTRY, TO GIVE THE YOUNGER BEFORE THE FIRSTBORN.

(27) "FULFILL HER WEEK, AND WE WILL GIVE YOU THIS ALSO FOR THE SERVICE WHICH YOU SHALL SERVE WITH ME YET SEVEN OTHER YEARS.

(28) "AND JACOB DID SO, AND FULFILLED HER WEEK: AND HE GAVE HIM RACHEL HIS DAUGHTER TO WIFE ALSO.

(29) "AND LABAN GAVE TO RACHEL HIS DAUGHTER BILHAH HIS HANDMAID TO BE HER MAID.

(30) "AND HE WENT IN ALSO UNTO RACHEL, AND HE LOVED ALSO RACHEL MORE THAN LEAH, AND SERVED WITH HIM YET SEVEN OTHER YEARS."

The diagram is:

1. As Jacob had deceived his father Isaac, he is now deceived.

2. The deception he practiced upon Isaac cost him at least 14 years of servitude.

3. *"The way of the transgressors is hard"* (Prov. 13:15).

THE AGREEMENT IS MADE

Verse 21 reads: *"And Jacob said unto Laban, Give me my wife, for my days are fulfilled, that I may go in unto her."*

His *"days being fulfilled"* simply means that the contract had been agreed upon, that he was to serve Laban seven years for Rachel. This is proven by Verse 30.

THE BARGAIN SEALED

Verse 22 reads: *"And Laban gathered together all the men of the place, and made a feast."*

After everything had been agreed upon as it regards Jacob serving Laban for seven years, Laban will now make a great feast, and invite all of the notables of the area to the wedding. But Laban, as we shall see, has something else in mind altogether.

LEAH

Verses 23 through 25 read: *"And it came to pass in the evening, that he took Leah his daughter, and brought her to him; and he went in unto her.*

"And Laban gave unto his daughter Leah Zilpah his maid for an handmaid.

"And it came to pass, that in the morning, behold, it was Leah: and he said to Laban, What is this you have done unto me? Did not I serve with you for Rachel? Wherefore then have you beguiled me?"

When Leah went in to Jacob, she no doubt was wearing a veil, and as well, the room was probably dark.

She evidently said nothing that night, but the next morning, to Jacob's surprise, it was not Rachel who had been given to him, but rather Leah.

The question, *"Did not I serve with you for Rachel?"*, could have been translated, *"Did not*

I agree to serve with you for Rachel?" In this is *"Election."*

ELECTION

In Romans, Chapter 9, we have the Doctrine of *"Election."* Jacob and Esau are mentioned in this scenario. Concerning Election, Mackintosh has, I think, an excellent statement. He said:

"It is deeply interesting to the spiritual mind to mark how sedulously the Spirit of God, in Romans 9, and indeed throughout all Scripture, guards against the inference which the human mind draws from the Doctrine of God's Election. When He speaks of 'vessels of wrath,' He simply says, 'fitted to destruction;' He does not say that God 'fitted' them. Whereas, on the other hand, when He refers to 'vessels of mercy,' He says, 'whom He had afore prepared unto glory.' This is most marked.

"If the Reader will turn for a moment to Matthew 25:34-41, he will find another striking and beautiful instance of the same thing."

Mackintosh continues: *"When the King addresses those on His right hand, He says, 'Come, you blessed of My Father, inherit the kingdom prepared for you from the foundation of the world' (vs. 34). But when He addresses those on His left, He says, 'Depart from Me, you cursed.' He does not say, 'cursed of My Father.' And further, He says, 'Into everlasting fire, prepared (not for you but) for the Devil and his angels'" (vs. 41).*

And then: *"In a word, then, it is plain that God has 'prepared' a kingdom of glory, and 'vessels of mercy' to inherit the kingdom; but He has not prepared 'everlasting fire' for men, but for 'the Devil and his angels;' nor has He fitted the 'vessels of wrath,' but they have fitted themselves.*

"The Word of God as clearly establishes 'Election' as it sedulously guards against 'reprobation.' (The idea is) everyone who finds himself in Heaven will have to thank God for it, and everyone who finds himself in Hell will have only himself to thank."

SEVEN OTHER YEARS

Verses 26 through 30 read: *"And Laban said, It must not be so done in our country, to give the younger before the firstborn.*

"Fulfill her week, and we will give you this also for the service which you shall serve with me yet seven other years.

"And Jacob did so, and fulfilled her week: and he gave him Rachel his daughter to wife also.

"And Laban gave to Rachel his daughter Bilhah his handmaid to be her maid.

"And he went in also unto Rachel, and he loved also Rachel more than Leah, and served with him yet seven other years."

Concerning Laban's contention that the custom in his country was that the younger must not be married before the firstborn, of that there is no proof. It seems to be something that Laban concocted on his own. There was some evidence of such in India, but not in his part of the world.

Laban now offers Rachel to Jacob for seven more years, now making 14 total. However, Jacob did not complain about the situation, perhaps seeing that he had little choice in the matter. His actions seem to suggest that he knew that he was now paying for his deception regarding Isaac and his brother. Consequently, he accepts the situation.

CHASTISEMENT

The Lord actually doesn't punish His children, but He definitely does chastise His children. And what is the difference?

Chastisement is designed to teach us something, while punishment contains no instruction, only hurt. Jacob is being chastised. He seems to recognize this, and accepts it.

This in no way meant that Laban was right in what he did, and to be sure, the Lord would deal with him, as the Lord deals with all. But Jacob suffered such, with there being no evidence that he sought to take matters into his own hands.

(31) "AND WHEN THE LORD SAW THAT LEAH WAS HATED, HE OPENED HER WOMB: BUT RACHEL WAS BARREN.

(32) "AND LEAH CONCEIVED, AND BEAR A SON, AND SHE CALLED HIS NAME REUBEN: FOR SHE SAID, SURELY THE LORD HAS LOOKED UPON MY AFFLICTION; NOW THEREFORE MY HUSBAND WILL LOVE ME.

(33) "AND SHE CONCEIVED AGAIN, AND BEAR A SON; AND SAID, BECAUSE THE LORD HAS HEARD I WAS HATED, HE HAS

THEREFORE GIVEN ME THIS SON ALSO: AND SHE CALLED HIS NAME SIMEON.

(34) "AND SHE CONCEIVED AGAIN, AND BEAR A SON; AND SAID, NOW THIS TIME WILL MY HUSBAND BE JOINED UNTO ME, BECAUSE I HAVE BORN HIM THREE SONS: THEREFORE WAS HIS NAME CALLED LEVI.

(35) "AND SHE CONCEIVED AGAIN, AND BEAR A SON: AND SHE SAID, NOW WILL I PRAISE THE LORD: THEREFORE SHE CALLED HIS NAME JUDAH; AND LEFT BEARING."

The structure is:

1. As the Lord saw what was being done to Leah, He sees everything.

2. In the sons born to Leah, we have a diagram of the Plan of Salvation, even as we shall see.

3. All of this was to prove that *"the origin of Israel was to be a work not of nature but of Grace"* (Keil).

WHAT THE LORD SAW

Verse 31 reads: *"And when the LORD saw that Leah was hated, He opened her womb: but Rachel was barren."*

The word *"hated"* here means *"loved less."*

There is no indication that Jacob mistreated Leah, but there is indication that Rachel did. The Lord saw all of this, and as a result, He made Leah fruitful, and at the same time, He made Rachel barren.

In fact, Leah was the ancestress of both David and Jesus. And there could have been no greater honor than that!

We learn from all of this the minute involvement of the Lord in all things. He knows all, sees all, and involves Himself in all!

All of this shows that whatever Laban did, Leah was not a party to the deception. She had no choice but to do as she did, but none of this was her idea.

And it certainly wasn't Rachel's idea, but as well, she had no say in the matter either. Her wrong comes in by taking out the situation on Leah, who was not to blame. In fact, the situation had to be very difficult for all three, Jacob, Rachel, and Leah. But it seems that Leah suffered the brunt of this scenario, and unjustly. As noted, the Lord didn't take kindly to what was happening.

REUBEN

Verse 32 reads: *"And Leah conceived, and bear a son, and she called his name Reuben: for she said, Surely the LORD has looked upon my affliction; now therefore my husband will love me."*

Reuben means, *"see, a son."*

Considering that in those days being barren was a reproach, and that having children was a great blessing, she evidently hoped that her having this child, in effect, giving Jacob his firstborn, would increase his affection for her. To be unloved, or even loved less, presents a very unsavory situation. It's very hard for anyone to function in such a climate. From the information given in the next Verse, it doesn't seem that the situation was ameliorated.

SIMEON

Verse 33 reads: *"And she conceived again, and bear a son; and said, Because the LORD has heard I was hated, He has therefore given me this son also: and she called his name Simeon."*

Simeon means, *"hearing."* She is functioning from the position that the Lord has heard her petition. However, at the moment it didn't change, but ultimately it would.

LEVI

Verse 34 reads: *"And she conceived again, and bear a son; and said, Now this time will my husband be joined unto me, because I have born him three sons: therefore was his name called Levi."*

Levi means, *"joined."*

She names her son accordingly in the hopes that her husband will be joined to her with greater love. There is evidence that this ultimately did happen (Gen. 31:4, 14; 49:31).

JUDAH

Verse 35 reads: *"And she conceived again, and bear a son: and she said, Now will I praise the LORD: therefore she called his name Judah; and left bearing."*

Judah means, *"praise."* From this Tribe would come both David, and above all, Christ.

Throughout, in the midst of her melancholy, there is a tone of fervent piety and

NOTES

Faith, and that not merely to God, but to the Covenant Jehovah. And now slowly she parts with her hope of human affection, and finds comfort in Jehovah Alone.

This time, she says, *"I will praise Jehovah."* And it was this son of the despised one, whose birth called forth from her this hymn of simple thanksgiving, who was foreordained to be the ancestor of the Promised acob two more sons, and a daughter.

In her six sons, we find the Plan of Salvation outlined so dramatically, as well as these men being Types of Christ. In fact, all of the sons of Leah and Rachel were Types of Christ, with each son portraying a particular Ministry of our Lord to Believers. In other words, He was our Substitute in all things. We will look first at the six sons of Leah, and how their names draw out the Plan of Salvation:

1. Reuben: *"See, a son."* This represents the child that is born into the world, whomever that child may be.

2. Simeon: *"Hearing."* When the child is old enough, it is to hear the Gospel.

3. Levi: *"Joined."* The child is born, it hears the Gospel, and it is joined to Christ.

4. Judah: *"Praise."* The child is born, it hears the Gospel, it is joined to Christ, and it praises the Lord.

5. Issachar: *"Reward."* The son is born, it hears the Gospel, it is joined to Christ, it praises the Lord, and the Lord gives the reward of Eternal Life.

6. Zebulun: *"Dwelling."* The child is born, it hears the Gospel, it is joined to the Lord, it then praises the Lord, it has reward, and now it will dwell with the Lord forever and forever.

Thus is the Plan of Salvation wrought out in the six sons of Leah.

The names of all of these sons also portray Christ, and a particular Work and Ministry which He has carried out for Believers, which we will address in the body of the next Chapter.

All of these children born to Leah, her maid Zilpah, Rachel, and her maid, Bilhah, including the two sons of Joseph, were the heads of the 13 Tribes of Israel, which were recipients of the Word of God, and as well, served as the womb of the Messiah. So we're seeing here the birth of a people, totally unlike any other people on the face of the Earth, who has ever been, or ever will be. As Christians, we are a part of Israel, but only in the spiritual sense.

"It was down at the Feet of Jesus,
"O the happy, happy day!
"That my soul found peace in believing,
"And my sins were washed away."

"It was down at the Feet of Jesus,
"Where I found such perfect rest,
"Where the light first dawned on my
    spirit,
"And my soul was truly blessed."

"It was down at the Feet of Jesus,
"Where I brought my guilt and sin,
"That He cancelled all my transgres-
    sions,
"And Salvation entered in."

CHAPTER 30

(1) "AND WHEN RACHEL SAW THAT SHE BEAR JACOB NO CHILDREN, RACHEL ENVIED HER SISTER; AND SAID UNTO JACOB, GIVE ME CHILDREN, OR ELSE I DIE.

(2) "AND JACOB'S ANGER WAS KINDLED AGAINST RACHEL: AND HE SAID, AM I IN GOD'S STEAD, WHO HAS WITHHELD FROM YOU THE FRUIT OF THE WOMB?

(3) "AND SHE SAID, BEHOLD MY MAID BILHAH, GO IN UNTO HER; AND SHE SHALL BEAR UPON MY KNEES, THAT I MAY ALSO HAVE CHILDREN BY HER.

(4) "AND SHE GAVE HIM BILHAH HER HANDMAID TO WIFE: AND JACOB WENT IN UNTO HER.

(5) "AND BILHAH CONCEIVED, AND BEAR JACOB A SON.

(6) "AND RACHEL SAID, GOD HAS JUDGED ME, AND HAS ALSO HEARD MY VOICE, AND HAS GIVEN ME A SON: THEREFORE CALLED SHE HIS NAME DAN.

(7) "AND BILHAH RACHEL'S MAID CONCEIVED AGAIN, AND BEAR JACOB A SECOND SON.

(8) "AND RACHEL SAID, WITH GREAT WRESTLINGS HAVE I WRESTLED WITH MY SISTER, AND I HAVE PREVAILED: AND SHE CALLED HIS NAME NAPHTALI.

(9) "WHEN LEAH SAW THAT SHE HAD LEFT BEARING, SHE TOOK ZILPAH HER MAID, AND GAVE HER JACOB TO WIFE.

(10) "AND ZILPAH LEAH'S MAID BEAR JACOB A SON.

(11) "AND LEAH SAID, A TROOP COMES: AND SHE CALLED HIS NAME GAD.

(12) "AND ZILPAH LEAH'S MAID BEAR JACOB A SECOND SON.

(13) "AND LEAH SAID, HAPPY AM I, FOR THE DAUGHTERS WILL CALL ME BLESSED: AND SHE CALLED HIS NAME ASHER."

The composition is:

1. Rachel pictures Israel; Leah, the Church. Rachel is first loved, but not possessed — sorrowful and childless; Leah, blessed with children and triumphant.

2. Rachel has children afterwards, Joseph and Benjamin. Joseph, a beauteous Type of Christ rejected by his brethren, but glorified among the Gentiles.

3. Benjamin, a Type also of Christ, the son of his mother's sorrow, but of his father's right hand; that is, the Messiah was to be born of Israel, and that is why Israel had to drink so great a cup of sorrow; but He becomes the Lord Messiah reigning in power in the Heavens at the Right Hand of God.

GIVE ME CHILDREN, OR ELSE I DIE

Verses 1 and 2 read: *"And when Rachel saw that she bear Jacob no children, Rachel envied her sister; and said unto Jacob, Give me children, or else I die.*

"And Jacob's anger was kindled against Rachel: and he said, Am I in God's stead, Who has withheld from you the fruit of the womb?"

Concerning this situation, Keil said: *"If not warranted to infer that Rachel's barrenness was due to lack of prayer on her part and Jacob's, we are at least justified in asserting that her conduct in breaking forth into angry reproaches against her husband was unlike that of Jacob's mother, Rebekah, who, in similar circumstances, sought relief in prayer."*

The brief period of some four or five years that had elapsed since Rachel's marriage, in comparison with the 20 years of Rebekah's barrenness, signally discovers Rachel's sinful impatience.

In this thing, she seems to blame Jacob, but she should have known that God Alone could remove sterility; but to this fact jealousy of Leah appears for the moment to have blinded her (Pulpit).

As we have stated, Rachel here pictures Israel, while Leah pictures the Church. In a sense, Paul addressed this very thing, even though he actually is writing about Sarah. The Apostle said: *"For it is written, Rejoice, thou barren who bears not; break forth and cry, you who travails not: for the desolate has many more children than she which has an husband"* (Gal. 4:27).

In a sense, Leah was not loved very much by her husband, but she had many more children than the one who had the greater love of the husband. And the Church, of which Leah is a Type, has many more children than Israel, of which Rachel is a Type.

Jacob's anger is kindled against Rachel, because she should have been taking the matter to the Lord, instead of blaming him.

BILHAH

Verses 3 through 5 read: *"And she said, Behold my maid Bilhah, go in unto her; and she shall bear upon my knees, that I may also have children by her.*

"And she gave him Bilhah her handmaid to wife: and Jacob went in unto her.

"And Bilhah conceived, and bear Jacob a son."

All of this shows little Faith in God. Jealousy, envy, and superstition, seem to have guided these affairs. To be sure, as sinful as it was, Sarah's resorting to Hagar, was much more understandable than Rachel resorting to Bilhah.

Both of these women, Rachel and Leah, seem to trust God, but only to a certain degree. It was somewhat a mixture of faith and fancy, not unlike the modern Church.

Trust in Christ, at least to a certain degree, and trust in other things, marks the modern Church. It leans partly on God and partly on the world!

At this stage, I'm not certain that Leah and Rachel properly understood the significance of all that was going on. They somehow understood that the bearing of children, and a goodly number, was of great significance. But there is little indication that they fully understood why.

NOTES

DAN

Verse 6 reads: *"And Rachel said, God has judged me, and has also heard my voice, and has given me a son: therefore called she his name Dan."*

Dan means *"to judge, or one decreeing justice."*

Calvin said, *"Jacob began with polygamy, and is now drawn into concubinage. Though God overruled this for the development of seed of Israel, He did not thereby condone the offence of either Jacob or Rachel."*

Calvin went on to say: *"So God often strives to overcome men's wickedness through kindness, and pursues the unworthy with His Grace."*

Exactly what Rachel meant by naming the child Dan, which means, *"judging,"* is open to question. The indication seems to be that she felt that God had vindicated her, that is, had judged her righteous, by giving this son to Bilhah, her maid. Whether God saw it that way, is also open to question.

As someone has well said, *"Men rule, while God overrules."* While He in no way ever condones evil or wrongdoing, not even to the slightest degree, at times, He does use such to bring about His Will. There had to be 13 sons born to Jacob, in order to found the nation of Israel. Twelve would be for the regular Tribes, while one would be for the Priestly Tribe.

To be sure, God had many ways of doing this, but at the same time, He has purposely limited Himself to work through human instrumentation; consequently, He is either limited or expanded according to the faithlessness or faith of the individual or individuals. Many years later He would say of Israel: *"Yea, they turned back and tempted God, and limited the Holy One of Israel"* (Ps. 78:41).

NAPHTALI

Verses 7 and 8 read: *"And Bilhah Rachel's maid conceived again, and bear Jacob a second son.*

"And Rachel said, With great wrestlings have I wrestled with my sister, and I have prevailed: and she called his name Naphtali."

Naphtali means *"wrestling."*

The contention between Rachel and Leah evidently was great. Rachel likens it as to a *"wrestling match."* Due to the births of both Dan and Naphtali, she considers herself to have prevailed.

Concerning this, Ellicott says: *"Rachel's was a discreditable victory, won by making use of a bad custom, and it consisted in weaning her husband still more completely from the unloved Leah. Now that Bilhah and children were added to the attractiveness of her tent, her sister, she boasts, will be thought of no more."*

GAD AND ASHER

Verses 9 through 13 read: *"When Leah saw that she had left bearing, she took Zilpah her maid, and gave her Jacob to wife.*

"And Zilpah Leah's maid bear Jacob a son.

"And Leah said, A troop comes: and she called his name Gad.

"And Zilpah Leah's maid bear Jacob a second son.

"And Leah said, Happy am I, for the daughters will call me blessed: and she called his name Asher."

Gad means, *"good fortune,"* while Asher means, *"happy."*

Ellicott said: *"By ceasing to bear, Leah had lost her one hold upon Jacob's affection, and to regain it, she follows Rachel's example."*

The struggle of these two women gives us an idea of their Faith, or the lack of such. It seems that neither one of them actually understood, at least as they should have, what the path of Faith actually was. In other words, their faith was riddled with self-will. They had a great tendency to *"help God!"* And of course, when they helped Him, it was always from the vantage point of jealousy, envy, malice, or some other passion gone awry. As previously stated, this picture drawn out here before us is not totally unlike our modern actions. Despite the Lord appearing to Jacob and giving him great Promises, we find that the Patriarch still has a long way to go.

And yet, placed in his same position, I wonder would we have done any better, or even as well? From our sanctimonious perches, we far too often ask with a sneer, *"Would you buy a used car from Jacob?"*

We must never make the mistake of judging the work before it is finished. And that we far too often do! We must not forget that one of the greatest appellatives in history

belongs in part to Jacob, *"The God of Abraham, of Isaac, and of Jacob."*

(14) "AND REUBEN WENT IN THE DAYS OF WHEAT HARVEST, AND FOUND MANDRAKES IN THE FIELD, AND BROUGHT THEM UNTO HIS MOTHER LEAH. THEN RACHEL SAID TO LEAH, GIVE ME, I PRAY YOU, OF YOUR SON'S MANDRAKES.

(15) "AND SHE SAID UNTO HER, IS IT A SMALL MATTER THAT YOU HAVE TAKEN MY HUSBAND? AND WOULD YOU TAKE AWAY MY SON'S MANDRAKES ALSO? AND RACHEL SAID, THEREFORE HE SHALL LIE WITH YOU TONIGHT FOR YOUR SON'S MANDRAKES.

(16) "AND JACOB CAME OUT OF THE FIELD IN THE EVENING, AND LEAH WENT OUT TO MEET HIM, AND SAID, YOU MUST COME IN UNTO ME; FOR SURELY I HAVE HIRED YOU WITH MY SON'S MANDRAKES. AND HE LAY WITH HER THAT NIGHT.

(17) "AND GOD HEARKENED UNTO LEAH, AND SHE CONCEIVED, AND BEAR JACOB THE FIFTH SON.

(18) "AND LEAH SAID, GOD HAS GIVEN ME MY HIRE, BECAUSE I HAVE GIVEN MY MAIDEN TO MY HUSBAND: AND SHE CALLED HIS NAME ISSACHAR.

(19) "AND LEAH CONCEIVED AGAIN, AND BEAR JACOB THE SIXTH SON.

(20) "AND LEAH SAID, GOD HAS ENDUED ME WITH A GOOD DOWRY; NOW WILL MY HUSBAND DWELL WITH ME, BECAUSE I HAVE BORNE HIM SIX SONS: AND SHE CALLED HIS NAME ZEBULUN.

(21) "AND AFTERWARDS SHE BEAR A DAUGHTER, AND CALLED HER NAME DINAH.

(22) "AND GOD REMEMBERED RACHEL, AND GOD HEARKENED TO HER, AND OPENED HER WOMB.

(23) "AND SHE CONCEIVED, AND BEAR A SON; AND SAID, GOD HAS TAKEN AWAY MY REPROACH:

(24) "AND SHE CALLED HIS NAME JOSEPH; AND SAID, THE LORD SHALL ADD TO ME ANOTHER SON."

The construction is:

1. These Passages present a perfect picture of prayer mixed with superstition. And let not the Reader think that this foolish practice died with the wives of Jacob.

2. These two women were mostly functioning from the position of jealousy or envy. God's purposes were considered, but less than their own passions.

3. The idea of true Faith is that we think like God, instead of on the far lower level of our own passions.

MANDRAKES

Verses 14 through 16 read: *"And Reuben went in the days of wheat harvest, and found mandrakes in the field, and brought them unto his mother Leah. Then Rachel said to Leah, Give me, I pray you, of your son's mandrakes.*

"And she said unto her, Is it a small matter that you have taken my husband? And would you take away my son's mandrakes also? And Rachel said, Therefore he shall lie with you tonight for your son's mandrakes.

"And Jacob came out of the field in the evening, and Leah went out to meet him, and said, You must come in unto me; for surely I have hired you with my son's mandrakes. And he lay with her that night."

Reuben at this time was probably four or five years old. According to Oriental superstition, the mandrake possessed the virtue of promoting fruitfulness and fertility. It was an apple-like fruit.

Somehow, Rachel found out about the situation, and asked for some of the mandrakes.

The request, seemingly, didn't set well with Leah. So Rachel, who held the dominant hand, made a bargain with Leah. For some of the mandrakes, she would not stand in the way of Leah spending the night with Jacob.

ISSACHAR AND ZEBULUN

Verses 17 through 20 read: *"And God hearkened unto Leah, and she conceived, and bear Jacob the fifth son.*

"And Leah said, God has given me my hire, because I have given my maiden to my husband: and she called his name Issachar.

"And Leah conceived again, and bear Jacob the sixth son.

"And Leah said, God has endued me with a good dowry; now will my husband dwell with me, because I have born him six sons: and she called his name Zebulun."

Issachar means, *"reward,"* while Zebulun means, *"dwelling."*

From Verse 17, we know that Leah sought the Lord as it regards her conceiving another son, which she did. The Lord heard and answered her prayer, and this despite the fact that superstition had been involved regarding the mandrakes. How so much the Lord overlooks in answering prayer for all of us.

Even though Rachel and Leah, it seems, were not as knowledgeable of the things of the Lord as they should have been, it still seems that they were influenced by the Promises of God to Abraham, on whose posterity were entailed the richest blessings, and from whom the Messiah, in the fullness of time, was to descend. It was the belief of these Promises that rendered every pious female in those times desirable of being a mother.

Little did Leah realize that at this time, the child which had been born to her two or three years earlier, Judah, would head up the Tribe from whom the Messiah would come. Near Jacob's dying day, the great Patriarch prophesied: *"The Sceptre* (ruling power) *shall not depart from Judah, nor a Lawgiver from between his feet, until Shiloh* (another name for the Messiah) *come; and unto Him shall the gathering of the people be"* (Gen. 49:10).

Leah thinks that God has heard her prayer regarding her fifth conception, because she had given her maid, Zilpah, to Jacob, who had brought forth two sons for Jacob, Gad and Asher.

Leah conceived again, and brought forth a sixth son, which she thought would give her preeminence over Rachel, meaning that Jacob would look at her as the favorite wife, especially considering that Rachel personally had not been able to conceive at all.

DINAH

Verse 21 reads: *"And afterwards, she bear a daughter, and called her name Dinah."*

Even though Dinah is the only daughter mentioned in the entirety of this family, there is a possibility that Jacob had other daughters as well, as seems to be evidenced in Genesis 37:35. Although the word *"daughters"* here could in fact refer to granddaughters, etc.

At any rate, Dinah is mentioned here because of the incident in her history afterwards related (Gen. 34:1).

JOSEPH

Verses 22 through 24 read: *"And God remembered Rachel, and God hearkened to her, and opened her womb.*

"And she conceived, and bear a son; and said, God has taken away my reproach:

"And she called his name Joseph; and said, The LORD shall add to me another son."

That the mandrakes could not remove sterility the Lord demonstrated by allowing Rachel's barrenness to continue at least two years longer, though she had made use of this supposed remedy, and by opening Leah's womb without them.

We should learn from all of this how useless superstition is, and that the Lord rules in all things. As well, I think it is obvious here that Rachel only exacerbated her situation, instead of helping it.

I wonder how much superstition is presently involved in the prayers and faith of many modern Christians? Let me give you at least one example:

CONFESSION

While memorizing Scriptures and confessing the Word of God are good things, and should be practiced by all Christians, still, if we think that by confessing certain Scriptures over and over, such will work some type of favor with God, or some type of magic, we are doing nothing less than engaging in superstition, exactly as Rachel used her mandrakes in order to bring about conception, which of course didn't work. But yet, many in the modern Charismatic world have been taught that endless repetition will bring about things from God, etc.

I happened to be with a man sometime back, who was, and is a dear friend. He had some particular problems which I will not now relate. Another well-meaning brother gave him two or three particular Scriptures, told him to memorize them, and to quote them over and over, and this would address his problem.

Pure and simple, even though the Scriptures definitely are the Word of God, quoting them over and over, thinking that such will bring about some type of help, is the wrong type of faith, and actually, as stated, is no more than superstition.

I will emphasize again that every Christian ought to memorize Scriptures constantly, and quote them constantly, *"For the Word of God is alive, and powerful, and sharper than any two-edged sword, piercing even to the dividing asunder of soul and spirit, and of the joints and marrow, and is a discerner of the thoughts and intents of the heart"* (Heb. 4:12). But we must be careful that we do not reduce the Word to superstition.

Believers receive from the Lord, which is always according to His Word, due to what Christ has done for us at the Cross. It is the Cross that makes it all possible, and it is the Cross which must always be the object of our Faith (I Cor. 1:17-18, 21, 23; 2:2; Col. 2:14-15). With our Faith rightly placed, then the Word functions in our lives as it should.

Let me say it again: The use of the Word in this wrong manner is not new. It was used by the Jews in such a way during the time of Christ, and even long before. Of this practice, Jesus said: *"But all their works* (Pharisees) *they do for to be seen of men: they make broad their phylacteries, and enlarge the borders of their garments"* (Mat. 23:5).

The *"phylacteries"* were sort of a little leather case worn around the wrist or the forehead. In the small case, they placed particular Scriptures printed on pieces of leather, or even the Ten Commandments. They thought of these things as amulets or charms, which would bless them, especially considering that it was the Word of God. As is obvious, Jesus condemned this practice.

RACHEL

Ultimately, God answered Rachel's petition, and *"opened her womb."*

She named her son *"Joseph,"* which means, *"He shall add,"* which in effect was a prophecy referring to the birth of another son, who in fact would be Benjamin.

It seems by now that Rachel had advanced somewhat in the Spirit, and had by now forsaken human devices such as resorting to mandrakes, etc. She now evidenced a complete dependence on the sovereign Grace of the Covenant God of Abraham and Isaac and Jacob.

Concerning this, Horton says of her: *"When God remembers it does not mean He had forgotten. Rather it means that it was God's time and He actively entered the situation to do something about it. This intervention was to answer Rachel's prayers that He had been listening to the entire time of Leah's childbearing years. God, not the mandrakes, made it possible for Rachel to have a son. Barrenness was considered a disgrace. Now that disgrace was removed by the birth of a son. But she was not satisfied, since Leah had six sons. So she named the boy Joseph, meaning 'He shall add,' and she asked for another son. Unfortunately, the fulfillment of that prayer would cause her death (35:16-19)."*

The following is how these sons are Types of Christ:

1. Reuben: Jesus is the *"Son"* of God.

2. Simeon: Through Jesus we *"hear"* God.

3. Levi: Through Jesus we are *"joined"* to the Father.

4. Judah: Through Jesus, God has accepted our *"praises."*

5. Dan: Jesus has taken the *"judgment"* due us.

6. Naphtali: Jesus has *"wrestled"* the powers of darkness, all on our behalf, and has defeated the foe.

7. Gad: Jesus is the *"troop"* Who has fought on our behalf, and has brought us *"good fortune."*

8. Asher: Jesus has made us *"happy."*

9. Issachar: Jesus is our *"reward."*

10. Zebulun: Jesus has made it possible for Believers to *"dwell"* in the House of the Lord forever.

11. Joseph: Jesus has *"added"* all Believers to the Kingdom.

12. Benjamin: Jesus is the Father's *"strong right hand,"* and sits with Him in Heavenly Places.

(25) "AND IT CAME TO PASS, WHEN RACHEL HAD BORNE JOSEPH, THAT JACOB SAID UNTO LABAN, SEND ME AWAY, THAT I MAY GO UNTO MY OWN PLACE, AND TO MY COUNTRY.

(26) "GIVE ME MY WIVES AND MY CHILDREN, FOR WHOM I HAVE SERVED YOU, AND LET ME GO: FOR YOU KNOW MY SERVICE WHICH I HAVE DONE YOU.

(27) "AND LABAN SAID UNTO HIM, I PRAY YOU, IF I HAVE FOUND FAVOR IN

NOTES

YOUR EYES, TARRY: FOR I HAVE LEARNED BY EXPERIENCE THAT THE LORD HAS BLESSED ME FOR YOUR SAKE.

(28) "AND HE SAID, APPOINT ME YOUR WAGES, AND I WILL GIVE IT.

(29) "AND HE SAID UNTO HIM, YOU KNOW HOW I HAVE SERVED YOU, AND HOW YOUR CATTLE WAS WITH ME.

(30) "FOR IT WAS LITTLE WHICH YOU HAD BEFORE I CAME, AND IT IS NOW INCREASED INTO A MULTITUDE; AND THE LORD HAS BLESSED YOU SINCE MY COMING: AND NOW WHEN SHALL I PROVIDE FOR MY OWN HOUSE ALSO?

(31) "AND HE SAID, WHAT SHALL I GIVE YOU? AND JACOB SAID, YOU SHALL NOT GIVE ME ANYTHING: IF YOU WILL DO THIS THING FOR ME, I WILL AGAIN FEED AND KEEP YOUR FLOCK.

(32) "I WILL PASS THROUGH ALL YOUR FLOCK TODAY, REMOVING FROM THENCE ALL THE SPECKLED AND SPOTTED CATTLE, AND ALL THE BROWN CATTLE AMONG THE SHEEP, AND THE SPOTTED AND SPECKLED AMONG THE GOATS: AND OF SUCH SHALL BE MY HIRE.

(33) "SO SHALL MY RIGHTEOUSNESS ANSWER FOR ME IN TIME TO COME, WHEN IT SHALL COME FOR MY HIRE BEFORE YOUR FACE: EVERY ONE THAT IS NOT SPECKLED AND SPOTTED AMONG THE GOATS, AND BROWN AMONG THE SHEEP, THAT SHALL BE COUNTED STOLEN WITH ME.

(34) "AND LABAN SAID, BEHOLD, I WOULD IT MIGHT BE ACCORDING TO YOUR WORD."

The composition is:

1. The principles of Grace may be professed, but the real measure of our experience of the power of Grace is quite another thing.

2. Jacob's vision portrayed to him the story of Grace; but God's Revelation at Bethel takes time to act. It's called *"Progressive Sanctification."*

3. Character and conduct prove the real measure of the soul's experience and conviction, whatever the profession may be.

FOURTEEN YEARS

Verses 25 and 26 read: *"And it came to pass, when Rachel had borne Joseph, that*

Jacob said unto Laban, Send me away, that I may go unto my own place, and to my country.

"Give me my wives and my children, for whom I have served you, and let me go: for you know my service which I have done you."

Jacob's terminology, *"For whom I have served you, and let me go,"* proves that both Leah and Rachel became his wives immediately, and then he served the 14 years for them.

It is highly unlikely that 11 sons and one daughter could have been born to this family in just seven years, as some claim. No, this number of children played out over the last 14 years.

Having served the 14 years which had been agreed upon, he tells Laban that he now wants to go back to Canaan.

THE BLESSING

Verses 27 and 28 read: *"And Laban said unto him, I pray you, if I have found favor in your eyes, tarry: for I have learned by experience that the LORD has blessed me for your sake.*

"And he said, Appoint me your wages, and I will give it."

Laban doesn't at all desire that Jacob leave. He readily admits that since Jacob has been with him, the Lord has blessed the entirety of all that he was and all that he had. He admits this! So in order to keep Jacob, and as well, to keep the blessing, he tells Jacob to name his wages, and he will pay it.

While Laban knew about the Lord, there is no evidence that he really knew the Lord. But he did know that Jehovah was real, and that the Blessings of God were definitely upon Jacob. This he readily observed and recognized. So for material benefits alone, he desires that the Patriarch remain with him as long as possible.

We should learn a lesson from all of this. Any person who is truly a Believer is a blessing to all who are in his employ, or else whoever employs him. The only time that possibly wouldn't hold true is when the Believer is out of the Will of God, as was Jonah.

A PERSONAL EXAMPLE

I call to mind an event similar to this, which took place when I was a kid.

Our little Church was very small, perhaps averaging 30 to 35 people. There was a dear

Sister in the Church who loved the Lord supremely. She had a large family. Her husband was in prison, so it was very difficult to make ends meet.

She had a job in a local five-and-dime store.

At a particular point in time, the manager of this store requested of her that she stop talking to people about their problems, in other words, talking to them about the Lord, during her working hours.

She tried to conduct herself in that fashion, but soon found that she was unable to do so. After two or three warnings, he terminated her.

After about 30 days, if that, he came to her house, requesting that she come back to work. His reason was as follows:

Whenever he terminated her, his business was cut about in half. He found out that many of the people were coming into the store, and while they would buy something, sometimes purchase quite a few things, they mainly wanted to talk to this dear lady. She was always kind and gracious, and had a word for each one, as she gently and kindly talked to them, whomever they may have been, about the Lord.

This man realized that this woman, in fact, was his business.

So when he hired her back, he told her explicitly, to conduct herself as she felt like she ought to and nothing else would be said.

Pure and simple, this dear lady, who was very Godly to say the least, was a great blessing to this business establishment. That's the way the Lord intends for it to be. Unfortunately, there are many who profess to know Christ, but really have very little relationship with Him, if any. These people are not a blessing to anyone, but rather a curse.

So what I'm speaking of, and who I'm speaking of, refers to those who truly love the Lord, and the blessing they are to all concerned.

THE BLESSING RECALLED

Verses 29 and 30 read: *"And he said unto him, You know how I have served you, and how your cattle was with me.*

"For it was little which you had before I came, and it is now increased into a multitude; and the LORD has blessed you since my coming: and now when shall I provide for my own house also?"

Jacob knows that the Hand of the Lord is upon him. He also knows, that being the case, that the Lord will bless all that he touches. Inasmuch as he is now working for Laban, then Laban is the one who is the recipient of the blessings; however, even as we have addressed, Jacob's time of servitude is now over and a different arrangement must be entered into.

THE AGREEMENT

Verses 31 through 34 read: *"And he said, What shall I give you? And Jacob said, You shall not give me anything: if you will do this thing for me, I will again feed and keep your flock.*

"I will pass through all your flock today, removing from thence all the speckled and spotted cattle, and all the brown cattle among the sheep, and the spotted and speckled among the goats: and of such shall be my hire.

"So shall my righteousness answer for me in time to come, when it shall come for my hire before your face: every one that is not speckled and spotted among the goats, and brown among the sheep, that shall be counted stolen with me.

"And Laban said, Behold, I would it might be according to your word."

Some have criticized Jacob as it regards this particular agreement. They have once again attributed such to devious ways, trickery, and even dishonesty. However, it would appear that he acted honestly.

The tenor of this agreement seems to me that he is referring his cause to God, rather to enter into any stipulated agreement for stated wages with Laban, whose selfishness, one would have to acknowledge, was very great.

Laban selfishly concluded that his cattle would produce few different in color from their own, and in the natural he would be correct; however, I think we may consider all of this, at least that which happened with Jacob, as a miracle from God. And this we do know:

The Lord will never bless sin and dishonesty, or even the slightest hint of evil. So if the Lord is involved, we must conclude that the acts, whatever they may have been, had been righteous.

NOTES

(35) "AND HE REMOVED THAT DAY THE HE GOATS THAT WERE RINGSTRAKED, AND SPOTTED, AND ALL THE SHE GOATS THAT WERE SPECKLED AND SPOTTED, AND EVERY ONE THAT HAD SOME WHITE IN IT, AND ALL THE BROWN AMONG THE SHEEP, AND GAVE THEM INTO THE HAND OF HIS SONS.

(36) "AND HE SET THREE DAYS' JOURNEY BETWIXT HIMSELF AND JACOB: AND JACOB FED THE REST OF LABAN'S FLOCKS.

(37) "AND JACOB TOOK HIM RODS OF GREEN POPLAR, AND OF THE HAZEL AND CHESTNUT TREE; AND PILLED WHITE STRAKES IN THEM, AND MADE THE WHITE APPEAR WHICH WAS IN THE RODS.

(38) "AND HE SET THE RODS WHICH HE HAD PILLED BEFORE THE FLOCKS IN THE GUTTERS IN THE WATERING TROUGHS WHEN THE FLOCKS CAME TO DRINK, THAT THEY SHOULD CONCEIVE WHEN THEY CAME TO DRINK.

(39) "AND THE FLOCKS CONCEIVED BEFORE THE RODS, AND BROUGHT FORTH CATTLE RINGSTRAKED, SPECKLED, AND SPOTTED.

(40) "AND JACOB DID SEPARATE THE LAMBS, AND SET THE FACES OF THE FLOCKS TOWARD THE RINGSTRAKED, AND ALL THE BROWN IN THE FLOCK OF LABAN; AND HE PUT HIS OWN FLOCKS BY THEMSELVES, AND PUT THEM NOT UNTO LABAN'S CATTLE.

(41) "AND IT CAME TO PASS, WHENSOEVER THE STRONGER CATTLE DID CONCEIVE, THAT JACOB LAID THE RODS BEFORE THE EYES OF THE CATTLE IN THE GUTTERS, THAT THEY MIGHT CONCEIVE AMONG THE RODS.

(42) "BUT WHEN THE CATTLE WERE FEEBLE, HE PUT THEM NOT IN: SO THE FEEBLER WERE LABAN'S, AND THE STRONGER JACOB'S.

(43) "AND THE MAN INCREASED EXCEEDINGLY, AND HAD MUCH CATTLE, AND MAIDSERVANTS, AND MENSERVANTS, AND CAMELS, AND ASSES."

The synopsis is:

1. Laban required that there should be an interval of between 30 and 40 miles between *"himself,"* that is, his flocks, and those of Jacob. His wealth in sheep and goats must

have been enormous to require so large a separate feeding ground.

2. All of this, we learn from Verse 30, had been the result of Jacob's care.

3. The great question is, did God give this idea to Jacob as it regards the animals being born spotted, etc.? I believe He did!

THE PLAN GIVEN TO JACOB BY GOD

Verses 35 through 39 read: *"And he removed that day the he goats that were ringstraked and spotted, and all the she goats that were speckled and spotted, and every one that had some white in it, and all the brown among the sheep, and gave them into the hand of his sons.*

"And he set three days' journey between himself and Jacob: and Jacob fed the rest of Laban's flocks.

"And Jacob took him rods of green poplar, and of the hazel and chestnut tree; and pilled white strakes in them, and made the white appear which was in the rods.

"And he set the rods which he had pilled before the flocks in the gutters in the watering troughs when the flocks came to drink, that they should conceive when they came to drink.

"And the flocks conceived before the rods, and brought forth cattle ringstraked, speckled and spotted."

Whenever Jacob proposed his plan, which would give him all of the spotted and mingled sheep and goats, Laban reasoned, and rightly so under normal circumstances, that the number of animals falling into this category, would be small indeed. As he looked at his vast herd, even as Jacob made the proposal, he didn't see how he could lose.

It is my contention that the Lord told Jacob what to do in this situation.

It is said to have been frequently observed that, particularly in the case of sheep, whatever fixes their attention in copulation is marked upon the young. That Jacob believed in the efficacy of the artifice he adopted is apparent; but the multiplication of parti-colored animals it will be safer to ascribe to Divine Blessing than to human craft (Pulpit).

INCREASE

Verses 40 through 43 read. *"And Jacob did separate the lambs, and set the faces of*

the flocks toward the ringstraked, and all the brown in the flock of Laban; and he put his own flocks by themselves, and put them not into Laban's cattle.

"And it came to pass, whensoever the stronger cattle did conceive, that Jacob laid the rods before the eyes of the cattle in the gutters, that they might conceive among the rods.

"But when the cattle were feeble, he put them not in: so the feebler were Laban's, and the stronger Jacob's.

"And the man increased exceedingly, and had much cattle, and maidservants, and menservants, and camels, and asses."

Incidentally, the term *"cattle"* as used in the Old Testament, can refer to all domestic animals, such as lambs, goats, oxen, or heifers, etc. In the Passages of our study, it seems to refer to all types.

I think we must conclude that the proposal of such a singular condition on the part of Jacob was an act not of folly, but of Faith, being tantamount to a committal of his cause to God instead of Laban. The acceptance of it on the part of Laban was a display of greed, and a proof that the bygone years of prosperity had only increased that greed.

That impressions made upon the minds of sheep at rutting time affect the unborn animal seems a well-established fact; but the extraordinary rapidity with which brown and speckled animals were produced appears to point to the intervention of a special providence on Jacob's behalf. There was nothing fraudulent in what Jacob did and may be inferred from the fact that he acted under the Divine approval (Gen. 31:12). I don't see how we can do anything but come to this conclusion.

Increase in the best sense is God's Promise. It will be sent as He wills and when He wills, but will be found the true answer to prayer and the true manifestation of love. On all that belongs to us the blessing rests. We must understand that, and treat it accordingly.

"The Church of God is one:
"As Brethren here we meet;
"For us Salvation's work is done,
"In Christ we stand complete."

"The Church of God is one:
"One only Lord we know;

*"We worship Jesus, God's Own Son,
"Who came God's love to show."*

*"The Church of God is one:
"All, sinners saved by Grace;
"Our plea, the Precious Blood alone;
"The Cross, our meeting place."*

*"The Church of God is one:
"The Bible we revere;
"By it all saving truth is known,
"And God to man brought near."*

*"The Church of God is one;
"One blessed hope have we;
"Our dear Redeemer's sure return
"His Saints to glorify."*

CHAPTER 31

(1) "AND HE HEARD THE WORDS OF LABAN'S SONS, SAYING, JACOB HAS TAKEN AWAY ALL THAT WAS OUR FATHER'S; AND OF THAT WHICH WAS OUR FATHER'S HAS HE GOTTEN ALL THIS GLORY.

(2) "AND JACOB BEHELD THE COUNTENANCE OF LABAN, AND, BEHOLD, IT WAS NOT TOWARD HIM AS BEFORE.

(3) "AND THE LORD SAID UNTO JACOB, RETURN UNTO THE LAND OF YOUR FATHERS, AND TO YOUR KINDRED; I WILL BE WITH YOU.

(4) "AND JACOB SENT AND CALLED RACHEL AND LEAH TO THE FIELD UNTO HIS FLOCK,

(5) "AND SAID UNTO THEM, I SEE YOUR FATHER'S COUNTENANCE, THAT IT IS NOT TOWARD ME AS BEFORE; BUT THE GOD OF MY FATHER HAS BEEN WITH ME.

(6) "AND YOU KNOW THAT WITH ALL MY POWER I HAVE SERVED YOUR FATHER.

(7) "AND YOUR FATHER HAS DECEIVED ME, AND CHANGED MY WAGES TEN TIMES; BUT GOD SUFFERED HIM NOT TO HURT ME.

(8) "IF HE SAID THUS, THE SPECKLED SHALL BE YOUR WAGES; THEN ALL THE CATTLE BEAR SPECKLED: AND IF HE SAID THUS, THE RINGSTRAKED SHALL BE YOUR HIRE; THEN BEAR ALL THE CATTLE RINGSTRAKED.

NOTES

(9) "THUS GOD HAS TAKEN AWAY THE CATTLE OF YOUR FATHER, AND GIVEN THEM TO ME.

(10) "AND IT CAME TO PASS AT THE TIME THAT THE CATTLE CONCEIVED, THAT I LIFTED UP MY EYES, AND SAW IN A DREAM, AND, BEHOLD, THE RAMS WHICH LEAPED UPON THE CATTLE WERE RINGSTRAKED, SPECKLED, AND GRISLED.

(11) "AND THE ANGEL OF GOD SPOKE UNTO ME IN A DREAM, SAYING, JACOB: AND I SAID, HERE AM I.

(12) "AND HE SAID, LIFT UP NOW YOUR EYES, AND SEE, ALL THE RAMS WHICH LEAP UPON THE CATTLE ARE RINGSTRAKED, SPECKLED, AND GRISLED: FOR I HAVE SEEN ALL THAT LABAN DOES UNTO YOU.

(13) "I AM THE GOD OF BETH-EL, WHERE YOU ANOINTED THE PILLAR, AND WHERE YOU VOWED A VOW UNTO ME: NOW ARISE, GET YOU OUT FROM THIS LAND, AND RETURN UNTO THE LAND OF YOUR KINDRED."

The diagram is:

1. The Lord told Jacob that it was now time to return to the land of Canaan.

2. I think we must conclude from Verses 10 through 12 that Jacob's actions here were of the Lord, as it regards his acquiring the great number of lambs and goats.

3. The Lord reaffirms the Promises He had given to Jacob at Beth-el.

THE ATTITUDE OF LABAN

Verses 1 and 2 read: *"And he heard the words of Laban's sons, saying, Jacob has taken away all that was our father's; and of that which was our father's has he gotten all this glory.*

"And Jacob beheld the countenance of Laban, and, behold, it was not toward him as before."

Two factors are involved here:

1. As long as Jacob was increasing the wealth of Laban, and he (Jacob) remained poor, Laban had no problem with that. But once Jacob begins to prosper, and begins to do so in a grand way, this creates jealousy in Laban. He thinks in his mind that everything Jacob acquires is actually his. He wanted all the blessings of the Lord which rested upon

Jacob, to fall out totally to his increase and not Jacob's.

2. It was time for Jacob to leave. He had spent 20 years away from Canaan, and it was now time, according to the Lord, for him to go home. The Lord had other plans for Jacob, and those plans did not include Laban.

The Lord now lifts His Hand from the attitude of Laban, as it regards Jacob. While the Lord certainly was not the cause of his anger toward Jacob, due to the Hand of the Lord being lifted, the natural heart of Laban begins to show itself. The Lord can cause even our enemies to be at peace with us, but He can also lift His Hand, to where the peace is dissolved (Prov. 16:17).

COMMAND OF THE LORD

Verse 3 reads: *"And the LORD said unto Jacob, Return unto the land of your fathers, and to your kindred; and I will be with you."*

The Lord now moves upon Jacob's heart that it is time to return to Canaan.

It is so pleasing to the heart to note the minute leading of the Lord in the life of the Patriarch. At this stage, I'm not certain how much Jacob actually knew regarding his part in the great Plan of God, which would more and more unfold as time went on; however, one can certainly see spiritual progress in Jacob's life. In other words, these 20 years with Laban weren't wasted. He is a different man now than he was when God spoke to him at Beth-el those long years before. You can sense it in his demeanor, his manner, his attitude, and his spirit.

Exactly how the Lord appeared to the Patriarch, we aren't told. Perhaps it was in a dream, as mentioned in Verse 10, concerning other matters.

The Promise of the Lord to be with him is, in fact, the greatest Promise that anyone could ever have.

In fact, the Lord is always with every Believer; however, He is speaking here of being with Jacob in a special way, which does not hold true with everyone.

Jacob's role in the great Plan of God was to bring the necessary sons into the world, who would head up the Tribes of Israel, who would be the people of God in the world. In other words, they would be God's special, chosen people. Of the 13 required sons, 11

have already been born. A little later Benjamin would be born, which will be the last one as it regards the sons of Jacob. However, even as we shall see, Joseph will be used in another context, actually as a Type of Christ, with his two sons, Ephraim and Manasseh, becoming a part of the Tribes of Israel, numbering 13, which were the desired number.

JACOB'S DECISION

Verses 4 through 9 read: *"And Jacob sent and called Rachel and Leah to the field unto his flock,*

"And said unto them, I see your father's countenance, that it is not toward me as before; but the God of my father has been with me.

"And you know that with all my power I have served your father.

"And your father has deceived me, and changed my wages ten times; but God suffered him not to hurt me.

"If he said thus, The speckled shall be your wages; then all the cattle bear speckled: and if he said thus, The ringstraked shall be your hire; then bear all the cattle ringstraked.

"Thus God has taken away the cattle of your father, and given them to me."

From these Passages, we learn a little more concerning what had taken place between Jacob and Laban. For instance, the Patriarch says that Laban had changed his wages ten times, which probably refers to *"many times,"* instead of the actual number ten. As used in the Old Testament, the number 10 contains the idea of completeness, and not necessarily the exact amount, unless accordingly specified.

When he saw that Jacob's flocks were increasing according to the bargain originally made, he then changed the rules. But as we see, God overruled that particular change, and whatever it is that Laban said that Jacob could have, which was reduced from the original agreement, the Lord had them all to turn out in that particular manner.

We should see from this that the Lord doesn't take kindly to His children being put upon. Sometimes He will step in, even as He did with Jacob; other times He doesn't; nevertheless, one can be doubly certain that the Lord knows all things, and keeps account of all things.

So that his conversation will not be overheard, the Patriarch asks both Rachel and Leah to come out into the field where he is, in order that he might talk to them. His words to them consisted of three parts:

1. He relates to them the change in Laban's manner towards him, and his consequent fear of violence.

2. He justifies his own conduct towards their father, and accuses him of repeated injustice.

3. Finally, he announces to them that he has received the Divine command to return to Canaan.

THE DREAM

Verses 10 through 13 read: *"And it came to pass at the time that the cattle conceived, that I lifted up my eyes, and saw in a dream, and, behold, the rams which leaped upon the cattle were ringstraked, speckled, and grisled.*

"And the Angel of God spoke unto me in a dream, saying, Jacob: And I said, Here am I.

"And he said, lift up now your eyes, and see, all the rams which leap upon the cattle are ringstraked, speckled, and grisled: for I have seen all that Laban does unto you.

"I am the God of Beth-el, where you anointed the pillar, and where you vowed a vow into Me: now arise, get you out from this land, and return unto the land of your kindred."

I don't see how that one can look at these Passages, and then come to the conclusion that what Jacob did regarding the animals was immoral, fraudulent, or dishonest.

Some expositors claim that this dream was had by Jacob at the conclusion of his six years of service to Laban, but I personally feel that it was given to the Patriarch at the beginning. In any case, it would require to be understood as a Divine intimation to Jacob that whatever would be done was not to be ascribed to the success of his own stratagems, but to the Blessings of God.

The Lord gave Jacob a dream, and in this dream several things are said and done:

1. The Lord told Jacob what to do about the spotted animals.

2. He told him that He had seen all that Laban had done unto him.

3. He reaffirmed that He was the God of Beth-el, which proclaims the fact that every promise given there to Jacob still held true.

NOTES

4. He reminded Jacob that he anointed the pillar, which spoke of the Holy Spirit and of Christ.

5. He reminded Jacob of the *"vow"* which had been made, about giving a tenth to the Lord. Most probably, these were animals which should be offered up in sacrifice.

6. He now tells Jacob that it's time to leave Syria, and go back to Canaan.

(14) "AND RACHEL AND LEAH ANSWERED AND SAID UNTO HIM, IS THERE YET ANY PORTION OR INHERITANCE FOR US IN OUR FATHER'S HOUSE?

(15) "ARE WE NOT COUNTED OF HIM STRANGERS? FOR HE HAS SOLD US, AND HAS QUITE DEVOURED ALSO OUR MONEY.

(16) "FOR ALL THE RICHES WHICH GOD HAS TAKEN FROM OUR FATHER, THAT IS OURS, AND OUR CHILDREN'S: NOW THEN, WHATSOEVER GOD HAS SAID UNTO YOU, DO.

(17) "THEN JACOB ROSE UP, AND SET HIS SONS AND HIS WIVES UPON CAMELS;

(18) "AND HE CARRIED AWAY ALL HIS CATTLE, AND ALL HIS GOODS WHICH HE HAD GOTTEN, THE CATTLE OF HIS GETTING, WHICH HE HAD GOTTEN IN PADAN-ARAM, FOR TO GO TO ISAAC HIS FATHER IN THE LAND OF CANAAN.

(19) "AND LABAN WENT TO SHEAR HIS SHEEP: AND RACHEL HAD STOLEN THE IMAGES THAT WERE HER FATHER'S.

(20) "AND JACOB STOLE AWAY UNAWARES TO LABAN THE SYRIAN, IN THAT HE TOLD HIM NOT THAT HE FLED.

(21) "SO HE FLED WITH ALL THAT HE HAD; AND HE ROSE UP, AND PASSED OVER THE RIVER, AND SET HIS FACE TOWARD THE MOUNT GILEAD."

The structure is:

1. Both Rachel and Leah understood completely the duplicity of their father. He not only had done Jacob wrong, but he had wronged them as well.

2. Jacob now leaves, which probably took several days of preparation, or else he had already prepared when he called his wives to him, which was probably the case.

3. The images which Rachel stole from her father had to do with her inheritance, of which we will momentarily address.

RACHEL AND LEAH

Verses 14 through 16 read: *"And Rachel and Leah answered and said unto him, Is there yet any portion or inheritance for us in our father's house?*

"Are we not counted of him strangers? For he has sold us, and has quite devoured also our money.

"For all the riches which God has taken from our father, that is ours, and our children's: now then, whatsoever God has said unto you, do."

There is a marked severity towards their father in the answer of Jacob's wives. They are recalling that they received no dowry whatsoever, when they married Jacob. So they are upset with their father not only as to how he has treated Jacob, but in the manner in which he has treated them as well. So they tell Jacob, *"Whatsoever God has said unto you, do."*

It's a shame that Laban figures so prominently in the Gospel Message, but yet, never came to know the Lord. His sister and two daughters would be instrumental in bringing into the world those who would be the heads of the great Tribes of Israel, and to whom God would make all the Promises. He was so close, but yet so far away. He saw the Hand of God move mightily, but never came to know the Lord.

JACOB DEPARTS

Verses 17 through 21 read: *"Then Jacob rose up, and set his sons and his wives upon camels;*

"And he carried away all his cattle, and all his goods which he had gotten, the cattle of his getting, which he had gotten in Padan-aram, for to go to Isaac his father in the land of Canaan.

"And Laban went to shear his sheep: and Rachel had stolen the images that were her father's.

"And Jacob stole away unawares to Laban the Syrian, in that he told him not that he fled.

"So he fled with all that he had; and he rose up, and passed over the river, and set his face toward the mount Gilead."

The Scripture says that Jacob is leaving, *"For to go to Isaac his father in the land of Canaan."* These 20 years that Jacob has been gone are silent regarding Isaac. How so much he must have grieved for his son.

While Esau no doubt provided some comfort, there was no spiritual bond whatsoever between Isaac and his oldest son. Esau simply did not know God.

He knew of course that God had laid His Hand on Jacob, but these 20 years pass in silence. Did he hear from Jacob during this time? Did Isaac send any news to Jacob from home?

It is believed that Rebekah died while Jacob was away, but no one knows when. The Scriptures are silent regarding her death, only saying that she was buried with Isaac in the tomb of Abraham (Gen. 49:31).

The great Plan of God regarding the formation of Israel as a nation will now begin. From the time of Abraham when he arrived in Canaan, to Jacob when he went into Egypt, was 215 years. When he left Syria, he was about 100 years old. When he went into Egypt, he was 130 (Gen. 47:9). So he would spend about 30 years in Canaan before going into Egypt, about 20 years of that grieving for Joseph, whom he thought was dead.

THE IMAGES

From Verse 19, some have concluded that Rachel was an idol-worshiper, because she had stolen the images which belonged to her father.

Concerning this, Horton says: *"Rachel had a reason for stealing the teraphim. These were small idols (like figurines) considered the family gods and were kept on a god-shelf, probably in the corner of the main room of the house.*

"When there was any question about the inheritance, the person who had the teraphim was considered to have the right to the double portion of the primary heir. When Jacob first came, he was welcomed into the family and adopted as the heir, since Laban had no sons at the time. But Laban had sons born shortly after, and that normally would invalidate Jacob's claim unless he possessed the teraphim. Rachel felt Jacob deserved more than he was getting, so she stole them for his benefit, and for the benefit of Jacob's family. There is no evidence she wanted to worship these images."

This was evidently sheepshearing time, and Laban was busy in this endeavor. Consequently, Jacob, while Laban was busy, took his vast herds, and fled. He passed over the

Euphrates River, and then set his face toward Mount Gilead.

(22) "AND IT WAS TOLD LABAN ON THE THIRD DAY THAT JACOB WAS FLED.

(23) "AND HE TOOK HIS BRETHREN WITH HIM, AND PURSUED AFTER HIM SEVEN DAYS' JOURNEY; AND THEY OVERTOOK HIM IN THE MOUNT GILEAD.

(24) "AND GOD CAME TO LABAN THE SYRIAN IN A DREAM BY NIGHT, AND SAID UNTO HIM, TAKE HEED THAT YOU SPEAK NOT TO JACOB EITHER GOOD OR BAD.

(25) "THEN LABAN OVERTOOK JACOB. NOW JACOB HAD PITCHED HIS TENT IN THE MOUNT: AND LABAN WITH HIS BRETHREN PITCHED IN THE MOUNT OF GILEAD.

(26) "AND LABAN SAID TO JACOB, WHAT HAVE YOU DONE, THAT YOU HAVE STOLEN AWAY UNAWARES TO ME, AND CARRIED AWAY MY DAUGHTERS, AS CAPTIVES TAKEN WITH THE SWORD?

(27) "WHEREFORE DID YOU FLEE AWAY SECRETLY, AND STEAL AWAY FROM ME; AND DID NOT TELL ME, THAT I MIGHT HAVE SENT YOU AWAY WITH MIRTH, AND WITH SONGS, WITH TABRET, AND WITH HARP?

(28) "AND HAVE NOT SUFFERED ME TO KISS MY SONS AND MY DAUGHTERS? YOU HAVE NOW DONE FOOLISHLY IN SO DOING.

(29) "IT IS IN THE POWER OF MY HAND TO DO YOU HURT: BUT THE GOD OF YOUR FATHER SPOKE UNTO ME YESTERNIGHT, SAYING, TAKE YOU HEED THAT YOU SPEAK NOT TO JACOB EITHER GOOD OR BAD.

(30) "AND NOW, THOUGH YOU WOULD NEED BE GONE, BECAUSE YOU SORE LONGED AFTER YOUR FATHER'S HOUSE, YET WHEREFORE HAVE YOU STOLEN MY GODS?

(31) "AND JACOB ANSWERED AND SAID TO LABAN, BECAUSE I WAS AFRAID: FOR I SAID, PERADVENTURE YOU WOULD TAKE BY FORCE YOUR DAUGHTERS FROM ME.

(32) "WITH WHOMSOEVER YOU FIND YOUR GODS, LET HIM NOT LIVE: BEFORE OUR BRETHREN DISCERN YOU WHAT IS YOURS WITH ME, AND TAKE IT TO YOU. FOR JACOB KNEW NOT THAT RACHEL HAD STOLEN THEM."

NOTES

The exegesis is:

1. For Jacob to leave in this manner shows that the situation had become intolerable.

2. Just before Laban caught up with Jacob, the Lord warned him in a dream not to harm the Patriarch. This tells me that Laban was definitely intending harm to Jacob, as well as taking his flocks, plus the wives and the children.

3. Jacob had no knowledge that Rachel had taken the images of her father, Laban.

THE DREAM

Verses 22 through 24 read: *"And it was told Laban on the third day that Jacob was fled.*

"And he took his brethren with him, and pursued after him seven days' journey; and they overtook him in the mount Gilead.

"And God came to Laban the Syrian in a dream by night, and said unto him, Take heed that you speak not to Jacob either good or bad."

Laban, busy shearing the sheep, did not hear of Jacob's departure for some three days. He immediately set out, evidently with a group of armed men, to overtake the Patriarch. It took some seven days for Laban to overtake Jacob, considering that he had traveled now for some 10 days, covering approximately 300 miles.

Every indication is, Laban meant to do Jacob harm. The Lord would not have warned him in a dream, had that not been the case. He probably intended to take the herds, his two daughters, and all the children, and maybe even kill Jacob. But what he doesn't know is that Jacob, no doubt, was surrounded by a band of Angels (Gen. 32:1-2). So, had he disregarded the admonition given to him by the Lord in the dream, Laban no doubt, would have met with a violent end. While it would not have been at the hand of Jacob, it would definitely have been at the hand of the Angels.

THE CHASE

Verses 25 through 32 read: *"Then Laban overtook Jacob. Now Jacob had pitched his tent in the mount: and Laban with his brethren pitched in the mount of Gilead.*

"And Laban said to Jacob, What have you done, that you have stolen away unawares to me, and carried away my daughters, as captives taken with the sword?

"Wherefore did you flee away secretly, and steal away from me; and did not tell me,

that I might have sent you away with mirth, and with songs, with tabret, and with harp?

"And have not suffered me to kiss my sons and my daughters? You have now done foolishly in so doing.

"It is in the power of my hand to do you hurt: but the God of your father spoke unto me yesternight, saying, Take you heed that you speak not to Jacob either good or bad.

"And now, though you would need be gone, because you sore long after your father's house, yet wherefore have you stolen my gods?

"And Jacob answered and said to Laban, Because I was afraid: for I said, Peradventure you would take by force your daughters from me.

"With whomsoever you find your gods, let him not live: before our brethren discern what is yours with me, and take it to you. For Jacob knew not that Rachel had stolen them."

Laban accuses Jacob of carrying away his daughters as captives, but that is totally untrue. Rachel and Leah voluntarily accompanied their husband in his flight.

The idea that Laban would have tendered a great going away party for Jacob is crassly hypocritical. More than likely, the Lord told Jacob to depart as he did, and because of Laban's hostile intentions.

One thing is certain: There is no way that Laban would have allowed Jacob to take the herds with him, and probably he would not have allowed his daughters or any of the children to go with Jacob. So his accusations and his claims hold no merit.

He then accuses Jacob of having stolen his gods, which Jacob vehemently denies, and rightly so. He had no idea that Rachel had taken these things, and as it would prove out, they were of no consequence anyway as far as the inheritance was concerned. After this meeting, Rachel would never see her father again.

(33) "AND LABAN WENT INTO JACOB'S TENT, AND INTO LEAH'S TENT, AND INTO THE TWO MAIDSERVANTS' TENTS; BUT HE FOUND THEM NOT. THEN WENT HE OUT OF LEAH'S TENT, AND ENTERED INTO RACHEL'S TENT.

(34) "NOW RACHEL HAD TAKEN THE IMAGES, AND PUT THEM IN THE CAMEL'S FURNITURE, AND SAT UPON THEM. AND LABAN SEARCHED ALL THE TENT, BUT FOUND THEM NOT.

(35) "AND SHE SAID TO HER FATHER, LET IT NOT DISPLEASE MY LORD THAT I CANNOT RISE UP BEFORE YOU; FOR THE CUSTOM OF WOMEN IS UPON ME. AND HE SEARCHED BUT FOUND NOT THE IMAGES.

(36) "AND JACOB WAS ANGRY, AND CHODE WITH LABAN: AND JACOB ANSWERED AND SAID TO LABAN, WHAT IS MY TRESPASS? WHAT IS MY SIN, THAT YOU HAVE SO HOTLY PURSUED AFTER ME?

(37) "WHEREAS YOU HAVE SEARCHED ALL MY STUFF, WHAT HAVE YOU FOUND OF ALL YOUR HOUSEHOLD STUFF? SET IT HERE BEFORE MY BRETHREN AND YOUR BRETHREN, THAT THEY MAY JUDGE BETWEEN US BOTH.

(38) "THIS TWENTY YEARS HAVE I BEEN WITH YOU; YOUR EWES AND YOUR SHE GOATS HAVE NOT CAST THEIR YOUNG, AND THE RAMS OF YOUR FLOCK HAVE I NOT EATEN.

(39) "THAT WHICH WAS TORN OF BEASTS I BROUGHT NOT UNTO YOU; I BEAR THE LOSS OF IT; OF MY HAND DID YOU REQUIRE IT, WHETHER STOLEN BY DAY, OR STOLEN BY NIGHT.

(40) "THUS I WAS; IN THE DAY THE DROUGHT CONSUMED ME, AND THE FROST BY NIGHT; AND MY SLEEP DEPARTED FROM MY EYES.

(41) "THUS HAVE I BEEN TWENTY YEARS IN YOUR HOUSE; I SERVED YOU FOURTEEN YEARS FOR YOUR TWO DAUGHTERS, AND SIX YEARS FOR YOUR CATTLE: AND YOU HAVE CHANGED MY WAGES TEN TIMES.

(42) "EXCEPT THE GOD OF MY FATHER, THE GOD OF ABRAHAM, AND THE FEAR OF ISAAC, HAD BEEN WITH ME, SURELY YOU HAD SENT ME AWAY NOW EMPTY. GOD HAS SEEN MY AFFLICTION AND THE LABOR OF MY HANDS, AND REBUKED YOU YESTERNIGHT."

The composition is:

1. How foolish for Laban to call those things his gods to which could be stolen! Could he expect protection from things that could neither resist nor discover their invaders?

2. Happy are they who have the Lord for their God, for they have a God of Whom they cannot be robbed. Enemies may steal our goods, but not our God.

3. Here Laban lays to Jacob's charge things that he knew not. Those who commit their cause to God are not forbidden to plead it themselves with meekness and fear.

THE IMAGES

Verses 33 through 35 read: *"And Laban went into Jacob's tent, and into Leah's tent, and into the two maidservants' tents; but he found them not. Then went he out of Leah's tent, and entered into Rachel's tent.*

"Now Rachel had taken the images, and put them in the camels' furniture, and sat upon them. And Laban searched all the tent, but found them not.

"And she said to her father, Let it not displease my lord that I cannot rise up before you; for the custom of women is upon me. And he searched but found not the images."

To explain the significance of all of this, let us say it again: The idea was, whoever had the small image could, at a given point in time, claim the inheritance. This is at least one of, if not the most important reason for Laban's diligence in searching for this little idol. And as well, it's the reason that Rachel had taken it, but which would do her no good. She would never see her homeland again, or her father for that matter, after he left.

"The camel's furniture," actually was a saddle riding affair, made of wickerwork, and had the appearance of a basket or cradle. It was usually covered with carpet, and protected against wind, rain, and sun by means of a canopy and curtains, while light was admitted by openings in the side. When riding a camel, this was the apparatus which served as a saddle-like affair, at least for women.

Rachel had hidden the images under this saddle, and was sitting on it. She apologized for not standing, claiming that she was having her *"period."* Whether this was correct or not, we have no way of knowing; but there is a good possibility that it was.

She reasoned in her mind that her father surmised that she was having some type of a problem, and would not inquire further, which means he would not search under the

camel saddle, which proved to be correct. At any rate, Laban did not find them, so Rachel's ruse worked.

THE ANGER OF JACOB

Verses 36 through 42 read: *"And Jacob was angry, and chode with Laban: and Jacob answered and said to Laban, What is my trespass? What is my sin, that you have so hotly pursued after me?*

"Whereas you have searched all my stuff, what have you found of all your household stuff? Set it here before my brethren and your brethren, that they may judge between us both.

"This twenty years have I been with you: your ewes and your she goats have not cast their young, and the rams of your flock have I not eaten.

"That which was torn of beasts I brought not unto you; I bear the loss of it; of my hand did you require it, whether stolen by day, or stolen by night.

"Thus I was; in the day the drought consumed me, and the frost by night; and my sleep departed from my eyes.

"Thus have I been twenty years in your house; I served you fourteen years for your two daughters, and six years for your cattle: and you have changed my wages ten times.

"Except the God of my father, the God of Abraham, and the fear of Isaac, had been with me, surely you had sent me away now empty. And God has seen my affliction and the labor of my hands, and rebuked you yesternight."

The contention between Jacob and Laban had gone on for many years. By now, it had reached a fever pitch. No doubt, if the Lord had not spoken to Laban in a dream, he without doubt would have taken everything Jacob had, including his wives and children, and possibly would have even killed him. But he was afraid to lift a hand against him in any manner at this particular time, and because of what the Lord had told him.

Jacob was now very angry. Instead of the father being sad regarding his two daughters and all of his grandchildren leaving, and knowing that he would possibly never see them again, he was more interested in material things than anything else. It is interesting that Jacob referred to these images as *"stuff"* (vs. 37).

Jacob then rehearses his twenty years with Laban, and in effect, is saying that Laban has absolutely no reason to be angry with him. He has treated Laban fair in every respect, and in fact, that was correct.

He then reminds Laban that he (Laban) knows that God is with him (Jacob), and he had best conduct himself toward the Patriarch accordingly.

The loss of Laban's manufactured deities was a ridiculous commentary on the folly of worshipping or trusting in a god that could be stolen. What a spectacle of infinite humor, if it were not so sad — a man seeking for his lost gods! The Gospel presents us with the opposite picture — the ever-present God seeking for His lost children.

(43) "AND LABAN ANSWERED AND SAID UNTO JACOB, THESE DAUGHTERS ARE MY DAUGHTERS, AND THESE CHILDREN ARE MY CHILDREN, AND THESE CATTLE ARE MY CATTLE, AND ALL THAT YOU SEE IS MINE: AND WHAT CAN I DO THIS DAY UNTO THESE MY DAUGHTERS, OR UNTO THEIR CHILDREN WHICH THEY HAVE BORN?

(44) "NOW THEREFORE COME YOU, LET US MAKE A COVENANT, I AND YOU; AND LET IT BE FOR A WITNESS BETWEEN ME AND YOU.

(45) "AND JACOB TOOK A STONE, AND SET IT UP FOR A PILLAR.

(46) "AND JACOB SAID UNTO HIS BRETHREN, GATHER STONES; AND THEY TOOK STONES, AND MADE AN HEAP: AND THEY DID EAT THERE UPON THE HEAP.

(47) "AND LABAN CALLED IT JEGAR-SAHADUTHA: BUT JACOB CALLED IT GALEED.

(48) "AND LABAN SAID, THIS HEAP IS A WITNESS BETWEEN ME AND YOU THIS DAY. THEREFORE WAS THE NAME OF IT CALLED GALEED;

(49) "AND MIZPAH; FOR HE SAID, THE LORD WATCH BETWEEN ME AND YOU, WHEN WE ARE ABSENT ONE FROM ANOTHER.

(50) "IF YOU SHALL AFFLICT MY DAUGHTERS, OR IF YOU SHALL TAKE OTHER WIVES BESIDE MY DAUGHTERS, NO MAN IS WITH US; SEE, GOD IS WITNESS BETWEEN ME AND YOU.

(51) "AND LABAN SAID TO JACOB, BEHOLD THIS HEAP, AND BEHOLD THIS PILLAR, WHICH I HAVE CAST BETWEEN ME AND YOU:

(52) "THIS HEAP BE WITNESS, AND THIS PILLAR BE WITNESS, THAT I WILL NOT PASS OVER THIS HEAP TO YOU, AND THAT YOU SHALL NOT PASS OVER THIS HEAP AND THIS PILLAR UNTO ME, FOR HARM.

(53) "THE GOD OF ABRAHAM, AND THE GOD OF NAHOR, THE GOD OF THEIR FATHER, JUDGE BETWEEN US. AND JACOB SWEAR BY THE FEAR OF HIS FATHER ISAAC.

(54) "THEN JACOB OFFERED SACRIFICE UPON THE MOUNT, AND CALLED HIS BRETHREN TO EAT BREAD: AND THEY DID EAT BREAD, AND TARRIED ALL NIGHT IN THE MOUNT.

(55) "AND EARLY IN THE MORNING LABAN ROSE UP, AND KISSED HIS SONS AND HIS DAUGHTERS, AND BLESSED THEM: AND LABAN DEPARTED, AND RETURNED UNTO HIS PLACE."

The composition is:

1. At Beth-el Jacob was to learn what God was; at Haran, what man was. And what a difference! At Beth-el God enriched him: at Haran, man robbed him!

2. The Lord speaking to Laban in a dream should have taught him that idols were vain and wicked inventions of man's folly, but yet he clings to them!

3. The parting of Laban and Jacob sadly illustrates the mutual suspicion which grips men's hearts when governed by the spirit of the world.

4. So Laban passes from the scene, not to be mentioned again, except in passing (Gen. 46:18, 25). He had seen the Hand of God greatly so in the life of Jacob, with the Lord, as stated, even speaking to him in a dream; however, he has no heart for God, and thereby, the opportunity of Heaven has been eternally lost.

THE PROTECTION OF GOD

Verse 43 reads: *"And Laban answered and said unto Jacob, These daughters are my daughters, and these children are my children, and these cattle are my cattle, and all that you see is mine: and what can I do this day unto these my daughters, or unto their children which they have born?"*

Laban wrongly claims everything that Jacob has, but recognizes, due to the Power of God, that there is nothing he can do regarding the taking of them. In fact, were he to try anything, he would no doubt forfeit his life. He knows this, but still doesn't relinquish claim.

How hard is the heart of man; how so difficult to turn, even in the face of the exhibition of the Power of God!

This whole scenario tells us that God is always in charge. Men rule, but God overrules!

Laban had little regard for Jacob, despite the fact that at this particular time he was a very rich man, and all because of the Patriarch. His greed would not allow him to see that, and as well, he only grudgingly gave God the glory. Instead of allowing Jacob to show him the one True God, and service for Him, he instead saw only worldly wealth.

How similar this entire spirit is, with many in the modern Charismatic movements, who claim the Word of Faith doctrine, etc. The emphasis is not at all on Righteousness and Holiness, but rather on material things. And let the Reader hear and know; if we labor for the meat that perishes, we will perish along with it. That's why Jesus said:

"Labor not for the meat which perishes, but for that meat which endures unto everlasting life, which the Son of Man shall give unto you: for Him has God the Father sealed" (Jn. 6:27).

Without a doubt, the situation presented before us regarding Jacob and Laban is at least one of the greatest hindrances to the Child of God. Why do we serve God? Is it for worldly accoutrements, or is it for the joy of Christ Himself?

THE COVENANT

Verses 44 through 48 read: *"Now therefore come you, let us make a covenant, I and you; and let it be for a witness between me and you.*

"And Jacob took a stone, and set it up for a pillar.

"And Jacob said unto his brethren, Gather stones; and they took stones, and made an heap: and they did eat there upon the heap.

"And Laban called it Jegar-sahadutha: but Jacob called it Galeed.

"And Laban said, This heap is a witness between me and you this day. Therefore was the name of it called Galeed."

The Covenant was a suggestion of Laban, or even a demand. Jacob is the one who has been wronged, so if one of the two needed a covenant, it was the Patriarch; however, the evidence is, Laban wanted this covenant because he was afraid, relative to what the Lord had told him in the dream (vs. 24). Jacob had a dream as well (vss. 10-13). In this dream, God, in essence, had promised to be with Jacob. So, the Patriarch needed no covenant, because his trust was in the Lord to take care of him. But evil men need covenants or contracts, simply because their word is no good. So, Laban claims that the heap of stones which they had erected, and over which they had broken bread, was to be a *"witness between me and you this day."*

THE GOD OF ISAAC

Verses 49 through 55 read: *"And Mizpah; for he said, The LORD watch between me and you, when we are absent one from another.*

"If you shall afflict my daughters, or if you shall take other wives beside my daughters, no man is with us; see, God is witness between me and you.

"And Laban said to Jacob, Behold this heap, and behold this pillar, which I have cast between me and you:

"This heap be witness, and this pillar be witness, that I will not pass over this heap to you, and that you shall not pass over this heap and this pillar unto me, for harm.

"The God of Abraham, and the god of Nahor, the gods of their father, judge between us. And Jacob swear by the fear of his father Isaac.

"Then Jacob offered sacrifice upon the mount, and called his brethren to eat bread: and they did eat bread, and tarried all night in the mount.

"And early in the morning Laban rose up, and kissed his sons and his daughters, and blessed them: and Laban departed, and returned unto his place."

At this stage, Laban makes a show of piety as it regards his daughters, but his actions have spoken much louder than his words. He is more concerned about material things than anything else.

Laban now adds an oath to the covenant, calling on the God of Abraham, and the gods of Nahor, the gods of their father, to judge between Jacob and Laban. All of this proves that Laban worships many so-called gods. He really doesn't know the God of Abraham, but only puts him into the mix, and on the same level as the gods of Nahor, etc. So Verse 53 should have been translated:

"The God of Abraham, and the gods of Nahor, the gods of their father. . . ."

Jacob ignored the gods of Nahor, and took his oath only in the name of the one True God Who was the *"Fear"* of, or *"the One Reverenced"* by Isaac (Horton).

As well, the Scripture says that *"Jacob offered Sacrifice upon the mount, and called his brethren to eat bread"* (vs. 54).

The Sacrifice meant nothing to Laban, even though he was well acquainted with this practice, but everything to Jacob. In essence, he was saying that he was placing his faith and confidence in what the Sacrifice represented. The very purpose and reason for his grandfather Abraham being called out of Ur of the Chaldees, and the actions of his father Isaac, and his own life for that matter, were to bring the One into the world, of Whom the Sacrifices represented. As the Lamb gave its life, pouring out its blood, with its carcass then being offered on the Altar, likewise Christ would give His Life, offering up Himself on the Cross as a Sacrifice in order that man might be saved. The terrible sin debt must be paid, and there was no other way to pay it. God would have to become man, Whom Paul would refer to as the *"Last Adam,"* and the *"Second Man"* (I Cor. 15:45, 47).

Verse 55 says that *"Laban departed, and returned unto his place."*

Regrettably and sadly, that *"place,"* at least as far as we know, was eternal darkness, forever without God. In essence, he sold his soul for a few flocks and herds. What a sorry trade!

"O thou my soul bless God the Lord,
"And all that in me is,
"Be lifted up, His Holy Name
"To magnify and bless."

"Bless, O my soul, the Lord my God,
"And not forgetful be

"Of all His gracious benefits
"He has bestowed on thee."

"All your iniquities Who does
"Most graciously forgive,
"Who your diseases all and pains
"Does heal and thee relieve."

"The Lord Jehovah gracious is,
"And He is merciful,
"Long-suffering and slow to wrath,
"In kindness plentiful."

"O bless the Lord, all ye His Works,
"Wherewith the world is stored,
"In His dominions everywhere;
"My soul, bless thou the Lord."

CHAPTER 32

(1) "AND JACOB WENT ON HIS WAY, AND THE ANGELS OF GOD MET HIM.

(2) "AND WHEN JACOB SAW THEM, HE SAID, THIS IS GOD'S HOST: AND HE CALLED THE NAME OF THAT PLACE MAHANAIM.

(3) "AND JACOB SENT MESSENGERS BEFORE HIM TO ESAU HIS BROTHER UNTO THE LAND OF SEIR, THE COUNTRY OF EDOM.

(4) "AND HE COMMANDED THEM, SAYING, THUS SHALL YOU SPEAK UNTO MY LORD ESAU; YOUR SERVANT JACOB SAYS THUS, I HAVE SOJOURNED WITH LABAN, AND STAYED THERE UNTIL NOW:

(5) "AND I HAVE OXEN, AND ASSES, FLOCKS, AND MENSERVANTS, AND WOMENSERVANTS: AND I HAVE SENT TO TELL MY LORD, THAT I MAY FIND GRACE IN YOUR SIGHT.

(6) "AND THE MESSENGERS RETURNED TO JACOB, SAYING, WE CAME TO YOUR BROTHER ESAU, AND ALSO HE COMES TO MEET YOU, AND FOUR HUNDRED MEN WITH HIM.

(7) "THEN JACOB WAS GREATLY AFRAID AND DISTRESSED: AND HE DIVIDED THE PEOPLE THAT WAS WITH HIM, AND THE FLOCKS, AND HERDS, AND THE CAMELS, INTO TWO BANDS;

(8) "AND SAID, IF ESAU COME TO THE ONE COMPANY, AND SMITE IT, THEN

THE OTHER COMPANY WHICH IS LEFT SHALL ESCAPE."

The construction is:

1. The second Vision concerning the Angels corresponds to that at Beth-el in Chapter 28.

2. Then his possessions consisted of a staff, but now he has become a host; and he calls this place Mahanaim, i.e., *"two camps — his feeble camp and the encircling camp of God's mighty Angels."*

3. Like many today, Jacob first makes his plans and then he prays! He should have reversed the action. But the sense of having acted wrongly those years ago regarding his brother Esau, fills the heart with a thousand fears, and robs the Christian of confidence toward God and dignity before man (Williams).

THE ANGELS OF GOD

Verse 1 reads: *"And Jacob went on his way, and the Angels of God met him."*

Jacob was now about to cross over the brook into the Promised Land, to where God had called him. There would be many dangers, toils, and snares; however, for a few moments, and the Holy Spirit does not inform us as to exactly how, He pulls back the cover of the spirit world, and allows Jacob to see an Angelic host, which was ready to accompany him. And yet, strangely enough, as wonderful as this was, and as much as it should have spoken unto Jacob, he seemingly did not recognize its significance. Despite the fact of being surrounded by Angels, he begins to scheme and plan as it regards the coming of Esau. He had wronged his brother some 20 years before, and now he must face him.

The Angels appearing, and Jacob not quite realizing their significance, point to the fact that all the great manifestations, as wonderful as they might be, cannot bring us to the place where we ought to be in the Lord. That can only come when the sentence of death is written on the flesh, which only the power of the Cross can bring about. And that's one of the great problems of the modern Church.

For the last decade, the Church has been looking for manifestations. Mostly what they've seen has not been anything, and in some cases, it's literally been the powers of darkness. But even if the manifestations are real, which means they are genuinely of God,

NOTES

just as the Angels which made themselves visible to Jacob, that within itself will not bring about the victory for which we seek.

The following is a short article written by A. W. Tozer. It is titled, *"The Old Cross and the New."*

I could easily rewrite this, and put it in my own words; however, I feel that the article as written by our dear Brother, is so appropriate, so needful, so necessary, and so Scriptural, that I want to make certain that everything he has said comes to you exactly as he said it; hence, I will give it word for word.

THE OLD CROSS AND THE NEW

All unannounced and mostly undetected there has come in modern times a new Cross into popular evangelical circles. It is like the old Cross, but different: the likenesses are superficial, the differences, fundamental.

From this new Cross has sprung a new philosophy of the Christian life, and from that new philosophy has come a new evangelical technique — a new type of meeting and a new kind of preaching. This new evangelism employs the same language as the old, but its content is not the same and its emphasis not as before.

THE WORLD

The old Cross would have no truck with the world. For Adam's proud flesh it meant the end of the journey. It carried into effect the sentence imposed by the Law of Sinai. The new Cross is not opposed to the human race; rather it is a friendly pal and, if understood aright, it is the source of oceans of good clean fun and innocent enjoyment. It lets Adam live without interference. His life motivation is unchanged; he still lives for his own pleasure, only now he takes delight in singing choruses and watching religious movies instead of singing bawdy songs and drinking hard liquor. The accent is still on enjoyment, though the fun is now on a higher plane morally if not intellectually.

A NEW APPROACH

The new Cross encourages a new and entirely different evangelistic approach. The Evangelist does not demand abnegation of the old life before a new life can be received. He preaches not contrasts but similarities.

He seeks to key into public interest by showing that Christianity makes no unpleasant demands; rather, it offers the same thing the world does, only on a higher level. Whatever the sin-mad world happens to be clamoring after at the moment is cleverly shown to be the very thing the Gospel offers, only the religious product is better.

ACCEPTABLE TO THE PUBLIC

The new Cross does not slay the sinner; it redirects him. It gears him into a cleaner and jollier way of living and saves his self-respect. To the self-assertive it says, *"Come and assert yourself for Christ."* To the egotist it says, *"Come and do your boasting in the Lord."* To the thrill-seeker it says, *"Come and enjoy the thrill of Christian fellowship and entertainment."*

The Christian message is slanted in the direction of the current vogue in order to make it acceptable to the public.

FALSE

The philosophy back of this kind of thing may be sincere, but its sincerity does not save it from being false. It is false because it is blind. It misses completely the whole meaning of the Cross.

A SYMBOL OF DEATH

The old Cross is a symbol of death. It stands for the abrupt, violent end of a human being. The man in Roman times who took up his cross and started down the road had already said good-bye to his friends. He was not coming back. He was not going out to have his life redirected; he was going out to have it ended. The Cross made no compromise, modified nothing, spared nothing; it slew all of the man, completely and for good. It did not try to keep on good terms with its victim. It struck cruel and hard, and when it had finished its work, the man was no more.

A DEATH SENTENCE

The race of Adam is under a death sentence. There is no commutation and no escape. God cannot approve any of the fruits of sin, however innocent they may appear or beautiful to the eyes of men. God salvages the individual by liquidating him and then raising him again to newness of life.

NOTES

That evangelism which draws friendly parallels between the ways of God and the ways of men is false to the Bible and cruel to the souls of its hearers. The Faith of Christ does not parallel the world; it intersects it. In coming to Christ we do not bring our old life up onto a higher plain; we leave it at the Cross. The corn of wheat must fall into the ground and die.

PUBLIC RELATIONS AGENTS?

We who preach the Gospel must not think of ourselves as public relations agents sent to establish goodwill between Christ and the world. We must not imagine ourselves commissioned to make Christ acceptable to big business, the press, or the world of sports, or modern education. We are not diplomats but Prophets, and our message is not a compromise but an ultimatum.

LIFE

God offers life, but not an improved old life. The life He offers is life out of death. It stands always on the far side of the Cross. Whoever would possess it must pass under the rod. He must repudiate himself and concur in God's just sentence against him.

What does this mean to the individual, the condemned man who would find life in Christ Jesus? How can this theology be translated into life?

Simply, he must repent and believe. He must forsake his sins and then go on to forsake himself. Let him cover nothing, defend nothing, excuse nothing. Let him not seek to make terms with God, but let him bow his head before the stroke of God's stern displeasure and acknowledge himself worthy to die.

JESUS CHRIST

Having done this let him gaze with simple trust upon the risen Saviour, and from Him will come life, rebirth, cleansing, and power. The Cross that ended the earthly life of Jesus now puts an end to the sinner; and the power that raised Christ from the dead now raises him to a new life along with Christ.

To any who may object to this or count it merely a narrow and private view of truth, let me say God has set His hallmark of approval upon this message from Paul's day to the present. Whether stated in these exact words or not, this has been the content of all preaching that has brought life and power to the world through the centuries. The mystics, the reformers, the revivalists have put their emphasis here, and signs and wonders and mighty Operations of the Holy Spirit gave witness to God's approval.

Dare we, the heirs of such a legacy of power, tamper with the truth? Dare we with our stubby pencils erase the lines of the blueprint or alter the pattern shown us in the Mount? May God forbid. Let us preach the old Cross and we will know the power.

The above message by A. W. Tozer is that which is so desperately needed by the modern Church. And let me say it again:

We can have all the manifestations in the world, and as good as they might be, and as much of a blessing as they may be temporarily, if we do not understand the Cross of Christ, we will find ourselves in the same condition after the manifestation, as we were before. Only the Cross can change men, not manifestations! Only the Cross can put an end to the terrible works of the flesh, and bring about the Fruit of the Spirit! Only the Cross can properly place self into Christ, and as someone has well said, Jesus died on the Cross, not only to save us from sin, but as well, from self!

THE TWO CAMPS

Verse 2 reads: *"And when Jacob saw them, he said, This is God's Host: and he called the name of that place Mahanaim."*

There is some disagreement as to exactly what Jacob meant by the name *"Mahanaim."* It means *"two armies or camps."*

Some claim there were two camps of Angels, one directing him from Syria, and the other into the Promised Land. Others suggest that Jacob was speaking of his camp or host, and the Angels as another camp, which was God's Host.

"God's Host" in the Hebrew is *"Mahaneh Elohim,"* which means, *"the army or camp of the Lord,"* as opposed to the Mahanoth, or hosts of Jacob himself. More than likely, the latter is what Jacob was meaning.

The statement from Verse 1, *"And the Angels of God met him,"* can mean, *"appeared*

to him." More than likely, these Angels had been with Jacob ever since they appeared to him in Beth-el some 20 years before.

I think one can say without any fear of Scriptural contradiction or exaggeration, that Angels surround every Believer in some capacity (Heb. 1:14; 12:1).

But again allow me to emphasize that as wonderful as manifestations may be, and as much as all of us desire to have them, and I speak of course of those which are truly from God, those things will not change us, as powerful as they may be in their own right. It is only the Cross which can change the Child of God. The Believer must understand that he is baptized into the death of Christ, buried with Him, and raised with Him in newness of life (Rom. 6:3-5). Until he understands that, thereby understanding that the Cross is the key not only to his Salvation, but as well to his Sanctification, he will never know a victorious life. God cannot give victory to the flesh, of which we will have more to say momentarily, but only to His Son, the Lord Jesus Christ.

At any rate, Jacob is shown that he has a host of Angels around him.

GRACE

Verses 3 through 6 read: *"And Jacob sent messengers before him to Esau his brother unto the land of Seir, the country of Edom.*

"And he commanded them, saying, Thus shall you speak unto my lord Esau: Your servant Jacob says thus, I have sojourned with Laban, and stayed there until now:

"And I have oxen, and asses, flocks, and menservants, and womenservants: and I have sent to tell my lord, that I may find grace in your sight.

"And the messengers returned to Jacob, saying, We came to your brother Esau, and also he comes to meet you, and four hundred men with him."

During this some 20 years that Jacob had been away from home, he must from time to time, have received some word as to the happenings there, for the simple reason that he knew Esau now lived in *"the land of Seir, the country of Edom."*

Incidentally, some believe that Esau was the founder of the ancient city of Petra, and may have been there when Jacob sent for him.

Knowing that he has done Esau wrong, he feels that the first thing he must do is to address this situation. And to be sure, if we have wronged anyone, it is absolutely imperative as a Christian that the matter be handled Biblically. It doesn't matter what they have done. Whatever that may have been gives us no excuse to wrong them. And if we have wronged anyone for any reason, no matter how legitimate it may seem on the surface, it we want to be where God wants us to be, the wrong must be set aright, at least as far as lies within our power.

The messengers whom Jacob had sent to Esau now return, and their news is not exactly positive. Esau is coming to meet Jacob, but he has 400 men with him. Common sense tells us that one doesn't bring that many men, as it regards a mere greeting. It is almost positive that Esau had other things in mind, and they were not exactly meant to be pleasant.

Jacob has asked for grace, and in the immediate sense, this was not to be granted; however the Lord, as we shall see, would beautifully and wondrously change things.

FEAR

Verses 7 and 8 read: *"Then Jacob was greatly afraid and distressed: and he divided the people that was with him, and the flocks, and herds, and the camels, into two bands;*

"And said, If Esau come to the one company, and smite it, then the other company which is left shall escape."

Jacob, upon hearing this news concerning his brother Esau, immediately begins to make plans, and then he prays. He should have prayed first.

Once again we come back to the *"manifestation"* of Angels. As wonderful as that was, it didn't have much effect on Jacob, because manifestations cannot change an individual. In other words, despite this great vision, Jacob was unchanged, and in reality, Jacob was the problem. In this problem of the flesh, he tries to manage Esau, instead of leaning on God.

Jacob's first thought, as we see the first years of his life, which in fact spanned over half, was always a plan, and in this we have a true picture of the poor human heart. True, he turns to God after he makes his plan, and cries to

Him for deliverance; but no sooner does he cease praying than he resumes the planning.

Concerning this, Mackintosh said: *"Now, praying and planning will never go together. If I plan, I am leaning more or less on my plan; but when I pray, I should lean exclusively upon God. Hence, the two things are perfectly incompatible, they virtually destroy each other. When my eyes fill with my own management of things, I am not prepared to see God acting for me; and, in that case, prayer is not the utterance of my need, but the mere superstitious performance of something which I think ought to be done, or it may be, asking God to sanctify my plans. This will never do. The life of faith is not asking God to sanctify and bless my means, but it is asking Him to do it all Himself."*

In other words, we don't make our plans and then ask God to bless them, but rather ask God to make the plans, which are guaranteed then of blessing.

VICTORY

A few paragraphs back, we made the statement, *"God cannot give victories to the flesh, but only to His Son, the Lord Jesus Christ."* Perhaps we could say it a little differently, and make it a little more understandable:

"God cannot give victories to man, but only to His Son, the Lord Jesus Christ."

Now that statement is very simple, but if you the Reader properly understand it, you will understand a great deal of the entirety of the New Covenant. In brief it means this:

Jesus Christ was and is our Substitute, and that means our Substitute in all things. He did for us what we could not do for ourselves, and undid all that was wrong, which we did do.

For instance, He kept the Law of Moses in every respect, which of course, we did not do, and in fact, could not do. But as our Substitute, He addressed every nuance of the Law, kept it perfectly and as the Scripture says, *"Blotted out the handwriting of ordinances that was against us, which was contrary to us, and took it out of the way, nailing it to His Cross"* (Col. 2:14).

When He did this, and which He did so by the giving of Himself in Sacrifice, this atoned for all sin, past, present, and future. And by atoning for all sin, He took away Satan's legal right to hold man in captivity, at least for all who will believe (Jn. 3:16; Col. 2:15).

Consequently, all the victories were purchased and won by the Lord Jesus Christ, which was done at the Cross. Therefore, the way that we obtain victory is by simply trusting in what Christ has done for us at the Cross, placing all our Faith there, which then gives the Holy Spirit the latitude to work within our hearts and lives (Rom. 6:3-14; 8:1-2, 11; I Cor. 1:17-18, 21, 23; 2:2, 5; Gal. 6:14).

So all victory has already been won by Christ, all done for us, and we obtain this victory by simply trusting in what Christ has done. Considering that He did all of this at the Cross, this is why the Cross is so very, very important.

Consequently, God will not give victories to man, and because such would have been and is impossible at any rate. The victories were given to Jesus Christ, simply because He is the One Who paid the price for victory in every capacity; therefore, we simply believe Him, trust in Him, place our Faith in Him and what He did for us in His sufferings, and His victory becomes ours, which it is intended to do.

ACTIVITY OR POSITION?

Many Christians erroneously think that victory comes by activity. And what do we mean by that?

Millions of Christians are constantly doing this and doing that, many of these things being very good things, and thinking that all of this *"doing"* will gain them victory, or whatever it is they seek. It won't!

Everything we have in Christ is not at all because of our religious activity, but it is altogether ours because of our position in Christ, which we attain simply by Faith, and I speak of Faith in Him and what He did for us in His great Sacrifice. But it's very hard for many Christians to accept that which I've just said. They want to think that their activity is what gives them place and position in Christ. But again I emphasize, it doesn't!

Our doing all these religious things, and whatever they may be, and even though they are good in their own respect, if our faith and trust is in that, and this is the key, then we are in effect saying, whether we realize it or not,

that what Jesus did at the Cross did not suffice, and we have to add something to His Work. Now we can't have it both ways. What He did is either a *"Finished Work,"* or it isn't, and if it isn't, then we really have nothing at all.

To be frank, whenever we place our faith and confidence in our activity, we are insulting Christ to the highest degree. We may not think of such as doing that, but that's exactly what is happening. The writer of the following song is right:

> *"Nothing in my hands I bring,*
> *"Simply to the Cross I cling!"*

What do we mean by *"position"*?

I am what I am in Christ, and I have what I have in Christ, because of my position in Christ. I gain this position by simply believing Him, and what He did for me at the Cross. That's why we constantly speak of the Cross, constantly extol the Cross, and constantly lift up the Cross. That's why Paul said: *"But God forbid that I should glory* (boast), *save in the Cross of our Lord Jesus Christ, by Whom the world is crucified unto me, and I unto the world"* (Gal. 6:14).

I lift up the Cross, or boast of the Cross, exactly as Paul, because that's where I was able to attain my position as it regards Christ. I place my Faith and trust in Him, and what He did, never divorcing Him from the Cross, and thereby am granted instant position in our Lord.

Now once again, that's very difficult for most Christians to accept. They want to think that they have earned their place, or else they have attained this position, whatever it is they think they have in the Lord, simply because they belong to a certain Church or Denomination, etc. For them to be told that none of that has anything to do with place and position in Christ doesn't set well. As we have previously stated, it was very grievous for Abraham to have to give up Ishmael; likewise, it's very grievous for most Christians to have to give up their *"works religion."* However, please understand this:

As a Believer, there is no position in Christ attained by *"works"* of any nature. It simply cannot be done. Paul also said:

"Christ is become of no effect unto you, whosoever of you are justified by the Law; you are fallen from Grace" (Gal. 5:4). He

had just said that if the Believers in Galatia trusted in circumcision, or anything else of that nature, *"Christ shall profit you nothing"* (Gal. 5:2). So Jacob makes his plans, and then prays, typical of most modern Christians, but little solving anything.

(9) "AND JACOB SAID, O GOD OF MY FATHER ABRAHAM, AND GOD OF MY FATHER ISAAC, THE LORD WHICH SAID UNTO ME, RETURN UNTO YOUR COUNTRY, AND TO YOUR KINDRED, AND I WILL DEAL WELL WITH YOU:

(10) "I AM NOT WORTHY OF THE LEAST OF ALL THE MERCIES, AND OF ALL THE TRUTH, WHICH YOU HAVE SHOWED UNTO YOUR SERVANT; FOR WITH MY STAFF I PASSED OVER THIS JORDAN; AND NOW I AM BECOME TWO BANDS.

(11) "DELIVER ME, I PRAY YOU, FROM THE HAND OF MY BROTHER, FROM THE HAND OF ESAU: FOR I FEAR HIM, LEST HE WILL COME AND SMITE ME, AND THE MOTHER WITH THE CHILDREN.

(12) "AND YOU SAID, I WILL SURELY DO YOU GOOD, AND MAKE YOUR SEED AS THE SAND OF THE SEA, WHICH CANNOT BE NUMBERED FOR MULTITUDE."

The overview is:

1. *"The heart is deceitful above all things, and desperately wicked."* It is often hard to detect what is the real ground of the heart's confidence. We imagine that we are leaning upon God, when we are, in reality, leaning upon some scheme of our own devising.

2. Jacob's prayer is the first recorded in the Bible.

3. His prayer was correct, but his faith as of yet wasn't!

THE PRAYER

Verses 9 through 12 read: *"And Jacob said, O God of my father Abraham, and God of my father Isaac, the LORD which said unto me, Return unto your country, and to your kindred, and I will deal well with you.*

"I am not worthy of the least of all the mercies, and of all the truth, which you have showed unto your servant; for with my staff I passed over this Jordan; and now I am become two bands.

"Deliver me, I pray you, from the hand of my brother, from the hand of Esau: for I fear

him, lest he will come and smite me, and the mother with the children.

"And You said, I will surely do you good, and make your seed as the sand of the sea, which cannot be numbered for multitude."

There is no fault with Jacob's prayer. It is sincere, honest, straightforward, and as well puts self into its proper place, and God in His proper place.

But as we have stated, it is often hard to detect what is the real ground of the heart's confidence. We think that we are leaning upon the Lord, trusting exclusively in Him, when, in reality, we are leaning on some scheme of our own devising.

Jacob asks the Lord to deliver him, but then turns right around and tries to appease Esau with a present. Was he placing more confidence in a few lambs than he did Jehovah, to Whom he had just been committing himself?

These are the questions which naturally arise out of Jacob's actions in reference to Esau. But the hurtful part is that we can more readily answer them by looking into the glass of our own hearts. There we learn, as well as on the page of Jacob's history, how much more apt we are to lean on our own management rather than on that of God.

But it's not that simple. We must be brought to see the end of our own efforts, that they are perfect folly, and that the true path of wisdom is to repose in full confidence upon God. But as previously stated, we do not come there readily, quickly, easily, or without price. This fits perfectly with what Paul said in his second Letter to the Corinthians:

"And lest I should be exalted above measure through the abundance of the Revelations, there was given to me a thorn in the flesh, the messenger of Satan to buffet me, lest I should be exalted above measure.

"For this thing I besought the Lord thrice, that it might depart from me.

"And He said unto me, My Grace is sufficient for you: for My strength is made perfect in weakness" (II Cor. 12:7-9).

Having made the above statements, we find Jacob closer now than he had been 20 years earlier at Beth-el. By him addressing the Lord as the *"God of my father Abraham, and God of my father Isaac,"* portrays the fact that he understood the tremendous responsibility which was upon him, which included greatly his Grandfather and his Father. He claims, and rightly so, that his journey back to Canaan was in obedience to the Lord, even as it was.

He then disavows all self-worthiness, claiming, and rightly so, that he did not deserve even the least of the mercies of God. Plainly, despite his present problems, this is not the same Jacob of 20 years before. He thanks God for the Truth, and claims that the Lord has shown him great things, which was no doubt true. But there was still more to be learned, as there is always more to be learned.

The *"two bands"* of which he speaks was of his own doings, and not that which the Lord had told him to do. That's what we meant about trying to manage the situation, instead of letting the Lord take care of what needed to be done.

He asked for deliverance from the hand of his brother, and gives us the greatest reason, *"the mother with the children."* He knew, which was a part of the truth that God had revealed to him, that these children were the beginning of this great nation which God would raise up; consequently, he realized their significance.

He closes his prayer by reminding the Lord of the Promises which Jehovah had made. In fact, and as stated, the prayer was excellent; however, even though the Patriarch had come a long way, he still had a way to go as it regards his faith.

(13) "AND HE LODGED THERE THAT SAME NIGHT; AND TOOK OF THAT WHICH CAME TO HIS HAND A PRESENT FOR ESAU HIS BROTHER;

(14) "TWO HUNDRED SHE GOATS, AND TWENTY HE GOATS, TWO HUNDRED EWES, AND TWENTY RAMS.

(15) "THIRTY MILK CAMELS WITH THEIR COLTS, FORTY KINE, AND TEN BULLS, TWENTY SHE ASSES, AND TEN FOALS.

(16) "AND HE DELIVERED THEM INTO THE HAND OF HIS SERVANTS, EVERY DROVE BY THEMSELVES; AND SAID UNTO HIS SERVANTS, PASS OVER BEFORE ME, AND PUT A SPACE BETWEEN DROVE AND DROVE.

(17) "AND HE COMMANDED THE FOREMOST, SAYING, WHEN ESAU MY BROTHER

MEETS YOU, AND ASKS YOU, SAYING, WHOSE ARE THESE? AND WHERE ARE YOU GOING? AND WHOSE ARE THESE BEFORE YOU?

(18) "THEN YOU SHALL SAY, THEY BE YOUR SERVANT JACOB'S; IT IS A PRESENT SENT UNTO MY LORD ESAU: AND, BEHOLD, ALSO HE IS BEHIND US.

(19) "AND SO COMMANDED HE THE SECOND, AND THE THIRD, AND ALL THAT FOLLOWED THE DROVES, SAYING, ON THIS MANNER SHALL YOU SPEAK UNTO ESAU, WHEN YOU FIND HIM.

(20) "AND SAY YOU MOREOVER, BEHOLD, YOUR SERVANT JACOB IS BEHIND US. FOR HE SAID, I WILL APPEASE HIM WITH A PRESENT THAT GOES BEFORE ME, AND AFTERWARD I WILL SEE HIS FACE; PERADVENTURE HE WILL ACCEPT OF ME.

(21) "SO WENT THE PRESENT OVER BEFORE HIM: AND HIMSELF LODGED THAT NIGHT IN THE COMPANY.

(22) "AND HE ROSE UP THAT NIGHT, AND TOOK HIS TWO WIVES, AND HIS TWO WOMENSERVANTS, AND HIS ELEVEN SONS, AND PASSED OVER THE FORD JABBOK.

(23) "AND HE TOOK THEM, AND SENT THEM OVER THE BROOK, AND SENT OVER THAT HE HAD."

The exegesis is:

1. These gifts from Jacob to Esau, in 2002 currency, would amount to nearly $100,000. For him to give this much as a gift shows how large his main herds must have been.

2. Though he had prayed for deliverance from Esau, it seems he had no real confidence in his prayer being answered, and he says: *"I will appease him with a present."*

3. As to his dignity before man, his language is: *"My lord Esau,"* and *"Your servant Jacob."*

A PRESENT FOR ESAU

Verses 13 through 23 read: *"And he lodged there that same night; and took of that which came to his hand a present for Esau his brother;*

"Two hundred she goats, and twenty he goats, two hundred ewes, and twenty rams,

"Thirty milk camels with their colts, forty kine, and ten bulls, twenty she asses, and ten foals.

"And he delivered them into the hand of his servants, every drove by themselves; and

said unto his servants, Pass over before me, and put a space between drove and drove.

"And he commanded the foremost, saying, When Esau my brother meets you, and asks you, saying, Whose are these? And where are you going? And whose are these before you?

"Then you shall say, They be your servant Jacob's; it is a present sent unto my lord Esau: and, behold, also he is behind us.

"And so commanded he the second, and the third, and all that followed the droves, saying, On this manner shall you speak unto Esau, when you find him.

"And say you moreover, Behold, your servant Jacob is behind us. For he said, I will appease him with the present that goes before me, and afterward I will see his face; peradventure he will accept of me.

"So went the present over before him: and himself lodged that night in the company.

"And he rose up that night, and took his two wives, and his two womenservants, and his eleven sons, and passed over the ford Jabbok.

"And he took them, and sent them over the brook, and sent over that he had."

The idea was that there would be a space between the droves, and when Esau came upon a drove, he was to be told that this was a present from Jacob. A half a mile or so further on, he would meet another drove, and would be told the same thing. Thus, Jacob hoped to appease his brother.

As stated, considering the number of animals which Jacob gave to Esau as a gift, tells us how large his flocks must actually have been.

The Brook Jabbok crosses the Jordan about 30 miles north of the Dead Sea.

THE BROOK JABBOK

On our 1998 trip to Israel, we visited Jordan as well. Coming up on the eastern side of the Jordan River, intending to cross near the Sea of Galilee over into Israel, which we did, we of course, had to pass over the Brook Jabbok. I asked the driver if he would stop, which he did, with all of us getting out of the bus.

Most of the people with us had little idea as to why we had stopped, or the significance of this Brook.

From where the modern road runs, at least where we crossed, where Jacob would have

crossed, and as well would have had the wrestling match with the Lord, is approximately five or six miles west toward the Jordan River.

As I stood there that day looking at this Brook, which incidentally is quite large, at least as Brooks go, my mind went to that moment which took place about 3,700 years ago. Jacob figures so prominently in the great Plan of God, that everything he did was of vast spiritual significance. And this which took place by the side of the Brook Jabbok was one of the most important events of all.

(24) "AND JACOB WAS LEFT ALONE; AND THERE WRESTLED A MAN WITH HIM UNTIL THE BREAKING OF THE DAY.

(25) "AND WHEN HE SAW THAT HE PREVAILED NOT AGAINST HIM, HE TOUCHED THE HOLLOW OF HIS THIGH; AND THE HOLLOW OF JACOB'S THIGH WAS OUT OF JOINT, AS HE WRESTLED WITH HIM.

(26) "AND HE SAID, LET ME GO, FOR THE DAY BREAKETH. AND HE SAID, I WILL NOT LET YOU GO, EXCEPT YOU BLESS ME.

(27) "AND HE SAID UNTO HIM, WHAT IS YOUR NAME? AND HE SAID, JACOB.

(28) "AND HE SAID, YOUR NAME SHALL BE CALLED NO MORE JACOB, BUT ISRAEL: FOR AS A PRINCE HAVE YOU POWER WITH GOD AND WITH MEN, AND HAVE PREVAILED.

(29) "AND JACOB ASKED HIM, AND SAID, TELL ME, I PRAY YOU, YOUR NAME. AND HE SAID, WHEREFORE IS IT THAT YOU DO ASK AFTER MY NAME? AND HE BLESSED HIM THERE.

(30) "AND JACOB CALLED THE NAME OF THE PLACE PENIEL: FOR I HAVE SEEN GOD FACE TO FACE, AND MY LIFE IS PRESERVED.

(31) "AND AS HE PASSED OVER PENUEL THE SUN ROSE UPON HIM, AND HE HALTED UPON HIS THIGH.

(32) "THEREFORE THE CHILDREN OF ISRAEL EAT NOT OF THE SINEW WHICH SHRANK, WHICH IS UPON THE HOLLOW OF THE THIGH, UNTO THIS DAY: BECAUSE HE TOUCHED THE HOLLOW OF JACOB'S THIGH IN THE SINEW THAT SHRANK."

The exegesis is:

1. In this Chapter, and in Hosea, Chapter 12, this Man is called God, the Angels, Elohim Sabaoth, and Jehovah.

2. In this scenario, we find that it was not with Esau his brother with whom he had to contend, but with Jehovah Himself. This is always the case with every Believer.

3. The great principle that God cannot give victory to *"the flesh,"* appears in this night scene.

4. It is the broken heart that begins to experience what Divine power means. Better for the sun to rise upon a limping Israel than to set upon a lying Jacob.

5. Jacob, for his misconduct, was exiled from the Promised Land, having nothing but his staff. He returns a wealthy prince, but lamed. So Israel cast out of Jehovah's land because of her sin will return with abundance, and we speak of the time of the Second Coming, but broken and contrite in spirit (Williams).

THE WRESTLING

Verse 24 reads: *"And Jacob was left alone; and there wrestled a Man with him until the breaking of the day."*

In the *"making of a man"* we find here a turning point in the history of this very remarkable person. To be left alone with God is the only true way of arriving at a just knowledge of ourselves and our ways. We can never get a true estimate of nature and all its operations until we have weighed them in the balance of the Sanctuary, so to speak, and there we ascertain their real worth. No matter what we may think about ourselves, nor yet what man may think about us; the great question is, what does God think about us? And the answer to this question can only be heard when we are *"left alone."* Away from the world; away from self; away from all the thoughts, reasonings, imaginations, and emotions of mere nature, and *"alone"* with God; thus, and thus alone, can we get a correct judgment about ourselves.

Please note it was not Jacob wrestling with a man, but a Man wrestling with Jacob. My wrestling with a man, and a man wrestling with me, present two totally different ideas to the mind. In the former case, I want to gain some object from him; in the latter, he wants to gain some object from me. In Jacob's case, the Divine object was to bring him to see what a poor, feeble, worthless creature he was (Mackintosh).

This *"Man"* Who wrestled with Jacob, was none other than Jehovah, i.e., *"a preincarnate appearance of the Lord Jesus Christ."*

THE WRESTLING OF GOD WITH US

Two things are brought here into play:

1. The struggle, whatever direction it might take as it regards the Believer, is always on the part of God with us. This we must never forget. The initiative is always with Him, and it begins immediately at conversion.

2. This struggle is to bring us to a particular place in the spiritual sense. In other words, we must come to the end of self, to where our trust and Faith is always in God, and for everything. While most all Believers think of themselves in this capacity, the truth is, the *"flesh"* is far more predominant in us, than even the best of us realize, whoever that might be. So the purpose is away from self-reliance to total reliance on God. And to be sure, the Believer is not brought to that place quickly or easily.

As we have stated, the Holy Spirit through Abraham showed us *"Justification by Faith."* It took about 12 Chapters in this great Book of Genesis to do that. Jacob showed us *"Sanctification by Faith,"* and it took about 25 Chapters, nearly double the amount of the former. This means that it's much easier to *"receive this life,"* than it is to *"live this life."*

THE FLESH

Verse 25 reads: *"And when He saw that He prevailed not against him, He touched the hollow of his thigh; and the hollow of Jacob's thigh was out of joint, as he wrestled with Him."*

The sentence of death must be written on the flesh — the power of the Cross must be entered into before we can steadily walk with God.

We have followed Jacob so far, amid all the windings and workings of his extraordinary character — we have seen him planning and managing during his 20 years sojourn with Laban; but not until he *"was left alone"* did he get a true idea of what a perfectly helpless thing he was in himself.

The dislocating of Jacob's hip reduced his strength to little more than zero. This is what it was meant to do. All of his life, Jacob had depended on his scheming and ability. By the Lord crippling him, this was to serve as a symbol of the eradication of the flesh, and total dependence on the Lord. As Jacob was left a cripple, so must the flesh in all of us be crippled to the extent that it can no longer be leaned upon.

WHAT IS THE FLESH?

Paul uses this term *"flesh"* very often (Rom. 3:20; 6:19; 7:5, 18, 25; 8:1, 3, 5, 8).

When he speaks of the *"flesh,"* he is speaking of our own ability, strength, acumen, power, etc. In other words, what we can do as a human being, apart from the Holy Spirit.

Of course, as human beings we are made of flesh, and we have to live our lives in the flesh, even as Paul said (Gal. 2:20).

However, when it comes to living for God, which refers to Holiness and Righteousness, and Christlikeness in every respect, such cannot be produced by our own strength, ability, etc. All of these things are works of the Holy Spirit, and can, accordingly, be carried out exclusively by Him.

But this is the hardest thing for the Believer to learn. We keep trying to make ourselves holy, to make ourselves righteous, all by our efforts, actions, and ability. It's hard for us to learn that it cannot be done. But regrettably, probably about 90 percent of all the actions of Believers present that which are functions of the flesh.

So if we do not attain to Holiness and Righteousness by our own efforts and ability, whatever that might be, how in fact do we come to these places and positions in Christ?

WALKING AFTER THE SPIRIT

Paul said: *"There is now no condemnation to them who are in Christ Jesus, who walk not after the flesh but after the Spirit"* (Rom. 8:1).

So how does one *"walk after the Spirit,"* which alone can bring the person to the desired place in Christ?

Let us give the answer first. Walking after the Spirit is simply looking totally and completely to Christ and what He has done for us at the Cross, which is always the domain of the Holy Spirit. In other words, the Holy Spirit works exclusively within the parameters of the Finished Work of Christ. The Cross made it possible for Him to function within us as He does. He demands that we have Faith in that Finished Work, which of course is the Sacrifice of Christ, which is

referred to as *"His Sufferings."* To explain this, Paul said: *"For the Law* (a Law devised by the Godhead) *of the Spirit* (Holy Spirit) *of life* (all life comes from Christ through the Spirit) *in Christ Jesus* (meaning that everything the Spirit does within our lives is all done through and by what Jesus did at the Cross) *has made me free from the law of sin and death"* (Rom. 8:2).

This one Verse tells us how the Holy Spirit works. It is all *"in Christ Jesus,"* which refers to His great Sacrifice. So, simple Faith in that constitutes *"walking after the Spirit."*

Unfortunately, many Believers think that doing spiritual things constitutes walking after the Spirit. It doesn't!

While doing spiritual things may be very good, and I speak of reading the Bible, witnessing to the lost, engaging in prayer, giving money to the Work of the Lord, etc., these things in fact, should be a result of walking after the Spirit, but do not, within themselves, constitute walking after the Spirit.

DEAD TO THE FLESH

Since the Early Church, I suppose, Christians have been trying to *"die to the flesh,"* or whatever type of terminology one would like to use. Growing up as a child, I heard this statement I suppose untold numbers of times.

Any Christian who is trying to die to the flesh always (and I use *"always"* advisedly) tries to do so by the flesh. And to be sure, the flesh cannot subdue the flesh. All of this results in such a Christian being about one of the meanest Christians you've ever met in all of your life.

The only way that one can *"die to the flesh"* is by simply looking to Christ, and what Christ did at the Cross. Our Faith is to be in Him and His Finished Work. This means that we are not trusting in ourselves, but totally in what He has done for us.

This is something that we must actually do on a daily basis, hence Jesus saying: *"If any man will come after Me, let him deny himself, and take up his cross daily, and follow Me"* (Lk. 9:23).

This is something we work at day-by-day, even as the Master said. We die to the flesh by being in what He has done, and only what He has done.

THE BLESSING

Verse 26 reads: *"And He* (the Lord) *said, Let Me go, for the day breaks. And he* (Jacob) *said, I will not let You go, except You bless me."*

When sore broken by that mighty Hand, he ceased to wrestle and clung with weeping and supplication to the very God Who wounded him, then it was that he got the victory and the glorious name of Israel (Williams).

Up to this point he had held fast by his own ways and means; but now he is brought to say, *"I will not let You go."* Now, let the Reader understand that Jacob did not express himself thus until *"the hollow of his thigh was touched."* May we learn to cling more simply to God Alone, that so our history may be more characterized by that holy elevation above the circumstances through which we are passing. It is not, by any means, an easy matter to get to the end of *"flesh,"* in every shape and form, so as to be able to say, *"I will not let You go except You bless me."* To say this from the heart, and to abide in the power of it, is the secret of all true strength. Jacob said it when the hollow of his thigh was touched; but not until then. He struggled long, ere he gave way, because his confidence in the flesh was strong. *"The Power of Christ"* can only *"Rest on us"* in connection with the knowledge of our infirmities. Christ cannot put the seal of His approval upon nature's strength, its wisdom, or its glory: all these must sink that He may rise. Nature can never form, in any one way, a pedestal on which to display the Grace or Power of Christ; for if it could, then might flesh glory in His Presence; but this, we know, can never be.

The *"Blessing"* which Jacob had schemed and planned to get, and for so many years, he now knows can only be given to him by God. And so, many presently, and possibly all of us at one time or the other, have tried to gain the Blessing in all the wrong ways. It can only be obtained through the Cross, and our Faith in that Finished Work. There is no other way!

ISRAEL

Verses 27 and 28 read: *"And He* (the Lord) *said unto him* (Jacob), *What is your name? And he said, Jacob.*

"And He said, Your name shall be called no more Jacob, but Israel: for as a prince have you power with God and with men, and have prevailed."

It should be readily understandable that the Lord already knew Jacob's name. So why did He insist on Jacob pronouncing his name?

He wanted Jacob to admit who and what he actually was. And to be sure, that just might be the hardest task for the Lord to perform within our lives. We do not yield easily to the truth. We like to think of ourselves in glowing terms, and whatever our problems, we minimize them, while at the same time, almost always we magnify the problems of others. But it was not until Jacob fully admitted what he actually was, which was a deceiver, a trickster, and a supplanter, that the Lord then blessed him.

Grace is a peculiar thing. We must be disqualified and admit that we don't deserve it, before we are qualified to receive it. To say it another way, the qualification for Grace is to be disqualified.

Upon the admittance as to what he actually was, the Lord then instituted the change. It was symbolized by his name being changed from *"Jacob the deceiver,"* to *"Israel the prince with God."* What a change!

And yet, as we shall see, Jacob's change was instant, but yet gradual. What do we mean by that?

PROGRESSIVE SANCTIFICATION

Possibly we are witnessing here both *"positional Sanctification"* and *"conditional Sanctification."* As far as God was concerned, Jacob's new position regarding Sanctification had now been established, and would be unmovable, because it is established in Christ. However, his *"condition,"* as will be painfully obvious through the remainder of the Book of Genesis, will not always be up to his *"position."* So during the times that the *"condition"* falls short, the Lord refers to the Patriarch as *"Jacob."* The times it reaches up to his *"position,"* he is referred to as *"Israel."* Consequently, we will find, as Jacob's life goes forward, that little by little through the years, he is more and more referred to as *"Israel."* And so it is prayerfully with us. We grow in Grace and the knowledge of the Lord, or at least that should be the idea (II Pet. 3:18).

PENIEL

Verses 29 through 32 read: *"And Jacob asked him, and said, Tell me, I pray You, Your name. And He said, Wherefore is it that you do ask after My name? And He blessed him there.*

"And Jacob called the name of the place Peniel: for I have seen God face to face, and my life is preserved.

"And as he passed over Penuel the sun rose upon him, and he halted upon his thigh.

"Therefore the children of Israel eat not of the sinew which shrank, which is upon the hollow of the thigh, unto this day: because he touched the hollow of Jacob's thigh in the sinew that shrank."

As is obvious here, Jacob asks the name of the One with Whom he wrestled. The Lord's answer is revealing. He responded with another question:

"Wherefore is it that you do ask after My name?" The idea is, Jacob by now ought to know Who the One is with Whom he has been struggling. And the next statements prove that he did.

When the Scripture says that the Lord *"blessed him there,"* He was in effect giving Jacob at that moment *"power with God and with men."*

Showing that Jacob now knew the One with Whom he had struggled, he names the place *"Peniel,"* which means, *"the face of God,"* or *"I have seen God face to face, and my life is preserved."*

Man, whomever he might be, and whatever he might be, must have a Revelation from God, exactly as did Jacob. It may be somewhat different, and it may not be quite as dramatic as that which Jacob experienced; however, to the individual involved, it will definitely be dramatic and, therefore, life-changing.

Now please understand, we're not speaking here of manifestation nearly as much as we are speaking of Revelation.

I can say without fear of contradiction that every single person down through history, who has truly been Born-Again, has always come by this tremendous, life-changing experience, by a Revelation from God. If there has been no Revelation, there has been no *"born*

again" experience. And please believe me, if there has truly been a Born-Again experience, the individual will know that of which I speak.

The Church is too full of individuals who have mentally accepted the Lord, at least after a fashion. They have been somewhat intellectually moved, but they've never really had a Born-Again experience. In other words, there's never been a Revelation of God to their souls. Therefore, while they might be religious, they aren't truly saved.

The means by which the Lord has chosen to make evident this Revelation is the Cross, always the Cross! Unless the Cross enters the picture, there can be no Revelation, simply because the Cross is the means by which the Grace of God is extended to undeserving souls. And whenever the believing sinner sees the Cross, to be sure, he will see Christ, and the Revelation will be evident.

A NEW DAY

The sun is now rising, but upon a crippled Jacob. The crippling did not bring about instant Sanctification, at least as far as the conduct of Jacob was concerned. But it brought about the possibility of such, which was ultimately made real in Jacob's life.

As Believers, we have to first of all understand that all victory, all solutions, and whatever the need might be, stem totally and completely from the Cross of Christ. Once we learn this Divine truth, which is the foundation of truth, then we will begin to properly see ourselves, i.e., *"the flesh."* Blessed be the day that the sun rose upon Jacob, for he has passed a milestone in the *"making of a man."*

THE SINEW WHICH SHRANK

This particular sinew is the proper name for the large tendon which takes its origin from the spinal chord, and extends down the thigh unto the ankle. It was called by the Greeks the *"tendo Achillis,"* because it reaches to the heel. So, the *"heel catcher"* became a *"Prince with God."*

Whether Jacob remained crippled all of his life, or was this way for a short period of time, we aren't told. Nevertheless, this was so prominent in Jewish thinking that it became a symbol of Jacob's tryst with God, or perhaps it could be better said, *"God's tryst with Jacob."*

"Jesus, wondrous Saviour! Christ, of kings, the King!

"Angels fall before Thee, prostrate, worshipping;

"Fairest they confess Thee in the Heaven above.

"We would sing Thee fairest here and hymns of love;"

"All Earth's flowing pleasures were a wintry sea,

"Heaven itself without Thee dark as night would be.

"Lamb of God! Thy glory is the light above.

"Lamb of God! Thy glory is the life of love."

"Life is death, if severed from Your throbbing heart.

"Death with life abundant at Your touch would start.

"Worlds and men and Angels all consist in Thee:

"Yet You came to us in humility."

"Jesus! All perfections rise and end in Thee;

"Brightness of God's glory Thou, eternally.

"Favored beyond measure they Thy face who see;

"May we, gracious Saviour, share this ecstasy."

CHAPTER 33

(1) "AND JACOB LIFTED UP HIS EYES AND LOOKED, AND, BEHOLD, ESAU CAME, AND WITH HIM FOUR HUNDRED MEN. AND HE DIVIDED THE CHILDREN UNTO LEAH, AND UNTO RACHEL, AND UNTO THE TWO HANDMAIDS.

(2) "AND HE PUT THE HANDMAIDS AND THEIR CHILDREN FOREMOST, AND LEAH AND HER CHILDREN AFTER, AND RACHEL AND JOSEPH HINDERMOST.

(3) "AND HE PASSED OVER BEFORE THEM, AND BOWED HIMSELF TO THE GROUND SEVEN TIMES, UNTIL HE CAME NEAR TO HIS BROTHER.

(4) "AND ESAU RAN TO MEET HIM, AND EMBRACED HIM, AND FELL ON HIS NECK, AND KISSED HIM: AND THEY WEPT.

(5) "AND HE LIFTED UP HIS EYES, AND SAW THE WOMEN AND THE CHILDREN; AND SAID, WHO ARE THOSE WITH YOU? AND HE SAID, THE CHILDREN WHICH GOD HAS GRACIOUSLY GIVEN YOUR SERVANT.

(6) "THEN THE HANDMAIDENS CAME NEAR, THEY AND THEIR CHILDREN, AND THEY BOWED THEMSELVES.

(7) "AND LEAH ALSO WITH HER CHILDREN CAME NEAR, AND BOWED THEMSELVES: AND AFTER CAME JOSEPH NEAR AND RACHEL, AND THEY BOWED THEMSELVES."

The synopsis is:

1. The action of Esau shows how groundless were Jacob's fears, and how needless his plans.

2. The straight path of Faith and obedience is free from the tormenting apprehensions which wear out the doubting heart.

3. It is obvious that Esau is a powerful Chieftain. How so sad that this man did not see the great spiritual truths. In that case, it would have been, *"The God of Abraham, Isaac, and Esau."* But such was not to be!

ESAU

Verse 1 reads: *"And Jacob lifted up his eyes, and looked, and, behold, Esau came, and with him four hundred men. And he* (Jacob) *divided the children unto Leah, and unto Rachel, and unto the two handmaids."*

The time has come that Jacob and Esau will now meet. Jacob sees him coming with his cortege of some 400 men.

Esau, at this particular time, must have been a powerful Chieftain, at least one of, if not the most powerful in that part of the world.

But while Esau had 400 men, armed no doubt, Jacob had a host of Angels, while unseen, but yet, so powerful!

Some have criticized Jacob as it regards the preparation concerning his family, especially considering that he has just had this great visitation from the Lord, with great promises further extended to him. I think, however, we do wrong when we always judge Faith according to perfection. No man's faith is perfect. Even the best of us, whomever that might be, are always in a growing process. If we demand perfection out of Jacob, why don't we, especially considering that we are now living under a better Covenant, demand perfection of ourselves? While never condoning wrongdoing, or even a lack of faith, still, if in his shoes, would we have done any better, or even as well? Armchair generals and Monday morning quarterbacks are a dime a dozen. But until you've been there, it is best to withhold judgment, and rather try to learn the lesson which the Holy Spirit desires to teach us from the Text.

Many, many years ago, one of the Pilgrim Fathers preached a message, containing the following points, which we would do well to heed presently. They are:

1. When we hear something bad about someone, we should realize that what we are hearing is gossip, and treat it accordingly.

2. Even if we actually know the facts of the case, the truth is, still, we little know the degree of spiritual warfare involved.

3. If we were placed in their shoes, as stated, would we do any better, or even as well?

HIS BROTHER

Verses 2 through 4 read: *"And he put the handmaids and their children foremost, and Leah and her children after, and Rachel and Joseph hindermost.*

"And he passed over before them, and bowed himself to the ground seven times, until he came near to his brother.

"And Esau ran to meet him, and embraced him, and fell on his neck, and kissed him: and they wept."

If it is to be noticed, Jacob put the ones he thought the least important in the forefront, followed by Leah and her children, and then bringing up the very rear were Rachel and Joseph, whom Jacob looked at the most favorably. As it all proved out, all of this was unnecessary.

As Jacob was approaching Esau, his brother, the Scripture says, *"run to meet him."* He embraced him, kissed him, with both of them weeping.

It was the Lord Who had mellowed Esau, and I think that is obvious. This should be a lesson to us as well.

The Holy Spirit gave to David the following formula, which he gave to us, and if

followed, will lead to spiritual prosperity. It is:

"Trust in the LORD, and do good; so shall you dwell in the land, and verily you shall be fed.

"Delight yourself also in the LORD: and He shall give you the desires of your heart.

"Commit your way unto the LORD; trust also in Him; and He shall bring it to pass.

"Rest in the LORD, and wait patiently for Him" (Ps. 37:3-5, 7).

To abbreviate what is said here, we can reduce it to four words. They are:

1. Trust
2. Delight
3. Commit
4. Rest.

A proper adherence to these Passages will solve any problem.

THE MEETING

Verses 5 through 7 read: *"And he lifted up his eyes, and saw the women and the children; and said, Who are those with you? And he said, The children which God has graciously given your servant.*

"Then the handmaidens came near, they and their children, and they bowed themselves.

"And Leah also with her children came near, and bowed themselves: and after came Joseph near and Rachel, and they bowed themselves."

All of this proclaims the fact that the entirety of the family of Jacob showed great respect to Esau, which they should have done. Little did the older brother know (older by a few moments) that this family was the seedbed of the great nation of Israel, to whom would be given the great Promises of God. Here they stand by the Brook Jabbok, and if the mighty men of the world had taken notice of this retinue, they would have scarcely given it a second glance.

From the time that God had called Abraham out of Ur of the Chaldees, to this particular time of Jacob, had been a little less than 200 years. The boys upon whom Esau looked would be the beginning of great Tribes, and from one of these, Judah, would come the Prince of Glory, of Whom Esau had no knowledge. This, in effect, was the *"birthright"* of which he had no interest. In fact, he never did understand spiritual things, and because he couldn't understand spiritual things.

(8) "AND HE SAID, WHAT DO YOU MEAN BY ALL THIS DROVE WHICH I MET? AND HE SAID, THESE ARE TO FIND GRACE IN THE SIGHT OF MY LORD.

(9) "AND ESAU SAID, I HAVE ENOUGH, MY BROTHER: KEEP THAT YOU HAVE UNTO YOURSELF.

(10) "AND JACOB SAID, NO, I PRAY YOU, IF NOW I HAVE FOUND GRACE IN YOUR SIGHT, THEN RECEIVE MY PRESENT AT MY HAND: FOR THEREFORE I HAVE SEEN YOUR FACE, AS THOUGH I HAD SEEN THE FACE OF GOD, AND YOU WERE PLEASED WITH ME.

(11) "TAKE, I PRAY YOU, MY BLESSING THAT IS BROUGHT TO YOU; BECAUSE GOD HAS DEALT GRACIOUSLY WITH ME, AND BECAUSE I HAVE ENOUGH. AND HE URGED HIM, AND HE TOOK IT.

(12) "AND HE SAID, LET US TAKE OUR JOURNEY, AND LET US GO, AND I WILL GO BEFORE YOU.

(13) "AND HE SAID UNTO HIM, MY LORD KNOWS THAT THE CHILDREN ARE TENDER, AND THE FLOCKS AND HERDS WITH YOUNG ARE WITH ME: AND IF MEN SHOULD OVERDRIVE THEM ONE DAY, ALL THE FLOCK WILL DIE.

(14) "LET MY LORD, I PRAY YOU, PASS OVER BEFORE HIS SERVANT: AND I WILL LEAD ON SOFTLY, ACCORDING AS THE CATTLE THAT GOES BEFORE ME AND THE CHILDREN BE ABLE TO ENDURE, UNTIL I COME UNTO MY LORD UNTO SEIR.

(15) "AND ESAU SAID, LET ME NOW LEAVE WITH YOU SOME OF THE FOLK WHO ARE WITH ME. AND HE SAID, WHAT NEEDS IT? LET ME FIND GRACE IN THE SIGHT OF MY LORD."

The diagram is:

1. In Eastern countries, the acceptance of a gift is equivalent to the striking of a Covenant of friendship. If it is declined, there is no friendship.

2. Esau took the gift proposed by Jacob, signifying his acceptance of friendship.

3. He mentioned about coming to where Esau lived at Seir, but there is no record that he ever went there.

NOTES

THE GIFT

Verses 8 through 11 read: *"And he said, What do you mean by all this drove which I met? And he said, These are to find grace in the sight of my lord.*

"And Esau said, I have enough, my brother; keep that you have unto yourself.

"And Jacob said, No, I pray you, if now I have found grace in your sight, then receive my present at my hand: for therefore I have seen your face, as though I had seen the face of God, and you were pleased with me.

"Take, I pray you, my blessing that is brought to you; because God has dealt graciously with me, and because I have enough. And he urged him, and he took it."

In the Eastern countries of that particular time, the thing which Jacob proposed, as it regarded the giving of this gracious gift to Esau, was very, very important.

In the first place, the gift was to be a token signifying that the difficulty had been settled.

Second, if the problem was serious, the one offering the gift was to make it commiserate with the problem itself. In other words, the largeness of Jacob's gift signified that he felt that he had greatly wronged Esau.

Last of all, if the recipient took the gift, it means that the matter was dropped, forgiven, and would not cause further problems. So concerning the gift, when the Scripture says that Esau *"took it,"* this signified that the difference between he and Jacob had now been settled.

SEIR

Verses 12 through 15 read: *"And he said, Let us take our journey, and let us go, and I will go before you.*

"And he said unto him, My lord knows that the children are tender, and the flocks and herds with young are with me: and if men should overdrive them one day, all the flock will die.

"Let my lord, I pray you, pass over before his servant: and I will lead on softly, according as the cattle that goes before me and the children be able to endure, until I come unto my lord unto Seir.

"And Esau said, Let me now leave with you some of the folk who are with me. And he said, What needs it? Let me find grace in the sight of my lord."

Jacob, in a sense, mentions the fact that he would eventually come to Esau in Seir; however, there is no record that Jacob ever went to this particular place.

Despite the fact that they had settled their differences between them, the two, although twins, had nothing in common.

Whenever a person comes to the Lord, everything changes. That's why the Scripture says, *"Old things pass away, and all things become new"* (II Cor. 5:17).

(16) "SO ESAU RETURNED THAT DAY ON HIS WAY UNTO SEIR.

(17) "AND JACOB JOURNEYED TO SUCCOTH, AND BUILT HIM AN HOUSE, AND MADE BOOTHS FOR HIS CATTLE: THEREFORE THE NAME OF THE PLACE IS CALLED SUCCOTH.

(18) "AND JACOB CAME TO SHALEM, A CITY OF SHECHEM, WHICH IS IN THE LAND OF CANAAN, WHEN HE CAME FROM PADAN-ARAM; AND PITCHED HIS TENT BEFORE THE CITY.

(19) "AND HE BOUGHT A PARCEL OF A FIELD, WHERE HE HAD SPREAD HIS TENT, AT THE HAND OF THE CHILDREN OF HAMOR, SHECHEM'S FATHER, FOR AN HUNDRED PIECES OF MONEY.

(20) "AND HE ERECTED THERE AN ALTAR, AND CALLED IT EL-ELOHE-ISRAEL."

The structure is:

1. Jacob went to Succoth. But the Lord had not said *"I am the God of Succoth,"* but rather, *"I am the God of Beth-el."* Events will prove that he was not in the Will of God.

2. Jacob erects an Altar at Shechem, for the conscience is uneasy without religious forms, but the Divinely chosen place for the Altar was Beth-el.

3. The Altar was a Type of the Cross. While the Cross is the place for wrongdoing, and in fact, the only place; still, it is never to be used to condone wrongdoing, and it cannot cover wrongdoing which is the Believer has no intention of forsaking

SUCCOTH

Verses 16 through 20 read: *"So Esau returned that day on his way unto Seir.*

"And Jacob journeyed to Succoth, and built him an house, and made booths for his

cattle: therefore the name of the place is called Succoth.

"And Jacob came to Shalem, a city of Shechem, which is in the land of Canaan, when he came from Padan-aram; and pitched his tent before the city.

"And he bought a parcel of a field, where he had spread his tent, at the hand of the children of Hamor, Shechem's father, for an hundred pieces of money.

"And he erected there an Altar, and called it El-elohe-Israel."

Several things are wrong as presented in these Passages:

1. Jacob was not told by the Lord to go to Succoth.

2. This is the first mention of a house being built by a Patriarch. He was to be a pilgrim instead.

His *"buying a parcel of a field,"* only made a bad matter worse.

3. He built an Altar, but it was not in the right place.

4. He called it *"God, the God of Israel."* Its name given by him, however, couldn't atone for the Altar being built in the wrong place.

Some, if not all these things may seem to be innocent. In face, they very well may be; however, the idea which we wish to present proclaims the fact that if one is out of the Will of God, everything one does lends toward the wrong direction.

"Praise the Lord: ye heavens adore Him;
praise Him, Angels in the height;
"Sun and moon, rejoice before Him,
praise Him, all ye stars of light.
"Praise the Lord, for He has spoken;
worlds His mighty Voice obeyed:
"Laws which never shall be broken, for
their guidance He has made."

"Praise the Lord, for He is glorious;
never shall His Promise fail:
"God has made His saints victorious;
sin and death shall not prevail.
"Praise the God of our Salvation; hosts
on high, His power proclaim;
"Heaven and Earth and all creation,
laud and magnify His name."

"Worship, honor, glory, blessing, Lord,
we offer unto Thee;

"Young and old, Thy praise expressing,
in glad homage bend the knee.
"All the Saints in Heaven adore Thee;
we will bow before Thy Throne:
"As Thine Angels serve before Thee, so
on Earth Thy will be done."

CHAPTER 34

(1) "AND DINAH THE DAUGHTER OF LEAH, WHICH SHE BEAR UNTO JACOB, WENT OUT TO SEE THE DAUGHTERS OF THE LAND.

(2) "AND WHEN SHECHEM THE SON OF HAMOR THE HIVITE, PRINCE OF THE COUNTRY, SAW HER, HE TOOK HER, AND LAY WITH HER, AND DEFILED HER.

(3) "AND HIS SOUL CLAVE UNTO DINAH THE DAUGHTER OF JACOB, AND HE LOVED THE DAMSEL, AND SPAKE KINDLY UNTO THE DAMSEL.

(4) "AND SHECHEM SPAKE UNTO HIS FATHER HAMOR, SAYING, GET ME THIS DAMSEL TO WIFE.

(5) "AND JACOB HEARD THAT HE HAD DEFILED DINAH HIS DAUGHTER: NOW HIS SONS WERE WITH HIS CATTLE IN THE FIELD: AND JACOB HELD HIS PEACE UNTIL THEY WERE COME.

(6) "AND HAMOR THE FATHER OF SHECHEM WENT OUT UNTO JACOB TO COMMUNE WITH HIM.

(7) "AND THE SONS OF JACOB CAME OUT OF THE FIELD WHEN THEY HEARD IT: AND THE MEN WERE GRIEVED, AND THEY WERE VERY ANGRY, BECAUSE HE HAD WROUGHT FOLLY IN ISRAEL IN LYING WITH JACOB'S DAUGHTER: WHICH THING OUGHT NOT TO BE DONE."

The composition is:

1. Jacob is here personally responsible for the conduct of his children. This principle operates today as well.

2. Dinah goes out to see the daughters of the land. That seemed very innocent. But these daughters led to a companionship with shame. The Christian has to be very careful concerning the world and its ways.

3. Consequently, we see, in this Chapter, the bitter fruits of the sojourn of Jacob at Shechem.

NOTES

DINAH

Verse 1 reads: *"And Dinah the daughter of Leah, which she bear unto Jacob, went out to see the daughters of the land."*

It is believed that Dinah was about 16 or 17 years of age at the time. The thing which took place with her did not happen immediately after Jacob came to Succoth, but more than likely, several years later.

The evidence is, a festive gathering was taking place, and Dinah desired to be a part of the social entertainment.

Her going out to *"see the daughters of the land,"* is not meant to imply that she had not done this previously. This particular time is highlighted for the simple reason of what happened to her.

The Believer has to be very, very careful as far as the world is concerned. While we must not become legalistic, at the same time, we must understand that the world and its ways are not our friend. Satan has many temptations and snares in the world, which have tripped up many Believers, Dinah not being the first or the last.

Understanding these things, we are foolish if we ignore the allurement of the world and its dangers. While we as Believers are in the world, we must never be of the world. We believe in separation, but not isolation. And to be factual, separation is very, very important! The moment separation breaks down is the moment the problem begins, even as with Dinah.

SHECHEM

Verses 2 and 3 read: *"And when Shechem the son of Hamor the Hivite, prince of the country, saw her, he took her, and lay with her, and defiled her.*

"And his soul clave unto Dinah the daughter of Jacob, and he loved the damsel, and spake kindly unto the damsel."

The Pulpit Commentary says: *"Dinah paid the full penalty of her carelessness. She suffered the fate which Satan had planned for Sarah and Rebekah in the land of Pharaoh and Abimelech; she was seen and taken by the son of the prince, forcibly it seems, against her will, but yet with the claims of affection by her lover."*

It does seem that he actually loved her, and *"spoke kindly unto her,"* which probably refers to marriage.

Whatever it seemed at the moment, all of this was an attempt by Satan to spoil the Godly line with intermarriage, which both Abraham and Isaac sought so diligently to avoid.

The Believer must ever understand that Satan and his demon hosts are forever seeking to hinder and hurt in some way. That's the reason the Scripture plainly tells us to *"watch and pray"* (Mat. 26:41). When we speak of Christians doing certain things or not doing certain things, it's not a matter of legalism, but rather a matter of the possibility of Satan getting the advantage. Because of its great significance, let us say it again:

We as Believers must evaluate every single thing we do, every place we go, and all the things we propose. Can the Evil One use whatever it is we propose to do as an avenue to cause us problems? That's the basic reason that the Scripture also says that we are to *"abstain from all appearance of evil"* (I Thess. 5:22).

THE PLAN OF SATAN

Verses 4 through 7 read: *"And Shechem spake unto his father Hamor, saying, Get me this damsel to wife.*

"And Jacob heard that he had defiled Dinah his daughter: now his sons were with his cattle in the field: and Jacob held his peace until they were come.

"And Hamor the father of Shechem went out unto Jacob to commune with him.

"And the sons of Jacob came out of the field when they heard it: and the men were grieved, and they were very angry, because he had wrought folly in Israel in lying with Jacob's daughter: which thing ought not to be done."

The Scripture uses the phrase *"Jacob's daughter,"* in order to proclaim the fact that this was as bad as it could be. It would have been bad enough if one of Jacob's handmaids had been raped, but his daughter. . . .

Marriages were arranged in those days, so Shechem asked his father Hamor to work out the arrangement with Jacob that Dinah could now be his wife.

The account of all of this tells us that Dinah's brothers were extremely angry when they heard this sordid news about their sister.

In those times, it was thought that a brother was more dishonored by the seduction of his

sister than a man could be by the infidelity of his wife. A man may divorce his wife, and then she is no longer his, they reasoned, while a sister and daughter remain always sister and daughter.

In Verse 7, the word *"Israel"* is used for the first time to designate Jacob's descendants, which actually became the great nation of Israel. And the phrase *"folly in Israel"* became a standing expression for acts done against the sacred character which belonged to Israel as a separated and covenanted community, as the people of God. This expression was used more so for sins of the flesh than anything else (Deut. 22:21; Judg. 20:10; Jer. 29:23).

Pulpit Commentary says: *"The special wickedness of Shechem consisted in dishonoring a daughter of one who was the head of the theocratic line, and therefore under peculiar obligations to lead a holy life."*

Unfortunately, it becomes painfully obvious as to the sordid failure of almost all concerned, even as shortly we will read the account of Joseph's brothers seeking to kill him. Despite the fact that the Church is also a holy line in this world, and even more so one might say than Israel of old; still, the problem is just as acute, if not more so presently, than then.

Dinah was partly to blame here, but Jacob and Leah were far more to blame. They should not have allowed their daughter to frequent the festivities of the Canaanites.

It is understandable that young girls and young boys would want companionship of their own age, which more than likely Dinah lacked. And as well, it is almost certain that the festivities of that particular time were very enticing.

Perhaps Dinah went to this entertainment without the knowledge of her Mother and Dad; however, that is not likely. Not wanting to say *"no,"* to their daughter, the thought is probably correct that they allowed her to attend, but to their chagrin. As young girls would do, she no doubt pestered them for permission, wanting to go. In such a situation, it is much easier to say, *"yes,"* than it is to say *"no."* However, the results of saying *"yes,"* can be very painful, as the Holy Spirit here makes very plain.

(8) "AND HAMOR COMMUNED WITH THEM, SAYING, THE SOUL OF MY SON SHECHEM LONGS FOR YOUR DAUGHTER: I PRAY YOU GIVE HER HIM TO WIFE.

(9) "AND MAKE YOU MARRIAGES WITH US, AND GIVE YOUR DAUGHTERS UNTO US, AND TAKE OUR DAUGHTERS UNTO YOU.

(10) "AND YOU SHALL DWELL WITH US: AND THE LAND SHALL BE BEFORE YOU; DWELL AND TRADE YOU THEREIN, AND GET YOU POSSESSIONS THEREIN.

(11) "AND SHECHEM SAID UNTO HER (DINAH'S) FATHER AND UNTO HER BRETHREN, LET ME FIND GRACE IN YOUR EYES, AND WHAT YOU SHALL SAY UNTO ME I WILL GIVE.

(12) "ASK ME NEVER SO MUCH DOWRY AND GIFT, AND I WILL GIVE ACCORDING AS YOU SHALL SAY UNTO ME: BUT GIVE ME THE DAMSEL TO WIFE."

The structure is:

1. By the act of intermarriage, Satan would compromise and corrupt the sacred lineage.

2. The end result of this plan as fomented by Satan was to ultimately stop the Incarnation. This lineage must be kept pure.

3. The plan was, *"You shall dwell with us,"* meaning the Canaanites, and in a sense, that is still Satan's plan regarding Believers. That's why Paul said, and speaking in a spiritual sense, *"Wherefore come out from among them, and be ye separate, saith the Lord, and touch not the unclean thing; and I will receive you"* (II Cor. 6:17).

DWELL WITH US

Verses 8 through 10 read: *"And Hamor communed with them, saying, The soul of my son Shechem longs for your daughter: I pray you give him her to wife.*

"And make you marriages with us, and give your daughters unto us, and take our daughters unto you.

"And you shall dwell with us: and the land shall be before you; dwell and trade you therein, and get you possessions therein."

We shall see, when we come to Chapter 35, Jacob is led to take a higher and a wider view of God; but at Shechem he was manifestly on low ground, and he was made to smart for it, as is always the case when we

stop short of God's Own ground. So we see in Chapter 34, the bitter fruits of his sojourn at Shechem.

Due to being out of the Will of God, which means he was in the wrong place, he walks in constant apprehension of danger to himself and his family, and in the manifestation of an anxious, cautious, timid, calculating spirit, utterly incompatible with a life of genuine faith in God (Mackintosh).

The plan of Satan was to corrupt the sacred line, by intermarriage with the Canaanites, who were a part of the curse originally placed on Canaan, the son of Ham, regarding the situation with Noah (Gen. 9:23-27).

PAYMENT

Verses 11 and 12 read: *"And Shechem said unto her (Dinah's) father and unto her brethren, Let me find grace in your eyes, and what you shall say unto me I will give.*

"Ask me never so much dowry and gift, and I will give according as you shall say unto me: but give me the damsel to wife."

The *"dowry"* represented the price paid for a wife to her parents (Ex. 22:16; I Sam. 18:25).

In essence, Shechem was saying that whatever they asked, as far as monetary value was concerned, he would pay it.

(13) "AND THE SONS OF JACOB ANSWERED SHECHEM AND HAMOR HIS FATHER DECEITFULLY, AND SAID, BECAUSE HE HAD DEFILED DINAH THEIR SISTER:

(14) "AND THEY SAID UNTO THEM, WE CANNOT DO THIS THING, TO GIVE OUR SISTER TO ONE WHO IS UNCIRCUMCISED; FOR THAT IS A REPROACH UNTO US:

(15) "BUT IN THIS WILL WE CONSENT UNTO YOU: IF YOU WILL BE AS WE BE, THAT EVERY MALE OF YOU BE CIRCUMCISED;

(16) "THEN WILL WE GIVE OUR DAUGHTERS UNTO YOU, AND WE WILL TAKE YOUR DAUGHTERS TO US, AND WE WILL DWELL WITH YOU, AND WE WILL BECOME ONE PEOPLE.

(17) "BUT IF YOU WILL NOT HEARKEN UNTO US, TO BE CIRCUMCISED; THEN WE WILL TAKE OUR DAUGHTER, AND WE WILL BE GONE.

(18) "AND THEIR WORDS PLEASED HAMOR, AND SHECHEM HAMOR'S SON.

(19) "AND THE YOUNG MAN DEFERRED NOT TO DO THE THING, BECAUSE HE HAD DELIGHT IN JACOB'S DAUGHTER: AND HE WAS MORE HONORABLE THAN ALL THE HOUSE OF HIS FATHER.

(20) "AND HAMOR AND SHECHEM HIS SON CAME UNTO THE GATE OF THEIR CITY, AND COMMUNED WITH THE MEN OF THEIR CITY, SAYING,

(21) "THESE MEN ARE PEACEABLE WITH US; THEREFORE LET THEM DWELL IN THE LAND, AND TRADE THEREIN; FOR THE LAND, BEHOLD, IT IS LARGE ENOUGH FOR THEM; LET US TAKE THEIR DAUGHTERS TO US FOR WIVES, AND LET US GIVE THEM OUR DAUGHTERS.

(22) "ONLY HEREIN WILL THE MEN CONSENT UNTO US FOR TO DWELL WITH US, TO BE ONE PEOPLE, IF EVERY MALE AMONG US BE CIRCUMCISED, AS THEY ARE CIRCUMCISED.

(23) "SHALL NOT THEIR CATTLE AND THEIR SUBSTANCE AND EVERY BEAST OF THEIRS BE OURS? ONLY LET US CONSENT UNTO THEM, AND THEY WILL DWELL WITH US.

(24) "AND UNTO HAMOR AND UNTO SHECHEM HIS SON HEARKENED ALL THAT WENT OUT OF THE GATE OF HIS CITY; AND EVERY MALE WAS CIRCUMCISED, AND ALL THAT WENT OUT OF THE GATE OF HIS CITY.

(25) "AND IT CAME TO PASS ON THE THIRD DAY, WHEN THEY WERE SORE, THAT TWO OF THE SONS OF JACOB, SIMEON AND LEVI, DINAH'S BRETHREN, TOOK EACH MAN HIS SWORD, AND CAME UPON THE CITY BOLDLY, AND SLEW ALL THE MALES.

(26) "AND THEY SLEW HAMOR AND SHECHEM HIS SON WITH THE EDGE OF THE SWORD, AND TOOK DINAH OUT OF SHECHEM'S HOUSE, AND WENT OUT.

(27) "THE SONS OF JACOB CAME UPON THE SLAIN, AND SPOILED THE CITY, BE-CAUSE THEY HAD DEFILED THEIR SISTER.

(28) "THEY TOOK THEIR SHEEP, AND THEIR OXEN, AND THEIR ASSES, AND THAT WHICH WAS IN THE CITY, AND THAT WHICH WAS IN THE FIELD,

(29) "AND ALL THEIR WEALTH, AND ALL THEIR LITTLE ONES, AND THEIR WIVES TOOK THEY CAPTIVE, AND SPOILED EVEN ALL THAT WAS IN THE HOUSE.

(30) "AND JACOB SAID TO SIMEON AND LEVI, YE HAVE TROUBLED ME TO MAKE ME TO STINK AMONG THE INHABITANTS OF THE LAND, AMONG THE CANAANITES AND THE PERIZZITES: AND I BEING FEW IN NUMBER, THEY SHALL GATHER THEMSELVES TOGETHER AGAINST ME, AND SLAY ME; AND I SHALL BE DESTROYED, I AND MY HOUSE.

(31) "AND THEY SAID, SHOULD HE DEAL WITH OUR SISTER AS WITH AN HARLOT?"

The composition is:

1. The sons of Jacob practiced deceit in this situation, in which Jacob had no part therein.

2. They pledged an agreement with the Canaanites, but demanded that all the males in that area be circumcised. This proposal was sinful, since they had no right to offer the sign of God's Covenant to a heathen people.

3. Verse 23 proclaims the fact that Hamor was practicing deceit as well. In this Hamor said, they would ultimately have all the cattle and substance which then belonged to Jacob.

CIRCUMCISION

Verses 13 through 17 read: *"And the sons of Jacob answered Shechem and Hamor his father deceitfully, and said, because he had defiled Dinah their sister:*

"And they said unto them, We cannot do this thing, to give our sister to one who is uncircumcised; for that is a reproach unto us:

"But in this will we consent unto you: if you will be as we be, that every male of you be circumcised:

"Then will we give our daughters unto you, and we will take your daughters to us, and we will dwell with you, and we will become one people.

"But if you will not hearken unto us, to be circumcised; then will we take our daughter, and we will be gone."

The sons of Jacob are now beginning to show the traits which will lead to their desire to murder Joseph. They concoct a plan, an evil plan incidentally, to avenge their sister Dinah. They will have vengeance not only on the boy who did this and his father, but on all the men and boys of the city, who incidentally had no part in this thing. The sad thing is, this was the Church of its day!

Their proposal to the Shechemites is, if all of their men and boys will be circumcised, then all the people can be joined together. Of course, they had absolutely no intention of doing such a thing.

This thing which they would do would be so cruel, so ungodly, that Jacob, on his deathbed, could offer no excuse or reason for the atrocious cruelty practiced there. ———

This proposal was sinful for three reasons:

1. As stated, they had no right to offer the sign of God's Covenant to a heathen people.

2. They had less right to employ it in ratification of a merely human agreement.

3. They had the least right of all to employ it in duplicity as a mask for their treachery.

THE PROPOSAL ACCEPTED

Verses 18 through 24 read: *"And their words pleased Hamor, and Shechem Hamor's son.*

"And the young man deferred not to do this thing, because he had delight in Jacob's daughter: and he was more honorable than all the house of his father.

"And Hamor and Shechem his son came unto the gate of their city, and communed with the men of their city, saying,

"These men are peaceable with us; therefore let them dwell in the land, and trade therein; for the land, behold, it is large enough for them; let us take their daughters to us for wives, and let us give them our daughters.

"Only herein will the men consent unto us for to dwell with us, to be one people, if every male among us be circumcised, as they are circumcised.

"Shall not their cattle and their substance and every beast of theirs be ours? Only let us consent unto them, and they will dwell with us.

"And unto Hamor and unto Shechem his son hearkened all that went out of the gate of his city; and every male was circumcised, all that went out of the gate of his city."

In that Hamor agreed so readily, we must come to the conclusion that circumcision was something not unknown to them, and as well, something that they regarded as a small price to pay for what they believed they would receive.

It is obvious that the Hivites were few in number, and so the addition of Jacob's large family would make their tribe even stronger, or so they reasoned.

Jacob's sons were of the Semitic stock and, therefore, possessed of high physical and mental endowments; and as they were rich in cattle and other wealth, their incorporation with the people of Shechem, or so they reasoned, would raise it to a high rank.

So they agreed to Hamor's proposal.

THE TERRIBLE DEED

Verses 25 through 31 read: *"And it came to pass on the third day, when they were sore, that two of the sons of Jacob, Simeon and Levi, Dinah's brethren, took each man his sword, and came upon the city boldly, and slew all the males.*

"And they slew Hamor and Shechem his son with the edge of the sword, and took Dinah out of Shechem's house, and went out.

"The sons of Jacob came upon the slain, and spoiled the city, because they had defiled their sister.

"They took their sheep, and their oxen, and their asses, and that which was in the city, and that which was in the field,

"And all their wealth, and all their little ones, and their wives took they captive, and spoiled even all that was in the house.

"And Jacob said to Simeon and Levi, You have troubled me to make me to stink among the inhabitants of the land, among the Canaanites and the Perizzites: and I being few in number, they shall gather themselves together against me, and slay me; and I shall be destroyed, I and my house.

"And they said, Should he deal with our sister as with an harlot?"

There is nothing that would justify what these men did.

They murdered all the men and boys of the small town, and did so in cold blood, one might say. It was Simeon and Levi who committed this vile deed, but their brothers, it seems, helped them in the confiscating of the sheep and oxen, along with *"all their wealth."* Joseph didn't join in this debacle.

The Scripture says they also made captives of all the women and the little children. What they did with these, we aren't told. It even appears that they stripped the dead. In fact, the annals of uncivilized warfare scarcely record a more atrocious crime.

The sin of Shechem was avenged, but it was avenged by the commission of an even greater sin by Simeon and Levi. To say the least, this is certainly not the way that the Kingdom of God was to be spread.

"Not what these hands have done,
"Can save this guilty soul;
"Not what this toiling flesh has borne,
"Can make my spirit whole."

"Not what I feel or do,
"Can give me peace with God;
"Not all my prayers, or sighs, or tears,
"Can ease my awful load."

"Your love to me, O God,
"Not mine, O Lord, to Thee
"Can rid me of this dark unrest,
"And set my spirit free."

"No other work save Thine,
"No meaner blood, will do;
"No strength, save that which is Divine,
"Can bear me safely through."

"I praise the God of Grace,
"I trust His love and might;
"He calls me His, I call Him mine;
"My God, my joy, my light!"

—■—

CHAPTER 35

(1) "AND GOD SAID UNTO JACOB, ARISE, GO UP TO BETH-EL, AND DWELL THERE: AND MAKE THERE AN ALTAR UNTO GOD, THAT APPEARED UNTO YOU WHEN YOU FLED FROM THE FACE OF ESAU YOUR BROTHER.

(2) "AND JACOB SAID UNTO HIS HOUSEHOLD, TO ALL WHO WERE WITH HIM, PUT AWAY THE STRANGE GODS THAT ARE AMONG YOU, AND BE CLEAN, AND CHANGE YOUR GARMENTS:

(3) "AND LET US ARISE, AND GO UP TO BETH-EL; AND I WILL MAKE THERE AN ALTAR UNTO GOD, WHO ANSWERED ME IN THE DAY OF MY DISTRESS, AND WAS WITH ME IN THE WAY WHICH I WENT.

NOTES

(4) "AND THEY GAVE UNTO JACOB ALL THE STRANGE GODS WHICH WERE IN THEIR HAND, AND ALL THE EARRINGS WHICH WERE IN THEIR EARS; AND JACOB HID THEM UNDER THE OAK WHICH WAS BY SHECHEM.

(5) "AND THEY JOURNEYED: AND THE TERROR OF GOD WAS UPON THE CITIES THAT WERE ROUND ABOUT THEM, AND THEY DID NOT PURSUE AFTER THE SONS OF JACOB.

(6) "SO JACOB CAME TO LUZ, WHICH IS IN THE LAND OF CANAAN, THAT IS, BETH-EL, HE AND ALL THE PEOPLE THAT WERE WITH HIM.

(7) "AND HE BUILT THERE AN ALTAR, AND CALLED THE PLACE EL-BETH-EL: BECAUSE THERE GOD APPEARED UNTO HIM, WHEN HE FLED FROM THE FACE OF HIS BROTHER.

(8) "BUT DEBORAH REBEKAH'S NURSE DIED, AND SHE WAS BURIED BENEATH BETH-EL UNDER AN OAK: AND THE NAME OF IT WAS CALLED ALLON-BACHUTH."

The construction is:

1. Jacob is called back to the Altar, the True Altar!

2. He goes *"up"* to Beth-el. Physically and morally it was indeed a going-up.

3. When, therefore, he learns that he is to meet God publicly at Beth-el, he at once feels that idols cannot be brought into fellowship with that House, and accordingly he commands the surrender of all the strange gods that were in their hands and in their ears, and he buried them beneath the oak at Shechem.

THE ALTAR

Verse 1 reads: *"And God said unto Jacob, Arise, go up to Beth-el, and dwell there: and make there an Altar unto God, Who appeared unto you when you fled from the face of Esau your brother."*

Nearly ten years had passed since Jacob had come back to the land of Promise. At that time, those ten years ago, the Lord had said to Jacob, *"Return unto your land, I am the God of Beth-el."* The Lord did not say, *"I am the God of Succoth."* But how slow was he to obey this command! Had he gone immediately to Beth-el, and had he *"dwelt"* there, as commanded, what sin and sorrow would have been avoided! (Williams).

The Lord tells the Patriarch to build an *"Altar"* at Beth-el. He had built one at Succoth, but being out of the Will of God, the Grace of God was hindered.

The words of Paul, some 1,800 years before that great Apostle uttered them, come into play here. They are: *"Shall we continue in sin, that Grace may abound?"* The answer was instant: *"God forbid. How shall we, who are dead to sin, live any longer therein?"* (Rom. 6:1-2).

Jacob was out of the Will of God at Succoth, as I think is overly obvious. All the Altars in the world cannot rectify that. In fact, I think one can say without fear of contradiction that the Altar at Succoth was not recognized by God.

It is amusing that the Lord would pinpoint the place, by saying to Jacob, *"When you fled from the face of Esau your brother."*

It's like the Lord was saying to Jacob, *"I told you to go there ten years ago, but you didn't obey Me; consequently, you brought on yourself real trouble. Now I'm telling you the second time, 'Go up to Beth-el.'"*

This confirms the principle on which we have been dwelling. When there is failure or declension, the Lord calls the soul back to Himself. *"Remember, therefore, from whence you have fallen; and repent, and do the first works"* (Rev. 2:5).

This is the Divine principle of Restoration. The soul must be recalled to the very highest point; it must be brought back to the Divine standard.

GOD'S STANDARD

It is when thus recalled to God's high and holy standard, that one is really led to see the sad evil of one's fallen condition. What a fearful amount of moral evil had gathered around Jacob's family, unjudged by him, until his soul was roused by the call to *"Go up to Beth-el."* Shechem was not the place in which to detect all this evil. The atmosphere of that place was too much impregnated with impure elements to admit of the soul's discerning, with any degree of clearness and precision, the true character of evil. But the moment the call to Beth-el fell on Jacob's ear, *"then Jacob said unto his household, and*

to all who were with him, 'Put away the strange gods that are among you. . . .'"

STRANGE GODS

Verses 2 through 4 read: *"Then Jacob said unto his household, and to all who were with him, Put away the strange gods that are among you, and be clean, and change your garments:*

"And let us arise, and go up to Beth-el; and I will make there an Altar unto God, Who answered me in the day of my distress, and was with me in the way which I went.

"And they gave unto Jacob all the strange gods which were in their hand, and all their earrings which were in their ears; and Jacob hid them under the oak which was by Shechem."

As we've said some pages back, while the new Cross might be in vogue, it is the old Cross that brings one to Repentance. Jacob and all with him were to do five things:

1. Put away the strange gods that were among them.
2. Be clean.
3. Change your garments.
4. Arise, and go up to Beth-el.
5. Make there an Altar unto God.

The Hebrew Scholars claim, due to the manner in which this is written, there were many strange gods among them. These were objects of idolatrous worship, either brought by Jacob's servants from Mesopotamia, or adopted in Canaan, or perhaps possessed by the women taken captive during the problem of the recent past.

Regrettably, the modern Church is full of strange gods. We have with us the gods of humanistic psychology, the gods of contemporary, Christian music, the gods of false doctrine which promise material riches, etc. As the command was given to Jacob so long ago, it is given now as well.

THE THREEFOLD DANGER

While preaching a Campmeeting years ago (about 1961) with A. N. Trotter, he made a statement which I have never forgotten.

He brought out the fact that the Church was running aground, as he put it, on three things. Those three things are:

1. Education: He was actually referring to the wrong kind of education. More and

more, the Colleges built by Denominations, are less and less Bible, and more and more secular. Education is attained in the things of the world, but woefully lacking as it regards the Word of God. This is a sure way to destroy the people of God! In other words, the Church is too much depending on education, and not the Spirit of God.

2. Money: The Church is running aground on money. While, of course, money is needed, if we, however, compromise the Message for the sake of money, then we've sold out for the proverbial 30 pieces of silver.

3. People: If we sacrifice the Message in order to get people, then we have destroyed ourselves. Our primary purpose and goal are not people, but rather the Will of God.

He was right: the Church is running aground today on education, money, and people.

MUSIC

Some paragraphs back, I mentioned contemporary, Christian music as being one of the *"strange gods."* To try to justify this type of music, which incidentally is not of God, which means that it's ultimately of the Devil, the claim is made that this music reaches the young people, etc.

There are two answers to that:

1. It is only the Holy Spirit Who can reach anybody for God. Our problem is, we're reaching to many without the Holy Spirit, thereby filling our Churches with people who aren't even saved.

2. Our purpose in music must never be to reach people, but rather to please God. I have little interest in what the young people want, or what the older people want, but only what the Holy Spirit wants.

Now you know why most of the Church world doesn't too very much like Jimmy Swaggart. Irrespective of that, I must one day stand before God. And the bottom line then will not be whether people liked me or not, but whether I obeyed the Lord as it regards this Ministry. That's the only thing that counts.

The Scripture mentions *"their earrings which were in their ears."* These were employed for purposes of idolatrous worship, which were often covered with allegorical figures and mysterious sentences, and supposed

to be endowed with a talismanic virtue (Judg. 8:24; Isa. 3:20; Hos. 2:13).

The Scripture says that Jacob buried all of these *"strange gods"* under the oak which was by Shechem.

The cleansing and changing of garments were meant to symbolize moral and spiritual purification of the mind and heart (Pulpit).

EL-BETH-EL

Verses 5 through 8 read: *"And they journeyed: and the terror of God was upon the cities that were round about them, and they did not pursue after the sons of Jacob.*

"So Jacob came to Luz, which is in the land of Canaan, that is, Beth-el, he and all the people who were with him.

"And he built there an Altar, and called the place El-Beth-el: because there God appeared unto him, when he fled from the face of his brother.

"But Deborah Rebekah's nurse died, and she was buried beneath Beth-el under an oak: and the name of it was called Allon-bachuth."

The Scripture says, *"And they journeyed."* This is a journey that they should have taken when Jacob came back into the Land of Promise.

No doubt, the news got out among the various different tribes in that part of the world concerning what had happened at Shechem. But the Scripture says that no one touched Jacob as he and his retinue journeyed toward Beth-el, and because *"the terror of God was upon the cities that were round about them."*

What exactly the Lord did, we aren't told. But one thing is certain: Had the Lord not done this thing to protect Jacob and his family, they would no doubt have been slaughtered.

When Jacob arrived at Beth-el, in accordance with the Command of the Lord, *"He built there an Altar."* He called the place *"El-beth-el."* The name means, *"God of the House of God."* At Shechem he kept his Saviour and his Salvation to himself, and permitted his family and household to retain their idols. But this cannot be suffered if God is to be recognized and publicly confessed as the God of Beth-el, that is, the God of the House of God; for the elect are His House, and *"judgment must begin at the*

House of God." Then we can say, *"Holiness becometh Your House O Lord forever!"* When, therefore, he learns that he is to meet God publicly at Beth-el, he at once feels that idols cannot be brought into fellowship with that House, and accordingly he commands, as stated, the surrender of all the strange gods that were in their hands and in their ears.

The Divine command to Jacob some ten years back, and now renewed, was *"Go up to Beth-el and dwell there."* Disobedience preceded this command and followed it. In Beth-el itself there was victory, but before Beth-el was Shechem, and after Beth-el, Edar. The one, the scene of Dinah's dishonor; the other, and as we shall see, of Reuben's incest (Williams).

We're told here that Deborah, Rebekah's nurse died. The introduction of this aged servant is very affecting, and Jacob's excessive grief reveals an affectionate nature.

What no doubt sharpened his grief was that though he might close the eyes of his mother's servant, who was now when she died well over 150 years old, he, by his own misconduct, was not to see that mother herself! (Williams).

That she was now with Jacob may be accounted for by supposing that Jacob had paid a visit to his father at Hebron, and brought her back with him to Shechem.

She had left Padan-aram for Canaan along with Rebekah, upwards of 150 years ago. That the Holy Spirit would mention her passing proclaims to us the fact that she was faithful all of those years, and that she is now with Christ.

Little did she realize, as Abraham, Isaac, and Jacob kept account of these happenings, and that Moses years later, under the inspiration of the Holy Spirit, would place those accounts in the Holy Writ, and that thousands of years later, untold millions would read these Verses. But those who live for God, no matter how menial their task may seem to be, let them know and understand that what they do is eternal.

(9) "AND GOD APPEARED UNTO JACOB AGAIN, WHEN HE CAME OUT OF PADAN-ARAM, AND BLESSED HIM.

(10) "AND GOD SAID UNTO HIM, YOUR NAME IS JACOB: YOUR NAME SHALL NOT BE CALLED ANY MORE JACOB, BUT ISRAEL

NOTES

SHALL BE YOUR NAME: AND HE CALLED HIS NAME ISRAEL.

(11) "AND GOD SAID UNTO HIM, I AM GOD ALMIGHTY: BE FRUITFUL AND MULTIPLY; A NATION AND A COMPANY OF NATIONS SHALL BE OF YOU, AND KINGS SHALL COME OUT OF YOUR LOINS;

(12) "AND THE LAND WHICH I GAVE ABRAHAM AND ISAAC, TO YOU I WILL GIVE IT, AND TO YOUR SEED AFTER YOU WILL I GIVE THE LAND.

(13) "AND GOD WENT UP FROM HIM IN THE PLACE WHERE HE TALKED WITH HIM.

(14) "AND JACOB SET UP A PILLAR IN THE PLACE WHERE HE TALKED WITH HIM, EVEN A PILLAR OF STONE: AND HE POURED A DRINK OFFERING THEREON, AND HE POURED OIL THEREON.

(15) "AND JACOB CALLED THE NAME OF THE PLACE WHERE GOD SPOKE WITH HIM, BETH-EL."

The overview is:

1. The renewal of the name given to Jacob some ten years earlier at Peniel was most possibly done because the Patriarch feared that he had forfeited the Blessing. But the calling of the gifts is without Repentance.

2. Along with this renewal is revealed to Jacob the glorious title of *"El-Shaddai,"* i.e., *"God Almighty,"* the God Who is able to fulfill to him the promises made here.

3. In Verse 14 is found the first mention of a Drink-Offering.

THE APPEARANCE OF GOD

Verse 9 reads: *"And God appeared unto Jacob again, when he came out of Padan-aram, and blessed him."*

This was a visible manifestation. The appearance was similar to what had taken place with Jacob when he had wrestled with the Lord, which took place some ten years earlier.

The Lord blessed the patriarch, and we find the account of the Blessing, which follows.

The phrase, *"When he came out of Padan-aram,"* should have been translated, *"When he came from Padan-aram."* The word *"out"* is not in the Hebrew.

ISRAEL

Verse 10 reads: *"And God said unto him, Your name is Jacob: your name shall not be* called any more Jacob, but Israel shall be your name: and he called his name Israel."

I personally feel that the Lord reaffirmed this great Promise and action which He had taken with Jacob some years earlier. I have no doubt that the Patriarch was fearful that he had forfeited this great Blessing, because of not going to Beth-el when commanded to do so by the Lord, but rather going to Succoth, where had been the occasion of much failure.

The path of Faith is not one that we trod without mishap. I can remember a day some ten years ago from the time of this writing (1991), when I felt the same as Jacob must have felt. Had I forfeited the great Call of God upon my life? But then in a Prayer Meeting that October night, the Lord wondrously and graciously spoke to my heart, saying: *"I'm not a man that I should lie, neither the son of man that I should repent. What I have blessed nothing can curse."* The statement was taken from Numbers 23:19-20. There was no doubt in my mind then as to what I must do; and as well, there is no way that I have words to properly express the joy that filled my heart, that the Lord had spoken to me, reaffirming all that he had called me to do. Jacob must have felt the same way as the Lord spoke to him.

GOD ALMIGHTY

Verse 11 reads: *"And God said unto him, I am God Almighty: be fruitful and multiply; a nation and a company of nations shall be of you, and kings shall come out of your loins."*

The Lord repeats to Jacob substantially the promises made to Abraham.

Perhaps Jacob had many questions in his mind concerning his own conduct, in that many problems no doubt had arisen because of that. These tribes were bitterly opposed to him because of the action at Succoth. So the Lord not only reaffirms His Promise and action as it regards Jacob becoming *"Israel,"* but further tells him that whatever needs to be done, God is able to do it, for He is *"Almighty."*

Jacob's purpose, the very reason for his being, was to raise up a nation, all for the elect purpose of bringing the Redeemer into the world.

The *"kings"* of which the Lord spoke at this time began with Saul, but actually should

have begun with David. But the ultimate King will be the Lord Jesus Christ.

Could Jacob's Faith reach out and claim all of this? It not only could, but it did!

THE LAND

Verse 12 reads: *"And the land which I gave Abraham and Isaac, to thee I will give it, and to your seed after you will I give the land."*

While Jacob had purchased a piece of land close to Shechem (Gen. 33:19), due to the action of his sons, he had been forced to leave it; so in reality, he owned nothing of this Land of which the Lord promises to give him. In effect, it would be his seed which would inherit the land, and would do so about 275 years later.

For the people of whom the Lord spoke here, who would be raised up out of Jacob's loins, they would have to have a domicile, a place that would be specifically for them. Canaan was that land, hence the Lord calling Abraham to this place at the very beginning. As we've said, all of this was for the purpose of bringing the Redeemer into the world, Who would be the *"Seed of the woman,"* and Who would bruise Satan's head (Gen. 3:15).

THE PILLAR OF STONE AND THE DRINK-OFFERING

Verses 13 through 15 read: *"And God went up from him in the place where he talked with him.*

"And Jacob set up a pillar in the place where he talked with him, even a pillar of stone: and he poured a drink offering thereon, and he poured oil thereon.

"And Jacob called the name of the place where God spoke with him, Beth-el."

Williams says: *"In Verse 14 is found the first mention of a drink-offering. When God first revealed Himself to Jacob at this spot, which was some 30 years earlier, Jacob poured oil upon the pillar; now he pours both oil and wine. Then, there was Guilty fear; now, there is joy as well as fear.*

"This Stone figures Christ the Rock of Ages, anointed with the Holy Spirit, typified by the oil, and filled with the joy of God, typified by the 'drink-offering.'"

All of this which happened to Jacob at this particular time, this great manifestation of

God's Presence was more solemn than any of the previous occasions upon which the Deity had revealed Himself to Jacob. It was, in fact, the acknowledgement of the Patriarch as the heir of the Abrahamic Covenant.

The *"Drink-Offering"* used here was probably grape juice. It would then have been called *"wine"*; however, the word *"wine"* could mean either grape juice or the fermented variety. Considering that this represented Christ, it is highly unlikely that the fermented variety would have been used.

The *"Drink-Offering"* symbolized joy, but as well, it symbolized helplessness on the part of both the Redeemer and the Believer. It symbolized the Redeemer in His Incarnation, God becoming man, which meant that He would be helpless within Himself, but yet would do great and mighty things, because of the empowerment of the Holy Spirit (Lk. 4:18-19).

As it regards the symbolization of the Believer, the pouring out of a *"Drink-Offering,"* which was done before the Lord, or in essence, *"before His Face,"* pointed to the helplessness of the one doing the pouring, and that he recognized his helplessness. Consequently, Jacob pouring out the *"Drink-Offering"* here symbolized far more than meets the eye. At long last he is in essence saying, *"Lord, I cannot do this thing without You. Within myself, I am helpless, so I must have Your leading, Grace, and Power."*

THE CROSS

Jesus said: *"If any man will come after me, let him deny himself, and take up his cross daily, and follow Me.*

"For whosoever will save his life shall lose it: but whosoever will lose his life for my sake, the same shall save it" (Lk. 9:23-24).

In essence, as the Believer takes up his cross, and does so daily, which means that he renews his Faith each and every day, this specifies that he is looking to the benefits of what Jesus did there in the giving of Himself in Sacrifice. In looking to the Cross, and doing so on a daily basis, in essence, the Believer is saying that he cannot do this thing himself, cannot live this life by his own strength and power, and must have the power of the Holy Spirit, which is obtained by exhibiting Faith in the Finished Work of Christ.

In the doing of this, and as stated even on a daily basis, the Believer is in essence pouring out a *"Drink-Offering"* each and every day.

The doing of this, which loses one's life in Christ, in effect *"saves it."* This brings a joy unspeakable and full of glory, which as well, and as stated, the *"Drink-Offering"* symbolizes.

One cannot have the strength of the Lord, until one recognizes one's own weakness. As long as one is relying upon his own strength, acumen, ability, and power, he frustrates the Grace of God, simply because the *"Strength of the Lord is made perfect only in weakness"* (II Cor. 12:9).

In fact, this is the greatest struggle for the Christian, even as it was the greatest struggle for Jacob. The Patriarch depended long upon his on strength and cunning. It took much time, test, and trial, before he finally realized that he couldn't do this thing as it should be done, and that he must rely totally and wholly on the Lord.

Even in this age of Grace, and as one might say, this age of the Holy Spirit, this remains the biggest problem for the Believer. We talk about leaning totally on Christ, and solely trusting Christ, but the truth is, if the Believer is not looking exclusively to the Cross, then in some way, the Believer, whether he realizes it or not, is looking to himself. *"Self"* to be sure, is so very, very subtle. We know how to dress up self until it looks like the Lord, but in reality, it isn't. In this problem which plagues all Believers, and in effect, is the cause of every difficulty, the Cross of Christ becomes the bone of contention, so to speak.

THE CROSS AND UNBELIEF

Faith is judged by the Lord as it relates to the Cross (Rom. 6:3-5, 11; I Cor. 1:17-18, 23; 2:2, 5). Faith is either registered in the Cross, or it's registered in self. God will not honor the type registered in self. It is only Faith in the Cross which He honors and recognizes, which says that Jesus paid it all, and in fact, accomplished a Finished Work.

And let the Reader understand, while we may speak of having faith in Christ or in the Word of God, if it's not Faith in the Cross, in essence what Jesus did there, then it's not really Faith in Christ. That's why Paul spoke of *"another Jesus," "another spirit,"* and *"another gospel"* (II Cor. 11:4). If Christ is at all divorced from the Cross, then He becomes *"another Jesus."* And regrettably, that's where the majority of the modern Church actually is. It talks about Jesus constantly, but not about the Cross. In fact, the Cross is ignored in most circles, if not downright rejected. That is the blueprint for spiritual disaster.

So Jacob now pours out a *"Drink-Offering"* before the Lord, which represents something wonderful and glorious in his life. Of course, he did this at the behest of the Holy Spirit. But the Spirit had him to do such, simply because Jacob had now come to a place to where he is beginning to let the Lord plan for him, instead of him trying to do the planning himself. In other words, he is admitting that he is as weak as water; therefore, he needs the leading and guidance of the Lord in every aspect of his life. And so do we!

(16) "AND THEY JOURNEYED FROM BETH-EL; AND THERE WAS BUT A LITTLE WAY TO COME TO EPHRATH: AND RACHEL TRAVAILED, AND SHE HAD HARD LABOR.

(17) "AND IT CAME TO PASS, WHEN SHE WAS IN HARD LABOR, THAT THE MIDWIFE SAID UNTO HER, FEAR NOT; YOU SHALL HAVE THIS SON ALSO.

(18) "AND IT CAME TO PASS, AS HER SOUL WAS IN DEPARTING, (FOR SHE DIED) THAT SHE CALLED HIS NAME BEN-ONI: BUT HIS FATHER CALLED HIM BENJAMIN.

(19) "AND RACHEL DIED, AND WAS BURIED IN THE WAY TO EPHRATH, WHICH IS BETH-LEHEM.

(20) "AND JACOB SET A PILLAR UPON HER GRAVE: THAT IS THE PILLAR OF RACHEL'S GRAVE UNTO THIS DAY.

(21) "AND ISRAEL JOURNEYED, AND SPREAD HIS TENT BEYOND THE TOWER OF EDAR."

The exegesis is:

1. Rachel dies giving birth to Benjamin.

2. Strangely enough, Jacob is referred to here by the Holy Spirit as *"Israel,"* the first time this name has been used as it regards his person.

3. How strange all of this appears to human wisdom! Jacob is his name of weakness,

NOTES

Israel, of strength, and yet is he only named Israel in connection with suffering, wandering, and dishonor!

BENJAMIN

Verses 16 through 20 read: *"And they journeyed from Beth-el; and there was but a little way to come to Ephrath: and Rachel travailed, and she had hard labor.*

"And it came to pass, when she was in hard labor, that the midwife said unto her, Fear not; you shall have this son also.

"And it came to pass, as her soul was in departing, (for she died) that she called his name Ben-oni: but his father called him Benjamin.

"And Rachel died, and was buried in the way to Ephrath, which is Beth-lehem.

"And Jacob set a pillar upon her grave: that is the pillar of Rachel's grave unto this day."

The journey that Jacob was taking was probably to Mamre to visit Isaac. From the last Verses of this Chapter, it seems that Jacob made it there before the great Patriarch died.

In the journey to Mamre, they were close to Beth-lehem, when Rachel began to go into labor. Twice the Scripture says that she had *"hard labor."*

The baby was born, which occasioned the death of Rachel. But before she died, *"she called his name Ben-oni,"* which means, *"son of my sorrow."* She had asked the Lord for another son when Joseph was born, and the Lord had answered her prayer, but it occasioned her death.

In the culture of that day, the mother usually named the child, as here. If the father stepped in, it would be an unusual situation, even as it was here. Jacob felt that the name she had chosen was not appropriate, so the Patriarch countermanded her request, and *"called him Benjamin,"* which means, *"son of my right hand."* Rachel was buried near Beth-lehem.

ISRAEL

Verse 21 reads: *"And Israel journeyed, and spread his tent beyond the tower of Edar."*

It has possibly been some ten years since the Lord had spoken to Jacob about his name change, which took place at the great wrestling (Gen. 32:24-28). Even though the Lord at that time had said to him, *"Your name shall be called no more Jacob, but Israel: for as a prince you have power with God and with men, and have prevailed,"* in the intervening ten years, Jacob hadn't been referred to by that name at all. And now for the first time the Holy Spirit refers to the Patriarch as *"Israel."*

It is strange that this would be done at a time of great sorrow on Jacob's part, when he had lost his most wonderful possession, his Rachel. As we have stated, Jacob is his name of weakness, Israel, of strength, and yet he is only named Israel in connection with suffering, wandering, and dishonor. But yet, this illustrates exactly what happened to Paul, when the Lord said to him: *"My Grace is sufficient for you: for My strength is made perfect in weakness"* (II Cor. 12:9).

The point I wish to make is, if the modern Church would analyze Jacob at this point, they would see his failure at Succoth, which came about because he was out of the Will of God, and now the loss of Rachel, and would hardly think of him as *"Israel."* In fact, at this stage, he would be greatly depreciated in the eyes of the Church. His outward circumstances certainly don't look favorable. He seems to be in a state of disarray. He is brokenhearted, disconcerted, and in just a few days will lose his father as well. But yet, the Holy Spirit refers to him now as *"Israel."*

This means that we must be very careful as to how we judge people. Through many dangers, toils, and snares, Jacob was learning to lean totally on the Lord, and to trust Him completely. As stated several times, this position doesn't come quickly, easily, or without difficulty.

(22) "AND IT CAME TO PASS, WHEN ISRAEL DWELT IN THAT LAND, THAT REUBEN WENT AND LAY WITH BILHAH HIS FATHER'S CONCUBINE: AND ISRAEL HEARD IT. NOW THE SONS OF JACOB WERE TWELVE:

(23) "THE SONS OF LEAH; REUBEN, JACOB'S FIRSTBORN, AND SIMEON, AND LEVI, AND JUDAH, AND ISSACHAR, AND ZEBULUN:

(24) "THE SONS OF RACHEL: JOSEPH, AND BENJAMIN:

NOTES

(25) "AND THE SONS OF BILHAH, RACHEL'S HANDMAID; DAN, AND NAPHTALI:

(26) "AND THE SONS OF ZILPAH, LEAH'S HANDMAID: GAD, AND ASHER: THESE ARE THE SONS OF JACOB, WHICH WERE BORN TO HIM IN PADAN-ARAM.

(27) "AND JACOB CAME UNTO ISAAC HIS FATHER UNTO MAMRE, AND TO THE CITY OF ARBAH, WHICH IS HEBRON, WHERE ABRAHAM AND ISAAC SOJOURNED.

(28) "AND THE DAYS OF ISAAC WERE AN HUNDRED AND FOURSCORE YEARS.

(29) "AND ISAAC GAVE UP THE GHOST, AND DIED, AND WAS GATHERED UNTO HIS PEOPLE, BEING OLD AND FULL OF DAYS: AND HIS SONS ESAU AND JACOB BURIED HIM."

The synopsis is:

1. Jacob is again referred to as *"Israel,"* even in the midst of terrible wrongdoing, committed by Reuben.

2. The 12 sons of Jacob are listed here, who will head up the Tribes of Israel, with Manasseh and Ephraim taking the place of Joseph, making a total of 13. There would actually be 13 Tribes, counting Levi, which was the Priestly Tribe.

3. Isaac dies at 180 years old.

ISRAEL AND SINFUL FAILURE

Verse 22 reads: *"And it came to pass, when Israel dwelt in that land, that Reuben went and lay with Bilhah his father's concubine: and Israel heard it. Now the sons of Jacob were twelve."*

Understanding that Jacob is referred to as *"Israel,"* two times in this one Verse, considering the circumstances, again, it is incumbent upon us to see what the Holy Spirit is doing.

Why would the Holy Spirit refer to Jacob two times as *"Israel,"* considering the circumstances in which it is given? Reuben, his firstborn, commits incest with Bilhah, which is an abomination to say the least. And yet in this setting, the Holy Spirit will refer to Jacob in a very positive manner.

The only answer that one could give is that Jacob, during this very trying time, leaned on the Lord totally and completely, looking to Him for leading and guidance.

The old Jacob would no doubt have taken matters into his own hands upon hearing what Reuben had done, with very negative results. The new Jacob does what should be done and no more, and then puts everything into the Hands of the Lord.

For this sin, Reuben was afterwards disinherited (Gen. 49:4; I Chron. 5:1).

THE SONS OF JACOB

Verses 23 through 26 read: *"The sons of Leah; Reuben, Jacob's firstborn, and Simeon, and Levi, and Judah, and Issachar, and Zebulun:*

"The sons of Rachel; Joseph, and Benjamin:

"And the sons of Bilhah, Rachel's handmaid; Dan, and Naphtali:

"And the sons of Zilpah, Leah's handmaid: Gad, and Asher: these are the sons of Jacob, which were born to him in Padan-aram."

All except Benjamin were born in Padan-aram.

For all of its problems, this family consisted of the Church of that day, one might say.

These men, with the exception of Joseph and Benjamin, were anything but examples of Righteousness. In fact, they were examples of unrighteousness. But gradually over time, they would change, which change we will witness before the end of this account in the great Book of Genesis.

ISAAC

Verses 27 through 29 read: *"And Jacob came unto Isaac his father unto Mamre, unto the city of Arbah, which is Hebron, where Abraham and Isaac sojourned.*

"And the days of Isaac were an hundred and fourscore years.

"And Isaac gave up the ghost, and died, and was gathered unto his people, being old and full of days: and his sons Esau and Jacob buried him."

This account is not given in chronological order. The death of Isaac took place some 10 to 12 years after Joseph had been sold into Egypt.

Isaac was 60 when his sons were born. Jacob was 120 years of age at his father's death, and 130 when he appeared before Pharaoh (Gen. 47:9). As Joseph was 17 when sold into Egypt (Gen. 37:2), and 30 when raised to power in Egypt (Gen. 41:46), and as the seven years of plenty and two of the years of famine had passed before Jacob went

down into Egypt, it follows that the cruel deed, whereby he was robbed of Joseph, was committed about 10 to 12 years before the death of Isaac (Ellicott).

Esau comes from Mount Seir to pay the last service due to his deceased parent, and Jacob accords him that precedence which had once belonged to him as Isaac's firstborn, by placing his name first.

They laid Isaac beside his ancestral greats in the family burying-place of Machpelah, where already slept the lifeless bodies of Abraham and Sarah, awaiting the Resurrection, while his spirit went to company with theirs in the better country, even an heavenly.

Jacob was with Isaac when he died, and Esau came to the grave.

"Come, Christians, join to sing Hallelujah! Amen!

"Loud praise to Christ our King; Hallelujah! Amen!

"Let all, with heart and voice, before His Throne rejoice;

"Praise is His gracious choice: Hallelujah! Amen!"

"Come, lift your hearts on high; Hallelujah! Amen!

"Let praises fill the sky; Hallelujah! Amen!

"He is our Guide and Friend; to us He'll condescend;

"His love shall never end: Hallelujah! Amen!"

"Praise yet our Christ again; Hallelujah! Amen!

"Life shall not end the strain; Hallelujah! Amen!

"On Heaven's blissful shore His goodness we'll adore,

"Singing forevermore, Hallelujah! Amen!"

CHAPTER 36

(1) "NOW THESE ARE THE GENERATIONS OF ESAU, WHO IS EDOM.

(2) "ESAU TOOK HIS WIVES OF THE DAUGHTERS OF CANAAN: ADAH THE DAUGHTER OF ELON THE HITTITE, AND

AHOLIBAMAH THE DAUGHTER OF ANAH THE DAUGHTER OF ZIBEON THE HIVITE;

(3) "AND BASHEMATH ISHMAEL'S DAUGHTER, SISTER OF NEBAJOTH.

(4) "AND ADAH BEAR TO ESAU ELIPHAZ: AND BASHEMATH BEAR REUEL;

(5) "AND AHOLIBAMAH BEAR JEUSH, AND JAALAM, AND KORAH: THESE ARE THE SONS OF ESAU, WHICH WERE BORN UNTO HIM IN THE LAND OF CANAAN."

The diagram is:

1. Esau and his sons, as the men of the world, who have their portion in this life (Ps. 17:14), established themselves in power, with their kings and their dukes, and their riches and their possessions.

2. The heirs of Promise, that is, Jacob and his sons, are pilgrims and strangers.

3. This furnishes a prophetic picture (Williams).

ESAU

Verses 1 through 5 read: *"Now these are the generations of Esau, who is Edom.*

"Esau took his wives of the daughters of Canaan; Adah the daughter of Elon the Hittite, and Aholibamah the daughter of Anah the daughter of Zibeon the Hivite;

"And Bashemath Ishmael's daughter, sister of Nebajoth.

"And Adah bear to Esau Eliphaz; and Bashemath bear Reuel;

"And Aholibamah bear Jeush, and Jaalam, and Korah: these are the sons of Esau, which were born unto him in the land of Canaan."

In all of this we find that Esau is repeatedly called here Edom. This is the name which perpetuated the remembrance of his selling his birthright for a mess of pottage. Esau continued the same profane despiser of heavenly things.

We may wonder as to why the Holy Spirit deemed it necessary to have this genealogy of generations concerning Esau given to us.

It is given to us because Esau was the son of Isaac. Consequently, he was a member of the sacred family, the family that would bring the Redeemer into the world. As such, what he does is important, even if in a negative way, and negative it was.

No one is forced to live for God, and Esau chose to go the direction of the world. The Holy Spirit says of him:

"Lest there be any fornicator, or profane person, as Esau, who for one morsel of meat sold his birthright" (Heb. 12:16). That was the lifestyle he chose, and that was the lifestyle he had.

(6) "AND ESAU TOOK HIS WIVES, AND HIS SONS, AND HIS DAUGHTERS, AND ALL THE PERSONS OF HIS HOUSE, AND HIS CATTLE, AND ALL HIS BEASTS, AND ALL HIS SUBSTANCE, WHICH HE HAD GOT IN THE LAND OF CANAAN; AND WENT INTO THE COUNTRY FROM THE FACE OF HIS BROTHER JACOB.

(7) "FOR THEIR RICHES WERE MORE THAN THEY MIGHT DWELL TOGETHER; AND THE LAND WHEREIN THEY WERE STRANGERS COULD NOT BEAR THEM BECAUSE OF THEIR CATTLE.

(8) "THUS DWELT ESAU IN MOUNT SEIR: ESAU IS EDOM."

The structure is:

1. With the inheritance he received from the death of his father Isaac, Esau now was a very, very rich man.

2. His flocks and herds were so large in fact, that there wasn't room in that part of the country for both flocks.

3. So Esau colonized Edom.

EDOM

Verses 6 through 8 read: *"And Esau took his wives, and his sons, and his daughters, and all the persons of his house, and his cattle, and all his beasts, and all his substance, which he had got in the land of Canaan; and went into the country from the face of his brother Jacob.*

"For their riches were more than they might dwell together; and the land wherein they were strangers could not bear them because of their cattle.

"Thus dwelt Esau in Mount Seir: Esau is Edom."

The land of Edom extends from the southern extremity of the Dead Sea to the Gulf of Elath, and consists of a chain of mountains running parallel to the Akaba, or continuation of the deep depression through which the Jordan flows till it loses itself in the Dead Sea.

The hills are of limestone, with masses here and there of basalt; and though large portions are so covered with stones as to be barren, the rest is moderately fertile, not indeed in grain, but in figs, pomegranates, and other fruits.

The climate is pleasant, the heat in summer being moderated by cool winds, but the winters are cold. The border of it was distant only some 50 or 60 miles from Hebron, so that Esau's transference of himself thither was an easy matter.

Petra is located in Edom, and was probably originally settled by Esau.

(9) "AND THESE ARE THE GENERATIONS OF ESAU THE FATHER OF THE EDOMITES IN MOUNT SEIR:

(10) "THESE ARE THE NAMES OF ESAU'S SONS; ELIPHAZ THE SON OF ADAH THE WIFE OF ESAU, REUEL THE SON OF BASHEMATH THE WIFE OF ESAU.

(11) "AND THE SONS OF ELIPHAZ WERE TEMAN, OMAR, ZEPHO, AND GATAM, AND KENAZ.

(12) "AND TIMNA WAS CONCUBINE TO ELIPHAZ ESAU'S SON; AND SHE BEAR TO ELIPHAZ AMALEK: THESE WERE THE SONS OF ADAH ESAU'S WIFE."

The composition is:

1. The *"Amalek"* mentioned here is probably the Amalekite nation which attacked Israel at Horeb.

2. Amalek in Biblical typology could be looked at as a type of the flesh.

3. When Israel experienced the miracle of the water coming from the Rock, which was a Type of Christ and the Holy Spirit, the Scripture says, *"Then came Amalek, and fought with Israel in Rephidim"* (Ex. 17:6-8).

AMALEK

Verses 9 through 12 read: *"And these are the generations of Esau the father of the Edomites in Mount Seir:*

"These are the names of Esau's sons; Eliphaz the son of Adah the wife of Esau, Reuel the son of Bashemath the wife of Esau.

"And the sons of Eliphaz were Teman, Omar, Zepho, and Gatam, and Kenaz.

"And Timna was concubine to Eliphaz Esau's son; and she bear to Eliphaz Amalek: these were the sons of Adah Esau's wife."

There is some question among Scholars as to whether this was the Amalek which founded the powerful nation of the Amalekites, or

rather a nomadic group found in the Negeb and Sinai area. The discussion centers on Genesis 14:7, which predates Esau, which refers to *"the country of the Amalekites."* The distinction is unnecessary if we regard the phrase as a later editorial description. It is my contention that the Amalek mentioned in Genesis 36:12 is the founder of the Amalekites.

Israel first met the Amalekites at Rephidim in the wilderness of Sinai (Ex. 17:8-13; Deut. 25:17-18). Because of this attack, the Amalekites came under a permanent ban and were to be destroyed (Deut. 25:19; I Sam. 15:2-3). On that occasion Aaron and Hur held up Moses' hands and Israel prevailed. A year later, after the report of the spies, Israel ignored Moses' command and sought to enter Palestine. The Amalekites defeated them at Hormah (Num. 14:43, 45).

From the days of the Judges two encounters are recorded. The Amalekites assisted Eglon, king of Moab, to attack Israelite territory (Judg. 3:13), and later combined forces with the Midianites in order to raid Israelite crops and flocks. Gideon drove them out (Judg. 6:3-5, 33; 7:12; 10:12).

From the Exodus onwards, Amalekites were to be found in the Negeb, but for a time they gained a foothold in Ephraim (Judg. 12:15). Balaam, the false prophet, looked away to their lands from his vantage point in Moab, and described them as *"the first of the nations"* (Num. 24:20), which may mean in regard either to origin or to status.

Samuel commanded Saul to destroy the Amalekites. Even booty was forbidden. Saul pursued them from Havilah to Shur but captured their king alive. Later, Samuel slew Agag and rebuked Saul (I Sam., Chpt. 15).

David fought the Amalekites in the area of Ziklag which Achish, king of Gath, had given him (I Sam. 27:6; 30:1-20). The Amalekites declined later, and in Hezekiah's day the sons of Simeon attacked *"the remnant of the Amalekites that had escaped,"* taking their stronghold in Mount Seir (I Chron. 4:43).

(Bibliography: F. M. Abel, Geography of Palestine; D. Baly, The Geography of the Bible.)

TYPOLOGY

"Amalek" can be looked at as a type of the flesh. When Israel experienced the great

miracle of the water coming out of the rock, which was a Type of Christ and the Holy Spirit, the Scripture says, *"Then came Amalek, and fought with Israel in Rephidim"* (Ex. 17:6-8).

The entrance of the Holy Spirit occasioned the rising up of Amalek, i.e., *"the flesh."* What do we mean by that?

When the Believer is Baptized with the Holy Spirit, the entrance of the Spirit into this new dimension in the heart and life of such a Believer always arouses the flesh. The Believer will find the Spirit of God pointing out things in his life which are wrong, and which a severance is demanded. These things, whatever they might be, constitute *"the flesh,"* and create difficulties. In fact, the Seventeenth Chapter of Exodus closes with the statement: *"For he said, Because the LORD hath sworn that the LORD will have war with Amalek from generation to generation"* (Ex. 17:16).

In fact, this is a battle that actually never ends, and will not end, until the Trump sounds, or the Lord calls us home.

THE FLESH

Paul often referred to *"the flesh"* (Rom. 8:1, 8). He is speaking of our own ability, strength, power, and efforts, which means that it's us doing whatever is being done, and not the Holy Spirit.

Doing what, some may ask?

I am speaking of Believers attempting to be holy, to be righteous, in other words, our efforts to live for God. This can only be done by and through the Holy Spirit, and no other way. Unfortunately, it's very easy for man to attempt to do this on his own, which automatically pushes the Believer into this realm. While it's not the Law of Moses which we address here, it is definitely laws made up by men, whomever those men might be. As stated, the Holy Spirit cannot function in such a climate.

So what is the true way?

The Believer is to understand that everything he receives from the Lord comes to him exclusively through Christ and what Christ has done for him at the Cross (Rom. 6:3-14; 8:1-2, 11; I Cor. 1:17-18, 21, 23; 2:2; Gal. 6:14; Col. 2:14-15).

Understanding that it is the Cross which has made all things possible, and I speak of those things we receive from the Lord, and whatever they might be, we are to anchor our Faith in the Cross, and not allow it to be moved to other things. In other words, the Cross of Christ, which constitutes what Jesus did there, must ever be the object of our Faith. This being the case, the Holy Spirit will then work and perform mightily on our behalf. Only in this manner can we live a righteous, holy life.

Paul said concerning this: *"But if the Spirit* (Holy Spirit) *of Him* (God the Father) *Who raised up Jesus from the dead dwell in you, He Who raised up Christ from the dead shall also quicken your mortal bodies by His Spirit Who dwells in you"* (Rom. 8:11).

But we must never forget that the Work of the Holy Spirit within our lives is predicated on our Faith in the Cross (Eph. 2:13-18).

(13) "AND THESE ARE THE SONS OF REUEL; NAHATH, AND ZERAH, SHAMMAH, AND MIZZAH: THESE WERE THE SONS OF BASHEMATH ESAU'S WIFE.

(14) "AND THESE WERE THE SONS OF AHOLIBAMAH, THE DAUGHTER OF ANAH THE DAUGHTER OF ZIBEON, ESAU'S WIFE: AND SHE BEAR TO ESAU JEUSH, AND JAALAM, AND KORAH.

(15) "THESE WERE THE DUKES OF THE SONS OF ESAU: THE SONS OF ELIPHAZ THE FIRSTBORN SON OF ESAU; DUKE TEMAN, DUKE OMAR, DUKE ZEPHO, DUKE KENAZ,

(16) "DUKE KORAH, DUKE GATAM, AND DUKE AMALEK: THESE ARE THE DUKES THAT CAME OF ELIPHAZ IN THE LAND OF EDOM; THESE WERE THE SONS OF ADAH.

(17) "AND THESE ARE THE SONS OF REUEL ESAU'S SON; DUKE NAHATH, DUKE ZERAH, DUKE SHAMMAH, DUKE MIZZAH: THESE ARE THE DUKES THAT CAME OF REUEL IN THE LAND OF EDOM: THESE ARE THE SONS OF BASHEMATH ESAU'S WIFE.

(18) "AND THESE ARE THE SONS OF AHOLIBAMAH ESAU'S WIFE; DUKE JEUSH, DUKE JAALAM, DUKE KORAH: THESE WERE THE DUKES THAT CAME OF AHOLIBAMAH THE DAUGHTER OF ANAH, ESAU'S WIFE.

(19) "THESE ARE THE SONS OF ESAU, WHO IS EDOM, AND THESE ARE THEIR DUKES.

(20) "THESE ARE THE SONS OF SEIR THE HORITE, WHO INHABITED THE LAND; LOTAN, AND SHOBAL, AND ZIBEON, AND ANAH,

(21) "AND DISHON, AND EZER, AND DISHAN: THESE ARE THE DUKES OF THE HORITES, THE CHILDREN OF SEIR IN THE LAND OF EDOM.

(22) "AND THE CHILDREN OF LOTAN WERE HORI AND HEMAM; AND LOTAN'S SISTER WAS TIMNA.

(23) "AND THE CHILDREN OF SHOBAL WERE THESE; ALVAN, AND MANAHATH, AND EBAL, SHEPHO, AND ONAM.

(24) "AND THESE ARE THE CHILDREN OF ZIBEON; BOTH AJAH AND ANAH: THIS WAS THAT ANAH THAT FOUND THE MULES IN THE WILDERNESS, AS HE FED THE ASSES OF ZIBEON HIS FATHER.

(25) "AND THE CHILDREN OF ANAH WERE THESE; DISHON, AND AHOLIBAMAH THE DAUGHTER OF ANAH.

(26) "AND THESE ARE THE CHILDREN OF DISHON; HEMDAN, AND ESHBAN, AND ITHRAN, AND CHERAN.

(27) "THE CHILDREN OF EZER ARE THESE; BILHAN, AND ZAAVAN, AND AKAN.

(28) "THE CHILDREN OF DISHAN ARE THESE; UZ, AND ARAN.

(29) "THESE ARE THE DUKES THAT CAME OUT OF THE HORITES; DUKE LOTAN, DUKE SHOBAL, DUKE ZIBEON, DUKE ANAH.

(30) "DUKE DISHON, DUKE EZER, DUKE DISHAN: THESE ARE THE DUKES THAT CAME OF HORI, AMONG THEIR DUKES IN THE LAND OF SEIR.

(31) "AND THESE ARE THE KINGS THAT REIGNED IN THE LAND OF EDOM, BEFORE THERE REIGNED ANY KING OVER THE CHILDREN OF ISRAEL.

(32) "AND BELA THE SON OF BEOR REIGNED IN EDOM. AND THE NAME OF HIS CITY WAS DINHABAH.

(33) "AND BELA DIED, AND JOBAB THE SON OF ZERAH OF BOZRAH REIGNED IN HIS STEAD.

(34) "AND JOBAB DIED, AND HUSHAM OF THE LAND OF TEMANI REIGNED IN HIS STEAD.

NOTES

8 Dukes

(35) "AND HUSHAM DIED, AND HADAD THE SON OF BEDAD, WHO SMOTE MIDIAN IN THE FIELD OF MOAB, REIGNED IN HIS STEAD: AND THE NAME OF HIS CITY WAS AVITH.

(36) "AND HADAD DIED, AND SAMLAH OF MASREKAH REIGNED IN HIS STEAD.

(37) "AND SAMLAH DIED, AND SAUL OF REHOBOTH BY THE RIVER REIGNED IN HIS STEAD.

(38) "AND SAUL DIED, AND BAAL-HANAN THE SON OF ACHBOR REIGNED IN HIS STEAD.

(39) "AND BAAL-HANAN THE SON OF ACHBOR DIED, AND HADAR REIGNED IN HIS STEAD: AND THE NAME OF HIS CITY WAS PAU; AND HIS WIFE'S NAME WAS MEHETABEL, THE DAUGHTER OF MATRED, THE DAUGHTER OF MEZAHAB.

(40) "AND THESE ARE THE NAMES OF THE DUKES THAT CAME OF ESAU, ACCORDING TO THEIR FAMILIES, AFTER THEIR PLACES, BY THEIR NAMES; DUKE TIMNAH, DUKE ALVAH, DUKE JETHETH,

(41) "DUKE AHOLIBAMAH, DUKE ELAH, DUKE PINON,

(42) "DUKE KENAZ, DUKE TEMAN, DUKE MIBZAR,

(43) "DUKE MAGDIEL, DUKE IRAM: THESE BE THE DUKES OF EDOM, ACCORDING TO THEIR HABITATIONS IN THE LAND OF THEIR POSSESSION: HE IS ESAU THE FATHER OF THE EDOMITES."

THE HOLY SPIRIT AND HIS REASONS

Concerning this part of Chapter 36, we will depart from our usual procedure. But perhaps the following comments will shed a little more light on the reason for this information being given.

Concerning this Chapter, Matthew Henry said, *"In external prosperity and honor, the children of the Covenant are often cast behind, and those who are out of the Covenant seemingly got ahead. We may suppose it is a trial to the Faith of God's Israel, to hear of the pomp and power of the kings of Edom, while they were bond slaves in Egypt; but those who look for great things from God must be content to wait for them; God's time is the best time."*

Henry went on to say: *"Observe, Mount Seir is called the land of their possession.*

While the Israelites dwelt in the house of bondage, and their Canaan was only the land of Promise, the Edomites dwelt in their own habitations, and Seir was in their possession. The children of this world have their all in hand, and nothing in hope (Lk. 16:25); while the children of God have their all in hope, next to nothing in hand. But all things considered, it is better to have Canaan in Promise, than Mount Seir in possession."

"Thine arm, O Lord, in days of old, was strong to heal and save;
"It triumphed over disease and death, over darkness and the grave.
"To Thee they went, the blind, the dumb, the palsied, and the lame,
"The leper with his tainted life, the sick with fevered frame."

"And lo! Your touch brought life and health, gave speech, and strength, and sight;
"And youth renewed and frenzy calmed owned Thee, the Lord of light.
"And now, O Lord, be near to bless, Almighty as of yore,
"In crowded street, by restless couch, as by Gennesaret's shore."

"Be Thou our great Deliverer still, Thou Lord of life and death;
"Restore and quicken, soothe and bless, with Your Almighty breath;
"To hands that work and eyes that see, give wisdom's heavenly lore,
"That whole and sick, and weak and strong, may praise Thee evermore."

CHAPTER 37

(1) "AND JACOB DWELT IN THE LAND WHEREIN HIS FATHER WAS A STRANGER, IN THE LAND OF CANAAN.

(2) "THESE ARE THE GENERATIONS OF JACOB. JOSEPH, BEING SEVENTEEN YEARS OLD, WAS FEEDING THE FLOCK WITH HIS BRETHREN; AND THE LAD WAS WITH THE SONS OF BILHAH, AND WITH THE SONS OF ZILPAH, HIS FATHER'S WIVES: AND JOSEPH BROUGHT UNTO HIS FATHER THEIR EVIL REPORT.

(3) "NOW ISRAEL LOVED JOSEPH MORE THAN ALL HIS CHILDREN, BECAUSE HE WAS THE SON OF HIS OLD AGE: AND HE MADE HIM A COAT OF MANY COLORS.

(4) "AND WHEN HIS BRETHREN SAW THAT THEIR FATHER LOVED HIM MORE THAN ALL HIS BRETHREN, THEY HATED HIM, AND COULD NOT SPEAK PEACEABLY UNTO HIM."

The construction is:

1. The narrative continues with Jacob, but includes Joseph.

2. Joseph is one of, if not the most remarkable Type of Christ, found in the entirety of the Old Testament.

3. Inasmuch as the hearts of his brethren were not in communion with the touch of God in his heart, they hated him.

THE LAND OF CANAAN

Verse 1 reads: *"And Jacob dwelt in the land wherein his father was a stranger, in the land of Canaan."*

Having dispensed with Esau in the previous Chapter, and having mentioned him at all simply because he was a son of Jacob, we now pick up the narrative of Jacob, which includes the story of Joseph.

Jacob has spent some 20 years in Syria, and as well, approximately 10 years in Shechem, where he was out of the Will of God. However, he has now settled himself in Mamre in the Vale of Hebron, beside his aged and bedridden father Isaac.

We must realize that the families of Abraham, Isaac, and Jacob were in essence the Church of that day. Regrettably, it does not present a very pretty picture. The increase in numbers does not bring about an increase in holiness, but rather the very opposite. But ultimately the Grace of God will gain the upper hand, but the change will not come quickly or easily.

JOSEPH

Verse 2 reads: *"These are the generations of Jacob. Joseph, being seventeen years old, was feeding the flock with his brethren; and the lad was with the sons of Bilhah, and with the sons of Zilpah, his father's wives: and Joseph brought unto his father their evil report."*

The Second Verse in this Chapter sets Joseph forward as a shepherd, 17 years of age. It is believed that his mother Rachel was still living, but died within the year. It must be remembered that these accounts are not necessarily given in chronological order.

The story, which is about to unfold before us, is at least one of the most remarkable, one of the most powerful in the entirety of the Scriptures. It is a powerful testimony to the inspiration of the Word of God; for no man, either before or after the writing of the New Testament, could have composed such a story. As stated, it is one of the most remarkable in history.

Evidently, Jacob's vast herds were divided into at least two flocks, and perhaps even more. Joseph was with the sons of Bilhah and the sons of Zilpah, while the sons of Leah were evidently shepherding the other flock.

We aren't told exactly what the evil report was, which Joseph related to his father. But it probably had to do with the immoral Canaanite practices, in which his brothers were participating. There is some indication that he had spoken to them about these practices first of all, but that only aroused resentment against him in their hearts. While these men were in the Covenant so to speak, they were actually not a part of the Covenant. In other words, they knew about God, but they really didn't know God.

THE MODERN CHURCH

As one looks at this scenario, one is as well looking at the modern Church. Out of this family of brothers, the only one at the present who knew the Lord was Joseph, although all, as stated, were a part of the Covenant. And one must remember, merely being a part of the Covenant did not mean that one necessarily knew the Lord. They gained this position by natural birth; they could only gain the latter position of knowing the Lord by a new birth which is evident they had not yet experienced.

So we find here that only about one out of eleven truly knew the Lord. Benjamin had not yet been born, that is if our chronology is correct.

Out of the 11 brothers, the Church of that day, only Joseph knew the Lord. Considering

all the various Denominations of the modern Church, I'm not sure if the percentage is presently that high.

Out of the approximate one billion Catholics in the world, that is if we would conclude Catholicism to be Christian, which it really isn't, the number who are truly saved in that particular religion is abysmally small. And in fact, any Catholic who truly comes to Christ is going to have to leave out of Catholicism. It is not possible for a true Believer to remain in that ungodly, unscriptural system.

It grieved me to read sometime back where that a group of well-known so-called Protestant Preachers signed a concordant that they wouldn't try to evangelize Catholics. Their conclusion was, *"Catholics are already saved, and so our efforts must be spent on the unsaved."*

In the first place, Catholics aren't saved. If they are, the Bible means nothing. And as well, these Preachers, whomever they may be, aren't going to get anyone saved, Catholic or otherwise, because the gospel they preach is pure and simple, *"another gospel"* (II Cor. 11:4).

When we come to the Denominational world, and I speak of the Denominations which have rejected and even denounced the Baptism with the Holy Spirit with the evidence of speaking with other tongues, while there are some people who are truly saved in these ranks, that number is, as well, abysmally small. The reasons would be obvious. Having rejected the light given on the Holy Spirit, which has taken place, beginning approximately with the Twentieth Century, they have, for all practical purposes, shut the door to Christ. Understanding that every single thing done in this world as it regards the Godhead is done by the Holy Spirit, the Denominational world is left with little more than a philosophy of Christ.

These people, of course, claim that they haven't rejected the Holy Spirit; however, if we reject the *"Work"* of the Holy Spirit, and I speak of the Holy Spirit Baptism, we have in effect rejected the Holy Spirit (Acts 2:4; 10:44-47; 19:1-7).

Sadder still, most of the modern Pentecostal Denominations are such in name only. In fact, I am told that only about one-third of the people in Assemblies of God Churches, and Churches of God, the two largest Pentecostal Denominations, even claim to be baptized with the Holy Spirit. If that is in fact true, then these Denominations cannot even rightly and honestly claim to be Pentecostal. Sadly, many in the Pentecostal world have attempted to preach the Holy Spirit without the Cross, and they are left now with neither. Likewise, but in the opposite direction, the Denominational world has tried to preach the Cross without the Holy Spirit, and they are left with neither. To preach the Cross without the Holy Spirit leads to nothing but spiritual deadness, while to preach the Holy Spirit without the Cross leads to fanaticism. And that's exactly where the majority in the Pentecostal world actually is. They are chasing signs, that is, if they are chasing anything at all as it pertains to God.

The Charismatic world, for all practical purposes, has been rendered totally ineffective, and because it is shot through with false doctrine, especially the *"Jesus died spiritually doctrine."* This doctrine is, pure and simple, a repudiation of the Cross, which is a direct attack on the Atonement, and there could be no more serious offence than that.

Regrettably, the modern Church finds itself with the spirit of the Laodiceans. Jesus said of that Church:

"I know your works, that you are neither cold nor hot: I wish that you were cold or hot.

"So then because you are lukewarm, neither cold nor hot, I will spew you out of My mouth.

"Because you say, I am rich, and increased with goods, and have need of nothing; and know not that you are wretched, and miserable, and poor, and blind, and naked" (Rev. 3:15-17).

Coming from none other than the Lord of Glory, that is a powerful indictment! But that characterizes the modern Church to the proverbial *"T."*

THE MESSAGE OF THE CROSS

Considering that the Holy Spirit works exclusively through the Finished Work of Christ, which in effect makes His Work possible, He is raising up the Message of the Cross presently, equal to the days of the Apostle Paul.

NOTES

The story of the New Covenant is the story of the Cross. And one might say, the story of the Cross is the explanation of the New Covenant.

The Lord gave this explanation to Paul, which he gave to us in all of his Epistles, but especially in his Epistle to the Romans.

I believe that the Lord is raising up the Message of the Cross, which at the same time is the Message of the Holy Spirit, as a dividing line between the True Church and the apostate church. In other words, as one looks at the Cross, so will one be either in the True Church or the apostate church. That's how important all of this is.

In fact, the Cross has always been the dividing line; however, I personally believe the Holy Spirit is going to make it an even greater testimony today than ever before.

One can read the Book of Acts and see how the Church was brought in. I believe it's going to be taken out in the same manner. The facts are, most will be apostate; however, for those who embrace the Message of *"Jesus Christ and Him Crucified,"* they are going to portray the Book of Acts all over again. This means that the True Church will not be wretched, miserable, poor, blind, and naked, and we speak of the spiritual sense, but rather will have done what Christ said to do. We will *"buy of Him gold tried in the fire, that we may be* (truly) *rich; and white raiment* (true Righteousness), *that we may be clothed, and that the shame of our nakedness does not appear; and* (we will) *anoint our eyes with eyesalve, that we may see"* (Rev. 3:18).

The *"gold"* typifies Deity, in other words, that which is of God and not of man. The *"white raiment"* typifies the Righteousness of Christ, and not the righteousness of man. The *"eyesalve"* typifies the Anointing of the Holy Spirit, which can only come upon that which is of Christ.

Because it's so very important, please allow me to say it again:

The Message of the Cross has always been the Message, is the Message now, and will ever be the Message. To reject that Message is to reject the entirety of the Word of God. One cannot have it both ways; either what Christ did for us at the Cross suffices, or else it doesn't, and we must turn to other things.

But I know that it does suffice. Paul said:

"For Christ sent me not to baptize, but to preach the Gospel: not with wisdom of words, lest the Cross of Christ should be made of none effect.

"For the preaching of the Cross is to them that perish foolishness; but unto us which are saved it is the Power of God" (I Cor. 1:17-18).

THE COAT OF COLORS

Verse 3 reads: *"Now Israel loved Joseph more than all his children, because he was the son of his old age: and he made him a coat of many colors."*

If it is to be noticed, the Holy Spirit uses here the name *"Israel,"* signifying that what was done here regarding Joseph was totally of the Lord. Many have claimed that Jacob caused this problem among his sons, by favoring Joseph, etc. Not true!

The *"love"* expressed here had to do with the Lord laying His Hand on Joseph, while Jacob's other sons had rejected the Lord. Even though Jacob loved all of his sons, his love for Joseph had to do with the Will of God. While he was his youngest, Benjamin not yet having been born; still, that was not the primary reason.

Because of sin on the part of his other sons, there was no fellowship between Jacob and these sons. In fact, there couldn't be any fellowship, as would be obvious. There was fellowship with Joseph, and because of the touch of God on his life, and above all, his love for God.

He *"coat of many colors"* holds a special meaning. It was to be worn by the one who was to have the birthright, normally the first-born. But as it had been with Jacob and Esau, the firstborn, who was Reuben, would not have this position of leadership. The Holy Spirit proclaimed that it should go to Joseph. When Jacob left this mortal coil, Joseph, in essence, was to be the High Priest of the family, which the following years proved to be the case, and graphically so!

Jacob didn't want to make the mistake his father Isaac had made. Isaac didn't want to give the birthright to Jacob, even though the Lord had made it very plain, even at the birth of the two boys, that this was to be the case. Jacob coming by that position, as a result of Isaac's procrastination, was fraught with

difficulties and problems. Jacob was determined that this would not be the case with his actions. The moment the Lord told him that Joseph was to be the one, however that happened, Jacob immediately proclaims his position, by making Joseph this many-colored coat which he would wear at certain times. As we shall see, all of this didn't set well at all with his brothers.

HATRED

Verse 4 reads: *"And when his brethren saw that their father loved him more than all his brethren, they hated him, and could not speak peaceably unto him."*

This perfectly epitomizes Christ; of Whom Joseph was one of the most remarkable types found in the Word of God. God loved His Son, and showed it greatly by lavishing upon Him all the power of the Holy Spirit. As a result, the Jews, who were His brethren, so to speak, hated Him.

So what we see here regarding this scenario is a perfect picture of Christ.

This *"hatred,"* and hatred it is, follows down in the Church, regarding the same principles. What do I mean by that?

Those on whom the Lord has laid His Hand will ultimately be hated by the Church. As we have previously stated, this small family, which constituted the Church of its day, had little trouble with surrounding neighbors, although they were heathen; the greatest problems came from within, even as we are studying here. It is the same with the Church. The hatred and animosity little come from without, but rather from within.

A PERSONAL EXPERIENCE

In 1982, if I remember the year correctly, the Lord spoke something to my heart that was to come to pass in totality.

It was a Saturday morning. I had gone to a place close to the Mississippi River, which is not far from our home, in order to seek the Face of the Lord, even as I often did. That morning was not to be uneventful.

As my custom was, I would pray approximately 30 minutes, and then sit in the car and study the Word for approximately the same period of time. I would alternate doing this for most of the day.

It was sometime before noon, when the Spirit of God came over me greatly, actually telling me what the core of my Message was to be as it regarded our Ministry.

At that time, we were on Television over much of the free world. In fact, the Telecast was translated into several languages. As a result of all of this, and above all, the Anointing of the Holy Spirit, we had the largest audience in the world as it regards Gospel. Many people were being saved, with many lives being changed. At that time we were in the process of constructing Family Worship Center, as well as building the Bible College. And then the Lord that morning said this to me:

"You must use the platform of Television, which I have given you, to preach Justification by Faith to the Catholics. Tell them that their Church cannot save them. As well, you must tell the Denominational world that it must come to the Holy Spirit, and that the Pentecostal world must come back to the Holy Spirit."

I am not quoting verbatim that which the Lord gave to me, but what I have given is the gist of what was said.

And then the Lord spoke again to my heart, saying, *"If you preach what I tell you to preach, you will see many saved, but your own will turn against you."*

And then: *"Are you willing to do what I want you do, even though the price will be high?"*

Once again I emphasize that these are not the exact words, but basically the gist of what was said.

I knew what I was hearing was from the Lord, but I wondered as to what He meant by *"Your own will turn against you."*

After a short time of deliberation, I told the Lord that I would do my very best to preach what He gave me, not adding to or taking away from the Message.

THE FULFILLMENT

I'm so very glad, at the time, I didn't know the extent to what the Lord was speaking to my heart regarding my own turning against me. I'm not sure I could have stood it.

It all happened exactly as the Lord said it would. I began to preach what I felt God gave me to preach, which resulted in literally

hundreds of thousands all over the world being brought to a saving knowledge of Jesus Christ. As well, we saw tens of thousands baptized with the Holy Spirit, and untold numbers of lives gloriously and wondrously changed by the Power of God.

But at that time, while I understood the Cross of Christ, and graphically so, as it regarded the initial Salvation experience, and preached it powerfully and strongly, I didn't understand the Cross as it regards our Sanctification. In other words, I didn't know that the Cross plays a role just as important in our Sanctification as it does in the initial Salvation experience. Not knowing that, I found myself in the same situation as the Apostle Paul, which he reiterated in Romans, Chapter 7. And let me address that for a moment:

I don't care who the person is, or how much God is using them; if they do not understand the Cross according to Romans, Chapter 6, and the part it plays in their everyday living for God, it is absolutely impossible for that person to live a victorious life. In some way, the works of the flesh will be made evident in that person's life (Gal. 5:19-21).

Satan taking advantage of this Scriptural ignorance, which no doubt was also accompanied by much self-will on my part, he succeeded in bringing about a terrible rupture in my life. It would cause untold heartache.

Because of my strong stand on many issues as it regards the Word of God, I found to my dismay that many in the Church, and especially the leadership of the Denomination with which I was then associated, had developed a strong animosity against me. They took full advantage of my failure to express that animosity. Not at all attempting to be melodramatic, I can describe it as nothing but *"hatred."* And to boil it all down, their hatred for me was because of the Anointing of the Holy Spirit within my heart and life. They would use other things as an excuse, but what I've said is actually the truth of the matter. Sadly and regrettably, that hatred is no less today than it was then.

Now that the Lord has given me the Revelation of the Cross, which is actually the same Revelation that He gave to Paul, they are faced with a dilemma. It makes it very hard for them to accept the Message, when they so very much dislike the messenger. But unfortunately, the Church doesn't have any say as it regards who the messenger is. And that's one of the great problems!

The Lord has His messengers, and the Church, through carnal activity, has its messengers. So, between these two sets of messengers, the *"hatred"* continues. How sad!

(5) "AND JOSEPH DREAMED A DREAM, AND HE TOLD IT HIS BRETHREN: AND THEY HATED HIM YET THE MORE.

(6) "AND HE SAID UNTO THEM, HEAR, I PRAY YOU, THIS DREAM WHICH I HAVE DREAMED:

(7) "FOR, BEHOLD, WE WERE BINDING SHEAVES IN THE FIELD, AND, LO, MY SHEAF AROSE, AND ALSO STOOD UPRIGHT; AND, BEHOLD, YOUR SHEAVES STOOD ROUND ABOUT, AND MADE OBEISANCE TO MY SHEAF.

(8) "AND HIS BRETHREN SAID TO HIM, SHALL YOU INDEED REIGN OVER US? OR SHALL YOU INDEED HAVE DOMINION OVER US? AND THEY HATED HIM YET THE MORE FOR HIS DREAMS, AND FOR HIS WORDS.

(9) "AND HE DREAMED YET ANOTHER DREAM, AND TOLD IT HIS BRETHREN, AND SAID, BEHOLD, I HAVE DREAMED A DREAM MORE; AND, BEHOLD, THE SUN AND THE MOON AND THE ELEVEN STARS MADE OBEISANCE TO ME.

(10) "AND HE TOLD IT TO HIS FATHER, AND TO HIS BRETHREN: AND HIS FATHER REBUKED HIM, AND SAID UNTO HIM, WHAT IS THIS DREAM THAT YOU HAVE DREAMED? SHALL I AND YOUR MOTHER AND YOUR BRETHREN INDEED COME TO BOW DOWN OURSELVES TO YOU TO THE EARTH?

(11) "AND HIS BRETHREN ENVIED HIM; BUT HIS FATHER OBSERVED THE SAYING."

The composition is:

1. The Lord revealed the future to Joseph in a dream. While the dream definitely referred to him, it more so referred to Christ and Israel.

2. He told his brothers the truth, and they hated him even more. Thus was it with Joseph's great antitype. He bore witness to the truth, and his testimony to the truth was answered, on man's part, by the Cross.

3. The mention of Joseph's mother in Verse 10 is thought by some to be a mistake in the Sacred Text, Rachel being already dead. But she was still living at the time, and died shortly afterwards. As stated, these accounts are not necessarily given in chronological order.

NOTES

THE DREAMS

Verses 5 through 8 read: *"And Joseph dreamed a dream, and he told it his brethren: and they hated him yet the more.*

"And he said unto them, Hear, I pray you, this dream which I have dreamed:

"For, behold, we were binding sheaves in the field, and, lo, my sheaf arose, and also stood upright: and, behold, your sheaves stood round about, and made obeisance to my sheaf.

"And his brethren said to him, Shall you indeed reign over us? Or shall you indeed have dominion over us? And they hated him yet the more for his dreams, and for his words."

Looking at these dreams from the natural viewpoint, many have suggested that it was prideful arrogance which had Joseph to relate these dreams to his brothers; however, it was not done in pride, since there is no reason to suppose that Joseph as yet understood the celestial origin of his dreams, much less what they meant.

Pulpit Commentary says, *"He related this in the simplicity of his heart, and in doing so he was also guided, unconsciously it may be, but still really, by an overruling providence, Who made use of this very telling of the dream as a step toward its fulfillment."*

Pulpit Commentary continues, *"In the absence of information to the contrary, we are warranted in believing that there was nothing either sinful or offensive in Joseph's spirit or manner in making known his dreams. That which appears to have excited the hostility of his brethren was not the mode of their communication, but the character of their contents."*

In fact, due to the principle of Joseph being a Type of Christ, and without a doubt, the most powerful Type in the Old Testament, no sin whatsoever is recorded as it regards this brother. While he very definitely did commit sins at times, and simply because the Scripture says that *"all have sinned and come short of the Glory of God"*; still, these sins were not recorded because of his place and position.

And to be sure, if what Joseph did in relating these dreams was wrong, the Holy Spirit would have said so, or else ignored the incident.

While the dream definitely had to do with Joseph, as we shall see, Joseph's life and experiences far more portray Christ. Concerning the dream, while his brothers would definitely bow down to him, the greater meaning has to do with the time that is coming, when Israel will bow down to Christ, which will take place at the Second Coming. That is by far the greater meaning, and that which the Holy Spirit intends to present.

THE TRUTH

The hatred that Joseph's brethren exhibited toward him represents the Jews in Christ's day. *"He came to His Own, and His Own received Him not."* He had *"no form nor comeliness"* in their eyes. They would not own Him as the Son of God, or as the King of Israel. Their eyes were not opened to behold *"His Glory, the glory as of the only begotten of the Father, full of Grace and Truth."* They would not have Him; they hated Him.

REVELATION

Verses 9 through 11 read: *"And he dreamed yet another dream, and told it his brethren, and said, Behold, I have dreamed a dream more; and, behold, the sun and the moon and the eleven stars made obeisance to me.*

"And he told it to his father, and to his brethren: and his father rebuked him, and said unto him, What is this dream that you have dreamed? Shall I and your mother and your brethren indeed come to bow down ourselves to you to the Earth?

"And his brethren envied him; but his father observed the saying."

As it regards Joseph, we see that in no wise did he relax his testimony in consequence of his brothers' refusal of his first dream. He dreams another dream, and tells it, as well, to his brethren and his father.

This was simple testimony founded upon Divine Revelation; but it was testimony which brought Joseph down to the pit. Had he kept back his testimony, or taken off part of its edge and power, he might have spared himself. But no; he told them the truth and, therefore, they hated him even more.

Concerning this, Mackintosh said: *"Thus was it with Joseph's great Antitype. He bore witness to the truth — he witnessed a good confession — He kept back nothing — He could only speak the truth because He was the Truth, and His testimony to the Truth was answered, on man's part, by the Cross, the vinegar, the soldier's spear.*

"The Testimony of Christ, too, was connected with the deepest, fullest, richest Grace. He not only came as 'the Truth,' but also as the perfect expression of all the love of the Father's heart: 'Grace and Truth came by Jesus Christ.' He was the full disclosure to man of what God was, and was the full disclosure to God of what man ought to have been, but was not; hence man was left entirely without excuse. He came and showed God to man, and man hated God with a perfect hatred. The fullest exhibition of Divine love was answered by the fullest exhibition of human hatred. This is seen in the Cross; and we have it touchingly foreshadowed at the pit into which Joseph was cast by his brethren."

(12) "AND HIS BRETHREN WENT TO FEED THEIR FATHER'S FLOCK IN SHECHEM.

(13) "AND ISRAEL SAID UNTO JOSEPH, DO NOT YOUR BRETHREN FEED THE FLOCK IN SHECHEM? COME, AND I WILL SEND YOU UNTO THEM. AND HE SAID TO HIM, HERE AM I.

(14) "AND HE SAID TO HIM, GO, I PRAY YOU, SEE WHETHER IT BE WELL WITH YOUR BRETHREN, AND WELL WITH THE FLOCKS; AND BRING ME WORD AGAIN. SO HE SENT HIM OUT OF THE VALE OF HEBRON, AND HE CAME TO SHECHEM.

(15) "AND A CERTAIN MAN FOUND HIM, AND, BEHOLD, HE WAS WANDERING IN THE FIELD: AND THE MAN ASKED HIM, SAYING, WHAT DO YOU SEEK?

(16) "AND HE SAID, I SEEK MY BRETHREN: TELL ME, I PRAY YOU, WHERE THEY FEED THEIR FLOCKS.

(17) "AND THE MAN SAID, THEY ARE DEPARTED HENCE; FOR I HEARD THEM SAY, LET US GO TO DOTHAN. AND JOSEPH WENT AFTER HIS BRETHREN, AND FOUND THEM IN DOTHAN.

(18) "AND WHEN THEY SAW HIM AFAR OFF, EVEN BEFORE HE CAME NEAR UNTO

THEM, THEY CONSPIRED AGAINST HIM TO SLAY HIM."

The construction is:

1. Joseph is given more Revelation through another dream. Little did all of these men know, even Joseph or his father, as to exactly how important this Revelation actually was.

2. In these dreams, the Holy Spirit portrays Israel's acceptance of Christ, when in fact, at the time the dream was given, there was no Israel, at least as far as a nation was concerned.

3. The short phrase, *"Here am I,"* in reply to Jacob's request of Joseph, foreshadows the statement of Christ, *"Then said I, Lo, I come: in the volume of the Book it is written of Me,*

"I delight to do Your Will, O My God: yes, Your Law is within My heart" (Ps. 40:7-8).

4. The conspiracy against Joseph to murder him foreshadowed the conspiracy of the religious leaders of Israel to murder Christ.

THE SENDING OF JOSEPH

Verses 12 through 14 read: *"And his brethren went to feed their father's flock in Shechem.*

"And Israel said unto Joseph, Do not your brethren feed the flock in Shechem? Come, and I will send you unto them. And he said to him, Here am I.

"And he said to him, Go, I pray you, see whether it be well with your brethren, and well with the flocks; and bring me word again. So he sent him out of the vale of Hebron, and he came to Shechem."

Jacob sending Joseph to his brethren in order to find out how they were doing proves that he did not understand at all the depths of their hatred for Joseph. However, all of this foreshadows God sending His Son, the Lord Jesus Christ, to the nation of Israel, even as Israel was raised up for this very purpose. But the difference is, whereas Jacob was ignorant of the degree of hatred evidenced against Joseph, God was not ignorant at all, but knew totally of the hatred on the part of Israel, which would be evidenced toward Christ; nevertheless, this did not deter Him at all!

THE CONSPIRACY

Verses 15 through 18 read: *"And a certain man found him, and, behold, he was wandering in the field: and the man asked him, saying, What do you seek?*

"And he said, I seek my brethren: tell me, I pray you, where they feed their flocks.

"And the man said, They are departed from here; for I heard them say, Let us go to Dothan. And Joseph went after his brethren, and found them in Dothan.

"And when they saw him afar off, even before he came near unto them, they conspired against him to slay him."

Little does Jacob realize that his sending Joseph to his brothers will instigate a time of sorrow of unparalleled proportions. It will break his heart to such an extent that, in fact, there are no words that could describe, at least properly so, what Joseph's brothers did to him, and thereby, to their aged father, Jacob.

Such is sin. It has no heart. It truly steals, kills, and destroys.

The sons of Jacob were guilty of murder, for their hatred fostered such. The Scripture plainly says that *"whosoever hates his brother is a murderer"* (I Jn. 3:15), and this, even though the deed itself may not be carried out.

The sons of Jacob hated their brother because their father loved him. Joseph was a Type of Christ; for though He was the Beloved Son of His Father, and hated by a wicked world, yet the Father sent Him out of His bosom to visit us in great humility and love. He came from Heaven to Earth to seek and save us, and that despite our hatred toward Him.

He came to His Own, and His Own not only received Him not, but consulted, saying, *"This is the Heir, come, let us kill Him; crucify Him, crucify Him!"* This He submitted to, in pursuance of His design to redeem and save us.

As we go forward in this narrative, we will see Christ in the actions of Joseph, set out perfectly before us. As such, we must learn what the Holy Spirit is telling us through the life of this man.

Dothan was about 12 miles north of Shechem, with Shechem being about 50 miles north of Hebron. So Joseph would have to walk about 62 miles to find his brothers.

Even before he arrived there, that is when they saw him coming, they conspired to kill him. It was thus so with Christ as well. When He was born, Herod sought to kill Him (Mat., Chpt. 2).

If it is to be remembered, Shechem is the place where Simeon and Levi killed all the men of that small town, and because their sister Dinah had been raped.

Some period of time had now passed, but the greater reason that the brothers were not fearful of reprisal is probably due to their great strength.

That Jacob would have to send a part of his herds so far away as to Shechem, a distance of some 50 miles, tells us how large these herds were and, therefore, the power of Jacob. There is a possibility that there were quite a number of other men with the brothers at this time, actually serving in their employ, which would have made this group powerful indeed!

(19) "AND THEY SAID ONE TO ANOTHER, BEHOLD, THIS DREAMER COMETH.

(20) "COME NOW THEREFORE, AND LET US SLAY HIM, AND CAST HIM INTO SOME PIT, AND WE WILL SAY, SOME EVIL BEAST HAS DEVOURED HIM: AND WE SHALL SEE WHAT WILL BECOME OF HIS DREAMS.

(21) "AND REUBEN HEARD IT, AND HE DELIVERED HIM OUT OF THEIR HANDS; AND SAID, LET US NOT KILL HIM.

(22) "AND REUBEN SAID UNTO THEM, SHED NO BLOOD, BUT CAST HIM INTO THIS PIT THAT IS IN THE WILDERNESS, AND LAY NO HAND UPON HIM; THAT HE MIGHT RID HIM OUT OF THEIR HANDS, TO DELIVER HIM TO HIS FATHER AGAIN.

(23) "AND IT CAME TO PASS, WHEN JOSEPH WAS COME UNTO HIS BRETHREN, THAT THEY STRIPPED JOSEPH OUT OF HIS COAT, HIS COAT OF MANY COLORS THAT WAS ON HIM;

(24) "AND THEY TOOK HIM, AND CAST HIM INTO A PIT: AND THE PIT WAS EMPTY, THERE WAS NO WATER IN IT.

(25) "AND THEY SAT DOWN TO EAT BREAD: AND THEY LIFTED UP THEIR EYES AND LOOKED, AND, BEHOLD, A COMPANY OF ISHMEELITES CAME FROM GILEAD WITH THEIR CAMELS BEARING SPICERY AND BALM AND MYRRH, GOING TO CARRY IT DOWN TO EGYPT.

(26) "AND JUDAH SAID UNTO HIS BRETHREN, WHAT PROFIT IS IT IF WE SLAY OUR BROTHER, AND CONCEAL HIS BLOOD?

(27) "COME, AND LET US SELL HIM TO THE ISHMEELITES, AND LET NOT OUR

NOTES

HAND BE UPON HIM; FOR HE IS OUR BROTHER AND OUR FLESH. AND HIS BRETHREN WERE CONTENT.

(28) "THEN THERE PASSED BY MIDIANITES MERCHANTMEN; AND THEY DREW AND LIFTED UP JOSEPH OUT OF THE PIT, AND SOLD JOSEPH TO THE ISHMEELITES FOR TWENTY PIECES OF SILVER: AND THEY BROUGHT JOSEPH INTO EGYPT."

The composition is:

1. When we look at Joseph in the pit and in the prison, and look at him afterwards as ruler over all the land of Egypt, we see the difference between the thoughts of God and the thoughts of men; and so when we look at the Cross, and at *"the Throne of the Majesty in the Heavens,"* we see the same thing.

2. Nothing ever brought out the real state of man's heart toward God but the Coming of Christ.

3. The merchants who bought Joseph are called Midianites and Ishmeelites. They were sons of Abraham by Hagar and Keturah.

4. They sold Joseph to the Ishmeelites for 20 pieces of silver. Christ was sold for 30 pieces of silver.

REUBEN

Verses 19 through 22 read: *"And they said one to another, Behold, this dreamer comes.*

"Come now therefore, and let us kill him, and cast him into some pit, and we will say, Some evil beast has devoured him: and we shall see what will become of his dreams.

"And Reuben heard it, and he delivered him out of their hands; and said, Let us not kill him.

"And Reuben said unto them, Shed no blood, but cast him into this pit that is in the wilderness, and lay no hand upon him; that he might rid him out of their hands, to deliver him to his father again."

Partly through the personal character of Joseph, partly through the evil passions of his brethren, partly through the apparently casual incidence of the neighborhood, partly through the Spirit of Righteousness working in the heart of Reuben, partly through the weakness and fondness of Jacob, we see *"all things working together"* in God's Hands! He weaves the web composed of many single threads into one united, orderly pattern as a whole in which we are able to trace His Own thought and purpose.

Reuben was actually the firstborn; consequently, it was to him that the birthright should have come, which would have guaranteed him a double portion of Jacob's riches, when the Patriarch came down to die. So he would have had the most to gain from Joseph's death, who by now had been given the birthright instead. But Reuben seemed to have some conscience left, where his brethren did not. As such, the Scripture says, *"He delivered him out of their hands; and said, Let us not kill him."*

Several things greatly rankled these men.

The dreams angered them greatly, as did the coat of many colors. So they would kill the one who dreamed the dreams, and strip the coat from him, thinking to silence his voice. Little did they know what the future held!

Reuben suggested that they put Joseph in a pit, which they did, with him thinking that he would come back later and rescue the boy. Evidently he had to go some place. When he returned, he found that Joseph was gone. They had sold him to the Ishmeelites.

Along with Reuben, Judah is the one who saved the life of Joseph, suggesting that they sell him as a slave. However, this was little an act of mercy on the part of Judah, inasmuch as under normal circumstances, they were consigning him to a life worse than death.

TWENTY PIECES OF SILVER

Verses 23 through 28 read: *"And it came to pass, when Joseph was come unto his brethren, that they stripped Joseph out of his coat, his coat of many colors that was on him;*

"And they took him, and cast him into a pit: and the pit was empty, there was no water in it.

"And they sat down to eat bread: and they lifted up their eyes and looked, and, behold, a company of Ishmeelites came from Gilead with their camels bearing spicery and balm and myrrh, going to carry it down to Egypt.

"And Judah said unto his brethren, What profit is it if we kill our brother, and conceal his blood?

"Come, and let us sell him to the Ishmeelites, and let not our hand be upon him; for he is our brother and our flesh. And his brethren were content.

"Then there passed by Midianites merchantmen; and they drew and lifted up Joseph out of the pit, and sold Joseph to the Ishmeelites for twenty pieces of silver: and they brought Joseph into Egypt."

These brothers sitting down to eat bread, even after they had thrown Joseph into the pit, shows how hard their hearts were, indicating deplorable brutality on their part. In their minds, they had satisfactorily disposed of the young man and his dreams. This *"coat of colors,"* which signified that he had now been chosen for the birthright instead of Reuben, would be used to deceive his father.

Evidently, their idea was, when they put him in the pit, to let him starve to death. But now a change of events comes about, in that they spot a camel train coming near them, and going down to Egypt. They would sell Joseph as a slave to these Ishmeelites, and make some profit from the transaction. Judah was the one who suggested this. They would get 20 pieces of silver. This is a Type of Christ being sold for 30 pieces of silver.

As they stripped the coat from Joseph, likewise, they cast lots for Jesus' robe.

Verse 25 says they *"sat down to eat bread: and they lifted up their eyes and looked."* Likewise, Mathew said concerning the Crucifixion of Christ, *"And sitting down they watched Him there"* (Mat. 27:36).

Verse 27 speaks of Joseph being sold *"to the Ishmaelites"* (Gentiles). Likewise, Matthew said, *"When they had bound Him, they led Him away, and delivered Him to Pontius Pilate, the Governor"* (Mat. 27:2).

(29) "AND REUBEN RETURNED UNTO THE PIT; AND, BEHOLD, JOSEPH WAS NOT IN THE PIT; AND HE RENT HIS CLOTHES.

(30) "AND HE RETURNED UNTO HIS BRETHREN, AND SAID, THE CHILD IS NOT; AND I, WHITHER SHALL I GO?

(31) "AND THEY TOOK JOSEPH'S COAT, AND KILLED A KID OF THE GOATS, AND DIPPED THE COAT IN THE BLOOD;

(32) "AND THEY SENT THE COAT OF MANY COLORS, AND THEY BROUGHT IT TO THEIR FATHER; AND SAID, THIS HAVE WE FOUND: KNOW NOW WHETHER IT BE YOUR SON'S COAT OR NO.

(33) "AND HE KNEW IT, AND SAID, IT IS MY SON'S COAT; AN EVIL BEAST HAS

DEVOURED HIM; JOSEPH IS WITHOUT DOUBT RENT IN PIECES.

(34) "AND JACOB RENT HIS CLOTHES, AND PUT SACKCLOTH UPON HIS LOINS, AND MOURNED FOR HIS SON MANY DAYS.

(35) "AND ALL HIS SONS AND ALL HIS DAUGHTERS ROSE UP TO COMFORT HIM; BUT HE REFUSED TO BE COMFORTED; AND HE SAID, FOR I WILL GO DOWN INTO THE GRAVE UNTO MY SON MOURNING. THUS HIS FATHER WEPT FOR HIM

(36) "AND THE MIDIANITES SOLD HIM INTO EGYPT UNTO POTIPHAR, AN OFFICER OF PHARAOH'S, AND CAPTAIN OF THE GUARD."

The overview is:

1. The Scripture says they *"killed a kid of the goats,"* and then *"dipped Joseph's coat in the blood."* Rebekah used a *"kid of the goats"* to deceive Isaac, as it regards Jacob (Gen. 27:9).

2. Instead of taking the coat to Jacob, they sent it, evidently by a slave, and told the slave what to say.

3. Joseph was sold as a slave into Egypt, and the brothers thought they would never see him again.

THE DECEPTION

Verses 29 through 33 read: *"And Reuben returned unto the pit; and, behold, Joseph was not in the pit; and he rent his clothes.*

"And he returned unto his brethren, and said, The child is not; and I, whither shall I go?

"And they took Joseph's coat, and killed a kid of the goats, and dipped the coat in the blood;

"And they sent the coat of many colors, and they brought it to their father; and said, This have we found: know now whether it be your son's coat or no.

"And he knew it, and said, It is my son's coat; an evil beast has devoured him; Joseph is without doubt rent in pieces."

It seems like Reuben is genuinely sorry about the turn of events; however, they explained to him what they had done, and the record proclaims the fact that he did nothing further.

To be frank, he could easily have overtaken the Ishmeelites and Midianites and bought Joseph back. But he made no effort to do so.

In order to deceive their father, they evidently got an employee or slave to take the

bloody coat to Jacob, and to give him the story they had concocted. More than likely, the slave didn't know the truth of the matter either. He would in all good conscience have related to Jacob what they told him to say.

This being the case, he would not have had any knowledge of this coat of many colors, or that it had been given to Joseph by his father. The slave only knew what he had been told to say, so he hands Jacob the coat, with others probably with him, and asked Jacob if this coat actually belonged to Joseph.

He recognized it immediately, and then surmised what his evil sons wanted him to surmise, that a wild animal had killed Joseph.

Knowing how much Jacob loved Joseph, it seems that they took some glee in the suffering they caused the Patriarch at this time. However, even as the next two Verses portray, his grief, it seems, was even greater than they had anticipated it would be. It almost killed the old man!

WHY WOULD GOD ALLOW THIS TO HAPPEN TO JACOB?

Verses 34 and 35 read: *"And Jacob rent his clothes, and put sackcloth upon his loins, and mourned for his son many days.*

"And all his sons and all his daughters rose up to comfort him; but he refused to be comforted; and he said, For I will go down into the grave unto my son mourning. Thus his father wept for him."

As the test regarding Abraham concerning the offering of Isaac in Sacrifice, even as the Lord commanded him, was no doubt the most difficult test that God ever required of any man, to be sure, that which was demanded of Jacob wasn't far behind. In some ways, it was even worse.

As difficult was the test with Abraham, it was over in three days. Jacob's would last about 20 years. Isaac was alive during this three days and nights, but in the mind of Jacob, he thought that Joseph was dead.

He knew that the Lord had told him to give Joseph the birthright. That being the case, why would the Lord then allow his life to be taken by a wild animal, or so Jacob thought?

In fact, there was no answer to this question, plus a thousand others, at least as far as Jacob was concerned. But to his credit, despite the sorrow and the heartache, the aged Patriarch didn't give up, at least as far as his Faith in God was concerned. Despite questions which seemed to have no answers, he continued to believe. In fact, circumstances seemed to prove God wrong.

What a lesson for all of us. It is one thing to wait, but it is something else altogether to not even know that for which one is waiting.

There are questions in life for which we do not have any answers. And yet we know that the great Planner of all the ages, the Creator of all things, has everything under control. Not one single piece is out of place as it regards His Plan, or His Way.

In the next Chapter, we will observe the wickedness of Judah, and then pick up in Chapter 39 with Joseph, and ultimately come back to Jacob.

EGYPT

Verse 36 reads: *"And the Midianites sold him into Egypt unto Potiphar, an officer of Pharaoh's, and captain of the guard."*

It is said that in those days, the method for transporting slaves was to put each one in a wicker basket, where they would be placed in a cart, or strapped to the side of a camel. This would keep them from escaping.

So Joseph, on his way to Egypt, would have passed very close to his home in Hebron, but he was powerless to say or do anything. Bottled up in this awkward setting, and unable to stretch his legs, after awhile the pain would have become excruciating. But to be sure, those who had bought him little cared for his comfort, as would be obvious.

It is also obvious that the Lord was watching over him every mile of the way. Joseph sold to Potiphar, the captain of Pharaoh's guard, was no accident. It was planned by the Lord.

A TYPE OF CHRIST

One may wonder regarding Joseph, especially considering that he was a Type of Christ, and as well, considering his righteous life, as to why the Lord would submit him to such difficulties. Well, the same could be said for Jacob, and untold millions of other Believers down through the many centuries.

Faith must be tested, and great faith must be tested greatly. And, as it regards the Child

of God, every single thing with the Believer, even as we have stated some Chapters back, is a test.

As should be obvious, this hardly matches up to the modern gospel being preached, claiming that proper faith will exempt one from all difficulties. No, it doesn't match up, and because the modern gospel is wrong.

It is pathetic when one's faith is measured against the price of the suit he wears, or the model of car he drives. How would such foolishness have stacked up with Joseph, or Jacob for that matter?

The Christian life, at least according to the Bible, doesn't claim a life exempt from all problems and difficulties. In fact, the Lord definitely allows certain adverse things to come our way, in order for our faith to be tested.

When God blesses us, we learn about God, and how wonderful and glorious that He is; however, we learn nothing about ourselves. It takes adversity, trouble, and difficulties, for us to learn about ourselves, and most of the time, what we find is not very pleasant. So the blessings teach us about God, while adversity teaches us about ourselves.

This last Verse of Chapter 37 says that Joseph was *"sold into Egypt."* As the story will tell, Joseph will become the second most powerful man in Egypt. As well, Jesus Christ would rise from the dead and become the Head of the Church, which is, by and large, made up of Gentiles.

"I know of a Name, a beautiful Name,
"That Angels brought down to Earth;
"They whispered it low, one night long
　　ago,
"To a maiden of lowly birth."

"I know of a Name, a beautiful Name,
"That unto a Babe was given;
"The stars glittered bright throughout
　　that glad night,
"And Angels praised God in Heaven."

"The One of that Name my Saviour be-
　　came,
"My Saviour of Calvary;
"My sins nailed Him there, my burdens
　　He bears,
"He suffered all this for me."

*"I love that blessed Name, that won-
　　derful Name,*
"Made higher than all in Heaven;
*"'Twas whispered, I know, in my heart
　　long ago,*
"To Jesus my life I've given."

CHAPTER 38

(1) "AND IT CAME TO PASS AT THAT TIME, THAT JUDAH WENT DOWN FROM HIS BRETHREN, AND TURNED IN TO A CERTAIN ADULLAMITE, WHOSE NAME WAS HIRAH.

(2) "AND JUDAH SAW THERE A DAUGHTER OF A CERTAIN CANAANITE, WHOSE NAME WAS SHUAH; AND HE TOOK HER, AND WENT IN UNTO HER.

(3) "AND SHE CONCEIVED, AND BEAR A SON; AND HE CALLED HIS NAME ER.

(4) "AND SHE CONCEIVED AGAIN, AND BEAR A SON; AND SHE CALLED HIS NAME ONAN.

(5) "AND SHE YET AGAIN CONCEIVED, AND BEAR A SON; AND CALLED HIS NAME SHELAH: AND HE WAS AT CHEZIB, WHEN SHE BEAR HIM.

(6) "AND JUDAH TOOK A WIFE FOR ER HIS FIRSTBORN, WHOSE NAME WAS TAMAR.

(7) "AND ER, JUDAH'S FIRSTBORN, WAS WICKED IN THE SIGHT OF THE LORD, AND THE LORD SLEW HIM.

(8) "AND JUDAH SAID UNTO ONAN, GO IN UNTO YOUR BROTHER'S WIFE, AND MARRY HER, AND RAISE UP SEED TO YOUR BROTHER.

(9) "AND ONAN KNEW THAT THE SEED SHOULD NOT BE HIS; AND IT CAME TO PASS, WHEN HE WENT IN UNTO HIS BROTHER'S WIFE, THAT HE SPILLED IT ON THE GROUND, LEST THAT HE SHOULD GIVE SEED TO HIS BROTHER.

(10) "AND THE THING WHICH HE DID DISPLEASED THE LORD: WHEREFORE HE SLEW HIM ALSO."

The exegesis is:

1. This Chapter is a parenthesis introduced here as an actual picture of the sin, darkness, corruption, and self-will of Joseph's

NOTES

brethren during the whole period of his absence from them, and as the certain fruit of their rejection of him.

2. It is a fore-picture of the moral condition of the Jews today as the result of their rejection of the Messiah.

3. The Chapter is also placed here in order to show the connection between Christ and His predecessor Judah. Chapter 1 of Matthew shows how truly Christ made Himself of no reputation and by being born a member of the Tribe of Judah humbled Himself (Williams).

JUDAH

Verses 1 through 5 read: *"And it came to pass at that time, that Judah went down from his brethren, and turned in to a certain Adullamite, whose name was Hirah.*

"And Judah saw there a daughter of a certain Canaanite, whose name was Shuah; and he took her, and went in unto her.

"And she conceived, and bear a son; and he called his name Er.

"And she conceived again, and bear a son; and she called his name Onan.

"And she yet again conceived, and bear a son; and called his name Shelah: and he was at Chezib, when she bear him."

As we have already stated several times, we are reading here the account of the Church, so to speak, during Jacob's day. It is not a very pretty picture. Other than Joseph, and we have very little account of Benjamin, the sons of Jacob were grossly evil, to say the least. They were guilty of murder, adultery, and fornication, and about every other sin that one could imagine.

Chronologically, it is believed by some that Chapter 38 should follow Chapter 33, for a little over 30 years after Jacob left Haran, he went into Egypt. By that time, Judah's son's widow had given birth to twins, and they were old enough that one of them had married and become the father also of twins.

Chapter 38 of Genesis is just another proof of the veracity of the Bible. If man had written this account of his own accord, it is certain that such a Chapter would never have been included. But inasmuch as it is inspired by the Holy Spirit, the sacred writer, in this case Moses, had no choice but to include the narrative, because it's what the Holy Spirit desired. Why?

For one thing, it is meant to show us the awful condition of mankind. Even though exposed to the Word of the Lord, the sons of Jacob little cared for that Word. In fact, without a person being *"born again,"* and their having the Help and Power of the Holy Spirit, it is literally impossible for that person to live for God. And to be sure, these sons of Jacob at this stage were not Born-Again. There would be a time, years later, that they would be, but at this present time, they were extremely evil.

In all of this we see the special danger to which the theocratic family was exposed by their intermarrying with the Canaanites (Gen. 24:3; 28:6). To remove them from this constant temptation, they would be taken to Egypt, or else the line of Shem would have been absorbed into the line of Ham and Canaan, which was cursed by God.

Judah is the son of Jacob through whom the Redeemer would come.

When it says that *"Judah went down from his brethren,"* it means that he moved away from them, setting up a domicile of his own.

He became enamored with a Canaanite woman, whose father's name was Shuah. He took her for his wife. In rapid succession, it seems, she had three sons, *"Er," "Onan,"* and *"Shelah."*

The years pass, with *"Er"* becoming an adult, and marrying a girl by the name of *"Tamar."*

The Scripture says of this man, *"Judah's firstborn,"* that he *"was wicked in the sight of the Lord, and the Lord slew him."* Exactly as to how this happened, we aren't told.

It probably means that he became grossly involved in Canaanite idolatry. Now all of this is very important, simply because, as Judah's firstborn, he was to be in the lineage of the coming Redeemer. So we see Satan at work here, attempting to destroy that line, which line was necessary in order for the Redeemer to be born into this world.

After *"Er"* was slain by the Lord, however it happened, Judah demanded of *"Onan,"* his second son, who evidently was unmarried, to go in to Tamar, *"and raise up seed to his brother."* In this manner, the lineage would continue. But as we shall see, Onan in essence was saying by his actions, that he cared nothing about a Redeemer coming into the world. He didn't want Tamar for a wife, so he refused the command of his father, Judah.

Concerning this, the attitude of Onan, it greatly displeased the Lord, and the Scripture bluntly states, *"Wherefore He slew him also."*

QUESTIONS!

Many questions arise, as it regards these happenings. Had these men wanted to do right where, in fact, would they have found wives, if not among the Canaanites?

If they really wanted to do right, the example of Abraham regarding a wife for Isaac, and even of their father Jacob, was very evident before them. They each could have gone back to the area of Haran, to the family of Abraham, which was of the lineage of Shem, and there secured wives. But they had no interest in the things of the Lord, such action, and attitude, in fact, being a joke to them.

Another question looms: Did they really understand how important all of this actually was?

No! But at the same time, their lack of understanding was not because they had not been properly taught. It was because they had no concern or regard for the things of the Lord.

I think we can see here what the Lord thought of all of this, by Him taking the measures He did. In fact, what the Lord did in executing these two young men, which is exactly what happened, did have a marked effect on Judah, even as we shall see.

TAMAR

Verses 6 through 10 read: *"And Judah took a wife for Er his firstborn, whose name was Tamar.*

"And Er, Judah's firstborn, was wicked in the sight of the LORD, and the LORD slew him.

"And Judah said unto Onan, Go in unto your brother's wife, and marry her, and raise up seed to your brother.

"And Onan knew that the seed should not be his; and it came to pass, when he went in unto his brother's wife, that he spilled it on the ground, lest that he should give seed to his brother.

"And the thing which he did displeased the LORD: wherefore he slew him also."

So as not to break up the continuity, we dealt with the above Verses in previous Commentary. But as an aside, let us look at the following:

Five women are mentioned in the genealogy of Christ. They are in the following order: *"Tamar, Rahab, Ruth, Bathsheba* (but not by name), *and Mary"* (Mat. 1:3, 5-6, 16).

Three of these women were Gentiles, *"Tamar, Rahab, and Ruth."* Two were of the Jewish people; *"Bathsheba"* referred to as *"the wife of Urias,"* and *"Mary,"* the *"Mother of our Lord."*

The mix of both Jewish and Gentile, proclaims to all concerned that the Lord came for the entirety of the world, and not merely for the Jews. In fact, the Gentile women outnumbered the Jewish women, three above two.

Two of the women came by their place and position as a result of dubious means, but through no fault of their own. They are Tamar and Bathsheba. But yet, great faith characterized both of these women, even as we shall see in our study of Tamar, and which the record bears out as well, as it regards Bathsheba. In fact, the last Chapter of Proverbs (Chpt. 31) proclaims Bathsheba, even though she is not named. Solomon refers to himself as *"King Lemuel,"* and in this Chapter, he speaks of his Mother. Among many things, he refers to her as *"a virtuous woman"* (Prov. 31:10).

In the last Verse of that Chapter, the Holy Spirit through Solomon said of her, *"Give her of the fruit of her hands; and let her own works praise her in the gates"* (Prov. 31:31).

Once again when Satan attempted to subvert the Will of God as it regarded the one to take David's place, it was Bathsheba who stood her ground, and demanded of David and all concerned that Solomon be appointed king, and not Adonijah (I Ki., Chpt. 1).

As we shall see, Tamar, no doubt prodded strongly by the Holy Spirit, proved herself to be a much greater woman of faith, although a Canaanite, than even Judah.

(11) "THEN SAID JUDAH TO TAMAR HIS DAUGHTER IN LAW, REMAIN A WIDOW AT YOUR FATHER'S HOUSE, TILL SHELAH MY SON BE GROWN: FOR HE SAID, LEST

PERADVENTURE HE DIE ALSO, AS HIS BRETHREN DID. AND TAMAR WENT AND DWELT IN HER FATHER'S HOUSE.

(12) "AND IN PROCESS OF TIME THE DAUGHTER OF SHUAH JUDAH'S WIFE DIED: AND JUDAH WAS COMFORTED, AND WENT UP UNTO HIS SHEEPSHEARERS TO TIMNATH, HE AND HIS FRIEND HIRAH THE ADULLAMITE.

(13) "AND IT WAS TOLD TAMAR, SAYING, BEHOLD YOUR FATHER IN LAW GOES UP TO TIMNATH TO SHEER HIS SHEEP.

(14) "AND SHE PUT HER WIDOW'S GARMENTS OFF FROM HER, AND COVERED HER WITH A VEIL, AND WRAPPED HERSELF, AND SAT IN AN OPEN PLACE, WHICH IS BY THE WAY TO TIMNATH; FOR SHE SAW THAT SHELAH WAS GROWN, AND SHE WAS NOT GIVEN UNTO HIM TO WIFE.

(15) "WHEN JUDAH SAW HER, HE THOUGHT HER TO BE AN HARLOT; BECAUSE SHE HAD COVERED HER FACE.

(16) "AND HE TURNED UNTO HER BY THE WAY, AND SAID, GO TO, I PRAY YOU, LET ME COME IN UNTO YOU; (FOR HE KNEW NOT THAT SHE WAS HIS DAUGHTER IN LAW.) AND SHE SAID, WHAT WILL YOU GIVE ME, THAT YOU MAY COME IN UNTO ME?

(17) "AND HE SAID, I WILL SEND YOU A KID FROM THE FLOCK. AND SHE SAID, WILL YOU GIVE ME A PLEDGE, TILL YOU SEND IT?

(18) "AND HE SAID, WHAT PLEDGE SHALL I GIVE YOU? AND SHE SAID, YOUR SIGNET, AND YOUR BRACELETS, AND YOUR STAFF THAT IS IN YOUR HAND. AND HE GAVE IT TO HER, AND CAME IN UNTO HER, AND SHE CONCEIVED BY HIM.

(19) "AND SHE AROSE, AND WENT AWAY, AND LAID BY HER VEIL FROM HER, AND PUT ON THE GARMENTS OF HER WIDOWHOOD.

(20) "AND JUDAH SENT THE KID BY THE HAND OF HIS FRIEND THE ADULLAMITE, TO RECEIVE HIS PLEDGE FROM THE WOMAN'S HAND: BUT HE FOUND HER NOT."

The synopsis is:

1. The conduct of Tamar, though in every way reprehensible, is not to be attributed to mere lust, or inordinate desire for children,

but was most probably to assert her right to a place among the ancestresses of the Patriarchal family.

2. Even though the Lord did not condone the means by which all of this was done, He did accept the results with Pharez being the firstborn, being in the lineage of Christ.

3. Thankfully, this sordid scene which portrays Judah will ultimately change as it regards all the sons of Jacob. In other words, they will ultimately serve the Lord.

JUDAH AND TAMAR

Verses 11 through 14 read: *"Then said Judah to Tamar his daughter in law, Remain a widow at your father's house, till Shelah my son be grown: for he said, Lest peradventure he die also, as his brethren did. And Tamar went and dwelt in her father's house.*

"And in process of time the daughter of Shuah Judah's wife died; and Judah was comforted, and went up unto his sheepshearers to Timnath, he and his friend Hirah the Adullamite.

"And it was told Tamar, saying, Behold your father in law goes up to Timnath to sheer his sheep.

"And she put her widow's garments off from her, and covered her with a veil, and wrapped herself, and sat in an open place, which is by the way to Timnath; for she saw that Shelah was grown, and she was not given unto him to wife."

It is evident from this that Judah, for reasons which, in Verse 26, he acknowledged to be insufficient, wished to evade the duty of giving a third son to Tamar. It does not follow that he blamed her for their death; but the loss of two sons in succession must have frightened him.

A period of time had now passed, and Shelah, the last son of Judah, was grown. But Judah made no move to bring together this marriage.

Some say that the real reason for Tamar acting as she did is because she wanted her share of the inheritance, which the firstborn would receive. That may very well be the case, and more than likely, most definitely entered into the picture. Nevertheless, whatever her reasons, the Lord had other things in mind altogether. Her desire for a husband of the house of Judah, and as well a child,

the fruit of such a union, whatever the reasons, was placed there by God. So now she would carry out a scheme, which to her Canaanite mind was very plausible.

THE PLEDGE

Verses 15 through 20 read: *"When Judah saw her, he thought her to be an harlot; because she had covered her face.*

"And he turned unto her by the way, and said, Go to, I pray you, let me come in unto you; (for he knew not that she was his daughter in law.) And she said, What will you give me, that you may come in unto me?

"And he said, I will send you a kid from the flock. And she said, Will you give me a pledge, till you send it?

"And he said, What pledge shall I give you? And she said, Your signet, and your bracelets, and your staff that is in your hand. And he gave it to her, and came in unto her, and she conceived by him.

"And she arose, and went away, and laid by her veil from her, and put on the garments of widowhood.

"And Judah sent the kid by the hand of his friend the Adullamite, to receive his pledge from the woman's hand: but he found her not."

We find from all of this, and as should be obvious, that God will show that His choice is of Grace, and not of merit, and that Christ came into the world to save sinners, even the chiefest of sinners, and is not ashamed, upon their Repentance, to be allied to them.

Also, we must come to the conclusion as it regards all of this that the worth and worthiness of Jesus Christ are Personal, of Himself, and not derived from His ancestors. Humbling Himself to be made in the likeness of sinful flesh, he was pleased to descend from some who were infamous.

Tamar did not degrade herself, as is popularly thought, to the level of a harlot, but assumed to be a virgin devoted to the worship of the Phallus. This is shown by the Hebrew word *"Kesedah"* (which only appears here and in Hosea 4:14) (Williams).

Judah, not having any money it seems, gave her a *"pledge"* for her services, by which he would incriminate himself. His problem was lust, while hers was commitment.

(21) "THEN HE ASKED THE MEN OF THAT PLACE, SAYING, WHERE IS THE HARLOT, WHO WAS OPENLY BY THE WAYSIDE? AND THEY SAID, THERE WAS NO HARLOT IN THIS PLACE.

(22) "AND HE RETURNED TO JUDAH, AND SAID, I CANNOT FIND HER; AND ALSO THE MEN OF THE PLACE SAID, THAT THERE WAS NO HARLOT IN THIS PLACE.

(23) "AND JUDAH SAID, LET HER TAKE IT TO HER, LEST WE BE SHAMED: BEHOLD, I SENT THIS KID, AND YOU HAVE NOT FOUND HER.

(24) "AND IT CAME TO PASS ABOUT THREE MONTHS AFTER, THAT IT WAS TOLD JUDAH, SAYING, TAMAR YOUR DAUGHTER IN LAW HAS PLAYED THE HARLOT; AND ALSO, BEHOLD, SHE IS WITH CHILD BY WHOREDOM. AND JUDAH SAID, BRING HER FORTH, AND LET HER BE BURNT.

(25) "WHEN SHE WAS BROUGHT FORTH, SHE SENT TO HER FATHER IN LAW, SAYING, BY THE MAN, WHOSE THESE ARE, AM I WITH CHILD: AND SHE SAID, DISCERN, I PRAY YOU, WHOSE ARE THESE, THE SIGNET, AND BRACELETS, AND STAFF.

(26) "AND JUDAH ACKNOWLEDGED THEM, AND SAID, SHE HAS BEEN MORE RIGHTEOUS THAN I; BECAUSE THAT I GAVE HER NOT TO SHELAH MY SON. AND HE KNEW HER AGAIN NO MORE.

(27) "AND IT CAME TO PASS IN THE TIME OF HER TRAVAIL, THAT, BEHOLD, TWINS WERE IN HER WOMB.

(28) "AND IT CAME TO PASS, WHEN SHE TRAVAILED, THAT THE ONE PUT OUT HIS HAND: AND THE MIDWIFE TOOK AND BOUND UPON HIS HAND A SCARLET THREAD, SAYING, THIS CAME OUT FIRST.

(29) "AND IT CAME TO PASS, AS HE DREW BACK HIS HAND, THAT, BEHOLD, HIS BROTHER CAME OUT: AND SHE SAID, HOW HAVE YOU BROKEN FORTH? THIS BREACH BE UPON YOU: THEREFORE HIS NAME WAS CALLED PHAREZ.

(30) "AND AFTERWARD CAME OUT HIS BROTHER, THAT HAD THE SCARLET THREAD UPON HIS HAND: AND HIS NAME WAS CALLED ZARAH."

The diagram is:

NOTES

1. Judah was very quick to condemn Tamar, while just as guilty himself, or even more so.

2. Tamar gave birth to twins as a result of her union with Judah, and one of the twins was named *"Pharez,"* who would be in the direct lineage of Christ (Mat. 1:3).

3. Even though Christ was born of a woman from such wicked, sinful lineage, He was wholly free from all moral corruption, and because He was Virgin born.

CONDEMNATION

Verses 21 through 24 read: *"Then he asked the men of that place, saying, Where is the harlot, that was openly by the wayside? And they said, There was no harlot in this place.*

"And he returned to Judah, and said, I cannot find her; and also the men of the place said, that there was no harlot in this place.

"And Judah said, Let her take it to her, lest we be shamed: behold, I sent this kid, and you have not found her.

"And it came to pass, about three months after, that it was told Judah, saying, Tamar your daughter in law has played the harlot; and also, behold, she is with child by whoredom. And Judah said, Bring her forth, and let her be burned."

Tamar announces that she is now with child, but at this stage gives no indication, as to how this came about. It was automatically assumed that she had *"played the harlot."* Judah immediately said, *"let her be burned."*

He was very quick to condemn her, when in reality, he was just as guilty, and even much more so. According to the customs of that day, her intentions were honorable, while his intentions were no more than gutter lust.

Unfortunately, this problem did not die with Judah. We seem to continue to be plagued with this malady. It is so easy for us to condemn others, while at the same time, we are grossly guilty ourselves.

SIN

I would hope that we could see from all of this that it is *"sin"* which is the problem plaguing humanity. Unfortunately, the modern Church introduces every other problem, which perverts the Gospel.

Man is a sinner, and it is sin which separates him from God. There is only one solution, one answer, one remedy, for sin, and that remedy is *"Jesus Christ and Him Crucified"* (I Cor. 1:23; 2:2). So why does the modern Church have such a problem preaching *"Jesus Christ and Him Crucified"*?

While the problems may be many, the greatest problem of all is *"unbelief."*

Man attempts to address the problems of mankind by solutions he has devised himself, which God can never honor. He refuses to simply believe that the problem is sin, whatever other name he might give it, and that the only answer for sin is what Jesus did in the giving of Himself in Sacrifice (Gal. 1:4).

THE LINEAGE OF CHRIST

Verses 25 through 30 read: *"When she was brought forth, she sent to her father in law, saying, By the man, whose these are, am I with child: and she said, Discern, I pray you, whose are these, the signet, and bracelets, and staff.*

"And Judah acknowledged them, and said, She has been more righteous than I; because that I gave her not to Shelah my son. And he knew her again no more.

"And it came to pass in the time of her travail, that, behold, twins were in her womb.

"And it came to pass, when she travailed, that the one put out his hand: and the midwife took and bound upon his hand a scarlet thread, saying, This came out first.

"And it came to pass, as he drew back his hand, that, behold, his brother came out: and she said, How have you broken forth? This beach be upon you: therefore his name was called Pharez.

"And afterward came out his brother, who had the scarlet thread upon his hand: and his name was called Zarah."

When Tamar was brought before Judah, and no doubt others as well, she then displayed the items which Judah had given her some months earlier, proving that he was responsible for her condition. He immediately acknowledged that this was the case, but at the same time, how could he deny such a thing?!

He did conclude that she was more righteous than he was.

Twins were born to her, and the first one born was called *"Pharez,"* who was in the lineage of Christ.

Luther asks why such things were placed in Scripture, and answers:

1. That no one should be self-righteous.

2. That no one should despair. There is forgiveness for all who will humbly come to the Lord.

3. To remind us that Gentiles by natural right are brothers, mothers, sisters to our Lord; the Word of Salvation is a Word for the whole world.

"The Name of Jesus is so sweet,
"I love its music to repeat;
"It makes my joys full and complete,
"The precious Name of Jesus!"

"I love the Name of Him Whose heart
"Knows all my griefs and bears a part;
"Who bids all anxious fears depart
"I love the Name of Jesus!"

"That Name I fondly love to hear,
"It never fails my heart to cheer;
"Its music dries the falling tear
"Exalt the Name of Jesus!"

"No word of man can ever tell
"How sweet the Name I love so well;
"O let its praises ever swell,
"O praise the Name of Jesus!"

CHAPTER 39

(1) "AND JOSEPH WAS BROUGHT DOWN TO EGYPT; AND POTIPHAR, AN OFFICER OF PHARAOH, CAPTAIN OF THE GUARD, AN EGYPTIAN, BOUGHT HIM OF THE HANDS OF THE ISHMEELITES, WHICH HAD BROUGHT HIM DOWN THITHER.

(2) "AND THE LORD WAS WITH JOSEPH, AND HE WAS A PROSPEROUS MAN; AND HE WAS IN THE HOUSE OF HIS MASTER THE EGYPTIAN.

(3) "AND HIS MASTER SAW THAT THE LORD WAS WITH HIM, AND THAT THE LORD MADE ALL THAT HE DID TO PROSPER IN HIS HAND.

(4) "AND JOSEPH FOUND GRACE IN HIS SIGHT, AND HE SERVED HIM: AND HE MADE HIM OVERSEER OVER HIS

HOUSE, AND ALL THAT HE HAD HE PUT INTO HIS HAND.

(5) "AND IT CAME TO PASS FROM THE TIME THAT HE HAD MADE HIM OVERSEER IN HIS HOUSE, AND OVER ALL THAT HE HAD, THAT THE LORD BLESSED THE EGYPTIAN'S HOUSE FOR JOSEPH'S SAKE; AND THE BLESSING OF THE LORD WAS UPON ALL THAT HE HAD IN THE HOUSE, AND IN THE FIELD.

(6) "AND HE LEFT ALL THAT HE HAD IN JOSEPH'S HANDS; AND HE KNEW NOT OUGHT HE HAD, SAVE THE BREAD WHICH HE DID EAT. AND JOSEPH WAS A GOODLY PERSON, AND WELL FAVORED."

The structure is:

1. Some eight times in this Chapter, in one way or the other, it is said that the Lord was with Joseph. Eight speaks of Resurrection, so it tells us that whatever happened with Joseph, no matter how adverse it seemed at the moment, a Resurrection was coming.

2. In the story of Joseph, we will perceive a remarkable chain of events, all tending to one grand point, namely, the exaltation of the man who had been in the pit.

3. We will see that the leading object was to exalt the one whom men had rejected, and then to produce in those same men a sense of their sin as it regards this rejection.

POTIPHAR

Verse 1 reads: *"And Joseph was brought down to Egypt; and Potiphar, an officer of Pharaoh, captain of the guard, an Egyptian, bought him of the hands of the Ishmeelites, which had brought him down thither."*

It is ironic that this young man, sold as a slave, will ultimately be the Prime Minister of Pharaoh, will save from starvation the Patriarchal family, and finally will see them settled in Goshen.

This is something that only God could do. It is done to portray Christ, for Joseph was a Type of Christ, and perhaps the most beautiful Type of the entirety of the Old Testament. Studying his life, we will see Christ, and what would ultimately happen to Christ, and we will also see prophetic events, which have not even yet come to pass, but will do so shortly.

During the time of Joseph, it is believed that the Hyksos then ruled Egypt, having

defeated the Egyptians a short time earlier. This is the reason that Potiphar is identified as *"an Egyptian."* This means it was somewhat unusual for an Egyptian under the Hyksos to hold such a high position. They ruled, it seems, for about 100 years.

So now, Joseph, who is about 17 or 18 years old, is sold by the Ishmeelites to Potiphar, the captain of the guard. All of this was being guided, even down to the minute details, by the Hand of the Lord.

THE BLESSINGS OF THE LORD

Verse 2 reads: *"And the LORD was with Joseph, and he was a prosperous man; and he was in the house of his master the Egyptian."*

I want the Reader to note that despite the fact that Joseph had been thrown into a pit, had been sold as a slave, was now hundreds of miles from his home and family, and not knowing if he would ever see them again, the Scripture emphatically states, *"And the Lord was with Joseph."*

We find in all of these happenings that the finger of the Lord is guiding all the springs of the vast machine of circumstances, and that nothing functions without His knowledge, and as it regards the Blood-bought redeemed, *"all things work together for good to them who love God, to them who are the called according to His purpose"* (Rom. 8:28).

Due to so much false teaching, I doubt that many in the modern Church, if this scenario were set down in the Twenty-first Century, would hardly think that *"the Lord was with Joseph."* But He was! We are made to believe by this false teaching that only that which outwardly looks like great blessings, could be of the Lord. And what has that teaching produced?

For the most part, it has produced spoiled, Christian brats. But if the Lord wants *"Rangers,"* or *"Green Berets,"* or *"Navy Seals,"* they're going to have to undergo the same spiritual training as Joseph.

The Holy Spirit refers to him as *"a prosperous man,"* and yet he was a slave. This means that where he was, even as a slave, everything he touched was blessed by God. So this means that where he was, in this case, *"the house of the Egyptian,"* was blessed by God as well! Little did Potiphar know and realize just who Joseph was, when he was purchased. In fact, it would have been impossible for him to have put together the facts, that Joseph was blessed by God more so than any other human being in the world at that time, and yet was a slave. The questions which hang heavy over such a situation could not have been answered by Potiphar, or probably anyone else for that matter.

THE BLESSING

Verse 3 reads: *"And his master saw that the LORD was with him, and that the LORD made all that he did to prosper in his hand."*

Potiphar had more sense than most Christians. He saw that the hand of the Lord was on Joseph, and he took advantage of that, even as he should have done.

It is strange. The world will oftentimes see the Blessings of God upon an individual, and recognize it as such, while the Church far too often exhibits jealousy. Consequently, the Work of God is greatly hindered by such action and attitudes.

GRACE

Verse 4 reads: *"And Joseph found grace in his sight, and he served him: and he made him overseer over his house, and all that he had he put into his hand."*

This does not imply that Potiphar was acquainted with Jehovah, but simply that he concluded Joseph to be under the Divine protection (Pulpit).

Potiphar made Joseph the business manager over all of his holdings, whatever that might have been, which no doubt was considerable.

When the circumstances of Joseph's lot might have induced despondency, indifference, inaction, carelessness, and inattention, Divine Grace so upheld and cheered him that he was able to go about his duties with joy and cheerfulness, so that everything to which he turned his hand succeeded.

It is not our surroundings or circumstances which bring about happiness and joy. Unfortunately, the world thinks it does, but it doesn't! It is one's walk with the Lord, one's relationship with the Lord, one's nearness to the Lord, which makes a penitentiary into a palace, a Hell into a Heaven, sadness into gladness, etc. That's why the Scripture

tells us, *"The joy of the LORD is your strength"* (Neh. 8:10). If you'll notice, it said, *"the joy of the Lord."* It is His joy, not ours. But it becomes ours when we have the proper relationship with Christ which we ought to have. Unfortunately, the world, and even most of the Church, attempts to have joy without Christ. Such is not to be. He has the joy, and He will freely give it to us, if we will walk exclusively with Him (Jn. 10:10).

THE BLESSING OF THE LORD

Verses 5 and 6 read: *"And it came to pass from the time that he had made him overseer in his house, and over all that he had, that the LORD blessed the Egyptian's house for Joseph's sake; and the Blessing of the LORD was upon all that he had in the house, and in the field.*

"And he left all that he had in Joseph's hand: and he knew not ought he had, save the bread which he did eat. And Joseph was a goodly person, and well favored."

If it is to be noticed, the Scripture says that the blessing came *"for Joseph's sake."*

Joseph being a Type of Christ, this means that the Blessing comes upon us, given by God the Father, Who has all good things, *"for Jesus' sake."*

We must realize, and have it penetrate our hearts and lives, remaining there permanently, that all that Jesus did was done exclusively for us. Of all the things He did, not one of them was done for Heaven, Angels, God the Father, or Himself. Everything was done exclusively for us. Therefore, all that He did carries an eternal meaning, which we must come to know.

We must know and understand that Jesus is God, and has always been God, and will always be God. As God, He had no beginning, was not formed, made, created, or born. He always has been, always is, and always shall be.

However, He became man, with Paul referring to Him as *"The Last Adam,"* and *"The Second Man"* (I Cor. 15:45-47).

Even though becoming a man, He was a Man as there has never been a man. Born of the Virgin Mary, He was born without original sin, and in fact had no sin nature.

As Jesus, the Son of God, He kept the Law perfectly in every respect, all on our behalf. This

Perfect Man, this ideal Man, never failed even one single time in all that He did. And again I emphasize that this was done all on our behalf, actually as our Substitute. So this means that what He did was far more than simply doing it for us — He actually was the Substitute Man, doing for us what we could not do for ourselves.

And then when He kept the Law perfectly, all on our behalf, He then went to the Cross, which was planned from before the ages (I Pet. 1:18-20), thereby to atone for all sin, past, present, and future (Jn. 1:29).

Atoning for all sin, Satan had no way or means to hold Him in the death world; Jesus rose from the dead; however, the entirety of the Cross, exactly as His life, was all for us. Thereby, when the believing sinner comes to Christ, in the Mind of God, we are baptized into His death (Rom. 6:3-5).

Now this is not speaking of Water Baptism, as many believe, but rather the Crucifixion of Christ. The word *"baptize"* was used by the Holy Spirit through Paul, in order to impress upon us the totality of what happened to us when we came to Christ. We are literally placed *"in Christ"* (Rom. 8:1).

We were then buried with Him, which means that all that we once were, and I speak of the sin, the degradation, the bondage, the iniquity, etc., were buried with Him. We died when Christ died (Rom. 6:7-8). But it doesn't stop there:

We were then raised with Him in *"newness of life,"* which speaks of the *"born again"* experience (Jn. 3:3, 16).

Understanding all of this, our Faith is then to forever rest in Christ and what He did for us in His sufferings. We are to *"reckon ourselves to be dead indeed unto the sin nature, and alive unto God, through Jesus Christ our Lord"* (Rom. 6:11).

Continuing to exhibit Faith in Christ and what He did for us at the Cross, and forever continuing in that capacity, we can be assured that *"sin shall not have dominion over us, for we are no longer under Law, Jesus having satisfied that demand, but under Grace"* (Rom. 6:14).

So for Jesus' sake, God the Father gives us all things. But we must always remember that all of these great and glorious things come to us exclusively by and through what Jesus did for us at the Cross. As we've said repeatedly, Christ and the Cross must never be divided. Jesus, without the Cross, is actually *"another Jesus"* (II Cor. 11:4). All blessings, all victory, all Grace, in fact everything, comes to us *"for Jesus' sake."*

EVERYTHING IS IN JESUS

The Sixth Verse says, *"And he left all that he had in Joseph's hand."* Of course, this is speaking of Potiphar; however, Joseph being a Type of Christ, it means that the Father has put everything into the Hand of Christ. Of this Jesus said: *"All things that the Father has are Mine"* (Jn. 16:15).

So, individuals who think that one can be saved and go to Heaven by worshiping and serving Mohammed, or Buddha, etc., simply don't know what they're talking about. The Father has given nothing to these imposters, only to Jesus. In fact, and as stated, He has given everything to Christ. And once again, this was done because of what Jesus did at the Cross as it regards this great Redemption Plan.

As well, when it says in Verse 6, *"And Joseph was a goodly person, and well favored,"* the same can be said of Christ. In fact, it is of Jesus Alone that the Father has said, *"This is My Beloved Son, in Whom I am well pleased"* (Mat. 3:17). If it is to be noticed, the Lord is pleased only with Christ, and for all the obvious reasons. So, for Him to be pleased with us, this can only be said and done, providing we are *"in Christ."*

This is the reason that we must carefully do our best to understand Christ, and to always place our Faith squarely in Him, and what He did for us in the Sacrifice of Himself on the Cross.

(7) "AND IT CAME TO PASS AFTER THESE THINGS, THAT HIS MASTER'S WIFE CAST HER EYES UPON JOSEPH, AND SHE SAID, LIE WITH ME.

(8) "BUT HE REFUSED, AND SAID UNTO HIS MASTER'S WIFE, BEHOLD, MY MASTER KNOWS NOT WHAT IS WITH ME IN THE HOUSE, AND HE HAS COMMITTED ALL THAT HE HAS TO MY HAND;

(9) "THERE IS NONE GREATER IN THIS HOUSE THAN I; NEITHER HAS HE KEPT BACK ANYTHING FROM ME BUT YOU, BECAUSE YOU ARE HIS WIFE: HOW THEN CAN I DO THIS GREAT WICKEDNESS, AND SIN AGAINST GOD?

NOTES

(10) "AND IT CAME TO PASS, AS SHE SPOKE TO JOSEPH DAY BY DAY, THAT HE HEARKENED NOT UNTO HER, TO LIE BY HER, OR TO BE WITH HER.

(11) "AND IT CAME TO PASS ABOUT THIS TIME, THAT JOSEPH WENT INTO THE HOUSE TO DO HIS BUSINESS; AND THERE WAS NONE OF THE MEN OF THE HOUSE THERE WITHIN.

(12) "AND SHE CAUGHT HIM BY HIS GARMENT, SAYING, LIE WITH ME: AND HE LEFT HIS GARMENT IN HER HAND, AND FLED, AND GOT HIM OUT.

(13) "AND IT CAME TO PASS, WHEN SHE SAW THAT HE HAD LEFT HIS GARMENT IN HER HAND, AND WAS FLED FORTH,

(14) "THAT SHE CALLED UNTO THE MEN OF HER HOUSE, AND SPOKE UNTO THEM, SAYING, SEE, HE HAS BROUGHT IN AN HEBREW UNTO US TO MOCK US; HE CAME IN UNTO ME TO LIE WITH ME, AND I CRIED WITH A LOUD VOICE:

(15) "AND IT CAME TO PASS, WHEN HE HEARD THAT I LIFTED UP MY VOICE AND CRIED, THAT HE LEFT HIS GARMENT WITH ME, AND FLED, AND GOT HIM OUT.

(16) "AND SHE LAID UP HIS GARMENT BY HER, UNTIL HIS LORD CAME HOME."

The composition is:

1. The action of Joseph in resisting this temptation pressed upon him showed him to be the true firstborn.

2. His chastity rebuked the unchastity of Reuben who was the natural firstborn.

3. His language to the woman is very telling. He urged three reasons against wrongdoing: A. Gratitude to his master who had put everything into his hand; B. Respect for the woman, seeing that she was Potiphar's wife; and, C. Fear of God.

4. This is the second occasion that the Sacred History speaks of Joseph's garment. His brothers took the one; Potiphar's wife the other. They tried to hide their sin with that garment; she tried to hide hers as well.

THE TEMPTATION

Verse 7 reads: *"And it came to pass after these things, that his master's wife cast her eyes upon Joseph, and she said, Lie with me."*

Satan now institutes a very telling temptation against Joseph, and the Lord gives him certain latitude to do so. Faith must be tested, and great Faith must be tested greatly.

At times the Lord does the testing Personally, and at times He uses other things, even Satan, as noted here.

It is said that Joseph was one of the most handsome young men of his day. In fact, it is stated that his attractiveness was celebrated all over the East. Persian poets of the Twelfth Chapter of the Koran speak of his beauty as perfect.

Traditions say that Zuleekah, Potiphar's wife, was at first the most virtuous of women, but when she saw him, she was so affected that she lost all self-control and became a slave to her passions.

On one occasion, she supposedly made a dinner inviting forty of the most beautiful women in Egypt who, when they saw Joseph, were so moved with admiration that they exclaimed with one accord that he must be an Angel.

HOW TO HANDLE TEMPTATION

Verse 8 reads: *"But he refused, and said unto his master's wife, Behold, my master knows not what is with me in the house, and he has committed all that he has to my hand."*

Joseph refused the woman's advances, even though the temptation was great. He gave the reasons, which we will deal with a little later.

As the Bible student knows, Joseph's understanding of the ways of the Lord was that which his father Jacob had taught him. There was no Bible in those days, that first coming with Moses, with him writing the first five Books of the Bible approximately 200 to 250 years later.

As well, the knowledge of Joseph as it regards the Lord, at that particular time, as well as all others who then lived for the Lord, as few as they were, was wrapped up in the sacrificial system. The head of the house was to act as the Priest of the home, offering up sacrifices, with the Lord having given those directions to Adam and Eve, with it being passed down (Gen., Chpt. 4). I think it is obvious that they knew what the sacrifices represented, which was the Redeemer Who was to come into this world, and Who would die for lost humanity. This latter part was made clear to Abraham, when he was told to offer up Isaac, with the Lord staying his hand at the last moment.

From Abraham, this information went to Isaac, then to Jacob, with Jacob giving it to his sons, of whom it seems Joseph was the only one who heeded, at least at that particular time.

Considering that Joseph was now a slave of Potiphar, it is doubtful that he was able to offer up sacrifices at this particular time, although that would more than likely change with the change of his status in the near future.

The point I'm attempting to make is, Joseph had placed his Faith entirely in Christ and what Christ would do at the Cross, to the degree that he then understood the great Plan of God. This means that Joseph escaped this temptation, in the same manner in which we escape temptation presently. And how is that?

While Joseph definitely refused the advances of this woman, he was able to refuse by the help of God. Left to himself, I doubt very seriously that he would have passed this test.

The Believer faces temptation presently by exhibiting Faith in Christ and what Christ has done for us at the Cross. Unfortunately, most of the modern Church has the idea that once a person is saved, they then have the power (willpower) to say *"no"* to sin, etc.

If the Believer is functioning in that capacity, after awhile, he's going to say *"yes"* to sin, and because that is not God's Way. In other words, it has nothing to do with one's willpower (Rom. 7:18).

While the *"will"* is definitely involved, it is that we will subscribe to God's prescribed order. And what is that?

John said: *"This is the victory that overcometh the world, even our faith"* (I Jn. 5:4). It is not willpower; it is Faith.

WHAT DO WE MEAN BY THE WORD *"FAITH"*?

Most Christians instantly think they know what the meaning of Faith is; however, the truth is, most don't.

The Faith of which John spoke here, and which Paul addressed constantly, refers to Faith in Christ and what Christ did at the Cross, all on our behalf. As I've said already several times in this Volume, Faith in Christ and His Substitutionary Work on the Cross

is the only kind of Faith which God will recognize. While other types of faith may in truth be faith, it's not that which spends in the economy of the Kingdom of Heaven.

When the Believer places his Faith totally and completely in Christ and what Christ has done for him in His Sufferings, while Satan continues to tempt, the Holy Spirit, Who is God, and Who lives within the heart and life of the Believer (I Cor. 3:16), will then greatly help the Believer, and the temptation is easily overcome, because the Believer is not attempting to do this within himself, but all in Christ.

SIN

Verse 9 reads: *"There is none greater in this house than I; neither has he kept back anything from me but you, because you are his wife: how then can I do this great wickedness, and sin against God?"*

All sin is against God. Joseph refers to the suggestions of this woman as *"this great wickedness."*

Adultery is wrong in any capacity, and even though the Commandment against this sin had not yet been given, the moral law had already been placed in the hearts of those few who truly followed the Lord.

In all of this, we see that Joseph felt a keen responsibility toward his master, which he certainly should have, and more than all, toward God. To do such a thing which was suggested of him, he would be greatly betraying the man who had given him this great position of responsibility, which is a grievous sin. But above all, he would be sinning against God. The moral is, if we treat the Lord right, it is certain that we will treat our fellowman right.

CONTINUING TEMPTATION

Verse 10 reads: *"And it came to pass, as she spoke to Joseph day by day, that he hearkened not unto her, to lie by her, or to be with her."*

Unfortunately, Joseph's business took him repeatedly into the main house, which he could not avoid. At the same time, Potiphar's wife, knowing all of this, would lie in wait for Joseph. And so it was a continuing temptation, pressed upon day-by-day, with him continuing to resist.

The lengths to which she went, we can only imagine. But one can be very certain that the temptation increased day by day, which meant that it took the Grace of God, and exceedingly so, in order for Joseph to come out victorious each day. One can well imagine that Joseph greatly dreaded each day, knowing what he would face.

THE GARMENT

Verses 11 through 16 read: *"And it came to pass about this time, that Joseph went into the house to do his business; and there was none of the men of the house there within.*

"And she caught him by his garment, saying, Lie with me: and he left his garment in her hand, and fled, and got him out.

"And it came to pass, when she saw that he had left his garment in her hand, and was fled forth,

"That she called unto the men of her house, and spake unto them, saying, See, he has brought in an Hebrew unto us to mock us; he came in unto me to lie with me, and I cried with a loud voice:

"And it came to pass, when he heard that I lifted up my voice and cried, that he left his garment with me, and fled, and got him out.

"And she laid up his garment by her, until his lord came home."

All of this is very obvious as to what happened.

Matthew Henry said: *"Chaste and holy love will continue, though slighted; but sinful love is easily changed into sinful hatred. Those who have broken the bonds of modesty will never be held by the bonds of Truth."*

Evaluating Joseph, some would claim that after advances had been made, he should not have gone back into the house; however, of this he had no choice. His business demanded that he frequent the place. It is certain, he would have done anything to have avoided contact with this woman, but the situation actually presented itself as a trap. And so the trap is ultimately sprung.

The Devil would surmise that if he cannot get Joseph to do that which is wrong, he will have him locked up in prison for years. Now of course, the Lord could have stopped all of this, but the remainder of the Chapter tells us why not!

(17) "AND SHE SPOKE UNTO HIM ACCORDING TO THESE WORDS, SAYING, THE HEBREW SERVANT, WHICH YOU HAVE BROUGHT UNTO US, CAME IN UNTO ME TO MOCK ME:

(18) "AND IT CAME TO PASS, AS I LIFTED UP MY VOICE AND CRIED, THAT HE LEFT HIS GARMENT WITH ME, AND FLED OUT.

(19) "AND IT CAME TO PASS, WHEN HIS MASTER HEARD THE WORDS OF HIS WIFE, WHICH SHE SPOKE UNTO HIM, SAYING, AFTER THIS MANNER DID YOUR SERVANT TO ME; THAT HIS WRATH WAS KINDLED.

(20) "AND JOSEPH'S MASTER TOOK HIM, AND PUT HIM INTO THE PRISON, A PLACE WHERE THE KING'S PRISONERS WERE BOUND: AND HE WAS THERE IN THE PRISON.

(21) "BUT THE LORD WAS WITH JOSEPH, AND SHOWED HIM MERCY, AND GAVE HIM FAVOR IN THE SIGHT OF THE KEEPER OF THE PRISON.

(22) "AND THE KEEPER OF THE PRISON COMMITTED TO JOSEPH'S HAND ALL THE PRISONERS WHO WERE IN THE PRISON; AND WHATSOEVER THEY DID THERE, HE WAS THE DOER OF IT.

(23) "THE KEEPER OF THE PRISON LOOKED NOT TO ANYTHING THAT WAS UNDER HIS HAND; BECAUSE THE LORD WAS WITH HIM, AND THAT WHICH HE DID, THE LORD MADE IT TO PROSPER."

The composition is:

1. In one moment Joseph exchanged a palace for a prison.

2. But Jehovah was with him as much in the prison as in the palace.

3. Joseph accepted this position, without saying a word or attempting to justify or defend himself.

THE HEBREW SERVANT

Verses 17 through 19 read: *"And she spoke unto him, according to these words, saying, The Hebrew servant, which you have brought unto us, came in unto me to mock me.*

"And it came to pass, as I lifted up my voice and cried, that he left his garment with me, and fled out.

"And it came to pass, when his master heard the words of his wife, which she spoke

unto him, saying After this manner did your servant to me; that his wrath was kindled."

The Believer must understand that everything which happens to him is either caused by the Lord, or allowed by the Lord. Now we know and realize that the Lord did not cause this woman to do what she did, but it is evident that He did allow it.

Why?

Among other things, Joseph is being prepared for something. In fact, he is being prepared for the second most powerful position in the world, the Prime Minister of the greatest nation, at that time, on the face of the Earth. Of course, he knew not at all of such plans, but the point is this:

He trusted God. He didn't know why the situation had been allowed to play out in this manner. No doubt he asked himself the question many times, *"What did I do, that would warrant such?"*

The answer is simple: Joseph didn't do anything that was wrong or negative. But yet he was about to undergo several years of very severe circumstances.

THE LORD WAS WITH JOSEPH

Verses 20 through 23 read: *"And Joseph's master took him, and put him into the prison, a place where the king's prisoners were bound: and he was there in the prison.*

"But the LORD was with Joseph, and showed him mercy, and gave him favor in the sight of the keeper of the prison.

"And the keeper of the prison committed to Joseph's hand all the prisoners who were in the prison; and whatsoever they did there, he was the doer of it.

"The keeper of the prison looked not to anything that was under his hand; because the LORD was with him, and that which he did, the LORD made it to prosper."

Whereas Potiphar once had the best business manager he had ever known, the keeper of the prison now has the best jailor he had ever known.

We know that it was the Will of God for Joseph to be placed in this prison, for Verse 21 says, *"But the Lord was with Joseph."* And it is speaking of the Lord being with Joseph as it regards Grace, Mercy, Power, Leading, and Guidance, in a word, all things. Someone

who is out of the Will of God, or lacking in Faith, while the Lord most definitely might be with him, at the same time, He definitely is not with them in this capacity.

The Scripture further says of this event: *"He sent a man before them, even Joseph, who was sold for a servant:*

"Whose feet they hurt with fetters: and he was laid in iron:

"Until the time that his word came: the Word of the LORD tried him.

"The king sent and loosed him; even the ruler of the people, and let him go free.

"He made him lord of his house, and ruler of all his substance:

"To bind his princes at his pleasure; and teach his senators wisdom" (Ps. 105:17-22).

There is something else that must be considered in all of this:

Considering the advances of this woman, the Lord may have done Joseph the greatest favor by having him put in prison. Joseph, despite being a Type of Christ, was human, as all other men. Considering his attractiveness, as to exactly how long he could have withstood such temptation, is anyone's guess. We would like to think that he could have stood it indefinitely; however, I'm not so sure that was the case.

And then again, whatever part the seduction played, to prepare Joseph for the task ahead, the Lord would have to put Jacob's son through an extremely arduous course. And the Lord was with him in the prison, just as much, as stated, as He had been with him in the palace.

However, if Joseph had grown bitter, without the shadow of a doubt, this would have greatly hindered the Blessings of the Lord on the future Prime Minister. Let us say it again:

Everything that happens to the Believer, due to the great price that was paid for us, and that we are not our own, but that we belong entirely to the Lord, is either *"caused"* by the Lord or *"allowed"* by the Lord. Satan doesn't have free reign whatsoever with any Believer, even the weakest. In fact, he must ask permission from the Lord whatever it is that he does, and to the degree that it is done (Job, Chpts. 1-2).

So if in fact we have done something wrong, which Joseph didn't, we should realize that we deserve what is happening, and in fact, we deserve much worse. At the same time, we must learn the lesson which the Lord is thereby teaching us, for He is always teaching us, and because everything is a test.

"Oh, wonderful Name, how my heart thrills to hear it

"The Name of my Risen Redeemer and King!

"It falls like the music of Heaven on my spirit,

"And fills me with rapture Divine while I sing."

"When lost in my sin, 'twas the Name of my Saviour

"That banished my fear and brought peace to my soul;

"I'll sing it in Glory forever and ever

"With joy while the years of eternity roll."

"I think of the Cross where He suffered to save me,

"And Oh, how my heart thrills with glory Divine

"To know it is life everlasting He gave me,

"When, sinless, He died for a soul such as mine."

CHAPTER 40

(1) "AND IT CAME TO PASS AFTER THESE THINGS, THAT THE BUTLER OF THE KING OF EGYPT AND HIS BAKER HAD OFFENDED THEIR LORD THE KING OF EGYPT.

(2) "AND PHARAOH WAS WROTH AGAINST TWO OF HIS OFFICERS, AGAINST THE CHIEF OF THE BUTLERS, AND AGAINST THE CHIEF OF THE BAKERS.

(3) "AND HE PUT THEM IN WARD IN THE HOUSE OF THE CAPTAIN OF THE GUARD, INTO THE PRISON, THE PLACE WHERE JOSEPH WAS BOUND.

(4) "AND THE CAPTAIN OF THE GUARD CHARGED JOSEPH WITH THEM, AND HE SERVED THEM: AND THEY CONTINUED A SEASON IN WARD.

(5) "AND THEY DREAMED A DREAM BOTH OF THEM, EACH MAN HIS DREAM IN ONE NIGHT, EACH MAN ACCORDING TO THE INTERPRETATION OF HIS DREAM, THE BUTLER AND THE BAKER OF THE KING OF EGYPT, WHICH WERE BOUND IN THE PRISON.

(6) "AND JOSEPH CAME IN UNTO THEM IN THE MORNING, AND LOOKED UPON THEM, AND, BEHOLD, THEY WERE SAD."

The construction is:

1. In Chapter 39, Satan uses Potiphar's wife; and in Chapter 40, he uses Pharaoh's chief butler. The former he used to put Joseph into the dungeon; and the latter he used to keep him there, through his ungrateful negligence; but all in vain. God was behind the scenes. His finger was guiding all things.

2. One very lovely feature in Joseph's character was that he never murmured.

3. And another yet more beautiful one was his unselfish interest in the needs and sorrows of others.

THE BUTLER AND THE BAKER

Verses 1 through 3 read: *"And it came to pass after these things, that the butler of the king of Egypt and his baker had offended their lord the king of Egypt.*

"And Pharaoh was angry against two of his officers, against the chief of the butlers, and against the chief of the bakers.

"And he put them in ward in the house of the captain of the guard, into the prison, the place where Joseph was bound."

As we shall see, we will find the Hand of the Lord in these proceedings. While the butler will not do what he should have done, that is to remember Joseph, he will be used as the instrument to make Joseph known to Pharaoh, as we shall later see, at a very critical time.

It is remarkable to observe the Hand of God in all of this. We would do well to look at our own lives accordingly. Whatever it might be, whether good or seemingly bad, we must realize that we belong to Him, and that He is moving events and people to a particular destination, all on our behalf. To properly know and understand this should bring great comfort to the heart of the Believer.

It is only the unredeemed who *"rage as waves of the sea, foaming out their own shame; wandering stars, to whom is reserved the blackness of darkness forever"* (Jude, vs. 13).

To the contrary, the Believer has the sure Hand of the Lord constantly guiding him. If we can see that, understand that, and thereby place our faith and confidence in the knowledge of the Lord, which is expended on our behalf, knowing that it's all for our good, then whatever comes, it can be a blessing, even if it's a prison in which Joseph found himself, and through no fault of his own.

THE DREAM

Verses 4 through 6 read: *"And the captain of the guard charged Joseph with them, and he served them: and they continued a season in ward.*

"And they dreamed a dream both of them, each man his dream in one night, each man according to the interpretation of his dream, the butler and the baker of the king of Egypt, which were bound in the prison.

"And Joseph came in unto them in the morning, and looked upon them, and, behold, they were sad."

In studying the Word of God, it will become obvious that the Lord quite often uses dreams to carry forth His Work in some way.

Concerning these dreams had by the butler and the baker, as the events proved, the interpretation put on them by Joseph, showed the dreams to be no vague hallucinations of the mind, but Divinely-sent foreshadowings of the future fortunes of the dreamers, whether good or bad.

As one can see, the Lord is working in all of these situations, in order to bring about His desired Will. But of course, the Will of the Lord being brought about is predicated on the obedience of Joseph in all things. In fact, he is the only one who falls into this situation, and simply because he is the only one serving God. The others knew nothing about the Lord; therefore, whatever it is they did, whether good or bad, had little effect on the outcome as it regards the things the Lord desired to do.

Let the Believer understand the things which we are saying. While the Lord works with and through the unredeemed, as is obvious here, it is through Believers that His ultimate purpose is carried out. That's the reason that Jesus said: *"You are the salt of the Earth . . . You are the light of the world"* (Mat. 5:13-14).

In other words, in all of Egypt, for all of its knowledge, riches, etc., the only light in that land was that provided by Joseph. Before he came, there was no *"light."* And by *"light"* we're speaking of correct spiritual illumination that shows the right way in all things.

The more true Believers there are in any given place, the more of this *"light"* which is present.

Please observe the nations of the world which know God, and those which don't. Look at those first of all which do not espouse Christianity, but rather some other religion. Poverty and ignorance grip these poor, unfortunate people, with them little realizing that it's their religion which is the cause of this consternation.

ISLAM

For instance, let's look at Islam!

Any way that you look at this religion, it has produced nothing but a failed culture in every capacity. There is no such thing as the separation of Church and State in the Islam religion. This particular religion is the government, and rules everything, even down to the minute details of one's life. The point I'm making is this:

Considering that the religion of Islam has total sway in the countries where it rules, there is no excuse for its failures. But the truth is the following:

Islam has produced nothing but a failed culture in every single country over which it has authority. The culture has failed in every capacity, be it education, freedoms, prosperity, quality of life, etc. In fact, the nations of the world which boast of Islam are some of, if not the poorest on the face of the Earth. Take Saudi Arabia for instance:

It is at least one of the richest of the Muslim nations, and because of the United States purchasing billions of dollars worth of oil from this government. But even in this country, illiteracy is rampant, with the average income only approximately $1,600 per capita; while it's over $50,000 in the United States.

Looking at freedom for its people, and this goes for all Muslim countries, women are treated as little more than slaves. They have no rights, no freedoms, and are second-class citizens in every respect.

Even in countries where religion is not so oppressive, such as China, where Buddhism and Confucianism reigns, or India, where Hinduism is supreme, the poverty and/or lack of freedom are rampant.

Even though the political pundits wouldn't admit it, the secret of the prosperity of the United States is not its form of Government, its institutions of learning, or its industry, but rather its worship of the Lord Jesus Christ, which provides light and illumination for all of these other things to be done.

CHRISTIANITY

No, this is not an effort to make Christianity the State Church. In fact, no worse thing could be done than that. However, even though the separation of Church and State is one of the cornerstones of this democracy, that doesn't mean the separation of God and State.

Whether our Educators realize it or not, the entire fabric of proper education in this nation rests upon the Word of God. The moral tone of all that is right or wrong rests, likewise, upon these principles. In other words, the Word of God is the seedbed of the Constitution of this nation, as well as the Bill of Rights. As someone has well said, *"Much Bible, much freedom; little Bible, little freedom; no Bible, no freedom."* Think about the following:

Almost all the inventions which have brought the world into the modern technological age have been brought about since the turn of the Twentieth Century. As well, I would dare say that 90 percent of all technological advancement has had its beginning in the United States. Also, this country can probably boast the largest number of *"born again, Spirit-filled"* Believers on the face of the Earth. My contention is, with the mighty outpouring of the Holy Spirit comes even more *"light and illumination,"* and in every capacity, whether spiritual or otherwise. Yes, that's what I'm saying!

The technological advancement of the world during these modern times can be linked to the outpouring of the Holy Spirit and the fulfillment of the Prophecy of Daniel. The Lord spoke to the great Prophet-Statesman, and said: *"But you, O Daniel, shut up the words, and seal the Book, even to the time of the end: many shall run to and fro, and knowledye shall be increased"* (Dan. 12:4).

NOTES

(7) "AND HE ASKED PHARAOH'S OFFICERS WHO WERE WITH HIM IN THE WARD OF HIS LORD'S HOUSE, SAYING, WHEREFORE LOOK YOU SO SADLY TODAY?

(8) "AND THEY SAID UNTO HIM, WE HAVE DREAMED A DREAM, AND THERE IS NO INTERPRETER OF IT. AND JOSEPH SAID UNTO THEM, DO NOT INTERPRETATIONS BELONG TO GOD? TELL ME THEM, I PRAY YOU.

(9) "AND THE CHIEF BUTLER TOLD HIS DREAM TO JOSEPH, AND SAID TO HIM, IN MY DREAM, BEHOLD, A VINE WAS BEFORE ME;

(10) "AND IN THE VINE WERE THREE BRANCHES: AND IT WAS AS THOUGH IT BUDDED, AND HER BLOSSOMS SHOT FORTH; AND THE CLUSTERS THEREOF BROUGHT FORTH RIPE GRAPES:

(11) "AND PHARAOH'S CUP WAS IN MY HAND: AND I TOOK THE GRAPES, AND PRESSED THEM INTO PHARAOH'S CUP, AND I GAVE THE CUP INTO PHARAOH'S HAND.

(12) "AND JOSEPH SAID UNTO HIM, THIS IS THE INTERPRETATION OF IT: THE THREE BRANCHES ARE THREE DAYS:

(13) "YET WITHIN THREE DAYS SHALL PHARAOH LIFT UP YOUR HEAD, AND RESTORE YOU UNTO YOUR PLACE: AND YOU SHALL DELIVER PHARAOH'S CUP INTO HIS HAND, AFTER THE FORMER MANNER WHEN YOU WERE HIS BUTLER.

(14) "BUT THINK ON ME WHEN IT SHALL BE WELL WITH YOU, AND SHOW KINDNESS, I PRAY YOU, UNTO ME, AND MAKE MENTION OF ME UNTO PHARAOH, AND BRING ME OUT OF THIS HOUSE:

(15) "FOR INDEED I WAS STOLEN AWAY OUT OF THE LAND OF THE HEBREWS: AND HERE ALSO HAVE I DONE NOTHING THAT THEY SHOULD PUT ME INTO THE DUNGEON."

The overview is:

1. The Divine discipline permitted that Joseph should be tempted in all points, and so the chief cupbearer forgot him, although he knew his innocence, and that he possessed a mysterious relationship to God.

2. All these facts helped to build up Joseph as a very striking type of Israel's Saviour and the world's Redeemer.

3. It is an interesting and profitable study to examine all the Passages in the Sacred Scriptures which speak of dreams, and of how God used them as a channel of communication to men, whether inside or outside the Covenant of Grace (Williams).

THE INTERPRETATION

Verses 7 through 15 read: *"And he asked Pharaoh's officers who were with him in the ward of his lord's house, saying, Why do you look so sad today?*

"And they said unto him, We have dreamed a dream, and there is no interpreter of it. And Joseph said unto them, Do not interpretations belong to God? Tell me them, I pray you.

"And the chief butler told his dream to Joseph, and said to him, In my dream, behold, a vine was before me;

"And in the vine were three branches: and it was as though it budded, and her blossoms shot forth; and the clusters thereof brought forth ripe grapes:

"And Pharaoh's cup was in my hand, and I took the grapes, and pressed them into Pharaoh's cup, and I gave the cup into Pharaoh's hand.

"And Joseph said unto him, This is the interpretation of it: The three branches are three days:

"Yet within three days shall Pharaoh lift up your head, and restore you unto your place: and you shall deliver Pharaoh's cup into his hand, after the former manner when you were his butler.

"But think on me when it shall be well with you, and show kindness, I pray you, unto me, and make mention of me unto Pharaoh, and bring me out of this house:

"For indeed I was stolen away out of the land of the Hebrews: and here also have I done nothing that they should put me into the dungeon."

By this time, Joseph enjoys comparative freedom from corporeal restraint in the prison. But yet, he is still a prisoner, held in this dungeon.

Verses 9 through 19 tell of the dreams of the chief butler and the chief baker. It also tells of Joseph's interpretation of these dreams. In these interpretations, he preached faithfully the Word of the Lord, whether it

announced Grace or wrath — and so did the Lord Jesus Christ.

Verses 14 and 15 record the fact that Joseph never accused his brethren. He merely said, *"I was stolen away out of the land of the Hebrews."* Likewise, Jesus did not come to condemn, but to save.

After hearing the dream, Joseph predicted that in three days the butler would be restored to his place and position in the palace. Joseph then asked the butler, when he was free, that he would remember Joseph, and make mention of him unto Pharaoh, that he may be delivered out of this prison. Though required to endure this terrible time within his life, that incidentally which was laid on him by Divine Providence, which he would do with meekness and resignation, at the same time, he was under no obligation to stay a moment longer in prison than he could justly help, but was rather bound to use all legitimate means to ensure his deliverance, which he did. However, the Lord would not use the butler to effect Joseph's release. He had something far greater in mind than Joseph resuming his place as a slave.

Sometimes, through no fault of our own, and sometimes through fault of our own, we are placed by the Lord in severe straits, even as Joseph. And please understand, even as we have already said several times, the Lord is always in charge of all things. His power is so great, even as it regards knowledge, that a little sparrow falling to the ground does not escape His attention. As well, such detail is exacted, that *"the very hairs of our head are all numbered"* (Mat. 10:29-30).

It is impossible for mere mortals to grasp the significance of these statements, as given by Christ during His earthly sojourn. But it does give us an idea as to the magnificence of God Almighty, and especially His care for His Children.

The Lord allowed Joseph to be put in prison. He as well had him stay there for a particular period of time, and all for a distinct purpose.

As Joseph, in times of difficulty and problems, we should earnestly seek the Face of the Lord as to deliverance from these problems. That is not improper. But at the same time, we must understand that whatever situation we are in, the Heavenly Father has desired that we be there, and for excellent reasons. Consequently, we must seek to learn the lesson which He is trying to teach us.

WHAT DID JOSEPH LEARN?

The Scripture tells us: *"The trying of your faith worketh patience"* (James 1:3). To be sure, Joseph's faith was severely tested, but it was in order to perfect patience.

Second, it was to teach him the same lesson which the Lord, some 1,700 years in the future, would teach the Apostle Paul. I speak of the Grace of God. The Master told the great Apostle: *"My Grace is sufficient for you: for My strength is made perfect in weakness"* (II Cor. 12:9).

The development of the Child of God, whomever that person might be, even Joseph, even Paul, is brought about in ways totally contrary to the world.

Whenever the individual comes to Christ, that person is baptized into the death of Christ, buried with Him by baptism into death, and then raised with Him in newness of life (Rom. 6:3-5). And please understand, this is not speaking at all of Water Baptism, but rather the Crucifixion of Christ, with Christ serving as our Substitute. Our Faith places us literally in Christ, which refers to His death, burial, and Resurrection. By that means we came into Christ, the means of Faith, and by that means we remain in Christ.

As would be obvious, spiritually speaking, whenever you came to Christ, due to the Cross, and your Faith in that Finished Work, you literally died to what you were before being *"born again"* (Jn. 3:3). Paul said:

"Knowing this, that our old man is crucified with Him, that the body of sin might be destroyed (its power is destroyed and its guilt is removed), *that henceforth we should not serve sin."*

He then said: *"For he who is dead is freed from sin"* (Rom. 6:6-7).

All of this means that we are now dead to the sin nature which once ruled us; however, the Scripture doesn't say that the sin nature is dead, but that we are dead rather to the sin nature. Listen again to Paul:

"Likewise reckon (account) *ye also yourselves to be dead indeed unto sin* (the sin

nature), *but alive unto God through Jesus Christ our Lord"* (Rom. 6:11).

If we function as we should function, which refers to our Faith being maintained in the Cross, we will remain dead to the sin nature, and it will have no control over us whatsoever; however, if we shift our faith to other things, and irrespective as to what those other things might be, by the doing of such, we limit the Holy Spirit as to what He can do within our lives, which guarantees failure. For the Holy Spirit to work as only He can work, for He is God, our Faith must be maintained in the Finished Work of Christ (Rom. 8:1-2).

But the problem is, we have a tendency to allow our faith to drift to other things, and when this happens, the *"old man"* suddenly comes alive again, and we find ourselves in trouble. In fact, this particular fight of faith is a constant struggle (I Tim. 6:12).

Concerning this, the great Apostle also said: *"For the flesh* (self efforts) *lusteth against the Spirit* (Holy Spirit), *and the Spirit against the flesh: and these are contrary the one to the other: so that you cannot do the things that you would"* (Gal. 5:17).

The *"flesh"* pertains to our own self-efforts, our own ability and strength, which the Lord incidentally cannot use. Everything He does must be done by and through the Power of the Holy Spirit. To subdue the flesh, the following must be done:

SUBDUING THE FLESH

As stated, the *"flesh,"* as Paul used the word, pertains to our own ability and strength. In other words, it speaks of us trying to perfect Holiness and Righteousness by our own religious efforts, other than the prescribed order which the Lord has given unto us, which is the Cross. And if the Believer doesn't understand the Cross, and I speak as to how the Cross effects our Sanctification, then without fail, the Believer is going to attempt to subdue the flesh by his own machinations, ability, and strength. He will never succeed, but in fact, will only make the flesh, and thereby failure, more predominant.

The flesh is subdued only by the Believer understanding that everything he needs comes to him through what Jesus did at the Cross, and that he will receive nothing from God, but that it comes through the Finished Work of Christ. It is absolutely imperative that the Believer understands this. We have what we have from the Lord not because of our Denominations with which we are associated, or our Churches, as important as that may be, or good works, etc., but by and through what Jesus did at the Cross. Whenever the Believer anchors his Faith in the Cross, the flesh will automatically be subdued, and in fact, this is the only way it can be subdued.

But for the Believer to come to this place, and to remain in this place, oftentimes the Lord must bring the Believer through difficulties which force him to depend exclusively on Christ, and not at all on himself. The Lord oftentimes will put us in a position to where our own strength and ability are woefully insufficient. In other words, we have to trust Him, have to believe Him, and have to look to Him. Joseph was in that type of situation:

Unless the Lord brought him out of that prison, there was no way that he could be released. So, Joseph could grow bitter, blame God, and other people, or he could allow the Holy Spirit to mold him, make him, humble him, which he did, and which the Lord intended. Millions of Christians have tried to circumvent the *"prison experience,"* but to no avail. Sooner or later, in one way or the other, the Lord puts us in a difficult situation. It is all for purpose, and is intended to cut away the dead branches, in order that we may look more and more to the True Vine, that we might bring forth much fruit (Jn., Chpt. 15).

(16) "WHEN THE CHIEF BAKER SAW THAT THE INTERPRETATION WAS GOOD, HE SAID UNTO JOSEPH, I ALSO WAS IN MY DREAM, AND, BEHOLD, I HAD THREE WHITE BASKETS ON MY HEAD:

(17) "AND IN THE UPPERMOST BASKET THERE WAS OF ALL MANNER OF BAKEMEATS FOR PHARAOH; AND THE BIRDS DID EAT THEM OUT OF THE BASKET UPON MY HEAD.

(18) "AND JOSEPH ANSWERED AND SAID, THIS IS THE INTERPRETATION THEREOF: THE THREE BASKETS ARE THREE DAYS:

(19) "YET WITHIN THREE DAYS SHALL PHARAOH LIFT UP YOUR HEAD FROM OFF

NOTES

YOU, AND SHALL HANG YOU ON A TREE; AND THE BIRDS SHALL EAT YOUR FLESH FROM OFF YOU.

(20) "AND IT CAME TO PASS THE THIRD DAY, WHICH WAS PHARAOH'S BIRTHDAY, THAT HE MADE A FEAST UNTO ALL HIS SERVANTS: AND HE LIFTED UP THE HEAD OF THE CHIEF BUTLER AND OF THE CHIEF BAKER AMONG HIS SERVANTS.

(21) "AND HE RESTORED THE CHIEF BUTLER UNTO HIS BUTLERSHIP AGAIN; AND HE GAVE THE CUP INTO PHARAOH'S HAND:

(22) "BUT HE HANGED THE CHIEF BAKER: AS JOSEPH HAD INTERPRETED TO THEM.

(23) "YET DID NOT THE CHIEF BUTLER REMEMBER JOSEPH, BUT FORGOT HIM."

The structure is:

1. God Alone knows the future, and He is able to reveal it to men, should He so desire.

2. The manner in which the Holy Spirit used Joseph in this instance would come under the heading of three modern Gifts of the Spirit: *"discerning of spirits," "the Word of Knowledge,"* and *"the Word of Wisdom"* (I Cor. 12:8-10).

3. Even though the butler forgot Joseph, which was the Will of God, he would remember him some two years later, when it was God's time for him to be released. *"Waiting"* is a part of Faith.

THE CHIEF BAKER

Verses 16 and 17 read: *"When the chief baker saw that the interpretation was good, he said unto Joseph, I also was in my dream, and, behold, I had three white baskets on my head:*

"And in the uppermost basket there was of all manner of bakemeats for Pharaoh; and the birds did eat them out of the basket upon my head."

One thing was certain: the chief butler didn't have long to wait to see if Joseph's interpretation was correct — only three days.

Evidently, the chief baker had not been too anxious to relate his dream to Joseph, probably thinking that such was a waste of time. But upon hearing the interpretation given to the chief butler, and knowing that in three days Joseph's accuracy would be proven, he ventured forth to relate his dream.

THREE DAYS

Verses 18 through 23 read: *"And Joseph answered and said, This is the interpretation thereof: The three baskets are three days:*

"Yet within three days shall Pharaoh lift up your head from off you, and shall hang you on a tree; and the birds shall eat your flesh from off you.

"And it came to pass the third day, which was Pharaoh's birthday, that he made a feast unto all his servants: and he lifted up the head of the chief butler and of the chief baker among his servants.

"And he restored the chief butler unto his butlership again; and he gave the cup into Pharaoh's hand:

"But he hanged the chief baker: as Joseph had interpreted to them.

"Yet did not the chief butler remember Joseph, but forgot him."

I can well surmise that the chief baker was not at all pleased with Joseph's interpretation, and probably laughed it off. Nevertheless, in three days, a great feast was conducted by Pharaoh celebrating his birthday, and both the chief butler and the chief baker were released from prison. Thus far, it was exactly as Joseph had predicted.

At a given point in time, the narrative seems to indicate that Pharaoh suddenly announced that the chief butler was restored to his former position, but that the chief baker was to hang, which he was. So, in the exact manner that Joseph predicted, in that exact manner it was carried out.

But yet the chief butler forgot Joseph, which seems to indicate that it was the Will of God that this be done. It is certain that if the Lord had intended for Joseph to be released at that time, He would have pressed hard upon the mind of the chief butler. That not being the case, we must come to the conclusion that the Lord had other purposes in mind, which become very obvious in the next Chapter. While Joseph may have been forgotten by man, he definitely was not forgotten by God.

"Wonderful birth, to a manger He came,
"Made in the likeness of man,
"To proclaim God's boundless love for a world sick with sin,

"Pleading with sinners to let Him come in."

"Wonderful life, full of service so free,
"Friend to the poor and the needy was He;
"Unfailing goodness on all He bestowed,
"Undying faith in the vilest He showed."

"Wonderful death, for it meant not defeat,
"Calvary made His great mission complete,
"Wrought our Redemption, and when He arose,
"Banished forever the last of our foes."

"Wonderful hope, He is coming again,
"Coming as King over the nations to reign;
"Glorious promise, His Word cannot fail,
"His righteous Kingdom at last must prevail!"

CHAPTER 41

(1) "AND IT CAME TO PASS AT THE END OF TWO FULL YEARS, THAT PHARAOH DREAMED: AND, BEHOLD, HE STOOD BY THE RIVER.

(2) "AND, BEHOLD, THERE CAME UP OUT OF THE RIVER SEVEN WELL FAVORED CATTLE AND FATFLESHED; AND THEY FED IN A MEADOW.

(3) "AND, BEHOLD, SEVEN OTHER CATTLE CAME UP AFTER THEM OUT OF THE RIVER, ILL FAVORED AND LEANFLESHED; AND STOOD BY THE OTHER CATTLE UPON THE BRINK OF THE RIVER.

(4) "AND THE ILL FAVORED AND LEANFLESHED CATTLE DID EAT UP THE SEVEN WELL FAVORED AND FAT CATTLE. SO PHARAOH AWOKE.

(5) "AND HE SLEPT AND DREAMED THE SECOND TIME: AND, BEHOLD, SEVEN EARS OF CORN CAME UP UPON ONE STALK, RANK AND GOOD.

(6) "AND, BEHOLD, SEVEN THIN EARS AND BLASTED WITH THE EAST WIND SPRUNG UP AFTER THEM.

(7) "AND THE SEVEN THIN EARS DEVOURED THE SEVEN RANK AND FULL

EARS. AND PHARAOH AWOKE, AND, BEHOLD, IT WAS A DREAM.”

The construction is:

1. Joseph, while yet in humiliation, becomes the interpreter of the thoughts and counsels of God.

2. In his elevation, he executes with power those counsels, and subjects all Egypt to him who then sat upon the throne.

3. And in all this was Joseph wonderfully a full Type of Christ, Who, in the humiliation of His First Advent, revealed the counsels and affections of God's heart, and Who will, in the glory of His Second Advent, establish the Kingdom of God in power over the whole Earth.

THE DREAM

Verse 1 reads: *"And it came to pass at the end of two full years, that Pharaoh dreamed: and, behold, he stood by the river."*

This is two years after Joseph had given the interpretation to the butler and the baker.

This, to be sure, was another test for Joseph, and a difficult test at that. It was the *"test of delay."* But God's delays are not cruel. They all have a purpose (Horton).

Again, the Lord uses a dream in order to bring about several things. The dream will bring about the release of Joseph, but more importantly, while addressing itself to the present, it will more particularly address itself to the distant future, in fact, a time which has not even yet come to pass. Momentarily, we will go into detail as it regards this prediction of futuristic events, which in fact pertains to the great outpouring of the Holy Spirit in the last days, and as well, the coming time of great trouble, called *"the Great Tribulation Period,"* as it regards Israel (Mat. 24:21).

In the dream, Pharaoh stands by the river, which incidentally, is the Nile.

The Egyptians believed the Nile to be the giver of life; consequently, by the Lord giving this man such a dream, and having him in the dream to stand by the Nile, is at least a great part of the reason that Pharaoh placed such stock in these dreams. Otherwise, he might have passed it off as incidental.

THE DREAM AS IT WAS GIVEN

Verses 2 through 7 read: *"And, behold, there came up out of the river seven well*

favored cattle and fatfleshed; and they fed in a meadow.

"And, behold, seven other cattle came up after them out of the river, ill favored and leanfleshed; and stood by the other cattle upon the brink of the river.

"And the ill favored and leanfleshed cattle did eat up the seven well favored and fat cattle. So Pharaoh awoke.

"And he slept and dreamed the second time: and, behold, seven ears of corn came up upon one stalk, rank and good.

"And, behold, seven thin ears and blasted with the east wind sprung up after them.

"And the seven thin ears devoured the seven rank and full ears. And Pharaoh awoke, and behold, it was a dream."

According to some of the sages of old, the heifer was regarded by the ancient Egyptians as a symbol of the Earth, agriculture, and the nourishment derived therefrom. It was, therefore, natural that the succession of seven prosperous years should be represented by seven thriving cows (Pulpit).

That they are coming up out of the Nile is the same thing as God speaking to Pharaoh, at least in his heathen thinking.

We find that the dream was doubled by the Lord to Pharaoh, for of a certainty, it was the Lord who gave the Monarch these two dreams.

Both dreams are simple to Pharaoh, but yet he lacks understanding. Seven fat cows come up out of the river, and they begin to feed or graze in a meadow.

But then we have seven other cattle coming up out of the river, but rather lean and undernourished. These which are undernourished come up to the fat cattle, and eat them up.

Pharaoh then awoke, and then went back to sleep that same night, or else it speaks of the next night, etc. The dream is basically the same, but different ingredients are used.

The second dream portrays a stalk coming up containing seven sheaths of grain, fat and healthy. Then another stalk comes out of the ground, with seven thin sheaths, which then devoured the seven healthy sheaths.

As we shall see, in this simple dream given to this heathen Monarch, the future will be foretold concerning time soon to come, and as well, happenings into the distant future, which have not come to pass even yet.

NOTES

(8) "AND IT CAME TO PASS IN THE MORNING THAT HIS SPIRIT WAS TROUBLED: AND HE SENT AND CALLED FOR ALL THE MAGICIANS OF EGYPT, AND ALL THE WISE MEN THEREOF: AND PHARAOH TOLD THEM HIS DREAM; BUT THERE WAS NONE THAT COULD INTERPRET THEM UNTO PHARAOH.

(9) "THEN SPOKE THE CHIEF BUTLER UNTO PHARAOH, SAYING, I DO REMEMBER MY FAULTS THIS DAY:

(10) "PHARAOH WAS ANGRY WITH HIS SERVANTS, AND PUT ME IN WARD IN THE CAPTAIN OF THE GUARD'S HOUSE, BOTH ME AND THE CHIEF BAKER:

(11) "AND WE DREAMED A DREAM IN ONE NIGHT, I AND HE; WE DREAMED EACH MAN ACCORDING TO THE INTERPRETATION OF HIS DREAM.

(12) "AND THERE WAS THERE WITH US A YOUNG MAN, AN HEBREW, SERVANT TO THE CAPTAIN OF THE GUARD; AND WE TOLD HIM, AND HE INTERPRETED TO US OUR DREAMS; TO EACH MAN ACCORDING TO HIS DREAM HE DID INTERPRET.

(13) "AND IT CAME TO PASS, AS HE INTERPRETED TO US, SO IT WAS; ME HE RESTORED UNTO MY OFFICE, AND HIM HE HANGED.

(14) "THEN PHARAOH SENT AND CALLED JOSEPH, AND THEY BROUGHT HIM HASTILY OUT OF THE DUNGEON: AND HE SHAVED HIMSELF, AND CHANGED HIS RAIMENT, AND CAME IN UNTO PHARAOH."

The composition is:

1. Pharaoh dreams of seven cattle, and seven ears of corn. The Egyptian *"Book of the Dead,"* now in the British Museum in London with its sacred cows and mystic number *"seven"* — a book beyond doubt well known to Pharaoh — must have helped to convince the king that this double dream was supernatural.

2. Events now transpire which no human hand could manipulate. Only God could do such a thing. This should teach us that we should allow the Lord to plan for us.

3. Men forgot Joseph, but it is double certain that God didn't forget Joseph. And neither will He forget you. This is at least one of the reasons that we must look to God instead of men.

THE MAGICIANS OF EGYPT

Verse 8 reads: *"And it came to pass in the morning that his spirit was troubled: and he sent and called for all the magicians of Egypt, and all the wise men thereof: and Pharaoh told them his dream; but there was none who could interpret them unto Pharaoh."*

Considering that the Lord used the Nile River, cows, and stalks of grain out of the Earth as symbols in this dream, such made it very important to Pharaoh, who considered these things to be gods in their own right. Considering that the dream was doubled, and more than likely given in one night, the Monarch was most desirous of learning the meaning of what he had dreamed.

The *"magicians of Egypt,"* along with the *"wise men,"* were the most learned and knowledgeable of their kind in the world of that day. Concerning these individuals, history says that they claimed mysterious knowledge of magic, divination, and astrology; they knew all the ancient magical inscriptions and were skilled in deciphering and interpreting them.

That they could not explain the dream, though couched in the symbolical language of the time, was no doubt surprising; but *"the things of God knows no man, but the Spirit of God"* (I Cor. 2:11), and they to whom the Spirit does reveal them (I Cor. 2:10) (Pulpit).

It is no different presently. The only people in the world who have a blueprint for the future are the people of God, who know their Bibles. For it is the Bible alone which tells us what the future holds regarding the nations of this world. And yet, despite the fact of such startling information, precious few take the time to peruse the contents of the Word of God.

FUTURE

Concerning the future, in brief, the Bible teaches that the Rapture of the Church could take place at any moment (I Thess. 4:13-18). This will be followed at some point by seven years of Great Tribulation, which believe it or not, Pharaoh saw in his dreams (II Thess. 2:7-8). The Great Tribulation Period, lasting some seven years, will be concluded by the Second Coming of the Lord (Rev., Chpt. 19). It will be the fulfillment of Daniel's interpretation of the dream of Nebuchadnezzar. The great Prophet-Statesman said: *"Forasmuch as you saw that the stone was cut out of the mountain without hands, and that it broke in pieces the iron, the brass, the clay, the silver, and the gold; the great God has made known to the king what shall come to pass hereafter: and the dream is certain, and the interpretation thereof sure"* (Dan. 2:45).

That *"Stone"* is Christ. At the Second Coming, He will smash in pieces all of the governments of men, and thereby take control of the entirety of the world Himself. Isaiah said of Him: *"And the government shall be upon His shoulder: and His Name shall be called Wonderful, Counselor, The Mighty God, The Everlasting Father, The Prince of Peace."*

He then said, *"Of the increase of His Government and peace there shall be no end, upon the throne of David, and upon His Kingdom, to order it, and to establish it with judgment and with justice from henceforth even forever. The zeal of the LORD of Hosts will perform this"* (Isa. 9:6-7).

Under Christ, the world will then enter into one thousand years of peace, with Satan locked away in the bottomless pit. At the end of that thousand-year period, he will be loosed for a little season, but will be put down quickly, with the world then being renovated by fire, and the New Jerusalem coming down from God out of Heaven, to rest upon this Earth, with God literally changing His Headquarters from Heaven to Earth (Rev., Chpts. 20-22).

In fact, about one-third of the Bible is Prophecy, with another third being instruction, and the remaining third being history. No other book in the world even remotely compares with the Word of God. Without God and His Word, all the magicians and wise men of the world have no clue as to what the future holds. But as stated, the Bible portrays that future to us. Man would do well to heed its contents! The wise men of Pharaoh's day could not interpret the dreams or the times. Joseph could, and because the Lord revealed it to him.

The dreams which will be interpreted will, in a sense, be the very first glimpse into the future regarding nations, unless we would count that given by Enoch, which actually

wasn't given to us in the Old Testament, recorded only in the New (Jude, vs. 14).

JOSEPH

Verses 9 through 13 read: *"Then spake the chief butler unto Pharaoh, saying, I do remember my faults this day:*

"Pharaoh was angry with his servants, and put me in ward in the captain of the guard's house, both me and the chief baker:

"And we dreamed a dream in one night, I and he; we dreamed each man according to the interpretation of his dream.

"And there was there with us a young man, an Hebrew, servant to the captain of the guard; and we told him, and he interpreted to us our dreams; to each man according to his dream he did interpret.

"And it came to pass, as he interpreted to us, so it was; me he restored unto my office, and him he hanged."

As the great court of Pharaoh, the mightiest Monarch on the face of the Earth, comes to their proverbial wits end, which means that no one has the answer, the chief butler suddenly speaks up concerning Joseph, and his experience concerning the interpretation of his dream, as well as the dream of the chief baker, when they both were in prison.

The second and third pronoun *"he"* in Verse 13 refers to Pharaoh and not Joseph. While Joseph interpreted the dreams, it was Pharaoh who restored the man to his office, and hanged the other one.

As we observed the entirety of the scene unfolding before us, we see the Hand of God in all things. The Lord is getting the Earth ready for great harvest, which will be followed by famine. At the appropriate time, He will give dreams to Pharaoh, dreams incidentally, which the mighty Monarch cannot interpret, nor can anyone in his kingdom, at least as far as his wise men are concerned. The Lord then causes the chief butler to vividly remember the incident with Joseph concerning his dreams of some two years before.

As well, during these two years, the Lord was further educating Joseph in His Ways. The Scripture is not exactly clear as to how long Joseph actually stayed in prison. The two years mentioned only concerned the time from Joseph's interpretation of the dreams regarding the butler and the baker, to the time he was released from prison. How long he spent in prison altogether, we aren't told. Many think it was approximately seven years, which could well have been the case.

JOSEPH AND PHARAOH

Verse 14 reads: *"Then Pharaoh sent and called Joseph, and they brought him hastily out of the dungeon: and he shaved himself, and changed his raiment, and came in unto Pharaoh."*

During all of this previous time of preparation, and preparation it was, had Joseph become bitter, hateful, and haughty, had he held grudges against his brothers, or blamed God, he would never have come to this place to which the Lord will elevate him. This should be a great lesson for all of us.

As I've previously stated, everything as it regards the Child of God presents itself as a test. How do we act? How do we react?

The Believer is to do everything according to the Word of God, irrespective as to what my brother might do to me, or how bad it might be, I must not grow bitter in my heart toward him. I must pray for him, because that's exactly what Christ told us to do. He said: *"Love your enemies, bless them who curse you, do good to them who hate you, and pray for them which despitefully use you, and persecute you"* (Mat. 5:44).

This doesn't mean to condone their actions, nor does it mean to have fellowship with them. In fact, unless they repent, fellowship is impossible; however, none of that precludes the command of Christ that we love them, bless them, do good to them, and pray for them. And let the Reader understand the following:

While following the admonition of Christ will definitely bless the individual in question, it is actually done more so for the one who has been wronged, than anyone else. Obeying Christ will stop bitterness, ill will, rancor, and anger.

Whenever we harbor ill will against someone, thereby refusing to forgive them, in a sense, that person owns us. And let me explain that:

We think about them constantly, as to how we can get even with them, what we can do to

them, etc. As stated, they own our thoughts, in effect, owning us.

Whenever we properly forgive someone, even as Joseph forgave his brothers, we then release them to the Lord, letting Him take care of the situation. However, we should remember this as well:

Forgiveness, as stated, doesn't mean that fellowship can be restored. As we shall see when the time comes, when Joseph's brothers came before him, he did not immediately reveal himself to them. In fact, he tested them thoroughly to see if they were the same men who sold him into Egyptian bondage, or whether they had changed. We are obligated to do the same as well!

(15) "AND PHARAOH SAID UNTO JOSEPH, I HAVE DREAMED A DREAM, AND THERE IS NONE WHO CAN INTERPRET IT: AND I HAVE HEARD SAY OF YOU, THAT YOU CAN UNDERSTAND A DREAM TO INTERPRET IT.

(16) "AND JOSEPH ANSWERED PHARAOH, SAYING, IT IS NOT IN ME: GOD SHALL GIVE PHARAOH AN ANSWER OF PEACE.

(17) "AND PHARAOH SAID UNTO JOSEPH, IN MY DREAM, BEHOLD, I STOOD UPON THE BANK OF THE RIVER:

(18) "AND, BEHOLD, THERE CAME UP OUT OF THE RIVER SEVEN CATTLE, FATFLESHED AND WELL FAVORED; AND THEY FED IN A MEADOW:

(19) "AND, BEHOLD, SEVEN OTHER CATTLE CAME UP AFTER THEM, POOR AND VERY ILL FAVORED AND LEANFLESHED, SUCH I NEVER SAW IN ALL THE LAND OF EGYPT FOR BADNESS:

(20) "AND THE LEAN AND THE ILL FAVORED CATTLE DID EAT UP THE FIRST SEVEN FAT CATTLE:

(21) "AND WHEN THEY HAD EATEN THEM UP, IT COULD NOT BE KNOWN THAT THEY HAD EATEN THEM; BUT THEY WERE STILL ILL FAVORED, AS AT THE BEGINNING. SO I AWOKE.

(22) "AND I SAW IN MY DREAM, AND, BEHOLD, SEVEN EARS CAME UP IN ONE STALK, FULL AND GOOD:

(23) "AND, BEHOLD, SEVEN EARS, WITHERED, THIN, AND BLASTED WITH THE EAST WIND, SPRUNG UP AFTER THEM:

(24) "AND THE THIN EARS DEVOURED THE SEVEN GOOD EARS: AND I TOLD THIS UNTO THE MAGICIANS; BUT THERE WAS NONE WHO COULD DECLARE IT TO ME."

The overview is:

1. The Lord, once again, uses dreams to reveal His Will.

2. Joseph could have claimed great things, but instead, he gave all the glory to God for giving him the interpretation of these dreams.

3. The Lord is still using dreams to outline His Will, and to portray the future.

THE WORDS OF PHARAOH

Verse 15 reads: *"And Pharaoh said unto Joseph, I have dreamed a dream, and there is none that can interpret it: and I have heard say of you, that you can understand a dream to interpret it."*

The evidence is, Joseph, after shaving and changing his clothes, came immediately from the dungeon to the palace. I wonder what his thoughts were, as he walked into one of the most palatial settings in the entirety of the world. Had the Lord given him any clue at all as to what was about to happen? This one thing is certain:

Any Believer, who is truly right with God, is master of the situation, irrespective as to the setting, or how powerful the unsaved individuals present might be.

Any saved individual is a Child of God. As such, there is an authority which accompanies the position. Despite this being the palace of the mightiest Monarch on the face of the Earth, Joseph was supreme. He alone held the answer to the dilemma at hand.

GIVE THE GLORY TO GOD

Verse 16 reads: *"And Joseph answered Pharaoh, saying, It is not in me: God shall give Pharaoh an answer of peace."*

Joseph is quick to give the glory to God. He takes no credit for what is about to transpire, even as he shouldn't have taken any credit. This is very, very important.

It is hard for God to bless many people, and for the simple reason that they tend to think that they have made some contribution to the effort. None of us have. Anything and everything which is spiritual always comes totally and completely from the

NOTES

Lord. We are merely an instrument at best, and must always understand that.

Pharaoh, knowing little or nothing about Jehovah, gives Joseph the credit for these things he has heard concerning the interpretation of dreams, and especially the fact that what had been predicted came to pass exactly as predicted. Knowing that Pharaoh understood nothing about Jehovah, Joseph could have easily overlooked this part; but he was quick to correct the Monarch, saying, *"It is not in me,"* with him then telling Pharaoh that if the answer came, it would be God Who did it.

THE DREAMS RELATED

Verses 17 through 24 read: *"And Pharaoh said unto Joseph, In my dream, behold, I stood upon the bank of the river:*

"And, behold, there came up out of the river seven cattle, fatfleshed and well favored; and they fed in a meadow:

"And, behold, seven other cattle came up after them, poor and very ill favored and leanfleshed, such as I never saw in all the land of Egypt for badness:

"And the lean and the ill favored cattle did eat up the first seven fat cattle:

"And when they had eaten them up, it could not be known that they had eaten them; but they were still ill favored, as at the beginning. So I awoke.

"And I saw in my dream, and, behold, seven ears came up in one stalk, full and good:

"And, behold, seven ears, withered, thin, and blasted with the east wind, sprung up after them:

"And the thin ears devoured the seven good ears: and I told this unto the magicians; but there was none who could declare it to me."

The dreams had made such an impression upon Pharaoh, that he felt he had to have an answer as to their interpretation. This was not a case of mere curiosity, but rather a compulsion actually placed in the heart of the Monarch by the Lord. It's ironic: Pharaoh was looked at by the Egyptians as a *"god"* in any case, but yet the interpretation of a dream completely disproved this fallacy.

That which seemed to be more confusing to the Monarch was the fact that the lean cattle ate up the fat cattle, but showed no improvement. It was the same with the seven stalks of grain. The thin sheaths devoured the seven good sheaths, but were none the better. The Monarch then emphatically states to Joseph concerning the interpretation of all of this, *"There was none who could declare it to me."*

(25) "AND JOSEPH SAID UNTO PHARAOH, THE DREAM OF PHARAOH IS ONE: GOD HAS SHOWN PHARAOH WHAT HE IS ABOUT TO DO.

(26) "THE SEVEN CATTLE ARE SEVEN YEARS; AND THE SEVEN GOOD EARS ARE SEVEN YEARS: THE DREAM IS ONE.

(27) "AND THE SEVEN THIN AND ILL FAVORED CATTLE THAT CAME UP AFTER THEM ARE SEVEN YEARS; AND THE SEVEN EMPTY EARS BLASTED WITH THE EAST WIND SHALL BE SEVEN YEARS OF FAMINE.

(28) "THIS IS THE THING WHICH I HAVE SPOKEN UNTO PHARAOH: WHAT GOD IS ABOUT TO DO HE SHOWS UNTO PHARAOH.

(29) "BEHOLD, THERE COME SEVEN YEARS OF GREAT PLENTY THROUGHOUT ALL THE LAND OF EGYPT:

(30) "AND THERE SHALL ARISE AFTER THEM SEVEN YEARS OF FAMINE; AND ALL THE PLENTY SHALL BE FORGOTTEN IN THE LAND OF EGYPT; AND THE FAMINE SHALL CONSUME THE LAND;

(31) "AND THE PLENTY SHALL NOT BE KNOWN IN THE LAND BY REASON OF THAT FAMINE FOLLOWING; FOR IT SHALL BE VERY GRIEVOUS.

(32) "AND FOR THAT THE DREAM WAS DOUBLED UNTO PHARAOH TWICE; IT IS BECAUSE THE THING IS ESTABLISHED BY GOD, AND GOD WILL SHORTLY BRING IT TO PASS."

The synopsis is:

1. Discoveries about 100 years ago at the First Cataract, and at El-Kab, record the fact of this seven years famine. The date is given as 1700 B.C. This date accords with accepted Bible chronology.

2. The dream was doubled, in order, as Joseph says in Verse 32, to denote its Divine certainty, and as well, to portray its immediate happening, as well as its futuristic happening.

3. For those whom God would use, in some way, there must be a prison before there

can be a palace. The problem of *"self"* demands it!

WHAT GOD IS ABOUT TO DO

Verse 25 reads: *"And Joseph said unto Pharaoh, The dream of Pharaoh is one: God has shown Pharaoh what He is about to do."*

This one statement as given by Joseph proclaims the fact that God is over all. He controls the weather; He controls nations; He controls men. And by that, I do not mean to say, nor does the Scripture teach that everything is predestined; however, the idea is, God is in charge and not man. But it's hard for man to understand that, or even to agree to that.

Even though these two dreams had a double fulfillment, Pharaoh of course, would be interested in that which was coming in the immediate future, hence Joseph saying, *"God has shown Pharaoh what He is about to do."*

THE INTERPRETATION

Verses 26 through 32 read: *"The seven good cattle are seven years; and the seven good ears are seven years: the dream is one.*

"And the seven thin and ill favored cattle that came up after them are seven years; and the seven empty ears blasted with the east wind shall be seven years of famine.

"This is the thing which I have spoken unto Pharaoh: What God is about to do He shows unto Pharaoh.

"Behold, there come seven years of great plenty throughout all the land of Egypt:

"And there shall arise after them seven years of famine; and all the plenty shall be forgotten in the land of Egypt; and the famine shall consume the land;

"And the plenty shall not be known in the land by reason of that famine following; for it shall be very grievous.

"And for that the dream was doubled unto Pharaoh twice; it is because the thing is established by God, and God will shortly bring it to pass."

Exactly as to how the Lord moved upon Joseph as it regards this interpretation, we aren't told. More than likely, he revealed it to his spirit, and did it in such a way that Joseph knew beyond the shadow of a doubt, that what he was saying was correct. And as well, it was so right that Pharaoh accepted the interpretation immediately.

The seven fat cattle, and the seven fat sheaths of grain represented seven years of tremendous harvest which would come to Egypt, generating perhaps the greatest abundance the nation had ever known. This would begin immediately, possibly with the coming planting season.

And then immediately following the seven years of plenty would come seven years of famine, which would devour all the surplus of the seven years of plenty, and would do so to such an extent that it would leave nothing. The Scripture says, *"The famine shall consume the land"* (vs. 30).

THE PROPHETIC ANALYSIS

The interpretation as given by Joseph, and which greatly concerned Pharaoh, was to take place in the immediate future. But due to the fact of the dream being doubled, it has an Endtime meaning as well, and which will be of far greater magnitude than that which would take place in the near future. It is as follows:

We know that this terrible famine which would follow the seven years of plenty would bring Joseph's brothers to him, ultimately along with his father Jacob. This represents Israel coming to Christ, which they shall do at the conclusion of the seven-year Great Tribulation Period. So, the seven years of famine point to the coming seven-year Great Tribulation Period, prophesied by Daniel, and foretold by Jesus (Dan. 9:27; Mat. 24:21).

As well, the *"east wind"* mentioned in Verse 27 localizes the Great Tribulation Period that is coming, which will affect the entire Earth, but will have its beginnings in the Middle East.

As it regards the seven years of plenty which immediately preceded the seven years of famine, looking at it in the prophetic sense, we can take the number *"seven"* in two different ways.

The number *"seven,"* which is God's number of perfection could pertain to the Church, and it being completed, and then taken out of the world immediately before the seven years of Tribulation. Or, even as the seven years of famine correspond exactly with the

NOTES

coming seven years of great tribulation, the seven years of plenty could refer to a tremendous harvest of souls immediately preceding the Rapture, which will be followed by the Great Tribulation. Quite possibly, both particulars will come into play. There will be a great harvest of souls, fulfilling the prophecy of Joel, about the Lord pouring out His Spirit upon all flesh, which Peter infers will be in the last days, which will conclude the Church Age (Acts 2:16-21).

Regarding the Church, the Bible teaches two things taking place in the last days. It speaks of a great *"falling away,"* which corresponds with a falling away from the Faith, which in fact is happening now (II Thess. 2:3), which means that many will *"depart from the faith, giving heed to seducing spirits, and doctrines of devils"* (I Tim. 4:1).

So we have two things taking place in these last days, the outpouring of the Holy Spirit, and the falling away from the Faith.

THE CROSS

The dividing line between the two, which we've already stated, will be, and in fact is, the Cross of Christ. The Cross has always been the dividing line, but it will be, and is now more pronounced than ever. In other words, faith is either going to have to be placed in Jesus Christ and Him Crucified, or else in other things. And to place one's faith in something else means simply that *"Christ shall profit you nothing"* (Gal. 5:2). That means that all of this will end exactly as it began.

For the beginning we go to the Fourth Chapter of Genesis, and we find Abel offering up the sacrifice of an innocent victim, a lamb, and Cain offering up the work and labor of his own hands in sacrifice, which God would not accept. While both were sacrifices, only one was acceptable to God, because it spoke of man's sin and man's Redemption, which would be gained through the Sacrificial Offering of Christ Himself. In effect, Cain's sacrifice stated that he wasn't a sinner, and, thereby, didn't need a Redeemer. He was willing to acknowledge God, by offering up the sacrifice as he did, but not willing to admit what he was, and what he needed. It is the same presently! It is the Cross or nothing, as it has always been the Cross or nothing!

(33) "NOW THEREFORE LET PHARAOH LOOK OUT A MAN DISCREET AND WISE, AND SET HIM OVER THE LAND OF EGYPT.

(34) "LET PHARAOH DO THIS, AND LET HIM APPOINT OFFICERS OVER THE LAND, AND TAKE UP THE FIFTH PART OF THE LAND OF EGYPT IN THE SEVEN PLENTEOUS YEARS.

(35) "AND LET THEM GATHER ALL THE FOOD OF THOSE GOOD YEARS THAT COME, AND LAY UP CORN UNDER THE HAND OF PHARAOH, AND LET THEM KEEP FOOD IN THE CITIES.

(36) "AND THAT FOOD SHALL BE FOR STORE TO THE LAND AGAINST THE SEVEN YEARS OF FAMINE, WHICH SHALL BE IN THE LAND OF EGYPT: THAT THE LAND PERISH NOT THROUGH THE FAMINE.

(37) "AND THE THING WAS GOOD IN THE EYES OF PHARAOH, AND IN THE EYES OF ALL HIS SERVANTS.

(38) "AND PHARAOH SAID UNTO HIS SERVANTS, CAN WE FIND SUCH A ONE AS THIS IS, A MAN IN WHOM THE SPIRIT OF GOD IS?

(39) "AND PHARAOH SAID UNTO JOSEPH, FORASMUCH AS GOD HAS SHOWED YOU ALL THIS, THERE IS NONE SO DISCREET AND WISE AS YOU ARE:

(40) "YOU SHALL BE OVER MY HOUSE, AND ACCORDING UNTO YOUR WORD SHALL ALL MY PEOPLE BE RULED: ONLY IN THE THRONE WILL I BE GREATER THAN YOU.

(41) "AND PHARAOH SAID UNTO JOSEPH, SEE, I HAVE SET YOU OVER ALL THE LAND OF EGYPT.

(42) "AND PHARAOH TOOK OFF HIS RING FROM HIS HAND, AND PUT IT UPON JOSEPH'S HAND, AND ARRAYED HIM IN VESTURES OF FINE LINEN, AND PUT A GOLD CHAIN ABOUT HIS NECK;

(43) "AND HE MADE HIM TO RIDE IN THE SECOND CHARIOT WHICH HE HAD; AND THEY CRIED BEFORE HIM, BOW THE KNEE: AND HE MADE HIM RULER OF ALL THE LAND OF EGYPT.

(44) "AND PHARAOH SAID UNTO JOSEPH, I AM PHARAOH, AND WITHOUT YOU SHALL NO MAN LIFT UP HIS HAND OR FOOT IN ALL THE LAND OF EGYPT.

(45) "AND PHARAOH CALLED JOSEPH'S NAME ZAPHNATH-PAANEAH: AND HE

GAVE HIM TO WIFE ASENATH THE DAUGHTER OF POTI-PHERAH PRIEST OF ON. AND JOSEPH WENT OUT OVER ALL THE LAND OF EGYPT."

The diagram is:

1. Joseph was made the lord of Egypt, even as Christ was made the Lord of the Gentiles.

2. This famine was designed by God, not only to bless and instruct Egypt, but mainly to be the means of bringing Joseph's brothers in Repentance to his feet. It is all, as well, as stated, a picture of present and future facts.

3. The true Joseph in his present rejection by His brethren takes to Himself an election from among the Gentiles. The completion of that election, if this portrayal may be so interpreted, will be followed by *"the time of Jacob's trouble,"* the effect of which trouble will be to cause the sons of Israel to recognize Him Whom they had pierced, and to mourn and weep (Williams).

THE SUGGESTION OF JOSEPH

Verses 33 through 36 read: *"Now therefore let Pharaoh look out a man discreet and wise, and set him over the land of Egypt.*

"Let Pharaoh do this, and let him appoint officers over the land, and take up the fifth part of the land of Egypt in the seven plenteous years.

"And let them gather all the food of those good years that come, and lay up corn under the hand of Pharaoh, and let them keep food in the cities.

"And that food shall be for store to the land against the seven years of famine, which shall be in the land of Egypt; that the land perish not through the famine."

Joseph's suggestion to Pharaoh, as to addressing this coming situation, must have been given to him by the Lord as well. And as stated, the interpretation so satisfied the Monarch, that he never doubted, it seems, the words of Joseph. Of course, the Lord had prepared everything for this moment. This one thing is certain: Despite the fact that Joseph had been in prison for several years, not one person steps up to accuse him at this particular time. This proves beyond the shadow of a doubt the absolute falseness of the charges which had placed him in prison to begin with.

I wonder how Joseph felt, when Pharaoh sent for him. He had languished in prison for several years, and now he will go stand before Pharaoh. Regarding those who were sent by Pharaoh to retrieve Joseph, did they give him any hint as to why he was being called before the mightiest Monarch on the face of the Earth?

Whatever the situation may have been, it is absolutely certain that the Lord had prepared him minutely for this moment. In fact, he will go not only from the prison to the palace, but as well to the place and position of being the second most powerful man in Egypt, and thereby the world.

JOSEPH CHOSEN

Verses 37 through 45 read: *"And the thing was good in the eyes of Pharaoh, and in the eyes of all his servants.*

"And Pharaoh said unto his servants, Can we find such a one as this is, a man in whom the Spirit of God is?

"And Pharaoh said unto Joseph, Forasmuch as God has shown you all this, and there is none so discreet and wise as you are:

"You shall be over my house, and according unto your word shall all my people be ruled: only in the throne will I be greater than you.

"And Pharaoh said unto Joseph, See, I have set you over all the land of Egypt.

"And Pharaoh took off his ring from his hand, put it upon Joseph's hand, and arrayed him in vestures of fine linen, and put a gold chain about his neck;

"And he made him to ride in the second chariot which he had; and they cried before him, Bow the knee: and he made him ruler over all the land of Egypt.

"And Pharaoh said unto Joseph, I am Pharaoh, and without you shall no man lift up his hand or foot in all the land of Egypt.

"And Pharaoh called Joseph's name Zaphnath-paaneah; and he gave him to wife Asenath the daughter of Poti-pherah priest of On. And Joseph went out over all the land of Egypt."

After Joseph suggested to Pharaoh as to what should be done, the Monarch instantly suggested that Joseph be made the Prime Minister. He uses a term that is familiar to

us, but needs explanation. He said, *"A man in whom the Spirit of God is."*

The Hebrew would have been *"Ruach Elohim,"* and would have been understood by Pharaoh as referring to the sagacity and intelligence of a Deity. Other than that, he would have had no knowledge as to What of Who the Spirit of God actually was. And his understanding would have been far different than the understanding of Joseph, etc.

So in a moment's time, Joseph is promoted to the august position of the Prime Minister of Egypt, and is thus one of the most powerful men in the world.

Pharaoh made him greater than anyone else in Egypt, except himself, and made his authority to cover the entirety of the land of Egypt. Furthermore, he took off his ring from his hand, *"and put it upon Joseph's hand,"* which proclaimed the fact that his position was real and not merely honorary. The *"vestures of fine linen,"* made Joseph a part of the priestly class. The *"gold chain about his neck"* pertains to that which was worn by persons of distinction. Joseph's authority was to be absolute and universal, which it was. There was no part of Egypt over which he didn't have control.

The very name that Pharaoh gave Joseph, *"Zaphnath-paaneah,"* was prophetic. As his Hebrew name, Joseph, means, *"Jehovah shall add,"* his Egyptian name means, *"life more abundant."* So in essence, both of his names meant, *"Jehovah shall add life more abundant,"* which portrays Christ as well. Jesus said:

"I am come that they might have life, and that they might have it more abundantly" (Jn. 10:10).

(46) "AND JOSEPH WAS THIRTY YEARS OLD WHEN HE STOOD BEFORE PHARAOH KING OF EGYPT. AND JOSEPH WENT OUT FROM THE PRESENCE OF PHARAOH, AND WENT THROUGHOUT ALL THE LAND OF EGYPT.

(47) "AND IN THE SEVEN PLENTEOUS YEARS THE EARTH BROUGHT FORTH BY HANDFULS.

(48) "AND HE GATHERED UP ALL THE FOOD THE SEVEN YEARS, WHICH WERE IN THE LAND OF EGYPT, AND LAID UP THE FOOD IN THE CITIES: THE FOOD OF

THE FIELD, WHICH WAS ROUND ABOUT EVERY CITY, LAID HE UP IN THE SAME.

(49) "AND JOSEPH GATHERED CORN AS THE SAND OF THE SEA, VERY MUCH, UNTIL HE LEFT NUMBERING; FOR IT WAS WITHOUT NUMBER."

The structure is:

1. Joseph was 30 years old when he stood before Pharaoh, and Jesus was 30 years old when He began His public Ministry.

2. Concerning the seven years of plenty, Joseph's predictions proved to be exact.

3. The harvests were greater than Egypt had ever experienced, so great in fact, that it could not be counted or measured.

THIRTY YEARS OLD

Verse 46 reads: *"And Joseph was thirty years old when he stood before Pharaoh king of Egypt. And Joseph went out from the presence of Pharaoh, and went throughout all the land of Egypt."*

It was not without meaning that the Holy Spirit through Moses tells us that Joseph was thirty years old when he stood before Pharaoh. Joseph, as a Type of Christ, began his public Ministry, so to speak, at the same age that the greater Joseph would begin His public Ministry. Christ was thirty years old when He came forth to minister to the people (Lk. 3:23).

As Joseph *"went throughout all the land of Egypt,"* as it refers to his authority in carrying out the commands of Pharaoh, likewise, the Lord Jesus Christ, rejected by His brethren, has gone out over the entirety of the Gentile world, in order to gather the grain of souls.

THE SEVEN YEARS OF PLENTY

Verses 47 through 49 read: *"And in the seven plenteous years the Earth brought forth by handfuls.*

"And he gathered up all the food of the seven years, which were in the land of Egypt, and laid up the food in the cities: the food of the field, which was round about every city, laid he up in the same.

"And Joseph gathered corn as the sand of the sea, very much, until he left numbering; for it was without number."

Exactly as Joseph predicted, exactly as it happened. There were seven years of harvests as Egypt had never known. In fact, it was so

great, that the Scripture says that they quit trying to number or count the bushels, etc.

Quite possibly this seven-year period of time could stand for the entirety of the Church Age, and the tremendous number of souls which have been saved during the last nearly 2,000 years; however, it could as well speak of the last seven years of the Church Age, as we have mentioned. If so, many, many souls will find Christ in the very near future.

To be sure, that could very easily happen. The Holy Spirit being poured out upon all flesh has been fulfilled in measure; however, I personally do not think it has been fulfilled in totality. If the Spirit of God moves in certain ways, which He is very capable of doing, it could usher in untold thousands, and even millions, into the Kingdom of God. The Scripture does say concerning the last of the last days, *"And it shall come to pass, that whosoever shall call on the Name of the Lord shall be saved"* (Acts 2:21).

(50) "AND UNTO JOSEPH WERE BORN TWO SONS BEFORE THE YEARS OF FAMINE CAME, WHICH ASENATH THE DAUGHTER OF POTI-PHERAH PRIEST OF ON BEAR UNTO HIM.

(51) "AND JOSEPH CALLED THE NAME OF THE FIRSTBORN MANASSEH: FOR GOD, SAID HE, HAS MADE ME FORGET ALL MY TOIL, AND ALL MY FATHER'S HOUSE.

(52) "AND THE NAME OF THE SECOND CALLED HE EPHRAIM: FOR GOD HAS CAUSED ME TO BE FRUITFUL IN THE LAND OF MY AFFLICTION."

The construction is:

1. Joseph was given a Gentile wife, which was a type of the Gentile wife given to Christ, for the Church is mostly Gentile.

2. His two sons born during the time of the great harvests, *"Manasseh"* and *"Ephraim,"* are indicative of his spiritual condition. Manasseh means, *"forgetfulness,"* while Ephraim means, *"fruitfulness."*

3. Faith in God brought Joseph to this place of prominence and position.

TO FORGET AND BE FRUITFUL

Verses 50 through 52 read: *"And unto Joseph were born two sons before the years of famine came, which Asenath the daughter of Poti-pherah priest of On bear unto him.*

"And Joseph called the name of the first-born Manasseh: For God, said he, has made me forget all my toil, and all my father's house.

"And the name of the second called he Ephraim: For God has caused me to be fruitful in the land of my affliction."

The names given to the two sons of Joseph portray the spiritual struggle which he endured.

Naming his firstborn *"Manasseh,"* tells us something. He said, *"For God has made me forget."*

This shows us that it would not have been possible for Joseph to have forgotten what had happened to him, in other words, to allow the terrible scars to be healed as it regards what his brothers had done to him, unless God had helped him. Man left to his own strength is simply unable to come to this place that he forgets all the pain, suffering, sorrow, and in fact, the murderous intent of his brothers. As well, the wounds of loved ones are far worse than the wounds of others.

But at the same time, the Lord will help anyone who will sincerely seek His help as it regards such things. Unfortunately, life is not uneventful. The hurts and the harm come, and sometimes by those we love the most. In such situations, it is so easy to grow bitter. But if so, we actually hurt no one but ourselves.

Every evidence is, Joseph earnestly sought the Lord about this matter. He knew that he didn't have the strength to put this out of his mind. But the Lord answered his prayer, and helped him to *"forget."* This tells us what we must do, and it also tells us how it can be done.

When he was able to forget, which means he placed it in the Hands of the Lord, and in its entirety, then he was able to be fruitful. As it held true for Joseph, it holds true for every Believer.

We want to be *"fruitful,"* and we can be, but only if we *"forget!"*

(53) "AND THE SEVEN YEARS OF PLENTEOUSNESS, THAT WAS IN THE LAND OF EGYPT, WERE ENDED.

(54) "AND THE SEVEN YEARS OF DEARTH BEGAN TO COME, ACCORDING AS JOSEPH HAD SAID: AND THE DEARTH WAS IN ALL LANDS; BUT IN ALL THE LAND OF EGYPT THERE WAS BREAD.

(55) "AND WHEN ALL THE LAND OF EGYPT WAS FAMISHED, THE PEOPLE CRIED

TO PHARAOH FOR BREAD: AND PHARAOH SAID UNTO ALL THE EGYPTIANS, GO UNTO JOSEPH; WHAT HE SAYS TO YOU, DO.

(56) "AND THE FAMINE WAS OVER ALL THE FACE OF THE EARTH: AND JOSEPH OPENED ALL THE STOREHOUSES, AND SOLD UNTO THE EGYPTIANS; AND THE FAMINE WAXED SORE IN THE LAND OF EGYPT.

(57) "AND ALL COUNTRIES CAME INTO EGYPT TO JOSEPH FOR TO BUY CORN; BECAUSE THAT THE FAMINE WAS SO SORE IN ALL LANDS."

The composition is:

1. Once again, exactly as Joseph had predicted, and because it was the Word of the Lord, the seven years of famine began.

2. *"All lands"* of Verse 57 refers to all lands of the Middle East.

3. Joseph had stored so much grain as it regards the seven years of plenty, that he was able to sell grain to anyone from any nation who came to buy such.

THE FAMINE

Verses 53 and 54 read: *"And the seven years of plenteousness, that was in the land of Egypt, were ended.*

"And the seven years of drought began to come, according as Joseph had said: and the dearth was in all lands; but in all the land of Egypt there was bread."

All of this was for many reasons; however, the great reason at the moment was to bring the brothers of Joseph to Egypt. The ultimate goal, as superintended by the Lord, was that the entirety of the family of Jacob would come into Egypt, where they would remain for some 215 years, before being delivered by the Power of God. As we shall see, the family of Jacob numbered 70 when they came into Egypt; they would go out approximately three million strong.

THE EXTENT OF THE FAMINE

Verses 55 through 57 read: *"And when all the land of Egypt was famished, the people cried to Pharaoh for bread: and Pharaoh said unto all the Egyptians, Go unto Joseph: what he says to you, do.*

"And the famine was over all the face of the Earth: and Joseph opened all the storehouses,

and sold unto the Egyptians; and the famine waxed sore in the land of Egypt.

"And all countries came into Egypt to Joseph for to buy corn; because that the famine was so sore in all lands."

The great Plan of God would include bringing Jacob and his family into Egypt, where as stated, they would remain for many years before being delivered. Even though they would ultimately be made slaves in that land, all of this, their being in Egypt, would have a tendency to keep them together as a people, without them being disseminated into other cultures, which Satan had already tried previously.

But before the excursion into Egypt could come, there was the matter of reconciliation between Joseph and his brothers. This must be done, and to be sure, would shortly come to pass.

It seems, to which all evidence points, that these men, which had been so hateful and murderous years before, had now changed. In other words, they were not the same men that Joseph had known some 20-odd years before. Their reconciliation with Joseph presents one of the most memorable scenes in history, but not only for them, for Jacob as well, and especially for Jacob.

"I am the Lord's! O joy beyond expression,

"O sweet response to voice of love Divine;

"Faith's joyous 'yes' to the assuring whisper,

"Fear not! I have redeemed you; you are Mine."

"I am the Lord's! It is the glad confession,

"Wherewith the Bride recalls the happy day,

"When love's 'I will' accepted Him forever,

"'The Lord's' to love, to honor, and obey."

"I am the Lord's! Yet teach me all it meaneth,

"All it involves of love and loyalty,

"Of holy service, absolute surrender,

"And unreserved obedience unto Thee."

"I am the Lord's! Yes; body, soul, and spirit,

"O seal them Lord, forever I am Thine;

"As Thou, beloved, in Thy Grace and fullness

"Forever and forever more art mine."

CHAPTER 42

(1) "NOW WHEN JACOB SAW THAT THERE WAS CORN IN EGYPT, JACOB SAID UNTO HIS SONS, WHY DO YOU LOOK ONE UPON ANOTHER?

(2) "AND HE SAID, BEHOLD, I HAVE HEARD THAT THERE IS CORN IN EGYPT: GET YOU DOWN THITHER, AND BUY FOR US FROM THENCE; THAT WE MAY LIVE, AND NOT DIE.

(3) "AND JOSEPH'S TEN BRETHREN WENT DOWN TO BUY CORN IN EGYPT.

(4) "BUT BENJAMIN, JOSEPH'S BROTHER, JACOB SENT NOT WITH HIS BRETHREN; FOR HE SAID, LEST PERADVENTURE MISCHIEF BEFALL HIM.

(5) "AND THE SONS OF ISRAEL CAME TO BUY CORN AMONG THOSE WHO CAME: FOR THE FAMINE WAS IN THE LAND OF CANAAN."

The structure is:

1. Now it begins. Joseph's skill — that skill which only love can give — in leading his brothers step by step to a confession of their sin against him, and to a sense of its blackness in the sight of God, is a picture of the future action of the Lord Jesus Christ in bringing Israel to recognize her sin in rejecting Him, and the consequent enormity of that sin against God.

2. Now we find the real reason for the famine. Oftentimes, the Lord uses the elements, even in a negative way, to bring about His Will.

3. The sons of Jacob buying food in Egypt portrays the coming Great Tribulation, when Israel, no doubt, will lean heavily on America and other Gentile countries for help and sustenance.

EGYPT

Verses 1 and 2 read: *"Now when Jacob saw that there was corn in Egypt, Jacob said unto his sons, Why do you look one upon another?*

"And he said, Behold, I have heard that there is corn in Egypt: get you down thither, and buy for us from thence; that we may live, and not die."

The seven years of great harvests have now ended in Egypt, and no doubt the surrounding nations as well. The famine has set in, and is so severe that whatever surplus these other nations had, including Jacob's family, had been quickly used up.

Somehow, Jacob and his sons hear that Egypt has plenty of grain and other foodstuff, and is selling it to all who would desire to buy. Consequently, plans are made for the sons of Jacob, minus Benjamin, to travel to Egypt, in order to purchase a supply, which was no doubt desperately needed.

Jacob had no way of knowing that all of these things which were happening, the seven years of excellent harvests, and now the famine, were all being brought about by the Hand of God, and for a particular purpose, which centered up on this special family. Now think of what we're saying:

All of these great happenings which affected the entirety of the Middle East, which involved quite a number of nations, and untold thousands of people, were all for one purpose, and that was to bring about the Will of God, as it regarded Jacob and his sons. From this we must take a lesson.

Every happening in the world at the present time, and in fact, as it always has been, whatever those happenings might be, even though they will involve many things, the major purpose is to bring about the Will of God as it regards the Work of God and the people of God on Earth. Let's look for a moment at the greatest happening of all, at least in the last 100 years. I speak of World War II.

As is obvious, in one way or the other, this Great War involved the entirety of the world. But whatever happened militarily or economically, what were the spiritual reasons?

No doubt there were many reasons as it concerns the Lord, Who overrules all things. The first reason pertains to Israel.

The time was drawing close for the fulfillment of Bible Prophecy as it regards Israel once again, even after some 1,900 years, becoming a nation. Satan knew this as well; consequently, he moved upon Adolph Hitler

and his thugs to exterminate the Jews, at least all over whom they had control in Germany, and the occupied countries, which number was substantial to say the least. According to the thinking of the Evil One, if enough Jews could be slaughtered, Israel simply wouldn't have the strength to form a nation. And of course, Satan very well knew, if the prophecies concerning Israel were stopped, then in effect, God is defeated, and Satan has won. In fact, if any promise or prediction in the Word of God falls down, Satan has then won the agelong conflict.

As well, in this Great War, the United States would rise to world prominence in every capacity, and would be greatly instrumental in helping Israel to be formed once again as a nation. In 1948, this was carried out by a unanimous vote regarding the United Nations.

Due to America's prominence, a great Move of God was brought about in this country, which also resulted in the greatest missionary efforts the world had ever known, with the Gospel being taken, in one way or the other, to every nation on the face of the Earth. In fact, our own Ministry (Jimmy Swaggart Ministries) had a part to play in all of this, for which we are so grateful to the Lord for allowing us this privilege.

SPIRITUAL SIGHT

As well, the Child of God should realize that whatever happenings may be taking place in the world, and however they affect him personally, even though some may be very negative, all of this is the Plan of God, designed to fall out to our good. Thus it was with Jacob.

The Patriarch never dreamed that all of these things, as negative as some of them were, were designed by the Lord, and for the express purpose of bringing about the Will of God regarding his particular family. It would all ultimately fall out to Jacob's good.

This is where Faith comes in. The Holy Spirit through Paul said: *"And we know that all things work together for good to them who love God, to them who are the called according to His purpose"* (Rom. 8:28).

To be sure, God in His omnipotence, can bring all things out to the furtherance of His Will, even as it regards the entirety of the Church all over the world, and at the same time, deal with each particular individual accordingly. Man is limited, but God isn't limited.

Man has to do many things for the overall welfare of all concerned, which sometimes affects certain people in a negative way. But man reasons that the overall good is more important, which of course is correct; however, God is able to deal not only with the corporate body, but also each individual, and make everything come out to our good, that is, if we truly love the Lord, and we are striving to bring about *"His purpose."* Striving to bring about out own purposes, as should be obvious, cannot fall into the category of the blessings of God.

BENJAMIN

Verses 3 through 5 read: *"And Joseph's ten brethren went down to buy corn in Egypt.*

"But Benjamin, Joseph's brother, Jacob sent not with his brethren; for he said, Lest peradventure mischief befall him.

"And the sons of Israel came to buy corn among those that came: for the famine was in the land of Canaan."

Both Joseph and Benjamin were the sons of Rachel, and thereby special to Jacob. Even though he loved all his sons, it seems that these were the only two who, at least at this particular time, truly served the Lord.

Quite possibly, Jacob mused in his heart that with Joseph now being dead, or so he thought, the Lord would place the mantle on Benjamin; therefore, he would specifically watch over the young man, who was now about 20 years of age.

The Lord had not revealed to Jacob that these were His plans, but Jacob, not knowing what had actually happened, at least as it regards Joseph, can only see Benjamin taking Joseph's place. So he will not allow him to go into Egypt with his brothers.

(6) "AND JOSEPH WAS THE GOVERNOR OVER THE LAND, AND HE IT WAS WHO SOLD TO ALL THE PEOPLE OF THE LAND: AND JOSEPH'S BRETHREN CAME, AND BOWED DOWN THEMSELVES BEFORE HIM WITH THEIR FACES TO THE EARTH.

(7) "AND JOSEPH SAW HIS BRETHREN, AND KNEW THEM, BUT MADE HIMSELF STRANGE UNTO THEM, AND SPOKE ROUGHLY UNTO THEM; AND HE SAID UNTO

THEM, FROM WHERE DO YOU COME? AND THEY SAID, FROM THE LAND OF CANAAN TO BUY FOOD.

(8) "AND JOSEPH KNEW HIS BRETHREN, BUT THEY KNEW NOT HIM.

(9) "AND JOSEPH REMEMBERED THE DREAMS WHICH HE DREAMED OF THEM, AND SAID UNTO THEM, YOU ARE SPIES; TO SEE THE NAKEDNESS OF THE LAND YOU ARE COME.

(10) "AND THEY SAID UNTO HIM, NO, MY LORD, BUT TO BUY FOOD ARE YOUR SERVANTS COME.

(11) "WE ARE ALL ONE MAN'S SONS; WE ARE TRUE MEN, YOUR SERVANTS ARE NO SPIES.

(12) "AND HE SAID UNTO THEM, NO, BUT TO SEE THE NAKEDNESS OF THE LAND YOU ARE COME.

(13) "AND THEY SAID, YOUR SERVANTS ARE TWELVE BRETHREN, THE SONS OF ONE MAN IN THE LAND OF CANAAN; AND, BEHOLD, THE YOUNGEST IS THIS DAY WITH OUR FATHER, AND ONE IS NOT.

(14) "AND JOSEPH SAID UNTO THEM, THAT IS IT THAT I SPAKE UNTO YOU, SAYING, YOU ARE SPIES:

(15) "HEREBY YOU SHALL BE PROVED: BY THE LIFE OF PHARAOH YOU SHALL NOT GO FORTH HENCE, UNTIL YOUR YOUNGEST BROTHER COME HITHER."

The construction is:

1. Had Joseph thought of his own dignity and of his own affection, he would have revealed himself at once to his brothers. But such a Revelation would have produced confusion, but not Repentance. He loved them and, therefore, sought their spiritual welfare.

2. He acted so as to bring their sin to remembrance, to make them confess it with their own lips, and not just to him and in his presence, for he still concealed himself from them, but to God and in His Presence.

3. In all of this we see how God deals with us as it regards Repentance. For Repentance to truly be Repentance, it must always be sincere and total.

JOSEPH

Verse 6 reads: *"And Joseph was the governor over the land, and he it was who sold to all the people of the land: and Joseph's brethren came, and bowed down themselves before him with their faces to the Earth."*

Joseph had been Governor for eight years, before he saw the fulfillment of the dreams he had as a 17 year old boy.

The day finally arrived that the sons of Jacob came to Egypt, and thereby to Joseph, in order to purchase grain. They bowed down themselves to him as the lord of Egypt, and did not recognize him as their brother which they had sold as a slave over 20 years before.

Why didn't Joseph reveal himself to his brethren then? In fact, why didn't Joseph contact his brothers and his father once becoming Prime Minister of Egypt? He had the means to do so, and in grand style.

Joseph was doing what the Lord wanted him to do. If his brothers had not changed, a meeting with them would have done little good. He had to determine if they were still the same men they had been, or if time had effected a change, all brought about by the Lord.

Joseph had most definitely forgiven his brothers, but the circle couldn't be complete, until they truly repented of their former actions toward him. There is a great lesson in all of this for us.

FORGIVENESS

The Believer is to instantly forgive anyone who wrongs him in any way. He is to do this for several reasons, the least not being that Christ has forgiven us of so much more than we are called upon to forgive others. And if we have truly been forgiven ourselves, which refers to being *"born again,"* and truly living for God, we will always remember what the Lord has done for us, and be quick to forgive others.

As well, our forgiving others keeps down bitterness in our own hearts, and in fact, is more so for our good than the one to which we are extending forgiveness. This means we are to forgive them, even though they are wrong in what they have done, and even though they have not asked for forgiveness. Jesus said:

"For if you forgive men their trespasses, your Heavenly Father will also forgive you:

"But if you forgive not men their trespasses, neither will your Father forgive your trespasses" (Mat. 6:14-15).

NOTES

As should be obvious, there is a severe penalty here that is attached to the failure to forgive.

And we must understand as well that the type of forgiveness we extend to others must be the same type of forgiveness that God has extended to us. It cannot be a partial or half-hearted forgiveness. It must be total and complete, with no conditions attached. If conditions are attached, then this of which we are being engaged is not truly forgiveness, but something else altogether.

But yet we find here that even though Joseph, who incidentally is a Type of Christ, had definitely forgiven his brothers, and this we know because of the names given to his two sons; still, we find that he did not jump into their arms the moment that he saw them. In fact, even as we shall see, he submitted them to a very strenuous test, before revealing himself as their brother. What does this mean?

If someone has wronged us, and has not asked for our forgiveness, as stated, we are to forgive them just the same; however, this doesn't mean that we are to have fellowship with them. In fact, it's impossible to have fellowship with someone who hasn't truly repented. While we hold nothing in our heart against them, at the same time, there is no ground for fellowship, as would be obvious. What good would it have done Joseph to have revealed himself to his brothers, if they had been the same men as before? While they may have paid him lip service, simply because he was the Prime Minister of Egypt, their hearts would have been toward him the same as before, which could only be described as a murderous heart. And let it ever be understood that this entire scenario is a perfect picture of evil doings within the Church. These men had murder in their hearts toward Joseph. And any time we do something harmful to a fellow brother or sister in Christ, we are engaging a murderous heart toward them. We should remember that!

A PERSONAL EXPERIENCE

If I remember correctly, the year was 1958. Frances and I were in full time Evangelistic work, or at least we were getting started. Donnie was four years old.

A Preacher friend was dying with cancer, and my Dad and I went to visit him. Incidentally, the Lord graciously and wondrously healed him.

If I remember correctly, when we arrived, we were unable to see the Brother, in that he had been taken to the hospital. At least this seems to be my recollection of the incident.

At any rate, and for whatever reason, we were waiting in another Preacher's home for a few minutes, before we were to visit the Brother, which did not come about. As well, the Preacher, in whose home we were waiting, was not present as well. His wife greeted us warmly, and we waited in the living room. I don't recall why we stopped by this brother's house, but we did.

At any rate, while waiting there the few minutes, I saw a box of Promise Cards sitting on the table. Out of habit, for we had always had one of these little boxes of cards in our home when I was a child, I reached over and selected one. I read the Scripture written thereon. It said:

"No weapon that is formed against you shall prosper; and every tongue that shall rise against you in judgment you shall condemn. This is the heritage of the servants of the LORD, and their Righteousness is of Me, saith the LORD" (Isa. 54:17).

As I read this particular Scripture, all of the sudden the Presence of the Lord came all over me. I turned my head away from my Dad, fighting back the tears. I knew the Lord had instantly moved greatly upon me, but I really did not know why. Years later I would find out.

In 1988, some 30 years later, the man in whose home my Dad and I were waiting, sued me and this Ministry, plus 18 people in all, claiming a conspiracy against him. The truth is, no one had done anything to this man, least of all me. His problem was the same as the brothers of Joseph — jealousy.

To be sure, the legal action he brought against me was well thought out, and was designed to totally destroy our Ministry. Strangely enough, he sued the Denomination of the Assemblies of God as well, but it seems they settled their differences quickly, with that particular Denomination then setting about to help him against me with all the power they had.

The trial, which was the first time I had ever been in a court room, lasted for nearly three months, if I remember correctly.

One morning while praying, and right in the middle of this trial, and importuning the Lord to help us, He took me back to 1958.

He reminded me of the house in which we were waiting, where I had drawn the little Promise Card. He also reminded me, which I had forgotten, that the man's house in which we had been waiting was the same man who was suing me. He also reminded me of the Scripture that He gave me, and why His Presence had filled my heart at that time. Thirty years before it would take place, He was telling me that irrespective as to what this man or these men would do, *"no weapon formed against me would prosper."*

It came out exactly as the Lord said it would. Their weapon didn't prosper.

In my heart I forgave this man, even though he has never asked for forgiveness, or even admitted to his culpability and guilt. And because of that, even though I do forgive him, and God knows I harbor nothing in my heart against him, and if it lay within my power to help him, that I would definitely do; but still, I can have no fellowship with him, and because there has been no Repentance of any nature, of which I am aware.

HIS BRETHREN

Verses 7 and 8 read: *"And Joseph saw his brethren, and he knew them, but made himself strange unto them, and spoke roughly unto them; and he said unto them, From where do you come? And they said, From the land of Canaan to buy food.*

"And Joseph knew his brethren, but they knew not him."

As Joseph, a Type of Christ, was ruler over Egypt, likewise, the Lord Jesus Christ is Ruler over all. In fact, it is Christ Who is the Source of all Blessings in the United States. Consequently, when Israel accepts help from this country, whether she realizes it or not, she is bowing to the Lord Jesus Christ.

The Seventh Verse says that Joseph *"spoke roughly unto them."* In the Great Tribulation Period, the Lord Jesus Christ will deal *"roughly"* with Israel. It will be called the *"time of Jacob's trouble"* (Jer. 30:7).

The Eighth Verse proclaims the fact that while Joseph knew his brethren, they didn't know him. Christ knows Israel, but, sadly, *"they know not Him."*

Joseph's dealings with his brothers is a picture of the future action of the Lord Jesus Christ in bringing Israel to recognize her sin and rejecting Him and the consequent enormity of that sin against God. Had Joseph only been concerned about his own dignity, he would have revealed himself at once to his brothers. He had the power to do so, as would be obvious, and there was nothing they could do in any capacity, him being the Prime Minister of Egypt.

Likewise, Christ could easily reveal Himself presently to Israel, and do so immediately; however, as such revelation would have produced only confusion among Joseph's brethren, likewise, such revelation by Christ to Israel would as well, only produce confusion. There has to be Biblical Repentance before there can be a glorious Revelation.

THE DREAMS

Verse 9 reads: *"And Joseph remembered the dreams which he dreamed of them, and said unto them, You are spies; to see the nakedness of the land you are come."*

As these men bowed before Joseph, the dream that he'd had when only 17 years old now flashes before him. It is being fulfilled before his eyes. As someone has well said: *"The mills of God grind slowly, but they grind exceedingly fine."* In other words, the mills of God miss nothing!

And now begins the first procedure toward their Repentance. He accuses them of being spies, which was a most serious charge! To this charge, what would they say? Their answer would reveal much about themselves.

THEIR ANSWER

Verses 10 through 15 read: *"And they said unto him, No, my Lord, but to buy food are your servants come.*

"We are all one man's sons; we are true men, your servants are no spies.

"And he said unto them, No, but to see the nakedness of the land you are come.

"And they said, Your servants are twelve brethren, the sons of one man in the land of

Canaan; and, behold, the youngest is this day with our father, and one is not.

"And Joseph said unto them, That is it that I spake unto you, saying, You are spies:

"Hereby you shall be proved: By the life of Pharaoh you shall not go forth hence, except your youngest brother come hither."

The day the brothers of Joseph came before him, no doubt there were many other people present as well, all there, and from various countries, to buy food. So it must have seemed peculiar to the brothers of Joseph for him to single them out. Incidentally, he spoke to them in Egyptian, with his words translated to them by someone else.

He had only been 17 years of age when they saw him last. He was now about 38. As well, he was dressed as an Egyptian, so they had no inkling of knowledge that this was Joseph.

Abruptly he says to them, *"You are spies."* The charge was extremely serious. But yet, common sense would tell all concerned that if in fact their intention were spying, the entire family would not have come on such a mission. Irrespective, they were helpless before him.

They deny the accusations, and rightly so, and claim to be *"true men,"* i.e., *"honest men."* They then reveal some things about themselves:

They are 10 of the 12 sons of one man. One is at home, and the other is not, meaning that in their minds, Joseph was dead.

Over 20 years had passed since that fateful day of so long before, and they had not heard from Joseph in all of this time, so they reasoned that he was dead. Little did they realize that the man standing before them was indeed Joseph!

Reasoning that Jacob had probably transferred the birthright to Benjamin, he wanted to know the attitude of these men toward Benjamin. So he *"proves them."*

(16) "SEND ONE OF YOU, AND LET HIM FETCH YOUR BROTHER, AND YOU SHALL BE KEPT IN PRISON, THAT YOUR WORDS MAY BE PROVED, WHETHER THERE BE ANY TRUTH IN YOU: OR ELSE BY THE LIFE OF PHARAOH SURELY YOU ARE SPIES.

(17) "AND HE PUT THEM ALL TOGETHER INTO WARD THREE DAYS.

(18) "AND JOSEPH SAID UNTO THEM THE THIRD DAY, THIS DO, AND LIVE; FOR I FEAR GOD:

(19) "IF YOU BE TRUE MEN, LET ONE OF YOUR BRETHREN BE BOUND IN THE HOUSE OF YOUR PRISON: GO YOU, CARRY CORN FOR THE FAMINE OF YOUR HOUSES:

(20) "BUT BRING YOUR YOUNGEST BROTHER UNTO ME; SO SHALL YOUR WORDS BE VERIFIED, AND YOU SHALL NOT DIE. AND THEY DID SO.

(21) "AND THEY SAID ONE TO AN-OTHER, WE ARE VERILY GUILTY CON-CERNING OUR BROTHER, AND THAT WE SAW THE ANGUISH OF HIS SOUL, WHEN HE BESOUGHT US, AND WE WOULD NOT HEAR; THEREFORE IS THIS DISTRESS COME UPON US.

(22) "AND REUBEN ANSWERED THEM, SAYING, SPAKE I NOT UNTO YOU, SAYING, DO NOT SIN AGAINST THE CHILD; AND YOU WOULD NOT HEAR? THEREFORE, BEHOLD, ALSO HIS BLOOD IS REQUIRED.

(23) "AND THEY KNEW NOT THAT JO-SEPH UNDERSTOOD THEM; FOR HE SPOKE UNTO THEM BY AN INTERPRETER.

(24) "AND HE TURNED HIMSELF ABOUT FROM THEM, AND WEPT; AND RE-TURNED TO THEM AGAIN, AND COM-MUNED WITH THEM, AND TOOK FROM THEM SIMEON, AND BOUND HIM BEFORE THEIR EYES."

The composition is:

1. Verse 17 says, *"Into ward three days"*; likewise, Israel will be under tremendous pressure by the Antichrist for a little over three years.

2. Verse 21 speaks of the remorse of Joseph's brothers. The sin was a little over 20 years old, but it still lay heavily upon their consciences.

3. His detention of Simeon, and after-wards of Benjamin, was skillfully designed so as to find out if they still were indifferent to the cries of a captive brother and the tears of a bereaved father.

PRISON

Verse 16 reads: *"Send one of you, and let him fetch your brother, and you shall be kept in prison, that your words may be proved, whether there be any truth in you: or else by the life of Pharaoh surely you are spies."*

He proposes to keep nine of the brothers in prison, while one went back to their respec-tive home in order to fetch Benjamin. This must have come like a bombshell to them, as he spoke to them through an interpreter.

In a sense, all of these men are Types of Christ, but in a very limited way. As we've already stated, the meaning of their names points to Christ, and what He will do for dy-ing humanity.

But Joseph and Benjamin are Types of Christ in a much more pronounced way, and especially Joseph. Joseph's name means *"the Lord will add,"* and Benjamin's name means, *"a strong right arm."* Both meanings put together say, *"The Lord will add a strong right arm."* It refers not only to Joseph be-ing the Saviour of his family, as well as so many others during that trying time in Egypt of so long ago, but more than all, of the One of Whom he is a Type. In the Great Tribula-tion, which is yet to come, the Lord Jesus Christ, Who is the Strong Right Arm of the Father, will save Israel from the wicked hands of the Antichrist.

GOD

Verses 17 and 18 read: *"And he put them all together into ward three days.*

"And Joseph said unto them the third day, This do, and live; for I fear God."

Fear must have played havoc in the minds of these men, as they were placed under de-tention for three days. At this point, they had no idea as to what would happen next.

At the end of three days, Joseph came to them, with his interpreter. He will now make a different proposal to them, and will begin this proposal by evoking the name of Elohim.

Knowing and understanding Egypt and its worship of many gods, and knowing that Egypt little knew Jehovah, if at all, what must they have thought when Joseph proclaims to them through the interpreter that he knows and fears Elohim, who in fact, is the God of the Hebrews?

All of this had to be extremely strange to them, and because they knew that Elohim was little known, if at all, outside of their respec-tive family. Even though Joseph was speak-ing through an interpreter, and even though he may himself have used the Egyptian word for the supreme Deity, yet doubtless he would take care that the interpreter used the word *"Elohim,"* i.e. *"God."*

By Joseph proclaiming the fact that he *"feared God,"* in essence was saying to them that he would not do anything that would be displeasing to God. So they had nothing to fear as it regards the safety of the one left behind, which he will now demand.

Would to Heaven that every leader in the world feared God. But the sad truth is, precious few hold any fear of God whatsoever.

An excellent portrayal of this is found in the actions, attitude, and spirit of America. For instance, in the recent situation in Afghanistan, which in effect puts Christianity up beside Islam, we find care and concern for the lives and welfare of others in the actions of American soldiers. Little of that is found among those who fight for Islam. In fact, life is cheap in that false religion.

The United States, while having many faults, still retains a semblance of the fear of God. That and that alone serves as the Foundation of all truth. In Islam there is no truth, only that which is instigated by Satan, which is a lie, and because Satan is a liar, and the father of all lies (Jn. 8:44).

THE PROPOSAL

Verses 19 and 20 read: *"If you be true men, let one of your brethren be bound in the house of your prison: go ye, carry corn for the famine of your houses:*

"But bring your youngest brother unto me; so shall your words be verified, and you shall not die. And they did so."

Joseph now softens his demands, in that he at first stated that nine of the brothers would remain in Egypt, while one was sent to fetch Benjamin, but now he limits that to just one remaining in Egypt, while the nine go back home.

As well, he tells them to take grain back home. How different this is than when they had intended to leave him in a pit in order to starve. Actually, he now only has two demands:

1. Simeon must remain in Egypt.

2. When they return to buy more grain, Benjamin must come with them.

All of this was designed by the Holy Spirit. Joseph wanted to assure himself that

Benjamin was well. In fact, having been sold into Egypt shortly before Benjamin was born, he had never seen his younger brother.

THE SIN

Verses 21 through 24 read: *"And they said one to another, We are verily guilty concerning our brother, and that we saw the anguish of his soul, when he besought us, and we would not hear; therefore is this distress come upon us.*

"And Reuben answered them, saying, Spake I not unto you, saying, Do not sin against the child; and you would not hear? Therefore, behold, also his blood is required.

"And they knew not that Joseph understood them; for he spoke unto them by an interpreter.

"And he turned himself about from them, and wept; and returned to them again, and communed with them, and took from them Simeon, and bound him before their eyes."

Upon hearing this demand by Joseph, that one brother must be left behind, and knowing that this must be done, the men began to speak among themselves, not knowing that Joseph could understand them. We find in this Israel's actions in the latter day. As these men, they will be called to pass through deep and searching trial, through intensely painful exercises of conscience.

I must believe that in the coming Great Tribulation, when the Antichrist, whom Israel will think is the Messiah, will turn on them, and especially considering the 144,000 who will come to Christ, that Israel will think long and hard regarding the Lord Jesus Christ. I cannot see how that it can be otherwise.

This one thing is certain, the moment that Christ returns, which will take place at the Second Coming, and done so in power and glory such as the world has never experienced, Israel will accept Him immediately (Rev., Chpt. 19; Zech., Chpts. 13-14).

The first thing that the sons of Jacob think about as it regards what is demanded of them, is the sin they committed against their brother, little knowing that he is standing before them. They said, *"We are verily guilty. . . ."*

The idea that they recalled, graphically so, the anguish of his soul, when he earnestly besought them not to do the terrible thing they were doing, and we speak of them selling him to the Ishmaelites, but they would not hear — all points to the biting conscience.

Irrespective as to how long it has been, unless sin is duly repented of before God and forsaken, its biting torment will not go away. This is the reason for much physical breakdown, and worse yet, emotional distress, which plagues humanity. It is sin, which lies heavily upon the soul of the individual.

Reuben now reminds them that he had asked them not to sin against Joseph; but they would not hear.

Then he said, *"Behold, also his blood is required,"* meaning that they surmised that he was dead. So now they were going to have to pay.

To Noah, God had said so long, long before, *"Whoso sheds man's blood* (cold blood), *by man shall his blood be shed: for in the Image of God made He man"* (Gen. 9:6).

Because of man's terrible spiritual condition, the Lord Jesus Christ would have to shed His Life's Blood, which alone could atone for the sins of man. Paul said: *"But now in Christ Jesus you who sometimes were far off are made nigh by the Blood of Christ"* (Eph. 2:13).

John said: *"And the Blood of Jesus Christ His Son cleanses us from all sin"* (I Jn. 1:7).

The human race has sinned against God and against man, and as such, Atonement had to be made. It was Christ Alone Who could make such Atonement, and He did by the giving of Himself in Sacrifice, which necessitated the pouring out of His Own Precious Blood. That's why Peter said: *"Forasmuch as you know that you were not redeemed with corruptible things as silver and gold . . . but with the Precious Blood of Christ, as of a lamb without blemish and without spot"* (I Pet. 1:18-19).

Man has a choice: he can answer to God or he can answer to Christ. If he answers to Christ, this means that he accepts Christ and what Christ did for us at the Cross as the Sacrifice, and will thereby be saved. Refusing that, he will have to answer to God, which speaks of the Great White Throne Judgment, and means to be lost forever and ever (Rev. 20:11-15).

As they spoke among themselves, Joseph turned away from them and wept. As stated, they didn't know that he understood what they said. He wept simply because he knew that they were coming close to true Repentance.

He then took Simeon, and bound him before their eyes, which meant that he was the one that must be left behind. Why Simeon was chosen, we aren't told. More than likely, he was the ring leader in the terrible sin that had been committed against Joseph those long years earlier.

(25) "THEN JOSEPH COMMANDED TO FILL THEIR SACKS WITH CORN, AND TO RESTORE EVERY MAN'S MONEY INTO HIS SACK, AND TO GIVE THEM PROVISION FOR THE WAY: AND THUS DID HE UNTO THEM.

(26) "AND THEY LADED THEIR ASSES WITH THE CORN, AND DEPARTED THENCE.

(27) "AND AS ONE OF THEM OPENED HIS SACK TO GIVE HIS ASS PROVENDER IN THE INN, HE ESPIED HIS MONEY; FOR, BEHOLD, IT WAS IN HIS SACK'S MOUTH.

(28) "AND HE SAID UNTO HIS BRETHREN, MY MONEY IS RESTORED; AND, LO, IT IS EVEN IN MY SACK: AND THEIR HEART FAILED THEM, AND THEY WERE AFRAID, SAYING ONE TO ANOTHER, WHAT IS THIS THAT GOD HAS DONE UNTO US?

(29) "AND THEY CAME UNTO JACOB THEIR FATHER UNTO THE LAND OF CANAAN, AND TOLD HIM ALL THAT BEFELL UNTO THEM; SAYING,

(30) "THE MAN, WHO IS THE LORD OF THE LAND, SPAKE ROUGHLY TO US, AND TOOK US FOR SPIES OF THE COUNTRY.

(31) "AND WE SAID UNTO HIM, WE ARE TRUE MEN; WE ARE NO SPIES:

(32) "WE BE TWELVE BRETHREN, SONS OF OUR FATHER; ONE IS NOT, AND THE YOUNGEST IS THIS DAY WITH OUR FATHER IN THE LAND OF CANAAN.

(33) "AND THE MAN, THE LORD OF THE COUNTRY, SAID UNTO US, HEREBY SHALL I KNOW THAT YOU ARE TRUE MEN; LEAVE ONE OF YOUR BRETHREN HERE WITH ME, AND TAKE FOOD FOR THE FAMINE OF YOUR HOUSEHOLDS, AND BE GONE:

(34) "AND BRING YOUR YOUNGEST BROTHER UNTO ME: THEN SHALL I KNOW THAT YOU ARE NO SPIES, BUT THAT YOU ARE TRUE MEN: SO WILL I DELIVER YOU YOUR BROTHER, AND YOU SHALL TRAFFIC IN THE LAND."

The overview is:

1. Verse 25 says that he gave them *"provision for the way."* The Scripture says this concerning Israel during the Great Tribulation Period, *"Where she has a place prepared of God, that they should feed her there twelve hundred and sixty days"* (Rev. 12:6).

2. One says upon finding the money in his sack, *"What is this that God has done unto us?"* Sin may be committed in a moment; however, unless it is truly confessed to the Lord, repented of, and forsaken, it will weigh heavy on our conscience without reprieve, and do so forever.

3. The working of Joseph with his brothers was totally mysterious to them; likewise, the working of Christ with us falls into the same category; however, He has a Plan that He is attempting to work out within our lives, just as Joseph did with these brothers.

PROVISION

The phrase, *"Then Joseph commanded to fill their sacks with corn, and to restore every man's money into his sack, and to give them provision for the way: and thus did he unto them."*

The word *"corn"* should have been translated *"grain."* There was no corn, as we know such, in that part of the world at that time. To our knowledge, corn was first known by the pilgrims in America, which they learned from the Indians.

I would dare say that the story of Joseph and his brothers is the most remarkable incident in human history. I do not think that anything can even remotely equal the drama of such a happening.

Joseph is sold into Egypt as a slave, and now he is the Prime Minister of this nation, the greatest on the face of the Earth, which means that he is the second most powerful man in the world. And his brothers do not have the faintest idea that the man with whom they have been dealing is indeed their brother Joseph.

The reason it is so remarkable is because Joseph is a Type of Christ, and this which happened to him is a portrayal of what Israel would do to Christ. As Joseph was sold for 20 pieces of silver, likewise, Christ was sold for 30 pieces of silver. As Joseph's brothers

hated him, likewise, Israel, the brethren of Christ, hated Him. As Joseph became Prime Minister of Egypt, which was Gentile, likewise, Jesus is the head of the Church, which is by and large Gentile. As Joseph would save his brothers from starvation, as well, Christ will save Israel, although behind the scenes. As the brothers of Joseph finally accept Joseph, likewise, Israel will ultimately accept Christ.

WHAT HAS GOD DONE?

Verses 26 through 28 read: *"And they laded their animals with the grain, and departed thence.*

"And as one of them opened his sack to give his animal provender in the inn, he saw his money; for, behold, it was in his sack's mouth.

"And he said unto his brethren, My money is restored; and, lo, it is even in my sack: and their heart failed them, and they were afraid, saying one to another, What is this that God has done unto us?"

Actually, they were right! It was God Who was guiding these events, giving Joseph instructions all along the way as to how he should handle the situation. However, because of their sin, a sin committed well over 20 years before, they were thinking of God in a very negative way. It is no different presently.

Most all the world totally and completely misunderstand God. Because of the guilt of sin, which accompanies every single person who doesn't know Christ, or even the Christian who has failed to repent of his sin, such people think that God is *"out to get them."* Any negative thing which happens, or even that which on the surface seems to be negative, is attributed to God.

This is the *"guilt"* which caused Adam and Eve to hide from God after they had sinned (Gen. 3:9-10).

THE CROSS

There is only one way for the guilt of sin to be removed, and the power of sin to be broken, and that is by and through what Jesus did for us at the Cross. Let the Reader understand that there are no exceptions to this. It is the Cross and the Cross alone, which can address this problem. Paul said:

"Knowing this, that our old man is crucified with him (what Jesus did for us at the Cross),

that the body of the sin might be destroyed, that henceforth we should not serve the sin" (Rom. 6:6).

If the Reader is to notice, I have added the word *"the"* in front of the word *"sin."* Actually, this is the way it was originally written by Paul. In other words, the definite article (the) is placed in front of the word *"sin,"* signifying that Paul is not speaking of acts of sin, but rather the sin nature.

The destruction of the sin nature means here that it becomes inoperative. It no longer holds sway in our lives, as it did before we were Born-Again. While it does remain with us, even as Paul roundly proclaims in this Chapter, it is to be dormant, and in fact, will be dormant if our Faith is placed exclusively in the Cross and remains in the Cross. The Holy Spirit demands that (Rom. 8:1-2, 11).

With our Faith placed exclusively in the Finished Work of Christ, as stated, the guilt of sin is removed, and the power of sin is broken. Those two things are the greatest things that could ever happen to any human being. Guilt being gone, which can only happen by the Cross and our Faith in that Finished Work, peace then reigns. With the power of sin broken, we can then yield *"our members as instruments of righteousness unto God"* (Rom. 6:13). Once we were controlled by the sin nature, but now the sin nature is controlled by us. The *"Divine nature"* is now in control, which comes into the heart and life of every Believer at conversion. Peter said: *"Whereby are given unto us exceeding great and precious Promises: that by these you might be partakers of the Divine nature, having escaped the corruption that is in the world through lust"* (II Pet. 1:4).

With the *"Divine nature"* now controlling us, which is in effect the Holy Spirit and His Work, we know that God has only good things for us. In fact, that is true regarding God and all of humanity, but as stated, due to the guilt of sin, men do not think of God in a positive fashion.

JACOB

Verses 29 through 34 read: *"And they came unto Jacob their father unto the land of Canaan, and told him all that befell unto them; saying,*

"The man, who is the lord of the land, spoke roughly to us, and took us for spies of the country.

"And we said unto him, We are true men; we are no spies:

"We be twelve brethren, sons of our father; one is not, and the youngest is this day with our father in the land of Canaan.

"And the man, the lord of the country, said unto us, Hereby shall I know that you are true men; leave one of your brethren here with me, and take food for the famine of your households, and be gone:

"And bring your youngest brother unto me: then shall I know that you are no spies, but that you are true men: so will I deliver you your brother, and you shall traffic in the land."

From the terminology used by these men at this present time, it is obvious that a change has taken place in their lives; however, it is a change that is not quite yet complete.

For instance, even though their terminology is as it ought to be, in other words, they speak now with an entirely different spirit than they did those 20 odd years before when they sold Joseph, still, they haven't yet completely come clean with God and their father Jacob, concerning what they had done. As far as Jacob knew, Joseph was dead, killed by a wild animal. That's what his sons had told him, and they have never rectified this thing, as of yet.

But as we shall see, the Holy Spirit will force them into a position to where they have to *"come clean."* He will do the same with every single Believer, even presently, because sin can only be handled in one way, and that is by proper confession. And what does that mean?

It means that we confess our sin to God, and do so unequivocally (I Jn. 1:9). And as well, we must confess to every single person we have wronged, and seek their forgiveness. James said:

"Confess your faults one to another, and pray one for another, that you may be healed" (James 5:16).

Unfortunately, millions of Christians, and I think in the present tense, do not properly follow this Scriptural admonition. They try to justify their actions, whatever those actions may have been. Proper Justification, however, can only be brought about by proper confession to the Lord and to those we have wronged.

(35) "AND IT CAME TO PASS AS THEY EMPTIED THEIR SACKS, THAT, BEHOLD, EVERY MAN'S BUNDLE OF MONEY WAS IN HIS SACK: AND WHEN BOTH THEY AND THEIR FATHER SAW THE BUNDLES OF MONEY, THEY WERE AFRAID.

(36) "AND JACOB THEIR FATHER SAID UNTO THEM, ME HAVE YOU BEREAVED OF MY CHILDREN: JOSEPH IS NOT, AND SIMEON IS NOT, AND YOU WILL TAKE BENJAMIN AWAY: AND ALL THESE THINGS ARE AGAINST ME.

(37) "AND REUBEN SPOKE UNTO HIS FATHER, SAYING, SLAY MY TWO SONS, IF I BRING HIM NOT TO YOU: DELIVER HIM INTO MY HAND, AND I WILL BRING HIM TO YOU AGAIN.

(38) "AND HE SAID, MY SON SHALL NOT GO DOWN WITH YOU; FOR HIS BROTHER IS DEAD, AND HE IS LEFT ALONE: IF MISCHIEF BEFALL HIM BY THE WAY IN THE WHICH YOU GO, THEN SHALL YOU BRING DOWN MY GRAY HAIRS WITH SORROW TO THE GRAVE."

The exegesis is:

1. Verse 38 speaks of Jacob's great sorrow. The Great Tribulation Period is called, *"the time of Jacob's trouble"* (Jer. 30:7).

2. Jacob thinks that Joseph is dead; likewise, Israel thinks that Jesus is dead, denying that He rose from the dead.

3. Jacob is extremely sad because of events, but if he only knew the truth, he would be extremely glad. Paul said:

"But as it is written, Eye has not seen, nor ear heard, neither have entered into the heart of man, the things which God has prepared for them who love Him" (I Cor. 2:9).

FEAR

Verse 35 reads: *"And it came to pass as they emptied their sacks, that, behold, every man's bundle of money was in his sack: and when both they and their father saw the bundles of money, they were afraid."*

They now fear, and for many things. What does it mean that their money has been restored unto them in the sacks of grain?

Actually, there was no way they could do this themselves. But why would the lord of Egypt have this done, or so they reasoned in their minds? Actually, why did Joseph give

them back their money, charging them nothing for the grain?

While Joseph was definitely taking stern measures to ensure himself of the change in his brothers, at the same time, he held in his heart nothing but good for them.

Even when the Lord is forced to chastise us, as He does all Believers, during the chastisement, He always does good things for us at different intervals. That's the reason, or at least one of the reasons, that it is such a joy to live for the Lord. Even when He is stern, as He sometimes must be, He is at the same time tender.

JACOB

Verses 36 through 38 read: *"And Jacob their father said unto them, Me have you bereaved of my children: Joseph is not, and Simeon is not, and you will take Benjamin away: and all these things are against me.*

"And Reuben spoke unto his father, saying, Slay my two sons, if I bring him not to you: deliver him into my hand, and I will bring him to you again.

"And he said, My son shall not go down with you; for his brother is dead, and he is left alone: if mischief befall him by the way in the which you go, then shall you bring down my gray hairs with sorrow to the grave."

We should study carefully the actions of Joseph as it regards the entirety of this scenario. Remembering that he is a Type of Christ, we can learn from this, exactly how Christ loves us, teaches us, instructs us, leads us, and guides us. Joseph wanted only one thing from his brothers, and that was that they would *"do right."* That is all the Lord wants from us as well! He wants us to *"do right."*

While Jacob grieves over the situation, little does he realize just how close he is to the greatest and most wonderful happening of his life.

How often do we as well sorrow, when at the moment of our sorrowing, God in His Heaven, and on His Throne, is at that very moment planning great, wonderful, and beautiful things for us.

What a mighty God we serve!

"Sweet Name come down from Heaven above

"To win our heart's deep, tender love,

"As Bethlehem and Calvary prove,
"My Jesus!"

"Mysterious Name lies hid in Thee
"A balm for every malady,
"For deepest wound a remedy,
"My Jesus!"

"Thy Name to me is true delight,
"My rest and healing, food and light
"To guide my faltering steps aright,
"My Jesus!"

"For mankind all, Thy love is shown,
"Yet seems to be for me alone;
"I claim Thee for my very own,
"My Jesus!"

"Oh, grant my dying prayer may be
"What oft through life I whispered Thee,
"And which I'll sing eternally,
"My Jesus!"

CHAPTER 43

(1) "AND THE FAMINE WAS SORE IN THE LAND.

(2) "AND IT CAME TO PASS, WHEN THEY HAD EATEN UP THE CORN WHICH THEY HAD BROUGHT OUT OF EGYPT, THEIR FATHER SAID UNTO THEM, GO AGAIN, BUY US A LITTLE FOOD.

(3) "AND JUDAH SPOKE UNTO HIM, SAYING, THE MAN DID SOLEMNLY PROTEST UNTO US, SAYING, YOU SHALL NOT SEE MY FACE, EXCEPT YOUR BROTHER BE WITH YOU.

(4) "IF YOU WILL SEND OUR BROTHER WITH US, WE WILL GO DOWN AND BUY THEE FOOD:

(5) "BUT IF YOU WILL NOT SEND HIM, WE WILL NOT GO DOWN: FOR THE MAN SAID UNTO US, YOU SHALL NOT SEE MY FACE, EXCEPT YOUR BROTHER BE WITH YOU.

(6) "AND ISRAEL SAID, WHEREFORE DEALT YOU SO ILL WITH ME, AS TO TELL THE MAN WHETHER YOU HAD YET A BROTHER?

(7) "AND THEY SAID, THE MAN ASKED US STRAIGHTLY OF OUR STATE, AND OF OUR KINDRED, SAYING, IS YOUR FATHER YET ALIVE? HAVE YOU ANOTHER BROTHER? AND WE TOLD HIM ACCORDING TO THE TENOR OF THESE WORDS: COULD WE CERTAINLY KNOW THAT HE WOULD SAY, BRING YOUR BROTHER DOWN?

(8) "AND JUDAH SAID UNTO ISRAEL HIS FATHER, SEND THE LAD WITH ME, AND WE WILL ARISE AND GO; THAT WE MAY LIVE, AND NOT DIE, BOTH WE, AND YOU, AND ALSO OUR LITTLE ONES.

(9) "I WILL BE SURETY FOR HIM; OF MY HAND SHALL YOU REQUIRE HIM: IF I BRING HIM NOT UNTO YOU, AND SET HIM BEFORE YOU, THEN LET ME BEAR THE BLAME FOREVER:

(10) "FOR EXCEPT WE HAD LINGERED, SURELY NOW WE HAD RETURNED THIS SECOND TIME."

The synopsis is:

1. The First Verse says: *"The famine was sore in the land."* Likewise, the Great Tribulation Period will be *"sore in the land of Israel."*

2. In Verse 8, Jacob is referred to by the Holy Spirit as *"Israel."* However, it is noteworthy to look at the circumstances under which the Holy Spirit refers to him as *"Israel."* It was a time of total helplessness on Jacob's part, but yet a time when his faith, although weak, was about to bring forth eternal dividends.

3. The world, at this time, would have called Jacob *"Weak,"* but God called him *"strong."*

THE FAMINE

Verse 1 reads: *"And the famine was sore in the land."*

Considering the severity of this famine, and how that it affected several nations and untold numbers of people, we may very well ask the question, why would the Lord do all of this, in order to bring one family to a desired position? Could He have not done so in various other ways much less severe?

God can do anything. But there are several things which must be taken into account.

Famines during Old Testament times, and in fact, which continues unto this hour, are allowed by God because of the terrible wickedness and evil of the people.

For instance, in watching a newscast last week (Jan., 2002), the Newscaster remonstrated that war was not the only problem in

Afghanistan. Drought, which had now lasted for several years, was bringing famine on the land, causing tremendous hardship.

As I looked at the dry riverbeds, the barren landscape, the vineyards which had died or were dying, I knew the cause of this malady, even though it would only be chalked up by the political pundits, as the variances of the weather. The religion of Islam is evil. Fostered and nurtured by Satan, in Afghanistan, it is more evil than most. The drought resulting in famine is the result.

And as well, as it regards the famine in Jacob's time, and the thought that such was too severe, as it regards the manipulation of one family, we must remember the following:

There was nothing in the world more important than this one family, which means that the Work of God and the people of God are far, far more important, than anything else. In other words, the little Church on the corner, with only a few people attending, that is if the True Gospel is being preached from behind its pulpit, is far more important in the Eyes of God, than even the mighty Microsoft, or other industries, etc. While that certainly wouldn't be the case, as is overly obvious with the world, it definitely is the case with God. Those other things will perish with the using, but the Word of God abideth forever.

THE FOOD

Verse 2 reads: *"And it came to pass, when they had eaten up the grain which they had brought out of Egypt, their father said unto them, Go again, buy us a little food."*

It seems that the grain which they obtained in Egypt was used solely as their own personal food, with the flocks and herds evidently eating other things. So Jacob now admonishes his sons to go back to Egypt, in order that they might secure more grain, because what they bought on the first trip is now gone.

It may be thought peculiar that all of these men would go to Egypt as it regards such a transaction; however, travel was dangerous in those days, hence all going. There was greater safety in numbers.

JUDAH

Verses 3 through 5 read: *"And Judah spoke unto him, saying, The man did solemnly*

protest unto us, saying, You shall not see my face, except your brother be with you.

"If you will send our brother with us, we will go down and buy you food:

"But if you will not send him, we will not go down: for the man said unto us, You shall not see my face, except your brother be with you."

Reuben is the firstborn, and should have taken the lead in all of these matters, but it is Judah who in fact stands in the position of leadership. Quite possibly, the other brothers may have joined in as well, as it regards what they had to say; however, it is Judah alone, of which the Holy Spirit records.

Why?

Whatever happened that day which caused Judah to take the lead, and as well with Joseph during the second trip to Egypt, which we will study in Chapter 44, had to be the Moving and Operation of the Holy Spirit on his heart. Judah would head up the Tribe from which the Messiah would come; therefore, we see traits of leadership beginning to show themselves.

Judah explains to Jacob that despite their long trip to Egypt, they will not be able to buy food, unless Benjamin is with them.

ISRAEL

Verses 6 through 10 read: *"And Israel said, Wherefore dealt you so ill with me, as to tell the man whether you had yet a brother?*

"And they said, The man asked us straightly of our state, and of our kindred, saying, Is your father yet alive? Have you another brother? And we told him according to the tenor of these words: could we certainly know that he would say, Bring your brother down?

"And Judah said unto Israel his father, Send the lad with me, and we will arise and go; that we may live, and not die, both we, and you, and also our little ones.

"I will be surety for him; of my hand shall you require him: if I bring him not unto you, and set him before you, then let me bear the blame forever:

"For except we had lingered, surely now we had returned this second time."

If it is to be noticed, in Verses 6 and 8, the Holy Spirit refers to Jacob as Israel. As remembered, the name means *"prince with*

God." Whenever this name is used, it is always for purpose and reason. It shows an approval by God of Jacob. So the question we must ask is, what is Jacob doing now that would cause the Lord to think so highly of him?

I think the answer would be in several parts.

Jacob is obeying as it regards the sending of Benjamin, which of course is what the Lord wants and desires. As well. For Jacob to do this, he has to exhibit faith in God. And it is faith that is rightly placed, and that is always the criteria.

All of this will ultimately play out to the Redeemer coming into this world, Who would die on a Cross, thereby paying the terrible sin debt which man owed to God. Ultimately, it's the Cross! And ultimately, the Cross must always, in some way, be the object of our Faith, or else, it's faith that God will not recognize.

The problem or the question is never faith as such. Everyone has faith, but with few exceptions, it is faith in something else other than the Cross. Consequently, it is faith that God won't recognize. The faith that God honors, and what caused Him to refer to Jacob as *"Israel,"* is Faith in the Cross.

While, of course, Jacob would have known nothing about a Cross, all the things being done, that is if done properly, would ultimately lead to the Cross.

Judah remonstrates to his father that had it not been for this critical issue, the taking of Benjamin, which was demanded by the Lord of Egypt, due to the lack of food, they would have already returned. The situation has now reached the place to where they have no choice; they must go to Egypt.

(11) "AND THEIR FATHER ISRAEL SAID UNTO THEM, IF IT MUST BE SO NOW, DO THIS; TAKE OF THE BEST FRUITS IN THE LAND IN YOUR VESSELS, AND CARRY DOWN THE MAN A PRESENT, A LITTLE BALM, AND A LITTLE HONEY, SPICES, AND MYRRH, NUTS, AND ALMONDS:

(12) "AND TAKE DOUBLE MONEY IN YOUR HAND; AND THE MONEY THAT WAS BROUGHT AGAIN IN THE MOUTH OF YOUR SACKS, CARRY IT AGAIN IN YOUR HAND: PERADVENTURE IT WAS AN OVERSIGHT:

(13) "TAKE ALSO YOUR BROTHER, AND ARISE, GO AGAIN UNTO THE MAN:

NOTES

(14) "AND GOD ALMIGHTY GIVE YOU MERCY BEFORE THE MAN, THAT HE MAY SEND AWAY YOUR OTHER BROTHER, AND BENJAMIN. IF I BE BEREAVED OF MY CHILDREN, I AM BEREAVED.

(15) "AND THE MEN TOOK THAT PRESENT, AND THEY TOOK DOUBLE MONEY IN THEIR HAND, AND BENJAMIN; AND ROSE UP, AND WENT DOWN TO EGYPT, AND STOOD BEFORE JOSEPH.

(16) "AND WHEN JOSEPH SAW BENJAMIN WITH THEM, HE SAID TO THE RULER OF HIS HOUSE, BRING THESE MEN HOME, AND SLAY, AND MAKE READY; FOR THESE MEN SHALL DINE WITH ME AT NOON.

(17) "AND THE MAN DID AS JOSEPH BADE; AND THE MAN BROUGHT THE MEN INTO JOSEPH'S HOUSE.

(18) "AND THE MEN WERE AFRAID, BECAUSE THEY WERE BROUGHT INTO JOSEPH'S HOUSE; AND THEY SAID, BECAUSE OF THE MONEY THAT WAS RETURNED IN OUR SACKS AT THE FIRST TIME ARE WE BROUGHT IN; THAT HE MAY SEEK OCCASION AGAINST US, AND FALL UPON US, AND TAKE US FOR BONDMEN, AND OUR ANIMALS."

The synopsis is:

1. The Holy Spirit continues to refer to Jacob as *"Israel."*

2. It was a part of the Divine Plan that Jacob and his family should be settled for a long period in Egypt. So all of these proceedings are leading toward that conclusion.

3. Hence *"Jacob"* is now *"Israel,"* reminding us how the future is involved in all these events of this time.

THEIR FATHER ISRAEL

Verses 11 through 13 read: *"And their father Israel said unto them, If it must be so now, do this; take of the best fruits in the land in your vessels, and carry down the man a present, a little balm, and a little honey, spices, and myrrh, nuts, and almonds:*

"And take double money in your hand; and the money that was brought again in the mouth of your sacks, carry it again in your hand: peradventure it was an oversight:

"Take also your brother, and arise, go again unto the man."

In Verse 11, the Patriarch is referred to as *"Israel,"* making three times in succession (vss. 6, 8), without the name *"Jacob"* being mentioned once.

We have already addressed ourselves to this particular thought, but due to the great significance of what is happening here, please allow me the prerogative of covering the following point a little more thoroughly.

It is not so much here Jacob's great faith which is being applauded, but rather the correct object of his faith. The Plan of God for the removal of this family to Egypt is nearing the moment of fulfillment, and everything is now in readiness. Joseph is Prime Minister of Israel, but with Jacob unaware now of this fact. All he knows is that strange things have been happening. Simeon has been detained in Egypt, and for no apparent reason, except the ridiculous assertion that these men were spies. And as well, it is demanded, if the brothers return, they must bring Benjamin with them. Why was such a thing required of them?

Irrespective as to the *"why,"* Jacob acquiesces.

The Patriarch is trying to gather together a little gift for the lord of Egypt, and as well, taking care that there is enough money to pay not only for this order, but for the previous order as well. Little does he realize what is actually in store for him.

The little gift, which the brothers will present to Joseph, although precious to this family, and because of the famine, means nothing to Joseph, with the exception of sentimental value. It is the same with our gifts to Christ. It might look big to us, but its intrinsic worth means nothing to Christ, as should be obvious. But yet, our gifts are precious in His sight, just as this gift was precious in Joseph's sight, and because he loved his brothers, even as Christ loves us.

EL SHADDAI

Verse 14 reads: *"And God Almighty give you mercy before the man, that he may send away your other brother, and Benjamin. If I be bereaved of my children, I am bereaved."*

Jacob uses here the appellative *"God Almighty,"* which in the Hebrew is *"El Shaddai,"* and means, *"the all-sufficient One"* or *"the all-powerful One."* It refers to the Covenant

God of Abraham (Gen. 17:1), and of Jacob himself (Gen. 35:11).

Jacob in essence is saying, *"I do not understand all that is happening, but I know that God is able to protect both Simeon and Benjamin. I acquiesce to the Divine Will."*

While he is thinking only of the protection of his two sons, little does he realize just how able God actually is. In fact, Simeon and Benjamin are about the least of Jacob's concerns, if he only knew!

In effect, he says, *"If I lose my children, I lose them."* But the truth is, he will not only not lose his children, Joseph will be restored, and as well, the great Patriarch will even see his grandsons, the sons of Joseph.

JOSEPH

Verse 15 reads: *"And the men took that present, and they took double money in their hand and Benjamin; and rose up, and went down to Egypt, and stood before Joseph."*

But the thing is, they did not know it was Joseph.

They had brought double money, payment for the previous purchase and for the present purchase, and as well, they had their gift for Joseph. All of this was to prove that they were honest men. Little did they realize what Joseph's intentions actually were.

The Scripture says, *"And stood before Joseph."* He was their brother and their Saviour, but yet they did not know him. Likewise, Israel will stand before Christ at the Second Coming, and will not know Him. They will ask, *"What are these wounds in Your hands? Then He shall answer, Those with which I was wounded in the house of My friends"* (Zech. 13:6).

BENJAMIN

Verses 16 through 18 read: *"And when Joseph saw Benjamin with them, he said to the ruler of his house, bring these men home, and slay, and make ready; for these men shall dine with me at noon.*

"And the man did as Joseph bade; and the man brought the men into Joseph's house.

"And the men were afraid, because they were brought into Joseph's house; and they said, Because of the money that was returned in our sacks at the first time are we brought

in; that he may seek occasion against us, and fall upon us, and take us for bondmen, and our animals."

The union of Benjamin with Joseph points forward to the day when Christ, as Benjamin, will be the son of the right hand to Israel, and, as Joseph, king over all the Earth.

As the brothers arrive and stand before Joseph, and he sees his younger brother Benjamin, events once again become strange, and unexplainable to the brothers.

They were to be brought to the house of Joseph, which no doubt was a very palatial affair. As these men, in their crude shepherd's garments, were ushered in, they can only imagine something negative. Perhaps they are under arrest, and the first thing that goes to their minds is the money that they found in their sacks which they had paid for the first purchase. They imagined all of themselves being arrested.

(19) "AND THEY CAME NEAR TO THE STEWARD OF JOSEPH'S HOUSE, AND THEY COMMUNED WITH HIM AT THE DOOR OF THE HOUSE,

(20) "AND SAID, O SIR, WE CAME INDEED DOWN AT THE FIRST TIME TO BUY FOOD:

(21) "AND IT CAME TO PASS, WHEN WE CAME TO THE INN, THAT WE OPENED OUR SACKS, AND, BEHOLD, EVERY MAN'S MONEY WAS IN THE MOUTH OF HIS SACK, OUR MONEY IN FULL WEIGHT: AND WE HAVE BROUGHT IT AGAIN IN OUR HAND.

(22) "AND OTHER MONEY HAVE WE BROUGHT DOWN IN OUR HANDS TO BUY FOOD: WE CANNOT TELL WHO PUT OUR MONEY IN OUR SACKS.

(23) "AND HE SAID, PEACE BE TO YOU, FEAR NOT: YOUR GOD, AND THE GOD OF YOUR FATHER, HAS GIVEN YOU TREASURE IN YOUR SACKS: I HAD YOUR MONEY. AND HE BROUGHT SIMEON OUT UNTO THEM.

(24) "AND THE MAN BROUGHT THE MEN INTO JOSEPH'S HOUSE, AND GAVE THEM WATER, AND THEY WASHED THEIR FEET; AND HE GAVE THEIR ANIMALS PROVENDER.

(25) "AND THEY MADE READY THE PRESENT AGAINST JOSEPH CAME AT

NOTES

NOON: FOR THEY HEARD THAT THEY SHOULD EAT BREAD THERE.

(26) "AND WHEN JOSEPH CAME HOME, THEY BROUGHT HIM THE PRESENT WHICH WAS IN THEIR HAND INTO THE HOUSE, AND BOWED THEMSELVES TO HIM TO THE EARTH."

The diagram is:

1. The conduct of Joseph cannot be explained except on the ground of his inspiration. He is not acting. He is not trifling with human feelings. He is not merely following the dictate of his own personal affections. He is, under Divine direction, planning for the removal of his father's house to Egypt, that the people of God may pass through their season of trial in the house of bondage (Spence).

2. The tenderness, the pathos, the simplicity, the truthfulness, especially in the case of Joseph, proclaims the criterion of real greatness. The Bible histories help us to keep in mind that real Salvation does not suppress, but preserves and develops all that is best and noblest in the man.

3. Joseph's dealings with his brothers gradually prepared their minds for the great announcement, which was soon to be made.

THE STEWARD

Verses 19 through 23 read: *"And they came near to the steward of Joseph's house, and they communed with him at the door of the house,*

"And said, O sir, we came indeed down at the first time to buy food:

"And it came to pass, when we came to the inn, that we opened our sacks, and, behold, every man's money was in the mouth of his sack, our money in full weight: and we have brought it again in our hand.

"And other money have we brought down in our hands to buy food: we cannot tell who put our money in our sacks.

"And he said, Peace be to you, fear not: your God, and the God of your father, has given you treasure in your sacks: I had your money. And he brought Simeon out unto them."

Evidently, this steward could speak Hebrew, or else an interpreter was present, which was most likely the case. At any rate, the brothers began to explain to him the situation regarding the money that had been placed in their sacks, on their first visit.

It seems that the steward listened patiently, and then simply said something that must have sounded strange to their ears. He speaks of Elohim, Whom the Egyptians did not know. So it seems that Joseph had taught his steward to fear and trust the God of the Hebrews.

And yet, there is no indication that this man knew that these men standing before him were indeed the flesh and blood brothers of Joseph. But yet he was perfectly aware that they were innocent in the matter of the money. In fact, he relates to them that he was the one who had placed the money in their sacks.

All of this must have been exceedingly strange to them. What could all of it mean, they must have asked themselves?

And then Simeon is brought out to them, and none the worse for wear.

There is no indication whatsoever that Joseph communed with Simeon at all during those months, waiting for the brothers to return.

THE GIFT

Verses 24 through 26 read: *"And the man brought the men into Joseph's house, and gave them water, and they washed their feet; and he gave their animals provender.*

"And they made ready the gift against Joseph came at noon: for they heard that they should eat bread there.

"And when Joseph came home, they brought him the gift which was in their hand into the house, and bowed themselves to him to the earth."

The further it goes, the stranger it becomes. Surely, the Lord of Egypt didn't invite rank strangers from other nations of the Earth into his house to eat with him, and especially lowly shepherds! But yet here they were.

The steward had spoken kindly to them, as well, Simeon has been restored, and this somewhat allays their fears.

One thing is certain: they were not accustomed to the luxury and opulence of their surroundings. In fact, they had probably never seen such. And then Joseph comes into the room.

They bring him the gift which they had prepared, and then *"bowed themselves to him to the earth,"* again, fulfilling his dream.

(27) "AND HE ASKED THEM OF THEIR WELFARE, AND SAID, IS YOUR FATHER WELL, THE OLD MAN OF WHOM YOU SPOKE? IS HE YET ALIVE?

(28) "AND THEY ANSWERED, YOUR SERVANT OUR FATHER IS IN GOOD HEALTH, HE IS YET ALIVE. AND THEY BOWED DOWN THEIR HEADS, AND MADE OBEISANCE.

(29) "AND HE LIFTED UP HIS EYES, AND SAW HIS BROTHER BENJAMIN, HIS MOTHER'S SON, AND SAID, IS THIS YOUR YOUNGER BROTHER, OF WHOM YE SPOKE UNTO ME? AND HE SAID, GOD BE GRACIOUS UNTO YOU, MY SON.

(30) "AND JOSEPH MADE HASTE; FOR HIS BOWELS DID YEARN UPON HIS BROTHER: AND HE SOUGHT WHERE TO WEEP; AND HE ENTERED INTO HIS CHAMBER, AND WEPT THERE.

(31) "AND HE WASHED HIS FACE, AND WENT OUT, AND REFRAINED HIMSELF, AND SAID, SET ON BREAD.

(32) "AND THEY SET ON FOR HIM BY HIMSELF, AND FOR THEM BY THEMSELVES, AND FOR THE EGYPTIANS, WHICH DID EAT WITH HIM, BY THEMSELVES: BECAUSE THE EGYPTIANS MIGHT NOT EAT BREAD WITH THE HEBREWS; FOR THAT IS AN ABOMINATION UNTO THE EGYPTIANS.

(33) "AND THEY SAT BEFORE HIM, THE FIRSTBORN ACCORDING TO HIS BIRTHRIGHT, THE YOUNGEST ACCORDING TO HIS YOUTH: AND THE MEN MARVELED ONE AT ANOTHER.

(34) "AND HE TOOK AND SENT MESSES UNTO THEM FROM BEFORE HIM: BUT BENJAMIN'S MESS WAS FIVE TIMES SO MUCH AS ANY OF THEIRS. AND THEY DRANK, AND WERE MERRY WITH HIM."

The structure is:

1. The meal presented here is indicative of that which will take place at the Second Coming, when both Jews and Gentiles will fellowship with Christ, of whom Joseph was a Type.

2. They marveled that he knew their ages, and seated them accordingly. How could he have known this, they must have reasoned. Christ knows all things.

3. Benjamin was given five times as much food as the others, portraying the Grace of God, for the number *"five"* is God's number of Grace.

THE QUESTIONS

Verses 27 and 28 read: *"And he asked them of their welfare, and said, Is your father well, the old man of whom you spake? Is he yet alive?*

"And they answered, Your servant our father is in good health, he is yet alive. And they bowed down their heads, and made obeisance."

It must have seemed unusual to the sons of Jacob to hear the Lord of Egypt asking personal questions about their father and his health, etc. But according to the protocol of that time, they did not dare question this ruler of Egypt.

When Joseph asked this question concerning his father Jacob, it had been approximately 21 years since he had seen Jacob.

As well, we must understand Joseph's caution. Twenty-one years before, these men were murderers, that is, with the exception of Benjamin, who had not yet been born. The great question concerned what they were now! Consequently, Joseph's actions were designed to draw out their true character, and that it would. He would find that they were now changed men.

What had affected that change, we aren't told; however, it is now obvious that they are different men, with different attitudes. One might say that in the meantime they had been *"born again."*

BENJAMIN

Verse 29 reads: *"And he lifted up his eyes, and saw his brother Benjamin, his mother's son, and said, Is this your younger brother, of whom you spake unto me? And he said, God be gracious unto you, my son."*

As stated, this is the first time that Joseph had seen Benjamin. He had not yet been born when Joseph was sold into Egypt. While the other men were Joseph's half brothers, meaning that Jacob was their father, but they had different mothers. Benjamin's father was Jacob, even as Jacob was the father of them all, but his mother was Rachel, the mother of Joseph also.

The brothers had heard the steward of Joseph use the name of *"Elohim,"* and now they hear Joseph saying the same thing, *"God* (Elohim) *be gracious unto you, my son,"* as

he spoke to Benjamin. These were the first words that he said to the much younger boy. The tenderness of his terminology must have been extremely encouraging to all who were there.

WEEPING

Verses 30 and 31 read: *"And Joseph made haste: for his bowels did yearn upon his brother: and he sought where to weep; and he entered into his chamber, and wept there.*

"And he washed his face, and went out, and refrained himself, and said, Set on bread."

As Joseph looked at his younger brother, he was overcome by emotion. But yet, as the Prime Minister of Egypt, he couldn't let his brothers see him weeping; they simply wouldn't understand. So he slipped out of the room where they all had gathered, and going into another room where he could be alone, the Scripture says, *"And wept there."*

The scene was poignant not only as it expressed the feelings of the moment, but it presents itself in a much larger way, even as it typifies that coming day, when Christ will stand before Israel. At long last, the sons of Jacob will have come home. In fact, in all of history, there has never been anything so drastic as the Fall of Jacob, and I speak of the nation of Israel and their rejection of Christ. It eclipses every other happening. Paul said:

"For if the casting away of them (Israel) *be the reconciling of the world, what shall the receiving of them be, but life from the dead?"* (Rom. 11:15).

And their Fall has been so drastic, so all-encompassing, so total, and so complete, that it will take the Great Tribulation to finally bring them to their senses. The great Prophet Jeremiah referred to it as *"the time of Jacob's trouble,"* but then he said, *"But he shall be saved out of it"* (Jer. 30:7).

Finally, broken and humbled, just as the ancient sons of Jacob, they will stand before Christ. But then, exactly as Joseph, He will not be the lowly Nazarene, the *"meek and lowly One,"* but rather the *"King of kings and Lord of lords."*

THE FELLOWSHIP

Verses 32 through 34 read: *"And they set on for him by himself, and for them by themselves, and for the Egyptians, which did eat with him, by themselves: because the Egyptians might not eat bread with the Hebrews; for that is an abomination unto the Egyptians.*

"And they sat before him, the firstborn according to his birthright, and the youngest according to his youth: and the men marveled one at another.

"And he took and sent messes unto them from before him, but Benjamin's mess was five times so much as any of theirs. And they drank, and were merry with him."

The brothers were now thrust into an arrangement of luxury they had never previously known. In the first place, Egyptians didn't eat with Hebrews, or any other nationality for that matter, considering themselves to be superior. It was a matter of their religious beliefs. So the brothers ate by themselves, with Joseph eating with the Egyptians, who now considered Joseph as one of their own.

However, when the brothers of Joseph were assigned their places regarding the meal, they were astounded that he seated them according to their ages. Reuben was the firstborn, while Benjamin was the youngest, with all the others seated according to their age. How did Joseph know this, they must have reasoned? The Scripture says, *"They marveled,"* and no wonder!

As well, whenever the food was brought, Benjamin received five times as much as the others. Once again, they must have been astounded as to why Joseph had this carried out.

There was a Scriptural reason for this action. First of all, *"five"* is the number of the Grace of God. For instance, Christ was given five Names by the Holy Spirit (Isa. 9:6). As well, He suffered five wounds at the Crucifixion, *"whipped, nails in the hands, nails in the feet, thorns in the brow, and spear in the side."* Also, there is a fivefold calling, *"Apostles, Prophets, Evangelists, Pastors, and Teachers"* (Eph. 4:11).

The name *"Benjamin"* means, *"my strong right hand,"* typifying Christ. In a coming day, when Israel comes back to Christ, even though Christ has *"a strong right hand,"* He will deal with Israel in *"Grace,"* signified by the food given to Benjamin, which was five times more than his brothers.

"O Jesus King most wonderful!
"Thou Conqueror so renowned;
"Thou sweetest Name on mortal tongue,
"In Whom all joys are found."

"When once Thou comest in the heart,
"Then truth begins to shine;
"Then earthly vanities depart,
"Then kindles love divine."

"Jesus! Thy mercies are untold,
"Through each returning day;
"Thy love exceeds a thousand fold
"Whatever we can say."

"May every heart confess Thy Name,
"And ever Thee adore;
"And seeking Thee, itself inflame
"And seek Thee more and more."

"Thee may our tongues forever bless;
"Thee may we love alone:
"And ever in our lives express
"The image of Thine Own."

CHAPTER 44

(1) "AND HE COMMANDED THE STEWARD OF HIS HOUSE, SAYING, FILL THE MEN'S SACKS WITH FOOD, AS MUCH AS THEY CAN CARRY, AND PUT EVERY MAN'S MONEY IN HIS SACK'S MOUTH.

(2) "AND PUT MY CUP, THE SILVER CUP, IN THE SACK'S MOUTH OF THE YOUNGEST, AND HIS CORN MONEY. AND HE DID ACCORDING TO THE WORD THAT JOSEPH HAD SPOKEN.

(3) "AS SOON AS THE MORNING WAS LIGHT, THE MEN WERE SENT AWAY, THEY AND THEIR ANIMALS.

(4) "AND WHEN THEY WERE GONE OUT OF THE CITY, AND NOT YET FAR OFF, JOSEPH SAID UNTO HIS STEWARD, UP, FOLLOW AFTER THE MEN; AND WHEN YOU DO OVERTAKE THEM, SAY UNTO THEM, WHEREFORE HAVE YOU REWARDED EVIL FOR GOOD?

(5) "IS NOT THIS IT IN WHICH MY LORD DRINKETH, AND WHEREBY INDEED HE DIVINETH? YOU HAVE DONE EVIL IN SO DOING.

(6) "AND HE OVERTOOK THEM, AND HE SPOKE UNTO THEM THESE SAME WORDS."

The structure is:

1. None can teach like God. He Alone can produce in the conscience the true sense of sin, and bring the soul down into the profound depths of its own condition in His Presence.

2. The Lord was guiding Joseph in all of this.

3. Men run on in their career of guilt, heedless of everything, until the arrow of the Almighty pierces their conscience, and then they are led into those searchings of heart and intensive exercises of soul which can only find relief in the rich resources of redeeming love (Mackintosh).

THE SILVER CUP

Verses 1 and 2 read: *"And he commanded the steward of his house, saying, Fill the men's sacks with food, as much as they can carry, and put every man's money in his sack's mouth.*

"And put my cup, the silver cup, in the sack's mouth of the youngest, and his corn money. And he did according to the word that Joseph had spoken."

The casual reader may think that Joseph is being somewhat harsh respecting this next episode. But two things must be remembered:

1. Joseph is being led by the Lord in all that he does.

2. Due to the enormity of the sin these brothers, with the exception of Benjamin, he must make certain that there has been true Repentance in their hearts. Everything is at stake, and I speak of the future of the nation of Israel. If it is founded on murder and deceit, it cannot survive. It must be founded on true Repentance before God; hence Joseph taking the stern measures which he took.

THE FINAL PART OF THE PLAN

Verses 3 through 6 read: *"As soon as the morning was light, the men were sent away, they and their animals.*

"And when they were gone out of the city, and not yet far off, Joseph said unto his steward, Up, follow after the men; and when you do overtake them, say unto them, Wherefore have you rewarded evil for good?

"Is not this it in which my lord drinketh, and whereby indeed He divineth? You have done evil in so doing.

"And he overtook them, and he spoke unto them these same words."

If it is to be noticed in all of this, these brothers were guilty of many dreadful sins, and these are recorded in the Sacred Text, but they only think of this one great commanding sin, the rejection of their brother Joseph.

Some sins are worse than others, and what they did was the worst sin of all, hence it weighing heavily on their hearts.

It was exceedingly bad, not only because it was a sin against their own flesh and blood, but primarily because it was a sin against God's Will. It was the Lord Who selected Joseph for the birthright, and their actions proved that they despised what was done, which meant that their anger actually was against God.

While all sin is in some way against God, some sins strike directly at the throat of His Will, hence they are sins of great magnitude. In fact, the sins of Paul fell into that category. Before he was saved, he greatly opposed the Will of God, by opposing those who had accepted Christ. And when it comes down to the bottom line, all sin in one way or the other is in opposition to Christ, and what He did for us at the Cross. There rests every sin, every transgression, all iniquity, etc.

The fact of guilt does not have to be determined as it regards sin, because that is obvious. All sin carries with it its own guilt. It is Repentance which must be tested, and as always, it is tested by one's faith, and in no other way.

Had these men truly repented? Every evidence says they have, and I speak of their attitude, their actions, their spirit, etc; however, many will act one way in one place, and another way someplace else. In the face of Joseph, with his commanding authority, what else could they do? So he had to do one final thing, to prove to himself that what he hoped was evident in their lives, was in fact the truth. The test is now underway.

(7) "AND THEY SAID UNTO HIM, WHEREFORE SAITH MY LORD THESE WORDS? GOD FORBID THAT YOUR SERVANTS SHOULD DO ACCORDING TO THIS THING:

(8) "BEHOLD, THE MONEY, WHICH WE FOUND IN OUR SACKS' MOUTHS, WE BROUGHT AGAIN UNTO YOU OUT OF THE LAND OF CANAAN: HOW THEN SHOULD WE STEAL OUT OF THY LORD'S HOUSE SILVER OR GOLD?

(9) "WITH WHOMSOEVER OF YOUR SERVANTS IT BE FOUND, BOTH LET HIM DIE, AND WE ALSO WILL BE MY LORD'S BONDMEN.

(10) "AND HE SAID, NOW ALSO LET IT BE ACCORDING UNTO YOUR WORDS: HE WITH WHOM IT IS FOUND SHALL BE MY SERVANT; AND YOU SHALL BE BLAMELESS.

(11) "THEN THEY SPEEDILY TOOK DOWN EVERY MAN HIS SACK TO THE GROUND, AND OPENED EVERY MAN HIS SACK.

(12) "AND HE SEARCHED, AND BEGAN AT THE ELDEST, AND LEFT AT THE YOUNGEST: AND THE CUP WAS FOUND IN BENJAMIN'S SACK.

(13) "THEN THEY RENT THEIR CLOTHES, AND LADED EVERYMAN HIS ANIMAL, AND RETURNED TO THE CITY.

(14) "AND JUDAH AND HIS BRETHREN CAME TO JOSEPH'S HOUSE; FOR HE WAS YET THERE: AND THEY FELL BEFORE HIM ON THE GROUND.

(15) "AND JOSEPH SAID UNTO THEM, WHAT DEED IS THIS THAT YOU HAVE DONE? WOT YE NOT THAT SUCH A MAN AS I CAN CERTAINLY DIVINE?"

The composition is:

1. Events will prove true Repentance, and events will also prove a false repentance.

2. In all of this we greatly see the Grace of God, and it is beautiful to behold.

3. We also find in all of this that to the faithful heart, God can even turn evil into good, while never condoning the evil.

A DECLARATION OF INNOCENCE

Verses 7 through 9 read: *"And they said unto him, Wherefore saith my lord these words? God forbid that your servants should do according to this thing:*

"Behold, the money, which we found in our sacks' mouths, we brought again unto you out of the land of Canaan: how then should we steal out of thy lord's house silver or gold?

NOTES

"With whomsoever of your servants it be found, both let him die, and we also will be my lord's bondmen."

Once again, strange things are happening. They are now being accused of stealing a silver cup. Their actions, they feel, have proven that they wouldn't do such a thing, and in fact, they are right.

But again, they do not understand what is happening, as they have not understood the entirety of this scenario. But how could they?

Joseph, whom they knew as someone else, had been so kind to them, even inviting them to eat at his house, and then restoring their brother, Simeon. The atmosphere had been one of trust and kindness. And now this!

Why would he suddenly turn and accuse them of stealing something out of his house, which to say the least, would be a very serious crime.

Knowing they had not done such a thing, they suggest that if the silver cup is found in any sack, the one to whom that sack belongs, his life will be forfeited, and all of them will become slaves of Joseph.

They are right, and they are wrong! They are right in that they didn't steal the cup, but they are wrong in that it's not in one of the sacks.

BENJAMIN

Verses 10 through 15 read: *"And he said, Now also let it be according unto your words: he with whom it is found shall be my servant: and you shall be blameless.*

"Then they speedily took down every man his sack to the ground, and opened every man his sack.

"And he searched, and began at the eldest, and left at the youngest: and the cup was found in Benjamin's sack.

"Then they rent their clothes, and laded every man his animal, and returned to the city.

"And Judah and his brethren came to Joseph's house; for he was yet there: and they fell before him on the ground.

"And Joseph said unto them, What deed is this that you have done? Do you not know that such a man as I can certainly divine?"

The same steward who had greeted them previously now stands before them, as it regards the cup that is supposedly missing. He is the one who had placed the cup in Benjamin's sack, so he knew exactly where it was.

Knowing they had not taken the cup, they make brash statements concerning their situation. He takes them partially at their word.

Only the one in whose sack the cup would be found would be punished. He would be a slave, and the others could go free.

The cup, of course, was found in Benjamin's sack.

They are taken back to stand before Joseph.

(16) "AND JUDAH SAID, WHAT SHALL WE SAY UNTO MY LORD? WHAT SHALL WE SPEAK? OR HOW SHALL WE CLEAR OURSELVES? GOD HAS FOUND OUT THE INIQUITY OF YOUR SERVANTS: BEHOLD, WE ARE MY LORD'S SERVANTS, BOTH WE, AND HE ALSO WITH WHOM THE CUP IS FOUND.

(17) "AND HE SAID, GOD FORBID THAT I SHOULD DO SO: BUT THE MAN IN WHOSE HAND THE CUP IS FOUND, HE SHALL BE MY SERVANT; AND AS FOR YOU, GET YOU UP IN PEACE UNTO YOUR FATHER.

(18) "THEN JUDAH CAME NEAR UNTO HIM, AND SAID, O MY LORD, LET YOUR SERVANT, I PRAY YOU, SPEAK A WORD IN MY LORD'S EARS, AND LET NOT YOUR ANGER BURN AGAINST YOUR SERVANT: FOR YOU ARE EVEN AS PHARAOH.

(19) "MY LORD ASKED HIS SERVANTS, SAYING, HAVE YOU A FATHER, OR A BROTHER?

(20) "AND WE SAID UNTO MY LORD, WE HAVE A FATHER, AN OLD MAN, AND A CHILD OF HIS OLD AGE, A LITTLE ONE; AND HIS BROTHER IS DEAD, AND HE ALONE IS LEFT OF HIS MOTHER, AND HIS FATHER LOVES HIM.

(21) "AND YOU SAID UNTO YOUR SERVANTS, BRING HIM DOWN UNTO ME, THAT I MAY SET MY EYES UPON IM.

(22) "AND WE SAID UNTO MY LORD, THE LAD CANNOT LEAVE HIS FATHER: FOR IF HE SHOULD LEAVE HIS FATHER, HIS FATHER WOULD DIE.

(23) "AND YOU SAID UNTO YOUR SERVANTS, EXCEPT YOUR YOUNGEST BROTHER COME DOWN WITH YOU, YOU SHALL SEE MY FACE NO MORE.

(24) "AND IT CAME TO PASS WHEN WE CAME UP UNTO YOUR SERVANT MY FATHER, WE TOLD HIM THE WORDS OF MY LORD.

(25) "AND OUR FATHER SAID, GO AGAIN, AND BUY US A LITTLE FOOD.

(26) "AND WE SAID, WE CANNOT GO DOWN: IF OUR YOUNGEST BROTHER BE WITH US, THEN WILL WE GO DOWN: FOR WE MAY NOT SEE THE MAN'S FACE, EXCEPT OUR YOUNGEST BROTHER BE WITH US.

(27) "AND YOUR SERVANT MY FATHER SAID UNTO US, YOU KNOW THAT MY WIFE BEAR ME TWO SONS:

(28) "AND THE ONE WENT OUT FROM ME, AND I SAID, SURELY HE IS TORN IN PIECES; AND I SAW HIM NOT SINCE:

(29) "AND IF YOU TAKE THIS ALSO FROM ME, AND MISCHIEF BEFALL HIM, YOU SHALL BRING DOWN MY GRAY HAIRS WITH SORROW TO THE GRAVE.

(30) "NOW THEREFORE WHEN I COME TO YOUR SERVANT MY FATHER, AND THE LAD BE NOT WITH US; SEEING THAT HIS LIFE IS BOUND UP IN THE LAD'S LIFE;

(31) "IT SHALL COME TO PASS, WHEN HE SEES THAT THE LAD IS NOT WITH US, THAT HE WILL DIE: AND YOUR SERVANTS SHALL BRING DOWN THE GRAY HAIRS OF YOUR SERVANT OUR FATHER WITH SORROW TO THE GRAVE.

(32) "FOR YOUR SERVANT BECAME SURETY FOR THE LAD UNTO MY FATHER, SAYING, IF I BRING HIM NOT UNTO YOU, THEN I SHALL BEAR THE BLAME TO MY FATHER FOREVER.

(33) "NOW THEREFORE, I PRAY YOU, LET YOUR SERVANT ABIDE INSTEAD OF THE LAD A BONDMAN TO MY LORD; AND LET THE LAD GO UP WITH HIS BRETHREN.

(34) "FOR HOW SHALL I GO UP TO MY FATHER, AND THE LAD BE NOT WITH ME? LEST PERADVENTURE I SEE THE EVIL THAT SHALL COME ON MY FATHER."

The composition is:

1. This Forty-fourth Chapter contains one of the most impassioned pleas ever made by one man to another. Judah made this plea unto Joseph.

2. The distress of Judah and the others shows that they were no longer in heart the men of 21 years back.

3. As well, this portrays a future day. Zechariah 9:13 says: *"When I have bent Judah for me."* In that day, at the Second Coming of the Lord, Judah will repent.

Zechariah, as well, said, *"In that day there shall be a great mourning"* (Zech. 12:11).

The Eighteenth Verse of this Chapter says: *"Then Judah came near unto him."* Finally, at the Second Coming, Judah will *"come near unto Him."* Joseph's brethren had no conception of all that was to flow to them from their conduct toward him. *"They took him and cast him into a pit . . . and they sat down to eat bread."* The Prophet Amos said, *"Woe to them . . . who drink wine in bowls, and anoint themselves with the chief ointments: but they are not grieved for the affliction of Joseph"* (Amos 6:1, 6).

And then strange things begin to happen. At first they took it in stride, the seven years of plenty, but then the seven years of famine were worse than anything they had ever known. Little did they know or realize that all of this, despite the fact that it was touching many nations and untold numbers of people, was because of them.

And then the first trip to Egypt, with very strange things happening, which resulted in Simeon being left behind, actually held in prison, and with the command given them, that unless they brought their younger brother Benjamin back with them, there was no need in coming.

Jacob had been so chagrined at the thought of Benjamin leaving, that he did not agree that it could be done, until there was no alternative. Judah took responsibility, and now their worst fears had been realized. Benjamin has been accused of stealing a silver cup belonging to the lord of Egypt, and it is demanded by the lord of Egypt that Benjamin remain behind, in fact taking Simeon's place in prison.

At this demand, Judah now comes before Joseph, and he makes the most impassioned plea that has probably ever been recorded.

All of this has brought them to the feet of the injured Joseph. How marked is the display of God's Own Hand in all of this! There they stand, with the arrow of conviction thrust through and through their consciences, in the very presence of the man whom they had *"with wicked hands,"* cast into the pit. Surely their sin has found them out. But it is in the presence of Joseph. Blessed place!

Judah closes out his plea with the pathos of the others being felt as well, by saying to Joseph, *"For how shall I go up to my father, and the lad be not with me?"*

The tests have finally come to an end. Joseph is fully satisfied that these men are not the same men who sold him into Egyptian bondage. We must realize that the entirety of this scenario, which affected all of the Middle East, was all brought about in order to further the great Plan of God. Joseph would figure very prominently in all of this, along with Jacob. But so would these brothers. But they had to be what they ought to be, and Joseph is now satisfied that the miracle of transformation has definitely taken place. The distress of Judah, and all the others for that matter, shows that they were no longer, in heart, the men of those years ago. They declared that they loved their father too much to be indifferent to his tears, and their brother Benjamin to consent to his captivity.

"Jesus is all the world to me, my life, my joy, my all;
"He is my strength from day to day, without Him I would fall.
"When I am sad, to Him I go, no other one can cheer me so;
"When I am sad He makes me glad — He's my friend."

"Jesus is all the world to me, my friend in trials sore;
"I go to Him for blessings and He gives them o'er and o'er.
"He sends the sunshine and the rain, He sends the harvest's golden grain;
"Sunshine and rain, harvest of grain — He's my friend."

"Jesus is all the world to me, and true to Him I'll be;
"Oh, how could I this friend deny when He's so true to me?
"Following Him I know I'm right, He watches over me day and night;
"Following Him be day and night — He's my friend."

"Jesus is all the world to me, I want no better friend;
"I trust Him now, I'll trust Him when life's fleeting days shall end.

"Beautiful life with such a friend, beautiful life that has no end;
"Eternal life, eternal joy! He's my friend!"

CHAPTER 45

(1) "THEN JOSEPH COULD NOT REFRAIN HIMSELF BEFORE ALL THEM WHO STOOD BY HIM; AND HE CRIED, CAUSE EVERY MAN TO GO OUT FROM ME. AND THERE STOOD NO MAN WITH HIM, WHILE JOSEPH MADE HIMSELF KNOWN UNTO HIS BRETHREN.

(2) "AND HE WEPT ALOUD: AND THE EGYPTIANS AND THE HOUSE OF PHARAOH HEARD.

(3) "AND JOSEPH SAID UNTO HIS BRETHREN, I AM JOSEPH; DOES MY FATHER YET LIVE? AND HIS BRETHREN COULD NOT ANSWER HIM; FOR THEY WERE TROUBLED AT HIS PRESENCE.

(4) "AND JOSEPH SAID UNTO HIS BRETHREN, COME NEAR TO ME, I PRAY YOU. AND THEY CAME NEAR. AND HE SAID, I AM JOSEPH YOUR BROTHER, WHOM YOU SOLD INTO EGYPT."

The composition is:

1. The First Verse says: *"Joseph made himself known unto his brethren."* Zechariah said: *"And they shall look upon Me Whom they have pierced"* (Zech. 12:10). As well, he said: *"And one shall say unto Him, What are these wounds in Your hands?"* (Zech. 13:6).

2. The Third Verse says: *"I am Joseph."* Revelation to the brethren was made. What will Israel's reaction be when Christ says: *"I am Jesus"*?

3. Joseph now knows beyond the shadow of a doubt that there has been a genuine change in his brothers.

JOSEPH

Verse 1 reads: *"Then Joseph could not refrain himself before all them who stood by him; and he cried, Cause every man to go out from me. And there stood no man with him, while Joseph made himself known unto his brethren."*

Without a doubt, this is one of the most memorable, touching scenes in history. Even above the drama of this happening, we know it portrays that glad morning when Christ will reveal Himself to Israel, which will take place immediately after the Second Coming (Zech. 12:10).

In the first place, only God could bring about such a happening. A Hebrew boy, just 17 years of age, sold into Egypt as a slave by his brothers, being placed in prison in Egypt because of false charges, and then miraculously and instantly, elevated to the second highest position in that land, and thereby the world. As stated, only God could do such a thing.

As Judah finishes his impassioned plea, closing out with the words, *"For how shall I go up to my father, and the lad be not with me?"*, Joseph can refrain himself no longer.

Suddenly he states to the Egyptians who were with him in the room, that all should leave with the exception of himself and his brothers.

Once again, Joseph's reactions are strange. The brothers are still overly confused concerning the recent happenings about the silver cup. They knew that Benjamin was not guilty of taking the cup. The solemn tones of Joseph still ring in their ears, as he said that the person in whose hand the cup was found must be his slave, and, thereby, must remain in Egypt. They knew if this happened, it would kill Jacob. And then Judah, sick at heart, makes his impassioned plea to Joseph, and first of all refers to their terrible sin of some 22 years before of their selling Joseph into Egypt.

Not knowing what to expect, and burdened down with sorrow, the room must have been deathly quiet, as the Egyptian guards and attendants leave, as commanded by Joseph.

WEEPING

Verse 2 reads: *"And he wept aloud: and the Egyptians and the house of Pharaoh heard."*

Without warning, Joseph breaks into loud sobs and weeping. As stated, he can refrain himself no longer. As well, he doesn't want the Egyptians who are present to hear what he will have to say as it regards the sin of these men. Joseph's grace in covering up their sin directly they confessed it, and hiding it from Pharaoh, and in hasting to acknowledge them before Pharaoh as his brothers, illustrates the richer Grace of Him Who says: *"Your sins and iniquities will I remember no more."*

No stranger is allowed to witness this sacred scene. In fact, what stranger could understand or appreciate it? We are called here to witness, as it were, divinely-wrought conviction in the presence of Divine Grace; and, we may say, when these two, conviction and Grace, come together, such always presents a settlement of every question.

The Reader must understand these words, because they are very, very important! The problems may be many. The difficulties, and in whatever realm, may be insurmountable, or even impossible as it regards man; however, if Holy Spirit conviction is responded to properly by the individual, the Grace of God will always and without exception be made evident in such a case, which guarantees the solution of every problem.

Only God can do this, and it merely requires faith, surrender, and obedience on the part of the individual to bring it to pass. If man attempts, which he always does, to ameliorate a situation by other means, he, able to deal with the externals only, can effect no real change. But Holy Spirit conviction, weighing heavily on the heart, deals with the real problem, and its cause. And to be sure, in some way, the cause is always rebellion against God, and God's Way. Sin is not so much the act, although it is that, as it is rebellion. It's man attempting to function by his own means and machinations, which always lead to wreckage. God's Way is *"Jesus Christ and Him Crucified"* (I Cor. 1:23; 2:2; Gal. 6:14; Eph. 2:13-18; Col. 2:14-15).

Joseph weeps so loudly that the Egyptians, who have just left the room, cannot help but overhear his loud sobbing.

"The house of Pharaoh hearing," means that the officials, which had previously been in the room, reported the happenings to Pharaoh.

I AM JOSEPH

Verse 3 reads: *"And Joseph said unto his brethren, I am Joseph; does my father yet live? And his brethren could not answer him; they were troubled at his presence."*

Concerning this moment, Pulpit Commentary says, *"The effect of this announcement*

can be better imagined than described. Hitherto he had been known to his brethren as Zaphnath-paaneah."

At the sound of this name, and that Joseph himself says it, and no doubt spoke to them in Hebrew, would have first of all filled them with consternation. Perhaps this is the reason that Joseph, discerning their countenances, asked so abruptly after Jacob, especially considering that a short time before, they had mentioned that Jacob was well (Gen. 43:27-28).

The simple statement *"I am Joseph,"* explains all of the strange happenings. But yet, they can hardly believe their ears. How in the world could their brother, whom they sold into Egyptian bondage, now be the Prime Minister of Egypt, and, thereby, the second most powerful man in the world? How could such a thing have happened?

EGYPT

Verse 4 reads: *"And Joseph said unto his brethren, Come near to me, I pray you. And they came near. And he said, I am Joseph your brother, whom you sold into Egypt."*

The Text indicates that they don't know what to do. They are transfixed to the spot where they are standing, not knowing what to say, what to do, or how to act.

Joseph mentions quietly that they should now come closer to him, which they do. So as to make sure they understand exactly what he has said, he amplifies the statement by saying, *"I am Joseph your brother, whom you sold into Egypt."*

Quite possibly, he wondered if they understood when he first said, *"I am Joseph."* So now he identifies himself in such a way that there can be no misunderstanding. He is the brother who was sold as a slave.

(5) "NOW THEREFORE BE NOT GRIEVED, NOR ANGRY WITH YOURSELVES, THAT YOU SOLD ME HITHER: FOR GOD DID SEND ME BEFORE YOU TO PRESERVE LIFE.

(6) "FOR THESE TWO YEARS HAS THE FAMINE BEEN IN THE LAND: AND YET THERE ARE FIVE YEARS, IN THE WHICH THERE SHALL NEITHER BE EARING NOR HARVEST.

(7) "AND GOD SENT ME BEFORE YOU TO PRESERVE YOU A POSTERITY IN THE

EARTH, AND TO SAVE YOUR LIVES BY A GREAT DELIVERANCE.

(8) "SO NOW IT WAS NOT YOU WHO SENT ME HITHER, BUT GOD: AND HE HAS MADE ME A FATHER TO PHARAOH, AND LORD OF ALL HIS HOUSE, AND A RULER THROUGHOUT ALL THE LAND OF EGYPT.

(9) "HASTE YE, AND GO UP TO MY FATHER, AND SAY UNTO HIM, THUS SAITH YOUR SON JOSEPH, GOD HAS MADE ME LORD OF ALL EGYPT: COME DOWN UNTO ME, TARRY NOT:

(10) "AND YOU SHALL DWELL IN THE LAND OF GOSHEN, AND YOU SHALL BE NEAR UNTO ME, YOU, AND YOUR CHILDREN, AND YOUR CHILDREN'S CHILDREN, AND YOUR FLOCKS, AND YOUR HERDS, AND ALL THAT YOU HAVE:

(11) "AND THERE WILL I NOURISH YOU; FOR YET THERE ARE FIVE YEARS OF FAMINE; LEST YOU, AND YOUR HOUSEHOLD, AND ALL THAT YOU HAVE, COME TO POVERTY.

(12) "AND, BEHOLD, YOUR EYES SEE, AND THE EYES OF MY BROTHER BENJAMIN, THAT IT IS MY MOUTH THAT SPEAKETH UNTO YOU.

(13) "AND YOU SHALL TELL MY FATHER OF ALL MY GLORY IN EGYPT AND OF ALL THAT YOU HAVE SEEN; AND YOU SHALL HASTE AND BRING DOWN MY FATHER HITHER."

The construction is:

1. Joseph's heart beat true to God and to his brothers. He kept pressing upon them that it was God Who had taken him out of the pit and placed him upon the Throne.

2. The way he says all of this leads them to feel that it was against God that they had sinned, rather than against himself, which actually was true and made the sin even worse.

3. And yet he assured them that God loved them and overruled all for their Salvation, as He will do for anyone who will come to Him in humble Repentance.

A GREAT DELIVERANCE

Verses 5 through 7 read: *"Now therefore be not grieved, nor angry with yourselves, that you sold me hither: for God did send me before you to preserve life.*

NOTES

"For these two years has the famine been in the land: and yet there are five years, in the which there shall neither be earing nor harvest.

"And God sent me before you to preserve you a posterity in the earth, and to save your lives by a great deliverance."

Joseph attempts to lessen their grief and sorrow, by showing them that whatever it was they intended, God overruled it, and turned it around for good.

We must all grieve over our failures, for such must never be taken lightly; however, God can take that which is degrading, even gross sin, even as the brothers of Joseph, and bring good out of it, with no thanks to the sinner, as would be obvious.

We should look carefully at how Joseph responded to his brothers. He constantly dwells on how God has turned this thing around, and because it's true. But at the same time, it serves as encouragement for his brothers, even as it was meant to do. This is very important!

Dealing with those who have failed, but have truly repented, should be handled exactly as Joseph handles this situation. But the great question is, how many Christians, if placed in Joseph's shoes and in his time, would have conducted themselves exactly as Joseph did. I'm afraid that many would have taken the opportunity to exact their pound of flesh. Such, as should be obvious, is certainly not Christlike, and in fact, puts the wronged person in the position of committing sin by acting in that manner.

Verses 8 through 13 read: *"So now it was not you who sent me hither, but God: and He has made me a father to Pharaoh, and lord of all his house, and a ruler throughout all the land of Egypt.*

"Haste ye, and go up to my father, and say unto him, Thus saith your son Joseph, God has made me lord of all Egypt: come down unto me, tarry not:

"And you shall dwell in the land of Goshen, and you shall be near unto me, you, and your children, and your children's children, and your flocks, and your herds, and all that you have:

"And there will I nourish you; for yet there are five years of famine; lest you, and

your household, and all that you have, come to poverty.

"And, behold, your eyes see, and the eyes of my brother Benjamin, that it is my mouth that speaks unto you.

"And you shall tell my father of all my glory in Egypt and of all that you have seen; and you shall haste and bring down my father hither."

Now Joseph gives instructions as to his father Jacob. But with that, the brothers have another problem:

They're going to have to confess to Jacob as to what happened with Joseph those 22 years before. Even though the news is going to be wonderful and glorious, because of their culpability, and having to confess to Jacob what actually happened, it will have a bittersweet effect.

Joseph is telling his father that he must come down to Egypt. As we shall see, even though his beloved son Joseph says this, the great Patriarch will have to hear from the Lord before he will consent to make the move. But he will hear from Jehovah, and the command will be even more emphatic regarding his transfer to Egypt.

Once again, the Plans of God are much larger than anything we could ever begin to think. While Egypt would be very good to Jacob, it would not prove to be so good to those who would follow after, for the children of Israel would remain in Egypt for some 215 years, before being delivered by the mighty Power of God.

Even though they will fall from the lofty status of place and position, down to the far lower level of slavery, still, there were plusses in all of this as well, one of them guaranteeing that, for the most part, Israel would remain to themselves, and not intermarry with the Egyptians.

Verse 13 speaks of Joseph telling his brethren to tell Jacob of *"all my glory in Egypt."* Isaiah said: *"And they shall declare My glory among the Gentiles"* (Isa. 66:19). Thus will the glory of Christ be made manifest in that coming day.

(14) "AND HE FELL UPON HIS BROTHER BENJAMIN'S NECK, AND WEPT; AND BENJAMIN WEPT UPON HIS NECK.

(15) "MOREOVER HE KISSED ALL HIS BRETHREN, AND WEPT UPON THEM: AND

AFTER THAT HIS BRETHREN TALKED WITH HIM.

(16) "AND THE FAME THEREOF WAS HEARD IN PHARAOH'S HOUSE, SAYING, JOSEPH'S BRETHREN ARE COME: AND IT PLEASED PHARAOH WELL, AND HIS SERVANTS.

(17) "AND PHARAOH SAID UNTO JOSEPH, SAY UNTO YOUR BRETHREN, THIS DO YOU; LADE YOUR BEASTS, AND GO, AND GET YOU INTO THE LAND OF CANAAN;

(18) "AND TAKE YOUR FATHER AND YOUR HOUSEHOLDS, AND COME UNTO ME: AND I WILL GIVE YOU THE GOOD OF THE LAND OF EGYPT, AND YOU SHALL EAT THE FAT OF THE LAND.

(19) "NOW YOU ARE COMMANDED, THIS YOU DO; TAKE YOU WAGONS OUT OF THE LAND OF EGYPT FOR YOUR LITTLE ONES, AND FOR YOUR WIVES, AND BRING YOUR FATHER, AND COME.

(20) "ALSO REGARD NOT YOUR STUFF; FOR THE GOOD OF ALL THE LAND OF EGYPT IS YOURS.

(21) "AND THE CHILDREN OF ISRAEL DID SO: AND JOSEPH GAVE THEM WAGONS, ACCORDING TO THE COMMANDMENT OF PHARAOH, AND GAVE THEM PROVISION FOR THE WAY.

(22) "TO ALL OF THEM HE GAVE EACH MAN CHANGES OF RAIMENT; BUT TO BENJAMIN HE GAVE THREE HUNDRED PIECES OF SILVER, AND FIVE CHANGES OF RAIMENT.

(23) "AND TO HIS FATHER HE SENT AFTER THIS MANNER; TEN ANIMALS LADEN WITH THE GOOD THINGS OF EGYPT, AND TEN SHE ANIMALS LADEN WITH GRAIN AND BREAD AND MEAT FOR HIS FATHER BY THE WAY.

(24) "SO HE SENT HIS BRETHREN AWAY, AND THEY DEPARTED: AND HE SAID UNTO THEM, SEE THAT YOU FALL NOT OUT BY THE WAY."

The exegesis is:

1. It has taken 22 years to come to this place, and much suffering along the way. But patience has now been rewarded. In fact, trust in God is never unrewarded.

2. Joseph allowed the Spirit of God to work out this thing, and did not try to insert

his own efforts, as we all are so prone to do. When the Lord does it, it's done well!

3. In the main, trust in the Lord never brings anything but good news.

REUNION

Verses 14 through 16 read: *"And he fell upon his brother Benjamin's neck, and wept; and Benjamin wept upon his neck.*

"Moreover he kissed all his brethren, and wept upon them: after that his brethren talked with him.

"And the fame thereof was heard in Pharaoh's house, saying, Joseph's brethren are come: and it pleased Pharaoh well, and his servants."

This had to be extremely traumatic for Benjamin as well. He was born after Joseph was sold into Egypt, so he had never seen his brother. At some point in time, he was no doubt told the story that his father Jacob had been told, that Joseph had died as the result of wild beasts. The brothers would not have dared to tell him that they had sold him as a slave into Egypt.

Whether the correct information was given to him immediately, or the brothers told him on the way home, we aren't told. At any rate, *"Joseph is alive!"*

Joseph kissing all of his brethren portrays the seal of recognition, of reconciliation, and of Salvation.

Concerning this scene, Lange says, *"It has been thought that Benjamin stood when Joseph embraced him, and that the two wept upon each other's neck, but that the brethren bowed themselves at Joseph's feet, causing the expression to be, 'And he wept upon them.'"* More than likely that's exactly the way it happened. Him kissing them, in effect, stated that the past is done, and it must not mar the future.

PHARAOH

Verses 17 through 20 read: *"And Pharaoh said unto Joseph, Say unto your brethren, This you do; lade your beasts, and go, and get you unto the land of Canaan;*

"And take your father and your households, and come unto me: I will give you the good of the land of Egypt, and you shall eat the fat of the land.

"Now you are commanded, this you do; take you wagons out of the land of Egypt for your little ones, and for your wives, and bring your father, and come.

"Also regard not your stuff; for the good of all the land of Egypt is yours."

It has been told Pharaoh that the brothers of Joseph have come, but of course, Pharaoh knows nothing about the situation at hand.

The Monarch evidently called Joseph before him, and gave him special permission to bring his entire family into the land of Egypt. Every evidence is that he did this gladly.

In fact, they were to be given land in the area of Goshen, all at the expense of the State.

Pharaoh informs Joseph that he wishes so much to lavish good things upon Joseph's family, that he tells them not to even bother to bring their *"stuff,"* from Canaan, because everything that will be needed will be provided in Egypt. This, in effect, is a carte blanche proposal.

Pharaoh is very quick to do this, and very glad to do this, simply because Joseph has been the Saviour of Egypt. As it is, they have plenty of grain stored up to last out the famine, and as well to sell grain to surrounding nations. Had it not been for Joseph, Egypt would have been in dire straits, exactly as these other countries now were. So Pharaoh gladly provides this which Joseph's family will need.

THE CHILDREN OF ISRAEL

Verses 21 through 24 read: *"And the children of Israel did so: and Joseph gave them wagons, according to the commandment of Pharaoh, and gave them provision for the way.*

"To all of them he gave each man changes of raiment; but to Benjamin he gave three hundred pieces of silver, and five changes of raiment.

"And to his father he sent after this manner; ten animals laden with the good things of Egypt, and ten she animals laden with corn and bread and meat for his father by the way.

"So he sent his brethren away, and they departed: and he said unto them, See that you fall not out by the way."

When the brethren of Joseph leave this time, they are not fearful that some untoward thing will happen to them as it had before.

Now they understand the reason for the strange events which took place on the first trip, and the first part of this last trip.

They were going back to Canaan with wagons, sent for the very purpose of bringing all the goods of Jacob and the entirety of the families back to Egypt. So there must have been quite a number of wagons.

As well, they were given beautiful changes of clothing, with Benjamin being given three hundred pieces of silver as well. Think of the difference as to what they had done to Joseph those 22 years earlier.

They had taken his coat of many colors, stained it with the blood of a kid of the goats, and had sent it by the hand of a slave to convince Jacob that Joseph had been killed. As well, they had sold Joseph for 20 pieces of silver.

But the raiment that Joseph gives them, is beautiful beyond compare, in fact, such as they had never had in their lives, and never hoped to have. What an expression of love!

It is the same with Christ, for Joseph is a Type of Christ. The old song says:

"I traded my sins for Salvation.
"I traded my load for relief.
"What I got was so much more than
   what He received,
"I sure got the best of the trade."

When you put the two scenes together, you are then seeing what we have done to Christ, and then in turn, what He has done for us.

There is no way that one can properly grasp the fullness of the love of Christ. What He has done for us, and for which He paid such a great price on the Cross, will stand good forever and forever.

(25) "AND THEY WENT UP OUT OF EGYPT, AND CAME INTO THE LAND OF CANAAN UNTO JACOB THEIR FATHER,

(26) "AND TOLD HIM, SAYING, JOSEPH IS YET ALIVE, AND HE IS GOVERNOR OVER ALL THE LAND OF EGYPT. AND JACOB'S HEART FAINTED, FOR HE BELIEVED THEM NOT.

(27) "AND THEY TOLD HIM ALL THE WORDS OF JOSEPH, WHICH HE HAD SAID UNTO THEM: AND WHEN HE SAW THE WAGONS WHICH JOSEPH HAD SENT TO CARRY HIM, THE SPIRIT OF JACOB THEIR FATHER REVIVED:

NOTES

(28) "AND ISRAEL SAID, IT IS ENOUGH; JOSEPH MY SON IS YET ALIVE: I WILL GO AND SEE HIM BEFORE I DIE."

The synopsis is:

1. For 22 years Jacob had suffered. The suffering is now over; Joseph is yet alive. Christ is alive! What more can I say!

2. *"And Israel said!"* The change of name here is significant.

3. The sons of Jacob likewise betrayed Christ. But on a coming glad day, Oh happy day, the wrong will forever be made right.

JACOB

Verses 25 through 28 read: *"And they went up out of Egypt, and came into the land of Canaan unto Jacob their father,*

"And told him, saying, Joseph is yet alive, and he is governor over all the land of Egypt. And Jacob's heart fainted, for he believed them not.

"And they told him all the words of Joseph, which he had said unto them: and when he saw the wagons which Joseph had sent to carry him, the spirit of Jacob their father revived:

"And Israel said, It is enough; Joseph my son is yet alive: I will go and see him before I die."

If the scene with Joseph revealing himself to his brothers was in fact one of, if not the most poignant in history, then the scene with the brothers before their father Jacob had to be a close second.

For 22 years the old man has grieved. A thousand questions loomed large in his mind, but there were no answers. Why would God have him select Joseph for the birthright, and then allow him to be killed by wild animals?

Even though the account given here doesn't mention the brothers telling their father what actually happened as it regards Joseph, and that situation of some 22 years earlier, it is obvious that they had to do so.

All of this which we read about in the account of Joseph and Jacob, were superintended by the Patriarch. So the following is the way it might have happened:

THE TRUTH

When the brothers arrived back from Egypt, which must have taken them at least some three weeks, of course Jacob was glad to see them, and more than all, glad to see Benjamin. Whether he noticed anything different about them, for their demeanor most definitely must have been somewhat different, we aren't told.

As they all gathered together to give an account of their trip, the old man would have been eager to hear all the news. Quite possibly, one of them, maybe Judah, would have requested of his father that he sit down, for they had something to relate to him. If that's the way it happened, Jacob no doubt would have been somewhat puzzled as to what it might be. Simeon had been returned to them, and Benjamin was here, safe and sound. So what could it be?

More than likely, the brothers would have related to him first of all as to their evil intent of those 22 years before. It would have been very difficult to have related such a thing. They had to admit their culpability, their hard hearts, and their efforts to deceive their father, in which they were very successful, and as the Patriarch heard this, it must have cut deep, especially considering how much he had suffered all of these years.

They would have related how they put Joseph in a pit, and then sold him as a slave into Egypt for 20 pieces of silver. They would have told how they took the coat of many colors and dipped it in the blood of a kid of the goats, and had someone else to bring it to Jacob, and let him draw his own conclusions that Joseph had been killed by a wild animal.

As they laboriously relived this scene, Jacob, no doubt, felt the pain all over again, wondering why they are revealing this to him now.

And then, Judah said, if in fact it was Judah doing the speaking, which it probably was, *"Joseph is yet alive,"* and then he added, *"He is governor over all the land of Egypt."*

JOSEPH IS YET ALIVE

The old man sat there for a few moments, unable to grasp what he had been told, and coming on the heels of the horrible words which had just been revealed to him, he grows faint, and cannot find it in his heart to believe what he is being told.

And then very slowly, Judah tells his father Jacob, how that Joseph had revealed himself unto them, and had then received permission

from Pharaoh to bring the entire family back to Egypt. He had even sent the wagons to help them move.

Jacob slowly arises from where he has been sitting, walks to the front and looks outside, and sure enough, there are the wagons.

And then the Scripture says: *"And Israel said, It is enough: Joseph my son is yet alive: I will go and see him before I die."*

It is noteworthy that Jacob is referred to in Verse 28 as *"Israel."* Whatever the reasons, to be sure, it is linked to Faith.

It is enough to hear that Joseph is yet alive. That within itself is miraculous to say the least. But to think that he is now the governor of Egypt makes the story even more incredible. How could such a thing be?

And no doubt, in the coming years, Joseph will relate all of the happenings to his father, and do so in minute detail.

"I've found a Friend, Oh, such a Friend!
He loved me ere I knew Him;
"He drew me with the cords of love, and
thus He bound me to Him.
"And round my heart still closely twine
those ties which naught can sever;
"For I am His, and He is mine, forever
and forever."

"I've found a Friend, Oh, such a Friend!
He bled, He died to save me;
"And not alone the gift of life, but His
Own Self He gave me.
"Naught that I have my own I call, I
hold it for the Giver;
"My heart, my strength, my life, my
all are His, and His forever."

"I've found a Friend, Oh, such a Friend!
All power to Him is given,
"To guard me on my onward course,
and bring me safe to Heaven.
"The eternal glories gleam afar to
nerve my faint endeavor;
"So now to watch, to work, to war; and
then to rest forever."

"I've found a Friend, Oh, such a Friend!
So kind, and true, and tender,
"So wise a Counselor and Guide, so
mighty a Defender.
"From Him Who loves me now so well,
what power my soul can sever?

*"Shall life, or death, or Earth, or Hell?
No, I am His forever."*

CHAPTER 46

(1) "AND ISRAEL TOOK HIS JOURNEY WITH ALL THAT HE HAD, AND CAME TO BEER-SHEBA, AND OFFERED SACRIFICES UNTO THE GOD OF HIS FATHER ISAAC.

(2) "AND GOD SPOKE UNTO ISRAEL IN THE VISIONS OF THE NIGHT, AND SAID, JACOB, JACOB. AND HE SAID, HERE AM I.

(3) "AND HE SAID, I AM GOD, THE GOD OF YOUR FATHER: FEAR NOT TO GO DOWN INTO EGYPT; FOR I WILL THERE MAKE OF YOU A GREAT NATION:

(4) "I WILL GO DOWN WITH YOU INTO EGYPT; AND I WILL ALSO SURELY BRING YOU UP AGAIN: AND JOSEPH SHALL PUT HIS HAND UPON YOUR EYES.

(5) "AND JACOB ROSE UP FROM BEER-SHEBA: AND THE SONS OF ISRAEL CARRIED JACOB THEIR FATHER AND THEIR LITTLE ONES, AND THEIR WIVES, AND THE WAGONS WHICH PHARAOH HAD SENT TO CARRY HIM.

(6) "AND THEY TOOK THEIR CATTLE, AND THEIR GOODS, WHICH THEY HAD GOTTEN IN THE LAND OF CANAAN, AND CAME INTO EGYPT, JACOB, AND ALL HIS SEED WITH HIM:

(7) "HIS SONS, AND HIS SONS' SONS WITH HIM, HIS DAUGHTERS, AND HIS SONS' DAUGHTERS, AND ALL HIS SEED BROUGHT HE WITH HIM INTO EGYPT."

The synopsis is:

1. The two names, Jacob and Israel, are used here by the Holy Spirit with great emphasis. When the Patriarch does not believe (Gen. 45:26) he faints and is called *"Jacob"*; when he does believe (Gen. 45:28; 46:1), he takes courage and boldly steps out and is called *"Israel."*

2. God spoke to him in the visions of the night as *"Israel,"* but addressed him as *"Jacob, Jacob"*; just as many, many years later, He spoke to Peter, and said, *"Simon, Simon."* To arrest attention He repeats the name; and to kindle affection and confidence, He uses the personal name and not the official title.

3. God forbade Abraham and Isaac to go down into Egypt. He now encourages Jacob to go, saying: *"I will go with you."* When God promises His Company and Presence, there need be neither hesitation nor fear.

SACRIFICES

Verse 1 reads: *"And Israel took his journey with all that he had, and came to Beer-sheba, and offered sacrifices unto the God of his father Isaac."*

Several things are said here:

We find Jacob starting for Egypt with the Holy Spirit giving him the name *"Israel,"* which reflects a renewed confidence and faith in God Who had originally changed his name. In fact, great and mighty things are happening. He knows it's true, but it's still hard to make himself believe what has just happened. Joseph alive? Yes, not only alive, but the governor over all the land of Egypt. The old man reasons that only God could do such a thing! With those words, *"Joseph is yet alive,"* every question, in essence, has been answered.

As Jacob looks at the wagons, with their sides emblazoned with the seal of Egypt, his mind can hardly contain all that he knows, and no doubt, again and again, the tears of thankfulness and gratitude came freely.

And now he comes to Beer-sheba, where both Abraham, his grandfather, and Isaac, his father, had sojourned for considerable periods, and had erected Altars to Jehovah.

He feels moved upon by the Holy Spirit to *"offer Sacrifices unto God."* He either used the Altar which had been erected by his father Isaac, or else he constructed one himself, for Isaac's Altar could well have been destroyed by vandals.

The Scripture says that he offered *"sacrifices,"* which means that several lambs were offered at this particular time.

THE ALTAR

This Altar represented what all of this was all about. It is the reason for all that Abraham, Isaac, and Jacob were led to do. It is the reason for the miracle birth of Isaac, and the miracle change of Jacob. His sons will form the nucleus of the new nation, which will be called after the name which the Lord has given Jacob — Israel. They will one day, some 255 years later, occupy this land of Canaan, and will rename it, *"Israel."* From this nation will come the Prophets, who will give Israel and the world the Word of God, as well as the great Law of Moses.

All of this is being done for but one purpose, and that is for the entrance of the Son of God into this world, which was prophesied immediately after the Fall in the Garden of Eden (Gen. 3:15). And the very purpose for His Coming would be the Cross, represented by this Altar, and untold numbers of other similar Altars, where Jesus would bleed, suffer, and die, thereby atoning for all sin, that Adam's fallen race might be brought back to God.

So when Jacob kills the little animals, with their hot blood pouring out in a basin, which he no doubt poured out at the base of the Altar, and then placed the carcasses on the Altar, watching the flames consume each one, a picture is presented here of that coming day, when Jesus Christ, as the Lamb of God, will take away the sin of the world (Jn. 1:29; 3:16).

The manner in which the statement is used, *"The God of his father Isaac,"* proclaims the fact that all that Abraham had handed down to Isaac, likewise, Jacob's father had handed down to him. The Doctrine was unsullied, and untainted, which refers to the fact that *"Jesus Christ and Him Crucified,"* was the Foundation of this great Plan of God.

ISRAEL — JACOB

Verse 2 reads: *"And God spoke unto Israel in the visions of the night, and said, Jacob, Jacob. And he said, Here am I."*

This Verse says that: *"God spoke unto Israel."* And yet, when He spoke to him Personally, He said, *"Jacob, Jacob."* Why the seeming contradiction?

Actually, there is no contradiction. When we look at the Second Verse, we are looking at Sanctification in both its positional and conditional form.

The type of Sanctification which God gives to us, which takes place immediately at conversion, refers to our position in Christ, and never changes. Hence Jacob would be called *"Israel"* (*"but you are sanctified"* — I Cor. 6:11). The address by God, saying, *"Jacob, Jacob,"* spoke of Jacob's condition, *"sanctify wholly"* (I Thess. 5:23).

Positional Sanctification is given to us freely by Jesus Christ. We do not earn it or merit it; it is a work of Grace, hence Jacob being referred to as *"Israel."* As well, there is a conditional Sanctification, hence God saying, *"Jacob, Jacob."* This refers to the fact that the Holy Spirit is making every endeavor to bring our *"condition"* up to our *"position."* In fact, this is a lifelong process, and is gained basically in the same manner as our initial Sanctification at conversion — Faith in the Cross. Faith maintained in the Finished Work of Christ guarantees the progress which we as Believers must make, that is, if Christlikeness is to be developed within our lives.

EGYPT

Verses 3 and 4 read: *"And He said, I am God, the God of your father: fear not to go down into Egypt; for I will there make of you a great nation:*

"I will go down with you into Egypt; and I will also surely bring you up again: and Joseph shall put his hand upon your eyes."

The Lord says to Jacob:

• *"I am God"*: In essence, this says, *"I am the El, the Mighty One."* After what Jacob has seen in the last few days, he does not doubt the Power of God.

• *"The God of your father"*: The same Message that God gave to Isaac, He also gives to Jacob. As previously stated, the Message must not be changed in any fashion.

• *"Fear not to go down into Egypt"*: This was evidently said because Jacob obviously had apprehensions about going to Egypt, despite the fact that Joseph had sent for him. Isaac had been forbidden to go there (Gen. 26:2). But the spirit of Jacob is now satisfied, because the Lord tells him to go.

What a delightful episode in his life, that he would take no one's word for this, even his son Joseph, but must have the personal leading of the Lord.

• *"For I will there make of you a great nation"*: Twice it had been predicted by the Lord that Jacob would develop into a multitudinous people (Gen. 28:14; 35:11). The present Promise was an indication that the fulfillment of the prophecy was at hand (Pulpit).

• *"I will go down with you into Egypt"*: This is not the idea of a local deity following them when they change their abodes, and, thereby, confined to the district in which they happen, for the time being, to reside, but a metaphorical expression for the efficiency and completeness of the Divine protection (Kalisch).

• *"And I will also surely bring you up again"*: This spoke of the time that Jacob would die, and his body would be brought back to Canaan for burial.

• *"And Joseph shall put his hand upon your eyes"*: He had never thought to see Joseph again, but the Lord assures him here that he will not only see his son, but will live near him for quite some time, and at the last, Joseph will close Jacob's eyes in death.

EGYPT

Verses 5 through 7 read: *"And Jacob rose up from Beer-sheba: and the sons of Israel carried Jacob their father, and their little ones, and their wives, in the wagons which Pharaoh had sent to carry him.*

"And they took their cattle, and their goods, which they had gotten in the land of Canaan, and came into Egypt, Jacob, and all his seed with him:

"His sons, and his sons' sons with him, his daughters and his sons' daughters, and all his seed brought he with him into Egypt."

Jacob was 130 years old at this time, and this event was 215 years after the call of Abraham. The Children of Israel would stay in Egypt as well, for 215 years. They would also spend some 40 years in the wilderness, before finally going into the Land of Promise.

Pharaoh had told Jacob not to regard his goods, because the good of all the land of Egypt was before him; but the patriarch did not wish to take advantage of the offer, any more than he had to, which was a wise decision on his part.

Out of the great events in God's dealings with the human race, Jacob coming into Egypt with all his family, without a doubt stands high. A threshold is being crossed, and even though it will be some 255 years before Israel will actually possess the Promise, as it regards the land of Canaan, great strides are now being made.

(8) "AND THESE ARE THE NAMES OF THE CHILDREN OF ISRAEL, WHICH CAME INTO EGYPT, JACOB AND HIS SONS: REUBEN, JACOB'S FIRSTBORN.

(9) "AND THE SONS OF REUBEN; HANOCH, AND PHALU, AND HEZRON, AND CARMI.

(10) "AND THE SONS OF SIMEON; JEMUEL, AND JAMIN, AND OHAD, AND JACHIN, AND ZOHAR, AND SHAUL THE SON OF A CANAANITISH WOMAN.

(11) "AND THE SONS OF LEVI; GERSHON, KOHATH, AND MERARI.

(12) "AND THE SONS OF JUDAH; ER, AND ONAN, AND SHELAH, AND PHAREZ, AND ZARAH: BUT ER AND ONAN DIED IN THE LAND OF CANAAN. AND THE SONS OF PHAREZ WERE HEZRON AND HAMUL.

(13) "AND THE SONS OF ISSACHAR; TOLA, AND PHUVAH, AND JOB, AND SHIMRON.

(14) "AND THE SONS OF ZEBULUN; SERED, AND ELON, AND JAHLEEL.

(15) "THESE BE THE SONS OF LEAH, WHICH SHE BEAR UNTO JACOB IN PADAN-ARAM, WITH HIS DAUGHTER DINAH: ALL THE SOULS OF HIS SONS AND HIS DAUGHTERS WERE THIRTY AND THREE.

(16) "AND THE SONS OF GAD; ZIPHION, AND HAGGI, SHUNI, AND EZBON, ERI, AND ARODI, AND ARELI.

(17) "AND THE SONS OF ASHER; JIMNAH, AND ISHUAH, AND ISUI, AND BERIAH, AND SERAH THEIR SISTER: AND THE SONS OF BERIAH; HEBER, AND MALCHIEL.

(18) "THESE ARE THE SONS OF ZILPAH, WHOM LABAN GAVE TO LEAH HIS DAUGHTER, AND THESE SHE BEAR UNTO JACOB, EVEN SIXTEEN SOULS.

(19) "THE SONS OF RACHEL JACOB'S WIFE; JOSEPH, AND BENJAMIN.

(20) "AND UNTO JOSEPH IN THE LAND OF EGYPT WERE BORN MANASSEH AND EPHRAIM, WHICH ASENATH THE DAUGHTER OF POTI-PHERAH PRIEST OF ON BEAR UNTO HIM.

(21) "AND THE SONS OF BENJAMIN WERE BELAH, AND BECHER, AND ASHBEL, GERA, AND NAAMAN, EHI, AND ROSH, MUPPIM, AND HUPPIM, AND ARD.

(22) "THESE ARE THE SONS OF RACHEL, WHICH WERE BORN TO JACOB: ALL THE SOULS WERE FOURTEEN.

NOTES

(23) "AND THE SONS OF DAN; HUSHIM.

(24) "AND THE SONS OF NAPHTALI; JAHZEEL, AND GUNI, AND JEZER, AND SHILLEM.

(25) "THESE ARE THE SONS OF BILHAH, WHICH LABAN GAVE UNTO RACHEL HIS DAUGHTER, AND SHE BEAR THESE UNTO JACOB: ALL THE SOULS WERE SEVEN.

(26) "ALL THE SOULS THAT CAME WITH JACOB INTO EGYPT, WHICH CAME OUT OF HIS LOINS, BESIDES JACOB'S SONS' WIVES, ALL THE SOULS WERE THREESCORE AND SIX;

(27) "AND THE SONS OF JOSEPH, WHICH WERE BORN HIM IN EGYPT, WERE TWO SOULS: ALL THE SOULS OF THE HOUSE OF JACOB, WHICH CAME INTO EGYPT, WERE THREESCORE AND TEN.

(28) "AND HE SENT JUDAH BEFORE HIM UNTO JOSEPH, TO DIRECT HIS FACE UNTO GOSHEN; AND THEY CAME INTO THE LAND OF GOSHEN."

The structure is:

1. In the Eighth Verse, the Holy Spirit once again says, *"Israel,"* and this is because of what He will do with, and make, of this people. Through them, the Messiah will come; hence, *"the Children of Israel."*

2. The *"Church"* of that day began with Abraham and Sarah. By the time of Jacob, the grandson of Abraham, it is somewhat larger. At this present time (2002), it numbers into the tens of millions of people, and I speak of those who are truly saved.

3. Verse 28 says: *"And he sent Judah before him unto Joseph."* Judah had natural traits that made him an outstanding leader of men and one to be trusted. In prophecy, he was destined to have the chief place among the Brethren. His was to be the ruling Tribe through which the Messiah would come and rule all nations forever (Gen. 49:10).

In history, Judah had the ruling part in Israel from David to the Babylonian captivity, a period of nearly 500 years. This Tribe, along with Benjamin and multitudes from all the other Tribes, continued as a nation for about 133 years longer than the apostate northern kingdom of Israel. Judah was the leader in the return from captivity until the Messiah came the first time. Judah, as well,

will be the leading Tribe under the Messiah in the Millennium and forever.

THE CHILDREN OF ISRAEL

We will dispense with our usual procedure as it regards commentary on this genealogy, and will address it according to the following:

In tabulating the number of people given in this genealogy, which came into Egypt, we are actually given three numbers: 66, 70, and then Stephen in Acts 7:14 gives the number as 75.

The apparent confusion in these different numbers will disappear, if it be observed that the first takes no account of Jacob, Joseph, Manasseh, and Ephraim, but with these included in the second computation of 70. And then Stephen simply adds to the 70 of Verse 27 the five grandsons of Joseph who are mentioned in the Septuagint version, from which he quoted, thus making 75 in all. There is thus no irreconcilable contradiction between the Hebrew historian and the Christian Preacher (Pulpit).

THE LINEAGE OF CHRIST

It is from the Tribe of Judah that the Son of Man would come, the Redeemer of the world. Actually, it was through Jacob that the prophecy came, that the Redeemer would come through this particular Tribe (Gen. 49:10). At first, the Lord merely said that the Redeemer would come through the human race (Gen. 3:15). He then said the Redeemer would come through a particular people, all from the loins of Abraham (Gen. 12:1-3). He then predicted, as stated, that from this people, the Redeemer would come from a particular Tribe, Judah. The prediction then came forth that of these people, and from this certain Tribe, the Redeemer would come from a particular family, David (II Sam., Chpt. 7). And then in this family, it would be a Virgin who would bring forth this wondrous Child (Isa. 7:14).

Of the sons of Judah, it would be Pharez who would be in the sacred lineage.

JOB

The *"Job"* mentioned here, the son of Issachar, is the same Job of the Book which bears his name. It is believed that his Book was the first one written, probably written by both Moses and Job, while Moses was in

NOTES

the wilderness some 40 years before delivering Israel. It is known that Job was contemporary with Moses for a number of years, before Job died. In fact, the Book of Job is probably the oldest Book in the world, being written while Moses was in the wilderness, in collaboration with Job, and written before the Book of Genesis was written, etc.

The Book of Job explains the problem why good men are afflicted. It is in order to their Sanctification. It is interesting that this difficult question should be the first taken up and answered in the Bible.

At a point in time, it is obvious that Job left his father Issachar and the land of Egypt, and went into the land of Uz (Gen. 22:20). At what age Job left the land of Egypt, we aren't told; however, he was probably about 70 years of age at the time of his great trial. He lived to be 210.

In brief, the Book of Job proclaims the worthlessness of self, which is the first step in Christian experience, with the Song of Solomon proclaiming the worthfulness of Christ, which is the last step in the Christian experience. It takes awhile for the Believer to climb out over the problem of *"self,"* which must be done before one can fully realize the *"worthfulness of Christ."* But we must remember that the *"Song of Solomon"* can never be reached, until *"Job"* has been passed through.

Job does not symbolize an unconverted, but rather, a converted man. It was necessary that one of God's children should be chosen for this trial; for the subject of the Book is not the conversion of the sinner, but the consecration of the Saint. It is evident that an unconverted man needs to be brought to an end of himself; but that a man who feared God, who was perfect in his worship, and who hated evil should also need this, is not immediately clear. And here comes the mystery of the Book of Job.

God uses Satan, calamity, and sickness to be His instruments in creating character and making men partakers of His Holiness, but with the understanding that those things themselves do not, and in fact cannot create character, etc., but that they draw us to Christ, Who can.

JUDAH

The Twenty-eighth Verse, as stated, proclaims Judah as already taking the lead in the family, and under Joseph we might quickly add. The Tribe of Judah, as also stated, would be the Tribe through which the Prince of Glory would ultimately come.

(29) "AND JOSEPH MADE READY HIS CHARIOT, AND WENT UP TO MEET ISRAEL HIS FATHER, TO GOSHEN, AND PRESENTED HIMSELF UNTO HIM; AND HE FELL ON HIS NECK, AND WEPT ON HIS NECK A GOOD WHILE.

(30) "AND ISRAEL SAID UNTO JOSEPH, NOW LET ME DIE, SINCE I HAVE SEEN YOUR FACE, BECAUSE YOU ARE YET ALIVE.

(31) "AND JOSEPH SAID UNTO HIS BRETHREN, AND UNTO HIS FATHER'S HOUSE, I WILL GO UP, AND SHOW PHARAOH, AND SAY UNTO HIM, MY BRETHREN, AND MY FATHER'S HOUSE, WHICH WERE IN THE LAND OF CANAAN, ARE COME UNTO ME;

(32) "AND THE MEN ARE SHEPHERDS, FOR THEIR TRADE HAS BEEN TO FEED CATTLE; AND THEY HAVE BROUGHT THEIR FLOCKS, AND THEIR HERDS, AND ALL THAT THEY HAVE.

(33) "AND IT SHALL COME TO PASS, WHEN PHARAOH SHALL CALL YOU, AND SHALL SAY, WHAT IS YOUR OCCUPATION?

(34) "THAT YOU SHALL SAY, THY SERVANTS' TRADE HAS BEEN ABOUT CATTLE FROM OUR YOUTH EVEN UNTIL NOW, BOTH WE, AND ALSO OUR FATHERS: THAT YOU MAY DWELL IN THE LAND OF GOSHEN, FOR EVERY SHEPHERD IS AN ABOMINATION UNTO THE EGYPTIANS."

The construction is:

1. In Verse 29, the Holy Spirit refers to the Patriarch as *"Israel,"* as he meets Joseph for the first time in over 20 years. Among other things, the Holy Spirit refers to him as *"Israel"* because of the future meeting that will take place when Israel and the Lord Jesus Christ meet at the Second Coming after such a long estrangement.

2. The Thirtieth Verse portrays the Lord referring again to the Patriarch by using the name *"Israel."* It is because his mission is, by and large, now complete. Actually, he will live some 17 more years, and it will be in great victory.

3. Joseph will meet his father in great splendor and glory, that which was befitting to his station, and which portrays the manner

in which Christ will meet Israel on a coming glad day.

THE MEETING

Verse 29 reads: *"And Joseph made ready his chariot, and went up to meet Israel his father, to Goshen, and presented himself unto him; and he fell on his neck, and wept on his neck a good while."*

Joseph making ready his chariot, and going up to meet his father, tells us very little in the translation; however, in the Hebrew, such terminology is commonly used of the appearance of God or His Angels. It is employed here in this manner to indicate the glory in which Joseph came to meet Jacob.

Joseph's chariot was of the royal house, and was probably unlike anything that Jacob had ever seen. As well, it would have been pulled by the finest and the most beautiful horses. As well, there were probably many attendants and guards with Joseph, also riding in gilded chariots, and dressed in the finery of Egypt. We must remember that Joseph was second only to Pharaoh, and Egypt possibly being the greatest nation in the world, meant that Joseph was the second most powerful man in the world of that time.

As well, Joseph didn't do this solely for his father, but this is actually the manner in which this Prime Minister traveled, which served to exhibit his authority.

But in all of this, there is a greater spiritual meaning. When Jesus came the first time, He came in fact as a humble Peasant. Israel knew Him as the carpenter's son, which means that He definitely was not of the Jewish aristocracy.

But when He comes the second time, He will not come as a peasant, but rather as *"King of kings and Lord of lords."* In fact, as it refers to splendor and glory, there is absolutely nothing that can even remotely compare with that which will accompany Christ when He comes back to this Earth. So when Israel sees Him at that time, and accepts Him as Lord and Saviour, it will be in a glory that beggars all description. In fact, the very planetary bodies of the heavens will dance in glee, so to speak, when our Lord shall come back to Earth again (Mat. 24:29-30). The Creator has now come back to His creation, and we speak of planet Earth, where He will ultimately make

His eternal Headquarters (Rev., Chpts. 21-22). So the meeting of Joseph with his father Jacob is meant to portray that coming day, hence the glory which accompanied Joseph.

The evidence is that Jacob and all of his entourage went first of all to the area called *"Goshen."* It would have been in the area very close to modern Cairo.

How long Jacob had been settled there before Joseph came, we aren't told; however, it could not have been very long, probably only a few days.

When they informed Jacob that Joseph was coming, I wonder what the thoughts were of the great Patriarch. He had never hoped to see Joseph again, and it had been over 20 years since he had laid eyes on him. In fact, Joseph was only 17 years old when he last saw him. He is now about 38 or 39.

When Joseph came into the presence of Jacob, he fell on his neck, which means that he embraced him grandly, with him weeping, as no doubt Jacob did as well. But it was tears this time of joy. Faith has now been honored, as faith will always be honored. In a few moments time, all of the sorrow and heartache of the past 20 years have been wiped away. It's only now a dim memory. Joseph is here, and Joseph is yet alive.

Strangely and beautifully enough, this is the story of Israel. The meeting which we are describing here, prophetically speaking, is yet to take place; however, it is closer now than ever. The seven years of dark trouble are yet to come to Israel, typified by the seven years of famine, but come they shall. And at the end of that seven years of trouble, *"Jacob's trouble,"* Jesus Christ is coming back, and will in fact be the Saviour of Israel, just as Joseph was the Saviour of Israel.

ISRAEL

Verse 30 reads: *"And Israel said unto Joseph, Now let me die, since I have seen your face, because you are yet alive."*

Without a doubt, this was the happiest moment of Jacob's life. That which he never dreamed would happen, has, miracle of miracles, come true.

In the Patriarch's mind, his life's journey had now filled its course. The last earthly longing of his heart had been completely satisfied

He was now ready, whenever God willed, to be gathered to his fathers.

However, the Lord would see fit to allow this great man to live another 17 years, and to enjoy to the fullest the Blessings of God. The Lord had asked Jacob to go through a great sorrow. But He will now make up for that sorrow, and do so manyfold. The Lord will never owe any man anything.

The truth is, the Lord has never owed anyone anything; however, even if He asks us to do something which is difficult, He, and without fail, will always reimburse us, and will do so exactly as He did with Jacob.

Not counting the five grandsons of Joseph, there would have been 70 people there that day, counting all the children, when Joseph met Jacob. What questions the children must have had! Could they understand that Joseph was the lord of Egypt, and yet the son of Jacob, and in essence, their uncle?

The number *"70"* became afterwards a symbolic number among the Israelites — as in the 70 Elders of Moses, the 70 of the Sanhedrin, the 70 Disciples of the Lord, etc. There may be something in the combination of numbers. Seventy is seven times ten. Ten is the Biblical symbol of the complete development of humanity. Seven of perfection. Therefore, 70 may symbolize the elect people of God as the hope of humanity — Israel in Egypt. In the 12 Patriarchs and 70 souls, we certainly see the foreshadowing of the Saviour's appointments in the beginning of the Christian Church. The small number of Israel in the midst of the great multitude of Egypt is a great encouragement to Faith. *"Who has despised the day of small things?"* (Pulpit).

SHEPHERDS

Verses 31 through 34 read: *"And Joseph said unto his brethren, and unto his father's house, I will go up, and show Pharaoh, and say unto him, My brethren, and my father's house, which were in the land of Canaan, are come unto me;*

"And the men are shepherds, for their trade has been to feed cattle; and they have brought their flocks, and their herds, and all that they have.

"And it shall come to pass, when Pharaoh shall call you, and shall say, What is your occupation?

"That you shall say, Your servants' trade has been about cattle from our youth even until now, both we, and also our fathers: that you may dwell in the land of Goshen; for every shepherd is an abomination unto the Egyptians."

Goshen seemed to be the most fertile part of Egypt, at least as it referred to the grazing of cattle and sheep. The Nile River ran through this area, and finally it settled into the marshlands of the Nile Delta, which afforded it much grass, etc.

While flocks of cattle and herds of sheep were held by the Egyptians, and even by Pharaoh, those who attended these flocks and herds were looked down on by the Egyptians. As well, the word *"abomination"* used in Verse 34 as it regards shepherds means, as well, that there was some religious connotation to the attitude of the Egyptians toward shepherds.

At any rate, Joseph does not attempt to conceal from Pharaoh the low caste of the shepherds, his brothers, but he trusts in God that what was an abomination to the Egyptians will be made, by the Grace of God, acceptable.

As well, if they kept to themselves in Goshen, the Israelites were not likely to intermingle with the Egyptians, and thereby to intermarry.

Egypt was an agricultural nation, which meant that her population was made up of farmers. As such, they despised herdsmen. Their monuments picture shepherds as distorted, dirty, and emaciated figures.

"O come, O come, Emmanuel, and ransom captive Israel,
"That mourns in lonely exile here until the Son of God appear.
"Rejoice! Rejoice! Emmanuel shall come to thee,
"O Israel!"

"O come, Thou Rod of Jesse, free Thine Own from Satan's tyranny;
"From depths of Hell Thy people save and give them victory o'er the grave.
"Rejoice! Rejoice! Emmanuel
"Shall come to thee, O Israel!"

"O come, Thou Dayspring, come and cheer our spirits by Thine Advent here;
"And drive away the shades of night, and pierce the clouds and bring us light!
"Rejoice! Rejoice! Emmanuel
"Shall come to thee, O Israel!"

"O come, Thou Key of David, come,
and open wide our Heavenly Home;
"Make safe the way that leads on high,
and close the path to misery.
"Rejoice! Rejoice! Emmanuel
"Shall come to thee, O Israel!"

CHAPTER 47

(1) "THEN JOSEPH CAME AND TOLD PHARAOH, AND SAID, MY FATHER AND MY BRETHREN, AND THEIR FLOCKS, AND THEIR HERDS, AND ALL THAT THEY HAVE, ARE COME OUT OF THE LAND OF CANAAN; AND, BEHOLD, THEY ARE IN THE LAND OF GOSHEN.

(2) "AND HE TOOK SOME OF HIS BRETHREN, EVEN FIVE MEN, AND PRESENTED THEM UNTO PHARAOH.

(3) "AND PHARAOH SAID UNTO HIS BRETHREN, WHAT IS YOUR OCCUPATION? AND THEY SAID UNTO PHARAOH, YOUR SERVANTS ARE SHEPHERDS, BOTH WE, AND ALSO OUR FATHERS.

(4) "THEY SAID MOREOVER UNTO PHARAOH, FOR TO SOJOURN IN THE LAND ARE WE COME; FOR YOUR SERVANTS HAVE NO PASTURE FOR THEIR FLOCKS; FOR THE FAMINE IS SORE IN THE LAND OF CANAAN: NOW THEREFORE, WE PRAY THEE, LET YOUR SERVANTS DWELL IN THE LAND OF GOSHEN.

(5) "AND PHARAOH SPOKE UNTO JOSEPH, SAYING, YOUR FATHER AND YOUR BRETHREN ARE COME UNTO YOU:

(6) "THE LAND OF EGYPT IS BEFORE YOU; IN THE BEST OF THE LAND MAKE YOUR FATHER AND BRETHREN TO DWELL: IN THE LAND OF GOSHEN LET THEM DWELL: AND IF YOU KNOW ANY MEN OF ACTIVITY AMONG THEM, THEN MAKE THEM RULERS OVER MY CATTLE."

The overview is:

1. As far as we know, no one in Egypt ever knew anything about the wickedness of the past deeds of Joseph's brothers; such is true forgiveness. It not only forgives sin, but it forgets as well.

2. Though Joseph was a great man, and despite the fact that his brothers were shepherds,

NOTES

which means that the Egyptians despised such, yet he openly owned them. Despite what we were, our Lord Jesus is not ashamed to call us brethren.

3. That the brothers were shepherds, which Joseph had been as well, served as a Type of the Good Shepherd, Who would someday come!

PHARAOH

Verses 1 and 2 read: *"Then Joseph came and told Pharaoh, and said, My father and my brethren, and their flocks, and their herds, and all that they have, are come out of the land of Canaan; and, behold, they are in the land of Goshen.*

"And he took some of his brethren, even five men, and presented them unto Pharaoh."

In this appearance of Joseph before Pharaoh, it seems that he went in first and told Pharaoh that his father and brethren, with all their flocks, were now in the land of Goshen.

He then brought in five of his brothers, and presented them to Pharaoh, and last of all, he *"brought in Jacob his father, and set him before Pharaoh."*

Joseph wanted his family in Goshen, for that was the best place for pasture. In fact, they were there now; but Joseph must observe protocol and ask permission from Pharaoh before everything can be settled, which he did.

Of course, there was no way that Pharaoh would refuse Joseph. In fact, Joseph, as was overly obvious, was the Saviour of Egypt. Egypt, due to the provisions made by Joseph, in effect is now the Saviour of the world of the Middle East. No nation in that area, the area of the famine, had any sustenance, except Egypt, and this was because of Joseph. Pharaoh owed everything to Joseph, so his request was met with instant approval.

Joseph taking five of his brothers in to see Pharaoh, after he had the first conference, portrays the fact that his request had been granted, which of course I'm sure that he knew it would.

It is interesting as to why he took only five of his brothers. Why not all of them? Quite possibly, five was a very special number to the Egyptians, even as seven later became to Israel.

GOSHEN

Verses 3 through 6 read: *"And Pharaoh said unto his brethren, What is your occupation? And they said unto Pharaoh, Your servants are shepherds, both we, and also our fathers.*

"They said moreover unto Pharaoh, For to sojourn in the land are we come; for your servants have no pasture for their flocks; for the famine is sore in the land of Canaan: now therefore, we pray you, let your servants dwell in the land of Goshen.

"And Pharaoh spoke unto Joseph, saying, Your father and your brethren are come unto you:

"The land of Egypt is before you; and the best of the land make your father and brethren to dwell: in the land of Goshen let them dwell: and if you know any men of activity among them, then make them rulers of my cattle."

Occupations were hereditary among the Egyptians, and thus the five brothers answered Pharaoh that they were shepherds, and that their father and grandfather had been such before them. Consequently, Pharaoh would conclude that in their case no change was possible, or desired, in their mode of life.

They asked for permission to dwell in the land of Goshen, even though Joseph had already received such permission. They were as well merely following protocol.

Pharaoh answered in a bountiful way, telling them that *"the land of Egypt was before them,"* and that they could have anything they desired; however, if it was Goshen they desired, then that's what they would have.

He further added, that if desired, Joseph could give his brothers employment as being over the vast herds of Pharaoh. In other words, they would be working for the State, which more than likely they did, and which these jobs would have been excellent promotions in their case. In other words, they were well taken care of regarding finances.

(7) "AND JOSEPH BROUGHT IN JACOB HIS FATHER, AND SET HIM BEFORE PHARAOH: AND JACOB BLESSED PHARAOH.

(8) "AND PHARAOH SAID UNTO JACOB, HOW OLD ARE YOU?

(9) "AND JACOB SAID UNTO PHARAOH, THE DAYS OF THE YEARS OF MY PILGRIMAGE ARE AN HUNDRED AND THIRTY YEARS: FEW AND EVIL HAVE THE DAYS OF THE YEARS OF MY LIFE BEEN, AND HAVE NOT ATTAINED UNTO THE DAYS OF THE YEARS OF THE LIFE OF MY FATHERS IN THE DAYS OF THEIR PILGRIMAGE.

(10) "AND JACOB BLESSED PHARAOH, AND WENT OUT FROM BEFORE PHARAOH."

The exegesis is:

1. The moment when Joseph revealed himself in his glory to his brethren was when Judah took the sorrow of the aged Israel to heart, and put himself into it. It is a wonderful picture of Christ's revelation of Himself, when Judah, in the latter day, will voice the sorrow of Israel in connection with the rejection of Jesus, the true Joseph (Williams).

2. Joseph is not ashamed of his brethren. He presents them to the great king. Jacob, although he has to confess a short and troubled life, and is himself a despised shepherd, yet blesses the mighty Monarch; *"and without contradiction, the less is blessed of the greater."*

3. The least and most faltering of God's children is superior to the mightiest Monarch; and is conscious of the superiority.

JACOB

Verse 7 reads: *"And Joseph brought in Jacob his father, and set him before Pharaoh: and Jacob blessed Pharaoh."*

In the story of Joseph, we have had a series of meetings which have been astounding in their presentation, and far reaching in their consequences. After bringing in his five brothers to Pharaoh, last of all he brings in his father, Jacob.

What Jacob thought, when as a lowly shepherd he walks into what must have been one of the grandest buildings on the face of the Earth, the palace of Pharaoh, head of the mightiest nation of the world of that day. This is a setting which Jacob, in his wildest dreams, could never have imagined. But yet, it quickly becomes obvious that despite the glory and the splendor of this palatial empire, Jacob is the better. And Pharaoh knew that as well.

He no doubt imagined that the tremendous powers possessed by Joseph, which were

NOTES

unequalled anywhere in the world, had to have their seedbed in the life of this aged Patriarch who stood before them, and he was right. As Pharaoh looks at this aged man, little does he realize, but yet senses, that a power greater than anything he knows resides in the heart of this frail Patriarch. As he looks at Jacob, this heathen never dreams that the man standing before him will be thought of throughout eternal ages as the third one in the great appellative, *"The God of Abraham, Isaac, and Jacob."*

Knowing the protocol of the time, it would have to be that Pharaoh, despite the splendor and glory of his surroundings, and despite the frailty of this aged man, requests that Jacob would bless him. As stated, *"the less is blessed of the better."*

As Jacob reaches out and lays his gnarled, aged hand on the head of Pharaoh and proceeds to bless him, such typifies the coming glad day, when Israel, with Jesus standing by her side, will bless the Gentile world. It will happen at the beginning of the great Millennial Reign, and will last throughout that definite time.

PHARAOH

Verses 8 through 10 read: *"And Pharaoh said unto Jacob, How old are you?*

"And Jacob said unto Pharaoh, The days of the years of my pilgrimage are an hundred and thirty years: few and evil have the days of the years of my life been, and have not attained unto the days of the years of the life of my fathers in the days of their pilgrimage.

"And Jacob blessed Pharaoh, and went out from before Pharaoh."

This was a first for Egypt, for never before had such a prayer been heard within an Egyptian palace. Still, we must believe that the conduct of Pharaoh was mostly due to the effect of Joseph's life and Ministry. One true man is a great power in any country.

Jacob being 130 years old at that time was evidently much older than most, if not all of the people in Egypt as it regards longevity. I think the facts are, at least during this particular period of time, that those who served the Lord, as a whole, lived much longer than their contemporaries in the heathen world. I think this was true then in Egypt, and I think it was true in all other countries as well.

From the Text, it seems that Pharaoh knew that Jacob was very aged, just by looking at him; consequently, he asked him his age, with Jacob replying that he was 130. I doubt seriously that there was anyone in Egypt that was 100 years old, much less the age of Jacob.

But yet, as Jacob confesses, he is not as old as his fathers. In fact, he will die at 147 years of age, some 17 years after coming into Egypt. His grandfather Abraham died at 175, and his father Isaac at 180.

(11) "AND JOSEPH PLACED HIS FATHER AND HIS BRETHREN, AND GAVE THEM A POSSESSION IN THE LAND OF EGYPT, IN THE BEST OF THE LAND, IN THE LAND OF RAMESES, AS PHARAOH HAD COMMANDED.

(12) "AND JOSEPH NOURISHED HIS FATHER, AND HIS BRETHREN, AND ALL HIS FATHER'S HOUSEHOLD, WITH BREAD, ACCORDING TO THEIR FAMILIES.

(13) "AND THERE WAS NO BREAD IN ALL THE LAND; FOR THE FAMINE WAS VERY SORE, SO THAT THE LAND OF EGYPT AND ALL THE LAND OF CANAAN FAINTED BY REASON OF THE FAMINE.

(14) "AND JOSEPH GATHERED UP ALL THE MONEY THAT WAS FOUND IN THE LAND OF EGYPT, AND IN THE LAND OF CANAAN, FOR THE CORN WHICH THEY BOUGHT: AND JOSEPH BROUGHT THE MONEY INTO PHARAOH'S HOUSE.

(15) "AND WHEN MONEY FAILED IN THE LAND OF EGYPT, AND IN THE LAND OF CANAAN, ALL THE EGYPTIANS CAME UNTO JOSEPH, AND SAID, GIVE US BREAD: FOR WHY SHOULD WE DIE IN YOUR PRESENCE? FOR THE MONEY FAILETH.

(16) "AND JOSEPH SAID, GIVE YOUR CATTLE; AND I WILL GIVE YOU FOR YOUR CATTLE, IF MONEY FAIL.

(17) "AND THEY BROUGHT THEIR CATTLE UNTO JOSEPH: AND JOSEPH GAVE THEM BREAD IN EXCHANGE FOR HORSES, AND FOR THE FLOCKS, AND FOR THE CATTLE OF THE HERDS, AND FOR THE ASSES, AND HE FED THEM WITH BREAD FOR ALL THEIR CATTLE FOR THAT YEAR.

(18) "WHEN THAT YEAR WAS ENDED, THEY CAME UNTO HIM THE SECOND YEAR,

AND SAID UNTO HIM, WE WILL NOT HIDE IT FROM MY LORD, HOW THAT OUR MONEY IS SPENT; MY LORD ALSO HAS OUR HERDS OF CATTLE; THERE IS NOT OUGHT LEFT IN THE SIGHT OF MY LORD, BUT OUR BODIES AND OUR LANDS:

(19) "WHEREFORE SHALL WE DIE BEFORE YOUR EYES, BOTH WE AND OUR LAND? BUY US AND OUR LAND FOR BREAD, AND WE AND OUR LAND WILL BE SERVANTS UNTO PHARAOH: AND GIVE US SEED, THAT WE MAY LIVE, AND NOT DIE, THAT THE LAND BE NOT DESOLATE.

(20) "AND JOSEPH BOUGHT ALL THE LAND OF EGYPT FOR PHARAOH; FOR THE EGYPTIANS SOLD EVERY MAN HIS FIELD, BECAUSE THE FAMINE PREVAILED OVER THEM: SO THE LAND BECAME PHARAOH'S.

(21) "AND AS FOR THE PEOPLE, HE REMOVED THEM TO CITIES FROM ONE END OF THE BORDERS OF EGYPT EVEN TO THE OTHER END THEREOF.

(22) "ONLY THE LAND OF THE PRIESTS BOUGHT HE NOT; FOR THE PRIESTS HAD A PORTION ASSIGNED THEM OF PHARAOH, AND DID EAT THEIR PORTION WHICH PHARAOH GAVE THEM: WHEREFORE THEY SOLD NOT THEIR LANDS.

(23) "THEN JOSEPH SAID UNTO THE PEOPLE, BEHOLD, I HAVE BOUGHT YOU THIS DAY AND YOUR LAND FOR PHARAOH: LO, HERE IS SEED FOR YOU, AND YOU SHALL SOW THE LAND.

(24) "AND IT SHALL COME TO PASS IN THE INCREASE, THAT YOU SHALL GIVE THE FIFTH PART UNTO PHARAOH, AND FOUR PARTS SHALL BE YOUR OWN, FOR SEED OF THE FIELD, AND FOR YOUR FOOD, AND FOR THEM OF YOUR HOUSEHOLDS, AND FOR FOOD FOR YOUR LITTLE ONES.

(25) "AND THEY SAID, YOU HAVE SAVED OUR LIVES: LET US FIND GRACE IN THE SIGHT OF MY LORD, AND WE WILL BE PHARAOH'S SERVANTS.

(26) "AND JOSEPH MADE IT A LAW OVER THE LAND OF EGYPT UNTO THIS DAY, THAT PHARAOH SHOULD HAVE THE FIFTH PART, EXCEPT THE LAND OF THE PRIESTS ONLY, WHICH BECAME NOT PHARAOH'S."

NOTES

The overview is:

1. Joseph, raised from the pit to the throne, a Type of Christ, enriches his brethren with all the promises, which they, by their rejection of him, had forfeited, but which are now, upon the ground of Grace, restored to them.

2. At the same time they are given the richest province in Egypt.

3. The Egyptians, themselves representative of all the nations of the Earth, are saved from death by Joseph, and made by him the willing slaves of the throne, and their future assured to them. All of this is a striking picture of what has yet to come to pass, but most definitely shall! This is the subject of Romans, Chapters 9, 10, and 11, in which it is pointed out that Israel and the Gentile will inherit the Promises, in fellowship, solely upon the ground of pure Grace.

4. Joseph was the greatest benefactor Egypt ever had. In one day, by Divine wisdom, he destroyed slavery and landlordism. He set up only one master and one landlord in the nation, and that was the nation itself, as physically embodied in Pharaoh (Williams).

With this portion, we will as well dispense with our usual procedure.

THE SEVEN YEARS OF FAMINE

From this account, we learn just how severe this famine actually was. And had it not been for Joseph, no doubt, hundreds of thousands, if not millions, would have died of starvation. But because of the Divine wisdom given to him, he was able to forecast the famine, lay in store for that coming time, and then again by Divine wisdom was able to nourish the people as the famine became more and more severe.

The people seemed to have done fairly well the first year of the famine, and possibly even the second year, but by the time of the third year, the situation had become critical, and remained that way, even growing steadily worse, to the conclusion of this terrible seven year period.

When Joseph levied the 20 percent tax, this was one of the fairest arrangements that any people had ever known. In fact, it is seldom equaled in any country presently. For instance, at this particular time (2002), counting State, local, and Federal income taxes, it approximates 50 percent in the United States.

DIVINE WISDOM

Some have claimed that Joseph robbed the Egyptians of their liberties, and converted a free people into a horde of abject slaves. Nothing could be further from the truth.

In fact, had it not been for Joseph, and the Divine wisdom which he was given during this extremely trying time, as stated, millions of people would literally have starved to death. As it was, the people were looked after, and there is no record that anyone starved.

As well, when the famine ended, and once again crops could be grown with the assurance of a bountiful harvest, Joseph allowed all the people to go back to their original land plots, and even gave them seed, equipment, and animals to work the land, with Pharaoh only getting 20 percent. To be frank, and as stated, that was and is an excellent arrangement.

(27) "AND ISRAEL DWELT IN THE LAND OF EGYPT, IN THE COUNTRY OF GOSHEN; AND THEY HAD POSSESSIONS THEREIN, AND GREW, AND MULTIPLIED EXCEEDINGLY.

(28) "AND JACOB LIVED IN THE LAND OF EGYPT SEVENTEEN YEARS: SO THE WHOLE AGE OF JACOB WAS AN HUNDRED FORTY AND SEVEN YEARS.

(29) "AND THE TIME DREW NIGH THAT ISRAEL MUST DIE: AND HE CALLED HIS SON JOSEPH, AND SAID UNTO HIM, IF NOW I HAVE FOUND GRACE IN YOUR SIGHT, PUT, I PRAY YOU, YOUR HAND UNDER MY THIGH, AND DEAL KINDLY AND TRULY WITH ME; BURY ME NOT, I PRAY YOU, IN EGYPT:

(30) "BUT I WILL LIE WITH MY FATHERS, AND YOU SHALL CARRY ME OUT OF EGYPT, AND BURY ME IN THEIR BURYING PLACE. AND HE SAID, I WILL DO AS YOU HAVE SAID.

(31) "AND HE SAID, SWEAR UNTO ME, AND HE SWEAR UNTO HIM. AND ISRAEL BOWED HIMSELF UPON THE BED'S HEAD."

The synopsis is:

1. In Verse 27, the nation for the first time is called "Israel."

NOTES

2. Feeble as was his body, and imperfect as was his faith, as all faith regrettably is imperfect, yet did Jacob esteem God's land, the land of Canaan, and the promises connected therewith, as unspeakably superior to Egypt with all its glory!

3. He makes Joseph swear that when he dies, he will put his bones where his heart was, in the land of Canaan.

ISRAEL

Verse 27 reads: *"And Israel dwelt in the land of Egypt, in the country of Goshen; and they had possessions therein, and grew, and multiplied exceedingly."*

They came in 70 strong, and would leave out about 215 years later, upwards of three million people.

Horton says: *"This is a summary Verse letting us know that though Israel's family came to Egypt intending to stay temporarily, they continued to live in Goshen and settled down to stay. They were prosperous and kept increasing in number."*

After the death of Joseph, there would come a day that a Pharaoh would occupy the throne, who held no affection for Joseph, or the Hebrews; consequently, he would make slaves of them.

But had that not been done, Israel would have had no desire whatsoever to leave Egypt, and in fact, would not have left. The Lord has to allow many things which are negative to come our way, in order for us to desire to do His Will. However, we will save commentary on that particular thought until we reach that specific time.

CANAAN LAND

Verses 28 through 31 read: *"And Jacob lived in the land of Egypt seventeen years: so the whole age of Jacob was an hundred forty and seven years.*

"And the time drew nigh that Israel must die: and he called his son Joseph, and said unto him, If now I have found grace in your sight, put, I pray you, your hand under my thigh, and deal kindly and truly with me; bury me not, I pray you, in Egypt:

"But I will lie with my fathers, and you shall carry me out of Egypt, and bury me in their burying place. And he said, I will do as you have said.

"And he said, Swear unto me. And he swear unto him. And Israel bowed himself upon the bed's head."

As previously stated, Jacob lived some 17 years in Egypt after arriving in that land, dying at 147 years old. However, he had brought about the sons who would make up the great Tribes of Israel, which would ultimately give the world the Word of God, and as well, serve as the womb of the Messiah. They were also meant to evangelize the world, but failed in that prospect, but will fulfill that also in the coming Millennial Reign, after having accepted Christ as their Messiah, Lord, and Saviour, which they will do at the Second Coming.

Jacob's life had been lived in the following places:

Born in Canaan, he had lived 77 years in that land, then 20 years in Padan-aram. He then lived 33 years in Canaan again, and now 17 in Egypt, 147 years in all.

Now the great Patriarch comes down to die. But first, he will gloriously predict the future of his sons, or rather the Tribes over which they will serve as the head.

Mackintosh has a beautiful statement concerning Jacob's last days. He said: *"The close of Jacob's career stands in most pleasing contrast with all the previous scenes of his eventful history. It reminds one of a serene evening after a tempestuous day: the sun, which during the day had been hidden from view by clouds, mists, and fogs, sets in majesty and brightness, gilding with its beams the western sky, and holding out the cheering prospect of a bright tomorrow. Thus is it with our aged Patriarch. The supplanting, the bargain-making, the cunning, the management, the shifting, the shuffling, the unbelieving selfish fears, all those dark clouds of nature and of Earth seem to have passed away, and he comes forth, and all the calm elevation of faith, to bestow blessings, and impart dignities, in that holy skillfulness which communion with God can alone impart."*

Jacob realizes, and graphically so, that God has blessed him exceedingly. The son he never hoped to see again now stands by his side. And not only that, his son is the Prime Minister of the greatest nation on Earth.

NOTES

Along with that, the entirety of his family has been given the choice part of Egypt in which to dwell and to pasture their flocks. And for some 17 years, he has lived a life of serenity, peace, and blessing, all coupled with the Presence of the Lord.

However, as wonderful as all of this is, Egypt, with all its glory, is not his home. His heart is in Canaan land, that Promised Land which God promised to his grandfather Abraham, calling him out of Ur of the Chaldees, and then his father, Isaac. The Promise had been just as clear to him as well.

So he makes Joseph promise, even swear, that he will not bury him in Egypt, but that he will put his remains where his heart is — in the land of Canaan, which will one day be called *"Israel."*

The Twenty-ninth Verse refers to Jacob as *"Israel,"* and because his Faith shines brightly. He faces the prospect of death with his Faith in the Promise. It was so real to the Patriarch, so outstanding, that he even had Joseph to put his hand under his thigh, the procreative part of man, signifying that a birth will take place in that land of Promise, exactly as the Lord has stated. When Joseph did as his father demanded, promising that he would carry him out of Egypt, and bury him in the burying place of his grandfather Abraham, and his father Isaac, the Scripture says that Jacob, i.e., *"Israel,"* bowed down on the head of his bed in praise and worship, which indicates that he was now satisfied.

Hebrews 11:21 says Jacob *"worshipped leaning on the top of his staff."* But there is no contradiction. These are two different incidents.

Jacob's feelings concerning Egypt and the Promised Land should be our feelings as well as it regards this world and the portals of Glory. Even though this present world can have some attractions, just as Egypt did for Jacob and his family, we must understand that this present world is not our abode. Our future is not here, but rather with the Lord in Glory. No matter its present attractions, there is a *"better country,"* awaiting us on the other side. We must live our lives accordingly, with our roots in the Promises of God rather than in this fleeting world.

*"Oh, teach me what it means, that
Cross lifted high*
*"With One — the Man of Sorrows —
condemned to bleed and die!*
*"Oh teach me what it cost Thee to make
a sinner whole;*
*"And teach me, Saviour, teach me the
value of a soul!"*

*"Oh, teach me what it means — that
sacred crimson tide —*
*"The blood and water flowing from
Thine Own wounded side*
*"Teach me that if none other had
sinned, but I alone,*
*"Yet still, Thy Blood, Lord Jesus, Thine
only, must atone."*

*"Oh, teach me what it means — Thy
love beyond compare;*
*"The love that reaches deeper, than
depths of self despair!*
*"Yeah, teach me, till there gloweth in
this cold heart of mine,*
*"Some feeble, pale reflection of that
pure love of Thine."*

*"Oh, teach me what it means, for I am
full of sin;*
*"And Grace alone can reach me, and
love alone can win.*
*"Oh, teach me, for I need Thee — I have
no hope beside,*
*"The chief of all the sinners for whom
the Saviour died!"*

*"Oh infinite Redeemer! I bring no
other plea,*
*"Because Thou dost invite me, I cast
myself on Thee.*
*"Because Thou dost accept me, I love
and I adore;*
*"Because Thy love constraineth, I'll
praise Thee evermore!"*

CHAPTER 48

(1) "AND IT CAME TO PASS AFTER THESE THINGS, THAT ONE TOLD JOSEPH, BEHOLD, YOUR FATHER IS SICK: AND HE TOOK WITH HIM HIS TWO SONS, MANASSEH AND EPHRAIM.

(2) "AND ONE TOLD JACOB, AND SAID, BEHOLD, YOUR SON JOSEPH COMES UNTO YOU: AND ISRAEL STRENGTHENED HIMSELF, AND SAT UPON THE BED.

(3) "AND JACOB SAID UNTO JOSEPH, GOD ALMIGHTY APPEARED UNTO ME AT LUZ IN THE LAND OF CANAAN, AND BLESSED ME,

(4) "AND SAID UNTO ME, BEHOLD, I WILL MAKE YOU FRUITFUL, AND MULTIPLY YOU, AND I WILL MAKE OF YOU A MULTITUDE OF PEOPLE; AND WILL GIVE THIS LAND TO YOUR SEED AFTER YOU FOR AN EVERLASTING POSSESSION.

(5) "AND NOW YOUR TWO SONS, EPHRAIM AND MANASSEH, WHICH WERE BORN UNTO YOU IN THE LAND OF EGYPT BEFORE I CAME UNTO YOU INTO EGYPT ARE MINE; AS REUBEN AND SIMEON, THEY SHALL BE MINE.

(6) "AND YOUR ISSUE, WHICH YOU BEGETTEST AFTER THEM, SHALL BE YOURS, AND SHALL BE CALLED AFTER THE NAME OF THEIR BRETHREN IN THEIR INHERITANCE.

(7) "AND AS FOR ME, WHEN I CAME FROM PADAN, RACHEL DIED BY ME IN THE LAND OF CANAAN IN THE WAY, WHEN YET THERE WAS BUT A LITTLE WAY TO COME INTO EPHRATH: AND I BURIED HER THERE IN THE WAY OF EPHRATH; THE SAME IS BETH-LEHEM."

The structure is:

1. Hebrews 11:21 throws much light on the beautiful Forty-eighth Chapter of Genesis. In fact, in Chapters 48 and 49, Jacob shines as never before. If it is to be noted, the Holy Spirit refers to him again and again as *"Israel."* This is the great Faith action of his life. Feeble and dying, and having nothing except the staff on which he leaned and worshipped, he yet bestowed vast and unseen possessions on his grandsons.

2. In Verses 3 and 4, Jacob reiterates the great appearance of the Lord, as the Lord appeared to him on a bygone day. He calls Him *"God Almighty,"* which means, *"The Great Provider."* In this, he is telling Joseph that God will continue to provide. Jacob is dying, but God will not die, and neither will His Promises.

3. In Verse 5, he makes the two sons of Joseph, Ephraim and Manasseh, his own.

What an honor for those two boys, who would head up great Tribes in Israel. Faith can reach out and claim that which actually isn't, and make it so!

JOSEPH AND JACOB

Verses 1 and 2 read: *"And it came to pass after these things, that one told Joseph, Behold, your father is sick: and he took with him his two sons, Manasseh and Ephraim.*

"And one told Jacob, and said, Behold, your son Joseph comes unto you: and Israel strengthened himself, and sat upon the bed."

Several things are said here:

1. When Joseph is informed that his father Jacob is ill, he hastens to go to his side, knowing that the old man doesn't have long left. But the Spirit of the Lord impresses Joseph to take his two sons, Manasseh and Ephraim with him. In fact, great spiritual consequences will be involved. These boys must have been about 18 or 20 years old at the time.

2. Joseph wants his two sons to know and realize that even though they have been born in Egypt, and all they have ever known is Egypt, still, they aren't Egyptians, but rather of the house of Jacob, i.e., *"Israelites."*

Such is a portrayal of Believers born in this present world, but nevertheless not of this world, but rather of the world to come.

And finally, the significance of the change of name from *"Jacob"* to *"Israel,"* is not to be overlooked. By Faith (it is always Faith), the great Patriarch, moved upon by the Lord, will claim the Promises, and chart the course of Israel. Though the eyes of the Patriarch are, in the natural, very dim, even as we shall see, his Faith burns brightly, actually, brighter than ever, hence he is called *"Israel."*

GOD ALMIGHTY

Verses 3 and 4 read: *"And Jacob said unto Joseph, God Almighty appeared unto me at Luz in the land of Canaan, and blessed me,*

"And said unto me, Behold, I will make you fruitful, and multiply you, and I will make of you a multitude of people; and will give this land to your seed after you for an everlasting possession."

Jacob refers to God as *"El Shaddai,"* using the same name which God had used of

Himself, when He appeared to the Patriarch at Beth-el, which was after the sad experience of Shechem (Gen. 35:7-15).

Along with relating this glorious experience, Jacob will also bring the Promise in view. First of all, he proclaims to Joseph that even though the Promises of God may seem to be so grand and glorious that they are beyond our reach, God, in fact, will provide, and every single promise will be fulfilled.

As well, the Promise of which he speaks is not material blessings, for Joseph already had that, and so did his sons, and Jacob as well. He was looking beyond all of that, to something of far greater magnitude. He was looking toward the purpose and reason for which this family had been raised up, brought from the loins of Abraham and the womb of Sarah.

The *"Great Provider,"* God Almighty, El Shaddai, would provide a Redeemer, Who would come into this world to restore the lost sons of Adam's fallen race. This is what all of this is all about! This is the purpose and reason for the struggle! It is to look forward to the Light that will ultimately dispel the darkness, the Salvation which will ultimately dispel the sin, the Life which will ultimately dispel the death, and the freedom which will ultimately dispel the bondage. All of this will be wrapped up in one Man, *"The Man Christ Jesus."*

Jacob again reiterates the glorious appearing of the Lord to him at Beth-el, when the great Promises were affirmed and reaffirmed.

A great multitude of people will come from Jacob, even as the Patriarch reminds Joseph. In fact, about 200 years later, they would number approximately three million strong.

But as well, Jacob reminds Joseph that Egypt is not their everlasting possession, but rather only a temporal possession. Canaan is that everlasting possession, and Canaan they will have. Joseph is to understand this, and so are his two sons.

And let the Reader understand that as it regards the land of Israel, even presently (2002), it belongs to Israel and not the Palestinians, or anyone else, and will belong to them forever and forever. When God said, *"everlasting possession,"* He meant exactly what He said.

OPPOSITION TO THE PROMISE

Though God promises something, not at all means that Satan will not oppose the Promise, and actually the fulfillment of the Promise. He will do everything within his power to keep it from being fulfilled. And let the Reader understand that the one ingredient he will fight is Faith, and it is because it is Faith that will claim and possess the Promise.

However, as Faith possesses the Promise, Faith also dispels the opposition. And once again, allow us to state the fact that the faith of which we speak is always Faith in *"Christ and Him Crucified"* (I Cor. 1:23; 2:2). Even though Jacob would not have understood the terminology I have just used, still, this as well is what his Faith would ultimately produce, and in fact, what it was meant to produce all along.

In essence, one might say that all in the Old Testament had Faith in the Prophetic Jesus, while we now have Faith in the historical Jesus, as well as the prophetical Jesus. Historically, He has come, lived, died, ascended, and is now exalted at the Right Hand of the Father on high (Heb. 1:2-3). Prophetically, He is coming again, and is coming to rule and reign upon this Earth for 1,000 years, during which time Israel and every Saint of God will reign with Him. And to be sure, we speak of every Saint who has ever lived, even from the dawn of time (I Thess. 4:13-18).

THE STRUGGLE OF FAITH

Let the Believer always know and understand that the struggle in which he is engaged, and in fact will be engaged until the Trump sounds, or the Lord calls us home, is a struggle of Faith. That's the reason the great Apostle told Timothy: *"Fight the good fight of faith, lay hold on eternal life, whereunto you are also called, and have professed a good profession before many witnesses"* (I Tim. 6:12).

While it is a *"fight,"* it is at the same time a *"good fight,"* and because it is a fight that we will win. This *"fight"* lays hold on eternal life, and *"professes a good profession before many witnesses,"* meaning that we are fighting the same fight of faith that Jacob fought, and in fact, all others who have gone before us, and have been victorious in this conflict.

This means that in the final, it is not a struggle with finances, with physical well-being, with domestical situations, or social implications, but rather that which is spiritual. It all comes down to the Promises of God, which is ensconced in His Word, which proclaims our victorious supremacy, and all brought about because of Who Jesus is, and What He did, and I speak of His Finished Work on the Cross. That is the fight of faith we are called upon to engage. It transcends all other struggles, and if we succeed in that, we succeed in all.

THE MESSAGE OF THE CROSS

The story of the Bible is the story of the Cross, even as the story of the Cross is the story of the Bible.

About 170 times in his 14 Epistles, Paul uses the term *"in Christ,"* or one of its derivatives, such as *"in the Lord Jesus,"* or *"in Him,"* etc. Those two words, *"in Christ,"* in effect say it all.

It refers to Christ and what He did for us at the Cross, which He, in effect, did as our Substitute and Representative Man (I Cor. 15:45-50). Simple Faith in Christ places us in His Death, Burial, and Resurrection (Rom. 6:3-5). The Cross is where the victory was won, and it is where the victory is maintained.

THE RESURRECTION

While the Resurrection is extremely important, even as would be obvious, our Redemption does not rest in the Resurrection, but rather the Cross. Many things prove this.

Some people act as if the Resurrection of Christ was in doubt. It wasn't! On the Cross, Jesus atoned for all sin, past, present, and future. If He had failed to atone for even one sin, due to the fact that the wages of sin is death, He could not have risen from the dead, meaning that Satan, legally, could have kept Him in the death world. But Satan could not keep Him there, and because he had no legal right to keep Him there. With all sin atoned, Satan's legal right of death was abrogated.

So there was no doubt as to the Resurrection of Christ. Satan was not only not going to hold Him in the death world, he was not even going to try, and because he had no right to do so.

At the moment Jesus died on the Cross, there is every evidence that the Holy Spirit actually told Him when to die, which He did, by simply breathing out His life (Heb. 9:14). This means that His death was not an execution, but was rather a Sacrifice. No man took His life from Him; He offered it up freely (Jn. 10:17-18).

The moment He died, the Scripture says: *"And, behold, the Veil of the Temple was rent in twain from the top to the bottom"* (Mat. 27:51).

The *"Veil"* in the Temple separated the Holy Place from the Holy of Holies. No one was allowed to go into the Holy of Holies, with the exception of the High Priest, and he could only go in once a year, and not without blood from the sacrifice. But the Veil being ripped from top to bottom, and done so by God, proclaimed to the entirety of mankind, and for all time, that the price was now paid. Jesus had died on the Cross, atoning for all sin, that *"whosoever will may come and drink of the water of life freely"* (Rev. 22:17). In other words, anyone, the vilest sinner, due to what Christ did at the Cross, and our Faith in that Finished Work, can come directly to the Throne of God, where he will always find pardon and peace.

Now, if Redemption awaited the Resurrection to be complete, the Veil in the Temple would have rent or torn when Jesus was resurrected. But God did not wait for the Resurrection, and because, even though the Resurrection is of supreme significance, it was the Cross which afforded Redemption, and which afforded Redemption in totality (Eph. 2:13-18; Col. 2:14-15; Rom. 6:3-5).

We sometimes use the term that we are *"people of the Resurrection."* That is correct, but only as we properly understand what we are saying. Paul said:

"For if we have been planted together in the likeness of His death, we shall be also in the likeness of His Resurrection" (Rom. 6:5).

This means that all that His Resurrection affords cannot be had or held unless we first of all understand that we have this not because of His Resurrection, but rather because we know and understand that *"we have been planted together in the likeness of His death."*

Let not the Reader think that we are minimizing the significance of the Resurrection

in any fashion. We aren't! We are merely putting it in its proper place. In fact, the Death, Burial, Resurrection, Ascension, and Exaltation of Christ are all looked at as *"The Finished Work"* (Heb. 1:2-3). Correspondingly, we should think of His Finished Work in that capacity. But at the same time, we should know that it is the Cross which is the primary objective, and the Cross which made everything possible. That's the reason that Paul also said:

"But God forbid that I should glory, save in the Cross of our Lord Jesus Christ, by Whom the world is crucified unto me, and I unto the world" (Gal. 6:14).

He didn't say: *"But God forbid that I should glory, save in the Resurrection. . . ."*

As well, he said: *"For Christ sent me not to baptize, but to preach the Gospel: not with wisdom of words, lest the Cross of Christ should be made of none effect"* (I Cor. 1:17).

He didn't say: *"Lest the Resurrection of Christ should be made of none effect."*

He also said, *"But we preach Christ crucified"* (I Cor. 1:23). He didn't say, *"But we preach Christ resurrected."*

Again I emphasize that the Resurrection was of supreme significance. One might say that it was the ratification of all that had been done on the Cross. But still, it is the Cross to which we must look, and because it was at the Cross that Christ atoned for all sin, thereby satisfying the demands of the broken Law, which then abrogated Satan's legal right to hold man in captivity. His legal right is *"sin,"* but with all sin atoned, he has lost that legal right. So the bondage in which he now holds mankind is a pseudo-bondage, and he does so by a pseudo-authority, meaning that it's authority that we give him, whether in an unsaved state, or even as a Believer.

SATAN'S PSEUDO-AUTHORITY

What do we mean by the term *"pseudo-authority"*?

We are meaning that Satan really doesn't have the authority to hold a single soul in captivity, Jesus having finished the work of Atonement at the Cross. So if he doesn't have the authority to do so, how is it that most of the world is still under Satanic domination, with even most Christians falling into this category?

The unsaved are held in bondage by Satan, simply because they have not availed themselves of the great Redemption afforded by Christ at the Cross. They refuse to believe, and faith, being the means by which Redemption is afforded (Jn. 3:16), Satan can continue to hold them in bondage by and through a pseudo-authority.

When it comes to Christians, in fact, it is the same principle. Whenever you as a Believer came to Christ, you did so by simply evidencing faith in Christ, which means that you then received Salvation, because you were *"born again"* (Jn. 3:3). Satan's authority over you was then broken.

But regrettably, after conversion, many, if not most, Christians, and because of erroneous teaching, then try to maintain their Salvation by a system of works and performance, which means they are not continuing to evidence faith in Christ and the Cross. In effect, they are giving Satan a pseudo-authority over them, and because their faith is misplaced. Now remember this:

It is never the quantity of faith, but always the quality of faith. And the quality of faith is brought about by the correct object of faith, which must always be the Cross. When we evidence Faith in the Cross, and keep our Faith in the Cross, we rob Satan of any authority he might have. Jesus has atoned for all sin, and by keeping our Faith in the Finished Work of Christ, Satan has no more authority over us (Col. 2:14-15).

MY PERSONAL EXPERIENCE

While personal experiences are not to be taken as examples, that is within themselves, if, however, personal experiences line up totally with the Word of God, they most definitely then can serve as examples.

For some five years, even on a daily basis, and with tears, I sought the Lord, asking Him to reveal to me the way of victorious living. And when I speak of *"victorious living,"* I'm not speaking of victory some of the time, but victory all of the time.

In respect to this petition, I began to cry to the Lord in October of 1991. In 1996, the Lord began to answer that prayer. I use the word *"began,"* simply because the Revelation which He began to give to me has continued unto

this hour, and I speak of its expansion, and which I believe it will ever continue and ever expand. The reason is simple: this great Covenant of Grace is *"an Everlasting Covenant."* In fact, the term is used *"through the Blood of the Everlasting Covenant,"* proclaiming the fact that it is the Cross which made possible this great Covenant, and made possible its everlasting duration. The price was fully paid; therefore, it can be everlasting (Heb. 13:20).

The first thing the Lord showed me was an explanation of the *"sin nature,"* as Paul explained it in Romans, Chapter 6. He then showed me that total and complete victory over the sin nature is maintained by Faith in the Cross of Christ, and in fact, Faith continuing in the Cross of Christ. This is the way, and in fact, the only way, to the victorious, overcoming, Christian life. This is the manner in which we *"walk the walk,"* so to speak!

What the Lord gave me is exactly what he gave to the Apostle Paul, even as Paul explained it in Romans, Chapter 6. In Chapter 7 of Romans, the great Apostle went on to give his own personal experience, of trying to live for God with his faith misplaced. Instead of Faith in the Cross, it was rather faith in *"self,"* which God, the Holy Spirit, can never condone or honor. Paul bluntly said in Romans 8:8, *"So then they who are in the flesh cannot please God."* In fact, the great Apostle referred to Believers as *"spiritual adulterers,"* who try to live for God by placing their faith in something other than Christ and what He did for us at the Cross (Rom. 7:1-4). In other words, such a Christian is being unfaithful to his Lord. As should be obvious, that's quite an indictment!

As the Lord continued to open up this Revelation to me, I found that the manner in which the Lord explained the meaning of the New Covenant to me is the same way in which He gave it to Paul. It is obvious to all in Romans, Chapter 6. The Lord explained to Paul the meaning of the sin nature, and how to have victory through the Cross. And as by now should be obvious, that was not only for Paul, but as well for all other Believers.

THEOLOGICAL AND MORAL

Even though I have already addressed these things in this Volume, because of their great significance, please permit me to look again at the following:

The way of the Cross demands a change. And that change is total in its complexion and total in its movement.

Satan has been very successful at pulling the Faith of the Church away from the Cross to other things. He really doesn't care what the other things are, or how holy they might be in their own right, just so it's not the Cross. That's why Paul said, as stated, *"Christ sent me not to baptize"* (I Cor. 1:17). Paul wasn't denigrating Water Baptism, but rather telling Believers that their emphasis must always be on the Cross, and never on the side issues, as important as they might be in their own right.

I suppose that the greatest weapon that Satan has used in these last several decades to destroy Faith in the Cross, has been the *"Word of Faith Message."* Now that particular name or title may definitely include people who do not have erroneous doctrines, but for the most part, it refers to an erroneous direction.

As Judaism was the great hindrance to the Message of Grace during the time of Paul, the so-called *"Faith Message"* is the great hindrance presently. In fact, in my opinion, it is worse even than Judaism.

First of all, the faith which is proposed is really no faith at all, at least that which God will recognize. And let us say it again:

If it's not Faith in *"Jesus Christ and Him Crucified,"* then it's not Faith that God will recognize (I Cor. 1:17-18, 21, 23; 2:2; Col. 2:14-15; Eph. 2:13-18). The *"Word of Faith"* teaching totally denigrates the Cross. It is referred to as *"past miseries,"* or even as *"the greatest defeat in human history."* It also teaches that the Blood of Jesus Christ didn't atone. While it will say out of one side of its mouth that the Blood does atone, it will then turn around and say, but not within itself. And with that little hook, people are made to believe that they are teaching and preaching the Blood, which they aren't.

They teach that Jesus became a sinner while on the Cross, died as a sinner, which means that He died spiritually, thereby went to Hell, and we speak of the burning side of Hell, and there suffered for three days and

NOTES

nights the agony of the damned. At the end of the three days and nights, they continue to teach, God then said, *"It is enough,"* meaning that He had suffered enough. He was then *"born again,"* even as any sinner is Born-Again, and then resurrected. So when they talk about a person's faith in Christ in order to be saved, they're speaking of trusting Christ and what He did in the pit of Hell as a lost sinner. Incidentally, all of this is pure fiction, with not a shred of it being in the Bible. But sadly, untold millions believe it!

BLASPHEMY!

The teaching of the *"Word of Faith Message"* of which I have given in brief, is none other than blasphemy. It cannot be construed as anything else. To believe such a doctrine, which is the worst perversion of the Atonement that Satan has ever concocted, is none other than believing a lie. That's why Paul also said:

"Examine yourselves, whether you be in the faith (Jesus Christ and Him Crucified is 'the Faith')*; prove your own selves, know ye not your own selves, how that Jesus Christ is in you, except you be reprobates?"* (II Cor. 13:5).

As should be obvious, these are strong terms as given by the Holy Spirit through the Apostle. In effect, he is saying that any doctrine, any teaching, that eliminates the Cross, because this is what the term *"the faith"* actually means, can only be termed as a reprobate doctrine, which produces *"reprobates."* *"Reprobates"* in the Greek is *"adokimos,"* and means, *"rejected, worthless, cast away."* So in effect He is saying that any other type of faith is a *"worthless faith."* This means that if it's faith other than *"Jesus Christ and Him Crucified,"* then it is a worthless faith, irrespective as to what it might be, or what it might claim.

The truth is, anyone who takes unto themselves the false message of the *"Word of Faith"* doctrine has taken a path that will ultimately lead to spiritual ruin.

THE SPIRIT OF GOD

A lady wrote me the other day and asked this question: *"If the Word of Faith doctrine is wrong, why does the Spirit of God move in these meetings where it is preached and proclaimed?"* My answer to her was after the following:

In the first place, the Spirit of God is not moving in those particular services. The Spirit of God cannot condone erroneous doctrine. While there are many things which might be labeled as the Spirit of God, the truth is, it isn't.

What is being projected is that which looks like God, sounds like God, and at times, may even feel like God. But what is at work is that which Paul referred to as an *"angel of light."* He said:

"For such are false apostles, deceitful workers, transforming themselves into the Apostles of Christ.

"And no marvel; for Satan himself is transformed into an angel of light.

*"Therefore it is no great thing if his minis-*ters (Satan's ministers) *also be transformed as the ministers of righteousness; whose end shall be according to their works"* (II Cor. 11:13-15).

That's why he also said, *"Now the Spirit* (Holy Spirit) *speaks expressly, that in the latter times* (the times in which we now live) *some shall depart from the Faith* (Jesus Christ and Him Crucified), *giving heed to seducing spirits, and doctrines of devils"* (I Tim. 4:1).

Does all of this mean that no one is saved who believes this doctrine? No, not at all! In fact, there are many people who believe this doctrine who are truly saved; however, the truth is, if they continue in that doctrine, more and more their spiritual experience will be weakened. In fact, many will lose their souls because of this doctrine, as it is with any false doctrine, and which Satan intends!

It all goes back to Cain and Abel, as outlined in Genesis, Chapter 4. Cain didn't refuse to offer up a sacrifice, only the sacrifice which God demanded, which was a slain lamb, an innocent victim, which was a portrayal of Christ. He wanted to offer up the labor of his own hands, which meant his own concoction, which God would not accept, and in fact, could not accept. It hasn't changed from then until now.

There is one Sacrifice which God will honor, and that is the sacrifice of His Only Son, the Lord Jesus Christ, which was carried out at the Cross. He will accept nothing else. But Satan has pushed and promoted,

and done so through the Church, every other type of sacrifice that one could begin to imagine. These sacrifices look good, and to the unspiritual eye, it would seem that surely the Lord would want this; however, no matter how pretty the Altar, if it's not the slain Lamb on that Altar, so to speak, God will never accept it. And let the following also be understood:

If the sacrifice is rejected, then the sacrificer is rejected as well. If the Sacrifice is accepted, then the sacrificer is accepted. The latter places faith in the Sacrifice and not self, while everything else places faith in self or other things. And so is the *"Word of Faith"* doctrine. It is faith in faith, which in effect means faith in self, which God cannot accept. As we've said over and over again, and will continue to say, if it's not Faith in the Cross, which refers to what Jesus did there, then it's not faith which God will recognize.

IS IT WHO HE IS OR WHAT HE DID?

The question of my heading is far more important than meets the eye at first glance. Many, if not most, Christians think that everything we have from the Lord comes to us simply because of Who Jesus is. I refer to Him being the Son of God, etc. However, that's not the case at all.

If the mere fact of Jesus being God, which He definitely is, and in fact, always has been and always will be, could bring us Salvation from our sins, then He would never have had to be born of the Virgin Mary, and then die on a Cross. But the truth is, that fact cannot save us.

While the Lord definitely could have regenerated man without the Cross, His Righteousness, and Justice, and in fact, His very Nature, would not allow such. In other words, the terrible debt of sin owed by man to God must be paid. Inasmuch as man cannot pay this debt, if it is to be paid, God Alone must pay it, for He is the only One Who can.

God could have allowed man to have been eternally lost, but at the same time, love would not allow such. It was love which created man, and it was love which must redeem man (Jn. 3:16).

So, for the Nature and Righteousness of God to be satisfied, as it must be satisfied, the debt had to be paid.

There was only one way it could be paid, at least as far as we know, and that was by Jesus going to the Cross, where there He would shed His Life's Blood, which would affect payment, and in fact, atone for all sin, past, present, and future, at least for those who will believe (Eph. 2:13-18; Rom. 10:9-10).

While Jesus was the only One Who could do this, in fact, before Salvation could come to Adam's fallen race, He would have to go to the Cross, which refers to *"What"* He did. That's the reason I keep saying, even as Paul said, that it's always *"Jesus Christ and Him Crucified"* (I Cor. 1:23; 2:2; Gal. 6:14). If we try to separate Jesus from the Cross, irrespective as to whether we do it through ignorance or not, the results are always the same. We conclude by preaching *"another Jesus."*

ANOTHER JESUS

Paul, in writing to the Corinthians said: *"For if he who comes preaches another Jesus, whom we have not preached, or if we receive another spirit, which you have not received, or another gospel, which you have not accepted, you might well bear with him"* (II Cor. 11:4).

The Apostle, in effect, was saying that Preachers were coming into the Church at Corinth, and elsewhere as well, and were not preaching the Cross, but rather something else. He likened the something else to *"another Jesus,"* which produced *"another spirit,"* and which played out to *"another gospel."*

That being the case, what was being proclaimed was not truly Christ, and was not truly the Gospel, but something else altogether.

To make it easier to understand, if any Preacher separates Christ from the Cross, in other words placing emphasis on something else other than the Cross, he is in effect preaching *"another Jesus."* And regrettably, that's where the far greater majority of the modern Church presently is. The Cross has been ignored, laid aside, or disbelieved altogether, as it is by the Word of Faith people, which means that what is presently being produced is none other than *"another Jesus."*

As a result, no lives are changed, no one is baptized with the Holy Spirit, and no one is delivered, and no one is healed by the Power of God.

Very few attempts in modern Church circles are even made presently for the salvation of souls. Very little effort is made as well regarding Believers being baptized with the Holy Spirit. Also, deliverance from sin and shame is nonexistent. And, while grandiose claims are made regarding healings and miracles, the truth is, it's mostly sham and scam.

Yes, some few people definitely are being saved, and some few definitely are being baptized with the Holy Spirit, etc., but the truth is, that number is abysmally small. Why? It's small simply because it's *"another Jesus"* which is being promoted, which produces another spirit, and which plays out to another gospel.

When one turns on Christian television, with some few exceptions, what is seen is about the same as modern professional wrestling. In other words, what professional wrestling is to the sports world, the modern Church is, for the most part, to the spirit world. In other words, it's a joke! And the tragedy is, the Church has drifted so far away from the truth, and because it has drifted so far away from the Cross, that it anymore little knows the difference. That's the tragedy of it all! Far too often, it claims things to be of the Holy Spirit, which in fact, are of *"another spirit."*

SALVATION AND SANCTIFICATION

Many, if not most, Believers understand the Cross as it refers to the initial Salvation experience. However, even that knowledge is very sparse, which I will come back to in a moment. But as it regards the Cross and Sanctification, the modern Church is almost totally illiterate respecting this single-most important aspect of the Christian experience.

The modern Church little knows the part the Cross plays in our everyday living before God, which plays out to our overcoming, victorious, Christian experience. If this life is lived as it ought to be lived, it is the most wonderful, joyous, fulfilling life that man has ever known (Jn. 10:10). But not knowing and understanding how Sanctification works, most Believers set out, whether they realize it or not, to sanctify themselves, which is an impossible task. The truth is this:

What Jesus did at the Cross not only provides Salvation for the sinner, but as well, Sanctification for the Saint. This means that not one single Christian ought to be bound by any power of darkness in any capacity. In other words, if we follow the Word of the Lord, and do so as we should, *"sin shall not have dominion over you"* (Rom. 6:14).

But the facts are, sin or rather the sin nature, in some way, dominates most Christians. It does so simply because they do not know and understand God's prescribed order of victory. And what is that prescribed order?

Even though I've already given this previously in this Volume, simply because of the way the Commentaries are normally studied, and above all because it's so very, very important, please indulge my repetition.

GOD'S PRESCRIBED ORDER OF VICTORY

Even though the Bible is extremely short on formulas, still, I'm going to use one, that it hopefully will help us to understand a little better.

If the Believer can totally adhere to the following, the victory that Jesus procured at the Cross, and which He did it all for us, can be ours in totality. And to be sure, such a victory gained is, as Simon Peter said, *"joy unspeakable and full of glory."* As I proceed, I will use the headings as the formula.

FOCUS

The focus of the Believer must be entirely on the Cross of Christ. This means that we must understand, and understand totally, that every single thing that comes to us from God is all made possible by what Jesus did at the Cross on our behalf. That must be settled once and for all. You have not gotten anything from the Lord, except that it was made possible by the Cross. That's why Paul said:

"For Christ sent me not to baptize, but to preach the Gospel: not with wisdom of words, lest the Cross of Christ should be made of none effect" (I Cor. 1:17).

Even as we've previously stated, Paul wasn't denigrating Water Baptism. He was merely saying that the emphasis must never be on those particular ordinances, as important as they are in their own right. The emphasis must always be on the Cross, because it's the Cross which has made everything possible. That's why he also said:

"But God forbid that I should glory, save in the Cross of our Lord Jesus Christ, by Whom the world is crucified unto me, and I unto the world" (Gal. 6:14).

He plainly tells us here that victory over the world can be obtained only by what Jesus did at the Cross, and our Faith in that Finished Work.

THE OBJECT OF OUR FAITH

Understanding that our focus must be on the Cross, we must then make the Cross and the Finished Work of Christ the object of our Faith, and the object of our Faith solely. Now this is the hardest struggle for the Child of God. Satan will do everything within his power to shift your Faith from the Cross to other things. Also, as we've already stated, he doesn't really care what the other things actually are, just so it's not the Cross.

When Paul began to explain the manner in which we are to have victory in this life, and that means to walk in perpetual victory, he took us to the Cross. This is what he said:

"Know you not, that so many of us as were baptized into Jesus Christ were baptized into His death?

"Therefore we are buried with Him by baptism into death: that like as Christ was raised up from the dead by the glory of the Father, even so we also should walk in newness of life.

"For if we have been planted together in the likeness of His death, we shall be also in the likeness of His Resurrection" (Rom. 6:3-5).

Regrettably, most Christians read right past this, thinking that Paul is speaking of Water Baptism, and because he uses the word *"baptize."*

The truth is, he is not speaking of Water Baptism, and in fact, Water Baptism is not even on his mind. What is said here has no connection with Water Baptism, as important as that Ordinance is in its own right.

The *"baptism"* of which he is speaking is the Crucifixion of Christ, and how we become a part of that Crucifixion, which is by Faith. What do we mean by that?

It means that whenever you as a believing sinner accepted Christ as your Lord and Saviour, in the Mind of God, you were literally placed into Christ when He died on the Cross, and as Paul put it, *"baptized into His death."*

He used the word *"baptize,"* because that explains more perfectly what he is saying. Through the Apostle, the Holy Spirit is actually telling us that we are literally *"in Christ."* Jesus as our Substitute actually became us in a sense, as we by Faith actually become Christ, in a sense.

In the strict sense of the word, the word *"baptize"* means that *"you are in whatever it is you are being baptized into, and whatever you are being baptized into, is in you."* A perfect example is a ship that has been sunk in the ocean. The ship is in the water, and the water is in the ship, but not only in the ship, it literally fills the ship and is all around the ship. Now if you can see yourself in Christ in that fashion, you are seeing the *"baptism"* of which Paul speaks here.

As well, you were buried with Christ, which means the old you, with all of its sin and iniquity, in other words the entire past, is buried with Him, which means it no longer exists (Rom. 6:6).

We are then raised with Him in *"newness of life."* This refers to His Resurrection. But before we can have and enjoy Resurrection Life, we must first of all understand that *"we have been planted together* (Jesus and I) *in the likeness of His death."*

What I've just given you in brief presents the nuts and bolts of God's prescribed order of victory. But it's not over yet, please read the next heading:

POWER SOURCE

Once our focus is right, which is the Cross, and the object of our faith becomes the Finished Work of Christ, and we do not allow our Faith to be moved to other things, the Power Source then becomes the Holy Spirit. And this is the secret of it all (Rom. 8:11).

The Holy Spirit is God. Of course, there is nothing that He cannot do. He is in our hearts and lives in order to carry out the Will of the Father (I Cor. 2:12).

There are many things which are impossible to us, but there is nothing impossible with the Holy Spirit. However, the great secret is, which in fact ought not to be a secret but tragically is, the Holy Spirit works exclusively within the parameters of the Finished Work of Christ. And what does that mean?

It means that all He does within our hearts and lives He does through the legal means of what Jesus did at the Cross. In fact, before the Cross, He couldn't come into the hearts and lives of Believers to abide permanently, even the Old Testament greats. The reason was the blood of bulls and goats could not take away sins; therefore, the sin debt remained, and in fact did remain until Christ went to the Cross (Heb. 10:4). But since the Cross, the Holy Spirit comes into our hearts and lives at conversion, and does so to *"abide forever"* (Jn. 14:16-17).

However, if we as Believers shift our faith to something other than the Cross, whether we do it inadvertently or not, we greatly hinder the Holy Spirit by such action. Unfortunately, most Denominational Christians sort of take the Holy Spirit for granted. In other words, they don't know too very much about Him, or how He works. The Pentecostals on the other hand, think that being baptized with the Holy Spirit, and thereby speaking with other tongues, guarantees all things. It doesn't! If it did, no Spirit-filled Believer would ever fail, etc. But we know that's not correct. So what is happening here?

While it is definitely true that every single Believer desperately needs to go on and be baptized with the Holy Spirit, which will always be accompanied by the speaking with other tongues (Acts 2:4), that is only the first step. In other words, being baptized with the Holy Spirit definitely guarantees the potential for all things, but it is potential only. In other words, the Holy Spirit now has the potential to do all of these great things within our hearts and lives, but once again, only if we follow God's prescribed order.

The Holy Spirit demands of us, and it is a simple demand, that we place our Faith in the Finished Work of Christ, and maintain our Faith in that Finished Work. That's actually all that He asks of us.

This means that we understand, as we go back to the *"focus,"* that it is through the Cross that all good, great, and wonderful things come to us. It also means that we understand that what is needed, we cannot do ourselves. In other words, we cannot receive the great things of God by and through the *"flesh."* And what is the *"flesh"*?

The flesh actually pertains to our own personal strength, ability, and efforts. Which means we're trying to do it, whatever it is that we're trying to do, without the Power of the Holy Spirit. And this is one of the Believer's greatest problems.

Please notice the following:

"For the Law of the Spirit of Life in Christ Jesus, has made me free from the law of sin and death" (Rom. 8:2).

This one Verse of Scripture tells us how the Holy Spirit works within our lives, which guarantees our Power Source. And what he does, He actually refers to as a *"Law,"* which means that He is not going to break this Law. And what is this Law?

It is *"The Law of the Spirit of Life in Christ Jesus."*

This means that all the Holy Spirit does, He does strictly by and through what Jesus did at the Cross, hence Him using the term, *"in Christ Jesus."* Every time Paul used that term, or one of its derivatives, without exception, he was always referring to what Christ did at the Cross, all on our behalf.

It all boils down to this: It is the Cross, our Faith, and the Holy Spirit. As a Believer, you're not going to get anything done in your heart and life without the fact of the Holy Spirit doing it. He Alone can do these things, and to be sure, He can do all things. But the secret is that we understand how He works. And as I've repeatedly stated, He works exclusively through the Cross, which is what Romans 8:2 actually means.

Once you have your Faith anchored in the Cross, your Power Source becomes the Holy Spirit, which enables you to live a holy life.

RESULTS

Once this is done, meaning that your focus is on the Cross, which means that the object of your Faith is the Finished Work of Christ, then your Power Source becomes the Holy Spirit, which guarantees victory, and we mean perpetual victory.

This is God's prescribed order, and to be sure, He has no other means or way, and because no other means or way is needed.

This is what Paul gave us in Romans, Chapter 6, as well as Romans, Chapter 8. If

NOTES

we follow what He said, victory will be ours, and in every capacity.

THE WRONG DIRECTION

The formula that I've just given you, *"focus, object of faith, power source, and results,"* I want to continue to use, but yet to show you the wrong direction that most Christians have taken. I will be much more brief, but I'm certain you'll get the message.

Focus: Works. This means that the Christian's focus is not on the Cross, but rather on works of some nature, which could fall into any category.

Object of Faith: Now it's no longer the Finished Work of Christ, but rather our performance as it pertains to these particular *"works."* In fact, that's where the faith of most Christians actually is.

Power Source: With the focus on works, and the object of faith now our performance, the power source becomes *"self."* In other words, because your faith is misplaced, the Holy Spirit simply will not function in this capacity, and because if He did, He would be breaking the *"Law,"* which He won't do (Rom. 8:2).

No matter that we are saved, and even Spirit-filled, if our faith is misplaced, we're left on our own, which means that we are limited to our own personal strength, which I can assure you is no match for the powers of darkness. While the Holy Spirit in such a case definitely remains with us, He is curtailed in what He can actually do.

Results: Functioning within our own strength, which is exactly what happens when we place our faith in something other than the Cross, we are guaranteed of failure, and no matter how hard we try. At this very moment, there are millions of Christians who love the Lord supremely, and are trying with all of their strength and power, but trying in all the wrong ways. Despite their efforts, they are failing, and not only are they failing, but the failures are getting worse and worse as time goes by, which is what always happens in such situations.

If we go God's Way, which is the Way of the Cross, we are guaranteed victory, because Jesus truly paid it all. If we go in other directions, and no matter how religious those other directions might be, we're guaranteed of failure. So why not do what the Word of God tells us to do. That being the case, victory in totality will be ours.

EPHRAIM AND MANASSEH

Verses 5 through 7 read: *"And now your two sons, Ephraim and Manasseh, which were born unto you in the land of Egypt before I came unto you into Egypt are mine; as Reuben and Simeon, they shall be mine.*

"And your issue which you beget after them, shall be yours, and shall be called after the name of their brethren in their inheritance.

"And as for me, when I came from Padan, Rachel died by me in the land of Canaan in the way, when yet there was but a little way to come unto Ephrath: and I buried her there in the way of Ephrath; the same is Beth-lehem."

The Holy Spirit through Jacob will now claim the two sons of Joseph, in effect, as his own sons, even though they were actually his grandsons. He claims them on the same level as his first two sons, Reuben and Simeon. Concerning this, Horton said: *"By this, Jacob indicated he was bypassing the older sons and was making sure that Joseph would get the double portion of the birthright. This would apply only to Ephraim and Manasseh. Any other children Joseph might have would get their inheritance through Ephraim and Manasseh. Jacob named Ephraim first in anticipation of the leadership Ephraim would have."*

Jacob first recites the gift of the land of Canaan to him by God (vss. 3-4), then, making Joseph his firstborn (vs. 22), he adopts Joseph's two sons as his own, actually setting the younger above the elder.

In effect, Joseph had a double claim; he merited the birthright; and, also, he was the firstborn of Rachel who was Jacob's true wife.

By Jacob doing this, and I speak of taking Ephraim and Manasseh, Joseph's sons as his own, this filled out the complement of 13 sons. He had 11, and these two would make 13 as is obvious, which were needed to fill out the entirety of the 12 Tribes of Israel, plus the Priestly Tribe, totaling 13.

(8) "AND ISRAEL BEHELD JOSEPH'S SONS, AND SAID, WHO ARE THESE?

(9) "AND JOSEPH SAID UNTO HIS FATHER, THEY ARE MY SONS, WHOM GOD HAS GIVEN ME IN THIS PLACE. AND HE SAID, BRING THEM, I PRAY YOU, UNTO ME, AND I WILL BLESS THEM.

(10) "NOW THE EYES OF ISRAEL WERE DIM FOR AGE, SO THAT HE COULD NOT SEE. AND HE BROUGHT THEM NEAR UNTO HIM; AND HE KISSED THEM, AND EMBRACED THEM.

(11) "AND ISRAEL SAID UNTO JOSEPH, I HAD NOT THOUGHT TO SEE YOUR FACE: AND, LO, GOD HAS SHOWN ME ALSO YOUR SEED.

(12) "AND JOSEPH BROUGHT THEM OUT FROM BETWEEN HIS KNEES, AND HE BOWED HIMSELF WITH HIS FACE TO THE EARTH."

The composition is:

1. Pulpit says: *"That Jacob did not at first discern their presence shows that his adoption of them into the number of the theocratic family was prompted not by the accidental impulse of a natural affection excited through beholding these young men, but by the inward promptings of the Spirit of God."*

2. Even though Jacob was blind, or nearly so, the Tenth Verse portrays the Holy Spirit referring to him as *"Israel,"* because he could *"see"* by Faith.

3. The Eleventh Verse once again names him *"Israel,"* and because of his great Faith in God. Satan had told him, *"You will never see Joseph again,"* but now the Holy Spirit says, *"You have not only seen Joseph, but his sons as well."* True Faith in God is never disappointed.

WHO ARE THESE?

Verses 8 and 9 read: *"And Israel beheld Joseph's sons, and said, Who are these?*

"And Joseph said unto his father, They are my sons, whom God has given me in this place. And he said, Bring them, I pray you, unto me, and I will bless them."

None of this which Jacob was doing was contrived out of his own mind. He was led by the Holy Spirit in every action. In fact, making these two sons of Joseph his own finished out the complement which God intended of the 13 Tribes of Israel. They will stay in Egypt some 215 years, at least that's how long it was from the time that Jacob came into Egypt, and when they would go out under Moses, delivered by the mighty Power of God, they would go out approximately three million strong.

As Joseph stood that day before his father, his two sons, Ephraim and Manasseh are with him. The implication seems to be that Jacob could dimly see them, but not well enough to make out as to who they were. This shows, if in fact my statements are correct, that Jacob was not entirely blind, but nearly so. At any rate, he did not recognize the two boys, even though he had been speaking of them to Joseph.

In the Eighth Verse, the Holy Spirit refers to Jacob as *"Israel,"* and because what he is doing is a Work and Word of Faith.

The two sons of Joseph stand before the aged Patriarch, and as he blesses them, a further Work of the Spirit takes place.

THE EYES OF FAITH

Verses 10 through 12 read: *"Now the eyes of Israel were dim for age, so that he could not see. And he brought them near unto him; and he kissed them, and embraced them.*

"And Israel said unto Joseph, I had not thought to see your face: and, lo, God has shown me also your seed.

"And Joseph brought them out from between his knees, and he bowed himself with his face to the Earth."

A number of things are said in these Verses:

First of all, Jacob is referred to as *"Israel,"* once again signaling his great Faith. In fact, the entirety of this Chapter throbs with Faith. Jacob is referred to *"Israel"* nine times in this one Chapter. It speaks of Faith. It's not so much that Jacob's faith was perfect, for possibly that cannot be said of anyone, but that he had carried out, and was carrying out, all that God had called him to do, and without reservation.

His eyes, naturally speaking, may have been dim and because of age, but even though he could little see in the physical sense, concerning his Faith, he had never had greater Illumination. In effect, he could now "see" as he had never seen before.

He now recalls to Joseph that he had never thought to see Joseph again, but not only had he seen Joseph, but also he had seen Joseph's sons, his grandsons. He gives God all the praise and glory for this, even as he should have done.

As Jacob said these things, Joseph bowed low before his father, realizing the tremendous import of what was being said.

(13) "AND JOSEPH TOOK THEM BOTH, EPHRAIM IN HIS RIGHT HAND TOWARD ISRAEL'S LEFT HAND, AND MANASSEH IN HIS LEFT HAND TOWARD ISRAEL'S RIGHT HAND, AND BROUGHT THEM NEAR UNTO HIM.

(14) "AND ISRAEL STRETCHED OUT HIS RIGHT HAND, AND LAID IT UPON EPHRAIM'S HEAD, WHO WAS THE YOUNGER, AND HIS LEFT HAND UPON MANASSEH'S HEAD, GUIDING HIS HANDS WITTINGLY; FOR MANASSEH WAS THE FIRSTBORN.

(15) "AND HE BLESSED JOSEPH, AND SAID, GOD, BEFORE WHOM MY FATHERS ABRAHAM AND ISAAC DID WALK, THE GOD WHICH FED ME ALL MY LIFE LONG UNTO THIS DAY,

(16) "THE ANGEL WHICH REDEEMED ME FROM ALL EVIL, BLESS THE LADS; AND LET MY NAME BE NAMED ON THEM, AND THE NAME OF MY FATHERS ABRAHAM AND ISAAC; AND LET THEM GROW INTO A MULTITUDE IN THE MIDST OF THE EARTH.

(17) "AND WHEN JOSEPH SAW THAT HIS FATHER LAID HIS RIGHT HAND UPON THE HEAD OF EPHRAIM, IT DISPLEASED HIM: AND HE HELD UP HIS FATHER'S HAND, TO REMOVE IT FROM EPHRAIM'S HEAD UNTO MANASSEH'S HEAD.

(18) "AND JOSEPH SAID UNTO HIS FATHER, NOT SO, MY FATHER: FOR THIS IS THE FIRSTBORN; PUT YOUR RIGHT HAND UPON HIS HEAD.

(19) "AND HIS FATHER REFUSED, AND SAID, I KNOW IT, MY SON, I KNOW IT: HE ALSO SHALL BECOME A PEOPLE, AND HE ALSO SHALL BE GREAT: BUT TRULY HIS YOUNGER BROTHER SHALL BE GREATER THAN HE, AND HIS SEED SHALL BECOME A MULTITUDE OF NATIONS.

(20) "AND HE BLESSED THEM THAT DAY, SAYING, IN YOU SHALL ISRAEL BLESS, SAYING, GOD MAKE YOU AS EPHRAIM AND AS MANASSEH: AND HE SET EPHRAIM BEFORE MANASSEH.

(21) "AND ISRAEL SAID UNTO JOSEPH, BEHOLD, I DIE: BUT GOD SHALL BE WITH

YOU, AND BRING YOU AGAIN UNTO THE LAND OF YOUR FATHERS.

(22) "MOREOVER I HAVE GIVEN TO YOU ONE PORTION ABOVE YOUR BRETHREN, WHICH I TOOK OUT OF THE HAND OF THE AMORITE WITH MY SWORD AND WITH MY BOW."

The construction is:

1. The Blessing which Jacob bestowed upon these two boys was no empty blessing, but rather rich with eternal wealth, even as Faith very well knew.

2. Jacob fears the influence of Egypt upon his sons. His nature led him all his life to grasp at wealth and position, but now Faith shines brightly, and he earnestly points Joseph and his sons to the true riches promised by God.

3. In fact, they were in great danger. Joseph was viceroy of Egypt, and brilliant prospects were within his reach for his children. The aged Patriarch urges him not to make his home in Egypt, but to set his heart in Canaan.

THE BLESSING

Verses 13 through 16 read: *"And Joseph took them both, Ephraim in his right hand toward Israel's left hand, and Manasseh in his left hand toward Israel's right hand, and brought them near unto him.*

"And Israel stretched out his right hand, and laid it upon Ephraim's head, who was the younger, and his left hand upon Manasseh's head, guiding his hands wittingly; for Manasseh was the firstborn.

"And he blessed Joseph, and said, God, before whom my fathers Abraham and Isaac did walk, the God which fed me all my life long unto this day,

"The Angel which redeemed me from all evil, bless the lads; and let my name be named on them, and the name of my fathers Abraham and Isaac; and let them grow into a multitude in the midst of the Earth."

Just before Jacob blesses these young men, the aged Patriarch retakes his staff, and leaning upon it, so as not to fall, bows in grateful worship before God. This is the time of which Paul spoke when he wrote: *"By Faith Jacob, when he was dying, blessed both the sons of Joseph; and worshipped, leaning upon the top of his staff"* (Heb. 11:21). Strengthening

NOTES

himself once more upon the bed, he bids his grandsons yet again to come near him, and crossing his hands, he blesses them. As stated, it was no empty blessing, but rich with eternal wealth, even as Faith very well knew (Williams).

All of this shows that Jacob was not set upon the wealth of his luxurious bedchamber, which Joseph no doubt had provided for him, but was far away in God's chosen land. And if he, for a moment, did lay upon such a costly couch, yet was he a worshipper thereon.

Manasseh was the firstborn, and Joseph expected Jacob to give him the greater part of the blessing. But the Holy Spirit, Who Alone knows all the future, told Jacob to put his right hand, which pronounced the greater blessing, upon the head of Ephraim, who was the younger.

He specifies that the blessing about to be pronounced comes from God, Who had guided both Abraham and Isaac, and Who had also guided him all the days of his life.

He gives the Lord the praise for redeeming him from all evil, and then said, *"Let my name be named on them, and the name of my fathers Abraham and Isaac."* And finally, *"Let them grow into a multitude in the midst of the Earth."*

The first pertained to the Promise, and I speak of the God of Abraham, Isaac, and Jacob, while the second spoke of blessing. The Promise had to do with the coming Redeemer, Who definitely did come. The Blessing concerning the multitude is yet to be fulfilled, but definitely will be fulfilled in the coming Millennium, when Israel will be the leading nation on the Earth.

EPHRAIM

Verses 17 through 22 read: *"And when Joseph saw that his father laid his right hand upon the head of Ephraim, it displeased him: and he held up his father's hand, to remove it from Ephraim's head unto Manasseh's head.*

"And Joseph said unto his father, Not so, my father: for this is the firstborn; put your right hand upon his head.

"And his father refused, and said, I know it, my son, I know it: he also shall become a people, and he also shall be great: but truly his younger brother shall be greater than he, and his seed shall become a multitude of nations.

"And he blessed them that day, saying, In you shall Israel bless, saying, God make you as Ephraim and as Manasseh: and he set Ephraim before Manasseh.

"And Israel said unto Joseph, Behold, I die: but God shall be with you, and bring you again unto the land of your fathers.

"Moreover I have given to you one portion above your brethren, which I took out of the hand of the Amorite with my sword and with my bow."

Joseph, thinking that his father's dim eyesight had caused him to confuse the two boys, proceeded to take the right hand of the Patriarch from the head of Ephraim, and place it on the head of Manasseh, who was the firstborn. But Jacob refused to do this, and in effect, said that he knew what he was doing.

He had done this simply because the Holy Spirit had guided him accordingly. Ephraim, although the younger, would be the greater of the two Tribes, and in fact, would be greater than any of the 12 Tribes of Israel, with the exception of Judah.

Jacob wanted Joseph and his two grandsons, as well as all of his sons to know that even though they were greatly blessed in Egypt, Canaan was in fact, their home. He bids them to always look to yonder land.

Jacob tells Joseph that the land is a doubly precious land; first, because God gave it to him; and second, because there he buried Rachel. In effect, he said to Joseph: *"That land should be doubly precious to you, because of these two facts."*

All of this presents a scene of touching tenderness! The aged eyes of the dying Patriarch glow once more with the love of early manhood. He looks eagerly into Joseph's eyes, as much as to say: *"Joseph, I loved her; and she was your mother."* Thus he laid these two great pleas upon the heart of Joseph so that they should save him from making Egypt his country (Williams).

We aren't told exactly what Jacob meant by his statement, *"Which I took out of the hand of the Amorite with my sword and with my bow."* It could mean one of two things, or even both:

This very well could have been a conflict with the Amorites of which we are given no information. And as well, it could speak of

NOTES

the coming day when Israel would vanquish this foe, which is probably the meaning.

In effect, Jacob giving the blessing to the sons of Joseph, and especially the double blessing to Ephraim, in essence was giving it to Joseph. Esau sold his birthright, and Reuben forfeited his. Jacob, therefore, could bestow it on whom he would.

"'Tis midnight, and on Olive's brow
"The stars dim that lately shone;
"'Tis midnight, in the garden now
"The suffering Saviour prays alone."

"'Tis midnight, and from all removed,
"The Saviour wrestles lone with fears
"Even that Disciple whom He loved heeds
"Not his master's grief and tears."

"'Tis midnight, and for other's guilt
"The Man of Sorrows weeps in blood;
"Yet He Who has in anguish knelt is
"Not forsaken by His God."

"'Tis midnight, and from other plains
"Is borne the song that Angels know,
"Unheard by mortals are the strains that
"Sweetly soothe the Saviour's woe."

CHAPTER 49

(1) "AND JACOB CALLED UNTO HIS SONS, AND SAID, GATHER YOURSELVES TOGETHER, THAT I MAY TELL YOU THAT WHICH SHALL BEFALL YOU IN THE LAST DAYS.

(2) "GATHER YOURSELVES TOGETHER, AND HEAR, YOU SONS OF JACOB; AND HEARKEN UNTO ISRAEL YOUR FATHER.

(3) "REUBEN, YOU ARE MY FIRST-BORN, MY MIGHT, AND THE BEGINNING OF MY STRENGTH, THE EXCELLENCY OF DIGNITY, AND THE EXCELLENCY OF POWER:

(4) "UNSTABLE AS WATER, YOU SHALL NOT EXCEL; BECAUSE YOU WENT UP TO YOUR FATHER'S BED; THEN DEFILED YOU IT: HE WENT UP TO MY COUCH."

The overview is:

1. In Verses 1 and 2, the Holy Spirit impresses the use of both names, *"Jacob"* and *"Israel."* As the 12 sons gather in his presence, he is referred to as *"Jacob."* However,

when it refers to the prophecies that will be given, *"Hearken unto Israel your father,"* he is referred to by his princely name, *"Israel."*

2. The *"last days"* of Verse 1 are mentioned some 33 times in Scripture. It refers here to days before both the First and Second Advents of the Messiah.

3. The Holy Spirit through Jacob will now give the prophetic direction of the Tribes, from the day that Jacob gave them, to the eternal future.

THE LAST WORDS OF JACOB

Verses 1 and 2 read: *"And Jacob called unto his sons, and said, Gather yourselves together, that I may tell you that which shall befall you in the last days.*

"Gather yourselves together, and hear, you sons of Jacob; and hearken unto Israel your father."

At a point in time, probably very soon after the Patriarch had blessed the two sons of Joseph, he calls all of his sons together, sensing that he doesn't have long left. As well, he has a prophetic Word from the Lord, which he must give unto them.

Concerning this particular time, Henry says: *"His calling upon them once and again to gather together, intimated both a precept to them to unite in love, to keep together, not to mingle with the Egyptians, not to forsake the assembling of themselves together, but that they ever should be one people."*

Henry went on to say: *"We are not to consider this address as the expression of private feelings of affection, resentment, or partiality, but as the language of the Holy Spirit, declaring the purpose of God respecting the character, circumstances, and situation of the Tribes which should descend from them."*

Even though the information given would be very abbreviated, as is normally the practice of the Holy Spirit, still, in what few words which were used, tremendous information can be derived.

The great Plan of God as it involves Redemption for the human race, began with the Sacrifice, as portrayed in Genesis, Chapter.

4. Actually, the Sacrifice is paramount throughout the entirety of the Bible, which actually constitutes the Plan. Until Christ

came, it consisted of a clean animal, such as a lamb, etc. All of this pointed to Christ Who was to come, and in fact did come, and became the ultimate Sacrifice. So everything revolves around Jesus Christ and the Cross.

To get this great Work accomplished, the nation of Israel was formed in order that faith may be generated in the Earth. Fallen man has no Faith in God, as fallen man can have no Faith in God. God would reveal Himself in some way to Abraham, just as He did to Isaac and to Jacob; however, the Revelation to Isaac and Jacob, and all others following, was predicated on instruction being given first of all by Abraham.

The nation of Israel was to give the world the Word of God, which they did, and as well, was to serve as the womb of the Messiah, which they also did. But Israel lost her way, crucified her Messiah, and was, consequently, destroyed. The Church was raised up to take her place, even as Paul describes in Romans, Chapter 11. But miracle of miracles, this great Chapter, plus many others in the Old Testament, proclaim the fact that Israel will be brought back. This will take place at the Second Coming.

At that time the Son of Man shall take the reins of Government into His Own Hand, by Divine appointment, and rule over the whole redeemed creation; His Church — the Bride of the Lamb — occupying the nearest and most intimate place, according to the eternal counsels.

The House of Israel, fully restored, shall be nourished and sustained by His gracious Hand; and all the Earth shall know the deep blessedness of being under His Sceptre. Finally, having brought everything into subjection, He shall hand back the reins of government into the Hands of God, that *"He may be all in all"* (I Cor. 15:24, 28).

From all this we may form some idea of the richness and copiousness of Joseph's history. In short, it sets before us distinctly, in Type, the mission of the Son to the House of Israel, His humiliation and rejection, the deep exercises and final Repentance and restoration of Israel, the union of the Church with Christ, His exaltation and universal government, and, finally, it points us forward to the time when *"God shall be all in all."*

While we do not build all of this entirely upon Joseph's history, still, it is edifying to find such early foreshadowings of these precious truths in his own life and experience.

It proves to us the Divine unity which pervades Holy Scripture. Whether we turn to Genesis or to Ephesians — to the Prophets of the Old or those of the New Testament — we learn the same truths, *"All Scripture is given by inspiration of God"* (Mackintosh).

REUBEN

Verses 3 and 4 read: *"Reuben, you are my firstborn, my might, and the beginning of my strength, the excellency of dignity, and the excellency of power:*

"Unstable as water, you shall not excel; because you went up to your father's bed: then defiled you it: he went up to my couch."

Reuben had some admirable qualities in his character; unfortunately, they were offset by his incestuous act with Bilhah, his father's concubine (Gen. 35:22). It was Reuben who advised his brothers not to kill Joseph, and returned to the pit to release him (Gen. 37:21, 29). Later he accused them of bringing calamity upon themselves, when they were held in the Egyptian court as suspected spies (Gen. 42:22). Again, it was Reuben who offered his own two sons as sufficient guarantee for the safety of Benjamin (Gen. 42:37).

In the blessing of the sons of Jacob, Reuben is recognized legally as the firstborn, although in actual fact, the double-portion which went with the birthright (Deut. 21:17) was symbolically bequeathed to Joseph, through his two sons, Ephraim and Manasseh.

However, after a eulogy of Reuben, no doubt sincerely meant, there is added a significant and prophetic utterance by the Patriarch: *"Unstable as water, you shall not have preeminence."*

The Tribe of Reuben was involved in the rebellion in the wilderness (Num. 16:1). Its pursuits would be mainly pastoral, but those to the west of Jordan were mainly agricultural. This may have led to a separation of interests, for Reuben took no part in repelling the attack of Sisera (Judg. 5:15).

However, a place is reserved for the Tribe of Reuben in Ezekiel's reconstructed Israel

NOTES

(Ezek. 48:7, 31), and they are numbered among the 144,000, sealed out of every Tribe of the Children of Israel, in the Revelation of John (Rev. 7:5) (New Bible Dictionary).

(5) "SIMEON AND LEVI ARE BRETHREN: INSTRUMENTS OF CRUELTY ARE IN THEIR HABITATIONS.

(6) "O MY SOUL, COME NOT THOU INTO THEIR SECRET; UNTO THEIR ASSEMBLY, MINE HONOR, BE NOT THOU UNITED: FOR IN THEIR ANGER THEY SLEW A MAN, AND IN THEIR SELFWILL THEY DIGGED DOWN A WALL.

(7) "CURSED BE THEIR ANGER, FOR IT WAS FIERCE; AND THEIR WRATH, FOR IT WAS CRUEL: I WILL DIVIDE THEM IN JACOB, AND SCATTER THEM IN ISRAEL."

The exegesis is:

1. Simeon and Levi are perfect examples of those who take matters into their own hands, instead of putting it into the Hands of the Lord.

2. That's why Paul said, *"Whatsoever is not of faith is sin"* (Rom. 14:23).

3. These predictions describe the *"Church"* of that particular time. As we can see, the picture is not pleasant in most cases.

SIMEON AND LEVI

Verses 5 through 7 read: *"Simeon and Levi are brethren; instruments of cruelty are in their habitations.*

"O my soul, come not thou into their secret; unto their assembly, mine honor, be not thou united: for in their anger they slew a man, and in their selfwill they digged down a wall.

"Cursed be their anger, for it was fierce; and their wrath, for it was cruel: I will divide them in Jacob, and scatter them in Israel."

Because of the slaughter at Shechem, Simeon and Levi were truly divided and scattered in Israel. Actually, Simeon, when the land would be parceled out at the command of Joshua, upon the arrival across the Jordan, would receive no inheritance, but, in fact, would have their part in the inheritance of Judah.

As well, Levi would have no inheritance at all but would have their curse turned into a blessing as they became the Priestly Tribe of Israel.

In fact, it might even be said of Simeon that their curse was turned into a blessing, because of having the privilege of being in the inheritance of Judah, the Messianic Tribe.

Simeon and Levi are perfect examples of the human race in general. The wickedness and iniquity mark humanity. As such, it is cursed, cursed by the broken Law. But when the land was parceled out when Israel came into Canaan, Simeon was given an inheritance in the possession of Judah, which was a Type of Christ (Josh. 19:1-9).

Likewise, when the believing sinner comes to Christ, the curse is removed, because Jesus has paid the price at the Cross, and then we are given a possession, an inheritance, in Christ, our Heavenly Judah.

Verse 6 speaks of *"their secret"* and refers to the plans to murder the inhabitants of Shechem, which they carried out.

They assembled the other brothers in order to carry out this gruesome task. This, as would be obvious, greatly impacted the *"honor"* of Jacob. The Holy Spirit says that one must not be *"united"* with such people and such actions.

The phrase, *"In their anger they slew a man,"* in the Hebrew tenses, refers to many men.

Their *"digging down a wall,"* actually referred to them hamstringing the oxen of Shechem, which is the way it should have been translated.

The word *"divided"* pertains to Simeon, in that they were divided from their inheritance, meaning they had none. As stated, their inheritance was in the Tribe of Judah.

"Scatter" pertains to the Tribe of Levi, which became the Priestly Tribe, which saw the curse turned into a blessing, exactly as did Simeon. While their inheritance was scattered here and there, still, this Tribe was involved in the greatest blessing of all, that of caring for the Tabernacle and the Temple, and all their administration.

(8) "JUDAH, YOU ARE HE WHOM YOUR BRETHREN SHALL PRAISE: YOUR HAND SHALL BE IN THE NECK OF YOUR ENEMIES; YOUR FATHER'S CHILDREN SHALL BOW DOWN BEFORE YOU.

(9) "JUDAH IS A LION'S WHELP: FROM THE PREY, MY SON, YOU ARE GONE UP: HE STOOPED DOWN, HE COUCHED AS A LION, AND AS AN OLD LION; WHO SHALL ROUSE HIM UP?

(10) "THE SCEPTRE SHALL NOT DEPART FROM JUDAH, NOR A LAWGIVER FROM BETWEEN HIS FEET, UNTO SHILOH COME; AND UNTO HIM SHALL THE GATHERING OF THE PEOPLE BE.

(11) "BINDING HIS FOAL UNTO THE VINE, AND HIS ASS'S COLT UNTO THE CHOICE VINE; HE WASHED HIS GARMENTS IN WINE, AND HIS CLOTHES IN THE BLOOD OF GRAPES:

(12) "HIS EYES SHALL BE RED WITH WINE, AND HIS TEETH WHITE WITH MILK."

The synopsis is:

1. From the Tribe of Judah, the Messiah would come. There could be no greater honor than this as it regards one of the Tribes of Israel.

2. The name *"Judah"* means, *"praise,"* and it signifies the Lord Jesus Christ.

3. *"Judah is a lion's whelp,"* and Jesus is referred to by the Holy Spirit as *"The Lion of the Tribe of Judah"* (Rev. 5:5).

4. The Sceptre of power would not depart from the Tribe of Judah, which business it was to bring forth the Messiah, until He came, and when He came, He took the Sceptre.

5. Jesus would satisfy completely the demands of the broken Law.

6. The entirety of the business of all the Tribes of Israel, and more specifically the Tribe of Judah, was to bring forth the Lord of Glory, and when He was brought forth, *"Unto Him shall the gathering of the people be."*

7. He shall bring forth much fruit, hence the *"choice Vine."*

8. He would bring forth this copious fruit, by *"washing His garments in wine, and His clothes in the blood of grapes,"* which signifies the Cross of Calvary, and the shedding of His Precious Blood, which would bring forth Redemption, which is what God promised Abraham, Isaac, and Jacob.

9. He Who is Righteousness would provide Righteousness for all who would believe in Him, typified by the phrase, *"And His teeth white with milk."*

JUDAH

Verse 8 reads: *"Judah, you are he whom your brethren shall praise: your hand shall be in the neck of Your enemies; your father's children shall bow down before you."*

Of all the Tribes of Israel, the premiere Tribe was Judah, and because through this Tribe, the Messiah, the Redeemer, the Son of God would come, Who would lift the fallen sons of Adam's lost race. As the very name *"Judah"* means *"praise,"* the One Whom Judah would produce would be the object of continual praise. He is the Son of God, the Fairest of Ten Thousands, Who is worthy of all praise, and because *"He has redeemed us to God by His Blood out of every kindred, and tongue, and people, and nation;*

"And has made us unto our God kings and priests: and we shall reign on the Earth" (Rev. 5:9-10).

VICTORY

The phrase, *"Your hand shall be in the neck of Your enemies,"* speaks of the great victory that Christ would win over Satan and all the powers of darkness, which He would do through the Cross, typified by Verses 11 and 12.

The phrase means that He will put His foes to flight, literally grasping them by the neck, signifying that He would *"bruise the head"* of Satan.

Let the Reader understand that God doesn't give victories to fallen man, but only to His Son the Lord Jesus Christ. Now if you will think a moment, this statement speaks volumes:

1. It tells us that irrespective of our own efforts, and I speak of efforts outside of Faith in the Cross, we will win no victories by that method. It makes no difference how religious our efforts are, even how right they may be in their own way; victory can never be secured in this manner.

2. We obtain victory by placing our Faith exclusively in Christ, because God has given all victory to Him. We secure that victory by simple Faith, and never by works.

3. This victory has already been won by Christ, in other words, as they say on the street, *"It's a done deal!"* So that means that every single unbeliever in this world, and irrespective as to how pitiful his situation might be, if he will only turn to Christ and trust Him, all that Christ has purchased on the Cross can totally and instantly come to

such a person. In fact, that's the manner in which all people have been saved.

As well, it speaks to every Christian who at this moment is bound by the sin nature in some way, that you can be totally and completely free. It's already done. All you have to do is trust Christ, and be very careful that you are trusting that in which He did at the Cross, all on your behalf. If you will rest your Faith in the Cross of Christ, refuse to allow it to be moved, the Holy Spirit through Paul plainly said, *"Sin* (the sin nature) *shall not have dominion over you"* (Rom. 6:14).

JESUS CHRIST IS GOD

The phrase, *"Your father's children shall bow down before You,"* refers to the fact that the glorious One Whom Judah will produce, and we speak of the Incarnation, will in fact be the Son of the Living God. As such, and because He is God, untold millions bow down before Him, and rightly so!

"Bowing down before Him," is not merely a matter of paying homage, but rather an admission that the One before Whom we are bowing, is in fact the Son of God, the Saviour of the world, the Baptizer with the Holy Spirit, the Giver of eternal life, *"The Man, Jesus Christ."*

THE LION OF THE TRIBE OF JUDAH

Verse 9 reads: *"Judah is a lion's whelp: from the prey, my son, you are gone up: he stooped down, he couched as a lion, and as an old lion; who shall rouse Him up?"*

Even though Judah is addressed here, all of this actually, as is obvious, refers to Christ. He Alone is the *"Lion of the Tribe of Judah"* (Rev. 5:5). In the Hebrew language, four things are implied here:

A. Christ is likened to a young lion; B. He is described as *"an old lion,"* referring to one ripening into its full strength and ferocity; C. It roams through the forest in search of prey; and, D. It is heightened by the alternate image of a lioness, which is particularly fierce in defending its cubs.

The phrase, *"Judah is a lion's whelp,"* refers to a young lion, in the power of its youth, absolutely invincible. This represented Christ in the flower of His manhood, full of the Holy Spirit, healing the sick, casting out devils, raising the dead, doing great and mighty things, with every demon spirit trembling at His Feet.

A lion seeks out *"prey,"* meaning that Christ is always on the offensive. He never fights a defensive mode, so to speak, but only that which is offensive.

While it is true that the weapons of our warfare, as described in Ephesians, Chapter 6, are mostly defensive in nature, the idea is, as we wield the sword of the Spirit, which is the Word of God, and which is offensive, all are meant to protect us, while in the offensive mode, which we should be at all times.

ON THE OFFENSIVE AND NEVER DEFENSIVE

In fact, the Child of God should never be defensive. The lion was always seeking the prey, never the prey seeking the lion. The words *"defeat"* and *"defensive"* go hand in hand, while the words *"offend"* and *"offensive"* go hand in hand. It is my business as a Child of God to offend the Devil at all times.

The song says:

"We are able to go up and take the country,
"And possess the land from Jordan unto the Sea.
"Though the giants may be there our way to hinder,
"Our God has given us the victory."

THE SCEPTRE

Verse 10 reads: *"The Sceptre shall not depart from Judah, nor a lawgiver from between his feet, until Shiloh come; and unto Him shall the gathering of the people be."*

The word *"Sceptre"* in the Hebrew is *"Shebet,"* and means, *"a stick or baton for punishing, righting, fighting, ruling, walking, etc."* It is also defined as *"a staff of office and authority,"* which is the meaning in this Tenth Verse.

Due to the fact that the Tribe of Judah will bring forth the Messiah, it will hold the Sceptre of power until He comes, which this Tribe did. But when He came, the Sceptre was taken from Judah, and placed in the Hands of the Son of God, where it was intended all the time.

The Sceptre held by Christ, and which He still holds this power, and in fact, will ever hold this power, has reference to more than the fact that He is God, which He definitely is. To cut straight through to the bottom line, it refers to what He did at the Cross, which satisfied the demands of the broken Law, and which thereby took away Satan's legal right to hold mankind captive (Col. 2:14-15). Let the Reader understand that the Sceptre of power is now in the Hands of Christ, where it will remain in the Hands of Christ forever and forever. And due to the fact that every Believer is *"in Christ,"* that means as well that the sceptre of power is in our hands also. But it is there only as long as our Faith is anchored in Christ, and what Christ did at the Cross. It is the Cross which made it possible for us to have such power (Acts 1:8).

LAWGIVER

The phrase, *"Nor a lawgiver from between his feet, until Shiloh come,"* refers to the fact that Judah was meant to be a guardian of the Law, which they were. The Temple was in Jerusalem which was a part of the Tribe of Judah, and which had to do with the Law.

When Jesus came, typified by the name *"Shiloh,"* Who in fact was and is the True Lawgiver, He fulfilled the Law in totality, by His life, and His death, thereby satisfying all of its just demands. Now the Law is totally and completely in Christ, and every Believer becomes a Law-keeper, and does so automatically when Faith is expressed in Christ, Who has perfectly keep the Law. In other words, we don't try to keep the Law, but in fact it is kept, and because Christ has kept it perfectly, and our Faith in Him gives us His victory in totality. So in effect, we keep the Law by placing our Faith and trust in Him Who has kept the Law perfectly. As stated, we then become actually Law-keepers, instead of Law-breakers. Naturally, we're speaking of the moral Law.

UNTO HIM

The phrase, *"And unto Him shall the gathering of the people be,"* proclaims the fact that Christ is all in all. Israel was raised up for the express purpose of pointing the world to Christ. Unfortunately, they tried to make themselves bigger than Christ, and thereby fell by the wayside. Nevertheless, the objective of the Holy Spirit was Christ, and unto Him, not Israel, etc., *"shall the gathering of the people be."*

It didn't say that people would gather to Mohammad, or the Pope, or Buddha, or any other fake luminary, but unto Christ.

There are about two billion people in the world presently who claim Christ in one way or the other, whether Catholic or Protestant. The number truly Born-Again would be far, far smaller. Nevertheless, Biblical Christianity, with Christ as its Head, is the most powerful, driving force in the world, and in fact, always has been, even from the beginning of the Church. I speak of the True Church!

THE BLOOD OF GRAPES

Verse 11 reads: *"Binding His foal unto the vine, and His animal's colt unto the choice vine; He washed His garments in wine, and His clothes in the blood of grapes."*

The *"Vine"* speaks of fruit, and in fact, *"the blood of grapes,"* speaks of what He did on the Cross in the shedding of His Life's Blood, in order to bring forth this fruit. In John 15:1 He said: *"I AM the true vine, and My Father is the husbandman."*

The *"fruit"* He would bring forth would be those who are *"in Him."* In fact, He said: *"For without Me you can do nothing"* (Jn. 15:5). The fruit is made possible as it grows on the Vine, with us being *"in Him,"* due to the fact that He paid the price on the Cross. *"He washed His garments in wine,"* i.e., *"in Blood."*

RIGHTEOUSNESS

Verse 12 reads: *"His eyes shall be red with wine, and His teeth white with milk."*

This speaks of the Righteousness of Christ. It is Righteousness which He has always had, but now is made possible to us, due to what He did in His sufferings, i.e., *"the blood of grapes."*

These Passages have been applied to the coming Millennium, with others applying them to the judgments of the Tribulation, etc.

While all of those things definitely will happen, that, however, is not the thrust of these Passages. This speaks of the Redemption which

He affords, and because of Who He is and What He has done, and I speak of the Cross.

(13) "ZEBULUN SHALL DWELL AT THE HAVEN OF THE SEA; AND HE SHALL BE FOR AN HAVEN OF SHIPS; AND HIS BORDERS SHALL BE UNTO ZIDON.

(14) "ISSACHAR IS A STRONG ANIMAL COUCHING DOWN BETWEEN TWO BURDENS:

(15) "AND HE SAW THAT REST WAS GOOD, AND THE LAND THAT IT WAS PLEASANT, AND BOWED HIS SHOULDER TO BEAR, AND BECAME A SERVANT UNTO TRIBUTE.

(16) "DAN SHALL JUDGE HIS PEOPLE, AS ONE OF THE TRIBES OF ISRAEL.

(17) "DAN SHALL BE A SERPENT BY THE WAY, AN ADDER IN THE PATH, THAT BITETH THE HORSE HEELS, SO THAT HIS RIDER SHALL FALL BACKWARD.

(18) "I HAVE WAITED FOR THY SALVATION, O LORD.

(19) "GAD, A TROOP SHALL OVERCOME HIM: BUT HE SHALL OVERCOME AT THE LAST.

(20) "OUT OF ASHER HIS BREAD SHALL BE FAT, AND HE SHALL YIELD ROYAL DAINTIES.

(21) "NAPHTALI IS A HIND LET LOOSE: HE GIVETH GOODLY WORDS.

(22) "JOSEPH IS A FRUITFUL BOUGH, EVEN A FRUITFUL BOUGH BY A WELL; WHOSE BRANCHES RUN OVER THE WALL:

(23) "THE ARCHERS HAVE SORELY GRIEVED HIM, AND SHOT AT HIM, AND HATED HIM:

(24) "BUT HIS BOW ABODE IN STRENGTH, AND THE ARMS OF HIS HANDS WERE MADE STRONG BY THE HANDS OF THE MIGHTY GOD OF JACOB; (FROM THENCE IS THE SHEPHERD, THE STONE OF ISRAEL:)

(25) "EVEN BY THE GOD OF YOUR FATHER, WHO SHALL HELP YOU; AND BY THE ALMIGHTY, WHO SHALL BLESS YOU WITH BLESSINGS OF HEAVEN ABOVE, BLESSINGS OF THE DEEP THAT LIETH UNDER, BLESSINGS OF THE BREASTS, AND OF THE WOMB:

(26) "THE BLESSINGS OF YOUR FATHER HAVE PREVAILED ABOVE THE BLESSINGS OF MY PROGENITORS UNTO

THE UTMOST BOUND OF THE EVERLASTING HILLS: THEY SHALL BE ON THE HEAD OF JOSEPH, AND ON THE CROWN OF THE HEAD OF HIM WHO WAS SEPARATE FROM HIS BRETHREN.

(27) "BENJAMIN SHALL RAVIN AS A WOLF: IN THE MORNING HE SHALL DEVOUR THE PREY, AND AT NIGHT HE SHALL DIVIDE THE SPOIL."

The overview is:

1. This Chapter forms one of the great dispensational prophecies of the Word of God. It concerns the *"latter days"* and the *"last days"* (vs. 1). It is believed that these predictions give prophetic direction from the day that Jacob gave them to the eternal future.

2. It is said that Reuben, Simeon, and Levi contain the moral history of Israel up to the birth of Christ.

3. Judah portrays the time of the Messiah and His rejection.

4. Zebulun and Issachar, the dispersion and subjugation of the Jews among the Gentiles.

5. Dan, the appearing and kingdom of the Antichrist. It is even believed that the Antichrist may be from the Tribe of Dan.

6. Verse 18 portrays the cry of anguish of the elect sons of Israel for the Second Coming of Christ; Gad, Asher, and Naphtali, those who will cry.

7. Joseph and Benjamin together predict the Second Coming and glory of Israel's Messiah.

ZEBULUN

Verse 13 reads: *"Zebulun shall dwell at the haven of the sea; and he shall be for an haven of ships; and his borders shall be unto Zidon."*

This portrayal of Zebulun is not so much geographical, as it is occupational.

The closest that Zebulun came to the Mediterranean was about 10 miles; however, the great trade routes from north to south, etc., went through Zebulun, with them being very active in commerce.

As well, the phrase, *"And his borders shall be unto Zidon,"* should have been translated, *"And his borders shall be towards Zidon."*

ISSACHAR

Verses 14 and 15 read: *"Issachar is a strong animal couching down between two burdens:*

"And he saw that rest was good, and the land that it was pleasant, and bowed his shoulder to bear, and became a servant unto tribute."

The Tribe of Issachar bordered the Jordan River, and as a result, favored some of the best agricultural areas in all of Israel.

As well, the phrase, *"And became a servant unto tribute,"* has to do with its agricultural pursuits, and not subjugation by another nation.

DAN

Verses 16 and 17 read: *"Dan shall judge his people, as one of the Tribes of Israel.*

"Dan shall be a serpent by the way, an adder in the path, that biteth the horse heels, so that his rider shall fall backward."

Dan had the ability to bear rule, yet became a treacherous serpent. It is certainly observable that the first introduction of idolatry in Israel is ascribed to the Tribe of Dan (Judg., Chpt. 18), and that in the numbering of the Tribes of Revelation, Chapter 7, the name of Dan is omitted.

As well, it is believed that the Antichrist, who will be Jewish, will spring from the Tribe of Dan, once again likened to *"an adder in the path,"* a most venomous serpent.

GAD, ASHER, AND NAPHTALI

Verses 18 through 21 read: *"I have waited for your Salvation, O LORD.*

"Gad, a troop shall overcome him: but he shall overcome at the last.

"Out of Asher his bread shall be fat, and he shall yield royal dainties.

"Naphtali is a hind let loose: he gives goodly words."

As we mentioned in the overview, if it is correct that these Tribes portray Israel all the way from Jacob's day to the eternal future, then the cry, *"I have waited for your Salvation, O Lord,"* speaks of the Second Coming, when the Messiah will miraculously rout the Antichrist, thereby saving Israel from sure destruction.

This is the first time that the word *"Salvation"* is used in the Bible. As Jacob, and in fact all of Israel would see such, it pertains to the ancient people's most trying time, even yet to come. Jesus Himself said: *"For then shall be great tribulation, such as was* not since the beginning of the world to this time, no, nor ever shall be.

"And except those days should be shortened, there should no flesh be saved: but for the elect's sake (Israel) those days shall be shortened" (Mat. 24:21-22).

Jacob's ancient prayer will then be answered, and answered in such a graphic way, as to defy all description. For the Coming of the Lord will be the most cataclysmic happening the world has ever known in all of its history, or will ever know.

"Gad" will be overcome by the Antichrist during the Great Tribulation, but "shall overcome at the last," which speaks of the Second Coming.

"Asher" could well be the first of the Tribes to welcome Christ upon His Second Coming. The phrase, "yield royal dainties," pertains to an excellent presentation for the king. That King is the Lord Jesus Christ.

"Naphtali" will have wonderful words for Christ upon His return. They will be words of Repentance (Zech. 13:1).

While these predictions definitely had to do with the Tribes of Israel in their coming formation as a nation, which is borne out in the Old Testament, I have, by and large, ignored that, and dealt with the prophetic predictions, even as I believe the Holy Spirit gave to Jacob.

JOSEPH

Verses 22 through 26 read: "Joseph is a fruitful bough, even a fruitful bough by a well; his branches run over the wall:

"The archers have sorely grieved him, and shot at him, and hated him:

"But his bow abode in strength, and the arms of his hands were made strong by the hands of the mighty God of Jacob; (from thence is the Shepherd, the Stone of Israel:)

"Even by the God of your father, who shall help you; and by the Almighty, Who shall bless you with blessings of Heaven above, blessings of the deep that lieth under, blessings of the breasts, and of the womb:

"The blessings of your father have prevailed above the blessings of my progenitors unto the utmost bound of the everlasting hills: they shall be on the head of Joseph, and on the crown of the head of him who was separate from his brethren."

Joseph, as Judah, is a Type of Christ, hence, the flowing and glowing superlatives.

Judah is portrayed as Christ in His sufferings, while Joseph is portrayed as Christ in His Millennial Blessings. It is the same as David portraying Christ in His conquering mode, while Solomon portrays Christ in His rulership of peace and prosperity; consequently, this of Joseph portrays Christ in the coming Kingdom Age.

He is described first of all as a "fruitful bough," and greater still, "a fruitful bough by a well." In fact, the branches are so outspreading, and so full of fruit, that they "run over the wall," which means that in that coming Age, there will be an abundance of everything.

As Joseph's brethren hated him, likewise, Israel hated Christ, and in fact, crucified Him. However, what they didn't seem to know was, the One they hated was actually "The Shepherd, the Stone of Israel." As such, God would raise Him from the dead, with His "arms being made strong by the hands of the Mighty God of Jacob."

BLESSINGS

As Joseph is a Type of Christ, the Holy Spirit through the Patriarch is here actually referring to Christ. It is Christ Alone Who enjoys the Blessings of the Father. And those Blessings come upon Him in every manner. For instance, He has all Blessings from Heaven, and as well, the Earth will literally spew out Blessings upon Him. The "Blessings of the breasts and of the womb," proclaim the fact that untold numbers will be born into the Kingdom of God, all because of what Christ did at the Cross, and in effect, will be His brothers and sisters.

As well, He is blessed more than the Patriarchs, Prophets, and Apostles of old, and as long as the hills endure, His Blessings will endure.

These Blessings shall rest on the head of Christ, and shall settle on His crown, for He is "King of kings and Lord of lords."

BLESSINGS ON BELIEVERS

The Believer must understand that our Blessings are received only through Christ. Apart from Christ, God blesses no one, for apart from Christ, God cannot bless anyone.

Jesus is our Substitute, and in effect, the Representative Man (I Cor. 15:45-47). As the Federal Head of all Believers, He stands in our place. In other words, God does not really look to us or at us, but rather to Him and at Him. Whatever He is, we are.

And the way we obtain this is by Faith. And when we use that statement, we are referring to Faith in Christ, and what He did for us in His Finished Work. Faith in Him exclusively, which if it is proper faith, always refers to what He did on the Cross, guarantees to such a Believer all that Christ is.

Every Christian wants blessings, and rightly so! However, we must understand that God does not bless us because of our works, labors, enthusiasm, zeal, or efforts on His behalf, as dedicated as all of these things might be! Our blessings come exclusively through Christ, and are obtained strictly by faith.

And whenever our Faith is properly placed, all that is said here regarding Joseph, i.e., *"Christ,"* applies to us as well. It is blessings of every description, and from every direction.

Now what I've told you in these previous few paragraphs constitutes a great truth. As we've already stated, every Believer wants Blessings, but there is only one way those Blessings can be obtained. And because it's so important, let us say it again:

God does not really bless individuals per se, whomever they might be; at least He doesn't bless us apart from Christ. The Blessings rest upon Christ, and rests upon Christ exclusively. When we have Faith in Him, which refers to what He did at the Cross, then His Blessings become our Blessings.

A PERSONAL TESTIMONY

It is January 6, 2002 as I dictate these notes. Approximately a year ago, the Lord began to wondrously speak to me as it regards *"Blessings."*

It began as we were taping a Television special. As we began to tape the Program, we began by playing a Choir number, *"Your Blessings are coming through."*

As the song began to play, I strongly sensed the Presence of God, even as I sat there along with Frances and Donnie waiting for the song to end, so we could proceed with the balance of the program. In fact, I

felt the Presence of the Lord so strongly that I could hardly wait for the song to conclude.

The Holy Spirit greatly moved upon my heart that day, and I did my best to tell the Television audience how so very much the Blessings of God awaited them. But I sensed in my Spirit that the Lord was actually saying something else. In fact, He was saying something else.

He in effect spoke to my heart in the coming days, saying to me, that the Moving of the Spirit which we experienced in taping the Television special, while it definitely was meant for all who would believe, primarily, it was meant for this particular Ministry. I speak of Jimmy Swaggart Ministries.

There were a number of other Movings of the Spirit along this very line concerning the *"Blessings,"* in the following months, which have already begun to come to pass. Now let's analyze that just a little further.

According to the measure of Faith that a Believer has in Christ, and according to the proper placement of that Faith, which is the Cross, the Lord will always bless anyone who falls into such a category. But as it regards my own personal Ministry, beginning in 1996, the Lord has opened up the Message of the Cross to such an extent that it has changed my life. It has as well changed this Ministry. Even beyond that, the Revelation which the Lord has given me concerning the Cross, which in fact continues to expand even unto this hour, and I personally believe will never stop expanding, has opened up truths, which are clearly taught by the Apostle Paul, which the Holy Spirit has shown to me, but which I have not found elsewhere. What I am saying is this:

While there have been untold thousands of Preachers down through the Church Age who have preached the Cross, with some of them being given deep truths, in all of the Commentaries from which I have studied, and I speak of my own personal library, but more than all our Bible College Library, which contains many thousands of Volumes, I have not read these truths which the Lord has opened up to me in any of these Commentaries of which I speak. I can only give the Lord all praise and glory for this.

However, what I'm saying is not something new. The Revelation of God is always progressive. In other words, when the Lord begins to reveal something to someone regarding *"Truth,"* two things generally happen:

1. Anything revealed by the Lord in this fashion is always based squarely on the Word of God. In other words, the Lord will never give anything that goes beyond the Word. If some claim that He does, what they are hearing is not from the Lord, but rather from an angel of light.

2. That which He gives will always be progressive, meaning that it enlarges upon the truth, which had been previously given. It doesn't enlarge upon that which is already in the Word, but it opens up and reveals more light on that particular subject, whatever it might be. The Word of God doesn't change; however, the Holy Spirit can definitely throw more light on the Word, helping us to understand in a better way that which is being said. As I've stated over and over again, what we're saying about the Cross is not new; it is actually that which was given to the Apostle Paul, which I believe the Lord is helping us to bring out to those who would hear and heed. Now I've said all of that to say this:

While the Lord has always blessed my person and this Ministry, all because of Christ, until the Cross became the principle factor in my heart and life, that Blessing was limited, as would be obvious. The idea is, with Faith properly placed in Christ, and what He has done for us in His Finished Work, the Blessings can now come, exactly as Jacob prophesied so long, long ago.

BLESSINGS NOW

Since the Lord spoke to my heart in 2001 concerning *"Blessings,"* which I've just related to you, and which He continues to speak to my heart unto this hour, I have watched the Blessings become more and more pronounced.

I personally feel that the Lord is going to give us more souls, more people delivered, more lives changed, more Believers baptized with the Holy Spirit, more people truly healed by the Power of God, than we have ever previously known. I also believe that the Lord is going to give us the means, which in fact He has already begun to do so, to proclaim this Message of the Cross all over the world. The Message of the Cross is the Gospel. That's why Paul said:

"For Christ sent me not to baptize, but to preach the Gospel: not with wisdom of words, lest the Cross of Christ should be made of none effect.

"For the preaching of the Cross is to them who perish foolishness; but unto us which are saved it is the Power of God" (I Cor. 1:17-18).

BENJAMIN

Verse 27 reads: *"Benjamin shall ravin as a wolf: in the morning he shall devour the prey, and at night he shall divide the spoil."*

Benjamin is addressed last, and possibly because he was the youngest.

It concerns the conclusion of the Millennial Reign, when Satan will be loosed for a season; however, the Lord, at that time, will make short shift of Satan. The Tribe of Benjamin may very well be the leading Tribe to oppose the Evil One, even as the Scripture says: *"In the morning he shall devour the prey, and at night he shall divide the spoil."*

Concerning Benjamin, Jacob said, *"He shall ravin as a wolf."* It is plain by this that Jacob was guided in what he said by the Spirit of Prophecy, and not by natural affection; else he would have spoken with more tenderness of his beloved son Benjamin, concerning whom he only foresees and foretells this.

The warlike spirit of Benjamin carried over to Paul the Apostle, who was of this Tribe (Rom. 11:1; Phil. 3:5). Paul shared the Blessings of Judah's lion, and was the recipient of His victories. And so are we!

(28) "ALL THESE ARE THE TWELVE TRIBES OF ISRAEL: AND THIS IS IT THAT THEIR FATHER SPOKE UNTO THEM, AND BLESSED THEM; EVERY ONE ACCORDING TO HIS BLESSING HE BLESSED THEM.

(29) "AND HE CHARGED THEM, AND SAID UNTO THEM, I AM TO BE GATHERED UNTO MY PEOPLE: BURY ME WITH MY FATHERS IN THE CAVE THAT IS IN THE FIELD OF EPHRON THE HITTITE,

(30) "IN THE CAVE THAT IS IN THE FIELD OF MACHPELAH, WHICH IS BEFORE MAMRE, IN THE LAND OF CANAAN, WHICH ABRAHAM BOUGHT WITH THE FIELD OF EPHRON THE HITTITE FOR A POSSESSION OF A BURYING PLACE.

(31) "THERE THEY BURIED ABRAHAM AND SARAH HIS WIFE; THERE THEY

BURIED ISAAC AND REBEKAH HIS WIFE; AND THERE I BURIED LEAH.

(32) "THE PURCHASE OF THE FIELD AND OF THE CAVE THAT IS THEREIN WAS FROM THE CHILDREN OF HETH.

(33) "AND WHEN JACOB HAD MADE AN END OF COMMANDING HIS SONS, HE GATHERED UP HIS FEET INTO THE BED, AND YIELDED UP THE GHOST, AND WAS GATHERED UNTO HIS PEOPLE."

The structure is:

1. While Jacob died in Egypt, his heart was in Canaan, for this was God's Land. We are in this world, but our heart must ever be in the Heavenly Canaan.

2. His demand to be buried in Canaan presented itself as an act of Faith that one day, the entirety of the land would be his. Presently, as Paul said, we only *"have the Firstfruits of the Spirit,"* but the Firstfruits guarantee the remainder (Rom. 8:23).

3. Jacob was gathered to his people. If God's people be our people, death will father us to them (Henry).

THE TWELVE TRIBES OF ISRAEL

Verse 28 reads: *"All these are the Twelve Tribes of Israel: and this is it that their father spoke unto them, and blessed them; every one according to his blessing he blessed them."*

Even though Reuben, Simeon, and Levi were under the marks of their father's displeasure, yet he is said to bless them every one according to his blessing; for none of them were rejected as was Esau.

Whatever rebukes of God's Word or providence we are under at any time, yet as long as we have an interest in God's Covenant, a place and a name among His people, and good hopes of a share in the Heavenly Canaan, we must account ourselves blessed (Henry).

CANAAN

Verses 29 through 32 read: *"And he charged them, and said unto them, I am to be gathered unto my people: bury me with my fathers in the cave that is in the field of Ephron the Hittite,*

"In the cave that is in the field of Machpelah, which is before Mamre, in the land of Canaan, which Abraham bought with the field of Ephron the Hittite for a possession of a burying place.

"There they buried Abraham and Sarah his wife; there they buried Isaac and Rebekah his wife; and there I buried Leah.

"The purchase of the field and of the cave that is therein was from the children of Heth."

The Spirit of God concludes the prophecies given by Jacob concerning his sons, and actually the 12 Tribes of Israel, and now he charges his sons to surely bury him in the land of Canaan. He didn't even want his bones to remain in Egypt.

He had lived in this land for some 17 years, and had no doubt enjoyed ease and splendor. He was blessed to see Joseph as the second most powerful man in Egypt, and thereby the world of that day. But the great Patriarch never allowed all of this splendor and ease to turn his Faith from its correct object. It burned brightly to the end, and he says to his sons, *"Bury me with my fathers in the land of Canaan."* Him being buried in Canaan, just as it had been with his grandfather Abraham, and his father Isaac, proclaimed itself, and made a statement, that all of these were staking claim to the entirety of the land. God had promised it to them, and ultimately that Promise would be realized.

THE DEATH OF JACOB

Verse 33 reads: *"And when Jacob had made an end of commanding his sons, he gathered up his feet into the bed, and yielded up the ghost, and was gathered unto his people."*

The last hours of the great Patriarch were filled with prophecies and predictions concerning the 12 Tribes of Israel, which would ultimately bring the Redeemer into the world. He died when that prophecy was completed, but he did not die until it was completed. What a way to go!

The great Patriarch had ultimately realized that which God had called him to do. The main thing is, he had kept the Faith that was once delivered unto Abraham, and his father Isaac. He had not allowed that torch to fall to the ground, or even be dimmed. At his death, it burned brightly, and in fact, brighter than ever.

And so concludes the Ministry of the blessed trio, *"Abraham, Isaac, and Jacob."* But the *"God of Abraham, Isaac, and Jacob,"* will never conclude. And because He lives, they shall live also!

It was Faith that made these men great! It was Faith that burned their lives, testimonies, and experiences into our hearts. Despite their failures and their foibles, and they had those because they were human, it was Faith which shone so brightly at the last, and because Faith is ever greater than its counterparts.

What was said of Abraham, *"He believed God, and it was counted unto him for Righteousness,"* can be said of all three. Nothing could be greater than that!

"There's a wideness in God's Mercy
"Like the wideness of the sea;
"There's a kindness in His justice,
"Which is more than liberty."

"There is welcome for the sinner,
"And more graces for the good;
"There is Mercy with the Saviour;
"There is healing in His Blood."

"For the Love of God is broader
"Than the measure of man's mind,
"And the heart of the Eternal
"Is most wonderfully kind."

"If our love were but more simple
"We should take Him at His Word;
"And our lives would be all sunshine
"In the sweetness of our Lord."

CHAPTER 50

(1) "AND JOSEPH FELL UPON HIS FATHER'S FACE, AND WEPT UPON HIM, AND KISSED HIM.

(2) "AND JOSEPH COMMANDED HIS SERVANTS THE PHYSICIANS TO EMBALM HIS FATHER: AND THE PHYSICIANS EMBALMED ISRAEL.

(3) "AND FORTY DAYS WERE FULFILLED FOR HIM; FOR SO ARE FULFILLED THE DAYS OF THOSE WHICH ARE EMBALMED: AND THE EGYPTIANS MOURNED FOR HIM THREESCORE AND TEN DAYS."

The construction is:

1. Joseph closed his father's eyes, as predicted by the Lord to Jacob in Chapter 46, Verse 4.

2. Jacob's body was embalmed, but his soul and spirit went into Paradise, to be there with his grandfather Abraham, and his father Isaac, and every other Believer who had lived up unto this time, which included Enoch, Noah, and Abel, plus no doubt others.

3. They mourned for Jacob 70 days, for death is an enemy. It is the last enemy which will be defeated (I Cor. 15:26). Jesus took the sting out of death at the Cross, but at the end of the Kingdom Age, when Satan and all his minions shall be locked away in the Lake of Fire forever and forever, death will then be totally defeated (Rev., Chpt. 20).

DEATH

Verse 1 reads: *"And Joseph fell upon his father's face, and wept upon him, and kissed him."*

Verse 1 is a picture of Christ weeping over Israel. Jacob was dead physically and alive spiritually. Israel was alive physically and dead spiritually.

Of all the sons, Joseph knew and understood the Faith of his father as no other. He was standing there when the great prophecies were given those last hours, and as well, understood them to a degree that his brothers didn't. But yet, I'm not sure if Joseph, or anyone at that time, could have even remotely grasped the totality of what was happening, or the eternity of such.

When a man comes down to die, the only thing he can really take with him is his Faith. Faith characterized Jacob, as it characterizes every Saint of God. When it all comes down to the bottom line, it is Faith and Faith alone.

MOURNING

Verses 2 and 3 read: *"And Joseph commanded his servants the physicians to embalm his father: and the physicians embalmed Israel.*

"And forty days were fulfilled for him; for so are fulfilled the days of those which are embalmed: and the Egyptians mourned for him threescore and ten days."

The embalmers were not normally Physicians. So, it is more than likely that Joseph commanded the Physicians to superintend the process, which they no doubt did.

According to Pliny, the study of medicine originated in Egypt. The physicians employed by Joseph were those attached to his own household, or the court practitioners, which latter was probably the case.

Due to the fact that they were going to have to take Jacob's body the long distance back to Canaan, which would take several weeks, Jacob would have to have the most extensive process.

(4) "AND WHEN THE DAYS OF HIS MOURNING WERE PAST, JOSEPH SPOKE UNTO THE HOUSE OF PHARAOH, SAYING, IF NOW I HAVE FOUND GRACE IN YOUR EYES, SPEAK, I PRAY YOU, IN THE EARS OF PHARAOH, SAYING,

(5) "MY FATHER MADE ME SWEAR, SAYING, LO, I DIE: IN MY GRAVE WHICH I HAVE DIGGED FOR ME IN THE LAND OF CANAAN, THERE SHALL YOU BURY ME. NOW THEREFORE LET ME GO UP, I PRAY YOU, AND BURY MY FATHER, AND I WILL COME AGAIN.

(6) "AND PHARAOH SAID, GO UP, AND BURY YOUR FATHER, ACCORDING AS HE MADE YOU SWEAR.

(7) "AND JOSEPH WENT UP TO BURY HIS FATHER: AND WITH HIM WENT UP ALL THE SERVANTS OF PHARAOH, THE ELDERS OF HIS HOUSE, AND ALL THE ELDERS OF THE LAND OF EGYPT,

(8) "AND ALL THE HOUSE OF JOSEPH, AND HIS BRETHREN, AND HIS FATHER'S HOUSE: ONLY THEIR LITTLE ONES, AND THEIR FLOCKS, AND THEIR HERDS, THEY LEFT IN THE LAND OF GOSHEN.

(9) "AND THERE WENT UP WITH HIM BOTH CHARIOTS AND HORSEMEN: AND IT WAS A VERY GREAT COMPANY.

(10) "AND THEY CAME TO THE THRESHINGFLOOR OF ATAD, WHICH IS BEYOND JORDAN, AND THERE THEY MOURNED WITH A GREAT AND VERY SORE LAMENTATION: AND HE MADE A MOURNING FOR HIS FATHER SEVEN DAYS.

(11) "AND WHEN THE INHABITANTS OF THE LAND, THE CANAANITES, SAW THE MOURNING IN THE FLOOR OF ATAD, THEY SAID, THIS IS A GRIEVOUS MOURNING TO THE EGYPTIANS: WHEREFORE THE NAME OF IT WAS CALLED ABEL-MIZRAIM, WHICH IS BEYOND JORDAN.

NOTES

(12) "AND HIS SONS DID UNTO HIM ACCORDING AS HE COMMANDED THEM.

(13) "FOR HIS SONS CARRIED HIM INTO THE LAND OF CANAAN, AND BURIED HIM IN THE CAVE OF THE FIELD OF MACHPELAH, WHICH ABRAHAM BOUGHT WITH THE FIELD FOR A POSSESSION OF A BURYINGPLACE OF EPHRON THE HITTITE, BEFORE MAMRE."

The composition is:

1. The grandeur of Jacob's funeral procession must have been a wonder to behold. It is amazing to think of this great Patriarch, a pilgrim all his life, being carried to his final resting place by the grandeur of mighty Egypt. It is one of the few times in history that the world recognized the greatness that was among them.

2. The grandeur of Jacob's funeral procession speaks of the burial of Christ in the tomb of the rich (Jn. 19:41).

3. Abraham and Isaac, both very wealthy men, were buried in the tomb of Machpelah. Jacob was laid to rest, with all the glory and riches of Egypt; however, none of them took anything with them *"but their Faith."*

PHARAOH

Verses 4 through 6 read: *"And when the days of his mourning were past, Joseph spoke unto the house of Pharaoh, saying, If now I have found grace in your eyes, speak, I pray you, in the ears of Pharaoh, saying,*

"My father made me swear, saying, Lo, I die: in my grave which I have digged for me in the land of Canaan, there shall you bury me. Now therefore let me go up, I pray you, and bury my father, and I will come again.

"And Pharaoh said, Go up, and bury your father, according as he made you swear."

Joseph did not go in directly to Pharaoh, but rather spoke to the Monarch through the members of the royal household.

According to Egyptian custom, Joseph would have let his beard and hair grow during the time of mourning, which appearance forbade him approaching the throne. Pharaoh's answer would, of course, be conveyed through the courtiers.

A VERY GREAT COMPANY

Verses 7 through 13 read: *"And Joseph went up to bury his father: and with him went up all the servants of Pharaoh, the elders of his house, and all the elders of the land of Egypt,*

"And all the house of Joseph, and his brethren, and his father's house: only their little ones, and their flocks, and their herds, they left in the land of Goshen.

"And there went up with him both chariots and horsemen: and it was a very great company.

"And they came to the threshingfloor of Atad, which is beyond Jordan, and there they mourned with a great and very sore lamentation: and he made a mourning for his father seven days. '

"And when the inhabitants of the land, the Canaanites, saw the mourning in the floor of Atad, they said, This is a grievous mourning to the Egyptians: wherefore the name of it was called Abel-mizraim, which is beyond Jordan.

"And his sons did unto him according as he commanded them:

"For his sons carried him into the land of Canaan, and buried him in the cave of the field of Machpelah, which Abraham bought with the field for a possession of a buryingplace of Ephron the Hittite, before Mamre."

This funeral procession must have been one of the largest ever conducted in Egypt up to that time. Of course, all the family of Jacob were present, with the exception of the babies and little children. As well, the household of Pharaoh attended, and also the members of his Cabinet, all accompanied by chariots and horsemen.

Funeral processions in Egypt were generally headed up by servants which led the way, carrying tables laden with fruit, cakes, flowers, vases of ointment, wine, and other liquids, with three young geese and a calf for sacrifice, chairs and wooden tablets, napkins, and other things.

Then others followed bearing daggers, bows, fans, and the mummy cases in which the deceased and his ancestors had been kept previous to burial.

Next came a table of offerings, couches, boxes, and a chariot. After these things, men appeared with gold vases and more offerings. To these succeeded the bearers of a sacred boat and the mysterious eyes of Osiris, as the god of stability.

Placed on the consecrated boat, the hearse containing the mummy of the deceased was drawn by four oxen and by seven men, under the direction of a superintendent who regulated the march of the funeral. Behind the hearse followed the male relations and friends of the deceased, who either beat their breasts, or gave token of their sorrow by their silence and solemn steps as they walked, leaning on their long sticks; and with these the procession closed.

Of course the procession described was only for a short distance; consequently, the funeral procession of Jacob, while certainly having some of these trappings, of necessity would have been scaled down due to the long trip to Canaan.

Joseph had the entire procession to stop when they came to the *"threshingfloor of Atad"* where they underwent a second mourning of seven days. And then Jacob was taken to the *"cave of the field of Machpelah,"* where Abraham and Isaac were also buried. Sarah was also buried there, along with Rebekah and Leah.

While the inhabitants of the land of Canaan did not know or understand the significance of these burials, the Patriarchs readily understood what they were doing. God had promised them this land, and their burial in the land, by Faith, staked a claim, not merely to the buryingplace, but to the entirety of this country which would one day be called, *"Israel."*

As well, there was something else in mind, which did transcend all other principles, and I speak of Resurrection. Even though the subject was then dim, still their Faith was sure, as it regarded this miracle of miracles, which they believed that one day would happen. In fact, it has not yet happened, but we are 4,000 years closer than Abraham was when he was buried.

In fact, the Resurrection could take place at any moment. Concerning that coming event, the great Apostle Paul said:

"But I would not have you to be ignorant, Brethren, concerning them which are asleep, that you sorrow not, even as others which have no hope.

"For if we believe that Jesus died and rose again, even so them also which sleep in Jesus will God bring with Him.

"For this we say unto you by the Word of the Lord, that we which are alive and remain unto the Coming of the Lord shall not prevent them which are asleep.

"For the Lord Himself shall descend from Heaven with a shout, with the voice of the Archangel, and with the Trump of God: and the dead in Christ shall rise first:

"Then we which are alive and remain shall be caught up together with them in the clouds, to meet the Lord in the air: and so shall we ever be with the Lord.

"Wherefore comfort one another with these words" (I Thess. 4:13-18).

We do know that the Resurrection was known as early as Job, who was the son of Issachar. And as well, the Book of Job is probably the first Book written as it regards the Bible, and was probably written by Moses, in collaboration with Job, who was contemporary with Moses for some years. Job said:

"If a man, die shall he live again? All the days of my appointed time will I wait, till my change come" (Job 14:14).

Job would have learned of the Resurrection from his grandfather Jacob, who learned it from Isaac, who learned it from Abraham. No doubt, the Doctrine was known from the very beginning.

Enoch said, who lived about 1,200 years before Jacob, *"Behold, the Lord cometh with ten thousands of His Saints"* (Jude, vs. 14).

This speaks of Resurrection!

(14) "AND JOSEPH RETURNED INTO EGYPT, HE, AND HIS BRETHREN, AND ALL THAT WENT UP WITH HIM TO BURY HIS FATHER, AFTER HE HAD BURIED HIS FATHER.

(15) "AND WHEN JOSEPH'S BRETHREN SAW THAT THEIR FATHER WAS DEAD, THEY SAID, JOSEPH WILL PERADVENTURE HATE US, AND WILL CERTAINLY REQUITE US ALL THE EVIL WHICH WE DID UNTO HIM.

(16) "AND THEY SENT A MESSENGER UNTO JOSEPH, SAYING, YOUR FATHER DID COMMAND BEFORE HE DIED, SAYING,

(17) "SO SHALL YOU SAY UNTO JOSEPH, FORGIVE, I PRAY YOU NOW, THE TRESPASS OF YOUR BRETHREN, AND THEIR SIN; FOR THEY DID UNTO YOU EVIL: AND NOW, WE PRAY YOU, FORGIVE THE TRESPASS OF THE SERVANTS OF

THE GOD OF YOUR FATHER. AND JOSEPH WEPT WHEN THEY SPOKE UNTO HIM.

(18) "AND HIS BRETHREN ALSO WENT AND FELL DOWN BEFORE HIS FACE; AND THEY SAID, BEHOLD, WE BE YOUR SERVANTS.

(19) "AND JOSEPH SAID UNTO THEM, FEAR NOT: FOR AM I IN THE PLACE OF GOD?

(20) "BUT AS FOR YOU, YOU THOUGHT EVIL AGAINST ME; BUT GOD MEANT IT UNTO GOOD, TO BRING TO PASS, AS IT IS THIS DAY, TO SAVE MUCH PEOPLE ALIVE.

(21) "NOW THEREFORE FEAR YOU NOT: I WILL NOURISH YOU, AND YOUR LITTLE ONES. AND HE COMFORTED THEM, AND SPOKE KINDLY UNTO THEM.

(22) "AND JOSEPH DWELT IN EGYPT, HE, AND HIS FATHER'S HOUSE: AND JOSEPH LIVED AN HUNDRED AND TEN YEARS."

The overview is:

1. Joseph's brothers never did quite understand who their brother was or what he was. Now that Jacob was dead, they expected evil of Joseph. They did not, and even perhaps could not understand that Joseph, being a Type of Christ, would deal with them not with judgment, but with Mercy and Grace. How beautiful it would be if the Church could learn this simple and yet beautiful act of Joseph as well.

2. The Eighteenth Verse records the last of five times the brothers fulfilled the dreams of Joseph (Gen. 37:5-11). One day, in its greater fulfillment, which will be in the latter days, Israel will fall down at the Feet of the Lord Jesus Christ; of Whom Joseph was a Type.

3. The Twentieth Verse holds one of the greatest Promises found in the entirety of the Word of God. God can take the evil that is planned against the Believer, that is if the Believer will truly trust, and turn it to good.

4. As well, nothing can happen to a Christian but that God either causes it or allows it.

FORGIVENESS

Verses 14 through 17 read: *"And Joseph returned into Egypt, he, and his brethren, and all that went up with him to bury his father, after he had buried his father.*

"And when Joseph's brethren saw that their father was dead, they said, Joseph will

peradventure hate us, and will certainly re- quite us all the evil which we did unto him.

"And they sent a messenger unto Joseph, saying, Your father did command before he died, saying,

"So shall you say unto Joseph, Forgive, I pray you now, the trespass of your breth- ren, and their sin; for they did unto you evil: and now, we pray you, forgive the trespass of the servants of the God of your father. And Joseph wept when they spoke unto him."

Concerning this time, Williams said: *"The incurable unbelief of the heart is illustrated by the cruel thoughts of Joseph's brothers as to his affection for them. This unbelief moved Joseph to tears; and in his action and lan- guage he once more stands forth as, perhaps, the most remarkable type of Christ in the entirety of the Bible."*

Upon arriving back in Egypt, the Broth- ers sent a message to Joseph, as it regarded the great sin they had committed against him those many years before. They claimed that Jacob had said before he died that they should ask Joseph to forgive them of this sin.

Many Jewish Expositors consider that this was untrue, and that Jacob was never made aware of the fact that his sons had sold Jo- seph into slavery. However, there is too much evidence to the contrary.

It is almost impossible that the brothers could have told their father about Joseph being alive and the viceroy of Egypt, without further relating their culpability in Joseph's disappearance. It is almost imperative that they confess to their father at that time.

They knew that very soon, Jacob would see Joseph, and in their minds, they believed that Joseph would relate the truth to Jacob, whether in fact he would have or not. And once again, in their thinking, it would be much better for this terrible truth to first come from them, which it no doubt did.

And then again, it is highly unlikely that they would have lied to Joseph at this stage, claiming that Jacob had said such a thing, when in reality he hadn't.

The terminology sounds like Jacob, and be- cause the Patriarch knew that the brothers were no doubt very concerned about this. So he probably told them what to do, thereby, at least after a fashion, setting their minds at ease.

The messenger went before Joseph, with Joseph then sending for his brothers.

As he discussed with them what had hap- pened so long before, he began to weep. The answer he will give them is most beautiful to behold, and as stated, is one of the most Christlike statements ever made by a hu- man being.

GOD MEANT IT FOR GOOD

Verses 18 through 22 read: *"And his broth- ers also went and fell down before his face; and they said, Behold, we be your servants.*

"And Joseph said unto them, Fear not: for am I in the place of God?

"But as for you, you thought evil against me; but God meant it unto good, to bring to pass, as it is this day, to save much people alive.

"Now therefore fear you not: I will nour- ish you, and your little ones. And he com- forted them, and spoke kindly unto them.

"And Joseph dwelt in Egypt, he, and his father's house: and Joseph lived an hundred and ten years."

As the brothers bowed down before him, by now knowing that all was forgiven, most probably, Joseph asked them to stand, as he spoke the following to them:

His question, *"Fear not: for am I in the place of God?"*, in effect says, I'm not the Judge and, therefore, I do not punish. If any punishment is meted out, it will be God Who does it, and not me. You have nothing to fear from me.

He then makes a statement to them, which proclaims to us a great truth.

Literally, he said to them, *"And you were thinking or meditating evil against me; Elohim was thinking or meditating for good."*

This tells us that God can take the evil practiced against us, and can turn it around to our good, which He Alone can do.

In effect, Joseph is saying that God, long since before, had taken total charge of the affair, and everything was in His Hands. As a result, he dare not insert his own will into the mix, but rather should trust the Lord implicitly. In effect, he's telling the brothers to do the same.

It was not God Who caused Joseph's broth- ers to commit their foul deed against him, but He did permit it. And, as well, Grace turned the terrible ugliness to glorious beauty. However, He can do this, and in fact will do this, only if we put everything in His Hands. The moment we try to defend ourselves, thereby seeking vengeance, we have taken it out of His Hands, and the results will never be pleasant.

Joseph didn't talk down to his brothers. He told them that they must not fear: and furthermore, he promised to continue to see after them just as he had before their father Jacob had died. They were so fearful that once Jacob was dead, Joseph would use his great power to turn on them. In fact, he did use his great power, but it was to bless them and comfort them.

Out of all of this, one of the most beautiful statements is, *"And . . . Joseph . . . spoke kindly unto them."*

(23) "AND JOSEPH SAW EPHRAIM'S CHILDREN OF THE THIRD GENERATION: THE CHILDREN ALSO OF MACHIR THE SON OF MANASSEH WERE BROUGHT UP UPON JOSEPH'S KNEES.

(24) "AND JOSEPH SAID UNTO HIS BRETHREN, I DIE: AND GOD WILL SURELY VISIT YOU, AND BRING YOU OUT OF THIS LAND UNTO THE LAND WHICH HE SWEAR TO ABRAHAM, TO ISAAC, AND TO JACOB.

(25) "AND JOSEPH TOOK AN OATH OF THE CHILDREN OF ISRAEL, SAYING, GOD WILL SURELY VISIT YOU, AND YOU SHALL CARRY UP MY BONES FROM HENCE.

(26) "SO JOSEPH DIED, BEING AN HUNDRED AND TEN YEARS OLD: AND THEY EMBALMED HIM, AND HE WAS PUT IN A COFFIN IN EGYPT."

The exegesis is:

1. Joseph was 110 years old when he died. He lived in Egypt 93 years, and his father's descendants lived there 215 years. This man who was sold as a slave into Egypt became a viceroy of the most powerful and richest nation on the face of the Earth. He was without a doubt one of the most beautiful Types of Christ who ever lived.

2. Hebrews 11:22 draws attention to the double testimony of Joseph's Faith when dying:

A. God would surely redeem the Children of Israel out of Egypt.

B. And they were to carry his bones out with them when leaving.

3. The Book of Genesis begins with life and ends with death. It starts with creation and ends with a coffin. It begins with a Living God and ends with a dead man.

GREAT-GREAT-GRANDCHILDREN

Verse 23 reads: *"And Joseph saw Ephraim's children of the third generation: the children also of Machir the son of Manasseh were brought up upon Joseph's knees."*

Joseph lived to be 110 years of age, and saw not only Ephraim's children, but as well, his children's children, which were his great-great-grandchildren.

These Passages denote a happy time, as Joseph grew older. He was the greatest blessing that Egypt ever knew. During the time he held sway in that ancient land, little did Pharaoh know and understand what in fact was actually developing in his country.

Even though Egypt never really knew the Lord, and today she is steeped in Islam, with all of its attendant misery, in the coming Kingdom Age, Egypt will know the Lord Jesus Christ, and will accept Him as Lord and as Saviour.

The great Prophet Isaiah said: *"In that day shall there be an Altar to the LORD in the midst of the land of Egypt, and a pillar at the border thereof to the LORD.*

"And it shall be for a sign and for a witness unto the LORD of Hosts in the land of Egypt: for they shall cry unto the LORD because of the oppressors, and he shall send them a Saviour, and a great One, and He shall deliver them.

"And the LORD shall be known to Egypt, and the Egyptians shall know the LORD in that day, and shall do sacrifice and oblation; yea, they shall vow a vow unto the LORD, and perform it" (Isa. 19:19-21).

THE PROMISE

Verse 24 reads: *"And Joseph said unto his brethren, I die: and God will surely visit you, and bring you out of this land unto the land which He swear to Abraham, and to Isaac, and to Jacob."*

Joseph was 110 years old, and he knew that he was about to die. He called his brethren around him, which in effect were his relatives. How many of his brothers were yet alive, we aren't told. The word *"brothers"* or *"brethren"* in the Hebrew, can refer to actual brothers as we know such, or their sons or even sons' sons, etc.

He told them that God would surely visit them, and would bring them out of this land. He didn't say when, but the Promise was given, and in a sense, was prophetic, exactly as had been the prophecies of his father Jacob.

By his use of the names, *"Abraham, Isaac, and Jacob,"* portrays the fact that he was well acquainted with all the Promises made to the Patriarchs. Also, in a sense, he considered himself, and rightly so, to have had a great part to play in all of this. In fact, he will be the last luminary until Moses, who would be born about 60 years later.

THE OATH

Verse 25 reads: *"And Joseph took an oath of the Children of Israel, saying, God will surely visit you, and you shall carry up my bones from hence."*

Joseph heard and believed what God had said to Abraham, to Isaac, and to Jacob as to the gift of Canaan, which would most surely come to pass.

Whenever the Children of Israel left out of Egypt, some three million strong, Moses was careful to *"take the bones of Joseph with him"* (Ex. 13:19).

It was some 40 years before the Children of Israel would finally arrive in Canaan's fair land. By this time, Moses was gone, but Joshua would be very careful to bury the bones of Joseph in Shechem, *"in a parcel of ground which Jacob bought of the sons of Hamor the father of Shechem for an hundred pieces of silver: and it became the inheritance of the children of Joseph"* (Josh. 24:32).

So, some 200 plus years after he died in Egypt, he would finally come home, and to the place where he had been sold as a slave into Egypt. Joshua, no doubt, attended the burial.

JOSEPH

Verse 26 reads: *"So Joseph died, being an hundred and ten years old: and they embalmed him, and he was put in a coffin in Egypt."*

Likewise, Joshua, who attended Joseph's burial, was also 110 years old when he died.

Ellicott said: *"With the death of Joseph ends the preparation for the formation of a chosen race. Summoned from a remote city upon the Persian Gulf to Canaan, Abraham had wandered there as a stranger, and Isaac and Jacob had followed in his steps. But in Canaan the race could never have multiplied largely; for there were races already there too powerful to permit of their rapid increase.*

"Abraham and Lot, Esau and Jacob had been compelled to separate; but now, under Joseph, they had been placed in a large, fertile, and well-nigh uninhabited region. The few who dwelt there were, as far as we can judge, of the Semitic stock, and whatever immigrants came from time to time were also of the same race, and we speak of Shem, and were soon enrolled in the clan of some Hebrew chief. And thus all was ready for their growth into a nation; and when we next read of them they had multiplied into a people so vast that Egypt was afraid of them."

Joseph finished this course with joy, even as did Jacob his father, and so can we, if our Faith is totally and completely in Christ, to Whom the Patriarchs ever pointed.

"Alas, and did my Saviour bleed?
"And did my Sov'reign die?
"Would He devote that sacred Head
"For such a worm as I?"

"Was it for crimes that I have done,
"He groaned upon the tree?
"Amazing pity! Grace unknown!
"And Love beyond degree!"

"Well might the sun in darkness hide,
"And shut his glories in,
"When Christ, the mighty Maker, died,
"For man the creature's sin."

"But drops of grief can ne'er repay
"The debt of love I owe:
"Here, Lord, I give myself away,
"'Tis all that I can do!"

CONCLUSION

It is February 6, 2002 as I conclude our efforts regarding commentary on the great Book of Genesis, the Book of beginnings. While it has taken about five months to assemble these notes, in reality, it has taken nearly 60 years. Concerning notes on the

Bible, one must live what one is writing, before it can be written.

FAITH

The story of Genesis, that is if it can be summed up in one word, is the story of *"Faith."* And of course, when one mentions Faith, one is at the same time speaking of the Cross. No sooner does man fall, than God promises a Redeemer, and the Cross is the manner in which Redemption will come (Gen. 3:15). The theme is carried throughout Genesis, and in fact looms ever larger and larger as one goes through Book after Book of the Bible.

As I've stated several times in this Volume, the story of the Bible is the story of the Cross, just as the story of the Cross is the story of the Bible. To understand it as it should be understood, in fact, as it must be understood, one has to understand the Cross. Then and then only can one actually understand the Word of God.

GENESIS

Genesis, written by Moses, is probably the second oldest Book in the Bible, therefore, the world, Job probably being first. As I have gone through this Book, Chapter after Chapter, Verse after Verse, and even various phrases and words, in a sense, I have lived the lives of the individuals of whom I have attempted to portray. It must be that way, or we can never truly know the people we are writing about. I have tried my best to learn the lessons they taught, and above all, what the Holy Spirit taught through them. I've then tried to apply those lessons to our present day, even as I think the Holy Spirit intended.

If there are any blessings in these efforts, then all glory goes to the Lord. Otherwise, I would ask you to forgive our efforts which did not quite come up to par.

It's an awesome task, attempting to write commentary on the Word of God. The woeful inadequacy stares at the writer constantly, never ending, ever reminding one of one's insufficiencies. I feel that constantly, and then think, who am I to undertake such a task?

Our Commentaries are written from the standpoint of the Evangelist, and if they are different, that's what makes them different.

THE EVANGELIST

The Evangelist seldom sees things in a dull gray, but rather in a stark white or stark black. In other words, there are no in-betweens. It is *"Thus saith the Lord."*

The Evangelist is not a Diplomat; he rather delivers ultimatums! By their very design, his Messages anger, just as they are intended to do. He asks no quarter, and he gives none. If he compromises, then he ceases to function in his calling as an Evangelist.

It is my business as an Evangelist to prod, to push, to pull, to jab, even like a fighter who feints and parries, looking for an opening for the knockout punch.

This I do believe: while the words of this Commentary may anger you, may prod you, and will hopefully get you to think, at the least, I pray they do not bore you.

THE CROSS

If you by chance read these notes first, I will say up front that I have taken every opportunity presented me to portray the Cross. If you have read this conclusion last, you will, I'm sure, agree with me that the Cross has been amply presented. Whether we have been able to treat it as well as we should, I will have to let the Lord judge. But this I do know:

I see the Cross on every page in the Bible, in fact, in every Chapter, even in every Verse. As I have stated, it is the theme of the Word of God.

So this Commentary not only carries the history of the beginnings of the great Plan of God for the lost sons of Adam's fallen race, but in that Plan, it also carries the great Message of the Apostle Paul, as he outlined to us in his writings, the Message of the Cross. Had I not given this material, I feel like I would have shortchanged you, the Reader. Above all, I feel I would have grieved the Holy Spirit, and that I must not do.

Genesis begins with the Creator, and ends with a coffin, which speaks of man's terrible failure, which brought death. But thank God, the great Redemption afforded by Christ will ultimately get man out of that coffin.

"Not all the blood of beast
"On Jewish Altars slain
"Could give the guilty conscience peace,
"Or wash away the stain."

"But Christ, the Heavenly Lamb,
"Takes all our sins away;
"A sacrifice of nobler name
"And richer blood than they."

"My faith would lay her hand
"On that dear head of Thine,
"While like a penitent I stand,
"And there confess my sin."

"My soul looks back to see
"The burden You did bear,
"When hanging on the accursed tree,
"And knows her guilt was there."

"Believing, we rejoice,
"To see the curse removed;
"We bless the Lamb with cheerful voice,
"And sing His bleeding Love."

BIBLIOGRAPHY

The New Bible Dictionary.
The Pulpit Commentary.
Genesis to Deuteronomy by C.H. Mackintosh.
Ellicott's Commentary on the Whole Bible.
Matthew Henry's Commentary.
Josephus, The Essential Writings.
The Preacher's Homiletic Commentary.
The International Standard Bible Encyclopedia.
The Zondervan Pictorial Encyclopedia of the Bible.
Theological Wordbook of the Old Testament.
Vine's Expository Dictionary of New Testament Words.

NOTES

INDEX

The index is listed according to subjects. The treatment may include a complete dissertation or no more than a paragraph. But hopefully it will provide some help.

As well, even though extended treatment of a subject may not be carried in this Commentary, one of the other Commentaries may well include the desired material.

631

For all information concerning the *Jimmy Swaggart Bible Commentary,* please request a Gift Catalog.

You may inquire by using Books of the Bible.

- Genesis (639 pages) (11-201)
- Exodus (639 pages) (11-202)
- Leviticus (435 pages) (11-203)
- Numbers
  Deuteronomy (493 pages) (11-204)
- Joshua
  Judges
  Ruth (329 pages) (11-205)
- I Samuel
  II Samuel *(will be ready Spring 2009)* (11-209)
- Psalms (688 pages) (11-216)
- Isaiah (688 pages) (11-220)
- Jeremiah
  Lamentations (456 pages) (11-070)
- Ezekiel (508 pages) (11-223)
- Daniel (403 pages) (11-224)
- Hosea-Malachi (582 pages) (11-072)
- Matthew (625 pages) (11-073)
- Mark (606 pages) (11-074)
- Luke (626 pages) (11-075)
- John (532 pages) (11-076)
- Acts (697 pages) (11-077)

- Romans (536 pages) (11-078)
- I Corinthians (632 pages) (11-079)
- II Corinthians (589 pages) (11-080)
- Galatians (478 pages) (11-081)
- Ephesians (550 pages) (11-082)
- Philippians (476 pages) (11-083)
- Colossians (374 pages) (11-084)
- I Thessalonians
  II Thessalonians (498 pages) (11-085)
- I Timothy
  II Timothy
  Titus
  Philemon (687 pages) (11-086)
- Hebrews (831 pages) (11-087)
- James
  I Peter
  II Peter (730 pages) (11-088)
- I John
  II John
  III John
  Jude (377 pages) (11-089)
- Revelation (602 pages) (11-090)

For telephone orders you may call 1-800-288-8350 with bankcard information. All Baton Rouge residents please use (225) 768-7000. For mail orders send to:

Jimmy Swaggart Ministries
P.O. Box 262550
Baton Rouge, LA 70826-2550

Visit our website: www.jsm.org

NOTES

NOTES

NOTES

NOTES

NOTES

NOTES

NOTES

NOTES